The Princeton Encyclopedia of the World Economy

The Princeton

PRINCETON REFERENCE

Encyclopedia of the World Economy

Volume I

EDITORS IN CHIEF

Kenneth A. Reinert

Ramkishen S. Rajan

ASSOCIATE EDITORS

Amy Jocelyn Glass

Lewis S. Davis

PRINCETON UNIVERSITY PRESS

PRINCETON AND OXFORD

Copyright © 2009 by Princeton University Press

Published by Princeton University Press, 41 William Street,
Princeton, New Jersey 08540

In the United Kingdom: Princeton University Press, 6 Oxford
Street, Woodstock, Oxfordshire 0X20 1TW

The findings, interpretations, and conclusions expressed in this book
are entirely those of the authors writing in their personal capacities.
They do not necessarily represent the views or positions of the institutions with which the authors are affiliated, or of any other
person associated with those institutions.

Library of Congress Cataloging-in-Publication Data
The Princeton encyclopedia of the world economy / editors in chief,
Kenneth A. Reinert, Ramkishen S. Rajan ; associate editors, Amy
Jocelyn Glass, Lewis S. Davis.
    p.   cm.
  Includes bibliographical references and index.
    ISBN 978-0-691-12812-2 (hbk. : alk. paper)   1. International
trade—Encyclopedias.   2. International finance—
Encyclopedias.   3. International business enterprises—
Encyclopedias.   4. International economic relations—
Encyclopedias.   I. Reinert, Kenneth A.   II. Rajan, Ramkishen S.
III. Glass, Amy Jocelyn.   IV. Davis, Lewis S.
    HF1373.P75 2009
    337.03–dc22   2008020573

This book has been composed in Adobe Garamond and Myriad

Printed on acid-free paper.

press.princeton.edu
Printed in the United States of America
10 9 8 7 6 5 4 3 2 1

Contents

Introduction

The world economy, that collection of human activities spanning national borders, touches us all. The banking executive organizing global financial services and the poor agricultural worker cultivating an export crop are both strongly influenced by global economic forces beyond their control. The banking executive operates within a financial services protocol of the World Trade Organization and in financial markets that increase in importance with every passing year and yet remain stubbornly volatile in new and not always predictable ways. The agricultural worker sees her fortunes rise and fall with the world price of the export crop she produces and the remittances she receives from her son who works abroad in a country she will never visit. The value of these remittances changes with her country's exchange rate, as well as with the business cycle where her son works. The banking executive and the agricultural worker do not know one another, but both are participants in what we call the world economy.

This work conceives of the world economy as the interaction among countries in four broad areas: international trade, international finance, international production, and international economic development. Some decades ago, considerations of the world economy neatly fit into only two of these four areas, namely international trade and international finance. Not today. Significant changes in the way production is taking place in the world, the emergence of new regions as active locations of this production, and conceptual and theoretical advancements in our understanding of economic growth

necessitate a more inclusive view. What we conceive of as the "world economy" here is more than just traditional international economics. Integration among countries in the four broad areas considered here has progressed to the extent that it is appropriate to conceive of the world as having characteristics of a single global economy.

Despite the importance of the modern world economy, people around the globe face a number of challenges in their attempts to understand it. Foremost among these challenges is a tendency for the relevant published works to be either too general or too specialized to suit the needs of students in economics and the broader social sciences, public policy and public affairs, international studies, and business, as well as the large and growing number of professionals working in international economic policy. Works intended for a popular audience tend to focus on broad themes and theories, often with a political point of view. Articles in academic journals often use terminology and mathematics beyond the reach of the nonspecialist.

This encyclopedia is intended to bridge the gap between the general and the specialized. It explains the structure and workings of the world economy, summarizes issues and debates related to economic globalization, and provides suggestions for further reading on more than 300 topics. With a few necessary exceptions, the entries in this book eschew the broad sweep. Instead, we have chosen topics we consider essential to a real understanding of forces at play. The entries for the most part do not employ advanced mathematics or highly technical language. Their aim is to accurately educate and inform, not overwhelm.

Structure and Coverage

The entries fall into six major categories: concepts and principles; models and theory; institutions and agreements; policies and instruments; analysis and tools; and sectors and special issues. Our selection of topics in the last of these categories, sectors and special issues, was based on policy relevance rather than on theoretical considerations. We have not included biographical entries, but individuals who have played a significant role in the world economy are mentioned in the relevant topical entries; their names also appear in the index.

The *Encyclopedia* is informed by the modern history of international economic relations since the introduction of the gold standard in the late 19th century. This is widely considered to be the beginning of the modern era of economic relations and, as such, offers a useful starting point. We have tried to select topics that will continue to be important— essential concepts, perennial issues, and long-term trends—regardless of the particular future course of the world economy.

International Trade

Around 1980, our understanding of international trade—the exchange of merchandise and services among the countries of the world—began to change. In response to emerging patterns of trade within (rather than between) manufacturing and service sectors, new theories emerged based on imperfect competition and economies of scale, supplementing the old stories of comparative advantage based on factor or resource endowments in which, for example, a country with a relatively large amount of labor would export labor-intensive goods. At the same time, trade policy agendas rapidly expanded into new areas such as trade in services, intellectual property, a

new generation of preferential trade agreements, and the settlement of disputes. Trade economists and trade lawyers became acquainted. Unforeseen issues emerged out of or alongside of trade negotiations such as trade and the environment, trade and labor, and trade and public health.

Trade-related entries in this *Encyclopedia* reflect this new reality. Standard models of international trade (the Ricardian model, the Heckscher-Ohlin model, and the specific-factors model) are given their due by world-renowned trade theorists. New Trade Theory (i.e., based on oligopoly and monopolistic competition) also receives attention, as do its applications in areas such as the New Economic Geography. We supplement these core models with entries on a large set of basic concepts, from absolute and comparative advantage to terms of trade and fragmentation. A host of trade policy instruments are covered, from basic tariffs to nontariff measures, including quotas, tariff rate quotas, and technical barriers to trade. A large number of institutions and agreements are covered, from the obvious (e.g., the World Trade Organization) to the less well known (e.g., the Convention on Biological Diversity and the Convention on International Trade in Endangered Species). We also give attention to commonly used tools of analysis, such as revealed comparative advantage, effective protection, and gravity models. Finally, we cover a range of special issues such as access to medicines, gender, and the illegal drugs trade.

International Finance

Changes have been even more dramatic in the realm of international finance than in international trade. The liberalization and integration of global financial markets began in the 1980s, but accelerated significantly in the 1990s. For example, data from the Bank for International Settlements indicate that global foreign exchange turnover increased from U.S. $620 billion in 1990 to U.S. $3.2 trillion in 2007. Potential benefits that can emerge from these changes include improved resource allocation from countries specializing in financial services; increased portfolio diversification; improved competition in the financial sector; and increased market discipline on policymakers. Such changes can have positive effects on the overall growth and development of the countries involved.

That said, these changes in the landscape of global finance have also been associated with repeated episodes of significant turbulence. For example, in 1992–93, Europe was faced with the very real possibility of a complete collapse of the European Exchange Rate Mechanism (ERM). In 1994–95, the Mexican currency crisis involved a steep devaluation of the peso and brought Mexico to the brink of default, with spillover effects on Argentina and Brazil. Between July 1997 and mid-1998, the world experienced the effects of the East Asian crisis, which started somewhat innocuously with a run on the Thai baht, but spread swiftly to a number of other regional currencies, most notably the Indonesian rupiah, Malaysian ringgit, Philippine peso, and Korean won. Other large emerging economies, such as Russia and Brazil, also experienced periods of significant market weakness and required the assistance of the International Monetary Fund. The Russian ruble was devalued in August 1998, while the Brazilian real's fixed rate to the U.S. dollar was eventually broken in January 1999. A number of other smaller emerging economies, such as Turkey and Ecuador, also experienced currency and financial crises in the 1990s.

Another striking change has been the reversal of capital flows from developed to developing countries. Due in large part to the emergence of a significant current account deficit (i.e. spending in excess of national saving) in the United States and involving the official transactions of central banks, the developing world is now an *exporter* of capital to the developed world rather than an importer. In fact, the flow of international capital from developing countries to developed countries is now one of the key paradoxes of the global economy, as is the fact that foreign governments and central banks have become major participants in global financial markets via the creation of sovereign wealth funds.

Finance-related entries in the *Encyclopedia* reflect these important changes. Standard models of inter-

national finance and open-economy macroeconomics are covered, including the interest parity conditions and the Mundell-Fleming model, and a host of basic concepts such as balance of payments, capital flight, currency crisis, and sterilization. These are supplemented with more recent theoretical contributions such as the New Open Economy Macroeconomics. Entries on policy instruments include capital controls, hedging, and foreign exchange intervention, to name a few. Coverage also includes the basic analytical tools of the field, such as early warning systems and exchange rate forecasting, as well as special topics such as financial services, sequencing of financial sector reform, recycling of petrodollars, and money laundering.

International Production

As mentioned earlier, a key change in the world economy has been in the structures of international production of goods and services, as multinational enterprises (MNEs) engage in varieties of foreign direct investment (FDI) with managerial influence over foreign-based productive enterprises. Drawing on both the work of earlier theory in international business and new developments in trade theory, economists have incorporated MNEs and FDI into the theory and practice of international economics. At the same time, issues such as outsourcing and offshoring have attracted public attention and increased political interest in this area. This has occurred both in high-income countries, where outsourcing has moved to white-collar as well as blue-collar occupation categories, and in developing countries, where new income-generating possibilities have emerged outside of manufacturing.

When deciding to become a MNE, a firm chooses the mode that maximizes its profits, typically considering such options as exporting and licensing a local firm (outsourcing/offshoring) as alternatives. Consequently, models usually revolve around the trade-offs between FDI and at least one alternative. In these models, the location of production differs between FDI and exporting, and whether transactions occur within the firm differs between FDI and licensing.

Like trade, much FDI occurs between similar, developed countries and is often two-way, but FDI has grown even more rapidly than trade. A large share of world trade (about 30 percent) occurs *within* firms and is known as intrafirm trade. MNEs tend to arise in industries with large research and development expenditures relative to sales, significant product differentiation, and substantial intangible assets such as intellectual property and brand value. FDI is mostly horizontal—with MNEs creating local production facilities in each country and selling within each country or region—rather than vertical, in which MNEs allocate production processes across countries and ship the products back home.

Our coverage of international production begins with issues of theory, from long-standing pursuits such as location theory to emerging issues of importance such as FDI under monopolistic competition and oligopoly. These more formal considerations are again supplemented with a set of entries on basic concepts, from FDI and MNEs themselves to intangible assets and technology licensing. Coverage of policy instruments includes entries on domestic content requirements, foreign equity restrictions, and trade-related investment measures more broadly. We also cover specific analytic tools such as market size and exchange rates as they relate to FDI. Finally, the book addresses several special issues related to FDI, such as FDI and export performance and FDI and labor markets.

International Economic Development

Due to the huge disparities in standards of living around the globe and the tremendous impact, for good or ill, of international economic transactions in the development process, the ideas and policies that shape economic development are subject to ongoing and highly charged debates. In entries on influential development institutions, such as the World Bank, and policy frameworks, such as import substitution industrialization and the Washington consensus, our

goal is to explain these debates without attempting to resolve them. Entries on economic development and the evolution of development thinking are designed to provide the reader with a conceptual framework and a context for understanding the issues addressed in entries such as international migration, international trade and economic development, and technological progress in open economies.

Since the 1990s, development thinking has shifted toward recognizing the central importance of political processes in structuring and potentially limiting economic development. Reflecting this shift, the *Encyclopedia* attempts to view the economic processes of development in the broader context of political decision-making. This emphasis on political economy is apparent in many of the entries on economic policy and takes center stage in entries that address the linkages between economic and political systems, such as those on democracy and development, corruption, and international aid and political economy. Finally, while most of the development entries take the national economy as their starting point, entries on global poverty, global income inequality, and international income convergence take a deliberately transnational approach, reflecting the growing consensus that it is now meaningful to view some issues from the perspective of a single global economy.

Using the Encyclopedia

There are a number of ways to engage with the encyclopedia. Entries are arranged in alphabetical order. If you are uncertain of the particular entry that may be most appropriate to your interest, you can consult the Topical List of Entries, which groups the entry terms by category. You also can consult the index to find topics that are covered in related entries but do not have entries of their own.

At the end of most entries you will find "See also" references to other entries related to the topic at hand. Each entry concludes with an annotated Further Reading list to guide readers with an interest in additional research.

Acknowledgments

Our foremost debt related to this work is to the hundreds of contributors who took the time to craft entries to meet the needs of readers. We would also like to thank Anne Savarese, Senior Reference Editor at Princeton University Press, who conceived of this project and has been a full partner throughout. Jennifer Formichelli and Claire Tillman-McTigue managed the entries with aplomb, helping to keep the entire project on track. Natalie Baan supervised the copyediting. We would like to thank our Advisory Board, Jerry Cohen, Ian Goldin, Ron Jones, Peter Kenen, and Ted Moran, for their advice at critical junctures in the project. Finally, Ken Reinert would like to dedicate his work on this project to the memory of Anthony Wallace, a long-time educator on the world economy who is greatly missed by his colleagues and students.

Alphabetical List of Entries

free trade area
Free Trade Area of the Americas (FTAA)

gains from trade
gender
General Agreement on Tariffs and Trade (GATT)
General Agreement on Trade in Services (GATS)
Global Environment Facility
global imbalances
global income inequality
global public goods
globalization
gold standard, international
government procurement
gravity models
Group of Seven/Eight (G7/G8)
growth in open economies, neoclassical models
growth in open economies, Schumpeterian
    models
Gulf Cooperation Council

health and globalization
Heckscher-Ohlin model
hedge funds
hedging
HIV/AIDS
home country bias
hot money and sudden stops

illegal drugs trade
import substitution industrialization
impossible trinity
infant industry argument
inflation targeting
information and communications
    technology
infrastructure and foreign direct investment
intangible assets
intellectual property rights
intellectual property rights and foreign direct
    investment
interest parity conditions
internalization theory
international financial architecture
international financial centers

international income convergence
international institutional transfer
international investment agreements
International Labor Organization
international liquidity
International Monetary Fund (IMF)
International Monetary Fund conditionality
International Monetary Fund surveillance
international policy coordination
international reserves
intrafirm trade
intraindustry trade

J-curve effect
joint ventures

knowledge-capital model of the multinational
    enterprise

labor standards
Latin American debt crisis
lender of last resort
linkages, backward and forward
liquidity trap, the
location theory
Louvre Accord

Maastricht Treaty
market access
market size and foreign direct investment
Marshall-Lerner condition
mercantilism
Mercosur
mergers and acquisitions
migration, international
migration governance
Millennium Development Goals
monetary conditions index
monetary policy rules
monetary versus fiscal dominance
money laundering
money supply
monopolistic competition
multilateral environmental agreements
multilateral trade negotiations

Topical List of Entries

2. Models and Theory

International Trade
economies of scale
foreign direct investment under monopolistic
   competition
foreign direct investment under oligopoly
Heckscher-Ohlin model
monopolistic competition
New Economic Geography
New Trade Theory
nontraded goods
oligopoly models
political economy of trade policy
Ricardian model
specific-factors model

International Finance
Balassa-Samuelson effect
Feldstein-Horioka puzzle
forward premium puzzle
interest parity conditions
J-curve effect
Marshall-Lerner condition
Mundell-Fleming model
New Open Economy Macroeconomics
optimum currency area (OCA) theory
primary products trade
quantity theory of money
Swan diagram
Triffin dilemma

International Production
foreign direct investment: the OLI framework
foreign direct investment under monopolistic
   competition
foreign direct investment under oligopoly
internalization theory
knowledge-capital model of the multinational
   enterprise
location theory
pollution haven hypothesis
proximity-concentration hypothesis

International Economic Development
aid, international, and political economy
dependency theory
evolution of development thinking
growth in open economies, neoclassical models
growth in open economies, Schumpeterian
   models
infant industry argument
North-South trade
South-South trade

3. Institutions and Agreements

International Trade
African Caribbean Pacific–European Union
   partnership agreements (ACP-EU)
African Union
Agreement on Agriculture
Agreement on Trade-Related Aspects of
   Intellectual Property Rights (TRIPS)
agricultural trade negotiations
Andean Community
Asia Pacific Economic Cooperation (APEC)
Association of Southeast Asian Nations (ASEAN)
Basel Convention
Central American Common Market (CACM)
Central American–Dominican Republic Free
   Trade Area (CAFTA-DR)
Common Agricultural Policy
Common Market for Eastern and Southern Africa
   (COMESA)
Convention on Biological Diversity
Convention on International Trade in
   Endangered Species (CITES)
Doha Round
Economic Community of West African States
   (ECOWAS)
European Union
Free Trade Area of the Americas (FTAA)
General Agreement on Tariffs and Trade (GATT)
General Agreement on Trade in Services (GATS)
Global Environment Facility
Group of Seven/Eight (G7/G8)

dollar standard
dual exchange rate
expenditure changing and switching
foreign exchange intervention
hedging
inflation targeting
International Monetary Fund conditionality
International Monetary Fund surveillance
international reserves
lender of last resort
mercantilism
multiple currencies
special drawing rights
sterilization
Tobin tax

International Production
domestic content requirements
foreign equity restrictions
intellectual property rights and foreign direct
    investment
subsidies and financial incentives to foreign
    direct investment
trade costs and foreign direct investment
trade-related investment measures (TRIMs)

International Economic Development
aid, bilateral
aid, food
aid, humanitarian
aid, international
aid, military
capital accumulation in open economies
capital controls
domestic content requirements
export processing zones
export promotion
import substitution industrialization
migration governance
social policy in open economies
special and differential treatment
structural adjustment
technological progress in open economies
trade-related investment measures (TRIMs)
Washington consensus

5. Analysis and Tools

International Trade
applied general equilibrium models
effective protection
gravity models
partial equilibrium models
revealed comparative advantage
tariff-cutting formulas

International Finance
balance of payments
early warning systems
equilibrium exchange rate
exchange market pressure
exchange rate forecasting
Latin American debt crisis
monetary conditions index
monetary policy rules
real exchange rate

International Production
agglomeration and foreign direct investment
appropriate technology and foreign direct
    investment
exchange rates and foreign direct
    investment
factor endowments and foreign direct
    investment
fixed costs and foreign direct investment
infrastructure and foreign direct investment
market size and foreign direct investment
unions and foreign direct investment

6. Sectors and Special Issues

International Trade
access to medicines
air transportation
agriculture
child labor
corporate governance
digital divide
electronic commerce

Directory of Contributors

Rajat Acharyya
Reader, Department of Economics, Jadavpur University, Calcutta

    trade and wages (coauthor)

Charles Adams
Visiting Professor, Lee Kuan Yew School of Public Policy, National University of Singapore

    carry trade

Joshua Aizenman
Professor of Economics, University of California, Santa Cruz

    financial crisis; international reserves

Mark Allen
Director, Policy and Development Review Department, International Monetary Fund

    balance sheet approach/effects (coauthor)

Kym Anderson
George Gollin Professor of Economics, University of Adelaide

    distortions to agricultural incentives

Klaus Armingeon
Professor of Political Science and Director, Institute of Political Science, University of Berne

    Organisation for Economic Co-operation and Development (OECD)

Sven W. Arndt
Charles M. Stone Professor of Money, Credit, and Trade, Claremont McKenna College

    fragmentation

Nancy Neiman Auerbach
Associate Professor of International Political Economy, Scripps College

    financial liberalization; Latin American debt crisis; petrodollars, recycling of (coauthor)

Marc Bacchetta
Counselor, Economic Research and Statistics Division World Trade Organization

    tariff escalation; tariffs

Christopher M. Bacon
Lecturer, Departments of Latin American and Latino Studies, Sociology and Environmental Studies, University of California, Santa Cruz

    fair trade

Jennifer Bair
Assistant Professor of Sociology, Yale University

    commodity chains

King Banaian
Professor of Economics, St. Cloud State University

    currency substitution and dollarization

Subhayu Bandyopadhyay
Research Officer, Federal Reserve Bank of St. Louis
common market (coauthor)

Frank Barry
*Lecturer, School of Economics,
University College Dublin*
foreign direct investment and labor markets

Andrew L. Beath
*PhD Candidate in Government, Harvard
University*
migration, international (coauthor)

Hamid Beladi
*Professor of Economics, College of Business,
University of Texas at San Antonio*
nontraded goods (coauthor)

Paul Bergin
*Associate Professor of Economics, University
of California, Davis*
Balassa-Samuelson effect

Pradip Bhatnagar
*Economist, Technical Support Facility of the Group
of Fifteen (G-15), Geneva*
temporary movement of natural persons

Richard Blackhurst
*Professor of International Economics,
The Fletcher School, Tufts University*
General Agreement on Tariffs and Trade (GATT);
World Trade Organization

Robert A. Blecker
Professor of Economics, American University
steel

Clemens F. J. Boonekamp
*Director, Trade Policies Review Division,
World Trade Organization*
Trade Policy Review Mechanism

James M. Boughton
Historian, International Monetary Fund
International Monetary Fund surveillance

François Bourguignon
Director, Paris School of Economics
global income inequality (coauthor)

Paul Bowles
*Professor of Economics, University of Northern British
Columbia*
beggar-thy-neighbor policies; mercantilism

Russell S. Boyer
*Professor of Economics, University of Western
Ontario*
Mundell-Fleming model

Carlos A. Primo Braga
*Senior Advisor, International Policy and Partnerships
Group, World Bank*
World Trade Organizaton, accession to
(coauthor)

Mark R. Brawley
Professor of Political Science, McGill University
globalization

Drusilla K. Brown
Associate Professor of Economics, Tufts University
labor standards

Richard C. K. Burdekin
*Jonathan B. Lovelace Professor of Economics,
Claremont McKenna College*
commodity-price pegging; debt deflation;
quantity theory of money; seigniorage

Kenneth Button
*Professor of Public Policy and Director, Center for
Transportation Policy, Operations, and Logistics,
George Mason University*
air transportation; shipping

Fang Cai
Economist, Division of International Finance, Federal Reserve

   home country bias

Rui Castro
Associate Professor of Economics, Université de Montréal

   growth in open economies, neoclassical models

Tony Cavoli
Lecturer, School of Commerce, University of South Australia

   capital mobility (coauthor); inflation targeting; monetary policy rules

Avik Chakrabarti
Associate Professor of Economics, University of Wisconsin–Milwaukee

   nontraded goods (coauthor)

Maggie Xiaoyang Chen
Assistant Professor of Economics and International Affairs, George Washington University

   fixed costs and foreign direct investment; market access

Yin-Wong Cheung
Professor of Economics, University of California, Santa Cruz

   exchange rate forecasting; purchasing power parity

Menzie D. Chinn
Professor of Economics and Public Affairs, Robert M. La Follette School of Public Affairs, University of Wisconsin

   effective exchange rate; forward premium puzzle; interest parity conditions

Eric M. P. Chiu
Assistant Professor, Institute of National Policy and Public Affairs, National Chung Hsing University

   currency crisis (coauthor)

Christopher K. Clague
Emeritus Professor of Economics, University of Maryland

   democracy and development

Jennifer Clapp
CIGI Chair in International Governance and Professor, Faculty of Environmental Studies, University of Waterloo

   Basel Convention

Kimberly A. Clausing
Professor of Economics, Reed College

   intrafirm trade

Paul Collier
Professor of Economics and Director, Center for the Study of African Economies, University of Oxford

   aid, military (coauthor)

Brian R. Copeland
Professor of Economics, University of British Columbia

   pollution haven hypothesis

Germán Creamer
Center for Computational Learning Systems, Columbia University

   Andean Community

Edward Crenshaw
Associate Professor of Sociology, Ohio State University

   digital divide

Michael R. Curtis
Adjunct Professor of Public Policy, George Mason University

   petroleum

Lewis S. Davis
Assistant Professor of Economics, Union College

   development

xxvii

Harry de Gorter
Associate Professor, Department of Applied Economics and Management, Cornell University

  tariff rate quotas

James W. Dean
Ross Distinguished Professor, Department of Economics, Western Washington University

  Eurocurrencies; exorbitant privilege; money supply

Alan V. Deardorff
John W. Sweetland Professor of International Economics and Professor of Economics and Public Policy, University of Michigan

  Ricardian model

Gelaye Debebe
Assistant Professor of Organizational Sciences, George Washington University

  brain waste

Sirathorn Dechsakulthorn
PhD Candidate in Economics, Claremont Graduate University

  discipline (coauthor)

Robert Dekle
Professor of Economics, University of Southern California

  banking crisis

Desmond Dinan
Jean Monnet Professor, School of Public Policy, George Mason University

  European Union

Elias Dinopoulos
Professor of Economics, University of Florida

  growth in open economies, Schumpeterian models

Jonathan P. Doh
Associate Professor of Management and Operations, Herbert G. Rammrath Endowed Chair in International Business, and Director, Center for Global Leadership, Villanova School of Business, Villanova University

  nongovernmental organizations (NGOs)

Kathryn M. E. Dominguez
Professor of Public Policy and Economics, University of Michigan, and Research Associate, National Bureau of Economic Research

  sterilization

Brian Doyle
Senior Economist, International Finance Division, Federal Reserve Board

  New Open Economy Macroeconomics

Graham Dutfield
Professor of International Governance, School of Law, University of Leeds

  Agreement on Trade-Related Aspects of Intellectual Property Rights (TRIPS); World Intellectual Property Organization

Eric V. Edmonds
Associate Professor of Economics, Dartmouth College; Director, Child Labor Network, Institute for the Study of Labor (IZA); Faculty Research Fellow, National Bureau of Economic Research

  child labor

Andrew Elek
Independent Scholar

  Asia Pacific Economic Cooperation (APEC) (coauthor)

Kimberly Ann Elliott
Senior Fellow, Center for Global Development and Peter G. Peterson Institute for International Economics

  International Labor Organization

Korkut A. Erturk
Professor of Economics, University of Utah

bubbles; speculation

Wilfred J. Ethier
Professor of Economics, University of Pennsylvania

economies of scale

Simon J. Evenett
Professor of International Trade and Economic Development, Swiss Institute for International Economics and Applied Economic Research, University of St. Gallen; Research Fellow, Center for Economic Policy Research (CEPR)

competition policy; government procurement; World Trade Organization, accession to (coauthor)

David Favre
Professor of Law, Michigan State University College of Law

Convention on International Trade In Endangered Species (CITES)

Robert C. Feenstra
C. Bryan Cameron Distinguished Chair in International Economics and Director, Center for International Data, University of California, Davis; Director, International Trade and Investment Program, National Bureau of Economic Research

outsourcing/offshoring (coauthor)

Richard Feinberg
Professor of International Political Economy and Director, APEC Study Center, University of California, San Diego

Free Trade Area of the Americas (FTAA)

Susan Feinberg
Associate Professor of International Business, Rutgers Business School

location theory

Michael Ferrantino
International Economist, U.S. International Trade Commission

appropriate technology and foreign direct investment

Francisco Ferreira
Development Research Group, World Bank

global income inequality (coauthor)

Ben Ferrett
Research Fellow, Leverhulme Center for Research on Globalization and Economic Policy, School of Economics, University of Nottingham

foreign direct investment under oligopoly

Christopher Findlay
Professor of Economics, University of Adelaide

Asia Pacific Economic Cooperation (APEC) (coauthor)

Lionel Fontagné
Professor of Economics, Paris School of Economics, Université de Paris 1 Panthéon-Sorbonne

South-South trade

Joseph F. Francois
Professor of Economics, Johannes Kepler Universität Linz

partial equilibrium models (coauthor)

Michele Fratianni
Professor of Business Economics and Public Policy Emeritus, Indiana University, and Professor of Economics, Università Politecnica delle Marche, Ancona

Bank for International Settlements (BIS); dominant currency; Feldstein-Horioka puzzle; gold standard, international

Francis Fukuyama
Bernard L. Schwartz Professor of International Political Economy and Director, International

Development Program, Paul H. Nitze School of
Advanced International Studies, Johns Hopkins
University

    international institutional transfer

Andrea K. Gerlak
Visiting Professor, Department of Political Science,
University of Arizona

    Global Environment Facility (coauthor)

Chetan Ghate
Assistant Professor of Economics, Indian Statistical
Institute, New Delhi

    time inconsistency problem

Amit Ghosh
Assistant Professor, Department of Economics,
Illinois Wesleyan University

    exchange rate pass-through

Christopher L. Gilbert
Professor of Econometrics, University of Trento

    World Bank (coauthor)

Kate Gillespie
Research Associate Professor, Department
of Marketing, McCombs School of Business,
University of Texas at Austin

    smuggling

Amy Jocelyn Glass
Associate Professor of Economics, Texas
A&M University

    foreign direct investment and innovation,
    imitation (coauthor); infrastructure and foreign
    direct investment; vertical versus horizontal
    foreign direct investment

Linda S. Goldberg
Federal Reserve Bank of New York and National
Bureau of Economic Research

    exchange rates and foreign
    direct investment

Ian Goldin
Director, James Martin 21st Century School, and
Professorial Fellow, Balliol College, University
of Oxford

    aid, international; evolution of development
    thinking; migration, international (coauthor)

Holger Görg
Associate Professor and Reader, School of Economics,
University of Nottingham

    foreign direct investment and exit of local firms;
    linkages, backward and forward

Ashima Goyal
Professor of Economics, Indira Gandhi Institute
of Development Research, Mumbai, India

    assignment problem; hedging; hot money
    and sudden stops (coauthor); Swan diagram

Ilene Grabel
Professor of International Economics, Graduate
School of International Studies, University of Denver

    Tobin tax

Jean-Christophe Graz
Assistant Professor, Institute of Political and
International Studies, University of Lausanne

    World Economic Forum

Duncan Green
Head of Research for Oxfam GB

    anti-globalization (coauthor)

Joshua Greene
Deputy Director, IMF-Singapore Regional
Training Institute

    black market premium; dual exchange rate

Matt Griffith
Senior Advisor, Commission for Rural Communities
in London

    anti-globalization (coauthor)

Stephany Griffith-Jones
Executive Director of the Initiative for Policy Dialogue, Columbia University

   capital flows to developing countries

Nigel Grimwade
Principal Lecturer of Economics and Finance, Department of Business, Computing, and Information Management, London South Bank University

   competitive advantage

Alfred V. Guender
Associate Professor, Department of Economics, University of Canterbury

   monetary conditions index

Morley Gunderson
Professor, Center for Industrial Relations and Human Resources and Department of Economics, University of Toronto; CIBC Chair in Youth Employment

   social policy in open economies

Markus Haacker
Economist, African Department, International Monetary Fund

   health and globalization; HIV/AIDS; Millennium Development Goals

David M. Hart
Associate Professor, School of Public Policy, George Mason University

   brain gain

C. Randall Henning
Professor, School of International Service at American University and Visiting Fellow, Peter G. Peterson Institute for International Economics

   exchange rate weapon

Almas Heshmati
Professor of Economics and Head of Department of Economics and Finance, University of Kurdistan

Hawler; Research Fellow, Techno-Economics, Management and Policy Program, Seoul National University

   information and communications technology (coauthor)

Jack High
Professor, School of Public Policy, George Mason University

   balance of payments

Anke Hoeffler
Research Officer, Center for the Study of African Economics, Department of Economics, St. Antony's College, University of Oxford

   aid, military (coauthor)

Bernard Hoekman
Senior Advisor, Development Research Group, World Bank and Researcher, Center for Economic Policy Research (CEPR)

   Doha Round; Uruguay Round

Henrik Horn
Senior Research Fellow, Research Institute of Industrial Economics (IFN), Stockholm, and Research Fellow, Center for Economic Policy Research (CEPR)

   nondiscrimination (coauthor)

Brett House
Economist, Policy and Development Review Department, International Monetary Fund

   balance sheet approach/effects (coauthor)

Andrew Hughes Hallett
Professor, School of Public Policy, George Mason University

   Bonn Summit; international policy coordination; Smithsonian Agreement

Michael Hutchison
Professor of Economics, University of California, Santa Cruz

   Bank of Japan; exchange rate regimes

Barry W. Ickes
Professor of Economics, Pennsylvania State University

    political economy of policy reform

Asif Islam
Research Associate, Department of Agricultural and Resource Economics, University of Maryland

    trade and the environment (coauthor)

Hiro Ito
Associate Professor, Department of Economics, Portland State University

    expenditure changing and expenditure switching; financial repression; liquidity trap, the

J. Bradford Jensen
Associate Professor of Economics and International Business, McDonough School of Business, Georgetown University; Senior Fellow at Peter G. Peterson Institute for International Economics; Research Associate at National Bureau of Economic Research

    outsourcing/offshoring (coauthor)

Omotunde E. G. Johnson
Retiree, International Monetary Fund, and Adjunct Professor, School of Public Policy, George Mason University

    African Union

R. Barry Johnston
Assistant Director, Monetary and Capital Markets Department, International Monetary Fund

    international financial centers; money laundering; offshore financial centers; sequencing of financial sector reforms

Ronald W. Jones
Xerox Professor of Economics, University of Rochester

    specific-factors model

Philippe Jorion
Chancellor's Professor of Finance, The Paul Merage School of Business, University of California at Irvine

    hedge funds

Tim Josling
Senior Fellow, Freeman Spogli Institute for International Studies, Stanford University, and Visiting Professor, Imperial College, London

    Agreement on Agriculture; agricultural trade negotiations

Joseph P. Joyce
Professor of Economics, Wellesley College

    International Monetary Fund (IMF); International Monetary Fund conditionality

William H. Kaempfer
Vice Provost and Professor of Economics, University of Colorado, Boulder

    sanctions (coauthor)

Inge Kaul
Special Advisor, United Nations Development Program

    global public goods

Sydney J. Key
Lecturer, Graduate Program in Banking and Financial Law, Boston University School of Law

    financial services

Christopher Kilby
Associate Professor of Economics, Vassar College

    aid, bilateral

John Kirton
Associate Professor of Political Science, University of Toronto

    Group Of Seven/Eight (G7/G8)

Jörn Kleinert
Professor of Economics, Eberhard-Karls-University Tübingen

    market size and foreign direct investment

Vladimir Klyuev
Economist, Western Hemisphere Department, International Monetary Fund

    capital accumulation in open economies

Ulrich Koester
Professor of Agricultural Economics, University of Kiel, Germany

　Common Agricultural Policy

Michel Kostecki
Professor of Marketing, Enterprise Institute, University of Neuchâtel

　trade-related capacity building

Jan Kregel
Distinguished Research Professor in the Center for Full Employment and Price Stability, University of Missouri, Kansas City; Senior Scholar, Levy Economics Institute, Bard College

　Bretton Woods system; Triffin dilemma

Kala Krishna
Professor of Economics, Pennsylvania State University

　free trade area; rules of origin

Pravin Krishna
Chung Ju Yung Distinguished Professor of International Economics and Business, Paul H. Nitze School of Advanced International Studies, and Professor of Economics, Johns Hopkins University

　multilateralism; regionalism

Maurice Kugler
Center for International Governance Innovation Chair in International Public Policy and Professor of Economics, Wilfrid Laurier University, and Visiting Professor of Public Policy, John F. Kennedy School of Government, Harvard University

　factor endowments and foreign direct investment

Philip R. Lane
Professor of Economics, and Director, Institute for International Integration Studies, Trinity College, Dublin

　transfer problem

Minkyu Lee
PhD Candidate, Technology Management Economics and Policy Program, Seoul National University

　information and communications technology (coauthor)

James Lehman
Professor of Economics, Pitzer College

　Federal Reserve Board

Priscilla Liang
Assistant Professor of Business and Economics, California State University, Channel Islands

　contagion (coauthor)

Ramón López
Professor of Economics, Department of Agriculture and Resource Economics, University of Maryland

　trade and the environment (coauthor)

Eduardo Lora
Principal Advisor, Research Department, Inter-American Development Bank

　Washington consensus

Mary E. Lovely
Associate Professor of Economics, Syracuse University

　agglomeration and foreign direct investment

Anton D. Lowenberg
Professor of Economics, California State University, Northridge

　sanctions (coauthor)

Rodney Ludema
Associate Professor of Economics, Georgetown University

　multilateral trade negotiations

Ronald MacDonald
Adam Smith Chair of Political Economy and Director of PhD Programs, Department of Economics, University of Glasgow

equilibrium exchange rate; exchange rate
volatility

Alex Mandilaras
Lecturer in Economics, University of Surrey

 early warning systems; exchange market
 pressure

Andrea Maneschi
*Professor of Economics and Director, Graduate
Program in Economic Development, Vanderbilt
University*

 comparative advantage; gains from trade

Sugata Marjit
*Director and Reserve Bank of India Professor,
Center for Studies in Social Sciences,
Calcutta*

 trade and wages (coauthor)

Stephen Marks
Professor of Economics, Pomona College

 asymmetric information

James R. Markusen
*Professor of International Economics, University of
Colorado*

 foreign direct investment (FDI);
 internalization theory

Antoine Martin
*Senior Economist, Federal Reserve Bank of
New York*

 currency competition; multiple currencies

Philip Martin
*Professor of Agricultural and Resource Economics
and Chair, UC Comparative Immigration and
Integration Program, University of California, Davis*

 migration governance

Will Martin
*Lead Economist, Trade and Development Research
Group, World Bank*

 tariff-cutting formulas

Catherine Matraves
*Visiting Assistant Professor of Economics, Michigan
State University*

 pharmaceuticals

Xenia Matschke
*Assistant Professor of Economics, University
of Connecticut*

 New Trade Theory

Aaditya Mattoo
*Lead Economist, Development Research Group,
World Bank*

 General Agreement on Trade in Services (GATS);
 trade in services

Petros C. Mavroidis
*Edwin B. Barker Professor of Law, Columbia
Law School; Professor of Law, University
of Neuchâtel*

 nondiscrimination (coauthor)

Daniel Maxwell
*Associate Professor, The Fletcher School, Tufts
University*

 aid, food; aid, humanitarian

Joseph A. McCahery
*Professor of Corporate Governance, Center
for Law and Economics, University
of Amsterdam*

 corporate governance

Ronald I. McKinnon
*William D. Eberle Professor of International
Economics, Stanford University*

 conflicted virtue; dollar standard

Niall P. Meagher
*Senior Counsel, Advisory Center on World Trade
Organization Law, Geneva*

 World Trade Organization dispute settlement
 (coauthor)

Jose Mendez
Professor of Economics, W. P. Carey School of Business, Arizona State University

  Central American Common Market (CACM); Central American–Domincan Republic Free Trade Area (CAFTA-DR)

Mokhtar M. Metwally
Professor of Economics, University of Wollongong

  Gulf Cooperation Council

Klaus Meyer
Professor of Strategy and International Business, School of Management, University of Bath

  foreign market entry

Constantine Michalopoulos
Independent Consultant

  special and differential treatment

Branko Milanovic
Economist, Development Research Group, World Bank

  global income inequality (coauthor)

Chris Milner
Assistant Professor, School of Economics and Leverhulme Center for Research in Globalization and Economic Policy (GEP), University of Nottingham

  effective protection; export promotion

Eugenio J. Miravete
Associate Professor of Economics, University of Texas

  infant industry argument

Ajit Mishra
Senior Lecturer, Department of Economics and International Development, University of Bath

  corruption

Andrew Mitchell
Senior Lecturer, Melbourne Law School

  electronic commerce

Devashish Mitra
Professor of Economics and Gerald B. and Daphna Cramer Professor of Global Affairs, Maxwell School, Syracuse University

  trade and economic development, international

Pradeep K. Mitra
Chief Economist, Europe and Central Asia Region, World Bank

  transition economies

José G. Montalvo
Professor, Department of Economics, Universitat Pompeu Fabra

  aid, international, and political economy

Michael O. Moore
Professor of Economics and International Affairs and Director, Institute for Economic Policy, Elliott School of International Affairs, George Washington University

  anti-dumping

C. W. Morgan
Associate Professor and Research Fellow, Center for Economic Development and International Trade (CREDIT), School of Economics, University of Nottingham

  African Caribbean Pacific–European Union (ACP-EU) partnership agreements

Arijit Mukherjee
Associate Professor and Reader in Economics, University of Nottingham

  technology licensing

Jacob Wanjala Musila
Associate Professor of Economics, Athabasca University

  Common Market for Eastern and Southern Africa (COMESA); Economic Community of West African States (ECOWAS)

Ethan C. Myers
Teaching Associate, Department of Social Thought and Political Economy, University of Massachusetts

Global Environment Facility (coauthor)

Usha Nair-Reichert
Associate Professor of Economics and Undergraduate Director, School of Economics, Georgia Institute of Technology

proximity-concentration hypothesis

Rajneesh Narula
Professor of International Business Regulation, Department of Economics, University of Reading

multinational enterprises

Léonce Ndikumana
Associate Professor of Economics, University of Massachusetts at Amherst

capital flight

J. Peter Neary
Professor of Economics, University of Oxford and Research Fellow, Center for Economic Policy Research (CEPR)

foreign direct investment: the OLI framework

Douglas Nelson
Professor of Economics, Tulane University

political economy of trade policy

Richard Newfarmer
Economic Advisor, International Trade and Department and Prospects Group, World Bank

international investment agreements

Hildegunn Kyvik Nordås
Senior Economist, Organisation for Economic Co-operation and Development (OECD)

textiles and clothing

Ilan Noy
Associate Professor of Economics, University of Hawai'i, Manoa

capital controls (coauthor); hot money and sudden stops (coauthor); special drawing rights

Gianmarco I. P. Ottaviano
Professor of Economics, University of Bologna

New Economic Geography

David Palmeter
Senior Counsel, Sidley Austin LLP, Washington, DC

World Trade Organization dispute settlement (coauthor)

Alberto Paloni
Senior Lecturer, Department of Economics, and Director, Center for Development Studies, Glasgow University

structural adjustment

Arvind Panagariya
Professor of Economics and Jagdish Bhagwati Professor of Indian Political Economy, School of International and Public Affairs, Columbia University

Heckscher-Ohlin model

Letizia Paoli
Professor, Leuven Institute of Criminology, K.U. Leuven Faculty of Law, Belgium

illegal drugs trade

Giovanni Peri
Associate Professor of Economics, University of California, Davis

techonology spillovers

Emile-Robert Perrin
High Council on International Co-operation (HCCI), French Prime Minister's Office

regional development banks (coauthor)

Richard Pomfret
Professor of Economics, University of Adelaide

common currency; optimum currency area (OCA) theory

Helen Popper
Associate Professor of Economics, Santa Clara University

   foreign exchange intervention; real exchange rate

Susan Pozo
Professor of Economics, Western Michigan University

   remittances

Thitima Puttitanun
Assistant Professor of Economics, San Diego State University

   intellectual property rights and foreign direct investment

Horst Raff
Professor of Economics, Christian-Albrechts University of Kiel

   joint ventures; mergers and acquisitions

Ramkishen S. Rajan
Associate Professor, School of Public Policy, George Mason University

   capital controls (coauthor); capital mobility (coauthor); exchange rate pass-through (coauthor); fear of floating (coauthor); hot money and sudden stops (coauthor); sovereign wealth funds (coauthor)

Carlos D. Ramirez
Associate Professor of Economics, George Mason University

   convertibility; original sin

Priya Ranjan
Associate Professor of Economics, University of California, Irvine

   trade costs and foreign direct investment

Martin Ravallion
Director, Development Research Group, World Bank

   global income inequality (coauthor)

Kenneth A. Reinert
Professor, School of Public Policy, George Mason University

   applied general equilibrium models; gravity models; migration, international (coauthor); partial equilibrium models (coauthor)

Nola Reinhardt
Professor of Economics, Smith College

   primary products trade

Kara M. Reynolds
Assistant Professor of Economics, American University

   countervailing duties

Francisco Rivera-Batiz
Professor of Economics and Education, Teachers College, Columbia University

   economic development

Donna Roberts
Senior Economist, Economic Research Service, U.S. Department of Agriculture

   sanitary and phytosanitary measures

G. Chris Rodrigo
Independent Consultant

   revealed comparative advantage

Riordan Roett
Sarita and Don Johnston Professor of Political Science and Director of Western Hemisphere Studies, Paul H. Nitze School of Advanced International Studies (SAIS), Johns Hopkins University

   Mercosur

Christoph Rosenberg
Senior Regional Representative for Central Europe and the Baltics, European Department, International Monetary Fund

   balance sheet approach/effects (coauthor)

G. Kristin Rosendal
Senior Research Fellow, Fridtjof Nansen Institute

Convention on Biological Diversity

Roy J. Ruffin
*Anderson Professor of Economics,
University of Houston*

monopolistic competition; oligopoly

C. Ford Runge
*Distinguished McKnight University Professor of
Applied Economics and Law and Director, Center for
International Food and Agricultural Policy, University
of Minnesota*

multilateral environmental agreements

Kamal Saggi
*Dedman Distinguished Collegiate Professor
of Economics, Southern Methodist University*

foreign direct investment and innovation,
imitation (coauthor); foreign direct investment
and international technology transfer

Dominick Salvatore
*Distinguished Professor and Director of the PhD
Program, Department of Economics, Fordham
University*

euro; global imbalances; international liquidity;
reserve currency; vehicle currency

Carlos Santiso
*Governance and Public Finance Adviser, Department
for International Development (DFID),
United Kingdom*

regional development banks (coauthor)

John Sargent
*Assistant Professor of Management, College of
Business, University of Texas-Pan American*

export processing zones

Prabirjit Sarkar
*Professor of Economics, Jadavpur University,
Calcutta*

terms of trade

Frederic M. Scherer
*Aetna Professor of Public Policy Emeritus,
John F. Kennedy School of Government, Harvard
University*

access to medicines

Nicolas Schmitt
*Professor of Economics, Simon Fraser University;
Research Fellow, Center for Economic Studies, Ifo
Institute for Economic Research, Munich*

parallel imports

Patricia Higino Schneider
*Assistant Professor of Economics, Mount Holyoke
College*

intellectual property rights

Jeffrey J. Schott
*Senior Fellow, Peter G. Peterson Institute for
International Economics*

North American Free Trade Agreement (NAFTA)
(coauthor)

M. Fuat Sener
Associate Professor of Economics, Union College

technological progress in open economies

Brad Setser
*Fellow for Geoeconomics, Council on Foreign
Relations*

bail-ins; bailouts; international financial
architecture

Pierre L. Siklos
*Professor of Economics and Director, Viessmann
European Research Center, Wilfrid Laurier
University*

European Central Bank; European Monetary
Union; impossible trinity; Maastricht Treaty

Keith Sill
*Senior Economist, Federal Reserve Bank
of Philadelphia*

peso problem; sovereign risk

Slavi Slavov
*Assistant Professor of Economics,
Pomona College*

> currency board arrangement (CBA); fear of
> floating (coauthor)

James L. Smith
*Cary M. Maguire Chair in Oil and Gas
Management, Department of Finance,
Edwin L. Cox School of Business,
Southern Methodist University*

> Organization of the Petroleum Exporting
> Countries (OPEC)

Pamela J. Smith
*Associate Professor, Department of Applied
Economics, University of Minnesota*

> trade-related investment measures (TRIMs)

Servaas Storm
*Faculty of Technology, Policy and Management,
Department of Economics, Delft University of
Technology*

> import substitution industrialization

Deborah L. Swenson
*Associate Professor of Economics, University of
California, Davis*

> domestic content requirements;
> transfer pricing

Alan O. Sykes
Professor of Law, Stanford Law School

> safeguards

Wendy Takacs
*Professor of Economics, University of Maryland,
Baltimore County*

> nontariff measures; quotas

Evan Tanner
*Senior Economist, Western Hemisphere Division,
International Monetary Fund*

> monetary versus fiscal dominance

Vito Tanzi
*Former Director of the Fiscal Affairs Department,
International Monetary Fund*

> subsidies and financial incentives to foreign
> direct investment

David G. Tarr
*Consultant and former Lead Economist,
Development Research Group, World Bank*

> customs unions

Jonathan R. W. Temple
Professor of Economics, University of Bristol

> international income convergence

Willem Thorbecke
*Associate Professor of Economics, George Mason
University; Senior Fellow, Research Institute
of Economy, Trade, and Industry, Tokyo*

> Louvre Accord; Plaza Accord; twin deficits

Jose L. Tongzon
*Associate Professor of Economics, National University
of Singapore*

> Association of Southeast Asian Nations
> (ASEAN)

Farid Toubal
*Assistant Professor, Paris School of Economics,
University of Paris I, Panthéon-Sorbonne, CNRS,
France*

> intangible assets

John Toye
*Visiting Professor of Economics, St. Antony's College,
University of Oxford*

> United Nations Conference on Trade and
> Development

Dieter M. Urban
*Professor, Department of Business and Economics,
Johannes Gutenberg-Universität*

> knowledge-capital model of the multinational
> enterprise

Diego E. Vacaflores
Assistant Professor, Department of Finance and Economics, Texas State University

foreign direct investment and tax revenues

Hylke Vandenbussche
Professor of International Economics, Université Catholique de Louvain

footloose production

Charles van Marrewijk
Professor of Economics, Erasmus University Rotterdam

absolute advantage; intraindustry trade

Irene van Staveren
Associate Professor of Feminist Development Economics, Institute of Social Studies, The Hague; Professor of Economics and Christian Ethics, Institute for Management Research, Radboud University Nijmegen

gender

Anthony J. Venables
Professor of Economics, University of Oxford

foreign direct investment under monopolistic competition

Matias Vernengo
Assistant Professor of Economics, University of Utah

dependency theory

David Vines
Professor of Economics, Oxford University

World Bank (coauthor)

Peter Walkenhorst
Senior Economist, International Trade Group, World Bank

foreign equity restrictions

Howard J. Wall
Vice President and Regional Economics Advisor, Federal Reserve Bank of St. Louis

common market (coauthor)

Stefanie Walter
Researcher, Center for Comparative and International Studies, Swiss Federal Institute of Technology, Zurich

currency crisis (coauthor)

Joshua C. Walton
PhD Candidate, School of Politics and Economics, Claremont Graduate University

currency crisis (coauthor)

Howard White
Fellow, Institute of Development Studies, University of Sussex

poverty, global

Clas Wihlborg
Fletcher Jones Chair in International Business, Argyros School of Business and Economics, Chapman University

deposit insurance; lender of last resort

Thomas D. Willett
Director of the Claremont Institute for Economic Studies and Horton Professor of Economics, Claremont Graduate University and Claremont McKenna College

contagion (coauthor); currency crisis (coauthor); discipline (coauthor); petrodollars, recycling of (coauthor); sovereign wealth funds (coauthor)

John Williamson
Senior Fellow, Peter G. Peterson Institute for International Economics

band, basket, and crawl (BBC)

John S. Wilson
Lead Economist, Development Research Group, International Trade, World Bank

technical barriers to trade; trade facilitation

Peter Wilson
Independent Scholar

J-curve effect; Marshall-Lerner condition

L. Alan Winters
Professor of Economics, University of Sussex;
Research Fellow and former Program Director of
the Center for Economic Policy Research (CEPR)

   North-South trade

Paul Winters
Associate Professor of Economics, American
University

   agriculture

Kar-yiu Wong
Professor of Economics and Director, Research Center
for International Economics, University
of Washington

   brain drain

Jon Wongswan
Emerging Markets Researcher, International Active
Equities Group, Barclays Global Investors,
San Francisco

   spillovers

Kevin Honglin Zhang
Associate Professor of Economics, Illinois State
University

   foreign direct investment and export
   performance

Laixun Zhao
Professor, Research Institute for Economics and
Business, Kobe University

   unions and foreign direct investment

The Princeton Encyclopedia of the World Economy

■ absolute advantage

A country is said to have an absolute advantage over another country in the production of a good or service if it can produce that good or service (the "output") using fewer *real* resources (like capital or labor, the "inputs"). Equivalently, using the same inputs, the country can produce more output. The concept of absolute advantage can also be applied to other economic entities, such as regions, cities, or firms, but we will focus attention on countries, specifically in relation to their production decisions and international trade flows. The fallacy of equating absolute advantages with cost advantages is a never-ending source of confusion. Deviations between the two are caused by the fact that real resources may receive different remunerations in different countries.

In reaction to the mercantilist literature of the 17th century (which advocated state regulation of trade to promote wealth and growth), a doctrine of free trade emerged at the end of the 18th century, culminating in 1776 in Adam Smith's masterpiece, *An Inquiry into the Nature and Causes of the Wealth of Nations*. Drawing on the work of others, Smith was able to put many different arguments and elements together in a coherent and systematic framework, organized using a few general principles, and thus providing a new way of thinking about political economy (Irwin 1996). Smith thus provided the first *analysis* of economic reasons for advocating a policy of free trade and, according to Joseph A. Schumpeter (1954, 374), "seems to have believed that under free trade all goods would be produced where their absolute costs in terms of labor are lowest."

Smith's arguments can be summarized as follows. First, he points out that regulations favoring one industry draw away real resources from another industry, where they might have been more advantageously employed (opportunity costs). Second, he applies the opportunity cost principle to individuals in a society—for example, by pointing out that the tailor does not make his own shoes (which would cost him a lot of time) but buys them from the shoemaker (who can produce them more efficiently). Each individual is therefore specializing in the production of those goods and services in which he or she has some advantage. Third, Smith applies the same principles of opportunity costs and specialization to international commercial policy and nations. It is better to import goods from abroad where they can be produced more efficiently, because this allows the importing country to focus production on the goods it can itself produce efficiently. The primary (classical) reason for international trade flows is therefore a difference of technology between exporter and importer.

Principle of Absolute Advantage To illustrate the principle of absolute advantage, suppose that there are two countries (the United States and Japan) producing two goods (food and cars), using labor as the only input. Assume that goods can be traded without costs and workers are immobile between the two countries, but mobile between the two sectors within a country. All workers in a country are equally productive. Production technology in Japan differs from that in the United States (see table 1). We assume that Japan requires three units of labor to produce one unit of food, whereas the United States

Table 1
Productivity tables, an example of absolute advantages

	a. Units of labor required to produce one unit of output		b. Units of output produced with one unit of labor	
	food	cars	food	cars
USA	2	8	1/2	1/8
Japan	3	6	1/3	1/6

requires only two units of labor. Similarly, Japan needs six units of labor to produce one car, whereas the United States needs eight units of labor. Since Japan is more efficient in the production of cars and the United States is more efficient in the production of food, Japan has an absolute advantage in the production of cars and the United States has an absolute advantage in the production of food.

To show that specialization of production, coupled with international trade flows according to absolute advantage, can be advantageous, in our example suppose that the United States produces one car less. This frees up eight units of labor, which can now be used to produce $8/2 = 4$ units of food (opportunity cost of car production in the United States). The United States has now produced one car less and four units of food more. Suppose that the United States wants to consume the same number of cars as before. It must then import one car from Japan. To produce this car Japan needs six units of labor. These laborers must come from the food sector, where production therefore drops by $6/3 = 2$ units of food (opportunity costs of car production in Japan). Now note that the total production of cars has been unchanged (one car less in the United States and one car more in Japan), while the total production of food has increased by two units (four units more in the United States and two units less in Japan). These extra units of food reflect the potential gains from specialization if both countries concentrate in the production of the good they produce most efficiently. In principle, both countries can gain: for example, if they exchange three units of food for one car.

Complications and Limitations There are several caveats to the foregoing analysis, some of which we discuss now.

Absence of absolute advantage: The example discusses a situation where one country has an absolute advantage in the production of one good and the other country in the production of another good. It is frequently argued that developing countries may lack the technology to gain an absolute advantage in the production of *any* good, such that they cannot possibly compete on the global market and benefit from free trade (in table 1, for example, if the United States needs four laborers to produce one unit of food). This conclusion is wrong, however, according to David Ricardo's model of comparative advantage (which emphasizes labor as the primary production factor and attributes the costs and benefits of trade to the differences in opportunity costs among countries), since technologically disadvantaged countries can compete on the global market by paying lower wages. It turns out that absolute advantage is neither a necessary nor a sufficient condition for exporting a certain good and gaining from international trade.

More factors of production: In reality, goods are produced using several factors of production simultaneously, such as capital, land, and various types of labor. Usually, goods then cannot be ranked according to absolute advantage as their production in one country requires more of one input and simultaneously less of another input than in another country. These issues are analyzed in the Heckscher-Ohlin (factor abundance) theory of international trade.

Intra- versus interindustry trade: The example discusses interindustry trade, which is the exchange of one type of good (cars) for another type of good (food). Many countries engage in intraindustry trade, the exchange of similar types of goods (e.g., simultaneously exporting and importing car parts). This type of trade is becoming ever more important. It can be based on market power and economies of scale, as analyzed in New Trade Theory.

Absolute Advantage, Income, and Wages Despite the limitations and complications just discussed, absolute advantages (as reflected by differences in technology) *are* important for explaining current international trade flows and differences between countries in terms of income levels and wage rates. Daniel Trefler (1995) systematically analyzes these issues by combining the Heckscher-Ohlin model with technology differences, while taking into consideration the empirically observed home country bias (a consumer preference for domestically produced goods over otherwise identical imports). This combination explains about 93 percent of international trade flows. It also shows that technology differences are largely responsible for the deviations in income levels (and wage rates) between, say, the African countries and the high-income countries of the Organisation for Economic Co-operation and Development. For this reason absolute advantage does retain relevance for understanding the modern world economy.

See also comparative advantage; economies of scale; gains from trade; Heckscher-Ohlin model; intraindustry trade; new trade theory; revealed comparative advantage; Ricardian model; trade and wages

FURTHER READING

Irwin, Douglas A. 1996. *Against the Tide: An Intellectual History of Free Trade*. Princeton, NJ: Princeton University Press. A magnificent overview of the arguments for and against free trade throughout history.

Schumpeter, Joseph A. 1954. *History of Economic Analysis*. 12th printing, 1981. London: Allen and Unwin. Still *the* history of economic analysis.

Smith, Adam. 1776. *An Inquiry into the Nature and Causes of the Wealth of Nations*. Edited by R. H. Campbell and A. S. Skinner. The Glasgow Edition of the Works and Correspondence of Adam Smith 2. Reprint, 1981. Indianapolis, IN: Liberty Press. The starting point of economics as a science, using a coherent system of analysis favoring free trade.

Trefler, Daniel. 1995. "The Case of the Missing Trade and Other Mysteries." *American Economic Review* 85: 1029–46. Ingenious empirical tests of various trade theories with a prominent role for technology differences.

CHARLES VAN MARREWIJK

■ access to medicines

The term *access to medicines* encompasses the array of problems faced by the world's lowest-income inhabitants, who often cannot afford, or do not have access to, medications that could greatly reduce the disease burden under which they suffer. The problems include deficient medical infrastructure, imbalances between prices and ability to pay, and the lack of incentive to develop medicines that would treat diseases endemic to low-income nations.

During the 20th century, numerous technological breakthroughs in pharmaceutical therapy made it possible to cure or at least alleviate most of the diseases that have killed or debilitated millions of people each year. But the ability to purchase those medicines is concentrated in relatively affluent nations, where the vast majority of pharmaceutical sales occur. At the other extreme, roughly 60 percent of the world's population live in nations defined by the United Nations in 2000 as "low income," with per-capita gross national product averaging less than $530 (at prevailing exchange rates) a year in 1998. The World Health Organization (WHO) (2004, 61) estimates that in 1999 those nations made only 2.9 percent of the world's pharmaceutical purchases. The WHO has predicted that by expanding access to available health interventions, and especially essential medicines, 10.5 million lives could be saved annually by the year 2015. Lack of access to medicines and complementary health care in turn perpetuates a vicious spiral: poor health impairs productivity and economic development, while low productivity keeps the citizens of the least-developed nations too poor to afford appropriate health care.

Affordability The medicine access problem has several facets. The overriding problem is inability of individuals to afford medicines. Health insurance is an absent corrective; an estimated 90 percent of the people in developing nations lack such insurance. Inability to pay restricts not only the demand for medicines but also the supply of physicians able to diagnose diseases and recommend appropriate therapies. Nations classified as low income in 1998 by the United Nations had 70 physicians per 100,000 population; those classified as high income, 252. In many instances, the only advice available comes from traditional practitioners whose herbal remedies may work for some indications, but with at best erratic success due to the lack of evidence from controlled experiments. For diseases such as AIDS, malaria, and tuberculosis, carefully administered therapy regimens must be maintained to inhibit the emergence of resistant strains. Counterfeit versions of first-world drugs continue to be a significant problem, in part because third-world health-care authorities lack systematic testing and approval institutions.

In their efforts to combat the burden of disease, health authorities at the WHO and in individual less-developed nations have since 1977 published "model lists" of so-called essential drugs. Drugs have been included on the list in part because of their proven efficacy and partly because of their relatively low cost. Low cost in turn has been achieved by emphasizing generic drugs, that is, those on which patent rights restricting supply to a single firm have expired. Historically, more than 90 percent of drugs on the WHO's model lists have been generics. However, this emphasis was threatened by the emerging epidemics of HIV/AIDS and related opportunistic diseases such as resistant tuberculosis and cryptococcal meningitis. Virtually all of the drugs effective against those diseases were patented and, at least initially, available only at costs for a year's treatment exceeding total average incomes of citizens in low-income nations.

The Trade-Related Aspects of Intellectual Property (TRIPS) agreement culminating the World Trade Organization's (WTO) Uruguay Round Treaty, signed at Marrakech in April 1994 and implemented in 1995, exacerbated this situation. Up to that time, many less-developed nations, emulating some more prosperous countries, were able either to produce or, more likely, import patented drugs because they granted no patent rights on pharmaceutical product inventions. TRIPS required that signatories to the Marrakech treaty begin awarding such patents—within one year for the wealthiest nations, five years for middle-income countries, and ten years (later extended to the year 2015) for the least-developed nations. Transitional provisions also re-quired grants of marketing exclusivity for post-1994 inventions on which initial patent applications were filed. Especially for AIDS and AIDS-related diseases, this posed special problems. Up to that time, the newest and most effective drugs might be available generically from India and other nations that had not awarded pharmaceutical product patents. But as the TRIPS provisions began to bind on India, Brazil, South Africa, and other nations, their ability to continue supplying low-cost generics atrophied.

The combination of TRIPS and the AIDS epidemic precipitated a crisis. Two main solutions emerged. First, at a joint WHO–WTO conference in Høsbjør, Norway, in April 2001, a consensus emerged encouraging the world's leading research-oriented pharmaceutical companies to practice "differential" or "Ramsey" pricing. The companies would charge high prices in rich nations and make life-saving drugs available to consumers in low-income nations at prices approaching marginal cost. From what had been near parity of AIDS drug prices across rich and poor nations (Scherer and Watal 2002), wholesale prices were shown by Lucchini et al. (2003) and the UK Department for International Development (2005, 22) to have plummeted in the least-developed nations, in some cases by as much as 98 percent. One consequence of such discriminatory pricing was the reexport of low-price drugs to high-price nations, but steps to suppress this "parallel trade" were quickly implemented. Donations from multinational pharmaceutical firms to organizations providing health care in less-developed nations—in effect, sales at a zero price—also helped increase access to essential medicines.

Second, because of exceptions written into the original TRIPS agreement, nations were able to threaten or actually implement compulsory licensing of existing or new patents on AIDS and other epidemic disease drugs in order to authorize generic production. Threats of compulsory licensing induced multinational patent holders to reduce sharply the prices of their branded drugs in the third world and enter into voluntary agreements with such nations as Brazil and South Africa to permit generic supply. A limitation in the original TRIPS text was that production under a compulsory license was to be "predominantly for the supply of the [Member's] domestic market." However, many of the world's least-developed nations lacked both the technological know-how and sufficient market scale to produce generics for their own use. A permissive amendment to the TRIPS agreement accepted in August 2003 following a mandate issued at the Doha Round of international trade negotiations in 2002 alleviated this problem. The TRIPS agreement does not require nations formally to report compulsory licensing decrees, and as of 2006, only an AIDS drug license by Thailand to a government entity, minimally controversial under TRIPS, had come to light publicly. The existence of other unreported cases cannot be ruled out. Alternatively, post-2000 price and voluntary license developments may have been sufficient to satisfy the limited ability of low-income nations to distribute drugs effectively.

Incentives for Drug Development Another fundamental problem preventing access to medicines is the lack of innovative drugs targeted specifically toward diseases prevalent only in the third world, for instance, sleeping sickness, Chagas disease, and leishmanisais. Because low-income nations have limited purchasing power, multinational pharmaceutical firms lack demand-based incentives for research and testing on drugs targeted toward the so-called tropical diseases and the resistant strains that continue to evolve. A study for Medicins sans Frontières (2001) revealed that among 1,393 new drug chemical entities introduced into world markets between 1975 and 1999, only 13 (or 15 counting tuberculosis) drugs were indicated for tropical diseases. Also deficient has been the development of vaccines that could *prevent* diseases curable using modern medicines, but at costs too high to be sustained by overstressed third-world medical care providers.

Here too the AIDS crisis played an important role in inducing corrective initiatives. Some large multinational pharmaceutical companies, seeing the problem as a moral challenge, increased research and development (R&D) efforts targeted at third-world diseases and established new laboratories nearer the potential markets. Private philanthropic organiza-

tions such as the Gates Foundation have provided generous subsidies to support R&D on new drugs and vaccines to combat third-world diseases. Their efforts complemented the work of the UN AIDS initiative and similar programs by national governments. In 2005–6, delegates from the world's eight largest market economies (the G-8) approved in principle a program to stimulate the development of vaccines by agreeing to purchase at generous pre-specified prices $3 billion worth (in each category) of new vaccines effective against AIDS, malaria, and tuberculosis. However, as of 2006, the G-8 member nations were tardy in backing their good intentions with actual purchase guarantees and the national budget commitments necessary to implement them.

Progress is being made in increasing the supply of affordably priced medicines to low-income nations, but much remains to be done. Overcoming the remaining barriers to access to medicines could alleviate disease worldwide and contribute to economic development.

See also Agreement on Trade-Related Aspects of Intellectual Property Rights (TRIPS); health and globalization; HIV/AIDS

FURTHER READING

Granville, Brigitte, ed. 2002. *The Economics of Essential Medicines.* London: Royal Institute of International Affairs. A comprehensive collection of relevant articles, with emphasis on the consequences of TRIPS.

Levine, Ruth, Michael Kremer, and Alice Albright. 2005. *Making Markets for Vaccines: Ideas to Action.* Washington, DC: Center for Global Development. Investigates thoroughly how nations could join together to offer advance market commitments providing incentives for the development of new vaccines.

Lucchini, Stephane, et al. 2003. "Decrease in Prices of Antiretroviral Drugs for Developing Countries: From Political 'Philanthropy' to Regulated Markets?" In *Economics of AIDS and Access to HIV/AIDS Care in Developing Countries,* edited by Jean-Paul Moatti et al. Paris: Agence de Recherches sur le Sida, 170–211. Traces fall of AIDS drug prices from 1997 to 2002.

Medicins sans Frontières, Access to Essential Medicines Campaign and Drugs for Neglected Diseases Working

Group. 2001. *Fatal Imbalance: The Crisis in Research and Development for Neglected Diseases*. Geneva: Medicins sans Frontières (September). A careful study of deficient incentives for R&D on diseases prevalent mainly in poor nations.

Scherer, F. M., and Jayashree Watal. 2002. "Post-TRIPS Options for Access to Patented Medicines in Developing Nations." *Journal of International Economic Law* 5(4): 913–39. Prepared for the Høsbjør conference, explores theoretically and empirically the pricing of AIDS drugs in third-world nations and explores income tax incentives for drug donations.

UK Department for International Development. 2005. *Increasing People's Access to Essential Medicines in Developing Countries: A Framework for Good Practice in the Pharmaceutical Industry*. London: UKDID (March). Reviews the broad access problem and summarizes UK initiatives to relieve the problem.

World Health Organization. 2004. *The World Medicines Situation*. Geneva: WHO. An excellent overview with statistical data.

F. M. SCHERER

■ **affiliate**

See foreign direct investment (FDI)

■ **African Caribbean Pacific–European Union (ACP-EU) partnership agreements**

The trade and development relationship between the European Union (EU) and the African, Caribbean, and Pacific (ACP) countries has been shaped by a number of formal treaties and agreements since the end of World War II. The aim of these agreements has been to promote, with EU participation, opportunities for growth and development among the ACP countries by both direct and indirect policy measures. The more direct methods have included development funds, investment loans, and compensatory payments, while indirect methods have centered on trading arrangements and protocols that favor exports from ACP countries in a bid to generate growth. Underpinning these specific aspects, though, has been a more general focus on engendering wider social, political, and economic development as part of an understanding (often referred to as the *acquis*) between the EU and the ACP countries, which reflects the fact that the relationship is not only a trading club.

The Treaty of Rome, which established the European Economic Community (EEC) in 1957, included a section entitled "The Association of the Overseas Countries and Territories." This made specific provisions for the relationship between the EEC and the overseas territories and former colonies of member states under Articles 131 to 136. The association with former colonies of the six members of the EEC was designed "to promote the economic and social development of the countries and territories and to establish close economic relations between them and the Community as a whole" (Article 131, Treaty of Rome). In practice, these arrangements had their greatest effect on the former French colonies in West Africa and the Caribbean. Preferential trading arrangements formed the major part of the association with a commitment to review the policy after five years.

The Yaoundé Conventions The first review produced a new set of arrangements embodied in the first Yaoundé Convention (or Yaoundé I) signed on July 20, 1963, in the Cameroon capital by 18 countries of the Association of African States and Madagascar (AASM) and the six EEC states. Yaoundé I aimed to encourage the development of the AASM countries mainly by allowing preferential treatment of their manufactured exports into the EEC, but with only limited preference for agricultural exports. In return, the EEC was permitted to export limited volumes of manufactures to the AASM with similar duty arrangements. In addition to trade provisions, there was also agreement on technical and financial issues, on rights of establishment that allowed for, among other commercial features, the establishment of companies in associated states, and also on the institutions that would oversee the governing of the convention. The agreement ran from 1964 to the end of 1969.

Countries that were not part of the Yaoundé I sought associate status. Under the Arusha Agreement signed in Tanzania on September 24, 1969, Kenya, Tanzania, and Uganda negotiated associate status with the EEC. This came into force at the same time as the second Yaoundé Convention (Yaoundé II), which was in effect from 1971. While reenforcing the preferential and reciprocal trade arrangements, Yaoundé II also included provision for investment by the EEC in the associated states. Specifically, funds were provided mostly for the European Development Fund (EDF) with a small amount going to the European Investment Bank (EIB) for loan-supported project work. The specific aim was to broaden the relationship between the two groups, from trade policy to wider development areas. The Arusha Agreement only contained trading elements and none of the financial aid offered under Yaoundé II.

From Yaoundé to the ACP In 1975, the developing country signatories to the Yaoundé Conventions formed a new alliance with the 20 Commonwealth countries associated with the United Kingdom (UK). The new body was called the African Caribbean and Pacific (ACP) Group. The terms of this new body were established within the Georgetown Agreement. The main aim was to coordinate negotiations for ACP countries with the EEC, a process that had begun in 1973 as part of a review of Yaoundé II. The negotiations were concluded with the signing on February 28, 1975, of the first Lomé Convention (Lomé I) in Togo, by 46 ACP countries and the then nine EEC Member States.

Lomé I had a number of provisions but the key ones again related to trade. Free access for most ACP exports to the EEC, although unlike Yaoundé II without reciprocal terms, lay at the heart of it. In addition, the agreement introduced specific protocols for sugar, rum, bananas, and beef and veal. In the Sugar Protocol, for example, the EEC agreed to volume import quotas of raw (cane) sugar from ACP producers at a guaranteed minimum price. The protocol reflected the UK's entry into the EEC and its established trading agreements with its former colonies. ACP sugar producers were allocated quotas for exports with the aim of aiding their producers

without harming EEC producers of beet sugar. The other commodities had similar export quota and guaranteed price arrangements, although beef and veal saw refunds of tax at 90 percent on imports.

In addition to these trade arrangements, the convention also provided for a Council of Ministers. This body was drawn from members of the Council and Commission of Ministers for the EEC and representatives from each ACP country, with the presidency alternating between the two groups. The other significant innovation was a change in the nature of EDF financing. The STABEX (shorthand for stabilization of export earnings) scheme aimed to provide stabilizing finance when export earnings fell due to a decline in prices for a producer's main (often primary) exports. This reflected the concerns about volatility in world commodity prices and the impact on exporters and countries' macroeconomic planning and policies. Coupled with further EDF and EIB monies, the convention moved explicit financial aid more prominently into the relationship between the EEC and the ACP, albeit with a continued emphasis on expenditure on infrastructure.

Lomé II was agreed and signed in 1979. Although it did not offer new trading provisions, within its EDF provisions it did introduce SYSMIN (stabilization of export earnings from mining products), a system of loans for helping the mining industries in those countries that relied heavily on exports of minerals for revenue generation, to diversify into other sectors. Lomé III (1984) signaled a shift from direct encouragement of export-led growth to encouragement of self-sufficiency and especially security of food supplies. Rural development was promoted as a means of achieving these goals. Finally, Lomé IV (1990) covered a 10-year period with a five-year review of financial support. However, it also became apparent that wider social issues, such as the environment, women's roles, and diversification of the economy were given much greater prominence as the ACP countries continued to develop. The EU recognized a desire for greater self-determination of policy.

A major review of the Lomé Convention came in 2000. The Cotonou Agreement of 2000 was signed in Benin and built on the Lomé acquis but took a new, longer-term approach to the political, trade, and development aspects of ACP-EU relations. Globalization had appeared to pass many ACP countries by, with their share of foreign investment flows being very small and their trade shares equally limited. Tied to decreasing donor aid, this presented a problem that the Lomé IV had not dealt with. Indeed, compliance with World Trade Organization (WTO) rules meant protective trade arrangements could no longer provide an answer even if they were desired. Instead, focus on poverty reduction via good governance, macroeconomic stability, and new trading arrangements increased. To integrate ACP countries more fully with global markets, the EU liberalized virtually all imports from least-developed countries (LDCs), not just ACP countries, under a General System of Preferences (GSP). The protocols for sugar and beef and veal remained, however. Funding was now via grants totaling 11.3 billion euros and for risk capital, which totaled 2.2 billion euros.

In 2001 the EU concluded its amendment of the GSP and developed its "Everything but Arms" policy. This policy extended duty-free access to all LDC exports apart from arms and munitions, with some restrictions still applying over a longer period for bananas, rice, and sugar. Of the 48 LDCs, 39 were ACP (Cotonou signatory) countries.

The WTO continued to put pressure on the EU to move away from preferential treatment of ACP exports, and in 2002 Economic Partnership Agreements (EPAs) became the focus for ACP-EU trading relationships. The negotiations with regional groupings sought to encourage partnership, regional integration, development, and ultimately integration of the ACP countries into the WTO. EPAs were scheduled to be in place by 2008.

Given the scope, scale, and relative complexity of the various ACP-EU agreements, it is possible to view them as central to a continuing process of different countries working together for mutual benefit. Although not comprehensive in either geographic or economic coverage, ACP-EU agreements have played a major role in shaping trading policies for many countries and have offered possible options for others to follow.

See also European Union; international trade and economic development; World Trade Organization

FURTHER READING

European Commission External Relations Directorate. http://europa.eu/scadplus/leg/en/s05032.htm. This site provides a wealth of materials relating to the establishment and development of EU-ACP trade agreements as well as links to other helpful documents.

Secretariat of the African, Caribbean and Pacific Group of States. http://www.acpsec.org/. The ACP site offers a number of useful resources that provide greater detail on the trade agreements with the EU, as well as giving an overview of the structure of the ACP group and how it operates.

C. W. MORGAN

■ African Development Bank

See regional development banks

■ African Union

Open to all countries in the African continent, the African Union (AU) is an organization designed to foster political and economic cooperation and development among its member countries. To such ends, it stands ready to address any and all issues relevant to state building, security, and economic development and integration among countries on the African continent. Hence the AU can contribute to factors deemed essential to greater integration of the continent in the world economy. It was officially launched on July 9, 2002, replacing the Organization of African Unity (OAU), whose charter was signed on May 25, 1963, with an original membership of 33 countries; the AU has 53 members. The headquarters are in Addis Ababa, Ethiopia, although the various organs can be located in other member states; for example, the Pan-African Parliament is in Midrand, South Africa.

Political Stability and Security In order to advance political stability and security, the AU focuses on conflict resolution within and between states, peer review among the African states to facilitate state building and the democratization process, and building solidarity to increase the leverage exercised by African countries at the international level. Still, the AU has found it difficult to speed up democratic transition in the continent; impediments to this transition include the manipulation of institutions by elites or breakdowns in the democratic political process because of ethnic conflicts or political fragmentation. The AU has also been handicapped in dealing with the resolution of conflicts in which the sources of conflict are deep seated and the combatants well armed.

With few exceptions, the AU has supported the territorial integrity of the African states since independence from colonialism, as well as noninterference in the internal affairs of those states. Enshrined in the Constitutive Act of the AU are the "condemnation and rejection" of "political assassinations," "subversive activities," and "unconstitutional changes of governments." Moreover, the AU has pronounced resolutely in favor of human rights. Thus one of the tenets of the Constitutive Act is the "right of the union to intervene in a Member State pursuant to a decision of the Assembly in respect of grave circumstances, namely war crimes, genocide and crimes against humanity."

Economic Integration The economic integration program of the AU is contained in the June 1991 Treaty Establishing the African Economic Community (AEC) signed in Abuja, Nigeria. That treaty has been operational since May 1994. The plan contained in the treaty calls for the AEC to reach fruition after a period of 34 to 40 years from 1994. The consequence, among other things, would be a single domestic market and a Pan-African Economic and Monetary Union, a single African Central Bank, and a single African Currency. A number of regional economic communities (RECs) operate under the aegis of the AEC, as part of the transition to full, continentwide union, namely, the Arab Maghreb Union (AMU), the Economic Community of the Central African States (ECCAS), the Common Market for Eastern and Southern Africa (COMESA), the Southern African Development Community (SADC), and the Economic Community of West African States (ECOWAS).

Progress in economic integration has been hampered by certain political and economic strains, overlapping membership among the RECs, competing subregional groupings within RECs, and a lack of clear commitment to integration among the populations and the political leadership. Political difficulties have included personal animosity among heads of states and governments; ideological differences among leaders; deep-seated disputes such as that over the Western Sahara (independence for a Sahrawi Arab Democratic Republic), in the case of the AMU; and regional conflicts, as in the Great Lakes area for ECCAS. But prospects are improving in these respects: Increasing democratization and acceptance of market solutions to economic problems are reducing ideological differences. Conflicts involving many states simultaneously are diminishing in number and those that remain are being better handled by the AU. Moreover, proponents of integration have been working hard to ensure that institutions and organizations of regional economic communities can function in spite of temporary personal hostilities in high political circles.

There is need to rationalize membership of RECs by encouraging countries to join only one. Also, subregional organizations with the same goal of economic integration exist. The best example is the East African Community (EAC), the three members of which are also members of either COMESA or SADC. In addition, the Francophone African countries are apparently happy with their monetary union arrangements. But they have been expanding their cooperation objectives in the direction of general economic integration, despite their membership in ECOWAS and ECCAS.

Economic obstacles to integration include (1) fear of a loss of national sovereignty over macroeconomic policy to some union authority or body; (2) disagreements over the nature and content of protection of local industries through tariffs and nontariff barriers, which reduce certain imports of commodities and services from outside an REC; and (3) concern about unequal distribution of gains and losses of REC membership. The RECs continue to make progress toward resolving these issues.

For instance, a common external tariff is an important objective of the RECs, and the structure of a tariff system has important implications for the protection bestowed on different commodities. If a simple rule were established, such as equal protection for all commodities, then the determination of tariff rates could be left to technical experts to decide. But to assist infant industry and foster industrial development, African countries want differential protection. Given the economic structure and the state of development of the various countries concerned, different schedules of tariff rates have dissimilar implications for comparative advantage of the countries. Hence, such considerations seriously affect discussions of the detailed tariff schedules to be put into effect.

Many in the continent fear that gains to countries from economic unions will be positively related to the degree of their economic development and/or the size of their domestic economies. The allegedly "unfair" distribution of gains and losses is widely believed to have been at the root of the breakup of the first EAC, where it was felt that Kenya's industrialization was greatly helped but, in the process, Tanzania's may have been adversely affected. An attempt to use differential intraunion tariffs—designated transfer taxes—could not alleviate the problems, at least not to the satisfaction of Tanzania.

In general, many want some kind of internal (intraunion) tariff structure that protects some national domestic production activities from direct competition within an REC. But once the principle is accepted (and applied) that the location of industries among countries should be determined in a world of open competition and free mobility of all factors of production including labor, rather than in an arena of negotiated industrial planning buttressed by restricted mobility of factors, especially labor, the case for transfer taxes becomes weak.

A challenge would still remain as to how to balance such a market-oriented approach to the location of industries with permitting selective intervention of governments for economic development of the countries, as deemed useful by all the countries. The difficulty would be compounded by the need to observe certain macroeconomic constraints set by the union as a whole—for example, limits on government budget deficits and on government debt in relation to gross domestic product.

Differences in taxation systems and structures also continue to engender issues of unequal gains and losses. In particular, countries have different reliance on import taxes as sources of government revenue. This fact has slowed down reduction of intraunion tariffs, since a formula to compensate those who will lose tax revenue from large intraunion tariff reductions is not easy to negotiate. Thus countries realize they need to reform their tax systems to lessen their dependence on import taxes if substantial and rapid intraunion tariff reductions are to occur in practice. The attempts of countries to reform their tax systems and to move toward greater reliance on income, profits, and value-added taxes should be of help in this regard.

One theme in the integration debate in the African continent is the degree to which African leaders are committed to full economic integration in the foreseeable future. For many of the countries, intraregional trade is very small in relation to extraregional trade, and the countries in each of the regions often produce similar goods. Hence countries sometimes do not feel an urgent need for a common market, given the widespread belief that integration would not yield substantial economic benefits for some time.

Still, every single leader of the countries voices the view that, in time, the benefits of integration will be substantial, as the effective size of domestic markets will greatly enlarge, so that technological economies of scale can be realized and the returns to investment enhanced. Hence it is along these lines that the most fervent proponents of integration have argued their case. Those who prefer a slower pace are content to push now for (1) promotion of greater intraregional trade, employing the instrument of a common external tariff, probably supplemented by some form of transfer tax or *taxe de coopération regionale*, until full labor mobility becomes socially and politically feasible; (2) cooperation in infrastructure and industrial "regional" projects; and (3) some harmonization of policies (especially macroeconomic) as feasible. This could be followed, in the eyes of the gradualists, by some form of monetary union. Only later, when mass support for integration is strong and ideological obstacles are minor, according to this perspective, should full integration be pursued.

Governance and the African Peer Review Mechanism The AU aims at improving *governance* in African countries, in a context of enhanced country *ownership* of policymaking. In 2001, the AU launched the Millennium Partnership for the African Recovery Program (MAP). It was billed as a pledge by African leaders to take decisive steps to improve governance, reduce poverty, and enhance economic growth of their countries. In particular, it claimed that a new crop of leaders was emerging in Africa committed to democracy and the integration of their countries into the world economy. It called for "a new relationship" with the international community, especially the industrial countries: African countries would take charge of their own destiny, and the rest of the international community was called on to make a concerted effort to enhance resource flows to the continent via "improvements" in aid, trade, and debt relationships. Several goals were specified, including most notably achieving a 7 percent average annual growth rate of gross domestic product over the following 15 years. Among the "policy thrusts" to achieve the objectives would be negotiating "a new partnership" with the industrialized countries and multilateral organizations. African "ownership, leadership, and accountability" were thus highlighted as central elements of the MAP. The African peoples were henceforth going to set and direct their agendas and shape their own destinies. This, then, is the idea of the New Partnership for Africa's Development (NEPAD).

Within the NEPAD framework, the African countries have instituted the African Peer Review Mechanism (APRM). Participating countries will do self-assessments, using the services of domestic autonomous bodies and individuals who in turn involve business and civil society groups throughout the countries. The governments will then draw up programs of action to address weaknesses identified in the self-assessments in the areas of political governance, economic governance, corporate governance, and socioeconomic governance. Review teams of African experts will visit the countries to assess the integrity of the self-assessment exercise and make recommendations, including on the action plans of the governments. Future expert teams will visit to review progress in implementing the action plans. Central in this arrangement will be a panel of eminent persons of the continent, overseeing the APRM processes to ensure their integrity and guiding the preparation of the country reports drafted mainly by the experts to be presented to the African Peer Review Forum. This forum comprises heads of state and government of participating countries (the "peers").

If high and transparent standards are maintained, the APRM can be an effective means of separating those African countries committed to good policies from the rest, because only those countries whose leaders are committed to implementing good policies will want to have their progress continuously reviewed and made known to the global community. In this respect, the APRM could address a major credibility problem: Africa as a region is considered high-risk for investors, and the credit ratings of countries within the region are adversely affected simply by their being there. The APRM can contribute to separation of African countries into those with good policy environments and those without. In addition, if the reports get widely circulated within the continent, and especially in those countries that have chosen not to participate, the APRM will help provide essential information to potential actors in civil society.

Moreover, if the APRM is to have any effect on NEPAD, and especially influence the aid and debt relationships, it would be important that it become credible among aid donors, who then allow it transparently to influence their aid policies. Those of the international community interested in providing aid to support good policies may want to see evidence that the APRM is influencing governance in the right direction, for recent research in the social sciences has concluded that good policies emerge exogenously, when countries own such policies and voluntarily adopt them.

Future of the African Union The AU is poised to have an enhanced, though still limited, role in the world economy in the foreseeable future. Its efforts are bringing peace, political stability, and democratization to African states. Peace and political stability are good for economic growth and democratization improves governance. But good political leadership remains elusive and this ultimately is the route by which the political regime has its greatest influence on economic growth. The AU is not likely to have much influence on political leadership in individual African countries. Economic integration also will proceed more slowly than envisaged by official AU pronouncements. But economic cooperation will accelerate, leading to faster infrastructure development, policy harmonization within the regional economic communities, and more efficient and development-oriented industrial, agricultural, and service projects. Moreover, in arenas such as the International Monetary Fund, the World Bank, and the World Trade Organization, African countries more frequently will speak with one coherent voice under the aegis of the AU.

See also Common Market for Eastern and Southern Africa (COMESA); Economic Community of West African States (ECOWAS); European Union; regionalism

FURTHER READING

African Union. 2003. "African Peer Review Mechanism: Organization and Processes." Addis Ababa, Ethiopia: African Union. Downloadable from http://www.nepad.org/2005/files/documents/48.pdf. Describes the APRM processes.

El-Agraa, Ali M. 2004. "The Enigma of African Economic Integration." *Journal of Economic Integration* 19 (1): 19–45. The paper critically examines the aims of the AU, arguing that they were not carefully thought out.

Johnson, Omotunde E. G. 1995. "Regional Integration in Sub-Saharan Africa." *Journal of European Integration* 18 (2–3): 201–34. Discusses the central themes of debate on economic integration in sub-Saharan Africa.

———. 2004. "How Will Good Economic Policy Environments Emerge in Africa?" *Journal of Policy Reform* 7 (3): 151–64. Argues that the underlying problem of the policy environments in Africa can be found in weak societal demand for good economic policies and a lack of exogenous constraints to make it in the self-interest of political elites to pursue good policies even without domestic demand pressures.

Murithi, Timothi. 2005. *The African Union: Pan-Africanism, Peacebuilding, and Development.* Aldershot, UK: Ashgate. Analyzes the challenges faced by the African Union in achieving its objectives, arguing that the African Union is another manifestation of Pan-Africanism.

OMOTUNDE E. G. JOHNSON

■ **agglomeration**

See New Economic Geography

■ **agglomeration and foreign direct investment**

The spatial clustering of foreign direct investment (FDI) is clearly visible in the location of multinationals investing in the United States, the European Union, China, and other regions. This agglomeration is at least partly the result of policy, as in China's special economic zones, but spatial concentration is also characteristic of domestic firms and of FDI in economies with few controls. These observations suggest that market forces, as well as policy, lead to clustering.

That new establishments tend to go to the same locations as earlier entrants suggests that productivity rises with the level of economic activity, especially as firms often must pay higher land prices to locate in clusters. If such productivity-enhancing effects, or agglomerative economies, exist and spill over to domestic activities, a case may be made for government incentives to multinationals to induce local affiliate production. Indeed, dozens of countries favor FDI through tax breaks and subsidies. Through these incentives, governments hope to begin a self-reinforcing process whereby subsidized early entrants attract additional investment.

To better design such policies, researchers have sought evidence that agglomerative economies exist and, if they do, the extent of their benefits to local productive factors. Location-choice studies seek to measure the attractiveness of local characteristics for foreign investors and thus provide a way to estimate the self-reinforcing power of FDI. Virtually all location-choice studies find that the existing stock of foreign investment is a significant predictor of the location a multinational will choose for new local affiliates. However, most countries receive a relatively small number of new multinational affiliates in a given year and for these projects there is often limited information, constraining our ability to identify the specific sources of agglomerative economies.

Head and Ries (1996) observe a relatively large number of investment projects, 931 equity joint ventures in 54 Chinese cities from 1984 to 1991. Their study is noteworthy for its careful modeling of the agglomerative process, emphasizing local input sharing as the source of positive firm spillovers. Using conditional logit analysis to estimate the likelihood that a particular city is chosen as the investment site, Head and Ries find that agglomerative economies greatly magnify the direct impact of government incentives. Their simulation analysis suggests that two-thirds of the gains from incentives can be attributed to the self-reinforcing nature of earlier investments. Not all locations gained equally, however, as cities considered attractive for other reasons, such as infrastructure and industrial base, gained the most. Similarly, Devereux, Griffith, and Simpson (2007) find that firms are less responsive to government subsidies in areas where there are fewer established plants in their industry.

Evidence that past investment increases the likelihood of new investment does not necessarily imply the existence of agglomerative economies. Agglomeration arises because there are benefits to locating near similar firms and because certain locations have natural advantages—features of a location that are independent of firm location decisions. A common example of how natural advantages influence location choice is the North American steel industry, which concentrated in the Great Lakes region largely because of the location of iron ore and coal deposits. In measuring the extent of agglomerative economies, researchers confront an identification problem: Are firms choosing a common location because its inherent characteristics make them more productive or are they more productive because they have all chosen the same location?

Head and Ries (1996) try to separate the roles played by natural advantages and agglomerative economies in two ways. First, they include in their logit analysis a set of variables that attempt to control for local characteristics that influence firm productivity, particularly infrastructure. Second, they allow for spatially correlated errors by including provincial fixed effects. These two approaches are standard in the literature, and data limitations often make it difficult to do more to avoid bias caused by omitted local characteristics or endogeneity. For example, it is often impossible to include fixed effects at the same geographic scale as the unit of location choice (e.g., city fixed effects in the Head and Ries study) because they cannot be estimated for regions that received no investment. However, to fully control for all features of a location that attract investment is impossible, and even in the most careful studies omitted variables likely remain a problem.

Some studies have tried to assess the relative attractiveness of various kinds of prior investment for new entrants. Examining Japanese investment in the United States electronics industry from 1980 to 1998, Chung and Song (2004) ask whether firms agglomerate with their competitors or with their own prior investments. They find that firms tend to colocate only with their own prior investments, with the exception of firms that have little of their own experience, who do tend to colocate with competitors.

More recent work emphasizes the role of trade costs and market access as an alternative explanation for FDI clustering. Head and Mayer (2004) develop a theoretical model in which firms prefer to locate where demand is highest and serve smaller markets by exporting. They confront the data with this hypothesis, measuring market potential by a term that weights demand in all locations by its distance from the proposed investment site. Head and Mayer use standard logit techniques to analyze the European regions chosen as the sites of 452 Japanese investments. They decompose existing investment in each region into three firm counts distinguished by their relatedness to the new entrant: domestic establishments in the same industry, Japanese affiliates in the same industry, and Japanese affiliates with the same parent or network. They find that all three measures of prior investment have a large and positive influence on the likelihood that a region will be chosen by a new entrant, with this effect larger the closer the relations between firms. Thus there are strong agglomeration effects even when controls for market potential are included in the analysis.

An important issue for policy is whether domestic productivity is enhanced by the presence of foreign-owned firms. Most productivity-spillover studies are of specific industries or are case studies, both of which are limited as a guide to policy. Haskel, Pereira, and Slaughter (2007) offer evidence on domestic spillovers from FDI using a plant-level panel of all UK manufacturing firms from 1973 to 1999. Several previous studies using plant-level data find a negative or insignificant effect of industry-level FDI on local productivity. The UK data are unique in that they cover the whole of manufacturing in a developed country. Haskel, Pereira, and Slaughter estimate plant-level productivity and regress it on industry-level FDI, controlling for inputs and the level of competition. They estimate that a 10-percentage-point increase in foreign presence in a UK industry raises the total factor productivity of that industry's domestic plants by about 0.05 percent. They compare the value of these estimated spillover effects to per-job incentives offered in spe-

cific cases and find that these expenditures outweigh the benefits.

Haskel, Periera, and Slaughter (2007) use a variety of methods to deal with identification problems. In addition to explaining variation in gross output, they time-difference the data, explaining the change in output as a function of changes in inputs and foreign industry presence. This method accounts for plant-specific effects. The authors also include time, industry, and region fixed effects in their regression analysis. They also worry about the possibility that changes in industry FDI levels are correlated with changes in domestic productivity, and use instrumental variable techniques to minimize endogeneity bias. Their findings provide the strongest evidence to date that foreign investment does raise domestic productivity, but more work is needed before we have a clear guide to policy.

In sum, locations are more attractive the larger the existing stock of foreign investment, especially when the existing investments are by firms that are closely related (same industry, nationality, or parent firm). Government incentives are a significant determinant of multinational affiliate location choice but incentives are most effective when a location is desirable for other reasons. Although recent evidence suggests that foreign-owned firms enhance the productivity of local establishments, the value of these domestic spillovers appear to be less than the incentives used to attract foreign investment.

See also location theory; New Economic Geography; technology spillovers

FURTHER READING

Chung, Wilbur, and Jaeyong Song. 2004. "Sequential Investment, Firm Motives, and Agglomeration of Japanese Electronics Firms in the United States." *Journal of Economics and Management Strategy* 13 (3): 539–60. For the location choice of experienced firms, own prior investments matter more than competitors' investments.

Devereux, Michael P., Rachel Griffith, and Helen Simpson. 2007. "Firm Location Decisions, Regional Grants, and Agglomeration." *Journal of Public Economics* 91 (3–4): 413–35. Firms are less responsive to subsidies where there is little own-industry investment.

Haskel, Jonathan E., Sonia C. Pereira, and Matthew J. Slaughter. 2007. "Does Inward Foreign Direct Investment Boost the Productivity of Domestic Firms?" *Review of Economics and Statistics* 89 (3): 482–96. FDI raises domestic productivity.

Head, Keith, and Thierry Mayer. 2004. "Market Potential and the Location of Japanese Investment in the European Union." *Review of Economics and Statistics* 86 (4): 959–72. Prior investments matter more the closer the relations between firms.

Head, Keith, and John Ries. 1996. "Inter-City Competition for Foreign Investment: Static and Dynamic Effects of China's Incentive Areas." *Journal of Urban Economics* 40 (1): 38–60. Agglomeration economies magnify impact of incentives.

Rosenthal, Stuart S., and William C. Strange. 2006. "Evidence on the Nature and Sources of Agglomeration Economies." In *Handbook of Regional and Urban Economics*, vol. 4, edited by J. V. Henderson and J. F. Thisse. Amsterdam: Elsevier, 2119–72. A detailed and clear exposition of the sources and nature of agglomerative economies and a thorough review of evidence based on domestic investment.

MARY E. LOVELY

■ Agreement on Agriculture

The Uruguay Round Agreement on Agriculture (URAA) came into effect in 1995 as a part of the Marrakesh Agreement that established the World Trade Organization (WTO). Contained in Annex IA of the Marrakesh Agreement, the URAA both modifies and greatly elaborates on those Articles of the General Agreement on Tariffs and Trade (GATT) that specifically dealt with agricultural trade by specifying significant constraints on government behavior in this area. The scope of the URAA covers all agricultural products (defined as products in Chapters 1–24 of the Harmonized System of tariff headings, excluding fish and fish products but including cotton, wool, hides, flax, hemp, and a few other products as specified in Annex 1). The agreement, by internal reference, also includes the country schedules that were appended to the WTO Treaty (Articles 3.1, 4.1, and 6.1). These schedules contained maximum permitted levels for export subsidies and for certain types of domestic subsidies, as well as commitments for the reduction of "bound" tariffs (tariff levels that cannot be exceeded without negotiating compensation for effected exporters).

The central elements of the URAA are often referred to as the three "pillars"—market access, domestic support, and export competition. In all three areas, new rules and reductions in trade barriers form a comprehensive framework for the regulation of measures that restrict trade in agricultural products.

Market access rules include the conversion of all nontariff import barriers (quotas and restrictive licenses) to tariffs (Article 4.2), and a footnote to Article 4.2 specifies some of the nontariff measures that are prohibited. Moreover, it was agreed that tariff levels were to be bound and that tariff rate quotas (TRQs, or quantities that can be imported at a zero or low tariff) were to be established to maintain market access as tariffication (replacement of nontariff barriers with tariffs) took place. These TRQs were to represent "current access" in cases of existing trade or a "minimum access" of 3 percent of domestic consumption (rising to 5 percent over the implementation period) in cases where there were no imports in the base period. Tariffs were to be reduced from the base period (1986–90) by an (unweighted) average of 36 percent, with a minimum cut of 15 percent for each tariff line, over a six-year period (1995–2000). In addition, the agreement established a special safeguard regime that countries could use to counter import surges or price drops in markets in which they had newly established tariffs (Article 5).

Domestic support was defined to include payments to farmers in addition to the transfers from consumers through border policies. These included deficiency payments, direct income supplements, administrative price systems, and subsidies for agricultural research and government advisory programs for farmers for conservation compliance, and for other programs that benefited farmers directly. These elements of domestic support were put into three categories, which have become known as the Amber Box, the Blue Box, and the Green Box.

Amber Box measures were those tied to output or input prices or to current output levels. These were to be reduced by 20 percent (in aggregate) relative to the base period (1986–90) subject to de minimis amounts that were excluded from the commitment. The Blue Box contained subsidies that were tied to supply control programs: such subsidies were regarded as less obviously output-increasing. There was no reduction obligation for Blue Box policies, but such subsidies were restricted to payments based on fixed acreage and yield or paid on a maximum of 85 percent of production (Article 6.5). Green Box subsidies were defined (in Annex 2) as those unrelated to price and output ("decoupled"), which included research and extension, payments designed to compensate farmers for the cost of compliance with environmental regulations, and domestic food assistance programs. Both the general criteria (that they be provided from public funds and not act as price supports) and the specific criteria for each type of subsidy identified have to be met. Those subsidies that qualified as Green Box payments were not constrained, though they had to be notified by governments to the WTO Committee on Agriculture.

The domestic support commitments were implemented by means of a calculation of the Total Aggregate Measure of Support (Base AMS) (Article 6) for the base period. This included market price support given by administered prices (calculated by a price gap relative to a reference price), nonexempt direct payments, and other subsidies. Exemptions included the Blue Box and Green Box subsidies and a de minimis amount of 5 percent of the value of production for non-product-specific subsidies and 5 percent of the value of the output of an individual commodity for product-specific payments. The reduction commitments were applied to the Base AMS to give the annual commitment levels included in the country schedules, and each year the Current Total AMS is compared to this commitment.

The rules regarding export competition included a prohibition on new export subsidies (Article 8) and a reduction of existing subsidies by both volume and expenditure. A list of export subsidy practices that are covered is given in Article 9.1. Following the agreed modalities, country schedules were drawn up that provided for subsidy reductions relative to the base period of 36 percent by expenditure and 21 percent by quantity subsidized. In addition, rules were made more explicit with regard to food aid (Article 10.4), and countries agreed to negotiate limits on export credit guarantees (government underwriting of sales to purchasers that might lack creditworthiness) (Article 10.2).

To provide for "special and differential treatment" for developing countries, the level of reductions for tariffs and subsidies was set at two-thirds of that of developed countries, and the period of transition was extended from 6 to 10 years (i.e., 1995–2004). Developing countries were also allowed to exempt de minimis subsidies of up to 10 percent of product value for product-specific payments and 10 percent of total agricultural production for non-product-specific payments. In addition, certain additional categories of both domestic support (Article 6.2) and export subsidies (Article 9.4) were allowed. In the case of least-developed countries, no reduction commitments were required (Article 15.2). These least-developed countries are defined as the 48 countries eligible for World Bank/International Development Association assistance, and developing country status is self-declared.

In addition to the three pillars, the URAA mandated the formation of an Agricultural Committee (Article 17), charged with the monitoring of adherence to the agreement. Countries were to notify the committee in a timely fashion of their subsidy levels and any new subsidies that were introduced. Notifications have lapsed, however, and some major countries have not notified beyond the year 2001. The Agriculture Committee became the locus for new negotiations on the continuation of trade reform, meeting in special session.

In addition, the URAA provided a degree of shelter for domestic programs through a "Peace Clause" (Article 13) that limited the scope for the challenge of agricultural subsidies under the Agreement on Subsidies and Countervailing Measures. The Peace Clause was to operate for a period of three years after the implementation period; it expired in 2003.

A further innovation in the URAA was the inclusion of a clause (Article 20) that mandated a continuation of the process of reductions in support and protection. To this end, there were to be new negotiations by the end of the period of transition (in effect, before 2000). Negotiations did indeed start in March 2000, and were incorporated in the Doha Development Agenda (DDA) at the Doha Ministerial in November 2001. The DDA talks were suspended in July 2006 and revived in January 2007.

The need for the development of new rules for agricultural trade in the Uruguay Round reflected both the unsatisfactory nature of the constraints incorporated in the GATT articles and the "disarray" that had characterized these markets for decades. The three GATT articles that had caused the most conflict were Article XI, which prohibits nontariff measures; Article XVI (as modified in 1955), which limits export subsidies; and Article XX, which permits the use of trade barriers in support of a range of domestic health and safety measures.

The part of Article XI that was considered unsatisfactory was the clause (Article XI.2(c)(i)) that allowed an exception to the prohibition of nontariff trade barriers in cases where the domestic production of an agricultural product was subject to supply control. Many countries had relied on this clause to restrict imports by quantitative trade barriers when domestic markets were being managed. As it was difficult to monitor the extent to which the domestic supply control was effective, exporters of the products concerned claimed that the import restrictions were in effect the dominant policy rather than just an adjunct to help reinforce the domestic production limits. Examples were quotas on Canadian dairy and poultry imports and those imposed by the United States under Section 22 of the Agricultural Adjustment Act (as amended), which mandated quantitative restrictions on imports of a number of goods when domestic programs were "materially interfered with" by imports.

Another complication related to Article XI was whether a "variable levy" (a tariff that changed fre-quently depending on the level of import prices, so as to stabilize domestic markets) was an "ordinary customs duty." If not, then it would have been constrained by Article XI. The European Economic Community (EEC, later the European Union, EU) had built its Common Agricultural Policy on such an import policy instrument. So the question as to whether the EEC was acting within the limits of the GATT was continually raised by exporting countries—though it was never resolved.

In the case of export subsidies, the problems revolved around the ambiguous nature of Article XVI. Though the original GATT article subjected both primary and manufactured product export subsidies to the same notification and consultation procedures, in 1955 it was agreed to add an explicit prohibition on export subsidies on manufactured goods. Agricultural export subsidies were constrained only by the obligation not to use such subsidies to capture "more than an equitable share" of world markets. Successive GATT panels failed to come up with a satisfactory definition of this concept, and agricultural export subsidies in effect escaped any discipline.

The problems that had arisen in the application of Article XX centered on the difficulty posed by the need to distinguish between those measures that were legitimate and effective regulations to protect against disease and those that were largely inspired by the desire to protect the economic interest of domestic producers. The clarification of Article XX was addressed by the Sanitary and Phytosanitary (SPS) Agreement, which was complementary to the URAA. By requiring risk assessment in the case of all health and safety regulations related to trade in plants and animals, the SPS Agreement created a greater degree of accountability. Regulations that are clearly motivated by economic rather than health protection can now be (and have been) challenged in the WTO.

The URAA has rendered the provisions in Article XI regarding supply control moot, as quantitative import restrictions are now prohibited. Similarly, the variable levy is explicitly included in the list of import barriers that are not allowed. By banning new export subsidies and including existing subsidies in schedules to be reduced, the URAA has largely resolved the issue of the "exception" for primary products. And the constraints on domestic support have had the effect of restricting the ability of countries to reproduce by domestic subsidies the protection levels previously granted by reduced tariffs and export subsidies. Thus the rule changes have to a large extent met the need to incorporate agricultural trade in a rules-based trade system.

The impact that the URAA has had on individual countries varies greatly. All countries converted nontariff barriers to tariffs and bound those tariffs—with the sole exception of rice quotas in Japan and Korea, which were allowed as temporary exceptions. Developing countries were allowed to declare "ceiling bindings" in place of product-by-product calculations of tariff equivalents, however. These ceiling bindings were commonly set at levels up to 100 percent or more, and thus had little impact on the actual level of tariffs used and the degree of market access. Tariffication had more impact in developed countries, where the quantitative restrictions were usually associated with sensitive products. In these cases the degree of market opening depended on the size of the TRQ agreed upon and the administration of that quota. Many countries considered the increased trade generated by the market access provisions of the URAA disappointing, and this increased the pressure for substantial market opening in the Doha Round.

The constraints on export subsidies have generally been successful, in that countries have appeared to stay within their scheduled limits for those subsidies included in their schedules. WTO panels have found (notably in the Canada dairy, U.S. cotton, and EU sugar cases), however, that there have been subsidies that were not included in the schedules, and the panels have declared these to be prohibited. Domestic subsidy constraints have also been generally respected, mainly because domestic policies in developed countries have tended to switch away from Amber Box subsidies. But there is continued concern that such subsidies cause considerable harm to other countries, and this has been confirmed by the panel in the U.S. cotton case.

Agreeing on disciplines on agricultural trade (as well as ending the quota system for textile imports) was a major step in completing the agenda embodied in the GATT of bringing all sectors in goods trade under the same regime. All agricultural tariffs are now bound, though they remain at a level several times higher than for manufactured goods. Nontariff barriers are no longer used, though TRQs still restrict market access. Though it does not directly mandate the type of policy instruments countries can use, the URAA has in effect provided a template for domestic policymakers: if they use WTO-compatible policies for their farm sectors they will be free from the constraints of the URAA. Export subsidies are still used but in much more restricted ways. The agricultural talks in the DDA have attempted to build on the achievements of the URAA.

See also agricultural trade negotiations; agriculture; Doha Round; multilateral trade negotiations; tariff rate quotas; Uruguay Round; World Trade Organization

FURTHER READING

Josling, Timothy E., Stefan Tangermann, and Thorald K. Warley. 1996. *Agriculture in the GATT*. Basingstoke, UK: Macmillan. A fuller account of the treatment of agriculture in the GATT.

Organisation for Economic Co-operation and Development (OECD). 2001. *The Uruguay Round Agreement on Agriculture: An Evaluation of its Implementation in OECD Countries*. Paris: OECD. A useful study on the implementation of the URAA.

World Trade Organization. 1996. *The Results of the Uruguay Round of Multilateral Trade Negotiations: The Legal Texts*. Geneva: WTO. The full text of the URAA and other agreements.

———. 2000a. "Domestic Support." Background Paper by the Secretariat. G/AG/NG/S/1 (13 April). Geneva: WTO. A useful paper on the compliance of countries with domestic support commitments.

———. 2000b. "Export Subsidies." Background Paper by the Secretariat. G/AG/NG/S/5 (11 May). Geneva: WTO. A useful paper on the compliance of countries with export subsidy commitments.

TIM JOSLING

■ Agreement on Trade-Related Aspects of Intellectual Property Rights (TRIPS)

The Agreement on Trade-Related Aspects of Intellectual Property Rights (TRIPS) has become the most important and far-reaching international accord in the field of intellectual property. It establishes workable global standards of protection and enforcement for virtually all of the most important intellectual property rights, such as patents, copyrights and related rights, and trademarks, in a single agreement. As such, it has major implications for knowledge-based industries seeking to trade profitably in many different countries.

History Strictly speaking, TRIPS is annex 1C of the Agreement Establishing the World Trade Organization, which was the main outcome of the Uruguay Round trade negotiations held under the auspices of the General Agreement on Tariffs and Trade (GATT). It resulted from a considerable amount of lobbying by certain industries that were keen to expand their activities in emerging economies where intellectual property protection was either lacking or was weakly enforced.

The first attempt to frame intellectual property as an issue to be discussed in wider trade negotiations was made by a group of trademark-holding firms organized as the Anticounterfeiting Coalition, which lobbied for the inclusion of an anticounterfeiting code in the 1973–79 GATT Tokyo Round. Although this initial attempt was unsuccessful, the copyright, patent, and semiconductor industries decided during the early 1980s to frame the lack of effective intellectual property rights protection in overseas markets as a trade-related issue *and* a problem for the U.S. economy that the government ought to respond to. By the time the contracting parties of the GATT met in Punta del Este, Uruguay, in September 1986 to launch another trade round, U.S. corporations had forged a broad cross-sectoral alliance and developed a coordinated strategy.

For those seeking high standards of intellectual property protection and enforcement throughout the world by way of the GATT, the strategy had three advantages. First, if successful, the strategy would globalize these standards much more rapidly than could be achieved through the conventions administered by the World Intellectual Property Organization (WIPO). This is because it allowed for the possibility of including all the main rights in a single agreement, which could also incorporate by reference provisions of the major WIPO conventions. Also, once it was agreed that the Uruguay Round agreements had to be accepted as a package (i.e., a "single undertaking"), countries could not opt out of any one of them and be a member of the new World Trade Organization (WTO). Second, the GATT already had a dispute settlement mechanism. WIPO has no enforcement or dispute settlement mechanisms except through the treaties that it administers, and these treaties do not provide much recourse for countries concerned about the noncompliance of other parties. Third, the broad agenda of the Uruguay Round provided opportunities for linkage-bargain diplomacy that WIPO, with its exclusive focus on intellectual property rights, did not allow. Hard bargaining by the United States, Europe, and Japan on intellectual property could thus be linked to concessions in such areas as textiles and agriculture, where exporting countries in the developing world were eager to achieve favorable settlements.

The Punta del Este Declaration of September 1986 included "trade-related aspects of intellectual property rights, including trade in counterfeit goods" as a subject for negotiations in the forthcoming trade round, which became known as the Uruguay Round. In full, the declaration's provisions on intellectual property were as follows:

> In order to reduce the distortions and impediments to international trade, and taking into account the need to promote effective and adequate protection of intellectual property rights, and to ensure that measures and procedures to enforce intellectual property rights do not themselves become barriers to legitimate trade, the negotiations shall aim to clarify GATT provisions and elaborate as appropriate new rules and disciplines.
>
> Negotiations shall aim to develop a multilateral framework of principles, rules and

disciplines dealing with international trade in counterfeit goods, taking into account work already underway in GATT.

These negotiations shall be without prejudice to other complementary initiatives that may be taken in the World Intellectual Property Organization and elsewhere to deal with these matters.

According to Susan K. Sell (2003), TRIPS is a case of 12 U.S. corporations making public law for the world. This makes sense only if one takes it to mean that the active engagement of these firms was a necessary, but not a sufficient, condition for there being a TRIPS Agreement. And actually she does not claim that the alignment of so much economic power and political influence made their victory inevitable or complete. Similarly, as John Braithwaite and Peter Drahos (2000) have noted, "It was a remarkable accomplishment to persuade 100 countries who were net importers of intellectual property rights to sign an Agreement to dramatically increase the cost of intellectual property imports."

So how was such a difficult feat achieved? Certain individuals played a decisive part in mobilizing support for the inclusion of trade-related intellectual property rights as a major Uruguay Round agenda item with the aim of formulating a legal instrument that would bind all members of what would become the WTO. These included chief executive officers of major corporations, lawyers, and a private consultant, all of whom were instrumental in conceptualizing intellectual property as a trade-related issue and then developing the political strategy that would ultimately result in TRIPS.

The interest groups succeeded in influencing the development of trade law and policy by incorporating their demands in the relevant legislation and by working closely with the key government agencies engaged in trade policy, especially the Office of the United States Trade Representative (USTR). Once the USTR had been persuaded that it was in the interests of the country to pursue the intellectual property demands coming from these groups, at least for the time being, at GATT rather than at WIPO, the next task was to form an international alliance including the businesses and governments of Western Europe and Japan while neutralizing resistance from opposing countries.

Initially, the Group of Ten developing countries within the GATT—India, Brazil, Argentina, Cuba, Egypt, Nicaragua, Nigeria, Peru, Tanzania, and Yugoslavia—took a determined stand against the use of GATT as a forum for negotiating global intellectual property standards. But from 1985 and especially 1989 onward, the United States used its own trade rules to publicly criticize, threaten, and punish individual countries whose intellectual property standards were lower than its own and therefore "inadequate." Section 301 (Actions by U.S. Trade Representative) of the U.S. Trade Act was amended in 1984. The amended section 301 specifically included failure to protect intellectual property as one of the "unfair trade practices" that could result in a USTR investigation and possible sanctions, and authorized the USTR to initiate its own cases so as to protect U.S. firms from retaliatory action by foreign governments.

The 1988 Omnibus Trade and Competitiveness Act in its special 301 provision further strengthened the authority of the USTR in order to insulate decision-making on trade retaliation from foreign policy or national security considerations, and required the USTR annually to "identify those foreign countries that deny adequate and effective protection of intellectual property rights, or deny fair and equitable market access to United States persons that rely upon intellectual property protection." It is largely due to the mandate of the USTR to actively pursue the complaints of U.S. firms and business associations that the developing countries eventually accepted TRIPS.

Nonetheless, representatives of the United States, Europe, and Japan did not just sit down together and write the TRIPS Agreement themselves. Not only did divisions emerge between Europe and the United States that required compromises, but developing countries were much more involved in the drafting than they are often given credit for. As Jayashree Watal (2001) explains, they achieved favorable language in 10 of the 73 articles, albeit with the necessary support of a few developed countries. The 10 include those dealing with the objectives and principles of TRIPS, limitations and exceptions to copyright, exceptions to patents and compulsory licensing, and control of anticompetitive practices in contractual licensing.

The Agreement's Key Provisions The preamble affirms the desire of member states "to take into account the need to promote effective and adequate protection of intellectual property rights," while "recognizing the underlying public policy objectives of national systems for the protection of intellectual property, including developmental and technological objectives." Dealing with counterfeiting is clearly considered as important. Its main importance lies in the fact that the trade in counterfeit goods is what makes intellectual property most clearly trade related. The preamble indicates that members recognize "the need for a multilateral framework of principles, rules and disciplines dealing with international trade in counterfeit goods." Yet the objectives as stated in Article 7 make no reference to the eradication of counterfeiting. Rather, TRIPS is explicitly aimed at promoting public policy objectives, the nature of such objectives presumably being left to national governments, though technological development is given priority.

Article 8.1 allows member states implementing their intellectual property laws and regulations to "adopt measures necessary to protect human health and nutrition, and to promote the public interest in sectors of vital importance to their socio-economic and technological development." These measures are not obligatory but, again, they highlight the socio-economic welfare implications of intellectual property. On the other hand, the proviso that such measures be consistent with the provisions of TRIPS appears to narrow their possible scope quite considerably.

By virtue of Article 3, members accept the principle of national treatment, that is, that each country must treat nationals of other members at least as well as it treats its own nationals. In other words, intellectual property protection and enforcement must be nondiscriminatory as to the nationality of rights holders.

Article 4 upholds the principle of most-favored-nation. This means that any concession granted by one member to another must be accorded to all other members "immediately and unconditionally." So if country A agrees to take special measures to prevent the copying of the products of a company from country B, but turns a blind eye when the company is from country C, D, or E, such inconsistency of treatment will violate this principle. Although this principle of international law dates back in history, TRIPS is the first multilateral intellectual property treaty that refers to it.

Part II of TRIPS deals with the actual rights. These are very comprehensive, comprising the following:

1. Copyright and related rights
2. Trademarks
3. Geographical indications
4. Industrial designs
5. Patents
6. Layout-designs (topographies) of integrated circuits
7. Protection of undisclosed information
8. Control of anticompetitive practices in contractual licenses

To some extent the provisions are based on existing agreements. Thus WTO members are required to implement substantial parts of the Paris Convention on the Protection of Industrial Property and the Berne Convention of Literary and Artistic Works whether or not they are signatories to them. Nonetheless, while most developed countries were required only to make cosmetic changes to their intellectual property laws, most developing countries needed to reform their laws quite drastically. This is not surprising since the intellectual property standards provided in TRIPS tend to be modeled on the laws of the United States, Europe, or are a hybrid of the rules of the two jurisdictions.

All countries had to apply Article 3, on national treatment and on most-favored-nation status, and Article 5, concerning multilateral agreements on acquisition or maintenance of protection, within one year of the entry into force of the WTO Agreement. But the developing countries and the former centrally planned socialist states were allowed a period of five years from the date of entry into force of the WTO Agreement, that is, until January 1, 2000, to apply the full provisions of TRIPS. Developing country members that were required to extend patent protection to areas of technology not hitherto covered in their laws were permitted to delay such extension until January 1, 2005. The least-developed countries (LDCs) were allowed until January 1, 2006, to apply TRIPS in full. Countries that have joined the WTO since then are required also to comply with these deadlines.

However, the LDCs have managed to secure two extensions. The 2001 Doha Declaration on the TRIPS Agreement and Public Health allowed them to delay implementation of patent protection for pharmaceutical products and legal protection of undisclosed test data submitted as a condition of approving the marketing of pharmaceuticals until January 1, 2016. In November 2005, the TRIPS Council extended the deadline to LDCs for fully implementing the rest of TRIPS by a further seven and a half years to July 1, 2013.

TRIPS places much emphasis on enforcement. With respect to the general enforcement obligations, procedures must be fair, equitable, and not unnecessarily complicated, costly, or time consuming. The judicial authorities must be granted the power to require infringers to pay damages adequate to compensate the right holder for the injury suffered due to the infringement. Members are required to provide for criminal procedures and penalties "at least in cases of willful trademark counterfeiting or copyright piracy on a commercial scale."

The agreement sets out the role of the Council for Trade-Related Aspects of Intellectual Property Rights (TRIPS Council). Accordingly, the council is responsible for:

 Monitoring the operation of TRIPS, and in particular members' compliance;

 Affording members the opportunity to consult on matters relating to trade-related intellectual property rights;

 Assisting members in the context of dispute settlement procedures; and

 Carrying out other duties assigned to it by the members.

The council is supposed to review the implementation of TRIPS at two-year intervals from January 2000. Article 71.1 states in addition that "the Council may also undertake reviews in the light of any relevant new developments which might warrant modification or amendment of this Agreement."

TRIPS-Related Developments at the WTO
TRIPS was, and continues to be, highly controversial. Indeed, for both developing and developed countries, it represents unfinished business. Developing country representatives continue to express concerns that TRIPS raises prices of drugs and educational materials in poor countries, legitimizes the "biopiracy" of genetic resources and traditional knowledge, and blocks transfers of much-needed technologies. They have successfully resisted the further tightening of TRIPS rules and have had some small victories along the way. They have enhanced their capacity to put forward substantial counter-proposals relating to such matters as public health, least-developed countries, traditional knowledge, and the compatibility between TRIPS and the Convention on Biological Diversity's provisions concerning benefit sharing, protection of traditional knowledge, and technology transfer. As for the developed countries and international business, which are constantly seeking ever higher levels of intellectual property protection and enforcement, TRIPS has to some extent been a disappointment.

It is in fact far from clear that making the intellectual property rules more or less identical whether you are a very rich country with enormous balance of payments surpluses in intellectual property protected goods, services, and technologies, or a poor country with highly burdensome trade deficits, is beneficial for the latter type of nation. While it is impossible to reliably calculate the long-term economic impacts of TRIPS on developing countries and their populations, we can be certain that they will incur short-term costs in such forms as rent transfers and administration and enforcement outlays, and that these will outweigh the initial benefits. The cost-benefit balance will vary widely from one country to another, but in many cases the costs will be extremely burdensome.

At the November 2001 Doha Ministerial Conference of the WTO, members agreed on the texts of two very significant documents with provisions concerning intellectual property: the Ministerial Declaration, and the Declaration on the TRIPS Agreement on Public Health. The former declaration's TRIPS-related matters concerned geographical indications, the relationship between TRIPS and the Convention on Biological Diversity (CBD) and the protection of traditional knowledge and folklore, and technology transfer. The latter declaration dealt exclusively with TRIPS, primarily its public health provisions relating to compulsory licensing and parallel importation.

TRIPS Article 27.3(b) concerns exceptions to patentability in the area of biotechnology. It permits WTO members to exclude from patentability "plants and animals other than micro-organisms, and essentially biological processes for the production of plants or animals other than non-biological and microbiological processes." At Doha, ministers representing WTO members clarified their commitment to opening up negotiations on issues relating to Article 27.3(b) to include the relationship between the TRIPS Agreement and the CBD, and the protection of traditional knowledge and folklore.

The key challenge for developing countries is that many of them remain unclear about how to tailor their patent regulations to promote their interests in the acquisition, development, and application of biotechnology, and therefore how best to exploit the flexible language of Article 27.3(b). Understandably, though, much of the discussion has focused not specifically on this issue, but on how best to address a wide range of moral, political, and economic concerns about "patenting life" and "biopiracy."

The CBD-TRIPS relationship and the protection of traditional knowledge and folklore have proved to be quite controversial. One key developing country demand that has been pushed quite strongly is that of disclosure of origin. Disclosure of origin would re-

quire inventors to disclose the source of genetic resources and/or traditional knowledge relevant to an invention being patented. In May 2006, Brazil, India, Pakistan, Peru, Thailand, and Tanzania proposed in the WTO General Council that new text be incorporated into the TRIPS Agreement under Article 29, which deals with conditions on patent applicants, to require such disclosure.

Geographical indications (GIs) are defined in the TRIPS Agreement as "indications which identify a good as originating in the territory of a Member, or a region or locality in that territory, where a given quality, reputation, or other characteristic of the good is essentially attributable to its geographical origin." In November 2001, the WTO members attending the Doha Ministerial Conference agreed "to negotiate the establishment of a multilateral system of notification and registration of geographical indications for wines and spirits by the Fifth Session of the Ministerial Conference." With respect to the possible extension of the enhanced protection of geographical indications to products other than wines and spirits, it was agreed that issues related to this matter would be addressed in the Council for TRIPS, an indication of the lack of consensus.

Despite the fact they are in TRIPS largely at the instigation of the European Commission, GIs have for several years been promoted as a concession to developing countries that they ought to take advantage of. Supposedly, they provide the means by which developing countries can use intellectual property to protect categories of local rural knowledge that they possess in abundance. In particular, the European Union and the Swiss government are very keen to promote GIs worldwide by arguing that this part of TRIPS can potentially provide substantial gains for developing countries. This seems plausible when one considers that GIs are especially appropriate for the produce of small-scale producers and cultivators, and, it should be underlined here, not just for foods and beverages but also handicrafts and other handmade items.

Many developing countries are rich in traditional knowledge having applications in agriculture, food production, and small-scale manufacturing. So GIs would appear to have real potential in terms of developing and exploiting lucrative markets for natural product–based goods, including those manufactured by resource-poor farming communities. Such countries tend to favor the extension of the additional protection to cover all products, not just beverages. Are they right to be so pro-GI with respect to products they wish to export? Possibly they are, but caution should be exercised. GIs are useless without good standards of quality control and marketing, and up-to-date information on markets including foreign ones if the products are to be exported. At present the potential of geographical indications for developing countries is somewhat speculative because this type of intellectual property right has been used only in a few countries outside Europe. Moreover, many GIs have quite small markets, and a relatively small number are traded internationally.

Other developing countries do not have an abundance of traditional knowledge and are key exporters of products that compete with well-established GI-protected goods coming from Europe. For those countries, GIs may be more of a threat than an opportunity.

Multilateralism, Bilateralism, and the Future of TRIPS Developing country WTO members have been very reluctant to engage in negotiations to raise levels of intellectual property protection at the WTO. In order to hold these countries to more rigid and higher standards of intellectual property protection than TRIPS compliance requires, the United States and the European Union have gone outside the multilateral WTO forum. One of the most effective strategies being employed is that of bilateral and regional free trade agreements, which generally contain so-called "TRIPS plus" intellectual property right provisions, which place obligations on governments to provide more extensive protection than TRIPS actually requires. A growing number of developing countries seeking to enhance access to developed world markets for goods produced in their nations have proved willing to overcome their reservations about strengthened intellectual property rights through such deals in order to achieve this.

As a WTO agreement, and one which deals with arguably the most valuable assets of modern corporations, intangible ones, the importance of TRIPS to the world economy is immense and will remain so for several years. However, there are early signs that it is outliving its purpose for those corporations that successfully lobbied for an intellectual property agreement in the Uruguay Round and the governments that took up their demands. There are three reasons for this. First, the WTO system of trade governance currently does not make it easy to achieve radical revision of existing agreements or, for that matter, consensus on the need for new ones. Second, developing countries have tended not to implement TRIPS with much enthusiasm, and enforcement measures continue to be inadequate from the view of the intellectual property owners. Third, for the developed countries and transnational industry, other forms of trade diplomacy including those presented above seem to further their interests more effectively. Thus one may reasonably question whether TRIPS in the coming years will continue to be such an important agreement as it is today.

See also access to medicines; intellectual property rights; nondiscrimination; parallel imports; World Intellectual Property Organization; World Trade Organization

FURTHER READINGS
Braithwaite, J., and P. Drahos. 2000. *Global Business Regulation.* Cambridge: Cambridge University Press. Contains an excellent chapter explaining the political background to the incorporation of intellectual property in the Uruguay Round and the drafting of the resulting agreement.
Matthews, Duncan. 2002. *Globalizing Intellectual Property Rights: The TRIPS Agreement.* London: Routledge. Useful empirical study on various aspects of TRIPS from the viewpoint of European and global business interests and the developing countries.
Ryan, Michael P. 1998. *Knowledge Diplomacy: Global Competition and the Politics of Intellectual Property.* Washington, DC: Brookings Institution Press. The first book-length account of how powerful political and business actors, based mainly in the United States,

organized a successful campaign that resulted in TRIPS.

Sell, Susan K. 2003. *Private Power, Public Law: The Globalization of Intellectual Property Rights*. Cambridge: Cambridge University Press. Empirical and theoretical study that explains why the developed countries decided to push for a comprehensive intellectual property agreement in the Uruguay Round and not at WIPO. It also considers some of the economic and social welfare implications of TRIPS.

UN Conference for Trade and Development and International Center for Trade and Sustainable Development. 2005. *Resource Book on TRIPS and Development*. Cambridge: Cambridge University Press. Definitive guide to TRIPS from a development perspective, which covers the negotiating history of the various articles, provides a technical interpretation of their language, and analyzes the WTO disputes relating to TRIPS. The chapters are separately downloadable from http://www.iprsonline.org/unctadictsd/ResourceBookIndex.htm

Watal, Jayashree. 2001. *Intellectual Property Rights in the WTO and Developing Countries*. New Delhi: Oxford University Press. Excellent insider account of TRIPS from a former Indian government trade negotiator and present WTO staff member.

World Bank. 2001. *Global Economic Prospects and the Developing Countries 2002: Making Trade Work for the World's Poor*. Washington DC: World Bank. Chapter 5 provides a detailed study of the economic costs and benefits of intellectual property rights and the TRIPS Agreement.

GRAHAM DUTFIELD

■ agricultural trade negotiations

Opening up markets for agricultural products has proved a stumbling block for trade negotiations at both the regional and the multilateral levels. The primary reason is the political sensitivity of more open markets for farm and food products. Most governments share a concern for the security of their countries' food supply and the income level and stability of their rural sectors. In importing countries, this concern has led to caution about relying on imports for basic foodstuffs and a conviction that protection from overseas competition is necessary for the health of the rural economy. Those countries with export potential have long decried such sentiments, arguing that they can provide a regular supply of foodstuffs at lower prices and that supporting inefficient domestic production is not a sound basis for development. But, as one might expect in a sector where governments still have considerable control over markets, negotiations to open up trade in farm products have tended to proceed at the pace of the most reluctant importers.

Since the 1980s, this cautious attitude toward trade in farm goods has begun to give way to a more confident approach that sees imports as complementary to domestic production and exports as a natural extension of domestic markets. Consumers are becoming used to the greater choice of foodstuffs that comes with trade, and producers are setting their sights increasingly on foreign markets for new sources of revenue. In the process, many countries have become both importers and exporters of farm products and foodstuffs. This has blurred the easy categorization of a country's trade policy by its trade balance. Developing country importers often join with developing country exporters in voicing concerns about trade issues, particularly about the subsidies given to domestic producers in rich countries. Developed country exporters have "sensitive" sectors that apparently need to be sheltered even while they advocate more open markets for other products. Developed country importers with high protection barriers are often major importers of farm products needed for processing or for animal feed. Perhaps only in the market for tropical agricultural products is it still possible to identify typical "importer" and "exporter" views, but even in this case there are clear distinctions between those that have preferential access to markets in industrialized countries and those that do not benefit from such preferences, and between those that sell the raw materials and those that successfully add value in the domestic economy.

Along with this shift in political perceptions on agricultural trade has come a change in the nature of trade in farm products. In the 1980s, much of the trade in primary agricultural products passed through sales or purchasing agents for producers and wholesalers, or of companies whose function was to distribute temperate-zone and tropical products through established channels. The role of state trading has shrunk markedly, with the adoption of policies to allow more private activity in marketing. Large companies now have a considerable role in the processing and marketing of farm products, as they have had for some time in the trading function. Most of these private actors operate in several countries, and thus food trade has become much more of a global business. The share of such trade that is categorized as "high value added" has correspondingly increased, leaving the trading of commodities and raw materials a smaller part of agricultural trade. Such trends explain the growing interest by large food and retail firms in removing trade barriers that act to inhibit worldwide marketing. As a result of these changes, in both political perception and structural reality, agricultural trade negotiations have been somewhat more successful in recent years in opening markets and have even made some progress in the past decade in reducing trade-distorting subsidies.

The change in the attitudes toward trade negotiations in agriculture is closely tied to reform of domestic policies. In developed countries, such policies were usually built on (and have been facilitated by) tariff and nontariff protection at the border and have employed a wide range of instruments to manage domestic markets and supplement farm incomes. Thus trade reform and market liberalization could not proceed as fast as in manufactured products in the postwar period. Domestic policies would have been impossible to maintain if trade liberalization had extended to agriculture. Reform of the domestic farm policies in developed countries started in the mid 1980s and continued apace for more than a decade. Policies that lowered support prices and substituted direct payments to farmers were found to be more easily amended to meet new targets, such as environmental stewardship, and tended to lower the incentive to produce unwanted surpluses. Developing countries, for different reasons, also relaxed their

control over domestic markets and lowered trade barriers. In this case the motive was to correct macroeconomic and structural problems that were inhibiting development.

These reforms allowed countries to institute, as part of the Uruguay Round in 1994, a wide-ranging Agreement on Agriculture, which acted as a framework in which domestic policies could operate. This framework was consistent with lower protection at the border and less trade-distorting subsidies at home. It helped to lock in domestic reforms and put pressure on countries that were lagging in the reform process. But it also simplified the task of negotiating reductions in trade barriers and importantly changed the dynamic of such negotiations.

The same reform of developed-country farm policies also made it easier to negotiate bilateral and regional trade pacts. For years, most of these agreements had avoided the problem of negotiating reductions in tariff barriers for agriculture by explicitly excluding sensitive agricultural sectors from the full impact of market opening. This became insupportable when agricultural export interests, even in net importing countries, began to ask for market access (and preferences) within the regional or bilateral agreement. In addition, the rules of the World Trade Organization (WTO) (Article XXIV of the General Agreement on Tariffs and Trade 1994) oblige countries to grant tariff-free access on "substantially all trade" within bilateral and regional trade agreements. As a result, the inclusion of agriculture in such agreements is now the norm rather than the exception. Safeguards and slowly increasing tariff quotas still give some protection to sensitive domestic farm sectors, but few agreements exclude agriculture altogether.

It would be misleading, however, to suggest that these processes of globalization in farm and food trade and of reform of domestic policies have removed all the obstacles to open trade in agricultural goods. The process of reform has taken place at different speeds in different countries. So the pace of trade negotiations is still controlled to a large extent by the slowest reformers. Among the developed countries this includes Japan, Norway, and Switzerland. Not only is protection high in these countries but the types of policies used still rely heavily on protection at the border. Hence they have been prominent members of the Group of 10 in the context of the WTO Doha Round, arguing for generous exclusions for "sensitive products," more modest tariff cuts, and no cap on the height of tariffs. Among the developing countries, the reluctant importers have formed the Group of 33, which emphasizes the need for adequate provision for "special products" and the inclusion of a "special safeguard mechanism" to allow them to reimpose tariffs if domestic markets are disrupted. These two groups, though negotiating actively, have effectively limited the "level of ambition" of the market access talks on agriculture.

Importantly, the process of trade and domestic reform has been uneven among sectors. The so-called white goods—rice, cotton, sugar, and milk—have among the highest tariff barriers and the most pervasive domestic subsidies. The sensitivity of these goods extends to exporting countries. The United States, normally a supporter of low tariffs, has come under pressure to reduce subsidies on each of these products. This has complicated the position of the United States in trade talks, arguing for others to open up markets but being more cautious in offering to cut support or lower tariffs where domestic interests are vocal. The European Union (EU) also has its sensitive products, including dairy and beef, though it has modified its domestic policies for rice, sugar, and cotton. The Uruguay Round did relatively little to improve the situation in the "white goods" markets, and their inclusion in regional trade agreements has often been politically sensitive. Sugar, for instance, was left out of the U.S.-Australia Free Trade Agreement, and was given a "temporary" exclusion from the Mercosur trade arrangements.

The implications of these changing political and economic forces can be seen with respect to the Doha Round of trade talks. Agriculture has been the biggest hurdle to an agreement, and the principal reason why talks were suspended for a time in July 2006. But the agricultural negotiations themselves are quite different from those in 1986, at the start of the Uruguay Round. At that time, the main protagonists were the United States and the EU, and the issues were whether to bring agricultural trade under the disciplines of multilateral rules and how to include rules for domestic policy that would be consistent with the trade disciplines. The United States, as a prominent exporter of temperate-zone farm products, favored such a move, in large part to circumscribe the Common Agricultural Policy of the EU. The EU had previously argued against this, on the grounds that domestic policy was a national issue and that the trade rules should give adequate scope for such internal choices. By the end of the talks, seven years later, the EU had agreed to rules that covered domestic policy instruments, categorizing them into "boxes" depending on their degree of trade distortion, and that eliminated quantitative trade barriers and limited export subsidies. The United States had achieved its objective of introducing binding rules but had to settle for only modest tariff reductions. The EU had to reform its own Common Agricultural Policy in 1992 in order to be able to live within the new constraints of the WTO.

The Doha Round is not about whether to develop rules for agricultural trade, or whether to extend trade rules to cover domestic policy. It was intended as a more "traditional" trade negotiation, to complement the outcome of the Uruguay Round by reducing tariffs by a substantial amount and by agreeing on a further reduction in subsidies. There is no longer any objection to the inclusion of domestic support in the trade talks and of curbing export subsidies. The focus has been on the depth of the tariff cuts and the extent to which certain "sensitive" products could be sheltered from the full cuts. In this sense it is much more in keeping with the negotiations in manufactured trade in the Kennedy Round (1963–67).

But one aspect of the Doha Round has made for more complex and difficult negotiations on agricultural trade. In contrast to the Uruguay Round, where with the exception of those in the Cairns Group few developing countries played a major role, the number of such countries that have been active has been remarkable. Spurred by the attempt (in August 2003) by the United States and the EU to develop a common position, Brazil, India, and China, together with South Africa and a number of other developing countries, formed the Group of 20. The main demand from these countries was that the EU and the United States commit themselves to significant cuts in domestic support (subsidies) as well as eliminating export subsidies and cutting tariffs on farm goods. This coalition has stayed together and played a major role in the search for solutions to the agricultural negotiations.

Multilateral negotiations on agricultural trade have changed in nature as globalization has broken down the easy categorization of countries as reluctant importers and aggressive exporters. The scope for talks to open markets has been enhanced by the conversion of nontariff trade barriers to tariffs and the move to direct subsidies to support farm income. But the emergence of the major developing countries as players has moved the emphasis from transatlantic tensions to North-South conflicts. And so 21st-century trade negotiations, both in the WTO and in regional and bilateral trade pacts, have revolved around the extent to which developing countries need special rules to reflect their development status, how to continue the reduction of trade-distorting subsidies, and when to finally end the exception to normal trade rules that has allowed the continuation of export subsidies for primary products.

See also Agreement on Agriculture; agriculture; Doha Round; multilateral trade negotiations; tariff rate quotas; Uruguay Round; World Trade Organization

FURTHER READING

Coleman, William, Wyn Grant, and Tim Josling. 2004. *Agriculture in the New Global Economy*. Cheltenham, UK: Edward Elgar. Discusses the dimension of globalization that has begun to dominate agricultural trade from the viewpoint of political science.

International Center for Trade and Sustainable Development (ICTSD). http://www.ictsd.org/about/index.htm. A source for current information on WTO agricultural negotiations and related issues, often from the viewpoint of developing countries.

Josling, Timothy E., Stefan Tangermann, and Thorald K. Warley. 1996. *Agriculture in the GATT*. Basingstoke,

UK: Macmillan. The history of the place of agriculture in the General Agreement on Tariffs and Trade negotiations prior to and including the Uruguay Round.

Sumner, Daniel A. and Stefan Tangermann. 2002. "International Trade Policy and Negotiations." In *Handbook of Agricultural Economics*, vol. 2B, *Agricultural and Food Policy*, edited by Bruce L. Gardner and Gordon C. Rausser. Amsterdam, Netherlands: North Holland Press, pages 1999–2055. An overview of agriculture in trade negotiations.

World Trade Organization (WTO). http://www.wto.org/english/tratop_e/agric_e/negoti_e.htm. The progress of negotiations in the Doha Round can be followed at this Web site.

TIM JOSLING

■ agriculture

Agriculture is the systematic raising of plants and animals for the purpose of producing food, feed, fiber, and other outputs. Historically, agricultural production has been linked to the use of the land and the tillage of the soil, and it is agriculture that allowed humans to initially establish permanent settlements. Such establishments were possible because agriculture provided the food necessary to meet human nutritional requirements. Because of its connection to the development of human societies, agriculture is closely associated with culture through the food that it produces and the manner in which it alters the landscape. This tie to culture gives agriculture special status in society and has led it to be treated differently from other commodities in international economic relations.

With economic development, the share of agriculture as a percentage of a country's gross domestic product (GDP) tends to decline (Chenery and Syrquin 1975). This trend is magnified on a global level. As countries have developed, the importance of agriculture in the global economy has declined, with agriculture in the early 21st century representing approximately 6 percent of global GDP.

This aggregate measure, however, masks the continued importance of agriculture for many countries and households, particularly in developing countries. Because of its social, cultural, and economic importance, the treatment of agriculture in global economic relations has always been controversial. In Latin America, for example, approximately 20 percent of export earnings comes from agricultural products; in Africa it is 14 percent. Additionally, more than 40 percent of the world's economically active population still works in agriculture, with these workers mostly concentrated in developing countries (FAO 2005). Therefore, the operation of the global economy and its influence on the agricultural sector can influence the lives of billions of people.

Disputes over agricultural trade and domestic agricultural policies have continued to plague trade negotiations, including recent meetings of the World Trade Organization (WTO). These disputes have come at a time when agricultural markets have undergone significant changes, particularly in developing countries. A clear understanding of the role of agriculture in the global economy requires consideration of the importance of agriculture in global trade, its role in multilateral trade negotiations, its particular importance to developing countries, and recent trends that have transformed agricultural markets.

Agriculture in Global Trade The value of world agricultural trade nearly doubled between 1980 and 2000, from U.S. $243 billion to U.S. $467 billion. While average annual growth in agricultural exports was substantial during this period—4.9 percent in the 1980s and 3.4 percent in the 1990s—it occurred at a time of generally increasing trade volumes and at a slower pace than growth in the manufacturing sector, particularly in the 1990s when manufacturing grew at an annual rate of 6.7 percent. This difference was even greater in developing countries, where agricultural export growth was 5.3 percent in the 1990s compared to 10.9 percent for manufacturing growth (Aksoy and Beghin 2005). Thus, while agricultural trade continues to expand and is clearly important to the world economy, there has been a general decline in its relative significance over time. For both the world in general and for

developing countries in particular, the share of agriculture in global trade has declined to just around 10 percent.

Along with a decline in the relative importance of agriculture, the composition of agricultural trade has shifted. First, there has been a movement away from the export of raw materials to greater export of processed products. Final agricultural products made up a quarter of world exports in 1980–81, but by 2000–2001 they had increased to 38 percent. Second, the commodities being produced and exported have changed from traditional tropical products (such as coffee, cocoa, tea, nuts, spices, fibers, and sugar) and temperate products (meats, milk, grains, feed, and edible oils) to nontraditional, higher-value products (seafood, fruits, and vegetables) and other products such as tobacco and cigarettes, beverages, and other processed foods. Tropical products, in particular, have declined from 22 percent of agricultural exports in 1980–81 to 12.7 percent in 2000–2001 (Aksoy and Beghin 2005). The expectation is that there will be a continued shift away from raw materials and traditional products toward these nontraditional higher valued products and processed items.

These overall trends in agricultural trade and volumes also mask the fact that much of the trade in agricultural commodities occurs within key trading blocs, particularly within the European Union (EU) and the member countries of the North American Free Trade Agreement (NAFTA). Table 1 shows the flows of global agricultural trade between different sets of countries in 2000–2001. Of the U.S. $181 billion in agricultural exports from the EU countries, U.S. $131 billion—or 73 percent—went to other EU member countries. Similarly, of the U.S. $90 billion in agricultural exports from the NAFTA countries, 39 percent occurred between Canada, Mexico, and the United States.

Agricultural policies account for part of the reason why agricultural trade stays within trading blocs. Historically, developing countries have often taxed agriculture, whereas developed countries have protected agriculture from outside competition and subsidized agricultural production. During the past two decades, changes in policies in many developing

Table 1
Global agricultural trade flows, 2000–2001 (US$ billion)

Importers	Exporters							
	Low income countries	Middle income countries	Developing countries	EU-15	Japan	NAFTA	Other industrial countries	Total imports
Low income countries	1.50	4.48	5.98	2.01	0.06	1.99	1.78	11.82
Middle income countries	9.20	48.44	57.64	22.85	1.74	23.42	10.71	116.36
Developing countries	10.70	52.92	63.63	24.86	1.80	25.41	12.49	128.18
EU-15	9.65	37.81	47.46	131.33	0.15	9.57	9.38	197.89
Japan	2.52	19.21	21.73	4.48		17.61	5.11	49.28
NAFTA	3.72	21.95	25.67	12.60	0.54	34.80	4.77	78.38
Other industrial countries	0.54	3.24	3.79	7.22	0.08	2.15	1.70	14.94
Total exports	27.14	135.13	162.27	180.84	2.57	89.55	33.45	468.67

Source: Aksoy and Beghin (2005) using COMTRADE data

countries—such as the devaluation of overvalued exchange rates, the reduction of import restrictions on manufactured goods, and the elimination of agricultural export taxes—have removed the anti-agricultural bias in these countries, leading to greater incentives to produce agricultural products. Developed countries, however, have continued to protect and promote agriculture through price supports and tariffs as well as direct subsidies. Within trading blocs, these protections are either not applied or are less restrictive and thus lead to greater agricultural trade within these regions.

The protection and subsidies to agriculture in developed countries influence their competitiveness in domestic and foreign markets. As discussed in the next section, this has become an important point of contention in trade negotiations. To calculate the degree of agricultural protection for farmers in these countries, the Organisation for Economic Cooperation and Development (OECD) has developed a method for estimating the total support to agricultural producers provided by a range of policies. The OECD's producer support estimate (PSE)

measures the monetary value of total gross transfers to agricultural producers arising from agricultural policies (OECD 2006). Compared with total gross farm receipts, this measure can be used to identify the share of farmer revenue that results from government policies. Table 2 provides the estimated percent PSE in farmers' revenue for selected OECD countries as well as for the OECD as a whole. The table also shows the share of support coming from market price supports, such as border tariffs, and the share coming from direct payments to farmers. The data indicate that with the exception of Australia, a significant share of farmers' revenue in developed countries is the result of agricultural policies in those countries. Furthermore, a substantial portion of the PSE is due to market price supports such as tariff and other forms of trade protection. However, there has been a decline in the PSE for each country in the table and the OECD as a whole between 1986–88 and 2003–5, and with the exception of Japan, there has been a shift away from market price supports toward direct subsidies. These agricultural policies, however, continue to influence the trade flows of agriculture into

Table 2
Producer support in selected OECD countries

	PSE as a percent of gross farm receipts		Market price support (share of PSE)		Direct subsidy (share of PSE)	
	1986–88	2003–05	1986–88	2003–05	1986–88	2003–05
Australia	8	5	50	0	50	100
Canada	36	22	52	46	48	54
European Union	41	34	87	50	13	50
Japan	64	58	90	91	10	9
United States	22	16	37	26	63	74
All OECD	37	30	77	57	23	43

Source: OECD (2006)

and out of developed countries. The sheer size of the economies where these policies are in place means they have a significant impact on global agricultural trade.

Agriculture and the World Trade Organization
The protection and support of agriculture in a number of developed countries has been justified on the grounds that agriculture deserves special consideration because it is linked to national culture. This special status has been recognized by the multilateral trade negotiations that have occurred under the General Agreement on Tariffs and Trade (GATT) and later under the WTO. Under the GATT, at the initial urging of the United States, certain agricultural sectors were exempted from the general prohibition in the agreement against quantity restrictions, as were export subsidies. As the EU took shape, it developed a Common Agricultural Policy (CAP) that provided general protection and support to farmers in all member countries and led to strong and increasing support by the EU for the special status of agriculture in multilateral trade negotiations.

The EU, the United States, and Japan remain strong supporters of the special status of agriculture. Countries that wish to export their agricultural products to these markets, however, argue that these policies are unfair since not only is access limited for certain commodities, but the subsidies provided to producers in these protected markets give them an advantage over producers in countries without such subsidies. Developing countries tend to be particularly critical of agricultural supports since they are not in a budgetary position to support agriculture and believe agriculture is one area where they may have a comparative advantage.

When the WTO was created as part of the Marrakesh Agreement in 1994, a specific Agreement on Agriculture was designed to align agricultural trade rules with those of other products. The Agreement on Agriculture dealt with three general issues that influenced global agricultural trade: market access, domestic support, and export subsidies. For market access, the agreement required countries to convert quantity restrictions to tariffs. Once tariff equivalents of quantity restrictions were established, they were to be reduced. For domestic support, the agreement distinguished between trade distorting measures, which countries were required to reduce, and nontrade distorting measures. As part of the Agreement of Agriculture, developed countries agreed to reduce the total aggregate measure of support (AMS) by 20 percent by 2000, while developing countries agreed to reduce it by 13 percent by 2004. Nontrade distorting measures were exempt from reduction commitments. A final special category of domestic support measures was also exempt from reductions. These measures, which were used especially in the

EU, covered payments under programs designed to reduce the overproduction that occurred under other traditional market support payments. For export subsidies, no new subsidies could be introduced and existing subsidies had to be reduced by 36 percent in value by 2000 for developed countries and by 24 percent by 2004 for developing countries, although special conditions applied in some cases (Ingno and Nash 2004). The changes in the rules governing agriculture are reflected in the data presented in table 2, which shows a general reduction in producer support among OECD countries and a shift from market price support to direct subsidies.

The Agreement on Agriculture has generally been viewed as a step forward for trade negotiations; although it did not bring about substantial changes in the short run, it did set up a framework that aligned agriculture with other products. Its supporters hoped that setting up this framework would lead to further liberalization of agricultural markets in future rounds of WTO negotiations, particularly in the current Doha Round of trade negotiations. In fact, the Ministerial Declaration launching the Doha Round put agriculture as the first item on the agenda, indicating its priority in the negotiations. However, the Doha Round has failed to make substantial progress and the negotiations have faltered largely because of disputes over agricultural issues. For example, prior to a WTO meeting in Cancun in 2003 a group of developing countries, referred to as the G21, stated clearly the importance of dealing with agriculture issues such as protectionism and farmer subsidies. The Cancun meeting made no progress on these agricultural issues and was generally viewed as a failure. Following a WTO General Council meeting in July 2006 and the continued failure to make progress, the chairman of the WTO's Trade Negotiation Committee noted that agriculture is "key to unlocking the rest of the agenda" and that there was "no visible evidence of flexibilities" that would help solve existing problems (WTO 2006). Agriculture, thus, remains the principal stumbling block to further trade liberalization.

Complicating the disputes over protection and support of agriculture are additional issues that have emerged as the Doha Round of negotiations has progressed. First are market access barriers that have been put in place because of domestic concerns about methods used for production. While this is a broader concern for trade negotiations, it is particularly important for food products where health and safety concerns are significant and where countries may legitimately claim a right to protect their consumers. Although international agreements and standards exist, separating legitimate from illegitimate standards imposed by particular countries is not straightforward. The case of genetically modified organisms (GMOs) is a good example. Because of concerns over the health and environmental impacts of such products, the EU has enacted laws requiring the labeling and traceability of GMOs. However, the United States has challenged these policies as illegitimate restrictions on trade, arguing there is no evidence to support such concerns. The dispute remains unsettled (Zarrilli 2005). A second issue is the protection of geographical indications (GIs), names or labels used to indicate the geographic origin of certain products and, by extension, to indicate that these products have certain qualities or meet certain standards of production because they are from a certain region. Many food and beverage terms—such as Parmesan and Gorgonzola cheeses, Parma ham, Chianti, and Champagne—have come to be used generically although they have specific geographic origins. The EU and a number of developing countries argue that if the products are produced through a traditional, controlled manner in a specific region, their names should be protected and that existing protection is insufficient. The EU has proposed amending the current protection under the Trade-Related Aspects of Intellectual Property (TRIPS) agreement in favor of a mandatory multilateral system of registering these types of products (Evans and Blakeney 2006).

Food, Agriculture, and International Development Of the 1.2 billion poor people in the world, 75 percent live in rural areas (IFAD 2001). Therefore, although the contribution of agriculture to global GDP continues to decline in importance, it remains a fundamental component of the livelihood strategies of these households and is critical to the advancement of the less-developed countries. Not only does agriculture provide food for the survival of the rural poor, it may be an important path out of poverty, particularly if the poor can take advantage of opportunities to produce nontraditional, high-value crops, which tend to be labor-intensive. The manner in which the global economy operates can alter the prices farmers fetch for their products, thus offering them incentives to produce more or less depending on the direction of price effects. Trade policies in developed countries therefore have an impact not only on developing economies, but potentially on the level of rural poverty in those countries.

Other than altering the incentives for farmers in developing countries, the policies of developed countries affect developing countries' agriculture through food aid. As a result of incentives for over-production in their agricultural policies, many developed countries have food surpluses. A portion of these surpluses is often used as food aid to developing countries. Although this seems a reasonable response to hunger, critics of food aid have argued that the provision of food creates disincentives for local production and policy. Increasing the supply of food commodities may cause prices of food to decline, thereby leading to lower incentives for farmers, rich and poor alike, to produce. The provision of food aid may also limit investment in agriculture by developing country governments that count on a regular supply of food aid to overcome limitations in food availability. This can limit the development of the rural economy and perpetuate a state of dependency. Most of these issues can be overcome with the judicious use of food aid in emergency situations and the careful management of aid programs when implemented, but the use of surpluses for food aid has the potential to cause significant problems for developing economies (Barrett and Maxwell 2005).

Given the importance of agriculture as a productive activity in developing countries, particularly in the poorest countries, the manner in which it is treated in global economic relations, and the agricultural policies enacted by key players in devel-oped economies, can have a profound impact on economic development. Trade controversies are then closely linked to broader global issues of poverty and equity.

The New Agricultural Economy in Developing Countries In recent years, agricultural production in many developing countries has undergone profound changes, leading it to become increasingly oriented toward high-value global and urban product markets. These changes have mirrored many of the changes that occurred in developed countries earlier and have been driven largely by changes within developing countries. On the demand side, these include increased urbanization, the expanded entry of women into the workforce, and the development of a middle class—all of which have led to greater demand for higher-quality and processed foods (Reardon et al. 2003). On the supply side, the opening of markets to foreign direct investment (FDI) influenced not only manufacturing sectors but also the domestic food market and the role of agro-industry in those markets. These domestic changes, combined with the expanded trade in processed and nontraditional products, have had a profound effect on the workings of the agricultural sector in many developing countries.

Referred to by some as the "new agricultural economy," these changes have led to new organizational and institutional arrangements within the food marketing chain as evidenced by new forms of contracts as well as by the imposition of private grades and standards for food quality and safety. Where open markets with a variety of sellers of different food commodities used to operate, there are now frequently supermarkets. Where small-scale processors of goods for the domestic consumer market—such as potato chips—used to exist, multinational corporations have taken over. Other multinationals have invested in the production of high-value crops—such as fresh flowers and vegetables—for immediate export to foreign markets. These supermarkets, processors, and exporters have specific requirements for the commodities they wish to purchase in terms of the quality of the goods and the timing of receipt. Products destined for the food market, in particular, often must meet certain sanitary and phytosanitary standards. To ensure those requirements are met, these buyers often procure their goods through contracts with producers rather than through spot markets.

These rapid changes have brought new challenges and opportunities to farmers and policymakers in developing countries. These new markets provide significant opportunities because they tend to provide a price premium for quality and high-value products. But they also may be difficult to access and, in some cases, involve substantial risk. Often, new inputs and varieties are required and farmers must have sufficient information on grades and standards to be successful. Governments can play a critical role in facilitating access to information as well as providing assistance with the transition into these markets. This is particularly important for poorer farmers who often lack the resources to take advantage of new opportunities. Governments also play a critical role in verifying and certifying that sanitary and phytosanitary measures are in place. Furthermore, since such standards are often used as a mechanism to limit trade, governments may be called on to ensure that limits to market access are legitimate under the WTO rules.

The Role of Agriculture in the World Economy
While agriculture continues to decline in its overall economic importance in global trade, its special status in trade negotiations and its critical role in economic development and global poverty alleviation make it a sector that will continue to play a critical role in the world economy. In the short run, agricultural issues are likely to dominate trade negotiations. In the long run, global and domestic agricultural policies will influence the ability of countries to develop, and for the poor within those countries, to exit poverty. Agriculture will continue to be part of any discussion of global economic relations.

See also Agreement on Agriculture; agricultural trade negotiations; Common Agricultural Policy; distortions to agricultural incentives; primary products trade; sanitary and phytosanitary measures

FURTHER READING

Aksoy, M. Ataman, and John Beghin, eds. 2005. *Global Agricultural Trade and Developing Countries.* Washington, DC: World Bank. An edited volume that provides a broad overview of the issues related to global agricultural trade and developing countries.

Anderson, Kym, and Will Martin. 2005. "Agricultural Trade Reform and the Doha Development Agenda." World Bank Policy Research Working Paper 3607. Washington, DC: World Bank. Evaluates how the various regions of the world and the world as a whole could gain from agricultural trade reform.

Barrett, Christopher, and Daniel Maxwell. 2005. *Food Aid after Fifty Years: Recasting Its Role.* London: Routledge. An overview of the history of food aid, its impact on recipient countries, and its potential role.

Chenery, Hollis, and Moises Syrquin. 1975. *Patterns of Development, 1950–70.* London: Oxford University Press for the World Bank. Describes the structural changes that tend to occur over time as countries experience economic growth.

Evans, G. E., and Michael Blakeney. 2006. "The Protection of Geographical Indications after Doha: Quo Vadis?" *Journal of International Economic Law* 9 (3): 575–614. Discusses the possible steps forward for resolving the dispute over protection of geographical indications.

FAO. 2005. *The State of Food and Agriculture 2005: Agricultural Trade and Poverty, Can Trade Work for the Poor?* Rome: Food and Agriculture Organization of the United Nations. Assesses how agricultural trade can help reduce poverty and food insecurity.

IFAD. 2001. *Rural Poverty Report 2001: The Challenge of Ending Rural Poverty.* Oxford: Oxford University Press for International Fund for Agricultural Development. Examines rural poverty in the world and policies that may be used to reduce it.

Ingno, Merlinda, and John Nash. 2004. *Agriculture and the WTO: Creating a Trading System for Development.* Washington, DC: World Bank. An edited volume that examines the WTO agreement and the issues in the agreement facing developing countries.

OECD. 2006. *Agricultural Policies in OECD Countries: At a Glance –2006 Edition.* Paris: Organisation of Economic Co-operation and Development. Estimates of support to agriculture for OECD countries.

Reardon, Thomas, C. Peter Timmer, Christopher B. Barrett, and Julio Berdegué. 2003. "The Rise of Supermarkets in Africa, Asia, and Latin America." *American Journal of Agricultural Economics* 85 (5): 1140–46. An overview of the transformation of the agri-food system in Africa, Asia, and Latin America.

WTO. 2006. "Report by the Chairman of the Trade Negotiations Committee." http://www.wto.org/english/news_e/news06_e/tnc_chair_report_10oct06_e.htm. Report on the problems facing the Doha Round of WTO negotiations.

Zarrilli, Simonetta. 2005. *International Trade in GMOs and GM Products: National and Multilateral Legal Frameworks. Policy Issues in International Trade and Commodities Study Series No. 29.* Geneva: United Nations Conference on Trade and Development. Discusses the national and international legal frameworks for managing GMOs and the current issues being confronted in trade negotiations.

PAUL WINTERS

■ aid, bilateral

Bilateral aid is official development assistance that flows directly from a donor country government to a recipient country. This is in contrast to multilateral aid, in which many donor governments pool their contributions via intermediary institutions that then disburse aid to recipient countries. Yet another category is private aid that individuals, corporations, and foundations donate voluntarily, often through nongovernmental organizations (NGOs). Typically, bilateral aid accounts for two-thirds to three-quarters of all official aid; estimates of private aid put it at about one-tenth the size of official aid.

Although bilateral aid of one form or another is as old as the nation-state, the modern era of bilateral aid began with U.S. aid to reconstruct Europe under the Marshall Plan following World War II. Over time, governments of other major developed countries joined the United States in providing bilateral aid, sometimes following U.S. pressure to share the burden. In some cases, aid programs developed out of colonial administrations during the 1960s as more and more colonies became independent. In other cases, notably Japan, the bilateral aid program evolved from war reparation payments. A number of developing countries—notably China, India, and Venezuela—are also aid donors.

Bilateral aid is most often government-to-government, although in some circumstances donors may fund NGOs directly. Many aid donors are members of the Organisation for Economic Cooperation and Development (OECD). The Development Assistance Committee (DAC) of the OECD is the international body that sets aid reporting standards, monitors aid flows, and urges donors to improve the quality and quantity of their aid. The DAC's main focus is on official development assistance (ODA), which it defines as official concessional flows for developmental purposes to low-income countries. This includes grants as well as loans that are at least 25 percent concessional as compared to a commercial alternative (35 percent for "mixed credits," where aid is used to finance a commercial venture). Over the life of an ODA loan, repayments of principal and interest must be at least 25 percent lower than for a comparable commercial loan. ODA normally excludes grants and loans for military purposes and funds not directed to poor countries. In contrast to multilateral aid, most bilateral aid is given as grants; Japanese aid is the exception. The DAC's long-standing goal is for donors to contribute seven-tenths of 1 percent of gross domestic product (GDP) as ODA, though only a few of the most generous donors attain this target. In general, the United States has been the largest donor but among the least generous as a share of GDP. Under the Marshall Plan, U.S. aid was as high as 2 percent of GDP, but it has been one-tenth of that in recent times. France, Germany, and Japan also have been major donors, while the Netherlands and the Scandinavian countries have been the most generous DAC donors relative to their GDPs.

Bilateral aid can fund a specific project (project aid), provide more general budgetary support for the recipient government (program aid), or flow through an NGO. Although reconstruction aid to Europe was often program aid, bilateral aid to developing countries has more often been project aid. Since the 1980s, multilateral aid agencies, particularly the World Bank, have become heavily involved in program aid, which aims to promote policy and institutional reform in developing countries; most bilateral donors put less funding into program aid.

Controversies Despite its apparent humanitarian nature, aid—especially bilateral aid—has been heavily criticized as insufficiently humanitarian and relatively ineffective. Critiques begin with the low volume of aid, both relative to the size of donor economies and relative to the need of the recipients. Critics also point to donor behavior that suggests that need can take a backseat to more narrowly defined donor interests such as geopolitics and commercial advantage. The geopolitical imperative is particularly pronounced for the United States with top recipients (Israel, Iraq, South Vietnam, South Korea) reflecting U.S. military interests rather than recipient need. For European donors former colony status dominates need, while Japanese aid often flows to countries rich in raw materials that Japan lacks.

The composition of aid also undercuts its development potential, as much bilateral aid is tied to purchases of donor products that are often expensive and inappropriate. Where aid funds projects, researchers have documented a bias toward large import- and capital-intensive undertakings that suit donors' needs but fail to reflect the relative scarcity of capital and foreign exchange in recipient countries. Aid levels are generally contingent on the donor's budget position so that aid tends to increase when the world economy is doing well. The result for many developing countries is procyclical aid fluctuations that can have the unintended consequence of destabilizing the recipient economy. The multiplicity of donors, each with their own priorities, procedures, and teams of visiting experts, can create a huge operational burden on a developing country government. All of these factors can reduce the development effectiveness of bilateral aid.

In response to the shortcomings of bilateral aid, the DAC and others have pushed for more multilateral aid. But if the main developmental short-comings of bilateral aid arise from its use as a geopolitical and commercial tool, why would donors be willing to redirect funds from bilateral to multilateral agencies? One argument is that the greater apparent independence of multilateral agencies makes them more efficient at some tasks (e.g., promoting sensitive institutional changes and providing a credible signal to private capital markets about the investment climate in the recipient country). A second argument is that donor country taxpayers favor developmental rather than geopolitical aid and that the donor government can demonstrate its developmental orientation most clearly through multilateral contributions. Neither argument, however, explains why some donors both contribute to and then work to undermine the independence of multilateral agencies. In any event, supporters of bilateral aid argue that the multiplicity of domestic interests served by bilateral aid helps to maintain a coalition in favor of larger budgets so that the net developmental impact of catering to domestic donor interests may be positive.

A recent trend in aid allocation has been toward selectivity. Research from the World Bank has argued that aid generally fails to promote growth and development when recipient government policies are poor and also that aid fails to promote policy change. Thus the implication is that more aid should be directed to countries that have already adopted appropriate (i.e., progrowth) policies. The empirical basis for these conclusions has proven weak. The original approach to estimating the link between aid and growth conditional on policy is not robust to small changes in specification or in which countries and years are examined. Other approaches have found a variety of results: aid has no impact regardless of policy; aid has a positive impact regardless of policy; aid has positive but diminishing returns regardless of policy; aid has a positive impact everywhere but the effect is larger when policies are good; and aid has a greater impact when policies are bad. Competing studies use different measures of aid, different approaches to deal with the potential for reverse causation, and different time horizons. The estimated impact of aid ranges from zero to economically substantial (a several percentage point increase in the growth rate of GDP).

Despite this uncertainty, many bilateral donors have increased the country selectivity of their aid programs. In the United States, the Millennium Development Account is a direct application of aid selectivity with 16 indicators of good governance used as criteria for aid eligibility. Other donors, including Scandinavian countries, have moved toward using governance criteria to reduce the number of countries receiving funds. Although such a policy might seem to abandon poorly governed countries to their fate, advocates of selectivity maintain that incentive effects (the desire to qualify for aid) will induce better governance so that eventually all would benefit. In the past, however, political changes in donor governments have led to changes in bilateral aid allocation. If developing country governments expect such changes to continue, the incentive effects of current selectivity criteria will be undermined.

Opponents of aid have frequently rallied behind the slogan "trade not aid," pointing out that protectionist trade policies in donor countries cost developing countries far more than they receive in foreign aid. In addition, they argue that trade is likely to improve the efficiency of developing country economies whereas aid could introduce perverse incentives and promote rent seeking or corruption. Yet the arguments in favor of more trade do not weaken the case for aid as the slogan's "either/or" dichotomy seems to suggest. The distributional impact of trade is likely very different from that of aid, as the poorest in most need of aid are unlikely to be the main beneficiaries of increased trade.

See also aid, international; aid, international, and political economy; HIV/AIDS; nongovernmental organizations (NGOs); political economy of policy reform; regional development banks; World Bank

FURTHER READING

Burnside, Craig, and David Dollar. 2000. "Aid, Policies and Growth." *American Economic Review* 90 (4): 847–68. World Bank researchers present evidence in favor of greater aid selectivity; extremely influential even though the results were later shown to be fragile.

Lancaster, Carol. 2007. *Foreign Aid: Diplomacy, Development, Domestic Politics.* Chicago: University of Chicago Press. Provides an overview as well as a more detailed treatment of five major donors.

Minoiu, Camelia, and Sanjay Reddy. 2007. "Aid Does Matter, After All: Revisiting the Relationship between Aid and Growth." *Challenge* 50 (2): 39–58. Summarizes the literature on aid and growth and presents evidence that the long-run impact of developmental aid on growth is large and positive regardless of the policy environment.

Organisation for Economic Co-operation and Development. Yearly. *Development Cooperation Report.* Paris: OECD. Downloadable from http://www.oecd.org/dac. Information on aid issues, statistics, and practices.

Radelet, Steven. 2006. "A Primer on Foreign Aid." Center for Global Development Working Paper 92. Downloadable from http://www.cgdev.org/content/publications/detail/8846. Readable overview of foreign aid history and issues, including bilateral and multilateral aid.

Tendler, Judith. 1975. *Inside Foreign Aid.* Baltimore: Johns Hopkins University Press. Classic treatment of institutional biases reducing the effectiveness of aid. Uses evidence from U.S. bilateral aid programs.

CHRISTOPHER KILBY

■ aid, food

Food aid is a resource provided on concessionary terms in the form of, or for the provision of, food. In accounting categories, international food aid is a cross-border flow that is an entry into a country's balance of payments. National governments do provide food aid within their own borders, however. Generally, food aid is thought of as assistance provided by donor governments and humanitarian agencies to address the problems of hunger, food insufficiency, and malnutrition—and indeed *some* food aid is expressly for this purpose. Over the history of modern food aid, however, substantial amounts of food aid have had little to do with addressing hunger.

History and Origins Food assistance throughout history has included attempts to address famine in

Venezuela in the 1830s, Ireland in the 1840s, and the Ukraine in the 1930s—all of which involved significant shipments of food. The India Famine Codes in the late 19th century may have been the first systematic attempt to balance market forces and free food distribution. But the origin of large-scale contemporary food aid traces to the post–World War II period in North America, when technological advances led to dramatic increases in production that resulted in significant surpluses and declining prices for farmers. Politically obligated to purchase the surpluses, the U.S. and Canadian governments found it less costly to give away the surplus food than to store it. United States Public Law 480, enacted in 1954, formalized this process. Hence the origin of modern food aid was a means of addressing domestic surplus production—not a means of addressing hunger or poverty. Over the past 50 years food aid has served multiple objectives: disposing of surplus production, supporting farm income, maintaining a maritime shipping fleet, supporting domestic agribusiness and food processing industries—as well as addressing hunger in foreign countries.

Types of Food Aid Classically there have been three kinds of food aid. *Program food aid*, for almost 40 years the largest single category, is subsidized deliveries or free grants of food on a government-to-government basis. The recipient government usually sells the food and uses the proceeds for many purposes—not necessarily for food assistance or anything to do with addressing hunger. The main purpose of program food aid has been to provide budgetary support or balance-of-payments relief for recipient governments.

Project food aid provides support to field-based projects in areas of chronic need through deliveries of food, usually on a grant basis, to a recipient government, a nongovernmental organization, or the U.N. World Food Programme. The recipient agency then uses the food either directly in projects such as mother and child health, school feeding, or food-for-work projects that provide an employment guarantee using food for wages, or by "monetizing" the food aid—selling it in the recipient country market and using the proceeds for project activities that require cash as an input rather than food.

Emergency or humanitarian food aid consists of deliveries of free food to populations affected by conflict or disaster, with a host country government, the World Food Programme, or a nongovernmental organization acting as the distributing agency.

Trends in Food Aid The total annual flow of food aid in the years 1981 through 2005 was around 8–10 million metric tons (see figure 1)—a relatively tiny amount compared to the more than 300 million tons of commercially traded food of the same commodity groups. Since 1980, humanitarian food aid has become the most dominant form, amounting to about 60 percent of the total, whereas prior to 1980, it was in the range of 10–15 percent. Since the beginning of the 21st century, program food aid or government-to-government food assistance has declined sharply, and by 2007 seemed likely to be phased out altogether soon. Project food aid tended to be relatively stable in volume terms in the period 1980–2005. In the post–World War II years, food aid comprised as much as 15 percent of total overseas assistance—in the early 21st century, by contrast, it accounted for only 2–3 percent of the total.

Food Aid Policy Debates International food aid has been subject to weak regulatory mechanisms, many of which are outdated or dysfunctional. As a result, many of these mechanisms were being renegotiated as of 2007, or their roles were being taken over by other, newer institutions. The Food Aid Convention—originally signed in 1967 and renewed

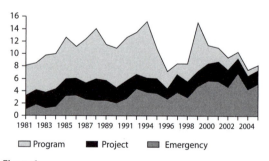

Figure 1

Global food aid deliveries, 1981–2005 (MMT). Source: WFP Interfais.

in 1998—existed on one-year extensions for several years in the first decade of the 21st century, and was up for a major renegotiation by 2007. Much of the impact of food aid on trade has come up for negotiation at the World Trade Organization.

The extent to which food aid undermines international trade or local incentives for agricultural production is also a subject of controversy. Overall, there appears to be no significant impact of food aid on domestic production, but different kinds of food aid have different effects—well-managed emergency food aid can actually lead to an increase in food production (with a lagged time effect, because well-managed emergency food aid can enable farmers to cultivate a crop when they might otherwise be unable, thus resulting in a greater harvest available at the end of the season). But poorly targeted food aid that ends up being consumed by people who would otherwise be able to grow or purchase food may undermine production or trade incentives. Open "monetization" (the sale of food aid in the recipient country) is thought to be one example that causes trade or production displacement.

Traditionally food aid was provided in kind by donor governments, to be used or distributed either by recipient country governments or by humanitarian agencies. Beginning in the 1990s, food aid from some donors has been "untied" from market sources in donor countries, meaning that a proportion of food aid budgets are now in cash for purchasing food either within the country where food aid is needed, or in a nearby developing country— called local and regional purchase. European donors and Canada devote significant proportions of their funding to local or regional purchase of food, which is believed to save both time and expense when responding to acute need, thus enabling more rapid response and a relatively greater volume of response within fixed budgets. United States food aid continued to be tied to procurement in U.S. markets as of late 2007, and the extent to which "aid-tying" of food assistance continued to be allowed was a subject of considerable controversy in World Trade Organization negotiations over a new Agreement on Agriculture. In addition to pressure for untying

food assistance, there was also considerable evidence that cash transfers are a more effective and efficient means of ensuring access by poor or disaster-affected populations to adequate food under some circumstances.

See also Agreement on Agriculture; aid, international

FURTHER READING
Barrett, Christopher, and Daniel Maxwell. 2005. *Food Aid after Fifty Years: Recasting its Role*. London: Routledge. Traces the origins and history of food aid, current applications and problems, and policy proposals for addressing many contemporary problems with food aid.
Clay, Edward, and Olaf Stokke. 2000. *Food Aid and Human Security*. London: Frank Cass. An edited volume dealing with many of the issues related to food, including the right to food.
Harvey, Paul. 2007. *Cash-based Responses in Emergencies*. HPG Paper. London: Humanitarian Policy Group. A state of the art review of using cash transfers in emergencies, to fulfill food security or other objectives.
The Sphere Project. 2004. *The Humanitarian Charter and Minimum Standards in Disaster Response*. Geneva: The Sphere Project. A humanitarian charter made up of key points from international human rights law, international humanitarian law, and refugee law. The "Sphere guidelines" also lay out minimum standards for assessment, service delivery, monitoring and evaluation, and participation in seven sectors of humanitarian intervention, including food aid and food security.
UN Food and Agriculture Organization (FAO). 2006. *The State of Food Insecurity in the World, 2006*. Rome: Food and Agriculture Organization. An annual report, the 2006 edition is devoted entirely to the subject of food aid.
UN World Food Programme. WFP Interfais. Available at http://www.wfp.org/interfais/index2.htm. Offers tables that detail recent allotment of food aid.

DANIEL MAXWELL

■ aid, humanitarian

Humanitarian aid is assistance provided directly to people affected by conflict or disasters. Traditionally it is in-kind material assistance—food, shelter, or medical care—but it also can take the form of cash assistance. The primary intent of humanitarian aid is to save lives, reduce suffering, and protect human dignity in times of crisis. Often, additional objectives are to protect people's livelihoods and assets or other indirect life-saving goals. Humanitarian aid is different from development aid, which has longer-term objectives and sometimes greater conditionality—but the distinction is not always clear, and in chronic emergencies may become quite blurred.

History and Origins Although there are humanitarian antecedents in many different religious and cultural traditions, the history of modern independent humanitarian aid traces to the Battle of Solferino in 1859. There, Swiss businessman Henri Dunant was horrified by the impact of industrialized warfare and organized a local effort to assist wounded soldiers on the battlefield. Dunant essentially struck a deal with the belligerent armies that he would not interfere with their conflict provided they would grant him safe passage to assist the wounded who were incapable of continuing to fight. In 1863, Dunant founded the International Committee of the Red Cross (ICRC) in Geneva, based on the same principle. The ICRC is the organization mandated by international humanitarian law to provide protection and assistance to wounded or captured soldiers, and especially to civilians and other noncombatants caught in conflict. National chapters of the Red Cross soon grew up as well, usually mandated by law in the host country. In Islamic countries, these are known as Red Crescent societies. The International Federation of Red Cross and Red Crescent Societies (IFRC) is made up of these national chapters.

Other Humanitarian Agencies Under international law, the state has the first responsibility for the protection and provision of assistance to citizens within its borders. But often the government of an affected country either cannot provide adequate assistance or, in some cases, may be one of the parties causing a humanitarian emergency in the first place. In such cases, other agencies may be called on (or take it on themselves) to provide assistance. Following each of the major crises of the 20th century, other agencies were founded to provide humanitarian

assistance for the victims of war as well as people affected by natural disasters or other crises. These include specialized UN agencies and nongovernmental organizations (NGOs). UN agencies—mostly formed in the aftermath of World War II—include the United Nations Children's Fund and the Office of the UN High Commissioner for Refugees. The largest of the UN humanitarian agencies, the World Food Programme was founded in 1963, and the Office for the Coordination of Humanitarian Affairs was founded in 1998, reorganized from the former Department of Humanitarian Affairs.

Major NGOs were also formed in response to the crises of the 20th century: Save the Children was formed in the aftermath of World War I, CARE and Oxfam in response to World War II, and World Vision in response to the Korean War. Médecins sans Frontières was formed in 1969 after French doctors split with the ICRC over the issue of raising public awareness about the plight of civilians during the Biafran war. More recent crises have seen the advent of increasing numbers of nontraditional providers of humanitarian aid—including the military, private for-profit companies, and contractors.

Defining Characteristics In principle, humanitarian assistance is based on the premise that no human caught in a life-threatening situation should be denied assistance (or conversely—and more controversially—that all humans in a life-threatening situation have a right to receive assistance). This was formalized by the ICRC in 1965 as the principle of *humanity* or the *humanitarian imperative*. This principle now informs humanitarian assistance across most if not all humanitarian agencies. The ICRC also formally articulated six other principles on which it had based its work for nearly a century and which followed logically. The first is *impartiality*, or the imperative to provide assistance on the basis of need alone, without respect to nationality, race, religion, gender, or political point of view. The second is *neutrality*, or a refusal to take sides in a conflict or to engage in "political controversies." This was seen as a principle in its own right and the means to gain access to conflict-affected populations. A third principle is *independence*, meaning that the offer of humanitarian assistance should be independent of government policies or actions. *Voluntary service*, *unity*, and *universality* are the other principles. These principles are codified for the entire humanitarian community in the Red Cross Code of Conduct and the Sphere Guidelines.

Humanitarian Policy Debates Up to the 1980s, humanitarian action was seen to be largely beyond reproach—a form of altruism that was neither a threat nor of serious political consequence. After the end of the cold war, humanitarian action became, for a time, a substitute for major powers' political engagement in problems affecting other countries—for example, in the Balkans wars of the 1990s. Since the onset of the global war on terrorism, humanitarian action has come to be seen, both by major powers and, in some cases, by popular perception in host countries, as part of a larger political and security agenda. Most humanitarian agencies still refuse to take sides in conflicts, but neutrality—especially the admonition against "political controversy"—is the subject of intense debate and many humanitarian agencies do not claim to be apolitical (although the ICRC still does). And as public sources of funding for humanitarian aid become more and more dominant, the capacity for independent humanitarian action has declined.

The principle of impartiality is intended to govern the provision of humanitarian aid in all circumstances, but political considerations often trump humanitarian principles in practice, and there are large discrepancies in the level of response by the humanitarian community to similar levels of human suffering by affected populations—from as little as a few dollars per person in some forgotten crises in Africa to more than $7,000 per person affected by the Indian Ocean earthquake and tsunami emergency in late 2004.

With larger budgets and greater scrutiny have come calls for the humanitarian enterprise to be more accountable—not only to the donors that provide funding, but for the behavior of agency staff in emergencies, for the development of industry standards for humanitarian response to which all actors should be held responsible, and to the recipient communities that are affected by war and disaster. To this end, in the early 21st century several interagency initiatives, including the Sphere Project, the Action Learning Network for Accountability and Performance, and the Humanitarian Accountability Partnership International, developed to hold humanitarian action to higher standards of accountability.

See also aid, international

FURTHER READING

Darcy, James, and Charles-Antoine Hofmann. 2003. *According to Need? Needs Assessment and Decision-Making in the Humanitarian Sector*. HPG Report. London: ODI. A landmark report highlighting the fact that humanitarian response is not impartial (i.e., not according to the level of humanitarian need). The international humanitarian community has no means for independently assessing comparable levels of needs, and the donor community does not believe most humanitarian needs assessments.

Development Initiatives. 2006. *Global Humanitarian Assistance 2006*. Somerset, UK: Development Initiatives. A summary report on the level of funding, the types of emergencies encountered, and the types of agencies responding to humanitarian emergencies in 2006.

International Committee of the Red Cross. 1983. *Understanding Humanitarian Law: Basic Rules of the Geneva Conventions and their Additional Protocols*. Geneva: ICRC. A primer on international humanitarian law, for the "law of war," which governs all humanitarian action in times of war and spells out the obligations of all parties.

———. 1995. *Red Cross/NGO Code of Conduct*. Geneva: IFRC. The code of conduct that lays out the basic humanitarian principles for all agencies, whether affiliated with the Red Cross or not. The code of conduct goes beyond just the four main ICRC principles. The Code of Conduct has been signed by more than 400 agencies.

Rieff, David. 2002. *A Bed for the Night: Humanitarianism in Crisis*. New York: Simon and Schuster. A critique that is at once sympathetic to the humanitarian movement but harsh in its judgment of the loss of vision, direction, and principle in humanitarian action during the late 20th century. Published just after the attacks of September 11, 2001, it doesn't deal with humanitarian action in the context of the global war on terrorism.

The Sphere Project. 2004. *The Humanitarian Charter and Minimum Standards in Disaster Response*. Geneva: The Sphere Project. A humanitarian charter made up of key points from international human rights law, international humanitarian law, and refugee law. The "Sphere Guidelines" also lay out minimum standards for assessment, service delivery, monitoring and evaluation, and participation in seven sectors of humanitarian intervention.

DANIEL MAXWELL

■ aid, international

International aid, or official development assistance (ODA), comprises a wide range of financial and nonfinancial components. These may take the form of cash transfers as well as grants of machinery, technical advice, and analysis and assistance in capacity-building support. Although foreign aid is often envisaged as transferring resources from rich to poor countries, the reality is more complex, with more than half of all ODA actually going to middle-income countries.

Early Foreign Aid The history of modern aid and colonialism are in many ways intertwined. In order to extract raw materials and exploit economic activity abroad, the colonial powers provided investment capital, technology, and personnel to colonies. Examples include the Belgian-initiated railroads in the Congo, the French design of the Suez Canal, and railroads and roads built under British rule to transport primary commodities in southern and eastern Africa.

Explicit reference to aid became more widespread in the 1940s. During this period, the wealthier countries began considering broader economic development as a goal, focusing on aspects of engagement that were not directly or exclusively related to extraction and exploitation. This reflected an evolution of economic and strategic interests (and in part was associated with the decline of mining relative to other sectors and also with the development of air and other military capabilities). It also reflected a changing understanding of human dignity in which

human rights and self-determination emerged in strong opposition to earlier Darwinian notions, which had reinforced colonial notions of superiority. The 1940s also brought to the fore arguments for the need to invest in strategic alliances and in peace.

The period immediately following World War II saw a concerted effort to avoid a repeat of the post–World War I peace process and reparations, which had served at best as a short-term palliative. It was recognized that peace required economic integration and this required both financial flows and policy changes to bring about closer economic integration. The new vision for sustained peace through economic opportunity gave rise to the Marshall Plan, as well as to the Bretton Woods conference and the creation of multilateral institutions such as the United Nations (UN), the World Bank, and the International Monetary Fund, whose goal was to increase international cooperation and assistance. This architecture largely remains in place today.

Increasingly, broad goals such as education were supported by emergent foreign aid programs and endorsed in parliamentary acts of the time, such as the 1948 British Overseas Development Act. In 1949, President Truman's inaugural address proposed the creation of a program for development assistance. The UN's 1951 report on *Measures for the Economic Development of Under-developed Countries* (with Arthur Lewis as the lead author) advocated the creation of a dedicated UN fund to support development, as well as an International Finance Corporation (IFC) to underpin private investment (five years later the IFC was established as part of the World Bank Group). In the 1950s and early 1960s, following the granting of independence to most colonies, many former colonial civil servants were employed in newly established aid projects, so that while the expatriate personnel remained, the nature of the relationship changed.

The initial focus of these institutions was on rebuilding war-torn Western Europe and Japan and on stabilizing the world financial system, rather than on broader notions of development. Indeed, the first four of the World Bank's loans were devoted to postwar reconstruction. In addition to supporting the activities of the multilateral agencies, the wealthiest countries began to set up their own bilateral initiatives to provide aid flows and technical assistance to developing countries. In 1960, Canada created an External Aid Office, and in 1961 the United States created the United States Agency for International Development, France inaugurated a Ministry for Cooperation, Japan created the Overseas Economic Cooperation Fund to provide loans for developing countries, and Germany established its development bank, the Reconstruction Credit Institute (KfW). Sweden and the United Kingdom established bilateral aid agencies in 1962 and 1964, respectively. These agencies at first focused on former colonies, leaving broader global reconstruction and development to the multilateral institutions such as the World Bank. Over time, however, the objectives and strategy of multilateral institutions and national agencies converged, and there is now a significant degree of overlap.

From the outset, nongovernmental and other groups had ambitions that were often ahead of governments' views on aid. For example, the World Council of Churches in 1958 called on the rich countries to allocate 1 percent of their national income to aid for developing countries. This was later taken up by the Development Assistance Group, which was established in 1960 as a forum for consultation among aid donors at the Organisation for European Economic Co-operation (OEEC), which became the Organisation for Economic Co-operation and Development (OECD) later that year. A target of 0.7 percent was agreed by the UN General Assembly in 1970, but by 2006 it had been reached by only five countries, despite the fact that rich countries are much wealthier and poor countries are much better managed than when the pledge was made.

Foreign Aid during the Cold War Chilling relations between the West and the Soviet Union meant that from the 1950s to the fall of the Berlin Wall in 1989, Cold War politics became a key determinant in all foreign policy, and not least aid. Increasingly aid was used as a means to support and bolster friendly states. Where geopolitical interests

were involved, economic and military support were often closely interconnected.

In Zaire (now Democratic Republic of the Congo), for example, aid was used as a strategic tool. Between 1960 and 1990, more than $10 billion was disbursed in aid to Zaire in support of an increasingly brutal and corrupt dictatorship. Maintaining a strategic alliance, rather than development effectiveness, was the objective. Similarly, political and economic factors were the main drivers of large aid donations in support of the transition to a market economy in Eastern Europe and Central Asia. Not surprisingly, such aid was not correlated with long-term poverty reduction. Such cases have lent support to aid skeptics.

A key characteristic of foreign aid during the Cold War period was its "tied" nature: aid was allocated to the purchase of specific goods and services from the donor country. In this way, much aid never left the donor countries, as it ended up paying for consultants or services (such as foreign-language radio broadcasts).

Food aid also became prevalent. In part this reflected the growing agricultural subsidies in Western Europe, the United States, and Japan, which rose to more than $300 billion per annum. These rich countries protected their markets from competitive imports and subsidized their farmers, dumping surpluses on world markets, often as food aid. Poor countries were unable to compete in agriculture and trade, and the dumping of food on world markets undermined and destabilized agricultural prices and production in developing countries. As outlined by Goldin and Knudsen (1993) and Sen (1982), the distortion of markets and policy failures contributed to price instability, long-term decline in agricultural prices facing developing country farmers, and even famines. While protectionist trade policies in the rich countries undermined the potential for sustainable growth in many developing countries, rich countries' aid policies provided at best a partial response to short-term humanitarian needs. Similarly, while significant quantities of aid were directed into investments in irrigation and other agricultural infrastructure in developing countries, the undermining of the rural economy as a result of protectionism by rich countries provides a classic example of a failure to achieve policy coherence.

Although there has been some progress in untying aid since the end of the Cold War, tying persists in many aid programs today. Meanwhile, agricultural protectionism continues to have a pernicious influence on world agricultural markets and trade, with the negative impact far exceeding the aggregate poverty-reduction impact of aid (Goldin and Reinert 2007).

Adjustment Programs Adjustment (or macroeconomic policy-based) aid was developed in the 1970s. This was designed to respond to the severe macroeconomic imbalances experienced by many poor countries, characterized by ballooning deficits and debt that were aggravated by exogenous shocks from oil prices, interest rates, and other sources. The constellation of conservative political leadership in the United States (Reagan), the United Kingdom (Thatcher), and Germany (Kohl) was also important, with aid acting as an agent of reform and bolstering the private sector. By the late 1970s, aid was increasingly predicated on the recipient country's acceptance of conditions that sought to enforce macroeconomic and trade reforms, and to facilitate private (particularly foreign) investment. The focus on structural economic reforms was not accompanied by corresponding attention to institutional reform or investments in education and health, and neglected demands of social cohesion. This limitation, along with the mounting assertions of self-determination by rapidly democratizing governments, as well as the pendulum swing in rich countries away from their former preoccupation with market solutions, meant that by the mid-1990s, following the end of the Cold War, adjustment lending had become far less common.

Poverty Reduction and Recent Development Models The reform of aid policies in the 1990s responded to a range of factors. These included the end of Cold War preoccupation with strategic allies, the success of the growth paradigms in China and India, the failure of major aid efforts (not least in Africa),

and intellectual evolution—particularly in the areas of understanding around economic growth, poverty reduction, and development. Perhaps the most striking belated change was the recognition that to reduce poverty, aid should be focused on those countries where poor people lived and in which the governments were willing and able to act to overcome poverty. In addition, as poverty increasingly was recognized as multifaceted, the policy discussions and interventions around poverty reduction became more nuanced.

By the late 1990s, the goals of development began to embrace the elimination of poverty in all its dimensions, by improving education, health, and other human capacities, not simply focusing on income. Scholars such as Sen (1999) gave intellectual form to the emerging understanding that development means increasing the control that poor people have over their lives. This is derived through a combination of education, health, and greater participation in politics and community decisions, as well as from improvements in access and income. It is also clear, and beginning to be reflected in aid policy, that the various dimensions of poverty are related, and that income growth generally leads to progress in the nonincome dimensions of poverty and vice versa.

From the early 1990s, this rethinking of development was associated with an increase in aid flows to health, education, and infrastructure. Due mainly to improvements in two countries, China and India, where government policies are largely but not entirely independent of aid, social indicators such as health and education on average have improved very quickly since the mid-1970s in developing countries.

Direct targeting of health and education goals, rather than waiting for improvements to follow income gains, has led to a virtuous circle that has improved the welfare of individuals and families. On average, at every level of income in developing countries, infant mortality fell sharply during the 20th century, and life expectancy increased by 20 years (from mid-forties to mid-sixties) over a period of only 40 years. The global trend in life expectancy remains very positive, although HIV/AIDS has dramatically reversed this trend in a number of countries, particularly in southern Africa.

Developing countries also experienced dramatic improvements in literacy: whereas in 1970 nearly two in every four adults were illiterate, now the proportion is only one in four. Particularly important is the greater focus on female literacy, as this has been shown to be pivotal in improving the health and human development levels of children and communities. These achievements cannot solely or even primarily be attributed to aid, but rather to a combination of national policies (not least in China and India) along with growing integration and the adoption of new health and other technologies.

The unevenness of the performance of developing countries, and ability of some very poor countries to grow despite resource constraints and others to squander abundant resources, has led to a growing focus of the aid community on governance and institutions. Increased attention to governance and institutions also has been associated with growing interest among academics in this topic. In the pragmatic world of aid agencies, attention to governance, and to institutional development more broadly, has been translated into growing budget allocations for the development of civil servants and building of regulatory authorities and judiciaries. It also has been associated with a growing emphasis on the allocation of aid in light of the performance of the recipients.

Millennium Development Goals In 2000 heads of state of both rich and poor countries committed themselves to achieving the Millennium Development Goals (MDGs). These are:

- eradicate extreme poverty and hunger
- achieve universal primary education
- promote gender equality and empower women
- reduce child mortality
- improve maternal health
- combat HIV/AIDS, malaria, and other diseases
- ensure environmental sustainability
- develop a global partnership for development

The Millennium Declaration marked a major step in the history of aid. For the first time, the international community came together to establish clearly defined common goals with a set of agreed measurable targets and results for developing countries, donor agencies, and the multilateral institutions. Building on this declaration, the 2002 Monterrey Conference established a new partnership for development in which the rich countries promised to increase both the volume and the quality of aid in return for commitments from developing countries to undertake vital reforms to enhance aid effectiveness. Despite the remarkable achievements in many countries, not least in China, it is becoming clear, however, that many or most of these goals will be missed, except perhaps that of halving income poverty, which will be met at the aggregate global level. Many developing countries have failed to live up to their Monterrey commitments on poverty reduction and good governance. Similarly, the rich countries have fallen well short of their commitments. Aid flows have increased, but these remain far short of the agreed targets, and the Doha Development Round of trade negotiations appears to be a long way from meeting even minimal expectations. The tremendous achievements of the MDGs, not least in terms of mobilizing public opinion in many rich countries, are therefore at risk of dissipating due to inadequate political will.

Types of Aid and Harmonization As figure 1 shows, only around 20 percent of bilateral aid in fact ends up as a cash transfer into the hands of the recipient country ("other bilateral"). Around 80 percent takes the form of aid to multilateral organizations, debt relief for countries such as Afghanistan and Iraq, administrative costs, costs for refugees living in donor countries, and technical cooperation—including support to students from developing countries studying in donor countries (imputed student costs). Although this indirect assistance may make an important contribution, it is often driven by the priorities of the donors and is no substitute for predictable, multiyear flows of aid mobilized behind government programs that are agreed upon by governments and across the donor community. Such

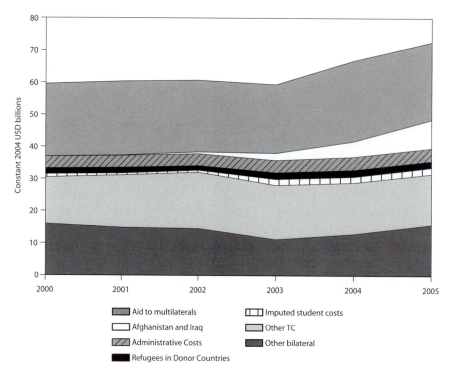

Figure 1

Aid components, 2000–2005. Source: OECD Development Aid Committee (DAC) data.

harmonization and coordination are vital to reduce the currently high transaction costs of aid, which divert scarce resources—including the time demands on the most competent civil servants—into projects and activities that have too often been donor priorities rather than recipient national priorities.

Considerable progress has been made in harmonizing approaches to aid. The 2005 Paris conference and subsequent Declaration on Aid Effectiveness brings together multilateral and bilateral donor agencies around common standards. While the MDGs provided a landmark in terms of defining common goalposts for development, the harmonization agenda aimed to ensure that the donors played as one team. Significant improvements in coordination among a number of the traditional major donors point the way forward. As diverse aid flows are increasingly combined into broad multidonor activities, the challenge for donors is

to convince their skeptical voters that their taxes have been spent wisely. Although attributing the impact of aid to individual donors may be counterproductive, in that it suggests that development is not a national responsibility, aid—like all public expenditures—requires accountability.

Levels of Aid, Aid Quality, and Evaluation Aid flows increased markedly between 1945 and 1960, but subsequently slowed and from 1990, when it averaged 0.34 percent of the gross national income (GNI) of the donor countries, declined to around 0.22 percent of the GNI of high-income countries in 2001, as shown in figure 2. The recommitment to aid at the Monterrey Conference in 2002 finally arrested this decline, with ODA reaching a record high in 2005. Subsequently, aid flows again slipped back, reflecting the fact that the inclusion of Iraq and Nigerian debt write-offs had temporarily inflated the numbers earlier. Going forward, the key uncer-

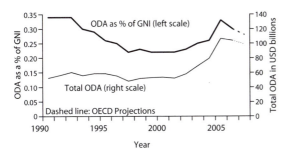

Figure 2

Aid flows. Source: OECD Development Aid Committee (DAC) data.

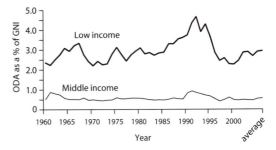

Figure 3

Foreign aid receipts as a percentage of low and middle income GNI, 1960–2006. Source: OECD Development Aid Committee (DAC) data.

tainty is the extent to which donors will honor the pledges made at Monterrey and reiterated at the 2005 Gleneagles G8 Summit, where it was agreed to double aid to Africa and to achieve the 0.7 percent commitment.

In comparison with domestic investment and government expenditure, aid flows are small. Development aid to developing countries in 2005 was a record $107 billion, but even without taking account of the fact that most of this was not transferred to developing countries, aid remained less than one-third of foreign direct investment in developing countries ($334 billion), which itself was only a small fraction of total investment in developing countries (more than $2 trillion). Although increasing the volume of aid is vital, improving its quality is even more important.

Both the relatively small levels of aid and the instability of these flows for middle- and low-income countries are reflected in figure 3. Since aid is typically small compared to budget and private investment flows, and more unstable, the key challenge is to ensure that aid effects systemic changes such as introducing ideas and improving practices. These in turn have positive effects on growth and poverty reduction. Such indirect effects are difficult to measure and attribute, however, and, as indicated earlier, attribution risks undermining government leadership and harmonization. It is important that aid be provided not solely for short-term and relatively easily measurable objectives.

A growing body of literature had sought to use randomized techniques to provide improved rigor to the evaluation of aid. Impact evaluation and other evaluative methods may be expected to become a necessary part of the toolbox of aid agencies as they and the recipient governments seek to enhance the effectiveness of pubic expenditures. These techniques yield powerful insights when applied through carefully designed studies of projects or programs but typically they are less helpful at the macro policy level, where there is limited scope for randomization or associating single actions or actors with particular outcomes.

The complexity of social and economic change means that the impact of foreign aid cannot be easily separated from other factors. The most successful projects are ones in which recipients are strongly committed and in charge of the development process, and where there is good partnership among donors and with local leadership. Recipients are then particularly well placed to draw on foreign aid, with a view to both learning lessons from international experience and funding well-defined investments that can underpin growth and poverty reduction. For such recipients, the objective is to become self-sustaining and to turn from being net aid recipients to donors, as has been the experience of China.

The increasing focus of aid on countries with relatively sound policies has meant that the estimated poverty-reduction productivity of ODA is significantly better than it was in the early 1990s. Countries with poor policies and poor institutional quality cannot simply be isolated, however. Some recent studies have found that the impact of aid on growth is strong regardless of institutions and policies, and it is necessary to be cautious about the evidence in this area.

Weak States If viable institutions and policies are conducive to effective use of aid, what should be done in weak or failed states where these do not exist? Such states usually lack the governance, institutions, and necessary leadership for successful reform. Each incompetent government has its own specific problems, and aid interventions must be tailored to addressing and overcoming these. A growing specialist literature has examined the lessons of interventions in weak states, and a number of pointers to supporting such countries have emerged. It has been shown that knowledge transfer and capacity building are more effective than large-scale financial transfers and that improving basic services such as health and education is also important. In such situations, the potential role for the United Nations, in particular in terms of coordination, is often underestimated and tends to be inadequately resourced in terms of personnel and funds. While Ethiopia, Mozambique, and Uganda are postconflict success stories, unfortunately many other countries have seen little significant progress in the past decade. The challenge for aid agencies is to remain engaged but not to throw good money after bad policies. Part of the response lies in attention to coherence between aid and other policies, especially in weak states and in countries beset by conflict, as emphasized by Collier (2007).

Global Public Goods Although much of the attention in the aid debate has been on support to countries and national projects, global initiatives are also significant beneficiaries of aid. An important step in development is supporting what are known as global public goods. These are public goods whose benefits are felt beyond the border of any one country, benefiting the poor in many countries and even all humanity. The pooling of resources and coordination across national boundaries, and between the public and private sectors, is vital in addressing such global issues. These include combating major infectious diseases such as HIV/AIDS and malaria, developing better crops, managing intellectual property, and dealing with climate change.

An example of a global aid initiative is the Consultative Group on International Agricultural Research (CGIAR). This is a partnership working toward sustainable food security and poverty reduction through scientific research in the fields of agriculture, forestry, fisheries, policy, and environment. The partnership includes countries, international and regional organizations, private foundations, national agricultural research systems, civil society, and the private sector, all of which support the work of 15 international research centers. The CGIAR significantly helped the Green Revolution, which began in South Asia in the 1970s and has led to impressive gains in production of basic food crops across the developing world. Between 1970 and 1997, yields of cereals in developing countries rose more than 75 percent, coarse grains 73 percent, root crops 24 percent, and pulses nearly 11 percent.

Private Initiatives and New Donors The Global Alliance for Vaccines is an example of aid in support of a global public good. It is also indicative of the rapidly growing contribution of private donors. The Bill and Melinda Gates Foundation and other relatively recently established private aid donors, as well as privately launched campaigns such as the Clinton Global Initiative, are adding to the contribution and in terms of financial flows overtaking the more traditional nongovernmental aid institutions such as the Ford and Rockefeller Foundations, civil society groups such as Oxfam and Save the Children, and religious foundations. Together, these nongovernmental flows are channeling aid that in many countries, and perhaps also in aggregate, now exceeds the public flows. This greatly increases the potential as well as the complexity of aid (see Klein and Harford 2005). In addition to the rapid growth of private flows, interesting experiments are under way that seek to build on public-private partnerships and leverage official flows. One such example is the pilot Innovative Funding Facility for Immunization. The

French-led actions to increase aid flows through a levy on airline travel and the British-led securitization of future aid flows to raise finance from capital markets are indicative of the way that innovation and partnership are beginning to change the shape and potential of the traditional aid architecture.

The transformation of traditional aid recipients, notably China, into highly significant aid donors has challenged the aid establishment. The thrust of the OECD official donors has been closer coordination and ensuring that the recipients conform to governance and other standards. China's and other new aid donors' perspectives and objectives are not necessarily aligned with those of the traditional donors, and these new donors have not been part of the OECD Development Aid Committee coordination process. The growth in these new aid flows, both from private foundations and from governments such as China and Venezuela, has meant that there have been significant increases in the volume of aid. The key questions concern the coordination and quality of this aid and the extent to which it will be able to avoid the dangers of tied aid and aid fragmentation that undermined previous surges in aid. The ending of the Cold War and the ability of countries to access aid together with a range of development ideas and technologies have made the biggest difference to development outcomes in recent years.

A New Way Forward The polarization of the aid debate between the strong advocates, such as Sachs (2005), and deep skeptics, such as Easterly (2006), reflects an oversimplification of the complexity of the development challenges and the need for strong domestic and international actions. Resources alone will not be sufficient to ensure that poverty goals are met. Level of commitment and quality of policies and institutions in recipient countries are the primary determinants of progress. It is also evident that, when a country is committed to reform and poverty reduction, external support (which may not be limited to aid) can have substantial payoffs. An important area in which rich countries can provide support is through reforms of their own trade and other policies. As important as robust global growth is reform of the protectionist policies of rich countries (such as

in agriculture and textiles), which are so damaging to poorer countries. As Goldin and Reinert have shown (2007), changes in trade, investment, migration, environment, security, and technology policies in rich countries would pull many out of poverty. The Commitment to Development Index and associated analysis by the Center for Global Development provides an indicative summary of the importance of coherence between aid and other policies.

Coherence between aid policies and other policies is vital. For example, aid donors' support for health and educational systems is undermined by the recruitment of teachers, doctors, and nurses to work in the rich countries. Similarly, support for agricultural programs is undermined by protectionism and subsidies that prevent developing countries from competing on world markets. With continued reform momentum and steady external support, past experience suggests that developing countries can extend and deepen the progress of the last half-century. Despite the progress made in the past 50 years, an immense poverty challenge remains. Approximately 1 billion people still live on less than one dollar per day. Aid has never been more effective in supporting growth and reducing poverty, and returns on aid have increased sharply. Raising the volume and the quality of aid is a moral, strategic, and economic imperative.

See also aid, bilateral; aid, food; aid, humanitarian; aid, military; evolution of development thinking; Millennium Development Goals

FURTHER READING

Collier, P. 2007. *The Bottom Billion: Why the Poorest Countries Are Failing and What Can Be Done About It.* Oxford: Oxford University Press. Seeks to identify the primary processes trapping the world's poorest people and suggests means to overcome their predicament.

Collier, P., and D. Dollar. 2004. "Development Effectiveness: What Have We Learnt?" *The Economic Journal* 114 (496): F244–F271(1). An overview and assessment of aid that seeks to identify determinants of aid effectiveness.

Easterly, W. 2006. *The White Man's Burden: Why the West's Efforts to Aid the Rest Have Done So Much Ill and So Little*

Good. New York: Penguin. Condemns top-down aid planning as a failure of utopian social engineering.

Goldin, I., and O. Knudsen. 1993. *Trade Liberalization: Global Economic Implications.* Paris and Washington, DC: OECD and World Bank. Explores the implications of trade protectionism and potential for trade reform to enhance development.

Goldin, I. and K. Reinert. 2007. *Globalization for Development: Trade, Finance, Aid, Migration and Policy.* Washington, DC: World Bank and Palgrave Macmillan. Identifies key economic flows and recommends policies to ensure that globalization supports development.

Goldin, I., H. Rogers, and N. Stern. 2002. *A Case for Aid: Building a Consensus for Development Assistance.* Washington, DC: World Bank. Evaluates evidence on aid and includes readings related to the MDGs.

Hansen, H., and F. Tarp. 2000. "Aid Effectiveness Disputed." *Journal of International Development* 12 (3): 375–98. Examines the literature on the aid-growth relationship, concluding aid works even in countries hampered by unfavorable policy environments.

Kaul, I., I. Grunberg, and M. A. Stern. 1999. *Global Public Goods: International Cooperation in the 21st Century.* Oxford: Oxford University Press. UNDP-edited collection of papers arguing that development cooperation has moved beyond aid and poverty reduction toward wider provision of global public goods.

Klein, M., and T. Harford. 2005. *The Market for Aid.* Washington DC: IFC. Introductory account of the mechanics and rapid evolution of the global aid industry.

OECD, Development Assistance Committee (DAC). Various Years. *Development Co-operation Report.* Paris: Organisation for Economic Co-operation and Development. The authoritative source of information on the foreign aid policies and programs of donor countries, published annually.

Reinert, K. 2005. *Windows on the World Economy: An Introduction to International Economics.* Mason, Ohio: South-Western Thomson. Provides an analytic understanding of the concepts of international trade, production, finance, and development.

Riddell, R. 2007. *Does Foreign Aid Really Work?* Oxford: Oxford University Press. An extensive overview of aid, examines where aid has failed and why, and identifies practical changes needed to make aid effective.

Sachs, J. 2005. *The End of Poverty: Economic Possibilities for Our Time.* New York: Penguin. Argues extreme poverty can be ended by 2025 through nine specific steps to help the poorest onto the first rung of the "development ladder."

Sen, A. 1982. *Poverty and Famines: An Essay on Entitlement and Deprivation.* Oxford: Clarendon Press. Develops an "entitlement approach" to development, focusing on the causation of starvation, and a general analysis of the characterization and measurement of poverty.

———. 1999. *Development as Freedom.* New York: Knopf. Argues that open dialogue, civil freedoms, and political liberties are vital dimensions of sustainable development.

Szirmai, A. 2005. *The Dynamics of Socio-Economic Development: An Introduction.* Cambridge: Cambridge University Press. A nontechnical introduction to development studies, exploring the dynamics of development and stagnation in developing countries.

Taylor, L. 1993. *The Rocky Road to Reform: Adjustment, Income Distribution, and Growth in the Developing World.* Cambridge, MA: MIT Press. A collection of case studies set in a broader context of examining why nations grow at different rates with inequitable patterns of wealth and income distribution.

United Nations Conference on Trade and Development (UNCTAD). 2006. *World Investment Report.* Geneva: United Nations. Provides global trends in foreign direct investment and identifies measures to improve investments contribution to development.

World Bank. 1994. *Reducing the Debt Burden of Poor Countries: A Framework for Action.* Development in Practice Series. Washington, DC: World Bank. Early discussion of the policies which aimed to reduce debt subject to performance improvements in highly indebted countries.

———. 2005. *World Development Report 2006: Equity and Development.* Washington, DC: World Bank. Concludes that inequality of opportunity sustains extreme deprivation and recommends ensuring more equitable access to health care, jobs, capital, secure land rights, and political freedoms.

IAN GOLDIN

■ aid, international, and political economy

International donors provided more than U.S. $2.4 trillion in the form of foreign aid from 1960 to 2004. In many African countries, for example, the size of the official development assistance (ODA) divided by gross domestic product (GDP) exceeded 10 percent during that period. Despite this large amount of financial aid, the economic performance of the recipient countries has been disappointing. The poor macroeconomic impact of foreign aid raises questions about its efficiency. Political economy considerations can provide explanations for the scarce effectiveness of foreign aid. By the term *political economy* we mean the allocation of markets and other economic institutions subject to the political environment in which these institutions work. In particular, the process of decision and delivery of foreign aid present multiple agency problems, derived from the existence of asymmetric information (the donor and recipient do not have access to the same information) and moral hazard (receipt of aid causes the recipient to exert less effort to solve its own problems), and inappropriate institutional designs.

Most of the academic research finds that international aid is ineffective in fostering economic growth. For instance, Boone (1996) finds that aid does not significantly increase investment or any human development indicator, but it increases the size of the government. Burnside and Dollar (2000) find that aid works, but only when there are good fiscal, monetary, and trade policies. Easterly, Levine, and Roodman (2003) dispute these results, however, since they are sensitive to changes in the sample period or filling in the missing observations.

One of the basic reasons that development aid does not seem to work is the presence of perverse incentives and faulty institutional designs. The political economy perspective treats foreign aid as the result of the incentives and motivations of the donors, the response of country recipients, and the interaction between donors and recipients.

The Incentives of Donors and Aid Agencies

Efficient public programs are supported by the existence of sufficient (perfect) information and the accountability of the representatives. Households in developed countries are, at the same time, clients and citizens. As clients, they have information about the programs intended for their benefit and as citizens in democratic countries they can hold politicians accountable for their poor performance. In the case of foreign aid this feedback loop is absent: taxpayers in donor countries (citizens) are not the beneficiaries of the aid, and they do not have information about its effectiveness; and the intended beneficiaries (clients) do not have the right to vote in donors' countries and, therefore, cannot affect the politicians in charge of approving the aid programs. We can describe this situation as a broken information feedback loop (Martens et al. 2002). In the absence of effective feedback from the intended beneficiaries of aid, the interests of consultants and suppliers of goods shape many decisions of aid agencies: these groups are the direct beneficiaries (control the information about the programs) and have direct influence on the decision-makers of donor countries.

Donors and aid agencies also have multiple objectives and represent multiple principals that often do not share the same objectives. For these reasons the institutional design of official aid agencies is difficult even if donors have good intentions. First, the multiplicity of objectives and the difficulty of performance measurement make it complicated to link the salaries of workers in aid agencies to their performance. Therefore, aid bureaucracies tend to define their output in terms of money disbursed (or volume of loans) instead of the rate of poverty reduction or economic development of recipient countries (Easterly 2003). Second, aid bureaucracies tend to develop their own procedures and increase the complexity of tenders and contracts (see Easterly 2006). Finally, aid agencies will tend to choose projects that minimize the risk of bad publicity, not the ones that maximize, for instance, the reduction of poverty.

Donor countries may also have objectives that undermine the effectiveness of foreign aid. In fact, almost half of the foreign aid provided by the members of the Organisation for Economic Co-operation and Development does not have as basic objectives poverty alleviation and economic development. Alesina and Dollar (2000) find that while some donors have the right incentives (raising income level, poverty reduction, institutional improvement), many others are driven by political and strategic considerations. The wrong incentives include targeting aid to inefficient and nondemocratic former colonies or developing countries that vote in favor of the proposals of the donor at the UN. The strategic interest in the Middle East explains why Egypt and Israel receive so much economic support from Western countries.

Another possible reason for the ineffectiveness of foreign aid is the so-called warm glow effect. Donor citizens may be interested only in the fact of giving itself and not in its effects on the recipient countries. Therefore, the utility of donors does not depend on the well-being of the citizen of recipient countries but rather on the satisfaction the donors derive from providing aid to developing countries. This interpretation is consistent with the evaluation of policies based on inputs (money disbursed) rather than on outcomes (effect of the aid on poverty and economic development). It is also consistent with voters who are worried about the total amount of money that is dedicated to foreign aid (say 0.7 percent of GDP) and not about the results that aid produces in recipient countries.

Finally, since there are multiple principals (donors and agencies), the effectiveness of foreign aid depends also on the degree of coordination among them. The need for coordination has increased over time because the level of fractionalization, or diversity, of donors (many donors with a small share of aid) has increased from 0.25 in 1960 to 0.68 in 2003. Fractionalization is measured as 1 minus the sum of the squares of the shares of different donors. Empirical evidence suggests that higher donor fragmentation is associated with a reduction in the bureaucratic quality in recipient countries.

The Interaction between Donors and Country Recipients The relationship between donors and country recipients is usually subject to principal-agent problems and moral hazard. The relationship between a principal (the donor) and an agent (the country recipient) can lead to problems when the

interests of the principal and the agent do not coincide and the principal has less than perfect information about the actions of the agent. The usual game theoretical solution to these types of problems is to write a contract, or design an incentive mechanism, to force the agent to perform as the principal wants. This incentive mechanism usually takes the form of aid conditionality: the requests associated with the concession of some types of foreign aid. The credibility of the threat to retire aid if the conditions of development of the projects are not satisfied is critical for the effectiveness of the conditionality, however. Recipient countries realize that these threats are not credible because donors do not have strong commitment ability. Donors may want to punish countries that do not fulfill their promises but, at the same time, they are pressed by their own constituencies to continue helping poor countries. The problem is reinforced by the fact that the status of the managers within the aid agencies is determined by the size of their budget and the disbursement of funds. Empirical studies show this lack of commitment technology. For instance, Burnside and Dollar (2000) do not find evidence of a significant positive relationship between aid flows (ODA) and good policies. Other studies find that there is no relationship between the developing countries' score on quality of governance (corruption, democracy, service delivery, etc.) and who receives adjustment loans, for instance, from the World Bank.

Some authors have proposed alternative institutional designs to overcome the lack of credibility of donor threats. Svensson (2000) shows that, when there is no commitment technology available for donors, the delegation of the aid budget to an institution with less aversion to poverty (underdevelopment) than the donor will improve the welfare of the citizens of the recipient country since it makes the threat credible. This theoretical result has yet to be implemented, however. If the aid game implies a donor and several recipients' countries, or a pool of projects that are disbursed to each individual country depending on its relative performance, it is possible to design an aid tournament in which potential aid recipients compete for funds. In a bilateral relationship the recipient country has more bargaining power and, therefore, the credibility of the donor's threats is weak. If the donor can choose between different recipients, however, then recipient countries have to commit to a high level of reform effort if they want to win the aid tournament. In fact, donors can impose a cost on the recipients (for instance, they may ask for a set of reforms even to get considered in the tournament). This is the traditional "stick and carrot" type of strategy. In addition, having alternative countries to receive the aid of a donor reduces the ability of one particular recipient country to use hold-up strategies.

Another problem associated with the moral hazard present in the relationship between donors and developing countries is the so-called Samaritan's dilemma (Gibson et al. 2005), which can be represented as a two-person game. The donor (Samaritan) wants to help a poor country to get out of poverty. Therefore, it gets a higher payoff from helping, or giving a large amount of help, than from not helping (or providing less aid). The recipient has to decide how much effort to exert. Obviously, the donor prefers the big-effort action. The recipient country, however, prefers to exert little effort. If the game is repeated, as happens in real interactions between donors and developing countries, then we get little effort and high levels of foreign aid. There are many examples of this situation. Donors give large amounts of food aid to developing countries with food crises. Recipient countries know this and, therefore, they have incentives to relocate their own resources away from agriculture. This action will increase the likelihood of food shortages in the recipient country, which will generate constant food aid from the donor. Then the recipient country produces less food than necessary, and the developed country sends food aid on a regular basis.

The solution to this principal-agent problem is to monitor the recipient country. However, the lack of information and the absence of accountability of the bureaucracies of recipient countries make monitoring a nonviable solution. Another possible solution for this type of problem is to threaten to withdraw the aid in the future. If this threat is credible

it can support the best outcome (high level of aid and high level of effort, which economists describe as a Pareto efficient equilibrium). In game theoretical terms the donor threatens the recipient country with ending in the worst situation for both agents (low level of aid and low level of effort, which economists call, in this case, Nash equilibrium). However, donors are usually unable to make this type of credible threat.

The Delivery of Aid in the Recipient Countries
The distribution of aid at the operational level is also subject to a principal-agent relationship and to a moral hazard problem. The moral hazard problem exists because the benefit of the contract to the donor depends on the actions taken by the recipient, and the recipient may not have incentives to behave properly after the donor has provided the funds. The recipient will take the action most beneficial to his own preferences. Therefore, the terms of the contract must be modified to provide the recipient enough motivation to behave properly. Bureaucracies are even more important in recipients' countries than in donors' agencies. The civil servants of the public bureaucracies of developing countries have a long-term contract with a low wage. Public regulation makes it difficult to fire government workers even if their performance is not appropriate. One particularly important consequence of this lack of incentives in the provision of education and health in developing countries is the so-called missing doctors and teachers. For example, Banerjee and Duflo (2006) report that, in India, the absence rate for teachers is more than 24 percent and for health providers is more than 40 percent. This is the usual shirking behavior predicted by the principal-agent theory.

In addition, since salaries for workers in the public bureaucracies of developing countries are low, they tend to run private moneymaking activities or extract side payments from citizens (extort payment for free health services, demand money for a license, etc.). Corruption and rent-seeking behavior are often the result of severe moral hazard problems combined with the absence of clearly defined property rights. One important explanation for the lack of effect of foreign aid on growth and social development is the capture of aid by government officials and politicians. The measurement of the extent of corruption in the allocation of foreign aid in developing countries is difficult because accounting systems work poorly and local accountability is weak. The World Bank has used Public Expenditure Tracing Surveys (PETS) to calculate how much money is diverted from the time the central government receives the funds until they reach the final beneficiaries. The proportion of funds that reach the intended beneficiaries tends to be very low. For instance, Reinikka and Svensson (2004) analyze a large public educational program (a capitation grant to cover schools' nonwage expenditures) in Uganda financed by the central government using district offices for its distribution. They find that many schools received nothing. On average, schools got only 13 percent of the government spending in the program. In Tanzania the analysis of the Primary Education Development Plan launched in 2002 by the World Bank and bilateral donors shows that, on average, only 20 percent of the funds disbursed at the central level finally reached the schools.

Rent-seeking activities may even produce negative consequences in the recipient countries. Djankov, Montalvo, and Reynal-Querol (2006) provide empirical evidence that a sudden windfall of resources in the form of foreign aid can damage the political institutions of the receiving country by reducing checks and balances in government and democratic rules. They label this effect the curse of aid. Other authors provide evidence that Somalia's civil war was caused by the desire of different factions to control the large amount of food aid that the country received.

The Market for Aid Some authors have argued that a possible solution to the agency problems in the aid industry is to increase competition among aid agencies (Klein and Harford 2005) and recipient countries (Svensson 2003) and use competition to make the market work better. Aid agencies should compete to fund the best projects, enabling donors to channel funds through the agencies that produce the best results; and developing countries should compete to receive official aid. This increase in competition, if accompanied with improved monitoring and

benchmarking of aid agencies and proper evaluation of outcomes for the projects, may alleviate some of the incentive problems originated by the multiple layers of delegation in the delivery of foreign aid.

Notice that this does not contradict the need for coordination among the donors. Competition is good in the sense that recipient countries will choose the most efficient project, and therefore will end up with the best donor for them. So, the existence of many donors competing for recipients does not imply that many donors will be delivering money to the same project, but only the most efficient one.

See also aid, international

FURTHER READING

Alesina, Alberto, and David Dollar. 2000. "Who Gives Foreign Aid to Whom and Why." *Journal of Economic Growth* 5: 33–63. Studies the pattern of allocation of foreign aid from various donors to receiving countries.

Banerjee, Abhijit, and Esther Duflo. 2006. "Addressing Absence." *Journal of Economic Perspectives* 20 (1): 117–32. Presents evidence on a number of innovative strategies to reduce absenteeism in government- and nongovernmental-organization–run schools and health facilities.

Boone, Peter. 1996. "Politics and the Effectiveness of Foreign Aid." *European Economic Review* 40: 289–329. Finds that aid does not significantly increase investment and growth, nor benefit the poor as measured by improvements in human development indicators, but does increase the size of government.

Burnside, C., and D. Dollar. 2000. "Aid, Policies, and Growth." *American Economic Review* 90 (4) (September): 847–88. One of the most influential papers on the recent literature of the effectiveness of foreign aid. It finds that aid has a positive impact on growth in developing countries with good fiscal, monetary, and trade policies but has little effect in the presence of poor policies.

Collier, Paul, and David Dollar. 2002. "Aid Allocation and Poverty Reduction." *European Economic Review* 46: 1475–1500. Reallocating aid is politically difficult, but it may be considerably less difficult than quadrupling aid budgets, which is what the authors estimate would be necessary to achieve the same impact on poverty reduction with existing aid allocations.

Djankov, Simeon, José G. Montalvo, and Marta Reynal-Querol. 2006. "Does Foreign Aid Help?" *Cato Journal* 26 (1): 1–28. Concludes that improving the effectiveness of aid requires increasing the responsibility of aid-receiving countries (by providing loans instead of grants in a credible environment), reducing the cost of remittances to developing countries, and improving the coordination among donors.

Easterly, William. 2003. "The Cartel of Good Intentions: The Problem of Bureaucracy in Foreign Aid." *Journal of Policy Reform* 5 (2): 67–91. Concludes that policymakers in rich and poor countries should experiment with decentralized markets to match those who want to help the poor with the poor themselves freely expressing their needs and aspirations.

———. 2006. *The White Man's Burden*. New York: Penguin Press. Should be compulsory reading for anybody interested in economic development.

Easterly, William, Ross Levine, and David Roodman. 2003. "Aid, Policies, and Growth: A Comment." *American Economic Review* 94 (3): 774–80. Finds that the results of Burnside and Dollar (2000) are not robust to extending the sample period, nor to filling in missing data for the original period 1970–93.

Gibson, Clark, Krister Andersson, Elinor Ostrom, and Sujai Shivakumar. 2005. *The Samaritan's Dilemma: The Political Economy of Development Aid*. Oxford: Oxford University Press. Suggests ways to improve aid's effectiveness.

Klein, Michael, and Tim Harford. 2005. *The Market for Aid*. Washington: International Financial Corporation. Argues for rigorous methods of evaluation and creative use of the private sector to produce a more effective aid industry that encourages new experiments.

Martens, Bertin, Uwe Mummert, Peter Murrell, and Paul Seabright. 2002. *The Institutional Economics of Foreign Aid*. Cambridge: Cambridge University Press. Examines the institutions, incentives, and constraints that guide the behavior of people and organizations involved in the implementation of foreign aid programs.

Reinikka, Ritva, and Jakob Svensson. 2004. "Local Capture: Evidence from a Central Government Transfer Program in Uganda." *Quarterly Journal of Economics* 119 (2): 679–705. Using panel data from a unique survey of primary schools, the paper assesses the extent to which government grants actually reach the intended end-user (in this case schools). The survey data reveal that during 1991–95, the schools, on average, received only 13 percent of the grants.

Svensson, Jakob. 2000. "When Is Foreign Aid Credible? Aid Dependence and Conditionality." *Journal of Development Economics* 61: 61–84. Shows that an aid contract, as proposed in the literature, is not time-consistent. The paper also provides some evidence supporting the basic idea that aid induces weak fiscal discipline and that increased fiscal difficulties lead to higher inflow of aid.

———. 2003. "Why Conditional Aid Does Not Work and What Can Be Done About It?" *Journal of Development Economics* 70: 381–402. Studies a simple reform that introduces ex post incentives for the donor to reward good policies.

JOSÉ G. MONTALVO

■ aid, military

Military aid can take many different forms, including grants, loans, or credits to purchase defense equipment, services, and training. Often military aid is "tied," in that recipients must use the funds to buy defense goods and services from the donor. The aim of military aid is to assist recipients with a variety of security problems. The recipient countries may face a number of different security threats, such as international war, internal rebellion, or terrorism. Military assistance is often supplied to help not only with the recipient's national security but with regional and global security threats. These international considerations make the study of military aid controversial.

Military aid may imply that this is part of a donor's official development assistance (ODA). However, *aid* as defined by the Organisation for Economic Co-operation and Development (OECD) explicitly excludes military aid. The OECD definition of ODA to developing countries includes grants or loans to countries that are undertaken by the official sector in order to promote economic development and welfare. Grants, loans, and credits for military purposes are excluded.

Rather than being part of a donor's aid budget, military aid is part of the defense budget. Defense expenditure is typically one of the least reliable components of a government's budget. The level and composition of military expenditures are often treated as state secrets and sizable portions are not open to public scrutiny. Generally, it is hard to study the effect of military aid since data are scarce and unreliable (Brzoska 1995).

Military and Development Aid Military and development aid are both targeted at foreign nations. An interesting question is how much of foreign assistance is allocated to the seemingly different purposes of overseas security on the one hand and development on the other. This analysis requires data on the different components of aid. Development aid data are available through national governments and the OECD. Few countries, however, make military aid data available, the United States being a notable exception. When one sums up U.S. military and development aid to "total aid," it is interesting to see how the composition of total aid changed over time. From 1970 until 1975 the share of military aid was larger than the share of development aid; it accounted for 53 percent of the total aid figure. After the end of the Vietnam War the composition of total aid changed, and by the early 2000s the share of military aid in total aid was only 23 percent.

Military aid data for the other major donors are not readily available but if the shares of military and development aid are similar to those of the United States, a rough estimate of global military aid can be calculated. In 2006 the sum of all development aid was U.S. $85 billion; therefore, globally military aid was probably around $26 billion. Not all of this military aid is provided to poor countries. Much of this military aid goes to developed countries such as Israel and Turkey. A large proportion of low-income countries' military expenditure is provided through foreign assistance, however. Since this is precisely the aim of military aid, there does not seem to be any problem with financing other countries' military budgets. But is all of the development aid used for the purpose of economic development for which it is intended or is some of it leaking into military spending, which is explicitly excluded from the definition of development aid?

A large number of studies examine what determines the allocation of aid to the different recipient countries (Alesina and Dollar 2000). The literature distinguishes between recipient need, recipient merit, and donor self-interest as motivations for development aid. It seems that, for example, U.S. aid allocation over the past few decades has been predominantly driven by geostrategic interests rather than by recipient needs (McKinley and Little 1979). In this sense donors use development aid for purposes other than assisting economic development in the recipient country. If donors do not always use development aid for its stated purposes, what about the recipient countries? In the development aid literature there is a large debate on fungibility—that is, there is concern that funds that are earmarked for a specific purpose are being used to finance projects and programs for which they were not originally intended (Feyzioglu, Swaroop, and Zhu 1998). It has been estimated that about 11 percent of development aid leaks into military expenditure (Collier and Hoeffler 2007). In 2006 this would have amounted to about $9 billion. Taking this leakage into consideration, we can state that the share of military aid in total aid is greater than the officially reported 23 percent; it is about 32 percent.

Military Spending in Low-Income Countries Is this explicit and implicit funding of military expenditure in low-income countries a problem? After all, these countries have security concerns, and without security no state can provide basic services to its citizens. Without security, economic development is not possible. Studies show that higher military expenditure in poor countries hinders their development (Deger and Smith 1983), suggesting that these countries should spend more on basic services such as infrastructure, health, and education rather than on the military. There is also evidence that higher military expenditure does not lower the risk of civil war, which is the most common form of large-scale violent conflict. It may even be the case that higher military expenditure in postconflict situations is particularly damaging because it increases the risk of a recurrence of civil war. Rebels may not trust the government to stick to a peace settlement if they observe an increase in armament (Collier and Hoeffler 2006). They are then more likely to restart a rebellion. To summarize, many developing countries receive direct and indirect military aid, but the evidence so far suggests that it neither helps them to develop economically nor increases their security.

See also aid, bilateral; aid, international; aid, international, and political economy

FURTHER READING

Alesina, A., and D. Dollar. 2000. "Who Gives Foreign Aid to Whom and Why?" *Journal of Economic Growth* 5: 33–63. Empirical examination of how donors allocate aid to poor countries.

Brzoska, M. 1995. "World Military Expenditures." In *Handbook of Defense Economics*, vol. 1, edited by K. Hartley and T. Sandler. Elsevier: North Holland, 45–67. Overview of the definition of military expenditure and the difficulties in compiling statistics across countries and time.

Collier, P., and A. Hoeffler. 2007. "Unintended Consequences: Does Aid Promote Arms Races?" *Oxford Bulletin of Economics and Statistics* 69: 1–28. Provides a general estimation of the demand for military expenditure and how aid changes this relationship.

———. 2006. "Military Expenditure in Post-Conflict Societies." *Economics of Governance* 7: 89–107. Theoretical and empirical analysis of the impact of military expenditure in postconflict situations.

Deger, S., and R. Smith. 1983. "Military Expenditure and Growth in Less-Developed Countries." *Journal of Conflict Resolution* 27: 335–53. Empirical cross-country analysis of how military expenditure affects growth.

Feyzioglu, T., V. Swaroop, and M. Zhu. 1998. "A Panel Data Analysis of the Fungibility of Foreign Aid." *World Bank Economic Review* 12: 29–58. Empirical examination of the use of foreign aid.

McKinley, R. D., and R. Little. 1979. "The US Aid Relationship: A Test of the Recipient Need and the Donor Interest Models." *Political Studies* 27: 236–50. Statistical analysis of how the United States distributes foreign aid.

Organisation for Economic Co-operation and Development. http://www.oecd.org/dataoecd/42/30/1860571.gif. A source for data about overseas development aid.

Stockholm International Peace Research Institute. http://www.sipri.org/contents/milap/. A source for data on worldwide military expenditures.

U.S. Census Bureau. http://www.census.gov/compendia/statab/foreign_commerce_aid/foreign_aid/. A good source for data about American military aid.

PAUL COLLIER AND ANKE HOEFFLER

■ aid for trade

See trade-related capacity building

■ air transportation

Air transportation is part of a service supply chain that moves both passengers and cargo. Although commercial airlines offer the immediate form of transportation, they are tied to airports for their takeoffs and landings and to air navigation services for guidance and control in route. Passengers and cargo also need to move to and from the airport. Air transportation, therefore, is a sector that caters to the transportation of passengers overall but especially those going the shortest distances and to the movement of high-value, low-bulk freight.

Air transportation is a major industry in its own right and acts as a lubricant for many other economic activities. In broad terms, air transportation accounts for about 1 percent of the gross domestic product of the European Union and slightly less for the United States economy. Globally, in 2005 there were about 18,000 commercial aircraft, carrying 1.6 billion passengers and more than 43 million tons of freight annually, and serving more than 10,000 airports. These statistics, however, ignore the role that air transportation can play in stimulating economic growth and trade (it is estimated that between 35 and 40 percent of international trade by value is moved by air transportation), linking together diverse communities, and fostering particular types of industry such as tourism and specialized agricultural sectors such as exotic fruits and flowers.

Although air transportation played a role in providing mail service, and some limited passenger and cargo service before 1939, it has gained significance only since the end of World War II with major technological advances in aircraft design and enhanced air traffic navigation systems. The advent of commercial jet aircraft in the 1950s provided faster and cheaper long-haul services, and in the 1960s the development of wide-bodied aircraft increased carrying capacity, which cut the costs of air travel considerably, reduced environmental concerns, and improved safety. Radar and improved communications, together with institutional changes and accompanying new management practices beginning in the late 1970s, resulted in further cost reductions and the expansion of airline service networks.

Modern scheduled air transportation networks take a variety of forms. To meet social or political objectives, governments stipulate certain types of service that must be supplied either by state-owned airlines or through financial support to private airlines from the taxpayer. Although government interventions in the market are considerable, they have diminished in many countries since the 1980s. As a consequence, profit is the motivating factor for an increasing portion of the air transportation system worldwide.

Where the market plays a dominant role, three broad types of scheduled service are common. Many services are essentially point-to-point with the airline serving a set of individual origins and destinations, often in a linear network akin to a bus service. This approach may be refined into radial networks with a carrier concentrating services from a base airport but offering no coordinated services involving a change of plane that allow passengers who want to continue on to another destination from that base. Finally, hub-and-spoke operations involve a major airport serving as an interchange facility (a little like a postal sorting office) that consolidates passengers or freight from diverse origins on flights to a range of destinations. This type of operation allows economies of scope (the ability to offer a range of services at lower costs than if they were provided individually) and density (the lowering of costs as larger flows can be channeled into each route), but suffers from potential congestion at the hub airports as traffic converges. From the airlines' revenue perspective, hub-and-spoke operations also allow them to enjoy economies of market presence—the ability to offer direct and indirect services between numerous airports.

These various network types overlap to a considerable extent with the types of commercial airlines that provide the bulk of services. The linear and radial services are features of low-cost or "no-frill" airlines such as Southwest in the United States and Ryanair in Europe. These carriers can standardize their fleets, fly from secondary airports, avoid scheduling difficulties by minimizing the number of connecting services they offer, and provide limited onboard and ground services because of the short duration of flights. In contrast, the "legacy," or full-service, carriers focus on channeling their traffic through hubs—for example, Delta Airlines through Atlanta and Northwest Airlines through Detroit—and deploy a mixed fleet to meet the needs of a more complex network, wide variations in flight lengths, and long-haul international services. To enhance the range and frequency of services, the legacy carriers often form global alliances. The Star Alliance, for example, includes United, Lufthansa, SAS, British Midlands, and other airlines. This allows for easier ticketing and fight connections as well as larger frequent flyer programs that reward passengers for loyalty to an airline or alliance.

Globally, the scheduled airline industry as a whole has not, at least since the 1980s, earned what would normally be seen as an economically viable return. Even in good years the operating margins of most airlines has been below the return offered by bank savings accounts. Excessive competition and, at least for a time, inflated costs account for this. This situation contrasts with most other elements in the air transportation value chain, with airports, air navigation systems, and global distribution systems all often making significant financial returns.

Besides scheduled airlines services, there are also charter services. These involve an entire aircraft's capacity being sold usually to a tour operator who then sells these seats, often in conjunction with hotel rooms, rental cars, and the like, to leisure travelers. Until the 1990s, because their activities were less regulated than those of scheduled airlines, these operators were important in Europe, taking up to 20 percent of the air travel market. Regulatory reforms have reduced the importance of charter carriers and also their nature: many offer near scheduled services with regular flights, and seat-only sales, not requiring the addition of a hotel purchase, are common. There are also air taxis and business aircraft that offer personal air transportation, usually to business executives. In addition to civilian air services, the military in most countries operates large fleets of aircraft to move equipment and personnel, in addition to any direct combat-related activities, and these flights must be integrated into the overall air traffic control system.

Regulation Air transportation traditionally has been regulated very heavily. Economic regulation of fares, cargo rates, market access, and capacity became widespread after World War II, both internationally as countries tried to develop their own commercial air fleets, and domestically as air transportation became a mechanism for greater mobility and political cohesion within countries. Notions that airlines, airports, and air navigation services, if left unchecked, would become monopolies that would penalize users were used to justify economic regulation of fares and access. Social regulation was also widespread and often aimed at providing otherwise unremunerative services to remote regions as well as to ensure adequate safety.

Internationally, the UN International Civil Aviation Organization, established at the end of World War II at the Chicago Convention, regulates air transportation. The resultant agreements give sovereignty to countries regarding their own air space and set down the basis of negotiations between nations over international routes, called air service agreements. Until the late 20th century, most international traffic was severely controlled: often, only one carrier from each country could offer international services at a regulated fare, with a limited capacity, and with the revenues shared equally between the two countries. Many domestic markets were also strictly controlled, and in some cases a state-owned airline was the only supplier of services at a regulated fare.

From the late 1970s on, there has been a global movement to introduce more market-based structures into the air transportation sector. This began when U.S. airlines removed rate and market entry controls (other than those retained for safety and security reasons) for domestic air cargo services in 1977 and from passenger services in 1978. The United States also initiated a large number of "Open Skies" agreements in the 1980s and 1990s that removed route access and fare controls from bilateral air service agreements with other countries but retained cabotage, the freedom of external airlines to operate within another country, and ownership controls. Parallel to this, by 1997 a gradual relaxation of international bilateral air service agreements within the European Union freed airlines services, both domestic and international, from economic regulation, including ownership rules within the EU.

The result of these changes has been an expansion in the number of commercial airlines and an increase in the diversity of services provided, not only by low-cost carriers on short-haul routes, but also by specialist airlines that offer only business class service on long-haul flights. In markets where regulatory reforms have been enacted, fares have been brought more closely into line with costs. At the same time, competition has lowered fares and forced airlines to become more efficient.

Airports The vast majority of the world's airports are either nationally owned or owned by a local (city or state) authority. The original reason for this was that airports, because of the large capital costs involved in establishing them, often are not commercially viable but nevertheless are important for strategic or local economic development reasons, and as a way to tie remote communities to larger cities. From the mid-1980s, airports have had to comply with strong regulations related to the noise, safety issues, and traffic congestion associated with them. Private sector involvement, however, has become more common under the state or local government ownership umbrella, with airlines financing, leasing, or owning parts of airports (such as terminal buildings) or directly providing services (such as ticketing and ground handling). In some cases, airports have allowed private caterers, retailers, and the like to offer services on their sites.

Since the 1980s, many countries have moved to privatize entire airports, or to distance their ownership and operations from political processes. The British Airports Authority, which owns seven airports in the United Kingdom, including the three major airports serving London, was privatized with equity capital. Other airports have been bought out as going concerns by commercial companies with no equity holdings. Privatization, however, often brings with it challenges of regulating monopoly power; most cities only have one airport, or at most two. The approach pursued in many cases involves "price-capping," with a regulator controlling the ways in which prices charged by airports for take-offs and landings may change.

In South America and some parts of Africa, various forms of concessions have allowed states to retain their ownership of an airport but hand their entire management and investment strategy over to private companies for long periods. Such approaches are aimed at bringing private capital and expertise into airport development where public finance is limited and the local market does not have an adequate supply of skilled workers and managers.

Air Navigation Systems Providers Air transportation involves the movement of aircraft along corridors akin to three-dimensional railway tracks. In some cases the traffic flows freely with air navigation system providers (ANSPs) supplying navigation and weather advice. Most commercial aviation, especially in congested air space, is subjected to air traffic control to prevent accidents. These involve en route controls at higher altitudes and tower controls around airports.

Reforms in air transportation infrastructure have been slower to materialize than for airlines. Most ANSPs traditionally have been state owned but in recent years a number have been privatized or "corporatized" (turned into nonprofit entities either in-

dependent or government-owned but not managed). For example, NAV CANADA became a private not-for-profit corporation in 1996; Airservices Australia became a government corporation in 1988; and the UK air transportation system, NATS, became a public-private partnership in 2001. France retains state ownership of its ANSP but allows Direction des Services de la Navigation Aérienne access to private financial markets and to levy user fees. The Federal Aviation Administration in the United States outsources some activities but is financed by taxes. Because of the increase in international air transportation and the need for greater integration of systems, some countries are developing coordinated strategies for delivering air navigation systems (ANSs). Within Europe, for example, EUROCONTROL has the remit for creating a Single European Sky that ultimately links the various national ANSs.

The changes have come about as new ways are being sought to finance the modernization of facilities and to improve their efficiency. ANSs are highly capital intensive and are continually being improved, but adopting the new technology is expensive and often has to be tailored to the peculiarities of the existing system rather than using generic hard- and software.

One of the main difficulties in enhancing air traffic management performance through regulatory reform has been the concern with aviation safety. Academic studies show a greater aversion to being killed in a plane crash, for example, than in an automobile accident. The evidence to date is that, although there are some geographical areas where the record is poor, the overall safety of air transportation has continually improved over the years in terms of both mortalities and morbidity per passenger mile flown.

Overall, air transportation is the fastest-growing transportation mode in the world for both passenger and freight traffic. It has traditionally been highly regulated but since the late 1970s, the removal of economic regulation from many markets has led to improved efficiency, innovation, and lower costs and fares, without any reduction in safety standards. There is now diversity in the types of airlines that offer services and also in the forms of infrastructure that is required to support flights.

See also shipping; trade in services

FURTHER READING

Airline Business. Monthly. Offers articles on the state of the air transportation industry and regularly provides detailed information at the global level on issues such as the membership of airline alliances, the scale and operational features of airports, and safety matters.

Boeing Commercial Airplane Group. Annual. *Current Market Outlook*. Provides reviews of the state of the air transportation market and long-term forecasts of traffic levels.

Doganis, R. 2006. *The Airline Business*. 2d ed. London: Routledge. Explains how the airline market works and the issues that confront both operators and policymakers.

Journal of Air Transport Management. Six times a year. Provides analysis at an academic and professional level of all aspects of air transportation.

KENNETH BUTTON

■ **Andean Community**

The Andean Community (CAN), as this organization is currently known, is a regional integration agreement among Colombia, Ecuador, Peru, and Bolivia. The community was originally known as the Andean Pact and was created in 1969 to reverse the stagnation of the Latin American Association of Free Trade and address the integration and development needs of the Andean countries (Venezuela, Colombia, Chile, Ecuador, Peru, and Bolivia). Venezuela became part of the Andean Pact in 1973, and Chile withdrew from the pact in 1976 to pursue more liberal trade policies. Initially, the pact sought to harmonize policies, define a common external tariff, liberalize intraregional trade, regulate foreign direct investment in the region, and organize production across member Andean countries by encouraging the development of promising industries. Later on, the pact supported the agenda of becoming part of wider economic agreements such as Mercosur—a regional economic agreement among Argentina, Brazil, Paraguay, and Uruguay—and the Free Trade Area of the Americas (FTAA) to be consistent with the General Agreement on Tariffs and Trade and the World Trade Organization principles.

The initial strategy of the Andean Pact was based on the import substitution, or closed regionalism, model that predominated in Latin America during the 1970s. According to this model, the government must coordinate economic policies and regional development plans in order to direct production toward the intraregional market. The consequence of this model is that protected rent activities (activities that generate rent because of government protection through tariffs or subsidies) develop, mainly in the industrial sector, which are financed in part by the revenues generated by primary-resource-intensive exports (agriculture, mining, and energy). Intraregional trade only increased from 1.7 percent of total exports in 1970 to 4.5 percent in 1979. This early stage of the Andean Pact failed for several reasons: many products were exempted from the tariff liberalization process; a clear consensus about the common external tariff was lacking due to significant differences in the level of protection of each Andean country; the production requirements established by the Andean Pact did not match the trade needs of each country, especially after the foreign debt crisis; the market was too small; and trade activity was directed mainly to the members of the Andean Pact. Therefore, the Andean countries were limited in their capacity to generate new foreign exchange, which became very important for paying the increasing foreign debt (Edwards 1993). The lack of coordination of macroeconomic policies led to exchange rate imbalances and to differences of protection among the Andean countries. (In 1980, about 25 percent of items included initially in the tariff list were exempted.)

These macroeconomic imbalances partially generated by the closed regionalism model contributed to the foreign debt crisis that exploded in the early 1980s. The adjustment policies applied to solve the crisis led to a contraction of the trade preferences among the Andean countries, thereby reducing the trade during the mid-1980s. By 1985 the Andean Pact was practically moribund. Intraregional trade did not follow the initial industrial planning, and only about a third of the investment programs (machine tools, petrochemical, and automobile sectors) were approved. Nevertheless, the Andean Pact was revived with the Quito Protocol, which was signed in 1987 and later modified over the course of several presidential meetings. The most important modification, the Trujillo Protocol of 1996, resulted in the name change from the Andean Pact to the Andean Community of Nations, a new structural organization, and a shift in emphasis from closed regionalism (inward integration) to open regionalism (outward integration with the rest of the world) (Reynolds 1997; and ECLAC 1994). The establishment of the Andean Free Trade Zone (AFTZ) in 1993, and the Andean customs union in the form of an Andean common external tariff in 1995, spurred private initiatives and innovative rent-seeking activities (instead of protected rent activities) aimed at achieving an efficient allocation of resources and exploiting the competitive advantages of the region. This increased efficiency and innovation is the main reason behind the shift toward the open regionalism model. The AFTZ was completed in 2006 with the full incorporation of Peru.

Using CAN as an example, Creamer (2003) demonstrated that economic integration by stages into wider regional agreements may lead to an improvement of intraregional trade and total trade, and not to a contraction of extraregional trade as during the period 1980–97. Taking a simple indicator, the trade balance of CAN—exports minus imports—with the rest of the world increased from U.S. $1.196 trillion in 1969 to U.S. $31.435 trillion in 2005 (Andean Community 2006). However, this growth is mostly explained by the significant improvement of the trade balance of Venezuela. Venezuela accounts for 90 percent of CAN's trade surplus with the rest of the world. This trade balance may be substantially affected because of the withdrawal of Venezuela from CAN in 2006, although this effect may be partially compensated by the integration

of CAN with Mercosur and the incorporation of Chile. The Andean Council of Foreign Affairs Ministers and the Andean Community Commission accepted Chile as an associate member in September 2006.

Governance During the 1990s, CAN changed its emphasis from a trade-oriented agreement into a political, social, and economic integration agreement in the spirit of the European Union. This transformation required the creation of the Andean Presidential Council and the conversion of the Cartagena Agreement into a General Secretariat in 1997. The set of all institutions that support the mission of CAN is the Andean Integration System (SAI). The political institutions that are part of SAI and have representatives of each member country are the Andean Presidential Council, composed of the presidents of member countries, which defines the strategic priorities of CAN; the Andean Council of Foreign Affairs Ministers, organized by the foreign affairs ministers of member countries, which is responsible for the foreign policy of CAN, agreements with third parties, and the election of the general secretary; the Andean Community Commission, in coordination with the Andean Council of Foreign Affairs Ministers, which is responsible for the intraregional policies of CAN; the Andean Community General Secretariat, which is the executive body of CAN; the Andean Community Court of Justice, which is the judicial body that interprets the Andean Community laws and solves internal disputes; the Andean Parliament, the legislative arm of CAN, which harmonizes member countries' laws; and the Business and Labor Consultative councils, which represent business and labor organizations, respectively, and advise the Andean Council of Foreign Affairs Ministers. Additionally, the Andean Development Corporation, which is responsible for promoting trade, investment, and economic growth in the region, and the Latin American Reserve Fund, which provides funds to the member countries to correct short-term macroeconomic imbalances and coordinates monetary and fiscal policies, also are part of the SAI. Finally, institutions of SAI responsible for social policies are the Simón Rodríguez Agreement, which coordinates social and labor policies; the Andean Health Organization–Hipólito Unanue Agreement, which coordinates health policies; and the Simón Bolívar Andean University, which promotes academic activities that are relevant to the integration and development of CAN.

Most of CAN's political institutions have not had a major impact on the internal policies of the Andean countries. These countries are still very much under the influence of the major financial multilateral organizations. Hence, CAN's political integration has been very limited. The Andean Development Corporation, however, has become a major source of funds to support the development policy of CAN. This organization has also had an impact in social areas, providing funds for projects that generate employment, support microentrepreneurs, and improve the productivity of the region. The Simón Rodríguez Agreement has helped to integrate educational systems in the Andean countries, and the Simón Bolívar Andean University has been invaluable in supporting the professional training of social scientists. However, major regional challenges include the development of human capital in technical areas and a significant increase in research and development investment to attract foreign capital and outsourcing opportunities to the region.

Andean Customs Union and Free Trade Zone
The Andean customs union, as it has functioned since 1995, establishes four basic tariff levels: 5 percent for raw material and industrial output, 10 percent for intermediate output, 15 percent for capital goods, and 20 percent for final goods. There are some exceptions to this common external tariff. For agricultural products, price bands help protect Andean agricultural products from subsidies and price variations in the international market. In 1997, Peru decided to join the Andean customs union and started a program of tariff reduction with Columbia and Ecuador. The Andean common external tariff covers about 90 percent of imports. The Declaration of Santa Cruz of the Andean Community, signed in

January 2002, introduced a new structure of the common external tariff that includes Peru. However, the new common external tariff had not been implemented and was still under review by a high level advisory group since August 2007.

CAN represented the Andean countries in the FTAA negotiations and lobbied the U.S. government for the extension of the Andean Trade Preference Act of 1991 into the Andean Trade Promotion and Drug Eradication Act of 2002. Also, CAN renewed the Generalized System of Preferences with the European Union for the period 2006–15 and at the time of this writing was negotiating a trade association agreement. In April 1998, CAN signed an agreement with Mercosur to create a free trade zone. As a result of this agreement, 80 percent of the trade between Mercosur and CAN was freed in January 2005. The remaining 20 percent will be liberated during the next 14 years. Additionally, the members of Mercosur became associate members of CAN, and Mercosur reciprocally conferred associate membership on the members of CAN.

The withdrawal of Venezuela in 2006, the potential signing of free trade agreements between the United States and Columbia, Ecuador, and Peru, and the formation of a South American free trade zone as agreed during the South American presidential meeting of 2004 are signs of the difficulties facing CAN. As long as CAN maintains its own identity, free trade agreements with the United States or with the other South American countries may indicate the success of the open regionalism process that has characterized the Andean Group since the 1990s. In fact, a South American free trade zone will open a market of 377 million inhabitants with a gross domestic product of U.S. $1.493 trillion and exports of U.S. $305.3 billion for 2005.

CAN offers significant advantages to its members, especially once the Andean Common Market is established. This market will enable the free movement of goods, services, capital, and people. CAN envisions that, in this way, it gradually will integrate itself into the world market, either through its participation as a subregion in a South American free trade zone or in a free trade agreement with the United States.

See also customs unions; free trade area; Free Trade Area of the Americas (FTAA); import substitution industrialization; Mercosur; regionalism

FURTHER READING

Andean Community. 2006. "37 Años de Integración Comercial, 1969–2005." http://www.comunidadandina .org. A compendium of the relevant trade statistics of the Andean Community since its foundation.

Creamer, Germán. 2003. "Open Regionalism in the Andean Community: A Trade Flow Analysis." *World Trade Review* 2 (1): 101-18. An analysis of Andean Community trade that demonstrates a pattern of open regionalism.

ECLAC (Economic Commission for Latin America and the Caribbean). 1994. *Open Regionalism in Latin America and the Caribbean.* Santiago, Chile: ECLAC. A policy analysis of the Latin American integration process from the open regionalism perspective.

———. 2006. *Panorama de la Inserción Internacional de America Latina y el Caribe. Tendencias 2005–6.* Santiago, Chile: ECLAC. Annual publication about Latin American international trade with a chapter on Latin American economic agreements such as the Andean Community.

Edwards, Sebastian. 1993. "Latin American Economic Integration: A New Perspective on an Old Dream." *The World Economy* 16 (3): 317–39. A macroeconomic explanation of the limited success of Latin American economic agreements.

Reynolds, Clark W. 1997. "Open Regionalism: Lessons from Latin America for East Asia." Kellogg Institute Working Paper No. 241. Notre Dame: University of Notre Dame. Available at http://kellogg.nd.edu/publications/workingpapers/WPS/241.pdf. Presentation of the open regionalism experience in Latin America and East Asia. This working paper is based on Clark W. Reynolds, Francisco Thoumi, and Reinhart Wettmann's "A Case for Open Regionalism in the Andes: Policy Implications of Andean Integration in a Period of Hemispheric Liberalization and Structural Adjustment" (1994), a typescript report prepared for the Friedrich Ebert Stiftung Foundation and USAID. North America Forum. Palo Alto: Stanford University. This is the first research that applies the term *open regionalism* to the Andean integration process and shows how the Andean Community can change its emphasis from inward integration to outward integration with the rest of the world.

GERMÁN CREAMER

■ anti-dumping

Many countries reserve the right to impose import taxes on foreign products that have been found to be "dumped" into their domestic economies (that is, sold at less than their "normal" prices). These tariffs, known as anti-dumping duties, have become a critical but controversial part of the multilateral trading system that has developed first under the General Agreement on Tariffs and Trade (GATT) and then under its successor, the World Trade Organization (WTO). Anti-dumping duties are one of the few ways consistent with international obligations by which governments may increase tariffs beyond levels negotiated in international trade talks.

WTO rules allow its members to impose these duties if the individual governments determine that foreign firms "dump" a product that damages a domestic industry producing a similar product. In common usage, anti-dumping duties are used to counteract "unfair" import pricing practices by foreign competitors.

Dumping is defined in two principal ways within the WTO system. The first is when a foreign firm sells in a domestic market at a price below the price it sets for the same good in its home market, known as "price-based" dumping. In others words, international price discrimination is an actionable practice under multilateral trade rules. The second basic definition, known as "cost-based" dumping, involves a foreign firm selling its product in the domestic market below its cost of production. In practice, this usually means that foreign firms are selling below the average total cost of producing the item. Anti-dumping duties may be imposed under WTO only if the dumping margin exceeds a de minimis level of 2 percent (i.e. the percentage difference between the "normal" value and the price charged in the export market); dumping below this level is not subject to duties.

It is important to note that dumping is based on the pricing practices of individual firms in specific countries. Consequently, anti-dumping duties may vary across firms within a particular exporting country. This means that customs officials in a country that has imposed anti-dumping duties must pay very close attention to which particular foreign firm is exporting the product and from which country. This can impose important administrative burdens and in principle may provide incentives for foreign firms to try to circumvent the duties by mislabeling the product's country of origin.

Anti-dumping duties are a recognized exception to a number of core WTO principles. For example, the "most-favored-nation" (MFN) principle means that a member commits to impose the same tariff on the same product for all WTO member countries. Anti-dumping duties, in contrast, can vary across countries for the same product. WTO rules also normally require governments not to raise duties beyond the tariff levels agreed to through multilateral negotiations. Members are freed from this obligation, however, if foreign firms are found to be dumping. Finally, WTO rules require "national treatment" so that foreign firms and domestic firms are treated in similar ways. Under anti-dumping rules, foreign firms selling below average total cost (i.e., total revenue is below total cost) may be subject to sanction while a domestic firm that does not cover its costs will not face similar fines. The fact that anti-dumping is a WTO-allowed exception to these critical principles of the multilateral trading system suggests the importance that member governments place on discouraging this type of foreign pricing behavior.

Administration of Anti-dumping Rules Anti-dumping investigations are usually initiated by domestic firms concerned about foreign competition. The importing country's government then must undertake two separate investigations, one to determine whether there is evidence of dumping and the other to find out whether the imported products are harming the domestic industry. The former requires information about foreign firm pricing and the latter data on the competing domestic firms' economic conditions.

A domestic administering agency responsible for calculating dumping margins requires different detailed information about foreign firm behavior. For example, it must collect pricing data in the foreign firm's home market if it uses price-based methods. If it uses cost-based methods, it must obtain information about the foreign firm's production costs. Both methods require foreign firm cooperation if precise dumping margins are to be calculated. Some foreign firms may be reluctant to open their books to another country's investigating agencies and may decide not to cooperate. WTO rules allow for an administering agency to use other sources of information, including allegations of the domestic import-competing firms, to complete the investigation. The threat of using domestic allegations serves as an inducement to the foreign firm to cooperate by providing needed data.

Calculating dumping margins can also be complicated if there is pervasive involvement of the government in the economic life of a country. For example, before the demise of the Soviet Union, an agency investigating a charge of dumping by a Soviet firm would not be able to use any information based on administratively determined prices. The multilateral trade system consequently recognizes different anti-dumping procedures in cases of "nonmarket economies" (with the People's Republic of China as the most prominent current example). In order to conduct an investigation involving such an economy the domestic agency may collect information about the quantities of inputs used by the Chinese firm. The agency will then apply the input prices of a third country deemed to be at a similar stage of development (e.g., Bangladesh or India) to calculate a proxy cost of production. This can then be used to determine the dumping margin by comparing the constructed value with the price charged in the export market.

The second part of an anti-dumping investigation requires that a domestic agency determine whether the dumped import causes "material injury" to a domestic industry producing the "like product." This requires that the domestic industry provide critical information about its current condition. Various indicators of material injury are used, including declines in domestic sales, employment, and profits, or the degree to which the dumped import prices are below domestic prices. In addition, the "threat" of material injury can also be a basis of imposing anti-dumping duties. Such a threat might be found if a firm found to be dumping has recently added significant export capacity.

According to WTO rules, anti-dumping duties finally imposed can be calculated in two distinct ways. One is that the import duties are equal to the dumping margins (i.e., difference between the "normal value" and the export price). This procedure is used in many jurisdictions, most notably in the United States. Those favoring this approach argue that anti-dumping duties are allowed because dumping itself is the ultimate problem, so the policy response must eliminate any dumping. The other approach is that the anti-dumping duties can be limited to the lesser of the dumping margin or the minimum duty required to eliminate injury to the domestic industry. This second version, the so-called "lesser-duty rule," is used in the European Union. Supporters of the latter approach often argue that the main goal of the anti-dumping process is to eliminate injury, not dumping itself.

WTO rules also allow alternatives to increased duties in anti-dumping cases. "Price undertakings" involve a settlement between the foreign firms accused of dumping and the importing country government. Typically, foreign firms offer to raise their export prices to eliminate any dumping in order to avoid duties placed on their products. If the investigating domestic government agrees to the offer, it will suspend the anti-dumping investigation as long as the foreign firms keep their exports prices sufficiently high. Price undertakings are particularly common in the European Union.

Anti-dumping orders may be in place for long periods. There is no specific time frame for their removal as there is with safeguard measures, which

have an eight-year maximum. WTO members did agree in the Uruguay Round to require governments to review anti-dumping orders every five years after the original imposition of duties. In particular, duties must be taken off unless an investigation determines that their removal likely would lead to lead to a resumption of dumping and material injury to the domestic industry.

Anti-dumping actions, like other aspects of the multilateral trading system, are subject to the WTO review. This means that member governments can ask the WTO dispute settlement bodies to rule whether countries imposing anti-dumping duties have lived up to their obligations. This setup allows WTO signatories to develop and use their own systems and procedures to protect their domestic industries against imports found to be dumped and causing injury but allows exporting countries some recourse if they believe that the anti-dumping duties are unjustified or implemented inappropriately.

WTO rules give governments the right to impose duties on injurious dumped imports but do not require it. WTO obligations allow governments to impose anti-dumping tariffs only if doing so would be in the "public interest." This provision reflects the fact that import taxes raise the price paid by domestic consumers, including industrial users that import intermediate inputs. For example, the European Union's procedures require that national representatives evaluate the impact of anti-dumping duties on broader EU interests. In sharp contrast, other countries such as the United States prohibit administrators from considering consumer interests when making the decision of whether to impose anti-dumping duties.

Anti-dumping procedures are similar to another WTO-consistent method to impose import restrictions. Countervailing duties (CVDs) are allowed by WTO rules if exports have been subsidized by a foreign government and those exports cause material injury to a domestic industry. Such subsidies are deemed to be unfair to domestic competitors since it involves competition with a government, not just with a private company. Thus, CVDs procedures have a structure similar to anti-dumping duty systems (i.e., "unfair" competition plus material injury) but involve foreign government actions rather than private firm pricing decisions as in the case of anti-dumping.

Supporters and Critics Anti-dumping duties are a controversial part of the WTO. Many supporters argue that anti-dumping is a necessary response to unfair trade. Critics regard it as simple protection with a rhetorical flourish.

Many of those who support anti-dumping's role in the international trading system argue that it counteracts foreign predatory pricing practices. *Predatory pricing* refers to a strategy under which a firm charges very low prices in order to drive out competitors so that it can later increase prices after achieving a monopoly position. Domestic antitrust and competition policy are at least partially built on these ideas. In the case of international competition, supporters of anti-dumping argue that international price discrimination or pricing below average total cost is akin to predatory pricing by foreign firms.

Supporters also argue that anti-dumping duties are necessary to counteract foreign firms operating from a "sanctuary market." This refers to the possibility that formal and informal trade barriers allow foreign firms to receive higher-than-normal profits in their own market, which they then use to offset losses in the export market as they try to drive out domestic competition. This also is sometimes seen as a part of a predatory pricing strategy.

Anti-dumping is often criticized by those favoring trade liberalization. One of the most important criticisms is that anti-dumping is a just another form of protectionism since it involves an increase in duties on imports. In this view, anti-dumping duties reduce access of domestic consumers to foreign goods and result in greater damage to consumers than any benefits accruing to the domestic producing industry. Critics also note that anti-dumping investigations are extremely complicated, especially regarding the calculation of dumping margins. Domestic agencies must make a myriad of decisions about how to treat transactions of an individual foreign firm and how to calculate foreign costs of production. Uncertainty about how the investigating agency will calculate those margins means that it is difficult for foreign firms to know what margin they will finally face. One reaction by foreign firms is to raise their prices even in the absence of an anti-dumping allegation; the mere presence of an anti-dumping system may result in higher prices for consumers. Critics also point out that there is no requirement to determine whether or not there is any evidence of a sanctuary market or predatory intent by foreign firms before imposing anti-dumping duties. Finally, they note that domestic firms that sell their goods for different prices in different cities domestically (i.e., engage in domestic price discrimination) or sell domestically below average total cost (i.e., losing money on domestic sales) are not subject to sanction by the domestic government. In other words, anti-dumping duties punish foreign firms for undertaking practices acceptable if done by domestic firms.

Some observers, even among those who doubt whether international predatory pricing is an important threat, believe that the presence of anti-dumping rules may allow politicians to engage in broader trade liberalization than would otherwise be possible. This view holds that anti-dumping rules can act as a kind of safety valve; governments may be able to deflect pressures for broader protectionist measures by giving domestic industries an administrative process under which they can petition for import restrictions. This could allow governments to raise duties on only a small number of narrowly defined products even as restrictions are lifted on a whole array of other imports.

Anti-dumping in Practice Anti-dumping has a long history, especially in the English-speaking world, but it has spread across much of the world in recent years. The world's first anti-dumping law came into effect in Canada in 1904, followed shortly by New Zealand (1905) and Australia (1906). The United States implemented its first anti-dumping law in 1916. The countries that would eventually make up the European Union were also early users of anti-dumping provisions. This group of countries constitutes the traditional users of anti-dumping; up until 1986, worldwide use of anti-dumping was almost exclusively restricted to this group. Beginning in the mid-1980s, countries such as Mexico, Argentina, and Brazil began to use the procedure more frequently. After the establishment of the World Trade Organization in 1995, many other countries began to use anti-dumping, including most notably India, the Republic of Korea, South Africa, and Turkey. Japan, though frequently a target of anti-dumping actions by importing countries, has only rarely used anti-dumping to restrict imports. The People's Republic of China has used anti-dumping more frequently in the post-2002 period but that country's involvement principally has been as the most frequent target of anti-dumping actions.

Anti-dumping duties have been imposed on a wide variety of manufactured, agricultural, and commodity products. The steel and chemical industries have been the most frequent users of the anti-dumping process. For the period between 1980 and 2002, approximately 50 percent of all anti-dumping petitions involved these two industries. This may reflect the very high fixed costs of both industries, which make them vulnerable to downturns in their industries and create incentives to expand production through exports to try to lower average production costs. The steel industry has been particularly active in the United States in supporting the role of anti-dumping in the multilateral trading system.

In short, the anti-dumping system receives strong support among some important members of the World Trade Organization but is controversial among nations especially reliant on exports.

See also countervailing duties; nondiscrimination; nontariff measures; World Trade Organization

FURTHER READING

Blonigen, Bruce, and Thomas Prusa. 2001. "Antidumping." In *Handbook of International Trade*, vol. 1, edited by Kwan Choi and James Hartigan. Oxford: Blackwell, 251–84. Provides a literature review of academic research on anti-dumping.

Finger, J. Michael, ed. 1993. *Antidumping: How It Works and Who Gets Hurt*. Ann Arbor: University of Michigan Press. Details administrative practices of agencies responsible for anti-dumping investigations.

Mastel, Greg. 1998. *Antidumping Laws and the U.S. Economy*. Amonk, NY: M. E. Sharpe. Analyzes some of the major arguments in favor of the use of anti-dumping laws in the world trading system.

MICHAEL O. MOORE

■ anti-globalization

The spectacular growth in the intensity, scope, and visibility of globalization (understood here as the increasing interconnectedness of individuals, groups, companies, and countries) since 1990 has been accompanied by a parallel growth in anti-globalization—a broad term used to characterize a public debate over the shaping, slowing, or rejecting of globalization.

Driven by the growth of international economic integration and international institutional arrangements and the spread of ever-denser networks of global communications, a debate has arisen since the 1990s around concerns regarding the distributional benefits of globalization, the desirability and impact of different types of policy, and the nature and representativeness of the political institutions that decide on global policy issues. The public face of this debate has been notable for the high-profile role of nonstate actors and for its focus on perceived shortcomings in current systems of global governance.

The terms most commonly used for this global debate, particularly with the involvement of nonstate actors—*anti-globalization* and *the anti-globalization movement*—were used most frequently between the failed World Trade Organization (WTO) Ministerial in Seattle in 1999 and the Group of Eight (G8) Summit held in Genoa in 2001 amidst violence by both police and demonstrators. These terms are misleading, as participants in this debate are neither solidly "anti-globalization," nor a single movement. Under the umbrella of these labels is a wide variety of actors with often sharply differing philosophies, objectives, and assumptions. Yet since the late 1990s they have proved a useful—if contested and in large part inaccurate—shorthand to describe what many identify as a new and important force in global politics.

In order to understand the nature of the current debate about globalization—as well as what might happen next to the "anti-globalization movement" and its actors—there is a need for disaggregation and a reflection on the context in which it exists.

Origins Although its political and social origins are diverse, anti-globalization in its broadest sense can be seen as a response to the economic and political events of the period since the early 1970s and their most visible symbols, the institutions of global economic governance. In the North, the oil crisis and the suspension of dollar convertibility in 1971 marked the end of the "long boom" of post-1945 Keynesianism. They also triggered the meteoric rise of global capital markets, which made earning and keeping "market confidence" an increasingly important determinant of government policies. In the South, the Mexican government's near-default on its foreign debt in 1982 marked the end of the postwar era of import-substituting industrialization and began a long and painful period for developing countries, characterized by the burden of massive foreign indebtedness and the rise in political influence of the International Monetary Fund (IMF), the World Bank, and international capital markets, all three of which ushered policymakers away from development policies focused on the domestic market and toward a strategy of export-led growth.

These developments helped drive the rapid expansion of trade and investment flows, as large parts of Latin America and Asia adopted export-led growth strategies, and the countries of the former Soviet empire were rapidly, if partially, absorbed into an increasingly integrated global economy. The term *globalization* quickly became the shorthand for this model of expansion—a heady and complex mix of technological, economic, political, and cultural change.

Globalization was accompanied and underpinned by a set of interlocking institutional developments at international and national levels. First, the existing structures of global economic gover-nance were overhauled. The World Bank and the IMF redefined their roles, moving swiftly away from Keynesian operating principles to become bastions of neoliberalism. A web of bilateral, regional, and global international trade and investment agreements, culminating in the creation of the WTO in 1995, bound the new system in place. These economic and political trends unified in opposition a diverse array of actors, however. Downsizing and corporate restructuring, privatization, the erosion of workers' rights, and the changing nature of production and supply chains activated opposition from the labor movement in both the North and the South. Global warming, unsustainable growth, and the depletion of resources created hostility from environmentalists, who were further outraged over the perceived threat to environmental legislation from trade rules in the WTO—for example, when four Asian nations successfully challenged provisions of the U.S. Endangered Species Act forbidding the sale in the United States of prawns caught in ways that kill endangered sea turtles. The erosion of the nation-state and of democratic institutions antagonized proponents of state-led development, democrats, and some on the political right. Increasing corporate power and social inequality galvanized the traditional left and a whole host of other left-of-center actors. Structural adjustment programs and growing Southern marginalization and inequality radicalized civil society (the term for nonstate civic and social organizations) and some political parties in the developing world.

The changed international institutional landscape also aided the growth of this opposition. This shift of power to international institutions and the growth in the range and reach of their activities were not well linked into the traditional accountability mechanisms of states. These inadequacies in global governance have raised the profile of attempts by nonstate actors to make these institutions more accountable. The increasing global reach of the World Bank and the IMF has provided common rallying points for protest, and the founding of the WTO in 1995 in particular put an institutional face on what had

anti-globalization

69

previously been an amorphous process—a gift to the protest movement.

Who's Who? At first glance, anti-globalization seems an incongruous political mix of contradictions, colors, and cultures, in part vocal and aggressive, in part quiet and conciliatory. Although it defies firm categorizations, the movement can be roughly divided into three strands: statists, alternatives, and reformists.

The statists believe the current process of globalization has been a disaster and seek to defend and rebuild the role of the state in economic management after the neoliberal assault that began in the 1980s. This group is dominated by the traditional left, some sections of the labor movement, and a large proportion of Southern activists. Through this group runs a strong sense of rejectionism and even conservatism. Some, such as a few of the U.S. labor unions protesting at the WTO Ministerial in Seattle, want to retain the state's ability to protect domestic industries from cheap imports. Others, such as the prominent Filipino activist Walden Bello, reject the terms of globalization outright, feeling that any alternative, including the abolition of the IMF and WTO, could not fail to be an improvement on present realities. Despite its focus on the nation-state, this group retains a strong sense of internationalism.

The alternatives are both highly visible and the hardest to define, though often labeled "anarchist." This element of the movement is strongly driven by cultural concerns and best understood in cultural terms. Its members—be they ecologists running organic businesses, followers of the *Small Is Beautiful* author E. F. Schumacher, activists seeking to "deconstruct" corporate power and global brands, or Zapatistas who wish to gain rights and land and make a statement about globalization's marginalizing effects—reject globalization in passing but concentrate more on building small-scale alternatives. These groups oppose the encroachment of the market or the market's power relations on their cultural or political spaces. Most are also small, decentralized, and strongly anticorporate.

The reformists make up the majority of formally structured groups involved in the movement, or at least dominate the thinking of the movement's leadership. Their aim is partial change to offset current injustices and inequalities. The reformists act within current political systems and advocate gradualism and peaceful change. Most accept a role for the market but believe it must be better regulated and managed in order to achieve socially just and sustainable outcomes. This group includes some trade unions, faith groups, charities and development organizations (such as Oxfam), and most mainstream environmental groups (including Friends of the Earth), as well as issue-specific campaigns such as Drop the Debt and the Tobin tax.

The reformist current has also made strong inroads into global and national politics, going far beyond "the usual suspects." The *Financial Times*, Gordon Brown, Nobel Prize–winning economists such as Amartya Sen and Joseph Stiglitz, Kofi Annan, the corporate social responsibility movement, Jeffrey Sachs, and George Soros could all be called reformists. As the economist Meghnad Desai puts it, "The reformists view themselves as the only true defenders of globalization. They believe that both isolationist calls to reverse the process and supporters' insistence on 'ultra-liberal' forms of global capitalism are bound to de-rail globalization, with tragic consequences" (Desai and Said 2001, 68).

This attempt to disaggregate the movement warrants several caveats, however. Many nongovernmental organizations (NGOs) and even individuals span more than one current: for example, Friends of the Earth is both reformist and alternative. Author Naomi Klein, one of the movement's most prominent figures since the publication of her book *No Logo*, may base her critique of globalization primarily in cultural terms and is a source of inspiration to the anticorporate wing of the movement, but is herself essentially a progressive reformist. Within mainstream NGOs, supporters and Southern partners often espouse more radical options than the full-time staff and leaders.

Nor does this picture do justice to the depth and breadth of the movement in the South. The largest protests against the WTO have been in India. Brazil is rapidly becoming a center of the movement, as evidenced by the huge gatherings of activists in Porto Alegre since January 2001 as part of the World Social Forum, held as a "people's response" to the World Economic Forum business summits in Davos. The movement in the North draws inspiration and guidance from a number of prominent Southern intellectuals such as Vandana Shiva (India), Martin Kohr (Malaysia), and Walden Bello (Philippines, but based in Bangkok) and the work of the NGOs to which they belong. Finally, none of these categories describes the nihilist currents, few in number in Seattle but significant at the G8 summit in Genoa in 2001, which used the protests as a platform for street violence rather than political debate.

Global institutions also play a key unifying role, both in providing focus to the movement and in creating the backdrop against which the movement has thrived. The movement is seen by some to be an important international player in its own right, helping to redefine public notions of democracy, accountability, and collective mobilization. The *Financial Times* identifies it as a "fifth estate," a valuable global counterbalance in a world of aging and often inadequate global institutions. The movement's reformist currents in particular have played an increasing role in what some academics have called "postsovereign governance."

But attitudes toward global institutions also mark a significant cleavage in the anti-globalization movement. For reformists, engagement is vital if change is to be achieved. Engagement has provided a small measure of greater transparency, participation, and popular pressure as NGOs enter policymaking channels and new mechanisms are created in an attempt to bridge gaps within highly imperfect existing structures. For rejectionists, by contrast, global institutions (in particular the WTO, IMF, and World Bank) are fundamentally illegitimate and unreformable, to be abolished rather than improved.

Main Concerns In general, the concerns of NGOs and civil society stem from an assertion that although globalization has led to benefits for some, it has not led to benefits for all. The benefits appear to have gone to those who already have the most, while many of the poorest have failed to benefit fully and some have even been made poorer. A linked concern of NGOs is that the drive for liberalization is based too much on dogma and ideology rather than on careful examination of the evidence and assessment of likely impact.

Equity and redistribution are seen as the missing link between globalization and poverty reduction. NGOs argue that improved equity within states leads not only to faster poverty reduction for a given amount of growth but also to faster growth. What is good for poor people is good for the economy as a whole. Yet up to now, globalization is seen to be frequently linked to increasing inequality, at both the national and the international levels. NGOs also argue for redistribution of wealth between developed and developing countries—through debt relief and increased aid flows.

NGOs highlight research that points to the importance of national differences. The same policy reforms have different outcomes in different countries, depending on the structure of the economy, the initial distribution of assets, and the nature of economic and political institutions. Policy responses to globalization should be appropriate to particular cases in terms of the instruments used, the sequencing of reforms, and the combination of policies implemented.

Even though the evidence points to the importance of diversity, however, developing country governments are pushed by international rule-making, whether under the auspices of the WTO, through the pressures exerted by structural adjustment packages, or by the need to reassure the markets, toward greater homogeneity of policy response. The challenge for policymakers is to find ways of ensuring that national and international rule-making accommodate appropriate diversity of policy rather than reduce diversity to a minimum.

One of the lessons of recent years is held to be that liberalization and deregulation have very different costs and benefits when applied to the three areas of financial flows, direct investment, and trade. There has been concern that the frequency and severity of financial crises in recent years demonstrate the need for serious reforms of the global financial architecture. Crises are seen to hurt the poor disproportionately and increase inequality, making the achievement of growth favorable to the poor harder thereafter.

One of the most high-profile areas of public concern (demonstrated by the impact and worldwide sales of Naomi Klein's *No Logo*) is that the increasing size and dominance of transnational corporations is making them more influential and less accountable. Public concern over excessive corporate power has led to calls for increased international regulation and has put pressure on companies to regulate themselves through the introduction of codes of conduct for themselves and their suppliers. In financial circles, this pressure has been accompanied by a greater awareness that successful companies must take into account a range of nonfinancial risks, including social, environmental, and ethical issues.

There are also fears that competition between countries wishing to attract foreign investment and technology could lead to a "race to the bottom" in terms of tax incentives and labor market suppression, thereby minimizing the potential social benefits offered by the private sector. Critics argue that the impact of foreign direct investment on employment, export performance, and domestic industry is not guaranteed, and that governments must be able to provide a regulatory framework to maximize the benefits and minimize the costs.

Finally, although most mainstream NGOs believe strongly that it is essential to have rules governing international trade, they severely criticize the particular set of rules established in the WTO. They see a multilateral trading system as necessary to ensure that weaker nations are not discriminated against by the strong in both North-South and South-South relations, but they argue that rule-making must proceed at a pace that is appropriate for the weakest members of the system, and the rules made in the WTO must be the right rules for development and poverty reduction. Current rules expose Northern governments to well-founded accusations of double standards on issues such as protection for domestic industries and support for domestic farmers, and are seen to provide insufficient

flexibility to enable Southern governments to pursue their development goals. The agenda being pushed by Northern countries is seen by many to militate against development and to be incompatible with the historical experience of the industrialized North.

Hegemonic Shifts In general terms, it is clear that significant changes have occurred in the thinking of policymakers since the mid-1980s. In part this has been a response to some of the more catastrophic results of gung-ho liberalization: the debacle of free market reforms in Russia, the Mexican crisis of 1994, and the Asian financial crisis of 1997–98 led to some serious soul-searching and admissions of mistakes, deflating the excessive self-confidence of the 1980s.

The growth of the anti-globalization movement fed off and accelerated this rethinking. Politicians recognized a need to respond to public disquiet, for example in the G8's decision to put debt on the agenda at its 1998 Birmingham summit, or when British prime minister Tony Blair used the 2005 Gleneagles G8 summit as a platform to gain further commitments for increased aid flows to Africa.

The emergence of a group of more economically powerful developing countries has also increased the political pressure for greater reform. For example, the creation of the G20 alliance of developing countries (including China, India, Brazil, and South Africa) at the WTO has shifted the balance of power within global trade relations and put greater pressure on the members of the Organisation for Economic Cooperation and Development to reform their agricultural sectors.

In recent years the movement has achieved some notable successes:

Jubilee 2000: This largely church-based coalition was credited by the British government with putting debt back on the international agenda. Initially started in the United Kingdom, Jubilee groups were set up in dozens of countries, North and South. Many, especially in the South, rapidly moved to campaign on wider globalization-related issues such as the impact of transnational corporations and structural adjustment programs.

Attac: This French-based network of intellectuals and activists has taken the lead in promoting the introduction of the Tobin tax (a small tax on currency transactions designed to curb speculative capital flows) and was influential in persuading the French government to support a study of the tax and oppose the Multilateral Agreement on Investment.

Corporate social responsibility: Public criticism and campaigning directed at corporate misconduct—for example, pollution or abusive labor practices—backed by increasing pressure from institutional investors, have prompted numerous initiatives to improve corporations' social and environmental performance. In the United States, student-led, grassroots, antisweatshop campaigns galvanized political life on campuses to a degree not seen since the Vietnam War.

These partial successes have strengthened the reformists within the movement and endangered its unity by heightening the points of difference between them and the rejectionists. The difficulties posed by partial victories were most clearly demonstrated in the Jubilee 2000 movement, when at the height of its policy successes at the Cologne G8 summit in 1999 the more radical "Jubilee South" wing, based in countries such as South Africa and Nicaragua, condemned the Northern Jubilee organizations for their reformist acceptance of the status quo.

Underlying the political debate has been a steady shift in public opinion, with messages on several fronts—press exposés of poor working conditions, public protest, and the growing availability and prominence of "fair trade" products—combining to make the public increasingly aware of the social impact of globalization.

It is easy to lose sight of how much has changed since the early 1980s in policy debates about globalization. There is now a much more nuanced understanding among decision-makers of the differences between liberalization of finance, direct investment, and trade; at the very least, most wings of the private sector pay lip service to notions of corporate social responsibility, and some of the most notorious excesses of free market zeal have been curbed.

The Future of Anti-globalization Understanding what may happen to this movement means exploring deeper questions about its political and social origins, the economic issues that it addresses, and the future of the international system to which it is a response. It also means looking at its component parts and their likely, and possibly differing, reactions to changing circumstances.

This brief overview suggests that much of this movement's coherence is contingent on external conditions. The strongest force in shaping its future development is therefore likely to be external, notably stemming from the pace and depth of change in the institutions of global governance and of the international system in which these institutions are based.

The success of the movement—and in particular its reformist current—in achieving change has been helped greatly by the multilateralism of the current international system. It has provided focus and coherence to otherwise disparate groups and allowed small gains in attempts to create a more balanced form of international governance.

Threats to multilateralism, however—either from a turn toward unilateralism by the most powerful states or from the increased strain put on the long-term effectiveness of global governance by the exclusion of the world's weakest nations—would strengthen the rejectionists and undermine the reformists, as well as the unity of the movement as a whole, and possibly the usefulness of the term itself.

See also fair trade; globalization; Group of Seven/Eight (G7/G8); Tobin tax; Washington consensus; World Economic Forum; World Trade Organization

FURTHER READING

Chang, Ha-Joon. 2007. *Bad Samaritans: Rich Nations, Poor Policies, and the Threat to the Developing World.* London: Random House. A readable and critical examination of the policy prescriptions of the Washington consensus and an argument for the potential merits of active state involvement in successful development strategies that draws upon the experience of southeast Asia.

Desai, Meghnad, and Yahia Said. 2001. "The New Anti-Capitalist Movement: Money and Global Civil Society."

In *Global Civil Society 2001*, edited by Helmut Anheier, Marlies Glasius, and Mary Kaldor. Oxford: Oxford University Press, 51–78. The Civil Society yearbook, based at the Centre for Civil Society at the London School of Economics, has been running since 2001 and provides a good overview of developments in the sector.

Fowler, Penny, and Kevin Watkins. 2003. *Rigged Rules and Double Standards: Trade, Globalisation, and the Fight against Poverty.* Oxford: Oxfam Academic. The benchmark publication that sets out the developmental case for fairer trade.

Green, Duncan, and Matthew Griffith. 2002. "Globalization and Its Discontents." *International Affairs* 78 (1): 49–68. An overview of globalization and anti-globalization movements, from which this entry draws.

Held, David. 2004. *Global Covenant: The Social Democratic Alternative to the Washington Consensus.* Oxford: Polity Press. In many ways the counterpoint to Martin Wolf's case for the global economy, Held argues for a "social democractic alternative" with greater attention to policies to compensate those who lose out from globalization, as well as the need for a stronger and more inclusive set of international institutions.

Klein, Naomi. 2001. *No Logo.* London: Flamingo. The best-selling critique of global business trends, which blends cultural analysis, political manifesto, and journalistic exposé.

Mallaby, Sebastian. 2004. *The World's Banker: A Story of Failed States, Financial Crises, and the Wealth and Poverty of Nations.* New Haven, CT: Yale University Press. A highly readable portrait of James Wolfensohn's presidency of the World Bank, which examines the struggles between the World Bank, its shareholders from the developed world, its clients in the developing world, and the NGOs that straddle both worlds.

Wolf, Martin. 2004. *Why Globalization Works: The Case for the Global Market Economy.* New Haven, CT: Yale University Press. A combative examination of the merits and faults of the different arguments from members of the anti-globalization movement.

WEBSITES
Third World Network, http://www.twnside.org.sg
Focus on the Global South, http://www.focusweb.org
World Social Forum, http://www.worldsocialforum.org
Global Policy Forum, http://www.globalpolicy.org
Oxfam, http://www.oxfam.org.uk

DUNCAN GREEN AND MATT GRIFFITH

■ applied general equilibrium models

In their single-country form, applied general equilibrium (AGE) models simulate the variety of markets that compose entire economies. In their regional or global forms, these models also simulate the market transactions among economies or groups of economies. In all these cases, AGE models account for the interactions in markets for goods, services, labor, physical capital, and other productive inputs. A large and growing body of evidence suggests that the indirect and economywide effects of policy changes captured in this framework are indeed important, and there is a well-established theoretical foundation for the approach. Economywide effects include upstream and downstream production linkages through input-output relationships; intersectoral competition for basic resources such as labor, physical capital, and land; reallocation of rents from quantitative restrictions; distributional effects across household types; and exchange rate changes. AGE models provide a means of explicitly accounting for these effects in a comprehensive and consistent manner.

The Notion of "Applied" What is meant by the notion of "applied" in AGE models? Francois and Reinert (1997) give the following four-part characterization:

Detailed policy orientation. Applied models use a broader set of policies than just ad valorem tariffs. The models involve an analytical commitment to the sectoral and institutional details of a policy, including the role of data nomenclatures and concordances among nomenclatures, as well as a commitment to the policymaking process itself and sensitivity to the kinds of results that are of interest to policymakers.

Nonlocal changes form distorted base equilibria. In most theoretical analyses of trade and other economic policies, the economy begins in a nondistorted state with no tariffs, quotas, or other taxes present. To this initial nondistorted equilibrium an infinitesimal tariff or tax is introduced, and a new, counterfactual equilibrium is solved for using the linear approximation of differential calculus. In applied policy models, by contrast, the initial or base equilibrium reflects the relevant set of policy distortions. Since the policy changes introduced into the model are those actually under consideration rather than infinitesimal, the resultant changes are nonlocal. Consequently, functional forms prove to be crucial to model results, and what economists term "second-best effects" play a role in these outcomes.

Accurate and current data. Given the close link between modeling and policymaking, both the accuracy and the currency of data are important. Unfortunately, there can be a trade-off between accuracy and currency; the most recent data may be only estimates or not entirely survey based. Consequently, professional judgment is needed, and there needs to be a willingness to revise published results as new and better information becomes available.

Model structure determined by the data. The functional forms used to construct applied models must be chosen to allow for important regularities observed in the data. For example, the classical structures of theoretical trade models assume that imports and domestic competing goods are perfect substitutes and that there are no barriers to trade. In this case, the model describes interindustry trade only, cannot support a number of goods that exceed the number of factors of production, and cannot explain *bilateral* patterns of international trade. To avoid this in applied work, steps are taken to specify alternative model structures that allow for bilateral patterns of intraindustry trade and numbers of goods in excess of numbers of factors of production.

As an illustration of the complexities of applied policy modeling in general and the role of AGE models in particular, consider the case of multilateral Doha Round trade negotiations as described by Francois, van Meijl, and van Tongeren (2005):

> Judging the economic impact of a WTO agreement is massively complex, even when it comes to issues as straightforward as tariff

cutting. The eventual Doha Round agreement should lower thousands of individual tariffs in each WTO member country and there are about 150 members. The result would be important shifts of resources among sectors in most nations in the world, along with attendant changes in the prices of goods and productive factors. Due to international trade, the supply and demand factors in each nation affect resource allocations in all other nations. How can economists evaluate the impact of these choices? The most practical way of proceeding is to employ a large-scale computable general equilibrium model that allows simultaneous consideration of all the effects. (352)

This speaks to the utility of AGE models and explains why the methodology has evolved from an obscure exercise in applied econometrics to being a key tool for applied policy analysis. Indeed, many national governments use single-country models to assess policy changes, and both national governments and multilateral financial institutions use global models (e.g., the GTAP model described in Hertel 1997 or variants of the linkage model described in van der Mensbrugghe 2006) to assess a large variety of international policy issues.

Overview of Model Structure In AGE models, it is generally the case that an equation system is solved for prices that equate supply and demand in all markets simultaneously and satisfy the accounting identities governing economic behavior. Exceptions to this approach exist that allow for disequilibria in some markets (e.g., labor markets). Once the equation system has been specified, the equilibrium is calibrated to a base-year data set (often in the form of a social accounting matrix, or SAM), and the model reproduces the base-year economy in the absence of any policy changes. The calibration ensures that subsequent policy simulations move from an initial position that describes the economy (be it national, regional, or global) and its accounting identities as accurately as possible.

After calibration, the AGE model is used to simulate the effects of alternative policy changes on the economy with reference to the base year (static) or a baseline scenario (dynamic). The model fully captures the flow of income from firms to labor, capital, and other inputs, from each of these inputs to households, and from households back to final demand of various types (household, government, investment, and rest of world or exports). Hence, it remains internally consistent even after introducing policy changes of various kinds.

The policy parameters of an AGE model include tariff rates, quotas, various domestic taxes and subsidies, and a number of behavioral elasticities. The behavioral elasticities play a central role in model results, and this represents an area of inquiry in which there is not always complete agreement with regard to appropriate values. Consequently, this is one aspect of AGE modeling that needs to be well documented and handled with care, including the analysis of the sensitivity of model outcomes to assumed elasticity values. Critical in this regard is what is known as the Armington (1969) elasticity, the elasticity of substitution between imports and domestic competing goods.

With a calibrated model in hand, an analyst can simulate the effects of proposed policy changes by comparing the base-year or baseline model solution with a counterfactual solution in which one or more of the policy parameters have been changed. A comparison of the base-year/baseline and counterfactual equilibria can reveal (depending on model specification) the effects of the policy changes on imports, exports, domestic production, employment, wages, aggregate economic welfare, disaggregated household welfare, and poverty and human development outcomes.

Standard Framework A standard framework of applied general equilibrium modes is that described by de Melo and Robinson (1989) and related to the previous contribution of Hazari, Sgro, and Suh (1980) on nontraded goods. In this framework, there are three varieties of goods: an export good (E), an import good (Z), and a nontraded, domestic good (D). Corresponding to these three goods, there are three different prices, P_E, P_Z, and P_D, and three dif-

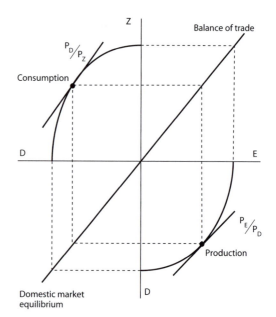

Figure 1

A graphical representation of a simple applied general equilibrium model

ferent quantities, E, Z, and D. The graphical representation of this framework is provided in the four quadrants of figure 1. In the southeast quadrant, the country produces two goods, E and D. The concave curve in this quadrant is the country's production possibilities frontier (PPF) and indicates that there are no economies of scale sufficient to outweigh the increasing opportunity costs of production. In practice, this part of AGE models is actually implemented in two stages, with a constant elasticity of substitution PPF and a constant elasticity of transformation allocation between exports and domestic supply, the latter following Powell and Gruen (1968). Under perfect competition, profit maximization, and full employment of resources, the country produces at a point on the PPF that is tangent to the relative price line P_E/P_D.

In the northeast quadrant of figure 1, we have a balance of trade line, which relates E and Z. This line tells us what level of imports can exist given the level of exports. As drawn, this balance of trade line is a 45-degree line, but changes in the terms of trade P_E/P_D will rotate the line either up or down. Capital inflows or outflows will shift the line up or down, respectively, without changing its slope.

In the southwest quadrant of figure 1, the vertical axis plots the supply of the domestic good from the PPF, while the horizontal axis plots the demand for the domestic good. The 45-degree line in this quadrant is simply a domestic market equilibrium condition.

Finally, the northwest quadrant of figure 1 addresses the consumption of goods Z and D. The concave curve in this quadrant is a consumption possibilities frontier (CPF). The consumption possibilities are determined by the PPF, the balance of trade constraint, and domestic market equilibrium. The choice of the point on the CPF will reflect utility maximization in the form of tangency with an indifference curve of a representative household based on product differentiation by country of origin and is typically modeled using a constant elasticity of substitution frameworks as in Armington (1969).

In standard trade theory with incomplete specialization and no transportation costs, bilateral trade patterns remain indeterminate. However, in the framework of figure 1, intraindustry trade is fully captured. In multicountry versions of the model, actual patterns of bilateral, intraindustry trade will be effectively described in both base and counterfactual equilibria. Finally, nontradability in the framework of figure 1 depends on the price line P_E/P_D. The higher is this ratio, the more of domestic output will enter into trade. Therefore, nontradability in the AGE framework is not fixed by sector but depends on relative prices. Further, unlike Salter (1959), the two traded goods, E and Z, are not aggregated into a single good, and this is more satisfactory for empirical implementation.

Dynamics The policy changes considered in AGE models have the potential to change both overall income levels and the returns to factors of production. As noted by Francois, McDonald, and Nordström, "To the extent that investment hinges on income levels and expected returns, the medium- and long-term results of changes in trading conditions will include induced shifts in the capital stock" (1997,

365). Incorporating these considerations into AGE models shifts the analysis from *static* to *dynamic* considerations. Dynamic specifications of AGE models can vary in a number of respects, but the research on these specifications is now fairly well developed.

When allowed for, dynamic effects show up in model results through a number of paths, including the following: increases in incomes due to trade liberalization and other policy changes raising savings rates, declines in the prices of capital goods increasing real investment, and increasing trade openness (typically measured by sectoral export-to-output ratios) causing sectoral productivity increases. The first and second of these dynamic gains are often referred to as "medium-run growth effects" as identified by Baldwin (1992) and do not depend on any dynamic externalities as emphasized in New Growth Theory. Therefore, they are best viewed as reflecting "classical" or "old" growth theory. In this respect, the first and second paths for dynamic gains are quite firmly reflective of received economic theory.

The third type of dynamic effect is often referred to as the "procompetitive effects of exporting" and can reflect economies of scale in production and trade, learning by doing, standards achievement, and network effects. These potentialities are less standard than the medium-run growth effects, and it is not clear whether they are as automatic as suggested by some model specifications. In addition, there is little empirical evidence with regard to the behavioral elasticities used to model these effects. For these reasons, it is prudent to separate out simulations based on these procompetitive effects as indicative of *potential* rather than as actual, realized gains.

Other Extensions The standard AGE model considered here has been extended in a number of relevant directions. These include environmental and natural resource issues (including climate change), industry structure (including imperfect competition), migration, capital flows (including foreign direct investment), financial crises, commodity prices, foreign aid, natural disasters, poverty, and human development. Given this broad coverage of issues that are paramount in assessing the world economy, as well as the more standard applications to trade policies, it is clear that AGE models will continue to be an important methodology to help us understand the role of national and multilateral policies in the world economy.

See also capital accumulation in open economies; gravity models; intraindustry trade; nontraded goods; partial equilibrium models; Swan diagram; terms of trade

FURTHER READING

Armington, Paul. 1969. "A Theory of Demand for Products Distinguished by Place of Production." *IMF Staff Papers* 16 (3): 159–76. The key contribution on product differentiation by country of origin used in most AGE modeling.

Baldwin, Richard E. 1992. "Measurable Dynamic Gains from Trade." *Journal of Political Economy* 100 (1): 162–74. A key contribution on the dynamic gains from trade.

de Melo, Jaime, and Sherman Robinson. 1989. "Product Differentiation and the Treatment of Product Differentiation in Computable General Equilibrium Models of Small Economies." *Journal of International Economics* 27 (1-2): 47–67. An introduction to the basic structure employed in many AGE models.

de Melo, Jaime, and David Tarr. 1992. *A General Equilibrium Analysis of U.S. Foreign Trade Policy*. Cambridge: Cambridge University Press. A thorough analysis of trade policy in a single-country using the AGE framework.

Francois, Joseph F., Bradley J. McDonald, and Håkan Nordtröm. 1997. "Capital Accumulation in Applied Trade Models." In *Applied Methods for Trade Policy Analysis: A Handbook*, edited by Joseph F. Francois and Kenneth A. Reinert. Cambridge: Cambridge University Press, 364–82. An introduction to dynamic issues in AGE modeling.

Francois, Joseph F., Hans van Meijl, and Frank van Tongeren. 2005. "Trade Liberalization in the Doha Development Round." *Economic Policy* 20 (42): 349–91. An application of AGE modeling to multilateral trade negotiations.

Francois, J. F., and K. A. Reinert. 1997. "Applied Methods for Trade Policy Analysis: An Overview." In *Applied Methods for Trade Policy Analysis: A Handbook*, edited by Joseph F. Francois and Kenneth A. Reinert. Cam-

bridge: Cambridge University Press, 3–24. A well-known introduction to the field of applied trade policy analysis.

Harrison, Glenn W., Thomas F. Rutherford, and David G. Tarr. 2003. "Trade Liberalization, Poverty, and Efficient Equity." *Journal of Development Economics* 71 (1): 97–128. An example of using household survey data in an AGE model to assess the distributional impacts of trade liberalization.

Hazari, Bharat R., Pasquale M. Sgro, and Dong C. Suh. 1980. "A Simple Geometric Treatment of Nontraded Goods in the Pure Theory of International Trade." *Keio Economic Studies* 17 (1): 91–104. A trade-theoretic treatment of nontraded goods that corresponds to a framework adopted in many AGE models.

Hertel, Thomas W., ed. 1997. *Global Trade Analysis: Modeling and Applications*. Cambridge: Cambridge University Press. A detailed description of a widely used, global AGE model known as GTAP.

Markusen, James R., Thomas F. Rutherford, and Linda Hunter. 1995. "Trade Liberalization in a Multinational-Dominated Industry." *Journal of International Economics* 38 (1/2): 95–117. An application of AGE modeling to foreign direct investment.

Powell, A., and F. Gruen. 1968. "The Constant Elasticity of Transformation Production Frontier and Linear Supply System." *International Economic Review* 9 (3): 315–28. The source for the functional form used in modeling the allocation of goods between exports and domestic supply in AGE models.

Reinert, Kenneth A., and David W. Roland-Holst. 1997. "Social Accounting Matrices." In *Applied Methods for Trade Policy Analysis: A Handbook*, edited by Joseph F. Francois and Kenneth A. Reinert. Cambridge: Cambridge University Press, 94–121. An introduction to social accounting matrices and their use in AGE models.

Salter, Wilfred E.G. 1959. "Internal and External Balance: The Role of Price and Expenditure Effects." *Economic Record* 35 (171): 226–38. A classic treatment of traded versus nontraded goods that has proved important in AGE modeling.

Shoven, John B., and John Whalley. 1984. "Applied General Equilibrium Models of Taxation and International Trade: An Introduction and Survey." *Journal of Eco-*

nomic Literature 22 (3): 1007–51. An early and noted review of AGE models in both trade policy and public finance.

van der Mensbrugghe, Dominique. 2006. *LINKAGE Technical Reference Document, Version 6.0.* Washington, DC: World Bank. A detailed description of a widely used, global AGE model that emphasizes development issues.

KENNETH A. REINERT

■ appropriate technology and foreign direct investment

Appropriate technology generally refers to technology that is suitable for local conditions. Although the term has sometimes been used very broadly to refer to technologies that support goals such as the preservation of nature, local culture, or life in small villages, economists typically speak of technological "appropriateness" in the context of technologies adapted for local conditions such as factor abundance—for example, capital-intensive technologies in capital-abundant countries and labor-intensive technologies in labor-abundant countries.

The discussion of appropriate technology in the context of foreign direct investment (FDI) arose from concerns that technologies developed under the economic conditions of developed countries could have harmful effects in developing countries—in particular, that multinational enterprises (MNEs) would not create enough jobs. This possibility is particularly likely if innovations are "induced" by cost-saving possibilities in the markets where they are first used (Kennedy 1964). Because developed countries are capital-abundant, the technologies developed there tend to be capital-intensive, labor-saving technologies, and thus tend to generate less employment in a developing country than do technologies tailored to the conditions of abundant, cheap labor present there. Similar arguments apply to other features of technology: for example, technologies requiring a steady supply of electric power may be inappropriate for countries that experience fre-

quent power outages. Thus there has been a general concern whether MNEs bring in the right type of technologies—whether the technologies that are in the best interest of MNEs to transfer are those that are in the best interest of the local economy.

Adaptation and Technology Transfer In simple models of the behavior of MNEs, the technology developed in the home market is often assumed to be reproduced identically in other countries, which is how the firm exploits its advantage of technological ownership. In fact, reproducing technology abroad is not easy; technology often must be adapted to local conditions for it to work. If the existing technology is not appropriate for local conditions in the host country, the MNE may have an incentive to adapt the technology.

Actual technology transfer is not simply a matter of shipping blueprints to another country, but involves a costly process of experimentation and trial and error (Teece 1977), during which the specifications of the technology adapt somewhat to local conditions. Some technologies may be more easily adaptable than others, such as ones where different techniques using different mixes of capital and labor are feasible. In some cases the costs of adaptation may be large enough that adaptation is not worthwhile to the MNE. The practical questions thus become a matter of how adaptable MNEs' technologies are to local conditions, how much adapting MNEs in fact decide to do, and whether local firms would in fact do a better job of adaptation (Lall 1978).

The degree to which MNEs adapt their technologies to local conditions has been widely studied. Since adapting technology is costly, and since the competitive advantage of MNEs lies in large part in their ability to replicate technologies they own in different countries, there can be a strong incentive to minimize adaptations to local conditions. For example, the basic type of machinery is likely to stay the same from country to country. Thus technologies initially created for local conditions may well be better suited for the local conditions than technologies created elsewhere and then adapted. However, the situations where technologies are ill adapted are apt to be those where adaptation is difficult, and hence local firms may be unable to do better than MNEs.

Empirical results on the observed degree of technological adaptation often defy easy generalization. Large statistical studies often include firms in different industries, and therefore the differences in capital intensity may be due to the industry rather than to individual firm choice. The effect of foreign firms' technological choices on domestic firms in developing countries depends in part on whether the local firms are suppliers, are competitors, or have some other relationship to foreign firms. It has been reported that MNEs impose particular technologies on their suppliers in developing countries, at least partially in an attempt to maintain quality control. There are many possibilities for developing country firms to learn and imitate the technology of MNEs, through reverse engineering, social networking among employees, or employees who leave to become entrepreneurs or are hired away by competitors. Sometimes, domestic imitators have been more successful adaptors than MNEs and have been rewarded by rising market shares. At the same time, one can observe cases in which managers in developing-country subsidiaries of MNEs from developed countries adapt technologies in the labor-intensive direction (Pack 1976; Lecraw 1977).

Multinationals from Developing Countries In the 1960s and 1970s, an increasing number of firms based in countries such as India, Hong Kong, Korea, Brazil, and Argentina became direct investors. These "third-world multinationals" tended to place the bulk of their investments in other developing countries. Since economists were accustomed to think of MNEs transferring capital and technology from the North to the South, new explanations seemed necessary for the phenomenon of South-South FDI. A widely offered idea was that developing-country firms had acquired "appropriate" technologies in their home markets, which gave their affiliates in other countries a competitive advantage.

The types of intangible firm advantages that could arise from operating in a developing-country environment are widespread. These could include managerial skills in dealing with severe bottlenecks in acquisition of materials and power, local labor conditions, and developing-country bureaucracies, and superior information about local product and factor markets in certain trading partners. Also, in some countries such as Korea and India, the largest domestic firms were organized as multiproduct conglomerates, and the managerial skills needed for such organization readily adapt to the multinational form.

The motivations for South-South FDI need not be limited to intangible appropriate-technology advantages. Informational advantages gained from a past history of exporting or migration suggest a transactions cost explanation rather than a technological one. Even in developing countries, firm-level efforts to promote efficiency might encourage capital intensity rather than labor intensity (Ferrantino 1992). By the early 21st century, some investors from developing countries were seeking to acquire developed-country technologies through mergers and acquisitions (e.g., Chinese investors in the United States), showing that home-country production experience need not be the only determinant of technological development in developing-country MNEs.

Appropriate Technology, Efficiency, and Spillovers From a policy standpoint, part of the idea of appropriate technology is that the technology chosen by markets might not be optimal for either economic growth or employment generation. This imperfection suggests a role for government either in technology choice or at least in undoing distortions such as those that might make labor artificially expensive. In the 1980s the skepticism about the benefits of FDI for developing countries began to wane, and the promarket ideas collectively called the Washington consensus tended to see FDI as enhancing productivity and growth rather than being an original source of distortions. Under this view, the most important feature of technologies bundled with FDI is their potential for enhancement of overall productivity, rather than their bias toward either capital or labor.

Nonetheless, the question of the conditions under which the activities of developed-country MNEs influence technological conditions in developing countries, and whether and under what conditions adaptation takes place, remains open. Much of the current research on technological spillovers from FDI is informed by the issues raised in the analysis of appropriate technology.

See also foreign direct investment and innovation, imitation; foreign direct investment and international technology transfer; location theory; technology spillovers

FURTHER READING

Ferrantino, Michael J. 1992. "Technology Expenditures, Factor Intensity, and Efficiency in Indian Manufacturing." *Review of Economics and Statistics* 74 (4): 689–700. Firm-level study examining whether the technological efforts of Indian firms, prominent among the early third-world multinationals, led to "appropriate" outcomes.

Kennedy, Charles. 1964. "Induced Bias in Innovation and the Theory of Distribution." *Economic Journal* 72 (295): 541–47. Early treatment of the response of innovation to relative resource prices.

Lall, Sanjaya. 1978. "Transnationals, Domestic Enterprises, and Industrial Structure in Host LDCs: A Survey." *Oxford Economic Papers* NS 30 (2): 217–48. A treatment of technological appropriateness and adaptation in the context of available evidence on linkages between transnationals and developing countries.

———, ed. 1983. *The New Multinationals: The Spread of Third World Enterprises*. Chichester: John Wiley and Sons. Case studies on multinationals from India, Hong Kong, Argentina, and Brazil.

Lecraw, Donald J. 1977. "Direct Investment by Firms from Less Developed Countries." *Oxford Economic Papers* NS 29 (3): 442–57. Demonstrates, for Thailand, that investors from developing countries have different motivations from developed-country investors and use more labor-intensive technology.

Pack, Howard. 1976. "The Substitution of Labor for Capital in Kenyan Manufacturing." *Economic Journal* 86 (341): 45–58. Firm-level study revealing that both domestic and foreign firms were capable of improving productivity without capital deepening.

Teece, David J. 1977. "Technology Transfer by Multinational Firms: The Resource Cost of Transferring Technological Know-how." *Economic Journal* 87 (346): 242–61. Evidence on the level and determinants of technology transfer costs within MNEs.

MICHAEL FERRANTINO

■ arbitrage
See interest parity conditions

■ Asia Pacific Economic Cooperation (APEC)

The Asia Pacific Economic Cooperation (APEC) process was the first structured forum for intergovernmental cooperation among the economies of East Asia and their main trading partners in North America, Australasia, and Russia. It was launched in Canberra, Australia, in 1989 to promote closer communications to help seize the opportunities for trade and investment among a diverse group of economies with different resources and comparative advantages, as well as to anticipate the inevitable tensions when comparative advantage changed as economies developed. APEC's central objective is to sustain the growth and development of the region by promoting mutually beneficial economic integration and by encouraging international flows of goods, services, capital, and technology. APEC has adopted the principle of open regionalism, seeking to reduce impediments to international economic transactions among participants without diverting economic activity away from other economies.

APEC was built on foundations laid during the preceding decades. Since the 1960s, the Association of Southeast Asian Nations (ASEAN) has demonstrated that a voluntary association of diverse nations with diverse economies can be valuable and effective. Since those years policy-oriented analysis by researchers and business people with a broad international outlook noted the growing, market-driven interdependence of Asia Pacific economies. This included the work of the Pacific Forum for Trade and Development, a group of policy-oriented researchers that has met annually since 1967 to assess the changing environment for economic development in the Pacific and its policy implications; the Pacific Basin Economic Council, a group of senior business people with a broad international outlook that also began to meet in the late 1960s; and the Pacific Economic Cooperation Council, established in 1980. APEC has also set up its own private-sector advisory group, the APEC Business Advisory Council.

In a January 1989 speech in Seoul, Australian prime minister Bob Hawke advocated the creation of a new intergovernmental vehicle of regional cooperation. The first ministerial-level meeting brought together representatives from twelve Asia Pacific economies. The initial participants were the then six members of ASEAN (Brunei, Indonesia, Malaysia, the Philippines, Singapore, and Thailand) together with Australia, Canada, Japan, the Republic of Korea, New Zealand, and the United States. Subsequently, APEC developed a comprehensive work program to promote economic integration and agreed on its main objectives and principles set out in the 1991 Seoul APEC Declaration.

APEC further distinguished itself from the legally binding and preferential arrangements adopted by the European Union (EU) and others by agreeing that Asia Pacific cooperation should be voluntary. APEC would not be a negotiating forum: instead it would seek to identify opportunities to promote mutual economic benefit through consultation, building consensus around a widening range of shared interests. APEC's nonformal structure made it possible to include all three Chinese economies. Taiwan participates as the economy of Chinese Taipei, and since 1997 Hong Kong has participated as Hong Kong, China. Membership has since expanded to 21: Chile, Mexico, Papua New Guinea, Peru, Russia, and Vietnam joined between 1993 and 1997. A subsequent moratorium on expanded membership was set to end in 2007.

Free and Open Trade and Investment APEC leaders met for the first time in 1993. At their 1994 meeting, in Bogor, Indonesia, they were able to make a political commitment to eliminating barriers to trade and investment by no later than 2010 for de-

veloped economies and 2020 for developing economies. A midterm stocktaking, conducted in 2005, showed considerable progress toward this goal. Average tariffs were considerably lower than in 1989 and border barriers to trade in most goods and many services were already set at zero or negligible levels. People and capital were moving much more freely around the region.

By harmonizing customs procedures, increasing the scope of mutual recognition of standards, adopting agreed principles for more transparent and competitive government procurement, and reducing impediments to international business travel, APEC made substantial progress in reducing other costs and risks of international commerce. This progress has led to the emergence of the Asia Pacific region as the engine of global economic growth, outpacing the rest of the world in terms of opening itself to international trade and investment and increasing its share of global output, trade, and investment (APEC 2005; Elek 2005).

Strengths and Weaknesses APEC's experience has also revealed some of the weaknesses as well as the strengths of voluntary cooperation among widely diverse economies. Coordinated unilateral actions have helped to bring down many impediments to trade and investment, but voluntary cooperation has not proved adequate to liberalize "sensitive sectors," such as agriculture, textiles, and clothing. APEC's limited ability to respond to the serious financial crises in East Asia in the late 1990s also demonstrated the value of attending to all of the foundations of sustained economic growth, not just the reduction of obstacles to international trade and investment.

By 2007, it was evident that one dimension of the vision of free and open trade and investment, the elimination of all traditional border barriers to trade, would not be achieved according to the 2010/2020 timetable. At the same time, there was growing realization that the removal of tariffs or quantitative restrictions on trade in goods, or even in services, would not be enough to promote deep economic integration. The experience of the EU had shown the value of a comprehensive program to reduce regulatory impediments to international movement, not only of products, but also of factors of production.

Facilitating economic integration by closer coordination or harmonization of policies on matters such as customs procedures or standards, adoption of compatible policies to encourage e-commerce, and reduction of the cost of international transportation have become relatively more important means of promoting economic integration. In these areas, the effective constraint on cooperation is not the short-term political cost of overcoming narrow vested interests but the capacity to implement more efficient policies. Facilitating trade by dealing with logistic or regulatory obstacles to trade is largely a matter of enhancing human, institutional, and infrastructure capacity.

The Busan roadmap for promoting progress toward free and open trade and investment, based on the 2005 midterm evaluation, takes account of these issues. Accordingly, the focus of attention is shifting from the remaining traditional border barriers to trade toward the sharing of information, experience, expertise, and technology to help all Asia Pacific economies build the capacity for designing and implementing better policies, which strengthen domestic as well as just international markets. At the same time, APEC economies would support traditional trade liberalization through the WTO. This could bring about a practical division of effort between APEC and the WTO, based on the comparative advantages of institutions for voluntary, rather than negotiated, cooperation.

Especially since 2000, APEC has needed to define its role alongside many other bilateral and subregional forms of economic cooperation. In response to the inability to make further significant progress on sensitive issues, such as agriculture, in either the WTO or APEC, combined with the need to address many new issues that influence international economic transactions, there has been a proliferation of mostly bilateral preferential trading arrangements. Yet bilateral preferential trading arrangements have also been unable to achieve significant liberalization of trade in sensitive products, while complicating all

international trade due to complex, and often overtly discriminatory, rules of origin. It remains to be seen whether that problem can be overcome by preferential trading arrangements among larger groups of economies.

Concurrently, reflecting the growing share of international production and trade in East Asia, several East Asia–centered forums have emerged. As in APEC, members of the wider networks of cooperation in East Asia will resist ceding powers to any supranational authority. This suggests that they might best focus on issues of perceived shared interests, rather than the negotiation and imposition of binding constraints on one another.

In summary, APEC members have moved toward their original goals but their institution has been redefining its own goals and operation. At the same time, other institutional developments in the region now create the prospect of competition and overlap with APEC (Soesastro and Findlay 2005). Progress on economic integration may prove easier in an East Asian, rather than in a wider trans-Pacific, forum. On the other hand, East Asia is itself a very diverse grouping and will face constraints quite similar to those encountered by APEC while the United States will seek to sustain trans-Pacific cooperation. One outcome may be "variable geometry," with APEC-wide consultations encouraging different groups of economies to pioneer cooperation on issues of shared interest, not necessarily in the institutional context of the APEC process itself.

See also Association of Southeast Asian Nations (ASEAN); free trade area; regionalism

FURTHER READING

APEC. 2005. "A Mid-term Stocktake of Progress toward the Bogor Goals—Busan Roadmap to Bogor Goals." (November) Busan, Korea: APEC. Downloadable from http://www.apec.org/apec/enewsletter/jan_vol7/publication.primarycontentparagraph.0009. A midterm report by APEC officials, based on research by a panel of economists from the region.

Elek, Andrew. 2005. "APEC after Busan: New Direction." APEC Study Series 05-01 (November) Seoul: Korean

Institute for International Economic Policy. Downloadable from http://www.kiep.go.kr/eng/std_data_view.asp?num=131907&sCate=013002&sSubcate=&lTp=r&nowPage=3&listCnt=15#. This paper sets out the reasons for adopting APEC's 2005 Busan roadmap and how that agenda could be realized.

Soesastro, Hadi, and Christopher Findlay, eds. 2005. *Reshaping the Asia Pacific Economic Order*. London: Routledge. A collection of papers including a review of APEC's contribution and analyses of the complementarities and conflicts among institutions in the region; includes a note on the contribution of Peter Drysdale to the development of the APEC concept.

ANDREW ELEK AND CHRISTOPHER FINDLAY

■ assignment problem

The assignment problem concerns the allocation of policy instruments to policy targets in order to improve policy effectiveness. Policy instruments are the variables or procedures that policy authorities directly control. Policymakers' use of these instruments to achieve objectives (i.e., policy targets) directly affects the welfare of their constituents. For example, government spending is an instrument that can be used to reduce unemployment. Assignment is important because in actual policymaking, competing government agencies can be given different instruments. The question then becomes—which is the appropriate allocation?

Trevor Swan (1960) noted the problem in the context of an open economy where the two objectives were full employment with price stability and a reasonable current account deficit (CAD) of the balance of payments. The first is the objective of internal balance and the second that of external balance, which is an essential part of participating in the world economy. External imbalances in one country can lead to imbalances for others with which it transacts. One country's delays and inefficiencies in achieving balance impinge on others, and when the country is large, can have repercussions for the global financial system.

The Tinbergen Rule In 1952, Jan Tinbergen demonstrated that to achieve policy objectives, governments must have policy instruments equal in number to the objectives. According to what is known as the Tinbergen rule, a government cannot achieve two objectives with just one instrument. If a country has unemployment and a CAD, for example, and the only instrument available is government spending, it can fix only one problem (Meade 1951). If the government spends more to stimulate the economy, it will lower unemployment but worsen the disequilibrium in the balance of payments as overall output and imports rise. If it reduces spending, the balance of trade improves, but unemployment rises. One objective is attained at the expense of the other. If the government uses two instruments—government spending and exchange rate policy—to achieve its objectives, the question is one of appropriate assignment: which instrument should it assign to control demand, output, and employment, and which to achieve trade balance?

Adjustment in the Swan Diagram Swan (1960) showed that an incorrect assignment can move the economy away from full equilibrium. Figure 1 shows a simple Swan diagram where the internal balance, or domestic market equilibrium schedule, IB_f is downward sloping in the space of real exchange rate

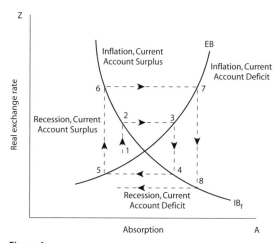

Figure 1
Assignment in the Swan diagram

Z and absorption, or domestic demand, A. Z is the ratio of external to domestic costs of production. Currency appreciation reduces demand for domestic goods so that government spending, a component of absorption, has to rise to maintain output unchanged. The external balance, or balance of payments equilibrium schedule, EB, is upward sloping. The current account will improve with real depreciation as imports fall and exports rise, so government spending must be raised to restore imports and prevent the balance of payments going into surplus. The four quadrants denote different types of disequilibria. Only at the point of intersection of the two schedules are the two instruments such that both the targets are achieved. Output is demand determined below the full employment IB_f schedule and otherwise limited by the factor of production labor.

Consider an economy at point 1 with a current account surplus and a recession. Policymakers assign the real exchange rate to achieve internal balance and government spending to achieve external balance, and sequentially adjust the two instruments. Depreciation at point 1 will lead to internal equilibrium at point 2 as exports raise demand. A rise in government spending raising imports to match will bring the economy to external equilibrium at point 3, and so on through points 3, 4, 5.... But instead of converging to the full equilibrium point, the economy diverges away from it. The opposite assignment leads to equilibrium. Reversing the arrows before point 8 shows the convergence to full equilibrium where the starting point is a recession and a CAD. Government spending then is raised to reach internal balance at point 8, and then the exchange rate depreciated to reach external balance at point 7, the process converging finally to the full equilibrium. Thus this is the correct assignment of instruments.

Note that the result depends on the relative steepness of the two schedules. Convergence to a stable equilibrium occurs because the internal balance schedule is steeper than the external balance. Depreciation has more of an effect on the current account than it does on aggregate demand since changes in imports and exports act in the same di-

rection on the CAD, but imports are a leakage from demand for domestic goods, and only the rise in exports raises output. Since a larger change in absorption is required to compensate for the relatively greater impact of depreciation on external balance, the EB schedule is flatter than the IB_f. That is, the exchange rate has a relatively greater impact on the external balance than it does on the internal balance. And government spending has a greater impact on internal balance than it does on external balance. It follows that exchange rate policy should be assigned to external balance, and government spending to internal balance.

Effective Market Classification Each policy instrument should be assigned to the target variable on which its relative effect is higher. Robert Mundell first formally stated this in 1962 as the principle of effective market classification. Consider a case where the two policy instruments are the interest rate and the budget deficit, with a fixed exchange rate. If the rate of interest has a larger effect on external balance, Mundell showed that the interest rate must be assigned to external balance and the budget deficit to internal balance in sequential adjustment; otherwise the economy will diverge from full equilibrium. The interest rate affects both the current and the capital account. Suppose government expenditure and interest rates rise, moving away from the unique equilibrium, but with internal balance satisfied. The rise in government expenditure tends to raise income, but the rise in interest rate reduces it, so that income remains at the full employment level. Since output is unchanged, the trade balance is unchanged as well, assuming exports are constant and imports depend only on income. But the rise in interest rates improves the capital account of the balance of payments, so that the balance of payments is now in surplus. Therefore the internal balance schedule must be steeper than the external balance schedule.

Starting from a position with recession and a CAD, if the government reduces spending to reduce the CAD, it will improve the CAD but worsen the recession. If it then decreases the interest rate to stimulate output, it will worsen the capital account as capital flows out, resulting in cumulative movements away from equilibrium. Adjustment converges to the full equilibrium if the opposite assignment is made. That is, the interest rate is directed to achieve external equilibrium and government spending to achieve internal equilibrium—each policy instrument is assigned to the target on which it has the greatest effect, or which it has a comparative advantage in achieving. In this simple model with fixed exchange rates, the implication is that monetary policy or the central bank should target external balance, while fiscal tax-expenditure decisions target full employment.

In practice, sequential policy adjustment is difficult since the economic system is simultaneous. In both models, since the full equilibrium is stable, it is attained with simultaneous adjustment of both instruments. Markets themselves also generate adjustment in response to disequilibrium. But optimal assignment is a useful feature to keep in mind when making a complex policy decision, especially if the two instruments are the responsibility of different institutions. The correct allocation of separate instruments to separate authorities may allow more efficient adjustment. In addition, since all models are a simplification of a complex reality, as international and domestic institutions change, the relevant model also changes or must be suitably adapted.

Allowing for Shocks In the simple deterministic models considered so far, there were no random shocks. Poole (1970) has an interesting variant of the assignment problem regarding the choice of the appropriate instrument for monetary policy. He showed that if aggregate demand was subject to more random shocks compared to the demand for money, money supply should be the operating instrument. Output fluctuations would then be lower, since procyclical interest rate movements would moderate the shocks. If the intensity of shocks to money demand was greater, interest rates should be the instrument, since automatic adjustment of money supply would smooth interest rates, reducing output fluctuations. The opposite assignment would magnify the impact of fluctuations.

See also balance of payments; comparative advantage; discipline; exchange rate regimes; expenditure changing and expenditure switching; money supply; Mundell-Fleming model; structural adjustment; Swan diagram; twin deficits

FURTHER READING

Agenor, Pierre-Richard, and Peter J. Monteil. 1999. *Development Macroeconomics*. 2d ed. Princeton, NJ: Princeton University Press. Detailed case studies of developing country experiences, which illustrate problems with the assignment of macroeconomic policy instruments.

Corbo, Vittorio, and Stanley Fischer. 1995. "Structural Adjustment, Stabilisation, and Policy Reform: Domestic and International Finance." In *Handbook of Development Economics*, edited by Jere Behreman and T. N. Srinivasan. Vol. 3. Amsterdam: North-Holland, chapter 44. An application of the Swan framework to modern stabilization and structural adjustment programs, which can be understood as assignment problems.

Meade, James E. 1951. *The Theory of International Economic Policy*. Vol. 1. *The Balance of Payments*. London: Oxford University Press. A classic of international economic policy.

Mundell, Robert A. 1962. "The Appropriate Use of Monetary and Fiscal Policy for Internal and External Stability." *IMF Staff Papers* 12 (9): 70–79. Examination of the dynamics of inappropriate assignment.

Poole, William. 1970. "Optimal Choice of Monetary Policy Instruments in a Simple Stochastic Model." *Quarterly Journal of Economics* 84 (2): 197–216. The effect of shocks on choice of policy instruments.

Swan, Trevor W. 1960. "Economic Control in a Dependent Economy." *Economic Record* 36 (March): 51–66. The seminal discussion of assignment.

Tinbergen, Jan, 1952. *On the Theory of Economic Policy*. Amsterdam: North-Holland. The original development of the Tinbergen rule.

van Marrewijk, Charles. 2007. *International Economics: Theory, Application, and Policy*. London: Oxford University Press. Simple clear textbook treatment of the assignment problem.

ASHIMA GOYAL

■ Association of Southeast Asian Nations (ASEAN)

The Association of Southeast Asian Nations (ASEAN) is an intergovernmental association that was formed to enhance cooperation among countries in the Southeast Asian region. Since its formation in August 1967, this association has grown in size to include 10 countries: Brunei, Cambodia, Indonesia, the Lao People's Democratic Republic (PDR), Malaysia, Myanmar, the Philippines, Singapore, Thailand, and Vietnam.

The formation of ASEAN was officially opened at the signing of the Bangkok Declaration on August 8, 1967, by five countries: Indonesia, Malaysia, the Philippines, Singapore, and Thailand. Brunei in 1984, Vietnam in 1995, the Lao PDR and Myanmar in 1997, and Cambodia in 1999 joined the grouping. Political and economic considerations have influenced these countries to form a regional cooperation. The original five signatory countries saw the need to foster their economic development and promote regional security in the face of a growing communist threat in Southeast Asia, precipitated by the fall of Indochina to communism and the declared intention of the West to withdraw its military forces from the region. Their common objectives could be best achieved through mutual cooperation in the economic, social, and cultural areas.

Political Cooperation During its early stages of development, ASEAN was mainly concerned with political cooperation to promote political stability and harmony in the region. Since 1976, however, the economic objective has grown in importance as economic development has become its main priority in view of, among other things, the increasing need to maintain economic competitiveness in the midst of growing international competition and sustain member countries' pace of economic development in light of rising expectations.

Economic Cooperation There have been two types of economic cooperation in ASEAN: market sharing and resource pooling. These types of economic cooperation have developed since the Bali Summit of 1976. At this summit, the ASEAN leaders signed a Declaration of ASEAN Concord that laid out a program of action for regional cooperation in political, economic, social, cultural, and security matters. But ASEAN economic cooperation of a market-sharing type has generally been unsuccessful mainly due to the significant differences in members' economic development levels and different economic priorities.

Economic Cooperation in Trade The most important form of market-sharing cooperation envisaged in the Bali Summit was the establishment of preferential trading arrangements to promote intra-ASEAN trade. The agreement on ASEAN Preferential Trading Arrangement, signed in February 1977, was the first attempt by ASEAN member countries to promote a higher level of intra-ASEAN trade. Five measures have been identified to achieve the objective of greater intra-ASEAN trade: exchange of tariff preferences, purchase of finance support at preferential rates for selected products of ASEAN domestic origin, long-term (three to five years) quantity contracts for basic commodities such as fuels and agricultural products, preference in procurement by government agencies, and liberalization of nontariff barriers on a preferential basis.

Economic Cooperation in Industry ASEAN countries have resolved that industrialization and economic development of their members can be largely facilitated through industrial cooperation. There is also a common realization that a significant increase in intra-ASEAN trade can occur only if the supply side of the market is also increased. Thus since 1976 five major schemes of ASEAN industrial cooperation (ASEAN Industrial Projects Scheme, ASEAN Industrial Complementation Scheme, Brand-to-Brand Complementation Scheme, ASEAN Industrial Joint Venture Scheme, and ASEAN Industrial Cooperation Scheme) have been established to create new industrial capacity jointly owned by member countries serving the regional market. Unlike trade liberalization, which raises apprehensions of uncontrolled trade flows and market disruption, industrial cooperation is linked to the creation of specific new production facilities, giving rise to much more predictable trade flows. Except for the ASEAN

Industrial Cooperation Scheme, the success of these initiatives was quite limited.

Economic Cooperation in Agriculture Given the importance of the agricultural sector in ASEAN, cooperation in this area has been one of the priority issues. All the cooperative undertakings in agriculture have so far been technical and developmental in nature, however. The Committee on Food, Agriculture, and Forestry (COFAF) is responsible for the identification and implementation of cooperative undertakings in the agricultural sector. Formed in March 1977, it (a) coordinates, reviews, and prepares studies on the prospects of the agricultural sector; (b) develops efficient methods for the exchange of information on agriculture; (c) identifies areas for cooperation; (d) maintains close ties with related committees in ASEAN and with other related organizations inside and outside the region; and (e) reports its progress to the ASEAN Economic Ministers.

Between 1978 and 1988, COFAF had identified 46 cooperative projects—7 in food, 10 in agriculture, 15 in forestry, 8 in livestock, and 6 in fisheries. By 1985, 13 of them were ongoing, 4 completed, and 29 not yet implemented. The largest number of projects was located in the Philippines, followed by Malaysia, Thailand, and Indonesia in descending order. Most of the funding for these projects came from sources outside the region and only a few projects were pursued on a long-term basis. One of them was the ASEAN Food Security Project, which established in 1979 an ASEAN Emergency Rice Reserve to be contributed to by each of the member countries. The objective was to create a stockpile of 50,000 metric tons of rice to meet shortfalls in domestic supply. This program is periodically reviewed for the purpose of creating a more dynamic food security arrangement to enhance intra-ASEAN trade and promote food production under the principle of comparative advantage. Others included the Food Handling and the Seed Technology projects. ASEAN cooperation in agriculture has also been fostered in the association's dealings with developed countries on matters of market access for member countries' primary exports, better terms of trade, stabilization

of export earnings, and other nonsensitive areas of cooperation.

ASEAN Free Trade Area The 1992 ASEAN Free Trade Agreement (AFTA) was a watershed in the history of ASEAN economic cooperation, as it represents a significant step in the economic policy orientation of the ASEAN countries. The main objective of AFTA is to increase the international competitiveness of ASEAN industries and the ASEAN region as an investment location. Specifically, the objectives are to increase intra-ASEAN trade by abolishing intraregional trade barriers while allowing member countries to keep their respective trade policies toward the rest of the world, attract local and foreign investors to invest in the region, and make their manufacturing sector more efficient and internationally competitive within a liberalizing global market. An integrated regional market is expected to produce economic benefits from greater consumer welfare, exploitation of economies of scale, competition-induced efficiency, industrial rationalization, interindustry linkages, and intraindustry trade.

To realize these benefits, AFTA seeks to reduce tariffs on all commodities traded within the member countries to no more than 5 percent ad valorem and remove all other trade restrictions by the year 2002 under the Common Effective Preferential tariff, the main instrument of AFTA. The agreement also lays down the rules for fair competition and identifies a number of measures to enhance economic cooperation such as harmonization of standards, macroeconomic consultations, improved reciprocal recognition of product testing and certification, coordination of foreign investment policies to enhance more investment flows, joint investment promotion strategies, and cooperation in transportation systems. Further, it contains measures of contingent protection and allows the reintroduction of trade barriers in case of balance of payments difficulties.

ASEAN Economic Community The Asian financial crisis of 1997 and 1998, the terrorist attacks of September 11, 2001, the Iraq war, and the SARS outbreak all dampened the outlook for greater trade liberalization and economic integration as envisioned under AFTA. Despite these unfavorable external events, the ASEAN countries have remained politically committed to the vision of transforming ASEAN into an economically integrated grouping within the framework of an ASEAN Economic Community (AEC). This AEC concept, which was first agreed on at the November 2002 ASEAN summit held in Phnom Penh, Cambodia, is based on the ASEAN Vision 2020, which foresees a more economically integrated ASEAN. The ASEAN Vision 2020 envisioned "a stable, prosperous and highly competitive ASEAN economic region in which there is a free flow of goods, services and investments, a freer flow of capital, equitable economic development and reduced poverty and socio-economic disparities" (ASEAN Vision 2020).

The AEC is built on the current initiatives under the ASEAN Free Trade Agreement, the ASEAN Framework Agreement on Services, and the ASEAN Investment Area, with clear timelines specified for removal of nontariff barriers, harmonization of product standards and technical regulations, and conclusion of mutual recognition arrangements for priority sectors.

Prospects for ASEAN Economic Cooperation
ASEAN faces a number of challenges in its journey toward greater economic integration. One major challenge is the widening economic gap within the grouping as ASEAN membership increased to 10 countries with significantly diverse economies and political regimes, and as the grouping is establishing more extra-ASEAN free trade agreements. The widening gap and the proliferation of extra-ASEAN free trade agreements, if not managed correctly, could lead to the weakening or marginalization of the ASEAN integration and, worse, to the irrelevance of ASEAN to the individual member countries' economic development.

See also Asia Pacific Economic Cooperation (APEC); free trade area; regionalism

FURTHER READING
ASEAN Secretariat. 1997. *ASEAN Economic Cooperation: Transition and Transformation*. Singapore: Institute of Southeast Asian Studies. A thorough review of the various schemes of ASEAN cooperation from the early stages of ASEAN to the 1990s.

ASEAN Vision 2020 (ASEAN Declaration at 13th ASEAN Summit). ASEAN Secretariat Website. Available at http://www.aseansec.org. The text of the 1997 summit statement.

Sjoholm, F., and J. L. Tongzon, eds. 2005. *Institutional Change in Southeast Asia*. New York: Routledge. A useful reference on the role of institutions in the ASEAN countries' economic development with a critical examination of key ASEAN institutions and their contributions to ASEAN economic performance, particularly during the 1997–98 Asian financial crisis.

Tan, G. 1996. *ASEAN Economic Development and Cooperation*. Singapore: Times Academic Press. An overview of the economic development experiences of the ASEAN countries up to the 1990s and the challenges faced in their process of economic development.

Tay, S., et al. 2000. *A New ASEAN in a New Millennium*. Jakarta: Center for Strategic and International Studies and Singapore Institute of International Affairs. A valuable reference on ASEAN as an institution with a critical analysis of ASEAN's major political achievements, governing principles, and future challenges.

Tongzon, Jose L. 2002. *The Economies of Southeast Asia: Before and after the Crisis*. Cheltenham, UK: Edward Elgar. An in-depth analysis of the economic development experiences of the ASEAN countries in the context of ASEAN economic cooperation before and after the Asian financial crisis of 1997–98.

———. 2005. "The Role of AFTA in an ASEAN Economic Community." In *Road Map to an ASEAN Economic Community*, edited by D. Hew. Singapore: Institute of Southeast Asian Studies, 127–47. An in-depth assessment of the role of AFTA in the building up of an ASEAN Economic Community, including the progress made in trade liberalization and the challenges faced in the next level of economic integration.

JOSE L. TONGZON

■ asymmetric information

An asymmetric information problem exists in a market if it is costly for some parties to observe the characteristics or behavior of other parties, and an inefficient outcome results. One problem that arises due to asymmetric information is moral hazard, which exists when an arrangement that relieves a party of some risk causes the party to engage in riskier behavior. In credit markets, for example, use of a loan to finance a project means that the gains to the borrower are reduced if the project succeeds, because the principal must be repaid with interest. If the project fails, however, the creditor absorbs the loss of principal and interest, net of any collateral provided by the borrower. Risks are thus shifted from the borrower to the creditor, much as would occur with an insurance contract. If the creditor could costlessly observe how the borrower used the loan, then it might be possible to give the borrower contractual incentives to work hard and avoid risky projects, in order to hold down the risk of default on the loan. For example, future disbursements of the loan could be conditioned on the borrower's using the loan responsibly. However, if it is costly to observe the borrower's behavior, then moral hazard may arise, particularly if the loan is not fully collateralized or it is costly to take legal action against a borrower in default.

Adverse selection occurs in a market if it is difficult to distinguish parties that are good risks from those that are bad risks, and the parties that represent bad risks are particularly attracted to the market. For example, consider a set of borrowers that wish to finance projects that are identical in all respects, including offering identical expected returns, except that the projects vary in their riskiness. It can be shown that borrowers with riskier projects will have higher expected profits than other borrowers, and thus will have stronger incentives to borrow, while the expected rate of return to banks from these borrowers is lower than it is from other borrowers (Stiglitz and Weiss 1981). Thus the borrowers that tend to select themselves into the market cause problems for it.

If it were obvious which parties were the bad risks, those parties could be offered more stringent terms or even avoided altogether. Absent such information, in markets subject to adverse selection, the normal function that prices play in determining who participates in the market can result in a perverse outcome. In credit markets, higher interest rates limit who will want to borrow by making borrowing more burdensome, but those with the least risky projects will be the ones driven out of the market first, all else being equal. Those who are less likely to pay back the loan will be less concerned about paying higher interest. Because the average quality of the loans actually made can then deteriorate, the adverse selection problem can be worsened. A higher interest rate will also exacerbate the moral hazard problem for a given borrower, because the higher interest rate is burdensome only in the event that the borrower actually repays the loan.

Given these drawbacks of raising interest rates to limit access to credit, banks may choose to ration credit, so that borrowers are not allowed to borrow as much as they want at a given interest rate (Stiglitz and Weiss 1981). It is also possible that credit rationing may not occur, in which case a small increase in interest rates can lead to collapse of the loan market (Mankiw 1986).

Asymmetric Information and Financial Crises
Problems related to asymmetric information can contribute to, and be exacerbated by, financial crises, such as those experienced by South Korea, Thailand, and Indonesia in 1997–98. Financial crises that lead to bank failures can have real economic costs because of the loss of the customer relationships that these banks had cultivated. In the course of repeated interactions with their loan customers, banks gain a considerable amount of information on the customers' creditworthiness and other characteristics. This information is lost in a bank failure, which can worsen the moral hazard and adverse selection problems (Mishkin 1999). Thus financial intermediation becomes less effective, and real economic activity can be harmed.

Currency depreciation can exacerbate a banking crisis because it tends to worsen the balance sheets of individuals and corporations within the country that have borrowed in foreign currencies. This reduces the value of the collateral that can be obtained from these borrowers in the event of default and thus exacerbates the moral hazard problem inherent in credit markets: borrowers with less to lose have weaker incentives to avoid default. Moreover, problems related to asymmetric information also limit how countries can respond to financial crises. For example, the higher interest rates required to combat inflation or stabilize the currency can aggravate adverse selection and moral hazard, as discussed earlier.

Information asymmetries can also exacerbate a tendency toward investor panic manifested by bank runs, capital flight, or asset price downturns, and can contribute to financial contagion between unrelated financial institutions or countries during crises.

Models of these phenomena typically posit that uninformed investors try to infer how asset prices will move based on the information revealed by these prices. Informed investors directly observe the fundamental determinants of asset prices, but the prices are also influenced by exogenous random factors. Moreover, informed investors are unable to drive asset prices directly to their equilibrium values dictated by the fundamentals because of various impediments to asset trading (such as trading costs, short-sale constraints, or borrowing constraints).

Now consider a negative shock to an asset price. Knowing that informed investors are limited in their ability to make trades, uninformed investors are uncertain whether the fundamental asset value is even lower, and therefore demand an additional risk premium to hold the risky asset, which forces its price down further. Thus asymmetric information exacerbates asset price movement.

For contagion between markets to occur, the simplest scenario is that the fundamental determinants of asset prices in two markets are correlated. Informed investors observe a shock to the fundamentals in one market, and in response reallocate their portfolios in the market that has experienced the shock and in other markets. The uninformed investor is uncertain whether asset price movements in either market are due to transactions by informed investors or due to random noise; given the greater uncertainties, uninformed investors demand a larger risk premium in both markets, which causes asset prices to move together.

Borrowing constraints can also trigger contagion, as shrinkage of investor assets in one country means that investors may be forced to sell their assets in other countries, as collateral requirements become binding (Yuan 2005). This contagion will also be exacerbated by the actions of uninformed investors. It will be stronger during asset price downturns than upturns and does not require that macroeconomic fundamentals in the countries be correlated. These findings are generally consistent with empirical evidence to date. Thus this model offers one explanation of why asset price shocks spread among East Asia, Latin America, and other parts of the world in 1998.

Lender of Last Resort Moral hazard becomes a policy issue in credit markets because of the lender-of-last-resort role played by various institutions. For example, central banks and other financial regulators are concerned about the possibility of a run on banks, which in turn could arise in part because it is difficult to distinguish solvent banks from insolvent ones. In order to lessen the risk of a run on banks, the central bank or other governmental institution usually provides implicit or explicit insurance to bank depositors. Bank liabilities may even be fully guaranteed on the grounds that the banks are too big or too politically important to be allowed to fail. The consequential moral hazard can give banks little reason to be cautious in their lending, or depositors little incentive to take the trouble to examine the financial soundness of one bank versus others. These problems can set the stage for a banking crisis.

Whether it is necessary or desirable for an international lender of last resort to assist countries in financial crises is a matter of some controversy. An argument in favor of such an institution is that the central bank of a country in crisis may have a limited capacity to restore the economy to health. For example, the provision of extra liquidity through monetary expansion could lead to currency depreciation and increases in inflationary expectations and interest rates (Mishkin 1999). Thus there may be an argument for an institution such as the International Monetary Fund (IMF) to lend foreign exchange to a country so that it can pay for imported inputs and intervene to support its currency, say, to alleviate the real economic harms that a financial crisis can cause. As critics have observed, however, IMF bailouts of countries in financial distress can also cause moral hazard by relieving the governments of those countries of the painful effects of the inadequacies of their economic policies and by relieving international investors of the adverse consequences of investing in inherently risky environments such as emerging markets.

Following the IMF decision not to bail out Russia in 1998, the amount by which interest rates on bonds in developing countries exceeded those in industrial countries increased, particularly for countries with weaker economic fundamentals, indicating that investors were increasingly taking into account the risks of lending to developing countries (Dell'Ariccia et al. 2002). It cannot be concluded, however, that this change was for the better, even if it indicated that moral hazard was reduced: IMF lending that reduces risks could be a good thing on balance, and its positive effects would also be reflected in interest differentials across countries. For example, an IMF intervention in a developing country could alleviate market failures such as coordination problems among creditors to the country, by acting as a catalyst that restores confidence and induces creditors to resume lending rather than waiting for other creditors to take the first step.

Measures to Limit Moral Hazard At all the levels at which moral hazard exists in financial markets, measures can be taken to lessen its impact. Individual loan contracts can include provisions that make it harder for the borrower to take excessive risks or to shirk repayment of the loan. For example, loans can be disbursed in increments, conditional on performance to date. One reason for the existence of financial intermediaries like banks is that they can perform these disciplining functions at lower cost than can individuals, such as by threatening to withdraw future business from recalcitrant borrowers.

At the level of the banking system, the dilemma for policymakers is how to contain moral hazard and yet prevent or at least mitigate financial crises. Most governments provide some form of implicit or explicit insurance for bank deposits. New Zealand does not, on the grounds that it eliminates depositors' incentives to monitor the riskiness of their banks, and because providing the deposit insurance at the same price to all banks implicitly subsidizes banks with riskier loan portfolios at the expense of those with more responsible ones. New Zealand instead tries to ensure that the public has complete and accurate information on banks' financial conditions. Some countries that provide deposit insurance, such as the United States, seek to lessen moral hazard by limiting deposit insurance to relatively small deposits, in order to provide larger depositors or other bank creditors with stronger incentives to monitor and price the risks embodied in banks' loan portfolios. In principle, the moral hazard from deposit guarantees can also be reduced through appropriate ongoing bank supervision and regulation. In practice, in many developing countries in particular, bank regulation remains problematic.

One approach to lessening the economic damage in the event of a crisis is for a lender of last resort to inject capital into financial markets. There may be merit in providing liquidity to the market in general rather than to particular distressed institutions, so that market forces can ultimately determine which institutions survive. If individual financial institutions are to be provided credit by the lender of last resort, Bagehot (1873) suggested that the terms should not be too attractive: the rate of interest should be higher than during normal times. Limiting moral hazard in this way is not without its own costs. Imposing a higher penalty rate can weaken the condition of the bank, signal to the market that the bank is in trouble, or induce bank managers to pursue a riskier strategy. However, Bagehot allowed that credit should be provided on collateral that would be marketable in normal times, so that a crisis-induced collapse of asset prices that caused collateral to shrink would not in itself limit the amount that could be lent.

If the crisis is due to a coordination failure, such as a panic-induced run on a bank, a lender of last resort may be able to suspend the obligations of the bank temporarily, in a way that the bank could not do on its own due to credibility problems. This approach would not diminish the risk to which creditors of the bank are exposed, and thus could limit moral hazard. The lender of last resort could also coordinate a private bailout of the bank, in an effort to limit moral hazard. If the coordination of private institutions is at all coercive, however, it will in effect provide a subsidy to the distressed institution, in which case moral hazard reappears in an alternative form. Indeed, the bailout of the Long-Term Capital Management (LTCM) hedge fund in 1998 raised questions about whether private investors were coerced by the central bank. The LTCM bailout under the guidance of the Federal Reserve has been criticized for causing moral hazard.

Parallel issues have arisen for the IMF as an international lender of last resort that has bailed out countries in financial crisis. For example, IMF loans of foreign exchange to countries in crisis are disbursed over time, and the institution monitors whether the recipient country is complying with the performance and policy conditions negotiated as part of the loan agreement.

To avoid the moral hazard that IMF bailouts can cause, an alternative approach is to rely more on private-sector solutions. Along these lines, Mexico, Brazil, and other countries have introduced collective action clauses into their sovereign bond contracts since 2003. Such clauses are intended to facilitate debt restructuring in the event of a crisis, primarily by making it harder for a small minority of bondholders to block debt restructurings endorsed by a large majority. Inclusion of these clauses appears to have lowered borrowing costs for these countries, despite concerns that the clauses might make it easier for some countries, particularly those that are less creditworthy, to avoid repaying their debts.

A degree of deliberate ambiguity in the actions of the lender of last resort may also limit moral hazard. If it remains unclear whether the lender of last resort will provide a bailout in all situations, the parties who might or might not be bailed out will have incentives to act more responsibly. The decision by the IMF not to bail out Russia in 1998, on the heels of its bailouts of South Korea, Thailand, and Indonesia in 1997–98, could be seen as creating such ambiguity.

A final restraint on moral hazard is for managers and owners of failed institutions to be punished: managers should lose their jobs and shareholders their capital. The argument may be applicable to national economies in crisis as well: a change of government tends to have a salutary effect in the recovery from a financial crisis, particular if mismanagement by the government was partly responsible for the crisis.

See also bail-ins; bailouts; balance sheet approach/ effects; banking crisis; contagion; currency crisis; deposit insurance; financial crisis; International Monetary Fund (IMF); International Monetary Fund conditionality; International Monetary Fund surveillance; lender of last resort; spillovers

FURTHER READING

Bagehot, Walter. 1873. *Lombard Street: A Description of the Money Market*. Reprint, 1919. London: J. Murray. An early observer of financial markets, on how a lender of last resort should operate.

Dell'Ariccia, Giovanni, Isabel Schnabel, and Jeromin Zettelmeyer. 2002. "Moral Hazard and International Crisis Lending: A Test." IMF Working Paper WP/02/181. Washington, DC: International Monetary Fund. Examines whether IMF decisions to intervene or not to intervene in a crisis can affect borrowing costs for developing countries.

Eichengreen, Barry, and Ashoka Mody. 2001. "Bail-ins, Bailouts, and Borrowing Costs." *International Monetary Fund Staff Papers* 47 (Special Issue): 155–87. Proposes measures to reduce moral hazard caused by IMF interventions through changes in international financial arrangements.

Mankiw, N. Gregory. 1986. "The Allocation of Credit and Financial Collapse." *Quarterly Journal of Economics* 101 (August): 455–70. Shows that adverse selection can cause a loan market to collapse.

Mishkin, Frederic S. 1999. "Global Financial Instability: Framework, Events, Issues." *Journal of Economic Perspectives* 13 (autumn): 3–20. Surveys international financial crises of recent years; includes a useful discussion of how moral hazard and adverse selection may be exacerbated during a crisis.

Stiglitz, Joseph E., and Andrew Weiss. 1981. "Credit Rationing in Markets with Imperfect Information." *American Economic Review* 71 (June): 393–410. A seminal analysis of information problems in bank loan markets, which includes an argument that collateral requirements can cause adverse selection.

Yuan, Kathy. 2005. "Asymmetric Price Movements and Borrowing Constraints: A Rational Expectations Equilibrium Model of Crises, Contagion, and Confusion." *Journal of Finance* 60 (February): 379–411. Offers a theory of how asymmetric information can contribute to contagion across countries during financial crises and provides a useful survey of related literature.

STEPHEN MARKS

■ bail-ins

A bail-in is an agreement by creditors to roll over their short-term claims or to engage in a formal debt restructuring with a troubled country. Bail-ins are usually done in conjunction with a broader program of International Monetary Fund (IMF) lending and policy changes to help restore a country's economic and financial health. In a bail-in, creditors with claims coming due are asked to defer repayment deadlines—and in some cases to agree to reduce their claims. In a bailout, by contrast, a country borrows hard currency reserves from the IMF, enabling it to pay off its maturing debt.

Academic models usually try to posit a clear choice between lender-of-last-resort financing and a standstill on all payments. In practice, though, policymakers rarely confront a binary choice between a complete standstill and lender-of-last-resort financing. Sources of existing or potential financial pressure on a crisis country are usually diverse: it is possible to bail in some creditors and bail out others. A strategy that combines a bailout (of some) and bail-in (of others) consequently can make sense. A successful bail-in of some creditors eliminates one potential source of financial strain. The benefits of securing additional financing from a set of private creditors, however, have to be balanced against the risk that attempting to bail-in some creditors will only prompt other creditors to run.

A bail-in is usually initiated when a country in financial trouble asks a set of its creditors to agree to roll over or reschedule their maturing claims. The debts coming due can be the obligations of the crisis country's government—for example, a maturing international sovereign bond—or they can be obligations of private borrowers (most often cross-border loans to the country's banks) in the crisis country. Convincing the country's creditors to defer payments, whether through a bond exchange or an agreement to roll over maturing bank loans, requires at least the implicit threat that the country will halt payments if the creditors do not agree on a restructuring. But the nature of the country's negotiations with its creditors can nonetheless vary. A country that tries to negotiate an agreement with its creditors to defer payments is acting quite differently from a country that just stops payments and demands that its creditors agree to reduce their claims.

Debt Restructuring and Burden Sharing Debt restructurings are a part of borrowing and lending; they would occur in the absence of any official-sector intervention. The trigger for a bail-in, however, is often a policy decision by the official sector not to provide a country with sufficient emergency financing to allow it to avoid a debt restructuring. The IMF, the Group of Seven (G7), and others can condition their lending on a requirement that a country keep its foreign exchange reserves above a designated level (effectively requiring the country to initiate a restructuring if it cannot find private sources of financing), refuse to lend in the absence of a restructuring, offer to provide financing to facilitate a consensual restructuring, or even help the country organize a rollover of its maturing loans. The Paris Club—a group of bilateral lenders—can also condition its willingness to restructure the debts a country owes to bilateral creditors on a country's willingness to seek a comparable restructuring of the debt the country's government owes to private creditors. (The official sector generally has leverage over the debtor, not the debtor's creditors. The official sector sometimes can, however, exert leverage directly on certain types of creditors—particularly banks. The official sector usually stops short of telling banks what to do. Nonetheless, major governments can make clear that it is in the banks' collective interest to cooperate to avoid default by agreeing to roll over their exposures.)

The line between a normal, voluntary market transaction—issuing a new bond, a voluntary debt exchange—and an involuntary concession to avert a crisis is not always clear. Some IMF programs rely on the expectation that the combination of financial support and policy adjustment will catalyze new private financial flows. Some debt exchanges done in the context of an IMF program occur at market rates and are altogether voluntary—the creditors who do not participate can expect to be treated as well as creditors who do participate. Because these exchanges must be done at market rates, they are often expensive. The most famous example is Argentina's megaswap in the summer of 2001: the swap extended the maturity of Argentina's bonds, but at an implied annual interest rate of close to 15 percent. This transaction allowed Argentina to avoid default only for six months, however. These voluntary exchanges are not a true bail-in: private creditors are extending credit at a market rate in the expectation of earning a commercial profit, not making a concession to help the country through a crisis.

Other debt exchanges are done at below-market rates to avoid an imminent default. These transactions are also voluntary in some loose sense. Creditors often are willing to defer payments at an interest rate lower than the prevailing market interest rate at the time of the exchange—as in Uruguay's 2003 exchange—or even accept a deep "haircut"—as in Argentina's 2005 exchange—rather than hold debt that the sovereign debtor is not willing (or able) to pay. A haircut typically involves a reduction in the face value, a reduction in the coupon (the amount to be paid at fixed intervals), or a reduction in both the face value and the coupon of the bond. The actual losses experienced by creditors who mark to market (that is, value the bond as an asset at its open-market price) depend on the price at which they bought the bond and the discount rate the market assigns to the payment stream on the restructured bonds. The decision to voluntarily agree to these kind of terms reflects the fact that the alternative to a restructuring is often default—and creditors lack the legal ability to force a sovereign debtor that is in default to resume payments.

Throughout the 1990s, the G7 and the IMF had trouble reaching agreement on the right term to use to describe efforts to secure the coordinated provision of emergency financing from a country's existing private creditors. Calls for more "burden sharing" were considered too heavy handed: no private creditor happily takes on a burden. Talk of "constructive engagement" with private creditors was considered a bit too diplomatic: private creditors generally preferred other forms of engagement. The relatively informal term *bail-in* drew attention to the bailouts that sometimes were provided to avoid bail-ins. The most widely used term—*private-sector involvement in crisis resolution*—suited the international bureaucracy well: it was easy to reduce to an acronym (PSI).

Acronyms can still generate impassioned debate. "Market fundamentalists" opposed all forms of official intervention. They wanted to scale back IMF lending. But they also opposed the official sector's efforts to facilitate the coordinated provision of emergency financing by private creditors. This group wanted both fewer bailouts and fewer officially organized bail-ins. A more pragmatic group—including many in the G7 and the IMF—hoped to combine official financing with attempts to involve private creditors. This group argued that commitments by prominent creditors not to take their money out would help to limit the distortions introduced by official crisis support. Many Europeans viewed efforts to involve private creditors as a direct substitute for large-scale official financing—they wanted more bail-ins to reduce the need for financial bailouts. They emphasized the need to change the institutions for debt restructuring in order to make restructurings less disruptive—whether through the introduction of collective action clauses in international sovereign bonds or the development of an international bankruptcy regime. Many emerging economies—sometimes with support from those in the U.S. Treasury who believed recent emerging market crises were overwhelmingly the product of an international analogue to bank runs—wanted to banish all talk of combining bailouts with bail-ins, arguing that any effort to bail in some groups of creditors would scare market participants and keep IMF financial support from generating the desired improvement in creditor confidence.

Bail-ins were rarely part of the official sector's initial response to market turmoil. Most countries approached their private creditors to seek emergency financing only after an initial (and sometimes limited) round of official financing failed to end their financial trouble. There have, nonetheless, been important successes. Korea convinced the international banks that had lent to Korean banks first not to demand payment on their maturing loans and then to reschedule these loans. The rollover agreement eliminated the immediate threat of default and—along with continued financing from the IMF—helped to pave the way for Korea's financial recovery. Uruguay successfully combined a very large credit line from the IMF with a bond restructuring. The credit line stopped Uruguay's bank run and provided Uruguay the time needed to execute the bond exchange; the exchange assured that the IMF's funds were not used to finance a reduction in the country's bond exposure. Pakistan and the Dominican Republic also restructured their international bonds without stopping payments.

Other bond restructurings came only after the country had fallen into general default. Such restructurings sought to clean up an existing financial mess rather than avert a deeper financial crisis. Russia's 2000 restructuring of its "London Club" debt was technically a restructuring of syndicated bank loans, but since most of these loans had been securitized and sold into the market, it resembled a bond exchange. Both the Ukraine and Ecuador restructured their international sovereign bonds in 2000. Argentina's restructuring, though, dwarfs the others in size and complexity: in 2005 Argentina sought to restructure 152 separate bond issues with a face value of more than $80 billion.

The legal challenges associated with a bond restructuring, though significant, have to date proved to be smaller than many initially feared. The difficulty in keeping a bond restructuring from leading to broader financial collapse—and specifically a domestic bank run—proved larger than expected, however. In practice, many "international" sovereign bonds (bonds governed by a foreign law) are held not by international investors, but by the domestic banking system.

Crisis Management: Finding the Right Balance
No single measure can gauge the success of efforts to obtain crisis financing from the country's private creditors. Success requires convincing private creditors to contribute, whether by deferring payments or by agreeing to reduce their claims on the crisis country. But success also requires that the private creditors' contribution not come at the expense of other goals—including preventing a sharp fall in output or triggering a broader run that leaves the country in a deep financial hole. Finding strategies that strike the right balance between these sometimes conflicting goals has been a constant challenge.

See also bailouts; banking crisis; currency crisis; financial crisis; international financial architecture; International Monetary Fund (IMF); International Monetary Fund conditionality; International Monetary Fund surveillance; Latin American debt crisis; lender of last resort

FURTHER READING

Blustein, Paul. 2005. *And the Money Kept Rolling In (and Out): Wall Street, the IMF, and the Bankrupting of Argentina*. New York: Public Affairs. The best account of Argentina's crisis.

Eichengreen, Barry. 2001. "Managing Financial Crises." Felix Neubergh Prize Lecture. Goteborg University, November 13. Downloadable from http://www.

econ.berkeley.edu/~eichengr/policy/crises_nov01.pdf. A concise summary of the policy debate from an influential economist.

———. 2002. *Financial Crises and What to Do about Them.* New York: Oxford University Press. A book-length examination of financial crises.

Haldane, Andrew, and Mark Kruger. 2001. "The Resolution of International Financial Crises: Private Finance and Public Funds." Bank of Canada Working Paper 2001-20 (November). Ottawa: Bank of Canada. An influential paper that made the case for using general payment standstills in a broader range of crises.

International Monetary Fund. 2000. Communiqué of the International Monetary and Financial Committee of the IMF Board of Governors (September 24). Downloadable from http://www.imf.org/external/np/cm/2000/092400.htm%20. The best example of the official sector's effort to reach consensus on how crises should be managed—and to spell out how private creditors might be "involved" in a range of different circumstances.

Krueger, Anne. 2001. "A New Approach to Sovereign Debt Restructuring." Speech given at the National Economists' Club Annual Members' Dinner, American Enterprise Institute, Washington (November 26). Downloadable from http://www.imf.org/external/np/speeches/2001/112601.htm. Proposed the creation of a new "statutory" international bankruptcy regime.

Rogoff, Kenneth, and Jeromin Zettelmeyer. 2002. "Bankruptcy Procedures for Sovereigns: A History of Ideas, 1976–2001." *IMF Staff Papers* 49 (3): 471–507. Washington, DC: International Monetary Fund. Downloadable from http://www.imf.org/external/pubs/ft/staffp/2002/03/pdf/rogoff.pdf.

Roubini, Nouriel, and Brad Setser. 2004. *Bailouts or Bail-ins.* Washington, DC: Institute for International Economics. Comprehensive survey of experience with debt restructuring; argues that bail-ins can be successfully combined with bailouts in some circumstances.

Sturzenegger, Federico, and Jeromin Zettelmeyer. 2006. *Debt Defaults and Lessons from a Decade of Crises.* Cambridge, MA: MIT Press. An up-to-date analysis of experience with debt restructuring, including calculations of investor losses in recent restructurings.

BRAD SETSER

■ bailouts

Bailouts broadly refer to large loans from the official sector—usually the International Monetary Fund (IMF)—to a country facing difficulties repaying its maturing debts or needing to intervene in the foreign exchange market to defend its exchange rate in the face of the withdrawal of foreign investment or domestic capital flight. These loans are provided directly to the crisis country to augment its reserves in the face of acute balance of payments difficulties. Augmenting a crisis country's hard currency (international) reserves often allows the country to avoid what otherwise would have been an almost certain default on its private debts and, in some cases, to intervene in the currency market to maintain an exchange rate peg at a level that would otherwise be unsustainable. Consequently, large loans that help a country try to avoid economic and financial collapse also help external and domestic creditors with foreign-currency debts coming due, as well as those looking to exchange local currency for dollars, euros, or another currency.

The term *bailout* could be applied to all loans provided for balance of payments support by the official sector. In practice, the policy debate over these loans focused primarily on the largest of these loans, and specifically those loans whose size exceeded the IMF's traditional lending limits of 100 percent of quota in a year, or 300 percent of quota over three years. (A country's quota determines the size of a country's contribution to the IMF as well as its voting and borrowing rights.) The first prominent loan to breach these limits was provided in 1995 to Mexico. By the end of 2007, the IMF had provided "exceptional" levels of IMF financing to an additional eight emerging market economies facing acute balance of payments difficulties. Indeed, "exceptional" financing—that is, financing in excess of the IMF's normal lending norms—effectively became the new norm for large emerging market economies that encountered balance of payments difficulties.

Using the size of an IMF loan relative to quota to distinguish between small and often uncontroversial IMF loans and those exceptionally large IMF loans creates some difficulties. First, the size of a country's

IMF quota maps only imperfectly to other relevant economic criteria—Korea in 1997 and Turkey in 2001 and 2002 got exceptionally large IMF loans relative to their quotas, in part because their quotas were quite small relative to their current gross domestic product (GDP). Second, in several prominent cases, the multilateral development banks and the Group of 10 countries (a group of economically advanced countries) provided large amounts of financing alongside the IMF, so looking only at IMF financing may understate the scale of official support. For example, the United States provided Mexico almost as much financing from its Exchange Stabilization Fund as the IMF and a group of bilateral creditors coordinated by the Bank for International Settlements (BIS) disbursed alongside the IMF in 1999. The World Bank and the Asian Development Bank—pushed by the United States—provided a large amount of emergency financing to Korea, and Japan provided additional bilateral funds to Thailand (the bilateral "second-line" commitments included in the initial packages for Korea and Indonesia were never disbursed). Loans that breached the IMF's own access limits also tended to be the largest loans when measured by other criteria. Those countries that got large amounts of financing from other official sources also tended to get large amounts of financing from the IMF.

How Does the IMF Differ from Domestic Lender of Last Resort? An IMF loan to a country is in some ways similar to emergency financing from a domestic lender of last resort (typically, the country's central bank). Both provide liquidity—cash—to those in need of it. Just as a loan from a domestic lender of last resort lets a troubled bank pay off its depositors, an IMF loan also lets some of the crisis country's creditors "off the hook" by financing the repayment of the debt. Just as support from a domestic lender of last resort can convince a troubled bank's creditors—its depositors—to give the bank time to try to work through its difficulties, international crisis financing can convince the country's creditors to give it time to work through its problems.

But there are also important differences between the IMF and a domestic lender of last resort. First, the IMF's lending capacity is constrained by the amounts members have placed on deposit with the fund. A domestic lender of last resort has no similar constraints, at least as long as it lends in the country's own currency. Second, IMF loans are usually tied to policy changes, and in order to encourage the country to implement those changes, IMF lending is rarely disbursed all at once; instead, IMF loans are usually disbursed in a series of tranches. A domestic lender of last resort can provide all necessary funds up front. Third, the IMF does not lend against collateral; rather, crisis countries, by long-standing convention, pay the IMF even if they are not paying their other creditors. This allows the IMF to lend to crisis countries at modest rates without taking losses. Finally, many domestic bank "bailouts" do more than just provide a cash-strapped domestic bank with emergency liquidity. They also typically require giving a troubled bank a government bond—a new financial asset—to prevent depositors (and sometimes even the shareholders) in the bad bank from taking financial losses. International bailouts, by contrast, do not increase the net assets of a troubled emerging economy. The country's external reserves rise, but so do its external debts. The international taxpayers who put up the money needed to make an IMF loan expect to get repaid in full.

Consequently the term *bailout* is perhaps too negative a term for emergency crisis financing, as it suggests that the crisis lender is picking up losses that otherwise would have been borne by the country and its creditors. The term *rescue loan* is probably too positive, however, as not all "rescues" have succeeded. Most neutral terms—such as *large-scale official crisis lending*—sound bureaucratic. The lack of an agreed term itself may be indicative of the ongoing debate about the wisdom of large-scale lending to crisis countries.

Debate Surrounding IMF Crisis Lending Proponents of large-scale IMF lending argue that financial integration is generally beneficial. But they also recognize that it can increase the risk that a country with correctable policy problems can be forced into a disruptive default by a self-fulfilling crisis of confidence. Concerns that other external creditors will not roll over their short-term debts as they come due can lead all external creditors to demand payment as soon as possible. A country's own citizens can also decide that they want to shift their savings abroad before the country runs out of reserves. Such a shift from domestic to foreign assets puts enormous pressure on the country's reserves if it has a fixed exchange rate regime, on its exchange rate if it has a floating exchange rate regime, or on both reserves and the exchange rate if it has a managed float. Sergei Dubinin, the chairman of Russia's central bank during the 1998 crisis, observed, "We can play games against the market, against the banks even, but we can't do anything if the entire population wants to change rubles into dollars" (Blustein 2001, 266–67).

Such crises of confidence have usually stemmed at least in part from doubts about a country's ability to put in place needed corrective policies, not just doubts about the willingness of other creditors to maintain their exposure. But as the run intensifies, a country can be pushed toward default well before it has time to show whether it can make the policy changes to ensure its long-run solvency.

Critics of large-scale lending have raised a host of objections. Some object to all official intervention in private markets. Official action that insulates a country and its creditors from paying the full price for their mistakes only encourages more bad policies and additional risk-taking—so called moral hazard. Others object to the conditions attached to IMF loans,

Table 1
How quickly were IMF (and bilateral first line) loans disbursed, and how fast were they repaid?

	Peak disbursement, $ billion (% of GDP)	Quarters to reach peak	Quarters to repay ½ peak disbursement	External debt precrisis (% of GDP)	Fiscal debt precrisis (% of GDP)
Mexico	27.6 (6.8)	4	9	34%	31%
Thailand	11.2 (6.2)	12	18[a]	60%	5%
Indonesia	10.8 (4.7)	13	35	43%	24%
Korea	19.4 (3.7)	4	8	32%	12%
Russia	5.1 (1.2)	2	4	35%	52%
Brazil (98–99)	17.5 (2.2)	3	7	25%	40%
Turkey (00–02)	23.2 (12.6)	13	24	57%	56%
Argentina	14.6 (5.1)	4	22	51%	45%
Uruguay	2.7 (14.6)	11	19	81%	38%
Brazil (01–02)	33.3 (5.7)	10	18	44%	65%

Sources: IMF and bilateral first line lending data from IMF, U.S. Treasury; debt data from Moody's (apart from Mexico's precrisis debt data, which is from the IMF). Moody's debt numbers for Brazil are higher than other sources. The IMF has Brazil's 1997 (precrisis) debt to GDP at 35% rather than 40%; and Brazil's 2000 (precrisis) debt to GDP at 49% rather 65%.

[a] Thailand's IMF exposure peaked after 9 quarters, and it repaid half of that exposure after 17 quarters. At that point in time, it had not repaid ½ its bilateral lending. However, we do not have data indicating Thailand's bilateral repayments after the end of 2001.

whether fiscal austerity, monetary tightening, or domestic financial and corporate reform. This criticism was particularly vociferous after the Asian crisis; many argued that the IMF's conditions themselves contributed to the cascading loss of confidence. Many argued that the large bailouts of the 1990s and the first few years of the new millennium were a marked change from the 1980s, when the typical IMF loan was smaller (in relation to quota, though quotas were larger in relation to GDP) and was combined with commitments by the country's largest creditors—the commercial banks—to roll over their claims.

Finally, some argued that the real problem was not that the IMF was lending too much, but rather that the IMF was not able to lend enough. The IMF risked providing enough money to allow a lucky few to exit, but not enough to assure that the run would stop and the country would have time to put in place corrective policies.

This highlights a key point: in practice, even the largest IMF loans typically fell short of providing sufficient funds to cover all potential drains on the country's hard currency liquidity. For example, Mexico received enough money to cover payments on the government's maturing short-term dollar-linked debt, the famous *tesobonos*, but not enough to cover all potential sources of capital flight. Even a loan large enough to cover the most obvious sources of payment difficulties works only if additional sources of financial pressure do not also materialize.

Has IMF Crisis Lending Been Successful? Several large IMF bailouts achieved most of their intended goals. Mexico, Korea, and Brazil (in 1999) all avoided default, recovered market access relatively quickly, and paid back their official creditors quite rapidly. Eight quarters after the onset of their crises, all had paid back more than one-half of their initial loans (see table 1). Brazil, however, is less obviously a success than Mexico and Korea, as the rise in its debt levels during the 1998–99 crisis laid the foundation for its 2002 crisis. Brazil did not pay its 2002 bailout loan back in eight quarters—in part because the large loan in 2002 came on top of an earlier loan in 2001. But it otherwise resembles the "success" stories: it fully repaid the IMF at the end of 2005, and its debt

levels were coming down through the end of 2007. Other rescues achieved their goals, but not as quickly. Thailand (1997), Turkey, and Uruguay all avoided default, regained market access, resumed growth, and eventually made significant payments back to the IMF. All these countries entered into their crises with higher debt levels and generally have taken longer to repay the IMF than Mexico, Korea, and Brazil (particularly in 1999).

Three bailouts clearly failed to achieve their initial goals, however: Russia, Argentina, and Indonesia— whether because the country failed to carry out its commitments to the IMF or because the IMF backed a flawed strategy. In 1998, Russia was cut off quite quickly, after one $5 billion disbursement from the IMF's new program—a decision prompted in part by the IMF's substantial exposure from its previous lending programs. Indonesia received only $4 billion in the early stages of its crisis. Most of the funds it received from the IMF came later on, after its corporate sector had fallen into general default. Argentina, in contrast, received almost $15 billion in an unsuccessful attempt to ward off default.

By the end of 2007, the IMF had not approved a new large loan—setting aside those loans extended to refinance existing IMF loans—since 2002. In retrospect, the period of large-scale IMF lending that followed Mexico's crisis may be viewed as facilitating the transition of many emerging economies from a point where they held too few reserves to navigate periods of financial volatility to a point where most emerging economies held more reserves than they needed. During the turbulent period between 1995 and 2003, the size of IMF lending was striking. By 2005, though, the size of even the largest IMF loans seemed fairly small relative to the reserves of the typical emerging economies. For all the criticisms leveled at the IMF, most emerging markets concluded that they needed to hold far more reserves than the IMF was ever willing to make available.

See also asymmetric information; bail-ins; banking crisis; capital flight; contagion; currency crisis; financial crisis; international financial architecture; international liquidity; International Monetary Fund (IMF); International Monetary

Fund conditionality; International Monetary Fund surveillance; international reserves; lender of last resort

FURTHER READING

Blustein, Paul. 2001. *The Chastening: Inside the Crisis that Rocked the Global Financial System and Humbled the IMF.* New York: Public Affairs. A readable—and critical—account of the IMF's response to the Asian financial crisis.

Fischer, Stanley. 1999. "On the Need for an International Lender of Last Resort." *Journal of Economic Perspectives* 13 (4): 85–104. The case for an international lender of last resort.

Jeanne, Olivier, and Jeromin Zettelmeyer. 2001. "International Bailouts, Moral Hazard, and Conditionality." *Economic Policy* 33: 409–32. Argues that IMF lending may sustain bad domestic policies since IMF lending—unlike domestic bailouts—is almost always repaid.

Ortiz, Guillermo. 2002. "Recent Emerging Market Crises—What Have We Learned?" Per Jacobsson Lecture. Basel: Bank for International Settlements. Downloadable from http://www.perjacobsson.org/lectures/2002-ortiz.pdf. A sympathetic treatment of the case for large-scale IMF lending.

Roubini, Nouriel, and Brad Setser. 2004. *Bailouts or Bail-ins.* Washington, DC: Institute for International Economics. A comprehensive survey of recent experience with crisis resolution along with the academic debate.

Rubin, Robert E., and Jacob Weisberg. 2003. *In an Uncertain World: Tough Choices from Wall Street to Washington.* New York: Random House. There is no better account of the U.S. decision to bail out Mexico—and the resulting policy debate.

BRAD SETSER

balance of payments

A balance of payments is an international accounting record. It records the economic transactions of the residents of one country with the residents of other countries during a fixed period (month, quarter, year). The payments are usually measured in a country's home currency, although the accounts are sometimes expressed in U.S. dollars to facilitate cross-country comparisons. The payments are broken down into categories—goods, services, transfers, investments, and official reserves. Inflows and outflows in each category are measured and a net figure for each is calculated. Strictly speaking, each category has a balance and, as a matter of practice, several balances are regularly reported by government agencies and the financial press. *The balance of payments* is a generic term that refers to payment flows in some or all of the different categories.

Although balance of payments accounts are constructed using sophisticated accounting principles, including double-entry bookkeeping, a country's cross-border transactions are not measured with the accuracy of a corporation's accounts. Balance of payments figures are statistically estimated based on sampling data gathered by government agencies. In the United States, business firms are required by law to provide information on international transactions. The Office of Management and Budget, the Customs Service, the Department of Commerce, and the Treasury Department gather or compile such information. Although these agencies do their utmost to provide reliable estimates, of necessity the accounts contain errors; the statistical estimates are based on data that are incomplete and otherwise imperfect.

Uses Business firms, labor unions, academics, lawyers, investors, and government officials take an interest in the balance of payments. Firms base financial and competitive decisions on the balance of payments. Firms and labor unions use balance of payments figures to argue for favorable tariffs or subsidies. Lawyers use information from the balance of payments to initiate cases in national courts or before the dispute resolution bodies of the World Trade Organization (WTO). Economists develop principles to explain the movement of goods and investments across borders, and they recommend policies based on those principles. Government officials are responsible for the policies that govern cross-border economic transactions. Some government policies, such as the trade restrictions imposed during the Cold War, discourage international transactions, while other policies, such as free trade agreements, encourage them. The balance of payments also helps us to understand how the world trading system is evolving. The flow of foreign aid from the United States to Europe in the 1950s, the increase in the exchange of services in the 1980s, and the rise of foreign direct investment in the 1990s all show up in the balance of payments accounts.

History The interest in international transactions goes back to at least the 14th century. The mercantilists, a group of British writers, urged government policies that encouraged exports and discouraged imports. They argued that a surplus of exports over imports would preserve the country's specie (metallic money supply) and enhance the wealth of the country. Borrowing the idea of an accounting balance from the double-entry bookkeeping of Italian merchants, the mercantilists introduced the term *balance of trade* into economic discussion in the 1600s. In the 18th century, David Hume pointed out that a country cannot run a permanent trade surplus (his famous price-specie flow mechanism), and Adam Smith roundly criticized the mercantilists for conflating money and wealth. The balance of payments received a great deal of theoretical attention in Britain's 19th-century monetary debates; the effects of fiduciary media (paper money) on the trade balance were especially controversial. European and U.S. governments collected international trade statistics in the 19th and early 20th centuries, but the modern system of payments accounting was not established until the end of World War II, when agreements at Bretton Woods empowered the International Monetary Fund (IMF) to gather and organize international trade data. World leaders recognized that the breakdown of the international trading system during the 1930s had exacerbated the Great Depression. They hoped that systematic gathering and presentation of trade data would enhance international cooperation.

Accounts All international economic transactions are divided into two main accounts—the current account and the awkwardly named capital and financial account.

Current Account The current account is broken down into four categories—goods, services, income, and transfers. Goods are the tangible items—

agricultural products, manufactured goods, and commodities such as copper and crude oil—that are traded across borders. For most countries, goods are the main component of the current account. In 2004, the United States exported slightly more than $800 billion in goods, about 50 percent of current account credits for the year. Japan exported $539 billion in goods, about 70 percent of its current account credits (see table 1). Services are the exchange of intangibles across borders. Travel, transportation, royalties and license fees, and financial (banking, investment, insurance) and military services are the main ones traded across borders. In 2004, the United States exported $340 billion in services, Japan $98 billion. Business and personal travel is an important component of services in many countries; $74 billion, or 21 percent, of U.S. service export revenue came from travel in 2004. Income in the current account is primarily the dividends and interest paid to residents of a country from their investments abroad. The income can result from a resident in one country holding securities in foreign companies or governments, or from interest earned on loans to residents of other countries. For a country that invests large sums abroad but discourages foreign investment into the country, inflows of income outweigh the outflows by a large margin—in Japan's case, $113 billion to $27 billion in 2004. Besides income from investments abroad, the income account also includes compensation to temporary workers, such as seasonal farmworkers and short-term business consultants. Compared to investment income, employee compensation is small for most countries; in 2004, the United States, for example, paid $9 billion to temporary workers from other countries, but $340 billion in interest and dividends to foreign investors.

The final item in the current account is unilateral transfers. The main items in this account are foreign aid (government grants of cash, food, clothing, etc. to the residents of other countries), charity (private donations to residents of other countries), and worker remittances (money sent home by workers employed abroad). Residents of wealthy economies usually spend considerable sums on government aid and charitable activities aimed at helping residents of

Table 1

Analytic balance of payments, United States and Japan (billions of U.S. dollars)

Line		U.S. 2000	U.S. 2004	Japan 2000	Japan 2004
1	A. Current Account	−416.00	−668.07	119.66	172.06
2	Goods: exports, f.o.b.	774.63	811.03	459.51	539.00
3	Goods: imports, f.o.b.	−1224.32	−1472.96	−342.80	−406.87
4	*Trade Balance*	−449.78	−661.93	116.72	132.13
5	Services: credit	296.85	340.42	69.24	97.61
6	Services: debit	−225.34	−296.07	−116.86	−135.51
7	*Balance on goods and services*	−378.27	−617.58	69.09	94.23
8	Income: credit	350.92	379.53	97.20	113.33
9	Income: debit	−329.86	−349.09	−36.80	−27.63
10	*Balance on goods, services, & income*	−357.22	−587.14	129.49	179.93
11	Current transfers: credit	10.83	17.92	7.38	6.91
12	Current transfers: debit	−69.61	−98.85	−17.21	−14.78
13	*Balance on current account*	−416.00	−668.07	119.66	172.06
14	B. Capital Account	−0.93	−1.65	−9.26	−4.79
15	Capital account: credit	1.08	1.13	0.78	0.44
16	Capital account: debit	−2.01	−2.78	−10.04	−5.23
17	*Total: Groups A plus B*	−416.93	812.16	110.40	167.26
18	C. Financial Account	486.66	581.79	−78.31	22.49
19	Direct investment abroad	−159.21	−252.01	−31.51	−30.96
20	Direct investment in U.S.	321.27	106.83	8.23	7.80
21	Portfolio investment assets	−127.91	−102.38	−83.36	−173.77
22	Equity securities	−106.71	−83.20	−19.72	−31.47
23	Debt securities	−21.19	−19.18	−63.64	−142.30
24	Portfolio investment liabilities	436.57	762.70	47.39	196.72
25	Equity securities	193.60	61.91	−1.29	98.22
26	Debt securities	242.97	700.79	48.67	98.44
27	Financial derivatives	...	...	−4.67	2.41
28	Financial derivatives assets	...	...	106.74	56.44
29	Financial derivatives liabilities	...	...	−111.41	−54.06
30	Other investment assets	−273.11	−503.92	−4.15	−48.01
31	Monetary authorities	...	...	...	...
32	General government	−0.94	1.22	−1.89	3.87
33	Banks	−133.38	−356.13	36.51	3.24
34	Other sectors	−138.78	−149.00	−38.77	−55.12
35	Other investment liabilities	289.05	570.58	−10.21	68.30
36	Monetary authorities	−2.52	52.77	...	...
37	General government	−0.39	1.39	−0.93	0.98
38	Banks	122.72	392.96	28.22	42.73
39	Other sectors	169.24	123.46	−37.49	24.59
40	D. Net Errors and Omissions	−69.44	85.13	16.87	−28.90
41	*Overall balance*	0.29	−2.80	48.95	160.85
42	E. Reserves and Related Items	−0.29	2.80	−48.95	−160.85
43	Reserve Assets	−0.29	2.80	−48.95	−160.85
	Conversion rates: yen per U.S. dollar			107.77	108.19

Source: Adapted from *Balance of Payments Statistics Yearbook*, International Monetary Fund, 2005.

other countries. In 2004, the residents of the United States disbursed foreign aid of $30 billion, private charitable contributions of $39 billion, and worker remittances of $30 billion to other countries. Residents of developing countries are usually net recipients of aid, charity, and remittances.

Financial Account Like the current account, the financial account is divided into four main kinds of transactions. The first of these is direct investment. Whenever residents in one country make an investment abroad that gives them a "substantial voice" in management, the investment is considered direct. A firm may do this by investing in plant and equipment or by purchasing enough stock (10 percent or more of outstanding shares) to influence the managerial decisions of an existing firm. In 2004, U.S. investors spent $252 billion on direct investments abroad, $176 billion of which was reinvested earnings. Foreign investors spent $106 billion on direct investment in the United States, $56 billion of which was reinvested earnings.

The second kind of investment transaction is portfolio investment, which is the purchase of bonds and equities in one country by residents of another. Although equities are issued mainly by private firms, bonds are issued by both firms and governments, so portfolio investment includes the purchase of government bonds by residents of other countries. In 2004, foreign residents invested $62 billion in U.S. equities and $701 billion in U.S. bonds, $458 billion of which was government bonds. By way of contrast, foreign residents invested $197 billion in Japan. The investment was split evenly, with $98 billion going into equities and $98 billion into bonds, of which $53 billion was government bonds. The government absorbed 60 percent of portfolio investment in the United States, compared to 27 percent absorbed by the Japanese government.

A third category of investment is a residual, named "other" in the accounts, which includes trade credit, bank loans and deposits, and currency exchanges. In 2004, foreign residents increased their residual investments in the United States by $570 billion, $407 billion of which represented an increase in the holdings of U.S. currency and bank deposits.

In Japan, the pattern was rather different. Foreign residents increased borrowing from Japanese firms and government agencies by $81 billion but reduced their holdings of the yen by $13 billion, so residual investment increased by $68 billion.

The fourth category of investment in the financial account is reserve assets, which are funds available to monetary authorities to finance payment deficits. Central banks and treasuries use gold, holdings with the IMF, and foreign exchange (currencies and deposits) for such financing. In 2004, monetary authorities in the United States financed an overall deficit of $2.8 billion, mainly by altering its reserve position within the IMF. Japan had an overall surplus of $161 billion, with which it acquired foreign exchange (i.e., international reserves).

Double-Entry Bookkeeping Every economic transaction entered into a country's balance of payments accounts contains both a debit and a credit. On the current account, debits and credits are apparent. When a country exports, the account shows a credit; when a country imports, the account shows a debit. On the capital account, the debits and credits can be somewhat confusing. When a company receives payment for its exports, it is recorded as a debit in the capital account; when a company makes a payment for an import, it shows up as a credit in the capital account. One way to make sense of credits and debits is to view them as sources and uses of funds, where *funds* means financial assets used in international transactions. Currencies, deposits in banks, trade credits and other forms of loans are examples of funds. In the balance of payments accounts, a source of funds is a credit; a use of funds is a debit. When a firm sells a bond to a foreign resident, the sale will show up as a credit (a source of funds) in the capital account of the home country. By selling a bond to a foreign resident, a firm has also increased its liabilities. An increase in liabilities is a source of funds and therefore a credit in the capital accounts. Conversely, when a firm redeems a bond, it reduces its liabilities by using funds. A decrease in liabilities is therefore a debit in the capital account. The opposite is true of assets. When a resident of one country purchases equity shares in a foreign firm, she uses funds; an increase in assets appears as a debit in the financial account. When this investor sells her shares, she decreases her assets and increases her funds. A decrease in assets appears as a credit in the capital accounts.

Balances If we accurately record all of the flows of payments between countries, they will always balance. Yet policymakers and others are often concerned with payment imbalances. Imbalances occur when we consider only particular types of transactions within the accounts, rather than all transactions. For example, if we consider only merchandise transactions, the resulting balance is officially called the balance on goods and is reported in the press as the trade balance. The trade balance for the United States, shown in line 4, was a negative $662 billion in 2004, while Japan's was a positive $132 billion. Although goods are usually the biggest item in a country's current account, services have become increasingly important. In 2004, the United States exported $340 billion and imported $296 billion in services. The United States' balance in services was a positive $44 billion, while Japan's was a negative $38 billion. The press does not usually report the services balance by itself, however. Instead, it reports the balance on goods and services, which for 2004 was negative $618 billion for the United States and positive $94 billion for Japan. This balance is particularly important, because it enters the national income accounts of each nation.

The gross domestic product of a country, measured in expenditures, equals consumption plus investment plus government expenditures plus exports minus imports, or $Y = C + I + G + (X - M)$. In this equation, $X - M$ is the balance on goods and services. Since U.S. residents spent more on imports than foreign residents spent on U.S. exports in 2004, the balance on goods and services subtracted from the gross domestic output of the United States. If we add to the balance on goods and services the balance on income and the balance on unilateral transfers, neither of which is widely reported, we get the current account balance, which is closely watched by policymakers. If this balance is negative, it means that a country's current transactions are being financed by investment from abroad (or from official reserves).

There is nothing wrong or even worrisome in this, as long as the investment is being used for productive purposes. If the investment does not produce a higher future income, however, then its repayment will lower a country's future standard of living.

Another balance closely watched is the overall balance. This is the sum of all current and financial account transactions, adjusted for errors and omissions, except for official reserve transactions, and is shown on line 41 of table 1. A negative overall balance means that a country is balancing its payments by draining its official reserves. If a country does not balance its current account deficit with a financial account surplus, or if it does not balance a financial account deficit with a current account surplus, then it must make up the difference by using its accumulated reserves. Governments will often use their reserves to balance the overall account over short periods, but they can do so only until their reserves are depleted. A large and persistent deficit in the overall balance indicates that a country's trade and financial policies are not sustainable.

The Effects of Monetary and Fiscal Policies on the Balance of Payments A country's balance of payments results from a large number of diverse transactions, conditions, events, and policies. Natural resources (copper in Zambia, oil in Saudi Arabia), comparative advantage (automobiles in Japan), entrepreneurial discovery (the computer industry in the United States), as well as exchange rates, interest rates, income levels and growth, savings rates, political stability, wars, tariffs, and subsidies all affect a country's balance of payments. Moreover, these influences affect different accounts in different ways, and they can operate at different speeds. Typically, economists and policymakers focus on only a few of the more important influences, among which are monetary and fiscal policies. Even within this restricted set of policies, the effects on the balance of payments are complicated. The effects of fiscal and monetary policies on a country's balance of payments will depend on its other policies—especially toward exchange rates and capital flows—and on the size and wealth of the country and the extent to which it trades with others.

See also aid, international; Bretton Woods system; convertibility; foreign direct investment (FDI); gold standard, international; International Monetary Fund (IMF); international reserves; mercantilism; money supply; Mundell-Fleming model; remittances; World Trade Organization

FURTHER READING

International Monetary Fund. *Balance of Payments Statistics Yearbook*. Washington, DC: IMF. Besides providing a wealth of statistical information on balance of payments, this volume explains the methods and rationale of modern balance of payments accounting.

Viner, Jacob. 1937. *Studies in the Theory of International Trade*. New York: Harper and Brothers. Historical exegesis and analysis of international trade and finance theory from the mercantilists to John Maynard Keynes.

JACK HIGH

■ balance sheet approach/effects

National authorities, market analysts, and the International Monetary Fund (IMF) traditionally have assessed the financial health of a country on the basis of *flow* variables, such as annual gross domestic product (GDP), the current account, and fiscal balances. Sudden and disruptive capital account crises in Mexico (1994–5), Southeast Asia (1997–8), Russia (1998), Turkey (2001), and Latin America (2001–2), however, called into question the capacity of such metrics to provide a full picture of an economy's vulnerabilities. Signs of impending trouble in these countries might have been spotted earlier through a more careful look at mismatches between the *stocks* of a country's assets and its liabilities; that is, by looking at imbalances within and between a country's sectoral balance sheets. Additionally, once a capital account crisis has begun, changes in the exchange rate, interest rate, and other asset prices can propagate the crisis through their effects on the relative valuations of assets and liabilities within and between sectors.

The balance sheet approach (BSA) represents a framework for identifying stock-based vulnerabilities

and the transmission mechanisms between sectors that can turn these weaknesses into full-blown capital account crises. Knowledge of sectoral balance sheet mismatches can aid policymakers in reducing vulnerabilities and identifying appropriate policy responses once a financial crisis unfolds.

Key Balance Sheet Concepts The BSA is principally concerned with providing a comprehensive assessment of the currency and maturity mismatches in a country's assets and liabilities that can trigger large adjustments in capital flows. Whereas traditional flow-based analyses of an economy have focused on the gradual buildup of unsustainable fiscal and current account positions over a defined period, the BSA looks at imbalances in the stocks of assets and liabilities, such as debt, foreign reserves, and loans outstanding at a certain point in time. Although the two approaches are obviously interrelated, since stocks are the product of both flows and valuation changes, the BSA focuses on how misalignments in stocks can lead to the sudden changes in flows that presage liquidity and even solvency problems.

An application of the BSA begins by looking at a country's consolidated external balance sheet; that is, its position vis-à-vis nonresidents. This consolidated balance sheet summarizes the external debts of a country's public and private sectors relative to their external assets. The consolidated balance sheet's level of aggregation can, however, mask considerable imbalances between and within sectors that could trigger disorderly adjustments. For instance, a country's consolidated balance sheet does not show foreign currency debt between residents, but such debt can trigger an external balance of payments crisis if the country's government needs to draw on its reserves to roll over its domestically held hard currency debt. In fact, one of the key insights of the BSA is that cross-holdings of assets between residents can create internal balance sheet mismatches that leave a country vulnerable to an external balance of payments crisis.

In order to implement the BSA, an economy can be disaggregated into a set of interlinked sectoral balance sheets. The exact disaggregation used should depend on the issues under analysis and the data available. A basic matrix of interrelated balance sheets would break down assets and liabilities by maturity and currency, and would include the public sector (i.e., central bank, government, and public corporations), the private financial sector (i.e., principally banks), and the nonfinancial private sector (i.e., companies and households), as well as an external (nonresident) sector to which all three of these domestic sectors are linked. Sectoral balance sheets are interrelated in that one sector's liabilities are by definition the assets of another sector (see figure 1).

Real assets, such as plants and materiel, which are often a major element of public assets, are not included in a BSA matrix since they are not sufficiently liquid to be called on in a crisis. Consequently, a BSA-style analysis provides a snapshot of an entity's net financial position and its capacity to draw on liquid assets in response to pressure for repayment of its liabilities. It is not intended as a method for calculating the net worth or solvency of an economy or sector, nor does it serve as a precise early warning system. Rather, the BSA reveals vulnerability to a sudden rebalancing of stocks without necessarily pro-

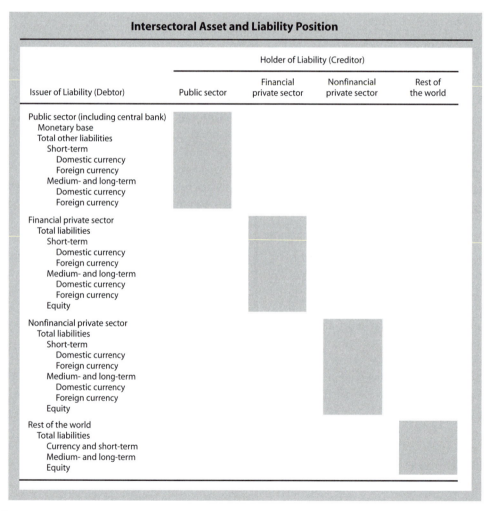

Figure 1
Intersectoral asset and liability position. Source: Rosenberg et al. (2005).

viding an indication of the probability that such an event could occur. In this regard, even partial data can provide useful insights into potential vulnerabilities.

Balance-sheet mismatches do not in and of themselves lead to crises. They simply create the conditions under which a random shock is likely to inflict damage on an economy. Maturity mismatches in Russia in 1998 left its balance sheets vulnerable to rollover and interest rate risks, but commodity price shocks and contagion from the Asian crisis were the actual triggers of the country's crisis. Conversely, Lebanon managed to avoid a financial crisis through 2007 despite years of marked exchange rate, rollover, and interest rate risks connected to gross public debt levels in excess of 180 percent of GDP. Unwavering investor confidence proved an effective shield against real shocks.

The particular vulnerability of emerging markets to sudden capital flow reversals has dictated an early BSA focus on these countries by the IMF and market analysts. The approach is increasingly used, however, to examine specific vulnerabilities, such as asset bubbles and unfunded pension schemes, in both emerging and more mature market economies.

Taxonomy of Balance Sheet Risks At least three major types of mismatch characterize the bulk of balance sheet risks:

1. Maturity mismatches. Mismatches between long-term, illiquid assets and shorter-term liabilities expose a balance sheet to risks related to both debt rollover and changes in interest rates. If liquid assets do not cover maturing debts, an economy or sector may be shut out of capital markets and unable to cover its debt-service liabilities. Similarly, a sharp change in interest rates can dramatically alter the cost of rolling over short-term liabilities, leading to a rapid increase in the cost of servicing debt.

2. Currency mismatches. A currency mismatch most often arises when a borrower's assets are mainly denominated in domestic currency, but its liabilities are denominated in foreign currency, leaving the borrower's balance sheet vulnerable to a depreciation or devaluation of the domestic currency. In many emerging markets, debtors have been motivated to borrow in foreign currency because it is often cheaper than borrowing in local currency. The choice to

borrow in foreign currency is sometimes related to deposit dollarization: banks need to match deposits in foreign denominations with loans in the same currency, increasing their incentive to lend to unhedged local borrowers. Following Argentina's crisis and default in 2001–2, many other highly dollarized countries in Latin America also experienced severe crises as a result of the pervasive currency mismatches created by their financial sectors' need to match dollar deposits with dollar loans.

3. Capital structure mismatches. In the context of the BSA, capital structure refers to the balance between debt and equity in an entity's financing. Compared with debt, equity provides a natural buffer during times of balance sheet stress since dividends can be reduced along with earnings, whereas debt payments remain unchanged regardless of circumstances. Capital structure mismatches can arise when a country finances current account deficits through external borrowing (including from official sources, some of which can be difficult to restructure in the event of a crisis) rather than through foreign direct investment or portfolio equity flows.

These mismatches often combine to increase vulnerabilities. For instance, maturity mismatches in foreign currency can create difficulties if market conditions change and domestic borrowers do not have enough liquid foreign currency reserves to cover short-term foreign currency debt. This is what happened in Uruguay in 2002, when domestic banks had difficulties meeting a run on foreign-exchange-denominated deposits. Similarly, financial entities that borrow short-term funds to invest in longer-term debt instruments would suffer from a rise in interest rates brought about, for example, by an exchange-rate defense or cyclical developments, as occurred in Turkey during 2001. Maturity, currency, and capital structure mismatches combined in the Asian crises of 1997–8. Prior to these crises, the Korean government had severely restricted foreign direct investment, and most capital inflows were financed through foreign-currency, shorter-maturity external debt. Similarly, Thailand's tax regime favored corporate debt over equity, which, combined with an implicit nominal exchange rate peg, also led the Thai nonfinancial private sector to build up foreign-currency denominated debt with nonresident creditors.

When current and expected liabilities exceed assets, a country, sector, or individual entity may face insolvency. Public-sector solvency is often assessed by looking at the ratio of sovereign debt to GDP or to revenue (as a proxy for the government's ability to service its debt). Similarly, a country's overall solvency is usually measured by the ratio of total debt to GDP or to exports. But such measures can indicate vulnerabilities only when combined with other measures of risk exposure and an assessment of related mismatches.

No single debt-to-GDP ratio indicates that a sovereign or balance of payments crisis is imminent. For instance, countries with identical debt-to-GDP ratios, but different currency and maturity mismatches, often face distinct balance sheet weaknesses. The recent literature on debt intolerance draws heavily on the BSA to explain why developing and emerging markets have tended to run into trouble at much lower debt-to-GDP ratios than advanced countries. On the asset side of the public balance sheet, this research has focused on weak revenue bases and poor expenditure control as probable explanations for such low sustainable public debt thresholds. On the liability side, the literature on "original sin"—the inability to borrow long term in local currency—highlights the vulnerabilities created by the predominance of foreign-currency debt in emerging markets' public borrowing.

Policy Implications The BSA can aid policymakers in preventing and resolving capital account crises. In support of crisis prevention, the approach systematically identifies balance sheet vulnerabilities and highlights sectors in which liquidity buffers may be wearing thin. The Brazilian authorities, for example, were able to head off a recession following the devaluation of the real in 1998 by shifting balance sheet risks away from the corporate and financial sectors, which were exposed to currency risks, and toward the public sector, which was relatively stronger at that time. They did so by issuing foreign-currency-denominated, interest-rate-indexed sovereign debt.

As overnight rates were hiked to defend the real, private domestic holders of these bonds stood to gain. The Brazilian operation also highlights the cost of such risk transfers: although it helped unhedged firms to weather the devaluation of the real, it burdened the public balance sheet for many years to come.

More generally, the BSA has guided policies to reduce vulnerabilities, such as building asset buffers (official reserves), promoting private-sector hedging instruments, strengthening banking supervision, conducting sound liability management operations, and—where appropriate—instituting flexible exchange rate regimes to reduce incentives for unhedged exposures. Once a country is in a capital account crisis, an awareness of balance sheet mismatches can help the authorities choose an appropriate policy response. The BSA can be useful in comparing, for example, the costs and benefits of letting a currency depreciate or of defending it with changes to interest rates.

Operationalizing and Extending the BSA Ideally, an application of the BSA begins with the compilation of the data needed to complete the basic 4×4 matrix shown in figure 1. Central banks in some OECD countries currently prepare and publish such balance sheet analyses of their economies. In emerging markets, data for the public and private financial sectors are usually easy to obtain, while data for the nonfinancial private sector are often harder to pin down. When national statistics are lacking, information from the Bank for International Settlements and the IMF on a country's international investment position can sometimes help in compiling the external position and deriving the rest of the matrix. In the context of its surveillance and program work, IMF staff has so far completed BSA-style analyses on more than 20 country cases. Furthermore, balance-sheet-related concepts underpin the IMF's frameworks for debt sustainability analysis and the Financial Sector Assessment Program, a key tool for identifying vulnerabilities in countries' banking sectors.

The basic BSA matrix can be further augmented by including off-balance-sheet items such as contingent claims and derivatives in the assessment of vulnerabilities. Additionally, a full assessment of the risks arising from balance sheet mismatches should factor in attempts to identify the likelihood of future shocks.

See also banking crisis; capital mobility; contagion; currency crisis; currency substitution and dollarization; early warning systems; financial crisis; global imbalances; hot money and sudden stops; international liquidity; International Monetary Fund (IMF); International Monetary Fund conditionality; International Monetary Fund surveillance; international reserves; original sin; spillovers

FURTHER READING

Allen, Mark, Christoph Rosenberg, Christian Keller, Brad Setser, and Nouriel Roubini. 2002. "A Balance Sheet Approach to Financial Crisis." IMF Working Paper No. 02/210. Washington, DC: International Monetary Fund. This paper launched a systematic application of the BSA to the assessment of countrywide vulnerabilities by the IMF, underpinned by insights from the second- and third-generation currency crisis models.

Eichengreen, Barry, and Ricardo Hausmann, eds. 2005. *Other People's Money: Debt Denomination and Financial Instability in Emerging Market Economies.* Chicago: University of Chicago Press. A comprehensive 10-essay survey of the balance-sheet problems created by the phenomenon of "original sin" in emerging markets.

Goldstein, Morris, and Philip Turner. 2004. *Controlling Currency Mismatches in Emerging Markets.* Washington, DC: Institute for International Economics. A wide-ranging survey of the problems associated with measuring and controlling currency mismatches in emerging countries that proposes a new measure of aggregate effective currency mismatch and argues that domestic policies can make a big difference in limiting currency mismatches.

Mathisen, Johan, and Anthony Pellechio. 2006. "Using the Balance Sheet Approach in Surveillance: Framework, Data Sources, and Data Availability." IMF Working Paper No. 06/100. Washington, DC: International Monetary Fund. A practical "how-to" guide to compiling a BSA-style analysis of countrywide and sectoral vulnerabilities.

Rosenberg, Christoph, Ioannis Halikias, Brett House, Christian Keller, Jens Nystedt, Alexander Pitt, and Brad Setser. 2005. "Debt-Related Vulnerabilities and Financial Crises. An Application of the Balance Sheet Approach to Emerging Market Countries." IMF Occasional Paper No. 240. Washington, DC: International Monetary Fund. A review of the evolution of balance sheet vulnerabilities in emerging market countries during the decade from the mid-1990s to 2005, and a collection of applications of the BSA to both emerging-market crises and potential crises that were averted.

Roubini, Nouriel, and Brad Setser. 2004. *Bail In or Bail Out? Responding to Financial Crises in Emerging Markets.* Washington, DC: Institute for International Economics. An analysis of possible responses to emerging-market crises informed and underpinned by the BSA.

MARK ALLEN, BRETT HOUSE, AND CHRISTOPH ROSENBERG

■ Balassa-Samuelson effect

It has become conventional wisdom in economics that richer countries tend to have higher overall costs of living than poorer countries. Typically this is measured in terms of the real exchange rate, which compares the consumer price indexes of two countries converted to a common currency using the nominal exchange rate. This empirical observation has been referred to as the Penn effect, after the Penn World Tables data used to measure it, or alternatively as the Balassa-Samuelson effect, after the economists who wrote about the observation and endeavored to explain it. One important implication of this observation is that it indicates a systematic deviation from the theory of purchasing power parity, which is a building block in exchange rate theory. It indicates that there is a role for economic fundamentals such as relative income levels in explaining long-run real exchange rate behavior.

Although numerous theories have been proposed over time to explain this systematic relationship between the real exchange rate and income levels, by far the most influential is that proposed in 1964 in two separate papers by Bela Balassa and Paul A. Samuelson. The theory is based on the divergence of productivity levels in a world of traded and nontraded goods, explaining that rich countries specialize in and produce goods that are characterized by higher productivity and that are easily traded internationally. (Because this basic idea is also found in an earlier book by Roy F. Harrod in 1933, the theory is sometimes referred to as the Harrod-Balassa-Samuelson effect. This entry will follow the convention of referring to the empirical observation and the theoretical explanation jointly as the Balassa-Samuelson effect.)

Many early empirical studies failed to find statistical support for the connection between relative prices and income levels. It was even more difficult to find statistical evidence of a linkage to the underlying causal factors that the Balassa-Samuelson hypothesis said should be at work, such as between exchange rates and relative productivity levels (see Officer 1982). It appears, however, that the strength of the Balassa-Samuelson effect has grown steadily over time. Recent statistical studies of the second half of the 20th century find that for a large sample of countries the relationship between relative national price levels and income levels became positive as well as statistically significant only in the 1960s, thus validating the Balassa-Samuelson hypothesis (for instance, see Bergin, Glick, and Taylor 2006). It may not be a coincidence that Balassa and Samuelson began writing on the subject at this time. Further, the correlation between these two variables appears to have quadrupled over the half-century since then, and it is very strongly significant statistically in current data.

The Theory of Balassa-Samuelson How exactly are positive correlations between national price levels and income levels related to the Balassa-Samuelson effect? There is a specific way of explaining these correlations, based on differences in productivity levels across countries and goods. Here is a simple version of the theory with an intuitive example to follow.

Consider two countries, home and foreign, where foreign variables are denoted with an asterisk (*). Let there be two goods produced in these countries, where one good (T) can be traded internationally, and the other is a nontraded good (N). Traditional,

albeit imprecise, examples of this distinction would be manufactured goods as traded and services as nontraded. For simplicity, suppose these goods are produced competitively in each country, using only labor as an input, with wages W and W^* in each country. Denote the labor productivity in each sector as A_T and A_N at home, and A_T^* and A_N^* in the foreign country.

If one assumes that trade is costless for the traded good, its price will be equalized in the two countries. Conveniently, this also pins down the relative wage levels in the two countries, since $W/A_T = P_T = P_T^* = W^*/A_T^*$. The wage levels, in turn, pin down the nontraded goods prices with $W/A_N = P_N$ and $W^*/A_N^* = P_N^*$. Now construct a simple consumer price index, say, where the share of expenditure on nontraded goods in consumption is constant at the value θ in both countries. Then the relationship between the price levels of the two countries is given by

$$\frac{P}{P^*} = \frac{(P_N)^\theta (P_T)^{1-\theta}}{(P_N^*)^\theta (P_T^*)^{1-\theta}} = \left(\frac{P_N}{P_N^*}\right)^\theta = \left(\frac{A_T/A_N}{A_T^*/A_N^*}\right)^\theta.$$

This equation predicts that a country will have a higher overall price level if it is highly productive in traded goods, relative to its own nontraded goods, and relative to the traded goods of the foreign country. If one country is richer than the other, this higher income level can be due to higher productivity in the nontraded goods, the traded goods, or some combination of the two. The theory says that the larger the role of productivity growth specifically in the traded sector, the more likely it will be that high relative income levels will be associated with high relative price levels. On the other hand, if a country is richer due to higher productivity in the nontraded sector, or high productivity equally over both sectors, then the model will not predict that the rich country will have a higher overall price level.

As an intuitive and commonly invoked example of the Balassa-Samuelson effect at work, suppose that the home country is rich because it is very good at producing a manufactured good like automobiles, but it has no productivity advantage relative to the foreign country in terms of a nontraded service like haircuts. The high productivity of home workers in the auto industry affords them a high wage. But it also requires that the wage be high for haircuts, or else no worker would be willing to provide this service, preferring instead to work in the auto industry. Given that a haircut requires the same amount of labor time in each country, but the wage rate paid to the haircutter is higher at home, it is clear that the price of haircuts will be higher at home. Since the purchase price of autos is the same across countries due to arbitrage through trade, the higher price of haircuts makes the overall cost of living higher in the home country.

Implications and Assessment of the Theory The Balassa-Samuelson theory is used regularly by economists and policymakers to interpret a range of applied issues. Note that a straightforward extension of the theory from levels to changes would imply that countries with faster growth rates in the traded sector would have real exchange rates that are appreciating over time. For example, it predicts that China or other rapidly developing countries might expect pressure for their real exchange rates to appreciate as a natural counterpart to their rapid growth in productivity. Similarly, the theory predicts that if new accession countries joining the European Monetary Union experience a period of accelerated growth as they catch up to richer European countries, they likewise should expect pressure for real appreciation. Since a monetary union effectively implies that the exchange rate is fixed, this pressure should be expressed in this case as a higher inflation rate for countries with higher growth rates. The principle remains the same: higher rates of growth are associated with a rise in the relative cost of living.

The prevalence of the theory behind the Balassa-Samuelson effect in economics owes much to its elegant explanation of the basic price-income relationship. But it has received criticism for the assumptions needed to derive it. There is evidence that productivity gains, especially recently, are not limited to manufactured goods, but that the wealth of relatively rich countries is in part attributable to significant productivity gains in many services, such as information technology and retail. Furthermore, it also appears to be true that many services, especially information services, are becoming more tradable due to new telecommunications technologies. As changes in technology and transportation costs lead to significant changes in the volume of trade and even the types of goods and services that are most traded, it is not entirely clear what the future holds for the Balassa-Samuelson effect.

See also equilibrium exchange rate; exchange rate forecasting; purchasing power parity; real exchange rate

FURTHER READING

Balassa, Bela. 1964. "The Purchasing-Power Parity Doctrine: A Reappraisal." *Journal of Political Economy* 72 (6): 584–96. One of two original sources for the theory.

Bergin, Paul R., Reuven Glick, and Alan M. Taylor. 2006. "Productivity, Tradability, and the Long-run Price Puzzle." *Journal of Monetary Economics* 53 (8): 2041–66. Documents empirically that the fundamental Balassa-Samuelson observation is only a modern phenomenon, but that it has strengthened steadily over time.

Officer, Lawrence H. 1982. *Purchasing Power Parity and Exchange Rates: Theory, Evidence, and Relevance.* Greenwich, CT: JAI Press. Documents weakness of the empirical support for the Balassa-Samuelson theory in early data.

Samuelson, Paul A. 1964. "Theoretical Notes on Trade Problems." *Review of Economics and Statistics* 46 (2): 145–54. One of two original sources for the theory.

———. 1994. "Facets of Balassa-Samuelson Thirty Years Later." *Review of International Economics* 2 (3): 201–26. A retrospective commentary on the theory by one of the original authors.

PAUL BERGIN

■ band, basket, and crawl (BBC)

BBC (basket, band, and crawl) constitute the three pillars of an intermediate exchange-rate regime. A currency that uses all three pillars has its central rate (and margins) defined in terms of a basket of currencies rather than a single currency such as the dollar. It has a wide band around the central rate, perhaps plus or minus 5, 10, or 15 percent, within which the currency floats, but at the edge of which the central bank is obligated to intervene to prevent the market rate going outside the band. Its central rate crawls rather than jumps; when it needs to move, it does so in a series of small, periodic steps rather than occasional abrupt changes. The three component elements were developed by different economists and were driven by different considerations, so they can be analyzed separately even though they tend to appeal to the same group of economists and to be used by the same set of countries. Although in practice there may be a strong complementarity among the three components, it is possible and helpful to consider them separately.

Baskets Before the break-up of the Bretton Woods system in the early 1970s there was no need to consider pegging to a basket of currencies since the major currencies were stable in relation to one another. It became clear that this was not going to continue after the advent of generalized floating in March 1973. Shortly thereafter the International Monetary Fund (IMF) redefined the value of its artificial reserve asset, the special drawing right (SDR), in terms of a basket of the 16 currencies of countries with more than 1 percent of world exports in the base period. When Jordan began to peg to the SDR, it was therefore indirectly pegging to a basket of currencies. This was the first instance of a peg to a basket.

The theoretical basis of the basket peg evolved shortly thereafter, in a number of papers that sought to develop rules for how developing countries should conduct their exchange-rate policies in a world where the major currencies were floating and therefore moving randomly against one another. The first major paper along these lines was that of Stanley Black (1976). He argued that in a context of generalized floating the strategic variable that affected a country's macroeconomic position was not its bilateral exchange rate with any single currency, but its effective (i.e., trade-weighted) exchange rate. According to Black, the weights in the effective exchange rate (EER) should reflect trade, both exports and imports, in goods and services—in other words,

the EER should be a concept broader than just commodity trade but narrower than all transactions that go through the foreign exchange market, in that it should not include capital flows. He also discussed whether the weights should reflect the currency of denomination or the direction of trade, preferring the latter on the ground that this was more relevant in the longer run. He recognized that there would be institutional costs in pegging to a basket, stemming from the fact that one could not intervene in a basket. (One can argue that the main cost of pegging to a basket accrues not—as Black assumed—because of the enhanced calculation costs of the monetary authority, but because it deprives traders of the possibility under normal circumstances of covering forward by utilizing the forward markets of the country's intervention currency.) If, but only if, a country decided that those institutional costs outweighed the macroeconomic benefits of pegging to a basket, then a country should peg to that single currency which minimizes the variance of its EER.

Several subsequent writers entered the debate. The possibility of a number of developing countries all pegging to the SDR was considered, the advantage being that this would avoid arbitrary changes in their cross-rates. Williamson (1982) argued that there was widespread agreement among the authors surveyed in the article that the peg should be chosen with a view to stabilizing something rather than optimizing anything. Specifically, the peg should be picked so as to minimize the instability in real income and inflation imposed by movements in third currencies that are noise to the domestic economy. This is the philosophy that lies behind the first B of BBC. It is perhaps best exemplified by the policy pursued for many years by the Monetary Authority of Singapore.

In recent years proposals for basket pegs have been advanced primarily in the context of East Asia. Several writers (e.g., Williamson 2005) have argued that the motivation to tie the region's currencies to the dollar arises not out of a mercantilist desire for export surpluses but as a response to the fear of losing competitiveness vis-à-vis one another. The way to overcome this collective action problem while avoiding wasting resources on large current account surpluses as a by-product of dollar depreciation is for all the countries of the region to use a *common* basket peg. (In the case of floating currencies, countries might treat the common basket as a *numéraire*, the unit in terms of which the value of the currency is defined, though this gives less assurance that the market exchange rate would move in parallel to the basket.)

Band Discussion of a wide band for the exchange rate (then called a widening of the gold points) can be traced back to some of John Maynard Keynes's writings in the interwar period, but in the postwar period it was revived by a Brookings Institution report (Salant et al. 1963) and an influential paper of George Halm (1965). Halm looked to a wide band with permanently fixed central rates to enable exchange rate movements to make a worthwhile contribution to the adjustment of balance of payments positions, while decreasing the need for identical monetary policies in different countries and therefore increasing the ability of monetary policy to achieve internal balance. It was this latter aspect on which most subsequent attention focused.

Later authors have differed sharply from Halm in viewing a wide band as complementary to, rather than competitive with, a crawl of the central rate. Few recent analysts have agreed with him in thinking that variations in the exchange rate within the band could be expected to make a worthwhile contribution to payments adjustment; it is changes in the central rate that were expected to do the heavy lifting in that regard. However, the freedom to vary monetary policy has been emphasized by many writers (McKinnon 1971). Williamson (2000) emphasized that this is one of four reasons for favoring a wide zone. A second reason is the difficulty in identifying the equilibrium exchange rate (a rate that is usually conceived as consistent with a sustainable balance of payments outcome) with any precision; there is no point in distorting macroeconomic policy in order to defend an exchange rate target if there is a chance that the rate is not misaligned in the first place. A third reason for a wide zone is to permit nontraumatic changes in the central rate. The analysis here goes back to Harry Johnson (1970), who showed that there would be no incentive to speculate if the change

in the central rate were sufficiently small that the new and old bands overlapped; the wider the band, the easier it is to satisfy this condition. The fourth reason is the desirability of being able to accommodate strong capital flows in part by changes in the exchange rate rather than compelling them to be met entirely by reserve changes.

In 1988 Paul Krugman showed that a credible band would help the authorities to enlist support from speculators in stabilizing the exchange rate (the definitive version was published as Krugman 1991). The intuitive argument was that as the exchange rate approached the margin, speculators would understand that it was increasingly likely to move back toward the central rate, because if it tried to move beyond the edge of the band this would merely provoke the central bank into intervention rather than lead to a further change in the rate. Speculators would therefore be induced to enter the market and help stabilize the rate. The mere promise of official intervention at the margin would suffice to stabilize the rate, without any need for the central bank to actually intervene. First tests of the experience of the European Exchange Rate Mechanism (ERM) were reassuring: it did indeed seem that expectations within the ERM were mean-reverting, in contrast to those that hold in a floating system. But further tests created doubts: Krugman's model predicted that exchange rates would spend most of their time close to the edges of the band, but this did not seem to have happened in the ERM (Svensson 1992). One could reconcile the findings, for example, by intramarginal intervention, but that cast doubt on whether the target zone was really fulfilling its key purpose of making expectations stabilizing. And the ERM was not altogether credible, as is required for Krugman's theorem to apply.

Crawl A central rate is said to be adjusted according to a crawl if its changes are "small." Just how small is best answered by the Johnson analysis cited earlier: a rate is crawling if the old band (prior to the change in central rate) overlaps with the new band. By that test one would count the pre-1987 ERM central rates as mostly crawling, since, although there was no legal obligation for the bands to overlap, in practice changes in the central rate were usually small enough to produce such an overlap.

A crawl may have several motivations. Probably the principal aim in practice has been to neutralize differential inflation and prevent a country that is inflating faster than the international norm from eroding its competitiveness. This is what led several Latin American countries (first Chile in 1965, then Colombia in 1967, and Brazil in 1968) to institute a crawl in the 1960s. Nowadays we tend to think that there is not much to be gained by running a high rate of inflation, but countries caught up in high inflation found difficulty in reducing it quickly and were acutely interested in preventing it from undermining their trade performance.

A much less common but surely more constructive purpose has been to neutralize biased productivity growth, for example, the bias in favor of tradables that typically comes as a by-product of rapid productivity growth (the so-called Balassa-Samuelson effect). Chile's crawl allowed 2 percent a year in real appreciation for this effect from 1995 until Chile floated in 1998.

Changes in the central rate may also be motivated by the desire to contribute to balance of payments adjustment. A country that wishes to improve its underlying balance of payments position will usually be advised to seek a more competitive exchange rate as one incentive for adjustment. Unless a government chooses to float its currency, it will have to accept a gradual adjustment, so that the incentive for capital flows can be offset by the interest differential. It was the desire to maintain a reasonable balance in international payments that motivated most of the parity adjustments in the early-phase ERM.

Why a BBC System? Perhaps the most basic argument in favor of the BBC regime is that this is the system best calculated to limit misalignments (defined as deviations of the market exchange rate from its equilibrium value), and that misalignments are the principal drawback of both of the alternative regimes. Fixed rates can become inappropriate through differential inflation, Balassa-Samuelson productivity bias, or a real shock that creates a need for balance of payments adjustment. Fixed rates are appropriate

only where there is reasonable certainty that none of these dangers will materialize: where the economy is small and open so as to satisfy the optimum currency area conditions; where it trades predominantly with the currency area to which it plans to peg; where it is comfortable with the inflation policy of that area; and where it is content to adopt institutional arrangements that will guarantee perpetuation of the fixed rate. Flexible rates follow a random walk: they are frequently pushed away from the level that would support a satisfactory evolution of the real economy. A BBC regime provides guidance as to what is considered the longer-run equilibrium rate and mandates action to bring the rate back to that vicinity when it deviates significantly from it. It is true that one advantage of a float, in comparison to the BBC regime, is that this permits a needed adjustment to be made instantaneously, rather than being strung out over time, with the need to retain an offsetting interest differential. There is no guarantee, however, that the private market will choose to make an adjustment at the right time or in the right direction. It is this fear that unguided markets will lead to misalignments that motivates support for the BBC regime.

See also balance of payments; Balassa-Samuelson effect; Bretton Woods system; effective exchange rate; equilibrium exchange rate; exchange rate regimes; exchange rate volatility; hedging; special drawing rights; speculation

FURTHER READING

Black, Stanley W. 1976. "Exchange Policies for Less Developed Countries in a World of Floating Rates." Princeton Essays in International Finance No. 119. Princeton, NJ: Princeton University.

Collignon, Stefan, Jean Pisani-Ferry, and Yung Chul Park. 1999. *Exchange Rate Policies in Emerging Asian Countries*. London: Routledge.

Halm, George N. 1965. "The 'Band' Proposal: The Limits of Permissible Exchange Rate Variations." Princeton Special Papers in International Finance No. 6. Princeton, NJ: Princeton University.

Johnson, Harry G. 1970. "A Technical Note on the Width of the Band Required to Accommodate Parity Changes of Particular Size." In *Approaches to Greater Flexibility of*

Exchange Rates: The Bürgenstock Papers, edited by G. N. Halm. Princeton, NJ: Princeton University Press, 280–82.

Krugman, Paul. 1991. "Target Zones and Exchange Rate Dynamics." *Quarterly Journal of Economics* 106 (3) (August): 669–82.

McKinnon, Ronald I. 1971. "Monetary Theory and Controlled Flexibility in the Foreign Exchanges." Princeton Essays in International Finance No. 84. Princeton, NJ: Princeton University.

Salant, Walter S., Emile Despres, Lawrence B. Krause, Alice M. Rivlin, William A. Salant, and Lorie Tarshis. 1963. *The United States Balance of Payments in 1968*. Washington, DC: Brookings Institution.

Svensson, Lars E. O. 1992. "An Interpretation of Recent Research on Exchange Rate Target Zones." *Journal of Economic Perspectives* 6 (4) (fall): 119–44.

Williamson, John. 1982. "A Survey of the Emergent Literature on the Optimal Peg." *Journal of Development Economics* 11: 39–61.

———. 2000. *Exchange Rate Regimes for Emerging Markets: Reviving the Intermediate Option*. Washington, DC: Institute for International Economics.

———. 2005. "A Currency Basket for East Asia, Not Just China." Policy Briefs in International Economics PB05-1. Washington, DC: Institute for International Economics.

JOHN WILLIAMSON

■ Bank for International Settlements (BIS)

The Bank for International Settlements (BIS) was established in 1929, when representatives of the World War I reparations conference set up a committee of experts to provide a definitive financial framework for German war reparations. The BIS was chartered the following year in Switzerland under an international convention. The new institution appealed to different constituencies with different interests. The Germans wanted to increase their exports and link the size of their obligations to capacity to pay; the French sought to replace a debt of the German government to private investors with a debt owed directly to the French government and, ulti-mately, to thwart German industrial development; the British were keen to secure enough payments to settle their debt with the United States; and the United States aimed to separate reparations from war debts. But war reparations were only one part of the BIS mission; the other involved extending and deepening cooperation among central banks.

From the beginning, the BIS was a club of central bankers interested in preserving their independence from finance ministries and governments in general. Emblematic of the distinction between central bankers and governments was the decision of the U.S. government not to allow the Federal Reserve System to join the BIS because membership was believed to conflict with the official U.S. position on reparations. Over time, the distinction between central bankers and governments became less sharp, although it still exists; for example, the chair of the Basel Committee on Banking Supervision must be a central bank governor.

The launching of the new institution suffered from poor timing, with much of the industrialized world sliding into economic depression. German war reparations certainly did not help the international economy. In 1931, the Credit-Anstalt, a large bank based in Vienna, went bankrupt, sparking a banking crisis that spread to Germany, Britain, the United States, and most of the countries on the gold standard. The BIS acted as a crisis manager and lent to the central banks of Austria, Hungary, Germany, and Yugoslavia, but the treatment was too feeble for the disease. At the core of the problem was an inability of policymakers to understand that feasible cooperation was inadequate to sustain the combination of a gold standard and high employment. The BIS remained a staunch supporter of the gold standard. This position, in addition to allegations that the institution had been too much under (Nazi) German influence before and during World War II, almost brought the BIS to extinction at the Bretton Woods conference in July 1944; it was saved by the Europeans (Toniolo 2005, chap. 8).

The BIS after World War II After World War II, the surviving BIS was out of step with the prevailing economic paradigm and policy prescriptions. The institution emphasized budget discipline, sound money, free trade, and international monetary co-operation, and had little sympathy for mechanical applications of the standard Keynesian model. Furthermore, central bankers, the BIS's clientele, had lost much of their luster and prestige because of their support of the gold standard in the interwar period. Inevitably, power shifted to finance ministers, who made central banks subordinate to government. Yet, despite this decline in power and prestige, the BIS remained an important forum for central bankers and the international financial community to discuss and find agreement on critical issues of monetary policy and financial stability.

The terms of reference for cooperation have changed over time. In the interwar period, cooperation meant to sustain and "lubricate" the mechanisms of the gold standard. In the 1950s, the focus was on the mechanism of the European Payments Union, in which member countries offset debits and credits in inconvertible European currencies on the books of the BIS and settled balances in convertible currencies. In the 1960s, the BIS became a central point for the discussion of the tensions that were developing in the gold-dollar exchange standard.

Arrangements were made by central banks and among central banks, sometimes using the BIS as the organizer. Central bankers were searching for ways to defend themselves against speculative attacks. The defense arsenal included mutual guarantees all the way to the prohibition of converting funds placed by foreign speculators. Guarantees were implemented by means of swap agreements among central banks and the stipulation that a central bank would repay borrowed funds at the original exchange rate. The techniques evolved over the years. In the mid-1960s, the BIS began to provide regular reviews and analysis of the Eurodollar and Eurocurrencies markets, as well as quarterly statistics on bank lending in the G10 group of countries (Belgium, Canada, France, Germany, Italy, Japan, the Netherlands, Sweden, the United Kingdom, and the United States) and Switzerland to approximately 100 individual countries.

The demise of the Bretton Woods system in 1973 did not spell the end of international financial crises and the role played by the BIS club. On the contrary, financial liberalization in many nations and the abolition of capital and exchange controls exposed the international financial community to more and bigger crises; large currency, debt, and banking crises occurred in Mexico in 1982 and 1994, Southeast Asia in 1997, Russia in 1998, Brazil in 1999, and Argentina in 2001.

The BIS after Bretton Woods The end of Bretton Woods rejuvenated the BIS through a different agenda: European monetary integration and financial regulation. European monetary integration was the natural extension of the European Payments Union. As to financial regulation, the BIS became involved in it after the failure of a German bank, Bankhaus Herstatt, in 1974. Before this date the fixed exchange-rate regime was buttressed by exchange controls and domestic regulation that reduced the risk of financial crises.

Some central banks are also bank regulators and supervisors (e.g., the Bank of Italy); others share this responsibility with other financial regulatory agencies (e.g., the Federal Reserve System); others retain some responsibilities but the bulk of these lies with other government agencies (e.g., Deutsche Bundesbank); and some have no regulatory role aside from that pertaining to the payments system (e.g., Bank of Canada). In practice, however, it is difficult to separate "narrow" central banking from regulation. Even a "narrow" central bank needs credit information on financial participants to prevent losses to either itself or participants in the payments system. Thus it is not surprising that central bank governors considered financial regulation as part of their mandate (Fratianni and Pattison 2001, 205–6).

The BIS acts as a host and secretariat for various committees on financial regulation, of which the best known is the Basel Committee on Banking Supervision (BCBS), which promulgates international standards and "best practices." The BCBS works with national banking regulators, among others, and also participates more broadly, where required, with securities regulators and insurance regulators. In 1988, a new regime, the Basel Capital Accord, or Basel I, went into effect: internationally active banks were subject to a somewhat common regime for minimum capital requirements. Basel I linked banks' capital requirements to their credit risk through mandated weights for different categories of bank credit. Basel I was ultimately adopted by more than 100 countries and was deemed a success, despite criticism of the crudeness and political bias of the mandated weights: for example, the preferential treatment given to government debtors and to industrial countries that were members of the Organization for Economic Cooperation and Development (OECD).

For several years now, the financial and prudential regulatory committees meeting in Basel have been working on Basel II, a new international agreement on bank capital measurement and minimum capital requirements (BCBS 2004). The main innovation of Basel II is to assess credit risk as the markets would, in contrast to mandated fixed weights. Market-sensitive credit risk assessment, however, requires expensive investments in sophisticated risk management systems and, in practice, can best be implemented by large and internationally active banks. These systems would pay off in terms of lower capital requirements. Smaller banks, instead, would rely on the cheaper and mechanistic formulas of Basel I. Basel II, which has yet to go into effect, got stuck because of U.S. opposition. Small U.S. banks perceive that large banks will gain a competitive advantage, through lower capital requirements, by the implementation of Basel II and have pushed for changes in it. The proposed changes, in turn, would make investment in sophisticated risk management systems cost ineffective and consequently would frustrate one of the main objectives of the new accord.

In sum, the BIS was created with two initial objectives: handling German war reparations payments and promoting and extending central bank cooperation. The first objective is long gone; the second remains central to the current activities of the BIS. The effectiveness of this institution rests on the confidence and commitments that can be made by a relatively small number of players who meet frequently and in relative seclusion to ensure a high degree of confidentiality. The geographical expansion of the BIS in Asia and Latin America, in the early part of the 21st century, suggests a strategy of enlarging the size of the club.

See also Bretton Woods system; capital controls; convertibility; currency crisis; euro; European Monetary Union; Federal Reserve Board; financial crisis; gold standard, international; international liquidity; International Monetary Fund (IMF); speculation

FURTHER READING

Basel Committee on Banking Supervision. 2004. *Basel II: International Convergence of Capital Measurement and Capital Standards: a Revised Framework*. Basel: Bank for International Settlements. Summarizes the work of the Basel Committee on Banking Supervision to revise capital standards for internationally active banks.

Fratianni, Michele, and John C. Pattison. 2001. "The Bank for International Settlements: An Assessment of its Role in International Monetary and Financial Policy Coordination." *Open Economies Review* 12 (2): 197–222. Reviews the role of the BIS and its adaptability to the changing international financial structure, from the gold standard to floating exchange rates.

Toniolo, Gianni, with the assistance of Piet Clement. 2005. *Central Bank Cooperation at the Bank for International Settlements, 1930–1973*. New York: Cambridge University Press. Offers the most comprehensive history of the BIS from inception to the end of the Bretton Woods system.

MICHELE FRATIANNI

■ Bank of Japan

The Bank of Japan was established in 1882, under the direction of the Ministry of Finance, to be the sole issuer of convertible notes in Japan. The first substantial revision of the Bank of Japan Law occurred in 1942, when the central bank was given the broad objective to conduct its operations "solely for the achievement of national aims" (article 2). There was no mention of financial or price stability, and the law was designed to support Japan's wartime military effort (Cargill, Hutchison, and Ito 1997 and 2000). In response to the triple-digit inflation in Japan immediately after World War II, in part due to monetization of government deficits, a change in the Finance Law was made in 1947 that provided the Bank of Japan a degree of independence from government deficit financing (e.g., prohibiting the bank from underwriting government bonds or making loans to the government except under some conditions).

In 1949 the Bank of Japan Law was again amended, mainly to provide an overall management structure to the bank by establishing a Policy Board consisting of five voting and two nonvoting members. The Policy Board was given primary authority for almost every aspect of monetary and financial policy operations of the Bank of Japan. Although the Ministry of Finance held a nonvoting position on the Policy Board, the Bank of Japan Law gave the ministry overall control over the bank and the ability to influence policy decisions, if not to determine them outright. For example, the cabinet had the authority to dismiss the governor and vice governor, and the minister of finance could dismiss executive directors, auditors, and advisors of the Bank of Japan "whenever it is deemed particularly necessary for the attainment of the objective of the Bank" (article 47).

New Bank of Japan Law The basic institutional and legal framework governing the Bank of Japan was unchanged during most of the postwar period until creation of the "new" central bank under the changes of the law in 1998 (Cargill, Hutchison, and Ito 2000). A number of economic and political events prompted the change in the law, including widespread dissatisfaction with the Ministry of Finance's handling of the serious banking problem. In particular, the Ministry of Finance was slow to address the bank's nonperforming loan problem (brought on by the collapse of the bubble economy, recession, and poor lending practices), the liquidation of the *jusen* industry (subsidiaries of financial institutions specializing in real estate loans), and other aspects of its response to the financial crisis that had burdened Japan since the early 1990s.

The 1998 Bank of Japan Law fundamentally changed the formal operating objectives of the central bank, its formal relationship to the government, its role in banking supervision, and other functions. Two elements are central to the reform. First, unlike the 1942 law, the new law specified two operating principles for currency and monetary control: the pursuit of price stability (article 2) and the maintenance of an orderly financial system (article 1). The law clearly states that the Bank of Japan is responsible for price stability and shares responsibility for financial stability with other parts of the government. Second, the bank was given much more autonomy from the government and in particular from the minister of finance. The new law states, for example, that autonomy for monetary and currency control shall be respected, and the Ministry of Finance's power to remove Bank of Japan officers was significantly limited. A number of other important changes were also made in the new law, including in the areas of governance and policy formulation, transparency and accountability, budgeting, lender-of-last-resort functions, exchange rate intervention, and government financing.

Conduct of Monetary Policy The conduct of monetary policy has gone through a number of distinct changes during the postwar period. The years immediately following the war were characterized by a chaotic environment and triple-digit inflation during 1946–48. From the mid-1950s to the early 1970s, Japanese monetary policy operated under the constraints of the Bretton Woods fixed exchange system, a period of very high growth, economic progress, and moderate inflation. The early 1970s were again a chaotic period: buffeted by the first oil-price shock and double-digit inflation (called "wild" inflation), Japan struggled to recover a nominal anchor following the breakdown of the Bretton Woods fixed exchange rate system.

The Bank of Japan then introduced a "money-focused" monetary policy in the mid-1970s that served to gradually lower inflation and then keep it at low levels, combined with very strong economic performance through the 1980s (Hutchison 1986). The Bank of Japan, despite its legal dependence on the Ministry of Finance, and facing the constraints imposed by the wartime conditions of the 1942 law, achieved an extremely successful policy record from 1975 to 1990. The price stabilization record of the Bank of Japan, combined with sustained real growth of the Japanese economy during this period, attracted international attention. The Bank of Japan appeared to be a stark exception to the conventional wisdom that the legal independence of central banks is necessary to generate good inflation records (Cargill, Hutchison, and Ito 1997). The biggest dilemma the Bank of Japan faced at the end of this period—the latter part of the 1980s—was how to respond to sharp increases in asset price inflation (in retrospect identifiable as an asset price bubble) without affecting other aspects of the economy, which otherwise seemed to be performing well, with strong economic growth and low price inflation overall.

The 1990s brought a completely new set of challenges for the Bank of Japan. The country faced a period of stagnation from 1991 to 2003, with real gross domestic product growth averaging only 1.5 percent, about half that of the rest of the members of the Organisation for Economic Co-operation and Development and much less than Japan's historical norm. During much of the stagnation Japan experienced prolonged deflation, or essentially zero price changes, and a sustained period of near-zero short-term interest rates when the central bank seemed unable to provide additional stimulus to the economy (Hutchison, Ito, and Westermann 2006). During this latter period, much of it when the Bank of Japan was operating independently under the new law, the bank came under severe criticism for not preventing price deflation and not doing more to stimulate the economy. Whether the Bank of Japan could have, or should have, operated differently during this period remains an open question.

See also Bretton Woods system; European Central Bank; exchange rate regimes; Federal Reserve Board; monetary policy rules; money supply

FURTHER READING

Cargill, Thomas, Michael Hutchison, and Takatoshi Ito. 1997. *The Political Economy of Japanese Monetary Policy.* Cambridge, MA: MIT Press. This detailed account of Japanese monetary and financial history from the postwar period through the mid-1990s also provides a historical overview of central banking in Japan, including the creation of the Bank of Japan in 1882 and the 1942 revision in the Bank of Japan Law.

———. 2000. *Financial Policy and Central Banking in Japan.* Cambridge, MA: MIT Press. A detailed history of the Bank of Japan, explaining how the change in the Bank of Japan Law in 1998 came about and why it represents the most fundamental change in the bank since its original charter. All of the quotations from various versions of the Bank of Japan Law come from this volume (chapter 4, titled "The New Bank of Japan"), where the specific sources translated into English are provided.

Hutchison, Michael. 1986. "Japan's 'Money Focused' Monetary Policy." (Federal Reserve Bank of San Francisco) *Economic Review* 3 (summer): 33–46. Explains the importance and economic effects of the Bank of Japan's new monetary policy implemented in the mid-1970s.

Hutchison, Michael, Takatoshi Ito, and Frank Westermann. 2006. "The Great Japanese Stagnation: Lessons for Industrial Countries." In *Japan's Great Stagflation: Financial and Monetary Policy Lessons for Advanced Economies*, edited by Michael Hutchison and Frank Westermann. Cambridge, MA: MIT Press. An account of Japanese monetary policy through the Great Stagnation (1990–2003) and the road to recovery.

MICHAEL HUTCHISON

■ banking crisis

In modern economies, banks play an important role in mediating between borrowers and lenders. Lenders, which are usually households, often do not have profitable investment opportunities on their own and seek high-quality borrowers from whom they can secure a higher rate of return. Households have difficulty finding high-quality borrowers because the financing needs of borrowers are such that the savings of numerous lenders must be aggregated. The coordination costs are simply too high for households to carry out this aggregation. Also, households usually do not have expertise in evaluating the quality of borrowers, so the lender-borrower relationship can be plagued by adverse selection problems (that is, lenders who lack sufficient information to make wise selections may be apt to select "bad" borrowers). Collecting the information on borrowers necessary for evaluating their quality is costly. Modern banks can aggregate the individual savings of lenders and, by developing expertise in evaluation of borrowers, can mitigate adverse selection problems, thereby smoothing the transfer of funds from households to borrowers.

Banks can play other important roles, such as lengthening the maturity structure of loans by borrowing short-term and lending long-term. Banks do this by taking short-term deposits of say, 1 month, and making loans of say 3 years. Moreover, financial markets such as stock and equity markets are volatile and expose households that invest their savings in them to market risk. By accumulating reserves, which are not typically linked to the stock market, banks can lessen the market risk for households that instead deposit their savings in banks.

There are times, however, when the banks' ability to serve this intermediary role is curtailed and banks actually raise the risk level in the financial system. Because banks have a mismatch between short-term liabilities (e.g., demand deposits) and long-term assets (e.g., loans), they are vulnerable to liquidity crises. Such vulnerabilities can lead to bank runs, as a critical mass of depositors suddenly withdraws funds, leaving the bank without liquid assets to carry on their normal business, which in turn may cause more depositors to panic and withdraw their funds.

In addition, when banks are improperly regulated, they are prone to excessive lending and loan creation, leading to a "bubble" in asset prices. The collapse of the bubble can result in defaults, which can lead to serious dislocation of the economy, as happened to Japan in the 1990s. Excessive loan creation abetted by improper regulation is also the root cause of the emerging market crisis of the late 1990s.

Causes of Banking Crises A banking crisis occurs when many depositors attempt to withdraw their funds all at once. In the past, banking crises happened with some frequency in Europe and the United States, particularly during the Depression in the 1930s. Banking crises occur with some frequency in emerging markets. For example, during the turbulent decade of the 1990s, many emerging markets—including Mexico, Thailand, Indonesia, Korea, Argentina, Russia, and Turkey—faced simultaneous banking and currency crises.

There are two traditional views of banking crises: the "fundamentals" view and the "random shocks" view (Allen and Gale 2000). The fundamentals view is that banking crises are a natural phenomenon of the business cycle. A recession will typically increase loan delinquencies and reduce bank equity, sharply lowering the value of bank assets. As depositors receive information about banking-sector weaknesses, they will withdraw their funds, leading to banking-sector insolvencies. According to this view, bank runs are not random events, but a result of the ups and downs of the business cycle.

The random shocks view is that banking crises are a result of herding or mob psychology. According to this view, bank runs are largely self-fulfilling prophecies (Diamond and Dybvig 1983). If depositors believe that a bank run is about to happen, they will withdraw their funds all at once and a bank run will occur. If depositors believe that bank runs will *not* happen, then they will stay put and a bank run will not occur. A good rendition of the random shocks view is a scene in the movie *It's a Wonderful Life*, in which depositors hear rumors about a failing savings and loan and mob its window. The depositors calm down and stay put when the character played by Jimmy Stewart confidently stresses that the savings and loan is actually doing fine.

In well-supervised jurisdictions, banking regulators promulgate rules and conduct inspections of banks to ensure that they are prudent in their lending, so that when a downturn inevitably comes, banks' balance sheets are not unduly impaired. A bank with an impaired balance sheet has many loans for which the collection of principal and interest is difficult. Thus, the loans will probably have to be written off as a loss. Should bank balance sheets become impaired, the country's central bank usually serves as the lender of last resort to banks, so that bank runs will not occur. Deposit insurance can serve the same role as "blanket insurance" by the central bank, since the government will "bail out" depositors at a failing bank.

The Late 1990s Banking Crisis in Japan Japan in the late 1990s had a fundamentals-driven banking crisis in which a crash in Japan's equity and real estate markets led to deterioration in bank balance sheets. Dekle and Kletzer (2006) explore the late-1990s crisis in the Japanese banking system and emphasize three key facts about the Japanese financial system at the time: (1) domestic investment was financed primarily by bank loans; (2) the government provided deposit insurance guarantees to the holders of domestic bank deposits; and (3) prudential regulation and enforcement were weak.

Weak prudential regulation in Dekle and Kletzer's model is interpreted as a failure of the government to enforce loan-loss reserve accumulations by banks against nonperforming corporate loans. Banks thus still make dividend payments to their shareholders against the interest collected on their performing and nonperforming loans, when banks should be foreclosing on firms that are in default on their loans. That is, the banks are paying dividends on even the loan repayments they have not yet received. Nonperforming borrowers are kept afloat by further borrowing from banks. Although the public is aware of the mounting nonperforming assets of the banks, they do not withdraw their deposits because of deposit insurance. In effect, deposit insurance allows the banks to transfer resources from the government to their shareholders. Deposit insurance makes the depositors feel safe, so they will keep their deposits even in a failing bank. In the eventuality that a bank fails, the depositors will be bailed out by the government.

If the government fails to intervene by closing banks before a critical date, then the banks' nonperforming loans will exceed the government's ability to borrow. At that point, there is a bank run by depositors, leading to a banking crisis. This appears to be the story of the Japanese banking crisis, from which Japan began to emerge only in 2006.

Twin Crisis in Emerging Markets Another example of a fundamentals-driven banking crisis is the emerging market crisis of the late 1990s. At that time, many emerging market countries were hit not only with a banking crisis but also with a currency crisis, which is characterized by a rapidly depreciating currency, a sharp outflow of foreign exchange, and a slowdown—in fact, almost a depression—in the domestic economy. The phenomenon of a banking crisis occurring simultaneously with a currency crisis is called a "twin" crisis.

Perhaps the best description of a twin crisis is by Diaz-Alejandro (1985), who discussed the Chilean crisis of the early 1980s. Like many emerging markets, Chile had a nationalized banking system. In the 1970s, Chile's banking system was privatized, even to the extent that authorities repeatedly warned the public that deposits were not guaranteed. In early 1981, however, following the cessation of credit payments by a troubled Chilean sugar company, the central bank bailed out several private banks to stem incipient bank runs. Realizing that the Chilean Central Bank stood ready to protect domestic bank deposits, foreign capital rushed in to take advantage of high Chilean interest rates.

By January 1983 the value of the peso fell as the official Chilean exchange rate rose from 39 pesos per U.S. dollar to 75 pesos. Chilean companies and banks with dollar-denominated debt came under great stress. Nonperforming loans of banks rose from 11 percent of their capital at the end of 1980 to 113 percent by May 1983. Foreign depositors became worried and started to withdraw their funds, rapidly depreciating the Chilean peso. The Chilean Central Bank had no choice but to intervene again, formally guaranteeing all deposits to stem the bank runs and injecting massive liquidity into the banking system to recapitalize the banks.

The Chilean experience illustrates the dangers of capital market liberalization with blanket government deposit guarantees. Such blanket guarantees can lead to moral hazard (in which a party insulated from risk engages in riskier behavior), with too much capital flowing in, excessive bank lending, a rise in nonperforming loans, bank failures, and finally, a currency crisis.

See also asymmetric information; bail-ins; bailouts; balance sheet approach/effects; Bank of Japan; capital controls; contagion; currency crisis; deposit insurance; financial crisis; financial liberalization; lender of last resort

FURTHER READING

Allen, F., and D. Gale. 2000. *Comparing Financial Systems.* Cambridge, MA: MIT Press. This is the classic graduate-level textbook and monograph on the theory of different financial systems.

Dekle, R., and K. Kletzer. 2006. "Deposit Insurance, Regulatory Forbearance, and Economic Growth: Implications for the Japanese Banking Crisis." In *Economic Stagnation in Japan*, edited by M. Hutchison and F. Westermann. Cambridge, MA: MIT Press, 345–415. This is the first general equilibrium model of the Japanese banking crisis.

Diamond, D., and P. Dybvig. 1983. "Bank Runs, Deposit Insurance, and Liquidity." *Journal of Political Economy* 91: 401–19. This is the classic and most referenced paper on bank runs.

Diaz-Alejandro, C. 1985. "Goodbye Financial Repression, Hello Financial Crash." *Journal of Development Economics* 19 (1–2): 1–24. Although largely descriptive, this is the first paper on how a banking crisis can lead to a currency crisis.

ROBERT DEKLE

■ Basel Convention

The Basel Convention on the Control of Transboundary Movements of Hazardous Wastes and their Disposal is an international agreement that governs cross-border shipments of toxic waste. Adopted in 1989 and entering into force in 1992, the agreement was a direct response to the growing problem of unregulated waste shipments in the 1980s, particularly between rich and poor countries. Waste exports to developing countries emerged at that time as a result of rising disposal fees in rich countries, the need for foreign exchange in poor countries, and an increasingly fluid global economy that facilitated the trade in waste.

The United Nations Environment Program sponsored negotiations on the Basel Convention in the late 1980s following public outcry in response to waste export scandals involving poor countries. The agreement covers toxic, poisonous, explosive, corrosive, flammable, eco-toxic, and infectious wastes. As of October 2007, there were 170 parties to the Basel Convention.

The objectives of the Basel Convention are to reduce the transboundary movement of hazardous wastes, encourage the treatment and disposal of hazardous wastes as close as possible to their generation, and minimize the generation of hazardous wastes.

The agreement governs the international trade in hazardous waste through a system of informed notification and consent. Exporting states must notify the importing country in writing before they ship hazardous waste and must receive consent in writing from the importing state before the shipment can be made. This system allows states to decide case by case whether they wish to accept a particular shipment. Parties to the agreement are prohibited from exporting hazardous waste to states that have banned its import. They are also prohibited from exporting waste to nonparties unless a bilateral or regional agreement allows such trade, provided it is disposed of in no less environmentally sound a manner than that called for in the Basel Convention. Parties to the agreement are encouraged to export hazardous wastes to other countries only if they themselves lack the capacity to dispose of it in an environmentally sound manner, or if the importing country considers the waste a raw material.

Immediately after the Basel Convention was adopted, a number of developing countries and non-governmental organizations (NGOs) criticized it for having a weak control mechanism. Critics had wanted the agreement to place an outright ban on the trade in hazardous waste between rich and poor countries, but the adopted agreement only regulated exports of waste between these groups of countries. In addition, some countries continued to export hazardous wastes to developing countries for the purpose of recycling, thereby evading the Basel Convention's control mechanism because the material was not identified as hazardous. Throughout the early 1990s environmental NGOs documented a significant number of toxic waste exports to developing countries for recycling purposes. Most of these exports were recycled in environmentally unsound ways, or were in fact not recycled at all and were simply disposed of.

Basel Ban In response to these concerns, developing countries and NGOs worked to strengthen the convention in the early 1990s. In 1995, at the second conference of the parties to the agreement, the parties adopted an amendment to the convention that bans outright the export of hazardous waste destined for either disposal or recycling from Annex VII countries (parties that are members of the European Union or the Organisation for Economic Co-operation and Development, and Lichtenstein) to non–Annex VII countries. This amendment, which has come to be known as the Basel Ban, required ratification by three-fourths of the parties in order to come into force. Many assumed that this number would be 62, as there were 82 parties to the Basel Convention when the Basel Ban amendment was adopted. Uncertainty emerged, however, over ratification procedures when the number of ratifications approached 62: whether the amendment required ratification by three-fourths of the parties at the time it was adopted, three-fourths of the parties present when it was adopted, or three-fourths of the current number of parties. It is expected that the 2008 Conference of the Parties to the Basel Convention will adopt a decision that will resolve this ambiguity. As of October 2007 there were 63 ratifications of the Basel Ban amendment.

In the late 1990s, the parties to the Basel Convention also adopted a classification system for hazardous wastes that delineates more clearly which wastes the treaty covers, including those destined for recycling operations. This system has clarified the scope of the convention considerably.

Challenges for Enforcement The Basel Convention has curtailed some types of hazardous waste exports to developing countries, but two major challenges have emerged that illustrate the difficulty of full enforcement.

The first of these challenges concerns the export of ships containing toxic materials to developing countries for scrapping. Since the mid-1990s, industrial countries have exported a number of ships to scrap yards in developing countries, most commonly India and Bangladesh, for decommissioning. These ships often contain highly toxic materials such as polychlorinated biphenyls (PCBs) and asbestos. In developing countries, ships are commonly dismantled in dangerous and environmentally unsound conditions. Because the ships are technically in use when exported and often not designated as waste material until on the high seas or until they reach their final destination, many have escaped control under the rules of the Basel Convention. Environmental NGOs such as the Basel Action Network (BAN) and Greenpeace have launched campaigns to halt this practice by exposing the failure of exporting states to enforce the Basel Convention when toxic ships are exported from their ports. These efforts have had some success, such as the 2006 decision of the French government to halt the export of the *Clemenceau*, which had been destined for scrapping in India.

The second challenge has to do with the export of electronic waste (e-waste), including discarded computers, mobile phones, and other electronic equipment. E-waste, which contains numerous toxic components, including heavy metals and polyvinyl chloride (PVC), is an especially fast-growing waste stream in industrial countries. Much of this waste has been exported to developing countries, such as China and Nigeria, without being subjected to the Basel Convention rules on notification and consent, and despite bans in those countries on the import of toxic waste. Often these wastes are exported under the pretense of reuse, when in practice they are recycled or simply land-filled. The conditions under which these wastes are recycled and disposed of in these locations are dangerous and environmentally unsound. Several factors have contributed to the continued export of e-waste to developing countries, including the facts that it can escape control when it is exported for reuse even if most of it is broken and beyond repair, and that customs officials lack knowledge about the hazardous nature of second-hand electronic components. Environmental groups such as BAN have called for pretesting of secondhand electronics before shipment to determine whether they are suitable for reuse or are simply hazardous wastes that would then be bound by the rules of the Basel Convention.

At the same time that the parties to the Basel Convention are considering ways to address these continuing problems with the transboundary movement of hazardous wastes, they have broadened the emphasis of the treaty for its second decade. Environmentally sound management of hazardous waste, as well as the prevention or minimization of such waste, has received more attention. Much of the work of the Basel Convention Secretariat now focuses on enhancing technical and administrative capacity to minimize waste generation and manage hazardous waste safely, especially in developing countries.

The Basel Convention has served an important role in the global economy by regulating the trade in what many consider to be "bads" as opposed to "goods." The parties to the agreement have taken considerable steps toward banning the export of toxic wastes from rich to poor countries. Although the difficulties of monitoring and enforcement allow certain types of toxic waste exports to continue, without the Basel Convention it is likely that the problem of unwanted hazardous waste exports to poor countries would be far worse.

See also multilateral environmental agreements; trade and the environment

FURTHER READING

Clapp, Jennifer. 2001. *Toxic Exports: The Transfer of Hazardous Wastes from Rich to Poor Countries*. Ithaca, NY: Cornell University Press. Outlines the economic aspects of the problem of hazardous waste trade between industrial and developing countries.

Kanthak, Judit. 1999. *Ships for Scrap: Steel and Toxic Wastes for Asia*. Hamburg: Greenpeace. First major report on the environmental impact of ship scrapping in developing countries.

Krueger, Jonathan. 1999. *International Trade and the Basel Convention*. London: Earthscan. Examines the legal relationship between the Basel Convention and international trade rules under the World Trade Organization.

Kummer, Katharina. 1995. *International Management of Hazardous Wastes: The Basel Convention and Related Legal Rules*. Oxford: Oxford University Press. Provides a comprehensive and authoritative account of the legal aspects of the Basel Convention.

O'Neill, K. 2000. *Waste Trading among Rich Nations: Building a New Theory of Environmental Regulation*. Cambridge, MA: MIT Press. Examines the particular problem of hazardous waste trade among industrialized countries.

Puckett, Jim, et al. 2002. *Exporting Harm: The High-Tech Trashing of Asia*. Seattle: Basel Action Network and Silicon Valley Toxics Coalition. First major study to document the environmental and social implications of e-waste recycling in Asia.

———. 2005. *The Digital Dump: Exporting Re-Use and Abuse to Africa*. Seattle: Basel Action Network. Major study by the leading environmental group working on waste issues revealing the extent of e-waste exports in Africa.

JENNIFER CLAPP

■ beggar-thy-neighbor policies

Beggar-thy-neighbor policies are those that seek to increase domestic economic welfare at the expense of other countries' welfare. What might be called the classic case of beggar-thy-neighbor policies occurs when one country devalues its currency in order to boost its domestic output and employment but, by so doing, shifts the output and employment problem onto other countries. This occurred in the 1930s when, faced with a worldwide recession, countries sought to increase their own output and employment by devaluing their currencies, a policy that would boost domestic output by reducing the demand for imports and increasing the demand for exports. This exacerbated the recessions in other countries, however, and invited the response of devaluations by other countries—and countries became locked into a series of competitive devaluations.

The experience of the 1930s played a significant part in the design of the Bretton Woods system. This system, by restricting the flow of capital internationally, provided countries with sufficient policy autonomy to target domestic output and employment levels without having to resort to changing the exchange rate. One of the aims of the Bretton Woods system in introducing fixed exchange rates was therefore to obviate the need for competitive devaluations and remove the temptation of beggar-thy-neighbor policies.

With the move to flexible exchange rate regimes since 1973 after the collapse of the Bretton Woods system, beggar-thy-neighbor policies—or the possibility of them—have occasionally resurfaced. For instance, following the Asian crisis of 1997, when the currencies of Thailand, Indonesia, Malaysia, and South Korea all plummeted, China came under considerable international pressure not to devalue the renminbi, which would likely have further destabilized the crisis-affected countries and led to a new round of currency depreciations. China maintained the value of the renminbi. Similarly, one of the arguments made for trading rivals adopting dollar or euro pegs is that it removes the possibility of beggar-thy-neighbor exchange rate policies. The creation of the euro provided similar benefits to its European members.

Historically, the classic term *beggar-thy-neighbor* has been associated with countries devaluing their currencies to increase domestic output and employment at the expense of other countries. More recently, however, the term has been used more generically to describe policies pursued by one country (or jurisdiction within one country) to increase its economic welfare at the expense of other countries (or jurisdictions), whether the mechanism is exchange rate policy, tax policy, competition policy, or foreign investment policy. Any policies that may have negative spillovers for other jurisdictions are now often referred to as beggar-thy-neighbor policies (Guha 2006).

The solution to the use of beggar-thy-neighbor policies in the 1930s was found in the international policy coordination instituted under the auspices of the Bretton Woods system. In the post–Bretton Woods period, the International Monetary Fund and the World Trade Organization face the challenge of providing of such coordination.

See also Bretton Woods system; currency crisis; dollar standard; euro; exchange rate regimes; financial crisis; International Monetary Fund (IMF); international policy coordination; World Trade Organization

FURTHER READING

Betts, Caroline, and Michael Devereux. 2000. "International Monetary Policy Coordination and Competitive Depreciation: A Reevaluation." *Journal of Money, Credit, and Banking* 32 (3) (November): 722–45. Argues that the case for international monetary policy coordination, and hence the avoidance of competitive depreciations, depends on the price-setting behavior of firms.

Bordo, Michael, and Barry Eichengreen, eds. 1993. *A Retrospective on the Bretton Woods System: Lessons for International Monetary Reform.* Chicago: University of Chicago Press. A comprehensive analysis of the origins and workings of the Bretton Woods system.

Guha, Krishna. 2006. "IMF Hits at 'Beggar Thy Neighbour' Policies." *Financial Times* (March 8). A discussion of new forms of beggar-thy-neighbor policies.

PAUL BOWLES

■ black market premium

Black market premium refers to the amount in excess of the official exchange rate that must be paid to purchase foreign exchange on an illegal ("black") market. A black market premium typically arises in two different cases: when the official exchange rate is not the rate that would prevail in the commercial market; and when a nation prohibits access to foreign exchange for specified purposes. In the first case, excess demand at the official exchange rate leads to the development of a parallel, unofficial ("black") market in foreign exchange to meet the demand, with the market rate exceeding the official rate. The difference between this rate and the official rate represents the black market premium, and it may exceed the difference between the official rate and the rate that would clear a legal market, because of the risks to sellers from participating in the unofficial ("black") market. In the second case, demand for foreign exchange for the prohibited activity induces the supply of foreign exchange in an illegal ("black") market, provided those seeking it will pay a sufficiently high price. Because of the risk involved in supplying foreign exchange for the illegal activity, sellers will demand a price higher than the official rate. The difference between this rate and the official rate will again represent a black market premium.

A black market premium has arisen most often in the context of fixed exchange rate regimes. The premium typically arises when a country fixes the value of its exchange rate in relation to another currency irrespective of the rate that would prevail in the commercial market. It is akin to the authorities' fixing a price for a commodity at a non-market-clearing level. Figure 1 depicts the situation.

In figure 1, schedule DD reflects demand for foreign exchange, while schedule SS reflects the supply. Under normal circumstances DD will be downward sloping, meaning that demand for foreign

exchange will be greater as the price (in units of domestic currency) declines. Similarly, SS will slope upward, since additional foreign currency will be supplied to the market only as the price (in units of local currency per unit of foreign currency) increases. Provided normal economic conditions prevail, the market can be expected to clear at price P^*, where the supply and demand schedules intersect. At this price, quantity Q^* of foreign exchange will be bought and sold.

When a nation fixes its exchange rate at a non-market-clearing rate, the normal market mechanism is disrupted. At the official exchange rate, P^{OFF}, demand for foreign exchange, Q^{DO}, exceeds the available supply, Q^{SO}. Those wishing to purchase foreign exchange cannot obtain it at the official price in the commercial market. If they seek to obtain foreign exchange from a private source, rather than using the queuing mechanism established by the authorities, they will need to pay more than the official price. The margin will reflect the scarcity value of the foreign exchange, plus a premium to compensate sellers for participating in an illegal ("black") market. This risk can be depicted by a leftward (upward) shift in the supply curve to $S'S'$, making the market-clearing exchange rate, P^B, likely to exceed the clearing rate in a legal market. The difference between the clearing rate in the illegal market, P^B, and the official exchange rate, P^{OFF}, is the black market premium.

In the second case, represented by figure 2, the premium arises because sales and purchases of foreign exchange for the specific activity are illegal. In this case, shadow demand and supply schedules, depicted by the lines DD and SS, occur. The difference between the clearing price in this market, again called P^B, and the official exchange rate will represent a black market premium. The size of this premium may differ from that in the previous case, depending on how the law affects the demand for and supply of foreign exchange for the restricted purpose. If the activity itself is illegal—for example, seeking foreign exchange to buy illegal drugs—risks for the buyer may drive down the price somewhat relative to the case where only the seller faces risks. If the restriction exists alongside a market-clearing exchange

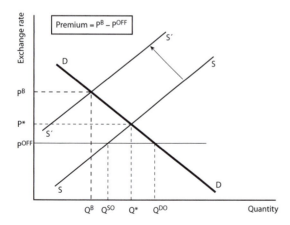

Figure 1
Black market premium when the official rate is not market-clearing

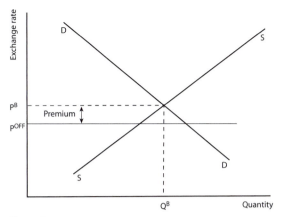

Figure 2

Black market premium for a restricted activity

regime for legal transactions, however, the opportunities for sellers to earn normal profits in the legal market may reduce the supply, and thus raise the price and the size of the black market premium, relative to what would prevail in the previous case of an official rate that is not market-clearing (figure 1).

Whichever situation applies, a black market premium signals a significant imperfection in the exchange market. This, in turn, typically has adverse implications for economic performance. Research has shown that countries with significant black market premiums tend, on average, to have lower rates of economic growth (Fischer 1993). Exchange market imperfections make it hard for foreign exchange to flow to the most productive activities, thus impairing the allocation of resources. In addition, when an overvalued exchange rate is the cause of the problem, firms and individuals must expend additional resources in obtaining foreign exchange. Thus economists typically advocate removing whatever restrictions may be leading to the emergence of black markets in foreign exchange.

See also convertibility; dual exchange rate; exchange rate regimes; foreign exchange intervention; peso problem

FURTHER READING

Fischer, Stanley. 1993. "Role of Macroeconomic Factors in Growth." *Journal of Monetary Economics* 32 (3) (December): 485–512. Argues that larger black market premiums are negatively correlated with economic growth.

Pozo, Susan, and Mark Wheeler. 1999. "Expectations and the Black Market Premium." *Review of International Economics* 7 (2) (May): 245–53. Shows that expectations of devaluation can also affect the size of the premium.

Shachmurove, Yochanan. 1999. "Premium in Black Foreign Exchange Markets: Evidence from Developing Economies." *Journal of Policy Modeling* 21 (1) (January): 1–39. Argues that the size of the black market premium appears to be affected by such factors as the (depreciation-adjusted) differential between the country's interest rates and those in major financial markets, and negatively by exports and the level of the official exchange rate.

JOSHUA GREENE

■ Bonn Summit

During the Bretton Woods era (1944–72), the proportion of dollars in world reserves rose steadily. As a result, it was in the countries with a persistent tendency to run balance of payments deficits (the United States and the United Kingdom) that the shortage of world liquidity was observed. In surplus countries (Germany, Italy, and the Netherlands), there was a widespread suspicion that deficit countries were all too ready to accept inflation rather than reduce growth and undergo the discipline needed to restrain their external trade to a position without deficits. In reality, however, world trade growth was not noticeably impeded by reserve shortages when the United States had run more conservative or restrictive policies. But the system was put under significant strain after 1967, when the United States followed policies that greatly increased the supply of dollars and necessitated devaluations. The expansionary policies of the United States, and the inflationary finance of the Vietnam War, are now generally credited with undermining the Bretton Woods system.

In this context, many governments responded to the oil price rise of 1973 by cutting taxes to maintain the level of demand. Governments did this to differing extents, and the industries of different countries also showed differing abilities to adapt to a new pattern of demand in world trade. This combination of policies led to large current account imbalances and, in particular, a weakness in the dollar. But despite those policies, unemployment rose generally—largely because profits bore the brunt of the adverse terms of trade shock, while wages did not adjust. At this point policymakers regarded unemployment as the more serious problem, and the view that potential growth had been permanently reduced was not widely accepted. Meanwhile, inflation, though subsiding from its 1974 peak, remained high in many countries.

Several years of discussion among governments in this climate led to the Bonn Summit agreement of 1978, which epitomized the period. Long discussions and careful staff work finally led to a wide-ranging agreement that embraced, but went beyond, macroeconomic policy. In an effort to offset what was seen as flagging growth, while contributing to better-balanced international payments, Japan and Germany were asked to take stimulative fiscal policy actions. In return, the United States agreed to liberalize its energy prices so that they would rise to world levels, dampen U.S. energy demand, and reduce prices for all oil importers.

This agreement has been extensively criticized. It has been viewed by many as the imposition of American power, pressuring Germany and Japan to accept inflationary policies in order to assist the United States. It was also widely criticized as an example of inappropriate and procyclical fine-tuning of aggregate demand. In fact, the Bonn Summit agreement helped each country to achieve the domestic policies it favored but had been unable to achieve because of political opposition at home (Putnam and Henning 1989). The summit may therefore have been necessary to bring about the policies at the time that they were implemented, but the governing groups in each country favored them anyway. Coordinated policies were not imposed on reluctant governments.

Indeed, given the priorities of the time, the summit measures were not mistaken. Policy preferences did change soon afterward, however. In 1978, the

German government wanted faster growth when faced with forecasts of 3.5 percent real growth and 3.5 percent inflation while unemployment was only 4 percent. Moreover, a strong but temporary surge of inflation, caused by the second oil shock, and the replacement of the governments of the United States and Germany in 1980 and 1982 by Republican and Christian Democratic administrations respectively, led to a substantial reordering of priorities (Holtham 1989).

In practice, the expansionary effects of the fiscal policy changes in Germany and Japan were modest at best. In Germany, they barely offset the automatic claw back through the tax system, and they were accompanied by a tightening of monetary policy. This was acceptable because the summit agreement did not cover monetary policy, although it was clear that any German expansions would have to be bond financed. The fiscal measures therefore had a negligible impact on inflation and a very small effect on the current account. As a result, the main effect of the summit was the deregulation of American oil prices—which most commentators now agree was beneficial.

The aftermath of the Bonn agreement looked rather different from the circumstances that brought it about. Unlike the first oil shock, it is implausible to ascribe the second oil shock (1979–80) to monetary expansions or loose policies in the industrial countries. Instead it was triggered by the fall of the shah of Iran. Although this did not lead to a substantial reduction in oil supplies, it caused a surge of speculative buying that drove up the oil price.

Nonetheless, by 1980 popular tolerance of inflation was exhausted, and the threat that a new surge in inflation could again ratchet up the trend inflation rate made for considerable uniformity of view in all countries. This reflected several changes of government, and resulted in a lack of interest in policy coordination plus a perception that each country should concentrate on putting its own house in order.

At this point, there was general agreement among governments on the need to reduce inflation and a much greater readiness to bear the costs in unemployment and recession—a readiness that had democratic endorsement. In part this readiness was disguised behind an assertion that there would be no lasting output or unemployment costs of eliminating inflation. Indeed, some analysts even suggested that there would be no costs at all so long as the authorities showed enough commitment to their policies, since the private sector would then adjust its expectations to the new regime. There was also some concern, however, that the Bonn Summit's attempt at coordination had failed because governments had failed to carry through their part of the bargain, preferring to free-ride on the stimulus provided by other governments. There is little evidence that this in fact happened. But it is a good example of the potential difficulties in negotiating and then sustaining a program of coordinated policies among sovereign governments.

See also balance of payments; Bretton Woods system; international liquidity; international policy coordination; international reserves; Plaza Accord; Smithsonian Agreement

FURTHER READING

Holtham, G. 1989. "German Macroeconomic Policy and the 1978 Bonn Summit." In *Can Nations Agree: Issues in International Economic Cooperation*, edited by R. N. Cooper, Barry Eichengreen, C. Randall Henning, Gerald Holtham and Robert Putnam, Washington, DC: Brookings Institution, 141–76.

Putnam, Robert D., and C. Randall Henning. 1989. "The Bonn Summit of 1978: A Case Study in Coordination." In *Can Nations Agree: Issues in International Economic Cooperation*, edited by Cooper et al. Washington, DC: Brookings Institution, 12–140.

ANDREW HUGHES HALLETT

■ brain drain

Brain drain is the emigration of skilled and professional workers (such as engineers, scientists, doctors, nurses, and university professors) from a country. These people emigrate legally, become residents or even citizens of a new country (the host or destination country), and stay there with no intention of returning to the source (sending) country. There are two main legal ways for skilled workers to move to another country permanently: direct immigration through official channels, and indirect migration through overseas education. Direct migration refers to obtaining permanent residency directly because the worker possesses a particular skill or is reuniting with family. Indirect, education migration occurs when a university graduate (or graduate of higher education or a training program that qualifies the worker as skilled) goes to another country to pursue further education, but later chooses to stay in the host country and apply for permanent residency after graduation.

One important feature of the current system of direct and indirect migration (except for family reunion) is that the governments of the host countries usually accept those workers with great skills and talent, because usually only those who are smart and perform well will be able to find new jobs in the host country to support their applications for permanent residency.

Brain drain is usually associated with developing countries, since most of the movement of skilled workers is from developing to developed countries. Many countries in Asia and Africa experience substantial outflow of skilled workers, both in absolute numbers and as a percentage of the initial stock of skilled workers, and this can have an adverse impact on the source countries. Furthermore, the big gaps between the wage rates of skilled workers in developed countries and those in developing countries make brain drain difficult to control.

It is not quite correct to regard brain drain as a problem only for developing countries. Many developed countries also experience outflow of some of their skilled workers. Canada, for example, has suffered a net loss of skilled workers and professionals to the United States, and some people have urged the Canadian government to do something to stem the loss. For developed countries such as Canada, however, while some local skilled workers are moving out, skilled workers from other countries, especially from developing countries, are moving in.

Both government policymakers and economists are interested in the impacts of brain drain on the local economy. A simple analysis of these impacts involves three steps: (1) determining the benefits that brain drain may bring, (2) determining the costs that brain drain may cause, and (3) comparing the benefits and costs of brain drain. This approach applies to both the host country and the source country.

Impacts on the Host Country Brain drain, as a form of permanent immigration, is usually not considered a problem by the host country, and in many cases it is regarded as a positive thing for the local economy. First, it gains workers, which contribute to the gross domestic product (GDP) and gross national product. Second, more skilled workers coming in usually drive down the marginal product of these workers, a phenomenon called the Law of Diminishing Returns. This phenomenon will lead to a drop in the market wage rates of these workers. At any point in time, each additional worker moving in will receive a wage rate equal to the value of his/her marginal product. However, the associated drop in the wage rate will mean that all the workers who moved in before will receive a new wage rate lower than their marginal products measured at the time they moved in. This means that the economy benefits from the gap between what these workers have contributed (their marginal products) and what they receive (the wage rate). Third, skilled workers could generate positive externalities for the society (such as increases in productivity and overall employment), and these immigrants can bring benefits to other parts of the economy not measured by the wage rates they earn.

Externalities (that is, the unintended effects of immigration of skilled workers) take two primary forms. By working with other skilled workers, new immigrants can raise the productivity of local workers through friendly competition and interactions. Also, there is usually some kind of complementarity between skilled workers and unskilled workers so that when a firm hires a skilled worker (such as a doctor or engineer) it also hires a certain number of less skilled workers (such as nurses or technicians) to work with the skilled worker. This means that the employment of skilled workers could generate demand for unskilled workers. This type of externality is especially helpful in solving the problem of unemployment of unskilled workers.

Brain drain, like other types of permanent migration, involves inflow of people, and thus it can have social and political effects. For example, the government may be concerned about any possible impacts of the inflow of foreign workers on crime, social order, and local education, or about cultural and language differences and conflicts between the new immigrants and local residents. Furthermore, the demographic distribution, the income levels, and the political views of the new immigrants may also have impacts on the local society.

Impacts on the Source Country The impacts of brain drain on the source country could be very different from those on the host country. Consider first the special case in which only one skilled worker moves out so that the local wage rate is not much affected. If before the move the worker is paid his/her value of marginal product, then the impact on *those left behind* (TLB, or the rest of the local economy) will be negligibly small because while the economy loses the contribution of the worker, it saves the payment to the worker. The nonharmful effect of brain drain will no longer hold if (1) the outgoing worker received a wage rate less than what he/she has contributed, or (2) more similar workers move out so that the wage rate rises.

If the outgoing worker received a wage rate less than his/her contribution, the emigration is harmful to TLB because the worker takes with him/her his/her previous contribution, which is bigger than what the rest of the economy is able to save. A worker receives less than his/her (value of) marginal product if there are distortions in the labor market. Two main types of distortion are monopsony (in which a single buyer has disproportionate influence in a market) and externality. A monopsonistic firm will tend to underemploy workers and underpay each worker. The existence of (positive) externality can lead to a wage rate less than the marginal product of labor. As explained earlier, a skilled worker can generate two types of externality: positive impacts on his/her co-workers through friendly competition and interactions, and complementarity between skilled workers and unskilled workers.

Brain drain can hurt TLB even if there are no distortions (such as monopsony or externality) in the economy. Suppose that a sufficient number of skilled workers move out so that the marginal product of labor increases, and thus the wage rate of the remaining workers increases. The gap between the new, higher marginal product and the original wage implies that TLB have experienced a net loss between the contribution of the emigrating workers and the wages saved by no longer paying them.

The impacts of brain drain on TLB in the source country are not all negative; some of them could be positive. For example, skilled workers working abroad may remit part of their income to their family, relatives, and friends back in the source country. They also serve as examples to younger generations of the benefits of acquiring high-level skills. Some of them may even bring back technologies and investment to the source country.

Brain drain can also have dynamic effects on the source country's economy. First, brain drain means that the country is losing human capital. Since human capital is an important growth factor, brain drain can adversely affect economic growth. Moreover, because skilled workers tend to earn high wages before their departure, they usually have saving rates higher than the average rate in the economy. Thus the outflow of some of these high-income workers could pull down the average saving rate of the remaining population, and this means that the local investment rate and thus economic growth will be hurt.

Emigration of these workers could have other impacts on the rest of the economy. One very important impact is that on education, especially higher education. The prospect of moving to other countries where higher wage rates are offered will increase the incentive of local students to seek higher education and in-depth training. This will in general raise the skill level of workers in the economy, and they could help the economy grow. There are,

however, some problems associated with this increase in the demand for higher education, sometimes referred to as a *brain gain*. First, the demand for higher education could be biased toward technical subjects such as engineering, medicine, science, and computer science, and away from other subjects such as the humanities. Second, there is always an excess demand for education, especially higher education. When there is an increase in the demand for higher education, it is not likely that the government will respond with an increase in the supply. As a result, brain drain may not imply an increase in higher education graduates although it may lead to an improvement in the quality of the graduates because talented children will have bigger incentives to get education.

Brain Drain as a Serious Issue for Developing Countries There are several reasons that the governments of developing countries regard brain drain as a serious problem for their economies. First, the wage gaps between developing countries and developed countries are wide, implying big incentives for the skilled workers in the developing countries to emigrate. Second, the externality associated with skilled workers could be high in these developing countries, mainly because there is usually widespread unemployment of unskilled workers. The complementarity between skilled workers and unskilled workers means that the loss of a skilled worker to another country could lead to a drop in the economy's demand for unskilled workers. Thus large outflow of skilled workers could substantially raise the unemployment rate of unskilled workers. Third, the outflow of different types of skilled workers may not be balanced, and the developing countries could very well be losing more of the types of skilled workers that they need the most—for example, doctors, engineers, and nurses, who can easily apply for immigrant visas to developed countries but also are in very short supply in the source countries. Fourth, most developing countries are in an early stage of development, and skilled workers are needed for the economy to take off. Losing some of these workers could seriously hinder the growth of the economy.

Policy Recommendations In view of the impacts of brain drain on local economies, many economists have suggested policies to protect the welfare of TLB.

Exit Tax One suggestion is that those who want to emigrate would have to pay a tax before leaving the country, and that the tax revenue collected would be distributed to the remaining population in some way. The amount of the tax could be set at a level so that TLB would be adequately compensated, and might include an amount to cover the subsidy on education the government provided to these emigrants. It has been argued in economic theory that the increase in the income of the emigrants should be big enough to cover the compensatory tax. For the emigrants the tax payment could come from their own funds, or loans from relatives, friends, and banks. For example, the former Soviet Union imposed exit taxes on some Jews who immigrated to Israel (although in this case the main reason for the tax may have been political deterrence of emigration rather than economic recovery of investment in the emigrants). China had a policy closer in essence to the exit tax suggested here: it required people who went abroad for education to put down deposits before they were allowed to go, and the deposits would be forfeited if after graduation they did not return to China.

Exit taxation is not common in developing countries, partly because it is difficult to calculate the right tax rate. Another reason is that the amount required to adequately compensate TLB could be big, and people who want to move out may not be able to raise that sum of money. Even though it is argued that the future earnings of the emigrants are big enough to cover whatever is required to compensate TLB, banks will not accept these future earnings to guarantee loans. Thus exit taxes, when implemented fully, could turn out to be prohibitive.

Host Countries to Collect Taxes for the Source Countries Since it is difficult to collect taxes before the emigrants actually earn the new wages, some economists have suggested that the host countries, notably the United States and other developed countries, could impose taxes on the new immigrants. The collected taxes would be returned to the source countries on a regular basis, with the purpose of compensating the remaining population. The merit of this argument is that taxes are collected only after the new immigrants have received income. However, it has a number of practical difficulties.

First, the administration of the tax scheme could be very costly, as a lot of information has to be collected in order to calculate the rates for immigrants from different countries. Second, strictly speaking, the tax scheme requires that people from different countries be subject to different rates. The problem of this requirement is that it could create a lot of administration problems, and it may generate feelings of unfairness among the immigrants. To respond to this point, it has been suggested that the source countries impose only one tax rate on the new immigrants, no matter where they came from. The required rate will be the one that is based on the average amount of compensation needed for all important source countries. The tax revenue collected will then be handed over to some international organization such as the United Nations to spend on programs that promote economic growth and development of developing countries.

Even if the high costs associated with administrating the scheme and the difficulty of implementing the scheme can be overcome, the tax scheme may be against the constitution of most developed countries: it requires that the initial residents in the host countries and new immigrants be subject to two different income tax rates, the higher being on the new immigrants. These developed countries are prohibited from imposing such a two-tier tax system, based on whether people emigrated from another country recently.

Other Policy Recommendations The fundamental way to solve the brain drain problem is to raise the local wage rates, so that skilled workers will have less incentive to emigrate. There are at least three possible ways to raise the local wage rates. First, the government can provide a general wage subsidy to all skilled workers to close the gap between what they may be able to get elsewhere and what they receive locally. This policy could be more effective in dampening brain drain, but it is costly because substantial subsidies will be needed. That could be beyond the budget capacity of the governments. Furthermore, the main reason why these skilled workers are able to earn higher wage rates is because they have higher marginal products in the host countries because of, for example, the availability of more and better capital and facilities. These can hardly be provided by the source country governments in the near future.

The second way is to substantially promote the growth of the economy so that the income levels of the population are raised. Economic growth of the country will boost not only the GDP and national income of the economy but also the wage rates of the skilled workers. The growth of the economy will substantially diminish the incentive of the skilled workers to move out.

This policy is only part of a long-term solution, as it takes a long time for the economy to have a substantial growth. Furthermore, brain drain has a negative impact on economic growth, as brain drain lowers the stock of human capital in the economy. To promote economic growth while skilled workers are moving out is not an easy task. To do that, the government can invest more in education and/or invest more in infrastructure. The first strategy seeks to slow the rate of depletion of the stock of human capital or even to increase the stock. The second one seeks to promote other growth factors, such as the infrastructure needed to attract foreign direct investment or support high-tech development.

The third policy is to implement a two-tier wage system for skilled workers: one at the prevailing rate in the economy, and a second, higher one for those who choose to come back from abroad, usually after graduation from a training program or higher education. The higher wage scale for the returning skilled workers is to attract them to come back. To carry out this policy successfully, either there must be a sub-stantially large public sector or the government must be willing to use widespread subsidies on the employment of these returning graduates. Many countries such as China have been using this policy to lure students who went abroad for education to come back after graduation.

The use of a two-tier wage system, however, has its own costs. This system requires subsidy payments to these returning workers, and the gap between the two wage scales could alienate those workers who were trained locally and are working with those returning skilled workers.

Another policy to slow the rate of brain drain and to encourage returning immigrants is to attract foreign direct investment. There are three channels through which the domestic demand for skilled workers can be raised. First, attract foreign firms to invest and produce locally. Because foreign firms usually have more advanced technologies than what local firms have, foreign direct investment could substantially raise the demand for skilled workers. Second, recent development of technologies allows local skilled workers (such as telephone operators, computer programmers, and accountants) to be employed by firms located in other countries, without having these workers moving out of the country—a phenomenon called offshoring. Third, local production of products to be exported can increase through a process called fragmentation and outsourcing. As firms in developed countries are able to fragment their production processes, they may move the production of some of the components and intermediate inputs of the final products to developing countries where labor costs are much lower. This will raise the demand for skilled workers in the developing countries.

See also brain gain; brain waste; migration governance; migration, international; remittances

FURTHER READING

Beine, Michel, Frederic Docquier, and Hillel Rapoport. 2001. "Brain Drain and Economic Growth: Theory and Evidence." *Journal of Development Economics* 64 (1): 275–89. A widely cited theoretical and empirical examination of the possibility of gains due to human capital formation of brain drain.

Bhagwati, Jagdish N. 1979. "International Migration of the Highly Skilled: Economics, Ethics, and Taxes." *Third World Quarterly* 1 (3): 17–30. An early consideration of using taxes as a policy tool to address brain drain.

Bhagwati, Jagdish N., and Koichi Hamada. 1974. "The Brain Drain, International Integration of Markets for Professionals and Unemployment: A Theoretical Analysis." *Journal of Development Economics* 1 (1): 19–42. An early theoretical examination of the brain drain phenomenon.

Chang, Shirley L. 1992. "Causes of Brain Drain and Solutions: The Taiwan Experience." *Studies in Comparative International Development* 27 (1): 27–43. A policy analysis of Taiwan's experience of and response to brain drain some decades ago with implications for other developing countries.

Martineau, Tim, Karola Decker, and Peter Bundred. 2004. "Brain Drain of Health Professionals: From Rhetoric to Responsible Action." *Health Policy* 70 (1): 1–10. A policy analysis of brain drain in the health professions that draws from case studies of Ghana, South Africa, and the United Kingdom.

Mountford, Andrew. 1997. "Can a Brain Drain Be Good for Growth in the Source Economy?" *Journal of Development Economics* 53 (2): 287–303. A theoretical examination of the effect of brain drain on productivity in the source economy.

Wong, Kar-yiu, and Chong Kee Yip. 1999. "Education, Economic Growth, and Brain Drain." *Journal of Economic Dynamics and Control* 23 (5–6): 699–726. An "overlapping generations" model of endogenous growth examining the effects of emigration on those left behind with a focus on human capital formation.

KAR-YIU WONG

■ brain gain

Brain gain refers to the hypothesis that the emigration of advanced students and highly skilled workers may produce domestic incentives for investment in education and skills that offset the human capital losses resulting from the departures. This hypothesis poses a challenge to the more widely held view that such emigration results in a net loss of human capital, or brain drain.

A brain gain may be realized only if several conditions are met. First, many emigrants must receive substantially higher returns on their education and skills than they would have done had they stayed home. Second, these gains must be perceived by individuals in the sending countries who have the interest and potential to acquire more education and skills, thereby inducing a demand for them. Third, domestic institutions must be able to respond effectively to this demand. Fourth, some of those who have been induced to acquire more education and skills, and thus add to their human capital stock, by the prospect of emigration, must be unable to emigrate. Finally, this group must be able to put their newly gained education and skills to good use at home.

The first condition is likely to be met quite often. Large international differences in compensation are a driving factor in many migration decisions. Although not all emigrants are able to put their education and skills to work in the receiving countries, many do. A quarter of all college-educated workers in science and engineering occupations in the United States in 2003, for instance, were born outside the country.

When emigrants experience employment success, reports are likely to filter back to interested communities in the sending countries, fulfilling the second condition. (Indeed, if these reports are exaggerated, so much the better for the brain gain hypothesis.) Electronic mail and the World Wide Web have expanded and accelerated the communication channels for such information. A case in point is the close association in the late 1990s and early 2000s between salaries in the U.S. information technology industry and foreign student enrollments at the graduate level in related fields.

The third condition may be the most difficult to fulfill. Effective institutions for education and training tend to be rigid. They require highly skilled teachers who may be difficult to recruit and retain. They may need substantial capital inputs for facilities and equipment. They may be burdened by red tape and political demands. Even when it is possible to expand such institutions, their quality may decline so significantly that their net contributions to human capital formation are far less than hoped for. New higher education franchises in India, for example, are a far cry from the Indian Institutes of Technology that have shaped high expectations among foreign employers.

If the educational bottleneck is surmounted by a large number of prospective emigrants, it does seem probable that a substantial fraction of them will be frustrated in their attempt to secure a better return on their investment in themselves by seeking skilled work abroad. This condition, the fourth for realizing a brain gain, is enacted through immigration quotas, labor market regulations, and other forms of protection for skilled workers in the receiving countries. Applicants for an employment-based "green card" for permanent residence in the United States, for instance, must typically wait several years for a decision.

The final question is whether these would-be emigrants can put their hard-won knowledge to effective use in the domestic economy. This condition, like the third one, is not necessarily easily met. The profile of the demand for skills, especially highly specialized skills, may be different at home than abroad. Nurses and doctors whose training prepared them to treat middle-class patients in comfortable surroundings provide an illustration; they may choose not to practice their professions rather than serve poor villages where the medical needs are greatest.

The data available for assessing the brain gain hypothesis, although they are improving, are still too poor to allow for anything other than tentative conclusions. The firmest of these conclusions is that a brain gain is more likely in countries with large populations than small ones. Beine et al. (2003), for example, find that China and India benefit from current levels of emigration of college-educated individuals and would benefit even more if outflows were to rise. At the other extreme, Guyana, Haiti, and Jamaica, which have lost more than 80 percent of

their college-educated to emigration, have been made worse off. Although more of the 50 developing countries in Beine et al.'s sample are "losers," the winners contain some 80 percent of the total population.

These tentative findings are intuitively appealing, given the conditions required to realize a brain gain. Large countries seem likely to more easily achieve the economies of scale required to support expansion of and new entry into higher education. They may also benefit more from competition among provinces and localities to provide public education and among private educational institutions as well. National quotas in receiving countries amount to a smaller fraction of the populations of large sending countries than small ones. (Citizens of Jamaica, for instance, are more than a hundred times more likely to be admitted as legal immigrants to the United States than those of India.) Finally, the more diversified economies of large countries may provide more opportunities for "surplus" human capital to be used productively.

Although the conditions for a brain gain may be more likely to be fulfilled in large countries, there are many policies that sending countries of all sizes might undertake to raise the odds of such an outcome. Chief among these are educational policies that provide general skills and economic policies that foster investment and entrepreneurship. Receiving countries, too, have a potential role to play, for instance, by linking their immigration policies to labor market conditions at home and abroad. Neither brain gain nor brain drain is, in the final analysis, an outcome of immutable laws of economics, but rather a construction of policy decision-making within institutional constraints.

See also brain drain; brain waste; migration governance; migration, international

FURTHER READING

Beine, Michel, Frederic Docquier, and Hillel Rapoport. July 2003. "Brain Drain and LDCs' Growth: Winners and Losers." IZA Discussion Paper no. 819. Bonn, Germany: IZA [Institute for the Study of Labor, University of Bonn]. The best available empirical assessment so far of the brain gain hypothesis at the national level of analysis.

Lucas, Robert E. B. 2004. "International Migration to the High Income Countries: Some Consequences for Economic Development in the Sending Countries." Paper presented at World Bank Conference on Development (April). A balanced and thorough review of the literature on brain gain, brain drain, and related issues.

Stark, Oded. 2004. "Rethinking the Brain Drain." *World Development* 32 (1) (January):15–22. A theoretical exposition of the brain gain hypothesis.

DAVID M. HART

■ brain waste

Brain waste refers to the underuse of migrant knowledge within a host country. In contrast, *brain use* refers to a situation in which migrants obtain jobs commensurate with their educational level and are in a position to make use of their knowledge and skills in the host-country labor market. Greater incidence of brain waste translates into lower levels of brain use and vice versa.

The 1990s were characterized by major geopolitical change and state reconfiguration. These changes put in motion new patterns in the movement of people across boundaries and gave rise to several new trends in international migration (International Organization for Migration 2005). An important new trend is that contemporary migration is concentrated in a few developed countries. In 1970, the developed world received 47 percent of all international migrants whereas 53 percent of migrants moved to developing countries. By 2000, the proportion of international migrants to developed countries had risen to 63 percent. The sharpest increase was in the United States, but Australia, Canada, France, Germany, and the United Kingdom also experienced substantial increases in their migrant populations (International Organization for Migration 2005).

In many of these receiving countries, family reunification has been an important vehicle of admission. In recent years, however, admission of skilled workers has gained prominence. In 2000, more than a half million skilled migrants were selected for admission to the United States, along with more than 100,000 in Australia and the United Kingdom, fewer than 100,000 in Canada, nearly 50,000 in New Zealand, and fewer than 10,000 in France (International Organization for Migration 2005). The growing use of skill level as an admission criterion in destination countries is important to the effective use of labor resources in the world economy.

National Origin and Brain Waste Migrants to Europe and especially the United States tend to be highly educated (Özden 2006). Those who migrate to the United States from Africa, the Middle East, Asia, and Eastern Europe are more educated than their counterparts that set out for Western Europe. In contrast, the United States is by far the destination of preference for Latin American migrants, and their educational levels tend to be lower than the average levels in their home countries (Özden 2006).

A key issue in brain waste research is the extent to which migrants' knowledge and skills are employed in destination countries. Some researchers have indicated that, despite the same level of educational attainment, migrants from different regions show significant differences in job placements in the U.S. labor market. One can discern three categories relating to the incidence of brain waste—low, moderate, and high—from Özden's (2006) study.

The first category is composed of professional migrants from Asia and Western Europe. It also includes migrants from Japan and Australia. Using 2000 U.S. Census data, Özden (2006) concluded that, in general, migrants from Asia tend to do better in terms of brain use than those from Western Europe. Brain use is lowest (and thus the incidence of brain waste is highest) among migrants from the Republic of Korea (33 percent) and Pakistan (38 percent); comparatively moderate for migrants from the Philippines (40 percent), Taiwan (46 percent), and China (51 percent); and highest among those from India (76 percent). For migrants from Western Europe, Japan, and Australia, brain use is estimated at between 38 percent for migrants from Italy to 69 percent for migrants from Ireland. Migrants from

Japan, the United Kingdom, Germany, Canada, and Australia also do relatively well, with between 59 percent (Japan) and 65 percent (United Kingdom). In this study, brain waste and brain use were measured by assessing the gap between educational attainment and job description in the destination country.

The second category of migrants, characterized by moderate brain waste, is composed of those from various African countries. The incidence of brain use is lowest among professional migrants from Ethiopia (37 percent), and highest among those from South Africa (62 percent). For immigrants from countries such as Nigeria, Ghana, and Kenya, brain waste is in the middle of this range, between 40 percent and 52 percent.

The third category of migrants, characterized by a high degree of brain waste, is composed of professional migrants from Eastern Europe, Latin America, and the Middle East. Although the incidence of brain waste is highest in this category, important differences between regions can be discerned. For migrants from Eastern Europe, brain use is estimated at between 31 percent (former Yugoslavia) and 57 percent (Hungary). For migrants from Latin America, brain use is estimated at between 32 percent (Guatemala) and 51 percent (Brazil). Of all groups, migrants from the Middle East experience the greatest incidence of brain waste, with brain use estimated at between 25 percent (migrants from Morocco) and 46 percent (migrants from Lebanon).

Factors Contributing to Differences in Brain Waste What explains the pattern of brain use among migrants from different regions of the world who possess the same educational credentials? Some brain waste researchers attribute the differences to quality and selection variables (Özden 2006; Matto, Neagu, and Özden 2005). *Quality variables* affect the extent to which an immigrant's human capital is valued within the host country. Two such variables are the source country's expenditure on tertiary education and whether the English language is used in the host country. The greater the expenditure on tertiary education, the better the schools and therefore the better the knowledge and skill level of the migrant. Proficiency in the English language can facilitate

migrant communication in the United States since it is the primary language of business.

Selection variables relate to differences in the abilities of immigrants from different countries. Selection variables predict whether immigrants from a particular country represent the highly educated and therefore professionally competitive, or the minimally educated and therefore professionally uncompetitive, members of their own society. Özden (2006) considers three selection variables (gross domestic product—GDP—per capita, distance, and conflict) that relate to the source country and one selection variable (migration policy) that relates to the destination country.

The higher the GDP per capita of the source country, the higher the opportunity cost of migration. Therefore, those who might wish to migrate are those who expect to get higher monetary returns on their knowledge and skills overseas. Less-educated individuals from high GDP per capita countries are unlikely to migrate because the costs of migration are greater than the expected returns. In contrast, both highly educated and less-well-educated individuals from low GDP per capita countries may want to migrate to high GDP per capita countries because of the expected economic rewards. Migration from low GDP per capita countries tends to favor the highly educated, however, because they are likely to possess the financial resources required to make a move. The implication of this for differentiating the abilities of migrants from different source countries is that we can expect migrants from high GDP per capita countries to be educated and skilled, while, in general, there is greater uncertainty about the abilities of those from low GDP per capita countries since they represent an education and skill mixture that has to be sorted out in the host country labor market. Further, the process of sorting between skilled and unskilled migrants can be costly for organizations.

Distance between source and destination countries can also have an impact on migrant ability through a self-selection process. Migrants are likely to select a distant destination over a closer one if they believe that they will obtain higher returns on their knowledge and skills in the former. Thus highly skilled migrants from Africa and the Middle East who expect higher rewards in the U.S. labor market are likely to migrate to the United States rather than to the closer destination of Western Europe. Even in Western Europe, where migration policy has favored family reunification and political asylum seekers, there is a trend toward policies that favor economic migration, making the distance explanation more widely applicable.

Military conflict can have at least two impacts on differences in abilities among migrants. The presence of political instability and military conflict creates an incentive for people with varying educational levels to migrate. This, in turn, contributes to a migrant population with a varying skill and knowledge composition. Military conflicts also affect the allocation of scarce resources from education to military efforts in source countries. This, in turn, diminishes the quality of education and the abilities of migrants from affected countries.

The only selection variable that relates to the destination country is migration policy (Özden 2006). This relates to the openness of immigration policies to migrants from particular countries. The more open the migration policies of destination countries, the more varied the skill composition of migrants. In contrast, migration policies can range from being open to migrants from countries perceived to have highly educated migrants in targeted industries, to being relatively restrictive toward migrants from countries perceived to have a low level of educational attainment among their populations.

Destination Country Labor Markets Although quality and selection variables may play an important role in brain waste, they mask destination-country labor market characteristics that may play an even greater role in explaining the differential patterns of brain waste among migrant professionals. The presumed efficiency of the labor market can hold only if employers in the destination country have perfect information relating to the quality and selection variables pertaining to the source countries of each immigrant. Furthermore, they would also have to use this information rationally to assess the value of identical educational credentials of migrants from different source countries. Research in organizational studies, migration, and cross-cultural adaptation, however, suggest that both structural and cognitive biases on the part of employers and migrants alike play a significant role in shaping perceptions of migrants from different parts of the world and affecting hiring decisions.

Research on diversity in organizations in the U.S. context identifies a wide range of structural barriers faced by nonmajority group members. These include discrimination and prejudice based on a variety of differences (Cox 1993), institutional barriers such as the organizational history in relation to diversity practice, formal hiring practices, and informal organizational processes (Nkomo 1992; Cox 1993). There are reasons to believe that these barriers would also be relevant to other destination countries (de Beijl 1996). Although diversity research has provided significant insight into the impact of these types of barriers on minority members in general, it has generally ignored the unique circumstances of migrants. Research on migration and cross-cultural adjustment suggests that many of the barriers identified in the diversity literature are important in understanding migrant work adjustment. There are other barriers faced by migrants, however, such as language, culture clash, lack of information and knowledge about the labor market, and the inability of potential employers to assess migrant credentials (de Beijl 1996). These barriers affect migrants' ability to adapt and become effectively integrated into the work context as well as the employment and promotion decisions of employers. Most important, these employment decisions on the part of employers fly in the face of any rational calculation regarding the migrants' qualifications. Thus exploring the cognitive and structural biases that play a role in migrant work adjustment would give us greater insight into the factors that may contribute to the differential pattern of brain waste among migrants from different parts of the world identified by Özden (2006).

See also brain drain; brain gain; migration governance; migration, international

140

FURTHER READING

Cox, T. 1993. *Cultural Diversity in Organizations: Theory, Research, and Practice*. San Francisco, CA: Berrett-Koehler. Describes the impact of cultural diversity on organizations, including the social psychological dynamics of prejudice and discrimination in organizations.

de Beijl, R. Z. 1996. "Labor Market Integration and Legislative Measures to Combat Discrimination against Migrant Workers." International Migration Papers No. 8. Geneva, Switzerland: International Labor Office. Describes the various sources of discrimination within host countries that inhibit the ability of migrants to integrate effectively into the labor market.

International Organization for Migration. 2005. "International Migration Data and Statistics." In *World Migration 2005: Costs and Benefits of International Migration*, edited by Population Division of the Department of Economics and Social Affairs, UN World Secretariat. Geneva, Switzerland: IOM, 379–421. Provides a wealth of statistical information concerning trends in international migration in general and for specific regions of the world.

Matto, Aaditya, Ileana Cristina Neagu, and Çağlar Özden. 2005. "Brain Waste? Educated Immigrants in the U.S. Labor Market." World Bank Policy Research Working Paper 3581. Washington, DC: World Bank. Useful empirical exploration of variables that explain brain waste among migrants from different regions and countries in the world.

Nkomo, S. M. 1992. "The Emperor Has No Clothes: Rewriting Race in Organizations." *Academy of Management Review* 17 (3): 487–513. Offers a theory for studying racial dynamics within organizations that takes the unique cultural and historical factors of a setting into account.

Özden, Çağlar. 2006. "Educated Migrants: Is There Brain Waste?" In *International Migration, Remittances and the Brain Drain*, edited by Ç. Özden and Maurice Schiff. Washington, DC: World Bank and Palgrave Macmillan, 227–44. Excellent empirical exploration of migration patterns of highly skilled individuals from select countries and explanation of differences in brain utilization of individuals from select countries.

GELAYE DEBEBE

■ Bretton Woods system

The Bretton Woods agreements negotiated at the United Nations Monetary and Financial Conference held in Bretton Woods, New Hampshire, in 1944 laid the groundwork for the creation of the International Monetary Fund (IMF) and the International Bank for Reconstruction and Development, now known as the World Bank. These institutions provided the framework for the postwar international trade and financial system that came to be known as the Bretton Woods system.

In the early 1940s the Allied powers started to consider the shape of the post–World War II international financial and trading system. Influencing their decision on measures to be taken was the assessment of why the trading system had broken down in the 1920s and the causes of the economic depression that had plagued the United States and the United Kingdom in the 1930s. The period had been characterized by record levels of unemployment, excessively onerous war reparations payments imposed in the Treaty of Versailles, and volatile international capital flows, as well as the collapse in the prices of primary commodities.

The response to these problems had been the introduction of policies to protect domestic producers by restricting imports, placing controls on the access to foreign exchange used to purchase imports, introducing preferential tariffs on imports from selected countries, and bilateral clearing and payments arrangements to ensure that imports balanced exports. Other measures included international schemes restricting supplies of primary commodities, as well as national import restrictions, export subsidies, and agricultural price supports. The objective of these policies was to defend domestic income and employment and the stability of domestic financial institutions. Instead, the attempted return to the gold standard was thwarted by sustained financial crises.

Postwar planners recognized the need to coordinate national policy objectives in an interdependent international system and concluded that multilateral institutional structures could eliminate the financial factors that had caused international trade to be viewed as a threat to national economic welfare. It was generally agreed that a stable international financial and exchange rate system was a prerequisite to successful restoration of free international trade.

The United States and the United Kingdom played the major role in the discussions of the shape of the new system, and both governments contributed proposals of what was to be the first step in this process. The UK proposal, authored by John Maynard Keynes, called for an international clearing union based on an internationally created and managed unit of account. The U.S. proposal, devised by U.S. Treasury official Harry Dexter White, proposed an international stabilization fund, similar to the U.S. Federal Reserve System on an international scale, that would hold reserves of the currencies of all members, from which countries could borrow to support their exchange rates.

The difference in the two proposals reflected the different motivations of the two countries. The United Kingdom was concerned that large payments imbalances under the gold standard had required debtor countries to reverse their balance of payments deficits and protect their declining gold stocks by reductions in domestic income and employment. Surplus countries, on the other hand, were accumulating gold and could easily postpone any action to reduce their surpluses through policies to expand their imports from the deficit countries. The goal of the United Kingdom, as a postwar debtor country, was thus to eliminate this asymmetric adjustment to trade imbalances by ensuring full participation of creditors in the international adjustment process.

The United States, on the other hand, was more concerned by the breakdown in free trade and the manipulation of exchange rates that had occurred in the interwar period as countries attempted to protect themselves from the exchange rate instability caused by large payments imbalances and the instability of international financial flows. The U.S. concern, as the major creditor country, was to prevent deficit countries from resolving their debt positions by using protection and exchange rate manipulation to create trade surpluses.

Article VII of the Atlantic Charter, negotiated by Winston Churchill and Franklin D. Roosevelt at the Atlantic Conference in August 1941 during a secret shipboard meeting, set out the conditions for U.S. support of the British war effort. It reflected U.S. concerns that the postwar trade and financial system be built on a rules-based system of relatively free multilateral trade as opposed to the British approach of trade preferences. The differences were worked out at the Bretton Woods Conference in 1944. The trade and commercial policy aspects of the new system were the subject of discussions at the UN Conference on Trade and Employment held in Havana in 1947.

Creation of the Bretton Woods Institutions
The Bretton Woods Conference created the IMF, largely on the lines proposed in the White plan. On a proposal from the United States, concerned to separate the financing of the postwar reconstruction of Europe from the financing of exchange rate stability, an International Bank for Reconstruction and Development (IBRD) was also created to deal with the longer-term problem of development finance for postwar reconstruction in Europe. The unanimously adopted Havana Charter, proposing the creation of an International Trade Organization (ITO) that would deal with the regulations on commercial policy, create a Commodity Stabilization Fund, and meet the British concerns for symmetric balance of payments adjustments, was never ratified by member states. Instead, a single chapter, the General Agreements on Tariffs and Trade (GATT), which dealt with commercial policy, was the only part of the charter that survived as a series of bilateral treaties to eliminate subsidies and reduce tariffs in support of world trade.

The role of these multilateral institutions with complementary mandates to ensure favorable international trade and financial conditions to support rapid income growth and employment is reflected in their stated objectives. The IMF was created "to facilitate the expansion and balanced growth of international trade, and to contribute thereby to the promotion and maintenance of high levels of employment and real income and to the development of the productive resources of all members as the primary objectives of economic policy." The ITO charter (Chapter 2, Article II) was even more explicit: "The Members recognize that the avoidance of unemployment or underemployment, through the achievement and maintenance in each country of useful employment opportunities for those able and willing to work and of a large and steadily growing volume of production and effective demand for goods and services, is not of domestic concern alone, but is also a necessary condition for the achievement of . . . the expansion of international trade, and thus for the well being of all other countries." Finally, the role of the IBRD was "to promote the long range balanced growth of international trade and the maintenance of equilibrium in balances of payments by encouraging international investment for the development of the productive resources of members, thereby assisting in raising productivity, the standard of living and conditions of labor in their territories."

This ambitious project of negotiating a new, coherent, and coordinated set of international institutions for the postwar period was never completed, however. The IMF and the IBRD became specialized agencies within the UN system, which allowed them to maintain independent governance mechanisms with representation based on each country's economic weight and financial contribution instead of on the UN General Assembly's rule of one country, one vote. In 1996 the GATT was transformed into the World Trade Organization, an ad hoc international body outside the UN system and without the wider mandate to eliminate discriminatory bilateral agreements as the third pillar of Bretton Woods originally intended for the ITO.

As a result, no multilateral institution was created to deal with the stabilization of primary commodity prices or to oversee trade in agriculture. Instead, official intervention in support of the prices of primary commodities continued in the form of ad hoc agreements dependent on controls over supply, and national and (in the case of European Union countries) regional schemes for the support of agricultural prices and incomes. The most important and most costly examples of the latter were found in industrial countries, and, as in the earlier period, they were generally supported by tariffs and other restrictions on imports, as well as by subsidies and other methods of export promotion. The responsibility for the consequences of fluctuations in developing country export earnings caused by volatility in commodity prices was left to the IMF.

The IBRD, although it was commonly referred to as a "world bank," was not a "bank" because it could not create money, and the majority of the financing for European reconstruction effort was provided by the Marshall Plan. As a result most European countries delayed full observance of their obligations in the international trading system, while the need for finance for reconstruction and trade was met by official aid or through regional multilateral monetary arrangements such as the European Payments Union. The financing problems facing the growing number of newly created democratic developing countries were addressed by the creation of special institutions in the World Bank such as the International Development Association and regional development banks. In addition, the UN Conference on Trade and Development, which had no financing capabilities, provided a forum for the formulation of financing policies designed to benefit developing countries.

Membership in the IMF required a country to maintain a fixed parity for its national currency relative to gold or the dollar. If necessary, countries were to maintain these rates by borrowing reserves temporarily from the IMF and by implementing policies to ensure external equilibrium. Only in the case of a "fundamental disequilibrium," where such adjustment would have meant insupportable domestic hardship, could a country contemplate a change in exchange rates, and such a change was to be negotiated with the other members of the IMF.

Dollar Standard Since most countries did not have the requisite gold stocks after World War II, they chose to fix their exchange rates to the dollar. The United States, with most of the global gold stocks, fixed its parity relative to gold. Nonetheless, the weak external positions of most European countries meant that convertibility at fixed parity for imbalances created by commercial account transactions was not implemented until the end of the 1950s. By 1960 the Bretton Woods fixed exchange rate system came under pressure when gold traded above its official dollar peg of $35 an ounce on the London gold market. Several years earlier, Yale economist Robert Triffin had suggested that this was the inevitable result of the decision made at Bretton Woods to require members to fix their exchange rates relative to gold or the U.S. dollar. Since all countries except the United States had fixed their currencies relative to the dollar, this created a system that resembled the prewar gold standard that the Bretton Wood system was supposed to replace, as the dollar had simply taken the place of gold.

When U.S. external deficits created a stock of international claims on the dollar that exceeded the U.S. gold stock, the United States could no longer ensure the exchange of dollars for gold at the rate of $35 per ounce. This is precisely what occurred in 1960 when the value of U.S. gold stocks at the official parity of $17.8 billion fell short of the $18.7 billion of outstanding liquid foreign dollar claims. To avoid changing the dollar parity, a series of ad hoc measures to prevent dollar conversion into gold and to increase foreign demand for dollars were introduced during the decade of the 1960s. These included a two-tier gold market separating official and private conversions of currencies into gold; an interest equalization tax on borrowing in the U.S. capital market; Operation Twist, which attempted to produce an increase in short-term rates while keeping long-term rates low in order to support U.S. growth prospects; and new methods of calculating the U.S. balance of payments on the basis of liquidity balances.

In 1966, to provide a supplement to the dwindling U.S. gold stocks and an alternative to the dollar in countries' reserves, the Group of 10 (composed of the ministers of finance of the 10 major industrialized countries) proposed a "special reserve drawing right," which was implemented by the IMF in 1967 with the creation of a facility based on "special drawing rights" (SDRs) in the fund. The SDRs, also known as "paper gold," were simple credit entries in the IMF accounts, distributed to members in proportion to their existing membership quotas in the IMF. They could be used in place of dollars or gold to settle payments imbalances. The value of the SDR was initially defined as the gold equivalent of the dollar (0.888671 grams of fine gold), but after the collapse of the Bretton Woods system the SDR was initially redefined as a basket of 16 currencies. In 1981 it was reduced to 5 currencies, with a revision of the weights and currencies that comprise the basket conducted every five years. Rather than a transaction currency that can be used to finance purchase and sale, it is a unit of account to be used by deficit countries losing foreign exchange reserves in defense of their parity to acquire currencies of other members.

Despite all these attempts to shore up the system, U.S. gold stocks by 1971 had fallen to just over $10 billion against outstanding claims of more than $60 billion. In August of that year the United States suspended convertibility of the dollar to gold at the fixed $35-an-ounce parity and introduced an import surcharge. This represented the de facto confirmation of Triffin's prediction and the end of the Bretton Woods system.

From 1971 to 1974 an ad hoc Committee of the Board of Governors on Reform of the International Monetary System and Related Issues (composed of the 20 executive directors of the IMF and known as the Group of 20) worked on proposals for the resurrection and reform of the Bretton Woods system. This attempt was abandoned, however, after the outbreak of the oil crisis in 1973, and negotiations focused instead on interim arrangements such as a quota increase, the creation of a new governance structure in the form of an "Interim Committee" and a "Development Committee," abolition of an official price of gold, and regulations for the valuation of gold held by the IMF on behalf of its members. The changes were finally completed at a special meeting held in Jamaica in 1976 that eliminated the formal obligation under Article IV for members to fix a parity relative to gold or the dollar. Under the new arrangement each member was bound to "collaborate with the Fund and other members to assure orderly exchange arrangements and to promote a stable system of exchange rates." In particular, each member was encouraged to "avoid manipulating exchange rates or the international monetary system in order to prevent effective balance of payments adjustment or to gain an unfair competitive advantage over other members"

Changing Roles of the Bretton Woods Institutions After the reform there was no longer a need for countries to borrow from the IMF in order to support their exchange rates. In theory, under flexible exchange rates countries no longer needed to hold exchange reserves since adjustment to external imbalances would take place through the changes in the relative prices of tradable and nontradable goods produced by exchange rate adjustment. IMF operations were thus concentrated on orderly adjustment by ensuring that flexible currency exchange rates reflected underlying economic forces.

The World Bank's mandate has also changed. As the need for European reconstruction finance disappeared, attention shifted to the financing of large economic infrastructure projects to support developing countries. The bank is an active borrower in private capital markets to finance its projects in developing countries. Dissatisfaction with the development impact of these projects, however, and criticism of widespread corruption in their implementation during the 1980s, led the bank to focus on supporting the creation of markets and institutions in developing countries that would eliminate poverty and support their more active participation in the international trading system.

Thus the two Bretton Woods institutions have lived on beyond their original mandates negotiated in 1944 to become complementary and sometimes conflicting institutions that aim to finance development and eliminate poverty in developing countries.

See also currency crisis; dollar standard; exchange rate regimes; Federal Reserve Board; financial crisis; foreign exchange intervention; gold standard, international; international financial architecture; international liquidity; International Monetary Fund (IMF); international policy coordination; international reserves; special drawing rights; Triffin dilemma; World Bank; World Trade Organization

FURTHER READING

Beyen, Johan W. 1949. *Money in a Maelstrom*. New York: Macmillan. Reflections of a participant in the official international monetary discussions on reform of the international financial system.

Gardner, Richard N. 1956. *Sterling-Dollar Diplomacy*. Oxford: Clarendon Press. Classic history of the negotiations between the United States and the United Kingdom that led to the Bretton Woods institutions.

Meier, Gerald M. 1974. *Problems of a World Monetary Order*. New York: Oxford University Press. Presents narrative and important documents involved in the creation and evolution of the Bretton Woods system.

Skidelsky, Robert. 2001. *John Maynard Keynes: Fighting for Freedom, 1937–46*. New York: Viking Penguin. Biography containing an account of Keynes's formulation of his proposal for the postwar international monetary system and his participation in the Bretton Woods Conference.

Tew, Brian. 1970. *International Monetary Co-operation, 1945–70*. London: Hutchinson. Historical survey of the various stages of evolution of the international monetary system under fixed exchange rates.

van Dormael, Armand. 1978. *Bretton Woods: Birth of a Monetary System*. New York: Holmes and Meier. Personal account of the discussions and negotiations that produced the Bretton Woods agreements.

Williamson, John. 1977. *The Failure of World Monetary Reform, 1971–74*. Sudbury-on-Thames, UK: Thomas Nelson. A history and criticisms from a participant in the 1970 Group of 20 discussions on the reform of the Bretton Woods system.

JAN KREGEL

■ bubbles

Bubbles are situations in which asset prices persistently deviate from their fundamental values—that is, the prices warranted by the true earning potential of firms. Until recently, economists believed that asset prices as a rule reflected fundamental values, and that bubbles were highly implausible. This view relied on an argument of backward induction: the worth of any asset in the period before the final payoff date would simply be equal to the discounted value of its face value in the period it expired—that is, terminal value. Extending this argument backward, the value of an asset at any period would be equal to the discounted present value of its future stream of revenue. Otherwise, it was argued, an arbitrage opportunity would arise and the price would be pushed back to its fundamental value by the exploitation of this opportunity by informed traders.

Both the rise of rational expectations theory in economics and the idea that assets prices (such as shares and exchange rate) always incorporate all available public information (efficient market hypothesis in its most widely accepted *semistrong* form) went hand in hand with the backward induction argument, underpinning the view that the best way to understand asset prices changes was by focusing on information about fundamental values.

With the rise of behavioral finance theory since the mid-1980s, however, the view that asset prices equal discounted present value of future streams of revenue has come under critical scrutiny (Shiller 2003). In fact, with the growing skepticism about the efficient market hypothesis, much of the theoretical literature on asset pricing has been in a "vibrant flux" (Hirshleifer 2001). Given this change of paradigm in finance theory, it is hardly surprising that conceptual understanding of bubbles has been changing as well. In fact, in many of the new models with risk-averse traders that have asymmetric expectations it has become next to impossible to define what "fundamental value" is (Allen et al. 1993).

The older, standard view argued that all major asset price variations, including famous historical episodes of bubbles such as the Dutch Tulip Mania (1634–37), the Mississippi Bubble (1719–20), and the South Sea Bubble (1720), were not really "bubbles" in the sense that they were caused by changes in fundamental values (Garber 1990). Although it was always recognized that less than fully rational behavioral traders exist in financial markets, defenders of the standard view have held that informed arbitrageurs would undo any mispricing caused by them even when they did not cancel out each other's effect

(Fama 1970; Malkiel 2003). In this setting, bubbles could arise only in assets that had an infinite horizon (and thus lack a terminal value) because in this instance the backward induction argument did not apply. This case has largely defined the limits of initial theoretical interest in bubbles, going back to the economist Paul Samuelson (1958), and is the foundation of more recent work that now goes under the name of "rational" bubbles (also see the comprehensive survey by Santos and Woodford 1997).

With the rise of behavioral theory, however, the effectiveness of arbitrage became a central issue of contention. Behavioral theorists have produced numerous examples where arbitrage is severely limited in its ability to prevent persistent deviations of asset prices from their fundamental values, bolstering the view that major asset price variations are caused by mispricing as opposed to changes in fundamental values (De Long et al. 1990a, 1990b; Shleifer and Vishny 1997; Allen and Gorton 1993).

Contrary to what is often argued, bubbles are not necessarily the result of irrational trading behavior. A body of more recent work suggests that the main cause of bubbles is the uncertainty about higher-order beliefs, that is, rational agents not knowing what other rational agents will do, where irrationality is not a necessary ingredient (Allen et al. 2006). For instance, in Abreu and Brunnermeier (2003) fully rational traders know that the bubble will eventually burst, but in the meantime generate profits by riding it. They cannot individually bring down the price for lack of sufficient funds, but collectively can if they act in tandem. They all know that a common arbitrage opportunity exists, yet they are uncertain when other traders will begin to act on it. Thus each trader has to determine the right time to exit the market without knowing the exit strategies of other traders, and the varied opinions about the right time to exit cause the bubble to persist. In this setting, some news events can have a disproportionately strong effect beyond what their intrinsic information value would warrant by having the effect of causing traders to synchronize their exit strategies, and thus lead to a precipitous fall in price.

The idea that a bubble bursts only when rational traders' subjective expectations begin to coalesce provides an interesting connection to some of the currency crisis models with self-fulfilling expectations. But the linkages between the new body of work on bubbles by behavioral theorists and international finance so far remain few, despite the rich potential for fruitful connections between the two literatures. Such linkages are made in many economic models (e.g., Allen and Gale 1999; Morris and Shin 1999; Shin 2005), where it is argued that financial liberalization has led to asset price bubbles in numerous countries around the world, and the banking crises that usually accompany currency crises are seen to result from the bursting of the asset price bubble.

See also asymmetric information; banking crisis; carry trade; currency crisis; financial crisis; financial liberalization; interest parity conditions; lender of last resort; speculation

FURTHER READINGS

Abreu, D., and M. Brunnermeier. 2003. "Bubbles and Crashes." *Econometrica* 71: 173–204. Shows that a bubble can exist despite the presence of rational arbitrageurs.

Allen, F., and D. Gale. 1999. "Bubbles, Crises, and Policy." *Oxford Review of Economic Policy* 15 (3): 9–18. Argues that in many recent cases financial liberalization has led to a bubble in asset prices, the bursting of which resulted in banking crises and recession.

Allen, F., and G. Gorton. 1993. "Churning Bubbles." *Review of Economic Studies* 60: 813–36. Argues that agency problems caused by asymmetric information in financial markets cause financial assets to trade at prices different than fundamentals.

Allen, F., S. Morris, and A. Postlewaite. 1993. "Finite Bubbles with Short Sales Constraints and Asymmetric Information." *Journal of Economic Theory* 61: 206–29. Examines the conditions under which asset price bubbles emerge even when all agents are assumed to be rational.

Allen, F., S. Morris, and H. S. Shin. 2006. "Beauty Contests, Bubbles, and Iterated Expectations in Asset Markets." *Review of Financial Studies* 19 (2): 719–52. Shows that higher-order expectations in a fully rational asset pricing model can give rise to bubbles.

De Long, J. B., A. Schleifer, L. Summers, and R. Waldmann. 1990a. "Noise Trader Risk in Financial Markets." *Journal of Political Economy* 98 (4) (August): 703–38. Shows that short trading horizons and risk aversion of informed traders can cause bubbles.

De Long, J. B., A. Schleifer, L. Summers, and R. Waldmann. 1990b. "Positive Feedback Investment Strategies and Destabilizing Rational Speculation." *Journal of Finance* 45 (2) (June): 379–95. Shows that rational speculation might cause rational traders to act as noise traders, jumping on the bandwagon of an asset price bubble the latter might create.

Fama, E. 1970. "Efficient Capital Markets: A Review of Theory and Empirical Work." *Journal of Finance* 25 (1): 283–417. Gives a comprehensive review of theoretical and empirical work on capital markets based on the efficient market hypothesis.

Garber, P. 1990. "Famous First Bubbles." *Journal of Economic Perspectives* 4: 35–53. Argues that the famous bubbles in history can all be explained by changes in fundamentals.

Hirshleifer, D. 2001. "Investor Psychology and Asset Pricing." *Journal of Finance* 56 (4): 1533–97. Reviews theoretical arguments and capital market evidence bearing on the importance of investor psychology for security prices.

Malkiel, B. 2003. "The Efficient Market Hypothesis and Its Critics." *Journal of Economic Perspectives* 17 (1): 59–82. Defends the efficient market hypothesis against the criticisms leveled at it by the proponents of behavioral theory of finance.

Morris, S., and H. Shin. 1999. "A Theory of the Onset of Currency Attacks." In *Asian Financial Crisis: Causes, Contagion, and Consequences*, edited by P. R. Agenor, M. Miller, D. Vines, and A. Weber. Cambridge, UK: Cambridge University Press, 230–61. Examines the role of uncertainty about other agents' beliefs in currency crises.

Samuelson, P. 1958. "An Exact Consumption-Loan Model of Interest with or without the Social Contrivance of Money." *Journal of Political Economy* 66: 467–82. Gives an early discussion of bubbles that can arise in assets that have an infinite horizon lacking a terminal value.

Santos, M., and M. Woodford. 1997. "Rational Asset Pricing Models." *Econometrica* 65 (1): 19–57. Gives a comprehensive survey of the work based on the notion of "rational" bubbles.

Shiller, R. J. 2003. "From Efficient Markets Theory to Behavioral Finance." *Journal of Economic Perspectives* 17 (1): 83–104. Discusses the evolution of finance theory since the 1980s.

Shin, H. 2005. "Liquidity and Twin Crises." *Economic Notes* 34 (3): 257–77. Explores the role of liquidity in crises where a currency crisis and a banking crisis occur simultaneously and reinforce each other.

Shleifer, A. and Vishny, R. 1997. "The Limits of Arbitrage." *Journal of Finance* 52 (1) (March): 35–55. Discusses how anomalies in financial markets can appear and why arbitrage would fail to eliminate them.

KORKUT A. ERTURK

■ **capital account reversals**

See hot money and sudden stops

■ **capital accumulation in open economies**

Capital accumulation increases the amount of machinery, equipment, and structures available to workers in the economy, thus raising their productivity. Moreover, new capital often embodies technological progress. Hence capital accumulation can be viewed as the most direct way of raising the standard of living.

An open economy enjoys opportunities for capital accumulation that are not available in the absence of international transactions. For one, it does not have to produce all the equipment employed in that country. Importing capital equipment allows a country to take advantage of international specialization in the manufacture of capital goods. For example, East and Southeast Asia produce the bulk of semiconductors and computers, while North America and Europe make most of the airplanes. More generally, a country does not have to specialize in capital goods at all, as trade gives it opportunities to acquire machinery and equipment in exchange for commodities or consumption goods. China is perhaps the most prominent current example of the latter case. Although some researchers have suggested that specialization according to comparative advantage in, say, agriculture, may deprive an economy of the benefits associated with learning by doing, it should be noted that importing capital goods gives a country access to sophisticated technologies, helping it to advance its own technological frontier and learn by imitation.

In addition to the classical static gains from trade, opportunities for trade over time are also important. In a closed economy capital goods have to be manufactured domestically, and resources for their production have to be diverted from other uses, in particular from making consumption goods. This constraint is relaxed in an open economy, where first, capital goods can be purchased from abroad, and second, current consumption does not necessarily have to be sacrificed to make room for investment, since foreign borrowing can partially finance both.

Canonical View Traditionally, the relaxation of the intertemporal budget constraint has been viewed as a great benefit of openness. This is particularly true of emerging markets. A prototypical emerging market country is one where current output per worker is relatively low because there is not enough capital. The diminishing marginal productivity of capital means that if such a country has access to the same technology as industrial countries, the rates of return on investment in the emerging market will be high. The country will be poised for growth, but it faces a dilemma. On the one hand, investment today would raise productivity and therefore the standard of living tomorrow. On the other hand, impatience and intergenerational equity considerations create pressures to bring some of that future prosperity into the present, generating high consumption demand today. Since both consumption and investment goods have to be produced from current resources, however, it is impossible to manufacture more of both, and hard choices have to be made.

The trade-off is much less stark in an open economy. Either consumption or investment goods or both can be imported. Moreover, the total value of everything that the country produces does not have to equal the value of its absorption (the sum of consumption and investment), as long as the country can finance its trade deficit by borrowing or selling its assets abroad. Of course, debts have to be serviced, and opportunities offered by openness are not unlimited. What happens is that the autarkic requirement that domestic output equal absorption at every point in time is replaced with just one intertemporal constraint—that the present discounted value of output equal that of absorption. Hence when new investment opportunities arise and the future looks bright, it is possible to increase both investment and consumption, thus laying the foundation of future prosperity and at the same time enjoying some of its fruits in the present.

Foreign financing of trade deficits can take many forms, all of which, being manifestations of intertemporal trade, involve a gain today for a loss tomorrow. The country's residents can take out foreign loans. They can also sell bonds or shares in their enterprises to foreign portfolio investors. A form of foreign financing particularly important for capital accumulation is foreign direct investment, whereby a foreign investor either builds a new plant in the host country or purchases a substantial enough share in a host country enterprise to participate in its management. In any case, some degree of openness in the capital account is required to realize this benefit, which relies on exchanging not only different goods, but also goods delivered at different points in time and thus can be viewed as a generalization of gains from trade.

Of course, intertemporal trade requires the existence of willing partners. In the canonical view, the counterparts of capital-hungry emerging market countries are advanced economies, where capital-labor ratios are high and, because of diminishing returns, the marginal product of capital may be low. These countries (Japan being one example) may not

have enough profitable investment opportunities at home, and they may seek opportunities for investment abroad, particularly as aging residents of these countries save for retirement.

To recapitulate, in the canonical view, when a low-income country has in place conditions for high return on investment and rapid growth and opens up to international trade and capital flows, it will experience an investment boom while also increasing consumption. This is possible because the country is able to finance the resulting trade deficit by borrowing abroad or selling its assets to foreigners. Over time, as its productivity catches up with that in advanced countries and returns to investment decline, its growth decelerates, and trade surpluses replace trade deficits. This description fits broadly the experiences of many countries that experienced rapid growth, including Japan and continental Europe after World War II, South Korea from the mid-1960s through the mid-1980s, and the Central European economies during postcommunism transition.

Dynamics of Growth and Capital Accumulation in an Open Economy Abstracting from technological progress, the rate of growth of output per worker is determined by the pace of "capital deepening," or increases in capital per worker. In a closed economy, that rate depends on available investment opportunities and the residents' preferences regarding the choice between investing and consuming their income. Capital accumulation is gradual, and the standard of living, measured by consumption per capita, converges slowly to a steady-state value determined by available technology. Greater impatience—an unwillingness to sacrifice current consumption for the sake of investment—implies slower convergence. The presence of technological progress does not alter the essence of this progression, except that the economy converges to a steady-state growth rate rather than a steady-state level of output.

As discussed in the previous section, openness relaxes the budget constraint and could accelerate capital accumulation dramatically. Exactly how much is a contentious question in the open-economy macroeconomic literature. If one extends the classical growth model—the Ramsey-Cass-Koopmans model, where rational, forward-looking households and profit-maximizing firms operate in a perfectly competitive environment—to an open-economy setting by assuming free trade and perfect capital mobility, the result will be instantaneous convergence. Perfect capital mobility implies unlimited borrowing at a constant interest rate, so domestic residents will immediately borrow enough money and install enough capital equipment to equalize the domestic rate of return on new investment with that available in the advanced economies they are borrowing from. Assuming they have access to the same technology, output per worker would immediately jump to its steady-state level, equal to that in the most advanced countries. Consumption per capita would permanently remain below the level of advanced countries, reflecting the need to service the debt, but it would also stay constant after a momentary upward transition (or grow at a constant rate in the presence of technological progress).

Needless to say, instantaneous income convergence is not observed in practice. In reality, countries cannot borrow unlimited amounts at a constant interest rate, purchase unlimited amounts of capital equipment, and install it costlessly and instantaneously. Many things get in the way. Borrowing over a certain limit may raise the probability of default or result in too much concentration in the lender's portfolio. Lenders may respond by charging the borrowing country a higher interest rate or by cutting off additional funding. Poor legal systems and the risk of government intervention give rise to doubt about the enforcement of contracts and make lending institutions in advanced economies hesitant to commit overly large sums to emerging market borrowers. Lack of information about local investment opportunities also hinders flows of external finance, and underdeveloped financial systems in emerging markets have a limited capacity to process these flows. In addition, some types of capital, such as buildings, may not be tradable internationally, or at least require some local nontradable inputs, such as construction labor, for their installation. Therefore, if some items in the consumption basket (e.g., services) are also nontradable, the trade-off between

consumption and investment is still relaxed by openness, but less than a model with a single tradable good would imply.

These and other obstacles have been incorporated into open-economy macroeconomic models to moderate the rate of convergence. Details of these frictions and other model assumptions have implications for the evolution of other macroeconomic variables, such as domestic interest rates and the exchange rate. For example, combined with the assumption that production in the tradable sector is more capital intensive than in the nontradable sector, friction in the financial markets such that the interest rate charged on foreign borrowing increases with the amount borrowed in a given period results in gradual convergence of interest rates in emerging and advanced countries and in gradual real exchange rate appreciation in the former, a phenomenon known as the Balassa-Samuelson effect.

Recent Experience The canonical view suggests that capital should flow from advanced countries to emerging markets, where returns are higher. Over the first decade of the 21st century, however, a new pattern has emerged, where trade surpluses in China and some other fast-growing emerging economies are financing trade deficits in a number of advanced economies, most notably the United States. The investment rates are very high in the surplus economies, exceeding 40 percent of gross domestic product (GDP) in China, but national saving is even higher, reflecting the relatively low share of consumption in GDP. While China has attracted a lot of foreign direct investment, it has been purchasing foreign financial assets on a grand scale.

Several explanations have been offered for this reversal of the traditional pattern. Among the factors cited are the relatively weak social safety net in China and some other emerging economies, creating the need for high precautionary private saving; the relatively underdeveloped financial systems in these countries, resulting in the flow of these savings abroad, particularly to the United States, whose innovative financial system has been able to generate attractive assets; and government policy of preventing the exchange rate from appreciating despite the trade surpluses in order to promote exports and to accumulate international reserves as insurance against external shocks.

The canonical view still holds in many instances. Many advanced economies, for example Germany and Japan, are running current account surpluses, and many emerging market countries, including Central and Eastern European economies and many Latin American economies, are running deficits. High commodity prices, which boost the incomes of many developing countries and reduce their reliance on external finance, may have disrupted the traditional pattern, although this explanation clearly does not pertain to China. On the other hand, the fact that capital does not flow to the poorest developing countries does not really contradict the canonical view, as these countries, for many reasons, do not promise high return on investment despite having little capital.

See also capital flows to developing countries; economic development; foreign direct investment (FDI); growth in open economies, neoclassical models; international income convergence

FURTHER READING

Barro, Robert J., and Xavier Sala-i-Martin. 2004. *Economic Growth*. 2d ed. Cambridge, MA: MIT Press. An introduction to growth models and empirics.

Brock, Philip L., and Stephen J. Turnovsky. 1994. "The Dependent-Economy Model with both Traded and Nontraded Capital Goods." *Review of International Economics* 2 (3): 306–25. A somewhat involved model of growth and capital accumulation in a small open economy.

Klyuev, Vladimir. 2004. *Imperfect Capital Mobility in an Open Economy Model of Capital Accumulation*. IMF Working Paper No. 04/31. Washington, DC: International Monetary Fund. A model that combines capital accumulation dynamics with a financial market friction.

Obstfeld, Maurice, and Kenneth Rogoff. 1996. *Foundations of International Macroeconomics*. Cambridge, MA: MIT Press. A standard open-economy macroeconomics text.

Prasad, Eswar, Raghuram Rajan, and Arvind Subramanian. 2006. "Foreign Capital and Economic Growth." Paper presented at a Symposium sponsored by the Federal Reserve Bank of Kansas City. Available at http://www.kc.frb.org/publicat/sympos/2006/pdf/Prasad RajanSubramanian.0811.pdf. An account of the changing pattern of international capital flows and possible explanations.

Rodrik, Dani. 1995. "Getting Interventions Right: How South Korea and Taiwan Grew Rich." *Economic Policy* 10 (20): 53–107. A fascinating account of the period of growth takeoff in East Asia, with a focus on the investment boom.

VLADIMIR KLYUEV

■ capital controls

Capital controls are public policies that aim to curb or redirect flows of financial assets (e.g., bonds, loans, stocks, and foreign direct investments) across international borders, through taxes or various types of quantity restrictions. Governments use these policies as a means to generate fiscal revenues and for other economic and/or political reasons.

From an economic efficiency perspective, an important economic rationale for capital controls usually revolves around a "second-best" argument, that is, a distortion of the operation of free markets that cannot be eliminated. These distortions may be due to asymmetric information (when the two sides of a transaction do not have access to the same information), externalities (unaccounted for consequences of agents' decisions), financial sector problems, or other market pathologies. In such cases when the distortion cannot easily be eliminated, a policy that would have been clearly inferior to free markets (such as capital controls) can be used to counter the cost of the initial distortion.

The first modern era that was to a large extent free of capital controls and in which international financial markets became highly integrated occurred prior to World War I (1880–1914). During the war, and during most of the interwar period that followed, numerous countries, including all of the major participants in the international economy, relied on the heavy use of capital controls. During the post–World War II era of 1945–72, capital controls were also used, based on a set of agreements signed at Bretton Woods in 1944. This usage was supported by the International Monetary Fund (IMF). Under the Bretton Woods system, fixed exchange rates and capital controls protected countries from destabilizing external shocks. The IMF Articles of Agreement allowed countries to retain capital controls, stipulating that countries could not draw on IMF resources to meet a "large or sustained outflow of capital" (IMF Articles of Agreement, Article VI, Section 1a).

The countermovement, which began with the breakdown of the Bretton Woods system in the 1970s, sought to remove government controls and allow markets to operate freely. Most developed countries removed the bulk of their restrictions on capital flows in the 1970s and 1980s, with the United States removing its main capital controls in 1974. A number of countries in Asia moved in the same direction during this period and were followed in turn by several South American economies at the end of the 1980s. The majority of African and Middle Eastern countries did not progress as far in liberalizing their capital accounts at the time. This process gained momentum in the early 1990s, with many developing countries removing most of their control on international capital flows. In the developing economies, this trend was seen as part of the neoliberal "Washington consensus," a set of liberalizing policies that included the decontrol of foreign direct investment.

The Asian financial crisis of 1997–98 fostered a wave of analyses that sought to determine its causes. Many analysts charged that the Asian countries that were hit the hardest had liberalized their capital accounts prematurely under pressure from the IMF. This criticism gave rise to intense skepticism about the wholesale removal of capital controls. This debate has spawned an extensive literature striving to evaluate the economic impact of the various types of capital controls.

Classifying Restraints on Capital Movements

Restraints on capital flows may broadly be divided into those that focus on capital account transactions (*capital controls*) and those that focus on foreign currency transactions (*exchange controls*).

Capital Controls These involve constraining one or more elements of the balance-of-payments capital account. In principle they can cover foreign direct investment (FDI), portfolio investment, borrowing and lending by residents and nonresidents, transactions making use of deposit accounts, and other miscellaneous transactions. Within each of these categories, there may be a wide range of possible controls. For example:

FDI by residents abroad or nonresidents domestically can be directly restricted, or restrictions can influence the repatriation of profits and initial capital, and the structure of ownership.

Portfolio investment restrictions can take the form of regulations on the issuance or acquisition of securities by residents overseas or by nonresidents domestically. Limitations on the repatriation of dividends and capital gains and transfers of funds between residents and nonresidents may also exist, as may "market-oriented" tax measures.

Regulations on external debt transactions largely take the form of ceilings or taxes on external debt accumulation by residents and firms (financial and nonfinancial institutions). Special exemptions are often provided in the case of trade-oriented enterprises or on a case-by-case basis, as determined by the regulatory authorities.

Restrictions on deposit accounts may be imposed on foreign currency deposits held locally by residents and nonresidents, or deposits held in local currency by residents abroad or by nonresidents overseas or locally.

Other capital controls entail restrictions on real estate, emigration allowances, and other forms of capital transfers.

Some Key Distinctions Mechanisms for seeking to restrain international capital flows may be applied on a *selective* or *comprehensive* basis; they can be based on *outflows* or *inflows*; they can be either *temporary* or *permanent*; and they can focus on direct *quantitative* controls or on using the *price mechanism* via explicit or implicit taxation.

Selective versus Comprehensive Curbs on capital movements may be more or less extensive. At one end of the range, the capital account could be virtually inconvertible (i.e., comprehensive capital controls). India and China are notable examples in Asia. This being said, it is more typical for a country to impose controls selectively, on one or more items within the capital account. Of the 155 countries surveyed in an IMF study, 119 were reported to have imposed some type of restrictions on certain capital account transactions (Ariyoshi et al. 2000). Of the 119 countries with some controls, 67 were reported to use comprehensive controls. The distinction between selective and comprehensive controls may not be precise, however. For instance, even India and China have relative freedom in some forms of capital movements (such as FDI). The distinction is therefore more of degree than of kind. A generally illiberal regime, that is, one with comprehensive controls, typically has a "positive list" of exceptions to the controls. A generally liberal regime, that is, one that imposes controls selectively, is likely to have a "negative list" of items to be controlled.

Outflows versus Inflows What is the purpose of restraints on capital outflows? First, restraints can slow the speed of capital outflows when a country is faced with the possibility of a sudden and destabilizing withdrawal of capital during a time of uncertainty. Second, they are supposed to break the link between domestic and foreign interest rates, recognizing that a country cannot maintain a flexible exchange rate regime, monetary policy autonomy, and an open capital account all at once (i.e., "impossible trinity"). Thus, crisis-hit economies could conceivably pursue expansionary monetary and credit policies as a means of growing their way out of debt or a recession without having to worry about possible capital flight and the weakening of the currency.

Controls on capital inflows have become more common since the mid-1990s and are meant to minimize the chances of an abrupt and sharp capital reversal (bust) in the future. These are sometimes referred to as "speed bumps" or "sand in the wheels" of the international financial system. Empirical studies have indicated that capital controls have been more effective at preventing "excessive" capital inflows than at stemming capital flight (Mathieson and Rojas-Suarez 1993).

The most prominent example of these controls is the Chilean *encaje*, implemented between 1991 and 1998. The *encaje* was the requirement that a fixed percentage (initially 20 percent) of any short-term capital inflow be deposited in a non-interest-bearing account at the Chilean Central Bank for at least three years. The *encaje*'s aim was to slow down capital inflows, prevent an appreciation of the Chilean peso, and discourage short-term flows and shift more flows into less destabilizing inflows with longer maturities.

Temporary versus Permanent Restraints Temporary restraints are seen as a deterrent to excessive outflows or inflows during an "extraordinary" period. When a country is facing the possibility of capital flight, for example, temporary restraints give policymakers time to make appropriate changes in economic policy. Conversely, temporary restraints may be imposed when an economy experiences unsustainably large capital inflows, due to excessive confidence in the growth prospects of the economy (i.e., "irrational exuberance").

The rationale behind temporary restraints arises from the fear that such capital surges could lead to a loss of competitiveness through a real exchange rate appreciation (sometimes referred to as the "financial Dutch disease phenomenon") (Calvo et al. 1996). In addition, the literature on optimal sequencing of economic liberalization has emphasized the need to reform the financial sector in conjunction with putting in place adequate prudential regulation so as to limit the possibility of systemic risks, before attempting to decontrol capital account transactions. As such, temporary controls may allow reforms to be phased (for instance, see Eichengreen et al. 1999).

Permanent controls are seen as necessary even during "normal" times. The rationale here is that even if all the microeconomic distortions are eliminated and macroeconomic policies are generally sound, certain inherent market failures will cause suboptimal decisions to be made in a decentralized and free market economy. Insofar as these market failures are prevalent in a laissez-faire economy, they may provide a rationale for permanent, rather than event-specific or transitory, capital restraints.

Direct/Administrative versus Market/Price-Based Restraints Restraints can either directly control market movements or they can be a market-based mechanism that alters the structure of price incentives market participants face, thereby inducing them to modify their behavior. Direct controls can generate such problems as bribery and corruption, high enforcement costs, and the inevitable creation of a black market. These drawbacks have generally led economists to prefer cost-based levies, which also may generate tariff revenues, over quantitative restrictions.

Exchange Controls Exchange controls regulate the rights of residents to use foreign currencies and hold offshore or onshore foreign currency deposits. They also regulate the rights of nonresidents to hold domestic currency deposits onshore. In addition, they may be defined to include taxes on currency transactions and multiple exchange rate practices that are aimed at influencing the volume and composition of foreign currency transactions. Exchange controls are not necessarily aimed at restricting capital flows; they are occasionally intended only to restrict the current account (trade in goods and services). Yet, strictly speaking, currencies are simply another type of financial asset, and therefore these controls amount to restrictions on trade in assets. Furthermore, whatever their original intention, exchange controls generally have a significant impact on the capital account.

Data on Capital Controls The primary source for internationally comparable data on capital controls is the IMF *Annual Report on Exchange Arrangements and Exchange Restrictions* (AREAER). The publication contains a detailed description of the legal framework that governs the capital account and is published annually, providing data relating to a large number of countries. Prior to 1996 the IMF reported only whether the country had imposed restrictions; after 1996 the publication includes a much more detailed description of the legal regime governing the capital account.

A number of researchers have devised various numerical indicators of the degree of capital account openness/controls, using the IMF AREAER dataset in addition to primary country sources (e.g., Miniane 2004; Edwards 2006). Several researchers alternatively focus on stock markets and detail various aspects of their actual or de jure state, such as when stock markets are open to trading by foreigners, or when domestic companies are allowed to cross-list abroad (e.g., Henry 2003; Edison and Warnock 2003; Bekaert et al. 2005).

This research agenda is still in its infancy, with little agreement among researchers on the appropriate measures and wide agreement on their respective drawbacks. As data quality improves economists should be better able to analyze and distinguish among the effects of various types of controls.

See also asymmetric information; balance of payments; Bretton Woods system; capital mobility; convertibility; currency crisis; exchange rate regimes; financial crisis; financial liberalization; hot money and sudden stops; impossible trinity; International Monetary Fund (IMF); Tobin tax; Washington consensus

FURTHER READING

Ariyoshi, A., K. Habermeier, B. Laurens, I. Otker-Robe, J. Canales-Kriljenko, and A. Kirilenko. 2000. "Country Experiences with the Use and Liberalization of Capital Controls." Occasional Paper No. 190. Washington, DC: International Monetary Fund. Details cross-country experiences with various types of capital controls.

Calvo, G., L. Leiderman, and C. Reinhart. 1996. "Inflows of Capital to Developing Countries in the 1990s." *Journal of Economic Perspectives* 10: 125–39. Discusses the macroeconomic implications of large-scale capital inflows into a developing country.

Bekaert, Geert, Campbell R. Harvey, and Christian Lundblad. 2005. "Does Financial Liberalization Spur Growth?" *Journal of Financial Economics* 77 (1): 3–55.

Bird, G., and Ramkishen S. Rajan. 2000. "Restraining International Capital Flows: What Does It Mean?" *Global Economic Quarterly* 1 (2): 57–80. Describes the various types of capital and exchange controls. Surveys the main arguments for and against the use of capital controls.

Edison, Hali J., Michael W. Klein, Luca Antonio Ricci, and Torsten Sløk. 2004. "Capital Account Liberalization and Economic Performance: Survey and Synthesis." *IMF Staff Papers* 51 (2): 220–56. Surveys the literature on the economic effects of capital account openness and stock market liberalization. Also discusses the various empirical measures used to gauge the presence of controls on capital account transactions.

Edison, Hali J., and Francis E. Warnock. 2003. "A Simple Measure of the Intensity of Capital Controls." *Journal of Empirical Finance* 10 (1–2): 81–103.

Edwards, Sebastian. 2006. "Capital Controls, Capital Flow Contractions, and Macroeconomic Vulnerability." *Journal of International Money and Finance* 26 (5): 814–40. Along with Edison and Warnock (2003), introduces new measures of the intensity of capital account openness and/or restrictions.

Eichengreen, B., M. Mussa, G. Dell'Ariccia, E. Detragiache, and G. Milesi-Ferretti. 1999. "Liberalizing Capital Movements: Some Analytical Issues." *Economics Issues No. 17* (February). Washington, DC: International Monetary Fund. Discusses the analytical issues surrounding the imposition of capital controls.

Henry, Peter Blair. 2003. "Capital Account Liberalization, the Cost of Capital, and Economic Growth." *American Economic Review* 93 (2): 91–96. One of several research projects that estimates the economic consequences of capital controls.

Mathieson, D., and L. Rojas-Suarez (1993). "Liberalization of the Capital Account: Experiences and Issues." Occasional Paper No. 103. Washington, DC: International Monetary Fund. Discusses cross-country experiences with capital account liberalization.

Miniane, Jacques. 2004. "A New Set of Measures on Capital Account Restrictions." *IMF Staff Papers* 51 (2): 276–308.

Stiglitz, Joseph E. 2000. "Capital Market Liberalization, Economic Growth, and Instability." *World Development* 28 (6): 1075–86. Offers a critical analysis of the economic impact of capital account liberalization.

Wright, Mark L. J. 2006. "Private Capital Flows, Capital Controls, and Default Risk." *Journal of International Economics* 69: 120–49. Offers a theoretical examination of the conditions that make capital controls beneficial.

ILAN NOY AND RAMKISHEN S. RAJAN

■ **capital flight**

Today's world economy is characterized by large movements of capital across countries and regions. Cross-border financial movements include legal transactions that are duly recorded in national accounts as well as the illicit smuggling of capital referred to as *capital flight*. Capital flight is the residual difference between capital inflows and recorded foreign-exchange outflows. Capital inflows consist of net external borrowing plus net foreign direct investment. Recorded foreign-exchange outflows comprise the current account deficit and net additions to reserves and related items. The difference between the two constitutes the measure of capital flight (Erbe 1985).

Measuring Capital Flight Capital flight (KF) for a country in a given year is calculated as:

$$KF = \Delta DEBT + FDI - (CA + \Delta RES)$$

where $\Delta DEBT$ is the change in total external debt outstanding, FDI is net direct foreign investment, CA is the current account deficit, and ΔRES is net additions to the stock of foreign reserves.

A number of refinements are made to the capital flight formula to obtain a measure of capital flight to take into account the various channels and factors that affect capital flight. First, as countries' debts are denominated in various currencies, the reported U.S. dollar value needs to be adjusted to take into account fluctuations in the exchange rates of these currencies against the dollar (Boyce and Ndikumana 2001). Second, trade misinvoicing constitutes an important channel of capital smuggling (Gulati 1987; Lessard and Williamson 1987). Export underinvoicing and import overinvoicing inflate the current account deficit recorded in the balance of payments, while import underinvoicing leads to understatement of the true deficit. Thus the capital flight estimate obtained using balance of payments trade data is likely either to overstate or understate the actual volume of capital flight. The refined measure of capital flight is the following:

$$KF = \Delta ADJDEBT + FDI \\ - (CA + \Delta RES) + MISINV$$

where *ADJDEBT* is debt flows adjusted for exchange rate fluctuations and *MISINV* is net trade misinvoicing. Additionally, a measure of the opportunity cost of capital flight or the losses incurred by the country through capital flight is obtained by imputing interest earnings on capital that left the country in early years.

Significance of Capital Flight from Developing Countries The problem of capital flight from developing countries deserves serious attention for several reasons. First, capital flight reduces domestic investment directly by reducing the volume of savings channeled through the domestic financial system, hence retarding economic growth. Second, capital flight affects the government's budget balance indirectly by reducing the tax base through reduced domestic economic activity. Moreover, capital flight forces the government to increase its borrowing from abroad, which further increases the debt burden and worsens the fiscal balance. Third, capital flight is likely to have pronounced regressive effects on the distribution of wealth. The individuals who engage in capital flight generally are members of a country's economic and political elites. They take advantage of their privileged positions to acquire and channel funds abroad. The negative effects of the resulting shortages of revenue and foreign exchange, however, fall disproportionately on the shoulders of the less wealthy members of society. The regressive impact of capital flight is compounded when financial imbalances result in devaluation of the national currency because those wealthy individuals who hold the external assets are insulated from its negative effects, while the poor enjoy no such cushion. Fourth, capital flight exacerbates the resource gaps faced by developing countries and forces them to incur more debt, which worsens their international position and undermines overall economic performance.

What Causes Capital Flight? The empirical literature has identified a number of factors that are associated with high levels of capital flight (Ndikumana and Boyce 2003; Murinde, Hermes, and Lensink 1996). The single most consistent finding in empirical studies on capital flight is that the annual flows of external borrowing are strongly associated with capital flight. The causal relationship between capital flight and external debt can run both ways: that is, foreign borrowing can cause capital flight, and capital flight can lead to more foreign borrowing. Foreign borrowing causes capital flight by contributing to an increased likelihood of a debt crisis, worsening macroeconomic conditions, and causing a deterioration of the investment climate. This is referred to as *debt-driven capital flight*. Foreign borrowing may provide the resources as well as a motive for channeling private capital abroad, a phenomenon called *debt-fueled capital flight* (Boyce 1992). Capital flight also induces foreign borrowing by draining national foreign-exchange resources and forcing the government to borrow abroad.

Good economic performance, measured in terms of higher economic growth, and stable institutions are associated with lower capital flight. Strong economic growth, for example, is a signal of higher expected returns on domestic investment, which induces further domestic investment and thus reduces capital flight. High and sustained economic growth also gives confidence to domestic investors about the institutional and governance environment of the country, which encourages domestic investment while reducing incentives for capital flight. The political and institutional environment is also an important factor in capital flight. In particular, political instability and high levels of corruption encourage capital flight as savers seek to shield their wealth by investing in foreign assets.

Policy Responses to Capital Flight Private assets held abroad by residents of developing countries include both illicit and legally acquired assets. Different strategies are required to repatriate the two types of assets. Presumably, savers choose to hold legally acquired assets abroad to maximize risk-adjusted returns. These assets will be repatriated as domestic returns rise relative to foreign returns. In order to prevent further transfers of resources abroad and to entice repatriation of legally acquired assets, therefore, governments in developing countries must implement strategies to improve the domestic investment climate.

Illegally acquired assets are held abroad not so much to maximize the returns on assets as to evade the law. Owners of these assets will be enticed by higher domestic returns only if they have guarantees of immunity against prosecution for fraud and penalties for unpaid taxes. Such guarantees, however, would have perverse incentive effects by rewarding malfeasance. Alternatively, these assets could be impounded and repatriated by force. However, the identity of the owners of capital that has been illegally smuggled out of a country can be difficult to obtain from the major financial centers, which have strong customer privacy legislation. In order to recover the proceeds of capital flight, therefore, developing countries will need the cooperation of the international financial centers and their governments.

See also balance of payments; capital controls; capital flows to developing countries; foreign direct investment (FDI); international reserves; money laundering; offshore financial centers

FURTHER READING

Boyce, J. K. 1992. "The Revolving Door? External Debt and Capital Flight: A Philippine Case Study." *World Development* 20 (3): 335–49. Explains in detail the two-way causation between capital flight and external borrowing.

Boyce, J. K., and L. Ndikumana. 2001. "Is Africa a Net Creditor? New Estimates of Capital Flight from Severely Indebted Sub-Saharan African Countries, 1970–1996." *Journal of Development Studies* 38 (2): 27–56. Provides a detailed description of the methodology for measuring capital flight and covers a representative sample of African countries.

Erbe, S. 1985. "The Flight of Capital from Developing Countries." *Intereconomics* (November/December): 268–75. Provides a concise definition of capital flight, which was extended by subsequent studies.

Gulati, S. K. 1987. "A Note on Trade Misinvoicing." In *Capital Flight and Third World Debt*, edited by D. R. Lessard and J. Williamson. Washington, DC: Institute for International Economics, 68–78. Describes the mechanisms of trade misinvoicing, which is an important channel for capital flight.

Lessard, D. R., and J. Williamson, eds. 1987. *Capital Flight and Third World Debt.* Washington, DC: Institute for International Economics. Discusses capital flight and its relationship with external debt.

Murinde, V., N. Hermes, and R. Lensink. 1996. "Comparative Aspects of the Magnitude and Determinants of Capital Flight in Six Sub-Saharan African Countries." *Saving and Development* 20 (1): 61–78. Attempts an empirical analysis of the causes of capital flight.

Ndikumana, L., and J. K. Boyce. 2003. "Public Debts and Private Assets: Explaining Capital Flight from Sub-Saharan African Countries." *World Development* 31 (1): 107–30. Provides a comprehensive survey of the literature on the determinants of capital flight and investigates the causes of capital flight by exploring the role of conventional portfolio-theory factors as well as institutional and policy-related factors.

LÉONCE NDIKUMANA

■ capital flows to developing countries

Since the 1970s, business cycles in many developing countries have been characterized by fluctuations in international capital flows. This has been particularly true for economies integrated into world financial markets. Fluctuations in capital flows lead to variations in the availability of financing (absence or presence of credit rationing) and in length of loans (maturities). This involves short-term volatility, such as the very intense upward movement of spreads (margin over basic interest rate that reflects perceived risk) and the interruption (rationing) of capital flows observed during the Mexican (1994–95), Asian (1997–98), and Russian (1998) crises. They also involve *medium-term* cycles, as the experience of the past few decades (since the last quarter of the 20th century) indicates.

The developing world experienced two full medium-term cycles between 1970 and 2000: a boom of external financing in the 1970s, followed by a major debt crisis, mainly in Latin America, in the 1980s; and a new boom in the 1990s, followed by a sharp reduction in net flows after the Asian and Russian crises of 1997–98. By 2007, international capital flows to developing countries had recovered, but new sources of potential procyclicality had emerged, particularly related to the explosive growth of derivatives worldwide. Derivatives, at their simplest, allow two parties to agree on a future price for a given asset, for example, a purchase of foreign exchange. Derivative contracts have become increasingly important in developing economies as instruments for firms and others to hedge risk and for international hedge funds and investment banks to speculate. Large parts of these derivative markets are not regulated, nor have existing regulations fully incorporated the risks that derivatives pose in situations of stress, when they can add to systemic risk.

During booms, developing countries that markets view as success stories are almost inevitably drawn into a capital flows boom, inducing private-sector deficits and risky balance sheets (Ffrench-Davis 2001). For example, when Mexico joined both the North American Free Trade Agreement (NAFTA) and the Organisation for Economic Co-operation and Development (OECD) in the 1990s and was seen as a "successful reformer," it initially attracted huge inflows of capital. Even countries with weak macroeconomic fundamentals, such as low current account deficits, may be drawn into the boom, however, and all countries, again with some independence from their fundamentals, will suffer sudden stops of capital flows. There is also widespread evidence that ample private capital flows encourage expansionary macroeconomic policies during booms, such as excessive growth of government spending. Ample private capital flows encourage expansionary responses by individuals (who consume more) and companies (which invest more), as well as by macroeconomic authorities. When capital inflows fall sharply or turn into outflows, consumers, companies, and governments in developing countries have to reduce their spending. Thus unstable external financing distorts incentives that both private agents and authorities face *throughout* the business cycle, inducing a procyclical behavior of economic agents *and* macroeconomic policies (Kaminsky et al. 2004).

Although procyclicality is inherent in capital markets, domestic financial and capital account lib-

eralization in the developing world, as well as technological developments, such as very rapid communications, have accentuated its effects. A lag in developing adequate prudential regulation and supervision frameworks increases the risks associated with financial liberalization.

The costs of such financial volatility in the developing world in terms of economic growth are high. There is now significant evidence that capital flows have not encouraged growth and rather have increased growth volatility in emerging economies (Prasad et al. 2003). Whatever the efficiency gains from financial market integration, they seem compensated by the negative effects of growth volatility. During and after financial crises, major falls in output, employment, and investment have occurred (Eichengreen 2004). Volatility in financial markets is partly transmitted to developing countries through public-sector accounts, especially through effects of the availability of financing on government spending, and of interest rates on public sector debt service payments. In commodity-dependent developing countries, links between availability of financing and commodity prices reinforce the effects on public sector accounts. The most important effects of capital account fluctuations are on private spending and balance sheets. Capital account cycles, their domestic financial multipliers, and their reflection in asset prices (such as stock markets and property prices) became an important determinant of growth volatility.

Different types of capital flows show different volatility patterns. The higher volatility of short-term capital indicates that reliance on such financing is highly risky (Rodrik and Velasco 2000), whereas the smaller volatility of foreign direct investment (FDI) vis-à-vis all forms of financial flows is considered safer. FDI also can bring valuable benefits related to technology transfers and access to management expertise and to foreign markets. Use of risk management techniques by multinationals, via derivatives, may make FDI in critical moments as volatile as traditional financial flows, however (Griffith-Jones and Dodd 2006).

Countercyclical Prudential Regulation and Supervision Managing countercyclical policies for developing countries in the current globalized financial world is no easy task. For this, it is essential that international cooperation in the macroeconomic policy area be designed to overcome incentives and constraints. This means that the first role of international financial institutions, from the point of view of developing countries, is to mitigate the procyclical effects of financial markets and open policy space for countercyclical macroeconomic policies, that is, policies that can attenuate the economic cycle, for example, by expanding government spending when the economy is slowing down so as to accelerate recovery and by contracting government spending in boom times, to avoid overheating of the economy. This can be achieved partly by smoothing out boom-bust cycles at the source through regulation.

One of the major problems seems to be the focus of prudential regulation on microeconomic risks and the tendency to underestimate risks that have a clear *macroeconomic* origin (see BIS 2001, chap. 7). For example, in times of rapid economic growth, a portfolio of bank loans may seem very safe; when the economy slows down or goes into recession, however, that same portfolio of bank loans may become highly problematic. This dimension of changing risk through time is not usually sufficiently perceived by individual banks or even by bank regulators. The basic problem in this regard is the inability of individual financial intermediaries to internalize collective risks assumed during boom periods.

Moreover, traditional regulatory tools, including both Basel I and Basel II international standards for bank regulation on capital adequacy, have a procyclical bias. The basic problem is a system in which loan-loss provisions are tied to loan default or to short-term expectations of future loan losses. Precautionary signals may be ineffective in hampering excessive risk-taking during booms, when expectations of loan losses are low, effectively underestimating risks and the counterpart provisions for loan losses. The sharp increase in loan delinquencies during crises reduces financial institutions' capital and, hence, their lending capacity, potentially triggering a credit squeeze; this would reinforce the downswing

in economic activity and asset prices and, thus, the quality of the portfolios of financial intermediaries.

Given the central role all of these processes play in the business cycles of developing countries, and the important influence of banking regulation on credit availability in the modern economy, the crucial issue is to introduce a countercyclical element into prudential regulation and supervision. The major innovation is the Spanish system of forward-looking provisions, introduced in 2000 and later adopted by Portugal and Uruguay. According to this system, provisions are made when loans are disbursed based on the expected ("latent") losses; such latent risks are estimated on the basis of a full business cycle.

Under this system, provisions build up during economic expansions and are drawn on during downturns. Moreover, many regulatory practices aimed at correcting risky practices shift underlying risks to nonfinancial agents (e.g., companies). This is why capital account regulations aimed at avoiding inadequate maturity structure of borrowing in external markets by all domestic agents, and at avoiding currency mismatches in the portfolios of those agents operating in nontradable sectors, may be the best available option (Ocampo 2003). Also, as long as there is no international central bank that could provide unconditional official liquidity in times of crisis, international rules should continue to provide room for the use of capital account regulation by developing countries.

More broadly, the Basel II Accord to regulate banks internationally has a number of problems that require attention: it is complex where it should be simple; it is implicitly procyclical when it should be explicitly countercyclical; and although it is supposed to more accurately align regulatory capital with the risks that banks face, in the case of lending to developing countries it ignores the proven benefits of diversification. In particular, by failing to take account of the benefits of international diversification of portfolios, capital requirements for loans to developing countries will be significantly higher than is justified on the basis of the actual risks attached to such lending. There are thus fears that Basel II creates the risk of a sharp reduction in bank lending to developing countries, particularly during crises (thus enhancing the stop-go pattern of such lending).

One clear way in which Basel II could be improved to reduce these problems would be to introduce the benefits of diversification. One of the major benefits of investing in developing and emerging economies is their relatively low correlation with mature markets. This has been tested empirically using a wide variety of financial, market, and macro variables. Different simulations that compared estimated losses of portfolios that were diversified across both developed and developing countries with the losses of portfolios in developed countries only indicate that the former were from 19 to 23 percent lower (Griffith-Jones, Segoviano, and Spratt 2002). If risks are measured precisely, this should be reflected in lower capital requirements.

An additional positive effect of taking account of the benefits of diversification is that this makes capital requirements far less procyclical than otherwise. Indeed, if the benefits of diversification are incorporated, simulations show that the variance over time of capital requirements will be significantly smaller than if they are not.

Adequate Official Liquidity for Crises At the country level, central banks have acted for many decades as lenders of last resort, providing liquidity automatically to prevent financial crises and avoid their deepening when they occur. Equivalent international mechanisms are still at an embryonic stage, with International Monetary Fund (IMF) arrangements, as of 2007, providing credit only with policy conditions attached and not automatically (Ocampo 2003). Despite some moderation in this area in the early 2000s, the general trend in IMF financing was toward increased conditionality, even in the face of external shocks, including those that involve financial contagion. Enhanced provision of emergency financing at the international level in response to external shocks is essential to lowering unnecessary reduction of economic growth or recession within a country and to avoiding the spread of crises to other countries.

Between the 1980s and the early 2000s, capital account liberalization and large capital account volatility greatly increased the need for official liquidity

to deal with large reversals in capital flows. There is increasing consensus that many of the crises in emerging markets in the late 1990s and early 2000s have been triggered by self-fulfilling liquidity runs (Hausmann and Velasco 2004). Indeed, capital outflows could be provoked by many factors not related to countries' policies. The enhanced provision of emergency financing in the face of capital account crises is thus important not only to manage crises when they occur but to prevent such crises and to avert contagion (Cordella and Yeyati 2005; Griffith-Jones and Ocampo 2003).

To address this obvious need, the IMF has made efforts to improve its lending policy during capital account crises. In 1997, the Supplemental Reserve Facility was established.

The evidence that even countries with good macroeconomic fundamentals might be subject to sudden stops of external financing also gave broad support to the idea that a precautionary financial arrangement, closer to the lender-of-last-resort functions of central banks, had to be added to existing IMF facilities. In 1999 the IMF introduced the Contingent Credit Line (CCL). The facility was never used and was discontinued in November 2003. Contrary to what was desired, the potential use of the CCL was seen as an announcement of vulnerability that could harm confidence.

After the expiration of the CCL, the IMF explored other ways to achieve its basic objectives. A move in that direction was proposed by the managing director of the IMF and approved by the International Monetary and Financial Committee in April 2006. Interestingly, as the IMF recognized, by offering instant liquidity, a well-designed facility of this sort "would place a ceiling on rollover costs—thus avoiding debt crises triggered by unsustainable refinancing rates, much in the same way as central banks operate in their role of lenders of last resort" (IMF 2005). Approval of such a facility within the IMF, however, seems difficult to achieve.

Implications Volatility and contagion in international financial markets increased the incidence of financial crises and growth volatility in the developing world, and reduced policy space to adopt countercyclical macroeconomic policies. Therefore, a major task of a development-friendly international financial architecture is to mitigate procyclical effects of capital flows and open a debate about countercyclical macroeconomic policies in the developing world. To achieve these objectives, a series of useful policy instruments can be developed, including explicit introduction of countercyclical criteria in the design of prudential regulatory frameworks; designing market mechanisms that better distribute the risk faced by developing countries throughout the business cycle; and better provision of countercyclical official liquidity to deal with external shocks. Such measures would make capital flows better support development.

See also asymmetric information; balance sheet approach/effects; banking crisis; capital controls; capital flight; capital mobility; contagion; convertibility; currency crisis; financial crisis; financial liberalization; global imbalances; hot money and sudden stops; international financial architecture; International Monetary Fund (IMF); International Monetary Fund conditionality; international reserves; Latin American debt crisis; lender of last resort; twin deficits

FURTHER READING

Bank for International Settlements. 2001. *71st Annual Report* (June). Basel: BIS. Annual report by the BIS on ongoing macroeconomic and financial issues in the global economy.

Cordella, Tito, and Eduardo Levy Yeyati. 2005. "A (New) Country Insurance Facility." IMF Working Paper No. 05/23 (January). Washington, DC: International Monetary Fund. Proposes the creation of a country insurance facility to deal with liquidity runs and financial crises and how such a facility might be designed.

Eichengreen, Barry. 2004. "Global Imbalances and the Lessons of Bretton Woods." NBER Working Paper No. 10497 (May). Washington, DC: National Bureau of Economic Research. Excellent overview of the various analytical debates about the ongoing global macroeconomic imbalance.

Ffrench-Davis, Ricardo. 2001. *Financial Crises in "Successful" Emerging Economies*. Washington DC: Brookings Institution Press and Economic Commission for Latin America and the Caribbean (ECLAC). Focuses on developing countries in Asia and Latin America that have been impacted by a "new variety" of crises and discusses the main factors that might increase a country's vulnerability to such crises.

Griffith-Jones, Stephany, and Randall Dodd. 2006. "Report on Derivatives Markets: Stabilizing or Speculative Impact on Chile and a Comparison with Brazil." Santiago, Chile: Economic Commission for Latin America and the Caribbean (ECLAC). Available at http://www.cepal.org.ar/publicaciones/xml/2/28572/2007-282-W134-GriffithJones.pdf. Discusses the growth of the derivatives markets in Chile and Brazil and analyzes their role in the economy.

Griffith-Jones, Stephany, and José Antonio Ocampo. 2003. *What Progress on International Financial Reform? Why so Limited?* Stockholm: Expert Group on Development Issues. Offers a stock-take of the progress in international financial reforms and why such progress has been fairly limited to date.

Griffith-Jones, Stephany, Miguel Angel Segoviano, and Stephen Spratt. 2002. "Basel II and Developing Countries: Diversification and Portfolio Effects." Capital Market Liberalization Program, December. Available at http://www.ids.ac.uk/ids/global/finance/pdfs/FINALBasel diversification2.pdf. Discusses the impact of Basel II on developing countries.

Hausmann, Ricardo, and Andrés Velasco (2004). "The Causes of Financial Crises: Moral Failure versus Market Failure." December. Available from http://ksghome.harvard.edu/~rhausma/new/causes_of_fin_crises.pdf. Discusses reasons behind crises in many developing countries in the 1990s and early 2000s with emphasis on Latin America.

Kaminsky, Graciela L., Carmen M. Reinhart, and Carlos A. Vegh. 2004. "When it Rains, it Pours: Procyclical Capital Flows and Macroeconomic Policies." NBER Working Paper No. 10780. Using a sample of 104 countries, the paper documents some stylized facts about the nexus between net capital flows, fiscal policy, and monetary policy.

Ocampo, José Antonio. 2003. "Capital Account and Counter-Cyclical Prudential Regulation in Developing Countries." In *From Capital Surges to Drought: Seeking Stability for Emerging Markets,* edited by Ricardo

Ffrench-Davis and Stephany Griffith-Jones. London: Palgrave Macmillan, 217–44. Highlights the role of capital account regulations and countercyclical prudential regulation of domestic financial intermediaries in managing a country's macroeconomic risks associated with capital account–induced boom-bust cycles.

Prasad, Eswar S., Kenneth Rogoff, Shang-Jin Wei, and M. Ayhan Kose. 2003. "Effects of Financial Globalization on Developing Countries: Some Empirical Evidence." IMF Occasional Paper 220. Washington, DC: IMF. Comprehensive discussion of the empirical evidence regarding the impact of financial globalization on developing countries in terms of economic growth and macroeconomic volatility. Also considers what countries need to do to exploit the benefits of financial globalization.

Rodrik, Dani, and Andrés Velasco. 2000. "Short-Term Capital Flows." In *Proceedings of the Annual World Bank Conference on Development Economics 1999.* Washington DC: World Bank, 59–90. Emphasizes the role of short-term debt to reserves ratio as a robust predictor of financial crises and discusses ways in which countries can reduce their financial vulnerability.

STEPHANY GRIFFITH-JONES

■ capital mobility

Capital mobility refers to the ease with which financial flows can occur across national borders. High capital mobility implies that funds are transferred relatively seamlessly from one country to another. Low capital mobility implies that financial capital does not flow as easily into or out of a particular country, and that there may be barriers hindering the capital flow. In the world of international finance there are many types of financial flows, including foreign direct investment (FDI), portfolio flows, and flows processed through the banking sector. In order to capture the mobility of such a broad range of financial flows, economists use many different ways to measure capital mobility. No single measure will capture all the essential characteristics of capital mobility. The best results are probably obtained by using several measures together. This entry groups

the many types of measures into four main categories: arbitrage measures (for debt flows), quantity-based measures, measures of equity market integration, and regulatory/institutional measures (figure 1).

Arbitrage Measures The first category refers to arbitrage conditions, which involve returns on debt instruments. These are largely embodied in the interest parity conditions: the covered interest parity (CIP), the uncovered interest parity (UIP), and the real interest parity (RIP). The basic idea behind parity conditions is that in a perfectly integrated financial market, investors will detect any gaps between the domestic currency return on a domestic asset and the domestic currency return on a foreign asset and will seek to close that gap. In other words, arbitrage should equalize the prices of identical assets traded in different markets—that is, the law of one price holds—and participants in the market will behave in such a way as to remove any differences in the exchange rate adjusted returns on assets in different markets. There are important differences between these measures: the CIP is the narrowest of measures; the UIP is a somewhat broader measure; and the RIP is the broadest of arbitrage measures. The arbitrage conditions seek to equate rates of returns of comparable assets across different markets/economies. If capital mobility is high, then any differences in (exchange rate adjusted) rates of return will be alleviated through arbitrage in those markets. Hence, high capital mobility implies that the various interest differentials will be low; perfect capital mobility implies a zero differential; while nonzero differentials suggest that there are barriers to capital flows.

Arbitrage conditions are probably a more appropriate way of measuring integration for certain sectors, such as banking, than for the whole economy. The perennial problem with using such arbitrage measures, especially in developing economies, is the question of what interest rate to use, and to what extent the available interest rates are comparable across countries.

Quantity-Based Measures A growing body of literature has explored quantity-based measures of financial integration. These measures provide an

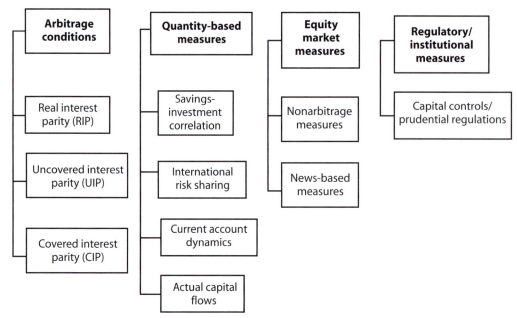

Figure 1
Categorizing measures of capital mobility: A simple framework

alternative to the traditional arbitrage conditions as a way of measuring capital mobility. Four such measures include savings-investment correlations, consumption correlations, current account dynamics, and actual capital flows.

Savings-Investment Correlations Feldstein and Horioka (1980) pioneered the use of savings-investment correlations as a measure of capital mobility. The argument regarding savings-investment correlations is that in a closed economy, by definition, savings must equal investment (i.e., the correlation between savings and investment should be very high). At the other extreme, with highly integrated capital markets and a single world interest rate, domestic investment should be largely independent of domestic savings since the former can be financed through foreign savings. There are significant empirical and theoretical shortcomings with the Feldstein-Horioka criterion and it remains a controversial measure of financial integration. The so-called Feldstein-Horioka puzzle is discussed in a separate entry.

International Risk Sharing Although savings-investment correlations are the most popular quantity measure of financial integration, a more theoretically elegant measure is examination of consumption patterns within and across economies (Obstfeld 1989). Essentially, agents access capital markets to save or dissave based on how they wish to smooth levels of consumption over time. If two agents in different countries have similar consumption patterns, this implies that they use the same capital markets and that the markets are equally accessible to both. More specifically, a high level of correlation of consumption between two economies is an indication that each country is accessing the same capital market to choose a time path for consumption that is outside the path implied by available domestic resources, thus implying access or openness to international capital flows.

The intuition behind tests of consumption correlations ("international risk sharing") is that financial openness ought to afford individuals the opportunity to smooth consumption over time as they can borrow and lend on international financial markets. Thus consumption in any one country should co-move less with income over time, and if their preferences over consumption are similar, consumption should be correlated across countries.

Conceptually, although consumption-based tests of capital mobility are attractive when attempting to discern whether a region is ready for monetary union (as the degree of business cycle synchronization may be less relevant as long as agents can share consumption risks across borders), they are based on a number of restrictive assumptions that limit their practical usefulness.

Current Account Dynamics A related strand of the literature has focused on current account dynamics and, in particular, whether the current account is stationary (i.e., its mean and variance do not change over time). Simply put, the argument here is that if savings and investment are cointegrated (i.e., a linear combination of the two is stationary), their difference, which is the current account, ought to be stationary (Ghosh 1995). The problem with this line of reasoning is that a finding of stationarity could imply either that an economy is not financially integrated (thus suggesting the existence of a long-run relationship between savings and investment) or that the open capital market is imposing a solvency constraint on the country in the sense that the financial market will penalize a country that is viewed as being profligate by persistently running current account deficits (i.e., spending more than it is producing).

Actual Capital Flows A fourth quantity-based measure of capital mobility is observation of the actual magnitude of capital flows (FDI, portfolio flows, bank flows). All other things being equal, the higher the levels of capital inflows and outflows, the greater the level of capital market integration. Although examination of cross-border capital flows is useful in examining the composition of flows, insofar as there is no yardstick by which to gauge high versus low capital mobility, it tends to be of limited use as a measure of financial integration.

Measures of Equity Market Integration Another measure of the integration of international capital markets involves examining equity market returns. This measure essentially refers to those nonarbitrage price-based measures that include stock market correlations (both direct correlations as well as the extent to which risky assets can be priced using the international capital asset pricing model), or news-based measures (i.e., the extent to which interest rates and other financial market variables are affected by common shocks versus country-specific ones).

Papers measuring nonarbitrage measures examine the bivariate properties of the data and how movements in the equity markets in one country influence the series in another country. In general, the methodological applications range from simple correlations and covariances to value-at-risk-based approaches such as Granger causality and variance decompositions for the short-run analysis and vector error correction models and cointegration tests for the long-run scenario. Essentially, these approaches examine the effect of changes in stock markets in major financial centers (the United States, Japan, the United Kingdom, etc.) on local stock markets. In addition, the use of test of asset pricing models has gained popularity. Asset pricing models allow for risk characteristics to be considered when evaluating market data for different countries. The variance of stock returns provides very useful information about the extent of capital mobility, in that a variance that decreases as the international portfolio increases would imply that correlations between markets are low enough for benefits to diversification to be realized. This is evidence against integration between these markets.

The news-based measures tend to be analyzed in a multivariate setting. The objective is to test for the existence of common trends and common sources of variation among a group of markets. A single common trend, for instance, implies a high level of integration. The existence of country-specific sources of variation would imply the opposite.

Regulatory, Institutional, and Other Measures The degree of capital mobility can also be measured by observing the extent to which a country has imposed capital controls. The types of controls that might be in place are numerous, including legislative control over deposit rates, restrictions on capital account transactions such as restrictions on term or currency, regulations relating to the entry and exit of foreign financial services, and exchange controls. An obvious limitation of these measures is the difficulty of obtaining good proxies to measure such barriers or regulatory impediments that prevent financial integration. A fundamental assumption with all indexes of capital controls is that the removal of capital controls may, in some way, result in a more financially integrated economy. A situation could exist, however, in which a country has very few capital controls and yet is not regarded as being integrated with other economies. This could be due to legal or political factors, cultural variables, business practices, or the economy's simply not having been noticed by others as a potential place to export capital flow—that is, it "escaped the radar" of the international financial community.

Going Forward It is generally believed that innovations in communications and market access, including reduction in barriers to capital flows, have increased the extent of international capital mobility worldwide. Obtaining empirical evidence of this is difficult, however. There is no single measure of capital mobility. Each measure offers only a partial indication of the extent of integration. Given the multiplicity of definitions of capital mobility, an important area for future research would be to develop a multivariate methodology to reduce the multidimensionality of the concept of capital mobility to an operational univariate measure. It is equally important to undertake more detailed studies on the legal, institutional, and other barriers that hinder the free movement of cross-border capital.

See also balance of payments; capital controls; capital flows to developing countries; convertibility; exchange rate forecasting; exchange rate volatility; Feldstein-Horioka puzzle; home country bias; interest parity conditions; purchasing power parity

FURTHER READING

Bayoumi, T. 1997. *Financial Integration and Real Activity.* Manchester, UK: Manchester University Press. Good reference for several measures of financial integration.

Feldstein, M., and C. Horioka. 1980. "Domestic Saving and International Capital Flows." *Economic Journal* 90: 314–29. The seminal reference for the literature on saving/investment correlations.

Flood, R., and A. Rose. 2003. "Financial Integration: A New Methodology and an Illustration." NBER Working Paper No. 9880. Washington, DC: National Bureau of Economic Research. A recent extension of the equity market integration literature using a general intertemporal asset pricing model.

Ghosh, A. 1995. "International Capital Mobility amongst the Major Industrialized Countries: Too Little or Too Much?" *Economic Journal* 105: 107–28. A good reference on theoretical and empirical underpinnings for consumption correlations.

Obstfeld, M. 1986. "Capital Mobility in the World Economy: Theory and Measurement." *Carnegie-Rochester Conference Series on Public Policy* 24: 55–104. A good reference on theoretical and empirical underpinnings for consumption correlations.

———. 1989. "How Integrated Are World Capital Markets? Some New Tests." In *Debt, Stabilization, and Development*, edited by G. Calvo. Oxford: Basil Blackwell, 134–55. A reading on consumption correlations.

Phylaktis, J., and F. Ravazzolo. 2005. "Stock Market Linkages in Emerging Markets: Implications for International Portfolio Diversification." *Journal of International Financial Markets, Institutions, and Money* 15: 91–106. A useful reference for the more recent financial integration literature involving equity markets.

TONY CAVOLI AND RAMKISHEN S. RAJAN

■ carry trade

The term *carry trade*, or *currency carry trade*, refers to trades in which funds are borrowed in a relatively low-yielding currency to invest in a higher-yielding currency. In the process, a "short" position is established in the low-yielding currency and a "long" position is created in the other currency. The degree of leverage depends on the amount of capital (or the required margins) put up against the borrowing in the relatively low-yielding currency. The borrower benefits not only from the difference in yields but, more important, from any favorable change in the exchange rate. In principle, carry trades can take place between any assets that offer different expected rates of return. This entry covers carry trades in currencies.

The considerable recent attention paid to carry trades reflects the judgment of some market analysts that these trades can significantly influence exchange rate dynamics. Surprisingly, however, there is little quantitative evidence on their importance. This, in large measure, reflects the opaqueness of the over-the-counter (OTC) markets in which the bulk of currency trading takes place, along with the difficulties of identifying the size of such trades from balance of payments data. Much of the evidence on carry trades tends to be anecdotal and based on the assessments of currency market analysts or participants.

The possibility of systematically earning higher-than-normal returns from carry trades is closely linked to whether foreign exchange markets are informationally efficient. In an efficient market, such trades would not be expected to systematically produce above-average returns (adjusted for risk), and any abnormal returns would be a matter of chance. Either because foreign exchange markets are not informationally efficient or on account of differences in view about the appropriate underlying equilibrium model of returns, the carry trade literature assumes that market players seek to systematically earn superior returns.

Market Efficiency The *informational efficiency* of financial markets refers to whether asset prices fully reflect all available information. The concepts of informational efficiency and rational expectations are closely related, and the term *rational expectations* is also used to characterize situations in which expectations (and markets) are informationally efficient.

Since the move toward generalized floating in the early 1970s there has been an extraordinary amount of empirical work on the efficiency of major foreign exchange markets. For the most part, the work has not been successful in unambiguously determining whether major foreign exchange markets are informationally efficient. Largely because efficiency tests are joint tests of both informational efficiency and an assumed underlying model of equilibrium returns, statistical findings invariably are open to different interpretations. As applied to the foreign exchange market, a common assumption in many tests has been that interest-earning assets denominated in different currencies are perfect substitutes and carry

the same expected rate of return (uncovered interest rate parity). Based on this assumption—together with the assumption of covered interest rate parity, which allows the forward rate to be used as a proxy for the unobserved expected future spot rate—many early tests considered whether forward exchange rates were biased predictors of future spot exchange rates (see equation [1]) or whether the difference between the realized spot rate and the lagged forward rate could be predicted on the basis of the available information set $I(t)$ (see equation [2]).

Under the null hypothesis of market efficiency, the parameter α in equation (1) should be equal to zero and the parameter β equal to unity, while the error term should be white noise. Alternatively, informational efficiency can be considered with relation to equations such as (2) where—depending on the assumed content of the information set $I(t)$—the market is either weakly or strongly efficient when $\Gamma = 0$ and the error term is white noise. Here lower case s and f refer to the natural logarithms of the spot and forward rates, respectively, $I(t)$ is the information set at time t, v and η are error terms, and Δ is the first difference operator. The term $f(t, k)$ refers to the period t forward rate for period k.

$$\Delta s(t + k, k) = \alpha + \beta(f(t, k) - s(t)) + v(t + k) \quad (1)$$
$$s(t + k) - f(t, k) = \Gamma I(t) + \eta(t + k) \quad (2)$$

Almost without exception, tests based on equations such as (1) and (2) have rejected the informational efficiency of foreign exchange markets under the maintained assumption of interest rate parity. In particular, a relatively robust finding across many major currencies and time periods—sometimes referred as to the negative forward bias puzzle—is that β in equation (1) is closer to negative unity than to positive unity as implied under efficiency. In addition, it is not uncommon for available information—including lagged values of forward and spot exchange rates—to be found useful in helping predict the difference between forward and spot exchange rates in equations such as (2). In short, forward premiums appear to be biased predictors of future exchange rate changes and forecast errors tend to be predictable.

These findings are open to a number of different interpretations with regard to whether it is informational efficiency or uncovered interest rate parity that is rejected. Hence the underlying equilibrium model of returns is not conclusive. This issue has not been resolved, but recent tests of efficiency have increasingly moved beyond the assumption of uncovered interest rate parity to incorporate both constant and time-varying risk premiums. In addition, a number of studies have used survey data to measure exchange rate expectations in place of forward rate data.

Carry Trades and Exchange Rate Regimes The extent to which large carry trades can be built up is likely to be influenced importantly by the exchange rate regime. Under a pure floating regime, uniformity in exchange rate expectations across agents would be expected to exclude the possibility of a very large buildup in carry positions. Negative sentiment toward a currency would be expected under floating rates to be reflected relatively quickly in adjustments in interest rates and exchange rates as individuals sought to build up their short-long currency positions. As a result, risk-adjusted expected returns on assets denominated in different currencies would tend to be equalized. Any substantial buildup in carry positions under flexible exchange rates could arise when agents hold very different exchange rate expectations or there are differences in risk appetites. In such circumstances, one individual's "long" carry position on a currency would be matched by an equal and offsetting position on the part of other individuals.

When there is substantial exchange market intervention and sterilization, the emergence of large carry positions seems more plausible. Such positions would represent bets of the private sector vis-à-vis the official sector about the future time path of the exchange rate. The positions would be facilitated by the official sector intervening in the foreign exchange market and providing increased supplies of the currency in which the private sector sought to go "long." Of particular interest in this latter connection are situations in which the buildup in "long" positions in a currency is matched by the authorities' sterilization of their exchange market interventions. In these cases, the long carry position of the private sector would effectively be matched by the authorities assuming the short position in the currency.

Carry Trades and Asia Notwithstanding the large amount of attention paid to carry trades, the evidence of their importance in particular episodes is largely in the eye of the beholder. In analyzing the 1997–98 Asian financial crisis, international organizations such as the International Monetary Fund took the view (based largely on market intelligence) that carry trades had been important determinants of exchange market dynamics. Spurred by sterilized intervention that led to interest rates in many Asian emerging markets remaining well above those in the United States and Japan even as currencies were expected to appreciate, carry trades were seen as contributing importantly to the surge in short-term capital flows to the region before the crisis. Subsequently, the unwinding of these trades during the 1997–98 crisis was seen as contributing to significant downward pressure on many regional currencies. No attempt was made, however, to quantify the importance of these trades.

More recently, many market analysts expressed concern about a possible disorderly appreciation of the Japanese yen during 2006 related to a possible earlier buildup of large carry trades that had been funded in yen during the period when short-term interest rates in Japan were effectively zero. As the Bank of Japan began to raise interest rates in 2006, the possibility that these trades might be unwound led to concerns that the Japanese yen would appreciate sharply. In the event, the yen continued to remain weak even as short-term interest rates in Japan were increased modestly during the first half of 2006. Subsequently, there has been debate among private sector financial analysts as to how large the buildup in yen-funded carry trades during the zero interest-rate period had been and whether its importance had been exaggerated.

Carry trades can be viewed as one of a large number of ways in which individuals can speculate on currency movements. The absence of data on the quantitative significance of carry trades precludes a systematic evaluation of their potential importance, but many market analysts regard them as potentially important influences on exchange markets dynamics during particular episodes.

See also Bank of Japan; capital flows to developing countries; conflicted virtue; currency crisis; exchange rate regimes; exchange rate volatility; foreign exchange intervention; hedging; interest parity conditions; international reserves; peso problem; speculation; sterilization

FURTHER READING

Anderson, Jonathan. 2006. *Japan, Free Money, and the World: Asian Economic Perspectives.* Hong Kong: UBS Investment Research. Provides a critical review of the role of the yen carry trade in 2005 and 2006 and concludes that its significance was limited.

Bank for International Settlements. 2007. "International Banking and Financial Market Developments." *BIS Quarterly Review* Part 4 (December). Basel. Discusses the role of the carry trade and its potential significance for exchange market dynamics.

Fama, E. F. 1970. "Efficient Capital Markets: A Review of Theory and Empirical Work." *Journal of Finance* 25: 383–417. The definitive original overview of efficient capital markets theory and the early empirical evidence.

Hallwood, C. Paul, and Ronald MacDonald. 2000. "Spot and Forward Exchange Rates and the Efficient Market Hypothesis." In *International Money and Finance*, edited by C. Paul Hallwood and Ronald MacDonald. Malden, MA: Blackwell, chapter 12. A comprehensive survey of the literature on the efficiency of the foreign exchange market.

International Monetary Fund. 1998. *International Capital Markets: Developments, Prospects, and Key Policy Issues.* World Economic and Financial Surveys. Washington, DC: International Monetary Fund. Discusses the role of the carry trade in the lead-up to the Asian financial crisis and in the subsequent crisis dynamics.

CHARLES ADAMS

■ Central American Common Market (CACM)

The Central American Common Market (CACM) was established by the General Treaty of Central American Economic Integration signed on December 13, 1960, by Guatemala, Honduras, El Salvador, and Nicaragua. Costa Rica joined on July 23, 1962. The treaty was the principal economic component of a series of measures adopted during the 1950s and early 1960s that were designed to facilitate the political and economic integration of the five nations of the Central American isthmus. The General Treaty also created two regional institutions: the Secretariat for Regional Economic Integration and the Central American Bank for Economic Integration. The political component of this integration process was to be carried out through the Organization of Central American States (ODECA), which was formed on October 14, 1951.

Integration Efforts in the 1950s and 1960s The notion of a unified isthmus has a long history in Central America. It dates back at least to 1821 and the formation of the Federation of Central American States shortly after the region's independence from Spain. The federation lasted only 15 years, but the ideal of unification continued to prevail throughout the next century and finally led to concrete unification measures in the 1950s. During this period, regional integration was driven in part by the example of the European Community and by the views of economists at the UN Economic Commission for Latin America (ECLA). According to their import-substitution industrialization (ISI) strategy, poor nations should eschew international trade and turn inward by closing their internal market to foreign products. The resulting boost to their domestic industry would lead to higher living standards. Since the ISI strategy does depend on the size of internal markets, however, ECLA economists believed that the strategy would be more effective in the region if the five nations formed a free trade area that expanded the market size for local firms but still protected them from international competition. Prompted by these ideas, the five nations signed the Multilateral Treaty on Free Trade and Economic Integration in Central America on June 10, 1958. That same day, they also signed the Regime for Central American Integration Industries (RII), which permitted member countries to identify firms that due to economies of scale would be granted monopoly right to supply the entire region. To ensure balanced development, each nation would be allocated an equal number of these industries.

The ECLA approach led to opposition from the United States and other groups concerned with its protectionist bent. Responding to this pressure, the five nations reached a new agreement—the General Treaty—that altered the direction of the proposed common market from one focused on protection to one intended to be more encouraging of trade. For instance, whereas the Multilateral Treaty required that products eligible for free trade intraregionally be listed within the treaty, the General Treaty freed all products unless specifically exempted and identified by the treaty.

By most criteria, the CACM was considered a dramatic success, especially during its first decade of operation. According to Bulmer-Thomas (1998, 314–16), the elimination of duties on intraregional trade and the creation of a common external tariff (CET) was done rapidly and efficiently: 74 percent of goods listed on the tariff schedule traded freely immediately on the General Treaty's entry into force and, by the end of 1966, 94 percent of all listed products were assessed no duty when trading intraregionally. In addition, by 1967, 90 percent of traded goods were covered by the CET. As a consequence, intraregional trade expanded by a factor of nine, from $31.3 million in 1960 to $285.2 million in 1970, and the share of intraregional trade as a percentage of total exports rose from 7.0 percent in 1960 to 26 percent in 1970. For more details see Bulmer-Thomas (1998, table 1).

Despite these successes, deficiencies in the integration model soon became evident. The General Treaty was biased toward freeing up intraregional trade in consumer goods manufactured regionally and left in place barriers to intraregional agricultural trade. This contributed to sizable intraregional trade imbalances among the less-developed members such as Honduras and Nicaragua, which had small or nonexistent manufacturing sectors. It also led to sizable trade diversion as third-country manufactured consumer goods, which faced high protectionist CETs, were replaced by more expensive, lower-quality regional goods. Yet the mechanisms

established to address imbalances were either incapable of reaching a consensus or nonexistent. For instance, the RII was suspended when Costa Rica permitted the establishment of a tire factory to compete with an integration industry already operating in Guatemala. Finally, since the structure of the regional agreement still maintained elements of the ISI model, tariff revenues fell sharply as a percentage of total government revenues. Not only did consumer goods trade duty-free, since they were manufactured regionally, but also imports of intermediate and capital goods from outside the region entered duty-free to avoid harming these regional manufactures. To address this problem, the five nations agreed to a 30 percent increase in the CET under the San Jose Protocol of 1968.

Finally, regional integration collapsed when a dispute over the attempted expulsion by Honduras of Salvadoran immigrants during the summer of 1969 led to a four-day war between the two neighbors and the eventual withdrawal of Honduras from the CACM in December 1970. Relations between the two nations would remain suspended for a decade.

A Revival of Integration Efforts in the 1990s As a by-product of efforts to restore peace to Central America, the Central American presidents' meeting in Antigua, Guatemala, in 1990 called for reviving the integration process. In response, the five nations, including Panama as a new member, signed the Tegucigalpa Protocol to the ODECA Charter on September 13, 1991. The protocol amended the existing integration framework and established a new institution, the System of Central American Integration (SICA), which was to oversee the integration process. As an umbrella institution, SICA oversaw 4 thematic areas (economic, political, social, and environmental) and incorporated 27 other regional institutions, more than 200 treaties or protocols existing among the member nations, and 3 regional bodies: the Central American Court of Justice, the Central American Parliaments, and the Secretary General of SICA.

It is worth underscoring that the protocol called for the creation of an economic union and the positioning of the region within the global economy.

This was one of a number of important indicators that views within the region regarding the appropriate development model had shifted dramatically. The integration efforts were now to be guided by an export-led development model whose orientation was outward, as opposed to the inward-oriented, import-substitution framework that dominated the views of the early architects of the CACM. Regionalism was now to be open, not closed. Moreover, several of the member countries had adopted a neoliberal trade strategy that focused on lowering tariffs, eliminating quantitative trade barriers, and employing more market-friendly measures.

The next important step in the revival of economic integration was taken on October 29, 1993, when the six member nations of SICA signed the Guatemala Protocol to the General Treaty. This protocol focused on economic integration and committed the six nations to the formation of a customs union.

Since these steps were taken, the momentum toward integration has ebbed and flowed, buffeted by a host of factors internal (such as the election of presidential candidates opposed to further integration) and external to the region. For instance, Hurricane Mitch in 1998 dampened enthusiasm for integration, the prices of the region's commodity exports deteriorated sharply, and SICA was confronted with a severe funding crisis.

Nonetheless some progress has occurred and the enthusiasm for integration appeared to be on the rise by about 2005. By early 2007, all but a handful of regional goods traded freely within the region and, according to data provided by SICA, 94 percent (5,846 out of 6,198) of the products in the tariff schedule had been harmonized into a CET. Additionally, the CET was far less protectionist than during the earlier integration period and was applied as follows: 0 percent to capital goods and raw materials produced outside the region, 5 percent to raw materials produced regionally, 10 percent to intermediate goods produced regionally, and 15 percent to final goods. Moreover, the recent implementation of the Central American–Dominican Republic Free Trade Agreement (CAFTA-DR), which establishes a free trade area (FTA) that includes the United States, the five Central American countries, and the Dominican Republic, has great potential for deepening the region's integration.

Following a comprehensive comparison of the FTA with existing integration instruments, Gonzalez (2005) concludes that among the most important features of the new FTA is that the Central American countries opted to make its requirements apply in a plurilateral fashion, as opposed to only bilaterally between the United States and each country. This contrasts with the FTA agreements signed earlier by the region with Chile and with Mexico, which were hub-and-spoke in nature. A second important feature identified by Gonzalez is that the FTA agreement sets a "floor" on disciplines in a host of existing areas (e.g., trade in goods) and new areas (e.g., services, investment, intellectual property, dispute settlement, etc.). As a result, the new FTA essentially deepens and updates the regional integration instruments.

See also Central American–Dominican Republic Free Trade Area (CAFTA-DR); common market; free trade area; Free Trade Area of the Americas (FTAA); import substitution industrialization; regionalism; tariff rate quotas

FURTHER READING

Bulmer-Thomas, Victor. 1998. "The Central American Common Market: From Closed to Open Regionalism." *World Development* 26 (2): 313–22. Contains a useful bibliography and updated analysis of the new integration efforts by the leading scholar on economic integration in the region.

Cline, William R., and Enrique Delgado, eds. 1978. *Economic Integration in Central America*. Washington, DC: Brookings Institution. Excellent, comprehensive analysis of the initial period of integration.

Gonzalez, Anabel. 2005. *The Application of the Dominican Republic–Central America–United States Free Trade Agreement*. OAS Trade, Growth, and Competitiveness Studies. Washington, DC: Organization of American States. Principally a legal analysis, but also provides excellent insights on the economic implications of CAFTA-DR for regional integration.

Solis, Luis G., and Patricia Solano. 2001. *Central America: The Difficult Road towards Integration and the Role of*

Canada. Ontario, Canada: Canadian Foundation for the Americas. Provides a useful overview of SICA's early history and outlines measures Canada may adopt to support integration efforts in the region.

JOSE A. MENDEZ

■ Central American–Dominican Republic Free Trade Area (CAFTA-DR)

On May 28, 2004, after a year and a half of intense negotiations, the United States and five Central American countries (Costa Rica, El Salvador, Guatemala, Honduras, and Nicaragua) signed the Central American Free Trade Agreement (CAFTA). The Dominican Republic joined the agreement on August 5, 2004, and to reflect this, the acronym was changed to CAFTA-DR. Like other recent free trade agreements (FTAs) signed by the United States, CAFTA-DR is a comprehensive agreement that goes far beyond traditional FTAs. Once fully implemented the agreement will bring about the elimination of barriers to virtually all trade and investment, and each member country will have implemented legal and regulatory reforms designed to protect intellectual property, raise and enforce labor and environmental standards, improve customs administration, and open up government procurement.

By December 2007, the treaty had been implemented between the United States and four countries and implementation with the Dominican Republic was imminent. Costa Rica had yet to submit the treaty to its congress for a vote, but ratification was certain following approval on October 7, 2007 by 51.6 percent of Costa Rican voters of a referendum supporting the treaty.

Challenges and Opportunities For the Central American (CA) countries, the FTA offered an opportunity to enhance their protrade, market-oriented development strategy by locking in the strategy with a trade agreement with the United States, their principal trading partner as well as the world's largest market. In 2004, the United States accounted for 56 percent of the region's exports and 44 percent of the region's imports. The agreement would also secure access on a reciprocal and more permanent basis. Eighty percent of the region's exports to the United States already entered duty free, but under the Caribbean Basin Initiative and General System of Preferences, tariff programs are one way, highly limited, and subject to periodic review and approval by the U.S. Congress.

U.S. policymakers saw an opportunity to improve national security because boosting regional prosperity would strengthen the region's ability to cooperate on security. They also saw an opportunity to pry open global markets for U.S. exporters and investors. The U.S. Trade Representative (USTR) notes that in 2004 the region represented the 2nd largest U.S. export market in Latin America behind Mexico and the 14th largest worldwide, ahead of India, Indonesia, and Russia combined.

The treaty posed two major challenges. First, it had to be perceived as balanced and not one in which the United States used its large economic size to gain the bulk of concessions. In 2004, the six countries had a combined population of about 45 million and a joint gross domestic product (GDP) of $90.7 billion, whereas the U.S. population stood at 294 million and GDP amounted to $11.7 trillion. Second, the treaty needed to balance the beneficial competitive pressures that come from freer trade with a recognition that the burden of adjustment would fall heaviest on the Central American countries since their economies were relatively more closed. Their average rate of protection was estimated to be more than three times that for the United States. Also, a high share of their economy was vulnerable. In 2004, the trade exposure index (the ratio of exports and imports to GDP) ranged from a low of 49.4 percent for Guatemala to a high of 94.3 and 95.8 percent, respectively, for the Dominican Republic and Costa Rica. Yet the Central American countries were least able to counteract the harmful adjustment effects. In 2004, per capita incomes (valued at purchasing power parity, or PPP) ranged from a high of $9,887 for Costa Rica to a low of $2,677 for Nicaragua, whereas the U.S. per capita GDP (valued at PPP) was $39,710.

Agreement Highlights The treaty commits the signatories to the elimination of import tariffs on nearly all goods traded among member countries. The only products exempted from tariff reductions are imports of sugar by the United States, white maize by El Salvador, Guatemala, Honduras, and Nicaragua, and potatoes and onions by Costa Rica.

The majority of products will receive zero-duty status immediately on the treaty's entry into force. According to estimates provided by USTR (2005), nearly 80 percent of U.S. exports of consumer and industrial goods to the region and 50 percent of its agricultural exports will receive immediate duty-free access. The tariffs on the remaining exports of industrial goods would be phased out in 10 years, whereas those facing U.S. agricultural products would be subject to tariff phase-out periods ranging from 5 to 20 years. For regional exporters, nearly 100 percent of their exports to the United States will receive immediate duty-free access, with only 19 products restricted to a 10-year phase-out period.

In addition to the lengthy transition provisions for duty reductions in order to lessen adjustment effects, the treaty permits tariff-rate quotas (TRQs) to be established for sensitive agricultural products. TRQs provide immediate zero-duty access to the quota amount of imports, but above-quota imports are assessed a higher, prohibitive rate. A special temporary safeguard rule was also established to prevent harm to domestic agriculture during the transition.

The United States made two important concessions in terms of market access. First, it agreed to double the region's sugar quota allocation over a 15-year period. Second, it relaxed the rules of origin pertaining to apparel, allowing certain apparel to enter duty-free even if the fabric was not produced in the United States. Eligible textile and apparel imports would also receive duty-free treatment retroactively to January 1, 2004.

In the services area, the treaty commitments go beyond those under the World Trade Organization's General Agreement on Trade in Services. Most industries receive broad market access. United States negotiators were also successful in opening access to sensitive sectors such as the telecommunications and insurance industries in Costa Rica. By late 2007 all that remained was passage of the necessary implementing legislation, considered a virtual certainty given the composition of the legislature. The related investment provision locks in rights for foreign investors that are already recognized in the region, such as the right to national treatment and nondiscrimination, fair compensation for expropriation, free transfer of profits, third-party arbitration, etc. A unique feature of this FTA is that it provides for a tribunal to review decisions by arbitration panels to ensure that foreign investors are not using them to circumvent domestic judiciaries (World Bank 2006).

The treaty includes detailed rules for improvement of customs procedures, enhancing transparency and access to government procurement bidding, and the monitoring and enforcement of labor and the environment standards. Unique aspects of the treaty related to the latter include: (1) establishing the right of citizens to request investigations if they believe environmental laws have been violated, (2) a commitment from the United States to strengthen the region's capacity to monitor labor and environment standards, and (3) the establishment of fines of up to $15 million for each instance of nonenforcement of labor laws.

Several studies have developed estimates of the likely economic effects on member countries of forming CAFTA-DR. Despite differences in techniques and scope, the conclusions are broadly similar. For the United States, they show that the aggregate economywide effect will be positive, but negligible. According to the largest estimate of the economic effects, by Brown et al. (2005), liberalizing trade in goods improves U.S. economic welfare by 0.04 percent of U.S. gross national product (GNP), while liberalization in services adds an additional 0.13 percent of U.S. GNP. The remaining studies, though limited to the effects of removing barriers to trade in goods, project a positive and even smaller impact on the U.S. economy. Two other studies (surveyed in Brown et al. 2005) project an improvement of GDP of 0.02 and 0.01 percent, whereas USITC (2004) obtains a positive impact on

U.S. welfare of $166 million which, when rounded, amounts to 0.00 percent of GDP.

The consequences for the regional economies are projected to be more significant. Brown et al. estimate an increase of 4.4 percent in Central American countries' GNP, whereas the other two studies calculate a rise of 2.4 and 1.5 percent in GDP.

It is important to note that the projections just cited for the Central American countries may be viewed as "minimum" estimates since they do not take into account the likely impact on foreign investment flows. Nor do they take into account the effects of locking in access to the U.S. market and providing a more stable regulatory environment. On the other hand, as underscored by the World Bank (2006), for these gains to be fully realized and spread equitably, the Central American countries will need to make complementary investments in areas such as infrastructure and create programs to assist the most vulnerable groups, that is, the poor, so they "have the means to take full advantage of the new opportunities."

See also Central American Common Market (CACM); free trade area; Free Trade Area of the Americas (FTAA); regionalism; tariff rate quotas

FURTHER READING

Brown, Drusilla K., Kozo Kiyota, and Robert M. Stern. 2005. "Computational Analysis of the U.S. FTAs with Central America, Australia and Morocco." World Economy 28 (10): 1441–90. Contains a useful outline of CAFTA's principal features and a valuable comparison of their own computations of CAFTA's economic impact to those developed by other authors.

Hornbeck, J. F. 2005. "The Dominican Republic–Central America–United States Free Trade Agreement (DR-CAFTA)." CRS Report RL31870. Washington, DC: Congressional Research Service. Exhaustive, but excellent, description of CAFTA-DR, including its history and the motives or issues driving the negotiators.

Salazar, Jose M., and Jaime Granados. 2004. "The U.S.–Central America Free Trade Agreement: Opportunities and Challenges." In Free Trade Agreements, U.S. Strategies and Priorities, edited by Jeffrey J. Schott. Washington, D.C.: Institute for International Economics,

225–75. Another thorough review of CAFTA-DR that identifies the key actors and their interests.

USITC. 2004. "U.S.–Central America–Dominican Republic Free Trade Agreement: Potential Economywide and Selected Sectoral Effects." Investigation No. 2104-13, USITC Publication 3717. Washington, DC: United States International Trade Commission.

USTR. 2005. "Free Trade With Central America and the Dominican Republic, Highlights of the CAFTA." CAFTA Facts. Washington, DC: Office of the United States Trade Representative.

World Bank, Latin America and the Caribbean Region. 2006. "DR-CAFTA: Challenges and Opportunities for Central America." Washington, DC: World Bank. Especially valuable for its analysis of CAFTA-DR's likely impact on the poor and its thoughtful assessment of the potential for trade policy changes to spur economic development.

JOSE A. MENDEZ

■ child labor

There are an estimated 191 million economically active children ages 5 to 14 in the world today (ILO 2006). This corresponds to 16 percent of this age group. The images that pervade the popular press of children chained in factories, forced into prostitution, or coerced into a country's military do not represent the conditions of most working children around the world. Most working children are at their parents' sides, helping in the family farm or business. A 2000 UNICEF (United Nations Children's Fund) project surveyed working children in 36 developing countries. The data represent more than 120 million children ages 5 to 14. Although nearly 70 percent of children in these countries spend time in some form of economic activity or domestic chores, less than 3 percent work in the formal wage labor market. Most of this wage employment, like most employment overall in the world's poorest economies, is in agriculture.

What Is Child Labor? There is no universally accepted definition of child labor. Some researchers view the phrase as referencing all nonschool, non-leisure activities of children. Others define "child labor" as referring to activities that harm the child in some sense.

Most quoted estimates of the incidence of child labor come from the International Labor Organization's (ILO) Statistical Information and Monitoring Program on Child Labor (SIMPOC). In their most recent global estimates of child labor, they define child labor as:

- An economically active child under 12 who works 1 or more hours per week;
- An economically active child 14 and under who works at least 14 hours per week or 1 or more hours per week in activities that are classified as a worst form of child labor;
- An economically active child 17 and under who works more than 43 hours per week or 1 or more hours per week in a worst form of child labor.

SIMPOC estimates that there are 218 million child laborers in 2004 under this definition (ILO 2006). This number is larger than the 191 million economically active children ages 5 to 14 because of older children in worst forms of child labor or working intensively.

This reference to *activities classified as a worst form of child labor* refers to activities that are considered either unconditional worst forms of child labor or hazardous work. *Unconditional worst forms of child labor* are activities that ILO convention C182 on the Worst Forms of Child Labor lists as inappropriate for children under 18: forced and bonded labor, prostitution, pornography, illicit activities, soldiering, and child trafficking. Each signatory country of C182 defines a set of industries and occupations that are classified as *hazardous work* and therefore a worst form of child labor. Hazardous work is defined as economic activity that, owing to the nature or circumstance of the work, is harmful to the child. There are an estimated 126 million children in hazardous work worldwide (ILO 2006), and 8.4 million children are involved in unconditional worst forms of child labor, 68 percent of whom are in forced or bonded labor (ILO 2002). A common bonded labor arrangement is when parents are paid an advance on the child's future

labor earnings, and the child is then committed to the employer until the advance is repaid.

The Child Labor Decision Poor families balance the child's potential economic contribution against alternative uses of child time. What is the child's potential economic contribution? Direct wage income paid to working children may be important in some contexts, but wage work is rare. In most contexts, working children's primary economic contribution comes through the help they offer their families. Most often, this help is providing domestic services that free up adult time for income-generating pursuits. When there is a family business or farm, the child and other family members often help, and working in the family business or farm is the most prevalent economic activity of children. The value of the child's economic contribution to family farms and businesses can be large. One recent study from Nepal estimates that children are responsible for nearly 9 percent of gross domestic product (GDP). Even when the net economic contribution of the working child is small, it may be important to the welfare of a poor family.

Schooling is typically viewed as the most important alternative use of a child's time outside of work. The net return to school will depend on how the family values future returns to schooling against the direct costs of schooling. Schooling is not the only alternative use of a child's time outside of work. Leisure and play are important components of how children spend their time and may be critically important for child development. In fact, the early Progressive-era arguments about child labor all focused on the value of leisure and play as reasons why children should not work.

Overall, children are most likely to work when the family's valuation of their net economic contribution is high or the perceived returns on alternative uses of the child's time are low. Empirically, poverty has stood out as a key factor influencing the allocation of children's time. Across countries, roughly three-fourths of differences in the economic activity rates of children can be explained by differences in GDP per capita. Within a country, some of the most compelling evidence is from Vietnam, which cut child labor nearly in half over a five-year period during its economic boom in the 1990s. A majority of this decline in child labor can be explained by improvements in living standards alone.

It is not clear whether the strong poverty–child labor connection that is generally observed reflects something about parental or child preferences, changes in the structure of household production, the weakening of credit constraints, a decline in insurance failures, or increases in the returns to activities outside of work such as schooling. All may play some role, and the importance of these factors should vary depending on country context.

Child Labor and International Trade One frequently hears anecdotes about children working in export industries. It is possible that if high-income countries increase labor demand for unskilled labor in low-income countries through international trade, then trade may increase the net economic contribution available to working children and thereby increase child labor. Also, trade can affect returns to education, prices of consumption goods, opportunities for household specialization, and the availability of substitutes for goods or activities involving children.

The cross-country data suggest that the most important connection between trade and child labor stems from the positive association between trade and family incomes. Child labor is lower in countries that trade more because incomes are higher in those countries. This income-driven positive association between trade and child labor holds when one considers all countries, only low-income countries, only trade between high- and low-income countries, and exports of unskilled labor–intensive products from low-income countries (Edmonds and Pavcnik 2006). The cross-country data provide no support for the claim that trade perpetuates high levels of child labor in poor countries.

The microeconomic evidence also emphasizes the importance of the effect of trade on family incomes. When income effects are negligible or transitory, children may work more, as apparently occurred in response to coffee price booms in Nicaragua and Brazil (Kruger 2007). When the income effects are positive and long-lived, children work less even when

labor demand has increased, as apparently happened with Vietnam's liberalization of its rice trade (Edmonds and Pavcnik 2005). Thus the microeconomic evidence illustrates both that child labor is primarily a facet of poverty and that ultimately decisions about child labor depend on the family's assessment of the relative value of the child's time in its alternative uses.

The End of Child Labor? There is no universally accepted definition of child labor. There is no consensus about how many of the world's 191 million working children are worse off because of their work. Evaluating whether work harms a child requires understanding what children would do in the absence of work. High-quality schooling is too rarely available as an alternative. Hence, it is not surprising that so many of the world's poor families choose to have their children help their families meet their basic needs. Most child work is not in the formal wage sector. In practice, international trade seems to have little influence on the propensity of children to work aside from trade's impact on living standards in low-income countries. Children will no longer work in today's poor countries when families can say that the returns to the child's time in other activities such as school or play are greater than the family's valuation of the child's potential economic contribution.

See also International Labor Organization; labor standards

FURTHER READING

Baland, Jean-Marie, and James A. Robinson. 2000. "Is Child Labor Inefficient?" *Journal of Political Economy* 108 (4): 663–79. After Basu and Van, probably the most frequently referenced theoretical paper in the modern literature on child labor. It emphasizes the potential importance of constraints on credit and intergenerational transfers in the parents' decision to have the child work.

Basu, Kaushik, and Pham Van. 1998. "The Economics of Child Labor." *American Economic Review* 88 (3): 412–27. The seminal paper in the child labor literature, framing the persistence of child labor as a coordination problem that could be solved by policy action against child labor.

Edmonds, Eric. 2007. "Child Labor." Working Paper No. 12929. Cambridge, MA: National Bureau of Economic

Research. A recent, comprehensive review of the empirical child labor literature.

Edmonds, Eric, and Nina Pavcnik. 2005. "The Effect of Trade Liberalization on Child Labor." *Journal of International Economics* 65 (2): 401–19. A study of Vietnam's liberalization of rice trade.

———. 2006. "International Trade and Child Labor: Cross-country Evidence." *Journal of International Economics* 68 (1): 115–40. Examines the cross-country data on trade and child labor in detail.

International Labor Organization. 2002. *Every Child Counts: New Global Estimates on Child Labor*. Geneva: ILO. Reports on the persistence of child labor into the 21st century.

———. 2006. *The End of Child Labor: Within Reach*. Geneva: ILO. The most recent estimates on the number of working children.

Kruger, Diane. 2007. "Coffee Production Effects on Child Labor and Schooling in Rural Brazil." *Journal of Development Economics* 82 (2): 448–63. About the effects of coffee prices on child labor and schooling.

ERIC V. EDMONDS

■ clusters

See New Economic Geography

■ commodity chains

Commodity chain refers to the linked set of processes involved in the design, production, distribution, and consumption of goods and services in the world economy. Many commodity chains are, and have long been, geographically extensive, spanning multiple countries and regions of the world. They are also often organizationally complex, involving multiple firms and economic agents connected to one another by a range of contractual and noncontractual relationships, including ownership ties, joint ventures, subcontracting networks, and strategic alliances. Because of the analytical leverage that the commodity chain construct provides for understanding the organization of global industries and the dynamics of the capitalist world economy, it has attracted considerable interest among social scientists from a range of disciplines. There are several varieties of global chain analysis, but each focuses on the networks linking people, places, and processes to one another across space, and seeks to underscore the importance of these networks as a critical infrastructure of economic globalization.

History of the Concept The term *commodity chain*, first defined by Terrence Hopkins and Immanuel Wallerstein as a "network of labor and production processes whose end result is a finished commodity," originates in world-systems theory. Three features characterize the world-systems tradition of commodity chain research. First, the focus is on how the global division and integration of labor into the world economy has evolved over time. Although some scholars argue that globalization is a relatively novel process facilitated by advances in information technology and transportation, historical reconstruction of commodity chains suggests that trade and production networks have been international in scope since modern capitalism's emergence. Second, the commodity chain concept enables analysis of the distribution of wealth and power in the world system by focusing on the differential returns to various actors linked through particular chains. Some links in a chain tend to be located in core (i.e., developed) countries of the world system, and others in the less-developed zones of the semiperiphery and periphery, although the particular geography of any chain changes over time. Third, the spatial and social configurations of chains are linked to cyclical shifts in the world economy. World-systems theorists contend that during phases of economic contraction, chains tend to shrink in size (as production volumes or the numbers of producers decline) and/or scope (with production becoming more geographically concentrated). During such periods, the degree of vertical integration along the chain also increases (i.e., a greater number of links become consolidated into fewer). The reverse is true for expansionary periods.

The first book in this field, *Commodity Chains and Global Capitalism*, edited by Gary Gereffi and

Miguel Korzeniewicz, appeared in 1994. This volume featured papers presented at an annual conference of the Political Economy of the World-System section of the American Sociological Association. Most of the essays, with the exception of those on the shipbuilding and wheat flour commodity chains during the 16th and 17th centuries, focus on contemporary manufacturing industries and, in particular, on trade and production networks linking developing country exporters to world markets.

In retrospect, the 1994 volume can be seen as having inaugurated a distinct approach to chain analysis, the global commodity chain (GCC) framework, which diverges somewhat from the world-systems research program on commodity chains. The GCC framework was first developed by sociologist Gereffi, who identified four dimensions with respect to which all commodity chains can be analyzed: (1) an input-output structure, describing the process of transforming raw materials and other inputs into final products; (2) a territoriality, or geographical configuration; (3) a governance structure, referring to the processes by which particular players in the chain exert control over others and appropriate and/or distribute the value that is created along the chain; and (4) institutional context, or the "rules of the game" bearing on the organization and operation of the chain.

Over the course of the 1990s, a substantial empirical literature on commodity chains accumulated, featuring studies of products such as cars, computers, clothing, chocolate, and coffee, among others. By the end of that decade, some scholars were beginning to reappraise the original GCC approach. Specifically, they questioned the very description of these networks as *commodity* chains, since the term commodity is generally taken to denote either primary products (e.g., agricultural staples) or basic manufactures (e.g., T-shirts as "commodity" garments). Others criticized the insularity of the GCC approach, noting that there was relatively little exchange between researchers working within Gereffi's paradigm and those who, although similarly interested in the organizational dynamics of the world economy, were using different concepts to describe interfirm networks in global industries. Some argued that a common terminology would foster dialogue and promote a sense of intellectual community among scholars of international trade and production networks. With the aim of selecting a neutral term that would encompass these various network constructs, *global value chain* (GVC) was chosen "because it was perceived as being the most inclusive of the full range of possible chain activities and end products" (Gereffi et al. 2001).

Governance of Global Chains As Gereffi explained in his contribution to *Commodity Chains and Global Capitalism*, the governance structure of a commodity chain is the set of "authority and power relationships that determine how financial, material, and human resources are allocated and flow within the chain." Gereffi proceeded to make what has become a seminal distinction in the GCC literature between "producer-driven commodity chains" (PDCCs) in heavy manufacturing or more capital-intensive industries such as motor vehicles, and "buyer-driven commodity chains" (BDCCs) in light manufacturing industries such as footwear and apparel. While producer-driven industries tend to be characterized by hierarchy (i.e., links in the chain are vertically integrated within the ownership structure of a firm or, in the case of international production, foreign direct investment), network (i.e., nonequity) forms of governance are characteristic of buyer-driven chains.

Gereffi's BDCC construct was a key theoretical innovation because it pointed to the changing role of commercial capital in establishing and managing global production networks. The lead firms of BDCCs, mostly retailers and brand name marketers, are able to exert control over firms involved in their production networks, although they generally have no equity relationship with the manufacturers and/or contractors making goods on their behalf. One of Gereffi's main interests was to show that even chains with more "marketlike" governance structures require coordination, and that these coordinating tasks are assumed by lead firms that determine much of the division of labor along the chain and define the terms on which actors gain access to it. In this sense, the distinction between PDCCs and BDCCs presented a new twist on the "markets versus hierarchies" formulation elaborated by Oliver Williamson and other contributors to the new institutional economics: lead firms in BDCCs are frequently connected to their suppliers by networks that differ from both arms-length, one-spot transactions (market) and ownership ties (hierarchy). Nevertheless, these networks are generally characterized by a power structure that gives the "buyers" in these chains leverage over other actors.

Although the analytical utility of these ideal types was confirmed by many studies using the PDCC/BDCC constructs as templates for analyzing various industries, the buyer-driven/producer-driven distinction was also faulted for being too narrow or overly abstract. Some critics suggested that these categories did not adequately capture the range of governance forms observed in actual chains. In his analysis of the electronics industry and the relationships between brand-name computer companies such as Dell and Compaq (so-called original equipment manufacturers, or OEMs) and their major component suppliers, Timothy Sturgeon identified a new governance structure, which he termed the *modular network*. Although modular value chains appear similar to BDCCs in the sense that OEMs typically have no equity tie to the companies manufacturing their components, Sturgeon argued that interfirm networks in the electronics industry are also different from the paradigmatic BDCCs characterizing industries such as apparel.

Sturgeon drew on transaction cost economics in elaborating his theory of value chain modularity. The question underlying transaction cost economics is, why are so many economic activities bundled within the firm instead of transacted on the market? For Williamson, the answer hinged largely on asset specificity; transactions are more likely to be internalized in the firm when they require particular, dedicated investments. This is because such investments foster mutual dependence between the actors in an exchange (for example, between buyer and supplier), which creates conditions for opportunistic behavior on the part of one or both parties to the transaction. To mitigate this risk, safeguards that are

capable of guarding against malfeasance must be built into the exchange, and this process increases the cost of the transaction. One way to deal with this problem is through hierarchy—that is, the acquisition and incorporation of asset-specific suppliers into the boundaries of a vertically integrated firm. But Sturgeon argues that modular value chains represent a different solution to the problem of transaction costs: in these networks, asset specificity remains relatively low because the codification of knowledge in industry standards allows a highly formalized link at the interfirm nexus between OEMs and their main suppliers.

Thus characteristics specific to the electronics industry—particularly the development of industry-wide standards permitting a high degree of codification—enable lead firms and highly competent "turnkey" suppliers to exchange rich information (such as detailed product or design specifications) without the kind of intense, face-to-face forms of communication associated with the interfirm networks documented by contributors to the "new economic sociology" literature. Economic sociologists, many influenced by Mark Granovetter's seminal statement regarding the embeddedness of economic activity in social life (1985), have tended to emphasize the "relational" feature of interfirm networks—that is, their particular value orientation as open-ended and trust-based. Sturgeon's work implicitly contrasts the relational networks described by sociologists such as Granovetter and Uzzi (1977) with the modular networks found in the electronics industry.

Sturgeon's work on value chain modularity challenged the adequacy of the PDCC/BDCC distinction and underscored the need for a more differentiated understanding of governance structures in global chains. This challenge was taken up by Gereffi, Humphrey, and Sturgeon (2005), who developed a formal theory of global value chain governance that aims to explain and predict the way that exchanges at the interfirm boundary are coordinated. The authors propose a continuum of five governance structures that describe the type of transactional linkage connecting firms in a global value chain. In addition to the poles of market and hierarchy, this continuum contains three distinct types of network linkages: (1) closest to the hierarchy pole is the captive network, which is characterized by a relatively large power differential between the stronger firm (usually the buyer) and the weaker firm (typically the supplier); (2) the relational network, which is in the middle of the continuum and characterized by complex interactions and greater mutual dependence; and (3) the modular network elaborated in Sturgeon's work on the electronics sector, which is closer to the market pole. Gereffi, Humphrey, and Sturgeon identify three independent variables which, they contend, explain a significant portion of the variation in governance structures across chains: the complexity of transactions, the codifiability of information to be exchanged, and the capabilities of the supply base.

Many GCC and GVC scholars focus on the governance dimension because they seek to understand how the dynamics of global chains can be leveraged into development outcomes, such as facilitating the shift of firms to more profitable links in the chain and fostering the creation of skills and competencies that would permit local producers to upgrade to higher-value-added activities within a chain (e.g., moving from assembly subcontracting to integrated manufacturing), or to switch to a new value chain (e.g., moving from apparel to electronics). For this reason, research on global chains has been supported by bodies such as the UN Commission for Latin America and the Caribbean as well as the U.S. Agency for International Development. The influence of the GCC and GVC literatures in the contemporary development field reflects an elective affinity between global chain frameworks, which analyze the way in which particular economic actors are inserted into international trade and production networks, and the paradigm of export-oriented development, which similarly focuses on the incorporation of local firms and workers into global markets. Chain-inspired development research also highlights, if not resolves, perennial units of analysis problems in development theory and policy: To what extent does increasing the participation of firms in global markets and their competitiveness in particular chains benefit local capital and labor? What is the relationship between firm-level upgrading at the micro level and the more macrolevel development of the regional or national economy?

Future Research and Complementary Approaches As analytical frameworks, the GCC and GVC approaches bring to the foreground the organizational dynamics of contemporary capitalism and their implications for local development in today's global economy. Some critics contend, however, that empirical analysis of commodity chains must pay greater attention to the historical and socio-institutional specificity of the contexts in which these networks are formed and operate. Although ideal types such as the producer-driven and buyer-driven constructs are useful abstractions, the study of commodity chains in situ reveals significant variation in the way that trade and production are organized across space and time, even within the same industry, thus reflecting the influence of the broader regulatory and political-economic frameworks which shape the linkages that emerge between places and processes in the world economy. The contingent and variable nature of international trade and production networks is underscored by recent contributions to an emerging subfield of historical research on commodity chains, with scholars describing and analyzing the centuries-old connections between geographically distant producers and consumers that world-systems theorists coined the term *commodity chain* to describe (Topik, Zephyr, and Marichal 2005).

In addition to the commodity chain concept, several related terms and frameworks have also been developed to analyze the geographical dispersion and organizational fragmentation of production in the global economy. These alternative but potentially complementary frameworks, such as global production networks, systems of provision, and the *filière* approach, draw inspiration from intellectual traditions that differ, to a greater or lesser extent, from those orienting GCC and GVC analysis. Furthermore, the GCC and GVC approaches are not identical to each other, as the former draws more from world-systems theory, organizational sociology, and the comparative political economy of development, while the latter borrows from the fields of institutional economics and industrial organization. Despite the different methodological and theoretical emphases of these various approaches, greater dialogue among them may facilitate a richer understanding of how international trade and production networks are organized, as well as their implications for a range of economic and developmental outcomes at the global-local nexus. Similarly, commodity chain analysis might be strengthened by dialogue with the New Economic Geography, since the latter's emphasis on spatial and institutional specificity could enrich the former's understanding of the processes by which the organizational dynamics of global industries become manifest in particular locations.

See also foreign direct investment (FDI); fragmentation; globalization; New Economic Geography; outsourcing/offshoring

FURTHER READING

Arrighi, G., and J. Drangel. 1986. "The Stratification of the World-Economy." *Review* 10 (1): 9–74. Applies the commodity chain concept to analysis of inequality and stratification among national economies in the context of world-systems theory.

Bair, J., ed. 2008. *Frontiers of Commodity Chain Research.* Palo Alto, CA: Stanford University Press. Collection containing chapters by several key figures including Gereffi, Sturgeon, and Wallerstein, as well as a comprehensive introduction by the editor that provides a broad overview of different approaches to commodity chain research and identifies key methodological and theoretical debates in the literature.

Bair, J., and G. Gereffi. 2001. "Local Clusters in Global Chains: The Causes and Consequences of Export Dynamism in Torreon's Blue Jeans Industry." *World Development* 29 (11): 1885–1903. Explains and evaluates the local implications of an export boom in a region of northern Mexico. Also discusses possible complementarities between the commodity chain and industrial districts literatures.

Gereffi, G. 1994. "The Organization of Buyer-Driven Global Commodity Chains: How U.S. Retailers Shape Overseas Production Networks." In *Commodity Chains and Global Capitalism,* edited by G. Gereffi and M. Korzeniewicz. Westport, CT: Praeger, 95–122. Seminal essay introducing the producer-driven/buyer-driven distinction.

Gereffi, G., J. Humphrey, R. Kaplinsky, and T. Sturgeon. 2001. "Introduction: Globalisation, value chains, and development." *IDS Bulletin* 32 (3): 1–8. Brief introduction to a special issue that introduces the global *value* chain terminology and explains the rationale for its adoption in place of global *commodity* chains.

Gereffi, G., J. Humphrey, and T. Sturgeon. 2005. "The Governance of Global Value Chains." *Review of International Political Economy* 12 (1): 78–104. Elaborates a theory of global value chain governance, including three types of network linkages.

Granovetter, Mark. 1985. "Economic Action and Social Structure: The Problem of Embeddedness." *American Journal of Sociology* 91 (3): 481–510. Widely regarded as a key contribution to the new economic sociology, argues that economic activity is embedded in networks of ongoing social relations.

Henderson, J., P. Dicken, M. Hess, N. Coe, and H. Wai-Chung Yeung. 2002. "Global Production Networks and the Analysis of Economic Development." *Review of International Political Economy* 9 (3): 436–64. Provides critical summary of the GCC approach and proposes alternative framework for analyzing dynamics and developmental implications of economic globalization.

Hopkins, T., and I. Wallerstein. 1977. "Patterns of Development of the Modern World-System." *Review* 1 (2): 11–145. Introduces the concept of commodity chain in the context of defining a research agenda for world-systems theory.

Lane, Christel, and Jocelyn Probert. 2006. "Domestic Capabilities and Global Production Networks in the Clothing Industry: A Comparison of German and UK Firms' Strategies." *Socio-Economic Review* 4 (1): 35–67. A comparative analysis of the apparel industry, combining global chain analysis with an institutionalist perspective on national capitalisms.

Ponte, S., and P. Gibbon. 2005. "Quality Standards, Conventions, and the Governance of Global Value Chains." *Economy and Society* 34 (1): 1–31. Insightful critique of GVC analysis, drawing on convention theory.

Sturgeon, T. 2002. "Modular Production Networks: A New American Model of Industrial Organization." *Industrial and Corporate Change* 11: 451–96. Analysis of turnkey suppliers and modular networks in the electronics industry; important precursor to the 2005 Gereffi, Humphrey, and Sturgeon article proposing a theory of GVC governance.

Talbot, J. 2004. *Grounds for Agreement: The Political Economy of the Coffee Commodity Chain.* New York: Rowman and Littlefield. Excellent comprehensive analysis of the coffee commodity chain, drawing on the world-systems and GCC traditions of chain research.

Topik, S., F. Zephyr, and C. Marichal, eds. 2005. *From Silver to Cocaine: Latin American Commodity Chains and the Building of the World Economy, 1500–2000.* Durham, NC: Duke University Press. This edited volume features studies of commodities that were Latin America's leading exports during various historical periods, including coffee, bananas, henequen, and rubber.

Uzzi, B. 1997. "Social Structure and Competition in Interfirm Networks: The Paradox of Embeddedness." *Administrative Science Quarterly* 42: 35–67. Representative of the "new economic sociology" approach to interfirm networks, emphasizing their embedded and relational nature.

Wallerstein, I. 2000. "Introduction to Special Issue on Commodity Chains in the World Economy, 1590 to 1790." *Review* 23 (1): 1–13. Updating 1986 special issue of *Review* (10, 1) on the same theme, contains analyses of the wheat flour and shipping commodity chains between 1590–1790.

JENNIFER BAIR

■ commodity-price pegging

Pegging the price of a broadly defined commodity basket would be an almost perfect means to achieve price stability. An adjustable commodity-based dollar was formally laid out in 1920 by the American economist Irving Fisher, who suggested adjustments in the number of resource units in the dollar to achieve price stability. If prices fell below a specific target by 1 percent, for example, the dollar value of the resource unit would be raised by 1 percent—at the same time automatically lowering the number of resource units in the dollar. But the larger the number of commodities involved, the more difficult it is to assign their relative weights. A single commodity price target would be more feasible than Fisher's system; however, it would be desirable only if this single commodity price were well correlated with the aggregate price level.

The principle that governments should intervene in commodity markets to maintain supplies and stabilize prices was endorsed by Confucius in China during the sixth century B.C., and stabilization of grain prices became an important part of early imperial Chinese policy. Communist anti-inflation policy during and after the Chinese Civil War also involved the buying and selling of surplus stocks. In this case, the state established trading companies to undertake large-scale commodity sales in the cities and bring prices down. Later, these same state trading companies used commodity purchases to offset deflationary pressures in 1950 and 1952. On a smaller scale, President Clinton employed the U.S. Strategic Petroleum Reserve (SPR) in a similar fashion in 1996, ordering the sale of a portion of these reserves in an attempt to combat rapidly rising gasoline prices. The SPR was subsequently tapped for limited interventions by the George W. Bush administration as well.

More recently, the economist Jeffrey Frankel suggested that policymakers in smaller commodity-dependent nations use a more dominant form of commodity-price pegging: specifically, policymakers should undertake monetary expansion whenever they face declining demand for that nation's key commodity (Frankel 2003). Under a pure commodity peg, oil producers would simply tie their monetary policy to the price of oil, expanding when oil prices fall and contracting when oil prices rise. Such a strategy has strong intuitive appeal given that it is almost inevitable that an oil-dependent country will face deflationary pressures if oil prices plunge and inflationary pressures if oil prices surge upward. Less specialized producers might enjoy analogous benefits by fixing the price of a basket of export commodities in terms of local currency. Once a target price range has been set, open market operations involving purchases or sales of foreign exchange or domestic securities could be used to keep the export price index within the band (Frankel 2005). Even larger economies could gain from a commodity-based strategy, at least in comparison to the more popular alternative of pegging to the U.S. dollar. For example, had Argentina adopted a wheat-peg rather than a dollar-peg during 1991–2001, the Argentine peso would have depreciated instead of appreciating as it did over the latter part of the period (Frankel 2003).

The dollar peg was deflationary for Argentina just as the gold peg was deflationary for the United States and many other countries in the late 19th century and during the Great Depression—and the authorities in each case ended up maintaining a fixed single-asset price while almost all other prices declined. Faced with very low interest rates and persistent deflation on a global scale during the Great Depression of the 1930s, a number of economists laid out proposals for a "commodity reserve standard" and intervention that would pull commodity prices up from their depressed levels. Some proponents saw this as an alternative to the old gold standard but others saw intervention in commodity markets as simply a means of achieving the desired expansionary end—as in, for example, the U.S. silver purchase program that began in 1934 under President Roosevelt.

Other Commodity-Based Proposals Although economists have argued that government warehousing of the commodities involved would not be necessary (see, e.g., Hall 1982), commodity-based proposals have more often been based on government stocks and direct government intervention in commodity markets. For example, one prominent proposal was for a commodity reserve currency to be established. Under this scheme, Federal Reserve banks would buy warehouse receipts for the chosen commodity units so as to "redeem their liabilities, on demand, in commodity units or gold at the option of the holder" (Graham 1941). The premise that a commodity reserve currency could be adopted as an alternative to the old gold standard received serious consideration in the 1930s and 1940s. Critics have pointed to the impracticality and cost of the proposed commodity-market interventions; the relatively narrow range of suitable standardized commodities, as well as high elasticity of supply, could force excessively large fluctuations in the stock of money under such a scheme (Friedman 1951).

Although few economists today would advocate an actual commodity-based monetary standard, commodity-price pegging may nonetheless merit consideration as a possible guide for monetary policy. Targeting commodity prices could provide for quantitative monetary easing in the face of deflation, for example, whereas pure interest-rate pegging soon runs out of room as interest rates cannot be driven below zero. In this case, implementation of commodity-price pegging could help secure an inflation or price-level target—or, at the very least, offer a complementary policy goal.

See also currency board arrangement (CBA); dollar standard; exchange rate regimes; Federal Reserve Board; gold standard, international; impossible trinity; money supply

FURTHER READING

Burdekin, Richard C. K., and Fang Wang. 1999. "A Novel End to the Big Inflation in China in 1950." *Economics of Planning* 32 (3): 211–29. Documents the commodity-market intervention that played a key role in Communist stabilization policy in China in the late 1940s and early 1950s.

Fisher, Irving. 1920. *Stabilizing the Dollar.* New York: Macmillan. Includes Fisher's original proposal for a commodity-based dollar.

Frankel, Jeffrey. 2003. "A Proposed Monetary Regime for Small Commodity Exporters: Peg the Export Price." *International Finance* 6 (1): 61–88. Makes the case for smaller resource-based economies fixing the local currency price of their chief commodity export.

———. 2005. "Peg the Export Price Index: A Proposed Monetary Regime for Small Countries." *Journal of Policy Modeling* 27 (4): 495–508. Generalizes Frankel's earlier proposal to provide for fixing the price of a broader basket of exports for countries with a more diversified pattern of production.

Friedman, Milton. 1951. "Commodity-Reserve Currency." *Journal of Political Economy* 59 (3): 203–32. Questions the feasibility of introducing a commodity-based currency standard and considers the large fluctuations in the stock of money that might result.

Graham, Frank D. 1941. "Transition to a Commodity Reserve Currency." *American Economic Review* 31 (3): 520–25. A representative proposal for a commodity-based currency backed by warehouse receipts for the selected commodity units.

Hall, Robert E. 1982. "Explorations in the Gold Standard and Related Policies for Stabilizing the Dollar." In *Inflation: Causes and Effects*, edited by Robert E. Hall. Chicago: University of Chicago Press, 111–22. Shows that a particular mix of ammonium nitrate, copper, aluminum, and plywood would have closely tracked the U.S. cost of living over the 1946–80 period.

RICHARD C. K. BURDEKIN

■ Common Agricultural Policy

The Common Agricultural Policy (CAP) of the European Union (EU) is called "common" because the main agricultural policy decisions are made at the EU level, and these agricultural programs are financed for the most part from the EU's common budget. The functioning of the agricultural sectors in the member countries of the EU is widely determined by decisions at the Community level. Consequently, agriculture is perceived as one of the most integrated sectors in the EU and is sometimes viewed as a possible model for other sectors. Although the EU's agriculture sectors are politically integrated, however, they are less integrated economically than other sectors.

The creation of the CAP in 1962 was vital for the European Economic Community (EEC), the forerunner of the EU. The six founding countries—Belgium, France, Germany, Luxembourg, the Netherlands, and Italy—had their own national agricultural policies, which differed vastly. The individual countries were reluctant to remove their intervention in agricultural markets, or allow for free trade among member countries and to follow the rules of a customs union. It did not make sense to exclude one sector from market integration, however, and politically the stakes were high: France wanted access to the large German market for its agricultural products if it were to allow for German

industrial products to enter the French market. Hence, it became necessary to establish the organizational and institutional framework for agricultural policy at the Community level.

The institutional framework set up at the inception of the CAP was a compromise to satisfy the heterogeneous interests of the member countries. Under German pressure, the EEC decided on a common price level for agricultural products significantly higher than world market levels and introduced border regulations that completely disconnected EEC prices from those on the world market. The evolution of the CAP has proven that this initial framework constrained the CAP in adapting to changing conditions in the EEC and on the world market.

The Features of the CAP at the Time of Inception Common market organizations regulated the CAP for the main agricultural products. These market organizations are Community law and include the legal framework needed to administer the markets. The aim was to keep domestic farm prices above the level of world market prices. Variable levies were implemented as border measures to cover the gap between the domestic farm prices and the corresponding world market prices. The levies varied with the world price since the commonly agreed-upon prices were the lowest prices at which foreign supply was allowed to enter the European domestic market. From the start, the CAP provided for export subsidies in the event that domestic production was to surpass domestic use at domestic prices. The export subsidies were termed "export restitutions." Under the General Agreement on Tariffs and Trade (GATT) and later the World Trade Organization (WTO), export subsidies for industrial products were eliminated and import tariffs rates were bound by a ceiling rate negotiated by member countries. Thus the trading regime for agricultural products remained very different from that of industrial products.

In addition, market organizations included domestic measures of protection. The most important ones were guaranteed purchases by state agencies of selected products such as butter, skimmed milk powder, grains, and sugar at intervention prices, and facultative purchases for some other products if some additional conditions prevailed. The protection regime for sugar was exceptional as it included intervention prices for sugar, minimum purchase prices for sugar beets, and production quotas. For quantities above their allocated quotas, farmers received the world market price. The sugar market regime was the least in line with free market principles; it was more comparable to instruments used in centrally planned economies.

The Evolution of the CAP The institutional prices were the main instruments of the market regimes that constituted the Community law. The Community law or any changes to the law were generally proposed by the European Commission; in the case of agricultural law the decisions were made by the Council of Ministers, which is composed of agricultural ministers from member countries. The most important decision by the Council of Ministers was to make the agreed changes to the institutional prices. These changes were made annually up to the 1990s. Since no objective criteria guided the setting or changing of institutional prices, political considerations dominated these decisions. National interests diverged widely between member countries, partly because of differences in their national conditions such as inflation, overall growth in the economy, and productivity changes in agriculture. Moreover, the framework that was instituted to finance these policies accentuated the differences in national interests among the member countries. The EU had adapted the principle of financial solidarity, which stipulated that policies implemented at the Community level should be financed from a common budget. As the EU did not generate revenues, the contribution to the common budget came either from the member countries' budgets or from import tariff revenues, that is, member countries would deliberately forgo their own tariff revenue in favor of the Community budget. Not all countries benefited from these policies. For example, the Netherlands was traditionally a huge exporter of dairy products so decisions that resulted in higher dairy prices increased the income of Dutch dairy farmers much

more than it taxed its consumers. For the United Kingdom (UK), which was a huge importer of dairy products, an increase in dairy prices had the reverse effect. Hence, it is understandable that national interests diverged significantly.

The voting procedure made it even more difficult for member countries to come to an agreement. The Treaty of Rome (1957), from which the Community emerged, provided for majority voting for most decisions. The six founding members agreed in 1966, before the first market organization came into existence in 1967/68, to apply unanimity voting whenever there were vital interests at stake for any individual country. Thus agreements could be reached only if member countries for which common policies conflicted with national interests were compensated. The result was that an increase in the domestic price level was decided year after year, even in times where world market prices for agricultural products declined and the exportable surplus of the EU rose. The increase in agricultural protection, the enlargement of the EU, and unprecedented technological progress in EU agriculture contributed to a faster growth in EU agricultural production than consumption. For the Community, which had started as an importer of agricultural products, the changes in supply and demand reduced the import gap gradually over time and by the end of the 1970s generated export surpluses. Increasing exports and falling world market prices put pressure on the EU budget as outlays for export restitutions rose strongly. A new phase of the CAP began with even more governmental interference in the market. The milk market presented the most urgent problem. Milk production in the EU grew strongly as imports of concentrated feed could be imported free of duties due to the GATT. At the inception of the CAP, the EU had set its bound tariffs at zero or a very low level at a time when imports of these products were negligible. In return, the EU was allowed to introduce the variable levy system. The import regulation for concentrated feed became the Achilles' heel of the CAP. Low prices for feed, which were partly due to significant declines in transatlantic transport costs, and high support prices for CAP products, led to high effective rates of protection for meat and milk and increases of production. On the demand side, imported feed was substituted for domestically produced grain, and because of cheap imports of vegetable oil, margarine was substituted for butter. The consequence was the accumulation of stocks in the EU and accelerating budget outlays. The latter seemed to have been the main constraint for the CAP during this period.

In 1984, the council agreed on a quota system for milk. Farmers received a right to sell under the quota at guaranteed prices. Sales above the quota were taxed with a superlevy, which for many years was higher than the price paid for sales within the quota. Hence, production was curtailed and growth of production was stopped. Moreover, a set-aside program was offered to farmers in 1986. Grain farmers were offered a premium if they voluntarily took arable land out of production.

The first 25 years of the CAP were characterized by increases in border and domestic EU protection for agricultural products. The EU reacted to changes in the economic environment mainly by introducing new instruments to limit budgetary expenditure. The concerns of the trading partners were for the most part neglected.

1992 to 2003 The Uruguay Round (1986–94), the last round under the GATT, focused on agricultural trade. The EU had to reform the CAP in order to comply with the rules of the new round. The council decided to first reform the EU grain market in 1992. For the first time, the CAP prices of specific commodities were cut, some significantly: the council agreed to cut institutional prices for grain by 30 percent. Farmers were compensated entirely for their prospective income loss by direct payments. These payments were linked to the use of land for grain. In addition, farmers would qualify for payments if they set aside at least a politically determined percentage of their land. Although the effect on grain production was minimal, domestically produced grain became competitive against imported concentrated feed and, thus, the grain surplus vanished.

The decision on the grain sector contributed to a final agreement in the Uruguay Round. The agreement required further changes to the CAP, however. The EU's export subsidies were now constrained in two ways:

1. the quantity of well-defined products or product groups that was allowed to be subsidized was reduced by 21 percent (from their 1986–88 level); and
2. the amount of export subsidies had to be cut by 36 percent (from their 1986–88 level).

Moreover, like other GATT/WTO members, the EU had to accept concessions on the import side. Each country was to allow imports of specific products up to 5 percent of domestic consumption in the base period 1986–88; variable levies and other nontariff trade measures had to be converted to tariff equivalents (tariffication), and the tariff equivalents had to be reduced by 36 percent on average from the base period 1986–88, and by at least 15 percent for individual products. Thus, the EU was not allowed to apply the variable levy system anymore and had to take into account changes in world prices when setting domestic institutional prices. It was this international agreement that forced the EU to change its market organizations. Finally the EU reformed the CAP drastically in 2003, aiming at making a positive contribution to the Doha Round of trade negotiations, which was launched in November 2001. One of the reforms was of domestic support. The CAP direct payments were included in the "Blue Box." These are direct payments under production-limiting programs and hence they were exempted from reduction. This concession was given to the EU in return for price cuts and the realization that aid to the farmers was needed during the adjustment period. But the EU would have to give up these exemptions by the end of the Doha Round as adjustment compensations cannot be paid permanently, and the EU would have to look for alternatives for providing aid to farmers.

CAP Reform in 2003 and Thereafter The CAP reform of 2003 was a change in the paradigm of agricultural protection. Previously, support to agriculture took the form of price support to output and factors of production; and in the livestock sector, some kind of payments were made by head of animals. This support stimulated production and taxed consumption. Hence trading partners opposed this system and pressed for a change. The council decided in 2003 to reduce price support even more (for the main products from 2004 onward and for some products such as sugar, olive oil, tobacco, and cotton at a later time) and to decouple in principle all types of direct payments. The general proposal of the European Commission combined all income losses due to price cuts made until 2003 and all types of direct payments granted up to 2003 in one type of payment, the Single Farm Payment, to be made to individual farms based on historical levels. Entitlements to farm payments were made tradable and, thus, became decoupled completely from production, at least in principle. But the council allowed member countries a lot of flexibility. For example, countries were allowed to link part of the payments to production or to the use of factors of production during the transition period and to link them again to production in the future if regional or domestic production in a country fell too strongly. Payments could also be linked completely to land, either by granting a flat rate across the country or by differentiating between regions or between arable land and grassland. Finally, some payments were tied to environmental standards that farmers needed to meet, a process known as cross-compliance. Cross-compliance links payments to farmers to their respect of environmental and other requirements (such as animal and plant health and animal welfare) set at EU and national levels.

The 2003 reform also introduced a new classification of the CAP instruments: Pillar I for market and price support measures and Pillar II for rural development. In the reforms, a decline was imposed on Pillar I spending, while Pillar II spending was allowed to go up.

The distinction between the two types of measures may sound economically reasonable, but what justification could there be for increasing Pillar II's budget by about the same amount that Pillar I's decreases, given that in principle the two pillars have different purposes? Rural development should not focus mainly on agriculture. Rural development needs differ across regions and countries and they are not related to past agricultural support, so it is questionable that the changes in budget needs for rural development of each region and country (Pillar II) match widely the reduction made in agricultural support (Pillar I).

Hence critics suspect that Pillar II is a way for policymakers to continue providing support to farmers when they can no longer justify direct payments as adjustment compensation for price cuts that occurred more than a decade earlier. The framework of Pillar II seems suitable for hiding subsidies for agriculture. Pillar II measures require a higher quality of governance than Pillar I measures, but unfortunately, due to the enlargement of the EU from 15 to 25 member countries in 2004, and the further enlargement on the inclusion of Romania and Bulgaria in 2007, the competence to monitor and to enforce Pillar II measures has declined on average. The European Court of Auditors regularly finds irregularities and fraud in Pillar II measures.

The Future of the CAP The CAP has changed significantly over time. Changes have been driven by budgetary concerns rather than economic rationale, however. Up to the 1990s, budget constraints led to reforms, but they resulted in even more protective and trade-distorting policies. Finally, under the GATT/WTO multilateral trade negotiations, the CAP abandoned most of its border protection. Some products such as sugar and milk continue to be highly protected, however. Changes in the EU and other countries' policies and rising oil prices may result in higher world prices and may make further reforms of EU border measures unnecessary. But if these changes do not happen, the EU will need to cut its agricultural prices further in order to comply with the constraints imposed by the WTO.

The role of the CAP has become more important for the world food system over time as the EU has grown from 6 to 27 members as of 2007. The reduction in the CAP's external rate of protection contributes to less distorted agriculture. Two major concerns remain, however: first, as long as EU prices for food products are not completely linked to world market prices, the CAP does not buffer fluctuations in world market prices to the maximum possible extent. Thus further complete coupling of EU and world market prices is needed. Second, Pillar II of the CAP allows for hidden farm subsidies and causes distortions across EU member countries and worldwide. Hence, Pillar II measures have to be reconsidered and scrutinized with respect to distortive effects.

See also agricultural trade negotiations; agriculture; common market; distortions to agricultural incentives; European Union; political economy of trade policy

FURTHER READING

Borrell, B., and L. Hubbard. 2000. *Global Economic Effects of the EU Common Agricultural Policy*. Oxford: Institute of Economic Affairs, 18–26. An identification of the costs caused by CAP based on a quantitative model.

Brümmer, B., and U. Koester. 2004. "EU Enlargement and Governance of the CAP." In *European Union: Challenges and Promises of a New Enlargement*, edited by A. Puskas. New York. International Debate Education Association, 226–46. The focus is on governance problems of the CAP.

European Commission, Directorate General for Economic and Financial Affairs. 1994. "EC Agricultural Policy for the 21st Century." Reports and Studies No. 4. Brussels. An assessment of the evolution of the CAP and a proposal for change.

Frandsen, S., and A. Walter-Jorgenson. 2006. "The Common Agricultural Policy: A Review." In *WTO Negotiations and Agricultural Trade Liberalization: The Effect of Developed Countries' Policies on Developing Countries*, edited by E. Diaz-Bonilla, S. Frandsen, and S. Robinson. Wallingford Oxfordshire, UK: CAB, 34–56. A nontechnical survey of the evolution and functioning of the CAP.

Koester, U., and A. El-Agraa. 2007. "The Common Agricultural Policy." In *The European Union, Economics, and Policies*, edited by A. El-Agraa. 8th ed. Cambridge University Press, 2007, 373–410. A survey of the
functioning and evolution of the CAP, which can be used as classroom text.

ULRICH KOESTER

■ common currency

In the modern world economy, a common currency shared by a number of countries has been a rare phenomenon. At least since the 19th century, the rule has been that independent countries have independent currencies. Territorial currencies were established in the 1815–1914 period, a result of important technical advances—such as presses that could mint coins and print notes that were hard to counterfeit—combined with economic factors, such as the spread of the monetized economy and the state taking on more functions and casting its revenue net more widely. As new nations such as Italy, Canada, and Germany formed in the second half of the 19th century, they adopted national currencies.

The pattern of one country–one currency was reinforced with the decline of empires. Some former colonies were reluctant to discard shared currencies, but after a brief time lag, currencies became national. An example from the 1990s is the rapid introduction of national currencies following the dissolution of Yugoslavia, the USSR, and Czechoslovakia. The 12 Commonwealth of Independent States successors to the USSR recognized the increased transaction costs that would result from abandoning the common currency, but after less than two years the ruble zone had collapsed.

Most currencies are national, where N_m is the number of monies and N_c is the number of countries:
$$N_m \approx N_c \qquad (1)$$
In practice, however, the one country–one currency rule is not always the case and sometimes $N_m < N_c$. The exceptions to the rule fall into two categories: carrots and ministates (Pomfret 2005).

Carrots and Ministates The principal examples of currency union driven by carrots (i.e., incentives offered by an interested party) are the CFA franc zone in central and West Africa and the rand zone in southern Africa. The French Treasury, which acts as a guarantor of the fixed exchange rate, manages the CFA franc zone's reserves and settles the regional central banks' payments and receipts. The zone has existed for more than a half a century because of preferential French aid to zone members and balance of payments (BOP) support. In the rand zone, South Africa has formal arrangements to share seigniorage (i.e., the real resources obtained from printing money which can be spent on goods and services) with the countries in which the rand is legal tender (Lesotho and Namibia), and the South African central bank is prepared to act as lender of last resort in these countries. Similar carrots encouraged retention of the ruble zone in 1992–93, but Russia objected to the size of transfers to other members while some members opposed the political use of the levers. Ultimately, lack of agreement on monetary policy institutions made the ruble zone unstable. In the both the CFA franc zone and the rand zone, by contrast, members accept the institutions imposed by a dominant economic power. Even so, the membership of the CFA franc zone and the rand zone has not been entirely stable. Mali withdrew from the CFA franc zone in 1962 and rejoined in 1984; Mauritania withdrew in 1973; Equatorial Guinea, a former Spanish colony, joined in 1985; and Guinea-Bissau, a former Portuguese colony, joined in 1997. Botswana withdrew from the rand zone in 1976.

Other countries that lack independent currencies or those that participate in a shared currency arrangement are small and often special cases, known as ministates. Between 1970 and 1990, according to Rose (2000, 41), 82 countries were involved in currency unions, 15 of which were in the CFA zone and three in the rand zone. The remaining 64 countries were small economies using the currency of a neighboring or quasi-colonial power or ceding monetary policy control to a larger country. The Eastern Caribbean Currency Area (consisting of eight small island economies), the British Virgin Islands, Bahamas, Barbados, and Belize have tied their currencies' value to the U.S. dollar since 1976. Ireland-UK (pre-1979), Luxembourg-Belgium (pre-euro), and Brunei-Singapore are often described as

currency unions, but the second-named country in each pair had total control over monetary policy. The remainder of the 82 currency union members used another country's money for all or part of the twenty-year period. Most of these are tiny economies, such as Svalbard, Isle of Man, and Norfolk Island. The largest, Liberia, ceased using the U.S. dollar in the 1980s when a new government started issuing first coins and then paper currency. The next largest, Panama, has had a special status with the United States since it was created prior to construction of the Panama Canal.

Historically, some colonies have had separate currencies, although this typically involved large colonies of a kind that no longer exists. The status of some territories is not clear cut, because the ruler, occupier, or guardian is sensitive to the term *colony*, but territories such as Guam (and Panama, to a lesser extent), Northern Cyprus, or Western Sahara have a quasi-colonial relationship with the country whose currency they use. Other currency union members are integral parts of the larger nation. Scotland, for example, is part of the United Kingdom, not a member of a currency union, just as Christmas Island is part of Australia.

Apart from the CFA countries, Lesotho, Namibia, Swaziland, Ireland, Luxembourg, Brunei, Liberia, and Panama, all currency union members identified from 1970 to 1990 were small islands or territories without full sovereign status. An updated version of this list would include another exception: the eurozone. The euro, however, is a unique example of independent nation-states agreeing to use a common currency whose monetary policy is determined by a common institution.

Explaining Currency Domains The theoretical approach to explaining the use of a common currency has been dominated by the optimum currency area (OCA) literature initiated by the economists Robert Mundell and Ronald McKinnon in the early 1960s and continuing to Alberto Alesina and Robert Barro (2002). OCA theory, which emphasizes the trade-off between the macropolicy benefits of an independent currency and the microeconomic benefits from a common currency, is appealing in principle but has a poor record of explaining the composition of existing currency areas or predicting changes in currency domains.

Independent countries want their own currency because they want to set their own monetary policy. Economic stability is not always a primary concern. Ukraine left the ruble zone in 1992, for example, so that the government could print money to support inefficient producers. In many newly independent countries in all eras, monetary policy independence enabled rulers to finance expenditures. Fixed exchange rate arrangements and currency unions both involve some level of constraint on independent monetary policy, but all exchange rate regimes involve an important element of choice (over instrument and peg) and leave an option of reversal. Fixed exchange rate systems enable countries to make their own macroeconomic policy choices, while a currency union definitively cedes control over monetary policy.

OCA theory takes the position that very small nations, or microstates, cannot afford to have a national currency because the transaction costs would be too high. The threshold for such transaction costs is not so high as to prohibit small countries like Malta or Iceland from having independent currencies, however. Neither are transaction costs the reason for membership in the CFA franc zone and rand zone; these members use common currencies because France and South Africa provide carrots for them to do so, and even then the carrots were insufficient to keep Mauritania in the franc zone or Botswana in the rand zone.

What explains the use of a common currency by independent countries, and especially the case of the euro? The OCA theory does not explain the timing or composition of the euro because it ignores the importance of a common currency for public finance. For governments, seigniorage is a benefit of a national currency, but the benefit tends to be small, especially as cash declines in significance. More important is the need to have a common unit of account for the public finances; the concept of legal tender allows the government to set tax rates, approve expenditures, and similar functions. The use of multiple currencies within one country would undermine political

agreement over the allocation of the central budget. Internal exchange rate changes would reduce the tax burden and increase the relative value of expenditures for the users of one currency over another.

The Adoption of the Euro The emergence of single-currency areas paralleled the consolidation of the nation-state. The major currency unions of the second half of the nineteenth century, including those in Germany, Italy, and Canada, were associated with political unions. In 1990, German monetary union accompanied the reunification of the country. Although debates took place at the time over acceptance of the deutschmark in the former East Germany and the rate at which old Ostmarks would be exchanged, a common budget in common units played a key role in German reunification. The euro, first adopted for noncash transactions in the late 1990s before it became a cash currency, is a 21st-century example of public finance driving adoption of a common currency.

The adoption of the euro was preceded by a lengthy transition period during the existence of the European Monetary System, which began in 1979, and especially after the Maastricht agreement of the early 1990s. The process did not follow the predictions of the OCA theory. Although the EU did become more integrated with more open national economies and greater movement of labor and capital across national borders, the pace of monetary integration did not follow these trends, and in the end, restrictions on capital movements were abolished as a step toward monetary union rather than monetary union being driven by greater factor (e.g., labor or capital) mobility.

How to explain these outcomes? The European Monetary System began operation in 1979, and an important driving force was the difficulty of managing the Common Agricultural Policy based on agreed common prices when exchange rates were market-driven (Pomfret 1991; Basevi and Grassi 1993). The problems of the EU's agricultural policy may be reduced by reform, but any common policies based on political negotiations about financial contributions and monetary benefits will be undermined by changes in bilateral exchange rates. The more far-reaching the EU's common policies and the larger the EU's common budget became, the more severe the problems associated with lack of a common currency. Meanwhile, the desire for independent monetary policies was moderated by growing agreement on the primacy of price stability and on the desirability of central bank independence. In the 1990s, the crucial issues behind adoption of a common currency concerned who determines the conduct of monetary and fiscal policy, rather than the emphasis in OCA theory on private sector transaction costs and on whether macropolicy will be effective or not.

If the EU is becoming a territorial unit as Germany or Italy or Canada did in the 19th century, and this was a significant motive behind the introduction of the euro, then the euro as a common currency is sui generis in the current world economy. Apart from the euro, the only current examples of common currencies are the special cases of the CFA franc zone and the rand zone, where carrots encourage membership, and the extreme cases of ministates.

See also Bretton Woods system; dominant currency; euro; European Monetary Union; exchange rate regimes; impossible trinity; multiple currencies; optimum currency area (OCA) theory

FURTHER READING

Alesina, Alberto, and Robert J. Barro. 2002. "Currency Unions." *Quarterly Journal of Economics* 117 (2): 409–36. A survey of the theoretical literature.

Basevi, Giorgio, and Silvia Grassi. 1993. "The Crisis of the European Monetary System and Its Consequences for Agricultural Trade." *Review of Economic Conditions in Italy* 47 (June): 81–104. An analysis of the relationship between the EU's agricultural policy and its decision to push toward monetary union in 1978–79.

Bowles, Paul. 2007. *National Currencies and Globalization: Endangered Specie?* London: Routledge. An analysis of the threat posed by globalization to the national currencies of medium-sized countries like Norway or Canada.

Helleiner, Eric. 2003. *The Making of National Money.* Ithaca, NY: Cornell University Press. A historical account of the rise of national currencies over the last two centuries.

Mckinnon, Ronald I. 1963. "Optimum Currency Areas." *American Economic Review* 53 (September): 717–24. One of the pioneering papers on the OCA theory.

Mundell, Robert A. 1961. "A Theory of Optimum Currency Areas." *American Economic Review* 51 (November): 509–17. One of the pioneering papers on the OCA theory.

Pomfret, Richard. 1991. "The Secret of the EMS's Longevity." *Journal of Common Market Studies* 29 (December): 623–33. An analysis of why European monetary integration went off track in the 1970s but not in the 1980s, emphasizing the importance of fiscal considerations.

———. 2005. "Currency Areas in Theory and Practice." *Economic Record* 81 (253): 166–76. A review of the empirical applicability of the main theories of currency area formation.

Rose, Andrew. 2000. "One Money, One Market: The Effect of Common Currencies on Trade." *Economic Policy* 30 (April): 7–33. A seminal and controversial assessment of the impact of a common currency on bilateral trade.

RICHARD POMFRET

■ common market

A *common market* differs from other preferential trading arrangements, such as a free trade area or a customs union, in that, in addition to free trade in goods and services among members, there also is free mobility of factors, that is, free mobility of labor, capital, and other inputs used in producing goods and services. The European Union (EU) is a prominent—although imperfect—example of this form of integration.

Global free trade and global factor mobility allow the most efficient allocation of resources and, therefore, yield the best situation. In contrast, a common market, which restricts trade and factor mobility between members and nonmembers, has to be seen in a *second-best* context. As in any preferential trading arrangement, a common market leads to welfare-reducing trade-diversion effects to go along with its welfare-enhancing trade-creation effects. Trade diversion occurs when an importing country buys a good at a higher price from a member of the common market, while this same good was previously imported at a lower price from a nonmember nation. This can happen because of the tariff preference that is granted to the members. As a result, trade is diverted from a low-cost nonmember to a high-cost member, and this is efficiency reducing. These effects apply to factor mobility as well. To the extent that intrabloc capital movement or labor migration might improve factor allocation within the union, it is efficiency enhancing. On the other hand, if factor mobility within the union leads a country to replace factor inflows from nonmembers with less-efficient factors from members, it will be welfare reducing. Finally, as with goods, the prices for mobile factors might differ in a common market, thereby conferring terms-of-trade losses or gains to member nations.

In the presence of foreign factors of production, many of the conventional welfare results of international trade break down. Brecher and Bhagwati (1981) highlight the role of the *differential trade volume* phenomenon and the *differential trade pattern* phenomenon in leading to apparent paradoxes. The trade volume for the home nation as a whole will, in general, differ from the corresponding volume for the nationals (excluding the immigrant factors of production) only. This is referred to as the *differential trade volume*. It is also possible that, while the country is a net exporter of (say) a capital-intensive good, the nationals are net importers of the same good. Brecher and Bhagwati (1981) call this the *differential trade pattern*. A terms-of-trade improvement for the country can be an adverse movement for the nationals because of this effect. Similarly, even with the same trade pattern, an adverse terms-of-trade movement will be amplified if the nationals' volume of trade is disproportionately large (compared to the country's as a whole). This can reduce the income of the nationals, even if the aggregate income (including that of the immigrants) rises. Overall, they conclude that even if standard trade theory may suggest that a nation will gain (or lose) from a certain change, the effect on its citizens might be ambiguous in the presence of immigrant factors. In light of this discussion, we infer that factor mo-

bility can lead to conflicts between member-nation interests. Policies that might be good for the union need not raise the national income of each member. In such a situation, welfare-enhancing policies might be feasible only if members can coordinate and set up compensation mechanisms that allow for appropriate intrabloc transfers.

Wooton (1988) considers the effects of moving from a customs union to a common market. To the extent that factor mobility leads to superior resource allocation within the union, efficiency rises. However, given that trade taxes exist between the union and the rest of the world, factor mobility can amplify or reduce distortions. For example, consider a good that is subject to an import tariff by the union. When factors move within the bloc, production of the good will fall in some nations and rise in others—through changes in their respective production possibility frontiers. If the net effect is such that production of the good falls at the union level, more will be imported by the union, thereby moving the outcome closer to the free-trade level. In such a situation, a common market will improve on a customs union. If not, then the opposite will occur. The welfare issue is more complicated at the national level: even if the union as a whole gains, some member nations might lose because of adverse terms-of-trade movements in product and/or factor markets. For an individual member nation, the extent of gains or losses from such movements will depend on its volume of trade. Furthermore, because a common external tariff restricts trade, a member nation will gain if factor mobility induces an expansion of trade with nonmembers. Kowalczyk (1993) focuses on related issues and, in addition to the terms-of-trade and volume-of-trade issues related to trade taxes, considers the role of nontariff barriers (NTBs). He points out that intraunion trade in goods or factors is often subject to NTBs that do not generate revenues. Consequently, the welfare gains related to NTB removal depend on the initial volume of trade and not the change in the volume, which is scaled by the tariff rate. Viewed in this context, a union that already has a large volume of trade in factors is likely to gain significantly from the removal of impediments to factor mobility.

Issues of tax competition and coordination also arise when there is factor mobility between union members (see Haufler 2001). Broadly speaking, as long as there are differences in national policies within a union, there will be incentives for labor and/or capital to move to take advantage of the differences. By the same token, nations can anticipate such movements and adjust their policies accordingly. In the absence of coordination at the union level, factor mobility can lead to tax competition between nations and to inefficient policy outcomes for an individual member and perhaps for the union as a whole. Competition for mobile capital is an example: Consider two nations that are competing to have capital locate within their borders. Assume also that capital-tax revenues go toward financing a public good. If one nation raises its tax rate on capital, the other nation will benefit as some of the capital will relocate to it. In other words, the tax imposed by one nation causes a positive externality on the other, which experiences an increase in tax revenue, and public-good provision, without increasing its tax rate. In a noncooperative Nash taxation equilibrium, this leads to tax rates and public-good provision that are too low from the perspective of a union of these two nations. At a noncooperative Nash taxation equilibrium, each country sets its capital tax unilaterally to maximize its objective function, assuming that the other country's tax rate is fixed at a certain level. In addition, at this equilibrium, the tax rates of the two nations (say A and B) must be such that, given A's tax rate, B's tax rate maximizes its objective function, and vice versa. Tax coordination between the nations will help to alleviate this problem. However, asymmetry between nations can make such coordination difficult. It is possible that the coordinated outcome is not superior for a nation that stands to benefit from tax competition. Therefore, for heterogeneous unions, coordination can be harder to achieve.

Although capital and labor mobility have been treated symmetrically in our discussion so far, there is evidence that actual movements of labor within a common market are relatively small compared to the movement of capital. Dustmann et al. (2003) note that the introduction of mobility between Greece, Portugal, and Spain and existing EU members did not lead to large migration flows from these nations to the rest of the EU. This is significant, because these acceding countries differed substantially in their economic conditions (for example, much lower per capita incomes) relative to the existing EU nations. Qualitatively similar conclusions are reached by Zaiceva (2004) regarding accession of East European nations to the EU. No major jumps were anticipated and, indeed, as income levels converge over the long run, migration flows are expected to fall. As an explanation for the low levels of labor migration following integration, Dustmann et al. suggest that it is not only current conditions but also expectation of future conditions that can determine such flows. To the extent that agreements such as that for EU expansion create optimism in a new member nation about its own economy, it may dampen the desire of a potential migrant to incur the costs associated with migration.

Harris and Schmitt (2005) contrast intra-EU mobility with the relatively high mobility between states in the United States and note that labor market shocks in the EU generate changes in the labor market participation rate without affecting migration significantly. The EU experience may not immediately generalize to other groupings of nations. For example, mobility between Canada and the United States has been high historically and is likely to strengthen with potentially deeper labor market integration under the North American Free Trade Agreement (NAFTA) (see Harris and Schmitt 2005). Similarly, labor market integration that includes Mexico might also lead to large flows. The migration pressure between Mexico and the United States is readily seen in the large existing stock (and flow) of legal and illegal immigration across the U.S.-Mexican border. At least in the context of NAFTA, however, the recent immigration reform proposals, and the debate surrounding them, suggest that a common market with full mobility of labor seems unlikely to be politically feasible in the near future.

See also customs unions; European Union; free trade area; North American Free Trade Agreement (NAFTA); regionalism

FURTHER READING

Brecher, Richard A., and Jagdish N. Bhagwati. 1981. "Foreign Ownership and the Theory of Trade and Welfare." *Journal of Political Economy* 89 (3): 497–511. A theoretical contribution qualifying standard trade theoretic results in an economy with immigrant factors of production.

Dustmann, Christian, Maria Casanova, Michael Fertig, Ian Preston, and Christoph M. Schmidt. 2003. "The Impact of EU Enlargement on Migration Flows." Home Office Online Report 25/03. Center for Research and Analysis of Migration (CReAM), UK. Assesses potential migration flows to the UK due to EU enlargement.

Harris, Richard G., and Nicolas Schmitt. 2005. "Labour Mobility and a North American Common Market: Implications for Canada." In *Brains on the Move: Essays on Human Capital Mobility in a Globalizing World*, edited by S. Easton, R. G. Harris and N. Schmitt. Toronto: C. D. Howe Institute, 133–74. Focuses on greater labor mobility within NAFTA and its implications for Canada.

Haufler, Andreas. 2001. *Taxation in a Global Economy*. Cambridge: Cambridge University Press. Brings together different policy coordination issues that may arise within an economic bloc like the EU.

Kowalczyk, Carsten. 1993. "Integration in Goods and Factors: The Role of Flows and Revenue." *Regional Science and Urban Economics* 23: 355–67. Compares revenue generating barriers to trade to NTBs, in the context of a common market type of trading bloc.

Wooton, Ian. 1988. "Towards a Common Market: Factor Mobility in a Customs Union." *Canadian Journal of Economics* 21 (3): 525–38. Assesses efficiency gains for members of a customs union, who plan to move to a common market type of integration.

Zaiceva, Anzelika. 2004. "Implications of EU Accession for International Migration: An Assessment of Potential Migration Pressure." CESifo Working Paper #1184. Empirical forecast of migration flows from accession nations to EU member states due to eastern enlargement.

**SUBHAYU BANDYOPADHYAY
AND HOWARD J. WALL**

■ Common Market for Eastern and Southern Africa (COMESA)

The Common Market for Eastern and Southern Africa (COMESA) is a regional trade organization consisting of 20 African states in the eastern and southern regions of Africa and a small number of countries in central and northern Africa. In 2007 its membership included Angola, Burundi, Comoros, Democratic Republic of Congo, Djibouti, Egypt, Eritrea, Ethiopia, Kenya, Libya (since June 2005), Madagascar, Malawi, Mauritius, Rwanda, Seychelles, Sudan, Swaziland, Uganda, Zambia, and Zimbabwe. Its objective is to strengthen the institutions of member states to help them achieve collective and sustained development.

Origin and Background COMESA, also known simply as the common market, traces its origin to the pan-African vision of economic integration of the African continent that gained prominence between the late 1950s and early 1960s. The consensus then was that the smallness and fragmentation of postcolonial African national markets would constitute a major obstacle to the development of the continent. Accordingly, it was agreed that the newly independent African states should promote economic cooperation among themselves. In the mid-1960s, the countries of eastern and southern Africa initiated the process toward the formation of an eastern and southern African cooperation arrangement. After the preparatory work had been finalized, the Preferential Trade Area (PTA) Treaty was signed in 1981 and ratified in 1982, giving birth to the Eastern and Southern African PTA.

COMESA was created by treaty in 1994 to replace the PTA. Its formation was a fulfillment of the requirements of the PTA Treaty, which provided for the transformation of the PTA into a common market. The common market was intended to strengthen the progress of regional integration that had begun under the PTA. The COMESA Treaty had two notable provisions that the PTA Treaty lacked: (1) the concept of multiple speed or variable asymmetry, which allows some countries to progress faster in the regional economic integration process than other countries, and (2) the use of sanctions (financial penalty, suspension, or expulsion) to discipline member states that fail to implement COMESA programs or to settle disputes arising from the interpretation or implementation of the treaty. These two innovations helped to expedite the process of economic integration in the region.

The affairs of the common market are managed by a number of institutions, including those organs (the Authority of Heads of States and Governments, the Council of Ministers, the Court of Justice, and the Committee of Governors of Central Banks) responsible for making decisions on behalf of the common market; the COMESA Trade and Development Bank, which provides capital for development; the COMESA Re-Insurance Company, which is responsible for providing insurance for trade, investment, and other productive activities, and for promoting trade in insurance and reinsurance business; the COMESA Association of Commercial Banks, which is responsible for promoting and strengthening links between banks in the region; the COMESA Clearing House, which is responsible for settling payments with respect to all transactions in commodities conducted within the common market; and the COMESA Leather Institute, which is responsible for promoting productivity, competitiveness, trade, and regional integration in the leather subsector.

Member countries of the common market are diverse in terms of socioeconomic development and resource endowments. According to 2004 data, gross domestic product (GDP) per capita ranged from as little as US $90 for Burundi to more than US $8,600 for Seychelles. The United Nations Development Program ranked only two countries (Seychelles, followed by Mauritius) as high-human-development countries, six as medium-human-development countries, and 12 as low-human-development countries. The population levels range from less than a million in Comoros to more than 70 million each in Egypt and Ethiopia, with a total of 380 million people in the entire region. Resource endowments vary from agricultural products to crude oil (in Libya) to mineral ores. COMESA was intended to take advantage of the larger market size, to share the region's

common heritage and destiny, and to allow greater social and economic cooperation with the ultimate goal of creating a regional economic community. This regional economic community would then form one of the building blocks on which the creation of the African Economic Community (AEC) would be erected, as envisaged by the Lagos Plan of Action of 1980 and the Abuja Treaty of 1991.

Key Elements and Procedures The COMESA integration strategy comprises the following four phases: (1) the establishment of a free trade area (FTA) through the abolition of all tariff and nontariff barriers on commodities imported from member countries by 2000; (2) the establishment of a customs union with a common external tariff structure by 2004; (3) the adoptions of common investment practices and visa arrangements, and the establishment of a payments union; and (4) the establishment of a common monetary union by 2025. The FTA phase was achieved in 2000 when Djibouti, Egypt, Eritrea, Ethiopia, Kenya, Madagascar, Malawi, Mauritius, Sudan, Zambia, and Zimbabwe eliminated tariffs and nontariff barriers on goods produced in the common market. Burundi and Rwanda eliminated theirs in 2004 and became FTA partners. At the end of 2007, the common market was still operating as an FTA.

The common market has five key provisions. First, there are no custom duties or charges of equivalent effect imposed on goods from one FTA member to another unless it is for protecting an infant industry or against dumping. Second, member states are allowed to impose full national tariff rates on goods from nonmember states. Third, there are no nontariff barriers against goods from one FTA member to another unless such goods are deemed to pose a health or security risk. Fourth, member states follow the COMESA rules of origin in determining whether or not a good is eligible for preferential treatment. Strict local content requirements have been established to prevent nonmember countries from establishing assembly operations in one member country in order to gain duty-free access to the common market. Fifth, member states that are not yet FTA partners but have met the 60 percent tariff reduction target are granted trade preferences by the FTA partners on the basis of the tariff reductions they have attained. For instance, countries such as Comoros, Eritrea, and Uganda that have reduced their tariff rates on products originating from the common market by at least 80 percent qualify to receive an equivalent reciprocal preferential treatment from the FTA partners. Other COMESA member states that have not implemented the 60 percent minimum tariff reduction do not get any preferential rate from the FTA partners or from those that have reduced their tariffs by at least 60 percent.

Besides market integration, the COMESA integration strategy has been expanded to include transport and communications infrastructure development. More specifically, the focus is on development and implementation of transit traffic facilitation programs; identification and coordination of regional investments in the transportation, communications, and energy sectors; and the promotion and coordination of institutional and policy reforms in the transportation, telecommunication, postal, energy, and environment sectors.

Impact on Member States Economists separate the welfare effects of a regional economic integration into static and dynamic effects. Static effects are short-run effects that relate to productive efficiency and consumer welfare. Static effects are further delineated into trade creation and trade diversion effects, à la Jacob Viner (1950). Trade creation is associated with increase in trade among member states of a regional organization owing to the reduction in tariff and nontariff barriers. Trade diversion occurs when trade with nonmember countries declines as a result of the formation of a regional organization. A regional economic arrangement is welfare-increasing if the trade creation effects more than compensate for the trade diversion effects.

There is evidence of trade creation in the CO-MESA region. Trade among member countries (intra-COMESA trade) has expanded substantially since the creation of COMESA. Intra-COMESA trade increased from US $1.7 billion in 1994 to US $5.5 billion in 2003. The formation of the FTA has played a major role in facilitating this trade. More specifically, trade among the FTA partners alone increased from US $1 billion in 2000 to more than US $5 billion in 2005. Jacob W. Musila (2005) investigated the static effects of the COMESA regional trade agreement and concluded that it is welfare-increasing. More specifically, Musila estimated the relative sizes of the trade diversion and trade creation effects for COMESA and found that the trade creation effects exceed the trade diversion effects.

The dynamic effects of regional economic integration relate to the long-run growth rates of the member countries due to increased efficiency as a result of market enlargement. It is believed that large markets permit economies of scale to be realized on certain export goods and, therefore, may lead to specialization in particular types of goods. The net impact of the dynamic effects, like that of the static effects, is not obvious, however. Whether or not regional economic integration increases welfare in the long run depends on the scope of liberalization in member countries and the type of goods in which countries specialize. Athanasios Vamvakidis (1999) shows that growth is faster in economies that liberalize broadly than in those that merely join regional trade agreements and do not liberalize. Augustin K. Fosu (1990) finds that primary commodity exports do not have a significant impact on long-run economic growth.

For COMESA, the approach to regional integration is open regionalism—that is, it liberalizes trade without crowding out the world economy. COMESA member countries specialize mainly in primary commodities, however. As a result, the trade commodity base among member states is narrow and similar. The trade pattern of the common market is such that manufactured goods are imported from outside the region (mainly from rich nations) while primary commodities dominate the exports of the region. And Antonio Spilimbergo (2000) has shown that the importation of manufactured goods may not necessarily result in dynamic gains for less-developed countries (the South). The learning-by-importing models suggest, however, that imports of high-technology goods lead to transfer of technology that stimulates domestic innovation and economic growth in the importing country.

The experience for the common market region has been a slight improvement in economic growth since the creation of COMESA in 1994. The average growth rate of real GDP per capita per annum increased from about 0.01 percent during 1980–94 to 1.35 percent during 1995–2005. It is likely that the improvement in economic growth in the common market is partly due to the trade liberalization programs implemented under the auspices the CO-MESA Treaty. Together, the static and dynamic effects determine the overall welfare gains or losses associated with regional economic integration. The evidence appears to suggest that there are overall welfare gains in the case of COMESA.

Relation with External Actors COMESA and other African regional trade blocs seek to augment and deepen regional integration on the African continent with a view to creating an AEC. Accordingly, COMESA supports and has signed cooperation agreements with several other African regional undertakings such as the Intergovernmental Authority on Development and the Economic Community of West African States (ECOWAS) and allows overlapping memberships with other regional organizations. Robert Sharer (1999) has observed, however, that overlapping memberships with internal inconsistencies, conflicting regulations and rules, and different strategies and objectives work to impede market expansion and, thus, discourage domestic and foreign investment. Indeed, some of the countries with dual or more memberships, such as Namibia and Tanzania, have been reluctant to implement COMESA programs in full or have quit the common market.

Non-African regional trade blocs are often seen as impeding Africa's regional integration. Jeffrey D. Lewis, Sherman Robinson, and Karen Thierfelder (2003) have observed that North-South trade is more attractive to African countries than South-South trade. Indeed, a majority of the member states of COMESA trade with the European Union (EU) more than with one another. The trade with the EU and the United States was set to increase even further

following the opening up of the EU and U.S. markets under the Everything-but-Arms and the African Growth and Opportunity Act initiatives, respectively. A 2001 WTO provision aiming at removing quotas and duties on a large number of goods originating from the world's poorest countries also promised to increase trade with non-African regional blocs and further reduce the advantages that the common market offers to its member states. Ironically, however, the very same processes of global trade liberalization and cooperation with non-African trade blocs have contributed to the evolution of COMESA. The EU directly encourages developing countries to form a group and speak with one voice. For the EU, dealing with a collective organization rather than with numerous individual countries reduces transaction costs. Indirectly, the success of the EU has inspired the hopes for creating the AEC, with COMESA being an intermediate step.

See also customs unions; Economic Community of West African States (ECOWAS); free trade area; regionalism; rules of origin

FURTHER READING

COMESA. COMESA Treaty. Downloadable from http://www.comesa.int/. Offers detailed insights about the establishment of COMESA, its objectives, and the various articles and protocols that govern the operation of the organization.

Fosu, Augustin K. 1990. "Export Composition and the Impact of Exports on Economic Growth of Developing Economies." *Economics Letters* 34 (1): 67–71. An empirical investigation suggesting that exporting of primary products does not have a significant influence on long-run economic growth rates of the producing country.

Lewis, Jeffrey D., Sherman Robinson, and Karen Thierfelder. 2003. "Free Trade Agreements and the SADC Economies." *Journal of African Economies* 12 (2): 156–206. A general equilibrium analysis of the impact of trade liberalization in the Southern African Development Community (SADC), which shows that trade with the EU is more beneficial to SADC countries than a SADC free trade area would be.

Musila, Jacob W. 2005. "The Intensity of Trade Creation and Trade Diversion in COMESA, ECCAS and

ECOWAS: A Comparative Analysis." *Journal of African Economies* 14 (1): 117–41. An estimation of the static gains/losses of selected examples of regional economic integration in Africa using the gravity model.

Sharer, Robert. 1999. "Trade: An Engine of Growth for Africa." *Finance and Development* 36 (4): 26–29. Examines regional integration initiatives and suggests that the overlapping memberships of regional trade blocs in Africa may work to prevent the attainment of dynamic gains.

Spilimbergo, Antonio. 2000. "Growth and Trade: The North Can Lose." *Journal of Economic Growth* 5 (2): 131–46. An analysis of North-South trade that suggests that rich nations (the North) may experience technological slowdown if they trade with poor nations (the South), and the South could also lose in such trade.

Vamvakidis, Athanasios. 1999. "Regional Trade Agreements or Broad Liberalization: Which Path Leads to Faster Growth?" *IMF Staff Papers* 46 (1): 42–68. An empirical analysis that suggests that economic growth is faster after liberalizing broadly and slower after joining a regional trade agreement.

Viner, Jacob. 1950. *The Customs Union Issue.* New York: Carnegie Endowment for International Peace. Examines the effects of regional trade agreements and introduces the concepts of trade creation and trade diversion for the first time.

JACOB W. MUSILA

comparative advantage

The term *comparative advantage* was first used in England in the early 19th century by economists of the classical school, which dates from the publication of Adam Smith's *An Inquiry into the Nature and Causes of the Wealth of Nations* (1776). Sometimes denoted by the synonymous term *comparative cost*, it expresses the principle by which a nation that opens to international trade is led to specialize in and export certain commodities and to import others. Whereas the former commodities are those in which it has a comparative advantage, the nation is said to have a comparative disadvantage in the latter. The concept of comparative advantage is vital for understanding the structure of world trade and how each country contributes to it. It underlies the whole field of international trade theory and policy, the earliest and arguably the most important of the applied fields of economics and of its predecessor, political economy. Textbooks of international trade devote successive chapters to exploring the reasons why nations have a comparative advantage in certain commodities, and the welfare implications of specialization in accordance with its dictates. Comparative advantage is also relevant to different regions of a country in studying the pattern of interregional trade.

Starting in England at the end of the 17th century with mercantilist writers such as Sir Dudley North and Henry Martyn, the sources of comparative advantage and the gains from the trade that it induces were explored by the luminaries of the nascent economics profession: Smith himself and the classical economists who followed him, such as David Ricardo, Robert Torrens, and John Stuart Mill. Ricardo (1817) enshrined comparative advantage as a key concept for economists by illustrating it with a numerical example relating to trade in wine and cloth between England and Portugal. In the first half of the 20th century the neoclassical school of thought added its own perspectives to the concept of Ricardian comparative advantage when it was generalized by Gottfried Haberler (1936) and critiqued by two Swedish economists, Eli Heckscher (1949) and Bertil Ohlin (1933). Heckscher and Ohlin postulated that the source of comparative advantage resides in the differential factor endowments of trading countries. The Heckscher-Ohlin theory became the mainstream theory of trade after World War II. Since the late 1970s, doubts that had been raised about the empirical validity of comparative advantage led some economists to formulate a New Trade Theory that harks back to another source of trade mentioned by Ohlin (1933), economies of scale, and explains why much of the trade between advanced economies consists of differentiated commodities produced under conditions of imperfect competition.

Despite the frequency with which the principle of comparative advantage is discussed, a precise definition is hard to find, and most authors cite particular economists or associate the concept with numerical examples, such as Ricardo's, based on two countries, two commodities, and a single input, labor. An algebraic definition along Ricardian lines can clarify the concept. Consider two commodities, 1 and 2, and two countries, A and B. Define L_i^C as the input of labor per unit of output of commodity i ($i = 1, 2$) in country C (C = A, B). Then country A has an *absolute advantage* in commodity 1 if $L_1^A < L_1^B$, and a *comparative advantage* in commodity 1 if

$$L_1^A/L_2^A < L_1^B/L_2^B. \qquad (1)$$

Inequality (1) is consistent with the possibility that $L_1^A < L_1^B$ and $L_2^A < L_2^B$, so that A has an absolute advantage in both commodities but a comparative advantage in the first. Absolute advantage in a commodity thus indicates a smaller absolute cost in terms of a factor such as labor, whereas comparative advantage implies that the ratio between the unit costs of production is lower in A than in B. What is being "compared" in comparative advantage are unit costs relating both to countries and to commodities: a double-barreled comparison. Since relative prices before trade conform to the ratios L_1^C/L_2^C in A and B according to the labor theory of value, the commodity whose relative cost of production is lower is exported in exchange for the other commodity. If $L_1^A < L_1^B$, $L_2^A < L_2^B$, and inequality (1) holds, specialization according to comparative advantage has important welfare implications for both countries: A is better off if it participates in international trade despite its greater efficiency in producing both goods, and B can participate gainfully in the international division of labor despite its absolute disadvantage in both commodities. If $L_1^A < L_1^B$, $L_2^A < L_2^B$, and (1) is changed to the equality $L_1^A/L_2^A = L_1^B/L_2^B$, A has an absolute advantage in both commodities and a comparative advantage in neither. Trade cannot take place since both countries face the same relative price. Comparative advantage clearly trumps absolute advantage as a cause of trade.

According to Jones and Neary (1984, 3), "While the principle of comparative advantage may thus be defended as a basic explanation of trade patterns, it is not a primitive explanation, since it assumes rather than explains inter-country differences in autarkic relative prices." Autarkic relative prices are those that prevail in a state of *autarky*, when a country is closed to trade. Successive models of international trade have been based on different "primitive explanations" for why relative prices differ in autarky, such as intercountry differences in technologies, factor endowments, or tastes. The specification of an autarky equilibrium is, for most countries, a thought experiment designed to ascertain the prices that would prevail in the unlikely event that an economy were isolated or self-sufficient. It is part of an exercise in "comparative statics," in which an economy's resource allocation and economic welfare in autarky are compared to their pattern under free trade. If transportation costs are neglected, free trade equates the prices of traded commodities across countries. Each country's export good rises in value while the import-competing good falls. Under free trade one can therefore no longer speak of a country being a "low-price" country for the goods in which it holds a comparative advantage.

18th-Century Views on the Causes of Specialization Before Ricardo, comparative advantage was interpreted in a looser way than that indicated earlier, namely, as the reason why particular economies show a tendency toward specialization in certain types of commodity. In 1752 the philosopher David Hume published a series of essays analyzing a variety of commercial issues including trade between more developed economies such as England and less developed ones such as his native Scotland. Lower wages give a competitive advantage to more backward economies, allowing them to compete successfully with more advanced ones in the simpler manufactures. In a similar vein the English pamphleteer Josiah Tucker argued that

It may be laid down as a general Proposition, which very seldom fails, That *operose* or *complicated Manufactures* are cheapest in rich Countries; and *raw Materials* in poor ones: And therefore in Proportion as any Commodity approaches to one, or other of these *Extremes*, in that Proportion it will be found to be cheaper, or dearer in a rich, or a poor

Country.... [Moreover] there are certain *local* Advantages resulting either from the Climate, the Soil, the Productions, the Situation, or even the natural Turn and peculiar Genius of one People preferably to those of another, which no Nation can deprive another of. (Tucker 1774, 188, 193)

Tucker not only spoke of national "advantages," but traced them to climate, soil, and even "the natural turn and peculiar genius" of the people, factors that were often subsequently cited as explanations of economic specialization by the classical school of economists. He engaged with Hume in what became known as the "rich country–poor country" debate, in which they argued whether poor countries could catch up with or even surpass the standard of living of richer ones. In opposition to Hume, Tucker maintained that the built-in advantages of rich countries are hard to reverse. Without citing Tucker, Adam Smith also anticipated the theory of comparative advantage by maintaining that "the most opulent nations ... generally excel all their neighbours in agriculture as well as in manufactures; but they are commonly more distinguished by their superiority in the latter than in the former" (Smith 1776, 16). This notion of a "natural" territorial division of labor between rich and poor countries was adopted by most 19th-century economists.

Ricardo's Example of Comparative Advantage
The principle of comparative advantage is contained in chapter 7 of Ricardo's *Principles of Political Economy and Taxation* (1817), which is devoted to foreign trade:

The quantity of wine which she [Portugal] shall give in exchange for the cloth of England, is not determined by the respective quantities of labour devoted to the production of each, as it would be, if both commodities were manufactured in England, or both in Portugal.

England may be so circumstanced, that to produce the cloth may require the labour of 100 men for one year; and if she attempted to make the wine, it might require the labour of 120 men for the same time. England would

therefore find it her interest to import wine, and to purchase it by the exportation of cloth.

To produce the wine in Portugal, might require only the labour of 80 men for one year, and to produce the cloth in the same country, might require the labour of 90 men for the same time. It would therefore be advantageous for her to export wine in exchange for cloth. This exchange might even take place, notwithstanding that the commodity imported by Portugal could be produced there with less labour than in England. Though she could make the cloth with the labour of 90 men, she would import it from a country where it required the labour of 100 men to produce it, because it would be advantageous to her rather to employ her capital in the production of wine, for which she would obtain more cloth from England, than she could produce by diverting a portion of her capital from the cultivation of vines to the manufacture of cloth.

Thus England would give the produce of the labour of 100 men, for the produce of the labour of 80. (Ricardo 1817, 135)

These paragraphs contain four numbers denoting the amounts of labor needed to produce wine and cloth in England (120, 100) and Portugal (80, 90). International trade textbooks interpret them as constant labor coefficients per unit of output of wine and cloth, and deduce from them linear production possibility frontiers and complete specialization in both countries (unless one of them happens to be "large" and remains nonspecialized). Ruffin (2002) and Maneschi (2004) show that this interpretation is incorrect. A close reading of the first three paragraphs of the foregoing passage reveals that the two numbers relating to each country refer instead to the amount of labor embodied in its *total exports* and the amount it would require to produce its *total imports* of the other commodity. In the second paragraph, Ricardo is able to assert which commodity England exports before even mentioning the two numbers relating to Portugal. It is clear that Portugal has an absolute advantage in both commodities since it uses less labor than England does to produce both traded amounts of wine and cloth. Ricardo did not justify the four numbers by referring to particular economic characteristics of the two countries. Economists have assumed that differences between them in the technology of production account for their respective comparative advantage.

Ricardo never specified the quantities exported by each country. If X is the amount of cloth exported by England and Y that of wine imported, the *terms of trade* (defined as the relative price of the export good) are Y/X units of wine per unit of cloth. Since England requires 100 units of labor to produce X and 120 units to produce Y, the unit labor coefficients are $100/X$ and $120/Y$ respectively, so that its opportunity cost of cloth in terms of wine is $(100/X)/(120/Y) = (5/6)Y/X$. The corresponding unit labor coefficients in Portugal are $80/Y$ for wine and $90/X$ for cloth, so that its opportunity cost of cloth in terms of wine is $(9/8)Y/X$. If these opportunity costs remain constant for all levels of output they are equal to the internal price ratios, so that Portugal has a comparative advantage in wine while England has it in cloth. Since $(9/8)Y/X > Y/X > (5/6)Y/X$, these opportunity costs lie on either side of the terms of trade Y/X, so that trade causes the price of the imported commodity to fall in each country.

Classical Perspectives on Comparative Advantage after Ricardo Another classical economist, Robert Torrens, is often mentioned with Ricardo as a codiscoverer of the comparative advantage principle. In his *Essay on the External Corn Trade* published two years before Ricardo's *Principles*, Torrens argued that even if England produces "corn" (grains) more efficiently than Poland, it may be to England's advantage to import it from Poland: "tracts of her territory, though they should be equal, nay, even though they should be superior, to the lands of Poland, will be neglected; and a part of her supply of corn will be imported from that country" (Torrens 1815, 264–65). Although England has an absolute advantage in corn, it has a comparative advantage in manufactures and specializes in them in order to import corn. Despite Torrens's two-year precedence in print with a passage that shows that he appreciated the dis-

tinction between absolute and comparative advantage, Ricardo deserves his reputation as the discoverer of the principle of comparative advantage since (unlike Torrens) he presented it in terms of a numerical example that allowed both the determination of the direction of trade and the gains from trade accruing to each country. Ruffin (2002) highlights other deficiencies in Torrens's formulation of this principle.

Torrens deserves to be remembered for another reason. In his comparative cost example, Ricardo postulated the existence of a trade equilibrium but never explained how the terms of trade, and hence the division of the gains from trade between the two countries, are determined. Torrens advanced the notion that they depend on the reciprocal demand of each country for the export goods of the other country. As O'Brien (2004) points out, Torrens was a pioneer in the theory of trade policy by proposing that a tariff can turn the terms of trade in a country's favor, and hence insisting on reciprocity with other countries in tariff policy. His argument for an aggressive trade policy was critiqued, and the theory of reciprocal demand developed more rigorously, by John Stuart Mill (1848), who among the classical economists ranks with Ricardo as a great innovator in international trade theory. Mill postulated that reciprocal demand determines the terms of trade in such a way that a country's exports match the value of its imports. He noted that the terms of trade are located between, and bounded by, the autarky price ratios of the two trading countries. The gap between the two countries' autarky price ratios, which indicate their respective comparative advantages, thus fixes the possible range of the terms of trade, while reciprocal demand determines their location in this range. Mill also analyzed how technical change in the export good of one of the countries alters the pattern of comparative advantage and turns the terms of trade against it.

The first professor of political economy in Ireland, Mountifort Longfield, took an important step in generalizing the Ricardian model to many commodities, observing that a commodity is exported by a country if and only if the productivity of the labor producing it, relative to the other country's, exceeds their relative wages. In his words, "That kind of labour will succeed in each country which is more productive in proportion to its price" (Longfield 1835, 56). Longfield realized the importance of reciprocal demand in determining the range of commodities exported, noting that "if a nation enjoyed an immense superiority in the production of two or three articles of very general demand, the wages of her labourers might be, in consequence, so high that she could not compete with the rest of the world in any other manufacture, under a system of free trade" (69). In the two-commodity Ricardian world, comparative advantage is determined entirely by techniques of production that dictate that one good is exported and the other imported. In a multicommodity world, a country's comparative advantage depends not only on technology but also on the reciprocal demand of each country for the other's commodities, such that commodities are exported (imported) when the ratios of their labor productivity are greater (smaller) than the ratio of their wage rates. As Longfield asserted, a country that enjoys a very high wage rate compared to its trading partner produces and exports very few commodities.

Neoclassical Perspectives on Comparative Advantage The classical school of thought gradually gave way to the marginalist economics of W. Stanley Jevons in England, Carl Menger in Austria, and Léon Walras in France and Switzerland, and then to the neoclassical school that originated with Alfred Marshall in England. Marshall achieved a "neoclassical" synthesis by combining insights derived from the marginalist economists on the important role played by demand in price determination with the supply-side view of the classical economists that price is determined by the cost of production. This spelled the end of the classical labor theory of value used to determine the autarky prices in the theory of comparative advantage of Ricardo and Mill. The prestige enjoyed by the theory of comparative advantage guaranteed its continued longevity for several more decades, as shown in Jacob Viner's (1937) scholarly *Studies in the Theory of International Trade*, which painstakingly analyzed and critiqued the achievements of the mercantilist, classical, and neoclassical writers in international trade theory and policy.

Marshall did not do much to advance the theory of international trade beyond graphically translating Mill's analysis of reciprocal demand and terms of trade determination by means of the two trading countries' offer curves. The latter show how much of the good in which each country holds a comparative advantage it is willing to export in exchange for alternative amounts of its import good. The slope of the ray joining the origin to the intersection of the offer curves yields the terms of trade. Offer curve analysis was developed in greater detail by Francis Edgeworth, who incorporated the two countries' comparative cost ratios in the offer curves and showed diagrammatically that they bound the terms of trade. Both Marshall and Edgeworth used offer curves to illustrate the impact of a tariff on the terms of trade and to investigate the stability of a trade equilibrium.

Considerably more progress was made by the Austrian-born economist Gottfried Haberler in a 1933 book that appeared in English translation three years later as *The Theory of International Trade with Its Application to Commercial Policy* (Haberler 1936), and by the Swedish economists Eli Heckscher (1949) and Bertil Ohlin (1933). Haberler generalized Ricardian comparative advantage to an economy in which price is defined by the opportunity cost of a commodity in terms of another, rather than by its constant "real cost" of production. He depicted by means of a transformation curve, or production possibilities frontier (PPF), the menu of outputs that can be produced with the economy's factors of production and the available technology. Whereas the PPF is linear in the textbook Ricardian case since real costs of production are constant for any level of output, the neoclassical PPF is concave to the origin. Its slope measures the opportunity cost of one commodity in terms of the other and increases with the level of output because of increasing unit costs. In autarky this slope differs for the two trading partners and signals their comparative advantage in the commodity that is cheaper there. Unlike in the Ricardian case, this slope is no longer independent of demand considerations, and the mix of factors used changes along the PPF together with its slope. Haberler thus generalized the comparative cost model while accepting most of its welfare conclusions.

In an article published in Swedish in 1919 and translated into English in 1949 as "The Effect of Foreign Trade on the Distribution of Income," Eli Heckscher set out to discover for the Ricardian trade model the hitherto missing rationale for why comparative advantage differs across countries and, as the title of his paper suggests, to explore how trade affects income distribution. The clue lies in the difference in the relative abundance of factor endowments across countries combined with differences in the intensities with which commodities use factors in production. Under autarky these features yield differences in commodity prices across countries that in turn lead to trade between them. Making the additional assumption that techniques of production are identical across countries, Heckscher argued that trade causes factor prices to converge and even become equal if neither country becomes fully specialized, a result that later became known as factor price equalization. As in the case of Haberler's PPF, the difference between comparative costs responsible for trade in the first place is erased by the very trade it engenders. After trade is established, and unlike the Ricardian constant-cost case, the difference in comparative costs disappears since it is no longer needed to ensure continued trade.

Haberler's generalization of the Ricardian model and Heckscher's rationale for comparative costs in the context of that model did not go far enough for Heckscher's student Bertil Ohlin, who in 1933 published a book-length critique of the Ricardian model. Together with Heckscher's 1919 article, whose assumptions and conclusions were adopted by Ohlin, it laid the foundations for what became known as the Heckscher-Ohlin theory, the mainstream theory of international trade after World War II. According to Ohlin's critique, the Ricardian model could not be reformed or generalized, but must be rejected as based on false assumptions in order to reconstruct the theory of trade on the new

foundations sketched by Heckscher and the neoclassical school. The association of the term *comparative advantage* with the theory of comparative costs that Ohlin wished to discredit explains why this term is hardly used in his 1933 book and disappears completely from the revised edition of 1967. When Paul Samuelson (1948) applied the Heckscher-Ohlin model to two countries, two commodities, and two factors of production and thereby made it more comprehensible and suitable for graphical representation, he was not deterred from using the term *comparative advantage* in connection with it. In fact, Samuelson formulated what became known as the Heckscher-Ohlin theorem: a land-abundant (labor-abundant) country has a comparative advantage in the land-intensive (labor-intensive) commodity and exchanges this commodity for the other since in autarky it is cheaper than in the other country. Its validity depends on numerous assumptions, including identical demands in the two countries such that at the same price ratio they consume goods in the same proportion. It is somewhat ironic that, following Heckscher's lead and despite Ohlin's objection to the term *comparative advantage*, Ohlin ultimately provided the first book-length explanation of the causes of comparative advantage based on international factor endowment differences and differential factor intensities for commodities.

Comparative Advantage and the New Trade Theory The Heckscher-Ohlin (H-O) theorem was tested empirically by Wassily Leontief (1953). Despite his surmise that the United States was then the world's most capital-abundant country, Leontief discovered that it exported labor-intensive and imported capital-intensive commodities! His finding became known as the Leontief paradox and gave rise to numerous articles that attempted to account for it. The underlying H-O theory was extended to more factors than the two (capital and labor) considered by Leontief, including natural resources and skilled labor. Later empirical tests that included these extensions sometimes reversed, sometimes reaffirmed the Leontief paradox. Moreover, contrary to what the H-O theory suggests, most trade flows were shown to occur between industrialized countries whose factor endowments are fairly similar. Much of this trade is intraindustry in nature, meaning that the same types of commodity (such as automobiles) are both exported and imported. Dissatisfaction with the underlying H-O theory led in the 1970s to the formulation of a *new trade theory*, some of whose models dispense altogether with the notion of comparative advantage. They allow instead for increasing returns to scale, external economies, differentiated products, and the associated imperfectly competitive market structures. Trade can arise even between economies that are identical with respect to factor endowments and technical knowledge. The new trade theorists later realized that Ohlin himself had partly anticipated them in 1933. In chapter 3 of his book, titled "Another Condition of Interregional Trade," Ohlin argued that a powerful secondary reason for trade is economies of scale, due to the indivisibility of certain factors of production. Ohlin remarked that trade and specialization are partly determined by history and accident, factors also stressed by Paul Krugman (1990). Emphasizing increasing returns and monopolistic competition in economies in which comparative advantage plays no role, Krugman showed that the New Trade Theory can provide a satisfactory explanation for intraindustry trade. Other models of the New Trade theorists combine comparative advantage with economies of scale to produce a rich variety of possible trade outcomes.

Comparative Advantage: An Enduring Legacy
Comparative advantage has been attributed to many causes in the trade literature, such as different techniques of production in the Ricardian model and differential factor endowments in the writings of Heckscher and Ohlin. The strategy adopted by the innovators of each theory was to discover a factor that differs between countries, hold everything else in them the same, and build a theory based on this difference. As the French put it, *c'est la différence qui compte.*

Although comparative advantage plays no role in a few models of the New Trade Theory, where the industries that countries adopt are immaterial as long as they end up specializing and thus reaping economies of scale, some of its other models combine such increasing returns with traditional comparative ad-

vantage. Models of the Ricardian or Heckscher-Ohlin type thus endure as significant explanations of comparative advantage in the world economy. The drastic changes in the structure of world trade since the mid-20th century and the emergence of new major exporters such as China and the countries of the "East Asian miracle" present economists and policymakers with the task of analyzing and keeping up with the rapid evolution of comparative advantage in the presence of multinational corporations and of phenomena such as outsourcing and the instantaneous transmission of technological knowledge across frontiers.

See also absolute advantage; economies of scale; gains from trade; Heckscher-Ohlin model; intraindustry trade; monopolistic competition; New Trade Theory; Ricardian model; terms of trade

FURTHER READING
Haberler, Gottfried. 1936. *The Theory of International Trade*. Edinburgh: William Hodge. A comprehensive outline of neoclassical international trade theory and policy by one of its chief contributors.

Heckscher, Eli F. 1949. "The Effect of Foreign Trade on the Distribution of Income." In *Readings in the Theory of International Trade*, edited by H. S. Ellis and L. A. Metzler. Homewood, IL: Irwin, 272–300. First published in Swedish in 1919, the original and remarkably sophisticated presentation of the Heckscher-Ohlin theory of trade.

Jones, Ronald W., and J. Peter Neary. 1984. "The Positive Theory of International Trade." In *Handbook of International Economics*, edited by Ronald W. Jones and Peter B. Kenen. Vol. 1. Amsterdam: North-Holland, 1–62. Two noted trade economists survey developments in trade theory from the 1960s to the 1980s.

Krugman, Paul R. 1990. *Rethinking International Trade*. Cambridge, MA: MIT Press. An anthology of articles based on the new trade theory by one of its most eminent exponents.

Leontief, Wassily W. 1953. "Domestic Production and Foreign Trade: The American Capital Position Re-examined." *Proceedings of the American Philosophical Society* 97: 331–49. The article that brought the Leontief paradox to the attention of the profession.

Longfield, Mountifort. 1835. *Three Lectures on Commerce, and One on Absenteeism.* Reprint, New York: A. M. Kelley, 1971. A remarkable anticipation in the early classical period of later developments in international trade theory.

Maneschi, Andrea. 1998. *Comparative Advantage in International Trade: A Historical Perspective.* Cheltenham, UK: Edward Elgar. An analysis of the genesis, evolution, and current significance of the concept of comparative advantage in the theory of international trade.

———. 2004. "The True Meaning of David Ricardo's Four Magic Numbers." *Journal of International Economics* 62 (2): 433–43. A challenge to the conventional interpretation of the numerical example that Ricardo used to illustrate comparative advantage.

Mill, John Stuart. 1848. *Principles of Political Economy.* Reprint, London: Longman, Green, 1920. The most popular 19th-century textbook of British classical political economy.

O'Brien, Denis P. 2004. *The Classical Economists Revisited.* Princeton, NJ: Princeton University Press. A thorough analytical survey of the contributions of the classical school of economics.

Ohlin, Bertil. 1933. *Interregional and International Trade.* Revised ed. Cambridge, MA: Harvard University Press, 1967. A comprehensive and literary elaboration of the Heckscher-Ohlin theory of trade.

Ricardo, David. 1817. *On the Principles of Political Economy and Taxation.* In *The Works and Correspondence of David Ricardo,* vol. 1, edited by Piero Sraffa. Cambridge: Cambridge University Press, 1951. A fundamental contribution to classical economic theory containing a numerical illustration of comparative advantage and the gains from trade.

Ruffin, Roy J. 2002. "David Ricardo's Discovery of Comparative Advantage." *History of Political Economy* 34 (4): 727–48. An exploration of the path that led Ricardo to the discovery of comparative advantage and a novel interpretation of the numbers he used to illustrate it.

Samuelson, Paul A. 1948. "International Trade and the Equalization of Factor Prices." *Economic Journal* 58 (230): 163–84. An article that expounds and illustrates the Heckscher-Ohlin-Samuelson theory of trade.

Smith, Adam. 1776. *An Inquiry into the Nature and Causes of the Wealth of Nations.* Oxford: Clarendon Press, 1976. The most famous book of the founder of classical political economy.

Torrens, Robert. 1815. *An Essay on the External Corn Trade.* 1st ed. London: Hatchard. Expounded the notion of comparative advantage in literary form two years before Ricardo's better-known numerical example.

Tucker, Josiah. 1774. *Four Tracts, on Political and Commercial Subjects,* tract I. In *Precursors of Adam Smith,* edited by Ronald L. Meek. Totowa, NJ: Rowman and Littlefield, 1973. A preclassical anticipation of the international division of labor and an analysis of the possibility of convergence in the per capita incomes of more and less developed nations.

Viner, Jacob. 1937. *Studies in the Theory of International Trade.* New York: Harper. A magisterial survey of preclassical, classical, and neoclassical trade theories.

ANDREA MANESCHI

■ competition for foreign direct investment
See subsidies and financial incentives to foreign direct investment

■ competition policy
The term *competition policy* is typically taken to include all government policies that influence the degree of competition in a nation's markets, including trade policy. Competition law, in contrast, refers to a specific set of legal provisions concerning the manner in which firms collaborate and compete with one another. That set usually includes measures on cartels, other forms of interfirm collaboration (including so-called vertical restraints), mergers and acquisitions, and abuse of market power. Competition law, therefore, is an element of competition policy but not vice versa.

The appropriate relationship between national trade and competition policies and the merits of different international initiatives on competition law have long been controversial matters both in economic analysis and in international deliberations.

Indeed, if Adam Smith's critique in *The Wealth of Nations* of granting monopolies on trade with Britain's colonies is considered, then these debates are of very long standing. The spread of competition law and the strengthening of existing laws during the current era of international market integration accounts for the renewed interest in the relationship between trade and competition policies.

Many argue that open borders and competition laws are substitutes. Bhagwati (1968) was among the first to show that the pricing power of incumbent firms would be restrained by foreign firms that are prepared to supply domestic customers at world prices. In recent years empirical support for this contention was first provided by Levinsohn (1993) and Harrison (1994). Both showed that the markups of domestic firms declined as tariff rates fell. It should be pointed out, however, that such findings need not imply that setting zero tariffs eliminates market power.

The case for complementing trade reforms with active competition law has been made on several grounds. In the 1980s and 1990s the claim was frequently advanced that prior reductions in tariffs on imports into Japan had not led to greater foreign access to its markets because agreements among Japanese manufacturers, wholesalers, and retailers effectively blocked distribution channels to foreign suppliers (Lawrence 1993; Saxonhouse 1993). More generally, the argument has been made that tariff reductions provide incentives to import-competing firms to take steps, including engaging in anticompetitive practices, that frustrate imports. Private barriers to trade, according to this argument, replace state barriers. A related but distinct argument is that sometimes these anticompetitive practices are facilitated by national unfair trade laws, in particular antidumping measures. The policy implications of the last two arguments are different, however: the former calls for enforcement action against private anticompetitive acts; the latter for reform, if not outright abolition, of unfair trade legislation.

The resurgence of national enforcement actions against international cartels that has taken place since 1993, when the U.S. antitrust authorities offered more generous terms to cartel members to "defect" and turn state's evidence, revealed other complementarities between open borders and competition law (Evenett, Levenstein, and Suslow 2001). Underenforcement of national cartel law creates safe havens where international cartel members can hide evidence, thereby creating a negative cross-border spillover for trading partners. Successful prosecution of an international cartel in one jurisdiction has often prompted investigations in other jurisdictions, creating a positive cross-border spillover. The case for international discipline requiring nations to properly enforce a cartel law can be justified by reference to the first spillover. The case for promoting cross-border cooperation among national competition agencies, which would include the sharing of evidence on cartel investigations, can be made on the basis of the second spillover. Both forms of international collective action would enhance the deterrent effect of national cartel law enforcement.

Since 1995 there has been another wave of cross-border mergers and acquisitions (Evenett 2003). These combinations can involve commercial operations in many jurisdictions and, under current merger review legislation, are often subject to investigations by many national competition agencies. Decisions by national competition agencies to allow or refuse proposed combinations can have cross-border ramifications and from time to time have become the subject of commercial disputes between nations (Muris 2001; Neven and Röller 2000). The adverse reaction of certain U.S. commentators and policymakers to the European Commission's decision on July 3, 2001, to prevent the merger of General Electric and Honeywell is an example. Suboptimal resource allocation is not just a matter of potentially poor analysis of mergers by competition agencies or of different substantive welfare standards, but is also due to the generalized practice of competition agencies of taking into account only those effects of a merger that fall within its jurisdiction's borders. The absence of any compensation mechanism to take account of all relevant cross-border spillovers, similar to the cross-sectoral bargaining in trade negotiations, is at the center of the inefficiency of simultaneous national merger enforcement. Economic analyses that endogenize the decision to engage in cross-border mergers and acquisitions (Horn and Persson 2001) and that examine the effects of such consolidation in a general equilibrium setting (Neary 2004) have also been developed.

Although considerable attention has been given to competition policy in international forums since the late 1990s, two significant international initiatives predate them. The first was the failed attempt to include binding disciplines on "restrictive business practices" in the postwar multilateral trading system. The chapter on such practices in the Havana Charter, elements of which subsequently provided much of the legal foundation for the General Agreement on Tariffs and Trade, was rejected by the U.S. Congress. Second, in 1980 the members of the United Nations (UN) adopted a nonbinding Set of Multilaterally Agreed Equitable Principles and Rules for the Control of Restrictive Business Practices. The latter remains the only multilateral instrument on competition law.

In July 2004, World Trade Organization (WTO) members decided not to act on proposals to negotiate a multilateral framework on competition policy. The proponents of such a multilateral framework advocated binding obligations to enact and enforce national anticartel law and to adhere to core WTO principles. In addition, provisions to promote both voluntary cooperation between competition agencies and technical assistance for developing countries were advanced (Clarke and Evenett 2003). Some of the strongest opponents to negotiating competition rules at the WTO were the leading competition agencies, fearful of a loss of discretion. These parties created the International Competition Network in 2001, and its numerous activities have contributed to the sharing of best practices in many aspects of competition law. The Organisation for Economic Co-operation and Development has developed a number of recommendations pertaining to competition law and its enforcement. Binding provisions on competition law have been included in more than 80 free trade agreements, but the evidence to date on these provisions' effectiveness is too sparse to draw any broad policy conclusions.

See also corporate governance; Organisation for Economic Co-operation and Development (OECD); United Nations Conference on Trade and Development; World Trade Organization

FURTHER READING

Bhagwati, Jagdish N. 1968. *The Theory and Practice of Commercial Policy.* International Finance Section, Department of Economics. Princeton, N.J.: Princeton University. Contains an early formulation on the effects that international competition can have on the exercise of domestic market power.

Clarke, Julian L., and Simon J. Evenett. 2003. "A Multilateral Framework for Competition Policy?" In *The Singapore Issues and The World Trading System: The Road to Cancun and Beyond*, edited by State Secretariat of Economic Affairs and Simon J. Evenett. Bern: World Trade Institute. Provides a comprehensive overview of the proposals and criticisms of a multilateral framework for competition policy.

Evenett, Simon J. 2003. "The Cross Border Mergers and Acquisitions Wave of the Late 1990s." In *Challenges to Globalization*, edited by R. E. Baldwin and L. A. Winters. Chicago: University of Chicago Press for the NBER, 411–67. Provides an overview of the huge cross-border mergers and acquisitions wave of the late 1990s and the economic questions raised thereby.

Evenett, Simon J., Margaret Levenstein, and Valerie Y. Suslow. 2001. "International Cartel Enforcement: Lessons from the 1990s." *World Economy* 24 (9): 1221–45. Provides both an account of the resurgence of cartel enforcement in the 1990s and an economic analysis of the deterrence effect of national enforcement efforts against international cartels.

Harrison, Ann. 1994. "Productivity, Imperfect Competition, and Trade Reform: Theory and Evidence." *Journal of International Economics* 36 (1–2): 53–73. An early study of the relationship between import competition and market power.

Horn, Henrik, and Lars Persson. 2001. "Endogenous Mergers in Concentrated Markets." *International Jour-*

nal of Industrial Organization 19 (8): 1213–44. An analysis that endogenizes the incentive to merge in international markets.

Lawrence, Robert Z. 1993. "Japan's Different Trade Regime: An Analysis with Particular Reference to *Keiretsu*." *Journal of Economic Perspectives* 7 (3): 3–19. Contends that Japan's industrial structure and potentially anticompetitive practices accounts for its low share of imports of manufactures in GDP.

Levinsohn, James. 1993. "Testing the Imports-as-Market Discipline Hypothesis." *Journal of International Economics* 35 (1–2): 1–22. Another early and much cited study of the relationship between import competition and market power.

Muris, Timothy J. 2001. "Merger Enforcement in a World of Multiple Arbiters." Prepared remarks before the Brookings Institution's Roundtable on Trade and Investment Policy (December 21). Washington, DC: Brookings Institution. A thoughtful analysis by a leading antitrust policymaker on the questions that arise when many competition agencies can review a single global merger transaction.

Neary, J. Peter. 2004. "Cross-border Mergers as Instruments of Comparative Advantage." Mimeo. Dublin, Ireland: University College. One of the few analyses of the effects of mergers on the underlying determinants of trade flows.

Neven, Damien, and Lars-Henrik Röller. 2000. "The Allocation of Jurisdiction in International Antitrust." *European Economic Review* 44 (4–6): 845–55. An economic analysis of the effects of many competition agencies reviewing a given merger transaction.

Saxonhouse, Gary. 1993. "What Does Japanese Trade Structure Tell Us about Japanese Trade Policy?" *Journal of Economic Perspectives* 7 (3): 21–43. A critique of Lawrence's viewpoint that recounts the empirical findings that Japan's trade structure is no different from that predicted by standard theory.

WEB SITES OF POTENTIAL INTEREST:

World Trade Organization. http://www.wto.org/.

International Competition Network. http://www.internationalcompetitionnetwork.org/.

United Nations Conference on Trade and Development. http://www.unctad.org/.

Organisation for Economic Co-operation and Development. http://www.oecd.org/.

SIMON J. EVENETT

■ competitive advantage

The concept of competitive advantage came into popular usage in the 1980s as an attempt to identify and define the strategic goals of the firm. In his now famous work *Competitive Advantage: Creating and Sustaining Superior Performance*, Michael Porter showed that the goal of all firms is to achieve a competitive advantage in relation to their rivals. This they do either by selling at a lower cost/price or by differentiating their product from those of their rivals (Porter 1985). Cost and differentiation advantages are frequently referred to as "positional advantages," as they determine the firm's position in an industry, such as whether it competes in the broad, mass market or a segment/niche. A competitive advantage enables a firm to earn profits that are higher than the average profit earned by competitors ("excess profits"). A *sustainable* competitive advantage is one that cannot be duplicated or imitated by other firms that may enter the industry in the long run and compete for the excess profits enjoyed by existing firms. For example, a firm may acquire a sustainable advantage through the creation of a brand name that comes to be associated with quality or "value for money" and is difficult for other firms to replicate. The St. Michael's label has enabled the British retailer Marks and Spencer to establish a reputation of this kind in the clothing and food retailing industry.

Acquiring a Competitive Advantage Firms acquire a competitive advantage by creating more value than their competitors in the value chain. The latter is the system of activities (both primary and support activities) that the firm undertakes in the process of value creation. As goods pass through the value chain, value is created at each stage, from upstream suppliers to downstream sales and marketing outlets. Equally important is the contribution made by nonproduction activities such as research and development (R&D) and management services. In this process, an important decision is how to configure each of the activities within the value chain and how to coordinate these activities. Configuration refers to decisions about where to locate each particular activity and how many locations to have for each activity. Coordination relates to the decisions about how to link together the same activity performed in different locations and how to coordinate that activity with other activities in the value chain.

National Competitive Advantage In a later work titled *The Competitive Advantage of Nations*, Porter introduced the notion of national competitive advantage to refer to "the decisive characteristics of a nation that allow its firms to create and sustain competitive advantage in particular fields" (Porter 1990, 18). Such a concept must be distinguished from the concept of comparative advantage used in classical trade theory to refer to the relative cost advantage that a nation enjoys when entering into trade with another country. In classical trade theory, such an advantage was measured in terms of the relative amounts of labor time that producers in different countries required to produce different goods. Later, neoclassical trade theorists explained such differences in terms of factor endowments and the different factor proportions required to produce different goods. While recognizing the usefulness of the concept of comparative advantage for explaining patterns of trade, Porter called for a "new paradigm" based on competitive advantage.

Porter argued that what matters when determining why a particular nation succeeds in a particular industry is the competitive environment of the nation, as this shapes the success of the firms based in that country. This is determined by a number of factors, including the following:

1. *Factor conditions.* These consist of human resources (quantity, quality, and skills of the workers), physical resources (abundance, quality, accessibility, and cost of land and other natural resources, including climatic conditions and location), knowledge resources (scientific, technical, and market knowledge), capital resources (amount and cost of capital to finance industry), and infrastructure (including transportation system, communications

system, health care system, housing, cultural conditions, and quality of life). While neoclassical theory explained national comparative advantage in terms of factor conditions, it assumed that countries were endowed with fixed amounts of these factors. However, although some factors are given (e.g., land and natural resources), countries can add to their stock of other factors through factor creation or investment by individuals or firms.

2. *Demand conditions.* Three broad attributes of domestic demand matter—its composition, its size and rate of growth, and the ways in which it is internationalized. With regard to the composition of domestic demand, the segment structure matters (by giving firms an advantage in segments where domestic demand is strong), as does buyer sophistication (with firms gaining an advantage in sectors where domestic buyers are among the world's most sophisticated and demanding) and the presence of anticipatory buyer needs (domestic buyers are ahead of buyers in other countries). With regard to demand size and the pattern of growth, a large market can enhance competitiveness through economies of scale and learning effects. Also, where demand is rapidly growing, firms may invest more and adopt new technologies more quickly. Finally, it matters how domestic demand is internationalized, pulling a nation's products or services abroad. This can happen as sales of the product to multinational buyers increase and through domestic needs being transformed into foreign needs. The latter can happen through travel and is particularly applicable to cultural goods, such as films or television programs.

3. *Related and supporting industries.* This refers to the presence within a country of internationally competitive supplier industries or other related industries. Porter identified two mechanisms through which a competitive advantage in one industry could benefit other related industries. First, a supplier industry may provide a downstream industry with regular supplies of low-cost inputs and possibly privileged access to these inputs. Second, close working relationships between suppliers and an industry will result in more sharing of information and may result in more rapid innovation within the entire industry.

4. *Firm strategy, structure, and rivalry.* First, the way firms are managed in a particular country and choose to compete matters a great deal. The country's managerial system, the management practices and training, the way in which firms are organized and run, and the extent to which firms are globally oriented and willing to compete internationally are all part of this. Second, the goals of firms within a particular country, along with the motivation of employees and managers, may also contribute to a country's being successful in a particular industry. Third, the more vigorously firms compete with one another in a particular industry, the more likely that a country will develop and successfully sustain a competitive advantage in that industry. Policies designed to create "national champions" by encouraging two or more firms to merge rarely succeed. An important aspect of domestic rivalry is also the ease with which new businesses can be set up in a country and the extent to which they are.

The Porter Diamond Traditionally, these factors are represented by the "diamond" diagram shown in figure 1. In addition to these four factors shaping the competitive environment of a country, Porter emphasized the importance of two other factors that may separately contribute to a country's acquiring a competitive advantage or prevent its doing so. The first is the role played by *chance* events, such as an invention, shortages of key inputs, a sudden rise in the costs of inputs, significant shifts in exchange rates, wars, or the political decisions of government. The second is the role of *government* policy, which may influence firms in a particular industry either positively or negatively. The extent to which government intervention has contributed to the emergence of a national competitive advantage in particular countries is hotly debated. Advocates of government intervention point to the experiences of Japan and Korea as examples of how such intervention can work. By contrast, the same policy largely failed when applied by West European governments to Europe's electronics industry. Government intervention is viewed by Porter as working through the four main determinants of the diamond rather than constituting a fifth factor.

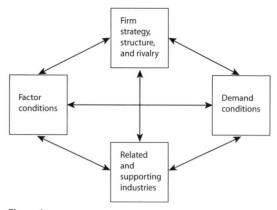

Figure 1
Porter's diamond

An important aspect of the phenomenon of national competitive advantage is that it is an evolving process, in which all the factors interact, with each determinant influencing the others. This process of interaction is as important as the presence or absence of each of the factors viewed separately. Thus factor conditions at any given time are determined by factor creation in the form of investment in education and infrastructure and, more important, investment in the creation and upgrading of advanced and specialized factors such as science and technology. Such investment is stimulated by a strong element of rivalry between domestic firms. Demand conditions are also affected by the existence of intense rivalry, which helps create a large domestic demand for the product through investment in marketing, aggressive pricing policies, and the introduction of more varieties of the same product. The development of related and supporting industries is affected by all of the other factors, as is the degree of domestic rivalry among firms.

Clustering and Sustainability An especially important role in this process is played by the geographical concentration of industries in a particular region, resulting in the phenomenon of clustering. Clustering is a readily observable feature of the economies of most countries. It exists because of the relationships among the four factors in the diamond and the need for firms to be close to exploit these advantages. Within a cluster, the competitive advantage enjoyed by one industry helps create or sustain the competitive advantage enjoyed by another in a mutually reinforcing process. An example of this is where competitive supplier industries enable a country to sustain a competitive advantage in downstream industries. The same dynamic process may equally well happen in reverse, however.

A further aspect of Porter's diamond model concerns the importance of sustaining a competitive advantage. It is not sufficient for firms in a country to obtain a competitive advantage in a particular industry; that advantage must be sustained by a processing of widening and upgrading. Some of the factors that give rise to a competitive advantage are also important in sustainability. These include investment in institutions that undertake research and generate new ideas, the composition of demand and the intensity of domestic rivalry, and the extent to which the different factors in the diamond interact.

A Multiple Diamond Approach One of the major criticisms leveled at Porter's model is that it fails to adequately address the role of multinational enterprises in the determination of national competitive advantage. In 1993, John Dunning argued that Porter was mistaken in arguing that the firm-specific advantages of multinational companies could be explained purely and simply in terms of the competitive advantages of their home countries (Dunning 1993). Multinational companies derive their advantage from the national diamond existing in a number of countries, not just the home country. If Porter's model is to be applied to international business, Alan Rugman has argued that a "multiple diamond" approach is needed (see Rugman and Verbeke 2001). The weakness of the Porter model, argue Rugman and Verbeke, is that it concentrates entirely on what they call "non-location-bound" firm-specific advantages that are developed by firms in home countries before they engage in foreign direct investment (FDI) and which can then be transferred to other branches of the firm. This ignores, however, the advantages that multinational companies, which have already engaged in FDI, enjoy from having value-added activities in several locations and from their common governance. Some of these advantages are "location bound," which means that they derive from a particular geographical area and cannot easily be transferred abroad.

The need for such a multiple diamond approach is especially relevant in the case of small countries, where firms are able to overcome the problems of a small domestic market by increasing their sales in the markets of other countries. Rugman and Collinson have illustrated how the Porter model could be applied to the analysis of the problem of international competitiveness with reference to firms in Canada (Rugman and Collinson 2006). Using a double diamond model, Rugman and Collinson show how Canadian firms have used exports to the United States and their rivalry with U.S. firms to develop a global competitive advantage in particular industries. In effect, the Canadian and U.S. markets served as two domestic markets through which Canadian firms could become globally competitive. Such an advantage may be acquired through developing new innovative products and services for consumers in both markets, drawing on support industries and infrastructures in both countries, and making freer and fuller use of the physical and human resources of both countries (Rugman and Collinson 2006).

Competitiveness One of the effects of the focus on competitive advantage since the 1980s has been an increased fascination with competitiveness rankings of countries. Two examples of this are the Global Competitiveness Report by the World Economic Forum (WEF), and the World Competitiveness Center's Yearbook. Such listings seek to rank countries in terms of competitiveness using a range of criteria such as economic performance, government efficiency, business efficiency, and infrastructure. The 2006 rankings of the WEF placed Switzerland, Sweden, and Finland respectively in the top three places in the world. It should be pointed out, however, that it is *comparative*, not *competitive*, advantage that determines what goods a country specializes in. This is because trade is a positive-sum game in which all countries gain, not a zero-sum game in which one country gains only at the expense of another.

This point is well made by Paul Krugman in a short essay first written in 1994, in which he comments on what he called the "dangerous obsession" with competitiveness (Krugman 1996). Using the example of Japan achieving a higher level of productivity than the United States, Krugman writes, "While competitive problems could arise in principle, as a practical, empirical matter, the major nations of the world are not to any significant degree in economic competition with each other. Of course, there is always a rivalry for status and power—countries that grow faster will see their political rank rise. So it is always interesting to *compare* countries. But asserting that Japanese growth diminishes US status is very different from stating that it reduces the US standard of living—and it is the latter that the rhetoric of competitiveness asserts" (Krugman 1996, 10).

Achieving a national competitive advantage is important in enabling some countries to grow faster than others. An obsession with competitiveness, however, is dangerous, as Krugman argues, because it can lead to protectionism and trade conflict, as well as misguided public spending designed to create and sustain a national competitive advantage over other trading partners and the promotion of national champions.

To summarize, acquiring and sustaining a competitive advantage can be seen as the primary strategic aim of firms in the modern world economy. The source of national competitive advantage is to be found in the competitive advantage obtained by the firms operating in the country, both domestically owned and foreign owned. This, in turn, is the product of a complex set of factors that interact with one another to shape the competitive environment of the country. Unlike comparative advantage, however, competitive advantage is a dynamic concept, in which national competitive advantage continuously evolves. In a world in which multinationals are dominant, the source of such advantage often results from firms operating in more than one country. Despite its usefulness in explaining why some countries develop a specialization in a particular industry or branch, an emphasis on attaining a competitive advantage can cause governments to pursue

misguided policies that lead to trade conflict. It remains the case that trade is a positive-sum game in which all can benefit.

See also commodity chains; comparative advantage; foreign direct investment (FDI); foreign direct investment: the OLI framework; New Economic Geography

FURTHER READING

Dunning, John H. 1993. "Dunning on Porter." In *The Globalisation of Business*, edited by John H. Dunning. London: Routledge. A useful and interesting paper criticizing Porter for not specifically including multinational activity as an element in the model shaping the competitive environment of a country and arguing for an extension to take into account multinational enterprises whose competitive advantage is derived from operating in several countries.

Krugman, Paul. 1996. *Pop Internationalism*. Cambridge, MA: MIT Press. A collection of short essays on the dangers of some popular ideas about trade, with the first chapter being a critique of the contemporary "obsession" with the notion of competitiveness and subsequent chapters further developing this theme.

Porter, Michael E. 1985. *Competitive Advantage: Creating and Sustaining Superior Performance*. New York: Free Press. An earlier work by Porter setting out and explaining the notion of competitive advantage as applied to firm strategy. It introduces the idea of generic strategy and distinguishes between competitive scope and competitive advantage.

———. 1990. *The Competitive Advantage of Nations*. London: Macmillan. A book presenting the basic "theory" of competitive advantage developed by the author and containing the results of extensive studies of competitive advantage in relation to both individual industries and countries. The final section examines the implications of competitive advantage for company strategy and government policy.

Rugman, Alan M., and Simon Collinson. 2006. *International Business*. 4th ed. Harlow, UK: Pearson Education. A leading textbook on international business containing a useful chapter titled "Corporate Strategy and National Competitiveness," which explains and evaluates the Porter diamond model and calls for a multiple-country diamond model. A particular attraction of the chapter is the use of several case examples to illustrate how this operates in practice.

Rugman, Alan M., and Alain Verbeke. 2001. "Location, Competitiveness, and the Multinational Enterprise." In *The Oxford Handbook of International Business*, edited by Alan M. Rugman and Thomas L. Brewer. Oxford: Oxford University Press, chapter 6. A chapter concerned with the influence of locational factors on international competitiveness, including an assessment of Porter's contribution to this through his work on national competitive advantage and introducing the authors' own conceptual framework. The latter dispenses with the single home base perspective of Porter's analysis and emphasizes the importance of foreign locations for the overall competitiveness of multinationals.

NIGEL S. GRIMWADE

■ competitive devaluation

See beggar-thy-neighbor policies

■ compulsory licensing

See access to medicines

■ computable general equilibrium models

See applied general equilibrium models

■ conflicted virtue

In the world's monetary system, only a few major currencies—mainly the U.S. dollar and the euro—dominate as units of account for the internationally liquid assets or debts of developing countries or emerging markets. The consequences of this international asymmetry among currencies are profound. It leads to the problems of original sin (the inability of a debtor country to borrow in its own currency) and conflicted virtue (the inability of a creditor country to lend in its own currency).

Any creditor country that cannot lend in its own currency cumulates a currency mismatch called con-flicted virtue—a concept introduced by McKinnon (2005). A country is "virtuous" if it has a high saving rate and tends to run surpluses in the current account of its balance of payments, that is, make loans to foreigners. Because the surplus country cannot lend in its own currency, however, it builds up claims on foreigners in foreign exchange, usually U.S. dollars. This situation has led foreign debtor governments—particularly the U.S. government—to complain that the surplus country's ongoing flow of trade surpluses and official reserve accumulation of dollars is an unfair result of having an undervalued currency. Debtor governments may then try to pressure the surplus country to appreciate its currency against the dollar in the often mistaken belief that an appreciation of the surplus country's currency will reduce its trade surplus.

The greater the foreign mercantile pressure for appreciation, the greater the concern of domestic private holders of dollar assets that they will suffer capital losses in their home currency. As holders of dollar assets switch into the domestic currency and out of dollars, the government is "conflicted." An appreciation would dampen exports and, if expected to be repeated, induce serious deflation with a zero percent interest liquidity trap (a situation in which the nominal interest rate is close to zero and the country's central bank is unable to stimulate the economy with monetary policy), as in Japan in the 1990s. But the American government may threaten trade sanctions if the creditor country under siege does not allow its currency to appreciate substantially. This is the essence of the syndrome of conflicted virtue.

Conflicted Virtue in East Asia Conflicted virtue would not arise in creditor countries whose money is the dominant vehicle currency in international finance. In the 19th century, Britain was the largest creditor country, with large current account surpluses financed by large net capital outflows. Most of the British claims on foreigners, however, were denominated in the pound sterling, the British currency. Thus British investors were happy to accumulate large sterling claims on foreigners without provoking a depreciation of their foreign claims against their domestic ones. Similarly, for 25 years after World War II, the United States had trade surpluses and was the world's biggest creditor. By then, however, the dollar had displaced sterling as the world's dominant vehicle currency. Because U.S. claims on foreigners were denominated mainly in dollars, there was no internal currency mismatch in U.S. private portfolios.

The East Asian economies (and, increasingly, oil-rich Middle Eastern countries) are unusual, however, in that they are significant international creditors whose currencies are relatively little used outside their own countries. In Japan, large current account surpluses have persisted since the late 1970s. Taiwan's and Singapore's current account surpluses have been significant since the 1980s. Since 1998, previous debtor economies such as Korea have run current account surpluses (reflecting their "virtuously" high saving rates), resulting in high net capital exports. Sometimes these are offset by foreign direct investments (FDI) abroad. But the common mode of finance is to build up liquid claims—either privately or as official exchange reserves—in international monies such as the dollar. Japan's current account surpluses continued into the new millennium. By 2005, Japan's net holdings of liquid claims on foreigners (largely in dollars) reached a new high of U.S. $1.7 trillion, of which about $830 billion were official exchange reserves (McKinnon and Schnabl 2006).

Although China's buildup of liquid dollar claims has a much shorter history than Japan's, it has been accentuated by large inflows of FDI—relatively illiquid long-term liabilities. By the end of 2005, China's liquid dollar-denominated assets were roughly $1 trillion, of which $819 billion were official exchange reserves—a higher proportion than in Japan. The cumulative joint holding of dollar claims of all East Asian countries amounts to nearly $3 trillion. In China, household consumption, wages, and claims on financial intermediaries such as banks (deposits) and insurance companies (annuities) are mainly in yuan. Thus private Chinese households and firms will hold dollar assets only if there is a substantial business convenience in doing so, or if the interest rate on dollar assets is higher, and if the im-

mediate threat of yuan appreciation (dollar devaluation) is absent.

Effects of Conflicted Virtue China and other East Asian governments worry about the sudden loss of export competitiveness should their currencies be forced to appreciate. Beyond this, when the world price level measured in dollars is stable, any such appreciation would be followed by a domestic deflationary spiral—as in Japan from the mid-1980s through the 1990s as a result of the erratically appreciating yen. McKinnon and Ohno (1997) describe the nature of an American mercantile pressure to appreciate the yen from the 1970s to the mid-1990s, then analyze the subsequent deflationary consequences for Japan.

Governments in creditor economies with conflicted virtue may cut domestic short-term interest rates to forestall or slow the conversion of privately held dollar assets into domestic currency. Insofar as people believe that low short-term rates will persist, domestic long-term interest rates also fall. At any given exchange rate, a new portfolio equilibrium can be found in which private agents would be willing to finance the nation's ongoing current account surplus by building up higher yield liquid dollar claims rather than the government accumulating official exchange reserves.

Japan has the longest experience with current account surpluses, and the associated buildup of dollar claims, from the early 1980s into the new millennium. Between 1978 and 2007, the interest rates on long-term (10-year) Japanese government bonds (JGBs) averaged about 3 to 4 percentage points less than those on long-term U.S. treasuries. Short rates are more volatile, but were bid down close to zero in the mid-1990s. In November 2006, when the American interest rate on overnight federal funds was 5.25 percent, the corresponding Gensaki rate in Tokyo was just 0.25 percent. As long as interest rates on yen assets are sufficiently below those on dollar assets, the Japanese private sector—banks, insurance companies, trust funds, and so on—can still be persuaded to fund Japan's ongoing current account surpluses by accumulating dollar assets with higher yields. This interest differential reflects both the expectation that the yen will appreciate on an upward trend, as was important from the late 1970s to the mid 1990s, and a negative risk premium that arises when the yen simply fluctuates against the dollar so as to make the ever-larger private holdings of dollar assets more risky in yen terms—as was the case in the first few years of the new millennium.

But there are limits on how negative this risk premium on yen assets, and on how wide the associated interest differential, can become. When American interest rates fell to abnormally low levels, with short-term rates down to just 1 percent in early 2004, the spread was not (could not be) big enough because Japanese nominal interest rates were bounded from below by zero. Then the Japanese private sector refused to keep acquiring enough dollar assets to finance the current account surplus. Indeed, private agents in Japan started dishoarding previously accumulated dollar assets in order to acquire near-zero-yield yen assets! In 2003–4, the Bank of Japan intervened massively in the foreign exchange markets to acquire more than $330 billion—mostly from private Japanese financial firms—in order to prevent the yen from appreciating sharply.

Since 2004, China has run a larger current account surplus, mainly financed by a huge buildup of official exchange reserves. This buildup has led to calls from the American government for China to appreciate its currency—the threat thereof leading to a fall in internal Chinese interest rates and the unwillingness of private Chinese wealth holders to acquire overseas assets. Therefore, the rapid accumulation of official exchange reserves becomes even larger. Conflicted virtue in creditor countries, with their overhangs of dollar assets, continues.

See also balance of payments; Bretton Woods system; carry trade; dollar standard; dominant currency; foreign exchange intervention; global imbalances; gold standard, international; interest parity conditions; International Monetary Fund (IMF); international reserves; mercantilism; original sin; reserve currency; vehicle currency

FURTHER READING

McKinnon, Ronald. 2005. Exchange Rates under the East Asian Dollar Standard: Living with Conflicted Virtue. Cambridge, MA: MIT Press. Focuses on East Asian exchange rate and monetary policy, with specific reference to Japan, China, and regional monetary cooperation. It elaborates on the concept of "conflicted virtue" as applied to East Asia.

McKinnon, Ronald, and Kenichi Ohno. 1997. Dollar and Yen: Resolving Economic Conflict between the United States and Japan. Cambridge, MA: MIT Press. Shows how forced appreciations of the yen in the 1980s to the mid-1990s deflated the Japanese economy and undermined subsequent economic growth.

McKinnon, Ronald, and Gunther Schnabl. 2006. "China's Exchange Rate and International Adjustment in Wages, Prices, and Interest Rates: Japan Déjà Vu?" CESifo Studies 52 (2) (June): 276–304. Analyzes the impact of China's exchange rate changes on the domestic economy and draws parallels with the Japanese experience.

RONALD I. McKINNON

■ contagion

In economics, *contagion* refers to the spread of a crisis from one country to others. Such a spread can show up in a variety of ways, such as its effects on interest rates, asset prices, exchange rates, capital flows, or the probability of a crisis. Economic usage of the word *contagion* draws on the analogy to the spread of contagious diseases. Thus the currency crisis in Thailand that spread to much of the rest of East Asia in 1997 was often referred to as the "Asian flu" or the "Asian contagion." The use of the term *contagion* became particularly popular with the crisis in Mexico at the end of 1994, which was felt throughout most of Latin America and became known as the "tequila crisis." Academic attention to contagion had been stimulated by the earlier crises in the European Monetary System in 1992 and 1993.

Defining Contagion There is considerable debate among economists about how to define contagion. Some hold that it refers to any general transmission of shocks from one market to another. Others argue that contagion exists only if there is a significant increase in cross-market relationships beyond what can be explained by the fundamental state of a country's economy ("fundamentals"). Still others contend that contagion spreads only through certain channels. In an influential analysis, the economist Paul Masson (1999) defined contagion as a consequence of sudden shifts in market expectations and investors' confidence. Such shifts are particularly relevant in the context of second-generation crisis models in which a country's fundamentals can be in an intermediate vulnerable zone between good and bad. In such situations, a crisis in one country can directly affect expectations of the situation in other countries, and hence move an economy from a good equilibrium to a bad one and end in a crisis. Masson distinguishes contagion from other types of shocks. He calls a common external shock that affects a group of countries "monsoonal effects," referring to the example of a monsoon season affecting several countries in a region. This type of effect, Masson argues, should not be considered contagion. Another example of a monsoonal effect is a shock to oil prices or supply that affects many countries at the same time. Still another is the effect on developing countries of major changes in the interest rates of large industrial countries. Both of the latter two examples helped contribute to the Latin American debt crises of the 1980s.

During noncrisis periods, contagion is usually related to the linkages of the economic fundamentals between one or more countries, and is typically called *interdependence*. Possible factors leading to contagion include trade linkages, common external shocks, and political or economic policies. Contagion is more frequent during crisis periods than noncrisis periods, however, and is an important explanation of emerging market crises of the late 20th and early 21st centuries. Crisis contagion beyond what can be explained by fundamental links is often called "pure contagion." "Unjustified" contagion refers to pure contagion resulting from panic and other forms of irrationalities and market imperfections. No commonly accepted name has yet been given to rational pure contagion that is transmitted through financial channels such as portfolio rebalancing. A country can be an "innocent victim" of fundamental-based contagion or of pure contagion. For example, the con-

tagion effect from Argentina to its small neighbor Uruguay in 2001 was due primarily to economic interdependence, while the spread of the Asian crisis has often been attributed to panic contagion. The degree of a country's innocence and the degree to which contagion is unjustified by fundamentals are often matters of considerable dispute.

Causes and Channels of Contagion Contagion can be transmitted through real or financial linkages, or through other channels such as global investors' behavior and market imperfection. Causes of contagion are often closely related to its transmission channels. Real linkages, such as trade, economic policies, shared fundamentals, and common shocks, all lead to increased interdependence among economic and financial markets. Contagion effects generally have a strong regional concentration (the Russian crisis in 1998 is a major exception). This has led many economists to stress the role of direct macroeconomic linkages, especially through international trade, as an important channel for contagion.

If contagion is taken to include the general interdependence among economic fundamentals, it can be measured using comovements of financial or economic variables. Pure contagion measurements typically test for cross-country relationships beyond fundamentals. Treatments of what are considered fundamentals also vary substantially. Typically, the broader the range of factors that analysts consider fundamentals, the less pure contagion they see.

Contagion also can spread through financial connections. Global portfolio diversification allows large capital flows to enter emerging markets but also makes inflows quickly become outflows during a crisis. Such abrupt reversals of capital flows are often called "sudden stops." In order to maintain the liquidity of their portfolios, institutional investors tend to sell their cross-border investments in one market when another market is in trouble. Portfolio diversification and rebalancing alone are often enough to explain contagion effects without invoking market imperfections. Similarly, common lender problems also lead banks to rebalance their assets portfolio and refuse to roll over debt to countries with risk characteristics similar to those countries in default. If several countries share the same type of investors, correlations among these countries' financial assets increase, even among countries with few economic similarities. If investors trade only certain categories of assets, the probability of selling out that type of asset during a crisis also increases.

Financial market imperfections, such as asymmetric information, a situation in which one party has more information than another, and ill-designed incentive structures for fund managers, can also contribute to the spread of a crisis from one market to another. When a market is less transparent and information is not readily available, investors are more likely to herd. When investors are relatively uninformed they may assume that if someone else takes an action, it is because that person has better information. Such behavior would increase the size of market swings.

Fund managers' compensation contracts, even if optimal at the firm level, may lead to inefficiencies at the macroeconomic level. Fund managers, for example, are usually evaluated on short time frames, which restrict them from taking advantage of mispricing. Moreover fund managers are typically evaluated against a benchmark, encouraging them to form a portfolio very close to that benchmark or to follow the actions of other fund managers. Such "separation of brain and resources" contributes to fund managers' pursuing short-term profits and herding, which can cause cross-border contagion.

Owing to similarities among the countries, their geographic proximity, and limited information, investors may not always be able to differentiate among common shocks and country-specific shocks. As a result, they might make heuristic decisions. Herding and rational ignorance are such "rule of thumb" responses to market imperfections, and contagion is the consequence.

Investors' sentiments—panic, overoptimism, overreaction, and shifts in expectation—can also lead to contagion. During a crisis, investors might panic and pull out funds in the entire crisis region regardless of each country's fundamentals. They can be overly optimistic before a crisis. A crisis in one country might force them to reevaluate investments that they initially should have investigated more thoroughly. Thus a crisis in one country can serve as a wake-up call prompting a reevaluation of investments in other countries with shared characteristics.

Of course, if markets were already fully efficient there would be no need for such reevaluations. However, many economists and finance experts are now giving much greater attention to ways in which financial markets may be less than ideally efficient. Such analysis is called behavioral finance. It varies from emphasis on external constraints such as the high cost of information to possible psychological biases. Behavioral analysis is still at an early stage of development, but it promises a number of fruitful insights into the behavior of actual financial markets that fall between the extremes of ideally efficient markets and wildly irrational ones (see Willett 2000).

Examples of Crisis Contagion Discussions of contagion often suggest that the spread of crises is especially associated with the effects of panic in financial markets. This panic contagion view has become particularly widespread in light of the 1997–98 Asian crisis as the countries hit had strong macroeconomic fundamentals. Subsequent analyses, however, showed that many of the countries in crisis had microeconomic and financial weaknesses that suggested some justification for the spread.

Since many crisis countries in Asia had impressive economic growth records, balanced government budgets, and conservative monetary policies, some economists started to analyze the role market psychology and investors' behavior played during the crisis. South Korea is a prime example. Despite its good macroeconomic fundamentals, Korea suffered devastating losses during the crisis largely because of financial and microeconomic weaknesses. Because of implicit guarantees against large depreciation of the exchange rate and the prospect of government bail out of failing institutions, the banking sector in South Korea had incentives to engage in excessively risky loans. As a result it became burdened with nonperforming loans while the corporate sector took on large dollar-denominated, short-term debt. Similarly, a large number of Indonesian and Thai corporations had been borrowing heavily in U.S.

dollars. They and their overseas investors had believed that their countries' exchange rates were safe from large depreciations. When this assumption proved false, there was a rush to cover their positions, which in turn generated large capital outflows.

Furthermore, while many initial analyses treated the whole set of crises as a single event, the crisis developed over a period of months and had several distinct phases. The first phase, between July and October 1997, started with the run on the Thai baht. Its subsequent depreciation spread mainly to Indonesia, Malaysia, and the Philippines, all of which were forced to allow large depreciations of their currencies. The financial markets of a much broader group of countries felt ripples, but did not experience strong speculative attacks or capital flight. In the second phase, which started in October 1998, the devaluation of the Taiwan dollar generated fears that the Hong Kong dollar would follow. The Hong Kong stock market lost 40 percent of its value, which led to the devastating devaluation of the South Korea won in less than two months. While Korea felt some immediate repercussions from the Thai crisis, they were relatively mild. The strong speculative attacks on the won did not occur until months later. Simple panic contagion would not explain such a protracted spread.

The Asian financial crisis drove down raw material prices. This had severe consequences for Russia, which was highly dependent on exports of raw materials. Even though interest rates soared to 150 percent to attract investors to buy government bonds, by mid-1998 Russia was in need of help from the International Monetary Fund (IMF) to maintain its exchange rate. However, the Russian government failed to implement a realistic budget and necessary legislation to meet IMF requirements. Fearing the IMF might pull the plug on its loans, global investors continued to flee Russia, and Russia soon after defaulted on its debt, sending shock waves through financial markets across the globe.

The financial market expected a substantial devaluation of the ruble, but most observers believed that Russia was too important geopolitically to be allowed to default. Thus markets were stunned.

Combined with the near collapse of the hedge fund Long-Term Capital Management in the United States, the Russian default set off a shift to extreme risk aversion among investors. Risk premiums rose substantially, and emerging market countries found it difficult or impossible to find investors for new international credit instruments for many months.

Policy Implications The best ways to prevent contagion and to deal with it when it occurs vary depending on its causes and channels. A number of policies that are good in their own right, such as the promotion of sound economic fundamentals and the development of better policies in both the public and private sector for assessing and managing risk, also help reduce problems from inflation. The role played by contagion during the crises of the 1990s prompted many proposals for greater national and international control over international financial flows.

Confusion has resulted from the tendency of the popular press to use the term *contagion* to describe any effects of a crisis in one country on currency or financial markets of other countries. The crisis in Iceland in 2006 was felt in currency markets as far away as Eastern Europe and Africa, but these fairly mild ripple effects from Iceland were of a quite different magnitude than the devastating crises that hit a number of Asian countries after Thailand's currency crisis. The global repercussions of the Russian default in 1998 fell between these extremes.

The available evidence clearly suggests that major shocks often do cause indiscriminant contagion in financial markets, but—with the exception of the Russian default—this tends to last for only a brief period, measured in hours, days, or weeks. Medium-term responses from the currency and financial markets tend to be much more differentiated, although the determinants of these more focused medium-term responses can be quite complex, including both trade and financial linkages and a broad range of fundamentals including financial and political as well as economic considerations. Since information is often quite imperfect, perception of the fundamentals can shift without any change in the actual fundamentals themselves. Thus a crisis in one country can act as a wake-up call that generates re-evaluations of conditions in other countries. The Thai crisis provides a vivid example.

In general, the fallout on other countries and markets from the crises occurring since the Russian default have been much milder, and as a consequence support for major reforms in the international financial architecture has fallen off. Many economists, however, still believe that there is a strong case for strengthening the capabilities of the IMF to act as an international lender of last resort to deal with liquidity crises, especially those that would have the potential to generate considerable contagion.

See also asymmetric information; banking crisis; capital flight; capital flows to developing countries; currency crisis; financial crisis; hedge funds; hot money and sudden stops; international financial architecture; International Monetary Fund (IMF); International Monetary Fund conditionality; International Monetary Fund surveillance; Latin American debt crisis; lender of last resort; sovereign risk; spillovers

FURTHER READING

Claessens, Stijn, and Kristin Forbes, eds. 2001. *International Financial Contagion: How It Spreads and How It Can Be Stopped.* Boston: Kluwer Academic Press. Examines the causes, channels, and measurement issues of international financial contagion.

Eichengreen, Barry. 1999. *Toward a New International Financial Architecture: A Practical Post-Asia Agenda.* Washington, DC: Institute for International Economics. Critically reviews proposals for reform of the international financial system and national policies to reduce the incidence of currency crises and contagion.

Masson, Paul. 1999. "Contagion: Monsoonal Effects, Spillovers, and Jumps between Multiple Equilibria." IMF working paper 98/142. Washington, DC: International Monetary Fund. Usefully distinguishes several concepts of contagion.

Rajan, Ramkishen S. 2003. "Unilateral, Regional, and Multilateral Options for East Asia." In *Financial Governance in East Asia*, edited by Gordon De Brouwer and Yunjong Wang. London: Routledge, 239-63. Considers a list of policy options to deal with financial crises and contagion.

Willett, Thomas D. 2000. "International Financial Markets as Sources of Crisis or Discipline: The Too Much, Too Late Hypothesis." Princeton Essays in International Finance No. 218 (May). Princeton, NJ: Princeton University. Discusses the usefulness of behavioral finance for analyzing the behavior of international financial markets that are neither fully efficient nor wildly irrational.

Willett, Thomas, Ekniti Nitithanprapas, Isriya Nitithanprapas, and Sunil Rongala. 2005. "The Asian Crises Reexamined." *Asian Economic Papers* 3 (3): 32–87. Analyzes hypotheses and evidence for the causes of the Asian crisis and reviews the contrasting views on the role of contagion in the Asian crisis. Offers extensive references.

PRISCILLA LIANG AND THOMAS WILLETT

■ Convention on Biological Diversity

The Convention on Biological Diversity (CBD) aims to promote the well-being of both nature and humans. Negotiated under the auspices of the UN Environment Program (UNEP), adopted on May 22, 1992, and entered into force on December 29, 1993, it is built on a threefold, interacting objective: "the conservation of biological diversity, the sustainable use of its components and the fair and equitable sharing of the benefits arising out of the utilization of genetic resources" (art. 1). The convention is comprehensive in scope, as it includes all species and ecosystems worldwide, as well as the genetic diversity within species. There are currently 188 parties to the convention, which is governed by a conference of the parties (COP) that is supported by a Subsidiary Body on Scientific, Technical, and Technological Advice. The CBD secretariat is located in Montreal and has about 60 professionals and support staff.

The background for negotiating and strengthening the CBD was an increasing awareness and agreement among scientists that the current rate of species extinction was (and remains) extremely high compared to the natural average rate (Wilson 1988; Heywood 1995, 232). A rapid loss of genetic diversity in domesticated plants, with risks of reduced food security, was another central concern. Of the estimated 7 to 30 million species on earth, only 1.9 million have been scientifically described—most of what is lost is scientifically unknown. Moreover, developments in the biotechnologies have increased economic interests in the world's genetic resources. Genetic resources constitute important input factors in biotechnology, including the pharmaceutical sector and all development and breeding of plants and animals. Wild relatives of domestic crops provide genetic variability that can be crucial in circumstances such as overcoming disease outbreaks or adjusting to climatic changes. Species may contain compounds (genes, proteins) that can generate valuable pharmaceuticals or other products at some future date (Laird and Wynberg 2005).

Provisions on access to genetic resources, including the equitable sharing of the benefits of their use, form a central element of the CBD and are regarded as a prerequisite for the two first objectives of conservation and sustainable use. The CBD reconfirmed national sovereign rights to genetic resources (art. 15.1) and equitable sharing of benefits from use of those resources (art. 15.7). Access to the resources is based on mutually agreed terms and subject to prior informed consent (art. 15.4 and 15.5).

The value of products derived from genetic resources worldwide has been estimated at between U.S. $500 billion and $800 billion (Ten Kate and Laird 1999). In addition to the direct economic values of genetic resources, biodiversity as a whole provides a great range of ecosystem services, such as local water and climate regulation, and materials for building and firewood. There is also a great range of noneconomic values attached to biodiversity, such as cultural and intrinsic values. The average annual loss of wild habitats and populations is estimated to deprive people of ecosystem services with a net worth of about U.S. $250 billion every year (Millennium Ecosystem Assessment 2005). The CBD parties have pledged to halt and reverse the loss of biodiversity by 2010.

To this end, the CBD parties have agreed to develop national biodiversity strategies, integrate biodiversity conservation in all policy levels and sectors, identify and monitor biodiversity, establish systems of protected areas, and identify activities that are likely to have adverse effects on biodiversity. Moreover, the parties must adopt economically and socially sound measures to act as incentives for conservation and sustainable use, establish programs for scientific and technical education and training for identification and conservation, and provide support for such training in developing countries. The CBD is equipped with a monitoring mechanism in the form of national reporting and an incentive mechanism in the form of the Global Environment Facility (GEF). The GEF has invested nearly U.S. $4.2 billion for biodiversity conservation in developing countries since its establishment in 1991.

In several respects, the CBD constitutes a framework agreement open for further developments and specifications. For example, article 19.3 commits parties to the CBD to consider the elaboration of a protocol to protect biodiversity from potential risks from genetically modified organisms. On this basis, the parties negotiated the Cartagena Protocol on Biosafety, which was adopted in 2000 and entered into force in 2003. The protocol builds on a precautionary approach and establishes an advance informed agreement (AIA) procedure to help countries make decisions before agreeing to the import of such organisms into their territory.

The COP has initiated work on seven thematic work programs. These address marine and coastal biodiversity, agricultural biodiversity, forest biodiversity, island biodiversity, the biodiversity of inland waters, dry and subhumid lands, and mountain biodiversity. In addition, work has been initiated on biosafety; access to genetic resources; traditional knowledge, innovations, and practices (art. 8[j]); intellectual property rights; indicators; taxonomy; public education and awareness; incentives; and alien species.

The ecosystem approach is the primary framework for action under the convention. It is a strategy for integrated management of land, water, and living resources that aims to promote conservation and sustainable use in an equitable manner. The ecosystem approach recognizes that humans, with their cultural diversity, are an integral component of ecosystems. As the greatest threat to biodiversity lies in the replacement of undeveloped land by alternative systems of land use, the approach recommends management in an economic context in order to reduce market distortions, which undervalue natural systems and provide perverse incentives and subsidies.

The COP has requested close collaboration with relevant international instruments and processes to enhance policy coherence. These include biodiversity-related conventions (Convention on International Trade in Endangered Species, Ramsar Convention on Wetlands, Convention on Migrating Species, and World Heritage Convention), the UN Framework Convention on Climate Change (UNFCCC), and the Convention to Combat Desertification (CCD), as well as intergovernmental organizations, such as the Food and Agriculture Organization, UNESCO, the Intergovernmental Oceanographic Commission, and the World Trade Organization (WTO). There is a joint Web site for biodiversity-related conventions (see Further Reading, at the end of this article).

The CBD and the Ramsar Convention on Wetlands are implementing a joint work plan, including the River Basin Initiative. The secretariats of the CBD and the CCD are developing a joint work program. The COP has also called for greater cooperation with the UNFCCC on issues such as drylands, forest biodiversity, coral reefs, and incentive measures. The Intergovernmental Panel on Climate Change examines linkages between climate change and biodiversity and prepares scientific advice on the integration of biodiversity considerations into implementation of the UNFCCC and its Kyoto Protocol. The Secretariat is collaborating with UNESCO on the development of a global initiative on biodiversity education, training, and public awareness. The COP also emphasizes the importance of developing a common understanding of the relationship between the CBD and the WTO agreements, including the Agreement on Trade-Related Aspects of Intellectual Property Rights (TRIPS). It has called for further work with respect to the relationship between intellectual property rights (IPRs), relevant provisions of TRIPS, and the CBD, in

particular those on technology transfer and on traditional knowledge and biological diversity. The COP has invited the WTO to explore the interrelationship between the CBD and the TRIPS. The COP has also sought to initiate cooperation with the World Intellectual Property Organization (WIPO) on the issue of IPRs arising from the implementation of the convention, such as those in access and benefit sharing and article 8(j) and related provisions. A memorandum of cooperation was signed with WIPO in 2003.

See also Agreement on Trade-Related Aspects of Intellectual Property Rights (TRIPS); Convention on International Trade in Endangered Species (CITES); Global Environment Facility; multilateral environmental agreements; trade and the environment

FURTHER READING

Convention on Biodiversity Handbook. 2003. Montreal: CBD Secretariat and UNEP. Complete text of agreement found in this publication.

Global Biodiversity Outlook. Periodic report. Montreal: CBD Secretariat and UNEP. www.biodiv.org/GBO2. Periodic report on the state of biodiversity worldwide.

Hendrickx, Frederik, Veit Koester, and Christian Prip. 1993. "Convention on Biological Diversity: Access to Genetic Resources, A Legal Analysis." *Environmental Policy and Law* 23 (6): 250–58. One of the first studies to spell out necessary legal policy measures for achieving access and benefit sharing among users and providers of genetic resources.

Heywood, Vernon H, ed. 1995. *Global Biodiversity Assessment.* Cambridge: Cambridge University Press. An early and central UNEP empirical examination of biodiversity loss.

Kloppenburg, J. R. 1988. *First the Seed.* Cambridge: Cambridge University Press. A central theoretical and empirical analysis examining global interdependence in plant genetic resources for food and agriculture.

Laird, Sarah, and Rachel Wynberg. 2005. *The Commercial Use of Biodiversity: An Update on Current Trends in Demand for Access to Genetic Resources and Benefit-Sharing, and Industry Perspectives on ABS Policy and Implementation.* UNEP/CBD/WGABS/4/INF/5. Nairobi: UNEP. A thorough empirical examination of present and future needs for access to genetic resources within different sectors.

Millennium Ecosystem Assessment (MEA). 2005. *Ecosystems and Human Well-Being: Biodiversity Synthesis.* Washington, DC: World Resources Institute. A comprehensive report and synthesis undertaken by more than 1,300 experts from 95 countries on the questions of how and why ecosystems change, and how this affects human well-being.

Swanson, Timothy, ed. 1995. *Intellectual Property Rights and Biodiversity Conservation.* Cambridge: Cambridge University Press. A detailed, interdisciplinary analysis of economic and scientific rationales for biodiversity conservation, including clarification of the property rights issue.

Ten Kate, K., and Sarah A. Laird. 1999. *The Commercial Use of Biodiversity: Access to Genetic Resources and Benefit-sharing.* London: Earthscan. The most comprehensive and practical guide to understanding the implications of and the implementation of the Convention on Biological Diversity.

Wilson, E. O., ed. 1988. *Biodiversity.* Washington, DC: National Academy Press. The earliest and most comprehensive book published on the issues of risk, value, and conservation of biodiversity, written in an accessible style.

Web sites for main biological diversity agreements and organizations are given below:

Convention on Biological Diversity. www.biodiv.org.

Global Environment Facility. www.gefweb.org.

The joint website for biodiversity-related conventions. http://www.biodiv.org/convention/partners-websites .asp.

G. KRISTIN ROSENDAL

■ Convention on International Trade in Endangered Species (CITES)

The Convention on International Trade in Endangered Species (CITES) is a mature international treaty that became effective in 1975. At the beginning of 2007, 169 sovereign states had ratified or acceded to the treaty.

Global trade in animals and plants is not measured by any one organization or individual; it occurs as $20 tourist items or as single blue fin tuna worth $40,000 for the Japanese sushi market, as well as reptile skin shipments worth more than $1 million. The total amount of trade in wild plants and animals is very difficult to determine, but one comprehensive estimate for the 1990s suggested an annual value of $15 billion, excluding timber and fisheries, which by themselves may have a value of $140 billion. Estimates of illegal trade in endangered species range between $5 billion and $10 billion per year. It is widely accepted that the value of illegal wildlife trade is second only to the illegal drug trade.

Approximately 5,000 species of animals and 28,000 species of plants are listed for some level of protection under CITES. Most well-known animals and plants are within the umbrella of the treaty: bears, elephants, whales, large cats, rhinos, sea horses, corals, orchids, and mahogany are but a sample of the species. The only group that is not well represented on the list is commercial fish from the open ocean. This absence has to do more with international politics than biological status.

The purpose of the treaty is to control the international movement of treaty-listed wild plants and animals, alive or dead, whole or parts thereof (specimens of species) in such a manner as to be assured that the pressures of international trade do not contribute to the endangerment of a species. This treaty does not deal with trade issues within a country or with the issues of habitat protection or preservation. CITES is implemented by way of permit requirements for the listed species. These permits are operative at the customs level as trade moves across national boundaries.

This is an active treaty regime; representatives of all the member states meet every two years to consider what adjustments need to be made to the list of protected species and what management and policy issues need to be addressed.

Listing of Species The treaty creates categories into which species of concern or at risk of extinction may be placed: appendix I and appendix II. Those on appendix I are species threatened with extinction and which are affected by international trade. Appendix II lists species that *may be* threatened with extinction and are part of international trade.

The placement of a species in appendix I or II is a group decision made at the conference of the parties (COP) and requires a two-thirds vote of the parties. Any state that disagrees with a listing decision may take a reservation on the species listing within 90 days of the vote. As of 2007, approximately 228 mammals and 146 bird species were listed on appendix I, and 369 mammal and 1,401 bird species on appendix II.

Since a consequence of listing a species on appendix I is that commercial trade in the species will be prohibited, proposals for placing new species on appendix I receive very close scrutiny by the delegates at the COP.

Permit Responsibilities Once a species is placed on either appendix I or II, then the protection of the treaty is triggered by the treaty requirement that each state must prohibit the transboundary movement of the species unless a permit has been issued by the relevant country. As there is no international police system to enforce the obligations of CITES, the treaty presumes that enforcement will be done at the national level. Indeed, a specific obligation of the treaty is for each state to adopt domestic legislation that will carry out the requirements of the treaty.

Appendix II species normally will be allowed in international trade so long as a CITES export permit has been issued by the state of export. Before issuing such a permit, the authorities of the state of export must make a key ecological finding: the scientific authority of the state of export must advise that such export will not be detrimental to the survival of that species. This is a particularly challenging requirement in developing countries where wildlife science for many species is nonexistent. If detrimental trade is allowed, knowingly or unknowingly, then the goal of the treaty is frustrated.

Appendix I species, those already identified as at risk of extinction, require two permits: an exporting permit and an importing permit. The criteria for the exporting permit are the same as with appendix II species. Note that the importing states must also make a finding that the purpose of the import will not be detrimental to the species. For the import permit the key requirement is that the management authority of the state of import must be satisfied that the specimen is not to be used for primarily commercial purposes. Although the determination of what is a primarily commercial purpose would seem to be straightforward in the main, on the margins it is a difficult question. Sport hunting trophies are generally not considered to have a commercial purpose even though they may have a market value. Importation of animals by zoos is likewise not prohibited by CITES custom even though the zoo will pay for the animal and generate money from its display.

The limitation on commercial use of appendix I species is controversial, in that some states argue that economic utilization of appendix I species would be useful for obtaining the resources and political motivation for the protection of the species—for example, the sale of elephant ivory could raise funds to help protect elephants. Additionally some states are troubled by the fact that the importing county (primarily the developed countries) can block trade that the exporting country (primarily developing countries) believes is acceptable. These issues have been settled by the language of the treaty and it would take an amendment of the treaty to change the existing approach. Although an amendment process is provided for in the treaty, it is highly unlikely to occur.

Enforcement The enforcement problems faced by CITES are not just the limitations of the treaty language but also limitations within individual party states:

Lack of adequate domestic laws.

Lack of an adequate number of government employees and lack of pay and training for the employees that do exist.

Lack of scientific experts within a country, unwillingness to give power to them, and a lack of resources for the scientists that are present.

Lack of support from the police and courts for wildlife crime prosecutions and lack of serious punishment when a prosecution is successful.

Lack of a public education component.

Wild plants and animals are important to both local and international economic activity. The overconsumption of these resources is a critical issue in many countries. The CITES treaty provides a legal mechanism and obligation to control trade in endangered species and to protect these resources. In an environment of limited government resources, however, enforcement is often difficult.

See also multilateral environmental agreements; trade and the environment

FURTHER READING

CITES, Secretariat. The language of CITES, the list of species, and adopted management resolutions are available at www.cites.org, the web site of the treaty.

———. 2003. *CITES Handbook*. Geneva: Secretariat CITES. Contains a detailed explanation of all the aspects of the treaty.

Oldfield, Sara, ed. 2003. *The Trade in Wildlife: Regulation for Conservation*. London: Earthscan. Presents a series of essays that focus on the nature of wildlife trade and how different regulatory systems, including CITES, affect the species at issue.

Robinson, John G., and Kent H. Redford, eds. 1991. *Neotropical Wildlife Use and Conservation*. Chicago: University of Chicago Press. Contains a number of chapters discussing the economic use of wildlife; although older, the ideas and examples are still fully relevant.

Traffic. Factual information about the nature and consequences of trade can be found at www.traffic.org. Traffic is a science-based organization that is a joint project of the World Wildlife Fund for Nature and the World Conservation Union.

DAVID FAVRE

■ convertibility

Convertibility refers to the ability of a currency to be freely transformed into foreign exchange. There are two types of convertibility: current account convertibility and capital account convertibility. The first term applies when the purpose of such transformation is to acquire foreign goods or services—activities that are typically recorded in the current account. The second term is used when the purpose is the acquisition of foreign assets, such as foreign stocks and bonds—activities that are typically recorded in the capital account.

Currency convertibility has direct consequences for international trade, capital mobility, and economic growth. When a country imposes restrictions on the conversion of domestic currency for foreign exchange, it necessarily impedes transactions between domestic residents or entities and foreign ones: most foreign counterparts will not accept a currency that is hard to convert into foreign exchange as a form of payment. Without current account convertibility, the cost of engaging in international transactions increases, leading to fewer transactions and to a lower level of trade. So important is current account convertibility that member nations of the International Monetary Fund (IMF) are required to fully adopt it under article VIII, sections 2, 3, and 4 of the Articles of Agreement.

Capital Account Convertibility and Growth A similar consensus, however, does not exist regarding capital account convertibility. The debate is more empirical than theoretical in nature. Theory tells us that in a perfect world, countries with full capital account convertibility can successfully exploit international capital markets to smooth out their consumption patterns over time; such countries can borrow from the rest of the world at a time when domestic consumption and investment are high relative to domestic income, and lend to the rest of the world when domestic consumption and investment are low relative to domestic income (Cole and Obstfeld 1991; Obstfeld and Rogoff 1995). Countries that have the ability to smooth out these income-expenditure patterns are theoretically better off than they would be otherwise. Without the ability to tap into international capital markets, a country would have to rely primarily on its own savings to fund domestic investment. Such a situation could limit future economic growth if domestic savings could not match the domestic level of investment demand.

According to the theory, countries that adopt and maintain full capital account convertibility should be able to grow faster than countries that do not. Empirical studies, however, have not been able to settle this issue convincingly. Some researchers have found that convertibility has a positive effect on growth; others argue that it has either no effect or a negative effect.

During the late 1970s, many countries systematically removed restrictions on—that is, liberalized—their capital accounts. The experiences of these countries presented an opportunity for researchers to test the hypothesis that liberalization is associated with subsequent output growth. Although some researchers found empirical support for this hypothesis (e.g., Quinn 1997), others found positive effects only for high-income countries, not for emerging-market economies (Edwards 2001). More recent research has examined the microeconomic consequences of capital account restrictions to ascertain whether they affect different industrial sectors or even firms differently.

A case study of capital controls in Chile during the 1990s found that these restrictions changed the way firms chose to do their financing. Specifically, firms in Chile switched from relying primarily on short-term debt to relying on internal funds for financing investment spending (Gallego and Hernandez 2003). This change is what one would expect to observe if capital controls introduced a cost wedge between domestic sources of funds and international capital markets. Although the results suggest that capital controls were costly for at least some firms, they cannot be used to judge the desirability of imposing or removing controls. Such policy decisions must be based on their effects on society as a whole rather than on a particular sector of society.

Although some evidence suggests that convertibility influences growth at some stages of development, research also suggests that such influence is limited at best and negative at worst. For example, one study estimates standard growth regression equations and does not find that capital account convertibility is associated with long-run growth (Rodrik 1998). Another study finds that many European countries enjoyed impressive growth rates during the 1950–73 period not despite having capital account restrictions, but instead precisely because they had them (Wyplosz 1999).

Theory versus Reality Why does research find capital account restrictions to be beneficial for growth when basic economic theory tells us otherwise? The discrepancy appears to stem from the fact that the "real world" is more complicated than basic theoretical models make it out to be. In a world with asymmetric information (i.e., buyers and sellers do not have the same information) and other capital market distortions, the conditions for smoothly operating markets do not exist. Many researchers note that with free capital mobility—or full capital account convertibility—a country is exposed to the whims and fads of investors and traders who make trading decisions for all kinds of reasons, some of them rational but many of them seemingly irrational. When enough of them decide to pull their investments out of a country, the sudden demand for foreign exchange may trigger a currency crisis with devastating consequences for the banking sector and the rest of the economy. Work by Kaminsky and Reinhart (1999) offers empirical evidence substantiating this effect.

The lack of consensus in the empirical literature reflects the beneficial effects of full capital account convertibility for some countries but not others (Prasad et al. 2003). As a result, the literature has shifted its focus to ask whether countries must have a set of institutions or economic conditions before they adopt full capital account liberalization, and whether the sequence of capital account liberalization matters. For the first question, researchers have hypothesized that sound macroeconomic conditions—such as low and controlled fiscal deficits or low and controlled inflation—are crucial for countries considering full capital account liberalization (Sen 2007; Williamson, Griffith-Jones, and Gottschalk 2005). Other researchers believe that countries must implement a set of reliable institutions in the financial sector, such as imposing minimum information requirements, prudential supervision and regulation of the banking sector, and investor protection, when pondering the adoption of full current account convertibility (Chinn and Ito 2002; Arteta et al. 2001; Gelos and Wei 2002).

Research has also investigated whether the method and timing of liberalization (or the sequencing of liberalization) matter as well. It is well known that short-term capital flows (such as portfolio investment) tend to be much more volatile than long-term flows (such as foreign direct investment). Given that this is the case, it is more prudent to liberalize long-term capital flows before liberalizing short-term ones. The idea is, of course, to reduce the country's exposure to what the literature has popularized as "hot money": short-term funds that enter and leave countries very suddenly and unexpectedly.

China and India are examples of countries that have considered adopting full capital account convertibility. Some commentators have argued that countries should always strive to adopt full capital account convertibility as soon as possible in order to reap all of its benefits (Forbes 2005). Others, however, argue that given the potentially disastrous consequences of implementing a liberalization program too rapidly, it is more prudent to go at it slowly and only when the country is "ready" (that is, when it has met all of the necessary preconditions). Given the theoretical complexities involved and the ambiguity of the empirical results, the advice that all researchers should probably offer to countries embarking on a full convertibility program is "proceed with caution."

See also asymmetric information; balance of payments; banking crisis; Bretton Woods system; capital controls; capital mobility; currency crisis; financial crisis; gold standard, international; hot money and sudden stops

FURTHER READING

Arteta, C., B. Eichengreen, and C. Wyplosz. 2001. "When Does Capital Account Liberalization Help More than It Hurts?" CEPR Discussion Paper No. 2910 (August). London: Centre for Economic Policy Research. Examines the evidence that capital account liberalization enhances growth and argues that correcting macroeconomic imbalances is a prerequisite for liberalizing the capital account.

Chinn, M., and H. Ito. 2002. "Capital Account Liberalization, Institutions, and Financial Development: Cross Country Evidence." NBER Working Paper 8967. Cambridge, MA: National Bureau of Economic Research. Investigates how capital controls affect the level of financial development.

Cole, H., and M. Obstfeld. 1991. "Commodity Trade and International Risk Sharing: How Much Do International Financial Markets Matter?" *Journal of Monetary Economics* 28: 3–24. Uses a general equilibrium model to quantify the social gains from having full capital account convertibility.

Edwards, S. 2001. "Capital Flows and Economic Performance: Are Emerging Economies Different?" NBER Working Paper 8076. Cambridge, MA: National Bureau of Economic Research. Studies the effect of capital mobility on economic growth.

Eichengreen, B. 2001. "Capital Account Liberalization: What Do the Cross-Country Studies Show Us?" *World Bank Economic Review* 15: 341–66. Summarizes the results of many studies that investigate the role of capital account liberalization in economic performance.

Eichengreen B., M. Mussa, G. Dell'Ariccia, E. Detragiache, G. M. Milesi-Ferretti, and A. Tweedie. 1999. "Liberalizing Capital Movements: Some Analytical Issues." *Economic Issues* 17 (February): 1–19. Summarizes the costs and benefits of having full capital account mobility, and touches on sequencing issues when countries decide to embark on a capital account liberalization program.

Forbes, Kristin J. 2005. "Capital Controls: Mud in the Wheels of Market Efficiency." *Cato Journal* 25 (1): 153–66. Argues that the use of capital controls brings microeconomic inefficiencies to capital markets, and hence that it may be prudent to eliminate all of them.

Gallego, F., and F. L. Hernandez. 2003. "Microeconomic Effects of Capital Controls: The Chilean Experience during the 1990s." *International Journal of Finance and Economics* 8: 225–53. Shows that Chile's experiment with capital controls resulted in an increase in the cost of capital for a sample of firms.

Gelos, R. G., and S. J. Wei. 2002. "Transparency and International Investor Behavior." NBER Working Paper 9260. Cambridge, MA: National Bureau of Economic Research. Finds that portfolio investment tends to be lower in countries that are less "transparent"—that is, where it is hard to obtain clear and reliable financial market information.

Kaminsky, G., and C. Reinhart. 1999. "The Twin Crises: The Causes of Banking and Balance-of-Payments Problems." *American Economic Review* 89 (3): 473–500. Studies the relationship between banking and financial crises.

Obstfeld, M., and K. Rogoff. 1995. "The Intertemporal Approach to the Current Account." In *Handbook of International Economics*. Vol. 3. Amsterdam: Elsevier/North-Holland, 1731–99. Develops a comprehensive open economy model in a dynamic setting that can be used to measure the welfare benefits from having full capital account convertibility.

Obstfeld, M., and A. Taylor. 2002. "Globalization and Capital Markets." NBER Working Paper 8846. Cambridge, MA: National Bureau of Economic Research. Documents and explains the evolution of world capital flows from the 19th century on.

Prasad, E., K. Rogoff, S. J. Wei, and M. A. Kose. 2003. "Effects of Financial Globalization on Developing Countries: Some Empirical Evidence." IMF Occasional Paper No. 220. Washington, DC: International Monetary Fund. Examines the empirical evidence behind the claim that financial globalization promotes economic growth.

Quinn, D. P. 1997. "The Correlates of Changes in International Financial Regulation." *American Political Science Review* 91: 531–51. Investigates the political and economic variables that appear to be best associated with international financial regulation.

Rodrik, D. 1998. "Who Needs Capital-Account Convertibility?" In *Should the IMF Pursue Capital Account Convertibility? Essays in International Finance No. 207*, edited by P. Kenen. Princeton, NJ: Princeton University Press, 55–65. Describes how full capital account convertibility may be more harmful than helpful to emerging market economies.

Sen, P. 2007. "Capital Inflows, Financial Repression, and Macroeconomic Policy in India since the Reforms." *Oxford Review of Economic Policy* 23 (2): 292–310. Provides a detailed analysis of the capital account liberalization process in India. The main conclusion is that, given the fragility of India's financial sector, full capital account convertibility for India may be premature.

Williamson, J., S. Griffith-Jones, and R. Gottschalk. 2005. "Should Capital Controls Have a Place in the Future International Monetary System?" In *The Future of the International Monetary System*, edited by M. Uzan.

Northampton, MA: Edward Elgar, 135–67. Provides a critical appraisal of the main arguments for and against capital controls and reports the main trends in the adoption and practice of capital controls across countries over the last 10 years.

Wyplosz, C. 2001. "Financial Restraints and Liberalization in Postwar Europe." In *Financial Liberalization: How Far? How Fast?* edited by G. Caprio, P. Honohan, and J. E. Stiglitz. New York: Cambridge University Press, 125–58. Looks at the evolution of financial repression and capital account liberalization in Europe.

CARLOS D. RAMIREZ

■ copyrights

See Agreement on Trade-Related Aspects of Intellectual Property Rights (TRIPS); intellectual property rights

■ corporate governance

Corporate governance determines, among other things, how control over the firm's resources is allocated, and how control and a monitoring hierarchy are created within a firm. Corporate governance acts as a facilitator, enabling managers and shareholders to move toward the optimal governance structure within the firm. Even though policymakers are often concerned with finding an optimal legal, institutional, and regulatory framework to protect the interests of investors and other stakeholders, it is difficult, in practice, to establish a single model that meets the needs of all parties. Given the broad and vague definition of *corporate governance*, there can be situations where the importance of other stakeholders such as employees and creditors may be central to a corporate governance system. Naturally, a corporate governance regime does more than regulate the ownership and control arrangements inside the firm. A "good" corporate governance system, for example, provides rules and institutions that enforce internal ownership and control arrangements, but it also contains measures that protect other stakeholders from the opportunistic behavior of insiders. Such a framework, which is mainly concerned with a company's investors but extends to wider interests, arguably provides a solid analytical basis on which a framework for understanding the key components of a good corporate governance system can be created.

What Is Corporate Governance and Why Does It Matter? The importance of corporate governance has become increasingly recognized for companies' and countries' prospects (Claessens 2006). As a consequence, regulators and policymakers in many countries diagnose weaknesses in their legal regimes and propose new arrangements said to foster higher firm performance, greater entrepreneurship, and better developed capital markets. Recent audit-based scandals in Europe and the United States have prompted investors to pay more attention to the institutions of corporate governance (Armour and McCahery 2006). Moreover, as allocation and monitoring of capital among competing purposes and investments have become more complex, financial instruments, corporate structures, and accounting have all become more sophisticated and often more risky. This has made monitoring of management by shareholders and other stakeholders more difficult, involving higher costs. The other side of the coin, of course, is that firms with good governance will benefit through higher market premiums (Gompers, Ishii, and Metrick 2003).

Corporate Governance Systems There are two main systems of corporate governance, which have significant differences: (1) the market-oriented corporate model, and (2) the relationship-based (or network-oriented) corporate system (Bratton and McCahery 1999; Roe 2003).

Market-oriented systems are characterized by dispersed equity holding through capital markets, a portfolio orientation among equity holders, and a broad delegation to management of discretion to operate the business. Two governance problems are said to result. The first is the shareholder–management agency problem. Collective action problems prevent close monitoring of management performance by widely dispersed shareholders of small stakes. Imperfect performance incentives result

for managers, who may rationally sacrifice shareholder value to pursue their own agendas. Market systems address this management incentive problem with three corrective mechanisms: the hostile takeover, shareholder legal rights against management self-dealing, and the inclusion of outside monitors on boards of directors. The second productive disadvantage of the market system is a time horizon cost that stems from shareholders' tendency to rely on short-term performance numbers. This problem has been attributed to information asymmetries. Management has superior information respecting investment policy and the firm's prospects, but this information tends to be soft or proprietary and therefore cannot credibly be communicated to actors in trading markets. At the same time, market systems fail to provide clear-cut protections to managers who make firm-specific investments of human capital, a failure due in part to these systems' reliance on takeovers, proxy fights, and boardroom coups to control agency costs.

Market systems have countervailing advantages. Their shareholders can cheaply reduce their risks through diversification. Compared to shareholders in relationship-based systems, they receive higher rates of return on their investment. Market systems' deeper trading markets facilitate greater liquidity. These capital markets also facilitate corporate finance, providing management with greater flexibility on the type and source of new capital than do the markets in relationship-based systems. More generally, they provide an environment relatively more conducive to management entrepreneurship, as reflected in increased investment in new technologies.

Relationship-based systems are characterized by a majority or near majority of stock held in the hands of one, two, or a small group of large investors who hold blocks of shares. Like market systems, relationship-based systems leave management in charge of the business plan and operations. But large block investments imply a closer level of shareholder monitoring (Becht, Bolton, and Röell 2003). In addition, the coalescence of voting power in a small number of hands means earlier, cheaper intervention in the case of management failure. The other primary benefit of relationship-based systems stems from the blockholders' access to information about operations. This decreased information asymmetry permits blockholders to invest more patiently. The longer shareholder time-horizon, in turn, frees management to invest for the longer term and creates a more secure management environment for firm-specific investment of human capital.

There are corresponding costs and benefits. Where the blockholder is a firm, internal agency costs can constrain its effectiveness as a monitor. Indeed, whatever the identity of the blockholder, its heightened oversight incentive does not appear to result in sharp oversight of management investment policy. Freedom to make long-term investments thus often means pursuit of growth in market share at the cost of suboptimal return on equity investment. Trading markets in relationship-based countries tend to be thinner and less transparent than in market-oriented countries. Meanwhile, the blockholders themselves forgo the benefits of diversification and, given the thin trading markets, the possibility of easy exit through sale. Finally, there is a shortage of loyalty. Blockholders, having sacrificed diversification and liquidity, extract a return in the form of private benefits through self-dealing or insider trading (Dyck and Zingales 2004). Legal regimes in network-oriented systems facilitate this quid pro quo with lax protection of minority shareholder rights and lax securities market regulation. The judiciary in network-oriented systems, unlike some market-oriented systems (which play a much more proactive role in shaping the actual contents of the corporate governance framework than in continental European jurisdictions), is more confined to interpreting the statutes and codes enacted by legislators (LaPorta et al. 1997).

Typology of Legal Strategies for Protecting Investors There is a wide collection of strategies for protecting shareholders and creditors from expropriation by managers and controlling shareholders. A basic division is between two categories: (1) regulatory strategies, through which the law mandates the terms of relationships among principals, agents, and the firm; and (2) governance strategies, through which the law channels the ongoing articulation of

the terms of corporate agencies (Kraakman et al. 2004). The strategies within each category are designed to provide different solutions to principal-agent problems ex post or ex ante.

On examination, it turns out that there are two categories of corporate law that pursue regulatory strategies. The strategies in the first category impose performance mandates on agents. These agent constraints apply on an ex ante basis by rule and on an ex post basis through open-ended standards of conduct. The strategies in the second category govern the terms of the principal's financial engagement with the firm. These affiliation terms apply on an ex ante basis when capital is transferred to the firm and on an ex post basis when capital is withdrawn or shares are sold. There are three other categories of corporate law measures that pursue governance strategies. The first category, appointment rights, concerns the ex ante selection of agents and their removal. The second, decision rights, concerns control over the terms of the firm's governing contracts and its business plan. Ex ante decision rights control the initiation and amendment of investments, divestitures, contracts, restructuring, and corporate legislation; ex post rights go to the ratification or veto of investments, divestures, contracts, restructuring, and legislation. The third set of governance strategies, agent incentives, concerns the incentives of the firm's agents. Ex ante these relate to the agents' qualifications as responsible fiduciaries; ex post they are related to the agents' financial rewards. From this analysis ten categories emerge, which are given in table 1.

A typology can be used to create indexes that capture the effectiveness of these five strategies to protect shareholders. The evidence shows that the strategy of giving shareholders strong legal rights in the appointment or removal of board directors has more measurable benefits for shareholders in common law countries such as the United Kingdom, which has tough rules on the removal of directors, than civil law regimes in continental Europe, where management has more discretion to address shareholder and creditor interests, and there are limited circumstances where a director can be removed. The evidence also points to potentially high benefits of

Table 1
Regulatory and governance strategies

	Regulatory strategies		Governance strategies		
	Agent constraints	Affiliation terms	Appointment rights	Decision rights	Agent incentives
Ex ante	rules	entry	selection	initiation	trusteeship
Ex post	standards	exit	removal	veto	reward

Source: Kraakman et al. (2004).

shareholder involvement in corporate decision-making, such as in the case of directors' remuneration. In the case of affiliation rights, the exit right of shareholders is addressed by corporate law strategies, developed albeit differently across Anglo-American jurisdictions, that effectively constrain management in frustrating a hostile bid and facilitate an exit right by ensuring shareholder approval of the bid. Changes in continental European takeover law to promote affiliation rights are still required, notwithstanding efforts by the European Commission to provide better constraints on target management in the Takeover Directive (McCahery and Renneboog 2003).

By comparison, the agent incentives strategies are often left to the contractual discretion of the board of directors. Codes of conduct set forth requirements in the area of board structure, the committee structure of the board, the role, monitoring and performance of the board and nonexecutive directors, and directors' remuneration. Codes of conduct and stock exchange rules draw up highly specific requirements concerning conflicts of interests and transactions where shareholder approval is necessary. According to a recent study that measures the board's independence from large shareholders, the legal strategies that deal with constraining the board and giving shareholders more authority are more effective in Anglo-American jurisdictions than civil law countries. Meanwhile, the empirical studies that focus on the reward strategy are voluminous (see, e.g., Jensen and Murphy 2004). This line of research reveals a number of problems in the design of appropriate criteria that link shareholder welfare to performance

criteria for directors and managers (Bebchuk and Fried 2004).

The above typology suggests a broad approach to corporate governance: (1) market value is the principal measure of shareholder interest; (2) other constituents should be protected by contract and outside regulation; (3) ultimate control should rest with the shareholders; (4) managers should be obligated to manage in the interests of the shareholders; and (5) noncontrolling shareholders should be strongly protected. These organizing factors, and the five corresponding regulatory strategies that constrain major shareholders and managers, provide a sufficient basis for evaluating corporate governance systems in differing jurisdictions and regions.

Good Corporate Governance In recent years, the increased focus on good corporate governance among academics, policymakers, and business leaders has given rise to investigations about how shareholders' rights and judicial enforcement vary across countries. This work has led to discussions which show that specific legal rules and practices are necessary to run a business and maintain corporate governance. Furthermore it shows that the best practices vary across countries (LaPorta et al. 1997). The impact of legal rules and institutions may vary, for example, depending on the judiciary's ability to quickly resolve disputes (Berglöf and Claessens 2004).

Similarly there is a growing awareness of how the variety of corporate governance arrangements and extralegal mechanisms are specific to firm type, industry sector, and sources of finance (Carlin and Mayer 2000). These findings suggest that a good corporate governance system requires, inter alia, legal rules that promote a system of disclosure and accounting and audit systems that function effectively to provide investors with timely and accurate information to make effective investment decisions. The key message for lawmakers is that the agenda for governance reform is broad and challenging, but delivering in the key areas will enhance performance (Black, Jang, and Kim 2006).

The positive impact of corporate governance can be felt not only on firm performance but also on the level of financial market development. Countries with better property rights and strong investor protection tend to have higher-valued securities and deeper capital markets. Enhanced creditor-protection rights are also associated with deeper and more developed banking and capital markets. Recent theoretical and empirical work highlights that countries with better investor protection are also less vulnerable to external economic shocks. In the end, corporate governance can induce countries to adopt higher standards which can have a major impact on realizing their objectives.

See also infrastructure and foreign direct investment; multinational enterprises

FURTHER READING

Armour, John, and Joseph A. McCahery, eds. 2006. *After Enron: Reforming Company and Securities Law in Europe and the United States.* Oxford: Hart Publications. A wide-ranging account of the recent corporate governance scandals and postscandal reform in Europe and the United States.

Bebchuk, Lucian, and Jesse Fried. 2004. *Pay without Performance: The Unfulfilled Promise of Executive Compensation.* Cambridge, MA: Harvard University Press. One of the most engaging and important discussions of the limitations of current executive pay practices in the United States, which provides a number of policy recommendations.

Becht, Marco, Patrick Bolton, and Ailsa Röell. 2003. "Corporate Governance and Control." In *The Handbook on the Economics of Finance*, edited by George Constantinides, Milton Harris, and Rene Stulz. Amsterdam: North-Holland, 1–109. The leading review of the main features of corporate governance in both blockholder and market-oriented regimes.

Berglöf, Erik, and Stijn Claessens. 2004. "Enforcement and Corporate Governance." World Bank Policy Research Working Paper No. 3409. Washington, DC: World Bank. Available at http://www.ssrn.com/. An exploration of the key variables that help explain what constitutes an effective system of enforcement and governance.

Black, Bernard, Hasung Jang, and Woochan Kim. 2006. "Does Corporate Governance Predict Firms' Market Values? Evidence from Korea." *Journal of Law, Economics, and Organization* 22 (2): 366–413. One of the more recent studies that provides a sophisticated empirical examination of the instrumental variables that affect the market value of companies.

Bratton, William W., and Joseph A. McCahery. 1999. "Comparative Corporate Governance and the Theory of the Firm: The Case against Global Cross-Reference." *Columbia Journal of Transnational Law* 38 (2): 213–97. One of the earliest articles to evaluate the tradeoffs between the blockholder and market-based system of governance.

Carlin, Wendy, and Colin Mayer. 2000. "How Do Financial Systems Affect Economic Performance?" In *Corporate Governance, Theoretical and Empirical Perspectives*, edited by Xavier Vives. Cambridge: Cambridge University Press, 137–68. A sophisticated theoretical and empirical analysis of the governance needs of different types of firms over their life cycle.

Claessens, Stijn. 2006. "Corporate Governance and Development." *The World Bank Research Observer* 21 (1): 91–122. A important look at the role of corporate governance in facilitating development and economic well-being.

Dyck, Alexander, and Luigi Zingales. 2004. "Private Benefits of Control: An International Comparision." *Journal of Finance* 59 (2): 537–600. The leading empirical study into the private benefits of control from a comparative standpoint.

Gompers, Paul, Joy Ishii, and Andrew Metrick. 2003. "Corporate Governance and Equity Prices." *Quarterly Journal of Economics* 118 (1): 107–55. An important empirical study of the way corporate governance provisions in the United States impact firm value.

Jensen, Michael, and Kevin Murphy. 2004. "Remuneration: Where We've Been, How We Got to Here, What Are the Problems, and How to Fix Them." ECGI Working Paper No 44/2004. Available at http://www.ecgi.org/wp. An interesting historical account of the system of executive compensation that provides a series of recommendation for reforming the system.

Kraakman, Reinier, Paul Davies, Henry Hansmann, Gerard Hertig, Klaus Hopt, Hideki Kanda, and Edward Rock. 2004. *The Anatomy of Corporate Law: A Comparative and Functional Approach*. Oxford: Oxford University Press. A lucid theoretical and comparative study of corporate law systems based on a typology of strategies that provides a way to compare the competing regimes.

LaPorta, Rafael, Florencio Lopez-de-Silanes, Andrei Shleifer, and Robert Vishny. 1997. "Legal Determinants of External Finance." *Journal of Finance* 52 (3): 1131–50. An early study that looks at 49 countries, showing that countries with poorer investor protections have smaller and narrower capital markets.

McCahery, Joseph A., and Luc Renneboog. 2003. *The Economics of the Proposed Takeover Directive*. Brussels: Centre for European Policy Studies. An economic account of the development of the Takeover Directive in Europe.

Organisation of Economic Co-operation and Development (OECD).1999. *Principles of Corporate Governance*. Paris: OECD. The key principles for OECD and non-OECD countries to evaluate and improve the legal and regulatory institutions for corporate governance within their countries and to provide guidance for other parties that play a role in the process of developing good corporate governance.

Roe, Mark J. 2003. *Political Determinants of Corporate Governance: Political Context, Corporate Impact*. Oxford: Oxford University Press. An important account of the theory of the firm and the variation in governance rules across systems.

JOSEPH A. MCCAHERY

■ corruption

Corruption is commonly defined as the abuse of public office for private gain. It involves bribe taking and deviation from public duties by officials in various governmental spheres such as the grant of licenses and permits, implementation of public programs, and enforcement of government policies. This view of corruption is meant to be a working definition only and it does not capture the context-specific and multidimensional nature of corrupt acts.

The difficulties in arriving at a commonly accepted definition are many. Corruption has moral, legal, and sociological dimensions. It need not be confined to the public sector. Corruption need not involve bribes or monetary payments. Moreover, in certain societies the culture of gifts, networking, and reciprocal favors is quite common, and these acts are socially acceptable.

Corruption, in one form or other, is present in most countries in varying degrees. Many poor and developing economies, however, are perceived to be highly corrupt, and the recent attention in academic as well as policy circles tends to focus on the type of corruption prevalent in these countries. Many development economists view corruption as a major problem.

Corruption is a fairly new field of inquiry in economics, although the earlier literature on rent-seeking activities is related and has influenced research in corruption. The phenomenon of corruption, however, is certainly very old. There are several accounts of governmental corruption in England, Italy, and China in the 18th and 19th centuries. References to bribery and the punishments for bribery can be found in many ancient sources, such as Babylon's Code of Hammurabi (22nd century B.C.), Egypt's Edict of Harmhab (14th century B.C.), and Kautilya's Arthasastra (14th century B.C.).

Types of Corruption Many scholars make a distinction between two types of corruption: grand corruption and petty corruption (e.g., Rose-Ackerman 1999). The latter category refers to bureaucratic corruption in which officials take bribes to grant favors in violation of their formal duties. Grand corruption refers to corruption by politicians and high-level decision-makers who accept payments from clients to influence policies or laws. This can be viewed as a form of state capture.

It is also useful to make a distinction between collusive and extortive corruption. Suppose an official is in charge of screening projects by granting approval only to socially desirable projects. Collusion occurs when the owner of an unqualified project manages to get approval by bribing the official. Extortion occurs when the official demands a bribe to approve qualified projects. The granting of permits and licenses by bureaucrats with near monopoly power resembles this type of corruption. Corruption can also take the form of embezzlement and appropriation of public funds. This is the more dominant form of corruption in many public education, health, and antipoverty programs.

Measuring Corruption Irrespective of their legal status, corrupt acts are always held in secrecy, and it is difficult to unearth systematic information on corruption. To a large degree research on corruption has suffered on this account. Early discussions of corruption tended to rely on journalistic accounts in newspapers and reports, on anecdotal evidence, or in a few cases, on prosecutorial evidence. Recently, there have been several attempts to construct more systematic measures of corruption.

Many authors have used perception measures of corruption. These measures are based on perceptions by various types of respondents such as local and multinational businessmen, country experts, and citizens. Two common measures are the corruption perception index (CPI) of Transparency International and the corruption control index (CCI) of the World Bank Institute. Transparency International has been publishing these indexes on an annual basis, and they now cover more than one hundred countries (Transparency International 2006). The CCI is more recent and it is available for selected years (Kaufmann et al. 2004). These indexes are based on many different polls conducted by several independent organizations. These polls use different methods and different sets of questionnaires about the business environment and corruption.

More recently, there have been attempts to use experience-based measures of corruption. The World Bank conducted a Business Environment and Enterprise Performance Survey (BEEPS) in 1999, in which selected firms in 26 East European and central Asian countries were asked various questions about the extent of bribe payments and the reasons for making such payments. In general, these surveys take care to elicit bribe-related information from the firms. Firms are seldom asked about their own payments; rather they are encouraged to talk about the average payment made by a similar firm in the industry.

Similar surveys have been conducted in some other countries to elicit information about corruption-related experiences of the general public. Despite their imprecise nature, these surveys convey useful information about corruption in different branches (police, judiciary, public services) of the government. There have been recent attempts to collect such information through field experiments.

In addition to the perception-based and experience-based measures, economists have also looked at several indirect measures. For example, by tracking government expenditure from its origin to the destination, one can get an estimate of the extent of leakage of public funds. This leakage may be viewed as a measure of corruption.

Causes Recent research into the causes of corruption focuses on the role of factors such as an oversized public sector, poor quality of regulatory institutions, the lack of democratic governance, low wages of public officials, and lack of economic competition. Researchers have used country-level perception measures to explore these causal links. Although there is disagreement about the nature and strength of these links, one can identify certain common features of the countries perceived to be highly corrupt.

In general, low levels of development (measured in terms of per capita income) and low human capital (measured in terms of years of schooling) are associated with high levels of perceived corruption. These two can be viewed as structural features, which could change only in the long run. But there are several other features that reflect the policy choices made by these countries.

For example, most of these countries also have a highly regulated business environment with a plethora of rules and bureaucratic procedures. A study by

Djankov et al. (2002) shows that in a cross section of countries the minimum official time required for a business startup varies from 2 business days in Canada and Australia to a high of 152 days in Madagascar. The association between the number of days required to start a legal business and the extent of perceived corruption is positive and robust. The presence of the rules allows bureaucrats to exercise monopoly power and extract bribes from private business.

A related feature is the absence of economic competition. The regulatory environment tends to discourage entry of new firms and helps to maintain the profitability of the few existing firms. These existing firms, in turn, transfer part of their profits as bribes to the politicians and bureaucrats. The concentration of economic power and wealth is more pronounced in smaller economies where economic activities rely on abundant natural resources or primary exports. The initially unequal distribution of assets (land, natural resources) leads to concentration of wealth in the hands of a few who use the corrupt system to increase their own wealth at the cost of others.

In many of these countries salaries of public officials are substantially lower than salaries in the private sector. This creates an inducement for the officials to seek illegal bribe income. Since in most cases the punishment for bribery involves loss of job and future income, low salaries also reduce the cost of engaging in corruption.

Other features such as lack of strong democratic traditions and lower level of press freedom are associated with higher levels of corruption. Among the democratic countries the forms of the government and the nature of electoral competition also seem to be associated with different levels of corruption. A presidential form of government is likely to be less corrupt than a prime ministerial form because of greater accountability, but this result crucially depends on the nature of checks and balances in place. Similarly, among electoral rules, a proportional representation system of voting tends to be associated with higher corruption. In a proportional representation system voters do not directly elect any particular political candidate, reducing the ability for voters to punish corrupt officials.

It is possible that noneconomic variables such as culture, values, religion, and geography also play roles in contributing to the levels of corruption. In a widely cited paper, Triesman (2000) finds support for the view that countries with histories of British rule and Protestant traditions tend to be less corrupt. Though such a result is by no means robust, it is a reminder that cultural determinants of corruption cannot be ignored altogether.

Consequences Some scholars argue that corruption can enhance efficiency. In the presence of a rigid bureaucracy and ill-planned regulations, corruption can facilitate speedy implementation of productive investment proposals. According to this view, corruption could grease the wheels of commerce and promote growth. There is very little support for this view in contemporary theoretical or empirical research, however. At best, corruption could result in a partial and temporary efficiency gain. Officials who benefit from such grease money would always have a tendency to increase red tape for their own benefit. Recent research has shown that corruption leads to inefficient allocation of resources with adverse effects on growth, investment, and foreign direct investment.

Mauro (1995) initiated one popular strand of empirical research on corruption by examining the link between corruption and growth in a cross section of countries. Using the CPI as an explanatory variable, he observed that growth and investment rates are adversely affected by corruption levels. Later studies tend to confirm this broad relationship, though the exact nature depends on several region-specific variables. One possible exception to this relationship is the experience of many high-growth Asian countries that are perceived to be highly corrupt. Though there is not enough evidence to suggest that corruption has promoted growth in these countries, it suggests that the corruption-growth link is quite complex.

Various studies have claimed that corrupt countries tend to have high inflation rates, greater military expenditures, and less public investment in education and health. The direction of causation is far from established, but the possibility that corruption distorts governmental spending programs cannot be ignored.

Corruption adversely affects inequality and poverty also. Poverty is affected because corruption tends to lower growth, affects the (pro-poor or otherwise) orientation of public spending, and undermines the implementation of many of the antipoverty programs. This issue has generated concerns among national governments, nongovernmental organizations, and international organizations such as the United Nations, the World Bank, and the European Union. Empirical research in this area is somewhat limited, however.

At a more micro level, corruption undermines enforcement policies in a variety of fields such as tax collection, environmental regulation, and policing. Hence a higher level of corruption would lead to lower tax revenues, poor environmental standards, and a deteriorating law and order situation.

Anticorruption Strategies Views on anticorruption strategies differ considerably, ranging from mild tolerance to advocacy of draconian measures. Even though corruption is perceived to be a problem associated with low levels of development, it is unlikely that corruption will fade out on its own with rising income levels in these countries. First, corruption might constrain the growth process itself. Second, corruption has a tendency to spread and persist across time. Third, apart from generating various economic inefficiencies mentioned earlier, corruption undermines people's faith in democracy and other human development objectives. Hence curbing corruption is both a goal in itself and an instrument for achieving other goals.

Anticorruption strategies involve design of suitable incentives and organizational structures and, at a more general level, improvements in institutional quality. To a large extent, a person's decision to be corrupt is based on calculations of associated costs and benefits. Hence many have proposed incentives measures that seek to reward honest behavior and punish the corrupt. This, of course, requires better monitoring and information gathering and a quick and fair judicial process. Such measures have proved to be successful in some of the recent tax enforcement

reforms exercises, such as those carried out by the Philippines, Singapore, and Brazil. Studies based on field experiments also support the view that better monitoring is effective.

Additionally, one can reduce the scope of corruption by increasing transparency, reducing discretion, and encouraging competition where appropriate. This involves measures such as simplification of laws and easier access to information by the public. There must also be ways to generate and transmit credible and hard information about governmental decisions where there is potential for corruption. A recent study shows how a newspaper campaign about the amount of funds allocated to schools in certain areas helped stakeholders (parents) to hold the disbursement officials accountable and reduce the leakage of funds. The role of local bodies, activists, and an independent press is quite vital in this respect. Last, bureaucratic and other forms of corruption are unlikely to thrive without corrupt politicians. As pointed out earlier, electoral competition and forms of democratic governance influence the scope and extent of corruption by political representatives. Hence a successful anticorruption strategy may require reforms in the political and electoral process as well.

See also aid, international; political economy of trade policy; smuggling

FURTHER READING

Bardhan, Pranab. 1997. "The Economics of Corruption in Less-Developed Countries: A Review of Issues." *Journal of Economic Literature* 35 (3): 1320–46. An excellent review of the issues and some of the early literature.

Djankov, Simeon, Rafael La Porta, F. Lopez-de-Silanes, and Andrei Shleifer. 2002. "The Regulation of Entry." *Quarterly Journal of Economics* 117 (1): 1–37. One of the first empirical exercises to capture the nature and impact of bureaucratic red tape across countries.

Kaufmann, Daniel, Aart Kraay, and Massimo Mastruzzi. 2004. "Governance Matters III: Governance Indicators for 1996, 1998, 2000 and 2002." *World Bank Economic Review* 18 (2): 253–87. Perception indexes for various aspects of governance including corruption in a large set of countries.

Klitgaard, Robert. 1988. *Controlling Corruption.* Berkeley: University of California Press. A popular book containing various case studies and proposals for anticorruption reforms.

Mauro, Paolo. 1995. "Corruption and Growth." *Quarterly Journal of Economics* 110 (3): 681–712. An important contribution evaluating the impact of corruption on investment and growth in a cross section of countries.

Mishra, A. 2005. *Economics of Corruption.* Oxford: Oxford University Press. A reader containing a survey of the literature and several important academic contributions in the field.

Rose-Ackerman, Susan. 1999. *Corruption and Government: Causes, Consequences and Reforms.* Cambridge: Cambridge University Press. An excellent commentary on various aspects of governmental corruption by one of the pioneers in the field.

———. 2006. *International Handbook on the Economics of Corruption.* Cheltenham, UK: Edward Elgar. An excellent collection of handbook style survey and research articles by leading scholars in the field.

Svensson, Jakob. 2005. "Eight Questions about Corruption." *Journal of Economic Perspectives* 19 (3): 19–42. An excellent discussion of the key issues in corruption.

Transparency International. 2006. *Global Corruption Report 2006.* London: Pluto Press. An annual report of Transparency International discussing its CPI, country analysis, and recent empirical research on corruption.

Triesman, Daniel. 2000. "The Causes of Corruption: a Cross National Study." *Journal of Public Economics* 76 (3): 399–457. An extensive cross-country analysis of determinants of corruption.

AJIT MISHRA

■ **corruption and foreign direct investment**
See infrastructure and foreign direct investment

■ **countervailing duties**
Countervailing duties (CVDs) are tariffs imposed by a country to offset a foreign subsidy. The General Agreement on Tariffs and Trade (GATT) has permitted the imposition of CVDs since 1947 to offset "actionable" subsidies if the government determines that these subsidized imports are causing or threatening to cause injury to the domestic industry. Actionable subsidies are subsidies that are not explicitly prohibited under the GATT but are subject to challenge if they cause adverse effects on another country.

CVDs are similar to anti-dumping duties, the tariffs imposed to protect domestic industries from products imported at unfairly low prices, in that both seek to counteract the "unfair" trade practices of a foreign trade partner. Anti-dumping duties are much more prevalent than CVDs in the world today, however. Between 1995 and 2005, World Trade Organization (WTO) members imposed 1,804 anti-dumping duties compared to just 112 CVDs. As a result, CVDs have provoked significantly less research and debate than anti-dumping duties.

Some economists emphasize that importing countries should welcome subsidized imports rather than punish the exporting country through the use of CVDs because foreign subsidies lower import prices and increase domestic welfare at the expense of the foreign government. Other economists and lawyers stress that CVDs can improve welfare by eliminating economic distortions caused by subsidies and discouraging the future use of these subsidies. It is unclear whether current CVD regulations are solely used to offset foreign subsidies; some empirical evidence suggests that CVDs are often geared more toward imposing additional trade protection rather than eliminating economic distortions that arise from foreign subsidies. In order to understand the current debate over CVDs, it is important to understand the economic arguments for and against the use of CVDs, the evolution of CVD regulations and their worldwide use, and how future international trade negotiations could alter the use of CVDs.

Economic Consequences of CVD Laws Economists generally agree that CVDs can improve global economic welfare, at least in principal. Consider, for example, Canadian lumber exports to the United States. Trade theory suggests that Canadian subsidies would lower the price of Canadian lumber exports to the United States. The United States would benefit from these lower prices as long as it is a net importer of lumber. In other words, U.S. consumers of lumber would gain more from the lower, subsidized prices than U.S. lumber producers would lose from lower prices and the loss of market share to Canadian producers. In this situation, the imposition of a CVD would increase the import price, restore the welfare of U.S. lumber consumers and producers to their pre-subsidy levels, and transfer money from the Canadian government to the U.S. government.

The imposition of the CVD causes total U.S. welfare to fall in this scenario because the gain to the U.S. government and U.S. lumber producers does not offset the loss that U.S. consumers experience from the higher prices. Even in this situation, however, the imposition of the CVD could result in an increase in global economic welfare. If the subsidy allows Canadian producers to export lumber to the United States even though U.S. producers harvest lumber more efficiently, then it creates an economic distortion. A CVD that offsets this subsidy should eliminate the unnatural advantage and the distortion, thus improving total economic welfare. By imposing the CVD, however, the U.S. government improves world welfare at the expense of a net decrease in U.S. economic welfare.

Since the late 1980s, most economists have agreed that under certain conditions CVDs can improve domestic welfare. Assume that there are two firms serving the world market for aircraft, one in the United States and a second in the European Union. Both firms, taking the output of their foreign competitor into consideration, choose output levels to maximize their profits. European production subsidies will artificially lower the cost of production, causing the European producer to increase its output. The U.S. producer will react by cutting its production level to try to maintain a higher price. The subsidy lowers the world price of aircraft, although not by the full amount of the subsidy as in the lumber example. It also increases European profits and lowers U.S. profits. The production subsidy can increase total European welfare as long as the gain to European consumers and producers offsets the cost

to the government. In contrast, the subsidy may decrease U.S. welfare if the loss of profits to the domestic aircraft producer is greater than the gain to U.S. consumers.

Using theoretical models, both Dixit (1988) and Collie (1991) show that the optimal response of the U.S. government in a situation like this is to retaliate with a CVD that partially offsets the subsidy. The CVD increases European production costs, thereby increasing the price of aircraft and transferring some of the profits of the European producer to the U.S. government and the U.S. producer. The CVD can increase U.S. welfare in this case because the gain to the U.S. producer and government will offset the loss to the U.S. consumer.

Collie also shows that a foreign country should be deterred from subsidizing exports when a domestic country uses CVDs. This theoretical prediction implies that the threat of the imposition of CVDs should be enough to eliminate subsidies. The continued use of subsidies and CVDs, however, reveals that this is not the case. Qiu (1995) develops a model to show that the coexistence of subsidies and CVD regulations can be explained by things such as lengthy delays in the imposition, and restrictions on the level, of CVDs.

Countervailing Duties from 1890 to the Present In 1890, the United States enacted the first CVD law, which applied only to certain grades of sugar. Belgium enacted the first CVD law targeting all subsidized imports in 1892, and the United States expanded its CVD coverage to all imports in 1897. By 1921, nine additional countries had passed CVD legislation.

The 1947 GATT formally sanctioned the use of CVDs to counteract foreign subsidies. The CVD portion of the 1947 GATT was largely based on the U.S. law at the time, with one important exception. The GATT allowed for the imposition of CVDs only if subsidized imports were causing or threatening to cause injury to a domestic industry. The United States was granted a grandfather provision and thus did not require proof of injury until 1974. International rules governing the imposition of CVDs remained largely unchanged until the 1979 Tokyo

Round GATT Agreement on Subsidies and Countervailing Measures and the 1994 revision of this agreement that resulted from the Uruguay Round of trade negotiations.

Under the version of the agreement finalized in 1994, governments may initiate a CVD investigation at the written request of the domestic industry. Prior to imposing a CVD, the government must determine that the imports from the country under investigation have (1) benefited from a prohibited or actionable subsidy, and (2) the subsidized imports have caused or threatened to cause "material" injury to the domestic industry. If the government makes a final determination that subsidized imports have injured the domestic industry, it may impose a CVD up to the calculated amount of the subsidy per unit of imported product.

In general, the agreement does not detail how countries should measure either the amount of the subsidy or the degree of injury to the domestic industry. The agreement does specify, however, that the amount of the subsidy should be consistent with some generally accepted guidelines, such as:

- The difference between the amount paid by the firm on a government loan or a government-guaranteed loan and the amount the firm would pay on a comparable commercial loan obtained in the private market; and
- The difference between the market price of a good and the price paid to the firm by the government in the purchase of goods, or the difference between the market price of a good and the price paid by the firm to the government in the provision of goods.

Injury determinations should be based on an examination of the volume of subsidized imports, the impact of these subsidized imports on domestic output and prices, and the subsequent impact of the imports on the domestic industry. In conducting this examination, the government should evaluate all economic factors associated with the industry, including the actual and potential decline in output, market share, profits, and capacity utilization, as well as other factors that may be causing injury to the domestic industry. No CVDs may be imposed if the government determines that the amount of the subsidy is less than 1 percent of the import price or the volume of subsidized imports is negligible.

Investigations must be concluded within 18 months of their initiation. CVDs should remain in force only for as long as necessary to counteract the subsidies causing injury. The duties must be eliminated after five years unless the government determines during a sunset review that revocation of the duties would be likely to lead to a recurrence of injury caused by the subsidies.

Countries have a great deal of latitude in the way they conduct CVD investigations. Most countries have either a bifurcated approach, in which the injury and subsidy investigations are conducted by two different governmental entities, or a single-track approach, in which both investigations are conducted by the same entity. For example, in the United States, the International Trade Administration of the Department of Commerce determines the level of subsidies, while the International Trade Commission determines whether the subsidies have caused injury to the domestic industry. In contrast, the Trade Directorate of the European Commission makes both determinations in the European Union.

In 1956, 20 countries had CVD legislation, although only 8 actually used the legislation. The United States, which has historically made much greater use of CVDs than other countries, imposed only 62 CVDs between 1897 and 1959. Under the Tokyo Round Agreement, however, the use of CVDs by a small subset of countries rose dramatically. For example, the United States imposed CVDs in more than 90 cases between 1980 and 1988 alone. Between 1989 and 1993, 7 signatories to the GATT initiated 150 CVD investigations, of which the United States accounted for slightly more than 45 percent.

Since the completion of the Uruguay Round Agreement, more countries have imposed CVD measures, although its use is still highly concentrated among a few countries. Seventeen WTO members initiated 182 CVD investigations between 1995 and 2005. Of these, 61.5 percent, or 112 investigations, eventually resulted in the imposition of CVDs. The United States and the European Union initiated 64 percent of all CVD investigations between 1995 and 2005. Half of all CVD investigations during this time period were filed against exports from India, Korea, Italy, Indonesia, and the European Union. Metals, particularly steel products, accounted for nearly 40 percent of all CVD petitions; other leading industries targeted for CVD actions include food products and footwear.

Some economists argue that many of these CVDs were used primarily to protect domestic industries from targeted imports, whether subsidized or not. For example, Marvel and Ray (1996) find that U.S. CVD petitions tend to be made against multiple nations simultaneously and are closely linked with anti-dumping petitions. Moreover, most CVD investigations define any financial contribution to the foreign firm as a subsidy, regardless of whether it lowers the foreign export price and creates an economic distortion. Based on these characteristics, Marvel and Ray conclude that CVDs are used primarily to provide the domestic industry with protection from imports rather than to counteract subsidies.

Other researchers have found empirical evidence that political pressure may explain the imposition of some CVDs. As summarized in Blonigen and Prusa (2003), there is a large literature that tests the economic and political determinants of the injury decisions in both CVD and anti-dumping investigations. Most research in this area has analyzed U.S. investigation outcomes and found that although economic factors significantly influence outcomes, political pressure also positively influences the likelihood that a CVD or anti-dumping investigation will result in the imposition of duties.

The Future of CVD Laws Stiglitz (1997) suggests that CVD laws can be beneficial as long as they are not used to protect domestic industries from import surges. He and others suggest that regulations be revised to include a higher standard of proof for establishing the existence of subsidies. In 2001, the members of the WTO agreed to "clarify and improve" CVD regulations during the Doha Round of trade negotiations, although the clarifications will not necessarily resolve the problems economists have with CVD laws. Negotiators developed a long list of proposals to consider, including specific changes to regulations governing the calculation of the amount of the subsidy and the injury determinations.

In summary, a countervailing duty is a tool that countries can use to offset the unfair use of production subsidies by foreign governments. The use of CVDs is relatively rare today compared to other trade remedy tools such as anti-dumping duties. There is no clear consensus among economists on the impact of CVDs on the economy. Although traditional international trade theory predicts that the imposition of a CVD will increase global welfare at the expense of the imposing country, more recent theoretical models have shown that CVDs can improve domestic welfare under certain conditions. Empirical evidence suggests that CVDs may be geared more toward imposing additional trade protection rather than offsetting foreign subsidies; therefore some economists have urged the WTO to revise current regulations governing the use of CVDs.

See also anti-dumping; Doha Round; fair trade; General Agreement on Tariffs and Trade (GATT); new trade theory; subsidies and financial incentives to foreign direct investment; Uruguay Round; World Trade Organization

FURTHER READING

Blonigen, Bruce A., and Thomas J. Prusa. 2003. "Anti-dumping." In *Handbook of International Trade*, edited by E. K. Choi and J. Harrigan. Oxford, UK: Blackwell, 251–84 . Includes a review of the literature testing the economic and political determinants of injury decisions in CVD and anti-dumping investigations.

Collie, David. 1991. "Export Subsidies and Countervailing Tariffs." *Journal of International Economics* 31: 309–24. Theoretical study that suggests that CVDs should deter subsidization.

Congressional Budget Office. 1994. *How the GATT Affects U.S. Antidumping and Countervailing Duty Policy.* Washington, DC: CBO. A thorough review of the history of GATT and U.S. CVD and anti-dumping regulations.

Dixit, A. K. 1988. "Antidumping and Countervailing Duties under Oligopoly." *European Economic Review*

32: 55–68. Theoretical study that proves that the optimal response of a country to a subsidy is a CVD.

Marvel, Howard P., and Edward John Ray. 1996. "Countervailing Duties." *Economic Journal* 105: 1576–93. A statistical analysis of the use of CVDs in the United States.

Qiu, Larry D. 1995. "Why Can't Countervailing Duties Deter Export Subsidization?" *Journal of International Economics* 39: 249–72. A theoretical study of the inability of CVDs to deter subsidization.

Stiglitz, Joseph E. 1997. "Dumping on Free Trade: The U.S. Import Trade Laws." *Southern Economic Journal* 64 (2): 402–24. A review of U.S. CVD laws before and after the Uruguay Round, and the policy objectives of these laws.

Viner, Jacob. 1923. *Dumping: A Problem in International Trade*. Chicago: University of Chicago Press. One of the earliest works to justify and describe anti-dumping and CVD laws.

KARA M. REYNOLDS

■ crisis prevention, management, and resolution

See bail-ins; bailouts; currency crisis; expenditure changing and expenditure switching; International Monetary Fund (IMF)

■ currency basket regime

See band, basket, and crawl (BBC)

■ currency board arrangement (CBA)

A currency board is a monetary arrangement based on two simple rules. First, the exchange rate between the domestic currency and an appropriately chosen foreign currency is fixed. Ideally, the fixed exchange rate is written into law in order to signal a long-term commitment. Second, there is full convertibility between the domestic monetary base and the foreign anchor currency. The currency board stands ready to exchange domestic into foreign currency, and vice versa, at the fixed rate, on demand, and without limit.

These two defining features have immediate and important implications. Under a currency board arrangement (CBA), every note or coin of the domestic currency in circulation is backed by foreign currency. Therefore, the currency board needs to hold a large amount of liquid foreign exchange reserves—at least 100 percent of the monetary base, and perhaps more—in order to provide a cushion against potential capital losses on the reserves. Domestic assets (also known as "domestic credit") on the balance sheet of the currency board should be zero or, more realistically, should be held constant. There should be no scope for creating money by expanding domestic credit. In practical terms, this prohibits the monetary authority from lending to the domestic government or commercial banks. In other words, the currency board is not allowed to monetize budget deficits or to act as a lender of last resort to troubled commercial banks. Therefore, in order to succeed, a CBA must go hand in hand with fiscal discipline and a healthy banking system.

On the continuum of exchange rate regimes, a CBA falls between a conventional fixed exchange rate and an outright monetary union. Under a conventional peg, there is only partial coverage of the monetary base by foreign reserves and there is no long-term commitment to the level of the exchange rate. Under a monetary union, a country gives up its currency altogether. A CBA is a more credible arrangement than a conventional peg but less credible than a monetary union.

Under a CBA, the adjustment mechanism for achieving external equilibrium is completely automatic. The monetary authority plays a passive role; it simply stands ready to exchange domestic notes and coins into foreign ones, or vice versa, as necessary. The money supply is endogenous and determined solely by market forces. If a country faces a balance of payments deficit (perhaps because private capital inflows are insufficient to cover the current account deficit), the monetary authority will face a loss of foreign exchange reserves. Under the operating rules of the currency board, the money supply will contract. In asset markets, this will push domestic interest rates up, which will attract greater private capital inflows into the country. In goods markets, the falling money supply will exert deflationary pressure, and prices and wages will tend to fall over time. This will make domestic tradable goods relatively cheaper in world markets, and the current account deficit may shrink. High interest rates and the real depreciation caused by deflation will stifle domestic aggregate demand, particularly the demand for imports, thus contributing further to the current account improvement.

This should sound familiar. It is very similar to the adjustment mechanisms operating under the classical gold standard. In fact, some economists have argued that the gold standard was a special case of a CBA, with a commodity (gold) replacing the foreign anchor currency. Given the key role of price and wage adjustment in the mechanism just described, a successful currency board needs flexible goods and labor markets.

History The history of currency boards spans approximately 150 years. There have been around 80 CBAs throughout the world. During the colonial era, various dominions of the British Empire operated more than 70 different CBAs. Currency boards combined centralized control by the colonial center with the retention of domestic monies in the periphery. They were designed to facilitate trade and financial flows within the British Empire. Currency boards fell into intellectual disfavor and were gradually replaced by conventional central banks after the demise of colonialism in the 1950s and 1960s. Central banks better fitted the political drive for national independence. The transition also reflected the period's intellectual climate, which was infused with a sunny optimism about the effectiveness of discretionary government policies.

Currency boards came back into fashion beginning in the early 1990s, due to a collapse of faith in discretionary monetary policy, especially in developing countries. A cursory look at some countries that have operated currency boards in the 1990s and early 2000s (Hong Kong, Argentina, Estonia, Lithuania, Bulgaria, and Bosnia and Herzegovina) shows

that CBAs have been successful in ending hyperinflation, facilitating the transition to a market economy or to national independence, assisting postwar reconstruction, and restoring stability in an international financial center plagued by political uncertainty and banking crises. CBAs were also proposed in the aftermath of macroeconomic crises in Indonesia, Russia, Brazil, and Turkey, although none of these proposals ultimately came to fruition. Modern CBAs have been subject to occasional speculative attacks—Hong Kong in 1997, and Argentina in 1995 and 2001. In general, exits from CBAs have been uneventful, with the single spectacular exception of Argentina in early 2002.

Most real-world CBAs have reserved some degree of discretionary powers, and thus deviate from the definition of an orthodox currency board. The ratio of foreign exchange reserves relative to the monetary base may be allowed to dip below 100 percent. This coverage ratio may also be allowed to go above 110–115 percent in order to sterilize capital inflows, finance a lender-of-last-resort function, or smooth fluctuations in domestic interest rates. The monetary authorities in almost all contemporary currency boards have reserved the right to change the required reserve ratio for commercial banks, which might thwart the operation of the automatic adjustment mechanism described earlier. (The monetary authority regains some degree of control over the broader money supply.) Almost all modern CBAs have volatile domestic assets on their balance sheets.

Argentina's CBA was the one with the most loopholes, which probably contributed to its ultimate demise. First, Argentina's CBA was allowed to lend to the government. Second, throughout 2001 the long-term commitment to the fixed exchange rate was undermined by switching the peg from the U.S. dollar to a currency basket, and by instituting a complicated scheme of export subsidies and import surcharges, which amounted to a sneak devaluation.

Debating the Pros and Cons Professional economists have advanced various arguments about the advantages and disadvantages of CBAs. Perhaps the single biggest advantage of a currency board is its simplicity and transparency. It may enable a government to commit credibly to monetary discipline at the expense of flexibility. In essence, through the currency board, the monetary authority can import the anti-inflationary credibility of the central bank issuing the anchor currency, typically the U.S. Federal Reserve or the European Central Bank. The domestic monetary authority becomes a mere warehouse for foreign cash.

A credible CBA reduces currency and default risk, which leads to lower domestic interest rates. It can boost the development of long-term financial markets, which are sorely lacking in many developing countries. By reducing transaction costs, the fixed exchange rate can promote trade and foreign direct investment. Finally, by establishing monetary discipline, a currency board can serve as a catalyst for a broad range of other reforms.

A serious drawback of currency boards is that they make the adopting country more vulnerable to external shocks, particularly terms-of-trade shocks, large capital inflows or outflows, or shocks emanating from the country issuing the anchor currency. Arguably, high interest rates in the United States and the strength of the dollar against the euro and the Japanese yen contributed to the demise of Argentina's CBA, in addition to lack of fiscal discipline within the country, especially at the provincial level.

As Argentina's experience with deflation in 1999–2001 also demonstrates, currency boards (or indeed fixed exchange rates in general) are probably not a good monetary arrangement for relatively closed economies. The less open the economy is, the larger the real depreciation necessary to eliminate a given balance of payments deficit. Under a fixed exchange rate, real depreciation can happen only through a fall in domestic prices. Such price adjustments can be slow and painful.

One reason to introduce a CBA is to arrest high inflation, but currency boards can generate overvalued real exchange rates and large current account deficits. Real appreciation results from the combination of a fixed nominal exchange rate and persistent domestic inflation. The introduction of a currency board can also be burdensome and time-consuming. In order to make the arrangement credible, policymakers must build political consensus, rewrite laws, and reorganize institutions.

Critics of CBAs have pointed out that countercyclical monetary policy is impossible under a CBA, and therefore output, employment, and prices would be more volatile under such an arrangement. Proponents of CBAs have countered that ending discretionary monetary policy is the intended purpose of such institutional arrangements: discretionary monetary policies in developing countries have been the prime source of macroeconomic instability, and currency boards have helped to restore macroeconomic stability by imposing a monetary straitjacket on the government. Monetary policy is an extension of fiscal policy—printing money is a government's revenue source of last resort. Therefore, a currency board can be beneficial in imposing a hard budget constraint on the country's treasury.

Opponents have noted that currency boards either abolish or sharply curtail the capacity of the monetary authority to serve as a lender of last resort to the banking system. Proponents counter that a lender-of-last-resort function is still possible under a CBA through assistance from the treasury, a deposit insurance scheme, or contingent credit lines from abroad. Bailing out domestic banks involves redistribution of income, and a currency board removes a nontransparent (and therefore politically cheap) tool of income redistribution. By making bank bailouts more politically costly and therefore less likely, a currency board limits the moral hazard problem of the banking system (the problem of a party insulated from risk engaging in riskier behavior). In essence, it imposes a hard budget constraint on domestic financial institutions.

Currency boards are unable, by definition, to create money by expanding domestic credit. Therefore, they cannot earn extra seigniorage through discretionary money creation. Currency boards still make profits on the difference between interest earned on their assets (highly liquid foreign securities) and their operating costs. Seigniorage revenues are somewhat lower under currency boards than under conventional central banks, however, both because CBAs cannot expand domestic credit and because foreign reserves may pay a somewhat lower interest rate than domestic assets. Of course, many economists would count the reduction in seigniorage as a *benefit* of CBAs, given that it is an inefficient and nontransparent way of raising revenue.

The Empirical Record Although theoretical arguments have dominated the debates about currency boards, little empirical work has been undertaken on the subject. The most authoritative empirical analysis available (Ghosh, Gulde, and Wolf 2000) finds that currency boards are associated with lower inflation than either floating or conventional fixed exchange rate regimes. This result is highly robust. Currency boards also appear to be associated with higher rates of gross domestic product (GDP) growth, although the reasons for this are not clear. It may be that countries with better overall economic policies self-select in choosing to establish a currency board. It may be that most countries introduce a currency board following a severe macroeconomic crisis, and the better growth performance observed in the first few years of the new arrangement reflects a postcrisis "rebound effect." At the very least, currency boards have not been associated with *lower* GDP growth rates, although there is some evidence that output tends to be more volatile. Finally, CBAs appear to be associated empirically with lower money supply growth rates, smaller budget deficits, and better export performance.

In conclusion, a CBA offers significant benefits but also has serious drawbacks. Although it is neither a quick fix nor a panacea for all economic ills, in some cases it can deliver monetary discipline and low inflation.

See also convertibility; currency substitution and dollarization; discipline; exchange rate regimes; expenditure changing and expenditure switching; foreign exchange intervention; gold standard, international; impossible trinity; international reserves; lender of last resort; money supply; quantity theory of money; reserve currency; seigniorage; sterilization

FURTHER READING

Ghosh, Atish, Anne-Marie Gulde, and Holger Wolf. 2000. "Currency Boards: More Than a Quick Fix?" *Economic Policy: A European Forum* 31: 269–321. A comprehensive and sober look at the history and the pros and cons of CBAs. Contains the best analysis of the empirical record of currency boards.

Hanke, Steve, and Kurt Schuler. 1994. *Currency Boards for Developing Countries: A Handbook.* San Francisco: ICS Press. A treatise on the defining features, history, and benefits of currency boards.

Roubini, Nouriel. 1998. "The Case against Currency Boards: Debunking 10 Myths about the Benefits of Currency Boards." Downloadable from http://www.rgemonitor.com/. A succinct and passionate summary of the cons of currency boards.

Schwartz, Anna. 1993. "Currency Boards: Their Past, Present, and Possible Future Role." *Carnegie-Rochester Conference Series on Public Policy* 39: 147–88.

Williamson, John. 1995. *What Role for Currency Boards?* Washington, DC: Institute for International Economics. Schwartz and Williamson each offer thoughtful and thorough analyses.

SLAVI SLAVOV

■ currency competition

Traditionally, *currency competition* refers to competition between privately issued monies or between privately issued and government-issued monies for use as means of payments. This entry will focus on such competition. Competition between government-issued monies—the pound sterling and the euro, for example—is discussed in the entry on multiple currencies.

Types of Money To understand the ideas related to currency competition it is useful to define a few terms. First, *commodity money* is money that has some intrinsic value. The value is embedded in the commodity that makes the coin. Gold and silver coins are examples of commodity monies. In principle, it is possible to melt such coins and the resulting metal would sell for a value approximately equal to that of the coins. In contrast, *fiat money* is intrinsically worthless. The paper on which a $20 bill is printed is worth very little. The value of such a bill comes from the belief that other people will accept it in exchange for goods or services. *Inside money* is a claim on the assets of the issuer of that money. It is a liability of the issuer. Traveler's checks are an example of inside money, as the issuer must, by law, repay such a check. Another example is bank deposits. In contrast, *outside money* is not a claim on its issuer. An issuer of outside money does not have a legal obligation to exchange its notes against some goods or services. Government-issued notes are examples of outside money. Central banks are not required to back the notes they issue with any kind of commodity.

Hayek and Currency Competition The economist Friedrich Hayek introduced the idea of currency competition in 1976. At that time, a number of countries were experiencing high inflation. The collapse of the Bretton Woods system of fixed exchange rates in 1971 had removed a constraint on the conduct of monetary policy for many monetary authorities. It also removed any remaining link between currencies and a metallic standard (gold in this case). Freed from these constraints, many central banks increased their money supply too quickly, spurring inflation.

Although there was broad agreement that inflation was undesirable, it was not clear how to give monetary authorities incentives to maintain the value of their currencies. Hayek reasoned that the lack of incentives came from the monopoly that monetary authorities held over the issuance of money. Competition from private issuers could force these authorities to maintain the value of their currencies. Indeed, if a money lost too much of its value, consumers and businesses would have the option to use another money. Hayek proposed to give banks the authority to issue notes that would compete with government-issued currency.

The interest generated by Hayek's proposal led a number of economists to study historical episodes during which banks were allowed to issue notes. Such episodes typically involved commodity money, however. Since the value of commodity money is intrinsic, there is not much scope for an issuer of commodity money to modify the value of its currency.

Economists have also been interested in competing inside monies. Such monies are typically denoted in some outside money, however. For example,

traveler's checks are often denominated in U.S. dollars. For this reason, it does not appear that inside money can affect the incentives of the issuer of outside money in the way Hayek intended.

What Hayek specifically had in mind was competition between *outside fiat* monies. He proposed to allow banks to issue intrinsically worthless notes that would not be liabilities of these institutions.

Private Issue of Outside Money For the kind of competition that Hayek proposed to occur, private institutions must be able to issue outside money. A number of economists have argued that a time inconsistency problem makes private issuance impossible. These economists point out that if a private institution could issue valued fiat outside money, profit maximization would induce the institution to issue money up to the point where the marginal benefit of an extra unit of money equaled its marginal cost. That is, since the cost of producing an additional unit of fiat money is negligible, the institution would issue money up to the point where it was worthless. Moreover, the issuing institution would have no obligation to redeem the note for something of value since it would be issuing outside money. Anticipating this outcome, nobody would want to hold the money in the first place.

Private issuance of fiat outside money may be possible provided agents hold certain expectations. The key is to find a way to prevent issuers from increasing their supply of notes to the point where the value of such notes is zero. Suppose everybody believes that the notes of a private issuer have value if the number of notes issued is less than some number. This threshold number is common knowledge. If the number of notes issued exceeds the threshold, then everyone believes that these notes are worthless. A serial number on a note indicates the quantity of notes issued previously.

Consider someone who is offered a note with a serial number that is greater than the threshold level above which notes are no longer valued. This person believes that nobody will be willing to accept the note in exchange for goods or services in the future. Hence, this person will not accept the note, and the belief that the note has no value is self-fulfilling. This kind of belief limits the ability of the issuer to print too many notes, which makes private issuance possible.

A Concept for the Future Although private issue of outside fiat currencies is possible in theory, there are few examples of such currencies. Some currencies used in online multiplayer games may be the best examples of fiat outside money. These currencies are almost costless to produce and are not backed by any asset. Moreover, online auction sites, such as eBay, provide a platform on which such currencies trade for U.S. dollars in a way that is similar to a currency exchange market. Although we are still far from Hayek's vision of currency competition, technological progress and new information technologies could make it happen.

See also discipline; dollar standard; dominant currency; money supply; multiple currencies; quantity theory of money; reserve currency; seigniorage; time inconsistency problem; vehicle currency

FURTHER READING

Martin, Antoine, and Stacey L. Schreft. 2006. "Currency Competition: A Partial Vindication of Hayek." *Journal of Monetary Economics* 53: 2085–2111. Provides a proof of the possibility of circulation of private outside money in the context of a formal model and a number of additional references.

ANTOINE MARTIN

■ currency convertibility

See convertibility

■ currency crisis

Currency crises are among the most dramatic events in global financial markets. They generally involve large outflows of funds from currencies that investors fear may devalue or sharply depreciate. When a government lowers the level at which a currency is pegged to other currencies this is referred to as a devaluation, while a fall in the value of a market determined exchange rate is called depreciation. To keep their currencies from depreciating in the face of exchange market pressure, governments must run down their foreign currency reserves, borrow from abroad, hike interest rates, and/or impose capital controls to slow down outflows. If they are successful, the speculation dies down, at least for a while, and the currency value is maintained. More often, exchange rates are eventually forced to adjust. Although the vast majority of currency crises involve downward pressure on currencies, sometime there are strong market pressures for surplus countries to let their currencies appreciate; a vivid example is China beginning in the early 2000s. Crises can vary in their effects as well as in their causes, but they have in common a high degree of exchange market pressure.

International speculators are widely blamed for generating crises, especially by government officials eager to shift the blame from themselves. In reality, however, much of the pressure usually comes from "normal" domestic and international firms that are trying to protect themselves against losses rather than to generate speculative gains. Even the speculators are more often the messengers that there are problems than the independent cause of currency crises. Speculative attacks occur when international businesses and investors anticipate a change in the value of the currency, thus adding speculative outflows to the underlying balance of payments deficit.

Crises, though always uncomfortable, can sometimes have good effects, stimulating policy reforms and promoting economic recovery. In other cases, however, especially in developing countries with weak financial systems and considerable debt denominated in foreign currency, the effects of crises can include large recessions and widespread suffering. This is particularly likely when a currency crisis either leads to or was generated by a domestic banking crisis—a so-called "twin crisis."

In general, the underlying causes of a currency crisis are inconsistencies between a country's exchange rate policy and its domestic economic policies so that the currency is either over- or undervalued relative to the currencies of other countries. Economists have developed a variety of theoretical models to explain currency crises, and most of these models can be classified into three types. First-generation models consider cases where the government is either unable or unwilling to correct inconsistencies between its exchange rate and other domestic policy goals. As these become more serious, a crisis eventually becomes inevitable. Second-generation crisis models analyze cases where these inconsistencies place the economy in a "zone of vulnerability," making a crisis possible but not inevitable. In these cases, the potential for a crisis outbreak depends critically on market perceptions of the government's willingness and ability to take corrective action. Finally, newer crisis models have focused on financial sector weaknesses and the role of politics in the emergence of currency crises.

First-Generation Crises: Fundamental Disequilibriums The classic theoretical explanations for currency crises—the so-called first-generation models—focus on fundamental economic disequilibriums such as large government budget deficits. In these models, governments are assumed to pursue fiscal and monetary policies that are inconsistent with maintaining their fixed or slowly adjusting pegged exchange rate regimes. The resulting balance-of-payments deficits are financed by running down foreign reserves. When the level of reserves falls to a certain threshold, there is a sudden balance-of-payments crisis. Capital flight by domestic residents escalates, even if the country has borrowed little from abroad. This leads to a loss of reserves and forces the government to devalue its currency or float the exchange rate. In these models, expansionary policies and the resulting bad economic fundamentals push the economy into crisis.

The particular causes of the fundamental disequilibriums in past crises have been varied. They often result from a lack of fiscal discipline, but first-generation-type currency crises have also been caused by budget deficits in the center country of a pegged exchange rate system (the center country is the nation to whose currency another country's currency is pegged) or external developments such as export slumps. These problems generally coincide with weak governments facing strong political pressures

that prevent them from addressing the emerging disequilibriums by cutting spending or raising taxes to keep monetary expansion under control. Very often, this inability to balance the budget results in high rates of inflation. When economic problems emerge, markets initially often give governments the benefit of the doubt, especially when they have large stores of international reserves. But as imbalances continue, market participants frequently realize well before governments do that the problems are not temporary. The capital outflows that result from this realization involve not only currency speculators but also businesspeople wanting to hedge against the risk of exchange rate adjustments. These flows in turn tend to increase payments imbalances further and eventually lead to a crisis and a forced adjustment.

Examples of first-generation-style crises include the currency crises of Latin American countries in the post–Bretton Woods period, such as Mexico in 1976 and Brazil on several occasions. In these cases, the government financed large deficits by creating more money, resulting in inflation. Combined with pegged or slowly adjusting exchange rates, such high levels of inflation led to progressive overvaluation of exchange rates and generated numerous currency crises. Inflation does not need to be in triple or quadruple digits in order to generate currency crises, nor are inflation-driven crises a threat only to developing countries, as demonstrated by Italy's crisis in 1992. As a member of the European Monetary System (EMS), Italy had pegged its exchange rate to the deutschmark. Although its inflation rate was far below triple digits, it was still well above the inflation rates of most of its partners in the EMS, and in particular higher than that of the center country, Germany. The resulting disparity eventually led to a currency crisis in 1992. Large budget deficits can at times cause currency problems even if they do not lead to monetary accommodation and rising inflation; one example of this is the 2001 crisis in Argentina. As part of a "shock therapy" program designed to break out of a cycle of high and rising inflation, Argentina had adopted a currency board in 1991 that took money creation out of the hands of the government by fixing the domestic currency to a foreign anchor currency, and maintaining full convertibility between domestic currency and the foreign anchor currency. This proved to be highly successful in bringing inflation under control but fiscal profligacy continued. As external developments contributed to a worsening of the situation, the result was a combined debt and currency crisis that ended in abandonment of the currency board and default on the government's foreign debt.

The collapse of the Bretton Woods system in the 1970s provides an example of an exchange rate system failing due to budget deficits in the center country (in this case the United States). For domestic political reasons, the U.S. government delayed tax increases required to pay for the large increases in expenditures associated with the Vietnam War. Seeking to prevent interest rates from escalating, the Federal Reserve Board financed a sizable portion of the resulting budget deficits with monetary accommodation. The consequent overheating of the U.S. economy led to increasing balance-of-payments deficits and ultimately to the currency crisis that was the final straw leading to the widespread abandonment of the Bretton Woods regime of adjustably pegged exchange rates.

Another type of first-generation crisis that need not be directly caused by bad domestic policies involves export slumps. Generally, monetary and fiscal policies that are sustainable under good circumstances become unsustainable when circumstances take a turn for the worse. In a country whose government's budget depends on export revenues, a sharp decrease in those revenues can cause a similarly sharp change in investor expectations of that country's ability to meet its debt-servicing obligations. A clear example of this is the 1998 Russian ruble crisis. By the mid-1990s Russia had tamed the runaway inflation that followed the breakup of the Soviet Union and its economic prospects had substantially improved. The domestic coalition favoring economic reform and stability was fragile, however. In the aftermath of the 1997 Asian crisis, oil prices fell to half of their precrisis levels due to decreased demand for oil in Asia. As a result, the Yeltsin government,

dependent as it was on oil revenues to fund its fiscal programs, found its treasury rapidly being emptied. Initially investors' belief that Russia was "too big to fail" and their perception that the Russian government was attempting to alleviate the situation by negotiating a loan package from the International Monetary Fund (IMF) and seeking to implement dramatic fiscal reforms caused most investors to give Russia the benefit of the doubt. After the IMF negotiations failed and the Russian legislature, the Duma, removed the most critical components of Yeltsin's proposed fiscal reform plan, however, it became clear that Russia was not going to be able to adjust its policy enough to avoid a fiscal crisis. In August 1998, there was a severe speculative attack on the ruble, and the Russian government announced that it would no longer support the crawling peg and would default on its foreign-held debt. The remaining investors immediately and frantically sought to divest themselves of the Russian liabilities and the ruble plummeted.

Second-Generation Crises: The Role of Expectations A surprising feature of a number of the currency crises of the 1990s was that they hit countries whose macroeconomic fundamentals were not particularly bad. First-generation models were unable to explain, much less predict, many of these crises. In response, a "second generation" of crisis models was developed that focused on investors' expectations and governments' conflicting policy objectives and predicted that speculative attacks could occur when a country's fundamentals were merely in an intermediate or vulnerable zone. Although these models retained the assumption that speculators would not attack countries with good fundamentals, they showed that once a country finds itself in a vulnerable zone, a change in the private sector's expectations about the future course of government policy can trigger a second-generation crisis.

In contrast to the passive role of policymakers in first-generation models, governments in second-generation models are able to take corrective measures, though they may prefer not to. For many governments, exchange rate stability is only one objective among many. Governments often make a trade-off between maintaining a pegged exchange rate and achieving other policy goals (such as low unemployment) that gain political salience when there is an economic downturn. In such situations speculators can lose confidence in the government's commitment to the exchange rate peg and can decide suddenly to attack the currency. The cyclical state of the economy can thus become an important factor in these models, since the tight monetary policies necessary to defend a currency are politically more costly when the economy is in recession than when it is booming.

Speculators are also collectively in a position to influence the future course of policy in second-generation models. The greater the proportion of speculators who expect the government to defend the peg at the expense of a worsening recession, the smaller the capital outflows and the more feasible a defense of the exchange rate peg. On the other hand, if most speculators bet against a defense, capital outflows will be larger and the costs of a defense will be higher. Since these outflows themselves can be detrimental to a government's ability to defend the pegged exchange rate, market expectations can thus prove to be self-fulfilling. Such speculation is not irrational, nor is it in itself destabilizing in the sense of going contrary to the fundamentals. It is, however, sometimes thought of as destabilizing in the sense that it can be the proximate cause of a crisis that may not necessarily have been inevitable.

In formal second-generation models, shifts in investor expectations from optimistic to pessimistic are treated as arbitrary. The resulting outcomes are therefore often referred to as "sunspot equilibria." This can give a misleading impression, however, since in the typical cases of major speculative attacks on currencies, certain events trigger the shift from a "good" to a "bad" equilibrium. In the past, such triggers have included the assassination of a presidential candidate (Mexico in 1994) and crises elsewhere that lead to a reevaluation of underemphasized fundamentals (the wake-up call concerning financial sector weakness that was a major aspect of the contagion in Asia in 1997).

An example of what many experts consider to be a second-generation crisis is the 1992–93 crisis in the EMS, particularly the speculative attacks on the French franc. The proximate cause of this crisis was the reunification of Germany, which led to a large increase in German government expenditures. As German policymakers were unwilling to offset this higher spending with higher taxes, a large budget deficit emerged. In response, the Bundesbank (Germany's central bank) raised interest rates. Since Germany was the EMS center country, the logic of the currency system required all other EMS members to tighten monetary policy as well, even though this ran counter to the requirements of their macroeconomic situation at the time. As we have already discussed, this generated crises that led to the breakdown of the EMS system. The crises in Italy and, arguably, the United Kingdom were quite consistent with first-generation models since both the lira and the pound appeared to be overvalued. The 1993 attack on the French franc was not as easy to explain, however, since some of France's fundamentals were even stronger than Germany's.

What proved to be more important was the lack of willingness of the individual EMS countries to adjust to the mutual payments imbalances that had emerged. Here Germany held the cards. Even so the EMS member states put considerable pressure on the Bundesbank to lower interest rates, but the independent German Bundesbank refused to back off its tight monetary policies. When it became known that Germany would also not continue providing short-term financing to maintain the pegged rates of the EMS, the only alternatives left for the other EMS members were depreciation or a substantial tightening of their own macroeconomic policies. Given the state of the economy in many of these countries, international financial market participants therefore increasingly questioned policymakers' willingness to implement policies that would further slow growth and increase unemployment. Eventually, financial markets launched speculative attacks, forcing governments to choose between unpalatable options: abandoning the peg, which they had worked hard to maintain, or facing a deepening recession. In the case of France, for example, the authorities withstood several bouts of speculative pressure before finally devaluing the franc in 1993.

The fact that France's fundamentals had not been particularly bad led many commentators, especially French officials, to conclude that France had been the innocent victim of destabilizing speculation. France was indeed an innocent victim in this case, but of geopolitical developments in Germany and its own commitment to the European pegged-rate system, not of capricious speculators. This illustrates that crises do not always fit neatly within one type of crisis model or another. Some economists consider France's crisis to be a classic second-generation example, but others argue that it was more of a first-generation crisis because of a fundamental disequilibrium generated by Germany's huge budget deficit. The crisis certainly had elements emphasized in both types of models, as did the 1997 Asian crisis, to which we now turn.

Financial Sector Weakness Most of the financial world and many economists were shocked in 1997 by the occurrence and the severity of the Asian financial crises. A crisis in the Thai exchange market had been at least partially anticipated, as there had been concerns about the possible overvaluation of the baht for some time. But the spread of the crisis to other countries was almost entirely unanticipated. Most—if not all—of the affected countries had enjoyed low inflation and robust economic growth for quite some time and appeared by and large to have strong enough economic fundamentals to preclude the type of crises predicted by first- and second-generation crisis models. In order to explain these events, economists developed what is sometimes referred to as the "third generation" of crisis models, which place a greater emphasis on the microfoundations of currency crises. Among these refinements are the considerations of financial sector weakness, moral hazard, contagion, and stock as well as flow disequilibriums.

Traditional macroeconomic models paid little attention to the financial sector, and the crises of the 1990s demonstrated that this was a major mistake. The discovery of serious weaknesses in financial

sectors can generate major changes in international capital flows, especially where countries have weak international liquidity positions (i.e., high short-term foreign debt relative to international reserves). Such a situation can quickly turn into a run on the currency without requiring any outright speculation; the scrabble to cover open positions could be sufficient. Indeed, many of the flows of funds during the Asian crisis were of this risk-covering nature.

One of the factors that can contribute to financial sector weakness is a high level of moral hazard, referring in the currency crisis context to the propensity to lend, borrow, or invest in enterprises under circumstances that would usually be considered excessively risky. In some cases, lending institutions or borrowers may have had either explicit or implicit guarantees that the government would cover any losses should the loan or investment fail to return a profit. In this way the contingent liability burden is shifted from the lender, investor, or borrower to the government, creating the situation described by economist Paul Krugman (1996) as a bet of "heads, I win; tails, the taxpayer loses." If this practice is sufficiently prevalent, even a minor shock to the economy could result in a dramatic increase in government financing to prop up banks whose nonperforming loans have suddenly rendered them insolvent.

Many of the other factors described earlier, most notably financial sector weakness, also played key roles in precipitating the Asian crises of 1997. Although public finances in all of the crisis countries were relatively strong by conventional measures, domestic financial sectors were in bad shape. Both the high levels of nonperforming loans and heavy unhedged foreign borrowing were generated at least in part by problems of moral hazard. The combination of moral hazard and weak risk management and regulatory systems had led to many ill-advised loans, so that in a number of countries the financial sectors were suffering from serious solvency and liquidity problems. While good statistics were not generally available to reveal these problems, international funds continued to pour into these emerging markets because of their apparently strong macroeconomic statistics and as a result of capital account liberalization.

In July 1997, the already overvalued Thai baht came under speculative attack when the severity of Thailand's problems with nonperforming loans in the financial sector became apparent. Highlighting Thailand's financial sector problems, this crisis served as a wake-up call to international financial markets, alerting them that Thailand's unhedged foreign borrowing was much riskier than many had believed. This in turn prompted foreign investors to reassess the vulnerability of their investments to financial sector risks. Thailand was not the only country found to have serious problems in the financial sector, and investors' assessments of some countries previously perceived to have well-aligned exchange rates, such as Korea and Taiwan, changed (those exchange rates were now seen as overvalued), prompting a run for the exits. Although financial sector problems were not the only contributing factors (as mentioned, the Thai baht was overvalued and political instability in Indonesia contributed importantly to the length and depth of the crisis there), the Asian crisis did highlight that crises could occur even when data on traditional economic fundamentals indicated a strong economic situation.

The Political Economy of Currency Crises Recent research has also recognized that political considerations can have an important influence on crises through a number of channels. Since economic policies are generally determined through the political process (one exception being when monetary policy is administered by an effectively independent central bank), political developments can have a strong influence on expectations about future economic policies. Thus political instability and expectations about the election of new administrations can have an important effect on capital flows even before there is any actual change in policy. Political considerations are also one of the major causes of the development of inconsistencies among policies that lead to fundamental disequilibriums. Because the costs of corrective action often show up faster than the benefits, short-run political pressures can lead to delays in undertaking needed policy adjustments, especially if elections are approaching (see Willett 2007).

One key example of how political considerations can play a role in the outbreak of crisis is the 1999 crisis in Brazil. Past fiscal excesses had left Brazil with a large public debt burden, which was substantial but manageable so long as interest rates remained moderately low. In 1999, polls increasingly indicated that leftist presidential candidate Lula da Silva and another leftist politician were likely to prevail in the impending elections. Lula's past as a trade unionist raised doubts among market participants over whether Brazil's sound economic policies would be continued after the election. Although a return to hyperinflation was not likely, the high debt levels meant that even a moderate loosening of fiscal policy might be sufficient to force default. As a consequence, a crisis of confidence and a speculative attack on the real ensued. It is important to note that this crisis was precipitated not by actually implemented policies, but rather on the evaluation of expected future policy.

The 1994 Mexican crisis provides another example of the importance of political events in understanding crises. The country had successfully brought down inflation from triple- to single-digit levels, but the combination of strong capital inflows and a slow rate of depreciation designed to limit domestic wage increases had resulted in a large current account deficit and a substantially appreciated real exchange rate. Thus although Mexico's domestic economic fundamentals were strong, the economy was vulnerable to a drop in capital inflows, and—as with the Brazilian crisis—to severe shocks to political stability. In this case, the shock was the assassination of the leading opposition (and proreform) presidential candidate, which prompted rapid reassessment on the part of investors as to whether necessary reforms in Mexico would be implemented, along with fears of a more volatile political climate. The combination of monetary tightening in the United States, temporary preelection loosening of fiscal policy in Mexico, and the emergence of domestic political instability brought the dreaded sharp fall in inflows and the crisis was on.

Political scientist Andrew MacIntyre (1999) has argued that Thailand and Indonesia illustrate ways in which different types of governments can exacerbate their vulnerability to crises. Thailand's political system with its large coalition governments tended to produce great policy stability (or paralysis) due to the difficulties in making policy changes. Intracoalitional politics caused budget and financial regulation reforms to be delayed, further weakening confidence in the Thai financial sector and generating uncertainty about the government's capacity to act once the crisis occurred. In contrast, Indonesia's political system was highly centralized and imposed little constraint on executive action. This led to its own set of problems by opening the way for erratic policy behavior. When crisis spread from Thailand to Indonesia in late July 1997, the Suharto government responded decisively and preemptively by widening the band within which the rupiah was allowed to fluctuate from 8 percent to 12 percent. As the rupiah continued to slide, Suharto appeared to be taking appropriate action by agreeing to a series of dramatic reforms as part of an IMF assistance program. Appearances can be deceiving, however, and in this case they certainly were, as Suharto quietly reneged on many of these reforms and as members of his government and family openly undermined others. It is not surprising that investor confidence in the Indonesian government plummeted, not because investors doubted whether Suharto *could* make the necessary reforms but instead because they doubted that he *would*. Where Thailand's case can be characterized as inaction in the face of a looming crisis, Indonesia's can be characterized as action—but of the wrong kind.

Crisis Prevention and Management There is widespread agreement that it is usually far easier to prevent crises than to fix them once they occur. Unfortunately, prevention is not easy to accomplish. Although analysis has often been able to identify sound reasons for crises after the fact, these reasons are not always easy to identify beforehand. The perception of crises as arising from the unjustified behavior of fickle financial markets doubtlessly stems at least in part from this dilemma. Significant advances have been made in the development of economic "early warning systems" for crises, though these tend to detect occasions when a country is vulnerable to a crisis rather than predict precisely when a crisis will occur.

Even when the threat of a crisis is unmistakable, however, countries often fail to take preventive actions in time. Sadly, it often takes the actual outbreak of crises to prompt major policy adjustments, as governments often find it politically difficult to take the actions needed to reduce vulnerability. Consequently, governments are often observed to initially respond to potential crises by addressing capital flows rather than macroeconomic fundamentals—by running down international currency reserves, increasing domestic interest rates to make the country a more attractive capital destination, or implementing restrictions on the flow of capital into or out of the country. When the country is facing a temporary liquidity crunch, such measures may be all that is required (see the 1997 case of Hong Kong, where some of these measures were successfully used to avoid the most serious potential repercussions of the crisis). If, however, the country faces a fundamental disequilibrium (such as is described in first-generation crisis models), such measures can only delay, not prevent, crises; borrowing and running down reserves cannot indefinitely offset the effects of a fundamental disequilibrium. In such cases, reserve cushions can only give countries the option of adjusting more gradually. Second- and third-generation models, however, provide insights into ways that strong reserve positions can help avoid crises. When countries are in vulnerable zones, shocks that would generate a run on the currency of a country with high levels of short-term foreign debt relative to its international reserves might not generate such a run if the country had a strong international liquidity position. In other words, although strong reserve positions can do little to deal with insolvency (fundamental disequilibrium) problems, they are a valuable instrument for countries with merely vulnerable fundamentals.

The effectiveness of high interest rate policies and capital controls has been the subject of considerable controversy. Because so many factors are typically at work during a crisis it is hard to accurately measure the effects of particular policies. High interest rates may send an ambiguous signal to currency markets, as excessively high interest rates may indicate to the markets that the country is in desperate need of capital—not an encouraging sign if the market is already concerned about the safety of investing in that country (Russia in 1998 provides an example of this dynamic). During the Asian crisis, high interest rates in Indonesia did not keep the rupiah from plummeting, because it was not clear at the time whether the high interest rates reflected tight monetary policy or premiums for inflation and political risk.

The effectiveness of capital controls also depends a great deal on how they are interpreted by the market. Capital controls can be seen as prudential measures taken to protect an otherwise stable economy from overly volatile international capital markets, in which case they can be effective in reassuring foreign investors. Capital controls can also be seen, however, as stopgap measures intended to prevent capital from flowing out of an already risky economy. In this case, the implementation of capital controls can itself be a signal to the market that the economy is in worse shape than previously thought. As with international reserves, the introduction of capital controls seems more promising when the economy is in a vulnerable zone than when it exhibits strong fundamental disequilibriums. The introduction of capital controls by Malaysia in 1998 has been the subject of different evaluations along these lines. Probably the best we can say about the Malaysian case is that the controls proved to be neither the disaster predicted by some critics nor the panacea envisioned by some advocates.

Recent crises also remind us that international financial flows can be fickle and that being the darling of international investors today is not a safe indicator of future stability. Although there remains considerable disagreement among economists about the conditions (if any) under which direct controls on international capital flows can be desirable, there is little disagreement that such flows and financial sectors more generally need to be subject to effective prudential regulation. Such policies need to be carefully crafted: in many countries, policies have contributed as much or more to the generation of crises (through moral hazard and other perverse incentives) as to good prudential oversight.

One of the most notable characteristics of recent currency crises has been the frequency with which they are associated with efforts to maintain various types of adjustably pegged exchange rate regimes. This phenomenon, which has been labeled "the unstable middle hypothesis," was a basic cause of the breakdown of the regime of adjustably pegged exchange rates of the Bretton Woods system. Few analysts dispute that without effective capital controls such adjustably pegged exchange rate regimes are highly prone to crises in the face of substantial international capital mobility. The debate is whether it is necessary to move all the way to one extreme or the other—hard fixes or relatively free floats—to substantially reduce vulnerability to crisis, or whether moving to crawling bands or managed floats is sufficient.

The role of the IMF in crisis prevention and management has been the subject of considerable controversy. Although far from perfect, its ability to identify emerging crisis situations has been much better than its ability to get countries to adopt the necessary preventative actions; the ability of its "seal of approval" to calm crisis situations has also suffered substantial erosion. The IMF has displayed considerable learning, but efforts at substantial reform of the international financial architecture have been largely unsuccessful, and the IMF's ability to act as a crisis manager and international lender of last resort has, so far, only marginally improved. This has resulted in greater self-help efforts undertaken by many countries, especially in Asia, to accumulate high levels of international reserves at both the country and the regional levels. Crisis liquidity is clearly most efficiently provided at the international level, but the failure of substantial reforms at that level makes these individual and regional efforts quite understandable.

See also asymmetric information; balance of payments; banking crisis; Bretton Woods system; capital controls;

capital flight; capital mobility; contagion; currency board arrangement (CBA); early warning systems; exchange market pressure; financial crisis; foreign exchange intervention; hot money and sudden stops; impossible trinity; International Monetary Fund (IMF); International Monetary Fund conditionality; International Monetary Fund surveillance; international reserves; lender of last resort; speculation; spillovers

FURTHER READING

Angkinand, Apanard, Jie Li, and Thomas D. Willett. 2006. "Measures of Currency Crises: A Survey." Claremont Working Papers 2006-06. Downloadable from http://www.cgu.edu/include/2006-06.pdf. Surveys a number of currency crisis indexes, compares their compositions, and discusses which indexes may be appropriately used under which circumstances.

Blustein, Paul. 2005. *And the Money Kept Rolling In . . . and Out: Wall Street, the IMF, and the Bankrupting of Argentina*. New York: Public Affairs. Intended for a general audience, this book provides an insightful account of the Argentine crisis and the roles played by the IMF and American investors.

Buiter, Willem H., Giancarlo Corsetti, and Paolo Pesetti, eds. 1998. *Financial Markets and European Monetary Cooperation: The Lessons of the 1992–93 Exchange Rate Mechanism Crisis*. Cambridge: Cambridge University Press. Provides a historical perspective on exchange rate stability in Europe and presents an interpretation of the European currency crisis of 1992–93.

Eichengreen, Barry. 1999. *Toward a New International Financial Architecture: A Practical Post-Asia Agenda*. Washington, DC: Institute for International Economics. Reviews proposals for reform of the international financial system and national policies to reduce the incidence of currency crises and contagion.

International Monetary Fund, Independent Evaluation Office. 2003. "The IMF and Recent Capital Account Crises: Indonesia, Korea, Brazil." Washington, DC: International Monetary Fund. Downloadable from http://www.imf.org/external/np/ieo/2003/cac/index.htm. Provides a useful critical analysis of the role of the IMF in recent crises and contains numerous references to the relevant literature.

Krugman, Paul. 1996. "Are Currency Crises Self-Fulfilling?" *NBER Macroeconomics Annual*. Washington, DC: National Bureau of Economic Research. Critically assesses the tenets and conclusions of the second-generation currency crisis models.

———. 1998. "What Happened to Asia?" Electronic document. Downloadable from http://web.mit.edu/krugman/www/DISINTER.html.

MacIntyre, Andrew. 1999. "Political Institutions and the Economic Crisis in Thailand and Indonesia." In *The Politics of the Asian Financial Crisis*, edited by T. J. Pempel. Ithaca, NY: Cornell University Press, 143–162. Offers an interesting comparison between the political attributes of Thailand and Indonesia, and traces their respective responses to the onset of the Asian crisis.

Pilbeam, Keith. 2006. *International Finance*. 3d ed. New York: Palgrave Macmillan. Chapter 17 of this introductory textbook contains an easy-to-read summary of currency crisis theory and provides some illustrative examples.

Rajan, Ramkishen. 2001. *(Ir)relevance of Currency-Crisis Theory to the Devaluation and Collapse of the Thai Baht*. Princeton Studies in International Economics No. 88 (February). Discusses the Thai crisis in the context of various generations of currency crisis models.

Saxena, Sweta C. 2001. "The Changing Nature of Currency Crises." *Journal of Economic Surveys* 18 (3): 321–50. Traces the changes in the currency crisis literature from 1979 through the post-Asia crisis models.

Willett, Thomas D. 2007. "Why the Middle Is Unstable." *The World Economy* 30 (5): 709–32. Discusses the political and economic reasons why delayed adjustments tend to make adjustable-peg exchange rate regimes particularly crisis-prone. It contains numerous references to the theoretical and empirical literature by both economists and political scientists.

Willett, Thomas D., Ekniti Nitithanprapras, Isriya Nitithanprapas, and Sunil Rongala. 2004. "The Asian Crises Reexamined." *Asian Economic Papers* 3: 32–87. Presents an overview of the various theories explaining the 1997–98 Asian crises and reexamines the evidence concerning the causes.

ERIC M. P. CHIU, STEFANIE WALTER, JOSHUA C. WALTON, AND THOMAS D. WILLETT

■ currency substitution and dollarization

Currency substitution refers to a broad set of conditions under which two or more currencies can be used as media of exchange. If currency substitution is a continuum within which domestic and foreign currencies cocirculate, dollarization occurs at one end of that continuum, when the foreign currency—most times, the U.S. dollar—is preeminent in domestic transactions in goods and/or assets. Since 2002, the term *euroization* has also emerged. Dollarization may occur either as a formal decision of governments or as the choice of most economic agents in a country. These are known as de jure (official) and de facto (unofficial) dollarization, respectively.

Currency Substitution Currency substitution may refer to foreign currency, deposits denominated in foreign currency units held in domestic banks, or to deposits of domestic residents at foreign banks. The currency reports of the U.S. Treasury are used to determine where U.S. dollars go abroad, but dollars that travel between countries outside the U.S. are not traced (see Feige et al. 2003.) Moreover, shipments of currency in amounts less than $10,000 are not recorded. Several estimates in a 2003 U.S. Treasury report put $300 billion to $400 billion of U.S. currency outside the country, with 25 percent elsewhere in the Western Hemisphere and about 40 percent in Europe and the former Soviet Union.

Motives for currency substitution can come from seeking money as either a store of value or as a medium of exchange. Often economic agents will hold U.S. currency for store-of-value considerations or for use in larger transactions, while the local currency cocirculates for smaller purchases. This characterizes most of the Latin American experience with currency substitution. At risk of loss of their monies due to confiscatory currency reforms of the past, many households in Eastern Europe in the late 1980s held wealth in foreign currencies because they had no alternative assets available. On the other hand, sometimes foreign currencies are needed to provide media of exchange because local currency is in short supply. This can occur, for example, when the central bank is defending an overvalued exchange rate peg.

Institutional factors play a major role in the evolution of currency substitution. In Latin America, for example, most countries have suppressed or limited the holding of foreign currency deposits for a time, only later to remove restrictions as the demand for foreign currency has grown. This has an obvious impact on the quantity of foreign currency held. Other countries have permitted foreign currency holdings from the start (the most extreme case being Panama's decision to adopt the U.S. dollar as the sole currency). A country's policies with regard to currency substitution can and do change over time. Increasing financial development leads to more alternatives to foreign currency as a store of value and removes the necessity of restrictions on its holding.

Once currency substitution occurs, it can become irreversible through what is sometimes referred to as *dollarization hysteresis*. In short, each agent holds currencies based on what it expects other agents to hold. Once other currencies are introduced, a substantial shock must occur to induce agents to return to holding just local currency (Feige et al. 2003).

Dollarization De jure, or official, dollarization most often occurs after a period of high inflation, when a country either finds itself unable to create a new domestic currency that would hold value or is unwilling to endure the output loss needed to create credibility. Unofficial, or de facto, dollarization could include currency as well as asset substitution. Feige (2003) provides a breakdown of the separate currency and asset dollarization channels and their relative sizes. For example, there is almost no currency substitution in the Former Yugoslav Republic of Macedonia, but foreign-denominated monetary assets in Macedonian commercial banks are 2.5 times the size of domestic-denominated monetary assets (excluding cash). In general, however, currency and asset substitution indexes are highly positively correlated (i.e., currency substitution and de facto dollarization). We therefore focus on de jure, or official, dollarization.

De jure dollarization benefits countries if they are small and well integrated into world markets, and if their capital is highly mobile (Mundell 2003). Many but not all of the smaller countries of Europe that are not part of the European Monetary Union—Andorra, Kosovo, Montenegro, Monaco, San Marino, and Vatican City—use the euro; only one (Kosovo) has a population of more than 1 million. Many of the island states of the Pacific use the U.S. dollar; a few use Australian or New Zealand dollars. Other states have granted legal tender status to the U.S. dollar and had their own currency circulate alongside. In Panama, which has the longest such history, the dollar is used for most transactions, but Panamanian coins circulate for minor trade. Panama is also highly integrated into the international capital markets. Guatemala and the Bahamas are other examples of de jure dollarized economies in the Western Hemisphere.

In many instances, de jure dollarization occurs through the creation of a currency board, such as in Argentina, but it need not be so. Ecuador makes an interesting example. The largest country by population to dollarize, it chose to abandon the local currency, the sucre, after that currency had depreciated precipitously at the end of 1999. The government declared the dollar legal tender, and the sucre was removed from circulation. The International Monetary Fund sent a technical assistance mission in support of dollarization.

Although official dollarization has helped many countries by imposing monetary discipline, its history in creating fiscal discipline is more mixed. Domestic currencies can gain revenue for a country through seigniorage; dollarization limits the ability of governments to collect an inflation tax (Willett and Banaian 1995), and so dollarization may remove any temptation for governments to resort to it. As a result, many economists have hypothesized that dollarization should produce fiscal discipline since additional spending would more likely be paid for with taxes. But as long as a government can borrow, fiscal discipline is muted. Moreover, if interest rates are reduced because of dollarization and greater monetary policy credibility, fiscal policy may become *more* lax. Fiscal deficits in dollarized Panama were higher than in nearby Latin American countries between 1970 and 1998 (Goldfajn and Olivares 2000). Additionally, dollarization through a currency board

did not help Argentina's fiscal authorities become more restrained. Therefore another expected benefit of dollarization—lower interest rates—has not always been realized.

The most ardent supporters of dollarization argue that when it comes from the decisions of individuals and is the result of a competition between note issuers, it provides benefits to an economy. Allowing the choice protects the property rights of households and ensures that their earnings cannot be confiscated by the inflation tax. Panama's adoption of the U.S. dollar as the sole legal tender in 1904 stands as the leading case of dollarization in most analyses.

Although many economists argue that the costs of dollarization are real and the benefits ephemeral, others argue that the benefits can be large only if the commitment to dollarization is made official, either through the abandonment of the domestic currency or through the creation of a currency board arrangement. But perhaps the biggest objection to dollarization is the country's lost pride. Few countries come into existence without some national fervor, and that fervor often seeks expression in historical pictures of the native landscape on paper, in the form of domestic currency. Many new currencies quickly become subject to inflationary pressures, but that seldom stops the next new country from thinking that it can do better and celebrating independence with new fiat money.

See also common currency; currency board arrangement (CBA); discipline; euro; exchange rate regimes; international reserves; money supply; multiple currencies; optimum currency area (OCA) theory; seigniorage

FURTHER READING

Calvo, Guillermo A. 2000. "Testimony on Dollarization." Presented before the Subcommittee on Domestic and Monetary Policy Committee on Banking and Financial Services, Washington, DC, June 22. A critical review of the discussion of using dollars in Latin America and the issues with remitting seigniorage revenues back to those governments.

Feige, Edgar L. 2003. "The Dynamics of Currency Substitution, Asset Substitution, and de Facto Dollarization and Euroization in Transition Countries." *Comparative*

Economic Studies 45 (3): 358–83. Provides a classification of types of dollarization with an application to transition economies.

Feige, Edgar L., Michael Faulend, Velimer Šonje, and Vedran Šošić. 2003. "Unofficial Dollarization in Latin America: Currency Substitution, Network Externalities, and Irreversibility." In *The Dollarization Debate*, edited by Dominick Salvatore, James W. Dean, and Thomas D. Willett. Oxford: Oxford University Press, 46–70. Contains an overview of the amount of dollarization that has happened in Latin America.

Goldfajn, Ilan, and Gino Olivares. 2000. "Is Adopting Full Dollarization the Solution? A Look at the Evidence." Working paper. Rio de Janeiro, Brazil: Pontifícia Universidade Católica do Rio de Janeiro. Reviews the history of complete dollarization in Panama.

Hanke, Steve H. 2003. "Money and the Rule of Law in Ecuador." *Policy Reform* 6 (3): 131–45. Reviews the decision of the Ecuadorian government to give up its local currency in order to solve chronic high inflation.

Mizen, Paul, and Eric J. Pentecost. 1996. "Currency Substitution in Theory and Practice." In *The Macroeconomics of International Currencies: Theory, Policy, and Evidence*, edited by Paul Mizen and Eric J. Pentecost. Cheltenham, UK: Edward Elgar, 8–43. An overview chapter for a book that studies currency substitution.

Mundell, Robert A. 2003. "Currency Areas, Exchange Rate Systems, and International Monetary Reform." In *The Dollarization Debate*, edited by Dominick Salvatore, James W. Dean, and Thomas D. Willett. Oxford: Oxford University Press, 17–45. A useful synopsis of how the optimal currency area approach is applied to the question of dollarization.

Schuler, Kurt. 2005. "Some Theory and History of Dollarization." *Cato Journal* 25 (1): 115–25. A number of economists have proposed dollarization in many developing economies; this article makes the case for its widespread use.

Willett, Thomas D., and King Banaian. 1995. "Currency Substitution, Seigniorage, and the Choice of Currency Policies." In *The Macroeconomics of International Currencies: Theory, Policy, and Evidence*, edited by Paul Mizen and Eric J. Pentecost. Cheltenham, UK: Edward Elgar, 77–95. Uses an optimal inflation tax approach to determine the effects of currency substitution on seigniorage revenues.

Williamson, John E. 2003. "Dollarization Does Not Make Sense Everywhere." In *The Dollarization Debate*, edited by Dominick Salvatore, James W. Dean, and Thomas D. Willett. Oxford: Oxford University Press, 172–76. A more skeptical look at the advice to central banks to give up domestic money issues.

KING BANAIAN

■ current account
See balance of payments

■ customs unions

Customs unions are arrangements among countries in which the parties do two things: (1) agree to allow free trade on products within the customs union, and (2) agree to a common external tariff (CET) with respect to imports from the rest of the world. Customs unions and preferential trade arrangements more generally have become increasingly important in recent years. The most famous example of a customs union is the European Union (EU). Trade among the member states of the EU flows tariff free, and regardless of which country in the EU imports a product, the same tariff is paid. The CET is what distinguishes a customs union from a free trade area. In a free trade area, trade among the member states flows tariff free, but the member states maintain their own distinct external tariff with respect to imports from the rest of the world. The North American Free Trade Agreement is the best known example of a free trade agreement. Canada, the United States, and Mexico do not share a common external tariff, despite allowing free trade on products traded among the three countries.

With the exception of high protection on agricultural products and some "sensitive" products, the EU generally has low tariffs, and the competitive markets of the EU in manufactures have been credited with improving the economic performance of the EU countries. The impact of customs unions among developing countries (or "South-South" customs unions) on the development of the participating countries has been ambiguous at best, however. There are many examples of customs unions among developing countries, including Mercosur (Argentina, Brazil, Paraguay, Uruguay, and, as of 2006, Venezuela), the Central American Common Market (Guatemala, Nicaragua, Costa Rica, Honduras, and El Salvador), the Eurasian Economic Community (Russia, Belarus, Kazakhstan, Kyrgyzstan, Tajikistan, and Uzbekistan), the East African customs union (Kenya, Tanzania, and Uganda), and the Southern African Customs Union, which is the oldest customs union in the world, comprising South Africa, Botswana, Lesotho, Namibia, and Swaziland.

Both economic theory and empirical evaluations of customs unions and free trade agreements are ambiguous regarding the usefulness of these arrangements for the growth and welfare of the participants. The reason these agreements can be harmful is that "trade diversion" can occur. Since the agreements are discriminatory, tariffs are paid on imports from the rest of the world but not from partner countries. Private individuals may import a tariff-free product from producers in partner countries, even though the price on world markets (the tariff exclusive price) of the goods is cheaper from suppliers in the rest of the world. For example, suppose a partner country will supply a product at $1.25, while a nonpartner will supply it at $1. If the same tariff is charged on imports from all countries, the home country will import from the cheapest source and pay $1. Under a customs union, however, if the tariff exceeds 25 percent, private individuals will have an incentive to import from partner countries; then the home country will lose the tariff revenue charged on nonpartner imports and will pay more in foreign currency for imports. This is known as trade diversion. When partner countries are the low-cost suppliers in the world, then lowering tariffs preferentially will result in benefits to the importing country from increased imports from the most efficient world suppliers—a phenomenon known as "trade creation." Excluding market access considerations, eco-

nomic theory tells us that nondiscriminatory tariff reduction would bring the country the gains of trade creation without the losses of trade diversion, and therefore nondiscriminatory tariff reduction dominates preferential trade arrangements on economic grounds. An additional important result of economic theory is that welfare-worsening customs unions (those where trade diversion dominates) can be made welfare improving if the external tariff of the customs union is lowered sufficiently. For example, in the case just discussed, if the tariff is lowered to less than 25 percent, the home country will import from the most efficient supplier on world markets and avoid the trade diversion.

The first incarnation of the Central American Common Market (CACM 1) is worthy of examination, in part because it resulted in an unusually large expansion of intracustoms union trade—from 7.5 percent of total trade in 1960 to about 22 percent between 1976 and 1982—and because it is an example of extensive trade diversion. Using high effective protection on manufacturing goods, the CACM countries significantly expanded their manufacturing industries during this period by selling manufacturing products to one another and reducing their imports of these products from the rest of the world. These products were not competitive on world markets, however, and traditional agricultural exports, such as coffee, remained the primary export products to the rest of the world. That is, the increase in intraunion trade in CACM was accomplished primarily by costly trade diversion. After the debt crisis of the early 1980s, many of these industries and intraunion trade went into decline. CACM 1 used the customs union to focus production inward, that is, for import substitution industrialization, and did not use the customs union as a means of fostering competition.

When the CET of the customs unions results in a significant amount of trade diversion or fails to protect influential domestic industries, countries often exclude these products from the CET of the customs union (such as the agriculture product exclusions in the customs union agreement between the EU and Turkey and the many exclusions in the

Mercosur agreement). In the case of the Eurasian Economic Community, the CET is reportedly applied to less than 60 percent of the tariff lines for most of the countries in the customs union through selective application of the CET without prior agreement on exclusions.

Although Kemp and Wan (1976) showed that it is theoretically possible to design a common external tariff (with lump sum transfers among partner countries) that leaves excluded countries no worse off and at least one partner country better off, numerical and econometric assessments indicate that countries that are excluded from preferential arrangements will typically lose. The reason is that due to the tariff-free intrablock trade, buyers within the preferential trade area divert purchases away from excluded countries toward partner countries. This reduces demand and the price that sellers from excluded countries may obtain in the preferential trade area.

An advantage of customs unions over free trade areas is that customs unions eliminate the need to have "rules of origin" schemes among the member countries. That is, in free trade areas, traders may import a product into a member country with a low tariff and then resell it to another member country with a high tariff. In order to prevent this kind of tariff rate arbitrage, traders must document that the product crossing borders within the free trade area is produced within the free trade area. Rules of origin are then typically established that determine the conditions under which the product may be considered as one produced within the free trade area. These rules of origin can be rather cumbersome and difficult to administer, and they often impede trade.

For a country that desires to use trade policy as a means of expanding exports and competing on world markets, a crucial disadvantage of a customs union relative to a free trade area is that the country cedes the power to lower its tariff to the customs union's tariff-setting authority. Some economic theory and empirical work suggests that tariff-setting authorities in customs unions are less likely to lower tariffs than individual countries. Faced with high-cost imports from a partner country, the individual country in a free trade agreement has the liberty to lower its ex-

ternal tariff to reduce or eliminate this trade diversion. For that reason, Chile refused to join the Mercosur customs union but has vigorously pursued free trade areas with most of its trading partners so that more than 90 percent of its imports enter tariff free, while also lowering its uniform tariff from 11 to 6 percent.

Customs unions are said to provide the advantage of political cooperation, which contributes to peace and security. Peace between France and Germany in the EU is the best example of this. But if there are costs to some of the participants, the customs union could have the opposite impact. The U.S. Civil War was partly motivated by resentment of the southern states over having to pay high prices for northern states' manufacturing products due to high tariffs on European imports. In the East African customs union, the Kenyan manufacturing sector was more developed than that in Tanzania and Uganda. The latter two countries complained of bearing most of the trade diversion costs due to having to pay high prices for manufactured products from Kenya, but they could not independently lower the tariff on these products. Reportedly resentment over the uneven costs of the customs union contributed to border hostilities between Tanzania and Uganda in 1979.

Although theoretically unambiguous conclusions about customs unions are difficult, a key rule of thumb is to use the customs union to increase competition. Crucially, tariff reduction can reduce the costs of trade diversion and foster competition. "Deep integration" that fosters competition is important. Notably, the customs union agreement can be used to reduce nontariff barriers, such as regulatory and administrative barriers to trade, and commitments to increase the rights of foreign investors can provide for competition in key sectors important for economic development, such as business services. Both Schiff and Winters (2003) and Harrison, Rutherford, and Tarr (2003) suggest that another rule of thumb is that developing countries are more likely to gain from customs unions with industrialized country ("Northern") partners. By virtue of their size, Northern countries are more likely to introduce competition in the markets of developing countries, and Southern countries are more likely to obtain technological advances from trade with Northern countries.

Customs unions form an important feature of the world economy as evidenced in the EU, Mercosur, and other examples of this kind of regional trade agreement. Consequently, the assessment of customs unions remains an important task for both theoretical and applied trade policy analysis.

See also common market; free trade area; multilateralism; regionalism; rules of origin

FURTHER READING

Harrison, Glenn H., Thomas F. Rutherford, and David G. Tarr. 2003. "Trade Policy Options for Chile: The Importance of Market Access." *World Bank Economic Review* 16 (1): 49–79. A numerical assessment, through a global computable general equilibrium model, of the impact of various regional trading arrangements involving Chile on partners and excluded countries.

Kemp, Murray, and H. Wan. 1976. "An Elementary Proposition Regarding the Formation of Customs Unions." *Journal of International Economics* 6: 95–97. A formal treatment of conditions under which a customs union can enhance efficiency.

Schiff, Maurice, and L. Alan Winters. 2003. *Regional Integration and Development*. Washington DC: World Bank and Oxford University Press. An excellent, clearly written, comprehensive treatment of theory and practice of preferential trading areas.

DAVID G. TARR

■ debt deflation

Debt deflation can occur if falling prices raise the real costs of repaying loans, thereby boosting the costs of debt service and leading to higher bankruptcy rates and debt defaults. Rising debt defaults then produce increasingly weaker business conditions, further fueling the downward spiral and leading to a vicious circle that the economist Irving Fisher believed to be an important element prolonging and deepening the Great Depression of the 1930s in the United States. Fisher's perspective represented a sharp departure from the earlier conventional wisdom that occasional deflation was a natural result of productivity gains and, as such, was to be more welcomed than feared. Such was clearly not the case with the contracting economy of the early 1930s, for which Fisher's mechanism emphasized the link between declines in goods prices and declines in asset prices. Although economists often discount the role played by the October 1929 Wall Street crash, under Fisher's debt-deflation mechanism an event like this serves as a catalyst for defaults that could, if widespread enough, induce deflation in the economy as a whole.

The role of balance sheet effects is also important in fueling a debt-deflation process (Bernanke 1983). Debtors who default forfeit their assets to banks. Sudden, large drops in the prices of the forfeited assets then hurt bank balance sheets and potentially threaten the solvency of the banking sector. If banks curtail lending as a result, firms dependent on bank credit could face a credit crunch that leads to further production cutbacks and intensifies the deflationary spiral. Firms' borrowing difficulties may be further exacerbated if declines in asset prices reduce the value of their loan collateral.

Country Experiences with Deflation During Japan's slide into deflation after 1989, land and equity price declines hurt firms' loan collateral at the same time that the banks' own direct exposure to the stock market weakened their balance sheets. Together, these factors made firms less creditworthy at the same time that banks became more reluctant to lend at all. Japan in 1989, like the United States in 1929, clearly suffered from a sudden decline in asset prices as the stock market crashed. In the U.S. case, the unprecedented debt buildup during the 1920s, coupled with a sudden shift from a stable price environment to a deflationary environment at the beginning of the 1930s, meant that firms and households may have faced an unexpected rise in their debt service costs at the very time that their ability to fund their debt diminished. The unanticipated nature of the rising real debt burden at the beginning of the 1930s would have been a key factor in the operation of a debt-deflation process during the Great Depression in the United States (Fackler and Parker 2005). The agricultural sector was especially vulnerable in the U.S. case, and as falling prices made it harder and harder for farmers to repay loans, banks dependent on farm credit suffered as well. It is much harder to make a case for the importance of the debt-deflation process outside the United States, however, given that other major economies such as the United Kingdom did not appear to face any such dramatic debt buildup during the 1920s.

In addition to the more familiar U.S. and Japanese experiences, a debt-deflation mechanism may have been at work in late 20th-century emerging market crises such as those experienced in Mexico, Russia, and Southeast Asia. Output declines can be fueled by credit constraints that limit firms' access to working capital. These binding credit constraints in turn trigger debt deflation under this approach, leading to the dumping of assets and falling asset prices that further tighten the existing credit constraints. Once under way, deflation then lowers the marginal product of—and real rates of return on—factors of production. Vulnerability to this process increases with leverage, and economist Enrique Mendoza (2006) points to a surge in leverage ratios (as reflected in the ratios of debt to firm sales, book value of firm equity, and market value of firm equity) of listed corporations in Indonesia, Korea, Malaysia, and Thailand in the period leading up to the 1997 Asian financial crisis. As with the earlier debt-deflation literature, the unfolding of this process requires a high debt buildup. Otherwise the binding collateral constraint would not come into play.

While the actual prevalence of debt deflation remains a subject of debate among economists, almost all would consider the potential triggers, or facilitating factors, for such a process undesirable. That is, it is hard to see how sudden asset price declines, the sudden onset of deflation, or high debt levels and leverage ratios could be considered desirable policy goals. The Federal Reserve in the 1920s and the Bank of Japan in the 1980s, in arguably fostering an extended period of easy credit policies followed by sudden tightening, may well have played a major role in producing these very conditions. The pattern of sudden collapse following an extended period of excess liquidity seems to have been repeated in Southeast Asia in the 1990s. Unfortunately, such patterns often become more obvious after the fact than they were before the declines began.

Moreover, even though sudden tightening may trigger a debt-deflation process, expansionary monetary and fiscal policy will not necessarily reverse it in the absence of expectations of recovery on the part of consumers, businesses, and banks. Consumer and business unwillingness to spend, and bank unwillingness to lend, may well become ingrained among survivors of a debt-deflation process. In the Japanese case, for example, the bad debt problems of many Japanese corporations and the risks of future loan defaults help to explain why, even with ample zero-interest-rate money available, banks remained reluctant to lend. At the same time, Japanese banks were seeking to bolster their own balance sheets, which had been hurt not only by nonperforming loans but also by the sharp drop in the market value of their equity holdings. The banks' reduced willingness to lend and to circulate the new money being created by the Bank of Japan meant that these funds were often simply held within the banking system, thereby doing little to fuel new spending and combat ongoing deflation in the second half of the 1990s.

Prevention May Be Easier Than Cure Debt-deflation concerns only add to the argument that the most effective way to fight deflation is to keep it from starting, or at least to keep it from lasting long enough to become entrenched in expectations. Indeed, once consumers come to anticipate continued falls in prices, they have an incentive to postpone nonessential purchases, to save now and consume later. Anticipation of deflation also encourages people to accumulate cash balances in the hope that their purchasing power will grow over time. All this further reduces the current demand for goods and services, adding to the problems that businesses face. And, once deflation has set in, even a zero *nominal* interest rate policy, as the Bank of Japan maintained for some years, cannot prevent real borrowing costs from rising in the face of further price declines. This reflects the fact that the purchasing power of the funds borrowed increases over the course of the loan, producing a gain for the lender and a loss for the borrower even if no nominal interest payment is collected. Indeed, the worse the deflation gets, the more the automatic rise in the *real* interest rate is likely to further curtail business spending and exacerbate the downward pressures on economic activity.

There certainly are a number of reasons for authorities in low-inflation environments to balance the risks of deflation against those of accelerating inflation. The onset of declining prices can be particularly dangerous for a highly indebted economy vulnerable to debt deflation. Sudden interruption of a long period of easy credit and rising asset prices certainly had dire consequences for the United States at the end of the 1920s and Japan at the end of the 1980s. The somewhat analogous boom-bust cycle in the emerging market economies of Southeast Asia in the 1990s, although it did not produce sustained deflation of goods prices, nevertheless led to an extended period of decline in both output and asset prices following the outbreak of the Asian financial crisis in 1997.

See also balance sheet approach/effects; currency crisis; Federal Reserve Board; financial crisis; hot money and sudden stops; liquidity trap, the; money supply; seigniorage

FURTHER READING

Bernanke, Ben S. 1983. "Nonmonetary Effects of the Financial Crisis in the Propagation of the Great Depression." *American Economic Review* 73 (3): 257–76. Points to the negative effects of the 1930–33 U.S. banking crisis on credit allocation during the Great Depression.

Burdekin, Richard C. K., and Pierre L. Siklos, eds. 2004. *Deflation: Current and Historical Perspectives.* New York: Cambridge University Press. Includes an overview of deflationary processes in chapter 1 and detailed analysis of the Japanese case by Michael Hutchison in chapter 9.

Fackler, James S., and Randall E. Parker. 2005. "Was Debt Deflation Operative during the Great Depression?" *Economic Inquiry* 43 (1): 67–78. Argues that a large, unanticipated increase in the real debt burden in the United States at the beginning of the 1930s provided the catalyst for debt deflation.

Fisher, Irving. 1933. "The Debt-Deflation Theory of Great Depressions." *Econometrica* 1 (4): 337–57. Fisher's original exposition of a debt-deflation process in which over-indebtedness is followed by attempted liquidation that leads to falling prices and still higher real debt burdens.

Mendoza, Enrique G. 2006. "Lessons from the Debt-Deflation Theory of Sudden Stops." *American Economic Review* 96 (2): 411–16. Points to debt deflation being operative in recent emerging market crises and triggered by credit constraints imposed on highly indebted firms.

RICHARD C. K. BURDEKIN

■ democracy and development

Although there is a strong positive association across countries between democratic governance and economic development, the exact nature of the relationship between these two concepts is less than perfectly clear and has been the subject of extensive study and intense debate. This entry will describe mechanisms by which democracy may or may not promote development, mechanisms by which development may or may not promote democracy, and causal effects from other variables on both development and democracy.

Democracy has many definitions, but recent scholarly literature has concentrated on variants of the following: democracy is the form of government in which political leaders are selected by periodic elections conducted reasonably honestly under conditions in which all political interests can compete. In addition to the right to vote, citizens have the rights to form political organizations, to try to influence public opinion, to put pressure on officeholders, and to compete for offices. This competition must take place under conditions of free expression through the media and the right of peaceful assembly. Note that this definition does not imply that all groups in the population, in particular the poor, are effectively represented in governmental decision making. Whether democracy results in implementation of the preferences and interests of the majority of citizens is an empirical question, not part of this definition of democracy.

Two widely used empirical measures of democracy are those of Freedom House and Polity IV. Since 1972, Freedom House has provided annual ratings of political rights and civil liberties for most of the countries of the world. Polity IV has combined measures of the competitiveness and openness of executive recruitment, the competitiveness of political participation, and constraints on the executive into annual scores of democracy and autocracy for some 140 countries; Polity IV's data go back to 1800 for some countries. Przeworski et al. (2000) constructed a dichotomous annual measure of democracy for the period 1950–90; their definition adds the requirement that an incumbent party has lost an election and turned over power to the opposition. Despite the differences in definition, there are generally high correlations among these and other similarly inspired empirical measures of democracy.

Democracy Promotes Development A considerable literature in institutional economics contends that the economic rise of the West is inextricably linked to the economic institutions of secure property rights and third-party contract enforcement through impartial courts, and that these economic institutions were founded on political institutions of separation of powers and representative government (North 1995). The contention is that autocratic governments, unconstrained by constitutional limitations backed by independent legislatures and courts, failed to provide secure property rights over the long term. The political institutions under which modern economic growth emerged in Europe and its offshoots (especially North America and Australasia) allowed the market system to flourish and the business class to invest and innovate, fairly secure from government predation and social unrest. The regimes also began to supply free public education, which further contributed to economic progress (Lindert 2004). The fact that these political regimes were able to provide a good investment climate despite substantial restrictions on the franchise owes something to the legacy of political and social deference by the lower classes, a deference that gradually disappeared. Prior to World War I the partial democracies of Europe and its offshoots were able to accommodate the rising demands of the middle and lower classes without a great deal of social unrest or harsh repression. By 1950 the political attitudes that tolerated restrictions on the franchise had virtually disappeared; in the postwar period, democracy essentially implies full adult suffrage.

This institutional economics literature claims that democracy promotes economic development by providing secure property rights, impartial third-party contract enforcement, social peace, and public education. There are exceptions to these generalizations, however, as some autocratic regimes have expanded educational opportunities far faster than the typical democracy, and a great deal of economic expansion has taken place under nondemocratic rule, presumably with secure enough property rights to encourage investment and innovation. A few autocracies in East Asia, namely South Korea, Taiwan, and Singapore, created institutions and followed policies that have fostered economic miracles, raising their populations from poverty to middle-income status in four decades, and it is arguable that their autonomy from democratic pressures was instrumental in their rapid growth in the early stages of industrialization. All of these regimes expanded educational opportunities and physical infrastructure more rapidly than similarly situated democracies. Strong bureaucracies provided contingent rents to entrepreneurial activities and withdrew privileges if performance did not match targets. Most other autocracies in the decades since World War II have not provided an environment conducive to growth, or they did so only for brief periods.

Well-functioning democracies have links between civil society and political parties that translate popular desires into government programs (Lipset and Lakin 2004) and civil services that can implement these programs. Countries meeting the definitional requirements of democracy may lack these institutional features of good government and fail to provide physical infrastructure, secure property rights, high-quality public education, and macroeconomic stability.

Economists have examined how inequality and type of regime affect economic growth. A high level of income and wealth inequality may promote growth by putting income into the hands of people who will save and take entrepreneurial risks, but inequality probably also inhibits growth through its effects on sociopolitical instability and inequality's adverse effects on the level of human capital (because of the inability of credit-constrained families to finance highly productive investments in human capital and because of the unwillingness of the rich to finance public education). Many models (e.g., Benabou 2000) incorporate the idea that democracy reduces inequality through redistributive fiscal policy; this redistributive policy has ambiguous effects on growth in the models. It inhibits growth through distortion of labor supply, saving, and risk-taking, but it promotes growth through its effects on human capital accumulation, especially if human capital generates positive externalities. The empirical literature finds little support for the proposition that democratic redistribution impairs growth through distortion of effort and saving incentives (Lindert 2004), but human capital accumulation probably does promote growth. A remaining question is whether the models are correct in assuming that democracy does in fact bring about redistribution of the growth-promoting variety. We take up this question later.

The econometric literature on economic growth in the postwar period has yielded mixed results on the effects of democracy on economic growth. No study prior to 1987 found in favor of democracy, and no study after 1988 found in favor of dictatorship (Przeworski et al. 2000, 178), but it is clear that growth can occur under either type of regime. Przeworski et al. (2000) find that democracy causes somewhat more rapid growth in output per worker, but regime type makes no difference to growth in very poor countries. There is some evidence that democracy reduces income inequality (Tavares and Wacziarg 2001), which is probably conducive both to economic growth and to the survival of democracy, but the same study finds that democracy inhibits investment, with a pronounced negative effect on growth.

The ambiguous effects of democracy on growth seem to be the result of multiple causal chains that offset one another. One of the ways democracy affects growth is through its effects on political instability. A regime change, such as from democracy to autocracy or vice versa, or the replacement of one dictator by another through unconstitutional means,

seems to have an adverse effect on growth, at least in the short run. At low levels of income regime change is no less likely under democracy than under autocracy, but as income level increases (either over time or in the cross-section) the failure of democracy becomes progressively less likely. Another aspect of political instability is social unrest, as manifested in strikes, antigovernment demonstrations, and riots. These events are actually more common under democracy than under dictatorship, but their occurrence has much more adverse effects on growth under dictatorship than under democracy (Przeworski et al. 2000). In other words, democracy accommodates this kind of social unrest without serious adverse effects on growth, but dictatorships in general do not.

Another channel through which democracy may affect economic growth is education. Many authors have asserted that extension of the franchise to all the people results in governmental support of mass education. This seems a very plausible statement when one looks at the spread of primary education and the franchise in Europe and the New World in the years before World War II (Lindert 2004). A landed elite, especially one that is ethnically different from the bulk of the population (as was the case in much of Latin America and the Caribbean), would not want to tax itself to provide mass education and might well fear that such education would threaten its hold on power. In fact, the extension of the franchise and the growth of primary education are fairly highly correlated across these countries in this period. The argument is less clear as applied to the postwar world, for while there is some econometric evidence showing a positive effect of democracy on primary and secondary enrollment rates while controlling for income level (e.g., Tavares and Wacziarg 2001), the evidence of a large effect is not strong. Moreover, one careful study failed to find a significant effect of democracy on the share of public expenditure on education in national output (Mulligan et al. 2004). This finding is not surprising, given the way democracy is defined in these studies.

Some countries that meet the empirical definition of democracy are so lacking in governmental capacity and in political parties and electoral institutions that reflect the popular will that the public investments in human capital and infrastructure are not forthcoming. But if one adopts a more substantive concept of democracy (as in, for example, Tilly 2007), it seems safe to say that fully democratic regimes will provide more of these investments than the average autocracy (leaving aside that small number of autocratic "developmental states" in East Asia, some of which have now become democracies).

In a surprising finding, Przeworski et al. (2000) note that fertility is lower under democracies than under dictatorships, after adjusting for many factors that affect fertility. One of these factors is the parents' desire for security in their old age, which might be provided by having a large number of children, or by having a smaller number of children who are more likely to survive and earn enough to assist their parents, or by accumulating financial assets or pension rights. Przeworski et al.'s interpretation is that democracy provides greater confidence in the continuity of economic policies, as well as lower infant and child mortality, and thus tips the balance in favor of having fewer, better-educated children rather than many offspring.

Development Promotes Democracy A large literature in political science and political sociology attributes the emergence and spread of democracy to various aspects of economic development. In traditional society a landholding or bureaucratically based elite is able to hold the reins of political power and preserve its privileges, but as development occurs, structural changes weaken the power of the traditional elite. Wealth accumulates in the hands of industrial and commercial interests, rural people move to the cities, an industrial labor force grows in factories and mines, and education expands at both primary and higher levels. Some scholars (e.g., Lipset 1959) contend that, in addition to these structural changes in the economy, modernization associated with economic development increases the level of rationality in individual decision making, encourages toleration of opposing points of view, and attenuates the struggle over economic resources. A pervasive theme in much of the literature is that, whether through structural changes or changes in political

culture, economic development makes authoritarian rule less viable and promotes the emergence and survival of democratic regimes. Strong versions of this perspective would contend that democracy is unlikely to survive in very poor countries and becomes inevitable as countries become highly developed. This modernization theory was heavily criticized as many relatively well-off democracies (especially in Latin America) succumbed to military coups and authoritarian rule and many other countries grew rich without showing any signs of democratization. The theory enjoyed a resurgence in the 1990s as the "third wave" of democratization around the world became manifest, and the empirical studies of that decade confirmed the association of income and democracy (Lipset and Lakin 2004).

An alternative view is that, rather than development leading more or less automatically to democratization, countries are on different paths of institutional and economic development. As a result of historical factors, some countries developed political institutions of constitutional government that encouraged economic development and led ultimately to full democracy, while other countries got onto paths of continuous or intermittent autocracy that have not evolved into stable democracy, despite considerable levels of economic development. A prominent idea is that experience with electoral contestation under a limited franchise established an institutional basis of political parties and civil society organizations that supported well-functioning democracy. As mentioned earlier, the representative governments of Europe and its overseas offshoots followed such a path, although less successfully in Latin America than in the United States, Canada, Australia, and New Zealand. Among the former colonies that achieved independence after World War II, there is a remarkable association between British colonial status and uninterrupted democracy, which is probably attributable to these colonies' experience with electoral contestation and independent judiciaries under British tutelage. Around 2000, there were eleven low-income countries—that is, with incomes less than Costa Rica's—that had been continuously democratic since independence; all were former British colonies.

A complementary approach that refines elements of modernization theory links democracy to structural changes in the economy that affect the power relationships among class-based interests. Democracy becomes more probable as the land-owning aristocracy loses political power to industrial interests and the middle class. An important study by Rueschemeyer, Stephens, and Stephens (1992) contends that in Europe, Latin America, and the Caribbean the working class was decisive in the push for full democracy. Some scholars doubt that interpretations based solely on the conflict of social classes are adequate explanations of democratic transitions; they stress elite choices and elite consensus on democratic rules, relatively independent of class interests. Collier (1999) analyzes the role of working-class organizations in Europe and Latin America and presents a rather mixed picture, with elites playing the dominant role in some of the cases.

In contrast to the nonformal approach of most of the sociological and political science literature, some economists and analytically minded political scientists have developed formal models of the determinants of democracy. A central question in these models is, under what circumstances will an authoritarian ruling social class decide to extend political rights to other social classes? In one type of model (Bourguignon and Verdier 2000), political participation depends on the individual's level of education; thus a decision to finance education for the lower classes may threaten the elite's political control. The elite benefits economically from the external effects of educating the lower classes, however, and hence may decide to finance public education, despite the fact that the new, larger electorate may impose redistributive fiscal policy to the detriment of the elite. In this model, the greater the initial inequality of income, the less likely is the elite to pursue a policy of public education that leads to a more democratic regime. In another type of model (Acemoglu and Robinson 2006), the ruling elite faces occasional threats of disruption or revolution by the middle or lower classes, who are demanding some redistribu-

tion of society's resources. These classes would not be satisfied with a promise by the elite to redistribute, because they know that the threat of disruption or revolution is temporary, and the elite could renege on their promise once the emergency has passed. The installation of democratic institutions, however, permits the elite to commit to redistribution and thereby avoid both the costs of repression and the danger of revolution. This framework gives rise to a very rich set of models describing precise mechanisms by which economic structures and social stratification may or may not lead to democratization and the survival of democracy.

The Econometric Literature By the 1990s abundant data had become available on national accounts and other economic and social indexes and on measures of democracy covering various periods from the 1950s to the present. Barro (1999) used democracy measured at five-year intervals as the dependent variable; independent variables included economic and social characteristics such as income and education and also the lagged value of democracy. His regression results suggest that a country's level of democracy will converge gradually to a level determined by the economic and social variables. The positive coefficients on income and life expectancy (viewed as a measure of standard of living) are consistent with the idea that these variables cause democracy to be more likely. In this particular study education does not have a statistically significant coefficient (but of course it is highly correlated with the other variables). A dummy variable for countries heavily dependent on oil exports has a negative sign, indicating that high income produced by petroleum exports does not have the same positive effect on democracy as income earned from other sources. It makes sense that the struggle to control large amounts of unearned government income would imperil democratic government.

Przeworski et al. (2000) studied the frequency of transitions from democracy to authoritarian rule and vice versa, and they related these frequencies to various country characteristics. A notable finding is that the probability of transition from authoritarian rule to democracy is only modestly positively related to income, but the transition from democracy to authoritarianism declines sharply as income rises. In fact, above an income level of Argentina in 1975, there were no transitions away from democracy during that period (or since). The authors conclude that the positive observed correlation between income and democracy at a point in time is primarily due to the fact that once democracies attain a moderately high level of income, they seldom fail, rather than to a tendency for countries to transition to democracy at higher rates as they become richer. They note that countries can remain under authoritarian rule for many years after attaining middle- or high-income status. (Their statement would have been even stronger if they had included six high-income oil-producing authoritarian countries in the Middle East.) These authors also find an independent effect of education: at each income level, democracies with higher levels of education are less likely to fail. They also find that a high level of income inequality or a small labor share in value added in manufacturing increases the failure rate of democracies.

Acemoglu et al. (2005) have presented an empirical challenge to the received wisdom that income causes democracy. The challenge is based on an econometric technique in which the estimated effect of income on democracy is determined solely by variations over time within countries. They find that changes in a country's income do not predict changes in that country's level of democracy. Their interpretation of the data is that prior to the Industrial Revolution some countries developed political institutions that constrained their monarchs and limited the powers of the elite, and these countries evolved along a path of prosperity and increasing democracy, while other countries with different historical characteristics evolved under autocratic and elite-dominant institutions. They report that for various periods from 1840 to the present, there is no tendency for countries that grew more rapidly to experience greater improvements in their democracy scores, compared to countries that grew more slowly. Similarly there is no tendency for countries with greater increases in education to experience greater improvements in their democracy scores. In those parts of the world where the disease environment encouraged European settlement and the displacement or extinction of the local population, the settlers demanded and obtained representative institutions that evolved into democracy, but in the tropics, where death rates of Europeans were high, the Europeans set up institutions designed to extract resources from the colonies for the benefit of the mother country. These extractive institutions were conducive neither to economic growth nor to an evolution toward democracy. They support their interpretation by noting that after adjusting for the rates of settler mortality in the 19th century and population density in 1500, they find that the apparently strong positive effect of income on democracy is severely attenuated.

The interactions between democracy and development have been the subject of much theoretical and empirical investigation. The recent availability of comprehensive data sets has permitted careful statistical studies, which have challenged interpretations derived from casual empiricism. The processes are complex, data limitations persist, and much remains unresolved, however. Scholarly opinion on causal effects is likely to continue to evolve, not least because the world will continue to throw up unexpected developments.

See also corruption; development; economic development; international institutional transfer; political economy of policy reform

FURTHER READING

Acemoglu, Daron, Simon Johnson, James A. Robinson, and Pierre Yared. 2005. "Income and Democracy." NBER Working Paper No. 11205. Cambridge, MA: National Bureau of Economic Research. Presents evidence against the popular hypothesis that economic growth leads to democratization.

Acemoglu, Daron, and James A. Robinson. 2006. *Economic Origins of Dictatorship and Democracy*. New York: Cambridge University Press. Presents a game theory model that spells out causal determinants of democracy. Contains case studies and an excellent review of literature.

Barro, Robert J. 1999. "The Determinants of Democracy." *Journal of Political Economy* 107: S158–S183. An important econometric study linking democracy to income, education, and a history of democracy.

Benabou, Roland. 2000. "Unequal Societies, Income Distribution, and the Social Contract." *American Economic Review* 90 (1): 96–129. Theoretical model of the evolution of inequality and democracy.

Bourguignon, François, and Thierry Verdier. 2000. "Oligarchy, Democracy, Inequality, and Growth." *Journal of Development Economics* 62: 285–313. A theoretical model in which the elite may be willing to trade political power for greater economic gains.

Collier, Ruth Berins. 1999. *Paths toward Democracy: The Working Class and Elites in Western Europe and South America.* New York: Cambridge University Press. Study by a political scientist of the spread of the franchise and democracy.

Lindert, Peter H. 2004. *Growing Public: Social Spending and Economic Growth since the Eighteenth Century.* An economic historian looks at the spread of education and democracy. Considers a less procedural and more substantive definition of democracy.

Lipset, Seymour Martin. 1959. "Some Social Prerequisites for Democracy: Economic Development and Political Legitimacy." *American Political Science Review* 53: 69–105. Classic article presenting a version of modernization theory.

Lipset, Seymour Martin, and Jason M. Lakin. 2004. *The Democratic Century.* Norman, OK: University of Oklahoma Press. Mature thoughts of an eminent political sociologist on political organization, civil society, political culture, and democracy in Latin America and the United States.

Mulligan, Casey B., Richard Gil, and Xavier Sala-i-Martin. 2004. "Do Democracies Have Different Public Policies than Nondemocracies?" *Journal of Economic Perspectives* 18 (1): 51–74. An empirical study that finds that democracy does not have much effect on economic and social policies.

North, Douglass C. 1995. "The Paradox of the West." In *The Origins of Modern Freedom in the West,* edited by R. W. Davis. Stanford, CA: Stanford University Press, 7–34. Argues that modern economic growth emerged in the West because of constitutional limitations on government power.

Przeworski, Adam, Michael E. Alvarez, Jose Antonio Cheibub, and Fernando Limongi. 2000. *Democracy and Development: Political Institutions and Well-Being in the World, 1950–1990.* New York: Cambridge University Press. Careful statistical study of determinants and consequences of democracy. Overturns much conventional wisdom.

Rueschemeyer, Dietrich, Evelyn H. Stevens, and John D. Stevens. 1992. *Capitalist Development and Democracy.* Chicago: University of Chicago Press. This study by a sociologist and two political scientists argues that the working class, more than the middle classes, has played an important role in pushing for democracy.

Tavares, Jose, and Romain Wacziarg. 2001. "How Democracy Affects Growth." *European Economic Review* 45: 1341–78. An econometric study of the channels through which democracy affects development.

Tilly, Charles. 2007. *Democracy.* New York: Cambridge University Press. A distinguished sociologist describes social processes that move polities toward or away from genuine democracy.

CHRISTOPHER CLAGUE

■ dependency theory

Dependency theory argues that the process of underdevelopment in the global economic periphery is intrinsically connected to the process of development in the center. Dependency theory appeared in the 1950s as a critical reaction to the conventional approaches to economic development that emerged in the aftermath of World War II. There are two dependency theory traditions (Dos Santos 2002). The first is the Marxist tradition, influenced by Paul Baran and Paul Sweezy and developed by André Gunder Frank with important ramifications in the works of Samir Amin, Theotônio dos Santos, Arghiri Emmanuel, and Aníbal Quijano. The second dependency tradition is associated with the structuralist school that builds on the work of Raúl Prebisch, Celso Furtado, and Aníbal Pinto at the Economic Commission for Latin America and the Caribbean. This structuralist approach is best represented by Fernando Henrique Cardoso and Enzo Faletto and by the subsequent contributions from Peter Evans, Osvaldo Sunkel, and Maria da Conceição Tavares. Other schools of thought were heavily influenced by dependency theory and espouse, in some respects, very similar views—in particular, the so-called world-systems tradition of Immanuel Wallerstein and his followers (Topik 1998).

Both groups would agree that at the core of the dependency relationship between center and periphery is the inability of the periphery to develop an autonomous and dynamic process of technological innovation. The lack of technological dynamism and the difficulties associated with the transfer of technological knowledge lead to underdevelopment of the periphery with respect to the center. The main contention between the two groups was ultimately related to the possibilities of economic development in the periphery. Marxists would argue that development in the periphery—meaning fundamentally catching up with the center—was impossible, while structuralists would argue that dependent development was feasible.

Vigorous growth in some parts of the developing world in the 1950s and 1960s seemed to justify the views of the latter group. The enduring process of stagnation after the 1980s debt crisis, however, has led to a reconsideration of the relevance of dependency situations. In particular, some authors argue that a new form of dependency has emerged, one in which technological backwardness and the international division of labor are of secondary importance, and the real obstacle to development is financial dependency, reflected in the inability of peripheral countries to borrow in international markets in their own currencies (Vernengo 2006). The following section discusses the main differences and similarities between the two dependency traditions, and the last one analyzes the financial dependency literature.

External versus Internal Limits to Development For Baran and other Marxists the origins of the center-periphery relation were strictly technological and determined by the international division of labor. The center produced manufactured goods for itself and the periphery, while the latter produced commodities mainly for the center, as well as maintaining a relatively large subsistence sector. Marxist *dependencistas* explained the lack of dynamism in the underdeveloped world as the result of its particular insertion in the world economy. In this view, the process of development depended on capital accumulation, which, in turn, hinged on surplus extraction. A larger surplus led to more accumulation of capital and a higher growth rate. Furthermore, for Marxists it was in the uses of the surplus that the differences between developed and underdeveloped regions were most evident. In the most backward countries, where the process of industrialization did not take hold and agriculture was still dominant, underdevelopment resulted from the patterns of land tenure that led to excessive concentration of ownership.

The predominance of large estates in plantation societies implied that a great part of the surplus remained in the hands of landowners, who emulated the consumption patterns of developed countries. Excessive and superfluous consumption of luxuries then reduced the potential for investment and capital accumulation. Conspicuous consumption implied that the surplus was not reinvested in the periphery, but ended financing investment in the center. Hence, conspicuous consumption was the cause of stagnation in the periphery. The international division of labor, which promoted the export-oriented plantation system in a large part of the developing world and reinforced the need for luxury imports, was at the core of the dependency relation.

If industrial development took place, then a new pattern of dependency would emerge. Industrialization would take place with participation of foreign capital, which would tend to control domestic markets. The periphery then would jump into the monopolistic phase of capitalistic development. The surplus extracted by monopolistic capital would not be reinvested in productive activities in the host country, however. Part of it would simply be sent abroad as profit remittances, while the other part would be spent on conspicuous consumption. Frank (1967) concluded that the only way to break with the circle of dependency would be a political revolution.

The significant economic development in a good part of the periphery during the 1950s and 1960s led to a critique of the Marxist tradition by structuralist authors. Cardoso and Faletto (1967) argued that not only was capitalist development in the periphery possible, but foreign capital also had a tendency to be reinvested in the host country so that foreign investment might in fact stimulate domestic investment. Hence the nature of dependency was such that partial or dependent development was viable. As a result, dependency was not a relationship between commodity exporters and industrialized countries, but one between countries with different degrees of industrialization.

Cardoso and Faletto also distinguished between political and economic variables in explaining dependent development. Development and underdevelopment were economic categories related to the degree of development of the productive structure, and to its level of technological advancement. On the other hand, dependency and autonomy referred to the degree of development of the political structure, and the ability of local political elites to take economic decision making into their own hands. As a result, dependent development in association with foreign capital was possible and occurred in countries such as Argentina, Brazil, and Mexico, and in parts of East Asia, one might add. These were the countries that corresponded to what world-systems authors refer to as the semiperiphery. These were countries in which the simple dualistic vision of a center and periphery, where development was impossible in the latter group, did not seem to fit the real experience.

Cardoso and Faletto emphasized the importance of domestic internal developments, in contrast to the external forces of the world economy, as the main determinant of the situation of dependency. It was the internal political process that led to outcomes that favored foreign actors in the process of development. Furthermore, national capitalist development was not incompatible with the absorption of

technological knowledge from multinational firms. Arguably, if the goal was to achieve development, dependent development was a reasonable road to it, even if autonomous development was politically more interesting.

In refuting the Marxist emphasis on the relevance of external factors, however, the structuralist version of dependency went to the other extreme and claimed that internal forces were the almost exclusive determinant of development. The inability to generate technical progress domestically, the domestic patterns of consumption, and the limitations of the domestic elites that opted for political dependency were to blame. If the successful industrialization of some parts of the periphery showed the weakness of the Marxist tradition, then the debt crisis of the 1980s and the failure to renew the process of development in the 1990s proved that the optimism of the structuralist approach was not necessarily warranted.

Financial Dependency and the Original Sin
The debt crises of the early 1980s indicated that the development possibilities in the periphery were not limited just by the inability to catch up technologically. Tavares (2000) argues that the technological division of labor in which the periphery concentrates in the production of commodities for the center, while the latter produces manufacturing goods for the former is of very limited historical relevance. Industrialization and technical progress in the periphery were not sufficient to break the dependency ties with the center. Financial dependency is reflected in the inability of peripheral countries to borrow in international markets in their own currencies and constitutes the real obstacle to development. The new interpretation of dependency situations puts "international money—and not technical progress—as the expression of financial capital domination over the periphery in the last 150 years" (Tavares 2000, 131–32).

The inability of domestic capitalists and governments to borrow in international markets in their own currencies reflects the inability of the domestic currencies of peripheral countries to acquire all the functions of money, as reserve of value, unit of account, and medium of exchange. The ability to function as international money is a question of degree. Cohen (1998) suggests that there is a pyramid that reflects the geography of money, with internationalized currencies at the top and fragile currencies, on the verge of currency substitution, at the bottom. The main problem associated with the inability to provide all the monetary functions is that financial markets remain underdeveloped in peripheral countries, and the process of capitalist accumulation is hindered.

Mainstream economists have also dealt with financial dependency. Eichengreen, Hausmann, and Panizza (2003), following previous contributions by Hausmann, argue that underdevelopment results in part from the so-called original sin, that is, the fact that the currencies of developing countries are inconvertible in international markets. In this view, the external instability of domestic currencies in the periphery hinders the process of capital accumulation. Although mainstream and dependency authors agree on the importance of currency inconvertibility, they disagree on the solutions. Mainstream authors emphasize the importance of sound fiscal policies and monetary rules that promote credibility, while dependency authors emphasize the need for capital controls and reduced integration with international financial markets.

See also original sin; Washington consensus

FURTHER READING

Cardoso, Fernando Henrique, and Enzo Faletto. 1967. *Dependency and Development in Latin America*. Berkeley: University of California Press, 1977. An interdisciplinary book that argues that associate-dependent development results from political rather than economic factors.

Cohen, Benjamin. 1998. *The Geography of Money*. Ithaca: Cornell University Press. An analysis of the power structure in international currency markets.

Dos Santos, Theotônio. 2002. *La Teoría de la Dependencia: Balance y Perspectivas*. Buenos Aires: Plaza and Janes. Takes stock of dependency theory and suggests that globalization has reinforced the types of problems that were originally raised in the 1960s.

Eichengreen, Barry, Ricardo Hausmann, and Ugo Panizza. 2003. "Currency Mismatches, Debt Intolerance, and Original Sin." NBER Working Paper No. 10036. Cambridge, MA: National Bureau of Economic Research. Discusses the volatility of emerging-market economies and the difficulty these countries have in servicing and repaying their debts.

Frank, André Gunder. 1969. *Capitalism and Underdevelopment in Latin America: Historical Studies of Brazil and Chile*. New York: Monthly Review. The closest to a dependency theory manifesto.

Tavares, Maria da Conceição. 2000. "Subdesenvolvimento, Dominação, e Luta de Classes." In *Celso Furtado e o Brasil*, edited by Maria da Conceição Tavares. São Paulo: Fundação Perseu Abramo. Suggests that international finance, and not technology, is at the center of the dependency situation.

Topik, Stephen. 1998. "Dependency Revisited: Saving the Baby from the Bathwater." *Latin American Perspectives* 25 (6) (November): 95–99. Provides a review of the dependency literature that emphasizes its connection to other schools of thought.

Vernengo, Matías. 2006. "Technology, Finance, and Dependency: Latin American Radical Political Economy in Retrospect." *Review of Radical Political Economics* 38 (4) (fall): 551–68. A critical assessment of the debates about dependency in Latin America.

Wallerstein, Immanuel. 1976. *The Modern World-System: Capitalist Agriculture and the Origins of the European World-Economy in the Sixteenth Century*. New York: Academic Press. The first of a three volume series that describes the rise of the world-system, a complex network of exchanges and production on a global scale.

MATÍAS VERNENGO

■ deposit insurance

Deposit insurance is part of the "safety net" for the banking system, but also can contribute to the system's instability, depending on its coverage and design. Deposit insurance has cross-border implications through its impact on banking crises that potentially spread to other nations.

In most countries, the regulatory structure for banks is much farther reaching than regulation of nonfinancial firms as well as of nonbank financial institutions. The case for regulation is based on special characteristics of banks and perceived market failures in banking. First, the double role of banks as liquidity providers and participants in credit and capital markets makes them potentially vulnerable to bank runs, since a large share of the assets cannot be liquidated quickly in case depositors want to convert their funds to cash. Second, banks are relatively opaque entities, making it difficult for depositors and other creditors to evaluate the default risk of each bank. The limited information among depositors about the risk and value of bank assets can lead to the spread (contagion) of bank runs from one bank to another (Diamond and Dybvig 1983). Third, there are generally substantial amounts of very short short-term interbank liabilities, which contribute further to the risk of contagion. The potential for contagion implies that the banking system is subject to "systemic risk" to a greater extent than other providers of credit. Fourth, banks play a key role in payment and settlement systems, with the implications that large failures can disrupt economic activity.

The risk of runs on a bank and contagion implies that speed of action is of the essence when a bank is perceived to be near failure. Conventional liquidation and restructuring procedures for corporations are too time-consuming to be applied to banks without modification.

Some economists argue that banks are not qualitatively different from other firms and that markets provide sufficient discipline on banks' risk taking. These economists, who generally are proponents of "free banking," are few, however. From a policy point of view it is most important which view dominates among policymakers. It can safely be said that in times of crisis they will not be willing to experiment in order to find out which group of economists is right.

The need for rapid intervention, lack of effective rules for dealing with a bank in distress, and fear of contagion work in tandem to compel governments to intervene in a crisis by issuing blanket guarantees to all creditors or bailing most or all of them out. Anticipating this government behavior, depositors, other creditors, and sometimes shareholders as well perceive themselves as implicitly insured even if there is no explicit deposit insurance.

The Safety Net for the Banking System The features of banking described earlier have led to the implementation of a number of measures in most countries that together constitute the safety net for the banking system. The typical components of the safety net are:

1. A lender of last resort (LOLR)
2. Deposit insurance
3. Supervision and regulation of banks' risk taking
4. Capital requirements

These aspects of the safety net should jointly protect the "safety and soundness" of the banking system while providing banks with the appropriate rules and incentives to allocate credit efficiently. Deposit insurance can limit the risk of bank runs by guaranteeing that depositors receive some, or all, of their deposited funds with reasonable speed in case their banks become insolvent or illiquid. The central bank can also act as a LOLR by lending to a solvent bank facing a liquidity squeeze as a result of a run by depositors. To limit the LOLR to cases of illiquidity, the central bank can require collateral to provide liquidity support.

Regulation of banks' behavior and asset allocation, and supervision of banks' credit allocation and risk management systems, have the purpose of limiting banks' risk taking, which can be excessive. In addition, capital requirements reduce risk-taking incentives by ensuring that there is always shareholder capital at risk. Capital also serves as a buffer against unanticipated losses.

International agreements with respect to capital requirements as well as principles for supervision are negotiated within the so-called Basel Committee. The first Basel Agreement was completed in 1988 (Basel I). After years of debate, a substantially revised Capital Adequacy Accord (Basel II) was completed in 2004. This accord was to be implemented in the European Union (EU) in 2007 and 2008, but it remains controversial, particularly in the United States.

Deposit Insurance, Risk Taking, and Banking Crises The flip side of the positive role of deposit insurance as a safeguard against bank runs and as a consumer protection device is its role in inducing banks to shift risk to a deposit insurance fund or tax payers. These risk-shifting incentives are caused by limited liability of shareholders and explicit or implicit protection of depositors and other creditors. The so called moral hazard problem caused by these factors implies that banks have incentives to take on excessive risk on the asset side or to keep the equity capital low. Thus deposit insurance systems can contribute to the very problem (systemic risk) they are designed to reduce.

One solution to the moral hazard problem would be to design a deposit insurance premium structure reflecting banks' risk taking. Risk-based pricing encounters the problem of defining banks' risk taking contractually. For this reason a private deposit insurance market is not likely to function well. The existence of explicit and implicit insurance also undermines the scope for private insurance. In the United States, the Federal Deposit Insurance Corporation (FDIC) sets insurance premiums based on levels of capital.

The substantial resources devoted to the design of a capital adequacy framework by central bankers and regulators in the Basel Committee indicate that there is a strong concern about incentives for excessive risk taking. Bank managers, by contrast, tend to deny that there are incentives for excessive risk taking because they do not deliberately set out to take "excessive" risk. Incentives need not reveal themselves as incentives for deliberate risk taking, however. Instead, it is the competition among banks with the opportunity to finance their lending activities at a near risk-free interest rate that induces them to prefer debt financing to equity financing. Furthermore, competition for funding will not be based on banks' risk evaluation and risk management skills. Increased resources devoted to regulation and supervision and increased sophistication of supervisors have done little to reduce the incidence of banking crises. For this reason several academic economists have called for increased reliance on market discipline in the regulatory framework for banks.

The existence of implicit insurance implies that it is not necessarily the extent of explicit insurance that determines creditors' and, indirectly, banks' behavior. Absence of explicit insurance does not constitute credible noninsurance if political realities require supervisors and governments to rapidly intervene in banking crises to protect creditors. On these grounds a deposit insurance scheme with limited coverage can maximize the market discipline by making it credible that noninsured deposits and creditors will not be bailed out (Angkinand and Wihlborg 2006). The appropriate coverage depends on a number of country-specific institutional factors affecting credibility of noninsurance. In particular, effective procedures for dealing with a bank in distress can reduce the likelihood of bailouts.

The empirical evidence on the relationship between the coverage of deposit insurance schemes and risk taking is ambiguous. Much work has been devoted to analysis of the relationship between deposit insurance coverage and the occurrence of banking crises around the world.

Differences in results across studies suggest that institutional differences matter greatly for the effect of deposit insurance on the likelihood of banking crisis. The economists Demirgüç-Kunt and Detragiache (2002) consider the effectiveness of prudential regulation and supervision, as well as the strength of the legal system, finding that deposit insurance contributes less to the probability of banking crisis in countries with a high level of institutional quality.

Banking crises and excess risk taking have also been analyzed at the bank level. On this level it is necessary to take into account that capital and risk taking are determined simultaneously. The economists Nier and Baumann (2006) found that bank capital is decreasing in deposit insurance coverage, increasing in uninsured deposits, and decreasing in government support. These results provide evidence that market discipline depends on explicit coverage as well as the credibility of noninsurance.

Dimensions of Deposit Insurance Systems
Several dimensions of explicit deposit insurance schemes can discourage bank runs and incentives for risk taking. In discouraging bank runs, speed and credibility of insurance compensation in case of a bank failure are particularly important.

Risk-taking incentives are influenced by the existence of groups of creditors with incentives to monitor banks and to withdraw funds if they find that a bank takes unacceptable risks. Demirgüç-Kunt and Detragiache (2002) constructed a "moral hazard index" for a large number of countries from data on coinsurance features, coverage of foreign currency and interbank deposits, type of funding, source of funding, management, membership, and the level of explicit coverage. Coinsurance implies that those insured are responsible for parts of the losses. Foreign currency and interbank deposits are not covered in most countries. Private participation in the deposit insurance system can also be required.

Funding can be through insurance premiums that are used to build up a fund, or governments can cover payments out of tax revenues when compensation is due. The existence of a fund enhances the credibility of the system and it implies that banks pay insurance premiums, which can be based on proxies for risk. Most countries either do not charge a premium or they charge a certain percentage of deposits. The method to replenish losses to a fund, and assign responsibility in case the fund is insufficient, also affects incentives. If banks are held responsible for the replenishment of a fund, the subsidy component to the insurance system is reduced and banks have stronger incentives to watch the soundness of the system. Finally, membership in the system can be voluntary or required.

The economists Hovakimian, Kane, and Laeven (2003) have estimated implicit insurance premiums for banks in a number of countries based on the insight that deposit insurance can be interpreted and valued as a put option on banks' assets (i.e. the right but not obligation to sell). The authors find that some risk-adjustment of the insurance premium for each bank, the existence of coinsurance, and the funding of the deposit insurance along with deposit insurance coverage affect the variation in implicit insurance premiums across countries.

Deposit Insurance in Cross-Border Banking
Banks are involved in cross-border activities through direct lending to foreign banks, companies, and governments; through subsidiaries; and through branches operating in foreign countries. In the first case the domestic deposit insurance system affects the incentives for lending to foreign entities and protects domestic depositors. Implicit insurance can also be provided by international financial institutions, in particular the International Monetary Fund (IMF). The IMF's role in helping Mexico during the crisis in 1995 has been widely blamed for contributing to the Asian crisis in 1997. The IMF does not protect banks directly but by helping countries such as Mexico in balance of payments crises, it indirectly provides protection for banks that have lent to banks and the government in a crisis country. As a result banks may consider loans to foreign governments and banks protected by the same governments to be relatively safe.

Foreign subsidiaries are separate legal entities. Depositors in subsidiaries are therefore protected by host country deposit insurance systems. Host countries are also responsible for supervision of the subsidiaries while home countries are responsible for supervision of the consolidated bank. Since subsidiary operations often are closely integrated with the parents in complex financial organizations, there are opportunities for shifting of risk between the entities. If a subsidiary or the consolidated bank fails there is scope for conflicts of interest between host and home countries with respect to the sharing of the burden for losses that are not clearly attributable to one of the entities. The absence of predetermined procedures for crisis resolution in banks makes conflicts more likely. It is common for home and host countries to have memoranda of understanding on crisis resolution for banks, but these memoranda are typically so general that they offer little guidance if a bank fails.

A bank can also run its host country operations through branches. Since branches are not separate legal entities, the challenges for authorities in home and host countries are different. The EU's Banking Directive provides banks with the opportunity to operate across borders within the EU through branches under home country supervision. Deposit insurance in the EU is also a home country responsibility. Thus banks of different nationalities can operate in the same country offering different levels of deposit insurance. If a host country has a higher coverage, local branches of foreign banks can be offered the opportunity to "top up" their deposit insurance. The EU rules with respect to deposit insurance and supervision are consistent in the sense that the responsibilities for insurance and supervision coincide. Nevertheless, there is substantial worry in host countries that their interests will not be well represented if a foreign bank fails. These concerns partly explain why the Banking Directive has not been put into large-scale practice; instead, most cross-border banking is organized in subsidiaries.

The situation in the United States is different. Branches of foreign banks must participate in the U.S. deposit insurance system, although they are foreign legal entities and formally relying on the same capital as buffer against losses. To protect the American interests in case a foreign bank fails, branches of foreign banks are "ring-fenced," meaning that the branches must hold separate capital for their activities in the United States. Therefore, the difference between a subsidiary and a branch in the United States is almost in name only.

See also asymmetric information; bailouts; contagion; discipline; financial services; International Monetary Fund (IMF); lender of last resort; spillovers

FURTHER READING

Angkinand, Apanard, and Clas Wihlborg. 2006. "Bank Insolvency Procedures as Foundation for Market Discipline." In *Cross-border Banking* (Proceedings from Federal Reserve Bank of Chicago–The World Bank Conference), edited by G. Caprio, D. Evanoff, and G. Kaufman. Chicago: World Economic Publishers, 423–44. Shows how a deposit insurance scheme with limited coverage can maximize the market discipline.

Barth, James R., Gerard Caprio Jr., and Ross Levine. 2006. *Rethinking Bank Regulation: Till Angels Govern*. Cambridge: Cambridge University Press. Provides an analysis of the effectiveness of banking regulation and supervision in many dimensions.

Benink, Harald, and George Benston. 2005. "The Future of Banking Regulation in Developed Countries: Lessons from and for Europe." *Financial Markets, Institutions, and Instruments* 14 (5): 289–328. Shows how banks' equity capital relative to total assets worldwide declined from a level similar to nonfinancial firms in the 1920s to a level of around 4 percent in the late 1980s when the Basel Committee began its work.

Benston, G. J., R. A. Eisenbeis, P. M. Horvitz, E. J. Kane, and G. G. Kaufman. 1986. *Perspectives on Safe and Sound Banking*. Cambridge, MA: MIT Press. Includes articles by several authors about different aspects of the safety net for banks.

Bhattacharya, Sudipto, and Anjan V. Thakor. 1993. "Contemporary Banking Theory." *Journal of Financial Intermediation* 3 (1): 2–50. Elaborates on the theory underlying principles for banking regulation and supervision.

Caprio, Jerry, and Daniela Klingebiel. 2002. "Episodes of Systemic and Borderline Financial Crises." Discussion Paper No. 428. Washington, DC: World Bank. Provides evidence of excess risk taking in the frequency of banking crises around the world. The documentation in this article is used in most empirical work on banking crises.

Demirgüç-Kunt, Asli, and Enrica Detragiache. 2002. "Does Deposit Insurance Increase Banking System Stability? An Empirical Investigation." *Journal of Monetary Economics* 49 (7): 1373–1406. Empirically analyzes the relationship between deposit insurance and banking crises.

Demirgüç-Kunt, Asli, B. Karacaovali, and Luc Laeven. 2005. "Deposit Insurance around the World: A Comprehensive Database." World Bank Policy Research Working Paper No. 3628. Washington, DC: World Bank. Database described in this article is used in most of the empirical work on deposit insurance.

Diamond, Douglas W., and Philip H. Dybvig. 1983. "Bank Runs, Deposit Insurance, and Liquidity." *Journal of Political Economy* 91 (3): 401–19. Classic article, which develops a theoretical model of bank runs and liquidity crisis.

Hayek, Friedrich. 1977. *Denationalisation of Money.* London: Institute for International Economics. Provides an argument for "free banking" without central bank monopoly on issuing money.

Hovakimian, Armen, Edward Kane, and Luc Laeven, 2003. "How Country and Safety Net Characteristics Affect Bank Risk-shifting." *Journal of Financial Services Research* 23 (3): 177–204. Estimates implicit deposit insurance premiums for banks in a large number of countries and analyzes how these premiums depend on characteristics of deposit insurance systems.

Kane, Edward J. 2000. "Designing Financial Safety Nets to Fit Country Circumstances." Policy Research Working Paper 2453. Washington DC: World Bank. Institutional features of deposit insurance systems and other aspects of the safety net are documented and discussed in this article.

Nier, Erlend, and Ursel Baumann. 2006. "Market Discipline, Disclosure, and Moral Hazard in Banking." *Journal of Financial Intermediation* 15 (3): 332–61. Examines the links between bank capital and deposit insurance coverage.

CLAS WIHLBORG

■ development

Development refers to a process that includes and goes beyond economic growth. Whereas growth is defined narrowly as an increase in real income per person, the Nobel laureate Amartya Sen (1999) defines development as the expansion of human freedom, including freedom from hunger, ignorance, political oppression, and disease. Although income clearly matters for development—a richer society can build and staff more schools, courtrooms, and hospitals—it is also clearly not all that matters.

In defining development the challenge is to find measures of social evolution that come closer to Sen's notion of expanding human freedom but are still concrete enough to permit meaningful measurement and study. Making choices about which social goals are emphasized and how their attainment is mea-

sured is of necessity a value-laden exercise, and because values vary sharply across cultures and individuals, no measure of development can safely claim to be either universal or entirely objective. Despite this inherent limitation, the inadequacy of economic growth as a measure of development has led to an ongoing effort to find alternative measures of development. Here we consider several dimensions of development—economic, human, and social—noting how each has been defined and measured and considering the relationship of development to economic growth.

Economic Development Economic development includes three dimensions that go beyond rising per capita incomes. The first involves the development of a country's economic system. Economic development is generally facilitated by a number of structural changes, including urbanization, the rise in the size of firms, the relative decline of the agricultural sector in terms of employment and output with expansion of manufacturing and services, the geographic expansion of markets, and increases in the diversity of goods produced and traded. These changes in the organization of economic activity are the hallmark of permanent shifts in economic activity. Income gains that are not accompanied by these changes, such as natural resource booms, are easily reversed. Furthermore, the expansion of markets and increases in the diversity of goods produced raises welfare by expanding the range of goods available to consumers and providing a form of insurance by diminishing the impact of dramatic changes to the local economy or particular industries.

The second dimension of economic development concerns the distribution of the gains from economic growth. A rise in the average income level means nothing more or less than a rise in national income divided by population size. As such, there is no guarantee that economic growth makes a majority of people better off or results in income gains for the poorest members of society. This point is particularly important for less-developed countries, in which calls for economic growth are motivated largely by the desire to reduce widespread poverty.

The perception that the gains from growth in the 1960s and 1970s were unequally distributed led to calls to redefine development in a manner that placed greater emphasis on poverty and inequality (see, e.g., Streeten 1981). Skepticism about the gains from growth also reflected the influence of economists such as the Nobel laureates W. Arthur Lewis and Simon Kuznets, who argued that industrialization was characterized by an initial period of rising inequality with limited benefits for the poor. In addition, many economists noted that the way in which growth rates are calculated gives greater weight to increases in the incomes of rich individuals: a 10 percent increase in an individual's income adds more to average income the richer that person is. One suggestion was to replace growth with a poverty-weighted index that measured the growth of the incomes of the poorest 20 to 40 percent of the population.

Although development economists remain concerned with the distribution of the gains from growth, the idea that growth is inherently biased against the poor is not supported by recent empirical work. For example, a study by Dollar and Kraay (2002) finds that on average the incomes of the poorest 20 percent of the population grow at the same rate as average income. Similarly, in a cross-country analysis of income inequality, Li, Squire, and Zou (1998) find that inequality is highly stable within countries over the postwar period. Prominent exceptions include rising inequality in the United States and falling inequality in several fast-growing East Asian economies. Although these results do not guarantee that the poor always benefit from growth, they undermine the presumption that growth is systematically biased against the poor.

The final dimension of economic development is sustainability (see, e.g., Goldin and Winters 1995). The UN's Brundtland Commission (1987) defined sustainable development as development that "meets the needs of the present generation without compromising the ability of future generations to meet their own needs." Viewed in terms of sustainability, income growth rates can be misleading measures of development, since consuming natural resources simultaneously increases income and reduces a country's stock of natural wealth. Correctly measuring sustainable development requires adjusting income levels to account for the depletion of natural resources and degradation of environmental quality. This has led to the development of "green" national accounting, in which the national saving rate is adjusted for resource depletion. Adjusting income levels for the negative impact of pollution is more difficult, since the value of environmental quality varies widely across individuals, societies, and time.

The relationship between economic growth and environmental quality is not clear cut. Economic growth clearly increases the pressure on natural resources and systems. The challenges to sustainability include the consumption of nonrenewable resources such as oil and coal reserves, loss of biodiversity, depletion of ocean fisheries, deforestation and desertification, and reductions in air and water quality, all of which reduce either the productivity or consumption of future generations. But rising income levels also increase a society's willingness to pay for environmental quality, its ability to mobilize political pressure, and the technologies and resources it has available to reduce or reverse environmental damage. Together these forces result in complex relationships between environmental quality and average income levels. For example, as income levels rise, access to clean water increases, carbon dioxide emissions worsen, and the output of industrial pollutants such as sulfur dioxide rises and then falls.

Human Development If income matters for development, it is because it measures the ability of individuals to satisfy their needs and create personally fulfilling lives. In brief, a higher income is at best a means to the end of greater development. Recognizing this led to several efforts to measure the "ends" directly, resulting in attempts to quantify numerous dimensions of consumption, including consumption of food, medical care, housing, and energy. Many of these measures were subsequently criticized as being based on Western norms and consumption patterns—larger houses counted but larger weddings did not—reducing their usefulness as general measures of development. A more generally accepted approach is the Human Development Index, which has been published annually since 1990 as part of the UN's Human Development Report.

The Human Development Index, or HDI, gives equal weight to three components measuring income, health, and educational attainment. For each component, a country's outcomes are graded on a scale from 0 to 1, where the ends of the spectrum are defined by the lowest and highest observation for other countries. Health is measured by life expectancy at birth. Life expectancy is highly sensitive to infant and child mortality rates. Since these depend on widespread access to nutrition and health care, life expectancy is highly sensitive to economic and social inequality. Education is a fundamental determinant of economic and social mobility, and as such plays an important role in determining the range of choices available to an individual. The educational index is calculated as two-thirds adult literacy and one-third current enrollment rates, making it sensitive to both educational inequality and future educational attainment. The HDI includes a measure of income to proxy for all aspects of human development not captured by health and education. The index of income levels uses the natural log of per capita income. This choice places greater weight on income increases among poor nations, since it implies that proportional increases in income are measured equally: the increase from $1,000 to $2,000 is equal to that from $10,000 to $20,000.

Although it is still clearly limited, the HDI is the most widely known and commonly used alternative to per capita income as a measure of development. To see how the HDI differs from per capita income as a measure of development, it is useful to compare country rankings using the HDI and per capita income levels. Using data from the 2007 Human Development Report, we find that major oil exporters and countries with significant AIDS crises do worse when ranked according to human development, results that probably reflect the HDI's sensitivity to inequality and life expectancy. Similarly, the United States ranks lower using HDI than it does using per capita income, an outcome that reflects inequalities in access to education and health care

relative to other wealthy countries. Alternatively, current and formerly socialist countries, such as Cuba, Venezuela, and the former Soviet countries, tend to rank higher using the HDI, reflecting both their commitment to the provision of education and health care and their relative inability to generate high incomes for their citizens. These differences aside, differences in per capita income explain more than 88 percent of the variation in the HDI, suggesting that income is the most important determinant of both health and educational outcomes. With higher incomes societies can build schools and hospitals and hire the teachers and doctors to staff them.

Social Development Social development refers to development of society as a whole. A number of dimensions of social development have been measured and subjected to analysis, often as part of the UN's Human Development Report, including political development, human rights, human security, and gender equality. Here we consider two aspects of social development: political development and gender equality. It should be noted that in attempting to define social development, it is impossible to escape from subjective value judgments that vary widely across individuals and cultures. In particular, the measures presented here have their roots in Western Enlightenment thinking that is both secular and individualistic. To the degree that other cultures emphasize competing values based on family or community or religious devotion, these measures may be inappropriate.

We measure political development along two dimensions, the extension of democratic political rights and freedom from corruption. Democratic political rights may be viewed both as an end in themselves and as the means to achieve other development goals. For example, democratic political rights and the civil rights that sustain them, such as the freedoms of speech, association, and the press, are central to self-expression and to full participation in the social life of a country. They may also play an instrumental role in reducing income inequality and raising incomes by securing access to health care and education. As Sen (1981) famously pointed out, despite instances of widespread crop failure, there has never been a famine in a democratic country: letting too many people starve is bad for reelection. Though it is difficult to measure democracy objectively, there appears to be a strong relationship between average income and democratic political rights. It is hard to disentangle cause from effect, and there appear to be important links in both directions. For example, democracies tend to have higher levels of education but also higher taxes, with conflicting implications for economic growth, and the demand for political rights may increase as rising incomes satisfy more basic physical needs (see, e.g., Barro 1996).

While democracy focuses on how political leaders are chosen, governance refers to their behavior once in office. Democracy may be seen as a means to the end of good governance. An important aspect of governance is corruption, defined as using public office for private gain. Measures of corruption are constructed using survey data and tend to be highly correlated with one another and with other measures of governance such as the quality of bureaucracy. Freedom from corruption tends to rise with per capita income, though less strongly than the Human Development Index. For example, using data from 2007, the correlation between the natural log of per capita income and Transparency International's Corruption Perceptions Index is 0.63. As with democracy, causality appears to run both ways. Clean government results in the better use of tax revenues and provision of public goods, and higher incomes increase the demand for good government and the ability to supply it.

Gender equality involves equal access for women and girls to economic opportunities and resources and full participation in the social and political spheres of life. Gender equality was first included in the Human Development Report in 1995. The Human Development Report now reports a Gender-related Development Index (GDI), which measures the inequality of health, education, and income outcomes by gender using the same indexes as the Human Development Index. Gender equality is both a fundamental measure of women's rights and opportunities and an important contributor in securing other development objectives. As with political development, there are complex relationships between gender equality and political and economic development. Expanding women's political participation may reduce corruption and increase the provision of education and health care, while women's economic participation both raises incomes directly and has important impacts on the well-being of future generations.

See also aid, international; economic development; evolution of development thinking; poverty, global

FURTHER READING

Barro, Robert J. 1996. "Democracy and Growth." *Journal of Economic Growth* 1: 1–27. Presents evidence on the relationship between economic and political development.

Dollar, David, and Aart Kraay. 2002. "Growth Is Good for the Poor." *Journal of Economic Growth* 7 (3): 195–225. Presents evidence on the growth of incomes among the poor.

Goldin, Ian, and Alan Winters, eds. 1995. *The Economics of Sustainable Development*. Cambridge: Cambridge University Press. An excellent introduction to sustainable development.

Li, Hongyi, Lyn Squire, and Heng-fu Zou. 1998. "Explaining International and Intertemporal Variations in Income Inequality." *Economic Journal* 108: 26–43. Argues that for most countries income inequality has been relatively constant in the post–World War II era.

Sen, Amartya. 1981. *Poverty and Famines: An Essay on Entitlement and Deprivation*. Oxford: Oxford University Press. A foundational analysis of famine in which Sen argues for the importance of democratic political rights.

———. 1999. *Development as Freedom*. New York: Knopf. An extended essay on development by the foremost thinker in this area.

Streeten, Paul. 1981. *First Things First: Meeting Basic Needs in Developing Countries*. Oxford: Oxford University Press. Argues that development should be defined in terms of poverty reduction rather than growth.

United Nations. 1987. "Report of the World Commission on Environment and Development." General Assembly Resolution 42/187. New York: UN. Known as the Brundtland Commission report, this paper did much to popularize the idea of sustainable development.

LEWIS S. DAVIS

digital divide

The term *digital divide* refers to the disparity between those who have the resources and capabilities to use telecommunications technologies and those who don't. This gap exists within nations (varying by geography, social class, age, and other social dimensions) and between nations (essentially reflecting more fundamental differences in social and economic development). Blending telecommunications with computer technology, the advent of the Internet constitutes one of the latest revolutions in how the world conducts its business, thereby making the digital divide ever more salient. Evolving from modest beginnings as a U.S. Defense Department project in the 1960s to a mass communications technology linking the world's cities, the Internet/World Wide Web has quickly outgrown its original role as a special tool of governmental and educational elites. As such, this new technology is simultaneously hailed as the fifth neo-Schumpeterian "long wave" of global economic expansion (Castellacci 2006) and cursed as a new, powerful tool of exploitation created by international capitalism (Parayil 2005). This debate, between those Norris (2001) labels as Internet "optimists" and "pessimists," animates much of the scholarly literature, but the truth about digital diffusion is probably more complicated (and less economically crucial) than many analysts suggest.

There is no doubt that the debate is driven by a real phenomenon. Although the number of Internet users has expanded exponentially from approximately 40 million in 1995 to more than a billion people in 2007, the Western world's share of the total number of users worldwide is still around 50 percent, even though the West makes up only about 17 percent of the world's population. On the other hand, the combined share of users from Africa, the Middle East, and Latin America (about a quarter of the globe's population) constitutes only about 13 percent of all users, suggesting a considerable disparity. Even more telling, as of 2007 about 70 percent of the populations of the United States and Canada used the Internet, while only 11 percent and 3 percent of Asia's and Africa's populations, respectively, did the same (Internet World Stats 2007).

For all intents and purposes, then, the Internet/World Wide Web is still very much a creature of well-developed markets. Although optimists hope that developing countries can use the Internet to "leapfrog" over the industrial phase of development and move directly into postindustrialism (Steinmueller 2001), the commodification of information is sufficiently different from material goods and other services to cast doubt on this proposition. Many goods and services are produced for final consumption, whereas information is typically produced as an intermediate commodity, something used to improve the efficiency of production or the distribution of goods and services, much like transportation (Mowshowitz 1992; Crenshaw and Robison 2006a). This explains why the need for information grows as social and economic complexity increases, and thus why demand for information as a commodity is contingent on large and complex markets.

Since it is clear that the Internet is firmly rooted in developed economies and is likely to remain so, it is the *diffusion* of Internet technology to the developing world that dominates the current scientific literature on the digital divide. Rogers (1983) defines cultural diffusion as "an innovation that is communicated through certain channels over time to a receiving society." Not surprisingly, the current literature focuses almost exclusively on these "receiving societies," attempting to gauge their *structural conduciveness* as adopters of complex information and communications technologies (ICT). The most consistent structural attributes that have been found conducive to Internet diffusion fall into a modest number of categories: (1) economic complexity, infrastructure, and income; (2) mass education and literacy; (3) public policies relating to the provision of telecommunication services; and (4) the relationship between government and civil society, with special emphasis on political rights and property rights. In general, higher incomes, a dominant services sector, more extensive telephone and electrical infrastructure, mass education and literacy, public policies related to telecommunications competition, reasonably priced telecommunications services, participatory democracy, and protection of property rights correlate positively with more rapid adoption of the Internet.

Diffusion theory stresses *contact* in addition to conduciveness, however. Indeed, the major reason Internet optimists think that "leapfrogging" is possible is that the Internet makes the world's most complicated economies accessible to a wide range of less-developed communities, even those that are relatively isolated. The thinking suggests that the Internet provides conduits that allow the populations of relatively undeveloped countries to access a complex global economy. In short, the optimistic view of Internet diffusion is predicated on a fairly benign view of globalization.

Globalization typically refers to a plethora of international networks composed of intergovernmental organizations, governments, multinational corporations, and many other actors. Although limited globalization has long been a part of human history, contemporary globalization is accomplished through unprecedented technological capacities, flows of material and information, and growth in international governance. Given this dynamism, it seems plausible to assume that globalization might "jump-start" Internet development in otherwise unlikely locations. The question is, therefore, whether globalization can ease the constraints placed on Internet diffusion by structural requisites (i.e., conduciveness).

Given that the Internet was created in the postindustrial West, contact with the West (and/or other advanced economies) may form postindustrial "bridges" or "beachheads" in developing countries (the choice of term depends on one's view of global capitalism). One interesting analogy is Crosby's (1986) notion that European colonialism was far more successful where local conditions allowed the formation of "neo-Europes"—territories where climates and disease regimes were conducive to the importation of European flora and fauna, which in turn displaced many native species and invited European settlement. The bridges (or beachheads) provided by the conduits of globalization may be creating something similar for ICT growth—islands of postindustrialism amid seas of the preindustrial.

Essentially, globalization creates postindustrial microcosms that generate *demand* for ICT where it would not otherwise exist.

The possible conduits of globalization should be familiar to students of international development. For instance, megacities (i.e., cities populated by millions of people) have proven to be important gateways for ICT diffusion (Crenshaw and Robison 2006a, 2006b). Urban areas generate extremely diverse labor and consumer markets and, as major service nodes, tend to host Internet service providers (ISPs) even in very poor nations. For instance, Nigeria is one of the world's poorer nations, and yet its capital of Lagos (a city of approximately 11 million people) had more than 90 ISPs in 2003. Thus such megacities can provide "islands" of postindustrial demand independent of a nation's other structural characteristics.

International investment and trade also provide conduits that create favorable environments for ICT development. One of the major reasons that a digital divide exists among developing nations is that trade and foreign investment are likewise unequally distributed. For instance, in the early 21st century, sub-Saharan Africa accounts for only 2 percent of the world's merchandising exports, and receives only about 8 percent of the foreign investment going to developing economies. If ICT diffusion tends to follow pathways blazed by trade and investment (Crenshaw and Robison 2006a), inequalities in Internet capacity and growth are probably inevitable.

While large commercial cities and international investment and trade probably play dominant roles in the spread of Internet traffic in the developing world, noncommercial/nonstate actors and flows of immigrants, some permanent and some temporary (i.e., tourists), also contribute to the diffusion of ICT. For instance, nongovernmental organizations (NGOs) and international nongovernmental organizations (INGOs) are carving ever-expanding niches in the world's cross-cultural networks. Indeed, the Union of International Associations estimates that around 70,000 NGOs and INGOs existed as of the mid-1990s (UIA 2008), and regardless of the myriad purposes of such organizations, the one thing they have in common is dependence on international telecommunications to spread their messages and coordinate their activities. As past research demonstrates, in all likelihood this growing web of nonstate organizations makes a substantial contribution to Internet connectivity in otherwise unlikely places (Drori and Jang 2003; Crenshaw and Robison 2006a).

Tourism also promotes Internet use in the developing world. Tourist destinations that cater to affluent visitors create nodes of strong demand for instant and up-to-date information and real-time communications, not only for the tourists themselves but also for the global travel industry. As with other global connections, however, global tourism is also unevenly distributed. For instance, American tourists disproportionately travel to the Caribbean and Europe, whereas Africa and many other destinations languish in relative obscurity. Western tourism has been found to promote Internet usage (Crenshaw and Robison 2006a, 2006b), and there is very little reason to expect this dynamic to equalize Internet capacity in the future.

On balance, then, what can be said is that structural conduciveness in the form of affluence, democracy, and political and property rights does invite the spread of digital technology. Moreover, other forces, particularly economic, political, and social globalization, contribute to the digital revolution, even in places where social structural conditions may be unsuitable (e.g., poor nondemocratic countries). None of these forces, however, easily lend themselves to policies that might "jump-start" the Internet revolution, nor does the current literature suggest that Internet development is crucial for economic growth in the developing world. Rather, the global digital network is an epiphenomenon of more fundamental economic, political, and social forces, and policies *focused* on Internet development are likely putting the cart before the horse. New technologies in laptop computers and wireless connectivity will ease the supply problem constraining Internet development, but solutions to the bedrock problem underlying the digital divide—the lack of demand that results from national poverty and isolation from the world economy—also depend on political reform, domestic production, economic trade, and tourism.

See also information and communications technology

FURTHER READING

Castellacci, Fulvio. 2006. "Innovation, Diffusion, and Catching Up in the Fifth Long Wave." *Futures* 38: 841–63. A discussion of how technological "waves" and global institutions are likely to influence the "digital divide."

Crenshaw, Edward M., and Kristopher K. Robison. 2006a. "Globalization and the Digital Divide: The Roles of Structural Conduciveness and Global Connection in Internet Diffusion." *Social Science Quarterly* 87: 190–207. An empirical, cross-national analysis of macro-social factors influencing the adoption of the Internet.

———. 2006b. "Jump-Starting the Internet Revolution: How Structural Conduciveness and Global Connections Help Diffuse the Internet." *Journal of the Association for Information Systems* 7 (1): 4–18. A cross-national pooled time series of the macro-social factors shaping the spread of the Internet.

Crosby, Alfred W. 1986. *Ecological Imperialism: The Biological Expansion of Europe, 900–1900*. Cambridge: Cambridge University Press. A detailed treatise on how biological/climatic compatibilities aided European colonization of non-European areas.

Drori, Gili S., and Yong Suk Jang. 2003. "The Global Digital Divide: A Sociological Assessment of Trends and Causes." *Social Science Computer Review* 21: 144–61. Research demonstrating that cultural commitment to science and education may be paramount in IT diffusion.

Internet World Stats. 2007. http://www.internetworldstats .com/stats.htm. A website that provides a variety of macrolevel statistics for most nations of the world.

Kiiski, Sampsa, and Matti Pohjola. 2002. "Cross-Country Diffusion of the Internet." *Information Economics and Policy* 14: 297–310. An empirical, cross-national analysis of internal factors that shape IT development.

Mowshowitz, Abbe. 1992. "On the Market Value of Information Commodities, I: The Nature of Information and Information Commodities." *Journal of the American Society for Information Science* 43: 225–32. A discussion of how and why the production and use of information is uniquely unlike other forms of economic activity.

Norris, Pippa. 2001. *Digital Divide: Civic Engagement, Information Poverty, and the Internet Worldwide.* Cambridge: Cambridge University Press. A treatise on the extent of the digital divide and how it may shape the economic and social future.

Parayil, Govindan. 2005. "The Digital Divide and Increasing Returns: Contradictions of Informational Capitalism." *The Information Society* 21: 41–51. An article emphasizing the "down-side" of IT diffusion.

Robison, Kristopher K., and Edward M. Crenshaw. 2002. "Post-industrial Trans-Formations and Cyber-Space: A Cross-National Analysis of Internet Development." *Social Science Research* 31: 334–63. An empirical, cross-national analysis of intranational forces that shape IT diffusion.

Rogers, Everett. 1983. *Diffusion of Innovations.* New York: Free Press. The "Bible" of diffusion theory.

Steinmueller, W. Edward. 2001. "ICTs and the Possibilities for Leapfrogging by Developing Countries." *International Labour Review* 140: 193–210. A discussion of the possibilities for less-developed countries to use ICTs to "skip" stages of economic development.

UIA (Union of International Associations). 2008. http://www.uia.be. A relatively comprehensive registry of nongovernmental associations around the world.

EDWARD CRENSHAW

■ discipline

There is a long history of arguments for the use of a fixed exchange rate regime as a source of discipline over domestic monetary and fiscal policies. Advocates of the view generally believed that governments had a tendency to debase their currencies (by generating inflation) as a way of financing their often excessive expenditures. Supporters of "sound money" were often opposed to the issuance of paper money for fear that it would lead to undisciplined money creation and hence inflation.

In the first decades of the post–World War II period, such arguments were made primarily by advocates of a return to a gold standard. Mainstream Keynesian economists claimed that these arguments reflected a conservative concern with inflation to the exclusion of other macroeconomic objectives. Indeed the mainstream view was that international monetary regimes, to the extent that they were consistent with other objectives, should be devised to minimize the constraint imposed on domestic macroeconomic policymaking.

By the 1960s, however, this mainstream consensus began to fray. The combination of unemployment and inflation ("stagflation") that developed in most industrial countries during the 1960s and 1970s prompted many to question the Keynesian premise that government policies would be operated predominantly in the public interest to help correct macroeconomic instabilities generated by the private sector. Often government policies seemed to be the cause of macroeconomic instability. Although politicians were quick to adopt the Keynesian perspective that favored cutting taxes and increasing government expenditures during a recession, they were much less interested in the other side of the strategy: that taxes be raised and expenditures be cut when the economy was overheating.

Such lack of government discipline provided fertile ground for a new generation of political scientists and economists who explored why governments might deviate from the pursuit of macroeconomic stability. One influential line of thinking argued that reelection objectives could generate incentives for political business cycles (see Drazen 2000; Keil and Willett 2004). Prices tend to adjust more slowly to changes in macroeconomic policies than does output. Thus a well-timed expansion before an election might boost employment and output in the short term but lead to higher inflation in the long term. On the other hand, restrictive policies to reduce inflation might generate a recession before most of the benefits of price stability were felt.

Theoretical developments and empirical evidence helped clarify views on the trade-offs between inflation and unemployment and the time inconsistency problems to which they can give rise. These arise from differences between short term and longer run effects that lead optimization of short run net benefits to generate greater longer run costs. In the short run, higher inflation and lower unemployment often do rise and fall together as emphasized in traditional Keynesian economics. Over the longer run, however, these effects disappear as higher or lower inflation becomes expected. Indeed, because higher inflation tends to generate greater uncertainty, over the longer term higher inflation is likely to depress employment and economic growth. Thus concerns with limiting inflation came to be seen more as a trade-off between short-term and long-term effects than between inflation and unemployment.

The new emphasis on the importance of credible commitment suggests that in addition to providing constraints over domestic macroeconomic policies the adoption of such commitments could substantially reduce the unemployment cost of disinflation by increasing the credibility of such policies. This gave rise to the popularity of exchange-rate-based stabilization strategies.

Exchange-Rate-Based Stabilization The traditional arguments for the adoption of pegged exchange-rate regimes as a means of keeping inflation low were based on the "discipline hypothesis," which proposes that pegged rates take away a government's ability to run inflating policies, or at least increase the costs of pursuing such policies.

The credibility argument, based on the theory of rational expectations, combined with the successful disinflations in the 1970s of a number of countries belonging to the pegged-rate-based European Monetary System (EMS), contributed to the popularity of exchange-rate-based stabilization (ERBS) in the 1980s. According to the credibility hypothesis, high-inflation countries can peg their exchange rates to the currency of a low-inflation country, thus sending a signal to the public that they intend to adopt and maintain a low-inflation policy. The track record of countries carrying through anti-inflationary policies to a successful conclusion had frequently been poor, so the initiation of such a program often failed to generate initial expectations that it would be successful. Therefore, there would be little initial adjustment in inflationary expectations, and the short-run effects of restrictive macroeconomic poli-

cies would show up primarily in higher unemployment and slower economic growth, which in turn made it more difficult for the government to maintain these policies. If the government could effectively signal a stronger commitment to maintaining these policies, then inflationary expectations would fall more quickly and the effects of the restrictive macroeconomic policies would show up more in lower inflation and less in higher unemployment. This in turn would enhance the odds of success.

A major focus of the credibility hypothesis is that adopting pegged exchange rates would discipline not only policymakers, but also private agents. Rational expectations theory suggests that credible institutional commitments would also discipline actions by influencing the expectations of private agents. Although some of the earlier discipline arguments for fixed exchange rates also posited that wage discipline would be enhanced since high wage increases would be less likely to be accompanied by expansionary monetary policies and hence would be likely to generate more unemployment, the emphasis on effects on private sector behavior is the focus of the rational expectations analysis (Tavlas 2000).

In the 1980s and 1990s many countries, especially in Latin America, adopted various forms of pegged exchange rates to counteract high inflation. Many academics and International Monetary Fund (IMF) officials advocated the ERBS policy, in part because of its touted ability to rapidly decelerate inflation while generating an initial boom. The advocates of ERBS, however, rarely acknowledged that the fall in inflation was often not rapid enough to prevent overvaluation of the currency. Once the currency becomes overvalued, a country's exports become less competitive, resulting in a recession and currency crisis. For ERBS to succeed, the government adopting it must also enact noninflationary fiscal and monetary policies, and convince speculators of the program's credibility.

Some advocates of ERBS have argued that such strategies should be abandoned before the need for large nominal devaluation after an excessive real overvaluation, in order to avoid a currency crisis. The propensity of ERBS to contribute to crises can easily be seen in Latin America. Faced with rapid rates of inflation in the 1990s, many Latin America countries, including Mexico, Chile, Brazil, and Argentina, turned to ERBS, hoping for salvation. In most cases, inflation did indeed fall substantially after the ERBS had been put in place. It typically did not fall sufficiently, however, to avoid exchange rate overvaluation and eventual currency crises.

Some economists therefore began to advocate premature exits from initial pegs without fully recognizing that the temporary nature of these pegs would likely undercut their credibility. Further analysis suggested that the same types of time inconsistency problems that created the need for discipline in the first place would also make it difficult for governments to exit from a peg in a timely manner (Willett 1998). Thus pegged exchange rates are less of a constraint on inflationary policies than genuinely fixed exchange rates and generate greater incentives to pursue those same policies.

Not only did many of the ERBS efforts of the 1980s and 1990s end in crises, but research also questioned whether the EMS countries had really been able to disinflate more effectively and at lower costs in the 1970s than other industrial countries that had adopted flexible exchange rates. We should not conclude from these experiences that ERBS never makes sense, but there is now widespread recognition that many early advocates oversold its benefits and underestimated its costs. The success of the credibility hypothesis rested on a government's ability to persuade the private sector that it would pursue sound macroeconomic policies to avoid the high exit costs associated with abandoning the peg.

Discipline from International Financial Markets In contrast, the foundation of the discipline hypothesis is coercion. In the 1970s many commentators argued that international financial markets could provide external discipline. The participants in these markets would carefully monitor national economic policies and provide early warning signals if policies started to go astray. If the warnings were ignored, the resulting capital outflows and increases in interest rates could force governments and the general public to take corrective ac-

tions. Because international financial markets may not always operate in such an efficient manner, however, some analysts argue that the discipline generated by international capital flows can be capricious rather than beneficial, and high international capital mobility may reduce rather than increase discipline, thus becoming a source of instability.

See also capital flows to developing countries; capital mobility; currency board arrangement (CBA); currency crisis; European Monetary Union; exchange rate regimes; expenditure changing and expenditure switching; financial crisis; gold standard, international; impossible trinity; inflation targeting; International Monetary Fund (IMF); monetary policy rules; seigniorage; time inconsistency problem

FURTHER READING
For discussion of political business cycles and other possible causes of undisciplined macroeconomic policy, see:
Drazen, Allan. 2000. *Political Economy in Macroeconomics.* Princeton, NJ: Princeton University Press.
Keil, Manfred, and Thomas D. Willett. 2004. "Political Business Cycles." In *Encyclopedia of Public Choice,* edited by Charles Rowley and Fredrich Schneider. New York: Springer-Verlag, 2:411–15.
For discussion of the possible discipline effects of pegged exchange rates and the use of exchange rates as nominal anchors, see:
Tavlas, George S. 2000. "On the Exchange Rate as a Nominal Anchor: The Rise and Fall of the Credibility Hypothesis." *The Economic Record* 76 (233): 183–201.
Willett, Thomas D. 1998. "Credibility and Discipline Effects of Exchange Rates as Nominal Anchors: The Need to Distinguish Temporary from Permanent Pegs," *World Economy* 21 (6): 803–26.
For empirical evidence on the effects of exchange rate regimes on fiscal policy, see:
Edwards, Sebastian. 2003. "Dollarization." In *The Dollarization Debate,* edited by Dominick Salvatore, James W. Dean, and Thomas D. Willett. New York: Oxford University Press, 111–29.
Tornell, Aarón, and Andrés Velasco. 1998. "Fiscal Discipline and the Choice of a Nominal Anchor in Stabilization." *Journal of International Economics* 46 (1): 1–30.

For analysis of the effects of international capital flows on monetary and fiscal policies, see:

Tytell, Irina, and Shang-Jin Wei. 2004. "Does Financial Globalization Induce Better Macroeconomic Policies?" IMF Working Paper WP/04/84. Washington, DC: International Monetary Fund.

Willett, Thomas D. 2000. "International Financial Markets as Sources of Crisis or Discipline: The Too Much, Too Late Hypothesis." Princeton Essays in International Finance No. 218. Princeton, NJ: Princeton University.

SIRATHORN DECHSAKULTHORN
AND THOMAS D. WILLETT

■ dispute settlement
See World Trade Organization dispute settlement

■ dissemination risk
See foreign direct investment and international technology transfer

■ distortions to agricultural incentives

The majority of the world's poorest households depend on farming for their livelihood. Two sets of policy interventions have depressed earnings from farming in many developing countries since the 1950s: own-country policies, which typically have had a prourban, antiagricultural bias, and high-income country policies, which typically assist and protect farmers with import barriers and subsidies. Governments in numerous developing countries have made considerable progress over the past two decades in reducing their own sectoral and trade policy distortions to market signals, and many of them now believe high-income countries should reduce their remaining protectionism that restricts market access for developing country exports of farm products. Indeed, developing country governments have called for such commitments on farm policies in the World Trade Organization's (WTO's) current round of multilateral trade negotiations (the

Doha Development Agenda, or Doha Round) before they consider any further reform commitments of their own.

Research reported in Anderson, Martin, and van der Mensbrugghe (2006) suggests that the agricultural protectionist policies of high-income countries harm many developing countries. That research, using the global economy–wide applied general equilibrium (AGE) model known as Linkage, along with similar research using the global GTAP Model (Anderson and Valenzuela 2007), also suggests full global liberalization of merchandise trade would raise value added in agriculture (that is, net farm incomes) in most developing country regions, and by more than it would raise value added in the rest of those economies (while doing the opposite in the protective high-income countries of the northern hemisphere).

Origins of Agricultural Protection While much of the government intervention in agricultural trade over the centuries has been aimed at stabilizing domestic food prices and supplies, such policy interventions tend to change in the course of a country's development from effectively taxing agriculture relative to other tradable sectors to effectively subsidizing farmers. From the late 1100s to the 1660s, prior to the first industrial revolution, Britain used export taxes and licenses to prevent domestic food prices from rising excessively. During 1660–90 a series of acts gradually raised food import duties (making imports prohibitive under most circumstances) and reduced the export restrictions on grain, provisions that were made even more protective by the corn law of 1815. The famous repeal of the corn laws in the mid-1840s heralded a period of relatively unrestricted food trade for Britain, but agricultural protection returned there in the 1930s and has been increasing since then. In many other Western European countries, similar tendencies have been observed, although on the Continent the period of free trade in the 19th and early 20th centuries was considerably shorter, and agricultural protection levels since the early twentieth century have been somewhat higher than in Britain (Kindleberger 1975). Gulbrandsen and Lindbeck (1973) estimate that the average nominal rate of agricultural protection in Western Europe (the proportion by which domestic prices are raised by import restrictions) increased from less than 30 percent in the 1930s through the early 1950s to around 40 percent in the late 1950s and 60 percent by the late 1960s. Meanwhile, tariffs on Western European imports of manufactured goods have progressively declined since the General Agreement on Tariffs and Trade (GATT) came into force in the late 1940s. This divergence in protection trends for farmers and industrialists in developed countries was foreshadowed, as early as 1958, as a potential problem for the GATT contracting parties by a high-level panel of experts chaired by Haberler (1958).

Japan provides an even more striking example of the increasing tendency to assist agriculture more than other industries. Its industrialization began later than in Western Europe, after the opening up of the economy following the Meiji Restoration in 1868. By the early 1900s Japan had switched from being a small net exporter of food to becoming increasingly dependent on rice imports. This was followed by calls from farmers and their supporters for rice import controls. Their calls were matched by equally vigorous calls from manufacturing and commercial groups for unrestricted food trade, since the price of rice at that time was a major determinant of real wages in the nonfarm sector. The heated debates were not unlike those that had led to the repeal of the corn laws in Britain six decades earlier. In Japan, however, the forces of protection triumphed, and a tariff was imposed on rice imports beginning in 1904. That tariff gradually rose over time, providing a nominal rate of protection for rice of more than 30 percent during World War I. Even when there were food riots because of shortages and high prices just after that war, the Japanese government's response was not to reduce protection but instead to extend it to its colonies and to shift from a national to an imperial rice self-sufficiency policy. That involved accelerated investments in agricultural development in the colonies of Korea and Taiwan behind an ever-higher external tariff wall that by the latter 1930s provided a nominal rate of

rice protection for the empire of more than 60 percent. After postwar reconstruction, Japan continued to increase its agricultural protection, just as countries in Western Europe did, but to even higher levels.

Meanwhile, in the 1950s a liberated South Korea and Taiwan adopted an import-substituting industrialization strategy that harmed agriculture. That strategy was replaced in the early 1960s with a more neutral trade policy that resulted in very rapid export-oriented industrialization in those densely populated economies. That export-led development strategy in turn imposed competitive pressure on the farm sector, which, just as in Japan in earlier decades, prompted farmers to lobby (successfully, as it happened) for ever-higher levels of protection from import protection in those newly industrialized economies as well (Anderson and Hayami 1986).

Policy Developments since the 1950s The historical tendency for countries to change gradually from taxing to subsidizing agriculture relative to other sectors in the course of their economic development has not been universal. The exceptions are rich countries with an extreme comparative advantage in agriculture (such as Australia and New Zealand) and poor countries with an extreme comparative disadvantage in agriculture (such as South Korea, as with Japan earlier, and some oil-rich states in the Middle East). Poor-country farmers also were disadvantaged by an antirural bias in public investments in infrastructure and human capital (education, health, agricultural research and development), and sometimes also by having to effectively finance urban consumer food subsidy programs (Pinstrup-Andersen 1988). Within the agricultural sector of each country, import-competing industries tended to enjoy more government support than those that were more competitive internationally (Krueger, Schiff, and Valdes 1988; Herrmann et al. 1992). The study by Krueger, Schiff, and Valdes also reveals that, at least up to the mid-1980s, direct disincentives for farmers such as agricultural export taxes were less important than indirect disincentives in the form of import protection for the manufacturing sector or overvalued exchange rates, both of which attracted resources away from agricultural industries producing tradable products.

This pattern of distortions to incentives is wasteful from a global viewpoint, and detrimental to the vast majority of the world's poorest people, who are small farmers in developing countries. Currently fewer than 15 million relatively wealthy farmers in developed countries, with an average of 78 hectares per worker, benefit at the expense of not only consumers and taxpayers in those rich countries but also the majority of the 1.3 billion relatively impoverished farmers and their families in developing countries, who have to earn a living from just 2.5 hectares per worker, on average. The evolution from taxing to subsidizing farmers as countries develop suggests that, if left unchecked, agricultural protectionism would continue to spread to newly industrializing countries in the decades ahead as governments sought to protect domestic producers from import competition as the farm sector came under pressure to shrink in relative terms and, eventually, in terms of absolute numbers of people engaged.

Such a prospect contributed to the resolve of several groups in the 1980s to try to counter those political forces. For example, agricultural-exporting countries formed the Cairns Group and succeeded in ensuring that GATT members included an agreement on agricultural trade and subsidy reform in the Uruguay Round outcome. Over the same period, international financial institutions made a more concerted effort to encourage developing countries to reduce unilaterally their distortions against agriculture. Accession to preferential trading agreements and to the WTO, and the demise of communism, have helped in some cases too.

Several groups have attempted to measure the extent of distortions to agricultural incentives since the 1950s. Anderson and Hayami (1986) report annual nominal rates of protection estimates for East Asian and high-income countries from 1955 to the early 1980s. Krueger, Schiff, and Valdes (1988, 1991) calculate both direct and indirect distortions to agricultural incentives for 17 developing countries from the early 1960s to the mid-1980s.

Tyers and Anderson (1992) estimate that the global welfare cost of agricultural protection doubled during the 1980s. And the Organisation for Economic Co-operation and Development (OECD 2006) has provided annual estimates in a consistent way since 1986, for developed countries plus Korea, Mexico, and some of Europe's transition economies, of what are now called producer support estimates (PSEs) and consumer subsidy equivalents (CSEs) for agricultural and food products. These efforts use somewhat different methodologies, so there was a clear need to provide a comparable set of estimates for both developed and developing countries using a standard methodology. A World Bank research project took on that task, covering the period since the late 1950s for as many as 73 large economies. Together those countries account for about 90 percent of both global income and farm output. Below the methodology is briefly described and the findings summarized, details of which can be found in Anderson (2008).

Methodology for Estimating Distortions to Incentives The simplest indicator of distortions to agricultural incentives is provided by the nominal rate of assistance (NRA), defined as the percentage by which a country's government policies have raised (or lowered if it is negative) gross returns to producers above (below) what they would be without the government's intervention. The NRAs are based on estimates of assistance to individual farm industries. Most distortions to industries producing internationally tradable products come from trade measures, such as a tariff imposed on the import price or a tax or subsidy imposed on exports at the country's border. An ad valorem tariff or export subsidy is the equivalent of a production subsidy and a consumption tax expressed as a percentage of the border price, and that is what is captured in the NRA (and can also be captured in a consumer tax equivalent, or CTE) at the point in the value chain at which the product is traded. To get the NRA for the farmer, it is necessary to determine the extent of pass-through back along the value chain to the farm gate (and likewise forward to the consumer at the retail level to get the CTE). The NRA thus differs from the OECD's PSE, since the PSE is expressed as a percentage of the distorted price and hence is lower than the NRA, which is expressed as a percentage of the undistorted price. But like the PSE, this NRA also captures any significant product-specific input price distortions by estimating their equivalence in terms of a higher output price and including that in the NRA for individual agricultural industries, and also adds non-product-specific distortions into the estimate for the overall sectoral NRA.

The degree of coverage of products for which NRA estimates are generated was 70 percent of the gross value of agricultural production (the same as for the OECD's PSE coverage). The OECD assumes the NRA for the residual noncovered products is the same as the average for covered products. However, in developing countries at least, policies affecting the noncovered products are often very different from those for covered products. The nontradables among them, for example, are often low-quality food staples that are subject to no distortionary policies. The World Bank project therefore provides three sets of estimates of the NRAs for noncovered farm products, one each for the import-competing, exportable, and nontradable subsectors. A weighted average for all agricultural products is then generated, using the values of production at unassisted prices as weights.

Since the late 1980s there has been a tendency in some high-income countries to move away from trade measures to more direct forms of assistance to farmers. This is largely in response to domestic pressures to reduce trade distortions to improve policy efficiency, as well as to pressures from abroad during and following the GATT's multilateral trade negotiations that resulted in the Uruguay Round Agreement on Agriculture. Some of those new measures are less decoupled from production incentives than others, so their production and trade effects have not entirely disappeared. And they still bestow a transfer on farmers. Hence it is helpful to show the NRA both with and without "decoupled" measures for those high-income countries adopting them.

It is not sufficient to look just at agricultural NRAs in isolation, because *relative* prices and hence relative

rates of government assistance are what affect producers' incentives. In a model of a two-sector economy, an import tax has the same effect on the export sector as an export tax, and this carries over to a model that also includes a third sector producing only nontradables, to a model with imperfect competition, and regardless of the economy's size (Vousden 1990). The reason the result carries over with nontradables is that if an import tax of rate t is replaced by an export tax at rate t, all traded goods prices are reduced by $1/(1 + t)$ and therefore the price of all nontradables has to also change by that same amount if the market for nontradables (in which the quantity supplied domestically has to equal the quantity demanded) is to remain in equilibrium. Thus if one can assume there are no distortions in the markets for nontradables, the overall distortion to agricultural incentives can be captured by the extent to which the tradable parts of agricultural production are assisted or taxed relative to producers of other tradables. By generating estimates of the average NRA for nonagricultural tradables, it is then possible to calculate a relative rate of assistance, RRA, defined as:

$$RRA = 100[(1 + NRAag^t/100)/ \\ (1 + NRAnonag^t/100) - 1]$$

where $NRAag^t$ and $NRAnonag^t$ are the average percentage NRAs for the tradable parts of the agricultural and nonagricultural sectors, respectively. Since an NRA cannot be less than -100 percent if producers are to earn anything, neither can the RRA. This measure is thus useful for providing an internationally comparable indication over time of the extent to which a country's policy regime has an anti- or proagricultural bias.

Caution is needed in interpreting the RRA. If it is negative for developing countries, and especially if it is positive for high-income countries, that probably indicates that farmers in developing countries effectively faced prices that were less than they would have been if there were no government distortions to goods markets. But there is the possibility that if all such distortions were removed globally—and even more so if they were removed only by developing countries—the international terms of trade could deteriorate for developing countries. Whether that would be so severe as to make developing-country farmers worse off than without such reform is a moot point. One would need a series of global economy–wide AGE models calibrated to each year in the time series to estimate the full general equilibrium effects on net farm incomes over time.

New Global Estimates of Distortions, 1955–2004 The World Bank research project's sample of 73 large economies comprises 22 high-income developed countries (HICs); 13 East European and Central Asian (ECA) economies in transition from socialism; and 17 African, 13 Asian, and 8 Latin American developing countries. Since these economies together account for around 90 percent of global income and of farm output, and since there are a similar number of developing countries as higher-income (including transition) countries, their NRAs and RRAs are very representative of each of those two groups and for the world as a whole.

Figure 1 illustrates the RRA estimates for the highest level of aggregation. It shows the strong upward trend in assistance to farmers in high-income countries from the mid-1950s to the late 1980s, rising from around 20 percent to 50 percent. Their rates have since come down somewhat, although less so when so-called decoupled assistance is included (the dashed uppermost line).

For developing countries there has also been a strong upward trend in the RRA estimate, but starting from a very low level. According to these estimates, the RRA averaged −50 percent in the latter 1950s, but this has risen steadily each half-decade since then. By the end of the 1990s the discrimination against agriculture by developing-country governments had virtually disappeared on average, and the RRA had even become slightly positive for the first time by the first half-decade of this century.

The weighted average for the two groups combined provides a global average RRA, shown as the middle line in figure 1, again with the so-called decoupled assistance included in the dashed upper part of that line. That line suggests global agricultural production was discouraged up to the mid-1980s, but

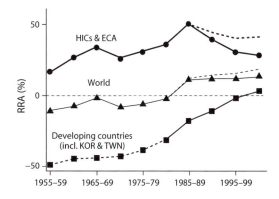

Figure 1

Relative rates of assistance to agricultural industries, showing weighted averages for high-income countries, developing countries, and the world, 1955 to 2004 (percent). Source: Anderson (2008).

has since been encouraged on average: even though in the past two decades agricultural protection has come down a little in high-income countries, agricultural taxation in developing countries has been replaced by positive assistance that has been more than offsetting. There thus appears to be a convergence toward a positive RRA in both sets of countries.

These weighted averages of RRAs of course hide a great deal of diversity among countries. Within the high-income group the estimated RRAs in 2000–2004 range from virtually zero in Australia and New Zealand to more than 10 percent in North America, more than 30 percent in the European Union, and more than 100 percent in both the rest of Western Europe and Japan (and in Korea and Taiwan). For developing countries, the RRAs in 2000–2004 averaged −5 percent in Africa, 0 percent in Latin America, 1 percent in China, 6 percent in South Asia, and 20 percent in Southeast Asia. With even more diversity within each of those developing country regions, these estimates suggest there are many countries that could boost their overall economies by reducing those RRAs.

Within most countries—including those with RRAs close to zero—there is also still much diversity in rates of assistance to different farm industries. Almost all countries assist their import-competing farmers more than their more competitive agricultural export industries. Given that exporters tend to be more productive and more innovative than other producers, this antitrade bias is slowing agricultural and overall economic growth.

As for the distribution across commodities, there is very strong support for the "rice pudding" products: rice, sugar, and milk. In high-income countries, rice has the dubious honor of being the most assisted, thanks especially to Japan. In 2000–2004 its NRA averaged 375 percent, compared with 125 percent for sugar and 65 percent for milk (with cotton and beef trailing close behind with NRAs of 55 and 45 percent, respectively). In developing countries the NRA for rice averaged "only" 17 percent in those years, but sugar and milk were higher at 41 and 32 percent, respectively. By contrast, developing countries continue to tax major export crops: their weighted average NRAs for cocoa, groundnuts, and cotton are still below zero.

Evidently there has been a great deal of reform in recent decades. The massive and widespread discrimination against farmers in developing countries that was identified empirically two decades ago in the seminal study by Krueger, Schiff, and Valdes (1988, 1991) has been much reduced and has even disappeared for some developing countries. Also, the growth in agricultural protection from the 1950s to the 1980s in high-income countries, identified empirically in Anderson and Hayami (1986), has slowed and, for the European Union, even reversed. There remains, however, plenty of scope for further welfare-enhancing reforms to policies distorting agricultural incentives. Reducing the remaining variance among rates of assistance to the various industries within each country's agricultural sector, and especially reducing the antitrade bias in current policies, would help. That in turn would reduce the wide range of NRAs across commodities globally, bringing down the present extreme positive rates for items such as rice, sugar, and milk and reducing the effective taxation of tropical cash crops such as cocoa.

The biggest uncertainty now is whether the RRAs for developing and high-income countries will continue their recent convergence and, if so, whether that will involve more reform by high-income countries

or a continuing upward long-run trend in RRAs for developing countries. Some commentators cite the tariffication and tariff bindings in the Uruguay Round Agreement on Agriculture as a reason to expect countries not to raise their agricultural assistance in the future. However, there is a great deal of "binding overhang" in those WTO commitments for many members and especially for developing countries (WTO, ITC, and UNCTAD 2007), meaning they could raise their applied import tariffs substantially on farm products before reaching the legally bound rates. It thus remains to be seen whether the forces of economic rationalism will be more or less powerful than the perennial agricultural protectionist forces in the decades ahead.

See also Agreement on Agriculture; agricultural trade negotiations; agriculture; Common Agricultural Policy; political economy of trade policy

FURTHER READING

Anderson, K., ed. 2008. *Distortions to Agricultural Incentives: Global Perspective.* London: Palgrave Macmillan. A synopsis of a new set of 75 country case studies providing annual estimates of agricultural protection and taxation over the past half-century.

Anderson, K., and Y. Hayami, eds. 1986. *The Political Economy of Agricultural Protection: East Asia in International Perspective.* London: Allen and Unwin. A set of empirical studies on the extent and causes of agricultural protection growth from the mid-1950s to the early 1980s in East Asia and other high-income countries.

Anderson, K., W. Martin, and D. van der Mensbrugghe. 2006. "Distortions to World Trade: Impacts on Agricultural Markets and Farm Incomes." *Review of Agricultural Economics* 28 (2): 168–94. A global economy–wide computable general equilibrium modeling analysis, using the World Bank's Linkage model, of the effects of agricultural subsidies and import tariffs as of 2005.

Anderson, K., and E. Valenzuela. 2007. "Do Global Trade Distortions Still Harm Developing Country Farmers?" *Review of World Economics* 143 (1): 108–39. Another global economy–wide computable general equilibrium modeling analysis, but using Purdue University's GTAP model, of the effects of agricultural subsidies and import tariffs as of 2005.

Gulbrandsen, O., and A. Lindbeck. 1973. *The Economics of the Agricultural Sector.* Stockholm: Almquist and Wicksell. An early empirical study of trends in agricultural protection in Europe from the 1930s to the 1960s.

Haberler, G. 1958. *Trends in International Trade: A Report by a Panel of Experts.* Geneva: GATT. An early analysis of the problems the GATT contracting parties would face if, as was feared, agricultural protection continued to grow as manufacturing protection was being phased down in successive multilateral trade rounds.

Hermann, R., P. Schenck, R. Thiele, and M. Wiebelt. 1992. *Discrimination against Agriculture in Developing Countries?* Tubingen: J.C.B. Mohr. An early assessment of agricultural pricing policy in developing countries.

Kindleberger, C. P. 1975. "The Rise of Free Trade in Western Europe, 1820–1875." *Journal of Economic History* 35 (1): 20–55. A seminal study of the differences across Europe in the evolution of agricultural protection in the 19th century.

Krueger, A. O., M. Schiff, and A. Valdes. 1988. "Agricultural Incentives in Developing Countries: Measuring the Effect of Sectoral and Economywide Policies." *World Bank Economic Review* 2 (3): 255–72. A synopsis of the extent of taxation of agriculture in developing countries reported more fully in Krueger, Schiff, and Valdes (1991).

———. 1991. *The Political Economy of Agricultural Pricing Policy.* Vol. 1, *Latin America*; Vol. 2, *Asia*; and Vol. 3, *Africa and the Mediterranean.* Baltimore: Johns Hopkins University Press for the World Bank. A milestone empirical study of 18 developing countries, analyzing the evolution of direct and indirect distortions to agricultural incentives from the early 1960s to the mid-1980s and the political economy forces behind them.

Lindert, P. 1991. "Historical Patterns of Agricultural Protection." In *Agriculture and the State*, edited by P. Timmer. Ithaca: Cornell University Press. The best summary available of the very long history of agricultural protectionism in the current high-income countries.

OECD. 2006. *Producer and Consumer Support Estimates, OECD Database 1986–2004.* Available at http://www.oecd.org/document/54/0,2340,en_2649_33727_35009718_1_1_1_1,00.html. The definitive annual report of PSEs and CSEs in all the OECD member countries during the past two decades, but treating the European Union as one entity.

Pinstrup-Andersen, P., ed. 1988. *Food Subsidies in Developing Countries: Cost, Benefits, and Policy Options.* Baltimore: Johns Hopkins University Press. A useful analysis of the consumer side of distortions to agricultural incentives in developing countries, complementing the majority of other studies that focus mainly on the producer impacts of agricultural policies.

Tyers, R., and K. Anderson. 1992. *Disarray in World Food Markets: A Quantitative Assessment.* Cambridge: Cambridge University Press. A model-based analysis of distortions to markets for grains, sugar, and livestock products, a preliminary version of which was used as the basis of the World Bank's *World Development Report 1986.*

Vousden, N. 1990. *The Economic Theory of Protection.* Cambridge: Cambridge University Press. A seminal textbook on the theory of protectionist international trade policies.

WTO, ITC, and UNCTAD. 2007. *World Tariff Profiles 2006.* Geneva: WTO, ITC, and UNCTAD. A new joint publication by these three international institutions that makes publicly available, in an easily accessible form, the WTO legally bound and the applied tariff structures of more than 100 countries.

KYM ANDERSON

Doha Round

The Doha Round, launched in 2001 and formally named the Doha Development Agenda (DDA), was the first round of global trade negotiations held under the auspices of the World Trade Organization (WTO). To understand the dynamics of the Doha Round, it is important to understand its genesis.

The creation of the WTO was one of the major results of the Uruguay Round of multilateral negotiations. The WTO began operations on January 1, 1995. Its early years were dominated by negotiations to finalize agreement on several services sectors (finance, telecommunications, maritime transportation) and to liberalize trade in information technology (IT) products. With the exception of the maritime services talks, these were successful: telecom and financial services agreements were concluded in 1996; the Information Technology Agreement (ITA)—a so-called zero-for-zero deal under which signatories abolished tariffs on a common set of IT products—entered into force in 1997.

Flush with these achievements, the first ministerial conference of the WTO, held in Singapore in December 1996, agreed to a work program for the following years. Members of the Organisation for Economic Co-operation and Development (OECD) proposed to put government procurement, trade facilitation, competition law, and policies on foreign investment on the WTO agenda. A minority (led by France and the United States) also sought to launch discussions on labor standards. Opposition by many developing countries kept labor standards off the WTO agenda, but members did agree to create working groups to discuss and study the relationship between trade and competition and investment policy disciplines, transparency in government procurement, and trade facilitation. These subsequently came to be known as the "Singapore issues."

In the years that followed, OECD members failed to agree on a Multilateral Agreement on Investment; furthermore the East Asian financial crisis and follow-on crises in other parts of the world added to skepticism on the part of many developing country governments and numerous vocal nongovernmental organizations that the WTO was a balanced and "fair" organization.

Research supporting aspects of this skepticism began to emerge in the late 1990s, concluding that the net benefits for many developing countries in narrow market-access terms were limited and may even have been negative as the result of the new requirements under the Agreement on Trade-Related Aspects of Intellectual Property Rights (TRIPS) to enforce patent rights and other forms of protection for intangible assets. TRIPS was the first example of a multilateral trade agreement that involved a significant element of policy harmonization. Although most economists accept that there is an economic logic to protection of intellectual property, both theory and economic history suggest that

harmonization is unlikely to be an optimal outcome for all countries, in particular poor economies. Whatever one's view of the economics, TRIPS greatly increased the awareness of many developing countries of the need to carefully scrutinize the likely impacts of agreements that entail regulatory harmonization.

A major feature of the WTO was that developing countries became subject to numerous rules of the game that they had not been affected by as members of the WTO's predecessor, the General Agreement on Tariffs and Trade. The costs of implementation of some of these WTO disciplines, if defined not just narrowly in terms of required legal and regulatory changes, but in terms of what is necessary to benefit from them, could be significant. Assistance to meet the costs of implementation was a matter for governments to request from national and international development agencies. Many developing countries argued that the provision of such assistance had been inadequate.

These considerations help explain why only a few years after the establishment of the WTO, efforts were made to initiate a new round of trade negotiations. The requirement in the Uruguay Round agreements on agriculture and services to initiate new negotiations in these two areas in 2000 provided an additional rationale for launching a broader round, as this would allow for cross-issue linkages and trade-offs.

Countries had very different objectives, with some (mostly developed countries) seeking to build on the Singapore ministerial and launch talks on the new areas as well as the core market-access agenda, and others (mostly developing nations) seeking to address implementation and related problems associated with existing agreements.

The attempt to launch a "Millennium Round" at the 1999 WTO ministerial meeting in Seattle failed to achieve the necessary consensus, largely reflecting opposition by many developing countries to engage in new negotiations when they had yet to digest the Uruguay Round and a perception that implementation concerns were not being taken sufficiently seriously, as well as resistance on the part of the

European Union (EU) and several other OECD countries to engaging in talks to significantly reduce support for their farmers. Many developing countries also opposed proposals to negotiate WTO disciplines for the Singapore issues, environmental policies, and (minimum) labor standards. Notwithstanding the deep differences in views, additional preparatory discussions in 2000–2001 allowed the first round of multilateral negotiations under WTO auspices to be launched at the 2001 Ministerial Conference in Doha, Qatar.

Major Players and Issues The name given to the round—the Doha Development Agenda—arose for two reasons. First, many WTO members held the view that a multilateral effort to reduce trade-distorting policies was part of an appropriate response to the terrorist attack on New York and Washington, DC, on September 11, 2001. The view that trade cooperation could help address some of the causes of terrorism by promoting economic growth was strongly espoused by the then U.S. trade representative Robert Zoellick and helped to change the political atmospherics that up to that point had not generated sufficient support for the launch of new trade talks. Second, the name reflected recognition of the view of many developing countries that the Uruguay Round had been "unbalanced." Making "development" a prominent goal of the round had a major impact on the subsequent negotiating dynamics.

Reflecting the differences in objectives of the participants, the negotiating agenda of the round was multidimensional. It spanned market access for goods and services, the WTO's existing rules, potential new disciplines on the Singapore issues, implementation problems, and a renewed emphasis on "special and differential treatment" (SDT) for developing countries.

The major protagonists were the EU and the United States on the side of OECD countries, and Brazil and India on the side of the developing countries. In addition to these four giants, a variety of coalitions played an important role, both in the run-up to the Doha Round and during the negotiations. Influential groups included the so-called Like Minded Group of developing countries, which argued for more SDT, for addressing implementation concerns, and for nonreciprocity in negotiations; the Africa Group, which espoused a similar position; the least-developed countries (LDC group) and a variety of "G-x" groups, where "x" is a number indicating how many countries were participants in the launch of the group. The most prominent of these was the G20, a group of countries led by Brazil and India that also included China and South Africa. The G20 had a fluctuating membership, with some countries leaving—sometimes as the result of pressure (inducements) offered by the United States (the departure of several Central American countries following the formation of the Central American Free Trade Agreement being an example)—and others joining. Other groups included the G90—comprising almost the totality of developing countries in the WTO—and the G11, a group of developing countries that were active in the nonagricultural market-access talks.

As many developing countries were not convinced that launching negotiations on the Singapore issues was in their interest, a last-minute compromise reached at the Doha Ministerial Conference was that negotiations on these four subject areas would commence at the 2003 meeting of WTO ministers. Based on an intervention by India, it was specified that a precondition for such negotiations was an "explicit consensus" among WTO members on their modalities.

The EU, Japan, and the Republic of Korea were the primary *demandeurs* for negotiations on all four Singapore issues. Three groups of developing countries—the African Union; the LDCs; and the African, Caribbean, and Pacific group of countries—had all agreed at the ministerial level in 2003 that they did not support launching negotiations on any of these topics. They were joined by a number of middle-income countries, such as Malaysia. Some countries argued that these were marginal issues, with only limited benefits for developing countries; that they could give rise to potentially significant implementation costs; and that they would divert scarce negotiating resources and political attention away from the more important market-access agenda. Although many middle-income economies, including most Latin American countries, did not have serious concerns about launching negotiations on the four subjects, it became clear in 2003 that an "explicit consensus" did not exist. As a result, the 2003 Cancún Ministerial Conference failed—the second one to do so in the WTO's short history.

The failure was not due solely to differences on the Singapore issues. Disagreements were particularly prominent on agriculture. Developed countries' farm subsidies—with the EU's Common Agricultural Policy (CAP) and the U.S. system of farm subsidies being the most prominent—were major bones of contention. Opposition by the EU to liberalization of its agricultural policies and stronger disciplines on farm subsidies was a fundamental factor impeding agreement. In addition, U.S. unwillingness to address demands by West African cotton producers to reduce production subsidies as a priority also played an important role in souring the atmosphere in Cancún.

A "Framework Agreement" negotiated in July 2004 removed three of the Singapore issues from the negotiating table (retaining only trade facilitation), specified that LDCs were not expected to make any market-access concessions (taking up then EU trade commissioner Pascal Lamy's call that these countries should benefit from the round "for free"), and established negotiating frameworks for the key areas of agriculture and nonagricultural market access. It was agreed that formulas were to be used to reduce trade barriers in both areas, and that export subsidies in agriculture were to be prohibited by a specific date to be negotiated.

One result of the decision to take three of the Singapore issues off the table was that to a much greater extent than in the Uruguay Round negotiations centered on tariffs. Although in principle services were another important market-access negotiation, WTO members were not willing to make significant liberalization commitments—in part because of a desire first to determine what the contours of a possible deal would be for merchandise trade, agriculture in particular. A major challenge

confronting negotiators was to agree to substantially lower remaining tariff peaks. As average tariff rates in most industrial countries are now relatively low, the main payoff from both a development and an economic efficiency perspective would come from reducing the dispersion in tariff protection by lowering the highest tariffs more than the average. A straightforward way of doing this is to apply a nonlinear tariff reduction formula to each country's prevailing tariffs.

WTO members agreed to make tariff-cutting formulas a core negotiating modality in the Doha Round, with eventual emergence of variants of the so-called Swiss formula—first used in the Tokyo Round (1973–79)—as the basis of discussion for merchandise trade liberalization. The Swiss formula is defined as $T_1 = MT_0/(M + T_0)$, where T_1 is the new tariff commitment, T_0 is the prevailing one, and M is a coefficient—the maximum level of the permitted tariff. The formula generates nonlinear cuts, with higher proportional reductions for higher tariffs. It was decided that (at least) two coefficients would be used, one for developed countries and another for developing nations, such that developed countries would reduce their tariffs proportionally more in accordance with the notion of SDT for developing countries. Limited exemptions would be permitted to allow governments to maintain higher levels of protection for a subset of "special" and "sensitive" products. Given that the major developing country coalitions such as the G20 spanned a differentiated set of countries, insistence on undifferentiated SDT for all members made it more difficult to agree on a coefficient and resulted in much attention also being given to the criteria that would apply for possible exemptions from the formula for "sensitive" products.

Disagreements on the specification of the formulas and the magnitude of allowable exceptions for specific products could not be overcome during 2004–7. Negotiations between the so-called five interested parties in agriculture—Australia and Brazil, representing export interests, the EU and India, representing the "defensive" interests, and the United States (both an exporter and a provider of substantial support to its farmers)—did not manage to identify a package of mutually acceptable reforms. Much of the discussion centered on technical issues such as how to go about converting specific tariffs (taxes that are based on volume rather than the value of imported products) into ad valorem equivalents. Although these were important, the fact that such technical matters needed to be addressed by ministers illustrated the depth of the political sensitivities that prevented lower-level officials from agreeing on negotiating modalities in Geneva.

The 2005 ministerial meeting in Hong Kong did not lead to any major breakthroughs, with the exception of (conditional) agreement to ban export subsidies for agricultural products in 2013, promises of an increase in development assistance ("aid for trade"), and a promise by rich countries to extend duty-free, quota-free access to their markets for at least 97 percent of exports originating in LDCs. As noted by many commentators, the last promise did little to go beyond the status quo, and the exclusion of 3 percent of tariff lines was enough to permit countries to maintain tariffs on the most competitive LDC exports if they desired to. Ministers renewed their commitment to conclude the DDA by the end of 2006. A roadmap for key decisions was agreed on, including a target date of April 30 to agree on modalities (formulas and liberalization parameters) for agriculture and nonagricultural merchandise trade. Comprehensive draft schedules based on these modalities were expected to be submitted by July 31, 2006. This was also the deadline for a second round of revised market opening offers in services.

As of mid-2006, the contours of a possible agreement on merchandise trade liberalization had emerged. It was described as a 20-20-20 package by the director general of the WTO. Under this proposal the EU would cut its bound agricultural tariffs by an estimated 54 percent (following the proposal made by the G20), the United States would cap its total trade-distorting agricultural subsidies at a maximum of $20 billion, and developing countries would agree to a maximum tariff on manufactures of 20 percent. A deal along the lines of the 20-20-20 package would have implied a significant reduction not only in tariff bindings but also in applied policies. Negotiators could not agree on a specific compromise, however. The G20 sought deeper cuts in EU tariffs and both the G20 and the EU wanted the United States to accept a lower ceiling on its domestic farm subsidies.

By this time the original endpoint envisaged for the Doha Round (January 1, 2005) had been missed by a wide margin, as were nearly all deadlines that had been set during the talks. This pattern extended into 2006–7. The inability of the major protagonists to make concessions led the director general of the WTO to suspend the negotiations in mid-2006. Despite efforts in early 2007 to resuscitate the process, which led to a high-profile meeting between four of the major protagonists (the EU, the United States, Brazil, and India) in Potsdam in June, no agreement could be reached on how much to cut farm subsidies and tariffs on agricultural and industrial goods. Developing countries remained disappointed by the United States' offer on agricultural subsidies and the EU's unwillingness to open its agricultural markets. Conversely, the EU and the United States were unsatisfied by what they regarded as inadequate offers by Brazil and India on industrial tariffs. At the time of writing (April 2008), prospects for an imminent conclusion of the Doha Round appeared dim. The expiry of Trade Promotion Authority—a provision previously called "Fast Track," which precludes the U.S. Congress from introducing amendments to a multilaterally negotiated deal—in June 2007 removed an important focal point for a timely conclusion of the talks. The political calendars of several major players suggested that the Doha Round was unlikely to conclude before 2009–10.

Progress and Prospects Despite the torturous negotiating process, some progress was made during the Doha Round to deal with several development-related concerns that had become prominent in the period immediately following the creation of the WTO. Thus in a Declaration on the TRIPS Agreement and Public Health, developing countries without the capacity to produce pharmaceuticals were permitted to import generics from countries that do have capacity under compulsory licensing arrangements.

A consensus also emerged around the notion that trade negotiations should be complemented by assistance for developing countries, both to help address implementation costs associated with specific WTO disciplines and, more generally, to bolster the competitiveness of domestic firms through actions to reduce the costs of trade and doing business. The recognition that trade negotiations must be complemented by actions to help address the prevailing constraints in many poor countries that inhibit exploitation of trade opportunities was an important development. Insofar as the Doha Round has led development organizations to focus greater attention on the trade agenda and constraints in developing countries, this should be counted as a positive outcome.

Why so little success in obtaining agreement? A number of reasons can be identified. Many of these revolve around the argument that there was not enough on the table to mobilize support within the OECD countries to accept greater agricultural liberalization. Concerns on the part of a number of smaller developing countries that they would suffer losses from the erosion of trade preferences following agreement among the larger WTO members to reduce tariffs on a most-favored-nation basis also played a role.

It is important to consider that the Doha Round took place during a period in which there was a boom in world trade, in part driven by trade liberalization that was implemented unilaterally by governments. World Bank research suggests that the uniform tariff equivalent of applied tariffs for merchandise products in 2007 was 7 percent in high-income countries and 15 percent in developing countries. The numbers are heavily influenced by the substantially higher protection of agricultural products, around 40 and 25 percent, respectively. They are much lower for manufactures (4 and 14 percent).

The implication of the relatively low levels of applied tariffs in many countries is that there is less

to play for. This translates into fewer export interests having an incentive to invest significant (political) resources in engaging in trade talks and providing the political support that is needed for liberalization. As most protection is now concentrated in agriculture, matters are complicated further by the fact that this sector is of significant export interest to only a subset of WTO members. Less than 10 percent of world trade is in agricultural products. Although trade volumes no doubt would be higher if rates of protection were lowered, it is trade in other merchandise that dominates, and much of this trade is relatively free.

Because WTO negotiations are barter exchanges, concessions in agriculture by high-income countries need to be balanced by concessions on the part of the agricultural exporting nations that will benefit in mercantilist, export volume terms. Although average levels of protection have fallen in these countries, there are still significant barriers to trade. The low prevailing averages mask relatively high tariff peaks in both agriculture and manufactures in many countries. In services, despite significant liberalization of trade and investment in recent years, numerous barriers persist. Finally, it is important to consider that the negotiating coin of the WTO is policy bindings—the levels of protection that a country commits itself not to exceed. These bindings are valuable even if a specific commitment does not imply much, if any, reduction in applied levels of protection, as they create greater certainty that past liberalization will not be easily reversed.

In principle it would appear therefore that even with the relatively narrow market-access (tariff) agenda that dominated the Doha Round after 2004, a bargain should have been feasible, with "payment" for OECD agricultural liberalization taking the form of traditional market-access liberalization by major developing countries. In practice, however, developing countries appeared unwilling to offer enough in terms of liberalization and bindings to induce the OECD countries to move enough to allow a deal to be struck. This in turn suggests that the major players perceived their best alternatives to a negotiated agreement to dominate an outcome under which they would have had to make additional concessions in order to get more liberalization from their major trading partners.

What the outcome of the Doha Round will be remains to be seen. The same is true regarding the consequences of the Doha Round for the WTO as an institution. The difficulty in attaining a consensus to negotiate on the Singapore issues, and the limited progress that was made on extending the coverage of services commitments, suggest there may be limits regarding the set of policies that can (should) be subject to binding multilateral disciplines.

See also agricultural trade negotiations; multilateral trade negotiations; special and differential treatment; Uruguay Round; World Trade Organization

FURTHER READING

Anderson, Kym, and Will Martin, eds. 2006. *Agricultural Trade Reform and the Doha Development Agenda*. Basingstoke, UK: Palgrave Macmillan. Analyzes the potential economic consequences of agricultural liberalization and the specific aspects of the Doha talks on agriculture.

Hertel, Thomas, and L. Alan Winters, eds. 2006. *Poverty and the WTO: Impacts of the Doha Development Agenda*. Basingstoke, UK: Palgrave Macmillan. Focuses on the potential impacts of global trade reforms on poverty within countries.

Hoekman, Bernard, Aaditya Mattoo, and Philip English, eds. 2002. *Development, Trade, and the WTO: A Handbook*. Washington DC: World Bank. A compilation of short papers that describe the WTO and the subjects that were on the Doha negotiating agenda.

Lee, Donna, and Rorden Wilkinson, eds. 2007. *The WTO after Hong Kong: Progress in, and Prospects for, the Doha Development Agenda*. London: Routledge. Provides an international relations perspective on the negotiations, including discussions of coalitions and negotiating strategies.

UN, Millennium Project. 2005. "Trade for Development." Task Force on Trade. New York: United Nations Development Program. Includes a comprehensive analysis of the issues on the Doha agenda and their importance from an economic development perspective.

World Trade Organization (WTO). http://www.wto.org/. The WTO home page is a primary source of information on developments in the negotiations.

BERNARD HOEKMAN

■ dollar standard

In the absence of a purely international form of money, a strong national currency is central to international commerce. Outside Europe, the dollar dominates as a vehicle currency in interbank foreign exchange, as an invoice currency in international trade and capital flows, and in official exchange reserves. How did the dollar establish its preeminent international role?

After World War II, the United States had the world's largest economy and the only stable financial system with open foreign exchange markets. Inflation and exchange controls proliferated throughout Europe—as well as in Japan and most developing countries. Thus the dollar naturally became the world's vehicle currency for (private) interbank transacting between any pair of national currencies and became the intervention currency that governments used for stabilizing their exchange rates. Foreign governments as well as private corporations could build up their dollar reserves knowing that they had a liquid market in which to sell them.

The Bretton Woods agreement of 1945 formally ratified the dollar as the dominant currency. Under Article IV, countries outside the communist bloc declared dollar parities, while, as center country, the United States had a passive foreign exchange rate policy—except for its residual tie to gold.

The Dollar as Facilitator of International Exchange But why does the dollar standard continue even when most other industrial countries, such as Japan and those in Europe, no longer have exchange controls—and Article IV was amended in 1976 so that member countries no longer need to declare dollar parities? Suppose there are 150 national currencies in the world economy. To facilitate international exchange, the markets themselves would always pick just one as the central money for intermediating nearly all international payments. Transaction efficiency increases because the number of active bilateral foreign exchange markets necessary for clearing international payments, both spot and forward, is thereby reduced.

A little algebra helps explain continued dollar predominance in a world of N national currencies. The total number of country pairs in the system is the combination of N things taken two at a time ($^{N}C_2$). If foreign exchange dealers tried to trade across each pair—say, Swedish kronor against Australian dollars, or Korean won against Japanese yen—there would be a huge number of active foreign exchange markets. With 150 national currencies in the world (N = 150), if dealers tried to trade each pair bilaterally that would lead to 11,175 different markets!

It is expensive for any bank to set up a foreign exchange trading desk. Thus, rather than trading all pairs of currencies bilaterally, in practice just one currency, the Nth, is chosen as the central vehicle currency. Then all trading and exchange takes place first against the vehicle currency before going to the others. By having all currency trading against that one currency, the number of markets in the system can be reduced to N-1. Thus, with 150 countries, we need just 149 foreign exchange markets against the U.S. dollar (instead of 11,175 bilateral exchange rates against each other). Unlike the Bretton Woods system, where all countries other than the United States set official dollar parities, this result does not depend on any formal agreement among governments. In private markets today, choosing one currency such as the dollar to be the intermediary currency is the most natural way of economizing on foreign exchange transacting.

But history is important. If one country starts to provide the central money, as the United States did in the late 1940s, it becomes a natural monopoly because of the economies of scale. The more countries that deal in dollars, the cheaper it is for any one of them all to deal in dollars as unit transaction costs fall—particularly in forward exchange markets that are much thinner and potentially much less liquid than spot markets. If you are a Japanese importer of

Swedish Volvos, to pay for the Volvos you would first have your bank convert your yen into dollars on the open market, then use the dollars to buy Swedish kronor. Volvo Corporation receives the Swedish kronor, and the importer gets the Volvos. But the dollar is the intermediary currency: two interbank transactions involving dollars are cheaper than trying to trade yen directly for Swedish kronor at different terms to maturity.

Using the standard textbook classification of the roles of money, table 1 summarizes our paradigm of the dollar's central role in facilitating international exchange. For both the private and government sectors, the dollar performs as medium of exchange, store of value, unit of account, and standard of deferred payment for international transactions on current and capital accounts—as it has done since 1945.

First, the dollar is a *medium of exchange*. Because the foreign exchange markets are mainly interbank, the dollar is the vehicle currency in interbank transactions serving customers in the private sector. The dollar is on one side or the other of about 90 percent of interbank transactions worldwide. Thus, when any government intervenes to influence its exchange rate, it also finds it cheaper and more convenient to use the dollar as the official intervention currency. (The major exception to this convention is a fringe of European countries to the east of the euro area, which mainly use the euro as their central money.) Although the dollar is the predominant money in foreign currency trading, London has the largest foreign exchange market—bigger than New York's. And large dollar-based markets also exist in Singapore and Hong Kong.

Table 1
The U.S. dollar's facilitating role as international money since 1945

	Private	Official
Medium of exchange	Vehicle	Intervention
Store of value	Banking	Reserves
Unit of account	Invoice	Peg
Standard of deferred payment	Private bonds	Sovereign bonds

Second, the dollar is an international *store of value.* Corporations and some individuals hold dollar bank accounts in London, Singapore, and other offshore banking centers—as well as in the United States itself. It is estimated that more than half the stock of coin and currency issued by the U.S. government circulates abroad in Latin America, Russia, Africa, and other financially distressed areas. In developing countries, as a whole, about two-thirds of their official exchange reserves are in dollars.

Third, the dollar serves as a *unit of account* for much of international trade. Trade in primary commodities shows a strong pattern of using the dollar as the main currency of *invoice.* Exports of homogeneous primary products such as oil, wheat, and copper all tend to be invoiced in dollars, with worldwide price formation in a centralized exchange. Spot trading, but particularly forward contracting, is concentrated at these centralized exchanges—which are usually in American cities such as Chicago and New York, although dollar-denominated commodity exchanges also exist in London and elsewhere.

Invoicing patterns for exports of manufactured goods are more complex. Major industrial countries with strong currencies tend to invoice their exports in their home currencies. Before the establishment of the European Monetary Union, more than 75 percent of German exports had been invoiced in deutsche marks, more than 50 percent of French exports invoiced in francs, and so on. (McKinnon 1979 provided a rationale for this difference in invoicing practices between primary commodities and manufactures.)

Within Asia, however, foreign trade is invoiced mainly in dollars. In Korea, for example, the proportion of imports invoiced in U.S. dollars is about 80 percent, and even higher for exports. Other less mature economies in East Asia, such as China, use dollars even more intensively in invoicing their foreign trade. In Japan, the most industrialized and richest economy in East Asia, almost half of its exports and three-quarters of its imports are invoiced in dollars.

Fourth, as *a standard of deferred payment*— which is also a traditional role of money—private

and sovereign bonds in international markets are heavily denominated in U.S. dollars, though the euro seems to be as important. The growth of a broadly based euro-denominated bond market within Europe has made it much more attractive for foreigners to borrow by issuing euro bonds. The euro area is unusual in that it is a net creditor in the world economy that can lend in its own currency. Other net creditors are more or less confined to lending in dollars.

Despite the increasing importance of the euro in international bond markets, U.S. Treasuries are still taken as the benchmark, or "risk-free" asset. That is, dollar-denominated sovereign bonds issued by emerging markets the world over have their credit ratings measured relative to U.S. Treasuries. Thus, risk premiums in interest rates on these bonds are typically quoted as so many percentage points over U.S. Treasuries.

The Dollar as Nominal Anchor Beyond the traditional roles of money outlined in table 1, the dollar has a second and complementary international function. Foreign monetary authorities may better anchor their own domestic price levels by choosing to peg, officially or unofficially, to the dollar. By opting to keep their dollar exchange rates stable, foreign governments are essentially opting to harmonize—without always succeeding—their monetary policies with that of the United States. This monetary harmonization has two avenues: (1) international commodity arbitrage—the *arbitrage avenue*, and (2) the *signaling avenue*, where other central banks take their cue from actions of the U.S. Federal Reserve Bank.

For the dollar to function successfully as nominal anchor, however, two important conditions must be satisfied: (1) The U.S. price level, as measured by a broad index of tradable goods prices, is stable and expected to remain so. (2) Most countries, and certainly neighboring ones, are on the same international standard, that is, they also fix their exchange rates to the dollar.

In the history of the post–World War II dollar standard, these two conditions were satisfied in some periods but not in others. Indeed, in contrast to the dollar's continued robustness as the facilitator of international exchange under either fixed or floating exchange rates, its function as nominal anchor has continually metamorphosed. It was strong in the Bretton Woods period of the 1950s and 1960s of fixed dollar parities, weakened greatly in the inflationary period of the 1970s into the 1980s, and then strengthened in the 1990s into the new millennium when the American price level again became fairly stable. The current proclivity of most Asian economies (with the major exception of Japan) and many emerging markets elsewhere to peg to the dollar, if only softly and informally, is sometimes called Bretton Woods II.

Consequences of International Currency Asymmetry Developing countries and a few industrial ones cannot borrow internationally in their own currencies—a phenomenon that has been dubbed *original sin*. Those developing countries that are dollar debtors live on sufferance: their domestic monies are only "provisional." Any economic or political disturbance at home provokes the suspicion that these foreign currency debts may not be repayable and that the domestic currency will depreciate against the dollar—as in the East Asian crisis of 1997–98.

But what about the biggest international debtor of all? After running trade deficits for more than 25 years, the United States is a net debtor: its liabilities in 2006 exceeded its claims on the rest of the world by about $4 trillion. At about 30 percent of U.S. gross national product (GNP) in 2006, America's net international indebtedness was higher than that of any other industrialized country—and higher than, say, Brazil's, which was only 20 percent of Brazilian GNP. Yet, unlike Latin American currencies today, and unlike East Asian currencies in 1997–98, the dollar is not threatened by a loss of confidence. As long as its purchasing power is seen to be stable, that is, as long as the Federal Reserve keeps price inflation very low, the dollar cannot be attacked in the usual sense. Default risk associated with foreigners holding dollar assets is virtually nonexistent. If need be, the Fed could always print more money to redeem U.S. Treasury bonds outstanding. Thus the United States has an indefinitely long line of credit with the rest of the world.

But this virtual invulnerability of the center country as debtor to foreign exchange risk means that this risk shifts to creditor countries that, Europe aside, cannot *lend* to the United States in their own currencies—a circumstance known as *conflicted virtue*. Creditor countries such as China and Japan with trade surpluses, reflecting their high domestic savings, simply accumulate large volumes of liquid dollar claims on the United States, leaving them vulnerable to unwanted currency appreciations. Conflicted virtue in creditor countries is the mirror image of original sin in debtor economies. Both creditor and debtor economies are exposed to serious currency risks should their currencies fluctuate against the dollar. The only country exempted from exchange risk is the United States itself.

See also Bretton Woods system; conflicted virtue; dominant currency; euro; exchange rate regimes; gold standard, international; interest parity conditions; international reserves; original sin; reserve currency; twin deficits; vehicle currency

FURTHER READING

McKinnon, Ronald. 1979. *Money in International Exchange: The Convertible Currency System.* New York: Oxford University Press.

———. 2005. *Exchange Rates under the East Asian Dollar Standard: Living with Conflicted Virtue.* Cambridge, MA: MIT Press. Introduces and describes in detail the concept of conflicted virtue.

RONALD MCKINNON

■ domestic content requirements

Domestic content requirements compel firms to purchase a certain percentage of their inputs from domestic firms as a precondition for local market access or preferential policy treatment. In general, domestic content requirements act as a protectionist measure, since they usually improve the competitive position of domestic firms in relation to foreign firms. Nonetheless, the ultimate effect of domestic content requirements depends on the form of the requirements, the characteristics of demand, market structure, and the nature of the production process.

Motives and Form In their simplest form domestic content requirements oblige firms to purchase a certain percentage of their inputs from domestic firms. If a firm fails to meet the requirement, it may be denied market access or its exports may be hit with additional tariffs. Alternatively, the firm may fail to qualify for policy benefits such as production subsidies. Although domestic content requirements usually apply to all firms, they typically have no impact on domestic firm production decisions, since domestic firms generally use a higher percentage of domestic inputs in their production than foreign firms do, and the political economy determinants of these measures generally result in domestic content requirements that surpass the natural domestic content selected by unconstrained foreign firms but are met or exceeded by the natural domestic content selected by domestic firms.

The implementation of domestic content or local content requirements is usually motivated by a country's desire to assist domestic firms or to increase the level of domestic economic activity. For example, many developing countries used domestic content regulations as an element of their import substituting industrialization policies. Domestic content regulations have also been imposed to influence the activities of foreign investors, with the goal of increasing foreign firm investment in the domestic economy or of increasing the domestic share of input purchases by foreign firms that already operate in the domestic market. Such policies have been especially common in large manufacturing industries, such as automobile assembly, where domestic countries preferred that investors provide many jobs in the local economy, rather than simply doing a small amount of local assembly using foreign materials. Since the imposition of local content requirements on foreign investors violates the national treatment principle of the General Agreement on Tariffs and Trade, however, the Uruguay Round included a trade-related investment measures agreement, which requires countries to remove domestic content re-

quirements on foreign investment. Nonetheless, such requirements may still remain in place, though in less transparent forms.

Content regulations have proliferated in a regional context as countries have entered into an ever-increasing number of free trade agreements. Since free trade agreements eliminate tariffs on all trade among member countries while leaving tariffs on nonmembers unchanged, free trade agreements create an incentive for tariff-shopping by nonmember exporters that wish to sell their products in the member market. To prevent tariff-shopping, free trade areas typically include rules of origin that stipulate the percentage of area content or area value added that the traded product must contain if it is to qualify for the preferential tariff treatment extended to member-country products.

Content preferences are generally implemented to protect domestic or regional markets. However, the Generalized System of Preferences (GSP), which provides tariff reductions for products exported from developing countries to developed countries, usually requires products to contain a minimum level of domestic content from the developing country. Finally, it is important to note that domestic content requirements are also imposed in service sectors, where regulations may require, for example, that a certain percentage of broadcast programming originates from domestic providers.

Impact of Content Requirements When domestic inputs are of similar quality and lower price than foreign inputs, firms will willingly meet or exceed the domestic content requirement and the requirement will have no effect on firm decisions. Since domestic content requirements are set in a political environment, however, they generally force foreign firms to purchase a larger fraction of their inputs from domestic sources than they would if they were unconstrained, while domestic content requirements usually have no effect on the sourcing choices of domestic firms. The best response for a cost-minimizing foreign firm is to exactly meet, though not exceed, the purchase criteria of the domestic content requirement. Alternatively, the foreign firm may decide to pay the tariff penalty that is associated with noncompliance if the tariff cost is less than the extra cost of purchasing more domestic inputs. Either way, since domestic content requirements raise the relative production costs of foreign firms, they benefit domestic producers of final goods by increasing domestic firm sales or profits. In addition, they may reduce competition in the final goods market if they reduce the volume of goods sold by the foreign firm in the domestic market.

Whether they are imposed by the domestic country or by an importing developed country that is administering its GSP tariff preferences, domestic content requirements protect domestic intermediates producers. Since these policies increase production costs, domestic content regulations harm domestic customers, who face higher prices for the goods they buy. In addition, programs such as the GSP have an ambiguous effect on developing country welfare, as the increased demand for imports of the final good from the developing country will be offset, and possibly even reversed, by the cost increases that are associated with the content requirement.

Domestic content requirements take many different forms. For this reason, the form of the requirement has great influence on its economic effects. For example, domestic expenditure on capital is often excluded, while domestic labor is generally counted toward the domestic content requirement. When this is the case, firms respond to the relative cost incentive by investing in more labor than they would if the treatment of labor and capital were uniform. Other common variations in implementation relate to the domestic content benchmark, and whether it is defined as a percentage of physical inputs, sales, costs, or value added.

The effects of domestic content regulations are also determined by firm responses. To begin, it is commonly understood that imports may impose market discipline. If the market that implements domestic content regulations is served by a monopoly input supplier, limits on the use of foreign inputs will reduce competition and allow the domestic input supplier to exploit its market power. In this case, domestic content requirements may even reduce domestic output of the final good, as the domestic input supplier reduces its production and consequent sales to take advantage of its market power. Second, if it is possible for firms to change the scale of their production at low cost, domestic content regulations may fail to shift consumption toward domestic varieties. Finally, if the domestic content requirement is at a level that is too high, foreign firms may reevaluate their decision to supply the domestic market.

The effects of domestic content requirements are also shaped by the nature of the production process. For example, when a content standard is based on value added, whether final good output increases or decreases depends in part on the relationship between labor and the intermediate inputs in production, and whether they are complements or substitutes. Similarly, depending on the relationship between the usage of labor and intermediate inputs, the imposition of a domestic content requirement based on value added may cause the volume of imported intermediate inputs to rise or fall. In addition, the composition of intermediate input imports may change. In particular, if there are many imported intermediate inputs, and the relative price of foreign inputs differs across inputs, a value-added requirement will shift purchases toward foreign inputs whose relative foreign price is the lowest.

In the case of foreign investment, the desire to foster greater domestic activity may be subverted by domestic content regulations. First, since foreign firms are placed at a disadvantage, they may place fewer of their activities in the local market. In addition, when the scale of their operations is reduced, the overall productivity of the foreign operation may suffer from a failure to achieve full economies of scale in production.

Due to the rise of vertically integrated production networks that cross national borders, the proliferation of free trade areas has created new difficulties in defining and meeting content requirements. In particular, when a hub country forms free trade areas with different associates, which are not linked to one another through any common partnership, the definition of content and rules of origin becomes increasingly complicated. The difficulties posed by multiple partnerships of differing membership groups is acknowledged, for example, by the European Union's creation of the Pan-European Cumulation System in 1997, which integrates bilateral rules into a multilateral framework that enables firms to determine "European" content.

See also rules of origin; trade-related investment measures (TRIMs)

FURTHER READING

Baldwin, Richard. 2006. "Multilateralizing Regionalism: Spaghetti Bowls as Building Blocs on the Path to Global Free Trade." *World Economy* 29 (11): 1451–1518. Addresses political economy forces driving regionalism and how to achieve greater multilateralism, with historical overview.

Corden, W. M. 1971. *The Theory of Protection.* Oxford: Oxford University Press. A key early work on trade policy, including domestic content requirements.

Grossman, Gene M. 1981. "The Theory of Domestic Content Protection and Content Preference." *Quarterly Journal of Economics* 96 (4): 583–603. Determines the effects of content protection, showing it to be equivalent to a combination of other commercial policies.

Krishna, Kala, and Motoshige Itoh. 1988. "Content Protection and Oligopolistic Interactions." *Review of Economic Studies* 55 (1): 107–25. Examines conditions that determine the effects of content protection in oligopolies and thus who might lobby for such protection.

Krueger, Anne O. 1999. "Are Preferential Trading Arrangements Trade-Liberalizing or Protectionist?" *Journal of Economic Perspectives* 13 (4): 105–24. Reviews effects of preferential trading areas and finds empirical evidence insufficient.

Lopez-de-Silanes, Florencio, James R. Markusen, and Thomas F. Rutherford. 1996. "Trade Policy Subtleties with Multinational Firms." *European Economic Review* 40 (8): 1605–27. Shows content requirements can be anticompetitive, reducing output and shifting rents to domestic firms, in oligopolies where foreign multinationals rely more on imported intermediates than domestic firms (applied to North American auto industry).

Moran, Theodore H. 1998. *Foreign Direct Investment and Development: The New Policy Agenda for Developing Countries and Economies in Transition.* Washington DC: Institute for International Economics. Reviews developing country policies toward foreign firms, including alternatives to domestic content requirements.

Munk, Bernard. 1969. "The Welfare Costs of Content Protection: The Automotive Industry in Latin America." *Journal of Political Economy* 77 (1): 85–98. An early work on domestic content requirements.

DEBORAH L. SWENSON

■ dominant currency

A currency dominates other currencies when it is used more frequently as a unit of account, medium of exchange, and store of value. Local currencies tend to dominate foreign currencies as means of exchange partly because the bulk of transactions is local and partly because governments discriminate in favor of the currency they issue. Legal tender laws and the fact that governments generally disburse funds and receive tax collections in the government-issued currency raise the cost of using other currencies as alternative means of payment in the domestic market. Currency substitution—the replacement of domestic money with a (better) foreign money—is a slow process even when it is permissible. Inflation must reach high rates before individuals switch out of a currency. For example, an inflation rate of 10 percent a month in the German hyperinflation of the 1920s led to a currency substitution of only 5 percent of the money stock.

At the international level, where legal restrictions matter much less and national currencies can freely compete, specific types of transactions tend to be denominated in international currencies to enhance market transparency, and international investments in different currencies are regularly held as a store of value. In the search for the preferred currency, transaction costs are one of the most relevant considerations. These costs decline as the transaction domain of a currency expands; call this the network value of money. Currencies that are not widely used have a low network value and are at a competitive disadvantage against widely used currencies. Once a currency reaches a dominant network value, it may gain from inertia: newer currencies with similarly low transaction costs may not be able to quickly upstage the dominant currency (Rey 2001).

Historical evidence indicates that one currency tends to dominate others as an international medium of exchange and a store of value. The Roman silver *denarius* was the first world currency; the Byzantine *solidus* was the unchallenged coin from the 5th to the 7th centuries. But the international role of the *solidus* was challenged by the Islamic *dinar*, which eventually made the crossover; both lasted until the 12th century. In the 13th century, Italian coins came to prominence: the Genoese *genoino*, the Florentine *fiorino*, and the Venetian *ducato*. All three coins circulated side by side for quite some time (Cipolla 1956). In the 19th century, Britain was the leading industrial economy in the world, and the British pound became the leading international currency. Britain's economic preeminence came to an end after World War I, but the key status of the pound lasted for more than four more decades (Eichengreen 2005). As late as 1965, 20 percent of official reserves were denominated in pounds, demonstrating how slowly a dominant currency can decline. The U.S. dollar emerged as the dominant international currency after World War II, but lost some ground toward the end of the 20th century, first with respect to the deutsche mark and the Japanese yen and later to the euro.

The U.S. Dollar and the Euro as Dominant Currencies Several different functions are subsumed under the label of "international role of a currency": to invoice internationally traded goods and services, to employ as a vehicle currency (that is, as neither the exporter's nor the importer's currency) in foreign exchange markets, to denominate assets held by monetary authorities and the private sector, and to serve as a reference currency in defining fixed exchange rates (Cohen 1971; Kenen 1983).

The dollar remains the dominant invoice currency, even though the extent of its dominance has declined since the advent of the euro (Goldberg and Tille 2006). Specifically, according to available data, the U.S. dollar remains the dominant invoice currency outside of Europe, where the euro has surpassed the dollar. The dollar is the largest currency traded in the foreign exchange markets, with a market share of 45 percent of daily transactions; the euro follows with a share of 20 percent (BIS 2005). These shares remained stable between 2001 and 2004. The greatest advances made by the euro as an international currency are in international bond issues. According to data published by the Bank for International Settlements (2006, table 13 B), international bonds and notes denominated in euros exceeded those denominated in dollars. The ascendancy of the euro coincides with the increased degree of efficiency, liquidity, and integration of the euro financial markets (Portes and Rey 1998).

Following the depreciation of the dollar relative to the euro after 2002, the financial press focused on the prospect that central banks with large and increasing stock of international reserves—especially those in Asia—may want to substantially diversify their holdings out of dollars and into euros and, in the process, bring an end to the dominance of the dollar in official portfolios. Yet, according to data published by the International Monetary Fund (2005, table I.2), the dollar still retained the same reserve share in 2005 that prevailed at the end of the Bretton Woods system. The novel aspect in the data is that the euro has gained at the expense of currencies other than the dollar (the euro share in official reserves has gone from 6.7 percent of the combined shares of the legacy currencies mark, franc, and guilder in 1973 to 25 percent in 2004). It is safe to say that the euro is becoming an established alternative to the dollar (Chinn and Frankel 2005).

With the United States and the euro area converging to similar economic and financial size, the race is now between two currencies that are backed by large and diversified regions and are integrated with the rest of the world both in trade and finance. Differences in policies will determine the outcome of the match for dominance. Hence the concern that the decline of the dollar may pick up speed if fiscal policy in Washington does not change.

Benefits of Currency Dominance The United States benefits from the dollar as the preeminent international currency in a number of ways. First, it earns a "foreign" seigniorage on the dollar currency held abroad; data indicate that as of 2005, $352 billion, approximately 50 percent of outstanding U.S. dollar currency, is in the hands of nonresidents (Survey of Current Business 2006). Second, the special role of the dollar has permitted the United States to issue liquid and short-term foreign liabilities and invest in illiquid and long-term foreign assets; that is, the United States is the "banker of the world" (Despres et al. 1966). By borrowing cheaply relative to rates of return achieved on foreign assets, the United States has relaxed the external constraint typically faced by other countries. This is one reason that, as of 2007, the United States had accumulated a staggering net foreign debt without yet incurring a financial crisis.

Finally, U.S. importers are largely insulated from exchange rate movements because virtually all U.S. imports are invoiced in dollars, and only a small fraction of a change in the exchange rate is passed through import prices. This reduction in exchange rate risk means that a depreciation of the dollar does not have the traditional effect of significantly reducing the demand for imports and does not lead to a deterioration of the terms of trade. The policy consequence of this benefit to U.S. consumers is that a dollar depreciation is a weak tool to produce a switch from imports to domestic goods and services and that a reduction of the trade deficit occurs mostly through the export side.

In sum, the dollar remains the dominant international currency; the euro is a distant second most important international currency. Whether the euro will eventually overtake the dollar depends on the inertia accorded to the dominant currency and on the policies that will be pursued on both sides of the Atlantic.

See also Bretton Woods system; common currency; convertibility; currency competition; currency substitution and dollarization; dollar standard; euro; exchange rate pass-through; exorbitant privilege; gold standard, international; multiple currencies; optimum currency area (OCA) theory; reserve currency; seigniorage; vehicle currency

FURTHER READING

Bank for International Settlements. 2005. *Triennial Central Bank Survey: Foreign Exchange and Derivative Market Activity in 2004.* Basel, Switzerland: Bank for International Settlements. Provides data on the size and currency breakdown of the foreign exchange and derivative markets.

———. 2006. *BIS Quarterly Review* (June). Gives developments in international banking and international financial markets.

Chinn, Menzie, and Jeffrey Frankel. 2005. "Will the Euro Eventually Surpass the Dollar as Leading International Reserve Currency?" NBER Working Paper No. 11510. Cambridge, MA: National Bureau of Economic Research. Analyzes the rise of the euro as an international currency and as a competitor of the U.S. dollar.

Cipolla, Carlo M. 1956. *Money, Prices, and Civilization in the Mediterranean World.* Princeton, NJ: Princeton University Press. Gives a historical account of early and dominant moneys.

Cohen, Benjamin J. 1971. *The Future of Sterling as an International Currency.* London: Macmillan. The first article to define the functions of an international currency.

Despres, Emile, Charles Kindleberger, and Walter Salant. 1966. "The Dollar and World Liquidity: A Minority View." *The Economist* (February 5). Advances the thesis that the United States acts as the world's banker, that is, borrows short and lends long.

Eichengreen, Barry. 2005. "Sterling's Past, Dollar's Future: Historical Perspectives on Reserve Currency Competition." NBER Working Paper No. 11336. Cambridge, MA: National Bureau of Economic Research. Underscores that it took a relatively long time for the UK pound to lose its status of key currency.

Goldberg, Linda, and Cédric Tille. 2006. "The International Role of the Dollar and Trade Balance Adjustment." NBER Working Paper No. 12495. Cambridge, MA: National Bureau of Economic Research. Quantitative study on the dominant role of the U.S. dollar in international transactions.

International Monetary Fund. 2005. *Annual Report of the Executive Board for the Financial Year Ended April 30, 2005.* Washington, DC.

Kenen, Peter B. 1983. *The Role of the Dollar as an International Currency.* New York: Group of Thirty. Elaborates on the different functions of an international currency.

Nguyen, Elena A. 2006. "The International Investment Position of the United States at Yearend 2005." *Survey of Current Business* 86 (7) (July): 9–19.

Portes, Richard, and Hèléne Rey. 1998. "The Emergence of the Euro as an International Currency." *Economic Policy* 26: 305–43. An early article advancing the thesis that the euro, the new European currency, can become a competitor of the U.S. dollar in international transactions.

Rey, Hèléne. 2001. "International Trade and Currency Exchange." *Review of Economic Studies* 68 (2): 443–64. Links the emergence of vehicle currencies to the pattern of international trade; also argues that inertia plays a role in the rise and fall of dominant monies.

MICHELE FRATIANNI

■ dual exchange rate

The term *dual exchange rate* refers to a situation in which more than one exchange rate applies between one currency and another. The term arises most often when a country's authorities establish one exchange rate for certain transactions involving foreign exchange/currency and a second rate governing other transactions. Many countries in Europe and the developing world use a fixed exchange rate for commercial (current account) transactions and another rate, either fixed or floating, for other (e.g., financial account) transactions. Another type of dual exchange rate occurs when a country's authorities require certain foreign exchange transactions to take place at a prescribed exchange rate, leaving other transactions to take place at the rate prevailing in the commercial market or driving other transactions into an illegal ("black") market, again at a more expensive (i.e., more depreciated) exchange rate.

For example, some countries with currencies that are not freely convertible have required exporters to sell ("surrender") their foreign exchange earnings to the country's central bank at one exchange rate and then buy the foreign exchange they need in the commercial market at the prevailing, and probably more depreciated, market clearing rate. In some other countries, tourists must exchange a certain amount of foreign currency at a set exchange rate on entering the country, the rate being different from, and usually more appreciated than, that in the commercial market. When the second market is illegal, the difference between the official rate and that in the illegal market is called the black market premium.

Dual exchange rates have been created for various reasons. Many European and Latin American countries, for example, have used dual rate regimes to ease the transition from a fixed to a floating rate regime or to limit downward pressure from capital flight on the rate for current transactions (Marion 1994). In some centrally planned or developing economies with nonconvertible exchange rates, they have been created to support activities or sectors said to yield special benefits to the economy. Authorities have sometimes argued that certain imports—goods used in the manufacture of exports or imports for official purposes such as development projects—are more valuable than imports of consumer goods and thus deserve priority, including access to cheaper foreign exchange. Accordingly, they have allowed importers of such goods easier access to foreign exchange at the official exchange rate, or allowed them to purchase foreign currency at a less expensive exchange rate. Dual exchange rates of this type have often been linked to systems of import licenses, in which importers request permission from the authorities to obtain foreign exchange, specifying the purpose(s) for which the foreign exchange will be used.

Despite their political appeal, dual exchange rate systems introduce serious inefficiencies to the foreign exchange market. Dual exchange rate systems artificially segment the market for foreign exchange. When some activities obtain foreign exchange at less expensive rates while others must pay more, the result is a nontransparent system of subsidies to favored sectors and taxes on those disfavored. This system distorts the allocation of resources and lowers output and real economic growth, as foreign exchange no longer flows to the most productive activities.

Dual exchange rate systems also create incentives to engage in wasteful activities (i.e., rent-seeking activities) as a way of obtaining foreign exchange at preferential rates. Importers, for example, may shift the composition of their imports or engage in illicit transactions to obtain a more favorable foreign exchange rate (Gros 1987). Exporters may engage in underinvoicing as a way to keep foreign exchange out of the country or to avoid having to "surrender" their foreign exchange earnings. Finally, dual exchange rate systems enable those in favored sectors to operate more cheaply, gain advantages relative to other sectors, or sell foreign exchange to those in less favored sectors, thus obtaining profits at the expense of others.

Because of the distortions created by dual exchange rate systems, economists typically discourage their adoption, and dual exchange rates have become far less common since the end of the 1980s. If national authorities wish to encourage certain activities, a more transparent system of subsidies and taxes has a less disruptive effect on the pricing signals created by exchange markets.

See also balance of payments; black market premium; capital controls; capital flight; convertibility; debt defla-tion; exchange rate regimes; foreign exchange intervention; peso problem

FURTHER READING

Gros, Daniel. 1987. "Dual Exchange Rates in the Presence of Incomplete Market Separation: Long-Run Effectiveness and Implications for Monetary Policy." IMF Working Paper No. 87/45 (July). Washington, DC: International Monetary Fund. Discusses the impact of dual exchange rates on domestic monetary policy.

Lai, Ching-Chong, and Yun-Peng Chu. 1986. "Exchange Rates Dynamics under Dual Floating Exchange Rate Regimes." *Southern Economic Journal* 53 (2): 502–8. Argues that eliminating a dual floating exchange rate system may trigger an overadjustment ("overshooting") of the primary (e.g., commercial) market exchange rate, so countries are urged to unify dual rates under appropriate safeguards, such as a (temporary) tightening of monetary policy.

Marion, Nancy P. 1994. "Dual Exchange Rates in Europe and Latin America." *World Bank Economic Review* 8: 213–45. Discusses the reasons why dual exchange rates have been created in European and Latin American countries.

JOSHUA GREENE

■ dumping
See anti-dumping

■ early warning systems

Early warning systems (EWSs) are used by policy-makers, ratings agencies, and many financial market participants to assess the vulnerability of countries to currency crises. Emerging markets have been in the eye of the storm several times in the late 20th and early 21st centuries: Mexico in 1994, Southeast Asia in 1997, Russia in 1998, and Argentina in 2001, among others. The effects of some of these episodes were not confined to the countries themselves but spread to other economies as well. In addition, the speculative attacks against currencies participating in the European Monetary System in the 1980s and the early 1990s showed that developed economies are not immune from such events either.

The scope, spread, and severity of crises originating in the foreign exchange market highlight the importance of understanding their causes and predicting where and when they may happen. This need cannot be overstated in an increasingly integrated world economy where free-flowing capital exposes the world's markets to greater risks. The so-called first-, second-, and third-generation models of currency crises constitute the theoretical framework for explaining the mechanisms underlying episodes of increased speculative pressure in the foreign exchange market. EWSs empirically test the implications of these models with the aim to predict currency crises and inform the relevant policy actions.

Basic Components of an EWS The first challenge in the construction of an EWS is how to define a crisis from an empirical perspective. A variety of methods have been used to identify such episodes,

ranging from straightforward measures of currency depreciation (e.g., Frankel and Rose 1996) to composite indexes incorporating changes in exchange rates, interest rates, and international reserves (e.g., Eichengreen et al. 1995). Measures focusing exclusively on developments in exchange rates can capture only the effect of successful speculative attacks, whereas wider market pressure indexes may, in addition, encapsulate failed attempts to destabilize an exchange rate regime or put downward pressure on a currency. This follows from the fact that policy-makers may choose to use the interest rate or part of the stock of the country's international reserves in order to prevent a devaluation of the currency. If such intervention is successful, then the movement in the exchange rate may be limited (or even zero), in which case a simple measure based solely on exchange rate movements will not register the foreign exchange market activity. In contrast, a wider pressure index will capture such activity through the changes in the international reserves and/or the interest rate components of the index.

A second issue relating to the construction of an EWS concerns the choice of sample, data frequency, and variables to be included in the model. Samples can be limited to economies that share certain characteristics (e.g., the stage of their development or their geographical proximity, among other things) or can be extended to include all economies for which data are available. There is a trade-off between the need to avoid overaggregation and the need to maximize the number of observations available for analysis.

An interrelated issue is that of the frequency of the data. Higher-frequency data (e.g., monthly) will provide more degrees of freedom but several economic variables are observed at lower frequencies (e.g., annual). Hence, adopting a monthly frequency increases the number of observations for the available variables but precludes the use of variables that are observed at lower frequencies. Adopting an annual frequency allows the use of a greater number of variables but reduces the number of observations per variable. Furthermore, selecting an annual frequency may have implications for identifying crisis episodes, as the effects of a—successful or unsuccessful—speculative attack may have played out within the twelve-month period. In such cases, annual data will miss the crises altogether.

Also, a choice must be made of the variables or indicators to be included in the EWS. The selection is usually informed by the relevant theory. First-generation models stress the importance of fiscal and monetary indicators (e.g., the fiscal deficit, the change in the amount of money in the economy); second-generation models emphasize the role of variables related to market expectations (e.g., the interest rate differential with respect to the United States); and third-generation models focus on, among others, the need to monitor indicators of the health of the banking system (e.g., the ratio of non-performing loans to performing ones).

The decisions on how to measure a crisis, and what sample, frequency, and variables/indicators to use constitute one reason for the different types of EWSs that have surfaced in the literature. The other reason concerns the distinct methodologies employed, which range from signal extraction to estimating discrete binary choice and structural models.

The "Signals" Approach One of the most influential approaches in EWSs is the "signals" approach, pioneered by the economists Graciela Kaminsky, Saul Lizondo, and Carmen M. Reinhart (see Kaminsky et al. 1998). This involves monitoring a set of key economic variables over time. Whenever a value of a variable exceeds (or, depending on the nature of the variable, falls below) a predefined critical threshold the model issues a warning signal that a crisis may be forthcoming within a specified time period. In order to assess the predictive ability of the model the incidence of signals needs to be compared with the incidence of actual crisis episodes.

Kaminsky et al. (1998) construct an exchange market pressure index using a weighted scheme involving changes in the exchange rate and the stock of international reserves. This is in turn converted into a binary crisis variable by assigning a value of one whenever a value exceeds the mean of the index by more than three standard deviations and assigning a value of zero otherwise. In that way, the ones correspond to crisis incidents and the zeros correspond to normal periods.

The critical thresholds for a signal to be issued are chosen on the basis of minimizing the ratio of "bad" to "good" signals, where a bad signal is one that is not followed by an actual crisis and a good signal is one that is followed by an actual crisis. Kaminsky et al. set a signaling horizon of 24 months, that is, if a signal has been issued that is followed by a crisis episode within this time window it will be considered a good signal. This is one of four possible outcomes. A second possible outcome is that a signal has been issued with no crisis occurring within the 24-month period. A third one is that a signal has not been issued but a crisis does take place within the specified time window. The final possible outcome is that a signal has not been issued and no crisis takes place.

We can summarize this information in a matrix. A is the number of months that a good signal was issued, B is the number of months that a bad signal was issued, C is the number of months that a signal should have been issued, and D is the number of months that a signal was, rightly, not issued. In terms

	Crisis (within 24 months)	No crisis (within 24 months)
Signal was issued	A	B
No signal was issued	C	D

Source: Kaminsky et al. (1998).

of this matrix, optimal thresholds are chosen so that $[B/(B+D)]/[A/(A+C)]$, the "noise-to-signal" ratio, is minimized. These thresholds are expressed relative to the percentiles of an indicator's distribution. Several threshold levels are examined in the vicinity between 10 percent and 20 percent and the one minimizing the noise-to-signal ratio is chosen as the optimal threshold. This is then used as a reference level for all countries in the sample (of course, a given percentile will correspond to different actual threshold values in different countries).

Kaminsky et al. use 15 indicators classified in the following categories: capital account, current account, debt profile, international variables, financial liberalization, other financial variables, real sector, fiscal variables, institutional/structural factors, and political variables. They find that a range of indicators contain useful information, including the deviation of real exchange rate from trend, banking crises, exports, equity prices, the ratio of M2 to international reserves, output, excess M1 balances, international reserves, the M2 multiplier, the ratio of domestic credit to gross domestic product, the real interest rate, and the terms of trade. These results have been partly replicated using a different sample of countries and time period by others (e.g., Berg and Patillo 1999).

The Discrete-Choice Approach Another type of EWS uses probit (or logit) econometric estimations to calculate the probability of a crisis conditional on a set of variables. The dependent variable is a binary indicator with unity indicating a crisis observation and zero indicating a noncrisis observation. The main advantage of this approach is that a variety of potential "triggers" can be used as explanatory variables of crisis episodes. For example, the predictive ability of economic and structural variables corresponding to the first-, second-, and third-generation theoretical models of currency crises can be assessed in this framework.

An example of the discrete-choice approach is Frankel and Rose (1996). They use annual observations for 105 countries between 1971 and 1992. Controlling for a range of macroeconomic indicators, they focus on the composition of debt and capital flows. They define a crisis as a reduction in the value of the domestic currency of at least 25 percent that also exceeds the previous year's depreciation by at least 10 percent. This measure would not capture a failed speculative attack as the crisis definition does not include measures of international reserves and/or the interest rate. Using a probit model, the authors find that crisis probabilities are significantly influenced by developments in foreign direct investment, international reserve levels, domestic credit, U.S. interest rates, and the real exchange rate.

Large sample studies can be useful in identifying potential crisis-triggering factors. Pooling observations from regions with different economic, historical, and structural characteristics, however, calls into question the general applicability of the model's implications: it may be necessary to focus on individual crisis incidents so that valuable information, which may be specific to an incident, does not go amiss. The following type of model is dedicated to a more structural approach.

The Structural Approach This type of model is used to examine a country's vulnerability to a currency crisis by assessing certain economic characteristics. An example of the structural approach is Sachs et al. (1996). These authors construct a market pressure index involving the exchange rate and international reserves but, unlike the signals and the discrete-choice approaches, they do not convert it into a binary variable. Instead, they use the index as the dependent variable in a regression. The right-hand side of the equation includes a measure of real exchange rate misalignment, a measure of liquidity in the economy, and a set of dummies capturing weaknesses in fundamentals and low international reserves. The sample consists of a cross-section of 20 emerging economies, and the time span for the calculation of the variables concentrates on the time around the Mexican crisis of 1994. Even though the results reveal that the indicators in question have explanatory ability with respect to the effects of pressure in the foreign exchange market on financial crises, subsequent efforts by Berg and Patillo (1999) to forecast the 1997 Asian crisis using this approach were not successful.

The Way Forward The definition of a crisis, the methodology employed, sample selection, and other factors can affect the predictive ability of the three main types of EWSs. But despite their limitations, EWSs of financial crises are a useful tool for policymakers. Although there is no consensus in the literature about a definitive list of predictors of crisis episodes, certain indicators, such as the misalignment of the real exchange rate and excess liquidity, are important factors in several models.

This is a literature that is constantly growing. Recent advances in econometrics have resulted in the construction of increasingly sophisticated models. The challenge for researchers and policymakers is that different crisis episodes appear to have different causes. It remains to be seen whether our current knowledge will be sufficient to enable us to predict the next crisis.

See also banking crisis; contagion; currency crisis; equilibrium exchange rate; European Monetary Union; exchange market pressure; financial crisis; financial liberalization; foreign exchange intervention; international reserves; money supply; real exchange rate; spillovers; sterilization

FURTHER READING

Berg, Andrew, and Catherine Patillo. 1999. "Are Currency Crises Predictable? A Test." *IMF Staff Papers* 46 (2): 107–38. Evaluates the out-of-sample predictive ability of models constructed prior to the 1997 Asian crisis.

Eichengreen, Barry, Andrew Rose, and Charles Wyplosz. 1995. "Exchange Market Mayhem: The Antecedents and Aftermath of Speculative Attacks." *Economic Policy* 21: 251–98. Employed for the first time a market pressure index, which in addition to the usual exchange rates and international reserves variables included interest rate differentials.

Frankel, Jeffrey, and Andrew Rose. 1996. "Currency Crashes in Emerging Markets: An Empirical Treatment." *Journal of International Economics* 41: 351–66. An example of a large-sample EWS based on probit analysis.

Kaminsky, Graciela, Saul Lizondo, and Carmen M. Reinhart. 1998. "Leading Indicators of Currency Crises." *IMF Staff Papers* 45 (1): 1–48. Regarded as the seminal work on signal-based EWSs and generated a number of citations and replications.

Sachs, Jeffrey, Aaron Tornell, and Andrés Velasco. 1996. "Financial Crises in Emerging Markets: The Lessons from 1995." *Brookings Papers on Economic Activity* 1: 147–215. Focuses on the 1994 Mexican crisis and adopts a structural approach to examine the vulnerability of countries to speculative pressures.

ALEX MANDILARAS

■ Economic Community of West African States (ECOWAS)

The Economic Community of West African States (ECOWAS), also known simply as the community, is a regional trade organization comprising countries in the West African region. As of late 2007, Benin, Burkina Faso, Cape Verde, Côte d'Ivoire, Gambia, Ghana, Guinea, Guinea-Bissau, Liberia, Mali, Niger, Nigeria, Senegal, Sierra Leone, and Togo (after Mauritania withdrew in 1999) are members. The aims and objectives of the community are to promote trade, cooperation, and self-reliance in West Africa and to assist in the creation of the African Economic Community (AEC).

Origin and Background Like other regional economic groups in Africa, the community was formed based on the pan-African vision of economic integration, which gained prominence during the late 1950s and early 1960s. It was believed that the small and fragmented postcolonial national markets would constitute an obstacle to the economic development of Africa. The pan-African solution was to create a single common market for the continent. The pan-African approach to integration was a "bottom-up" process that would begin at the regional levels (central, east, north, south, and the west) and evolve into a continentwide common market by welding the regional organizations together. It was against this background that the community was created to overcome the isolation of the small West African countries following the colonial and postindependence nationalism periods.

The community was created by treaty in 1975 as a preferential trade area for the transformation of the West African region. The original plan for the community was to establish a free trade area by 1980 followed by a customs union by 2000, and an economic and monetary union by 2005. Owing to a number of factors, however, including internal sociopolitical and economic instability in member countries, poor coordination of macroeconomic policies at the regional level, weaknesses in the operational procedures of the community's institutions, and lack of commitment on the part of member countries to implement the community's priority programs, implementation of the integration programs has proceeded very slowly.

The ECOWAS Treaty was revised in 1993 to expedite the process of economic integration and to increase political cooperation in the region. The revised treaty articulates comprehensive cooperation and integration programs, including trade promotion and liberalization; the provision of better roads and telecommunications infrastructure; and the development of agriculture, industry, and the energy sector. The implementation of the trade liberalization programs was planned to occur in three stages. The first involves the full liberalization of trade in unprocessed goods and traditional handicrafts. The second entails a phased liberalization of trade in industrial products whereby the most advanced member countries (Nigeria, Ghana, and Côte d'Ivoire) were to remove all trade barriers in a period of six years, middle-group countries (Benin, Guinea, Liberia, Sierra Leone, and Togo) within eight years, and third-group countries within ten years. The third stage concerns the establishment of a common external tariff.

In order to accelerate the regional integration process, the revised treaty allows for a double-track (fast-track) approach to economic integration whereby a group of countries can take measures to accelerate integration among themselves. The revised treaty also assigned to the community the additional responsibility of preventing and settling regional conflicts.

Various institutions have been formed to facilitate the achievement of the broad aims and objectives of the community. These institutions include the decision-making organs responsible for the smooth functioning of the community, the Mediation and Security Council (for maintaining peace and security in the region), and the Fund for Cooperation, Compensation, and Development (which provides development capital). The decision-making organs include the Authority of Heads of State and Government (i.e., the supreme policy organ), responsible for the general direction and control of the community; the Council of Ministers, responsible for making decisions on programs and the functioning and development of the community; the Parliament (without legislative powers), which acts in a consultative and advisory capacity; the Economic and Social Council, which plays an advisory role; the Court of Justice, which interprets the provisions of the ECOWAS Treaty and settles disputes among member states that are referred to it; and the Executive Secretariat, responsible for the smooth functioning of the community and for the implementation of the decisions of the supreme policy organ. The community also has specialized technical commissions that prepare projects and programs for consideration by the Council of Ministers on all key sectors of the economy.

The member states of the community have diverse backgrounds. Their heritages vary from Anglophone to Francophone states and to independent Liberia. The region consists of mainly two geographical zones—the Sahelian, semiarid, largely landlocked zone, and a more humid, forested coastal zone. Nigeria is a dominant economy in the region, accounting for more than half of the population and gross domestic product (GDP) of the region. Most of the other states are small in size (less than 5 percent) in terms of population and GDP. The region's resource endowments consist mainly of crude oil (in Nigeria) and agricultural products such as cocoa beans, coffee, and yams. The per capita GDP varies widely across the region. For example, in 2004, it was U.S. $141 for Liberia and U.S. $1,979 for Cape

Verde. In the same year, the UN Development Program ranked only Cape Verde and Ghana as medium human development countries and the rest as low human development countries.

Key Elements and Procedures Since the early 1990s, there has been some progress toward the establishment of a free trade area and a common market. For instance, visa and entry-permit requirements for ECOWAS nationals have been abolished and an ECOWAS passport has been adopted. In addition, ten countries (Benin, Gambia, Ghana, Guinea, Mali, Niger, Nigeria, Senegal, Sierra Leone, and Togo) have removed barriers on trade in unprocessed goods and three (Benin, Gambia, and Sierra Leone) have eliminated barriers on trade in industrial products. All member countries have abolished monetary nontariff barriers. Nonmonetary nontariff barriers still exist, however. A common external tariff was scheduled to be in place by the end of 2007.

In 1994, eight of the countries (Benin, Burkina Faso, Côte d'Ivoire, Guinea Bissau, Mali, Niger, Senegal, and Togo) took advantage of the double-track innovation and came together to create a customs union and a monetary zone called the West African Economic and Monetary Union (WAEMU). The WAEMU member states implemented a common external tariff in 1998 and have started to harmonize their policies in various fields. WAEMU has generally been perceived as successful. Intra-WAEMU trade as a share of the region's total world trade increased from about 10 percent in 1994 to about 16 percent in 2000. Also, the average annual GDP growth rate for the WAEMU subregion has been higher than that of sub-Saharan Africa as a whole. Six other countries of the community, Gambia, Ghana, Guinea, Liberia, Nigeria, and Sierra Leone, have followed suit and embarked on an initiative to form a second monetary zone with the aim to merge with the WAEMU and eventually create a single monetary zone for the ECOWAS region.

Until now, the community has operated as a preferential trade area. The member states apply tariff preferences under the common preferential tariff on goods originating from the community and charge national tariff rates on goods originating from nonmember countries. Member countries use the community's rules of origin to determine the tariff rate to levy on imported products. Products are deemed to originate from the community if (1) they are wholly obtained within a member state, (2) they have undergone sufficient processing in a member state (usually 40 percent value added), (3) 60 percent of the raw material used to manufacture the product comes from member states, or (4) they are local products or traditional handicrafts. Normally, a certificate of origin is not required for local products and traditional handicrafts of ECOWAS origin. For any other product, however, an importer who seeks to benefit from the preferential treatment must provide a certificate of origin.

Impact on Member States Regional economic integration agreements can be beneficial to member countries in both the static (short-run) and the dynamic (long-run) sense. In his analysis of static effects, Jacob Viner (1950) observed that while regional economic integration represents a movement toward free trade on the part of member countries (leading to trade creation), it can also lead to diversion of trade from low-cost nonmember sources that face tariffs to a high-cost member source that no longer faces tariffs. In the short run, member states can benefit as long as the trade creation effects exceed the trade diversion effects. Using the gravity framework, Jacob W. Musila (2005) estimated the two static effects for ECOWAS and found that trade creation exceeds the trade diversion effects. Therefore, member countries of the ECOWAS organization can be expected to obtain net gains in welfare. Céline Carrére (2004) also found that the formation of ECOWAS is associated with the increase in intra-ECOWAS trade and that the currency union, WAEMU, has helped to reduce trade diversion effects. The performance of intra-ECOWAS trade shows that its share in the region's total world trade increased from 2.4 percent in 1975 to more than 10 percent in the 1990s. During the period 1994–98, owing to the improvement of performance in the WAEMU zone, the share of intra-ECOWAS trade increased slightly but steadily from 10.7 to 11.9 percent.

The dynamic benefits of a regional integration occur through well-known channels, namely, increased efficiency through specialization, economies of scale, or increased trade and investment. Like static effects, however, the net impact of dynamic effects is not obvious. In the case of ECOWAS, exports comprise a limited range of agricultural commodities (only Nigeria is a net oil exporter), and manufactured goods are imported mainly from nonmember countries. Such pattern of trade can be a hindrance to long-term economic growth of the region since agricultural products are more prone to deterioration in terms of trade. Indeed, the sluggish growth that characterized the ECOWAS region in the late 1990s was partly attributed to the sharp fall in cocoa prices. Augustin Fosu (1990) finds evidence that supports the view that exporting primary commodities does not significantly improve a country's long-term economic growth rate. Antonio Spilimbergo (2000) shows that the importation of manufactured goods from rich countries (the North) by poor countries (the South) may not guarantee economic growth in the South. The learning-by-importing models, however, suggest that imports of high-technology goods can result in the transfer of technology which, in turn, stimulates domestic innovation and economic growth in the importing country.

Relation with External Actors The relation between ECOWAS and external actors in the world economy varies from region to region. ECOWAS and other African regional blocs seek to augment and deepen economic integration in their respective regions with a view to forming an AEC that will enable Africa to be in a stronger position when negotiating trade matters with other regional organizations such as the European Union (EU), the South American regional economic organization Mercosur, and the North American Free Trade Area. ECOWAS does not have overlapping memberships, which have been seen as an obstacle to market enlargement in some African regional integrations.

On the other hand, the relation between ECOWAS and non-African trade blocs is viewed by some analysts to be an impediment to regional integration. Jeffrey D. Lewis, Sherman Robinson, and Karen

Thierfelder (2003) have argued that North-South trade is more attractive to most African countries than South-South trade because of the structure of their economies or colonial heritage. Indeed, ECOWAS member states trade with the EU and the United States more than with one another. This trade is set to increase even more following the opening up of the EU and U.S. markets under the Everything-but-Arms and the African Growth and Opportunity Act initiatives, respectively. This may work to further reduce the relative importance of intra-ECOWAS trade. In addition, the World Trade Organization provision that substantially reduces quotas and duties on goods originating from the world's poorest countries will also increase the region's trade with non-ECOWAS countries and further reduce the advantages that the community offers to its member states. The very processes of global trade liberalization and cooperation with non-African trade blocs have contributed to the evolution of ECOWAS, however. To reduce transaction costs, the EU, for example, prefers developing countries to negotiate as one group (instead of as numerous individual countries). Furthermore, the success of the EU also inspires the evolution of ECOWAS. Indeed, the ECOWAS institutional design is fashioned after the EU.

See also customs unions; free trade area; regionalism; rules of origin

FURTHER READING

ECOWAS Treaty. 1975. Downloadable from http://www.ecowas.int/. Gives detailed insights about the establishment of ECOWAS, its aims and objectives, and the various articles and protocols about the operation of the organization.

Carrére, Céline. 2004. "African Regional Agreements: Impact on Trade with or without Currency Union." *Journal of African Economies* 13 (2): 199–239. Examines the impact of regional agreements on intraregional trade and on trade with the rest of the world, and compares the effects of the preferential trade agreements and currency unions in Africa.

Fosu, Augustin K. 1990. "Export Composition and the Impact of Exports on Economic Growth of Developing

Economies." *Economics Letters* 34 (1): 67–71. An empirical investigation suggesting that exporting primary products does not have a significant influence on long-run economic growth rates of the producing country.

Lewis, Jeffrey D., Sherman Robinson, and Karen Thierfelder. 2003. "Free Trade Agreements and the SADC Economies." *Journal of African Economies* 12 (2): 156–206. A general equilibrium analysis of the impact of trade liberalization in the Southern African Development Community (SADC) that shows that trade with the EU is more beneficial for SADC countries than a SADC free trade area.

Musila, Jacob W. 2005. "The Intensity of Trade Creation and Trade Diversion in COMESA, ECCAS and ECOWAS: A Comparative Analysis." *Journal of African Economies* 14 (1): 117–41. An estimation of the static gains/losses of selected regional economic integration in Africa using the gravity model.

Spilimbergo, Antonio. 2000. "Growth and Trade: The North Can Lose." *Journal of Economic Growth* 5 (2): 131–46. An analysis of North-South trade that suggests that rich nations (North) may experience technological slowdown if they trade with poor nations (South); and the South could also lose in such trade.

Viner, Jacob. 1950. *The Customs Union Issue.* New York: Carnegie Endowment for International Peace. Examines the effects of regional trade agreements and introduces the concepts of trade creation and trade diversion for the first time.

JACOB W. MUSILA

economic development

Economic development consists of socioeconomic changes that have the goal of raising economic welfare and the standard of living of a population. Chief among these objectives are higher income per capita and lower poverty, but others involve increasing protection of the natural environment, health and life expectancy, literacy and the educational attainment of current and future generations, and political freedom and civil liberties.

There are four major, proximate forces that influence economic development: population growth and demographic change; investment and physical capital accumulation; human capital and technological change; and land, agriculture, and geography. Underlying how these forces affect development, however, are policy choices. Three main areas of policy debates are discussed below: trade liberalization, international financial liberalization, and foreign aid. But these policies have underlying determinants as well. Public sector institutions and governance are influenced by political economy, social conflict, and the presence of large rents, among others. All of these forces have international linkages. The next sections highlight these connections of development to the world economy.

Population, Demographic Change, and International Migration The population in the developing world rose from 2.325 billion in 1960 to 5.489 billion in 2006. From Thomas Malthus to Robert Solow, a popular body of work has grown postulating how higher rates of population growth are linked to lower standards of living. Malthus focused on the impact of population growth on scarce food supplies. Solow postulated that increased population growth causes the amount of capital per worker to decline, reducing productivity and income per capita. Initial testing of Solow's hypothesis, such as that produced by Mankiw, Romer, and Weil (1992), showed that, holding other things constant, higher rates of population growth were indeed connected to lower income per capita.

But a more nuanced view of the relationship has emerged from recent research, one that is mediated by the economy's dependency rate, defined as the sum of people less than 15 years old and those older than 64, divided by those aged 15 to 64. As population growth expands, often as a result of the so-called demographic transition, dependency rates first rise in response to the larger proportion of children in the population. But as this wave of children becomes adults and enters the labor force it can lead to a surge in the saving rate, capital accumulation, and productivity growth. The result is a period of increased economic growth. Bloom and Williamson (1998) find this demographic dividend to be important in explaining the rapid growth of the

East Asian economies in the period 1960 to 1990, accounting for 1.9 percentage points out of the 6.9 percent average rate of growth of these economies. As the population ages, however, dependency rates increase and growth is negatively affected.

Population flows across countries have exploded in recent years and international migration has become a significant development force. In 1960, there was a stock of slightly over 75 million people residing in countries other than their country of birth. By 2005, this number had expanded to 190 million. Most of these migrants—65 percent of them—were born in developing countries.

The impact of emigration on developing countries has been a matter of debate. A partial-equilibrium approach would suggest that emigration reduces labor supply and raises wages in source countries. But in the Heckscher-Ohlin-Samuelson (HOS) general equilibrium framework used in trade theory, emigration has no lasting impact. As migrants leave and wages rise, production shifts away from labor-intensive products and into capital-intensive sectors. The overall demand for labor in the economy shrinks, matching the reduced labor supply induced by emigration (Rivera-Batiz 1983). But the assumptions of the HOS model under which this result is derived are stringent. Once these assumptions are relaxed, the theoretical analysis may yield complex and ambiguous effects of emigration on source countries (Rivera-Batiz 2008). The empirical evidence on the issue has grown in recent years, but remains exploratory (see, for example, Mishra 2006). In some countries, such as China, periods of emigration have been followed by a rise of reverse migration, which returns workers with accumulated skills to the source countries.

The impact of emigration in developing countries is often dominated by the flow of remittances. Measured in international purchasing power parity dollars, developing countries received more than $600 billion in 2005, and for some countries, such as Bangladesh, India, Mexico, Pakistan, and the Philippines, remittances are a major item in the balance of payments. Remittances raise households' standard of living, reduce poverty, and contribute to devel-opment. But whether they simply raise current consumption instead of stimulating investment and future growth varies by country (Adams 2007).

Physical Capital Accumulation and Foreign Direct Investment Most development models emphasize the role played by investment and physical capital accumulation in economic growth. For example, by raising capital per worker and productivity, the Solow model links increased savings and investment rates to higher income per capita.

Evidence on the role played by physical capital accumulation in economic growth varies by country, but it can be substantial. Young (1995) finds physical capital accumulation explains most of the miraculous economic growth of Singapore between 1966 and 1990. Recent work on China shows physical capital has also been key to its rapid growth since 1980 (see Riedel, Jin, and Gao 2007).

Most capital accumulation is financed through increased national savings. But in some countries, foreign capital contributes as well. Foreign direct investment (FDI) represents investments made by foreign residents (usually foreign firms) involving the acquisition of a lasting and significant control or ownership of the enterprise in which the funds are invested. Most FDI increases physical capital in the recipient countries and can stimulate economic growth. But until the early 1990s, FDI occurred mostly among high-income countries. In 1990, for example, developing countries accounted for only 12.1 percent of net FDI flows. This situation led the Nobel Prize winner Robert Lucas to write a paper in 1990 titled "Why Doesn't Capital Flow from Rich to Poor Countries?" The answer pointed mostly to restrictions and taxes imposed by developing countries on FDI inflows. This changed in the 1990s, with a massive wave of economic reforms that liberalized the flow of capital to developing countries. As a result, flows of FDI going to developing countries rose from $36.7 billion in 1990 to $314.6 billion in 2006 (measured in 2005 constant U.S. dollars).

Inflows of FDI have a direct, positive impact on employment. They can also accelerate the adoption of new technologies. If the FDI sector has significant forward and backward linkages with other industries in the economy, positive productivity spillovers will develop, further stimulating growth (Rivera-Batiz and Rivera-Batiz 1990). Forward linkages may emerge from other industries that use the products sold by the foreign firms (such as domestic pharmaceuticals using chemicals produced by foreign petrochemical companies) while backward linkages may be in the form of domestic suppliers of business services or other inputs used by the foreign firms in their productive activities (such as a multinational's use of local transportation services). The case of Ireland, the so-called Celtic Tiger, has been widely discussed as an example of the positive effects of FDI on development. As much as 50 percent of employment in Irish manufacturing is in foreign-owned firms and some simulations suggest that Irish growth would have been two percentage points slower each year since 1990 without the FDI inflows (Navaretti and Venables 2004). But the empirical evidence on the positive effects of FDI is mixed. There are potentially negative indirect effects, including the displacement of local firms, environmental damage, and the deterioration of working conditions, as present in sweatshops or in the employment of child labor, although the latter often occur due to lax domestic regulation and may apply as well to domestic firms (see Nunnenkamp 2004; and Moran, Graham, and Blomstrom 2005).

Technological Change, Human Capital, and Brain Drain William Easterly and Ross Levine have argued that, among developing countries, capital accumulation does not explain most economic growth (Easterly and Levine 2001). Indeed, the presence of diminishing returns in the accumulation of capital suggests that long-run economic development prospects must be aided by forces other than physical capital investment. Technological change is one such force.

But what factors foster technological change? Building on the work of Paul Romer, Robert Lucas, Philippe Aghion, and Peter Howitt, among others, on endogenous growth theory, research on this issue has multiplied since the early 1990s (see Aghion and Howitt 1997). Most of this research suggests that modern technological change is spurred by new product creation and imitation. Countries with high rates of research and development expenditures are able to create new products that allow—albeit temporarily—rents that are reflected in higher growth rates. Imitators destroy those rents but at the same time provide incentives for new products and niches that generate further growth. This process, called "creative destruction" by Joseph Schumpeter, is postulated by this literature as a major determinant of development (Helpman 2004).

In the development literature, some researchers initially developed so-called product life-cycle models that visualized developing countries as imitators, reproducing products originally created in high-income countries. More recently, however, research based on the cases of South Korea, China, and other countries indicates that, by expanding sectors of the economy that are technologically dynamic, developing countries can bypass product cycles and spur innovation, providing internationally competitive new products that can then act as an engine of exports and growth. In this context, the process of development is stimulated not by how much you export but what you export (see Rodrik and Hausmann 2006).

The work of Paul Romer focused on how the domestic supply of human capital dedicated to research and development is the key factor influencing technical change (Romer 1990). Empirical evidence confirms that increased human capital can have a major stimulating impact on growth. This was the case in the so-called East Asian miracle economies—Hong Kong, South Korea, Taiwan, and Singapore—where increased quantity and quality of schooling accompanied their development process (Hanushek and Kimko 2000). But the evidence also shows that increased schooling does not universally have a positive impact on development (Pritchett 2001). In countries where the quality of the public sector governance is low, many highly educated workers tend to end up employed in low-productivity sectors (Murphy, Shleifer, and Vishny 1991). In some countries, increased school enrollments have led to a deterioration of quality. In these cases, investments in human capital have a smaller impact on economic growth.

Domestic supplies of human capital can be severely depleted by emigration. The majority of migrants from developing countries are relatively unskilled but for some countries the emigration of professional and technical workers—the so-called brain drain—is most significant. The highest skilled emigration rates in the world are in the Caribbean, where as much as 43 percent of the region's labor force that has completed some tertiary (college) education currently resides outside its borders. There are also relatively high rates of skilled emigration in Africa, where the highest skilled-worker emigration rates include Cape Verde (68 percent) and Gambia (63 percent).

The emigration of skilled workers may not have a significantly negative impact on domestic consumers if it only causes a reduction in the output of sectors that produce tradable goods because these products can be imported from abroad when the laborers leave the country. But when the workers are employed in service sectors that produce internationally non-traded goods, the impact of emigration can be potentially disastrous because domestic consumers can only obtain those goods and services locally. If doctors and nurses emigrate, the supply of health services can collapse, resulting in higher prices and acute shortages. A brain drain can therefore reduce sharply the economic welfare of those left behind. Remittances may or may not offset these negative effects (Rivera-Batiz 2008).

If human capital flees an economy, then the ability of those left behind to sustain innovation may be compromised, thus reducing an economy's economic growth. On the other hand, the emigrants may generate international networks that enhance the scientific and technological capacities at home. Evidence on the relative significance of these two effects is not available.

Land, Agriculture, and Geography Geography can be a major barrier to development in several ways. First is the burden generated by diseases, which impose their cost more heavily in the tropics. Malaria, for example, is a disease that kills about 3 million people each year in tropical areas. It also weakens those who survive the disease. Countries that suffer from severe malaria epidemics grow more slowly than others and suffer from increased poverty (Gallup and Sachs 1999).

A second mechanism through which geography affects development is through transportation costs. Transportation costs act as a barrier to trade and, therefore, to development. Coastal economies or those close to navigable rivers generally have higher income per capita than landlocked economies without access to navigable waters. Indeed, outside of Europe, there is not a single high-income landlocked country. Much of the population in developing countries—particularly in Africa—lives in landlocked locations.

A third way geography influences development is through its impact on the agricultural sector. Tropical areas tend to suffer from climate influences that reduce agricultural productivity between 30 and 50 percent compared to temperate zones, holding other inputs constant (Gallup and Sachs 1999).

Public policies can be used to compensate for the impact of geography, whether through investments in health, transportation infrastructure, or irrigation schemes that can raise agricultural productivity. Land reform and rural market development policies are also essential for the development of agriculture. Despite the relatively scant attention paid to them by the World Bank and other international organizations, such policies have strong poverty reduction effects since rural areas are where the poor are concentrated. In the case of China, one of the most dramatic drops in poverty occurred in the early 1980s, before international trade became a major force in that country's development efforts. Rural poverty fell from 76 percent in 1980 to 23 percent in 1985, largely in response to comprehensive land reform initiatives and the growth of local agricultural markets. In the international arena, the Doha round of WTO negotiations begun in 2001 seeks to reduce agricultural subsidies and the non-tariff barriers to trade imposed by high-income countries, which hurt the exports of poor developing nations.

Governance and Institutions Although physical and human capital accumulation, technical change, demographics, land productivity, and so on are all proximate influences on development, they are all subject to the social, cultural, and economic environment within which individuals and firms live and function. This environment is closely connected to the country's government, which sets its legal and economic frameworks. Indeed, the quality of governance in a country is a major underlying determinant of development. High-quality governance includes, among other things, bureaucratic effectiveness and agility, institutions that assure the swift and strong accountability of government administrations, and a strong rule of law and control of corruption.

Since the mid-1990s, the World Bank has been collecting data on the public sector governance of most countries in the world. Based on these data, the evidence shows that good public sector governance is essential for development (Kaufmann, Kraay, and Mastruzzi 2007). A case in point is the acceleration of economic growth in India, which can be seen as the outcome of governance reforms in the 1980s (Rodrik and Subramanian 2005). Nations able to generate high quality of public sector governance—such as some of the East Asian miracle economies, including Singapore and Hong Kong—have been able to cultivate institutions that complement the process of economic development, introducing policies that foster higher investment in physical and human capital and provide incentives for entrepreneurship and innovation.

But what forces generate poor or good country governance? A major force is political power. Different interest groups or classes within a country have conflicting interests over the distribution of resources, and their policy prescriptions are informed by such interests. Political institutions then determine how various groups get—or do not get—access to government and its legislative powers. Overall, the quality of governance is substantially higher in more democratic countries, even after holding other variables constant. Transparent democratic institutions mean that, over the long run, inept and corrupt officials will be voted out of office, which is often more difficult under authoritarian regimes. More democratic institutions also facilitate the activities of the press and allow the dissemination of information to the public so that governments can be held accountable (Rivera-Batiz 2002). At the same time, there are cases of authoritarian regimes—such as Singapore and China—that have been able to provide high-quality public sector governance, spurring economic growth.

In many developing nations, a history of colonialism provides a backdrop for the creation of institutions that can hinder development efforts after independence (Acemoglu et al. 2006). Social conflict can also break down the government stability necessary for stable growth. Such conflict is endemic in the poorest developing countries and is fostered by relatively high proportions of poor young men with little education, ethnic or religious strife, and the presence of natural resources (such as diamonds or oil), which finance the armed conflicts (Collier 2007). Once social conflict starts, it generates a vicious circle, where conflict leads to poverty and poverty to more conflict. The more fragmented a country is—by ethnicity or social class—the lower its rate of economic growth. Many countries in Africa appear to follow this pattern (Easterly and Levine 1997).

Natural Resources and the Dutch Disease The presence of large rents can also give rise to poor governance and, as a result, constrain economic growth. Consider the case of countries that have rich endowments of natural resources. Surprisingly, the evidence shows that, despite their potential wealth, these countries have not grown faster nor have they been able to reduce poverty rates, holding other things constant (Sachs and Warner 1995b).

Consider the case of Nigeria, where massive oil reserves were discovered in 1965. The sum of oil revenues received by this country since that time has been more than $400 billion but its gross domestic product (GDP) per capita was about the same in 2000 as it was in 1970, when adjusted for inflation. In the meantime, poverty rates (using a $1 a day measure) rose from 36 percent in 1970 to 70 percent in 2000.

The lack of impact of natural resource exports on growth and poverty may be connected to the fact that, as countries pull resources into the exploitation of natural resources, they withdraw resources from other sectors. As a consequence, there is a crowding-out effect, with natural resource output crowding out manufacturing output, leaving no net impact on GDP. This has been called *Dutch disease*, referring to the case of natural gas exploitation in the Netherlands in the 1970s, which failed to generate sustained economic growth.

A second explanation links the increased exploitation of natural resources to a lower rate of technical change. The rewards for working in the natural resource industry are high and therefore a significant portion of a country's talent may end up employed in this industry. But the natural resources sector is not itself one that leads to great innovations or stimulates entrepreneurship. As a result, countries specializing in the production of natural resources may in fact have low rates of innovation and face lower long-run growth.

But in the case of Nigeria and many other countries, the culprit behind the lack of impact of natural resource exports on economic growth is poor public sector governance (Sala-i-Martin and Subramanian 2003). The consequence of massive economic rents is the emergence of a governance regime that permits those with greater political power to capture, by any means necessary, some of those rents. The result is corruption and slow growth.

The impact of natural resources on a country can be transformed from a curse to a blessing. For instance, some nations have been able to ameliorate the rent-seeking and corruption that is often associated with the export of natural resources. Part of the strategy has been to preempt possible corruption by earmarking or assigning a share of natural resource revenues directly to finance social programs, such as education and health. In the case of Indonesia, for example, revenues from oil exports were directed to a massive program of investment in education. More recently, Chile imposed a tax on copper production in order to finance a Competitiveness Innovation Fund that finances new technology projects. Through the use of innovative government policies, the exploitation of natural resources can have positive effects on development (Stiglitz 2005).

International Trade and Commercial Policy
The impact of international trade on economic development has been at the center of the debate on the consequences of globalization and is one of the most controversial issues in development economics. The key questions are whether trade liberalization reduces or increases poverty and inequality and whether it has a positive impact on economic growth.

The HOS model postulates that increased trade should reduce both poverty and inequality in developing countries. Trade induces a developing country to increase the production of goods in which it has a comparative advantage, that is, in sectors that use unskilled labor intensively. As production and export of these products rises, the demand for unskilled workers increases and this raises their relative wages. At the same time, the demand for—and the rewards received by—human and physical capital decline. Since unskilled workers are usually poor while the owners of both physical and human capital tend to be richer, the impact of international trade in the HOS framework is to reduce poverty and improve income distribution in developing countries.

The evidence on the impact of trade on poverty tends to support the HOS predictions. The data on extreme poverty, measured as people with consumption below the $1 a day level, show that world poverty has dropped sharply during the period 1981 to 2004, when globalization bloomed. Poverty declined from 40.1 percent in 1981 to 18.1 percent in 2004. This represents a halving of poverty rates and has meant a reduction in the number of poor in the world from 1,470,000 in 1981 to 969,480 in 2004 (Chen and Ravallion 2007). Furthermore, the two economies that have seen some of the sharpest increases in trade, China and India, are also the two economies where poverty has dropped the most. To cap off all of this, the region that has been the slowest to drop trade barriers, sub-Saharan Africa, is also the region where poverty failed to drop during the period.

On the other hand, the data show much less impressive drops in poverty when the poverty line rises to $2 a day. And metastudies that include a wide variety of developing countries show cases where poverty—particularly regional poverty—has risen as a result of trade (Harrison 2006). Furthermore, most of the estimates available suggest that the recent expansion of international trade in the world has been associated with a period of increased inequality. This inequality is displayed in both greater within-country inequality and higher cross-country inequality (Milanovic 2005).

The increasing inequality and declining poverty associated with globalization can be reconciled by the widespread evidence indicating that trade is linked to greater economic growth (Dollar and Kraay 2004; Wacziarg and Welch 2004). Economic growth tends to raise all boats and is associated with a reduction of poverty. But it has also been connected to rising inequality. One reason is that long-run growth in recent years has been closely linked to technological change. And this technological change has tended to be skill-biased, raising the demand for skilled labor at the expense of unskilled labor. Such a shift in demand raises the wages of skilled labor relative to unskilled workers, increasing inequality (Rivera-Batiz 2007).

For increased international trade to stimulate economic growth, domestic investment rates must be sufficiently high that new export industries can be developed. The evidence available suggests that, from South Korea to China, the implementation of active government policies designed to stimulate investment have been essential in allowing trade liberalization to generate growth and reduce poverty (Rodrik 1995). Without these—and other—complementary forces the impact of trade on growth is limited.

Financial Development and International Financial Markets One of the major forces that serves as a backdrop for economic growth is financial development. Although there is debate about the role of specific financial institutions, a growing body of empirical work shows that a well-functioning financial system has a strong, positive impact on economic growth and helps alleviate poverty by allowing the efficient transformation of savings into productive investments (Beck, Demirgüç-Kunt, and Levine 2007). The financial sector facilitates the trading, diversification, and management of risk, and it helps mobilize and pool savings by allowing savers to hold liquid assets and transforming those into higher-return long-term investments (Levine 2005).

While providing a solid, long-run basis for overall economic growth, the financial sector has nonetheless been prone to crises, with disastrous short-term consequences. In addition, traditional financial institutions have failed to fund the poor, who lack the collateral to access credit. In recent years, however, myriad microfinance institutions have emerged to provide credit to the poor. Microfinance institutions minimize the impact of a lack of collateral by pooling responsibility for loan repayment among communities of borrowers (Armendariz and Murdoch 2005). In addition, by having mobile operators who move among villages, they minimize transaction costs and mitigate adverse selection (which occurs when lenders cannot monitor the riskiness attached to borrowers' projects).

The conventional wisdom is that, as countries develop, the limits imposed by domestic savings may constrain development. From this perspective, international financial liberalization is a good thing for development, allowing developing countries with scarce capital to borrow in order to finance greater investment without the necessity of raising domestic savings. In addition, financial capital flows permit residents of different countries to pool risks, achieving more effective insurance than purely local arrangements would allow (Obstfeld and Taylor 2005; Prasad et al. 2003). International financial liberalization can also increase the efficiency of the domestic financial system, whether by enhancing the liquidity of local stock markets or by promoting contested markets and raising the efficiency of domestic banking.

But international capital market liberalization has its critics. Some argue that there is no systematic evidence that financial capital inflows cause greater growth. Others observe that unregulated capital inflows can be disastrous for developing countries, pointing to the rash of financial crises in Mexico, East Asia, Russia, Argentina, and a variety of other emerging markets during the 1990s and early 2000s (Stiglitz 2003). These crises occurred after capital flows to developing nations began to rise sharply in the late 1980s and early 1990s in response to the elimination of many restrictions on international capital movements.

There were very specific factors connected to the East Asian and other emerging market crises of the 1990s and early 2000s. Fragile domestic financial institutions were unable to handle efficiently the expansion of credit, partly because they lacked the appropriate expertise and partly because governments had failed to implement adequate regulatory and supervision systems. The result was overinvestment, in the form of excessive lending to risky projects with low short-term returns. In addition, the reliance on highly volatile, short-term debt led to liquidity crises that resulted in financial panics and bank runs. These problems were compounded by the fact that the capital inflows caused real currency appreciation by generating inflation in fixed exchange-rate regimes. As the value of the currency rose in real terms, the current account balance deteriorated and external borrowing climbed. These changes then led to expected currency depreciations that fueled capital flight. When central banks stubbornly defended prevailing currency values, their foreign exchange reserves were eventually depleted, precipitating a foreign exchange crisis that spilled over into a financial crisis as well (Rivera-Batiz 2001).

Most countries in financial crisis have benefited from massive loan packages provided by the International Monetary Fund (IMF). But the conditions imposed by the fund to disburse its loans were sometimes so stringent that they sharply increased poverty in the short run and may have undermined future growth. The next section examines the role in development played by international organizations.

Foreign Aid and Development Many of the poorest developing countries lack access to world private capital markets. For these countries, official development assistance (ODA)—grants and concessional loans made by governments and international organizations—constitutes a major source of capital. In 2005, a total of $120.4 billion of ODA flowed to developing nations. This foreign aid can originate in other, mostly high-income countries (bilateral aid) or in groups of countries (multilateral aid), including international organizations such as the United Nations, the World Bank, and the IMF.

The impact of foreign aid on development has been a source of controversy, with proponents of aid (such as Sachs 2005) arguing for much greater flows while critics (such as Easterly 2006) argue that such aid is largely a waste of resources. Evidence of the positive impact of specific foreign aid projects on development is widely available. International efforts that funded campaigns to rid developing countries from various diseases, including smallpox, polio, and guinea worm disease, among others, have been found to be successful (Levine 2007). The role played by country donors and international organizations in the development of new seed strains as well as technological innovations now referred to as the Green Revolution is well known. And recent studies have used random experimental designs to show the success of educational—and other—development projects (such as the Progresa/Oportunidades program in Mexico), projects which have received substantial foreign aid support.

But many foreign aid projects have failed miserably. For instance, World Bank educational projects in the 1980s and early 1990s often requested that countries introduce public school fees in order to raise additional funding. But the outcome of those policies was to sharply reduce school enrollment. Another example is the possibility that the various market-oriented policies adopted by the World Bank and IMF toward agricultural markets may have undermined rural development efforts in low-income countries, especially in sub-Saharan Africa. Even the World Bank's own operations evaluation department finds that in the period 1995 to 2004, at least one-third of all projects in sub-Saharan Africa failed to achieve their goals, more than half were unlikely to be sustained over time, and the great majority of projects did not have a substantial institutional impact on developing country governments. Some of this failure can be attributed to poor country governance. Nonetheless, systematically positive effects of foreign aid on overall economic growth have not been found (Rajan and Subramanian 2005).

A similar lack of support exists for the lending policies of the IMF. Despite the presence of apparently successful cases, such as Chile in the 1980s, South Korea in the 1990s, and Brazil in the 2000s, in other countries IMF-sponsored short-term reforms have not fared as well, including Bolivia in the 1980s, Indonesia in the 1990s, and Argentina in the 2000s. The evidence on the long-run growth effects of lending provided by the IMF under its conditionality agreements is mixed, with some studies finding negative impacts, especially among low-income countries (Vreeland 2003).

Macroeconomic Policies Notwithstanding the issue of the effectiveness of IMF stabilization policies, the IMF does not provide access to its lending facility unless asked by member countries in economic or financial distress. The available research suggests that macroeconomic mismanagement can be a major barrier to development (Montiel 2002).

Although the evidence on the relationship between low—or moderate—inflation and growth is mixed, the overwhelming evidence is that high inflation reduces growth and raises poverty (Barro 1995). By undermining the financial system and generating uncertainty, high and variable inflation rates inhibit investment and hurt growth. By acting as a tax on money balances, affecting especially those with fixed incomes, high inflation also hurts the poor.

Central banks, which manage the money supply, usually have as one of their goals the control of inflation. But a phenomenon economists refer to as time inconsistency means that, insofar as central banks are under the influence of the rest of the government, they may have an inflationary bias. This is associated with the fact that central banks have an incentive to break their own commitments to maintain low inflation rates because of the political

benefits of engaging in expansionary policies that provide greater output and employment in the short run (at the expense of higher inflation). As a result, countries that have more independent central banks also tend to have lower inflation (Cukierman 1992).

Government budget deficits can also act to constrain economic growth (Adam and Bevan 2005). Once the deficits rise over a certain level, the growing government financing needs can give rise to a wide array of negative consequences. Private investment may be crowded out by higher interest rates. And if the deficit is financed by borrowing, a ballooning external debt can raise country risk, leading to an expected currency depreciation and capital flight. If monetized, rising budget deficits can also lead to high inflation.

Currency regimes can provide a major boost to development or serve as a constraint. Both fixed and flexible exchange rate regimes have pros and cons (Agenor and Montiel 1999, chapter 7). Fixed exchange rates facilitate a stable trading environment that can foster exports and imports of goods and services. Therefore, among countries that are closely integrated, a fixed exchange rate regime—or maybe even a common currency—may be the optimal regime. But among countries that are not closely integrated, with substantial net flows of international capital, fixed exchange rate regimes become potentially subject to speculative attacks and to currency crises. Flexible exchange rates may allow the more stable management of capital flows and can serve as a policy instrument for the adjustment of relative prices. Furthermore, monetary policy loses its effectiveness in a regime of perfect capital mobility and fixed exchange rates. A mixture of fixed and flexible exchange rates may be the optimal outcome for some countries.

The variety of experiences with development policies reflects the complexity of development itself. As shown earlier, the links of development to the world economy are also complex and bring challenges as well as opportunities.

See also aid, international; capital accumulation in open economies; development; evolution of development thinking; foreign direct investment (FDI); global income inequality; migration, international; poverty, global; trade and economic development, international

FURTHER READING

Acemoglu, Daron, Simon Johnson, and James Robinson. 2006. "Understanding Prosperity and Poverty: Geography, Institutions, and the Reversal of Fortune." In *Understanding Poverty*, edited by A. V. Banerjee, R. Benabou, and D. Mookherjee. New York: Oxford University Press, 19–35. A survey of the historical and political factors that influence institutions and public sector governance in a country. The authors make the case that these factors explain more directly differences in poverty and prosperity around the world than geography or other determinants of prosperity.

Adam, Christopher S., and David L. Bevan. 2005. "Fiscal Deficits and Growth in Developing Countries." *Journal of Public Economics* 89 (3): 571–97. Examines the issue of whether government budget deficits affect a country's economic growth. Evidence is presented showing that fiscal deficits are indeed negatively related to growth in developing countries.

Adams, Richard. 2007. "International Remittances and the Household: Analysis and Review of Global Evidence." Policy Research Working Paper No. 4116. Washington, DC: The World Bank. Provides a survey of the literature on the determinants and consequences of migrant remittances in the world, including the role of these remittances in the economic welfare of the migrants, their families, and the countries involved.

Agenor, Pierre-Richard, and Peter Montiel. 1999. *Development Macroeconomics*. Princeton, NJ: Princeton University Press. A textbook on the theory and evidence of how macroeconomic factors affect development. It goes over a variety of theoretical models, describing them and providing evidence on a wide range of issues, including the effects of fiscal and monetary policies, credibility and disinflation, exchange rate regimes, currency substitution, speculative attacks, and political economy, among many others.

Aghion, Philippe, and Peter Howitt. 1997. *Endogenous Growth Theory*. Cambridge, MA: Harvard University Press. This book offers a technical review of the literature on endogenous growth, focusing on the various determinants of innovation and technological change and how research and development, education, competition, trade, policy, and other forces affect growth.

Armendariz, Beatriz, and Jonathan Murdoch. 2005. *The Economics of Microfinance*. Cambridge, MA: MIT Press. Presents a comprehensive survey of the theory of how microfinance institutions work and the empirical evidence on their worldwide growth and effectiveness. It examines the market failures and economic phenomena that plague lending for the poor—including capital market imperfections, moral hazard, and adverse selection—and the mechanisms used by microlending institutions to deal with them.

Barro, Robert. 1995. "Inflation and Economic Growth." NBER Working Paper No. 5326. Cambridge, MA: National Bureau of Economic Research. This paper presents research on how inflation is linked to growth. It includes a discussion of the various forces involved as well as empirical evidence from a cross-section of countries.

Beck, Thorsten, Asli Demirgüç-Kunt, and Ross Levine. 2007. "Finance, Inequality, and the Poor." *Journal of Economic Growth* 12 (1): 27–49. Presents the existing research on the links between financial development, growth, and poverty. The authors argue that, despite popular beliefs, there are a number of mechanisms through which financial development acts to reduce poverty and inequality.

Bhagwati, Jagdish N. 2004. *In Defense of Globalization*. Princeton, NJ: Princeton University Press. A wide-ranging review of the arguments in favor of and against globalization. The author argues that, overall, globalization has had a positive influence on both economic growth and the standards of living of the poor.

Bloom, David E., and Jeffrey Williamson. 1998. "Demographic Transitions and Economic Miracles in Emerging Asia." *World Bank Economic Review* 12 (3): 419–55. This paper presents research on how demographic forces affect economic development. The authors make the argument that a demographic dividend explains a significant part of the economic growth explosion in East Asia.

Chen, Shaohua, and Martin Ravallion. 2007. "Absolute Poverty Measures for the Developing World, 1981–2004." Development Research Group Working Paper No. 4211. Washington, DC: The World Bank. Presents the most recent World Bank estimates on poverty in the world and its behavior over time. The paper shows that absolute poverty has generally declined in the developing world since 1981, especially in certain countries and regions, such as East Asia. It also shows that specific countries and regions—such as sub-Saharan Africa—have failed to display any significant reductions in poverty.

Collier, Paul. 2007. *The Bottom Billion: Why the Poorest Countries Are Failing and What Can be Done About It.* Oxford: Oxford University Press. Arguing that poverty has dropped sharply in most of the developing world except for about 50 countries ("the bottom billion"), this book seeks to determine why these countries have been unable to prosper. The author discusses a set of traps that prevent economic development and shows how traditional policies—including foreign aid and globalization—have failed to improve matters.

Cukierman, Alex. 1992. *Central Bank Strategy, Credibility, and Independence: Theory and Evidence.* Cambridge, MA: MIT Press. A technical survey of the theory and evidence on how central banks function and how they affect the macroeconomy. Foremost among the various issues discussed is how central bank independence has been linked to lower inflation.

Dollar, David, and Aart Kraay. 2004. "Trade, Growth, and Poverty." *Economic Journal* 114 (2): F22–F49. This paper presents research showing that international trade reduces poverty by stimulating economic growth.

Easterly, William. 2006. *The White Man's Burden: Why the West's Efforts to Aid the Rest Have Done So Much Ill and So Little Good.* New York: Penguin. A wide-ranging study of how, after decades of financial aid valued at over $2.3 trillion, the development strategies forged in the West have failed to produce sustained development. The author argues that development efforts should refocus on specific microprojects in areas such as education and health, which have been found to be successful in reducing poverty.

Easterly, William, and Ross Levine. 1997. "Africa's Growth Tragedy: Policies and Ethnic Divisions." *Quarterly Journal of Economics* 112 (3): 1203–50. Dcuments the substantial racial and ethnic fractionalization in African countries and the negative impact such divisions have had on economic growth in the region.

———. 2001. "It's Not Factor Accumulation: Stylized Facts and Growth Models." *The World Bank Economic Review* 15 (2): 177–219. Presents research on the relative roles played by physical and human capital accumulation as well as technological change in explaining differences in growth among a cross-section of countries. The authors show that technological change appears to be the dominant factor.

Gallup, John Luke, and Jeffrey D. Sachs. 1999. "Geography and Economic Development." Center for International Development Working Paper No. 1, Cambridge, MA: Harvard University. Presents theoretical arguments and empirical evidence on how health, transportation costs, and agricultural productivity are affected by geography.

Hanushek, Eric A., and Dennis D. Kimko. 2000. "Schooling, Labor Force Quality, and the Growth of Nations." *American Economic Review* 90 (5): 1184–1208. Using the results of international assessments of education to measure the differences among various countries, this article offers a technical analysis of how the quantity and quality of schooling influence economic growth.

Harrison, Anne. 2006. *Globalization and Poverty.* Chicago, IL: University of Chicago Press. This volume provides a comprehensive survey of the various links between globalization, poverty, and inequality in the world. It shows that there exist diverse country experiences of the impact of rising trade on the poor and how it has affected income inequality.

Helpman, Elhanan. 2004. *The Mystery of Economic Growth.* Harvard, MA: Harvard University Press. This book offers a survey of the determinants of economic growth, including the roles played by physical and human capital, productivity growth, technological change and its determinants, interdependence across countries, inequality, and institutions and policies.

Kaufmann, Daniel, Aart Kraay, and Massimo Mastruzzi. 2007. "Governance Matters VI: Aggregate and Individual Governance Indicators for 1996–2006." Policy Research Working Paper No. 4280. Washington, DC: The World Bank. This paper presents the latest World Bank indicators on public sector governance in the world. It also shows the connections between improved governance and various indicators of economic development.

Levine, Ross. 2005. "Finance and Growth: Theory and Evidence." In *Handbook of Economic Growth*, edited by

Philippe Aghion and Steven Durlauf. The Netherlands: Elsevier Science, 865–934. A survey of how financial development affects economic growth. The author makes a strong case that policies that promote financial development have a significant positive impact on growth.

Levine, Ruth. 2007. *Case Studies in Global Health: Millions Saved.* Boston: Jones and Bartlett. This volume presents examples of successful foreign aid and domestic policy interventions in the field of global health in the developing world. It shows how international development assistance has been effective in some cases and draws lessons on how such assistance can work more effectively in other contexts.

Mankiw, N. Gregory, David Romer, and David N. Weil. 1992. "A Contribution to the Empirics of Economic Growth." *Quarterly Journal of Economics* 107 (2): 407–37. This paper presents empirical evidence showing how population growth and the accumulation of physical and human capital relate to income per capita and economic growth.

Milanovic, Branko. 2005. *Worlds Apart: Measuring International and Global Inequality.* Princeton, NJ: Princeton University Press. This book presents evidence on the disparities between poor and rich countries. Examining various measures of inequality, the author utilizes data from household surveys from over 100 countries to study the extent of global inequality and how it has changed over time.

Mishra, Prachi. 2006. "Emigration and Wages in Source Countries: Evidence from Mexico." Working Paper No. WP/86/06. Washington, DC: International Monetary Fund. Using data from 1970–2000, this paper examines the impact of emigration on the labor market and economy of Mexico. It shows that emigration has resulted in a rise of wages for those who remain in Mexico, including those with high levels of human capital.

Montiel, Peter. 2002. *Macroeconomics in Emerging Markets.* Cambridge, MA: Cambridge University Press. This volume provides an integrated, technical discussion of the main macroeconomic issues facing developing countries. It presents both theory and evidence, including discussions of high inflation episodes, central banking, financial repression, banking crises, and exchange rate management.

Moran, Theodore H., Edward M. Graham, and Magnus Blomstrom, eds. 2005. *Does Foreign Direct Investment Promote Development?* Washington, DC: Institute for International Economics. The authors present research on the diverse experiences that developing countries have had with the consequences of foreign direct investment. Ranging from Turkey to East Africa, they present a number of case studies, including an analysis of productivity spillovers to domestic firms and the impact on research and development and on country economic growth.

Murphy, Kevin M., Andrei Shleifer, and Robert Vishny. 1991. "The Allocation of Talent: Implications for Growth." *Quarterly Journal of Economics* 106 (2): 503–30. This paper presents research on how the sectoral allocation of educated and professional workers in developing countries can have positive or negative impacts on development. For example, if the talented persons in a country end up employed in profitable but static low-growth sectors due to poor governance and rent-seeking activities, then increased education may have a limited impact on development.

Navaretti, Giorgio Barba, and Anthony J. Venables. 2004. *Multinational Firms in the World Economy.* Princeton, NJ: Princeton University Press. A comprehensive survey of multinational firms, this book examines why multinationals exist, what makes them effective, their impact on both host countries and source countries, and their policy implications.

Nunnenkamp, Peter. 2004. "To What Extent Can Foreign Direct Investment Help Achieve International Development Goals?" *World Economy* 27 (5): 657–77. This paper examines the potential effects of foreign direct investment in developing countries. It shows that, despite high expectations, the impact of foreign direct investment varies by country and depends on the characteristics of host countries and their policies toward foreign direct investment.

Obstfeld, Maurice, and Alan Taylor. 2005. *Global Capital Markets: Integration, Crisis, and Growth.* Cambridge, MA: Cambridge University Press. Provides a historical view of international capital flows in the world. Showing that the recent globalization of capital flows constitutes a reversal to an earlier period of great capital mobility in 1880–1914, it examines the differences between these two golden periods for capital flows.

Prasad, Eswar, Kenneth Rogoff, Shang-Jin Wei, and M. Ayhan Kose. 2003. "Effects of Financial Globalization on Developing Countries: Some Empirical Evidence." IMF Occasional Paper No. 220. Washington, D.C.: International Monetary Fund. This report examines the impact of the liberalization of international financial flows on the economic growth and consumption volatility faced by developing countries. Both theoretically and empirically, the authors find that financial liberalization has mixed effects. The overall impact on growth may be tenuous and the impact on volatility could be negative for some countries. They suggest that more positive effects of international financial liberalization may be obtained by countries that have the adequate institutions and domestic absorptive capacity necessary to handle the liberalization.

Pritchett, Lant. 2001. "Where Has All the Education Gone?" *The World Bank Economic Review* 15 (3): 367–92. This paper presents research showing that increased educational attainment may not be connected to greater economic growth. Empirical evidence is presented along with possible explanations, including possible data problems, rent-seeking by educated workers, and issues with the quality of the increased schooling.

Rajan, Raghuram G., and Arvind Subramanian. 2005. "Aid and Growth: What Does the Cross-Country Evidence Really Show?" Working Paper No. 11513. Cambridge, MA: National Bureau of Economic Research. This article examines the empirical links between foreign aid and economic growth using panel data for a cross-section of countries. The authors fail to find any evidence that foreign aid has a positive effect on economic growth.

Riedel, James, Jing Jin, and Jian Gao. 2007. *How China Grows: Investment, Finance, and Reform.* Princeton, NJ: Princeton University Press. This volume examines the various factors that have been associated with the recent rise of economic growth in China. From increased savings and investment to policies toward technological change, the book argues that the Chinese economic miracle is related to a wide array of economic forces.

Rivera-Batiz, Francisco L. 1983. "Trade Theory, Distribution of Income, and Immigration." *American Economic Review* 73 (2): 183–87. This paper examines the theoretical arguments of how migration affects the distribution of income. It concludes that although in the short run immigration can reduce wages in the host country and emigration can raise wages in the source country, there are long-run forces that reverse these effects. As a result, the long-run impact of migration on wages in host and source countries may be minimal.

———. 2001. "The East Asian Crisis and the Anatomy of Emerging Market Disease." In *The Political Economy of the East Asian Crisis: Tigers in Distress*, edited by Arvid Lukauskas and Francisco L. Rivera-Batiz. Cheltenham, UK: Edward Elgar, 31–73. Examining the causes and consequences of the East Asian financial crisis, the authors argue that the crisis was precipitated by the impact of massive, unrestricted capital inflows in the late 1980s and the 1990s. These inflows generated inflation, a deterioration of domestic competitiveness in international markets, current account balance deficits, and increased indebtedness, all of which eventually led to expectations of devaluation and to the massive exodus of the foreign capital, precipitating exchange rate and financial crises.

———. 2002. "Democracy, Governance and Economic Growth: Theory and Evidence." *Review of Development Economics* 6 (2): 225–47. This article shows the theory and evidence on how democracy is related to growth. The conclusion is that the most important determinant of economic growth is the quality of the public sector governance in a country, independent of its political rights situation. However, evidence is also presented that, in the long-run, having a larger number of democratic institutions is connected to greater quality of governance.

———. 2007. "Trade, Poverty, Inequality, and Gender." Trade Policy Executive Program. Washington, D.C.: The World Bank. A survey of the literature on the impact of international trade on poverty and inequality, including its effects on gender inequities. The article concludes that although globalization has been associated with a general drop in poverty, it has also resulted in increased inequality. Furthermore, trade liberalization has had a negative impact on specific groups and sectors in developing countries. Its impact on gender inequities has been mixed and depends on the country and region being considered.

———. 2008. "International Migration and the Brain Drain." In *International Handbook of Development Economics*, edited by Amitava Krishna Dutt and Jaime Ros. Cheltenham, U.K.: Edward Elgar. Presents evidence on the extent of skilled emigration from developing countries in recent years and its consequences for the migrants themselves as well as for the source country and host country populations.

Rivera-Batiz, Francisco L., and Luis A. Rivera-Batiz. 1990. "The Effects of Direct Foreign Investment in the Presence of Increasing Returns Due to Specialization." *Journal of Development Economics* 34 (1): 287–307. This paper shows the theoretical connections between direct foreign investment and host country economic welfare. It demonstrates how foreign direct investment can provide positive gains to the host country through its employment effects as well as the potentially positive spillovers associated with the increased demand for local producer services by the foreign companies.

Rodrik, Dani. 1995. "Getting Interventions Right: How South Korea and Taiwan Grew Rich." *Economic Policy* 20: 55–107. This article examines why South Korea and Taiwan have been able to generate rapid growth. The author concludes that although the popular explanation has relied on export promotion and trade liberalization, the main factor that led to the economic miracles in these countries was increased investment rates (in physical and human capital), spurred by a wide array of government policies and incentives.

Rodrik, Dani, and Ricardo Hausmann. 2006. "What's So Special about China's Exports?" Working Paper RWP06-001. John F. Kennedy School of Government. Cambridge, MA: Harvard University. Examines the extent to which China's exports consist of products that have the technological sophistication of goods usually produced by higher-income countries. The authors find evidence that, despite the popular view of Chinese exports as cheap, low-technology products, a significant portion does consist of goods with substantial technological sophistication.

Rodrik, Dani, and Arvind Subramanian. 2005. "From Hindu Growth to Productivity Surge: The Mystery of the Indian Growth Transition." *IMF Staff Papers* 52 (2): 193–228. Although the popular explanation for the Indian growth spurt has been its trade liberalization measures, the authors of this paper argue that before trade was liberalized, India engaged in institutional, public sector reforms that allowed trade liberalization, as well as other economic changes, to take place.

Romer, Paul. 1990. "Endogenous Technological Change." *Journal of Political Economy* 98 (5): S71–102. Presents a theoretical framework examining the determinants of technological change. The focus is on how human capital employed in research and development sectors is the key to technological change and economic growth.

Sachs, Jeffrey D. 2005. *The End of Poverty: Economic Possibilities for Our Time*. New York: Penguin Press. This volume makes the case for increased worldwide aid in the developing world. It argues that such aid can be effectively used to reduce poverty by investing it in health, education, infrastructure, and other projects.

Sachs, Jeffrey D., and Andrew Warner. 1995a. "Economic Reform and the Process of Global Integration." *Brookings Papers on Economic Activity* 1: 1–118. This article examines the links between increased international trade and economic growth. By developing a comprehensive index of openness to international trade, the authors are able to examine empirically the connection between such openness and economic growth in a cross-section of countries. They find a strong, positive connection between openness and growth.

———. 1995b. "Natural Resource Abundance and Economic Growth." NBER Working Paper No. 5398. Cambridge, MA: National Bureau of Economic Research. This paper studies the empirical connection between exports of natural resources and economic growth. Surprisingly, it finds that countries that have a greater share of natural resources in their exports tend to grow more slowly, holding other things constant.

Sala-i-Martin, Xavier, and Arvind Subramanian. 2003. "Addressing the Natural Resource Curse: An Illustration from Nigeria." Working Paper WP/03/139. Washington, DC: International Monetary Fund. This article examines why the oil-exporting country of Nigeria has been unable to develop economically since oil reserves first began to be exploited decades ago. Although several hypotheses are explored, the authors conclude that the most significant factors were the low-quality public sector governance prevailing in the country and the increased corruption associated with the rent-seeking connected to the oil exports.

Stiglitz, Joseph. 2003. *Globalization and its Discontents.* New York: W. W. Norton. This book offers a dissection of the various effects that globalization has had on the world economy. Drawing on his extensive experience as a researcher and policymaker, the author presents a wide array of criticisms of the so-called Washington consensus, a set of market-oriented policies adopted by the United States which have favored free trade, deregulation, privatization, etc. According to the author, these policies have often had disastrous results in the developing world.

———. 2005. "Making Natural Resources into a Blessing Rather Than a Curse." In *Covering Oil*, edited by Svetlana Tsalikad and Anya Schiffrin. New York: Open Society Institute, 13–20. Presents a set of policies that can be used by countries with large endowments of natural resources to ensure that the revenues from the exploitation of such resources help—rather that hurt—the development process.

Stiglitz, Joseph E., and Andrew Charlton. 2005. "Trade Can Be Good for Development." In *Fair Trade for All: How Trade Can Promote Development*, edited by J. Stiglitz and A. Charlton. New York: Oxford University Press, 11–40. Shows how international trade can have positive or negative effects on development. It specifies the conditions under which trade can be harmful and those under which it can be more beneficial.

Vreeland, James R. 2003. *The IMF and Economic Development.* New York: Cambridge University Press. This book presents a wide-ranging discussion of the impact of IMF stabilization policies on economic development. Providing an analysis that ranges from the quantitative to the qualitative and from economics to political science, the book offers a comprehensive yet critical view of the effect that these policies have had on developing countries.

Wacziarg, Romain, and Karen Horn Welch. 2004. "Trade Liberalization and Growth: New Evidence." Working Paper No. 7. Stanford, CA: Center on Development, Democracy and the Rule of Law, Stanford Institute for International Studies. This paper reports research on the links between trade liberalization and economic growth. By looking at the experience of a wide array of countries before and after trade liberalization, it shows that, generally, trade liberalization is associated with greater economic growth, although a number of exceptions are also discussed.

Young, Alwyn. 1995. "A Tale of Two Cities: Factor Accumulation and Technical Change in Hong Kong and Singapore." *NBER Macroeconomics Annual 1995.* Cambridge, MA: MIT Press. This paper examines empirically the determinants of economic growth in Hong Kong and Singapore. The author concludes that Singapore grew primarily because of its investments in physical capital, while Hong Kong's growth drew more strength from productivity gains connected to technological developments and innovation.

FRANCISCO L. RIVERA-BATIZ

■ economic geography

See New Economic Geography

■ economies of scale

International trade theory recognizes three fundamental reasons for countries to trade: *comparative advantage* (to exploit differences in countries' tastes, technologies, or factor endowments), *economies of scale* (to concentrate on fewer tasks in order to produce more efficiently), and *imperfect competition* (to expose firms to more competition). Comparative advantage has always been dominant in trade theory, although economies of scale also long played a secondary role. This changed in the late 1970s, when economists realized that the lion's share of world trade consisted of the exchange of similar (manufactured) goods between similar (rich) countries.

A common reaction to this realization was that such trade could not be due to comparative advantage. But if similar countries trade similar goods, price elasticities (the sensitivities of demands and supplies of goods to price variations) are likely to be high since the traded products will likely be good substitutes. Similar countries would have similar relative prices in autarky (the absence of international trade), so comparative-advantage trade, establishing a world price between the two autarky prices, would imply a modest price change in each country. But, with high elasticities, this could still involve heavy trade. Likewise, dissimilar countries trading very distinct goods—manufactures for primary products, for example—could be expected to experience large price changes, but the resulting trade volumes could be small as price elasticities are likely to be low.

So, comparative advantage was not necessarily inconsistent with actual trade. Nevertheless, it was important to consider alternative possibilities because, although trade to exploit differences does *not* imply that the greater the differences, the greater the trade, it does imply, other things being equal, that the greater the differences, the greater the *gains* from trade. Thus one might conclude that the smaller part of world trade—that between dissimilar countries in quite different products—is more important for policy. But if trade patterns are significantly due to something other than comparative advantage, this conclusion need not follow.

Increasing returns to scale (IRS) and imperfect competition supply alternatives. This article considers the former, often also referred to as economies of scale.

Types of Scale Economies In practice, scale economies occur in great variety, so a classification of the more important attributes is useful.

Internal versus external (to the firm). Scale economies are internal if the individual firm can reduce average costs by operating at a higher scale (e.g., assembly-line operations and equipment made possible by large-scale production). They are external if the individual firm operates subject to constant returns to scale (CRS), but costs are lower the larger the industry in which the firm is located (e.g., well-developed infrastructure and a large supply of skilled workers consequent on a large industrial sector). Internal economies are inconsistent with a perfectly competitive equilibrium, and external economies are, well, externalities. Since the theory of compara-

tive advantage assumes perfect competition and no externalities, trade due to economies of scale alone *cannot* be comparative-advantage trade.

National versus international. Economies of scale may depend on the scale of operations within a nation (e.g., large plant size) or on the scale of operations globally (e.g., division of labor and free trade in intermediate goods). Either might be internal or external to the firm. An example of internal, international economies of scale is research and development (R&D) by a multinational firm that utilizes the results of the R&D in several countries.

Aggregative versus disaggregative. Increasing returns may be a property of manufacturing generally (e.g., the size of the industrial sector) or of individual manufactured goods (e.g., the number of red sedans).

These three considerations generate eight types of scale economies, each relevant in reality. Comparative-advantage trade can also be due to many causes, but they all matter *solely* in terms of how they influence differences in relative autarky prices. This imparts an attractive formal unity to that theory's predictions. Trade due to economies of scale is dramatically different: Basic implications are indeed very sensitive to the *type* of scale economy. Consider first national, aggregative, increasing returns external to the firm.

National, Aggregative Economies of Scale External to the Firm IRS can furnish a basis for trade independent of comparative advantage. Consider a simple model with two identical economies with two-good Ricardian technologies. Good A is produced with CRS, with one unit of labor required in each country to produce one unit of A. The B sector has IRS external to the firm: $B = k(L_B)L_B$, where $k(L_B) = k_0(L_B)^{\alpha - 1}$ for $\alpha > 1$. The individual firm takes k as a parameter.

Two such identical countries will have equal relative autarky prices. But there is still a basis for trade: with IRS in the B industry it is not globally efficient for both countries to produce both goods.

The no-trade case, with each country doing what it had done in autarky, is a free-trade equilibrium. But it will not be a very stable one. For suppose the home economy produces more B, and the foreign economy less. Then k is greater than k^*, the foreign analog, so home B firms can undersell their foreign rivals, while the two countries can still produce A on equal terms. Home B producers can increase their market share at the expense of their foreign competitors, so foreign resources move into the A sector. Thus k rises further and k^* falls, increasing the home B advantage still more. This continues until a new equilibrium is reached with the home economy producing only B and/or the foreign economy producing only A. Indeed there is more than just a second equilibrium: since the two countries are identical we can find a third equilibrium by simply reversing the home and foreign roles.

The basic idea behind comparative advantage is that countries should do what they can do relatively well; this implies some particular role in the world economy. Scale economies on the other hand require countries to concentrate on a small number of tasks; who does what is secondary. Thus scale economies introduce a bias toward a multiplicity of equilibria.

The other equilibria might involve one country specialized in B and/or one specialized in A. Consider an equilibrium in which the home country specializes in B, with the (identical) foreign economy producing both goods. Since $k > k^*$, foreign wages must be lower than home wages and also lower than wages in autarky, so foreign real income must have declined. Likewise, the home wage must have risen relative to autarky. Thus trade has benefited the home economy, but has made the foreign worse off. There is also a "mirror-image" equilibrium in which the roles of the two countries reverse. Thus potential international conflict is inherent. We might call this the Graham case since it corresponds to Graham's (1923) argument for protection.

Suppose now that, instead, the dynamic adjustment ends with the foreign economy specialized in A and the home economy producing both goods. Since both countries produce A, wages must be the same internationally, in sharp contrast to the Graham case. Thus residents of both countries fare the same, and that common fate must be an improvement over autarky, since the home B sector has grown. There will again be another "mirror image" equilibrium,

but unlike the previous case this is of no consequence, because everyone fares the same regardless of country of residence. With identical economies, a wage-equalization equilibrium is associated with a large world equilibrium demand for A, so that one country alone cannot satisfy it. But with dissimilar countries, it is easy to construct examples in which either the larger or the smaller country specializes in A, and in which both countries lose relative to autarky.

The final possibility is that both countries specialize. Then the international equilibrium is efficient, unlike the other cases, where too little B is produced. The various types of equilibria are not mutually exclusive. That is, if tastes, technology, and size imply multiple equilibria, the equilibria could be of different types. It is the possibility of wage equalization and (especially) Graham equilibria that produces the real value added that can come from consideration of IRS. These equilibria can produce positive and normative implications in sharp contrast to those of comparative advantage and can therefore be used in support of quite different policy recommendations. They are of direct relevance to the old debates in developing countries over the wisdom of participating in the international trading system.

But this analysis of national external economies of scale is less than fully satisfying and has accordingly had to play a role very much subservient to that of comparative advantage. The indeterminacy of results due to the likelihood of multiple equilibria renders the theory cumbersome to use. Also, this investigation of scale economies was motivated in large part by a desire to address more directly a world in which the lion's share of trade consists of the exchange of similar commodities between similar economies. But the influence of scale economies, enhancing the possibility of specialization, and perhaps causing initially similar economies to become very dissimilar, is to move the discussion in just the opposite direction. Additional methods of modeling scale economies are needed.

Disaggregative Economies of Scale Consider now the same model as above, *except* that the B sector now consists of n distinct varieties, B_i, each with the technology described above. Note the following concerning international trade in such a model.

1. Wage equalization equilibria will again feature both countries producing some A, but no variety of B in common, so that both are equally well off with free trade. If one country specializes in A all trade will consist of the *inter*industry exchange of A for B, but if both countries produce some varieties of B there will also be an *intra*industry exchange of B varieties. We would expect the latter to be relatively more important the more similar the two countries are: if the two are exactly alike, there will be an equilibrium with only intraindustry trade.

2. Graham equilibria can still emerge whenever the two countries produce some variety of B in common but in different amounts. The country with the larger production must have the higher wage and therefore cannot be producing any A. However this now seems like a much less likely outcome than before, since a smaller B sector than in autarky need not condemn a country to a lower wage: it can just produce a smaller number of varieties while fully supplying the world demand for each.

International Economies of Scale External economies have often been identified with an increased division of labor made possible by a larger market: Adam Smith's pin factory and the Swiss watch industry are the prominent hoary examples. Less common are examples having to do with a larger volume of public information generated by a larger industry. In principle none of these requires an industry to be physically located in one place. A dispersed industry can realize a great division of labor if intermediate components can be shipped from place to place; public information can be dispersed within the industry if communication is efficient. What matters, under these conditions, is the global size of the industry, not its geographical concentration.

This suggests that returns to scale may depend on the size of the *world* industry, not the national industry. This is what is meant by *international* returns to scale. Suppose that resources are used to produce A and m. A production is characterized, as in the above one-factor models, by CRS; m is an index of the scale of operations of the national B industry, subject to IRS. With *national* returns to scale, national B production B is related to m by

$$B = km \text{ where } k = k(m), k' > 0.$$

With *international* returns to scale, on the other hand, we have instead

$$B + B^* = k(m + m^*) \text{ where }$$
$$k = k(m + m^*), \ k' > 0.$$

Here an asterisk refers to the foreign country.

At first glance it might seem that we have complicated matters enormously. National production-possibility frontiers between final goods are not even defined, because productivity in each country's B industry depends on the size of the other country's B industry. But the situation becomes almost transparent as soon as we focus on patterns of resource allocation rather than on goods.

To see this, consider the world production-possibility frontier between A and B. A point on it can be found by maximizing world B production for a given feasible volume of world A production, that is, by choosing m, m^* to

maximize: $B + B^* = k(m + m^*)[m + m^*]$
subject to:
$T(m) + T^*(m^*) = \text{some specified value.}$

T and T^* denote the home and foreign production-possibility frontiers between A and m. Clearly, $B + B^*$ will be maximized by maximizing $m + m^*$: This problem has exactly the same solution as that of choosing m, m^* to

maximize: $m + m^*$
subject to:
$T(m) + T^*(m^*) = \text{some specified value}$

and the solutions to problems of the latter sort are just the comparative advantage predictions. Efficient patterns of world activity in A and B correspond to efficient patterns in A and m, ignoring the scale economies.

Productive efficiency is as with CRS, and firms behave competitively because the economies are external to them. The result is that the complex tendencies associated with Graham equilibria when scale economies are national disappear when they become international.

The second major implication of international IRS is that they imply a theory of the intraindustry exchange of intermediate goods between relatively similar economies. The essential idea behind international IRS is that a dispersed industry can realize the benefits of a large division of labor if intermediate goods can be shipped within the industry. Thus the more nearly equal in size m and m^* are, the greater the volume of intraindustry trade in B components.

All trade will be interindustry if the disparity between countries is great enough for the A exporter to specialize completely in A. Small international differences reduce the incentive for interindustry trade but cause the integrated B industry to be divided relatively evenly between countries, thereby inducing intraindustry trade. In the limiting case where the countries are identical, they will both be self sufficient in A. But they can gain from trade by establishing a single, rationalized B industry; all trade will be intraindustry.

Applications of Scale Economies Economies of scale can be a basis for trade, just like comparative advantage. But they can give a very different picture of the consequences of such trade. This has clearly emerged from recent work in the area.

The notion of international economies of scale, developed by trade theory, has been used to rejuvenate the theory of economic growth, as in the work of Romer (1986). If the division of labor is limited by the extent of the market, it is reasonable to suppose that indivisibilities in the production of intermediate goods is the reason why. So there is a role for imperfect competition with regard to the latter.

Imperfect competition and scale economies have been investigated in the context of both consumer goods, by Krugman (1979), Lancaster (1980), and Helpman (1981), and producer goods, by Ethier (1982a). As this literature does involve imperfect competition, it is beyond the scope of the present entry. More recently, scale economies have been central to the literature on trade with heterogeneous firms, as in the work of Melitz (2003).

Though scale economies were in trade theory from the beginning, their role was basically tangential until the late 1970s. Now it is central.

See also comparative advantage; intrafirm trade; intraindustry trade; monopolistic competition; New Trade Theory; Ricardian model

FURTHER READING

Ethier, Wilfred J. 1979. "Internationally Decreasing Costs and World Trade." *Journal of International Economics* 9 (1): 1–24. Discusses the implications of international economies of scale.

———. 1982a. "National and International Returns to Scale in the Modern Theory of International Trade." *American Economic Review* 72 (3): 389–405. Considers scale economies and trade in producer goods.

———. 1982b. "Decreasing Costs in International Trade and Frank Graham's Argument for Protection." *Econometrica* 50 (5): 1243–68. A discussion of how trade may or may not be harmful in the presence of scale economies.

———. 1998. "Regionalism in a Multilateral World." *Journal of Political Economy* 6 (106): 1214–45. An application of external, international economies of scale to regional integration.

Graham, F. 1923. "Some Aspects of Protection Further Considered." *Quarterly Journal of Economics* 37: 199–227. An early and forceful argument that economies of scale might cause trade to harm a country.

Helpman, Elhanan. 1981. "International Trade in the Presence of Product Differentiation, Economies of Scale, and Imperfect Competition: A Chamberlin–Heckscher–Ohlin Approach." *Journal of International Economics* 11: 305–40. A discussion of scale economies in the production of consumer goods.

———. 1984. "Increasing Returns, Imperfect Markets, and Trade Theory." In *Handbook of International Economics*, vol. 1, edited by Ronald W. Jones and Peter B. Kenen. Amsterdam: North Holland, 325–65. A useful survey of the early "new" trade literature emphasizing economies of scale.

Krugman, Paul. 1979. "Increasing Returns, Monopolistic Competition, and International Trade." *Journal of International Economics* 9 (4): 469–79. An influential discussion of scale economies in the production of consumer goods.

Lancaster, Kelvin. 1980. "Intraindustry Trade under Perfect Monopolistic Competition." *Journal of International*

Economics 10: 151–76. An early discussion of scale economies in the production of consumer goods.

Markusen, J., and J. Melvin. 1984. "The Gains-from-Trade Theorem with Increasing Returns to Scale." In *Monopolistic Competition and International Trade*, edited by H. Kierzkowski. Oxford: Oxford University Press, 10–33. An important treatment of the traditional gains-from-trade argument in the context of scale economies.

Matthews, R.C.O. 1949–50. "Reciprocal Demand and Increasing Returns." *Review of Economic Studies* 37: 149–58. A good example of the earlier literature on scale economies.

Melitz, Marc. 2003. "The Impact of Trade on Intraindustry Reallocations and Aggregate Industry Productivity." *Econometrica* 71: 1695–1725. Considers heterogeneous products and international trade.

Romer, Paul. 1986. "Increasing Returns and Long-Run Growth." *Journal of Political Economy* 94: 1002–37. A major application of "international" economies of scale to economic growth.

WILFRED J. ETHIER

■ effective exchange rate

The effective exchange rate is a summary measure of the rate at which a country's currency exchanges for a basket of other currencies, in either nominal or real terms. Effective exchange rates become relevant when a country conducts trade and investment transactions with a number of other countries. These rates can vary along several dimensions, including country coverage, weighting, and whether or not the effect of inflation is taken into account (i.e., the distinction between nominal and real). The final selection of the appropriate definition and calculation of the effective exchange rate depends on a rather complicated interplay of the theoretical model of interest and data availability and reliability.

The first issue to confront in calculating an effective exchange rate is how to attribute relative weights to each of the partner currencies. In many circumstances, the exchange rate plays the role of a relative price of traded goods; hence, the relevant weights involve trade weights. Asset trade has become more prominent in recent decades, suggesting that the appropriate weights may be related to the assets owed by, or liabilities owed to, other countries.

Trade-Weighted Effective Exchange Rates By far the most common means of calculating an effective exchange rate is to weight the currencies by trade weights. To fix concepts, consider a geometrically weighted average of bilateral exchange rates.

$$s_t^{effective} \equiv \sum_{j=1}^{n} w_j s_t^j \tag{1}$$

$$q_t^{effective} \equiv \sum_{j=1}^{n} w_j q_t^j \tag{2}$$

where $s^j (q^j)$ denotes the log nominal (real) exchange rate relative to country j. The weights w_j are usually based on bilateral trade volumes (the sum of exports and imports, expressed as a proportion of total exports and imports).

Trade weighting can take on a more complicated form to allow for competition in third markets, however. This goal is usually accomplished by adopting the Armington (1969) assumption that goods are differentiated by location of production. The third market weight is equal to the weighted average over all third-country markets of country j's import share divided by a weighted average of the combined import share of all of country i's competitors, with the weights being the shares of country i's exports to the various markets. This simple expression is based on the assumption that all the differentiated goods share the same constant elasticity of substitution, which may not necessarily be appropriate in all instances (Spilimbergo and Vamvakidis 2003). For instance, goods originating from less-developed countries may not be equally substitutable with goods originating from industrial countries. Moreover, these weights can change over time continuously or discretely and infrequently, with the choice depending in large part on the trade-off between convenience and accuracy.

Nominal versus Real Often the economist will encounter a model wherein the real, or inflation-adjusted, exchange rate plays a central role. There are a number of real exchange rates, or "relative prices," that appear in the literature, however, so there is ample scope for confusion. A decomposition of the most standard definition is useful. In this definition, the real exchange rate is given by:

$$q_t \equiv s_t - p_t + p_t^* \qquad (3)$$

where s is the log exchange rate defined in units of home currency per unit of foreign currency.

Most models of the real exchange rate can be categorized according to which specific relative price serves as the object of focus. If the relative price of nontradables is key, then using a broad price index encompassing tradables and nontradables is implied. One example of the use of a broad index is in productivity-based explanations of the real exchange rate such as the Balassa-Samuelson model. If, on the other hand, external balance (i.e., current account balance) is of paramount concern, some narrower index of traded goods may be the appropriate deflator. This variable is also what macroeconomic policymakers often allude to as price competitiveness—a weaker domestic currency (in real terms) means that it is easier to sell domestic goods abroad. A related concept is cost competitiveness. Assuming a cost-markup model of pricing (i.e., prices equal some markup over cost), one can calculate a measure of the real effective exchange rate where unit labor costs are used instead of prices (Golub 1994). This real exchange rate is best thought of as a measure of the relative *production cost*—rather than price—of goods.

In practice, one has a choice of only a few price deflators. At the monthly frequency, they include the consumer price index (CPI), the producer price index (PPI) or wholesale price index (WPI), or the export price index. At lower frequencies, such as quarterly data, the set of deflators increases somewhat, to include the gross domestic product (GDP) deflator and price indexes for the components of GDP, such as the personal consumption expenditure deflator. Typically, the CPI weights nontraded goods such as consumer services fairly heavily. Similarly, the GDP deflator and the CPI will weight expenditures on nontradables in proportion to their importance in the aggregate economy. In contrast, the PPI and WPI exclude many retail sales services that are likely to be nontraded.

The unit labor cost deflated index is in a sense the most relevant for many issues related to trade, as unit labor costs are a measure of cost competitiveness. Unfortunately, there are many difficulties with using such indexes. First, unit labor costs (ULCs) are not always available on a timely or consistent basis, and are subject to substantial revisions. Second, their greater covariation with the business cycle impedes discerning trends in the ULC deflated series. Third, measured ULCs usually pertain only to manufacturing sectors, and given the increasing tradability of services, measured ULCs may provide misleading inferences. Fourth and perhaps most important, ULCs are typically available on a consistent basis for developed economies, so that ULC deflated effective exchange rates can be calculated only against a reference group of countries that may not, in the end, be the relevant group.

Asset and Liability Weights In the preceding discussion, it has been taken as a given that the appropriate weights are those associated with trade flows. Yet there is no reason why trade weighting should be appropriate for all questions. The economists Cedric Tille, Hélène Rey, and Pierre-Olivier Gourinchas have pointed out that exchange rate changes have had substantial effects on the net international investment position of the United States. Tille (2003) noted that because U.S. assets are predominantly denominated in foreign currencies, while U.S. liabilities are mostly denominated in dollars, dollar depreciation induces a large upward effect on the dollar valuation of U.S. foreign assets. Hence, over the short to medium term, the net international investment position is heavily influenced by dollar movements.

See also Balassa-Samuelson effect; band, basket, and crawl (BBC); equilibrium exchange rate; exchange rate forecasting; exchange rate regimes; exchange rate volatility; nontraded goods; purchasing power parity; real exchange rate

FURTHER READING
Armington, P. S. 1969. "A Theory of Demand for Products Distinguished by Place of Production." *IMF Staff Papers* 16: 159–78. Provides the basis for the modeling of trade flows.

Bayoumi, Tamim, Jaewoo Lee, and Sarma Jayantha. 2006. "New Rates from New Weights." *IMF Staff Papers* 53 (2): 272–305. Describes the most recent incarnation of the IMF indexes.

Black, Stanley W. 1976. "Multilateral and Bilateral Measures of Effective Exchange Rates in a World Model of Traded Goods." *Journal of Political Economy* 84 (3): 615–22. One of the earliest descriptions of how to construct effective trade-weighted exchange rate indexes.

Chinn, Menzie. 2006. "A Primer on Real Effective Exchange Rates: Determinants, Overvaluation, Trade Flows, and Competitive Devaluations." *Open Economies Review* 17 (1) (January): 115–43.

Golub, Stephen. 1994. "Comparative Advantage, Exchange Rates, and Sectoral Trade Balances of Major Industrial Countries." *IMF Staff Papers* 41 (2) (June): 286–313. Links the idea of cost competitiveness to effective exchange rates.

Gourinchas, Pierre-Olivier, and Hélène Rey. 2005. "International Financial Adjustment." NBER Working Paper No. 11155 (February). Cambridge, MA: National Bureau of Economic Research. An important paper that implements the construction of asset-weighted effective exchange rate indexes.

Lane, Philip, and Gian Maria Milesi-Ferretti. 2005. "Financial Globalization and Exchange Rates." IMF Working Paper No. 05/03 (January). Washington, DC: International Monetary Fund. This paper notes that in a world characterized by increasing financial globalization (namely increasingly large cross-border holdings of assets and debt) exchange rate movements will have ever more pronounced effects on *net* asset positions in many countries, in addition to the United States.

Spilimbergo, Antonio, and Athanasios Vamvakidis. 2003. "Real Effective Exchange Rate and the Constant Elasticity of Substitution Assumption." *Journal of International Economics* 60 (2): 337–54. This paper drops the assumption that goods from developed and less-developed countries are not equally substitutable.

Tille, C. 2003. "The Impact of Exchange Rate Movements on U.S. Foreign Debt." *Current Issues in Economics and Finance* (Federal Reserve Bank of New York) 9 (1): 1–8.

MENZIE D. CHINN

■ effective protection

Effective protection measures the change in value added per unit of output induced by tariffs and other policy measures on competing imports and intermediate inputs. The concept has been widely used by trade economists and policy analysts interested in investigating trade policies' protective effects on domestic production activities. They recognize that trade policies affect both the price of a good produced domestically and the price paid for any inputs involved in producing that (final) good. The gross price of the final good is raised by a tariff on competing imports, giving rise to apparently positive protection in nominal terms and an incentive to increase production. The net price or value added in the activity may still be reduced even where there is positive nominal protection, however, if the price-raising effects of tariffs on intermediate inputs more than offset the effects of the final output tariff.

Economists had long recognized the danger of focusing on output tariffs to analyze the protective effects of a tariff structure, but it was Max M. Corden (1971) who systematically organized his and others' seminal contributions during the 1960s into an integrated theory of effective protection.

Modeling of the Concept Within a partial equilibrium modeling framework with fixed technologies (no scope to alter the mix of factor and material inputs) and tradable inputs only, effective protection can be measured using information on output (t_j) and input (t_i) tariff rates and technological or input share coefficients under free trade conditions (a_{ij}). The resulting measure of effective protection (e_j) summarizes the impact of the tariff structure on value added in each activity and indicates the corresponding production and resource allocation effects. For the single input and single output case:

$$e_j = \frac{t_j - a_{ij}t_i}{1 - a_{ij}} \qquad (1)$$

From equation (1) some key insights of the concept can be derived. Effective protection is positively related to the output tariff and negatively related to the input tariff—output tariffs implicitly subsidizing activity j and input tariffs taxing it. Effective protection can be positive or negative depending on the structure of protection (whether output tariffs are greater or smaller than input tariffs) and on the shares of intermediate inputs. Further, the effective rate of protection will exceed the nominal tariff rate if there is an escalating tariff structure, with output tariffs higher than input tariffs, the effects of tariff escalation being magnified the higher the share of intermediate inputs (or correspondingly the lower the degree of domestic value added). Indeed, with sufficiently steep tariff escalation and highly (imported) intermediate-dependent activities, value added at world prices (i.e., in the absence of tariffs) can be negative.

Measurement and Application The effective protection concept seeks to provide a framework for thinking systematically about the structure of tariffs and other trade policy measures, and the resulting structure of protection and incentives. It offers a coherent explanation of why tariff escalation is a widely observed feature of trade regimes. It offers an explanation also of why the degree of actual and perceived protection may vary substantially across different types of activities and sectors. Since a given product (e.g., steel) can be a final product of one set of producers (steel producers) and an input good for another set (e.g., car manufacturers), it is not possible to ensure an escalating tariff structure for all producers. Therefore, the effective rate of protection is an analytical tool that offers an explanation for both idiosyncratic features of trade policy regimes and systematic biases: the possibility of high rates of effective protection for many import-substituting activities but, at the same time, low negative rates for specific activities. Similarly, evidence has been found of systematic biases in favor of final goods production and against intermediate goods, as well as in favor of import-substitution activities and against export activities, both of which can be understood and quantified using the effective protection framework.

Following Corden's developmental work, a generation of applied trade economists sought to measure effective protection (mainly within the partial equilibrium modeling framework described earlier) and to use these measures for trade policy appraisal purposes, in particular but not exclusively in a developing country context. Its tractability was attrac-

tive for applied work. It can be applied at the firm or industry level, and it is relatively straightforward to allow for the complexities of multi-input and output activities, factor in nontraded inputs, distinguish sales of final goods to protected domestic markets from those to unprotected export markets, and account for a range of taxing and subsidizing effects induced by policy instruments other than tariffs. Compared with applied and economywide general equilibrium models, partial equilibrium estimates have relatively limited data requirements. In addition to tariff data (and possibly other policy information), the main data requirement is information on the technology or input share coefficients available from input-output tables or firm-level surveys.

Following the major multicountry studies by Anne O. Krueger (1978) and Bela Balassa (1982), there was an explosion of developing country studies that measured and analyzed effective protection within a partial equilibrium framework (reviewed by Greenaway and Milner 1993). Although there has been a significant liberalization of trade policies in developing countries since the late 1980s, effective rates of protection are still measured and analyzed, including in the World Trade Organization's Trade Policy Reviews. There has also been a renewal of interest in the role of transportation and other nontrade policy sources of international transaction costs. These costs also have implicit taxing and subsidizing effects that can be represented and analyzed within an effective protection framework.

Theoretical Criticisms From the outset trade theorists, such as Ronald Jones (1971), who were interested in whether the interpretation of partial-equilibrium measures survived in general equilibrium, closely scrutinized the concept of effective protection. A key assumption of the partial equilibrium approach is fixed technological coefficients, and therefore no substitutability among material inputs and between material and factor inputs. Defining and interpreting changes in value added becomes more problematic if substitution is possible. This, and the wider limitations of using differences between products or sectors in the scale of measured effective protection alone to comment on general equilibrium resource pulls, led some economists to conclude that the concept was "fatally flawed." Others have been more willing to distinguish between the theoretically possible and the probable problems in practice. Some applied general equilibrium (AGE) modeling has compared the resource allocation effects of tariffs under alternative substitution assumptions, and the rank correlations between effective protection measures and tariff-induced production changes are not necessarily low. Effective protection measures do not necessarily, therefore, provide poor guidance on the allocative effects of tariffs. Further, in a review of the arguments, Greenaway and Milner (2003) point out that many applied economists have been careful to avoid interpreting differences between sectors or changes over time in measured effective protection as providing detailed and precise guidance on resource allocation effects. Rather, they have used the overall pattern of estimates to comment on the likely systematic biases and distortions of a trade policy regime and to offer guidance on the general direction of policy reform.

The development and refinement of economy-wide AGE models, and the associated developments in software that have eased their construction, calibration, and solution, have extended their use in trade policy evaluation. Where they are available, AGE models clearly give direct information on the resource allocation effects of trade policy changes. But the data demands of such models are high, even at the relatively high levels of product aggregation typically involved. The effective protection concept, and estimates of effective protection interpreted judiciously, will continue to be useful for analyzing trade policy regimes and their potential effects on incentives, resource allocation, and incomes. This will help to shed light on patterns of protection in the world economy.

See also applied general equilibrium modeling; partial equilibrium modeling; tariff escalation; tariffs

FURTHER READING
Balassa, Bela, ed. 1982. *Development Strategies in Semi-Industrialized Economies.* Baltimore: Johns Hopkins University Press. A helpful summary of the empirical issues associated with measuring effective protection, with evidence for several industrializing countries.
Corden, Max M., ed. 1971. *The Theory of Protection.* Oxford: Oxford University Press. The first systematic exposition of the theory of effective protection.
Greenaway, David, and Chris R. Milner, eds. 1993. *Trade and Industrial Policy in Developing Countries.* London: Macmillan. Reviews the tools used to analyze trade policy and policy reform in developing countries.
———, eds. 2003. "Effective Protection, Policy Appraisal, and Trade Policy Reform." *The World Economy* 26 (4): 441–56. Reviews the empirical and theoretical literatures and offers a defense of the use of effective protection in applied work.
Jones, Ronald W., ed. 1971. "Effective Protection and Substitution." *Journal of International Economics* 1 (1): 59–82. An early example of the theoretical criticism of partial equilibrium measures of protection.
Krueger, Anne O., ed. 1978. *Liberalization Attempts and Consequences.* New York: National Bureau of Economic Research. A commonly cited, cross-country study of the costs of protection in developing countries.

CHRIS MILNER

■ electronic commerce

Electronic commerce, or *e-commerce*, has no settled definition. At its broadest, electronic commerce involves conducting business using most modern communication instruments: telephone, fax, television, electronic payment and money transfer systems, electronic data interchange, and the Internet. On September 25, 1998, the World Trade Organization (WTO) General Council adopted a broad view of electronic commerce in its work program on the subject: "The production, distribution, marketing, sale or delivery of goods and services by electronic means." In more recent times, the term *e-commerce* has become strongly associated with commercial activities on the Internet. For instance, the Organisation for Economic Co-operation and Development's discussions of e-commerce concentrate almost exclusively on Internet-based transactions.

In this article, electronic commerce is conceived of as conducting or facilitating business via electronic communications networks and computer systems. This includes buying and selling online, electronic funds transfer, business communications (including by telephone, facsimile, and internal data networks), and using computers to access business information resources. The WTO has recognized that commercial transactions can be broken into three stages: (1) advertising and searching, (2) ordering and payment, and (3) delivery. Common conceptions of electronic commerce involve business-to-consumer or business-to-business interaction at one or more of these three stages. Generally speaking, however, electronic commerce also encompasses activities that do not fit neatly into any one of these categories, such as electronic logistics tracking and business process outsourcing.

The Internet is of such critical importance to the world economy today that it necessarily dominates any discussion of electronic commerce. It offers greater possibilities for commercial interaction than do telephones or faxes, and has dramatically changed the way that information is exchanged and business conducted. The definition of electronic commerce adopted here deliberately extends beyond the Internet, however, not only to capture its predecessors, but also in anticipation of future technologies. If we have learned anything from the rapid development of computer and telecommunications technology over the last few decades, it is that what seems like an established technology today can quickly be replaced by another technology. The safest prediction about the future direction of technology is that it will be unexpected. Thus, as ubiquitous and permanent a feature of modern life as the Internet seems now, it may be replaced, and it is therefore appropriate to use a definition that is technologically neutral and forward looking.

The Economic Significance of Electronic Commerce Three factors contribute to the significance of electronic commerce to the world economy today: the rapid growth of the Internet, its ability to facilitate cross-border trade, and its ability to reduce transaction costs.

Although it became publicly accessible only with the inception of the World Wide Web in 1990, the Internet now has more than 1 billion users. In the early years of the World Wide Web, usage almost doubled from year to year, and it continues to grow. The benefit of conducting business online increases exponentially with the number of connections.

The Internet facilitates production and distribution across borders so that, for example, consumers in one country can respond to an advertisement published in another country for a product that was developed using a design team collaborating (using the Internet) in five other countries. Electronic commerce increases the range of services that can be traded internationally (e.g., medical, legal, educational, and gambling services) and can assist in opening markets that were previously closed. The dramatic increases in both online retail sales and advertising revenues are the most visible evidence of a much broader growth in electronic commerce in the global economy.

Electronic commerce has the potential to generate benefits beyond those of trade liberalization on its own. Benefits for suppliers and vendors include reduced transaction costs, reduced barriers to market entry, more rapid product innovations, and economies of scale. One source of reduced transaction costs is the possibility to dispense with traditional intermediaries (for example, in relation to the travel industry). In many cases, electronic commerce dispenses with the need for physical presence at the point of sale or for the provision of services, which can drastically reduce expenses relating to premises or personnel. Benefits for consumers include increased market transparency and reduced search costs, even if they make the final purchase in person. These benefits are particularly noticeable for consumers in smaller markets, who may not have enjoyed the same level of price and quality competition as consumers in larger markets. Challenges to increased consumer use of electronic commerce include concerns about information privacy and fraud, which have not been completely resolved. Governments also benefit from electronic commerce because it reduces the cost of providing services to their citizens, while offering greater transparency and accountability.

These three factors have certainly altered the conditions in many preexisting markets for goods and services, but two markets are particularly useful in demonstrating these factors. First, consumer-to-consumer commercial transactions, facilitated by accessible online financial services, community, and auction sites, now have the potential to operate on a global, cross-border level. It is difficult to draw a bright line between consumer-to-consumer and business-to-consumer transactions, as the removal of many barriers to entry have allowed some consumers to play a role that was once available only to established global players. This reveals one reason for the exponential benefit of growth in the Internet's user base: unlike previous communications technologies, which facilitated one-to-one or one-to-many marketing and sales, Internet-based e-commerce allows a many-to-many business paradigm to become practicable.

Second, the market for digital products and services (those that can be supplied to the purchaser electronically) is arguably the most substantially affected by the growth of electronic commerce. Once they are provided in a digital format, goods such as music, movies, and software have negligible production costs for additional units and equally negligible delivery costs. Over the Internet, their delivery time is limited primarily by bandwidth and connection speed rather than distance or the speed of physical transport. Services that can now be provided digitally across borders are increasingly being outsourced to take advantage of cheaper labor markets. This phenomenon, called business process outsourcing, began in its modern incarnation with the outsourcing of software development to India. India remains the market leader in business process outsourcing exports today and has moved into many other areas such as sales and customer service call centers as well as intrabusiness services—for example, information technology support and human resources. Other developing countries, such as Brazil and China, have also experienced strong growth in this area. As the uptake and speed of Internet con-

nections increase, the sale of digital products and services is likely to have a substantial impact on the world economy, not only in its own right, but also due to its disruptive effects on related "offline" industries.

Conversely, many factors militate against electronic commerce completely replacing traditional nonelectronic business models. Thus, despite its growth, the uptake of electronic commerce was slower than many expected. As mentioned earlier, the security of online payment and information transfer remains a primary concern. The market for digital products is especially affected by the lack of cost-effective micropayment methods (i.e., for low-value transactions). Additionally, due in part to the threat of fraud, or possibly more for sociological than economic reasons, many consumers and businesses prefer physical presence over electronic transactions, especially to conduct a physical inspection of goods before purchase. This has led to the perception that online retailers "freeload" off retailers with physical stock and showrooms, as customers can investigate the product in person in a retail store and then purchase it from an online store at a reduced price. Some manufacturers and suppliers refuse to sell to online retailers in order to protect their existing showroom-based retail outlets. Furthermore, although the growth of the Internet has been substantial, many use the Internet for recreational and communication purposes rather than commercial ones, and a majority of the world's population is still without regular Internet access.

Nevertheless, as electronic commerce matures and develops, it will undoubtedly play an increasingly important role in the world economy. Many of the impediments that it is presently facing are technological in nature, and given the speed at which new developments occur in information technology, it is only a matter of time before many of them are overcome.

The Role of the WTO Although electronic commerce involves new technology, at its heart it is simply another means of conducting international commercial transactions. Most countries have previously decided that such transactions should be dealt with in the WTO. The advantage of locating electronic commerce within the WTO framework is that it provides a system of transparent, predictable, and enforceable rules. These rules are based on principles of nondiscrimination (most-favored-nation treatment [MFN] and national treatment) and transparency, which are as relevant to electronic commerce as they are to other forms of international trade. The WTO also has an established record of trade liberalization and takes an economic and commercial focus. This means that it is not particularly concerned with technology matters; rather it is intent on creating a system of trade agreements that apply to transactions regardless of the form of technology used to produce or deliver the product. Many WTO members share this belief in the principle of technological neutrality. It is important to scrutinize deviations from neutrality: for example, those resulting from the goods and services distinction created by the General Agreement on Tariffs and Trade (GATT) and the General Agreement on Trade in Services (GATS). Technological neutrality should not be used as an excuse for protectionism, however. The primary purpose of the WTO remains trade liberalization. Thus, for example, practices that liberalize trade in a good only where it has been created using a certain technology (i.e., technologically discriminatory liberalism) should be preferred to practices that create or maintain barriers to trade in that good however created (i.e., technologically neutral protectionism).

On May 20, 1998, during its second Ministerial Conference in Geneva, the WTO adopted a Declaration on Global Electronic Commerce, recognizing the growth of electronic commerce and its potential to increase international trade. The declaration directed the General Council to establish a comprehensive work program to examine all trade-related issues of global electronic commerce and to produce a report on the progress of the work program and any recommendations for action at the third Ministerial Conference of the WTO. The Council for Trade in Goods, the Council for the Agreement on Trade Related Aspects of Intellectual Property Rights (TRIPS), the Committee on Trade and De-

velopment, and the Council for Trade in Services each produced a report for the General Council in July 1999. The general view of members emerging from these and subsequent reports is that the electronic delivery of services falls within the scope of GATS, and that all the provisions of GATS apply to trade in services through electronic means. Members have not reached a consensus on issues such as the treatment of certain digitizable products, however, and work continues on resolving these issues. The General Council has held a number of dedicated discussions on "cross-cutting" e-commerce issues, in recognition of the fact that many e-commerce problems cut across a number of WTO agreements such as the GATS, GATT, and TRIPS. These discussions have covered topics such as the classification of digital products and the fiscal implications of e-commerce. The Councils for Trade in Goods, Trade in Services, and TRIPS as well as the Committee on Trade and Development have also held discussions on e-commerce issues relating to their respective mandates.

The general view of WTO members that GATS applies to electronic delivery of services and trade in services through electronic means is consistent with the prevailing academic view that electronic commerce, for the most part, falls under the purview of GATS. Many WTO members have expressed the view that all digital products should be classified as services so as to fall under GATS. GATS extends the scope of international trade obligations to cover services, which represent a significant and growing proportion of global trade. It imposes general principles of MFN treatment and transparency to services (subject to some exceptions), and it also provides for individual commitments by members to liberalization of trade in services, including commitments to provide market access and national treatment in specified service sectors.

Once WTO members agree on how to handle electronic commerce, WTO agreements and dispute settlement have the potential to profoundly aid or curtail the growth and impact of e-commerce, especially as regards cross-border trade. Other international bodies will also have an effect on the future development of e-commerce, for instance the UN Working Group on Internet Governance. The proven effectiveness of the WTO in securing a degree of multilateral compliance with its international trade standards, however, makes it a key player in the regulation of electronic commerce.

Trends in Electronic Commerce A number of trends are evident in relation to electronic commerce that will affect the world economy. First, the value and number of digital products (e.g., music, books, and videos delivered electronically rather than physically) is likely to continue to increase. Second, communications technologies are gradually converging. If this trend continues, previously separate technologies such as the telephone, television, and the Internet may eventually be considered part of a single communications network. This would result in traditional media companies (such as television broadcasters) being compelled to shift to a more interactive, Internet-based model, and online vendors would benefit from greater reach to mobile and entertainment devices. Third, the Internet is continuing to affect consumer behavior. For example, consumers are spending more time and money online, and the value of their online purchases is increasing as they gain experience with online shopping and move to higher speed Internet. Fourth, transactions using notes and coins will continue to decline in favor of transactions using digital money. (Notes and coins make up only a small fraction of the total value of economic transactions, but they still comprise a significant proportion of the number of transactions.) Fifth, the growth in the business process outsourcing market has the potential to alter materially the structures and costs associated with many conventional businesses. Outsourcing specialized tasks to low-cost providers is becoming increasingly feasible, if not necessary, to compete on a global scale. This service, provided mainly by developing countries with cheaper labor, also has the potential to aid in integrating such countries into the global trading system.

The Role of Electronic Commerce in the Modern World Economy Electronic commerce will continue to play a significant role in the modern world economy in the coming years. Its potential will be limited, however, in the absence of a comprehensive understanding within the WTO or some other multilateral framework regarding how to treat international trade conducted using electronic commerce. So, too, may technological and regulatory limitations regarding issues such as privacy, financial security, and fraud hinder the development of electronic commerce beyond the level it has reached today. Experience with previous technologies and negotiations suggests that these hurdles will be overcome, however, particularly to the benefit of developing countries.

See also digital divide; General Agreement on Tariffs and Trade (GATT); General Agreement on Trade in Services (GATS); information and communication technology; trade in services; World Trade Organization

FURTHER READING

Borenstein, Severin, and Garth Saloner. 2001. "Economics and Electronic Commerce." *Journal of Economic Perspectives* 15 (1): 3–12. An effective introduction to many of the economic issues surrounding electronic commerce and to a symposium on economics and electronic commerce.

Mann, Catherine, Sue Eckert, and Sarah Knight. 2000. *Global Electronic Commerce: A Policy Primer*. Washington, DC: Institute for International Economics. Aimed at assisting policymakers, particularly those in developing countries, with formulating an appropriate response to e-commerce and to use it to facilitate development.

Organisation for Economic Co-operation and Development, Working Party on the Information Economy. *Online Payment Systems for E-Commerce*. OECD Doc DSTI/ICCP/IE(2004)18/FINAL (18 April 2006). Analyzes the recent development of online payment systems for e-commerce, covering different payment mechanisms, the extent to which these different systems are used, and the implications of industry characteristics and network effects. It discusses drivers and impediments to the uptake of payment systems and identifies some policy issues for further examination.

UN Information and Communication Task Force. 2005. *WTO, E-Commerce, and Information Technologies: From the Uruguay Round through the Doha Development*

Agenda (Series 7). Prepared by Sacha Wunsch-Vincent, this paper provides a comprehensive analysis of the WTO's engagement with e-commerce as well as some useful research into key areas of electronic commerce.

World Trade Organization, Secretariat. 1998. *Electronic Commerce and the Role of the WTO.* Lays out the relevant policy issues for electronic commerce and the WTO, including the legal and regulatory framework for Internet transactions, security and privacy questions, taxation, access to the Internet, market access for suppliers over the Internet, trade facilitation, public procurement, intellectual property questions, and regulation of content.

Wunsch-Vincent, Sacha. 2006. *The WTO, the Internet, and Trade in Digital Products: EC-U.S. Perspectives.* Oxford: Hart. A neutral and thorough reference work examining European Community and U.S. perspectives on digital products (that is, digitally delivered movies, music, and software), and the response of international trade rules, in particular those of the WTO.

ANDREW D. MITCHELL

■ endogenous growth theory

See growth in open economies, Schumpeterian models

■ equilibrium exchange rate

Ever since the advent of floating exchange rates for the principle currencies in 1973, exchange rate misalignment has been an important issue for academics, practitioners, and policymakers. In flexible exchange rate regimes, exchange rates can spend long periods away from their equilibrium, or fair value, levels (that is, they can take long swings). Consequently, in order to understand whether exchange rates are misaligned or not, analysts need an underlying measure of equilibrium. How then may the equilibrium exchange rate be defined?

Purchasing Power Parity (PPP) Reconsidered The equilibrium measure that many economists and policymakers first turn to is the concept of purchasing power parity (PPP). The PPP exchange rate is the ratio of some overall measure of domestic prices

relative to a comparable measure of foreign prices. Although there is controversy in the PPP literature regarding the correct measure of overall prices to use (e.g., consumer, wholesale, or some other measure) there is no longer a question about the "time dimension" of PPP. By this we mean how quickly exchange rates are expected to gravitate, or revert, to the PPP defined rate (MacDonald 2007).

Proponents of traditional PPP would argue that disturbances to PPP should be rapidly offset. But how rapidly should this be to be consistent with PPP? The classic disturbance that affects the relationship between the nominal exchange rate and relative prices is a liquidity disturbance, such as a monetary expansion. The latter, in the context of an economy in which there are sticky commodity prices, will not have an immediate effect on relative prices but would have their effect 18 months to 2 years thereafter. In this setting, therefore, a monetary shock is expected to move the real exchange rate in the short run, but the real exchange rate should revert to its mean value after around two years: a proponent of traditional PPP would argue that the so-called half-life of mean reversion would be one year.

There is now a huge empirical literature that indicates that the so-called half-life has a range of between three and five years, which is inconsistent with a traditional form of PPP; Rogoff (1996) labeled this the PPP puzzle. It is a puzzle because the stylized fact of the high volatility of real and nominal exchange rates is consistent with the interaction of liquidity shocks with sticky prices, but as we have seen, the slow mean reversion of real exchange rates is not.

Various attempts have been made to explain the PPP puzzle. One explanation, which is consistent with traditional PPP, is that the existence of transaction costs imparts a nonlinear process to exchange rate behavior, and when such nonlinear behavior is accounted for, real exchange rates behave in a manner that is consistent with traditional PPP—they have a half-life of around one year. Such nonlinear explanations, however, are really nothing more than black box interpretations and are equally consistent with other interpretations of the PPP puzzle (MacDonald 2007). A second key explanation of the PPP puzzle, which is not consistent with traditional PPP, is that real factors, such as productivity differences (usually motivated in terms of the Balassa-Samuelson effect) and a country's net foreign asset position, ultimately push real exchange rates away from their equilibrium values. A third key explanation of the PPP puzzle is the pricing-to-market behavior of multinational firms. Such firms, by altering their markup (in order to protect market share) as nominal exchange rates change, impart prolonged and persistent deviations from PPP. Although this latter view appears to capture an important determinant of the systematic behavior of real exchange rates, the second explanation may be more critical to understanding equilibrium exchange rates and, by implication, whether exchange rates are misaligned or not. We now consider these alternatives, all of which are based on an explicitly "real" interpretation of real exchange rate behavior.

Fundamental Equilibrium Exchange Rate The fundamental equilibrium exchange rate (FEER), developed by the economist Williamson (1983, 1994), is the rate at which both the internal and external balance are satisfied, where the internal balance is high employment and low inflation and the external balance is characterized as the sustainable desired net flow of resources between countries when they are in internal balance. The latter is usually derived by making some assumption about a country's net savings position, which, in turn, is determined by factors such as consumption smoothing and demographic changes. The use of the latter assumption, especially, has meant that the FEER is often interpreted as a normative approach and the calculated FEER is likely to be sensitive to the choice of the sustainable capital account. (The International Monetary Fund variant of the FEER approach attempts to remove the judgmental element in defining the desired capital account; see, e.g., Isard and Faruqee 1998; and Faruqee, Isard, and Masson 1998.) The FEER is an explicitly medium-run concept, in the sense that it does not need to be consistent with stock-flow equilibrium (the medium run is usually taken to be a period of about five years in the future).

There are essentially two widely used approaches to estimating a FEER. The first involves taking an estimated multicountry, macroeconometric model, imposing internal and external balance, and solving for the real exchange rate, which is then classified as the FEER. Such an approach is not very tractable and, consequently, by far the most popular method of generating a FEER involves focusing on a current account equation, setting it equal to a sustainable capital account, and then solving for the FEER (see Wren-Lewis 1992).

In addition to the difficulty in measuring a sustainable capital account, the calculation of trade elasticities has often meant that an extra layer of judgment has to be imposed before the FEER can be calculated. This is because the estimated trade elasticities often turn out to be effectively zero (see Goldstein and Khan 1985). Driver and Wren-Lewis (1999) assess the sensitivity of FEER calculations of the U.S. dollar, Japanese yen, and German mark to different formulations and assumptions. They find that two key factors impart a considerable amount of uncertainty into FEER-type calculations. For example, changes in the assumed value of the sustainable capital account (as a proportion of gross domestic product, GDP) of 1 percent can produce changes in the value of the FEER of around 5 percent. Since such changes in the capital account could easily be due to measurement error, this suggests caution in interpreting point estimates of the FEER. Although the FEER approach has been widely used by practitioners, the issues mentioned above often mean that it is used in conjunction with other measures of equilibrium.

Behavioral Equilibrium Exchange Rate The behavioral equilibrium exchange rate (BEER) approach of Clark and MacDonald (1998) is not based on any specific exchange rate model and, in that sense, may be regarded as a very general approach to modeling equilibrium exchange rates. As in the FEER-based approach, it takes as its starting point the proposition that real factors are a key explanation for the slow mean reversion to PPP observed in the data. In contrast to the FEER-based approach, the specific modus operandi of the BEER is to produce measures of exchange rate misalignment that are free of any normative elements and in which the exchange rate relationship is subject to rigorous statistical testing.

To illustrate their approach, Clark and MacDonald (1998) take the risk-adjusted real interest parity relationship, which has been used by a number of researchers to model equilibrium exchange rates (see, e.g., Faruqee 1995; MacDonald 1997), where it is assumed that the systematic component of the real exchange rate is a function of net foreign assets, a measure of relative productivity, and the terms of trade. The approach is estimated using a vector error correction mechanism (VECM), which incorporates both dynamic interactions and long-run effects, and plausible measures of equilibrium have been reported for a number of real effective exchange rates (plausible in the sense that coefficients in the long-run relationship are correctly signed and statistically significant and also fast adjustment to equilibrium is reported).

Comparing the actual real effective exchange rate with the computed equilibrium gives a clear and sharp measure of misalignment. For example, the approach shows that the U.S. dollar was massively overvalued in the period 1980–86. It is worth noting that this finding is common to other BEER estimates (see, e.g., Faruqee 1995; MacDonald 1997; Stein 1999). It is also possible to calibrate the BEER with some normative structure placed on the fundamentals, much as in the FEER approach. The big advantage of the BEER, however, is that the influence of the normative elements is explicit as is the nature of the estimated exchange rate model and the adjustment to equilibrium. The BEER approach has been widely and successfully used for industrial countries, developing countries, and emerging markets.

Natural Real Exchange Rate The natural real exchange rate (NATREX) approach of Stein (1994, 1999) may be considered to be grounded in elements of the FEER and the BEER. It has similarities with the FEER because it appeals to an internal-external balance approach to motivate the model, and shares with the BEER what is essentially a reduced form approach in the empirical estimation. In the NA-

TREX, the sustainable capital account term is assumed equal to social saving less planned investment, where the key determinant of social savings is the rate of time preference and the key determinant of investment is Tobin's q. Additionally, savings are assumed to be a function of net foreign assets and investment a function of the capital stock, k. The inclusion of stocks in the flow relationships enables an equilibrium to be derived that is stock-flow consistent.

Stein (1999) proposes two forms of NATREX equilibrium. In "long-run" equilibrium the following criteria have to be satisfied. First, net foreign assets are constant and, in a nongrowing economy, the current account is equal to zero. Second, the capital stock is constant and the rate of capacity utilization is at its stationary mean. Real interest rate parity prevails, in the sense that real interest rates are equalized (since the real exchange rate is also in equilibrium, the expected change in the real exchange rate is zero). Finally, there are no changes in reserves or speculative capital movements. The difference between the medium- and long-run NATREX relates to the evolution of net foreign assets and the capital stock. As in the BEER approach, Stein (1999) uses a VECM to empirically implement the NATREX in a single equation context. The misalignment is then calculated as the gap between the estimated value of the VECM and the actual value.

New Open Economy Macroeconomic Class of Models Obstfeld and Rogoff (2001) have demonstrated how the New Open Economy Macroeconomics (NOEM) class of model can be used to calculate the currency movement needed to satisfy internal and external balance (where the latter is taken as a zero current account position). Specifically, it asks the question: How much would the exchange rate have to move to reduce a current account imbalance to zero? There are two key elements in this calculation: knowledge of the consumption elasticity of substitution, which governs how much relative prices have to move in response to changes in the relative consumption of home to foreign goods, and the required movement of the consumption of traded to nontraded goods. If a country has a current account deficit as a proportion of GDP of 5 percent, for example, balance of payments statistics can be used to calculate how much the relative consumption of home to foreign goods has to move in order to return the ratio to zero. Given the elasticity of substitution, this adjustment can then be used to calculate by how much the exchange rate would have to move in order to facilitate the required consumption switch. The extent of exchange rate adjustment can be calibrated under different scenarios, such as sticky or flexible prices, pricing to market, or the inflation-targeting objectives of the central bank, and using different assumptions regarding the elasticity of substitution.

Since the NOEM approach requires little in the way of data, it would seem to offer a tractable way of calculating how much required exchange rate adjustment is necessary to achieve current account objectives. It may, therefore, be an appealing method of calculating equilibrium exchange rates for developing countries or transition economies where data constraints may make it difficult to implement some of the other approaches referred to earlier.

Other Approaches A somewhat different way of measuring equilibrium exchange rates is to use a time series estimator to decompose a real exchange rate into its permanent and transitory components and to interpret the permanent component as a measure of equilibrium and the distance between the permanent and actual exchange rate as the degree of misalignment. The permanent equilibrium exchange rate has been calculated using a variety of different econometric estimators. This approach often gives time series profiles of the equilibrium exchange rate, which are similar to those created using the BEER and NATREX methods, and is often used as a robustness check on estimates derived from these approaches.

To sum up, there is now a wide range of alternative real approaches to measuring equilibrium exchange rates. Indeed, central banks and practitioners often need to use a combination of these approaches when assessing whether a currency is over- or undervalued.

See also balance of payments; Balassa-Samuelson effect; capital mobility; exchange rate pass-through; exchange rate regimes; exchange rate volatility; interest parity conditions; new open economy macroeconomics; purchasing power parity; real exchange rate

FURTHER READING

Clarida, R., and J. Gali. 1994. "Sources of Real Exchange Rate Fluctuations: How Important Are Nominal Shocks?" *Carnegie-Rochester Series on Public Policy* 41: 1–56. Attempts to empirically identify the causes of real exchange rate fluctuations since the collapse of Bretton Woods.

Clark, P. B., and R. MacDonald. 1998. "Exchange Rates and Economic Fundamentals: A Methodological Comparison of BEERs and FEERs." IMF Working Paper 98/67 (March). Washington, DC: International Monetary Fund.

———. 2000. "Filtering the BEER: A Permanent and Transitory Decomposition." IMF Working Paper A0/144. Washington, DC: International Monetary Fund. Two papers that discuss the BEER and FEER approaches to modeling equilibrium exchange rates.

Cumby, R., and J. Huizinga. 1990. "The Predictability of Real Exchange Rate Changes in the Short Run and in the Long Run." NBER Working Paper, No 3468. Cambridge, MA: National Bureau of Economic Research. Examines whether real exchange rate changes are predictable.

Driver, R., and S. Wren-Lewis. 1999. *Real Exchange Rates for the Year 2000*. Washington, DC: Institute for International Economics. Monograph that defines what equilibrium real exchange rates are with emphasis on the FEER method and estimates FEERs for the G7 countries for 1995 and 2000.

Faruqee, Hamid. 1995. "Long-Run Determinants of the Real Exchange Rate: A Stock-Flow Perspective." *IMF Staff Papers* 42 (March): 80–107. Examines the long-run determinants of the real exchange rate from a stock-flow standpoint.

Faruqee, H., P. Isard, and P. R. Masson. 1998. "A Macroeconomic Balance Framework for Estimating Equilibrium Exchange Rates." In *Equilibrium Exchange Rates*, edited by R. MacDonald and J. Stein. Boston: Kluwer, chapter 4. Discusses and outlines the FEER approach.

Goldstein, M., and M. Khan. 1985. "Income and Price Effects in Foreign Trade." In *Handbook of International*

Economics, edited by R. Jones and P. B. Kenen. Amsterdam: Elsevier, 2:1041–45. Discusses the price and income elasticities of international trade.

Huizinga, J. 1987. "An Empirical Investigation of the Long-Run Behavior of Real Exchange Rates." In *Carnegie-Rochester Conference Series on Public Policy* 27: 149–214.

Isard, Peter, and Hamid Faruqee, eds. 1998. "Exchange Rate Assessment: Extensions of the Macroeconomic Balance Approach." IMF Occasional Paper No. 167. Washington, DC: International Monetary Fund. Discusses and outlines the FEER approach.

MacDonald, R. 1997. "What Determines Real Exchange Rates? The Long and the Short of It." *International Financial Markets, Institutions and Money* 8: 117–53. Presents a reduced-form model of the real effective exchange rates of the U.S. dollar, the deutsche mark, and the Japanese yen from 1974 Q1 to 1993 Q2.

———. 2007. *The Economics of Exchange Rates: Theories and Evidence*. London: Taylor Francis. Up-to-date and comprehensive textbook on exchange rate theory and empirics.

MacDonald, R., and P. Swagel. 2000. "Business Cycle Influences on Exchange Rates: Survey and Evidence." *World Economic Outlook* (*Supporting Studies*): 129–59.

Obstfeld, M., and K. Rogoff. 2001. "Perspectives on OECD Economic Integration: Implications for U.S. Current Account Adjustment." In *Global Economic Integration: Opportunities and Challenges*. Kansas City, MO: U.S. Federal Reserve Bank, 169–208. Demonstrates how the New Open Economy Macroeconomics (NOEM) class of model can be used to calculate the currency movements needed to satisfy internal and external balance.

Rogoff, K. 1996. "The Purchasing Power Parity Puzzle." *Journal of Economic Literature* 34: 647–68. Comprehensive paper on available evidence (till the mid 1990s) on PPP.

Stein, J. 1994. "The Natural Real Exchange Rate of the United States Dollar and Determinants of Capital Flows." In *Estimating Equilibrium Exchange Rates*, edited by J. Williamson. Washington DC: Institute of International Economics, 23–46.

———. 1999. "The Evolution of the Real Value of the U.S. Dollar Relative to the G7 Currencies." *Equilibrium Exchange Rates*, edited by R. MacDonald and J. Stein.

Amsterdam: Kluwer Press, chapter 3. Two papers that introduce and apply the NATREX approach to equilibrium exchange rate determination.

Williamson, J. 1983. *The Exchange Rate System*. Washington, DC: Institute for International Economics.

———. 1994. *Estimating Equilibrium Exchange Rates*. Washington, DC: Institute for International Economics. Two monographs that introduce and discuss the FEER.

Wren-Lewis, S. 1992. "On the Analytical Foundations of the Fundamental Equilibrium Exchange Rate." In *Macroeconomic Modelling of the Long Run*, edited by Colin P. Hargreaves. Aldershot, UK: Edward Elgar, 78–91. Discusses the analytical foundations of the FEER.

RONALD MACDONALD

■ euro

The euro is the currency of the European Monetary Union (EMU). The euro (€) came into existence as an accounting currency on January 1, 1999, for 11 of the then 15 member countries of the EMU (Austria, Belgium, Germany, Finland, France, Ireland, Italy, Luxembourg, Spain, Portugal, and the Netherlands). Greece officially adopted the euro at the beginning of 2001. Britain, Sweden, and Denmark chose not to adopt the euro as their currency, but left the door open to do so in the future. The introduction of the euro marks the first time that a group of sovereign nations voluntarily gave up their individual currencies in favor of a common currency, and it ranks as one of the most important economic events of the postwar period. Europe created the euro so that it could become a fully integrated economic market like the United States.

The official euro conversion rates for the currencies of the original 11 members of the EMU were decided on December 31, 1998, by the Council of the European Union based on the recommendation of the European Commission (see table 1). Greece adopted the euro on January 1, 2001, at the conversion rate of 340.750 drachmas to the euro. On January 1, 2002, the euro was introduced physically as a circulating currency, and by February 28, 2002, it became the sole currency of the 12 members of the EMU, also known as the eurozone, euro area, or euroland. From January 1, 1999, until their final withdrawal, the national currencies of the participating countries had been locked against one another at the fixed exchange rates given in table 1.

The euro was introduced in 1999 at the value of $1.18 but, defying almost all predictions that it would appreciate to between $1.25 and $1.30 by the end of the year, it declined almost continuously to a low of $0.82 at the end of October 2000. Starting in February 2002, however, the euro appreciated almost continuously, reaching parity with the dollar in mid-2002 and a high of $1.44 at the end of October 2007. The euro exchange rate with respect to the Japanese yen followed a similar pattern of high volatility.

Euro as Legal Tender The euro is printed and minted, managed, and administered by the European Central Bank (ECB) and the European System of Central Banks (ESCB—composed of the central banks of the member states) based in Frankfurt, Germany. The ECB has sole authority for determining the common monetary policy of the EMU.

Table 1
Official Currency Conversion Rates for the Euro (€)

Country	National currency	Currency units per euro
Austria	schilling	13.7603
Belgium	Belgian franc	40.3399
Finland	markka	5.94573
France	French franc	6.55957
Germany	Deutsche mark	1.95583
Ireland	Irish pound	0.787564
Italy	Italian lira	1936.27
Luxembourg	Luxembourg franc	40.3399
Netherlands	guilder	2.20371
Portugal	escudo	200.482
Spain	peseta	166.386

Source: Board of Governors of the Federal Reserve System

Euro banknotes come in €500, €200, €100, €50, €20, €10, and €5 denominations, with the first two seldom used in everyday transactions. Coins come in €2, €1, 50 cents, 20c, 10c, 5c, 2c, and 1c, with the last two denominations seldom used.

Outside the 12 countries of the eurozone, the euro is the legal tender also of the ministates of Monaco, San Marino, and Vatican City (all of which can mint their own coins by agreement with the ECB). Andorra, Montenegro, and Kosovo, as well as eurozone overseas territories of French Guiana, Guadeloupe, Martinique, Mayotte, Réunion, and Saint Pierre et Miquelon also adopted the euro as their currencies, but they do not participate in the ECB or the ESCB.

In May 2004, 10 additional countries joined the European Union (EU), thus increasing its membership to 25 countries. The new members were Poland, Hungary, the Czech Republic, the Slovak Republic, Slovenia, Estonia, Lithuania, Latvia, Malta, and Cyprus. Bulgaria and Romania joined on January 1, 2007, and Albania, Bosnia-Herzegovina, Croatia, Macedonia, Serbia, Montenegro, and Turkey were negotiating accession. The Accession Treaty for the 10 new member states requires them to adopt the euro when they meet some strict criteria, such as a budget deficit not exceeding 3 percent of GDP, a government debt not exceeding 60 percent of GDP, a low inflation rate, an interest rate close to the EU average, and a fairly stable exchange rate. Slovenia adopted the euro on January 1, 2007, but the other new members were not expected to adopt the euro for several more years.

Euro as an International Currency From its birth, the euro was destined to become an important international currency because the EU (1) is as large an economic and trading unit as the United States, (2) has a large, well-developed, and growing financial market, which is increasingly free of controls, and (3) is expected to have a good inflation performance that will keep the value of the euro stable. If the international use of the euro were to match the EU's share of world GDP, exports, and financial market, the euro would become as important as the dollar as an international currency. This would mean that the relative international use of the dollar would fall to 40–45 percent of the total (from 55–60 percent in 2007), with an equal share going to the euro and the remainder going mostly to the yen and a few other smaller currencies, such as the Swiss franc, the Canadian dollar, and the Australian dollar—but mostly the yen.

There are equally good reasons why the euro probably will not displace the U.S. dollar as the leading international currency in the short term. These are: (1) most primary commodities (especially petroleum) are priced in dollars, (2) most non-European countries are likely to continue to use the dollar for most of their international transactions for the foreseeable future, with the exception the former French colonies in West and Central Africa; and (3) sheer inertia, which favors the incumbent (the U.S. dollar).

See also common currency; dollar standard; dominant currency; European Central Bank; European Monetary Union; Maastricht Treaty; optimum currency area (OCA) theory; reserve currency; vehicle currency

FURTHER READING

Board of Governors of the Federal Reserve System. 1999. "The Launch of the Euro." *Federal Reserve Bulletin* (October): 655–66. Examines the process of launching the euro.

Issing, Otmar. 2005. "The ECB and the Euro." *Journal of Policy Modeling* (June): 405–20. Examines the operation and performance of the ECB since its creation.

Mundell, Robert A. 1961. "A Theory of Optimum Currency Areas." *American Economic Review* (November): 509–17. Analyzes the benefits and costs of adopting a single currency, such as the euro.

———. 2000. "The Euro and the Stability of the International Monetary System." In *The Euro as a Stabilizer in the International Economic System*, edited by Robert A. Mundell and Armand Clesse. Norwell, MA: Kluwer, 56–84. Examines the effect of the introduction of the euro on the dollar and on the functioning of the international monetary system.

Salvatore, Dominick. 1997. "The Unresolved Problems of the EMS and EMU." *American Economic Review* (May): 224–26. Examines the problems in the operation of the EMU and its precursor, the European Monetary System.

———. 2002. "The Euro: Expectations and Performance." *Eastern Economic Journal* (winter): 121–36. Evaluates the performance of the euro since its creation.

DOMINICK SALVATORE

■ Eurocurrencies

Eurocurrencies are domestic currencies of one country on deposit in a second country. More precisely, the term *Eurocurrency* means the currency denomination of a bank deposit or loan that is on the books of a bank situated outside the currency's country of origin. For example, large amounts of U.S. dollar deposits and loans are booked in banks located in London, Frankfurt, Tokyo, Singapore, and many other international financial centers. Eurocurrencies are on the books of major banks with international operations, but not necessarily banks headquartered in the Eurocurrency's country of origin. For example, Eurodollar deposits and loans are offered by banks of many home jurisdictions, not just by offshore branches and subsidiaries of American banks.

More than 70 percent of the world's Eurocurrencies are in U.S. dollars, with the rest in euros, yen, British pounds, Canadian dollars, Swiss francs, and Australian dollars. Individually they are often called Eurodollars, Euroeuros, Euroyen, and so on. The prefix *Euro* is an anachronism, since large amounts are booked in banks outside Europe. For a time, dollar deposits in Japan were called "Jurodollars," Singapore "Singdollars," and so on, but the generic term *offshore* for these deposits and loans has become more common.

Eurodollar deposits were first offered in the 1950s by London- and Paris-based banks (particularly the Moscow Narodny Bank in London and the Banque Commerciale pour l'Europe du Nord in Paris) in order to accommodate the desire of the Soviet Union and other communist countries to avoid holding their large dollar surpluses in the United States. But the Eurodollar market first expanded to international significance with the incursion of U.S. corporations into Europe in the 1960s. An added impetus was the imposition in the mid-1960s of a ban on U.S. corporations' borrowing in the United States for operations abroad, reflecting concern about a growing balance of payments deficit. U.S. firms quickly discovered that they could circumvent these regulations by borrowing in dollars from London-based banks. What began mostly in London with Eurodollars soon spread to the world's major financial markets and to other major currencies.

Causes of Growth The long-term growth of the Eurocurrency market was driven neither by politics nor by regulatory worries, but instead by economics. From the beginning, the British authorities set a precedent by not attempting to regulate Eurocurrency banking. To this day, in all of the world's major financial centers, neither home- nor host-country regulators impose any of the costly burdens that they place on domestic banks: requirements such as holding noninterest-bearing reserves, interest rate controls, deposit insurance, or high taxes. Typically also, restrictions on the entry of new banks are minimal. Moreover, "Eurobanks"—that is, the international departments of big banks that offer offshore deposits—accept only wholesale deposits, mostly $1 million or more. As a result of all these regulatory and economic advantages, Eurobanks are able to offer interest rates on deposits that are higher than in the currency's home country, and also interest rates on loans that are lower. In short, the "spreads" between loan and deposit rates are lower on Eurobanks' offshore deposits than at home.

A major impetus for growth of Eurobanking came with the virtual doubling of oil prices in the fall of 1973. In the context of heightened tension with the United States over its support for Israel, Middle Eastern oil exporters deposited much of their expanding oil revenues in Eurodollars in London. At the same time, oil-importing countries were hungry for hard currency loans. The Eurocurrency market expanded rapidly to meet this demand. Doomsayers had predicted disaster if the oil revenues were not "recycled." The International Monetary Fund (IMF) had until then been the conventional lender to deficit countries but lacked capacity to recycle such unprecedented amounts. The Eurocurrency markets grew seamlessly and saved the day.

By the late 1970s, the value of Eurodollar deposits exceeded the value of dollar deposits within the U.S. banking system. In December 1981, U.S. banking legislation was revised to allow U.S. banks to offer "international banking facilities" (IBFs)—that is, dollar deposits and loans to nonresidents of the United States and to other IBFs that are immune from U.S. regulatory requirements. Hence U.S. banks could offer deposit and loan rates competitive with the larger Eurodollar markets in London and elsewhere. More than 75 percent of U.S. IBF banking is in New York, with almost all the rest in California and Illinois.

Interest Rates The Eurocurrency markets virtually pioneered the offering of long-term loans with floating interest rates. They "unbundled" the usual package, which fixed loan rates for the term of the loan. Eurocurrency deposits typically mature every 30 to 90 days; so to induce rollover of existing deposits, or to attract new deposits, current deposit rates must be paid.

Eurocurrency loan rates are usually revised every three to six months, based on current deposit rates. This protects banks from the interest rate risks of long-term maturity mismatching. More precisely, loan rates (in London) are based on the London Inter Bank Offered Rate (LIBOR), which is reset daily at the median rate that top-tier London-based Eurobanks offer to pay other banks for short-term deposits. Other offshore financial centers quote rates close to LIBOR. LIBOR is usually slightly above the rate paid on deposits from nonbank customers since interbank deposits can be acquired on demand, within minutes. In effect, Eurocurrency loans are based on banks' marginal cost of raising new funds. The actual rates charged are LIBOR +, where the premium varies from borrower to borrower depending on credit risk. Very creditworthy customers can borrow at LIBOR or even, occasionally, slightly below. In this sense, LIBOR is like the "prime" rate in the United States and other domestic markets, with the major difference that it is marked to market daily. Much of the Eurodeposit market is securitized: they are certificates of deposit that are traded continuously; hence their yield varies continuously.

The practice of making long-term loans with variable rates was a key trigger for the so-called international banking crisis of 1982–89. In early 1980, the newly installed chairman of the U.S. Federal Reserve System, Paul Volcker, declared war on inflation, which had risen to double-digit levels in the United States and elsewhere. He more than doubled short-term interest rates, from about 10 percent to more than 20 percent. Because of the tight linkages to Europe and the rest of the world via competition between New York and London for Eurodollar deposits, short-term rates, based on LIBOR, doubled worldwide. By 1982, middle-income countries in East Asia, Eastern Europe, and especially Latin America had borrowed heavily via syndicated loan packages put together in the Eurocurrency markets. They were paying LIBOR + on their loans. By late 1981, their debt service burdens had doubled. This triggered a series of severe slowdowns and partial defaults, beginning with Mexico in August 1982.

Size of Market The size of the offshore markets including interbank loans as of 2007 was roughly $2 trillion in London, $1.5 trillion in New York, $1 trillion in Germany, and more than $0.5 trillion each in the Cayman Islands, Switzerland, and Japan. Net of interbank loans, the numbers are only about one-quarter of these. In other words, London Eurobanks had roughly $0.5 trillion worth of loans to nonbanks on their books in 2007. Nevertheless, interbank loans are important because they constitute the core of the world's trading in foreign currencies. Foreign exchange trading is part and parcel of the enormous offshore interbank market because Eurobanks typically find themselves with more deposits than loans in any particular currency, or vice versa. Also, unlike domestic retail banks, they often negotiate loan agreements before obtaining funding for them. For both reasons, Eurobanks trade trillions of dollars of deposits daily.

For example, a Japanese bank in London may find itself with $2 billion worth of yen deposits but only $1 billion worth of yen-denominated loans, with another $1 billion denominated in dollars. To avoid currency risk, the bank might "buy"—that is, borrow—$1 billion in dollar deposits (offering the going LIBOR interest rate for dollars) and "sell"—that is, lend—$1 billion in yen deposits. The transaction often takes the form of a "swap" of yen for dollars that is scheduled to be reversed in a few weeks or months when the $1 billion loan matures. In either case—whether it is structured as an outright sale of yen and purchase of dollars, or a swap—$1 billion of foreign exchange has been traded.

As another example, a London-based German bank that has already more or less matched the currency denominations of its loans and deposits may negotiate a $2 billion euro loan. In order to fund the loan it must buy deposits, offering the going LIBOR rate for euros on the interbank market. Because the largest volume of offshore interbank trading takes place in London, LIBOR is the international benchmark for short-term lending, with modifications for currency denomination, term to maturity, and risk.

In short, the Eurocurrency, or "offshore" interbank market for deposits, is the main means by which almost $2 billion of foreign exchange is traded daily. More fundamentally, the Eurocurrency market—which is in fact not just European but worldwide—is the main means by which the demands for and supplies of loanable bank funds are matched up internationally.

See also capital flows to developing countries; dominant currency; euro; International Monetary Fund (IMF); money supply; offshore financial centers; petrodollars, recycling of; reserve currency; vehicle currency

FURTHER READING

Dufey, Gunter, and Ian Giddy. 1994. *The International Money Market*. 2d ed. Upper Saddle River, NJ: Prentice Hall. An updated edition of a 1978 textbook that was a pioneering and eminently clear exposition of the evolving Eurocurrency markets, and much more.

Husted, Steven, and Michael Melvin. 2007. *International Economics*. 7th ed. Boston: Pearson Addison Wesley. Contains one of the best treatments of Eurocurrencies from a macroeconomic standpoint.

Moffett, Michael, and Arthur Stonehill. 2006. *Fundamentals of Multinational Finance.* 2d ed. Boston: Pearson Addison Wesley. Contains a good primer on the origins, institutions, and workings of Eurocurrency markets.

Rivera-Batiz, Francisco L., and Luis Rivera-Batiz. 1994. *International Finance and Open-Economy Macroeconomics.* Upper Saddle River, NJ: Prentice Hall. Theoretically sophisticated, clarifies links between the microeconomics of Eurocurrency markets and the macroeconomics of open economies.

JAMES W. DEAN

■ European Central Bank

The European Central Bank (ECB) is the central bank for the euro area. It opened its doors in June 1998 in Frankfurt, Germany. Together, the ECB and the national central banks that are members of European Monetary Union (EMU) form the European System of Central Banks (ESCB), also known as the eurosystem.

Before the ECB began to take responsibility for the conduct of monetary policy in the euro area, the member countries created the European Monetary Institute (EMI) in 1994 to facilitate the work toward transition to the era of the single currency. Its primary task was to address the technical needs for the switch to the euro. The EMI was responsible for reporting to the European Union (EU) on the progress toward convergence by individual member states, as prescribed by the Maastricht Treaty. The conduct of monetary policy remained under the responsibility of the individual member states. By the end of 1995, member governments approved a plan for change that focused on the need for rigorous acceptance of the convergence requirements. A legal basis for the single currency was necessary so that all who used the euro could be confident that it would be an accepted means of payment.

Objectives and Tasks of the ECB The primary objective of the ECB and, by implication, the ESCB, is to maintain price stability, a goal set but not defined by the Maastricht Treaty. The ECB defines price stability as an inflation rate close to 2 percent in

a Europewide index of consumer prices called the Harmonized Index of Consumer Prices over the "medium term." What is the medium term? The ECB does not provide a precise definition. It notes that monetary policy acts with long and variable lags, an idea made famous by Milton Friedman. Experience, however, suggests that inflation can be controlled within the objectives set out by the ECB within a two-year horizon. To achieve this objective, the ECB decided to give prominence to money growth as well as to a wide range of indicators such as the exchange rate, the yield curve, and various fiscal indicators. More precisely, the ECB's strategy involves a so-called two-pillars approach. This means that, in setting interest rates for the euro area, the ECB considers developments both on the real side of the economy, which are of a shorter-term nature, as well as on the monetary side, which captures the longer-run influences on monetary policy. Since current interest rate decisions have an impact on future decisions by individuals and firms, the ECB also receives guidance from forecasts of inflation and real economic activity for the euro area as a whole.

The ECB is headed by a president who serves a nonrenewable eight-year term. The first president of the ECB, Wim Duisenberg from the Netherlands, did not serve his full term, which would have ended in 2006; instead, Jean Trichet of France was appointed as the president of the ECB in 2003. Since the president and other senior officials of the ECB are appointed by "common accord" by the heads of state or governments of EU members, national political imperatives play an important role in such appointments. Therefore, it is unlikely that a country could have more than one representative on the executive board.

The principal decision-making body of the ECB is the governing council made up of the governors of the thirteen euro-area national central banks and the executive board. The executive board, which consists of six members chosen from the governing council, is responsible for the implementation of monetary policy and carrying out the day-to-day affairs of the ECB. The governing council of the ECB consists of members of the executive board and all the heads of the national central banks that belong to the euro area. The governing council is mainly responsible for formulating monetary policy. The general council, largely an advisory body, includes members from both euro-area and non-euro-area countries that are members of the EU.

Both the executive board and the governing council meet twice a month, generally in Frankfurt. During the first monthly meeting the governing council announces the monetary policy decision made by the executive board. The second monthly meeting is reserved for making decisions related to the other tasks of the euro system. The schedule of meetings is published in advance so financial markets can prepare for the announcement of the interest rate decision. Additionally, in an emergency or crisis the governing council can meet in an extraordinary session, as happened, for example, following the terrorist attack on the United States in September 2001. The president of the ECB announces the interest rate decision immediately after the meeting and holds a press conference, but the ECB does not release minutes of the meeting.

In addition to its responsibility for defining and implementing monetary policy in the euro area, the ECB conducts foreign exchange operations, holds and manages member states' foreign exchange reserves, and helps promote the Europewide payments system. This payment system is called TARGET (Trans-European Automated Real-Time Gross Settlement Transfer System). Finally, the ECB, together with the individual national central banks, collects and disseminates a large variety of financial and economic statistics.

The primary monetary policy instruments consist of open market operations followed by a marginal lending facility that permits select financial market participants to borrow overnight from national central banks against eligible assets. Finally, banks in the EMU are required to hold reserves against short-term deposits.

Enlargement In 2004, a historic enlargement took place. Ten new member states joined the EU on May 1: the Czech Republic, Estonia, Cyprus, Latvia, Lithuania, Hungary, Malta, Poland, Slovakia, and Slovenia. In 2007, Romania and Bulgaria joined the EU. All of these countries must fulfill the Maastricht Treaty convergence requirements. The enlargement of the EU in 2004 introduced a potential organizational problem for the ECB's governing council. With 15 national central banks and six executive board members, the main decision-making body of the ECB originally consisted of 21 members. Following enlargement, membership would rise to a total of 31 members and, potentially, a still larger number once other countries are admitted into the EU. Therefore, in 2002, the ECB recommended a voting system that would limit the number of voting national central bank members to a maximum of 15. This means that there would be a rotation system among members of the eurosystem. The rotation system is designed to ensure that the national central bank governors with the right to vote are from member states that, taken together, are representative of the euro-area economy as a whole.

In spite of the growing pains experienced by the ECB, it remains a grand experiment that shows every sign of success, durability, and future expansion. The euro, which is the most visible expression of the ECB's existence, is a currency that may someday rival the U.S. dollar as a reserve currency. Finally, the economic size of the euro area is now larger than that of the U.S. economy, and it is likely that economic performance in Europe will have repercussions worldwide.

See also common currency; euro; European Monetary Union; Federal Reserve Board; Maastricht Treaty; optimum currency area (OCA) theory

FURTHER READING

de Haan, Jakob, Sylvester Eijffinger, and Sandra Waller. 2005. *The European Central Bank*. Cambridge, MA: MIT Press. Provides a comprehensive historical analysis of the ECB, analyzes its policy functions, and provides an early general assessment of its performance.

European Commission. 1999. *Third Stage: Organization and Implementation (from 1 January 1999)*. Downloadable from http://europa.eu/scadplus/leg/en/s01030.htm. One of many official documents that provide the legal text defining the principal economic requirements for monetary union.

Padoa-Schioppa, Tommaso. 2004. *The Euro and Its Central Bank: Getting United after the Union.* Cambridge, MA: MIT Press. Written by an insider, a former governor at the ECB and Italy's finance minister from 2006 to 2008, who traces the creation of the ECB and its role in the project to create more integration in Europe.

Scheller, Hanspeter K. 2007. *The European Central Bank: History, Role and Functions.* Rev. ed. Frankfurt: European Central Bank. Downloadable from http://www.ecb.int/ecb/html/index.en.html. An official publication that provides background and other details about the structure, organization, and functions of the ECB.

PIERRE L. SIKLOS

■ European Monetary Union

The establishment of the European Monetary Union (EMU) was an event without historical precedent. Although monetary unions have existed in the past, the EMU was the first union of sovereign states to agree on a single currency and a single monetary policy, but not on a common fiscal policy. The development of the EMU was an evolutionary process. The drive for greater European integration began shortly after World War II, but the actual path to the EMU originated with the European Monetary System (EMS), an initiative led by France and Germany in 1978 to stabilize exchange rates within Europe following the end of the postwar Bretton Woods exchange rate system.

Even before the Bretton Woods system of exchange rates collapsed during the 1970s, six European countries—Belgium, France, West Germany (as it was then called), Italy, Luxembourg, and the Netherlands—signed the Treaty of Rome in 1957, which led to the creation of the European Community (EC). This was an ambitious attempt, first to integrate the economies in Europe, and then to use such integration to fix currencies among members of the EC. Although the EMS fixed exchange rates between the member states, the arrangement permitted bilateral exchange rates to fluctuate within a particular range or target zone. In practice, however, the rates were fixed to the German currency, the deutsche mark. When market-determined exchange rates came close to the permissible bands, central banks in the system intervened by buying or selling foreign exchange, usually German deutsche marks, to push the exchange rate back into the band.

Although most countries in the world participated in the Bretton Woods pegged exchange rate arrangement, almost immediately after the creation of the EMS, the original six members agreed that permissible exchange rate fluctuations would be limited to a band, or target range, narrower than that permitted by the International Monetary Fund at the time. The International Monetary Fund is one of two institutions, the other being what was eventually to be called the World Bank, that would govern the postwar international exchange rate system. The new European arrangement would be called the "snake within the IMF tunnel." In other words, the EMS was a miniature version of the Bretton Woods arrangement. The "snake," however, never functioned smoothly. (West) Germany and the Netherlands, for example, allowed their currencies to float temporarily. Eventually this system was abandoned in 1973, when a devaluation of the U.S. dollar led the EC to float all of its currencies for a time. Nevertheless, EC members reaffirmed their commitment to a fixed exchange rate system as a precursor to achieving eventual monetary and economic union.

Exchange Rate Mechanism In 1974, the second stage of the plan that would eventually lead to a currency union began when EC members pooled their foreign exchange reserves, increased short-term credit facilities to member states, and intensified coordination of members' economic and monetary policies. Despite a variety of setbacks and delays, the new and improved version of the EMS started operation in March 1979. Initially there were only six members in this club, namely the signatories of the original Treaty of Rome. Later, membership increased: Italy and Ireland joined in 1978, Greece in 1981, Spain and Portugal in 1986. The last holdout was the United Kingdom, which joined the

Exchange Rate Mechanism (ERM) in 1990, although it withdrew, along with Italy, in September 1992. Meanwhile, even nonmember countries, such as Sweden and later Denmark, effectively belonged to the EMS system by adhering to its rules, albeit not on a formal basis.

The system's monetary unit would be called the ECU or European Currency Unit. The ECU represented a basket of currencies weighted roughly by the relative importance of member countries' economies. The ECU would serve as a kind of *numéraire*, or unit of account, for the ERM, as there were no circulating ECU notes or coins. The EMS stipulated allowable movements of ±2.25 percent (±6 percent for Spain) in either direction of one another's currencies values, and an additional mechanism was added to provide economic support to the relatively less prosperous members of the EC. Allowable fluctuations were relative to a central parity, essentially the midpoint of the band around which the exchange rate was permitted to fluctuate. The EMS did permit an exchange rate realignment (revaluation) of the currencies that could not be sustained within the zone, but this was supposed to be only a last resort. For example, if one country experienced severe balance of payments difficulties, then by common agreement there would be a call for a realignment among the EMS members.

In spite of an agreement to fix exchange rates rigorously, there were 27 realignments of the currency relationships between 1979 and 1983, and 12 more during the 1984–87 period. After that, however, no further realignments were made, until September 16, 1992, known as "Black Wednesday," when the United Kingdom and Italy left the EMS. Also, Ireland, Spain, and Portugal all devalued their currencies against the German currency, the deutsche mark. The European exchange rate crisis of 1992 threatened to derail the whole EMU project. Instead, in August 1993, the bands were widened to ±15 percent, except for the Netherlands, which retained the narrower fluctuation band. This may have had the effect of reducing the incentive to test the resolve of the potential members of the single currency area to carry on with their project, although

economic recovery in Europe, assisted by an expansionary fiscal policy in Germany following reunification, also facilitated the return to a course toward the creation of the euro.

In principle, the chief advantage of the target zone system (ERM) is its ability to prevent large swings in a country's current account when there are sharp swings in the nominal exchange rate. Of course, the main drawback with EMS-type systems is that they may also be subject to speculative attacks. After all, the limits set by policymakers on exchange rate fluctuations will hold only if the policies of the countries that belong to the target zone system are credible and compatible with one another. Indeed, illustrations that advocates of floating rates point to, in favoring a more flexible exchange rate systems, are the impact of the large devaluation of the Mexican peso in early 1995 and the devaluations in several Asian countries in 1997. Advocates of pegged exchange rates reply by drawing attention to the sharp appreciation of the Japanese yen in 1992, the rapid appreciations of the Australian, New Zealand, and Canadian dollars in 2005–6, as well as the large swings in the euro–U.S. dollar exchange rate since its introduction in 2002.

The EMS continues to exist as ERM II, which took effect on January 1, 1999, and resembles the original ERM, except that the fluctuation band of 15 percent became the accepted norm. The countries that joined the European Union (EU) must adhere to its rules prior to being admitted into the EMU and must belong to ERM II for at least two years.

Although the EMS and ERM were intended to foster greater economic integration within Europe, the actual blueprint for the single currency area can first be traced to the Werner Report of 1970. This report followed on the heels of a summit of European heads of state and government in 1969 held at the Hague. This meeting led to a decision that, henceforth, the EMU ought to be an explicit goal for the EC. Werner was the prime minister of Luxembourg, who was entrusted to provide a way to create a common currency area. The Werner Report proposed a reduction in the size of the fluctuation bands for the currencies in the EMS in a first stage, a removal of all barriers to financial flows and enhancement of the integration of financial and banking sectors in a second stage, and an irrevocable fix in exchange rates in a third stage. Interestingly, the report was agnostic about the need for a single currency, as opposed to several currencies with a fixed exchange rate. Nevertheless, it called for greater fiscal harmony among the member states if the goal of a monetary union of some kind were to succeed. As mentioned earlier, the collapse of the Bretton Woods system interrupted the drive to the EMU, and problems with the EMS did not help matters either.

Delors Report and Beyond The next attempt to lay out a road map to monetary union was the Delors Report of 1989, named after the former French politician who is also a former president of the European Commission. Critical to achieving monetary union were the so-called convergence criteria. The goal, in principle, was simple: to ensure that the members of the area that would form a monetary union would have similar macroeconomic environments, as this would facilitate the introduction of a fixed exchange rate among the member currencies that would not be altered, which would pave the way for the introduction of a common currency.

One of the innovations of the Delors Report was its outline of the institutional environment under which monetary union would operate. A European System of Central Banks (ESCB) was to be formed and this body would formulate and implement monetary and exchange rate policy in Europe. The Maastricht Treaty would later enshrine the convergence criteria that were believed to be necessary for a successful monetary union, and it contained a recommendation to create a European Central Bank (ECB) that would bring together the ESCB under a separate institutional umbrella.

The need for economies that participate in a monetary union to look alike, in broad economic terms, is associated with the work of Robert Mundell, who was awarded a Nobel Prize for his work demonstrating the conditions that countries would have to fulfill to form an optimum currency area. In spite of the intellectual debt to Mundell's work, the EMU

project was fundamentally a political one, namely to encourage and enshrine integration among European countries, albeit underscored by the economic benefits of a single currency. These benefits are thought to include a reduction in transactions costs. Although tourists no doubt have seen the advantages of not having to exchange one currency for another as frequently, the evidence that the reduction of transactions costs is of macroeconomic significance is more dubious. As for the single currency fostering greater integration, the jury is still out, although there is evidence that participation in a currency area, or in a monetary union, can contribute to greater similarities in business cycle performance among the participants.

The establishment of the ECB was preceded by the European Monetary Institute (EMI). The creation of this institution marks the beginning of stage II toward the EMU. The EMI's task was to prepare the groundwork, at both the policy and the institutional level, until the ECB took over, that is, until the irrevocable exchange rates became a reality.

A second innovation of the Delors Report was the proposal for a single currency that would follow a transitional period leading up to the setting of irrevocable exchange rates. Unlike the Werner Report, however, there was considerably less emphasis on fiscal harmony within the proposed monetary union. The thinking was that the convergence requirements would represent sufficient discipline to bring the countries into line with one another. Events were to prove otherwise, as the Maastricht Treaty was later accompanied by the Stability and Growth Pact (SGP). The SGP was intended to generate a form of fiscal discipline that resembled the monetary discipline required of the Maastricht Treaty.

The original Delors Report called for European Monetary Union (EMU) by 1999. At the end of 1995, leaders of the EU announced in Madrid plans for a single currency that would be called the euro, and they reaffirmed the launch date of January 1, 1999. Events would delay the introduction of the euro but, in spite of considerable skepticism, the single currency project eventually saw the light of day. The goals of monetary policy for the euro area, and the conversion of accounting standards, were agreed to and implemented by 1999. Eleven EU member states initially became members of EMU in May 1998, marking the start of the third and final stage toward the EMU, which effectively came into being on January 2, 2002. Hence, between January 1, 1999, and December 31, 2001, the euro replaced the ECU at an exchange rate of one to one, while EMU member states' exchange rates were irrevocably fixed at rates announced on December 31, 1998.

See also band, basket, and crawl (BBC); Bretton Woods system; common currency; currency crisis; discipline; euro; European Central Bank; exchange rate regimes; fear of floating; international reserves; Maastricht Treaty; optimum currency area (OCA) theory

FURTHER READING

Bayoumi, Tamim, and Barry Eichengreen. 1993. "Shocking Aspects of European Monetary Integration." In *Adjustment and Growth in the European Monetary Union*, edited by Francisco Torres and Francesco Giavazzi. Cambridge: Cambridge University Press, 193–229. A somewhat technical study that asks whether greater monetary integration might be reflected in the pattern of economic shocks that hit prospective members of the monetary union.

De Grauwe, Paul. 1997. *The Economics of Monetary Integration*. Oxford: Oxford University Press. Covers both the economic and political aspects of the EMU project.

Delors Report, Committee for the Study of Economic and Monetary Union. 1989. *Report on Economic and Monetary Union in the European Community*. Luxembourg: Office for Official Publication of the European Communities. Text of the report that outlines a strategy for monetary integration, written in somewhat legalistic terms.

Eichengreen, Barry. 1993. "European Monetary Unification." *Journal of Economic Literature* 31 (September): 1321–57. A broad survey of the literature and the pros and cons of European monetary integration. Note that the publication date precedes actual monetary union in Europe.

Gros, Daniel, and Niels Thygesen. 1992. *European Monetary Integration*. New York: Longman. Like the De Grauwe volume, covers the essentials on the development of ideas and policies that would foster the dream of monetary union in Europe.

Padoa-Schioppa, Tommaso. 2000. *The Road to Monetary Union in Europe: The Emperor, the Kings, and the Genies*. Oxford: Oxford University Press. The story of the EMU written by an insider, a former member of the governing council of the ECB, and later, minister of finance for Italy.

PIERRE L. SIKLOS

■ European Union

The European Union is both a vague aspiration and a concrete organization. The aspiration, never held by more than a small minority of Europeans, is for a federation of European states to replace the hodgepodge of sovereign states that has characterized the continent in modern times. The organization—European Union (EU)—is a complex entity with federal features that is less than a full-fledged state yet far more than a traditional international grouping of states. After it acquired two new members in January 2007, the EU comprised 27 countries with a combined population of nearly 500 million and a combined gross national product of approximately €10 trillion. Perhaps it is best understood as an association of countries (member states) that have agreed to share sovereignty in a number of policy areas and to coordinate closely in others, in order to pursue jointly key objectives such as economic growth, social protection, regional stability, and global security.

The EU has grown in size and stature over the years but is increasingly beset by serious political problems. Buffeted by weak public support, poor leadership, the myriad challenges of enlargement, and widespread concerns about the impact of globalization on Europe's generous welfare states, the EU faces an uncertain future. Although hardly destined to wither away or collapse in ignominy, neither is the EU likely to evolve into a superstate, let alone a superpower, as some ardent advocates of European integration would like to see happen.

Origins Today's EU originated in the European Coal and Steel Community, an organization that, in our age of bits and bytes, sounds quaint or even archaic. In the early 1950s, however, coal and steel were essential ingredients for economic recovery and resurgence, and cherished symbols of industrial strength and vitality. The name of the organization denoted the political and economic importance of coal and steel in postwar Europe as well as the special nature of the relationship among its member states. Despite an apparently narrow emphasis on industrial restructuring and revival, the new entity was a "community" and not simply a functional international organization. As such, its members acknowledged the necessity of reconciling national interests with common, overarching security concerns in order to avoid a repetition of Europe's disastrous past and help ensure a more peaceful and prosperous future. By launching the Coal and Steel Community, the original member states also launched the process of political and economic integration that has continued in Europe, through various ups and downs, to the present day.

There was nothing inevitable about the form or content of the EU's precursor. Initial discussions about European unity in the postwar period focused on grandiose federal schemes. In a famous speech in Zurich in 1946, Winston Churchill, Europe's best-known statesman, endorsed the idea of a United States of Europe. Altiero Spinelli, a veteran Italian antifascist and ardent European federalist, advocated a "big-bang" approach to sharing national sovereignty. War weariness and popular disillusionment with the status quo seemed propitious for bold international initiatives. Yet when Europe's leaders met in The Hague in 1948 to discuss political integration, rhetoric clashed with reality. Few of them were willing to surrender sacred national sovereignty to an all-encompassing European federation. What emerged instead was the Council of Europe, an arena for exchanging ideas and information on European integration that lacked political clout.

Meanwhile, Europeans were grappling with the challenges of reconstruction. The Marshall Plan had provided the means, in the form of scarce American dollars, to fuel Western Europe's rapid economic recovery. Motivated in part by escalating East-West tensions, it also accelerated the onset of the Cold War. In view of rapid economic recovery and deepening Cold War hostility, the fate of Germany became more pressing than ever. In 1948 the Western Allies agreed to establish the Federal Republic of Germany. Nevertheless, France did not want the new West German state to become economically powerful, at least not yet. In particular, France coveted Germany's abundant coking coal and sought to modernize its own steel industry before German mills and market share could fully recover from the destruction of the war. Such a policy was unacceptable to the United States, which sought to reconstitute Germany politically and economically as the cornerstone of Western Europe's resurgence and a bulwark against the spread of communism. Under intense American pressure, France had little choice but to come up with a new approach toward its historical enemy.

In response, Jean Monnet, a senior French civil servant and confidant of leading American politicians, proposed the Coal and Steel Community. Rather than pursue a beggar-thy-neighbor policy toward each other, France and Germany would cede responsibility for managing the coal and steel sectors to a supranational High Authority. Robert Schuman, foreign minister of France, announced the proposal in May 1950 and pushed it through a skeptical French government. German chancellor Konrad Adenauer strongly supported what became known as the Schuman Plan, which provided a means of binding the new Federal Republic into Western Europe, promoting reconciliation with France, and lifting Allied controls on Germany's heavy industry.

In his public declaration, Schuman said that the plan was open to the other countries of Europe. With the onset of the Cold War, in effect that meant Western Europe. Britain, with its newly nationalized industries, different war experience, and unwillingness to share sovereignty, decided not to participate. A number of other countries followed suit, whereas Spain, an international pariah after the war, was excluded by default. That left only Italy, which saw

European integration largely in anticommunist terms, and the three Benelux countries (Belgium, Netherlands, and Luxembourg), which were tied economically to Germany, to take up Schuman's offer. As a result, the Coal and Steel Community came into existence in 1952 with six member states.

Monnet had wanted the institutional structure of the new community to comprise only the High Authority and a Court of Justice. In the event, governments successfully pressed for the inclusion as well of a Council of Ministers, to provide a direct national input into decision making, and an Assembly, to lend democratic credence to the organization. Thus the institutional design of today's EU took shape, with the High Authority changing its name to the European Commission in the late 1950s, following the establishment of the European Economic Community (EEC).

The Coal and Steel Community played an unglamorous yet essential role in the postwar European settlement. Its significance was more political than economic, notably by providing a diplomatic solution to the contentious question of German reconstruction and rehabilitation. Conversely, the emergence of the EEC later in the decade had less to do with Franco-German rapprochement than with the immediate economic interests of the contracting states. In particular, the explosive growth of international trade in the 1950s led the Dutch, traditional advocates of economic liberalism, to push for a Western European common market. Adenauer, enamored of any idea that would strengthen European integration, took up the call, despite the objections of Ludwig Erhard, his economics minister, who feared that the proposal would damage prospects for global trade liberalization. France was torn between accepting greater competition, albeit in a regional framework, and maintaining a policy of trade protectionism. Champions of the common market in the French government won the day by including in the proposed community provisions for EEC-level agricultural subsidies and a preferential regime for current and former colonies of the member states. With a huge, heavily subsidized agricultural sector

and a large, fragmenting empire, France stood to gain handsomely from such side payments. Hence the origin of the Common Agricultural Policy (CAP) and the Cotonou Agreement, two of the most controversial, trade-distorting policies of the EU.

The same six members of the Coal and Steel Community went on to establish the broader Economic Community in 1958, Britain again having refused to participate. The launch of the EEC, later known simply as the European Community (EC), was far from an earth-shattering event. Few Europeans had followed the negotiations, which were highly technical and conducted mostly in secret. News at the time was dominated by Soviet threats against Berlin, the deteriorating situation in Algeria, and the imminent collapse of the French Fourth Republic. The EC, which would later insinuate itself into everyday life in Europe and, in the form of the EU, occasionally dominate domestic politics, began with a whimper, not a bang.

Development of the EC Almost from the beginning, the EC developed along two lines: widening and deepening. Widening refers to enlargement, as more and more countries requested membership. Deepening refers to the acquisition by the EC of responsibility for or involvement in additional policy areas, as member states agreed to transfer more sovereignty to the organization. Conceptually, widening and deepening are contradictory: the larger the membership, the more cumbersome and less cohesive the organization. The EU may have reached that point by 2007, although even with 27 members the institutions operated surprisingly well. Historically, in any case, widening and deepening went hand in hand. Indeed, member states deliberately undertook institutional reform and increased the EC's policy scope in part to ensure that wider would not mean weaker.

The first opportunity to do so came almost immediately after the establishment of the EC. Having first dismissed European integration as unworthy of a victorious Great Power, and then having tried to subvert the EC by establishing the rival European Free Trade Association, Britain accepted the reality of growing economic interdependence with the

Continent and applied for membership in 1961. It would be another 12 years before Britain—together with Denmark and Ireland—joined, thanks largely to the policy concerns and personal spite of French president Charles de Gaulle. De Gaulle wanted to ensure that the EC was ready for Britain, meaning that the CAP, and with it the EC's budget, were fully fleshed out. Because of different agricultural preferences, Britain would have objected to the establishment of the CAP in the form in which it eventually emerged in the late 1960s. By the time Britain joined, the CAP was already in place. By contrast, Britain subscribed fully to the customs union, which finally came into being in 1968 following the eradication of tariffs and abolition of quotas among member states. As a corollary to the customs union, the EC developed a common commercial policy, the basis for collective member state action in successive rounds of multilateral trade liberalization under the auspices of the General Agreement on Tariffs and Trade and the World Trade Organization.

International strategic and financial developments in the late 1960s prompted the member states to move European integration in two new directions: monetary policy and foreign policy cooperation. In response to international currency fluctuations and Germany's overtures toward the Soviet bloc, national governments launched two separate initiatives. One aimed to achieve economic and monetary union by 1980; the other to coordinate member states' foreign policies as closely as possible. These were dramatic examples of deepening in the run-up to the EC's first enlargement, but European integration went through trying times in the years ahead. The reason was not enlargement itself, but the worldwide economic downturn that coincided with enlargement. In the recessionary 1970s and early 1980s, the economies of the member states diverged rather than converged; the ambitious and not well-thought-out goal of monetary union was scrapped; nontariff barriers proliferated in member states; and EC decision making ground to a halt.

The EC's fortunes revived in the mid-1980s when national governments, reeling from years of poor economic performance and facing intense interna-

tional competition, rediscovered the benefits of market integration. One of the main architects of the EC's revival was none other than British prime minister Margaret Thatcher. Though later dismissed as a Euroskeptic, or zealous opponent of European integration, Thatcher championed the importance of completing the single European market by ensuring the free movement of goods, services, capital, and people. Thatcher looked back to the future: to the original provisions of the treaty establishing the EC (the Treaty of Rome) as a means of breaking down economic barriers among member states in order to boost growth and employment. Thatcher was instrumental in forging a consensus across the political spectrum in favor of what became known as the single market program. Optimistic assessments of the likely economic impact of a borderless EC, notably the Cecchini Report of 1988, bolstered her position.

Whereas Thatcher did not think that completing the single market necessitated institutional reform in the EC, most of the other national leaders wanted to enshrine their commitment to the single market in a new treaty, which would include provisions for greater use of qualified majority voting, an instrument of supranational decision making. This was the genesis of the Single European Act, the first major overhaul of the Treaty of Rome. Negotiation of the Single European Act coincided with another round of EC enlargement, Greece having joined in 1981 and Portugal and Spain being about to join in 1986. In keeping with the recurring fear that wider would mean weaker, especially as the new member states were substantially poorer than the existing members, national leaders included in the Single European Act a promise to strengthen regional (cohesion) policy by substantially increasing spending on development projects in the EC's disadvantaged areas. Thatcher saw this as a betrayal of the liberal principles of the single market program and a shameful side payment to the EC's poorer member states. By contrast, most other national leaders, as well as Jacques Delors, the commission's new president, saw it as a manifestation of solidarity in a growing EC and an acknowledgement that, contrary to neoliberal belief, market forces alone would not guarantee the equitable or eventual spread of economic growth from the rich core to the poor periphery.

Thatcher and Delors fought their ideological battles in a series of speeches on the nature and purpose of European integration, delivered in the late 1980s. Embittered by the acceleration of integration beyond the single market program, and especially by the renewed momentum for economic and monetary union, Thatcher became increasingly isolated within the EC. Undisguised opposition to German unification set Thatcher further apart from her European counterparts. Battling fierce opposition at home to a proposed poll tax and growing hostility in Europe, Thatcher was forced from office by her own Conservative Party in 1990. Thatcher's departure and Delors's preeminence symbolized the remarkable transformation of the EC by the end of the 1980s, a period of profound change in the international system. With the end of the Cold War and the imminent collapse of the Soviet Union, a united Germany and a uniting Europe seemed to portend the triumph of European integration. As if to prove the point, the Maastricht Treaty of 1991, another far-reaching reform of the original Treaty of Rome, subsumed the EC into the EU, while pointing the way toward monetary union by the end of the 1990s, strengthening cohesion policy, launching a fledgling Common Foreign and Security Policy, and setting the stage for close cooperation in the policy areas of justice and home affairs.

The Overreaching EU It soon became apparent that the single market program was the zenith of European integration and that the Maastricht Treaty marked a profound turning point. The rejection of the treaty by a narrow majority of Danes in a referendum in June 1992 symbolized the EU's troubles. The result astounded Europe's political elites: how could a majority of citizens in any member state have rejected a carefully negotiated treaty intended to deepen European integration? Although there were many reasons why people voted against the treaty, the result reflected widespread public concern about the rapid pace of integration and, especially, the so-called democratic deficit—the seeming unaccountability and remoteness of EU institutions. Aware of the danger of the democratic deficit, EU leaders had already addressed the issue by giving more legislative power to the directly elected European Parliament and promoting the principle of subsidiarity or states' rights. Most Europeans were unimpressed by the European Parliament, however, as evidenced by the declining turnout in successive elections. Nor has subsidiarity, which is difficult to put into practice, grabbed the popular imagination.

Public disaffection with the EU has increased steadily since the early 1990s. Subsequent treaty changes—Amsterdam in 1997, Nice in 2001, and the Constitutional Treaty, signed by national leaders in 2005—failed to allay concerns about the democratic deficit or to endear the EU to the people. At the same time, poor economic performance in the big, continental member states further undermined public support, although responsibility for sluggish growth lay primarily with national leaders rather than the EU itself. Indeed, national leaders agreed at an EU summit in 2000 to undertake a series of labor market and other reforms—the so-called Lisbon Strategy—but governments in France, Germany, and Italy, in particular, were loath to antagonize volatile electorates by following through with concrete measures. The road to economic and monetary union in the 1990s may have made matters worse, as governments strove to reduce deficits and debts in order to meet the criteria for participation in the third stage of the process: adoption of a single monetary policy and a single currency. Regardless of its economic or political merits, the advent of monetary union in 1999—followed by the introduction of the euro in 2002—lacked popular enthusiasm. Most people in the eurozone miss their national currencies far more than they value the euro.

Europeans are especially concerned about enlargement, fearing that further expansion of the EU, following the accession of 10 Central and Eastern European states in 2005–7, is unsustainable. Economic arguments about the long-term benefits of enlargement—larger market size, economies of scale, increased competition—run counter to widespread worries about worker migration from east to west, downward pressure on wages, and possible job losses. Under the circumstances, Turkey's application for EU membership seemed doomed by late 2007. The accession negotiations, which formally began in 2004, were overshadowed in any case by disputes between both sides over the future of northern Cyprus and over the pace and durability of political reforms in Turkey. Lurking in the background was the generally unspoken but politically potent viewpoint that Turkey, a predominantly Muslim country located mostly across the Bosporus, is neither culturally nor geographically European.

The fate of the Constitutional Treaty, a political initiative to improve the EU's functioning and fortunes, illustrates the state of the EU itself. Drafted by a convention representing a wide range of political opinion from the existing members and candidate countries, the Constitutional Treaty included provisions to improve decision making in an enlarged EU, address concerns about the democratic deficit, and enhance the EU's ability to act internationally. Yet sizable majorities in France and the Netherlands, two of the EU's founding member states, rejected the Constitutional Treaty in referendums in mid-2005. Their reasons for doing so, like those of the Danes who rejected the Maastricht Treaty in 1992, were varied, but included a strong dislike of the EU's political pretensions. After a lengthy "period of reflection," EU leaders redrafted the Constitutional Treaty—dropping the word "constitution" or "constitutional" from the title and text and making other symbolic changes—and signed the Lisbon Treaty in December 2007. Until ratified by all member states, the Lisbon Treaty cannot come into effect. In the meantime, the EU is operating under the terms of the existing treaties, whose institutional provisions are hardly adequate for such a large and multifaceted organization.

Prospects The EU has been in existence, in one form or another, since 1952. During that time it has grown from 6 to 27 member states and in scope from a common market for coal and steel to a single market in goods, services, capital, and people, as well as a monetary union for countries that meet the conver-

gence criteria. Managing and perfecting the single market—facilitating free movement within its borders—is the core activity of the EU. It is an activity that requires constant vigilance, regulatory fine-tuning, and occasional intervention by the Court of Justice. It is also an aspect of the EU that enjoys public support, as Europeans have come to appreciate the benefits of unimpeded cross-border travel and shopping. Europeans appreciate as well the need for their governments to cooperate closely in the fight against terrorism and transnational crime, and to maximize their leverage by acting collectively on the global stage. Beyond that, Europeans appear to have little appetite for further enlargement and for extravagant constitutional schemes. There is a growing consensus that, at this stage in its history, the EU needs to focus on first principles and strengthen its fragile legitimacy by demonstrating its effectiveness in those policy areas in which it provides obvious added value.

See also common market; customs unions; European Central Bank; European Monetary Union

FURTHER READING

El-Agraa, Ali M., ed. 2004 *The European Union: Economics and Policies*. 7th ed. Upper Saddle River, NJ: Prentice Hall. A good collection of essays by leading authorities on a range of economic theories, debates, and policies related to the European Union.

Artis, Michael, and Frederick Nixson. 2002. *The Economics of the European Union: Policy and Analysis*. 3d ed. Oxford: Oxford University Press. A good account of economic policies and policymaking in the EU.

Baldwin, Richard. 2006. *The Economics of European Integration*. 2d ed. New York: McGraw Hill. A solid, accessible text on economic integration in Europe.

Calingaert, Michael. 1988. *The 1992 Challenge from Europe*. Washington, DC: National Planning Association. A classic assessment of the implications of the single-market program for the United States.

———. 1996. *European Integration Revisited: Progress, Prospects, and U.S. Interests*. Boulder, CO: Westview. A follow-up to Calingaert's 1988 assessment of the implications of the single-market program for the United States.

Cecchini, Paolo. 1988. *The European Challenge, 1992: The Benefits of a Single Market*. Aldershot, U.K.: Gower. A synopsis of the multivolume report by Paolo Cecchini on the "cost of non-Europe"—the cost of not integrating the European market.

Dinan, Desmond. 2004. *Europe Recast: A History of European Union*. Boulder, CO: Lynne Rienner. A comprehensive history of European integration.

———. 2005. *Ever Closer Union: An Introduction to European Integration*. 3d ed. Boulder, CO: Lynne Rienner. A classic textbook on the European Union, now in its third edition.

Eichengreen, Barry. 2006. *The European Economy since 1945: Coordinated Capitalism and Beyond*. Princeton, NJ: Princeton University Press. An excellent history of economic policymaking in Europe from the end of World War II to the early 21st century.

Gillingham, John. 2003. *European Integration, 1950–2003: Superstate or New Market Economy?* Cambridge: Cambridge University Press. A controversial book that characterizes the history of European integration as a struggle between economic centralizers and market reformers.

Molle, Willem. 2006. *The Economics of European Integration: Theory, Practice, Policy*. 5th ed. Aldershot, U.K.: Ashgate. One of the most popular and authoritative texts on the subject.

Neal, Larry. 2007. *The Economics of Europe and the European Union*. Cambridge: Cambridge University Press. A new version of a book with the same title originally written by Neal and Daniel Barbezat, published by Oxford University Press in 1998, that examines the EU economy collectively and the economies of the member states separately.

Pelkmans, Jacques. 2006. *European Integration: Methods and Economic Analysis*. 3d ed. London: Financial Times Press. A dense textbook on the economic principles and practices underlying European integration.

Wallace, Helen, William Wallace, and Mark Pollack. 2005. *Policy-Making in the European Union*. 5th ed. Oxford: Oxford University Press. An authoritative and comprehensive examination of key EU policy areas and of the policymaking process.

DESMOND DINAN

■ evolution of development thinking

In the international community, a focus on development emerged in the 1940s and 1950s, following the focus on reconstruction and development after World War II and the subsequent decolonization of former empires. As academics and senior civil servants turned their attention to how the newly decolonized regions could catch up to their richer counterparts, the arguments of development thinkers soon became caught up in the schisms of the Cold War.

In the heat of the postwar period, the spectrum of solutions offered by development thinkers ranged from solutions inspired by Marxist thought to those that advocated closer integration in the capitalist system. In the 1950s and 1960s, however, even the procapitalist economic orthodoxy placed the state at the heart of economic development, and the dominant paradigm across the spectrum was of state-led growth. For development thinkers, the lesson of the theories of John Maynard Keynes and the chastening experience of the Great Depression was that self-regulated markets could not be relied on to generate prosperity. This perception had been reinforced by what were regarded as the relatively effective planning processes of post–World War II Europe. Meanwhile, the small size and often enclave- or state-dependent private sector in developing countries meant that development thinkers had little evidence of, and heard only muted arguments for, more effective and open markets.

The broad aim of development thinkers was to raise growth in poorer countries to achieve the same income levels, on average, as developed countries. At first, even the non-Marxist development thinkers looked for universal models of development and theories that would initiate the growth process. The idea that growth, once initiated, would continue through virtuous circles or reinforcing effects gained wide currency. This was echoed in development thinkers' phrases that persisted into the 1960s, such as the "big push" (Rosenstein-Rodan), the "takeoff" (Rostow), and the "great spurt" (Gerschenkron) (see Hirschman 1981).

Development practitioners and thinkers observed that market failures were particularly prevalent in developing countries. The private sector, which was relatively poorly developed and driven by narrow interests, had shown itself to be an inadequate engine of growth. In newly decolonized Africa and in Asia and Latin America, new national states were determined to establish postcolonial models of development. Given that the majority of professionals were concentrated in public service and had limited knowledge of the private sector, and that the absence of democracy meant that the state exercised virtually all the levers of power, the preoccupation with the role of the state was not surprising.

Two strands of thought emerged, both of which reflected this heavy reliance on the state. The first was the dominant strand within developing countries, particularly on the political left. This was import-substitution industrialization (a policy intended to promote industrialization by protecting domestic producers from competition from imports), which informed government thinking in Latin America, Africa, and Asia. The second strand of thought was multilateralism (a policy of multiple nations working cooperatively to solve world problems), which was given added impetus in the strategic agenda of Western Europe and North America.

Industrialization plans aimed at getting around the problems of coordination of industry development became the dominant currency of development thinkers residing in developing countries and some developed countries, particularly the United Kingdom. Planning models, at times elaborated through input-output matrixes, provided a vision of an integrated chain in which domestically produced raw materials and local labor provided the building blocks of industries that met first domestic and then export requirements. To the extent that the concept of dynamic comparative advantage influenced thinking, it was within the constraint of perceptions regarding the unequal terms of trade and protectionism in rich countries, which were seen as effectively preventing the balanced integration of developing countries into a global trading system. Greater self-reliance and import-substitution indus-trialization, reinforced by fixed exchange rates, import tariffs, and exporting cartels, were seen by many as the appropriate response. These would prime the pump for a virtuous circle of increased employment and incomes, which would be coupled with improved health and education as well as rising consumer demand and investment. To the extent that the rich countries were seen to have a role, it was primarily as providers of capital and technology.

These ideas reflected the view that the prices for agricultural goods, expected to be primarily exported by developing countries, would fall in the long run and that the technological spillover effects from manufacturing were greater than those from agriculture (Prebisch 1950). Raúl Prebisch not only exercised a powerful influence in the evolution of development thinking but also was instrumental in the establishment of institutions that continue to carry his ideas forward, notably the Economic Commission for Latin America (ECLA) and the United Nations Conference on Trade and Development (UNCTAD).

The oil price increases of the 1970s also had important impacts on ideas about trade policy and development. Many developing countries considered that cartelization, as used by the Organization of the Petroleum Exporting Countries (OPEC), could be extended to other commodities to ensure that the gains from trade were more equally shared with developing countries. Government intervention at the national and supranational levels in markets and trade became a key element of what some termed the "New International Economic Order." UNCTAD and an array of marketing boards at the national and international levels (including the international coffee, cocoa, sugar, and commodity bodies established in the 1960s and early 1970s) were seen as providing the means to rebalance the international trading system for the benefit of developing economies.

While some thinkers continued to pursue global solutions, by the late 1970s many development specialists saw the evident constraints faced by bankrupt governments and narrowed their ambitions. Focus shifted toward filling needs such as those for food, education, and health and away from overall integrated frameworks that attempted to incorporate all sectors of an economy. This evolution largely reflected a lack of success in kick-starting growth and a growing realization that theories did not account for political economy factors related to institutions, governance, and conflict. There was also evidence that the benefits of growth were not necessarily trickling down to the poorest people in developing countries and that some types of growth were environmentally unsustainable.

Development thinkers recognized that state-led models, at least in the medium term, had failed to address poverty and that stubborn levels of high unemployment were endemic in many societies. Chenery and others argued that policies should be devised to specifically benefit the poor (Chenery et al. 1979). The Basic Needs Approach was adopted by the International Labor Organization and later by the World Bank. Rather than challenging the role of governments, it sought to ensure that governments adopted pro-poor policies that would ensure that minimum needs would be met to enable all citizens to lead productive lives. In the 1980s, the capability approach developed by Amartya Sen and others built on this understanding with the United Nations Development Program in its 1990 Human Development Report. This report went beyond the analysis of the World Bank's annual World Development Reports to provide a broad understanding of the issues and data required to address poverty (Stewart 2006). The shift in development aims was accompanied by an expanded set of measures by which to track development. In particular, the human development indicators published in 1990 covered poverty, health, education, and the status of women in many of the world's countries. A number of these indicators, as well as others covering environmental sustainability, are now part of the Millennium Development Goals.

Primacy of Markets By the late 1970s, the oil crises, interest rate hikes, and widespread macroeconomic instability had led to a reconsideration of the balance of state and market. Growing awareness that the pressure on public-sector finances was not

politically sustainable led to a reconsideration of governments' roles. The tension between the informational requirements of central planning and the increasing complexity and integration of developing economies was also becoming more evident. Macroeconomic instability associated, at least in part, with spikes in oil and interest rates led to deep crises, which in turn were seen by a new wave of development thinkers as symptomatic of a deeper malaise. By the 1980s, the global economic slowdown and the debt crisis had increasingly constrained the potential for state action in initiating development, and the voices of those who argued that governments should "get out of the way of development" were being heard more widely.

In the late 1970s, a new cohort of development thinkers, based mainly in the United States, was in the ascendant. They argued that state planners could not possibly possess all the knowledge required to make decisions reflecting efficiency as well as people's differing preferences. An influential World Bank study (Krueger et al. 1988) argued that import substitution often resulted in inefficient industries and an antiagriculture bias, undermining both growth and poverty reduction. Moreover, governments had revealed themselves to be collections of interests rather than the benevolent arbiters of the collective interest that the import-substitution industrialization model required. The development thinkers at the fore in the 1980s eschewed state-led development and focused on the removal of regulations, tariffs, and other government-induced economic and trade distortions. Governments were now viewed as a barrier to entrepreneurs and development, rather than as initiators of development. It was argued that the private sector, left to its own devices, would be the engine of economic growth.

The increasing market focus of development thinkers and practitioners reflected in part the economic experiences and the broader political climate of the time. Global economic growth slowed following the oil price shocks of 1974 and 1979. The second oil price shock was followed by higher U.S. interest rates to control inflation, which pushed the United States into recession. With falling demand for their exports and rising interest rates, many developing countries could not service the debts they had built up over the preceding ten years, resulting in the debt crisis that began in Mexico in 1982 and spread to other developing countries. The belief that government officials and bureaucrats would act in their own interest led many thinkers to push for rapid change. Jeffery Sachs and others argued that a crisis would provide only a limited amount of time for reform. Reforms would have to be pushed through quickly, despite attendant costs, to ensure that the rent seekers who sought to gain wealth through benefiting from the imbalances and lack of transparency in the legal and regulatory environment could not reestablish their interests (Sachs 1994; Lal 1997).

In the richer members of the Organisation for Economic Co-operation and Development (OECD), the oil shock and subsequent rise in interest rates and debt servicing costs also led to a growing appreciation for the need for fiscal adjustment. With the dominant political mood more open to the arguments of those economists who called for reductions in pubic expenditure, policies became more promarket in key developed economies.

The broader geopolitical context also contributed to this pendulum swing. The hardening of the Cold War caused a reaction against state-led growth models, with these models being seen as part and parcel of socialism. In this context, advanced economies such as the United States, Britain, and Germany began the wave of deregulation and privatization under the leadership of Ronald Reagan (United States), Margaret Thatcher (United Kingdom), and Helmut Kohl (Germany). Given the power that these governments exercised over the Bretton Woods institutions, and that the trend reflected a broad shift in economic thinking, it is not surprising that in this period the strongly promarket Anne Krueger replaced the long-serving development economist Hollis Chenery in the influential role as chief economist of the World Bank.

In this environment, Williamson (1990) identified a set of policies that he termed the "Washington consensus." These policies reflected the prevailing view of orthodox development thinkers, not least at the Washington-based World Bank and International Monetary Fund, in the 1980s and the first half of the 1990s. These policies included macroeconomic stabilization; liberalization of trade, exchange rates, and financial markets; deregulation of domestic industries; and privatization of government-owned businesses. What Williamson identified was not only the prevailing Washington view. It also was applied by a growing number of developing countries, often under the duress of fiscal adjustment, as these countries sought a prerequisite to sustainable growth.

The consensus broke down over the extent of liberalization required for growth. For the Washington-based multilateral lending institutions, this required the removal of regulations including trade barriers, freeing prices from controls, and the dismantling of marketing boards and similar state institutions to allow markets to work to achieve their reputed efficiency. Like the classical economists of the 19th century, these thinkers advocated a highly restricted role for the government involving the provision of public goods such as law and order, defense, and a sound currency, and when necessary, primary education, primary health care, and a social safety net.

The late 1980s saw improvements in macroeconomic stability and an opening to trade, financial, and other flows in much of the developing world. From the 1980s to 2005, trade barriers fell across developing economies from average levels of more than 30 percent to about 10 percent. The "tiger economies" of East Asia were held up as examples of the benefits of getting rid of government regulation and controls, promoting exports, and "letting markets work," and several studies appeared to confirm that these policies were responsible for the rapid growth of these economies (World Bank 1993). These studies were later shown to provide an inadequate explanation of the success of the "Asian Tigers." The interpretation of the industrialization of Asian economies has been challenged by a number of critics who argued that the state played a pivotal role in development (Amsden 2001; Wade 1990), and even the World Bank later developed a more nuanced view of the East Asian experience (Stiglitz and Yusuf 2001).

Importance of Institutions By the late 1990s, the failure of the rapid transition from centrally planned to capitalist economies to deliver broad-based benefits in Eastern Europe, together with the Asian crisis of 1997, in which institutional weakness played a part, and a growing perception that the distribution of globalization's gains was inequitable, led to a widening acknowledgment of the shortcomings of a purely "promarket" approach to development. In particular, it neglected the importance of institutions and the provision of public goods, not least good governance, both at the national and at the global level. The pendulum shift in development thinking built on the work of the 1993 Nobel laureate Douglass North, who noted that individual behavior was constrained by numerous rules and social norms of the society in which the individual lives (North 1990). It was argued that without studying these constraints, including how they arise and their impacts, attempts to promote development would be unlikely to succeed.

The constraints provided by history became particularly obvious following the attempted shock therapy in the former Soviet states. In contrast, China continued to implement market-oriented reforms while nevertheless holding to its core commitment to a powerful state and with only partial reform of key macroeconomic and institutional levers.

Development practitioners began promoting stable and effective government institutions, strong enforcement of property rights, the absence of bureaucratic harassment, a lack of corruption, and protection from organized crime—all things that matter for the functioning of markets and that had been previously neglected. In retrospect it was now considered naïve to think that the institutions that enable markets to work could evolve quickly and without state intervention.

The Asian crisis, Soviet transition, and Chinese experience highlighted the importance of sequencing, the order in which policies were put into effect. The orthodox position promoting liberalization of all aspects of the capital account was replaced by a

heterodox view that highlighted the importance of sequencing and country specificity.

Complementarity of Markets and Governments By the mid-1990s, the dominant development discourse had begun to move away from market-led approaches. In its place, a consensus was forming around the complementarities between markets and governments. Attention focused on how government and the private sector may best work together. A vibrant private sector was now seen as the driver of economic growth, but this required properly functioning state institutions to build a good investment climate and deliver basic services competently. Investment climate analysis was focused on the ease and cost of starting legitimate businesses, including the bureaucratic costs and access to credit and basic infrastructure and utilities. Indicators based on World Bank surveys provide a comparison of the performance of different countries (World Bank Doing Business Project and World Bank Investment Climate Surveys).

Countries that combined institutional improvements with market-oriented policy reforms and greater engagement with the world economy saw their per capita incomes grow in the 1990s at the historically very rapid pace of more than 5 percent per year. Some countries have achieved even faster growth, with China's per capita growth averaging 8.7 percent from 1990 to 2005. That a sound state is required for solid growth was shown in the uneven development outcomes of the former Soviet countries. Promarket policies could not be expected to succeed without strong market-based institutional foundations.

Important too is local "ownership" of the development agenda rather than imposition from outside. The countries that have achieved rapid development, such as China and India, have done so through the actions of their own people and government, and with very little development assistance.

Growth Theory and Development Thinking Growth has been a concern throughout the history of development thinking, albeit with a general decline in expectations of what development assistance and policies can do. Yet growth theory and development thinking diverged considerably in the 1960s, with growth theory identifying formal mathematical models—these were mainly focused on growth in advanced economies. Underlying these models were assumptions of well-functioning markets and a system of economic incentives.

In contrast, development theorists typically eschewed mathematical models and focused on the failure of the assumptions used in growth theory. Interest in input-output and later general equilibrium analysis has provided a heavily quantitative seam within the development literature, but such methods remain a relatively minor feature of development thinking (Goldin, Knudsen, and Brandao 1994).

With increasing macroeconomic stability has come a greater recognition of the importance of microeconomic and institutional development. To the extent that the focus of many development thinkers today is mainly on how to affect the actions of individuals and firms rather than on macroeconomic aggregates, interest in models based on broad aggregates of national accounts has diminished.

Both growth theory and development theory have had a considerable influence on development policy. The simplistic stories that emerge from growth models have encouraged theories of missing components of production and policies that fill these gaps. These have variously included capital, foreign exchange, human capital, and technology. Development thinkers have been more active than growth theorists in exploring the reasons why these factors may be missing. In this sense, recent development thinkers have focused on the incentives for people to accumulate physical and human capital, and on an efficient use of these types of capital.

Questions regarding the sustainability of growth have only recently begun to enter the mainstream of development theory. The oil price shocks of the 1970s and the rapid recovery of the 1980s, not least in East Asia, led to a growing recognition of the need to focus on resource degradation and what was termed (by the Club of Rome) as the Limits to Growth. The United Nations Commission on Environment and Development in 1987 published the widely cited Brundtland report, which defined sustainable development as meeting the needs of the present without compromising the ability of future generations to meet their own needs (WCED 1987). It would be 20 years, however, until the evidence of climate change became so overwhelming that the largely grassroots movement influenced by the Brundtland report could see sustainability becoming central to development thinking.

No Single Model for Development Development thinking has evolved rapidly since the 1950s and is continuing to change. Different development concepts have emerged in response to specific economic and political conditions and problems, attempting to address these challenges, but typically only partially succeeding. Concepts have been less useful when they have been exported without accounting for different economic, social, and cultural conditions, or when they have continued to be applied after economic and political conditions have changed. Development strategies have been most successful when they addressed the specific challenges facing a country at a particular point in time. This requires that countries have the capacity for policy formation in terms of skilled researchers and the relevant data. Both are vital to policy reform. Since the mid-1990s, development thinking has continued to evolve. Increasingly, development is seen not through the lens of actual outcomes but through the outcomes that a person is able to choose. This concept gives greater prominence to empowerment of the individual and the expansion of individual freedom; and individuals are seen as agents for change rather than as passive recipients of assistance.

It has become clearer since the 1950s that there is no development panacea or universal path for development. Development thinkers and practitioners can benefit from understanding the experiences of different countries and by drawing on the latest theory. There is, however, no shortcut. If anything, the evolution of development thinking shows how today's truths are replaced by tomorrow's wisdom. The application of development thinking requires an arsenal of knowledge that includes economic theory and is informed by comparative and historical analysis. The application also requires that the thinking respond to a country's specific priorities and circumstances. Greater investment in research is required to ensure that development thinking evolves even more rapidly in response to the enormous current challenges, many of which, such as global equity and climate change, go the heart of questions of sustainable development.

See also aid, international; development; economic development; Millennium Development Goals; poverty, global; Washington consensus

FURTHER READING

Adelman, I. 2001. "Fallacies in Development Theory and Their Implications for Policy." In *Frontiers of Development Economics: The Future in Perspective*, edited by G. M. Meier and J. E. Stiglitz. Oxford: Oxford University Press, 103–34. Discusses the impact of the narrow preoccupation of economics in the field of development economics.

Amsden, A. 2001. *The Rise of "The Rest"—Challenges to the West from Late-industrializing Economies*. New York: Oxford University Press. Challenges convergence theory and examines models of late industrialization, comparing the "independent" model of China, Korea, India, and Japan, and the "integrationist" model of Argentina, Brazil, Mexico, and Turkey.

Bruton, H. J. 1998. "A Reconsideration of Import Substitution." *Journal of Economic Literature* 36 (2): 903–36. Provides a critical view of import substitution and contrasts it to the "outward-oriented" approach to development.

Chenery, H., et al. 1979. *Redistribution with Growth*. Oxford: Oxford University Press. Coauthored with leading development thinkers of the time, this is a key statement of World Bank development strategy under Hollis Chenery.

De Soto, H. 2001. *The Mystery of Capital*. London: Black Swan. Argues that property rights and other reforms are required for the poor to turn "dead" into "liquid" capital.

Goldin, I., O. Knudsen, and A. Brandao. 1994. *Modeling Economywide Reforms*. Paris: OECD. Examines the impact of macroeconomic and sectoral reforms using a variety of economic models, comparing methodologies and outcomes.

Goldin, I., and K. Reinert. 2006. *Globalization for Development: Trade, Finance, Aid, Migration and Policy*. Washington, DC: World Bank and Palgrave Macmillan. Examines the key economic flows and shows how policies at the national and global level are required to make globalization work for development.

Hirschman, A. O. 1981. *Essays in Trespassing: Economics to Politics and Beyond*. Cambridge: Cambridge University Press. A collection of essays providing an overview of the author's scholarship, including work on economic development and its political repercussions, as well as on political participation, rational choice theory, and the history of economic thought.

Krueger, A., M. Schiff, and A. Valdes. 1988. "Agricultural Incentives in Developing Countries." *World Bank Economic Review* 2 (3): 255–71. Estimates the impact of sector-specific (direct) and economywide (indirect) policies on agricultural incentives for 18 developing countries for the period 1975–84.

Lal, D. 1997. *The Poverty of "Development Economics."* London: Institute of Economic Affairs. Argues for market-based economic management and less government intervention to address development challenges.

Lindauer, D. L, and Lant Pritchett. 2002. "What's the Big Idea? The Third Generation of Policies for Economic Growth." *Economia: Journal of the Latin American and Caribbean Economic Association* 3 (1):1–28. Puts the Latin American experience of reform in global context and offers policy advice on economic growth.

Myrdal, G. 1957. *Economic Theory and Underdeveloped Regions*. London: Gerald Duckworth. Based on a series of lectures delivered in Cairo in 1955, examining the basic principles of classical economic theory (particularly international trade) in relation to the problems of underdeveloped regions.

New Palgrave: A Dictionary of Economics. 1989. "Economic Development." Basingstoke: Palgrave Macmillan. Compendium of economics concepts and leading theorists.

North, D. 1990. *Institutions, Institutional Change, and Economic Performance*. Cambridge: Cambridge University Press. Develops an analytical framework for explaining the ways in which institutions and institutional change affect the performance of economies.

Prebisch, R. 1950. *The Economic Development of Latin America and its Principal Problems*. New York: UN Economic Commission for Latin America. Challenges comparative advantage as a basis for development, arguing that developing countries (the "periphery") are in a structurally unequal relationship with industrialized countries (the "center"), and that nonmarket solutions at the national and global level as a consequence are required to address development challenges.

Ray, D. 1998. *Development Economics*. New Delhi: Oxford University Press. Synthesizes literature in the field and raises policy questions, arguing that there is no single cause for economic progress, but that a combination of factors (physical and human capital, reduced inequality, and strong institutions) consistently favor development.

Rostow, W. W. 1990. *Theorists of Economic Growth from David Hume to the Present*. New York: Oxford University Press. Explores how growth theorists since the mid-18th century have dealt with variables and problems posed by the dynamics of economic growth.

Sachs, J. 1994. *Understanding Shock Therapy*. New York: Social Market Foundation. Motivation for rapid adjustment of the former Soviet Union to a market economy, and the need for radical reform of prices, liberalization, and privatization.

Sen, A. 1999. *Development as Freedom*. New York: Knopf. Argues that open dialogue, civil freedoms, and political liberties are vital dimensions of sustainable development.

Stern, N. H., J. Dethier, and F. Halsey Rogers. 2005. *Growth and Empowerment: Making Development Happen*. Cambridge, MA: MIT. Analysis of the interaction between growth and poverty reduction which emphasizes the importance of focusing on the "twin pillars" of investment and empowerment.

Stewart, F. 2006. "Basic Needs Approach." In *The Elgar Companion to Development Studies*, edited by D. Clark. Cheltenham: Edward Elgar, 14–18. Provides a synthesis of the basic needs approach and places it in the context of the evolution of development thinking.

Stiglitz, J. 2000. "Capital Market Liberalization, Economic Growth, and Instability." *World Development* 28 (6): 1075–86. Drawing lessons from the Asian crisis, highlights the importance of sequencing and of a nuanced approach to capital market liberalization.

Stiglitz, J., and S. Yusuf, eds. 2001. *Rethinking the East Asian Miracle*. New York: Oxford University Press. Compares the industrial policies of East Asian countries, including China, and sheds new light on the "East Asian Miracle."

Wade, R. 1990. *Governing the Market: Economic Theory and the Role of Government in East Asian Industrialization*. Princeton, NJ: Princeton University Press. Examination of industrial policy in East Asia focusing on the interaction of state and market.

Williamson, J. 1990. "What Washington Means by Policy Reform." In *Latin American Adjustment: How Much Has Happened?* Edited by J. Williamson. Washington, DC: Institute for International Economics, 5–20. The text that gave rise to the notion of the "Washington consensus" and which summarizes the orthodoxy of the time.

Wolf, M. 2003. "The Morality of the Market." *Foreign Policy* 138: 46–50. Argues for the ethical and equity basis of capitalism on the basis of superior outcomes.

World Bank. 1993. *The East Asian Miracle: Economic Growth and Public Policy*. New York: Oxford University Press. World Bank policy report which argues that strong macroeconomic policies, a focus on the market, narrowly targeted government interventions, and physical and human capital account for the success of the East Asian economies.

World Commission on Environment and Development (WCED). 1987. *Our Common Future*. Oxford: Oxford University Press. United Nations report that provided the first global attempt to locate environmental problems in the context of growth and development and to identify the long term implications of rising consumption and resource depletion.

IAN GOLDIN

■ **exchange controls**
See capital controls

■ **exchange market pressure**
Foreign exchange market pressure (EMP) indexes are weighted schemes of variables designed to gauge

speculative pressure on a country's currency. These variables normally include the exchange rate, the domestic interest rate, and/or a measure of international reserves available to the monetary authority. Crisis incidents in recent years, including the severance of the British pound from the exchange rate mechanism in 1992, the Asian crisis in 1997, and the abolition of the Argentinean peg with the U.S. dollar in early 2002, have shown that the potential for foreign exchange market pressure to result in currency crises is significant, and hence monitoring informative variables is crucial.

Investors may put downward pressure on a currency for several reasons: for example, they may have spotted a fundamental imbalance and believe that a given exchange rate is unsustainable; or they may observe and follow the actions of other investors/speculators. The reaction of policymakers depends on whether they want to accommodate the pressure and allow devaluation or, assuming a tough stance, they prefer to deter it. If the latter is the case, they may increase the short-term interest rate (hence offering a greater return than before on domestic currency investments) or spend international reserves (buying the domestic currency in the foreign exchange market with the aim of supporting its value). An EMP index is designed to capture this kind of activity in the foreign exchange market.

Theoretical Foundations The roots of the EMP index can be found in an analysis of demand and supply of national currencies in Girton and Roper (1977), where the term *exchange market pressure* was first used. A monetary model of the balance of payments is derived in which changes in the exchange rate and real international reserves for a small open economy are a function of changes in domestic credit expansion and real income, the money base and real income of a center currency country, as well as the inflation differential and the uncovered interest differential.

The widespread effects of the crises in the 1980s and the early 1990s highlighted the need to explain and predict such incidents. Girton and Roper's model provided the necessary insight for finding a solution to the problem of how to measure pressure

in the foreign exchange market. Whereas changes in the exchange rate can be easily used to capture the effects of a successful speculative attack, they cannot identify instances where in spite of speculative pressure being present no significant loss in the value of the currency has taken place. Furthermore, devaluation episodes may be voluntary on the part of policymakers attempting, for example, to boost exports. Clearly, in order to construct meaningful models of crisis prediction, also known as early warning systems, a robust definition of what constitutes a crisis needs to include a measure of international reserves.

Practical Issues The issue arises of how to weight the two variables—exchange rates and reserves—in an index of speculative pressure. One method commonly used is to employ the ratio of the standard deviation (σ) of the two components (Kaminsky and Reinhart 1999):

$$Index = \frac{\Delta e}{e} - \frac{\sigma_e}{\sigma_r}\frac{\Delta r}{r},$$

where $\Delta e/e$ stands for the percentage change in the nominal exchange rate and $\Delta r/r$ stands for the percentage change in the level of international reserves. The negative sign in front of the second term implies that losses in reserves are associated with a higher index value. Another weighting scheme could involve the inverse of the standard deviations. In addition, a third variable, namely, interest rate changes ($\Delta e \neq e$), is sometimes included in the computation. Thus another commonly used EMP index (Eichengreen, Rose, and Wyplosz 1995) is as follows:

$$Index = \alpha\frac{\Delta e}{e} + \beta\frac{\Delta i}{i} - \gamma\frac{\Delta r}{r},$$

where α is the inverse of the standard deviation of the percentage change in exchange rate divided by the sum of the inverses of the standard deviations of all three variables, β is the inverse of the standard deviation of the percentage change in the interest rate divided by the sum of the inverses of the standard deviations of all three variables, and γ is the inverse of the standard deviation of the percentage change in real reserves again divided by the sum of the inverses of the standard deviations of all three variables. This weighting scheme ensures that the most volatile components do not dominate the index. The variables are expressed relative to a reference country.

Advantages and Problems The advantage of EMP indexes over simple measures of exchange rates is that even if the exchange rate does not move in the presence of speculative pressure, the pressure is registered through the policy response of the authorities, which might be an increase in interest rates and/or a reduction in reserve levels. Very often the indexes are converted into a discrete binary variable so that observations can be classified as either crisis or noncrisis. It is commonplace to allocate a one whenever a value of the index exceeds the mean of the index by three standard deviations. Otherwise, a zero is allocated. It needs to be noted that the definition of a critical threshold for classifying an observation as crisis is rather arbitrary; as a result, a wide range of critical thresholds has been used in the literature.

The identification of crisis episodes is also sensitive to other factors, for instance, sample selection and data frequency. Extending a given sample by, say, incorporating a period of excess volatility will push the critical threshold up (as a result of a higher standard deviation in the sample), which may lead to different results: observations that were characterized as crisis in the original sample may now turn into noncrisis observations. The frequency of the dataset used in the construction of the index is also of importance, as crises in the foreign exchange market can be short lived, with exchange rates, interest rates, and reserves assuming their precrisis values soon after an episode. It may be the case that if an annual frequency is selected, crisis incidents may be missed. Higher frequency data increase the likelihood of spotting a crisis but these are not always readily available for all the components of the index, especially data on interest rates. A further issue relates to the fact that different exchange rate regimes may be in place over the time span of the index (de jure or de facto). This can have implications for the index. For example, the switch from a fixed regime to a flexible one may be followed by a sustained depreciation of the domestic currency, with the index failing to readily convey this information (due to the lower variability in the interest rate and reserves changes).

Overall, despite their deficiencies, EMP indexes have been widely used in the context of early warning systems to inform policymaking. The absence of components relating to capital controls and exchange rate regimes implies that they should be used in conjunction with relevant information about the implementation of the prevailing exchange rate policies.

See also balance of payments; capital controls; contagion; currency crisis; early warning systems; European Monetary Union; exchange rate regimes; exchange rate volatility; foreign exchange intervention; interest parity conditions; international reserves; monetary conditions index; money supply; speculation; spillovers; sterilization

FURTHER READING

Eichengreen, Barry, Andrew Rose, and Charles Wyplosz. 1995. "Exchange Market Mayhem: The Antecedents and Aftermath of Speculative Attacks." *Economic Policy* 21: 251–98. Interest rates are incorporated for the first time in the definition of the foreign EMP index.

Girton, Lance, and Don Roper. 1977. "A Monetary Approach of Exchange Market Pressure Applied to the Postwar Canadian Experience." *American Economic Review* 67(4): 537–48. Laid the theoretical foundations for the construction of EMP indexes.

Kaminsky, Graciela L., and Carmen M. Reinhart. 1999. "The Twin Crises: The Causes of Banking and Balance-of-Payments Problems." *American Economic Review* 89 (3): 473-500. Uses a measure of EMP in order to assess an early warning system.

ALEX MANDILARAS

■ **exchange-rate-based stabilization**
See discipline

■ **exchange rate forecasting**
While exchange rate changes can lead to significant gains or losses to private entities involved in international transactions, from a macroeconomic perspective they can also have important impacts

on inflation and output growth. Exchange rate determination has therefore been a topic much researched by central banks and financial markets. Two broad methods of exchange rate determination—fundamental analysis and nonstructural analysis—have been used by economists. Based on the evidence, however, it appears that no single model can forecast exchange rates for all currencies or at all times.

Fundamental Analysis Since the mid-1980s, a multitude of fundamentals-based models have been used to assess the predictability of exchange rates. The host of fundamentals-based or structural exchange rate models includes monetary models, portfolio balance models, behavioral (fundamental) equilibrium exchange rate models, productivity differential models, the interest rate parity equation, and the purchasing power parity specification. One general observation is that there is no consistent evidence of a complex structural model outperforming a simpler one.

For economists, the monetary model, of which money market equilibrium is an important component, has been the workhorse model of exchange rate determination. In their seminal work, however, economists Richard Meese and Kenneth Rogoff (1983) forcefully show that forecasts from the monetary model do not outperform the naïve forecast from a random model that uses current exchange rates to predict future exchange rates. The result has largely withstood the challenge of sophisticated exchange rate models and elaborate econometric techniques developed after its publication. Consequently, the Meese and Rogoff study has greatly shaped the subsequent empirical studies on forecasting exchange rates.

More recent empirical work rejuvenates the monetary model by showing that its forecasting performance can beat the random walk's over long horizons (Mark 1995). The intuition is that, despite its large short-term volatility, an exchange rate's long-run value is determined by economic fundamentals (also see Chinn and Meese 1995). These long-horizon results are, nonetheless, not that persuasive once they are subjected to close scrutiny. Besides the choice of sample periods and the method of con-

structing fundamental values, an issue is the interaction between short- and long-horizon forecasts. If long-horizon forecasts are constructed from a sequence of short-horizon forecasts, then the performance of these two types of forecasts should be linked (Berkowitz and Giorgianni 2001). Further, forecasting into the distant future usually involves a high level of uncertainty. These considerations plus some more recent studies cast doubts on the results that long-horizon forecasts from structural exchange rate models are better than those from a random walk.

Despite some setbacks, long-horizon forecasts are still the focus of some foreign exchange forecast exercises. Efforts to revive the monetary model's forecast ability include the uses of long history data, panel data, nonlinear dynamics, and nonparametric techniques. Notwithstanding all of these efforts, an extensive study shows that, despite some evidence of forecast superiority, it is difficult to find a fundamentals-based exchange rate model outperforming a random walk specification for all the sample periods, evaluation criteria, and currencies under consideration (Cheung, Chinn, and Pascual 2005).

Nonstructural Analysis Given the dismal performance of structural exchange rate models, researchers have explored the forecasting ability of nonstructural time series models. Various time series techniques have been used to model exchange rate behavior. Some common ones are standard autoregression-moving-average models, vector autoregression models, vector error correction models, fractional integration models, threshold autoregression models, Markov switching models, and nonparametric models. Again, there are reservations about the positive results of using a time series model to forecast exchange rates.

Technical analysis that relies on price patterns is also commonly used to forecast exchange rates. Technical analysis uses a range of tools from the relatively simplistic moving average rules to complicated neural network–based techniques. Despite the skeptics in academia, technical analysis is quite popular among professional foreign exchange traders (Cheung and Wong 2000). The performance of technical analysis has been quite unstable over time, however, and there has been a debate on whether the observed profits from technical analysis are compensations for trading risk or excess (abnormal) returns (Menkhoff and Taylor 2006).

Summing Up Since Meese and Rogoff reported the failure to beat the forecast performance of a random walk, there have been serious efforts to determine the predictability of exchange rates. Sophisticated exchange rate models—both structural and nonstructural—and refined econometric techniques have been developed to challenge the random walk forecast. In the process of finding the real contender, various reasons have been offered to explain the difficulty in forecasting exchange rates. The most commonly cited reasons include the time-varying relationship between exchange rates and their fundamentals, bad data quality, and incorrect model specification.

With the intense investigation since the mid-1980s, we are still waiting for convincing evidence that an exchange rate model can consistently outperform the random walk. In sum, exchange rate forecasting is still an elusive exercise, and the extant evidence confirms the adage that no single model can forecast exchange rates for all currencies or at all times.

See also balance of payments; equilibrium exchange rate; exchange rate volatility; interest parity conditions; purchasing power parity; real exchange rate

FURTHER READING

Berkowitz, J., and L. Giorgianni. 2001. "Long-Horizon Exchange Rate Predictability?" *Review of Economics and Statistics* 83: 81–91. Raised reservations about the reported positive performance of long-horizon forecasts.

Cheung, Y.-W., M. D. Chinn, and A. Garcia Pascual. 2005. "Empirical Exchange Rate Models of the Nineties: Are Any Fit to Survive?" *Journal of International Money and Finance* 24: 1150–75. Reported the difficulty of finding a model outperforming a random walk across currencies, forecasting periods, forecasting horizons, and evaluation criteria.

Cheung, Y.-W., and C. Y.-P. Wong. 2000. "A Survey of Market Practitioners' Views on Exchange Rate Dynamics." *Journal of International Economics* 51: 401–19.

One of a few survey papers that documents, among other things, the popularity of technical analysis among foreign exchange traders.

Chinn, M. D., and R. A. Meese. 1995. "Banking on Currency Forecasts: How Predictable Is Change in Money?" *Journal of International Economics* 38: 161–78. Showed that long-horizon forecasts from structural models can beat a random walk.

Engel, C., and J. Hamilton. 1990. "Long Swings in the Exchange Rate: Are They in the Data and Do Markets Know It?" *American Economic Review* 80: 689–713. Its result of a Markov model beating a random walk was called into question a few years later.

Mark, N. 1995. "Exchange Rates and Fundamentals: Evidence on Long Horizon Predictability." *American Economic Review* 85: 201–18. A noted exercise that, among other things, popularizes the examination of long-horizon forecasts.

Meese, R., and K. Rogoff. 1983. "Empirical Exchange Rate Models of the Seventies: Do They Fit Out of Sample?" *Journal of International Economics* 14: 3–24. Reported the difficulty in beating the forecast performance of a random walk.

Menkhoff, L., and L. P. Taylor. 2006. "The Obstinate Passion of Foreign Exchange Professionals: Technical Analysis." University of Warwick Working Paper. Warwick, UK. Surveyed the issues related to the use of technical analysis in foreign exchange markets.

YIN-WONG CHEUNG

■ exchange rate pass-through

Exchange rate pass-through can be defined as the degree of sensitivity of import prices to a one percent change in exchange rates in the importing nation's currency. A closely related term is *pricing to market*, which refers to the pricing behavior of firms exporting their products to a destination market following an exchange rate change. More to the point, *pricing to market* is defined as the percentage change in prices in the exporter's currency due to a one percent change in the exchange rate. Thus the greater the degree of pricing to market, the lower the extent of exchange rate pass-through.

At one extreme, if import prices change by the same proportion as the change in the exchange rate, the result is full or complete pass-through and hence no pricing to market. At the other extreme, if exporters adjust prices in their own currency by the same proportion as the exchange rate change but in the opposite direction, the result is full pricing to market but no or zero pass-through of the exchange rate change to the destination market prices. More generally, if exporters alter the export prices in their own currency by a proportion smaller than the exchange rate change, then exchange rate pass-through is said to be partial or incomplete.

The degree of exchange rate pass-through and pricing-to-market behavior has important bearings on economic policy. If pricing to market is high and exchange rate pass-through low, then any exchange-rate-based adjustments to improve the trade balance for economies may be ineffective, as nominal exchange rate changes do not translate into real exchange rate changes.

Although these concepts have been well known to economists for a long time, they attracted particular interest following the Plaza Accord in 1985 and the subsequent sharp appreciation of the Japanese yen in relation to the U.S. dollar. Following this strengthening of the yen, other things being equal, one would have expected the unit price of Japanese products sold in the United States (in U.S. dollars) to have risen sharply. In reality, however, the price of Japanese cars and electronic items sold in the United States rose only marginally or remained constant, and in some cases actually declined (Goldberg and Knetter 1997). This suggested that the Japanese firms exporting products to the United States may have been absorbing a large part of the exchange rate changes in order to maintain market share. Given this important empirical observation, economists began trying to estimate the extent of exchange rate pass-through, as well as to analyze the determinants of exchange rate pass-through and the corresponding pricing-to-market behavior.

What Determines Exchange Rate Pass-Through? Among the most important factors that determine the extent of exchange rate pass-through are the size of the export market and the degree of competition the exporter faces in that market. If the export market for the product is large, then exporting firms are often willing to absorb a proportion of the exchange rate change so as not to lose market share. This is particularly true if the industry is highly competitive. The presence of a large number of suppliers selling similar goods in the market provides domestic consumers with a choice of many substitutes, making them relatively price sensitive. Conversely, if the industry is highly differentiated and exporters do not face much competition for their products, then exporter prices may be somewhat less responsive to exchange rate changes. In this situation, pricing to market will be lower and the corresponding pass-through will be higher. For example, exports to certain competitive industries in the United States, such as autos and alcoholic beverages, show relatively high pricing to market and corresponding lower exchange rate pass-through as exporters try to preserve market share (Knetter 1993).

The direction, duration, and magnitude of exchange rate changes also affect pass-through. If the currency of the destination market depreciates, then exporters may be willing to absorb this exchange rate change in order to keep local currency prices of their products stable and retain market share. In this situation, exchange rate pass-through may be low or incomplete. If the currency of the destination market strengthens, however, the exporter's product will be relatively cheaper and the exporting firm may engage in complete exchange rate pass-through. In other words, the response of exporters to exchange rate changes may be asymmetric, depending on whether the currency rate appreciates or depreciates.

The high costs of changing prices, as well as the possibility that frequent changes in unit sales prices (in the destination market's currency) can adversely affect a firm's reputation, may prevent firms from passing through temporary fluctuations in exchange rates. When exchange rate changes are large or appear to be permanent, however, exporting firms are more likely to pass through the changes to avoid a sharp reduction in their profit margins.

Low and Declining Exchange Rate Pass-Through Exchange rate pass-through generally has a greater effect on import prices than on a nation's consumer price index. This is because the latter includes nontradables that are less responsive to exchange rate changes. Regardless of the price index used, however, exchange rate pass-through was lower in the 1990s than in the 1980s, and has continued to decline. Although most of the research has focused on developed countries, where more data are available, some studies suggest that the conclusion holds for developing countries as well (Ghosh and Rajan 2006).

Exchange rate pass-through may also depend on a country's monetary and exchange rate policies. The more stable a country's monetary policy and the lower its rate of inflation, the lower the extent of exchange rate pass-through will be, as it is less likely that foreign exporters will pass through exchange rate changes (Taylor 2000). This in turn helps to sustain low inflation and makes monetary policy more effective. Thus there may be a "virtuous cycle" between stable monetary policy and low exchange rate pass-through.

If exports are invoiced in the currency of the importing nation—known as consumer-currency pricing or local-currency pricing—then exchange rate changes have little effect on the destination market import prices, which leads to low exchange rate pass-through. On the other hand, if exports are invoiced in the currency of the exporters—referred to as producer-currency pricing—then exchange rate changes have a greater effect on prices in the importing nation, leading to higher pass-through. It has been argued that if exporters set their prices in the currency of the country that has the more stable monetary policy (i.e., local-currency pricing as opposed to producer-currency pricing), then exchange rate pass-through into import prices in local currency terms will be correspondingly low (Devereux and Engel 2001).

In an important paper, the economists Campa and Goldberg (2005) test the significance of changes in macroeconomic variables and the extent of exchange rate pass-through into aggregate import prices for 25 industrial nations for the period 1975–99. The authors find that the lower the average rate of inflation and the less variable the exchange rate, the lower the corresponding extent of exchange rate pass-through will be. These macroeconomic factors play a minor role in explaining the low exchange rate pass-through, however, compared to the changing composition of a nation's imports away from raw materials and energy imports toward manufactured imports. This changing composition of the basket of imports toward manufacturing goods (which tend to be characterized as being more competitive industries) may be behind the low and declining rates of exchange rate pass-through.

Another factor that may have affected the extent of pass-through is cross-border "production fragmentation," which refers to the dispersion of the production process among different countries. A country might export the final product but at the same time import the corresponding parts and components from another nation. A depreciation of the currency of the nation exporting the final good makes its imported components more expensive. Therefore, an exchange rate change affects the exporter's costs, which leads the exporting firm to raise its price denominated in its own currency, and subsequently pass through less of the exchange rate changes into the partner nation's currency denominated prices. Moreover, with dispersion of production processes, often more than one nation supplies parts and components, thereby increasing competition and lowering exchange rate pass-through (Ghosh and Rajan 2006).

Policy Relevance The low exchange rate pass-through in the United States may explain the persistence of the U.S. trade deficit despite declines in the U.S. dollar. Conversely, low exchange rate pass-through implies that economies may be less concerned about the potential inflationary consequences of exchange rate fluctuations. Although the extent of exchange rate pass-through has important macroeconomic implications, it is predominantly a microeconomic phenomenon and depends significantly on the types of goods being traded.

See also expenditure changing and expenditure switching; fragmentation; New Open Economy Macroeconomics; nontraded goods; Plaza Accord; real exchange rate

FURTHER READING

Campa, J. M., and L. S. Goldberg. 2005. "Exchange Rate Pass Through into Import Prices." *Review of Economics and Statistics* 87 (4): 679–60. This widely cited paper tries to empirically determine the reasons behind the low and declining exchange rate pass-through.

Devereux, M., and C. Engel. 2001. "Endogenous Currency of Price Setting in a Dynamic Open Economy Model." NBER Working Paper No. 8559. Cambridge, MA: National Bureau of Economic Research. Discusses how currency invoicing affects exchange rate pass-through.

Ghosh, A., and R. S. Rajan. 2006. "A Survey of Exchange Rate Pass-Through in Asia" *Asian Pacific Economic Literature* 21 (2): 13–28. An up-to-date review of empirical studies on exchange rate pass-through in various Asian economies.

Goldberg, P. K., and M. M. Knetter. 1997. "Goods Prices and Exchange Rates: What Have We Learned?" *Journal of Economic Literature* 35 (3): 1243–72. A useful and much cited literature review on the exchange rate pass-through with particular reference to the United States.

Knetter, M. M. 1993. "International Comparisons of Pricing-to-Market Behavior." *American Economic Review* 83 (3): 473–86. One of the earliest papers introducing the concept of pricing to market.

Taylor, J. B. 2000. "Low Inflation, Pass Through, and the Pricing Power of Firms." *European Economic Review* 44 (7): 1389–1408. The pioneering study linking stable monetary policy with the low and declining exchange rate pass-through in industrial countries.

AMIT GHOSH AND RAMKISHEN S. RAJAN

■ exchange rate regimes

The exchange rate regime is the characterization of the way a government manages its national currency in the foreign exchange market. The different forms of exchange rate regimes relate to how actively the government manages the foreign exchange rate, and how its actions are supported by institutional arrangements. At one end of the spectrum is an independently floating currency; at the other, a fixed exchange rate system, sometimes referred to as a "hard peg." Many varieties of exchange rate regimes exist between these two poles.

Floating Rate Regimes With an independent floating exchange rate regime the exchange rate is market determined and there is no explicit exchange rate target level or institutional commitment to influence the path of exchange rates. The purest form of independent floating is the "free float," in which the government neither intervenes in the foreign exchange market (buying or selling foreign currency from international reserves) nor directs monetary, fiscal, or regulatory policies to an explicit exchange rate objective. In free float regimes, the government allows the market-determined exchange rate to prevail and does not attempt to influence its value. Instead, the government directs macroeconomic policy entirely toward domestic stabilization objectives such as output and inflation levels.

Few countries follow purely free floats; even those that are independently floating occasionally intervene in foreign exchange markets and take into account the value of the exchange rate in making macroeconomic policy decisions. The countries with regimes most closely approaching pure free floats are the United States and the euro area (European countries that share the euro as a common currency). The United States has intervened in the foreign exchange market on only a few occasions since the mid-1990s with the objective of countering "disorderly" market conditions. The Federal Reserve System also puts little weight on exchange rates in its policy deliberations. Similarly, the European Central Bank has intervened in the foreign exchange market only a few times since the introduction of the euro in 1999 (Fatum and Hutchison 2002).

Other countries with independently but not freely floating regimes include Japan, Canada, New Zealand, Sweden, and many more. Countries that follow independent floats intervene in foreign exchange markets occasionally and at times quite heavily, but have no explicit exchange rate target level. Japan, for example, intervened to an unprecedented degree in 2003 and 2004, buying more than $300 billion in the foreign exchange market in an attempt to support the value of the U.S. dollar exchange rate against the yen (Fatum and Hutchison 2006).

Closely related to independently floating systems are "managed floating" exchange rate regimes. In these cases, the exchange rate is again largely market determined, with official foreign exchange market intervention aimed at slowing exchange rate movements or reducing volatility but without having a specific exchange rate path or target. These countries tend to undertake more active interventions in foreign exchange markets than independent floaters, with indicators for managing the rate being broadly judgmental (e.g., balance of payments position, international reserves, parallel market developments), and adjustments may not be automatic. In managed floating cases, however, the exchange rate is typically a secondary policy target with little constraint placed on the conduct of domestic monetary or fiscal policy. The International Monetary Fund (IMF) characterized 53 exchange rate regimes at the end of 2005 as "managed floating, with no predetermined path for the exchange rate." Most developing and emerging market economies fall within the managed floating group. Examples include the Czech Republic, Paraguay, and Indonesia.

National Legal Tender, Monetary Unions, and Currency Boards A "fixed" exchange rate regime is at the opposite end of the spectrum from an independent floating regime. In a fixed exchange rate system, the government is committed to maintaining a particular exchange rate value and pegs this rate by a combination of official foreign exchange market intervention, macroeconomic policies, and institutional arrangements such as international capital controls. The "hardest," or most durable and credible, exchange rate peg is supported by strong institutional arrangements, either by stringent controls on the flows of financial capital into and out of the country, when the country enters into a currency board arrangement, or when the national currency is replaced with a foreign currency ("dollarization").

Dollarization refers to a country's choice to circulate the currency of another country as its sole legal tender, without a separate national currency. The term *dollarization* does not necessarily refer to the

U.S. dollar; it is a generic term for any national currency that is the legal tender in a foreign country. Ecuador "dollarized" after currency turmoil, and the U.S. dollar has been in circulation in Panama for many years. Many small island nations are dollarized because it would be impractical for them to have independent national currencies. The IMF classified 29 countries (excepting members of the European Monetary Union) in the group "exchange rate arrangements with no separate legal tender" at the end of 2005. Dollarized countries have no control over the exchange rate, and typically little or no control over domestic monetary policy, since interest rates are largely determined abroad.

Countries that belong to monetary or currency unions have a legal tender that is shared by members of the union. As of 2006, 12 European countries had given up their national currencies since 1999, adopting the euro as a common currency. Previously separate (except in the case of Belgium and Luxembourg) national legal tenders have been replaced by one currency and one exchange rate, which is independently floating. Monetary unions have a common monetary and exchange rate policy. In the case of the euro, monetary policy is run by the European Central Bank (ECB) in Frankfurt. Unlike dollarized countries, however, countries in modern monetary unions participate in the exchange rate and monetary policy deliberations for their shared currency. The ECB has a decision-making structure representing all of the European Monetary Union (EMU) countries.

The "hardest" and most credible of the pegged rate systems (considering arrangements with no separate legal tender as a special case) is the currency board regime. Under this arrangement, all of the national currency in circulation is backed by the government's holding of foreign currency reserves, and the government stands ready to buy or sell as much foreign currency as necessary to maintain the exchange rate value. Currency boards are based on an explicit legislative commitment to exchange domestic currency for foreign currency at a fixed exchange rate. To enable the central bank to make this commitment, the board imposes restrictions on the issuance of domestic currency: new issuance of national legal tender is contingent on an inflow of foreign exchange reserves. The government has little or no control over monetary policy or short-term interest rates in a currency board institutional setting. The Hong Kong Special Administrative Region, China, has a long-standing currency board arrangement. Estonia, Lithuania, and several other countries also have currency board arrangements.

Pegged Exchange Rate Arrangements Pegged exchange regimes may take a variety of forms, including fixed peg arrangements, pegged rates in horizontal bands (e.g., the Danish krone vis-à-vis the euro), crawling pegs (e.g., Turkey), rates within crawling bands (e.g., Hungary, Israel, and Venezuela), and other fixed pegs (e.g., China, Egypt, and Malaysia). In a conventional fixed peg regime, the authorities attempt to maintain the value of the exchange rate within a narrow band (usually plus or minus 1 percent) around a central parity (or reference value) exchange rate. The authorities commit to intervene by buying and selling foreign exchange reserves, sometimes in cooperative arrangements with other central banks, or to adjust interest rates and other policies to maintain the exchange rate within the band. There is no legal or institutional commitment to maintain the central parity exchange rate irrevocably, and occasional adjustments to the central parity may occur. The central parity referenced exchange rate may be a single currency, a cooperative arrangement, or a currency composite. In the absence of capital controls, there is very limited monetary autonomy with a fixed rate peg, as foreign exchange interventions, and often interest rate changes, are necessary to maintain the value of the currency within a narrow range. Forty-five countries followed a fixed peg arrangement at the end of 2005, reflecting a wide range in level of development and geographic distribution. Examples include China, Malaysia, Nepal, and Saudi Arabia.

A pegged rate within horizontal bands is similar to a fixed peg but with more flexibility of the exchange rate around the central parity, typically plus or minus 2 percent. The wider band, compared to the fixed peg regime, allows somewhat greater monetary policy discretion. In general, the broader the band width, the greater the degree of monetary policy independence—in principle, monetary policy discretion is possible until the limits of the band are reached. As in the case of conventional fixed pegs, reference may be made to a single currency, a cooperative arrangement, or a currency composite. Target zones, such as the former exchange rate mechanism (ERM) of the European Monetary System, are a form of pegged rates within a horizontal band. Only six countries followed a pegged rate within horizontal band arrangement at the end of 2005, four of which were in the context of the ERM II arrangement with the EMU (Cyprus, Denmark, the Slovak Republic, and Slovenia).

Two other common forms of pegged exchange rate regime are the crawling peg and crawling band systems. The crawling peg refers to a case in which the currency is adjusted periodically in small amounts, either at a fixed increment or in response to indicators such as domestic inflation relative to trading partners or perhaps to expected future inflation differentials. Maintaining a crawling peg imposes constraints on monetary policy in a manner similar to a fixed peg system. Similarly, the crawling band regime maintains the currency within a band but adjusts the central reference rate or margins periodically in response to quantitative indicators.

Exchange Rate Regimes, Monetary Policy, and International Capital Controls One key feature distinguishing exchange rate regimes is the extent to which they constrain the conduct of monetary policy. Generally speaking, the greater the fixity of the exchange rate, the less room there is for monetary autonomy. On one side of the spectrum is an independently floating exchange rate, in which conduct of domestic monetary policy is under little constraint. On the other side of the spectrum is a currency board arrangement or a country that has no separate national legal tender. In these latter two cases, there is little or no room for independent monetary policy. If there is no separate legal tender, there is no national money and therefore no national monetary policy. In the currency board arrangement, changes in monetary policy follow the balance of payments and the rise and fall of official international reserves. Capital outflows that result in a decline of international reserves automatically trigger a contraction of the money supply, and the opposite is the case for capital inflows.

As the exchange rate regime moves along the spectrum from hard pegs toward independently floating, monetary authorities in principle have greater control over setting domestic interest rates and the path of monetary policy. The degree of international capital mobility, that is, the legal, institutional, or market-related constraints on the cross-border flow of financial resources, also affects a country's monetary policy. Monetary authorities frequently impose restrictions on capital flows in an attempt to gain more monetary autonomy in the face of constraints imposed, say, by fixed pegged exchange rates. The Bretton Woods system of fixed peg exchange rates (1946–71) lasted several decades because of pervasive capital controls, policies that led to low inflation in the United States, and the willingness of countries pegged to the U.S. dollar to accept limited monetary autonomy. Countries are more willing to give up monetary independence and link with the U.S. dollar if the monetary leadership of the reserve-currency country provides a stable macroeconomic environment.

The economics term *impossible trinity* means that countries cannot simultaneously follow an independent monetary policy, maintain a fixed peg exchange rate regime, and allow unrestricted international capital flows. Countries frequently face a dilemma if their domestic stabilization policy objectives and desired path of monetary policy (level of interest rates, for example) conflict with the monetary policy needed to maintain a pegged exchange rate. In these circumstances the country must abandon its desire to pursue its stabilization objectives, give up the exchange rate peg, or impose capital controls in the hope of gaining some flexibility in reconciling the two other objectives. Exchange rate regime changes frequently occur because of this dilemma, usually because countries cannot constrain monetary and fiscal policy effectively to curtail inflation and balance of payments imbalances. In a system with freely mobile international capital, this policy dilemma is often exacerbated by a sharp capital outflow as domestic asset holders, both foreign and national residents, anticipate devaluation (and associated capital loss on domestic assets) and move to sell the domestic currency before it occurs. In this circumstance, devaluation of the exchange rate is commonplace.

Optimal Exchange Rate Regimes and Regime Collapses A basic question in discussing exchange rate regimes concerns which regime is best suited to the particular circumstances of a given country. This topic is often referred to as "optimal" exchange rate regime choice. Much of the work in this area focuses on the nature of disturbances facing the country, whether they be foreign or domestic in origin, real or monetary, permanent or transitory, combined with the choice made by authorities of a particular systematic approach to intervention in the foreign exchange market or monetary policy rule to influence exchange rate developments (Marston 1985). The exchange rate arrangement must be consistent with the degree of monetary independence and international capital mobility to be sustainable. Traditional theory suggests that an intermediate regime usually is preferable to either a hard peg, such as a currency union or currency board arrangement, or a completely free floating exchange rate. The structure of the economy, the nature of economic disturbances, and the degree of capital mobility are some of the standard criteria in the choice of an exchange rate regime.

The choice of exchange rate regime, however, is more constrained than the traditional view would suggest. Speculative international capital flows can cause regime collapses very quickly, even when current fundamentals appear strong. Concerns about future policy choices, vulnerabilities in the banking sector, and similar factors may start a run on the currency. Self-fulfilling crises are also possible, with a seemingly random speculative attack causing so much economic disruption that the policy authorities may change course entirely, devalue the currency, and end up with higher inflation than otherwise would be the case. Clearly, exchange rate regime sustainability and choice are greatly complicated in an era of integrated financial markets and deregulated capital flows, and in response there has been a tendency for countries to move to one polar case or the other—either hard pegs or independently floating exchange rates.

See also band, basket, and crawl (BBC); Bretton Woods system; capital controls; capital mobility; common currency; currency board arrangement (CBA); currency crisis; currency substitution and dollarization; discipline; equilibrium exchange rate; European Central Bank; European Monetary Union; exchange rate forecasting; exchange rate volatility; Federal Reserve Board; financial crisis; foreign exchange intervention; hot money and sudden stops; impossible trinity; inflation targeting; International Monetary Fund (IMF); international reserves; monetary conditions index; purchasing power parity; real exchange rate; sterilization

FURTHER READING

Eichengreen, Barry, and Charles Wyplosz. 1993. "The Unstable EMS." *Brookings Papers on Economic Activity* 1. Washington, DC: Brookings Institution. Investigates the 1992 EMS crisis, offering four explanations and emphasizing the constraints of the "impossible trinity" on capital flows, fixed exchange rates, and monetary policy.

Fatum, Rasmus, and Michael Hutchison. 2002. "ECB Foreign Exchange Intervention and the Euro: Institutional Framework, News, and Intervention." *Open Economies Review* 13 (4) (October): 412–25. Explains the foreign exchange market policy of the newly established European Central Bank and the effect of reported intervention on the euro exchange rate.

———. 2006. "Effectiveness of Official Daily Foreign Exchange Market Intervention Operations in Japan." *Journal of International Money and Finance* 25: 199–219. Measures the effectiveness of large-scale intervention operations by the Bank of Japan using an event study approach with daily data.

Fischer, Stanley. 2001. "Exchange Rate Regimes: Is the Bipolar View Correct?" *Journal of Economic Perspectives* 15 (2) (spring): 3–24. Presents a broad survey of the history and theory of exchange rate regime failures and explores whether hard currency pegs or flexible rates are

the only practical alternatives for exchange rate regime choice.

International Monetary Fund. 2006. "De Facto Classification of Exchange Rate Regimes and Monetary Policy Framework, as of December 31, 2005." Downloadable from http://www.imf.org/external/np/mfd/er/index.asp. Presents data on the classification of exchange rate regimes and monetary policy frameworks for IMF member countries.

Krugman, Paul. 1979. "A Model of Balance-of-Payments Crises." *Journal of Money, Credit, and Banking* (August): 311–25. A classic, which shows how fundamental macroeconomic imbalances lead to predicable runs on central bank reserves.

Marston, Richard C. 1985. "Stabilization Policies." In *Handbook of International Economics*, vol. 2, edited by R. W. Jones, P. B. Kenen, G. M. Grossman, and K. Rogoff. Amsterdam: Elsevier, 859–916. A survey of macroeconomic policies in open economies with a section on the optimal exchange rate regime choice as a function of underlying disturbances, structure of the economy, and policy objective function.

Obstfeld, Maurice. 1996. "Models of Currency Crisis with Self-Fulfilling Features." *European Economic Review* 40 (April): 1037–47. A classic contribution demonstrating that currency crises may be associated with self-fulfilling speculative attacks and showing the existence of multiple equilibrium exchange rates when the policy authorities and private sector behave strategically.

MICHAEL M. HUTCHISON

■ exchange rate volatility

One of the key facts in international finance is that when exchange rates are flexible they are also highly volatile. Such volatility manifests itself in two key ways: inter- and intraregime volatility. *Intraregime volatility* refers to the volatility of exchange rates in floating exchange rate regimes relative to the volatility of macroeconomic fundamentals such as money supplies, interest rates, and output levels. A common, although by no means universal, belief is that exchange rates are excessively volatile compared to macroeconomic fundamentals. *Interregime vola-*

tility refers to the behavior of real and nominal exchange rates in the move from fixed to floating exchange rates: as a country moves from fixed to floating exchange rates the volatility of standard macroeconomic fundamentals remains unchanged, but the volatility of both real and nominal exchange rates increases dramatically. The key question that arises from this kind of regime-dependent behavior is: Can such exchange rate behavior be explained in a manner consistent with a macroeconomic framework (that is, using a model that relies on macroeconomic fundamentals such as money supplies), or does such a framework have to be abandoned and an alternative framework, such as a market microstructure approach, be adopted?

The first part of this entry analyzes the issue of intraregime volatility and, specifically, different explanations for the volatility result. All the explanations rely on some variant of the monetary model of the exchange rate. The second part of the entry focuses on interregime volatility, starting with empirical evidence and then considering some theoretical explanations for this phenomenon.

Intraregime Volatility: Monetary Model In trying to explain intraregime volatility in terms of macroeconomic fundamentals, the monetary model of the exchange rate has become something of a workhorse. In essence this model posits that exchange rates are determined by the interaction of money supply (usually assumed to be exogenous, i.e., predetermined by the central bank) and money demand (which is a function of interest rates and income levels) terms between the home country and its trading partners. Other things being equal, an increase in the home money supply leads to a proportionate depreciation in the exchange rate.

In the flexible price version of the monetary model, exchange rate volatility is explained in terms of a "magnification effect" that arises because of the link in the model between the current (spot) exchange rate and the future expected exchange rate (Bilson 1978). The model may be written simply as:

$$s_t = f_t + E_t s_{t+1}, \qquad (1)$$

where s_t denotes the nominal exchange rate, f_t is a composite fundamental comprising home and for-

eign money supplies and income terms (suitably weighted with income elasticities), and $E_t s_{t+1}$ is the expected exchange rate in period t+1. The expected exchange rate in each future period of the life of the underlying asset (money) is determined by expected money supplies and expected income levels and so the current spot exchange rate in this model becomes a function of current fundamentals (money and income)—in other words, period-t variables—and the expected fundamentals in all future periods. More formally, the current spot price is the present discounted value of all expected fundamentals. To the extent that a current change in the money supply signals to agents an expected increase in future period fundamentals, this can cause the exchange rate to move by more than the current change in the period-t fundamentals, f_t. By simply observing the current exchange rate and the current change in fundamentals, a magnified response of the former with respect to the latter will be seen. This is the so-called magnification effect.

The monetary model has also been used to demonstrate the implications that speculative bubbles or, more generally, any nonfundamental factor can have for exchange rate volatility. A speculative bubble or nonfundamental factor can be added to equation (1) as:

$$s_t = f_t + E_t s_{t+1} + b_t, \qquad (2)$$

where b_t represents a speculative bubble term and can impart exchange rate volatility over and above that generated by the macroeconomic fundamentals. The speculative bubble can be a rational bubble, which means it is consistent with the underlying model (i.e., equation 1), or nonrational and therefore not necessarily consistent with any model. The introduction of a speculative term into the monetary model can generate excessive volatility of the exchange rate with respect to the fundamentals (see MacDonald 2007).

Intraregime Volatility: Dornbusch Overshooting Model Perhaps one of the best-known explanations for intraregime volatility is the seminal overshooting model of the economist Dornbusch (1976). This model is also in the monetary class, but assumes that consumer prices are sticky in the short run (although flexible in the long run) while asset prices and yields (the exchange rate and interest rates) are continuously flexible. In the short run, income is assumed to be fixed. In this context, an increase in the domestic money supply upsets money market equilibrium and leads to a proportional depreciation of the long-run, or equilibrium, price level and exchange rate (which are flexible). In the short run, however, or in the immediate aftermath of the money supply increase, equilibrium can be restored only by a change in the interest rate (since the price level and income are held constant by assumption). But in a world of high, or complete, capital mobility the domestic interest rate is tied into the foreign rate through the uncovered interest rate parity condition and can change only if the expected change in the exchange rate is assumed to be nonzero.

The expected change in the exchange rate is, however, nonzero in the overshooting model because it is governed by a regressive expectations mechanism: a current depreciation of the exchange rate relative to its equilibrium, or long-run, value is expected to be reversed in the future. In other words, a current depreciation of the exchange rate produces the expectation of a future appreciation. So, in response to the increase in the money supply, what is required is the current exchange rate to move more than proportionally to the long-run, or equilibrium, exchange rate value (which moves in proportion to the increase in the money supply) to allow the domestic interest rate to fall below the world level: the exchange rate overshoots its long-run value and, by implication, the current change in the money supply. As in the magnification story, the current exchange rate is more volatile than current fundamentals. The extent of the overshooting is governed by how sensitive interest rates are to money supply changes (the less sensitive, the more the exchange rate will move) and the sensitivity of the expected change in the exchange rate with respect to the gap between the current and equilibrium exchange rates.

Intraregime Volatility: NOEM The variant of the monetary model used to derive both the magnification and overshooting results is regarded as ad hoc, in the sense that it is not based on an explicit microfoundations approach—that is, the starting point is not an explicit utility function, maximized subject to a budget constraint. Both Stockman (1980) and Lucas (1982), however, present variants of the monetary model founded on an explicitly optimizing framework in which agents maximize utility subject to a budget constraint and a cash-in-advance constraint. In this model the current exchange rate is, as in the ad hoc approach, a function of relative money supplies and output levels and also the ratio of home to foreign marginal utility. In this context exchange rate volatility with respect to current information (in this case, period-t relative prices) arises because both preference and technology shocks—real shocks—are highly volatile. More recent explanations for exchange rate volatility using an optimizing approach have exploited the New Open Economy Macroeconomics (NOEM) model of Obstfeld and Rogoff (1995) and we now provide a brief summary of these explanations.

By introducing uncertainty into the basic NOEM, Obstfeld and Rogoff (2000) generate a variant of the forward-looking monetary model in which a "level" risk premium term features. There are two key insights here. First, the risk premium can affect the level of the exchange rate, and not just the predictable excess return, which has been studied extensively in the literature (see, e.g., MacDonald 2007). This is important because it means that higher moments of economic variables can affect the volatility of the exchange rate and not just the first moment—if the forward risk premium is quite volatile, this could have important implications for exchange rate volatility. Second, the effect of the risk premium on the exchange rate may potentially be very large in this model because it enters the forward-looking model with a scaling factor that puts a large weight on the premium.

In the Obstfeld and Rogoff (2000) model a rise in the level of home monetary variability leads to a fall in both the level exchange risk premium and the forward exchange rate risk premium, and, given plausible values of the scaling factor, imparts an exchange rate appreciation and considerable exchange rate volatility. The appreciation of the exchange rate and fall in the risk premium are contrary to the standard intuition for the effect of increased monetary variability in which the common casual presumption is that financial markets attach a positive risk premium to the currency of a country with high monetary volatility. The effect is different in this model because in the sticky price variant, positive monetary shocks lead to increases in global consumption, which means that domestic money can be a hedge, in real terms, against shocks to consumption. Furthermore, higher monetary variability raises the expectation of the future real value of money (other things being equal) which is the convexity term (this effect also works in a flexible price model).

A further attempt to explain the excess volatility of exchange rates using a variant of the NOEM is made by Devereux and Engel (2001). They attempt to shed light on a conjecture of Krugman (1989) that exchange rate volatility is so great because fluctuations in the exchange rate matter so little for the economy. They use a variant of the NOEM in which there is a combination of local-currency pricing, heterogeneity in international price setting and in the distribution of goods (for example, some firms market their products directly in the foreign market and charge a foreign price while some exporters use foreign distributors, charging a price set in the exporter's currency), and crucially, the existence of noise traders (that is, traders who do not base their trades on fundamentals) who impart expectational biases into international financial markets.

Devereux and Engel (2001) demonstrate that in this setup the conditional volatility of the exchange rate depends on the volatility of the fundamentals (which in their case is the volatility in relative money supply terms) and the extent of local-currency pricing. With complete local-currency pricing, the conditional volatility of the exchange rate effectively rises without bound. This is because the combination of local-currency pricing, along with asymmetric distribution of goods and noise trading, implies a degree of exchange rate volatility that is far in excess of the underlying fundamental shocks.

Intraregime Volatility: Foreign Exchange Microstructure All of the foregoing research assumes that expectations are homogeneous. Bacchetta and

Wincoop (2003) build on the idea that the heterogeneity of investors may also be important for an understanding of exchange rate dynamics, however. In particular, they introduce two types of investor heterogeneity that have been associated with order flow into a standard variant of the monetary model. The first type is the heterogeneous information of market participants about future macro fundamentals—a dispersion effect—and the second is heterogeneity due to nonfundamentals. The latter includes noise traders and rational traders who trade for nonspeculative reasons, such as liquidity trades, or trades associated with differential access to private investment opportunities. Bacchetta and Wincoop demonstrate how information heterogeneity produces both a magnification effect on the exchange rate and endogenous persistence of the impact of nonfundamentals on the exchange rate. Using a simulation exercise and plausible parameter values, the authors demonstrate that there is a substantial magnification effect as a result of information dispersion, and a substantial part of this seems to be attributable to the role of higher-order expectations due to the infinite regress.

A number of economists have attempted to gauge the forward-looking monetary model as written in (1) and its speculative bubble variant given in (2) (e.g., see MacDonald and Taylor 1993). The evidence, in general, does not support the magnification story, although this could simply reflect the model specifications used. The research gives some support to the speculative bubbles hypothesis, although such tests could simply be picking up some other extraneous influence on the exchange rate (see, e.g., Engel and West 2004). More favorable empirical evidence has been reported for the overshooting model, while tests of the more recent NOEM variants of the monetary model have not yet begun. So, at best, we can conclude from this empirical evidence that the jury is still out on the validity of the various theoretical explanations for intraregime volatility (see also Arnold, MacDonald, and de Vries 2005).

Interregime Volatility Baxter and Stockman (1989) were the first to examine the variability of output, trade variables, and private and government consumption across the Bretton Woods and post–Bretton Woods experience, and they demonstrated that the behavior of macroeconomic fundamentals does not change in the move from fixed to floating exchange rates but that the behavior of the exchange rate (both real and nominal) does.

Flood and Rose (1995) reexamined the issue of interregime volatility using the monetary model. Specifically, they construct composite *f* terms using standard monetary and income variables and compare the conditional volatility of this term to the conditional volatility of the sum of the exchange rate and the interest differential for the Bretton Woods and post–Bretton Woods periods. The countries studied are the United Kingdom, Canada, France, Germany, Holland, Italy, Japan, and Sweden. The results of Flood and Rose show that the volatility of the exchange rate term increases dramatically as countries move from fixed to floating, but the volatility of the composite fundamental term does not. In their view, the standard monetary fundamentals cannot explain the volatility of exchange rates in the move from fixed to floating exchange rates and attention has to be focused on what does change in the fixed to floating move, namely the market microstructure of the foreign exchange market.

A number of papers have attempted to understand the interregime puzzle without abandoning a macroeconomics-based approach. For example, Duarte (2003) uses a variant of the two-country NOEM model in which asset markets are incomplete and prices are set one period in advance in the buyer's currency (i.e., local-currency pricing) to address the interregime volatility issue. Duarte studies the properties of this model in the context of a simulation exercise in which the utility function is fully specified, along with technology and monetary shocks. This exercise clearly generates a sharp increase in the volatility of the real exchange rate following a switch from fixed to flexible rates, with no similar change in the volatilities of output, consumption, or trade flows. The intuition for this result is quite simple: because prices are set one period ahead in the buyer's currency, allocation decisions are disconnected at the time of impact from unexpected changes in the

nominal exchange rate and so the volatilities of output, consumption, and trade flows are unaffected.

Arnold, MacDonald, and de Vries (2005) argue that to understand interregime volatility issues it is important to introduce distortions (such as trade and capital account restrictions and IMF support), which are likely to be prevalent in fixed rate regimes such as Bretton Woods, into the standard monetary exchange rate equations. Using a variety of measures for the distortion terms, the authors demonstrate that such terms can explain the interregime puzzle.

Reinhart and Rogoff (2002) argue that the interregime puzzle may not be such a puzzle after all. Specifically, they argue that empirical studies such as those of Flood and Rose (1995) and Baxter and Stockman (1989) use the IMF method of classifying an exchange rate regime as fixed or flexible. The de facto situation in the Bretton Woods and post–Bretton Woods eras, however, was in fact very different, with the majority of countries in Bretton Woods having much more flexibility in their exchange rate behavior than that portrayed in the official statistics, and in the floating rate period there is in practice much more evidence of exchange rate fixity than that indicated in the standard classification. Perhaps the neatest explanation for interregime volatility is that when exchange rates are de jure fixed they are often de facto flexible, and when they are flexible they are in practice fixed or quasi-fixed.

See also balance of payments; Bretton Woods system; exchange rate forecasting; exchange rate pass-through; exchange rate regimes; foreign exchange intervention; interest parity conditions; money supply; New Open Economy Macroeconomics; peso problem; quantity theory of money; real exchange rate; speculation; sterilization

FURTHER READING
Arnold, I., R. MacDonald, and C. de Vries. 2005. "Fundamental Volatility Is Regime Specific." Mimeo. University of Glasgow, Scotland. Revisits the evidence on intraregime exchange rate volatility.
Bacchetta, P., and E. van Wincoop. 2003. "Can Information Heterogeneity Explain the Exchange Rate Determination Puzzle?" NBER Working Paper No. 9498. Cambridge, MA: National Bureau of Economic Re-

search. Emphasizes the importance of investor heterogeneity in understanding exchange rate dynamics.

Baxter, M., and A. Stockman. 1989. "Business Cycles and the Exchange-Rate System." *Journal of Monetary Economics* 23: 377–400. Empirically investigates the differences in time-series behavior of output, consumption, trade flows, government consumption spending, and real exchange rates under alternative exchange rate systems.

Bilson, John F. O. 1978. "Rational Expectations and the Exchange Rate." In *The Economics of Exchange Rates: Selected Studies*, edited by Jacob A. Frenkel and Harry G. Johnson. Reading, MA: Addison-Wesley, 75–96. Classic paper on the flexible price version of the monetary model of exchange rate determination.

Devereux, M., and C. Engel. 2001. "Endogenous Currency Price Setting in a Dynamic Open Economy Model." Mimeo. University of Wisconson-Madison. Well-cited paper on the NOEM's rationalization of excess volatility of exchange rates.

Dornbusch, R. 1976. "Expectations and Exchange Rate Dynamics." *Journal of Political Economy* 84: 1161–76. Classic paper on the role of expectations and exchange rate overshooting.

Duarte, M. 2003. "Why Don't Macroeconomic Quantities Respond to Exchange Rate Variability?" *Journal of Monetary Economics* 50: 889–913. Examines why exchange rate movements do not respond to macroeconomic variables.

Engel, C., and K. D. West. 2004. "Accounting for Exchange Rate Variability in Present Value Models When the Discount Factor Is Near One." NBER Working Paper No. 10267. Cambridge, MA: National Bureau of Economic Research. Investigates why nominal exchange rates in low-inflation advanced countries are almost random walks.

Flood, R. P., and A. Rose. 1995. "Fixing Exchange Rates: A Virtual Quest for Fundamentals." *Journal of Monetary Economics* 36: 3–37. Revisits interregime exchange rate volatility.

Krugman, P. 1989. *Exchange Rate Instability*. Cambridge, MA: MIT Press. Highly readable monograph on the extreme volatility of exchange rates in the 1980s.

Lucas, R. E. 1982. "Interest Rates and Currency Prices in a Two-Country World." *Journal of Monetary Economics* 10: 335–60. Presents variants of the monetary model founded on an explicitly optimizing framework.

MacDonald, R. 2007. *Exchange Rate Economics: Theories and Evidence*. London: Taylor Francis. Offers an up-to-date and comprehensive overview of exchange rate measurement and determination.

MacDonald, R., and M. P. Taylor. 1993. "The Monetary Approach." *IMF Staff Papers* 40: 89–107. Reviews the monetary approach to exchange rate determination.

Monacelli, T. 2004. "Into the Mussa Puzzle: Monetary Policy Regimes and the Real Exchange Rate in a Small Open Economy." *Journal of International Economics* 62: 191–217. Revisits the issue of interregime exchange rate volatility.

Obstfeld, M., and K. Rogoff. 1995. "Exchange Rate Dynamics Redux." *Journal of Political Economy* 103: 624–60.

———. 2000. "Risk and Exchange Rates." NBER Working Paper No. 6694. Cambridge, MA: National Bureau of Economic Research. Two well-cited papers on the NOEM's rationalization of excess volatility of exchange rates.

Reinhart, C. M., and K. S. Rogoff. 2002. "The Modern History of Exchange Rate Arrangements: A Reinterpretation." NBER Working Paper No. 8963. Cambridge, MA: National Bureau of Economic Research. Well-cited paper that develops a new system of classifying historical exchange rate regimes.

Stockman, A. 1980. "A Theory of Exchange Rate Determination." *Journal of Political Economy* 103: 673–98. Present variants of the monetary model founded on an explicitly optimizing framework.

RONALD MACDONALD

■ exchange rate weapon

The concept of the *exchange rate weapon* refers to the use of the exchange rate by one state to secure policy change on the part of another. The weapon helps to explain important aspects of the international political economy of monetary relations, such as the behavior of governments and central banks during adjustment conflicts and the distribution of the costs of adjustment among countries. When collective management of the adjustment process has been required, the use or threat of use of the exchange rate weapon often underpinned international agreements.

The exchange rate weapon can take two forms, one *passive* and the other *active*. In the passive form, officials of a leading state within the system can allow the exchange rate of its currency to shift, perhaps even overshoot, in the knowledge that a more vulnerable partner country is thus subject to incentives to adjust its fiscal and/or monetary policy. Authorities can also actively promote a shift in the rate to induce the partner to shift macroeconomic policy. The two forms are deliberate, often coincide empirically, and have similar coercive effects.

Adjustment Conflict and Causal Mechanism
The exchange rate weapon can come into play particularly when current account imbalances become unsustainable and key states enter into political conflict over measures to reduce them. A large, closed economy is less sensitive to changes in the exchange rate compared to its smaller, more open partner(s), other things being equal. Under these circumstances, the smaller state will be subject to greater pressures to change macroeconomic policies in the face of a large shift in the exchange rate. The presence of a substantial asymmetry enables the large country to alter the incentives that confront the small country when setting macroeconomic policy.

Consider the example of a large country with a current account deficit locked in an adjustment standoff with a small partner, which runs corresponding surpluses. Domestic politics in both countries have dictated the macroeconomic policy preferences (e.g., for employment, growth, and inflation) that have given rise to the imbalances. The large state could eliminate the imbalance by shrinking its government budget deficit, for example, and the smaller state could accomplish the same through a fiscal expansion. For domestic political reasons, however, each government prefers that the other undertake the policy change.

When the imbalance becomes unsustainable—that is, private markets have become unwilling to finance it—the governments are confronted with politically difficult choices. The large, less vulnerable state could allow or encourage its currency to depreciate with relative equanimity. The corresponding currency appreciation of the small, more vulnerable state, however, sets in motion a chain of events that alters that government's incentives with respect to its macroeconomic policy. Specifically, the appreciation of the small country's currency will reduce the domestic price of imports, reducing inflation, and will shift the current account balance toward deficit, reducing growth and employment prospects. The reduction in inflation eases a constraint on stimulating domestic demand and the reduction in growth provides an incentive to do so. A change in macroeconomic conditions within the small country thus shifts the domestic political equilibrium toward providing a stimulus.

An asymmetry in exchange rate vulnerability enables the more insulated states to exploit cross-border economic effects in applying political pressure on their partners for policy adjustment. This generalization holds across a broad range of open economy macroeconomic assumptions, such as the degree of capital mobility. Three additional factors can reinforce the strength of the exchange rate weapon. First, a large, less vulnerable country might press the small country for policy change through diplomatic moral suasion, offering its support for currency stabilization in return. Second, the large country could deliberately act to shift the exchange rate in order to secure policy change on the part of the small country. Third, the large country could be reinforced in this effort by the international role of its currency, as in the case of the United States.

The active use of the exchange rate weapon hinges on the "exogeneity" of the exchange rate—that is, the ability of governments to influence currency values without altering underlying macroeconomic policies. Governments' scope for doing so is widely debated among international monetary economists. Professional consensus on the question has evolved over the decades. Recent studies generally find intervention to be more effective than did studies conducted during the 1980s. Suffice it to say that government action can be successful under a variety of circumstances, such as when it is publicly announced, conducted jointly by two or more central banks, and consistent with the underlying fundamentals, and when the exchange rate is far from equilibrium.

Historical Episodes The exchange rate weapon became a threat or a tactic during each of four episodes of conflict over international adjustment since the Bretton Woods regime: (1) the breakdown of that regime in the early 1970s, (2) the Bonn Summit of 1978, (3) the Plaza and Louvre accords of the mid-1980s, and (4) the early and mid-1990s. During each of these episodes, U.S. administrations pressed European and Japanese governments and/or central banks for expansionary measures and in some cases actively encouraged a depreciation of the dollar. U.S. authorities were more successful in some episodes, such as 1971–73, 1977–78, and 1985–87, than in others, such as during the 1990s.

Consider the Plaza-Louvre period as an example. During the first half of the 1980s, the U.S. current account deficit increased substantially under the macroeconomic and exchange rate policies of the first Reagan administration. In the summer of 1985, political pressure for trade protection in the U.S. Congress boiled over and Treasury Secretary James A. Baker III sought to defuse it with international policy coordination, among other measures. He and his counterparts among the Group of Five finance ministers signaled their support for dollar depreciation in the Plaza Accord of September of that year. A few months later, but prior to administering substantial stimuli to their economies, Japanese and West German officials indicated that the dollar had depreciated enough. By contrast, U.S. Treasury officials continued to "talk down" the dollar further and very large appreciations of the yen and mark occurred, prompting lobbying within Japan and West Germany for expansionary measures to offset the contractionary effects. At the meeting at the Louvre in 1987, U.S. officials agreed to stabilize currencies in exchange for European and Japanese policy stimuli. Changes in exchange rates and macroeconomic policy helped to nearly eliminate the U.S. current account deficit in subsequent years.

Structural Shift Because the effective use of this weapon hinges on the exploitation of an asymmetry by a large state, changes in the relative size and openness of the major countries could well affect the relevance of the weapon during adjustment conflicts in the future. Changes in the broad structure of the global economy—structural shift—derive from three main developments. First, the formation of the euro area in January 1999 created, in one fell swoop, a new monetary region of roughly equivalent weight to the United States—the most important change in the structure of the international monetary system since at least the Bretton Woods regime. Second, in East Asia the adjustment problem has been regionalized by foreign direct investment and cross-border production networks, as well as the practice by governments within the region of shadowing Chinese exchange rate policy vis-à-vis the dollar in order to preserve trade competitiveness. East Asian governments are advancing potentially important projects of regional financial cooperation. Finally, the U.S. economy is increasingly internationalized as measured by trade relative to gross domestic product and foreign investment relative to total U.S. financial assets.

The combined effect of these developments is to make Europe potentially less vulnerable to dollar depreciation, give pause to American officials when contemplating use of the exchange rate weapon in East Asia, and reduce the asymmetry in the effects of exchange rate changes between the United States and its partners. The exchange rate weapon could therefore be less useful to U.S. policymakers in the future than it has been in the past. Nonetheless, the United States will probably retain residual power while Europe's monetary union, Japan, and China could conceivably begin to exercise a similar form of influence through their currencies in geographically contiguous areas. The exchange rate weapon is thus likely to have continuing relevance as an instrument of economic conflict.

Critiques Some analysts find the notion of the exchange rate as a weapon to be troubling. Three specific objections can arise: (1) governments' ability to manipulate the exchange rate is limited; (2) the exchange rate should not be used coercively; and (3) the weapon is rarely used in practice. Consider each of these objections in turn.

First, the objection that governments are not generally effective in managing the exchange rate exogenously applies especially to the active form of the exchange rate weapon. But in the presence of high capital mobility, flexible exchange rates are often driven by herd behavior and expectations, and are thus frequently disconnected from the underlying economic fundamentals. In addition, the foreign-exchange markets often exhibit multiple equilibria—more than one exchange rate can be consistent with underlying fundamentals and the market rate is determined by private expectations. When private expectations are easily swayed—which is more often the case in the presence of large payments imbalances and conflicts over adjustment—governments are more likely to be able to induce a shift from one equilibrium to another. Particularly when the rate moves far from equilibrium, authorities might well coordinate the expectations of private participants by articulating an emerging consensus on the direction of movement.

Government officials can influence financial market expectations about rates and underlying policies, depending on market sentiment, by signaling their desire for a stronger, weaker, or stable currency; forswearing intervention; and intervening. Under some market conditions, such as a profound current account imbalance, an official's "no comment" in the face of a significant exchange rate movement can be interpreted by the market as a clear signal of approval. Conflict over trade policy and market access can enhance the markets' sensitivity to official statements. Thus, even if policymakers have only partial influence over the exchange rate, that influence can be substantial at particular junctures.

The second objection—that the exchange rate should not be used coercively—springs from the notion of the exchange rate as an economic variable whose movements allow consistency of internal and external balance across national economies. The main response to this objection is that simply ac-

knowledging that the exchange rate is sometimes used coercively does not mean that we endorse its use. The exchange rate weapon is a positive, explanatory concept, rather than reflecting a recommendation or prescription. The normative merit of the instrument depends on the use to which it is put and has varied from one historical case to the next.

As a positive concept, the weapon is an analytical tool of political economic analysis rather than of economic analysis per se. While acknowledging the economic function of the exchange rate, political analysis places the exchange rate in a larger context: an international struggle over the distribution of the costs of balance of payments adjustment. The variable is thus intermediate between the national politics of countries' macroeconomic policy, rather than intermediate simply between their economies. The exchange rate weapon is, in this conception, one of several means by which some states alter the payoffs to policy choices on the part of others.

Finally, in response to the objection that the instrument is rarely used, the exchange rate weapon has been employed at especially critical junctures in modern international economic relations. During the crises of the early 1970s, late 1970s, and mid-1980s, for example, U.S. administrations confronted strong protectionist pressures that were defused in part by the use of the exchange rate to secure adjustment. Had the U.S. Treasury simply let market forces bring adjustment in their own good time and in their own good measure, U.S. trade policy could have slowed the pace of liberalization or even become protectionist. Decisions to deploy or withhold the exchange rate weapon, therefore, can cast a long shadow into the future.

See also balance of payments; beggar-thy-neighbor policies; Bonn Summit; Bretton Woods system; exchange rate regimes; expenditure changing and expenditure switching; foreign exchange intervention; international policy coordination; Louvre Accord; Plaza Accord; Swan diagram

FURTHER READING
On the origin of the concept of the exchange rate weapon and its elaboration, see:

Henning, C. Randall. 1998. "Systemic Conflict and Regional Monetary Integration: The Case of Europe." *International Organization* 52: 537–73.

———. 2005. "The Exchange Rate Weapon and Macroeconomic Conflict." In *International Monetary Power*, edited by David M. Andrews. Ithaca, NY: Cornell University Press, 117–38.

For historical cases of macroeconomic conflict and cooperation, see:

Cooper, Richard N., Barry Eichengreen, C. Randall Henning, Gerald Holtham, and Robert D. Putnam. 1989. *Can Nations Agree? Issues in International Economic Cooperation*. Washington, DC: Brookings Institution.

Funabashi, Yoichi. 1988. *Managing the Dollar: From the Plaza to the Louvre*. Washington, DC: Peterson Institute for International Economics.

Helleiner, Eric. 1994. *States and the Reemergence of Global Finance: From Bretton Woods to the 1990s*. Ithaca, NY: Cornell University Press.

Henning, C. Randall. 1994. *Currencies and Politics in the United States, Germany, and Japan*. Washington, DC: Institute for International Economics.

Iida, Keisuke. 1999. *International Monetary Cooperation among the United States, Japan, and Germany*. Boston: Kluwer.

Broad treatments of international monetary power and influence by political scientists include:

Andrews, David M., ed. 2005. *International Monetary Power*. Ithaca, NY: Cornell University Press.

Kirshner, Jonathan. 1995. *Currency and Coercion: The Political Economy of International Monetary Power*. Princeton, NJ: Princeton University Press.

C. RANDALL HENNING

■ exchange rates and foreign direct investment

One of the many influences on foreign direct investment (FDI) activity is the behavior of exchange rates. Exchange rates, the domestic currency prices of foreign currencies, matter in terms of both their levels and their volatility. Exchange rates can influence the total amount of FDI that takes place and the allocation of this investment spending across a range of countries.

Understanding the effects of exchange rates on FDI is important for many reasons. For example, alternative exchange rate arrangements adopted by countries can reduce nominal changes in the relative values of currencies, sometimes even merging the currencies completely through a monetary union. For countries trying to attract more FDI, what roles do exchange rate levels and volatility play in determining the attractiveness of these countries for FDI? Can countries make themselves more or less attractive by manipulating the exchange rate?

Exchange Rate Levels When a currency depreciates, meaning that its value declines relative to the value of another currency, this exchange rate movement has two potential implications for FDI. First, it reduces that country's wages and production costs relative to those of its foreign counterparts. All else being equal, the country experiencing real currency depreciation has enhanced "locational advantage" or attractiveness as a location for receiving productive capacity investments. By this relative wage channel, the exchange rate depreciation improves the overall rate of return to foreigners contemplating an overseas investment project in this country.

The exchange rate level effects on FDI through this channel rely on a number of basic considerations. First, the exchange rate movement needs to be associated with a change in the relative production costs across countries, and thus should not be accompanied by an offsetting increase in the wages and production costs in the destination market. Second, the importance of the relative wage channel may be diminished if the exchange rate movements are anticipated. Anticipated exchange rate moves may be reflected in a higher cost of financing the investment project, since interest rate parity conditions equalize risk-adjusted expected rates of returns across countries. By this argument, stronger effects of exchange rate movements on FDI arise when unanticipated and not reflected in the expected costs of project finance for the FDI.

Some experts dismiss the empirical relevance of the interest-parity caveat. Instead, some argue that there are imperfect capital market considerations, leading the rate of return on investment projects to depend on the structure of capital markets across countries. For example, Froot and Stein (1991) argue that capital markets are imperfect and lenders do not have perfect information about the results of their overseas investments. In this scenario, multinational companies that borrow or raise capital internationally to pay for their overseas projects will need to provide their lenders some extra compensation to cover the relatively high costs of monitoring their investments abroad. Multinationals would prefer to finance these projects out of internal capital if possible, since internal capital is less expensive than borrowed capital.

Consider what occurs when exchange rates move. A depreciation of the destination market currency raises the relative wealth of source country agents and can raise multinational acquisitions of certain destination market assets. To the extent that source country agents hold more of their wealth in own currency-denominated form, a depreciation of the destination currency increases the relative wealth position of source country investors. As the parent company's wealth rises, more financing out of internal capital occurs. The reduced relative cost of capital allows these investors to bid more aggressively for assets abroad. Empirical support for this channel is provided by Klein and Rosengren (1994), who show that the importance of this relative wealth channel exceeded the importance of the relative wage channel in explaining FDI inflows to the United States during the period from 1979 through 1991.

Blonigen (1997) makes a "firm-specific asset" argument to support a role for exchange rates movements in influencing FDI. Suppose that foreign and domestic firms have equal opportunity to purchase firm-specific assets in the domestic market but different opportunities to generate returns on these assets in foreign markets. In this case, currency movements may affect relative valuations of different assets. While domestic and foreign firms pay in the same currency, the firm-specific assets may generate returns in different currencies. The relative level of foreign firm acquisitions of these assets may be affected by exchange rate movements. In the simple stylized example, if a representative foreign firm and domestic firm bid for a foreign target firm with firm-specific assets, real exchange rate depreciations of the foreign currency can plausibly increase domestic acquisitions of these target firms. Again, this channel predicts that foreign currency depreciation will lead to enhanced FDI in the foreign economy. Data on Japanese acquisitions in the United States support the hypothesis that real dollar depreciations make Japanese acquisitions more likely in U.S. industries with firm-specific assets.

Exchange Rate Volatility In addition to levels of exchange rates, volatility of exchange rates also matters for FDI activity. Theoretical arguments for volatility effects are broadly divided into "production flexibility" arguments and "risk aversion" arguments. To understand the production flexibility arguments, consider the implications of having a production structure whereby producers need to commit investment capital to domestic and foreign capacity before they know the exact production costs and exact amounts of goods that will be ordered from them in the future. When exchange rates and demand conditions are realized, the producer commits to actual levels of employment and the location of production. As Aizenman (1992) demonstrated, the extent to which exchange rate variability influences foreign investment hinges on the sunk costs in capacity (i.e., the extent of investment irreversibilities), on the competitive structure of the industry, and overall on the convexity of the profit function in prices. In the production flexibility arguments, the important presumption is that producers can adjust their use of a variable factor following the realization of a stochastic input into profits. Without this variable factor—that is, under a productive structure with fixed instead of variable factors—the potentially desirable effects of price variability on profits are diminished. By the production flexibility arguments, more volatility is associated with more FDI ex ante, and more potential for excess capacity and production shifting ex post, after exchange rates are observed.

An alternative approach linking exchange-rate variability and investment relies on risk aversion arguments. The logic is that investors require compensation for risks, and that exchange rate movements introduce additional risk into the returns on investment. Higher exchange-rate variability lowers the certainty equivalent expected exchange-rate level, as in Cushman (1985, 1988). Since certainty equivalent levels are used in the expected profit functions of firms that make investment decisions today in order to realize profits in future periods, if exchange rates are highly volatile, the expected values of investment projects are reduced, and FDI is reduced accordingly. These two arguments, based on "production flexibility" versus "risk aversion," provide different directional predictions of exchange rate volatility implications for FDI.

The argument that producers engage in international investment diversification in order to achieve ex post production flexibility and higher profits in response to shocks is relevant to the extent that ex post production flexibility is possible within the window of time before the realization of the shocks. This distinction suggests that the production flexibility argument is less likely to pertain to short-term volatility in exchange rates than to realignments over longer intervals.

When considering the existence and form of real effects of exchange rate variability, a clear distinction must be made between short-term exchange rate volatility and longer-term misalignments of exchange rates. For sufficiently short horizons, ex ante commitments to capacity and to related factor costs are a more realistic assumption than introducing a model based on ex post variable factors of production. Hence, risk aversion arguments are more convincing than the production flexibility arguments posed in relation to the effects of short-term exchange rate variability. For variability assessed over longer time horizons, the production flexibility motive provides a more compelling rationale for linking FDI flows to the variability of exchange rates.

As explained earlier, the exchange rate effects on FDI are viewed as exogenous, unanticipated, and independent shocks to economic activity. Of course,

to the extent that exchange rates are best described as a random walk, this view is a reasonable treatment. Otherwise, it is inappropriate to take such an extreme partial equilibrium view of the world. Accounting for the comovements among exchange rates, monetary demand, and productivity realizations of countries is important. As Goldberg and Kolstad (1995) show, these correlations can modify the anticipated effects on expected profits and the full presumption of profits as decreasing in exchange rate variability. Empirically, exchange rate volatility tends to increase the *share* of a country's productive capacity that is located abroad. Analysis of two-way bilateral FDI flows between the United States, Canada, Japan, and the United Kingdom showed that exchange rate volatility tended to stimulate the share of investment activity located on foreign soil. For these countries and the time period explored, exchange rate volatility did not have statistically different effects on investment shares when distinguished from periods where real or monetary shocks dominated exchange rate activity. Real depreciations of the source country currency were associated with reduced investment shares to foreign markets, but these results generally were statistically insignificant.

Although theoretical arguments conclude that the share of total investment located abroad may rise as exchange rate volatility increases, this logic does not imply that exchange rate volatility depresses domestic investment activity. In order to conclude that domestic aggregate investment declines, one must show that the increase in domestic outflows is not offset by a rise in foreign inflows. In the aggregate U.S. economy, exchange rate volatility has not had a large contractionary effect on overall investment (Goldberg 1993).

Overall, the current state of knowledge is that exchange rate volatility can contribute to the internationalization of production activity without depressing economic activity in the home market. The actual movements of exchange rates can also influence FDI through relative wage channels, relative wealth channels, and imperfect capital market arguments.

See also exchange rate regimes; exchange rate volatility; location theory

FURTHER READING

Aizenman, Joshua. 1992. "Exchange Rate Flexibility, Volatility, and Patterns of Domestic and Foreign Direct Investment." *International Monetary Fund Staff Papers* 39 (4): 890–922. Investigates the factors determining the impact of exchange rate regimes on the behavior of domestic investment and FDI, and the correlation between exchange rate volatility and investment.

Blonigen, Bruce A. 1997. "Firm-Specific Assets and the Link between Exchange Rates and Foreign Direct Investment." *American Economic Review* 87 (3): 447–965. Uses data on Japanese acquisitions of U.S. industries to show that dollar depreciation raises the likelihood of such acquisitions, especially in industries with high firm-specific assets.

Cushman, David O. 1985. "Real Exchange Rate Risk, Expectations, and the Level of Direct Investment." *Review of Economics and Statistics* 67 (2): 297–308. Shows U.S. annual bilateral direct investment to industrialized countries responds significantly to expected dollar depreciation and risk.

———. 1988. "Exchange Rate Uncertainty and Foreign Direct Investment in the United States." *Weltwirtschaftliches Archiv* 124 (2): 322–34. Attempts to clarify the ways that exchange rate uncertainty can affect FDI and tests for these effects on U.S. FDI inflows.

Froot, Kenneth A., and Jeremy C. Stein. 1991. "Exchange Rates and Foreign Direct Investment: An Imperfect Capital Markets Approach." *Quarterly Journal of Economics* 106 (4): 1191–1217. Model showing that when global capital markets have informational imperfections, depreciation lowers the relative wealth of domestic agents and leads to foreign acquisitions.

Goldberg, Linda S. 1993. "Exchange Rates and Investment in United States Industry." *Review of Economics and Statistics* 75 (4): 575–88. Shows how exchange rate level and volatility effects on real investment spending differ over time and across U.S. industries.

Goldberg, Linda S., and Charles D. Kolstad. 1995. "Foreign Direct Investment, Exchange Rate Variability, and Demand Uncertainty." *International Economic Review* 36 (4): 855–73. Model and empirical results show that shares of production capacity located abroad rise as exchange rate volatility rises and becomes more correlated with export demand shocks.

Klein, Michael W., and Eric S. Rosengren. 1994. "The Real Exchange Rate and Foreign Direct Investment in the United States: Relative Wealth vs. Relative Wage Effects." *Journal of International Economics* 36 (3–4): 373–89. Tests the Froot and Stein 1991 model, showing relative wealth effects stronger than relative wage effects of exchange rates on U.S. inward FDI.

LINDA S. GOLDBERG

■ exorbitant privilege

Exorbitant privilege refers to the ability of the United States to finance external deficits by printing its own currency. Countries incur external deficits by spending abroad more than they earn abroad. The conventional measure of this is a country's "current account deficit," which consists of three components: its export earnings minus its spending on imports; its earnings on foreign assets (interest payments on bank deposits and bonds, dividends on stocks, and profits on production abroad minus its payments to foreigners on their holdings of domestic assets), and its receipts of aid and private remittances from abroad minus its payments to foreigners for such aid and remittances.

Beginning in the late 1950s, the United States began running ever-larger external deficits: that is, it was "living beyond its means." By late 2007, the U.S. current account deficit was larger than ever before in its or any other country's history: about $850 billion per year, largely comprised of an excess of imports over exports.

Charles de Gaulle, ever envious of Anglo-American privilege, is widely credited with coining the term, but although he popularized it in speeches, it came, in fact, from Valery Giscard d'Estaing, de Gaulle's lieutenant during the 1960s.

The post–World War II arrangements designed by Britain and the United States at the Bretton Woods conference in 1944 placed the U.S. dollar at the core of the international monetary system. Almost all noncommunist countries agreed to peg their currencies to the dollar, which was in turn pegged to gold. Not only was the dollar literally as "good as gold"; it was for two decades almost the only currency that was freely convertible into other currencies (Canadian and Australian dollars were exceptions). It was also in goodly supply, given America's near-hegemony in world trade and finance from 1945 until the late 1950s. America produced more than 80 percent of world GDP and exports, and America's trade surpluses were invested in dollar-denominated assets issued by foreigners running trade deficits. Hence U.S. dollars became the world's preeminent choice for both trade and finance.

In short, all countries outside the Soviet sphere that aspired to import or export, or to borrow or lend internationally, had little alternative but to use U.S. dollars. America's exorbitant privilege derived from worldwide demand for a financial asset that could be created at near-zero cost. This led to the complaint that America was able to live beyond its means by simply printing money.

In 2007 almost all of the world's central banks still held at least three quarters of their "foreign exchange reserves" in U.S. dollars, usually in the form of bonds issued by the U.S. Treasury. By the time the Bretton Woods system collapsed in 1971–73, the United States was running a large external trade deficit. This was financed by the trade surpluses of large countries like Germany and Japan. Under Bretton Woods arrangements, these countries had kept their currencies pegged to the U.S. dollar at undervalued exchange rates by directing their central banks to sell deutsche marks and yen, and in the process to buy dollars. Trade surpluses accumulated as foreign exchange reserves in the coffers of their central banks.

After the Bretton Woods system collapsed, Germany, Japan, and other countries allowed their currencies to rise to market values. Nevertheless, global demand for dollar-denominated bonds and other dollar-denominated assets continued to grow. Although flexible-exchange-rate countries did not necessarily accumulate international reserves as rapidly as when they had fixed their rates, most countries returned to fixed- or managed-rate regimes. For ex-

ample, from 1979 to 1999 (before the introduction of the euro), core Western European countries fixed their rates against one another. International trade grew rapidly, as did central banks' appetite for foreign exchange reserves, mostly in the form of U.S. Treasury bonds. And in the 21st century, China's central bank has become the world's largest single buyer of U.S. Treasury bonds: since 1994, it has held its currency at a below-market exchange rate and has hence run current account surpluses that are mostly invested in U.S. government bonds, enhancing American "exorbitant privilege" as never before.

The United States has imported more than it has exported almost continuously since 1969. America enjoys the exorbitant privilege that it can finance part of this trade deficit simply by printing Treasury bonds, which are readily bought by the world's central banks. To be sure, the United States must pay interest on these bonds, but it is able to pay lower rates than on any other low-risk financial asset the world can offer. Because of the U.S. dollar's near-hegemony in international trade, and also because U.S. Treasury bonds are not only safe but quick and easy to sell (they are both default-risk-free and liquid), central banks and other investors are willing to hold Treasury bonds at rock-bottom interest rates relative to government bonds issued by other countries. This is likely to be true for the foreseeable future since no other country's government bonds are rivals for those of the United States in terms of both their default-free record and their sheer volume and hence liquidity.

Exorbitant privilege does not derive only from central banks' purchases of U.S. Treasuries. Private investors and institutions all over the world hold large parts of their portfolios in U.S.-dollar financial assets: in Treasury bonds, in corporate bonds, and in equities. This is partly because such assets yield good risk-adjusted returns, but it is partly also because the United States is a haven of free-market capitalism: it has never imposed currency controls, and (almost) never frozen funds (Iran's in 1978–79 were a notable exception).

In short, U.S. assets are virtually free from default risk and almost free from political risk. They are not, however, free from currency risk: the U.S. dollar can and does fluctuate widely against other currencies. Implicit in the term *exorbitant privilege* is that the United States has less incentive than other countries to assuage expectations of currency depreciation because it is assured of a "privileged" market for U.S.-dollar debt and equity, even when such assets seem likely to decline in value against other currencies.

See also Bretton Woods system; convertibility; currency substitution and dollarization; dollar standard; dominant currency; euro; foreign exchange intervention; gold standard, international; reserve currency; special drawing rights; vehicle currency

FURTHER READING

De Long, Brad. 2003. "'Exorbitant Privilege,' or, How Worrisome Is the U.S. Trade Deficit?" *Semi-Daily Journal* (August 6). http://econ161.berkeley.edu/movable_type/2003_archives/001993.html. De Long's "blog" is a continuing and very readable source of information and analysis of the U.S. external deficit.

Economist. 2004. "The Falling Dollar." (November 10). Discusses ongoing concern about U.S. external deficits and the dollar in the context of "exorbitant privilege."

Gourinchas, Pierre-Olivier, and Helene Roy. 2005. "From World Banker to World Venture Capitalist: U.S. External Adjustment and the Exorbitant Privilege." NBER Conference Paper (August). http://socrates.berkeley.edu/~pog/academic/exorbitant/exorb_privilege_0804.pdf. Links long-standing concern about the "exorbitant privilege" of the United States to its more recent role as a "venture capitalist." It also, in passing, gives due credit for the phrase to Giscard d'Estaing.

JAMES W. DEAN

■ expenditure changing and expenditure switching

In an open economy setting, policymakers need to achieve two goals of macroeconomic stability: internal and external balances. Internal balance is a state in which the economy is at its potential level of output—that is, a country's resources are fully employed and domestic price levels are stable. External balance is attained when a country is running neither an excessive current account deficit nor surplus (net exports are equal or close to zero). Attaining internal and external balances requires two independent policy tools: expenditure changing policy and expenditure switching policy.

Expenditure changing policy, which takes the form of fiscal or monetary policy, aims to affect income and employment with the goal of equating domestic expenditure, or absorption, and production. Expenditure switching is a macroeconomic policy that affects the composition of a country's expenditure on foreign and domestic goods. More specifically, it is a policy to balance a country's current account by altering the composition of expenditures on foreign and domestic goods. Not only does it affect current account balances, but it also can influence total demand, and thereby the equilibrium output level.

Internal and External Balances The interaction between internal and external balances can be demonstrated through a simple Keynesian model where consumption is a function of disposable income; the current account is related to the real exchange rate and disposable income (while foreign income that affects the domestic country's exports is assumed to be constant); and investment and government spending are exogenous. Internal and external balances are:

Internal balance (II):
$$Y = Y^f = C(Y^f - T) + I + G$$
$$+ CA(EP^*/P, Y^f - T)$$

External balance (XX):
$$CA = CA(EP^*/P, Y - T) = XX$$

where XX is a sustainable amount of current account deficit or surplus.

When the exchange rate is flexible, fiscal expansion—either government expenditure increase or tax cuts—raises output but worsens current account balances. Conversely, a fiscal contraction improves current account balances but lowers output. More specifically, if a country wants to raise its income level through fiscal expansion, it would have to experience a worsening in trade balances, because expansionary fiscal policy would lead to a rise in imports through improved disposable income and, therefore, worsens current account balances. Alternatively, if a country with a current account deficit attempts to reduce it, it could achieve that by implementing contractionary fiscal or monetary policy, so that as to reduce imports. When a country wants to achieve both internal and external balances simultaneously, it is most effective if the country lets the value of its currency change, so that change in the real exchange rate can affect both the economy's total demand and the demand for imports. Such policy to achieve current account balances by manipulating the demand for domestic and foreign goods through changes in the value of the currency is called expenditure switching policy.

When expenditure switching policy is not available—that is, when an economy is under the fixed exchange rate regime—expenditure changing policy through fiscal policy becomes the only available policy tool for attaining internal and external balances. In the fixed exchange rate system, monetary policy becomes unavailable because it affects the interest rate and the exchange rate. However, fiscal policy is insufficient to achieve both internal and external balances in such an environment.

Effects of Expenditure Changing Policy Although it is expected that expenditure changing policy with fiscal policy changes can affect output in the short run regardless of whether the exchange rate is flexible or fixed, its effect, or the "multiplier of fiscal policy," is smaller in an open economy than in a closed economy. When fiscal expansion is implemented, money demand and thereby the interest rate increase. This rise discourages, or "crowds out," private investment. This outcome arises as long as some degree of price stickiness is assumed. Hence some of the effect of fiscal expansion will be offset by the crowding out of investment, which makes the overall effect on income and also net exports (i.e., $EX - IM = S - I$) smaller than what could have been if the interest rate were assumed to be constant. Also, the multiplier is smaller the more open to international trade the economy is, because a greater portion of income "leaks out" of the system in the form of demand for foreign goods.

Expenditure changing policy with monetary expansion, on the other hand, involves a reduction in the interest rate in the short run, which expands income and worsens net exports. Both types of expenditure-increasing policies function in the same way: income rises while current account worsens in the short run. However, while monetary expansion favors private investment, fiscal expansion favors government spending.

Under the fixed exchange rate system, while monetary policy becomes ineffective, the effect of fiscal policy can be larger than under the flexible exchange rate system. When expansionary fiscal policy is implemented, the interest rate would rise because of the crowd-out effect. At the same time, however, the central bank would have to implement accommodative, that is, expansionary, monetary policy to cancel the rise in the interest rate. The action of canceling the effect on the money supply or interest rate is called sterilization. Otherwise, the interest rate would be affected, and that would affect the capital flows across the border (given the unchanged foreign interest rate) and therefore the exchange rate. Because fiscal expansion must be accompanied with sterilization, the effect of fiscal expansion on output is larger than that under the flexible exchange rate system where the exchange rate is allowed to fluctuate to reflect the change in the interest rate.

Effects of Expenditure Switching Policies Among possible expenditure switching policies, devaluation, or revaluation, is the most focused policy to affect current account balances and the equilibrium level of output. Devaluation increases the domestic price of imports and decreases the foreign price of exports; therefore, it decreases imports and increases exports. However, whether devaluation leads to an improvement in current account balances depends on the elasticities of demand for exports and imports. According to the Marshall-Lerner condition, if the sum of the elasticities of demand for exports and imports is greater than one, depreciation of the domestic currency leads to a current account improvement.

When an economy attempts to attain both internal and external balance, expenditure switching policy alone is insufficient. For example, if an economy is at the full employment level, in other words, internal balance is already attained, but if it is running current account deficits, policymakers in the economy could devalue its currency so that net exports rise. However, the improvement of current account balances would lead the economy to experience overheating so that internal balance would disappear. If an economy is experiencing an inflationary gap, or overheating, while maintaining a balanced current account, a revaluation policy may reduce total expenditure back to the full employment level, but lead to a current account deficit. Therefore, a mix of expenditure switching and changing policies is usually necessary to achieve both internal and external balances.

With the assumption that the Marshall-Lerner condition holds, for any given level of expenditure, devaluation leads to improvement of net exports, or current accounts, and therefore, a rise in output. However, when prices are assumed to be sticky in the short run, expenditure switching policy with devaluation involves the crowding-out effect. That is, the increase in output also raises the demand for money and consequently the interest rate, which discourages private investment. It is the crowding-out effect that offsets part of the income increase caused by devaluation. Hence, the new equilibrium income level will be a little lower than what could be achieved if the interest rate could remain constant.

Although devaluation policy is the most focused expenditure switching policy, it is not the only one. In general, expenditure policies take the form of trade (control) policy since they are aimed at affecting the volumes of exports and imports. Tariff policy can be implemented to discourage the inflow of imports, and export subsidy can be used to encourage exports, though these policies tend to be industry specific. The best-known tariff policy that has been actually implemented with macroeconomic ramifications is the infamous Smoot-Hawley Tariff Act of 1930. The goal of this policy was to switch demand for foreign goods to domestic ones at the expense of other countries to rescue domestic industries battered by the Great Depression. This policy, however, was followed by other countries that also tried to protect their domestic industries, eventually leading to rapid contraction of international trade.

See also assignment problem; balance of payments; capital mobility; exchange rate regimes; foreign exchange intervention; impossible trinity; Marshall-Lerner condition; money supply; Mundell-Fleming model; New Open Economy Macroeconomics; real exchange rate; sterilization; Swan diagram

FURTHER READING

Caves, Richard E., Jeffrey A. Frankel, and Ronald W. Jones. 2002. *World Trade and Payments—An Introduction.* Boston: Addison Wesley. The second half of this book presents theories and models for international macroeconomics. The effects of government macroeconomic policies are discussed from both the Keynesian and monetarist views as well as for economies with different degrees of capital account openness.

Corden, W. Max. 1969. "The Geometric Representation of Policies to Attain Internal and External Balance." In *Internal Finance,* edited by Richard N. Cooper. Harmondsworth, UK: Penguin Books, 256–90. A seminal paper where the models for expenditure switching and changing policies are introduced.

Krugman, Paul, and Maurice Obstfeld. 2006. *International Economics—Trade and Policy.* New York: Pearson/Addison Wesley. An introductory textbook for international trade and finance. In the international finance section, simple models for expenditure switching and changing policies are discussed. But for most parts of the book, free flows of capital are assumed.

HIRO ITO

export platform foreign direct investment

See vertical versus horizontal foreign direct investment

export processing zones

Export processing zones (EPZs) are locations where host countries have established special incentives to attract producers that import raw and intermediate components, process those items, and then export the final product. The regulatory structure governing EPZ operations in most zones is relatively straightforward. Participating firms are allowed to import inputs and equipment into the host country and export their final product duty free. Host countries may also provide zone firms incentives such as reduced income and property taxes, free or low-cost land, reimbursement for training expenses, and other benefits. In some countries, participating firms have to be located in a specific area. In others, producers qualifying for EPZ benefits can be located anywhere in the country. China, the Philippines, Malaysia, Mexico, Costa Rica, El Salvador, Honduras, Tunisia, Mauritius, and Madagascar are just a few of the many developing countries that have been able to dramatically increase exports through their EPZ initiatives. As a result, EPZs have become increasingly popular in the developing world. The International Labor Organization (ILO) reports that in 1997, 93 countries had established zones and total EPZ employment stood at 22.5 million. By 2002 these numbers had grown to 116 countries and 43 million jobs.

EPZs and Host Country Development EPZs are a controversial aspect of the global economy. On the positive side, they offer clear benefits to both producers and host countries. For producers, EPZs provide multinational companies (MNCs) and others easy access to a low-cost workforce in a developing country. For host countries, EPZs help create jobs, generate foreign exchange, and increase exports. EPZ opponents, however, contend that economic development strategies based on EPZ initiatives result in host countries voluntarily assuming an unattractive position within the global production system. MNCs have historically kept high-value-added, high-complexity links in the value chain close to the corporate center and delegated fragmented, low-value-added assembly tasks to their developing country operations. EPZ firms tend to be concentrated in labor-intensive industries such as apparel, footwear, toys, and electronics assembly, and to employ 18- to 25-year-old women with little education or formal training.

In developing countries where host country governments are struggling to provide the basic necessities of life to their population, low-value-added EPZ activity may represent a positive contribution to national development. To constitute a positive force in more advanced developing countries, the EPZ sector must transition toward a higher-value-added, higher-complexity production model. There are clear examples of countries where a significant percentage of EPZ firms have made this transition. This evolution can also include the transfer of knowledge-intensive support activities such as research and development and design engineering to the host country location. In other zones, the majority of firms have not evolved beyond basic assembly, and wages, especially for operating-level workers, have stagnated.

The quality of the jobs created through EPZ initiatives has been a consistent point of contention between EPZ proponents and their critics. The ILO, nongovernmental organizations, and academic researchers all express concerns about and actively monitor employment conditions in EPZs. In most countries it appears that zone firms provide at least equal if not better terms of employment than local companies, especially when compared to small businesses and the informal sector. There is, however, a clear need to develop appropriate regulatory structures and to aggressively monitor and enforce EPZ labor and environment standards. Of particular concern for the ILO, many developing countries restrict the opportunity for EPZ employees to join representative unions and engage in collective bargaining.

Critics also argue that the business model pursued by EPZ firms creates export enclaves with few if any linkages to other sectors of the host country economy. A closer look at day-to-day operations in successful zones shows that EPZs create numerous opportunities for construction companies, transportation firms, customs brokers, and a host of additional host country service providers. Local entrepreneurs also have the opportunity to supply raw and intermediate inputs that zone producers would otherwise import from global sources. For a variety of reasons, however, local firms have been unable to take full advantage of these opportunities in many developing regions. In Mexico, for example, inputs from national suppliers represent less than 4 percent of all raw and intermediate components used by the EPZ sector.

EPZs and Their Impact on the Developed World The use of EPZs by producers in many industry segments creates clear benefits for consumers in the developed world. Through accessing an abundant, low-cost workforce, companies are able to sell products at relatively low prices while still generating a profit. A number of well-known retailers such as Wal-Mart and Home Depot have increasingly turned to sourcing goods from EPZ plants in China as a core component of their business model. China's emergence as the world's premier EPZ location is frequently cited as one of the main reasons inflation has remained low in the developed world over the last decade.

As with so many other aspects of globalization, these benefits come at a cost. The argument has been made that EPZs represent one of the primary forces resulting in a so-called race to the bottom in global labor and environmental standards. Critics typically support this contention with three main points. First, EPZs clearly facilitate the exodus of manufacturing jobs from high-wage developed countries to low-wage developing regions. Second, the EPZ option also reduces the power of organized labor to bargain for improved wages and working conditions in industries where it is possible for companies to shift production to low-wage EPZs. By contributing to reduced demand for workers and the disruption in the bargaining power between management and unions, EPZs may be partially responsible for the recent stagnation in blue-collar wages in the United States and elsewhere. Finally, critics also contend that MNCs frequently move environmentally risky operations to developing country EPZs where appropriate standards are lacking and/or enforcement is weak. There is considerable, primarily qualitative evidence for the first two points, but little if any sound support indicating that large numbers of MNCs have moved to developing country EPZs to avoid strict environmental standards.

China's New Role in the Global EPZ Industry The primary location of EPZ-style production was very different in the early 2000s compared to prior decades. Starting from a very low base in the late 1970s China has rapidly become the world's preferred EPZ location. In 1997, the ILO estimated 18 million people were employed in Chinese EPZs. In December 2001, China gained full membership in the World Trade Organization (WTO) and with improved market access to the world's primary industrial and consumer markets EPZ employment increased to 30 million by 2002. This total represents close to 70 percent of the world's EPZ workforce.

EPZ producers are the main force responsible for China's increased prominence in world markets. It is estimated that EPZ firms account for more than half of all Chinese exports and 70 percent of Chinese exports to the United States. China's attraction as a production location is due to several factors: the undervalued Chinese currency, the availability of large numbers of very low cost workers as well as skilled middle- and upper-level engineers and managers, generous incentives provided by the Chinese government, considerable investment in export infrastructure, and the opportunity for firms to simultaneously engage in EPZ-style production and sell a percentage of factory output to the country's 1.2 billion consumers.

China's success is forcing countries in both industrialized and developing regions to rethink their export promotion strategies. A study by Lall and Albaladejo (2004) found higher-cost Asian countries were losing market share to China in the 1990s primarily in low-technology segments and were increasingly focusing on the production of intermediate components that were then exported to China for final assembly. Lall characterizes the trade relationship between China and its East Asian neighbors as complementary rather than competitive. This may change as China upgrades toward more technology-intensive, high-complexity sectors.

China does represent a direct threat for many EPZ producers in Mexico and the Caribbean Basin. The brief recession in the United States and increased competition from Chinese EPZ exports contributed to the loss of close to 300,000 jobs in *maquiladoras*, as Mexican EPZs are known, from 2000 to 2003. Mexican policymakers have argued that China's low-cost advantages will force Mexico's EPZ industry to shift from labor-intensive to more capital- and technology-intensive activities. The available evidence indicates, however, that *maquiladoras* have responded by adopting business models in which competitive advantage is based on proximity to industrial and consumer markets in the United States, such as mass customization, just-in-time delivery, low volume–high mix production systems, and re-manufacturing centers.

Policy Implications The historical record clearly shows both positive and negative outcomes associated with EPZs. Using scarce development resources to establish a zone in which participating firms employ a very young, unskilled, primarily female workforce at subsistence wages to perform low-value-added assembly work may be worthwhile only in the poorest of countries. This type of participation in the global economy is useful only if it represents a starting point leading to something better. Governments in Asia, Mexico, and elsewhere have employed EPZs as an integral component of much larger and more comprehensive upgrading strategies. Global competition as well as the evolution of the organizational capacity of MNCs present interesting new challenges for host countries with EPZ programs. In search of efficiency and profitability, MNCs continue to migrate entire industries from high- to low-wage locations. Companies are also improving their ability to divide value chains into smaller and smaller segments and place activities around the world where they can be performed most efficiently. The world's largest MNCs are also much more willing than they were in the past to delegate knowledge-intensive functions such as design engineering to their developing country subsidiaries. The offshore outsourcing of service functions is a closely related phenomenon that represents significant new opportunities for developing countries. In Mexico there are now locations where traditional EPZ activity, engineering centers, and call centers are all located in the same industrial park. Based on both the historical record and new opportunities, EPZs have a place in the policy kit of those in developing countries attempting to create wealth through open engagement with the global economy.

See also export promotion; fragmentation; International Labor Organization; outsourcing/offshoring

FURTHER READING

Cling, Jean-Pierre, Mireillie Razafindrakoto, and Francois Boubaud. 2005. "Export Processing Zones in Madagascar: A Success Story under Threat?" *World Development* 33 (5): 785–803. A firsthand account of EPZ activity in Madagascar since 1990.

Grunwald, Joseph, and Kenneth Flamm. 1985. *The Global Factory: Foreign Assembly in International Trade*. Washington, DC: Brookings Institution Press. One of the first relatively comprehensive studies of EPZs.

International Labor Organization. 2003. *Employment and Social Policy in Respect of Export Processing Zones (EPZs)*. BG.286/ESP/3. Downloadable from www.ilo.org. A summary of EPZ activity around the world and ILO labor concerns.

Kaplinsky, Raphael. 1993. "Export Processing Zones in the Dominican Republic: Transforming Manufacturers into Commodities." *World Development* 21 (11): 1851–65. A well-thought-out critique by a prominent development scholar.

Lall, Sanjaya, and Manuel Albaladejo. 2004. "China's Competitive Performance: A Threat to East Asian Manufactured Exports?" *World Development* 32 (9): 1441–66. An empirical study of the impact of China's exports on the exports of its neighbors.

Lemoine, Françoise, and Deniz Ünal-Kesenci. 2004. "Assembly Trade and Technology Transfer: The Case of China." *World Development* 32 (5): 829–50. An excellent study examining EPZ activity in China.

Romero, Ana Teresa. 1998. "Export Processing Zones in Africa: Implications for Labour." *Competition and*

Change 2 (4): 391–418. An interesting review of EPZs in Africa.

Steinfeld, Edward. 2004. "China's Shallow Integration: Networked Production and New Challenges for Late Industrialization." *World Development* 32 (11): 451–96. Examines the development challenges for China as a result of the emergence of modular production in EPZs.

JOHN SARGENT

■ export promotion

Governments often seek to promote exports from their country and to encourage national production of goods that might be exported. Export promotion can be viewed, therefore, as either an aim of economic policy (an export promotion strategy) or the set of policies and measures used by government agencies and the private sector to promote exporting and the production of exportable goods and services (export promotion policies).

Trade economists and policymakers have long been interested in how the trade policies, institutions, and trade strategy a country adopts affect its export and wider economic performance. The issues that generate this interest are controversial. Differences of opinion exist on the relationship between trade in general, and exports in particular, and economic growth; the influence of trade strategy in general, and an export-promoting strategy in particular, on export performance; and whether and how governments should interfere with market processes in general and in trade sectors in particular.

Traditional neoclassical theory represents trade as exposing domestic markets to greater competition, which induces efficient use and allocation of resources in line with relative world prices. In the absence of pervasive market failures, this representation provides a rationale for limiting government intervention and for adopting relatively neutral government interventions in the traded goods sectors. This resulting openness of the economy to international trade and competition implies in turn an outward orientation of the country's trade strategy, a willingness for as much specialization of domestic production and as much growth of imports and exports to occur as is consistent with the openness of the economy.

It is necessary, however, to recognize that the issues of trade orientation and degree of government intervention in markets are analytically separate. Outward orientation and export promotion can be led by markets or by policy intervention. An inward orientation can be removed by dismantling protectionist, import-substituting trade policies and moving to a free trade regime. The removal of import tariffs and other nontariff barriers can be seen as a market-led approach to export promotion. Alternatively, greater incentives to produce for export markets can be offered through additional government measures to subsidize exports and production in export sectors explicitly or implicitly. The relative merits of these alternative approaches to export promotion have been at the heart of the academic and policy debate in this area of international economics, in particular in the context of developing countries' policy options. Given the tendency of governments to use a mixture of import liberalization and direct export promotion measures to implement more outward-oriented trade strategies, controversy has developed over how to interpret the empirical evidence on the relationships among trade strategy, export performance, and economic growth or development.

The Case against Export Promotion There is a strong strand of the development economics literature that rejects the neoclassical focus on domestic supply conditions as an influence on export performance (see Evans 1990). This strand views the level of external demand as critical in influencing the export performance of developing countries. Pessimism about the growth of demand reflects the relatively low income elasticity of demand for primary products and the belief that the growth of manufactured imports by these countries would be met by protectionist responses in the industrial countries. Export pessimism provided a rationale for reducing reliance on external demand and export conditions for growth and development and led in the post–World War II period to the widespread adoption of interventionist and inward-looking policies.

Import restrictions were adopted to protect industries producing for the domestic market, with the aim of causing the demand for home goods to grow by replacing or substituting for imports. An import-substitution trade strategy was implemented through a range of direct and indirect means, which subsidized the production of importable goods, taxed the production of exportables, or did both. Taxes on imports, such as tariffs, or quantitative restrictions on importing (e.g., import licenses or quotas) implicitly subsidized importables production, while export taxes explicitly taxed exportables. Equivalent effects could be achieved also by less direct means. Export marketing boards might use their monopoly position to give commodity exporters less than the world price for their exports. Reluctance to alter a pegged exchange rate in the face of high inflation may cause currency overvaluation, reducing the price competitiveness of exports in foreign markets.

The Case for Export Promotion There are a priori arguments for encouraging outward orientation based on the benefits of more efficient allocation and use of resources due to greater competition. These may be one-time gains that raise per capita incomes but do not alter the steady-state or long-term growth rates of economies. More recently, theoretical support for export promotion has been provided by the so-called new or endogenous growth theories. In these, export growth may, in the presence of increasing returns and complementarities between physical and human capital accumulation, lead to permanent, positive growth effects.

It was not the advent of this new branch of theory, however, that caused most economists and policymakers to reject import-substituting trade strategies. In part they responded pragmatically to the revealed effects of import substitution and the evidence from developing countries of the resulting high costs of protection. Under import substitution, factories were underused, production technologies were often overly capital intensive, and the growth of

trade regulations created high returns to lobbying and other forms of rent-seeking. The move away from import substitution was also in part a reaction to the evidence that some developing countries, particularly in Southeast Asia, had developed an export capacity in manufactured goods and had brought about rapid growth and industrialization (Trindade 2005). This undermined the generality at least of the "export pessimism" arguments for inward orientation (Bhagwati 1990).

Finally, even where policymakers remained unconvinced by the relative performance of inward- and export-oriented countries or by the benefits of moving from one strategy to the other, the macroeconomic and debt problems of their economies forced them into accepting trade policy reform as part of the conditionality for the loans they needed from the World Bank. Structural adjustment programs that were required in order to access these loans were a major vehicle during the 1980s and 1990s in driving the import liberalization (reduction and/or elimination of nontariff barriers, and rationalization and lowering of tariff rates) and exchange rate adjustment (currency devaluation or depreciation). These reforms significantly lowered the large anti-export bias that had grown up in the trade regimes of many developing countries.

Export Opportunities and Mechanisms for Export Development Globalization and the growth of the global economy have brought increased export market opportunities. In addition, the successful newly industrializing and exporting countries demonstrate a "ladder of development" effect. There is evidence of the richer and more industrialized countries being displaced as exporters first of standardized labor-intensive manufactures and subsequently of less standardized and more capital-intensive products. This displacement has been by developing countries of varying size. The emergence of new, large-scale exporters such as China, India, and Mexico may cause other smaller, potential late entrants to worry that there are forces of agglomeration of international production that will make future entry into exporting more difficult. These new exporting countries, however, also offer additional market opportunities for final and intermediate goods. Furthermore, the increasing fragmentation of international production increases these market opportunities in both developed and developing country markets. Indeed, the key focus of the literature on export development has shifted away from concern about the absence of export opportunities when all countries try simultaneously to promote exports (often referred to as the "fallacy of composition" problem) to identifying the internal and external constraints on export development.

In the 1950s and 1960s attention tended to focus on external constraints, including on the issue of market access to the industrial countries. High trade barriers, especially against labor-intensive imports such as textiles, clothing, and footwear, were seen as constraining export growth in the developing countries. This led to the incorporation of "special and differential" treatment principles for developing countries in the General Agreement on Tariffs and Trade, which allowed the industrialized countries to offer preferential access to their markets for developing country exports. The benefits of preferences (lower tariffs than those applied to exports from non-preference-receiving countries) have been weakened subsequently by the multilateral trade liberalization that the industrialized countries have implemented. They have lowered their tariff and nontariff barriers significantly in general, though market access can still be highly constrained in specific products where contingent protection measures (e.g., anti-dumping controls) and regulations (e.g., technical and health standards) restrict imports.

The continuing small share of world trade of the developing countries led to the shift of attention after the 1970s to the role of the developing countries' own trade policies in constraining export development. As outlined earlier, high import barriers and other protectionist measures created major sources of antiexport bias. Unilateral and regional trade reforms in recent decades have significantly reduced this constraint on export development. Before they liberalized their imports, however, many developing countries experimented with trying to simultaneously import-substitute and export promote, that is, to supplement existing import-substitution measures with fiscal incentives for exporting.

In broad terms simultaneous promotion of import-substituting and exportables production may well be mutually offsetting, moving the economy toward similar relative prices as under free trade if the incentives to both sectors are of similar magnitude. Taxing imports and subsiding exports will, however, absorb resources to collect and spend the taxes. The costs of policy administration can be avoided with free trade. Nonetheless, governments were often reluctant to liberalize imports for ideological and political economy reasons.

One strategy pursued by reforming governments was to continue with a general import substitution regime, while creating enclaves of production for export markets. Domestic and potentially footloose foreign firms within these enclaves, or export processing zones, often gained access to duty-free imported inputs and capital goods or to subsidized inputs and were subject to preferential profits tax arrangements not applied to firms in the rest of the economy. Such arrangements tend to give rise to monitoring problems associated with trying to avoid leakage of subsidized production into the domestic market (Warr 1990). It is also increasingly recognized that exporting requires access to reliable and low-cost inputs and services, which is more likely where exporters are integrated into competitive, open economies.

Recently, attention has shifted from trade policy constraints to other policy and nonpolicy constraints on export development. Increasingly advocates of outward orientation of trade policies recognize that trade policy reform may not be a sufficient condition for improved export performance. Export promotion may well require improved institutions (to support better export marketing or provide cheaper trade credits) and improved infrastructure (better roads for internal sourcing of inputs and distribution or cheaper and more reliable international transportation services). There is growing evidence that the "taxing" effects on exports that arise from developing countries' own trade policies or from the trade policies of their trading partners are generally less important than those resulting from the inefficiencies or inadequacies of local services and input suppliers, of local institutions in both the private and public sectors, and of the national and regional communications and transport infrastructures (see Milner 2004). Export promotion is in fact recognized as being a much broader concept than that of the country's trade policy stance alone. It encompasses measures to reduce production costs in general and to reduce transportation (internal and international) costs in particular.

See also export processing zones

FURTHER READING

Bhagwati, Jagdish N. 1990. "Export-promoting Trade Strategy: Issues and Evidence." In *Export Promotion Strategies: Theory and Evidence from Developing Countries*, edited by Chris Milner. New York: New York University Press, 11–39. A clear statement of this proponent's case for export promotion.

Evans, H. David. 1990. "Outward Orientation: An Assessment." In *Export Promotion Strategies: Theory and Evidence from Developing Countries*, edited by Chris Milner. New York: New York University Press, 40–58. A critical assessment of the case for export promotion, with support for the case against.

Milner, Chris R., ed. 1990. *Export Promotion Strategies: Theory and Evidence from Developing Countries*. New York: New York University Press. A collection of essays on the theory and evidence relating to export promotion, with a section on alternative instruments of export promotion and on national case studies.

———. 2004. "Constraints to Export Development in the Developing Countries." In *The WTO and Developing Countries*, edited by Homi Katrak and Roger Strange. London: Palgrave, 213–32. Provides a useful broad evaluation of the relative importance of market access, trade policies, and other nontrade policy barriers in constraining export development.

Trindade, V. 2005. "The Big Push, Industrialization, and International Trade." *Journal of Development Economics* 78: 22–48. Provides a theoretical analysis of the industrialization of countries such as South Korea and Taiwan produced by export promotion policies.

Warr, P. 1990. "Export Processing Zones." In *Export Promotion Strategies: Theory and Evidence from Developing Countries*, edited by Chris Milner. New York: New York University Press, 130–61. A useful paper on the costs and benefits of export processing zones.

CHRIS MILNER

■ expropriation risk

See trade costs and foreign direct investment

■ factor endowments and foreign direct investment

International factor endowment differentials (FEDs) between home and host countries of multinational corporations (MNCs) setting up affiliate subsidiaries are one of the key determinants of foreign direct investment (FDI) flows. One reason that some corporate operations are geographically separated from headquarters activities is to minimize production costs. Aspects of production that are intensive in a particular factor (such as labor or a natural resource input) tend to be located where that factor is abundant.

Ascertaining how FEDs affect FDI is important for achieving a general understanding of the determinants of FDI. There is a broad concern, in developed countries, that production is fleeing high-cost industrialized countries for low-cost developing countries such as China—that FDI is motivated by firms trying to slash costs by shifting labor-intensive activities to countries where labor is cheap.

Yet it is important to recognize that to operate in a given host country, in addition to requiring abundant labor to make production costs low, the subsidiary of an MNC may also need to import machinery and employ engineers. Hence while relative labor abundance makes wage production costs low, the other production costs, such as for physical capital and human capital, cannot be exceedingly high for the country to be an attractive host for affiliate production. Moreover, the host location for affiliate operations must have nonproduction costs that also are sufficiently low. In fact, the poorest

countries attract almost no FDI. Considering all costs of bringing a good to market, not just labor production costs, poorer countries are often not cheaper locations.

This entry will consider theories of how FEDs affect FDI, and the empirical evidence. Understanding this issue will help form the basis for a better overall knowledge of why FDI occurs.

Global Firm Organization and Modes of FDI FDI occurs when a firm decides to locate production abroad and opts to maintain organizational, as well as financial, control over its foreign production. The first step in the choice to undertake FDI is the decision to relocate part of the production process offshore. The second step relates to organization—whether the foreign production is to be organized within the confines of the corporation or at arm's length. In the former case, the corporation is multinational and sets up an affiliate subsidiary outside the country where its headquarters are located. If the costs of setting up the affiliate subsidiary are financed via the MNC's headquarters, there is a financial inflow into the host country in the form of FDI. When the overseas production is at an arm's length operation rather than a subsidiary, there is foreign outsourcing rather than FDI.

In pursuing FDI, MNCs deploy various modes of entry, with the traditional ones being vertical and horizontal. The mode of entry will impinge on the role of FEDs in determining FDI, as each mode of entry seeks to minimize a particular cost to the MNC. First, *vertical* affiliate entry—breaking up stages across countries—seeks manufacturing cost minimization through production line fragmentation. Second, *horizontal* subsidiary entry—creating duplicate plants abroad—aims for transportation cost minimization by bringing production closer to customers. Third, using a host country as an *export platform* by a MNC—building a plant abroad to serve a third market—balances advantages emanating from FEDs enhanced by geographic location advantages minimizing trade impediments, including tariffs.

Vertical FDI involves different locations for the various parts of the production process of the MNC's final output. This type of organization involves international trade between the firm's subsidiaries with headquarters, and seeks to exploit international factor price differentials. As an example, a MNC might locate headquarters in a skilled labor–abundant home country and engage in unskilled labor–intensive production in an unskilled labor–abundant host country. In this case, there are foreign affiliate exports of final output from the host to the home country of the MNC. Vertical FDI is expected to be more prevalent the greater the FEDs across countries. Greater FEDs give rise to greater differences in factor prices and thus greater incentive for vertical FDI.

Horizontal FDI minimizes the costs of serving the market by producing locally rather than trading. It is more likely when trade costs are relatively high (e.g., tariff-jumping FDI). Establishing a plant in the host country incurs additional plant-level fixed costs but avoids per unit trade costs (including both tariffs and transportation costs), and hence is preferable when the host country market size is sufficiently large. Using a monopolistic competition model, Markusen and Venables (2000) demonstrate that multinationals are more likely to arise when countries are more similar in both relative and absolute endowments. At the same time, a reduction in transportation costs for intermediates can lead to either vertical FDI (when upstream activities are labor intensive) or horizontal FDI (when downstream activities are labor intensive).

The vertical and horizontal modes of FDI have been combined in the "knowledge-capital" model of the multinational firm by Carr, Markusen, and Maskus (2001). Barriers to investment and trade between countries give rise to endogenous FDI modes. The higher the relative costs imposed by trade barriers relative to investment barriers, the more likely MNCs are to engage in horizontal rather than vertical FDI. At the same time, MNCs need not view horizontal and vertical FDI as mutually exclusive strategies. In some cases, a host FDI country may play the role of export platform to serve a regional market.

When there is possible geographic fragmentation in the stages of production into intermediate input manufacturing and assembly, interesting complementarities emerge that give rise to more complex organizational forms.

First, Yeaple (2003) identifies one complementarity that results when the lower cost attainment associated with production relocation induces a rise in overall output, which in turn will give rise to further production relocation. Moreover, Grossman, Helpman, and Szeidl (2003) show that when transportation costs for final goods are moderate, there is a complementarity associated with the source of components: the cost savings from locating assembly in the low-cost region are higher when components are also produced there. This complementarity implies that FDI in assembly responds to changes in the costs of FDI in components. When transportation costs for components are high enough, there is also an agglomeration complementarity in FDI: firms conducting assembly abroad want to locate component production nearby to reduce the costs of shipping components. In addition, the interest in hybrid integration strategies has led to models with more than two countries, with emphasis not only on FEDs but also trade and investment costs across regions of the world.

When producing overseas raises MNC profitability, FDI rather than offshoring will be more likely, the more contractual difficulties the multinational corporation faces in the country where component production is most efficient. Hence the decision to engage in FDI jointly minimizes production and transaction costs for the investor. In this context, Antras and Helpman (2004) show that, other things equal, countries with a level of contractual frictions will receive more FDI inflows, the more abundant their endowment of the factor used intensively in production of intermediate inputs.

In terms of the financing of production once the offshoring decision is made, Antras, Desai, and Foley (2007) develop a model and provide evidence suggesting that the less developed investor protection is in a potential host country of FDI, the more of an outside stake by the MNC will be required in local capital markets to fund the affiliate subsidiary. More funding for the affiliate in the form of FDI will be forthcoming from headquarters, the less investor protection and financial development there is in the host country.

Thus given that relative factor abundance makes a country comparatively attractive to locate some stage of production activity, the inflow of FDI into that country should, controlling for other relevant country characteristics, increase with higher contractual frictions and lower investor protection. To some extent, FDI is a way to organize production within the confines of the MNC to substitute for poor institutions and incomplete markets in the host country where manufacturing can be most productive due to FEDs, or other motives for production relocation.

Evidence on FEDs and FDI Based on simple models of MNC behavior, FEDs should give rise to more vertical, but less horizontal, FDI. Brainard (1997) reports findings that are inconsistent with multinational activity depending on factor proportion differences. The finding is that increases in per worker income differences reduce affiliate sales (absolutely and relative to trade). Estimates of the knowledge-capital model of the multinational enterprise, which embeds both horizontal and vertical FDI, find support for horizontal FDI.

However, several recent studies do lend support to vertical FDI models based on FEDs. Hanson, Mataloni, and Slaughter (2005) find that demand for imported inputs increases when affiliates face lower wages for less-skilled labor. Braconier, Norback, and Urban (2005) find that more FDI is conducted in countries where less-skilled labor is relatively cheap.

Given the recent reductions in transportation costs, facilitating both international trade of goods and factor flows, traditional theories would predict that FEDs' importance in determining FDI would be mitigated. To the extent that FEDs play an important role in explaining recent FDI flows, this is likely to be due to the interaction, emphasized in more recent theories, of FEDs with some other determinant of FDI. For example, the complementarities discussed previously predict that a fall in transportation costs within an intermediate range may exacerbate the impact of FEDs on FDI flows.

More generally, theories on complex modes of FDI suggest that bilateral sales by MNCs between two countries are not determined solely by the characteristics of those two countries but are also affected by characteristics of other countries and regions. There is evidence consistent with bilateral FDI being complementary with exogenous bilateral and third-country determinants in the case of horizontal export-platform FDI. For vertical FDI, bilateral and third-country effects of changes in skilled and unskilled labor endowments tend to be substitutes for complex vertical FDI. Indeed, more recent evidence suggests that international FEDs matter for FDI not only at the bilateral level but in a more general sense.

Much of the recent expansion in trade flows would appear to be related to the growth of FDI. MNCs account for approximately half of U.S. exports. These are intrafirm transactions between the headquarters of U.S. MNCs and their foreign affiliates (Hanson, Mataloni, and Slaughter 2005). Helpman, Melitz, and Yeaple (2004) have shown that the effect of sector- and country-specific trade impediments in favoring FDI over exports is more pronounced under firm heterogeneity, both in theory and data. In addition, there is evidence that the most productive MNCs are able to atomize production facilities across countries and are not bound to central locations. In global markets, the organizational changes due to firm growth have overall been associated with higher FDI in response to international FEDs.

Taken together, these facts imply that the growth in tandem of FDI and exports reveals the increasing fair trade

global importance of MNC activities and their fragmentation across countries. The most productive MNCs have far reach across world markets both in intermediate input production organization and in assembly for global supply of final goods. The cost advantages conferred by certain locations due to FEDs are magnified for the select MNCs whose FDI flows, in their many modes, have global presence.

See also location theory; multinational enterprises

FURTHER READING

Antras, Pol, Mihir Desai, and Fritz Foley. 2007. "Multinational Firms, FDI Flows, and Imperfect Capital Markets." NBER Working Paper No. 12855. Cambridge, MA: National Bureau of Economic Research. Models and provides evidence on the host-country determinants of how MNCs finance offshore operations.

Antras, Pol, and Elhanan Helpman. 2004. "Global Sourcing." *Journal of Political Economy* 112 (3): 552–80. Develops a theoretical framework on the contractual environment, transaction cost, and production cost differences across countries in determining the organization of firms in a global economy.

Braconier, Henrik, Pehr-Johan Norback, and Dieter Urban. 2005. "Multinational Enterprises and Wage Costs: Vertical FDI Revisited." *Journal of International Economics* 67 (2): 446–70. Provides empirical evidence about the impact on FDI of the wage differential between MNC home and host countries.

Brainard, S. Lael. 1997. "An Empirical Assessment of the Proximity-Concentration Trade-off between Multinational Sales and Trade." *American Economic Review* 87 (4): 520–44. Analyzes empirically the link between FDI and MNC exports from the home country to the host country.

Carr, David L., James R. Markusen, and Keith E. Maskus. 2001. "Estimating the Knowledge-Capital Model of the Multinational Enterprise." *American Economic Review* 91 (3): 693–708. Lays out a framework in which MNCs choose the mode of FDI and provides empirical evidence.

Grossman, Gene M., Elhanan Helpman, and Adam Szeidl. 2006. "Optimal Integration Strategies for the Multinational Firm." *Journal of International Economics* 70 (1): 216–38. Models how the possibility of intermediate

input trade enriches the choices of MNC operation location including exports to third countries from host countries for FDI.

Hanson, Gordon, Raymond Mataloni, and Matthew Slaughter. 2005. "Vertical Production Networks in Multinational Firms." *Review of Economics and Statistics* 87 (4): 664–78. Provides an econometric analysis of the pattern of international trade and investment within U.S. MNCs.

Helpman, Elhanan, Marc Melitz, and Stephen Yeaple. 2004. "Exports versus FDI with Heterogeneous Firms." *American Economic Review* 94 (1): 300–16. Models and explores empirically how heterogeneous productivity across firms affects the trade-off for firms between export and FDI strategies.

Markusen, James R., and Anthony J. Venables. 2000. "The Theory of Endowment, Intraindustry and Multinational Trade." *Journal of International Economics* 52 (2): 209–34. Provides a model to assess the link between FEDs and the role of MNCs in international trade.

Yeaple, Stephen. 2003. "The Complex Integration Strategies of Multinationals and Cross Country Dependencies in the Structure of Foreign Direct Investment." *Journal of International Economics* 60 (2): 293–314. Provides a model in which vertical and horizontal FDI are not mutually exclusive and do not exhaust the range of market penetration strategies.

MAURICE KUGLER

■ **factor proportions**
See Heckscher-Ohlin model

■ **fair trade**

The concept of fair trade carries an implicit critique of the *unfairness* associated with the conventional North-South trade system and the proposition that an alternative *fairer* trade system is possible. Fair trade advocates reject the assumption that an unregulated, comparative advantage–based trade system provides a viable avenue for sustainable development with most artisans, small-scale farmers, and workers. The persistent poverty among small-scale agricultural commodity producers and artisans in the global South demonstrates the need for a different type of trading system. Since the 1940s, fair trade organizers have worked to create and expand an alternative trade system that starts with a set of commonly held principles codified into standards intended to support empowerment, gender equity, long-term partnerships, transparency, and sustainable community development (FLO 2007; Barratt-Brown 1993). According to an alliance among several international fair trade associations, "Fair trade is a trading partnership, based on dialogue, transparency and respect, which seeks greater equity in international trade. It contributes to sustainable development. Fair trade organizations (backed by consumers) are engaged actively in supporting producers, awareness raising and in campaigning for changes in the rules and practice of conventional international trade" (Krier 2005).

In practice, fair trade is an uneven global movement and an expanding market. The twin strategies for implementing fair trade principles are the creation of a market that offers better prices to small-scale producer organizations and support from international development nongovernmental organizations (NGOs) for business and social development. Fair trade organizations have established an international labeling system (Fair Trade Labeling Organizations International) and international associations of alternative trade organizations (IFAT) to implement these practices, expand awareness among in Northern countries, and build demand.

Although fair trade accounts for 1–5 percent of the global trade in specific agricultural commodities and handicrafts, the markets have expanded rapidly. As of October 2006, the global fair trade–certified network included 586 producer organizations and 1.4 million farmers, artisans, and workers in 58 developing countries from Latin America, Asia, and Africa (FLO 2007). Consumers worldwide spent U.S. $2.024 billion on fair trade–certified products (FLO 2007). The expanding list of fair trade products includes coffee, cocoa, tea, fruits, wine, sugar, honey, bananas, rice, crafts, and some textiles (Krier

2005). Although artisans and craft producers helped to pioneer the fair trade movement, coffee has emerged as the economic backbone of the certified fair trade system (Bacon et al. 2008).

Fair Trade History The historical roots of the global fair trade movement, like those of many international social movements, extend into many lives, organizations, and landscapes. The primary partnership consisted of impoverished small-scale producers and artisans selling high-quality goods to Northern volunteers, NGOs, and, later, businesses. The risk was often shared between producing and consuming ends of the movement: producers and artisans sometimes provided their products months or even years before receiving full payment after volunteers and alternative trade organizations sold them to distant markets. On the other hand, fair trade organizers from the North provided producers with loans that would otherwise be unavailable and bought crafts and coffee before they had developed markets.

The early alternative trade organizations emerged around handicrafts, often connecting religious and politically motivated Northern groups with groups of women artisans in impoverished communities. In 1946, Edna Ruth Byler, a church volunteer working with the Mennonite Central Committee in Pennsylvania, started buying quilts directly from seamstresses in Puerto Rico. Several years later, the church assumed this project and later created Ten Thousand Villages, an alternative trade organization that as of 2006 connected to some 100 artisan groups and had annual sales in excess of $20 million (DeCarlo 2007). Another early alternative trade organization, called SERVE International (Sales Exchange for Refugee Rehabilitation and Vocation), began as an income generation project in 1949 through the sale of wooden clocks carved by refugees in Germany. In 1959, Oxfam, UK, launched the Helping-by-Selling project to import and sell handicrafts (Oxfam 2007). Later that same decade, the first Worldshop opened in the Netherlands. By 2005, there were more than 2,800 Worldshops throughout Western Europe selling mostly fair trade products with annual sales of about $151.8 million (Krier 2005).

Coffee led the rise of fairly traded agricultural products, which followed a path similar to crafts until alternative trade organizations united with other NGOs and traders to create an international certification system in 1988. The emergence of a product certification system allowed the participation of more conventional companies, expanded fair trade markets, and shifted the ratio of global fair trade goods from crafts to foods and beverages. Dutch fair trade advocates were connected to fair trade coffee cooperatives from Guatemala and Mexico by the early 1970s. In the 1980s, two U.S.-based companies, the Equal Exchange workers cooperative and the Thanksgiving Coffee Company, imported Nicaraguan coffee through Canada in protest against the Reagan administration's embargo against the Sandinista government. During the same decade, a large cooperative of small-scale indigenous farmers in southern Mexico called the Unión de Comunidades Indígenas de la Región del Istmo began working with Frans VanderHoff Boersma, a liberation theology–inspired Jesuit priest from Holland (VanderHoff Boersma and Roozen 2003). VanderHoff Boersma and others soon identified that a core bottleneck in the fair trade movement was the lack of demand in Northern countries. The small volumes traded through these alternative networks limited revenue generation and community development impacts for small-scale producer organizations.

In response to the problem of how to expand fair trade product demand and distribution without compromising consumer trust, producer groups and Dutch organizers created a *product* certification and labeling system called Max Havelaar. Max Havelaar later united with European and North American NGOs to create Fairtrade Labeling Organizations International (FLO) in 1997. FLO is an international nonprofit multistakeholder association that seeks to establish fair trade standards; support, inspect, and certify disadvantaged producers; and harmonize the fair trade message across the movement (FLO 2007). The combination of activist push, the availability of a credible third-party product certification program (that adheres to ISO 65 standards), consumer demand, and growing public awareness

about the low commodity prices contributed to several large mainstream companies' decision to sell fair trade–certified products (Bacon et al. 2008). In an effort to support the alternative aspects within the fair trade movement and distinguish themselves from the large multinational companies, which include Starbucks, Procter and Gamble, and Nestlé, the International Fair Trade Association created a certification for alternative trade *organizations* that implemented fair trade principles throughout their operations.

Impacts, Debate, and Paradox Total sales figures, certification programs, and organizational histories tell us little about the ability of fair trade to deliver on its stated empowerment and sustainable development goals. A primary consideration in assessing fair trade impacts is the fact that as of 2006 only 20 percent of the agricultural goods produced by fair trade–certified organizations are sold according to generally accepted fair-trade terms (FLO 2007). Producers generally sell the remaining 80% of their products into lower-paying domestic and international markets. An important percentage is consumed within the household or traded locally. Furthermore, many producers have participated in this market for less than seven years. Most scholars agree that small-scale producers linked to fair trade are better off than producers that lack these connections (Jaffee 2007; Raynolds 2002). Many producers have advanced their sense of collective empowerment by building stronger organizations, and they have also conserved biological and cultural diversity through their farming practices (Bacon et al. 2008). However, the combination of fair trade sales and additional support from allied international development NGOs is not a panacea for eliminating poverty or stopping out-migration even within fair trade organizations (Bacon et al. 2008; Jaffee 2007; Hernández Navarro 2004). The minimum coffee prices are especially important when conventional market prices fall. Cooperatives used their links to fair trade networks to strengthen their capacity and grow as they outcompeted private exporters and transnational trading companies and helped to buffer small-scale farmers from consequences of the coffee crisis in 1992 and again in 1999–2004 (Bacon et al. 2008). Artisans have generally been able to sustain their crafts and cultures and partially support their livelihoods even as they have improved their organizations' business capacity through direct connections to better markets for their products (Leclair 2002).

Although fair trade has proven itself a useful tool for Southern producer organizations to strengthen their collective influence and for Northern social justice activists leading campaigns to declare fair trade towns and college campuses, it has yet to make significant contributions to international trade and development policy. Fair trade advocates have won voluntary support from the United Nations and the European Commission, and certified fair trade coffee is even served in the U.S. Capitol. No standards have been clearly adopted into global trade regulations, however. Small-scale producers have also used their participation in fair trade to strengthen their alliances and increase their visibility and negotiating power (Renard 2005). For example, the Latin American and Caribbean Network of Small-Scale Fair Trade Producers (CLAC), which represents more than 200,000 producer families, has used its participation in fair trade to win a seat on the FLO board of directors, to gain partial ownership of the certified fair trade system, and to advocate for minimum prices that keep up with inflation and cover the costs of sustainable production (CLAC 2006).

As a voluntary third-party certification system, fair trade contributes to debates about corporate social responsibility and the role of consumers, big business, and more cooperative economies in international sustainable development. One of the certified fair trade system's central paradoxes is that it sets out to achieve social justice and environmental sustainability within the same market that many believe impoverished small producers in the first place. There is also competition with a rapidly expanding array of sustainable product certification programs, such as the Rainforest Alliance and Utz Certified. Although this hybrid approach causes fair trade activists, producer organizations, NGO administrators, and business leaders to live in ideologically uncomfortable spaces, it may hold the potential to transform market-centered relationships from the inside out.

See also North-South trade; primary products trade; trade and economic development, international

FURTHER READING

Bacon, C. M., V. E. Méndez, S. Gliessman, D. Goodman, and J. A. Fox, eds. 2008. *Confronting the Coffee Crisis: Fair Trade, Sustainable Livelihoods, and Ecosystems in Mexico and Central America.* Cambridge, MA: MIT Press. Uses an action-oriented interdisciplinary perspective to analyze the global coffee industry and assess its effects on sustainable community development.

Barratt-Brown, Michael. 1993. *Fair Trade: Reform and Realities in the International Trading System.* London: Zed. One of the earlier books by a pioneer scholar and organizer within the fair trade movement.

CLAC. 2006. *Estudio de Costos y Propuesta de Precios para Sostener el Café, las Familias de Productores y Organizaciones Certificadas por Comercio Justo en América Latina y el Caribe.* Dominican Republic: Assemblea de Coordinadora Latinoamericana y del Caribe de Pequeños Productores de Comercio Justo. Available at http://www.claccomerciojusto.org/. The most recent study that analyzes the costs of sustainable coffee production and poses a substantial increase in the minimum price for fair trade certified coffee.

DeCarlo, Jacqueline. 2007. *Fair Trade: A Beginner's Guide.* Oxford, UK: One World. An excellent and accessible introduction to fair trade, with a strong focus on crafts.

Fairtrade Labeling Organizations International (FLO). 2007. *Shaping Global Partnerships: FLO Annual Report 2006/2007.* Bonn, Germany: FLO International. An annual report that offers an in-depth summary of the size, scope, and accomplishments within the certified fair trade system.

Hernández Navarro, L. 2004. "To Die a Little: Migration and Coffee in Mexico and Central America." Special Report. Silver City, NM: International Relations Center, Americas Program (December). Accessed December 16, 2006, http://www.americaspolicy.org/. Documents the high rates of out-migration from coffee growing regions.

Jaffee, Daniel. 2007. *Brewing Justice: Fair Trade Coffee, Sustainability and Survival.* Berkeley: University of

California Press. Combines a well-written review of the fair trade coffee industry with a case study among indigenous farmers in Mexico.

Krier, J-M. 2005. *Fair Trade in Europe 2005: Facts and Figures on Fair Trade in 25 European countries.* Brussels, Belgium: Fairtrade Labeling Organizations International, International Fair Trade Association, Network of European World Shops, and European Fair Trade Association Fair Trade Advocacy Office. Summarizes the fair trade markets and products (including both crafts and agricultural goods) in Europe.

Leclair, M. S. 2002. "Fighting the Tide: Alternative Trade Organizations in the Era of Global Free Trade." *World Development* 30 (6): 949–58. Summarizes the free trade debates and the role of alternative trade organizations' proposed response.

Oxfam UK, 2007. http://www.oxfam.org.uk/oxfam_in_action/index.html. Documents Oxfam's pioneering work in humanitarian assistance and fair trade.

Raynolds, Laura T. 2002. *Poverty Alleviation through Participation in Fair Trade Coffee Networks: Existing Research and Critical Issues.* New York: Ford Foundation. An early series of case studies documenting the qualitative impacts of fair trade coffee sales on poverty reduction.

Renard, Marie-Christine. 2005. "Quality Certification, Regulation, and Power in Fair Trade." *Journal of Rural Studies* 21: 419-31. An excellent summary of issues of quality, power asymmetries, and debates within the fair trade coffee movement.

VanderHoff Boersma, Franz, and Nico Roozen. 2003. *La Aventura del Comercio Justo: Una Alternativa de Globalización.* Mexico City: El Atajo. A chronicle of history, relationships, and debates in the fair trade movement, written by pioneers of fair trade certification.

CHRISTOPHER M. BACON

■ fear of floating

Since the end of the Bretton Woods system of fixed exchange rates in the early 1970s, the number of countries claiming to be running a flexible exchange rate regime has steadily grown. However, many of these countries appear to actively limit fluctuations in the external value of their national monies. Economists Calvo and Reinhart (2002) dubbed this behavior "fear of floating" and argued that this phenomenon appears pervasive in so-called "emerging markets" (middle-income countries with some access to global financial markets). Indeed, many self-proclaimed "floaters" often accumulate vast war chests of international reserves, which would not be necessary if their currencies were truly floating. In other words, many countries float with "a large life-jacket." Such behavior is puzzling not only because it does not match official pronouncements by policymakers, but also because emerging market economies are typically buffeted by larger and more frequent external shocks, which in theory necessitate more (not less) exchange rate flexibility.

Why Is Floating So Fearsome? Several interlocking factors underlie "fear of floating." First, while many industrial countries have operated fairly flexible exchange rates quite effectively, they have well-developed and diversified financial systems that are able to minimize real sector disruptions due to transitory exchange rate variations. Most important, industrial countries are able to borrow overseas in their domestic currencies. In contrast, many emerging economies are unable to do so, leading to an accumulation of foreign currency debt liabilities that are primarily dollar-denominated and unhedged (i.e., "liability dollarization"). This is commonly referred to as the "original sin" problem. In these countries, sharp depreciations in their currencies alter the domestic currency value of their external debt and therefore the net worth of the economies, with calamitous real sector effects. This in turn may explain why exchange rate stability is so important to emerging economies, and why many of these economies have an acute "fear of floating."

The inability to borrow overseas in one's own currency is related to the lack of hedging in a number of emerging economies. Even if a country has the ability to hedge, the transaction costs can be too high to make it an attractive option, especially in the short term. In view of this, it may be reasonable to expect some smaller domestic firms in emerging economies to be affected by exchange rate volatility (Bénassy-Quéré, Fontagné, and Lahrèche-Révil 2001). However, many economists argue that multinational firms can protect themselves from exchange rate fluctuations by maintaining diversified production facilities in different countries and by sourcing from a number of different countries.

Second, policymakers in emerging markets suffer from a chronic lack of credibility. They often have a poor track record in monetary and fiscal policy as a result of, for example, resorting to the inflation tax too often in the past. Consequently, an emerging economy might experience large and frequent shocks to exchange rate expectations or to interest rate risk premiums. A true floater would allow the spot exchange rate to absorb these shocks, while a true pegger would allow the interest rate to adjust in a way to keep the spot exchange rate stable. Governments struck by "fear of floating" allow for some flexibility in both variables, but by and large it is the interest rate that absorbs most of the shock. This might be why various empirical studies have found that emerging economies with officially floating exchange rates have domestic interest rates whose volatility is considerably higher than that in the developed world. Policymakers in these countries might be limiting exchange rate volatility as a way to gain credibility and in order to signal to financial markets their commitment to monetary discipline.

A third reason for "fear of floating" is that small and open economies are relatively more susceptible to exchange rate pass-through effects in domestic prices.

Fourth, countries with flexible regimes have experienced "excessive" volatility over the last few decades. It is difficult to define "excessive" with any precision, but evidence of excessive exchange rate variability comes in a number of forms. For instance, a number of surveys of foreign exchange ("forex") market participants clearly indicate that short-term/high-frequency exchange rate movements are caused by "speculative" or "trend-following" behavior rather than by underlying macroeconomic fundamentals. Indeed, destabilizing speculation is a particular problem in developing countries with thin markets (Indonesia's postcrisis experience since 1999 is a case in point). Of course, even if flexible exchange

rates exhibited greater volatility than would be warranted by underlying fundamentals, why might such excessive volatility be of concern? Studies suggest that institutionally fixed exchange rate regimes (i.e., common currency, currency boards, or dollarization) stimulate trade, which in turn boosts income. Proponents of the European Monetary Union (EMU) have used such an argument extensively in support of a single regional currency.

Fifth, some economists argue that access to global financial markets for developing countries is conditioned on currency stability. A sharp depreciation in the nominal exchange rate will often trigger an abrupt pause or even reversal of capital flows into the country (the so-called "sudden stop"). Empirically, such a reversal is associated with a sharp adjustment in the current account (from deficit to surplus), an output contraction, and a collapse in credit ratings.

Finally, there are political reasons behind "fear of floating." Sharp fluctuations in the nominal exchange rate combined with sticky prices translate into unstable relative prices for traded versus nontraded goods. This might cause political disruption in a country in which both the traded and nontraded sectors are large and have powerful lobbies.

Significance Given these explanations for fear of floating, it is reasonable to ask why emerging economies do not fix their currencies explicitly. One reason is that pegging the exchange rate constrains monetary independence. To be sure, some research casts doubt on the extent to which floating regimes in emerging economies provide insulation from foreign interest rate shocks (see Frankel, Schmukler, and Serven 2004; and Hausman, Panizza, and Stein 2001). However, a more recent study using de facto exchange rate regimes for 100 developing and industrial countries between 1973 and 2000 finds that the interest rates of the countries that operated pegged regimes followed the base country far more closely than nonpegs (Shambaugh 2004). There is also some evidence that emerging economies "learn to float" in the sense that as they adopt more flexible exchange rate regimes, they tend to adopt stronger monetary and financial frameworks (Hakura 2005). China appears to be a good example of a country engaging in this "learning to float" behavior. For example, as the Chinese authorities gradually allow for greater volatility of the currency, they are also putting in place the necessary infrastructure and institutions to ensure that the foreign exchange market functions well (i.e., is liquid) and that agents are able to hedge themselves against volatility. The loss of monetary-policy autonomy can have significant costs that must be carefully considered by policymakers.

See also balance sheet approach/effects; Bretton Woods system; common currency; contagion; currency board arrangement (CBA); discipline; European Monetary Union; exchange rate pass-through; exchange rate regimes; expenditure changing and expenditure switching; foreign exchange intervention; hedging; hot money and sudden stops; impossible trinity; international reserves; original sin; real exchange rate; speculation

FURTHER READING

Bénassy-Quéré, A., L. Fontagné, and A. Lahrèche-Révil. 2001. "Exchange Rate Strategies in the Competition for Attracting FDI." *Journal of the Japanese and International Economies* 15 (2): 178–98. Examines the impact of exchange rate volatility on FDI.

Calvo, G., and C. Reinhart. 2002. "Fear of Floating." *Quarterly Journal of Economics* 117 (2): 379–408. This paper, along with the following one, launched the debate on "fear of floating."

———. 2005. "Fixing for Your Life." In *Emerging Capital Markets in Turmoil: Bad Luck or Bad Policy?* edited by Guillermo Calvo. Cambridge, MA: MIT Press, 357–402.

Edwards, S. 2006. "The Relationship between Exchange Rates and Inflation Targeting Revisited." NBER Working Paper No. 12163. Cambridge, MA: National Bureau of Economic Research. Examines the impact of exchange rate pass-through in developing countries.

Frankel, J., S. Schmukler, and L. Serven. 2004. "Global Transmission of Interest Rates: Monetary Independence and Currency Regime." *Journal of International Money and Finance* 23 (5): 701–33. Examines the empirical validity of the impossible trinity.

Ghosh, A., and R. S. Rajan. 2007. "A Survey of Exchange Rate Pass-through in Asia: What Does the Literature Tell Us?" *Asia Pacific Economic Literature* 21 (2): 13–28. Examines the analytical and empirical literature on exchange rate pass-through into inflation in Asian economies.

Hakura, D. S. 2005. "Are Emerging Market Countries Learning to Float?" IMF Working Paper No. WP/05/98. Washington, DC: International Monetary Fund. Discusses how the underlying institutional exchange rate and monetary framework of a country changes as economies "learn to float."

Hausmann, R., U. Panizza, and E. Stein. 2001. "Why Do Countries Float the Way They Float?" *Journal of Development Economics* 66 (2): 387–414. An empirical study of "fear of floating," with a special focus on the role of exchange rate pass-through and currency mismatches.

Levy-Yeyati, E., and F. Sturzenegger. 2005. "Classifying Exchange Rate Regimes: Deeds vs. Words." *European Economic Review* 49 (6): 1603–35. Uses "cluster analysis" to disentangle what countries say versus what they do with regard to exchange rate management.

McKenzie, M. 1999. "The Impact of Exchange Rate Volatility on International Trade Flows." *Journal of Economic Surveys* 13 (1): 71–103. Surveys the literature on the impact of exchange rate volatility on trade.

Rajan, R. S. 2006. "Exchange Rate Policies in Asia since the 1997–98 Crisis." Mimeo (July). George Mason University, Arlington, VA. Examines the empirical trends on exchange rate regimes in Asia since the 1997–98 crisis and the analytical rationale behind the choice of various currency regimes.

Shambaugh, J. 2004. "The Effects of Fixed Exchange Rates on Monetary Policy." *Quarterly Journal of Economics* 119 (1): 300–351. Revisits the empirical validity of the impossible trinity.

SLAVI SLAVOV AND RAMKISHEN S. RAJAN

■ Federal Reserve Board

The Board of Governors of the Federal Reserve System (or the Federal Reserve Board, or "Fed," as it is more commonly known) is the central bank of the United States. It was created by an act of Congress, commonly known as the Federal Reserve Act, in 1913. It is a federal system, with its principal central entity, the Board of Governors, in Washington, DC, and 12 regional Federal Reserve Banks, one for each of the 12 Federal Reserve Districts, in Boston, New York, Philadelphia, Cleveland, Richmond, Atlanta, Chicago, St. Louis, Minneapolis, Kansas City, Dallas, and San Francisco.

The Federal Reserve System has five main sets of responsibilities: (1) the conduct of monetary policy, (2) bank supervision, (3) addressing systemic risk, (4) acting as the agent for the U.S. government and for foreign official institutions, and (5) operating the payments system of the United States. Generally, the goals of monetary policy, as established by Congress in a number of statutes passed since 1913, include economic growth, price-level stability, high employment, and moderate long-term interest rates.

The Board of Governors is intended to be an independent government agency as well. The board is not funded by congressional appropriations, and governors, once appointed, can be removed from office only "for cause." The Federal Reserve's decisions are not subject to approval by the executive branch, and its funding comes largely from the interest earnings of its portfolio of Treasury debt instruments.

Independence, however, does not mean isolation: members of the Board of Governors testify frequently before congressional committees, and the chairman is required by law to report in February and July of each year. The board has regular contact with the president's Council of Economic Advisors, and the chairman meets regularly with the secretary of the treasury and at times with the president.

Board Responsibility and Composition The Board of Governors has a staff of professionals (about 1,800) who analyze domestic and international economic and financial conditions. The board oversees the Federal Reserve Banks, regulates the operations of the nation's payments system, and administers laws regarding consumer credit protection.

The Board of Governors has seven members, appointed by the president subject to Senate confirmation, for nonrenewable terms of 14 years staggered so that one term would normally expire January 31 of each even numbered year. (A governor appointed to fill the balance of an unexpired term may still be appointed to a full 14-year term.) The chairman and the vice chairman are nominated by the president from the membership of the existing board, subject to Senate confirmation, for four-year terms, renewable through the end of their term as governor. The chairman is the chief executive of the board and is the public face and the spokesperson of the system.

The board and the system are meant to be apolitical: the law governing the board's composition allows for no more than one governor from any Federal Reserve District and calls on the president to make appointments with "due regard to a fair representation of the financial, agricultural, industrial, and commercial interests, and geographical divisions of the country." The staggered terms and fiscal independence provide a substantial measure of insulation from short-run political influence, as a president in the normal course of events would appoint only two governors during each four-year term in office.

Federal Reserve Banks The regional Federal Reserve Banks, which are the operating arms of the Federal Reserve System, include both public and private elements. Each Federal Reserve Bank has a separate board of nine directors, by law chosen from outside the bank. The boards are intended to represent a cross-section of interests within the district: commercial, agricultural, industrial, and public. Some are elected to their posts by the commercial banks in the district that are member banks in the Federal Reserve System, while others are appointed by the Board of Governors.

Conduct of Monetary Policy Responsibility for the conduct of monetary policy lies with the Federal Reserve System, using four mechanisms:

1. Open market operations—the purchase and sale of securities to raise or lower balances held by depository institutions at Federal Reserve Banks;
2. Reserve requirements: the percentage of deposits that depository institutions must hold in reserve as cash or as deposits at Federal Reserve Banks;

3. Contractual clearing balances: amounts that depository institutions agree to hold at Federal Reserve Banks in addition to required reserves; and

4. Discount Window lending: loans by the Federal Reserve Banks to depository institutions.

The Board of Governors is responsible for setting reserve requirements, and it must approve changes in the discount rate initiated by a regional Federal Reserve Bank. Open market operations are the province of the twelve-member Federal Open Market Committee (FOMC), which includes the seven members of the Board of Governors, the president of the New York Federal Reserve Bank, and 4 of the remaining 11 Federal Reserve Bank presidents. Those banks are arranged into four groups of districts—(1) Boston, Philadelphia, and Richmond; (2) Cleveland, Chicago, and Atlanta; (3) St. Louis, Dallas, and Minneapolis; and (4) Kansas City and San Francisco—and one Federal Reserve Bank president from each group serves a one-year term in rotation with the others from that group. The nonvoting presidents participate in the Open Market Committee deliberations and evaluation of the economy. Open market operations are conducted by the New York Federal Reserve Bank.

In deploying the tools of monetary policy, the Federal Reserve affects the demand for and supply of deposits held by depository institutions at the Federal Reserve Banks, and thus the federal funds rate, which is the interest rate depository institutions charge one another for overnight loans of deposits at the Federal Reserve banks. The most frequently used—daily, in general—instrument of monetary policy is open market operations, an activity that entails, in simple terms, the purchase (or sale) of U.S. Treasury securities by the Federal Reserve to increase (or decrease) aggregate deposits held by depository institutions at the Federal Reserve, and cause the federal funds rate to fall (or rise). Since 1995, the Federal Reserve has announced its target for the federal funds rate.

The discount rate applies to loans made via the Discount Window, a facility available to virtually all depository institutions that maintain reserves. The rate is usually set about 1 percentage point above the target federal funds rate for what is called primary credit, available to sound institutions for short periods, often overnight. All Discount Window loans are backed by collateral. The facility is an important supplement to open market operations when the supply of balances is less than demand. Further, in cases of natural disaster or other market disruption, the Discount Window provides an avenue for assuring credit availability in the financial system.

Bank Supervision The Federal Reserve Board supervises state-chartered banks that are member banks of the Federal Reserve System, bank holding companies, and the foreign activities of member banks. The board and the Federal Reserve Banks together supervise about 900 state banks and about 5,000 bank holding companies. Bank supervision is also provided by the Comptroller of the Currency (for national banks), and the Federal Deposit Insurance Corporation (for state banks that are not member banks of the Federal Reserve System).

International Responsibilities The chairman has international responsibilities, which include serving as the alternate U.S. member of the board of governors of the International Monetary Fund, a member of the board of the Bank for International Settlements, and a member of the National Advisory Council on International Monetary and Financial Policies. The chairman regularly attends the meetings of central bankers and finance ministers of the G7, and meetings of the Organisation for Economic Co-operation and Development in Paris. The board is also represented at international meetings such as the Finance Ministers' Process of the Asia Pacific Economic Cooperation Forum, meetings of the G20, and meetings of the Governors of Central Banks of the American Continent.

The Federal Reserve's foreign currency transactions are done under the direction of the FOMC and in consultation with the U.S. Treasury, which is responsible for U.S. international financial policy. The manager of the System Open Market Account at the Federal Reserve Bank of New York is the agent for both the Treasury and the Federal Reserve in conducting foreign exchange transactions. Since 1995, the Federal Reserve has only rarely intervened in foreign currency markets, though in principle it is ready to do so to counter disorderly market conditions. In 1985, when the governments of the five major industrial countries crafted an agreement on exchange rates known as the Plaza Accord, the United States began using foreign exchange market intervention more frequently than it had previously. That intervention, sometimes in concert with other countries' central banks, continued for about a decade, whenever the movement of dollar exchange rates against foreign currencies was deemed excessive.

Publications The board publishes information about the economy and its activities in publications such as the *Federal Reserve Bulletin* (quarterly) and the *Statistical Supplement* (monthly), the semiannual *Monetary Policy Report to the Congress,* and an *Annual Report.* The Federal Reserve Banks provide the board a variety of information from across their districts, used by the board to compile its assessments of the economy and by the FOMC in arriving at its decisions. This information is summarized and made publicly available in a document, popularly known as the Beige Book, issued about two weeks before each FOMC meeting.

See also Asia Pacific Economic Cooperation (APEC); Bank of Japan; deposit insurance; European Central Bank; foreign exchange intervention; inflation targeting; monetary policy rules; money supply; Plaza Accord

FURTHER READING

Friedman, Milton, and Anna Jacobson Schwartz. 1963. *A Monetary History of the United States, 1867–1960.* Princeton, NJ: Princeton University Press. Nontechnical in its exposition and accessible to the intelligent layperson, this monumental and influential book makes the case that "money matters" using case studies of a large variety of episodes rich in institutional detail, including a major focus on the Great Depression.

Hafer, R. W. 2005. *The Federal Reserve System: An Encyclopedia.* Westport, CT: Greenwood Press. Hafer's volume is aimed at nonspecialists and students, with a wide range of topics including biographical material, and an introduction dealing with the history of central banking in the United States.

Meltzer, Allan H. 2003. *A History of the Federal Reserve.* Chicago: University of Chicago Press. This highly detailed monetarist perspective on the U.S. central bank, from its inception to the Federal Reserve Treasury Accord of 1951, draws from official institutional records and is a complement to the Friedman-Schwartz volume.

JAMES LEHMAN

■ Feldstein-Horioka puzzle

There is a widely held perception that the world economy is highly financially integrated—in other words, a global finance village exists. However, the accumulated evidence suggests that national markets for physical capital (for example, plant and equipment) are much less integrated than national markets for financial capital (for example, bonds and equities). Martin Feldstein and Charles Horioka, in a well-known article of 1980, were among the first to challenge the view of an international capital market. Using data from 16 industrial countries for the period 1960–74, these authors showed that national investment in physical capital is primarily financed by national saving. Feldstein and Horioka used the following cross-section regression to test market segmentation:

$$I_i = \alpha + \beta S_i + u_i, \qquad (1)$$

where I denotes the ratio of national investment to gross domestic product (GDP), S the ratio of national saving to GDP, and the subscript i the country. If national markets are perfectly segmented, the estimated β is unity. National investment is fully financed by national saving, and capital is not mobile among countries. If, instead, national markets are perfectly integrated, the estimated β is zero. High national investment relative to national saving is financed by capital inflows; low national investment relative to national saving prompts an outflow of capital. Feldstein and Horioka tested and failed to reject the null hypothesis of $\beta = 1$ of zero physical capital mobility.

Interpreting the Feldstein-Horioka Results
The Feldstein-Horioka finding instigated a vast empirical literature, which found values of β lower

than unity but larger than zero, especially for the 1980s, but did not disprove the basic conclusion that the markets for physical capital are segmented. Just as important, this literature raised many questions and much criticism on what equation (1) means for capital mobility; three of the most significant criticisms are reviewed here.

The first pertains to the interpretation of parameter β. Consider a classical model in which investment and saving depend exclusively on the real rate of interest, r: r affects negatively I and positively S. In an open economy, an excess of saving over investment implies a net capital outflow or a current account balance surplus, denoted by B. In this model, β is the ratio of the interest sensitivity of investment to the sum of the interest sensitivity of investment, saving, and the current account balance:

$$\beta = I_r/(I_r + S_r + B_r), \qquad (2)$$

where I_r, S_r, and B_r are the slope coefficients of I, S, and B with respect to r (Coakley et al. 1998, 172–73). A simple inspection of equation (2) reveals that complete segmentation of national markets, meaning $\beta = 1$, occurs when both S and B are insensitive to the real interest rate. On the other hand, perfect capital mobility, meaning $\beta = 0$, occurs when either S or B is infinitely sensitive to r. What drives perfect capital mobility: an infinitely elastic saving rate or an infinitely elastic capital account? If we cannot discriminate between alternative causes of high or low β, the test suffers from what is known in jargon as an identification problem. The latter becomes more complex as the underlying models acquire more complexity.

The second criticism concerns the relationship between β and the size of the country. Recall that an excess of saving over investment spills over in a net capital outflow or in a current account surplus in a world of perfect capital mobility. Assume that an unforeseen increase in national saving takes place in a small open economy. The critical assumptions of a small open economy are that its real rate of interest is equal to the world rate of interest and that domestic events cannot influence the world rate of interest. It follows that the world rate of interest and the national investment demand will remain unchanged. The

increase in national saving spills over into larger net capital outflows; the relationship between I and S in equation (1) is such that β is zero. Suppose, instead, that the increase in saving occurs in an economy large enough to influence the world rate of interest. In this case, national I will rise because of the decline in r, and the relationship between I and S in equation (1) is such that β is positive. In sum, β is positively correlated with the size of the economies (Harberger 1980).

The final criticism deals with the use of cross-section data. In the Feldstein-Horioka test and in several subsequent studies, observations are averages of long annual time series. Given that the current account tends to be balanced over long periods of time, I and S tend to equal each other. It follows that the use of time series averages biases the estimate of β toward unity.

Persistence of the "Puzzle" Notwithstanding these criticisms, study after study has confirmed the positive association between investment and saving, to the point that the finding has been elevated to the rank of a "major puzzle" in international macroeconomics (Obstfeld and Rogoff 2001). It is a puzzle because our strong prior, or belief, is that capital is mobile, and our prior has been fed by the evidence on the integration of national markets for financial capital, especially short-term securities issued by industrial countries. Arbitrage tends to quickly eliminate yield differentials. But this parity does not hold for long-term portfolio capital or physical capital (Dooley et al. 1987, 522–23). For national markets of physical capital to be fully integrated, ex-ante real rates of interest in different national markets would have to be equalized; in other words, the following real interest rate parity would have to be satisfied:

$$r - r^* = (i - i^* - fp) + (fp - \Delta e) + (\Delta e - \pi + \pi^*) = 0. \qquad (3)$$

The new symbols in (3) are $\Delta e =$ the expected depreciation of the home currency and $\pi =$ the expected rate of inflation. The evidence overwhelmingly rejects (3), and not surprisingly. For (3) to hold, three conditions need to be simultaneously satisfied: covered interest rate parity (the first term in parentheses in the equation, the difference in national interest rates adjusted for the premium in the forward exchange market); the forward premium as an unbiased estimate of the expected depreciation (second term, the difference between the forward premium and the expected change in the future spot exchange rate); and expected purchasing power parity (third term, the difference between expected changes in national price levels adjusted for the expected change in the future spot exchange rate). The first of these three conditions, as we have noted, has empirical corroboration for selected currencies and a very narrow set of assets. The second and third conditions fail miserably. In sum, the failure of equation (3) supports the basic contention of Feldstein and Horioka that β is not zero.

Other Home Biases The Feldstein and Horioka finding seems to be consistent with two home biases, one in equities and the other in consumption. The domestic bias in equities is measured relative to the asset diversification predicted by the international capital asset pricing model. Given historical mean returns and variances, the model predicts that the weight of foreign equities should be much higher than the observed weight. The discrepancy between predicted and actual weight remains large even under the assumption of infinite relative risk aversion (Lewis 1999, table 2). The bias could stem from the failure of the capital asset pricing model to predict diversification, or from the failure of purchasing power parity, which is a standard assumption of the international capital asset pricing model, or from the failure of both; there is no way to distinguish between the two. Various attempts to justify the equity home bias have also failed.

The domestic consumption bias is measured relative to the prediction made by a model where markets are complete in the Arrow-Debreu sense and countries diversify risks due to idiosyncratic shocks (Obstfeld and Rogoff 1996, chapter 5). In this setting, the growth rate of domestic consumption is equal to that of foreign consumption. The data clearly refute the implication of complete markets (Lewis 1999, table 1).

In sum, financial capital is more mobile than physical capital. There is an obvious parallel between finance capital and traded goods, and between physical capital and nontraded goods. National borders are just as much an obstacle for the cross-border flows of many goods and services as they are for the flows of physical capital.

See also balance of payments; capital controls; capital mobility; forward premium puzzle; home country bias; interest parity conditions; international capital flows to developing countries; peso problem; purchasing power parity

FURTHER READING

Coakley, Jerry, Flarida Kulasi, and Ron Smith. 1998. "The Feldstein-Horioka Puzzle and Capital Mobility: A Review." *International Journal of Finance and Economics* 3: 169–88. Reviews the main issues of the Feldstein-Horioka puzzle.

Dooley, Michael, Jeffrey A. Frankel, and Donald J. Mathieson. 1987. "International Capital Mobility: What Do Saving-Investment Correlations Tell Us?" *IMF Staff Papers* 34: 503–29. Interprets the Feldstein-Horioka evidence as being consistent with a low degree of substitutability for claims on physical capital located in different countries; and physical capital need not be a perfect substitute of financial capital.

Feldstein, Martin, and Charles Y. Horioka. 1980. "Domestic Saving and International Flows." *Economic Journal* 90 (June): 314–29. The original article that shows that countries' investments are highly correlated with their national savings rates.

Harberger, Arnold. 1980. "Vignettes on the World Capital Market." *American Economic Review* 70: 331–37. Argues that capital does not move as freely across national borders as the world capital market view would have it.

Lewis, Karen K. 1999. "Trying to Explain Home Bias in Equities and Consumption." *Journal of Economic Literature* 37 (June): 571–608. Reviews the domestic equity bias and the domestic consumption bias.

Obstfeld, Maurice, and Kenneth Rogoff. 1996. *Foundations of International Macroeconomics.* Cambridge, MA: MIT Press. A graduate-level text on international macroeconomics.

———. 2001. "The Six Major Puzzles in International Macroeconomics: Is There a Common Cause?" In *NBER Macroeconomics Annual 2000*, edited by Ben Bernanke and Kenneth Rogoff. Cambridge, MA: MIT Press, 339–90. Reviews the major puzzles (or better outcomes inconsistent with widely held views) in international macroeconomics.

MICHELE FRATIANNI

■ financial crisis

The financial system is a set of institutions and markets that provides financial intermediation by transferring savings into productive investment. In most developing countries the bulk of financial intermediation has been done via the banking system, with the stock market gaining importance in countries with more advanced institutions. Financial intermediation entails maturity transformation— funding a longer-term tangible investment with shorter-term savings. As such, financial intermediation is exposed to financial fragility, in which heightened perceived risk may lead to liquidation, putting the financial system at risk.

Financial crisis refers to a rapid financial disintermediation due to financial panic. In practice, this involves a "flight to quality," where savers attempt to liquidate assets in financial institutions due to a sudden increase in their perceived risk, moving their savings to safer assets, such as foreign currency and foreign bonds in open economies, or currency, gold, and government bonds in closed economies. The ultimate manifestation of financial crises includes bank failures, stock market crashes, and currency crises, occasionally leading to deep recessions.

The economist Hyman Minsky (1964) theorized that financial fragility—which is related to the business cycle and to leverage—is a typical feature of any capitalist economy. These considerations are at the heart of the large literature propagated by the stock market crash of 1929 and the Great Depression (Bernanke 1995).

Financial Crises and Financial Integration
During the last quarter of the 20th century, observers focused attention on the growing role of international triggers for financial crises—an outcome of the collapse of the Bretton Woods system (the post–World War II framework for international trade and financial stability), the rapid increase in the importance of emerging markets in the global economy, and the growing financial integration of countries with the global financial system. The resumption of capital flows to developing countries in the early 1990s led to waves of "sudden stops" (the abrupt cessation of foreign capital inflows) and reversals of capital flows, starting with the Mexican crisis of 1994–95, continuing with the Russian and the East Asian crises in the second half of the 1990s, and culminating with the Argentinean meltdown in the early 2000s (Calvo 1998; and Edwards 2004).

Most of the financial crises in the 1990s and early 2000s affected developing and emerging markets, leading to a heated debate regarding their causes and the needed remedies. There is solid evidence that financial opening (that is, the dismantling of capital controls) increases the chance of financial crises. There is more tenuous evidence that financial opening contributes positively to long-run growth. Hence there may be a complex trade-off between the adverse intermediate run and the beneficial long-run effects of financial opening. These findings pose a challenge to policymakers: how to supplement financial opening with policies that would improve this intertemporal trade-off.

To place this issue in a broader context, the debate about financial opening is a reincarnation of the earlier immiserizing growth literature in economics. In particular, while financial opening increases a country's overall welfare when the only distortion is restricting intertemporal trade across countries, financial opening may be welfare-reducing in the presence of other distortions (an economic distortion occurs when an inefficiency prevents an economy from reaching its full potential). An example of such a distortion is moral hazard, which frequently acts as an implicit subsidy to borrowing and investment, ultimately leading to overborrowing and crisis

(McKinnon and Pill 1999; and Dooley 2000). Moral hazard arises when investors believe that they will be bailed out of their bad investments by the taxpayer and, therefore, have little incentive to undertake proper monitoring of their investments. This bailing out may be carried out by the treasury, the central bank, or by international agencies. In these circumstances, the taxpayer subsidizes the investment. A frequent rationale for the bailing out is the "too big to fail" doctrine—the fear that allowing large borrowers to go under will trigger a systemic crisis.

Key factors contributing to an exposure to financial crises are balance-sheet features in the form of maturity and currency mismatches between the assets and the liabilities of the banking system, leading to financial fragility. A currency mismatch occurs when residents of the country are not adequately hedged against a change in the exchange rate. This is frequently the case in countries with few foreign assets, serving large external debt denominated in foreign currency, so that a large depreciation generates a large increase in the domestic valuation of the foreign liability, inducing a fall in the economy's net worth, usually accompanied by a large fall in output and insolvencies on the part of firms and banks. Maturity mismatch occurs when the average duration of the liabilities differs from that of the assets. Frequently, banks' liabilities have shorter maturity than banks' assets; hence large withdrawals by consumers may lead to a bank run. Developing countries are more susceptible to balance sheet fragilities and are characterized by debt intolerance: the inability of emerging markets to manage levels of external debt that are manageable for developed, high-income countries (Reinhart, Rogoff, and Savastano 2003).

This literature has led to a spirited debate concerning the wisdom of unrestricted capital mobility between high-income countries and emerging markets. Advocates of financial liberalization in the early 1990s argued that external financing would alleviate the scarcity of savings in developing countries, inducing higher investment and thus higher growth rates. The 1990s experience with financial liberalization suggests that the gains from external financing are overrated—the bottleneck inhibiting economic growth has less to do with the scarcity of saving and more to do with other factors, such as the scarcity of good governance (Rodrik 1998; Gourinchas and Jeanne 2003).

Notwithstanding this debate, the strongest argument for financial opening is the pragmatic one. Like it or not, greater trade integration erodes the effectiveness of restrictions on capital mobility (see Aizenman 2004). Hence, for successful emerging markets that engage in trade integration, financial opening is not a question of if, but of when and how. Instead, the hope is that proper sequencing of policies (see McKinnon 1991) and improved coordination will reduce the severity of financial crises, thereby improving the odds of a positive long-run welfare effect of financial opening.

Financial Opening and Financial Crises: The Evidence The recent research has two common themes: it validates empirically the assertion "Goodbye financial repression, hello financial crash" (Diaz-Alejandro 1985). Yet it also has found tenuous evidence that financial liberalization tends to increase growth over time. Both observations suggest an intertemporal trade-off. In the short-run, the fragility induced by financial opening leads frequently to crises. Yet, if these crises force the country to deal with its structural deficiencies, financial opening may induce a higher growth rate in the long run (see Ranciere, Tornell, and Westermann 2005).

Kaminsky and Reinhart (1999) found that problems in the banking sector typically precede a currency crisis; that a currency crisis deepens the banking crisis, activating a vicious spiral; and that financial liberalization often precedes banking crises. Glick and Hutchison (1999) investigated a sample of 90 countries during 1975–97, covering 90 banking crises, 202 currency crises, and 37 twin crises. They found that banking and twin crises have occurred mainly in developing countries, and their number increased in the 1990s. Twin crises are mainly concentrated in financially liberalized emerging-market economies. The costs of these crises are substantial—currency (banking) crises are very costly, reducing output by about 5 percent–8 percent (8–10 percent) over a two- to four-year year period (Hutchison and Noy 2005).

A useful survey of financial liberalization is found in Williamson and Mahar (1998), which focused on 34 countries that undertook financial liberalization between 1973 and 1996. Overall, the authors found a mixed record of financial liberalization—the gains are there, but the liberalization carries the risk of a financial crisis. Financial liberalization has yielded greater financial depth and increased efficiency in the allocation of investment. Yet it has not brought the boost in saving. The main recommendations emerging from their study are akin to those in Hellman, Murdock, and Stiglitz (2000)—start with macroeconomic stabilization, improve bank supervision, while delaying capital account convertibility to the end of the process. Maintaining high spreads may be needed in a transition until banks are able to work off the legacy of bad debt inherited from the period of financial repression, preventing moral hazard associated with a "gamble for resurrection."

The overall effect of financial opening on growth remains debatable. Rodrik (1998) failed to detect any positive effects of financial opening on investment, growth, and inflation. Bekaert, Harvey, and Lundblad (2001) found that equity market liberalizations, on average, lead to a 1 percent increase in annual real economic growth over a five-year period. The investment/gross domestic product ratio increases postliberalization, with the investment partially financed by foreign capital, inducing worsened trade balances. The liberalization effect is enhanced by a large secondary school enrollment, a small government sector, and an Anglo-Saxon legal system.

In summary, recent financial crises affecting developing countries are the outcome of financial fragilities, reflecting the downside of growing financial integration. The challenge is mitigating the pain in ways that enhance growth and economic welfare.

See also asymmetric information; banking crisis; Bretton Woods system; capital flight; currency crisis; deposit insurance; financial liberalization; financial repression; international reserves; lender of last resort; original sin; sequencing of financial sector reform

FURTHER READING

Aizenman, Joshua. 2004. "Financial Opening and Development: Evidence and Policy Controversies." *American Economic Review* 94 (2): 65–70. Greater trade integration erodes the effectiveness of restrictions on capital flow. Thus, for a country that engages in trade integration, financial opening is not a question of if, but of when and how.

Bekaert, G, C. Harvey, and R. Lundblad. 2001. "Does Financial Liberalization Spur Growth?" NBER Working Paper No. 6724. Cambridge, MA: National Bureau of Economic Research. In a large sample of countries since 1980, financial liberalization leads to a 1 percent increase on average in a country's annual growth rate over a five-year period.

Bernanke, Ben S. 1995. "The Macroeconomics of the Great Depression: A Comparative Approach." *Journal of Money, Credit, and Banking* 27 (1): 1–28. Monetary shocks as aggregate demand force behind the Depression; the induced financial crisis and sticky nominal wages are supply mechanisms by which nominal shocks had real effects.

Calvo, Guillermo A. 1998. "Capital Flows and Capital-Market Crises: The Simple Economics of Sudden Stop." *Journal of Applied Economics* 1 (1): 35–54. Articulates mechanisms through which a sudden stop in international credit flows may bring about financial and balance of payments crises, and examines factors triggering sudden stops.

Catao, Luis, and Sandeep Kapur. 2006. "Volatility and the Debt-Intolerance Paradox." *IMF Staff Papers* 53 (2): 195–218. Differences in macroeconomic volatility account for debt intolerance of developing countries—the ability to borrow is constrained by higher default risk that volatility engenders.

Chang R., and A. Velasco. 1999. "Financial Crises in Emerging Markets." *Economic Review* (Federal Reserve Bank of Atlanta) 84 (2): 4–17. A bank collapse multiplies the harmful effects of an initial shock. Under fixed exchange rates, a run on banks becomes a run on the currency if the central bank acts as a lender of last resort.

Demigüc-Kunt A., and E. Detragiache. 1998. "Financial Liberalization and Financial Fragility." IMF Working Paper No. 98/83. Washington, DC: International Monetary Fund. Banking crises are more likely to occur in liberalized financial systems; the impact of financial liberalization on banking sector fragility is weaker where the institutional environment is strong.

Diaz-Alejandro, C. 1985. "Goodbye Financial Repression, Hello Financial Crash." *Journal of Development Economics* 19 (1/2): 1–24. Unintended consequences of financial liberalization: intrinsic imperfections in financial markets imply that lifting of financial repression leads frequently to financial crash.

Dooley, Michael. 2000. "A Model of Crises in Emerging Markets." *The Economic Journal* 110 (460): 256–72. Variety of shocks generate capital inflows to emerging markets followed by successful and anticipated speculative attacks, liquidating reserve assets accumulated as self-insurance.

Edwards, Sebastian. 2004. "Financial Openness, Sudden Stops, and Current Account Reversals." *American Economic Review* 94 (2): 59–64. Restricting capital mobility does not reduce the probability of experiencing a reversal; flexible exchange rate regimes are better able to accommodate shocks stemming from a reversal.

Glick R., and M. Hutchison. 1999. "Banking and Currency Crises: How Common Are Twins?" In *Financial Crises in Emerging Markets*, edited by Reuven Glick, Ramon Moreno, and Mark Spiegel. New York: Cambridge University Press, 35–69. Crisis phenomenon is most common in financially liberalized emerging markets; banking crises are a leading indicator of currency crises in emerging markets. The converse does not hold.

Gourinchas, Pierre-Olivier, and Olivier Jeanne. 2003. "The Elusive Gains from International Financial Integration." NBER Working Paper No. 9684. Cambridge, MA: National Bureau of Economic Research. Welfare gains from switching from financial autarky to perfect capital mobility in neoclassical models are negligible relative to the welfare gain of a take-off in domestic productivity.

Hellmann, F. Thomas, Kevin C. Murdock, and Joseph E. Stiglitz. 2000. "Liberalization, Moral Hazard in Banking, and Prudential Regulation: Are Capital Requirements Enough?" *American Economic Review* 90 (1): 147–65. Competition can undermine prudent bank behavior in the presence of moral hazard. Pareto-efficient outcomes can be achieved by adding deposit-rate controls as a regulatory instrument.

Hutchison, Michael, and Ilan Noy. 2005. "How Bad Are Twins? Output Costs of Currency and Banking Crises." *Journal of Money, Credit, and Banking* 37 (4): 725–52. Currency (banking) crises are very costly, reducing output by about 5 percent to 8 percent (8–10 percent) over a two- to four-year period, no additional feedbacks associated with twin crises.

Kaminsky, Graciela L., and Carmen M. Reinhart. 1999. "The Twin Crises: The Causes of Banking and Balance-of-Payments Problems." *American Economic Review* 89 (3): 473–500. Problems in the banking sector typically precede a currency crisis; currency crisis deepens the banking crisis, activating a vicious spiral; financial liberalization often precedes banking crises.

McKinnon, Ronald. 1991. *The Order of Economic Liberalization: Financial Control in the Transition to a Market Economy.* Baltimore: Johns Hopkins University Press. Financial control and macroeconomic stability are more critical to a successful transition than is any crash program to privatize state-owned industrial assets and the banking system.

McKinnon, Ronald, and Huw Pill. 1999. "Exchange-Rate Regimes for Emerging Markets: Moral Hazard and International Overborrowing." *Oxford Review of Economic Policy* 15 (3): 19–38. Investigates the overborrowing syndrome. A "good" exchange rate peg stabilizes the domestic economy while limiting moral hazard in the banking system.

Minsky, M. Hyman. 1964. "Longer Waves in Financial Relations: Financial Factors in the More Severe Depressions." *American Economic Review* 54 (2): 324–35. Firms' need to finance investment spending and capital externally explains longer and deeper swings in economic experience.

Ranciere Romain, Aaron Tornell, and Frank Westermann. 2005. "Systemic Crises and Growth." NBER Working Paper No. 11076. Cambridge, MA: National Bureau of Economic Research. Financial liberalizations facilitate risk-taking, increasing leverage and investment, leading to higher growth, but also to a greater incidence of crises.

Reinhart, C., K. Rogoff, and M. Savastano. 2003. "Debt Intolerance." *Brookings Papers on Economic Activity* 1: 1–74. Debt intolerance is the duress many emerging markets experience at debt levels that are manageable by advanced country standards, and is linked to default and inflation history.

Rodrik, Dani. 1998. "Who Needs Capital-Account Convertibility?" In *Should the IMF Pursue Capital Account Convertibility? Essays in International Finance No. 207* (May), edited by Peter Kenen. Princeton, NJ: Princeton University Press, 55–65. The magnitude of recent crises is not justified by changes in the fundamentals of the affected economies; capital account liberalization is not necessary as a tool for growth.

Williamson, John, and Molly Mahar. 1998. "A Survey of Financial Liberalization." *Princeton Essays in International Finance No. 211*. Princeton, NJ: Princeton University Press. Evidence that financial liberalizations lead to financial deepening and increase the efficiency of investment allocation, but frequently spawn financial crisis.

JOSHUA AIZENMAN

■ financial integration

See capital mobility

■ financial liberalization

Financial liberalization, or *financial reform*, in the most general sense, refers to the transition away from a financial system characterized by state intervention and ownership and toward a more market-oriented system. Not only does financial liberalization need to be considered in discrete historical phases that differ by region and level of development, it also can and should be understood as it applies to the domestic and international spheres. Sometimes this distinction boils down to the difference between banking reform and capital market reform. Outward, or externally oriented, financial liberalization involves lifting state controls on the flow of finance between the country in question and international financial markets, including allowing for competition from international banks operating within the country. Internally oriented financial liberalization focuses on removing restrictions on competition and other business practices within the domestic financial markets.

Internally Oriented Controls and Liberalization One of the most common forms of restrictions placed on domestic banks in both developed and developing countries has been interest rate ceilings—that is, restrictions on the interest rate banks are allowed to pay depositors in order to compete for their deposits, and/or limits on the interest rate banks are allowed to charge borrowers on their loans. Deregulation or liberalization in this case entails removing such ceilings.

Another form of interest rate regulation takes a more microeconomic form. Governments can set different interest rate ceilings depending on the economic sector of the loan. In this way, governments gain control over where banks choose to direct financial resources and who has access to credit. This is sometimes referred to as sector-specific allocation of finance, which has been much more common among newly industrializing economies (NIEs) in Asia than in Latin America or advanced industrial countries. Another method of sector-specific allocation is the manipulation of marginal reserve requirements on bank deposits. For example, monetary officials could control the allocation of private investment by altering the level of reserves private banks are required to hold in the central bank. Sometimes the reserve requirements would be adjusted depending on the sector of the economy to which loans were destined. (For a more detailed discussion of how this worked in Mexico, see Auerbach 2001). Especially in Asia, directed finance was part of a broader industrial policy strategy of state-led industrialization.

The most direct way that governments have controlled the flow of domestic finance, particularly in developing countries, is through ownership of banks. Thus privatization, that is, the process of selling off these banks to the private sector, often becomes the cornerstone of financial liberalization for the domestic market. Even after the domestic banking sector has been privatized, however, governments often and to varying degrees retain some control over where private sector banks direct their financial resources. This phenomenon, often called "window guidance," was mostly practiced in Asian economies by heavily interventionist developmental states such as South Korea and Japan that were unwilling to give up complete control over the allocation of finance despite the intense pressure to liberalize.

Another of the mechanisms by which governments have retained control over privatized banking sectors is through the authority to charter new banks. While this authority, much like the authority to print money, falls naturally under the purview of the state and would not necessarily be considered interventionist, the level of restrictions on new charters and the form that those restrictions take do fall under the umbrella of state intervention. Thus when restrictions on chartering are lifted altogether, or when preferential charter policies are replaced with neutrally applied charters that treat foreign and domestic owners alike, these policy reforms would be considered a form of financial liberalization.

Restrictions on banking competition have taken multiple and specific forms often related to particular national histories. In the United States, for example, legislation once mandated that banks could not take deposits in more than one state and that banks could not directly own stock in industrial firms. The repeal of this legislation in 1999 represented for the United States one of the last steps in a financial reform process that began in the 1970s with the lifting of interest rate ceilings.

External Financial Liberalization Externally oriented liberalization aims to remove restrictions of financial flows or price controls between the domestic financial market and international finance. The removal of capital controls in advanced industrial countries took place mostly by the 1970s primarily because of the ineffectiveness of these controls in the context of new technologies that allowed banks to transfer capital internationally at the touch of a button. Yet there have been notable exceptions to this rule. Chile imposed a significant tax on capital outflows, known as the "Chile tax," in the 1990s that effectively controlled the outflow of capital.

The second major type of external liberalization came in the form of allowing the entry of foreign banks into domestic banking markets that had been previously restricted to domestic ownership. This type of liberalization has been slow and piecemeal given the politically charged role that banking plays in most economies.

Liberalizing exchange rates has resulted in part from the pressures of increasingly mobile international capital. Most experts have agreed that managing exchange rates has become increasingly difficult and risky given the tendency for exchange rate speculation in international currency markets. While governments have continued to see the exchange rate as a key economic variable affecting trade competitiveness and foreign investment flows, their ability to manipulate that variable waned considerably in the 1990s.

Waves of Financial Liberalization Historically and globally, financial liberalization has come in waves. The 1970s saw a major wave of financial reforms among advanced industrial countries. Some authors frame the wave of market-oriented reforms among advanced industrial countries as part of the breakdown of the Bretton Woods system, which promoted state intervention through tight control over international financial flows. The end of the Bretton Woods system resulted in an immediate shift from pegged, or fixed, to floating exchange rates for most advanced industrial countries. Most attempted to maintain capital controls, but rapidly increasing financial flows aided by new computer technologies rendered these policies increasingly costly and difficult to monitor. Capital controls in the United States were permanently removed in 1974, and in Britain in 1979. The last European countries to lift controls were Portugal and Ireland in the early 1990s.

In contrast to the advanced industrial country experience, developing countries, especially the NIEs, maintained more state interventionist—or what some have called "repressed"—financial systems until the 1980s. Here the catalyst for the wave of reforms came as a result of the Latin American debt crisis. Again, interpretations of this wave of financial liberalization differ widely among proponents and opponents of financial liberalization. Proponents are apt to suggest that the debt crisis was the natural result of years of inefficient financial intervention or repression of financial markets. Opponents of financial liberalization, on the other hand, argue that the debt crisis put developing countries between a rock and a hard place: under international pressure from the United States and the International Monetary Fund (IMF), they had little choice but to liberalize their financial markets or face being permanently cut off from international capital flows. As a result, most Latin American countries and some Asian countries, to varying degrees, lifted interest rate ceilings, stopped using marginal reserve requirements to direct finance to specific sectors, loosened capital controls, and began privatizing the banking sector as part of the first rounds of financial reforms in the 1980s.

With the 1990s came a new set of financial crises that precipitated a new round of financial liberalization, this time focused on external capital markets and domestic banking. Lively debate over the pros and cons of financial liberalization has arisen among economists and political scientists as well. Particularly after the Asian financial crisis of 1997, proponents of financial liberalization blamed insufficient liberalization in the previous decade as the primary cause, while opponents blamed overly rapid and extensive liberalization, particularly the liberalization of external capital flows (see, e.g., Furman and Stiglitz 1998; and Rodrik 1996).

Most of the political economy literature on financial liberalization has focused on the causes of liberalization without differentiating between perverse and benign forms of liberalization. A growing political economy literature now rejects the notion that financial liberalization is either inherently beneficial or harmful, but instead describes the political conditions under which liberalization will promote growth and efficiency as opposed to perverse outcomes.

See also banking crisis; Bretton Woods system; capital controls; capital flows to developing countries; convertibility; currency crisis; exchange rate regimes; financial crisis; Washington consensus

FURTHER READING

Auerbach, N. 2001. *States, Banks, and Markets: Mexico's Path to Financial Liberalization in Comparative Perspective.* Boulder, CO: Westview Press. Discusses Mexico's experience with financial liberalization.

Furman, J., and J. Stiglitz. 1998. "Economic Crises: Evidence and Insights from East Asia." *Brookings Papers on Economic Activity No. 2*, 1–114.

Rodrik, D. 1996. "Understanding Economic Policy Reform." *Journal of Economic Literature* 34: 9–41. The Rodrik and Furman and Stiglitz articles argue that other economists oversold the benefits of the free movement of financial flows internationally as part of the benefits of financial liberalization.

Smith, P. H., K. Horisaka, and S. Nishijima. 2003. *East Asia and Latin America: The Unlikely Alliance.* Lanham, MD: Rowman and Littlefield. Articles in this book offer an interesting comparison of directed credit, industrial policies, and financial liberalization in Asia versus Latin America.

Williamson, J., and M. Mahar. 1998. "A Survey of Financial Liberalization." *Essays in International Finance No. 211.* Princeton: Princeton University, Department of Economics, International Finance Section. An excellent overview of the aspects of financial liberalization, including sequencing issues.

NANCY NEIMAN AUERBACH

■ financial repression

Financial repression refers to the notion that a set of government regulations, laws, or other nonmarket restrictions prevents an economy's financial intermediaries—such as banks and security markets—from functioning at their full capacity. The policies that cause financial repression include interest rate ceilings, liquidity ratio requirements, high bank reserve requirements, capital controls, restrictions on market entry into the financial sector, credit ceilings or restrictions on directions of credit allocation, and government ownership or domination of banks. Economists have commonly argued that financial repression prevents the efficient allocation of capital and thereby impairs economic growth.

The economists McKinnon (1973) and Shaw (1973) were the first to explicate the notion of financial repression. While theoretically an economy with an efficient financial system can achieve growth and development through efficient capital allocation, McKinnon and Shaw argue that historically, many countries, including developed ones but especially developing ones, have restricted competition in the financial sector with government interventions and regulations. According to McKinnon and Shaw's argument, a repressed financial sector discourages both saving and investment because the rates of return are lower than what could be obtained in a competitive market. In such a system, financial intermediaries do not function at their full capacity and fail to channel saving into investment efficiently, thereby impeding the development of the overall economic system.

Rationale for and Types of Financial Repression The control of fiscal resources is a key reason for the implementation of financially repressive policies by governments. By having a direct control over the financial system, the government can funnel funds to itself without going through legislative procedures and more cheaply than it could when it resorts to market financing. More specifically, by restricting the behavior of existing and potential participants in the financial markets, the government can create monopoly or captive rents (that is, economic profits that can arise from market imperfection) for the existing banks and also tax some of these rents so as to finance its overall budget, which may be economically attractive to both the existing banks and the government. Existing banks may try to collude with one another and to interrupt possible liberalization policies as long as they are guaranteed their collective monopoly position in the domestic market.

In some countries, governments require banks to meet high reserve ratios and seize some of these reserves as government revenues. Because reserves earn no interest, reserve requirements function as an implicit tax on banks and also restrict banks from allocating a certain portion of their portfolios to productive investments and loans. When high reserve ratios are required, the lending and borrowing rate spread must widen to incorporate the amount of no-interest reserves, which can reduce the amount of funds available in the financial market. If high reserve requirements are combined with interest ceilings and protective government directives for certain borrowers, savers—who are usually unaware of the requirement policy—become the main "taxpayers" because they face reduced rates of interest on their savings. Inflation can aggravate the "reserve tax" because it reduces the real rates of interest. Thus high reserve requirements make the best use of the government's monopolistic power to generate seigniorage revenue (the revenue monetary authorities can create by issuing currency) as well as to regulate reserve requirements. A variant of this policy includes required liquidity ratios—banks are required to allocate a certain fraction of their deposits to holding government securities that usually yield a return lower than could be obtained in the market.

Governments often impose a ceiling on the interest rate banks can offer to depositors. Interest ceilings function in the same way as price controls, and thereby provide banks with economic rents. Like high required reserve ratios, those rents benefit incumbent banks and provide tax sources for the government, paid for by savers and by borrowers or would-be borrowers. The rents borne by the interest ceiling reduce the number of loans available in the market—the real interest rates on loans and deposits are higher and lower, respectively, thereby discouraging both saving and investment. In return for allowing incumbent banks to reap rents, the government often requires banks to make subsidized loans to certain borrowers for the purpose of implementing industrial policy (or simply achieving some political goals). Interest ceilings in high inflation countries can victimize savers because high inflation can make the real interest rates of return negative.

Financial repression also takes the form of government directives for banks to allocate credit at subsidized rates to specific firms and industries to implement industrial policy. Forcing banks to allocate credit to industries that are perceived to be strategically important for industrial policy ensures stable provision of capital rather than leaving it to decisions of disinterested banks or to efficient securities markets. It is also more cost effective than going through the public sector's budgetary process. Government directives and guidance sometimes include detailed orders and instructions on managerial issues to financial institutions to ensure that their behavior and business are in line with industrial policy or other government policies. The Japanese Ministry of Finance (MOF) is a typical example of government's micromanagement of the financial industry. Till the 1980s, for example, the MOF segmented the banking industry into different types of banks and specified what kind of borrowers and depositors banks in each type can deal with, along with other specific directives and "administrative guidance" about the banking business allowed for each type of banks. The extreme example of direct state control of banks is the nationalization of banks as was observed in Mexico in the 1980s, when the government took control of all the banks to secure public savings.

Capital controls are restrictions on the inflows and outflows of capital, and are also financially repressive policies. Despite their virtues, the use of capital controls can involve costs. Because of their uncompetitive nature, capital controls increase the cost of capital by creating financial autarky (that is, restricting access to cheaper capital available outside the domestic market), limit domestic and foreign investors' ability to diversify their portfolios, and help inefficient financial institutions to survive by protecting them from international competition.

Impacts of Financial Repression Because financial repression leads to inefficient allocation of capital, high costs of financial intermediation, and lower rates of return to savers, it is theoretically clear that financial repression inhibits growth (Roubini and Sala-i-Martin 1992). The empirical findings on the effect of removing financial repression, that is, financial liberalization, on growth support this view. These findings suggest that liberalization spurs growth through various channels.

The possible negative effect of financial repression on economic growth does not automatically mean that countries should adopt a laissez-faire stance on financial development and remove all regulations and controls that create financial repression. Many developing countries that liberalized their financial markets experienced crises partly because of the external shocks that financial liberalization introduces or amplifies. Indeed, financial liberalization can create short-term volatility despite its long-term gains (Kaminsky and Schmukler 2002). Also, because of market imperfections and information asymmetries (in which one party to a financial transaction has better information than the other), removing all public financial regulations may not yield an optimal environment for financial development. An alternative to a financially repressive administration would be a new set of regulations to ensure market competition as well as prudential regulation and supervision.

See also asymmetric information; banking crisis; capital controls; capital flight; convertibility; financial liberalization; money supply; seigniorage

FURTHER READING

Ariyoshi, Akira, Karl Habermeier, Bernard Laurens, Inci Otker-Robe, Jorge Iván Canales-Kriljenko, and Andrei Kirilenko. 2000. "Capital Controls: Country Experiences with Their Use and Liberalization." IMF Occasional Paper 190 (May). Washington, DC: International Monetary Fund. Presents an overview of capital controls by discussing the role of capital controls and the current trend of capital account liberalization.

Beim, David, and Charles W. Calomiris. 2001. *Emerging Financial Markets*. New York: McGraw Hill. Discusses factors that contribute to the development of financial markets, especially those in emerging market countries. One of the chapters discusses the effect of financial repression.

Claessens, Stijin. 2005. "Finance and Volatility." In *Managing Economic Volatility and Crises: A Practitioner's Guide*, edited by J. Aizenman and B. Pinto. Boston: Cambridge University Press, 213–80. Reviews the academic literature on the determinants of financial markets; the role of financial markets in economic development; the potential impact of domestic financial deregulation; and the effect of financial volatility on the economy.

Kaminsky, Graciela, and Sergio Schmukler. 2002. "Short-Run Pain, Long-Run Gain: The Effects of Financial Liberalization." World Bank Working Paper No. 2912. Washington, DC: World Bank. Examines empirically the short- and long-run effects of financial liberalization on capital markets and finds financial liberalization can lead to pronounced boom-bust cycles in the short run, but more stable markets in the long run.

McKinnon, Ronald I. 1973. *Money and Capital in Economic Development*. Washington, DC: Brookings Institution. A seminal work along with Shaw (1973) in which the author defines financial repression and identifies it in the development of financial markets in countries.

Montiel, Peter. 2003. *Macroeconomics in Emerging Markets*. Cambridge: Cambridge University Press. Provides macroeconomic theories and models especially for emerging market countries. A few chapters in the book present academic discussions about financial repression and the impact of financial liberalization.

Roubini, N., and X. Sala-i-Martin. 1992. "Financial Repression and Economic Growth." *Journal of Development Economics* 39: 5–30. One of the first papers that empirically analyzes the negative effects of financial repression on economic growth.

Shaw, Edward. 1973. *Financial Deepening in Economic Development*. New York: Oxford University Press. Along with McKinnon (1973), this book is a seminal work that defines financial repression and examines the effect of financial development on economic development.

HIRO ITO

■ financial services

A nation's financial system provides an essential infrastructure for the functioning of the entire economy. A sound and efficient financial system is therefore imperative for economic growth and development. A sound financial system also increases the resiliency of a nation's economy, thereby helping it to withstand external shocks such as movements in exchange rates or a major increase in global interest rates.

International trade in financial services—in combination with enhanced prudential regulation and supervision and other basic structural reforms—can play an important role in helping countries build financial systems that are more competitive and efficient and therefore more stable. Trade in financial services can enhance capital market efficiency and improve the quality, availability, and pricing of financial services. Especially when a foreign financial firm operates through a commercial presence in a host country, trade in financial services can stimulate innovation through the dissemination of new technologies, know-how, and skills. Trade in financial services can also promote the use of international good practices—for example, with regard to risk management and disclosure of financial information.

Trade liberalization and strengthening domestic financial systems—the two major dimensions of the international framework for financial services—are complementary and mutually reinforcing. Indeed, in order to obtain the maximum benefits of liberalization while minimizing the risks, a host country must ensure adequate prudential regulation and supervision and put in place other elements of the institutional and legal structure necessary for a sound financial system. International work on strengthening domestic financial systems takes place in a variety of forums, ranging from the International Monetary Fund (IMF) to specialized bodies such as the Basel Committee on Banking Supervision.

Liberalization of trade in financial services is dealt with in the World Trade Organization (WTO) under the General Agreement on Trade in Services (GATS) and also in regional and bilateral trade arrangements.

International Trade in Financial Services Major financial firms now provide a wide range of services to customers in other countries. The GATS defines a financial service as "any service of a financial nature . . . including insurance and insurance-related services and all banking and other financial services" and provides a list of activities included in this definition. The list includes commercial banking activities such as lending and deposit-taking; investment banking activities, such as underwriting securities and advising on mergers and acquisitions;

trading activities, that is, brokering and dealing in securities and other financial instruments; and asset-management activities, including management of mutual funds and pension funds. Other noninsurance financial services on the list comprise financial information and data processing services; investment advisory services; payment and money transmission services, including credit cards; settlement and clearing for financial assets; and financial leasing. Insurance services on the GATS list include "direct" life and nonlife insurance, that is, insurance sold to the public and to noninsurance businesses; reinsurance and "retrocession" (reinsurance by reinsurers); and commercial insurance. The list also includes services auxiliary to insurance such as actuarial, risk assessment, and claims settlement services.

"Trade in services" as defined in the GATS covers both foreign direct investment (FDI) as well as cross-border trade, which is broadly analogous to trade in goods. FDI includes services provided through a "commercial presence" in a host country, such as a branch or subsidiary of a foreign bank. The GATS definition of commercial presence also includes representative offices, which are basically a marketing device and do not constitute FDI. Trade in services as defined in the GATS also includes services provided in a host country by "natural persons" (individuals) who are residents of another country. In the financial services sector, however, individuals usually provide services as employees of financial firms; exceptions are financial advisers and, in insurance, independent sales intermediaries.

A cross-border financial services transaction could be carried out in a number of ways. For example, a representative of a foreign bank might visit the customer's country to arrange a loan. Alternatively, the customer might travel abroad to visit the office of the foreign bank. Or, the transaction might take place via telephone, fax, or, increasingly, the Internet, which in this context is another technological means of carrying out a transaction. Although the GATS distinguishes between cross-border services provided to nonresidents "from" and "in" the country of the service supplier (referred to as "cross-border supply" and "consumption abroad," respectively), for financial services the line dividing these two modes of supply is not always clear.

Wholesale financial services—that is, services provided to "sophisticated" customers such as corporations and institutions, other financial services firms, and, under some definitions, wealthy individuals—are provided internationally both through FDI and across borders. Electronic transactions play a major role in the cross-border provision of wholesale financial services, including traditional financial services as well as newer types of services designed to facilitate business-to-business e-commerce activities. When wholesale financial services are provided through FDI, foreign financial firms typically prefer to use the branch form of organization. Branches, unlike subsidiaries, are not separately incorporated in the host country and, unless restricted by host-country regulations, operate using the firm's consolidated worldwide capital.

Retail financial services are still provided internationally primarily through FDI. Although the provision of some financial services over the Internet and through Web-enabled technologies, such as mobile telephony, is expanding dramatically *within* a number of countries, the cross-border provision of financial services to retail customers through these methods is still in its infancy. The lack of widespread development of cross-border retail banking and other financial services—whether through electronic transactions or more traditional methods—reflects host-country regulatory requirements aimed at ensuring adequate consumer protection, consumer preferences, and tax considerations. Some countries actually require the establishment of a commercial presence to provide retail financial services. Perhaps even more important, consumers may prefer dealing with a local commercial presence, particularly because redress against a local establishment is usually readily available through the domestic legal system. In addition, in a number of countries, consumers receive more favorable tax treatment on financial products that are provided through locally incorporated entities.

Strengthening Domestic Financial Systems

The financial services sector has an elaborate and intensively used framework of international forums that are used to address overall financial and regulatory policy issues, to promote cooperation and coordination among supervisors, to set voluntary but widely accepted international minimum standards and codes of good practices, and to provide "surveillance" of domestic financial systems. This international framework, which has been constructed over three decades and is still evolving, is a response not only to the internationalization of banking and other financial activities but also to the special characteristics of the financial sector, especially the phenomenon of "systemic risk" whereby problems with one financial firm can be transmitted to unrelated financial firms, both within and beyond a single country.

International minimum standards and codes of good practices for sound financial systems have been established in three broad areas: (1) transparency of macroeconomic policy and data; (2) institutional and market infrastructure, which covers insolvency, corporate governance, accounting, auditing, market integrity and functioning, and payment and settlement systems; and (3) prudential regulation and supervision, which covers both financial firms and regulatory and supervisory systems. Examples are the Code of Good Practices on Transparency in Monetary and Financial Policies promulgated by the IMF, the Principles of Corporate Governance issued by the Organisation for Economic Co-operation and Development (OECD), and the Core Principles for Effective Banking Supervision developed by the Basel Committee on Banking Supervision.

The international work on strengthening domestic financial systems includes financial sector surveillance conducted by the IMF and the World Bank under a joint Financial Sector Assessment Program (FSAP). The FSAP is designed to provide a "comprehensive health check-up of a country's financial sector" by identifying the strengths and vulnerabilities of a country's financial system, determining whether effective risk-management techniques are being used, and evaluating the observance of internationally accepted minimum standards and codes. A continuing challenge for the IMF is to integrate its financial sector surveillance more effectively into its so-called Article IV surveillance of the economic policies of its member countries. Technical assistance for a country that wishes to enhance its regulatory and supervisory capabilities is available under the auspices of the IMF and World Bank, or through programs established by national regulatory authorities.

Liberalization in the GATS The GATS, which was negotiated in the Uruguay Round (1986–94), is the first global trade agreement to cover financial and other services. The GATS has two major components. First, it establishes overall rules and disciplines for trade in services, both in the main text and in various annexes; the Annex on Financial Services deals with rules specific to financial services. Second, the GATS contains each WTO member's schedule of specific commitments and list of exemptions from the most-favored-nation (MFN) obligation. The results of the financial services negotiations—which were not concluded until December 1997, several years after the end of the Uruguay Round—are incorporated into these schedules and lists by the Fifth Protocol to the GATS. Although the expression "agreement on financial services" is widely used to refer to the results of the 1997 negotiations or, more broadly, to the GATS as it applies to financial services, from a legal point of view, a separate multilateral agreement for financial services does not exist.

The inclusion of the financial services sector in a multilateral trade agreement was a major milestone. Because of the special characteristics and sensitivity of the financial sector—in particular, the role of banks in monetary and payment systems and the phenomenon of systemic risk—finance officials in a number of countries were concerned about allowing financial sector issues to fall within the domain of trade officials and the multilateral trading system. Financial regulators made it clear that the inclusion of financial services in the GATS would be unacceptable without a specific carve-out from the obligations of the agreement for prudential measures. The regulators emphasized that such a carve-out was necessary to ensure that the agreement would not interfere with their ability to carry out their responsibilities for prudential regulation and supervision. Financial regulators also insisted that any dispute settlement panel dealing with financial services must have the appropriate expertise regarding the specific financial service at issue. Ultimately, provisions addressing both of these issues were included in the GATS Annex on Financial Services.

The prudential carve-out allows a country to take prudential measures "to ensure the integrity and stability of the financial system" or "for the protection of investors, depositors, policy holders or persons to whom a fiduciary duty is owed" even if the measures are inconsistent with other provisions of the GATS. The carve-out also contains an anti-abuse provision. As a result, not only the question of whether a particular measure is prudential in the first place but also the question of whether a seemingly "prudential" measure is being misused to avoid a country's obligations and commitments could be brought before a WTO dispute settlement panel. However, as of October 2007, there had been no dispute settlement proceeding and no request for consultation on a financial services issue. Therefore the scope of the prudential carve-out and its antiabuse provision remain untested in WTO jurisprudence.

A GATS commitment is permanent in the sense that it cannot be withdrawn without compensation of trading partners. Failure to honor a GATS commitment could open a country to a WTO dispute settlement proceeding and, ultimately, to WTO-sanctioned retaliatory measures by its trading partners. Thus backsliding in the face of domestic political pressures could be extremely costly. The GATS calls for periodic negotiating rounds to improve commitments for financial and other services to achieve "a progressively higher level of liberalization." The Doha Round, which was launched in November 2001 but as of October 2007 remained stalled, includes a new set of negotiations on trade in services.

Ideally, GATS negotiations can both reinforce and build on market and political forces that are creating pressures for liberalization within a host country. In this regard, a country's "readiness" for reform is critical. Indeed, undertaking commitments in the GATS can be an integral part of a country's longer-term policy reform agenda. For example, China's WTO accession commitment to open its banking market to FDI within five years (i.e., by December 11, 2006) in effect set a domestic political deadline for substantial progress in reforming China's banking system. During the 1997–98 Asian financial crisis, making commitments in the GATS to permit FDI in their domestic financial sectors offered an additional opportunity for Asian governments to try to reassure markets that they were committed to longer-term policy reform.

In the 1997 agreement on financial services commitments, most of the WTO members participating in that agreement "bound" the levels of liberalization for FDI that existed as the negotiations entered their final phase in late 1997. For a number of emerging market economies and other developing countries, such liberalization represented a substantial improvement over the liberalization that existed a few years earlier. Moreover, capturing existing levels of liberalization in binding commitments subject to WTO dispute settlement is important in its own right. In contrast to the commitments for FDI, the 1997 commitments for cross-border services provided "from" the country of the service supplier ("cross-border supply") were, even for OECD countries, relatively limited and did not always reflect existing liberalization. Most countries that have acceded to the WTO since its inception in 1995 have made strong financial services commitments, including new liberalization, for FDI and, in some cases, cross-border services.

Three Pillars of Liberalization The inclusion of financial services in the GATS and the negotiation of the 1997 agreement on financial services commitments constitute a significant step in the larger process of achieving international contestability of markets for financial services and strengthening domestic financial systems. "International contestability of markets" refers to the creation of markets that are competitive and efficient on a global basis—a goal that can be achieved by removing all types of barriers to foreign participation in host-country markets. International contestability is, in effect, based on three pillars of liberalization—namely, (1) opening markets by ensuring "national treatment" and "market access"; (2) removing nondiscriminatory structural barriers (domestic structural reform); and (3) liberalization of capital movements.

For financial services, the GATS has so far dealt mainly with first-pillar liberalization, that is, liberalization aimed at opening markets to foreign services and service suppliers and ensuring that they enjoy substantially the same treatment as their domestic counterparts. First-pillar barriers of particular importance for financial services include limitations on foreign ownership interests in domestic financial firms; restrictions on juridical form, for example, prohibiting a foreign financial firm from establishing a branch as opposed to a subsidiary; and prohibiting branches or subsidiaries of foreign financial firms from engaging in all of the activities that are permissible for their domestic counterparts.

One question for future negotiations on financial services is whether, or to what extent, they should extend into the second pillar. Second-pillar liberalization deals with nonquantiative structural barriers that do not discriminate between domestic and foreign services and service suppliers. In contrast to national treatment and market access—which ensure that foreign services and services suppliers can enter a host-country market as currently structured and enjoy equality of competitive opportunities vis-à-vis their domestic counterparts—second-pillar liberalization represents an effort to create maximum potential competitive opportunities in a host-country market. It may therefore require major domestic structural reform. Second-pillar barriers can be created by anticompetitive domestic policy measures, the inadequacy or absence of domestic regulation, differences in national rules that make it difficult to conduct operations on a global basis, or lack of regulatory transparency. Moreover, second-pillar barriers to trade in financial services are not limited

to financial sector regulation. They also include, for example, a host country's lack of an effective legal framework for corporate governance or insolvency; both of these areas are part of the international work on strengthening domestic financial systems.

The European Union's single-market program represents the most far-reaching effort to date to remove nondiscriminatory structural barriers among a group of nations. Predicated on political agreement on goals for economic liberalization, that effort is being carried out in the context of the unique supranational legislative, judicial, and administrative structure of the European Community. Even within the European Union, however, important nondiscriminatory structural barriers to trade in financial services among the member states still exist, especially with regard to retail financial services.

At present, the GATS addresses certain types of second-pillar barriers, including lack of transparency and barriers created by domestic regulation, in very general terms. Some second-pillar barriers are also dealt with in countries' schedules of commitments. For financial services, most of these commitments are simply "best efforts" commitments. Many believe that it is not realistic or appropriate to negotiate and bind in the GATS additional second-pillar liberalization for financial services. However, one type of second-pillar liberalization that involves procedural as opposed to substantive barriers—namely, regulatory transparency—is being discussed in the Doha Round for possible inclusion in the GATS. Disciplines on regulatory transparency, which might be designed to apply to all service sectors or only to financial services, would strengthen current GATS disciplines on transparency—for example, by requiring WTO members to establish a meaningful procedure for interested parties to comment on a proposed regulation prior to its adoption in final form. Such a requirement, together with other transparency disciplines, was included in China's Protocol of Accession to the WTO; similar disciplines have been included in the financial services chapters of bilateral free trade agreements to which the United States is a party.

The GATS deals with third-pillar liberalization only insofar as it affects countries' specific commitments to liberalize trade in services; in general, liberalization of capital movements is a matter of concern for the IMF. In particular, the GATS prohibits a WTO member from imposing restrictions on certain capital movements that would be inconsistent with its specific commitments to provide national treatment and market access. As a result, if a country makes a commitment to liberalize trade with respect to a particular financial service in the GATS, it is also making a commitment to liberalize most capital movements associated with the trade liberalization commitment. The country is not, however, making an across-the-board commitment to freedom of capital movements. The GATS provisions dealing with capital movements, like GATS-specific commitments to liberalize trade in services, are subject to a balance-of-payments safeguard. Both the capital movements and balance-of-payments safeguard provisions of the GATS refer to and are consistent with the IMF's responsibilities in these areas.

Trade Liberalization and Sound Financial Systems The financial services sector—including international trade in financial services—plays a vital role in the modern world economy. The adoption of international minimum standards and codes for sound financial systems and their implementation by individual countries make an important contribution to financial stability, both nationally and globally. These standards and codes also provide a strong foundation for liberalization of trade in financial services in the GATS and in regional and bilateral trade agreements. As the GATS explicitly recognizes, liberalization of trade in financial and other services is an ongoing process. For financial services, this process is being driven in large part by market forces and new technologies. It also reflects a growing recognition among policymakers that opening markets to foreign suppliers of financial services can both benefit host-country consumers and contribute to the resiliency of domestic financial systems.

See also capital controls; General Agreement on Trade in Services (GATS); International Monetary Fund (IMF); sequencing of financial sector reform; trade in services; World Trade Organization

FURTHER READING

Committee on Global Financial Systems. 2004. *Foreign Direct Investment in the Financial Sector of Emerging Market Economies.* Report of Working Group. Basel: Bank for International Settlements. Downloadable from http://www.bis.org/publ/cgfs22.pdf?noframes=1. Explores issues that financial sector FDI raises for investing institutions, home and host countries, and the global financial system.

Dobson, Wendy, and Pierre Jacquet. 1998. *Financial Services Liberalization in the WTO.* Washington, DC: Institute for International Economics. Examines benefits of financial reform, including pitfalls and transitional issues, and analyzes 1997 agreement on GATS financial services commitments.

Financial Stability Forum. 2002. "12 Key Standards for Sound Financial Systems." Downloadable from http://www.fsforum.org/compendium/key_standards_for_sound_financial_system.html. Twelve international minimum standards and codes of good practices are identified by the Financial Stability Forum (FSF) as key for sound financial systems and deserving of priority implementation, depending on country circumstances.

Graham, Edward M., and Robert Z. Lawrence. 1996. "Measuring the International Contestability of Markets: A Conceptual Approach." *Journal of World Trade* 30 (5): 5–20. Analytic framework for the concept of international contestability of markets.

International Monetary Fund, Independent Evaluation Office. 2006. *Report on the Evaluation of the Financial Sector Assessment Program.* Washington, DC: International Monetary Fund. Downloadable from http://www.imf.org/External/NP/ieo/2006/fsap/eng/index.htm. Analyzes effectiveness of Financial Sector Assessment Program (FSAP) from the perspective of the IMF.

Kampf, Roger. 1998. "Financial Services in the WTO: Third Time Lucky." *International Trade Law and Regulation* 4 (3): 111–123. Analyzes 1997 agreement on GATS financial services commitments.

Key, Sydney J. 1997. *Financial Services in the Uruguay Round and the WTO.* Occasional Papers 54. Washington, DC:

Group of Thirty. Analyzes issues and challenges in the Uruguay Round financial services negotiations.

———. 2003. *The Doha Round and Financial Services Negotiations*. Washington, DC: AEI Press. Downloadable from http://www.aei.org/book456. Analyzes the role of the GATS and the WTO in liberalization and regulation of the financial services sector from both trade and financial regulatory policy perspectives and identifies six broad goals for the Doha Round financial services negotiations. Current entry is adapted from this book.

Kono, Masamichi, Patrick Low, Mukela Luanga, Aaditya Mattoo, Maika Oshikawa, and Ludger Schuknecht. 1997. *Opening Markets in Financial Services and the Role of the GATS*. Geneva: World Trade Organization. Downloadable from http://www.wto.org/english/res_e/booksp_e/special_study_1_e.pdf. Examines benefits and challenges of liberalizing trade in financial services and the role of the GATS.

Mattoo, Aaditya. 2000. "Financial Services and the WTO: Liberalization Commitments of Developing and Transition Economies." *The World Economy* 23 (3): 351–86. Studies the financial services commitments made by nearly 100 developing countries and all Eastern European members of the WTO.

Rogoff, Kenneth S. 2002. "Rethinking Capital Controls: When Should We Keep an Open Mind?" *Finance and Development* 39 (4): 55–56. Downloadable from http://www.imf.org/external/pubs/ft/fandd/2002/12/rogoff.htm. Perspective on capital controls from former chief economist of the IMF.

Sato, Setsuya, and John Hawkins. 2001. "Electronic Finance: An Overview of the Issues." In *Electronic Finance: A New Perspective and Challenges*. BIS Papers 7. Basel: Bank for International Settlements. Downloadable from http://www.bis.org/publ/bispap07a.pdf. Overview of issues based on presentations and discussions at workshop on electronic finance organized by the Bank for International Settlements.

Skipper, Harold D., Jr. 2001. *Insurance in the General Agreement on Trade in Services*. Washington, DC: AEI Press. Overview of insurance and insurance markets, international trade in insurance services, and insurance commitments in the GATS.

SYDNEY J. KEY

■ **first-mover advantage**

See foreign market entry

■ **fixed costs and foreign direct investment**

Fixed costs are production costs, such as research and development (R&D) expenditures and rent of production facilities, that do not vary by the quantity of output. The existence of fixed costs often suggests increasing returns to scale in the production process: the average fixed cost borne by each unit of output decreases as output expands.

Fixed costs are a key element in a firm's decision to invest abroad and set up foreign subsidiaries. How motivated firms are to invest in a foreign country can be altered by the existence of fixed costs. Firms may decide to establish plants in foreign countries to avoid trade costs or to take advantage of lower factor prices. The former strategy leads firms to duplicate production across countries and undertake a horizontal type of foreign direct investment (FDI), while the latter motivates firms to locate different stages of production in different countries and engage in a vertical type of FDI. When fixed costs arise at the level of a plant, they create a disincentive to have duplicated plants, and thus a disincentive for horizontal FDI.

Firm-Level versus Plant-Level Fixed Costs Fixed costs may exist at the firm and/or the plant level. This distinction is particularly important to multiplant firms. Plant-level fixed costs include any fixed costs that accrue based on the number of plants, such as the cost of renting production facilities and the cost of equipment. These fixed costs provide physical capital for a specific plant and increase with the number of plants. By implication, they discourage firms from maintaining multiple plants and encourage geographic concentration of production.

Firm-level fixed costs, in contrast, include any fixed costs that accrue based on the number of firms, such as R&D and advertising costs. This type of fixed cost does not increase with the number of plants and thus raises firms' incentive to expand horizontally and spread the cost across multiple plants.

More specifically, the role of fixed costs in a firm's decision to invest abroad depends on whether the costs involve the supply of knowledge capital or physical capital. Knowledge capital such as technology know-how can be simultaneously supplied to multiple production locations and thus does not have to increase with the number of plants a firm operates. Physical capital such as production facility, however, is exclusively supplied to one location and thus requires additional investments when a firm establishes new plants. FDI is more likely to arise in industries where knowledge-based assets are important and scale economies in physical capital are less critical— that is, where firm-level fixed costs are important relative to plant-level fixed costs. In industries that are both knowledge- and physical-capital intensive, firms invest abroad when the benefit of proximity to consumers or lower factor prices in the host country dominate the plant-level diseconomies of scale.

Theoretical Considerations Numerous theoretical studies, led by the seminal work of Markusen (1984) and Horstmann and Markusen (1987, 1992), have investigated the role of these two types of fixed costs in a firms' decision to undertake FDI. Markusen (1984) was one of the first authors who showed from an international trade perspective that multinational enterprises may arise endogenously in equilibrium. In his model, firms may separate headquarter activities such as R&D from production. The headquarter activities require an up-front fixed cost and in turn provide knowledge-based assets, such as patents, blueprints, and trademarks. These assets then serve as a joint input that can be supplied to all the production facilities of a firm without lowering the value of the input. This approach is extended by Horstmann and Markusen (1987, 1992), who show, for instance, that two-way investment flows between pairs of countries can arise in equilibrium. These studies find that firm-level scale economy implies that it is best to have one firm produce for all markets as doing so avoids the need for duplication in headquarter services. A multiplant multinational firm with plants in both countries or a firm with a plant in one country that exports to the other would have cost efficiency over a single-plant

firm in each country selling locally. Furthermore, firms are motivated to set up local production plants in foreign countries rather than export from headquarters when the trade costs are high or the variable production cost in the foreign country is low.

The existing theoretical literature also shows that plant-level scale economies give rise to export-platform FDI. Ekholm, Forslid, and Markusen (2007), for example, find in both their model and empirical results that, in the presence of large plant-specific fixed costs, firms tend to adopt an export-platform strategy in which they concentrate their production in a low-cost country and export to other markets. A reduction in trade costs between the low-cost country and other countries would further augment firms' incentive to undertake geographically centralized FDI and achieve economies of scale.

Empirical Assessment The effect of fixed costs on multinational firms' decision to invest abroad has also been investigated empirically. In particular, Brainard (1997) and Yeaple (2003) examine the extent to which multinational production location decisions can be explained by a trade-off between maximizing proximity to consumers (or exploiting countries' difference in comparative advantage) and concentrating production to achieve economies of scale. Their analyses consider both firm-level and plant-level economies of scale. Firm-level scale economies are measured by the number of non-production workers in the average U.S.-based firm in each industry, while plant-level scale economies in each industry are measured by the number of production workers in the average U.S. plant. As predicted by the theory, these studies find that overseas production by multinational firms increases relative to exports when the scale economies at the plant level are lower than those at the firm level.

Ekholm, Forslid, and Markusen (2007) also confirm the role of scale economies in multinationals' investment decisions. They examine specifically export-platform FDI, a product of significant plant-level fixed costs and declining trade costs. They find that since the removal of trade barriers within the European Union and the North American Free Trade Area, multinational firms are increasingly motivated to concentrate their production in a low-cost member of the integrated region and supply the rest of the region through exports.

In sum, theories of the multinational firm suggest that firm-level fixed costs give rise to increased FDI, while plant-level fixed costs encourage export-platform FDI but deter horizontal FDI. Broad empirical support exists for these predictions.

See also footloose production; foreign direct investment and exit of local firms; foreign direct investment under monopolistic competition; foreign direct investment under oligopoly; foreign market entry; knowledge-capital model of the multinational enterprise; proximity-concentration hypothesis; subsidies and financial incentives to foreign direct investment

FURTHER READING

Brainard, S. Lael. 1997. "An Empirical Assessment of Proximity-Concentration Trade-off between Multinational Sales and Trade." *American Economic Review* 87 (4): 520–44. One of the earliest empirical studies that examine the role of trade costs and scale economies in multinationals' investment decisions.

Ekholm, Karolina, Rikard Forslid, and James Markusen. 2007. "Export-Platform Foreign Direct Investment." *Journal of European Economic Association* 5 (4): 776–95. An important study of the causes of export-platform FDI and the effect of free trade areas on multinationals' location decisions.

Horstmann, Ignatius, and James Markusen. 1987. "Strategic Investments and the Development of Multinationals." *International Economic Review* 28 (1): 109–21. A first theoretical analysis that investigates the sufficient production and transportation conditions for multinational corporations to arise.

———. 1992. "Endogenous Market Structures in International Trade." *Journal of International Economics* 32 (1–2): 109–29. A systematic investigation of market structure and the existence of multinational and exporting firms.

Markusen, James. 1984. "Multinationals, Multiplant Economics, and the Gains from Trade." *Journal of International Economics* 16 (3–4): 205–26. One of the first theoretical contributions on the efficiency and welfare implications of multiplant multinational firms.

Yeaple, Stephen. 2003. "The Role of Skill Endowments in the Structure of U.S. Outward Foreign Direct Investment." *Review of Economics and Statistics* 85 (3): 726–34. A careful account of the industry and country determinants of U.S. outward FDI with an emphasis on the role of skilled labor endowment.

MAGGIE XIAOYANG CHEN

■ floating exchange rate
See exchange rate regimes

■ footloose production

Multinational firms are increasingly important in the world economy. Since multinationals are usually firms with plants in more than one country they are considered "footloose" since they can shift their activities more easily from one country to another. At the end of 1997 the added value of all multinational enterprises (MNEs) in the world was approximately a quarter of the total added value in the world. In 2002, the stock of foreign investments worldwide was on average 22 percent of the gross domestic product of each country, and the corresponding percentages for West European countries were still higher, between 31.4 and 42.7 percent.

Increasingly, worldwide, more and more trade is in the hands of MNEs. The amount of intrafirm trade within MNEs accounts for almost one third of all worldwide trade. The number of MNEs also has increased substantially. Since the mid-1990s the amount of worldwide foreign direct investment has increased more rapidly than exports.

By the very act of becoming a multinational, the production of MNEs is potentially footloose in nature. A distinction can be made between horizontal MNEs, which produce the same goods and services in multiple countries, and vertical multinationals, which fragment production geographically by stages. While theoretically this distinction is easy to make, it is much harder to analyze empirically how much horizontal versus vertical MNE activity is involved

(Carr et al. 2001). Nonetheless, both types of multinational activity enable MNEs to shift production across countries.

MNEs are flexible in terms of geographically organizing their production structure. Optimizing their activities over different countries often results in vertical fragmentation of production, with activities of R&D, design, marketing, and distribution usually located in high-income developed countries and the production of intermediate inputs and assembly located in low-wage/low-tax countries (Hanson et al. 2005). This fragmentation of production results from endowment differences and falling transportation, tariff, and information costs across countries. In response to changes in any of these causes, MNEs may respond by shifting more (or less) production abroad. For example, improvements in information technology or increases in domestic wages may cause an MNE to shift the production of intermediate components abroad.

MNEs also often establish plants undertaking similar activities in multiple countries. A typical MNE may have several similar plants, with one in each major market, such as one in Asia, one in North America, and one in Europe. This duplication of plants is generally undertaken to avoid transportation costs, tariffs, and other trade restrictions. Although these plants are intended primarily to serve the immediate market (the country where located and neighboring countries), they can also be used to supply other markets if needed. A shock in demand or supply in one region could be offset by adjustments in production throughout the global network of plants.

How Footloose Is Production? Although all MNEs have the potential to shift production across countries, how easy it is to do so can differ. The ownership share that MNEs have in affiliates with plants abroad varies. While some studies consider ownership of 20 percent or more, other studies consider a higher cutoff for MNE ownership in the affiliate. For an MNE to be really footloose, however, arguably ownership in the affiliate by the MNE should exceed 50 percent or more of the shares. Only when the MNE has majority ownership in its affiliate

can it easily decide to "pack up and go" as typical for footloose production. Also, the higher the number of majority-owned affiliates, the more footloose the MNE is since it can relocate production activities from one affiliate to another.

There are two main reasons that production is becoming increasingly footloose. First, the production of MNEs is more footloose than that of domestic firms, so as the degree of multinational activity increases, production overall becomes more able to be moved across national borders. Second, changes may be occurring that make production by MNEs more flexible. New markets are joining the world economy and opening up to the inflow of foreign capital. This growth in market opportunities implies that MNEs geographically expand the scope of their networks with more plants in more countries.

Implications of Footloose Production The footloose nature of multinational production has implications for local product, labor, and capital markets. Whatever the type of MNE involved, its presence in the host country tends to increase the volatility of the local economy. MNEs' production tends to respond more quickly to upswings or downswings in economic conditions than does the production of domestic firms. Due to their footloose nature, MNEs are usually the first firms to come when conditions are favorable and the first to exit the market when fortune reverses. The increase in the number of MNEs worldwide therefore makes local economies more subject to shocks and volatility. Countries with flexible labor markets, that is, with low hiring and firing costs, are better equipped to cope with this new challenge since they can more quickly and at lower costs adjust to shocks.

In terms of local labor markets, MNEs usually have a stronger bargaining position with labor unions than domestic firms do, since MNEs always have the outside option of relocation. This does not imply that MNEs necessarily pay lower wages, however. Empirical evidence seems to suggest that MNEs pay higher wages and provide better working conditions than local firms in developing countries (Brown et al. 2003). In developed countries, wages in MNEs also tend to be higher. One reason is that MNEs tend to be larger and more productive; they also produce higher-quality goods than their local rivals, which gives them greater market power in product markets and allows them to charge higher prices. Higher product market rents are likely to result in higher wages. MNEs on average employ better-skilled workers to guarantee higher quality in production and a higher level of productivity. They often invest substantially in internal training. All these elements offer explanations for the wage gap between MNEs and local firms in the same country or region.

Theory suggests that MNEs in high-income countries export unskilled jobs to their affiliates in low-wage countries. There is some empirical confirmation; however, Braconier and Ekholm (2000) and Konings and Murphy (2006) find evidence of substitutability of labor among high-wage countries, but not between high-wage and low-wage countries. Employment effects may depend on the type of activity that is outsourced. Some suggest that in the long run the outsourcing of unskilled activities could create more job opportunities in developed countries. This subject is hotly debated, but more research is needed to understand the dynamic effects of MNEs on the labor markets of parent and host countries.

MNEs rely less on local capital markets. Typically MNEs and their affiliates benefit from internal capital markets. Recent evidence suggests that MNEs are less subject to credit constraints than other firms (Harrison et al. 2004). Hence MNEs suffer less from incomplete capital markets in developing countries than local firms since they can always turn to intrafirm financing. They depend less on local banking conditions and on the competition in the banking sector.

The footloose nature of multinational production implies that MNEs usually also have a strong bargaining position vis-à-vis governments that host their affiliates. Prior to choosing where to locate a plant, MNEs are often able to negotiate financial incentives with host governments. In recent years national governments have increasingly been using the corporate tax instrument as a tool to attract MNEs into their region. Small countries and countries that are otherwise less attractive may have to offer more favorable tax treatment to MNEs than to local firms. Vandenbussche and Tan (2005) found that in a small country such as Belgium, foreign-owned firms on average have lower effective tax rates than purely domestic firms.

In sum, the increasing prevalence of MNEs has caused production to become increasingly footloose in nature, with important implications for the world economy.

See also globalization; multinational enterprises

FURTHER READING

Braconier, Henrik, and Karolina Ekholm. 2000. "Swedish Multinationals and Competition from High- and Low-Wage Countries." *Review of International Economics* 8 (3): 448–61. Examines whether there is substitution between employment in different parts of Swedish firms.

Brown, Drusilla K., Alan V. Deardorff, and Robert M. Stern. 2003. "The Effects of Multinational Production on Wages and Working Conditions in Developing Countries." NBER Working Paper No. 9669. Cambridge, MA: National Bureau of Economic Research. Assesses evidence regarding the effect of multinational production and working conditions in developing countries.

Carr, David L., James R. Markusen, and Keith E. Maskus. 2001. "Estimating the Knowledge-Capital Model of the Multinational Enterprise." *American Economic Review* 91 (3): 693–708. Tests the horizontal versus the vertical multinational model.

Hanson, Gordon H., Raymond J. Mataloni, and Matthew J. Slaughter. 2005. "Vertical Production Networks in Multinational Firms." *Review of Economics and Statistics* 87 (4): 664–78. Studies intrafirm trade in intermediate inputs.

Harrison, Ann E., Inessa Love, and Margaret McMillan. 2004. "Global Capital Flows and Financing Constraints." *Journal of Development Economics* 75 (1): 269–301. Examines in a cross-section of countries the relation between inward foreign direct investment and domestic firms' financing constraints.

Konings, Jozef, and Alan Murphy. 2006. "Do Multinational Enterprises Relocate Employment to Low-wage Regions? Evidence from European Multinationals." *Review of World Economics* 142 (2): 267–86. Empirical analysis of employment substitution between parent firms and foreign affiliates.

Vandenbussche, Hylke, and Chang Tan. 2005. "The Taxation of Multinationals: Firm Level Evidence for Belgium." LICOS discussion Paper No. 160/2005, Catholic University Leuven. http://www.econ.kuleuven .be/LICOS/DP/DP2005/DP160.pdf. An empirical assessment of whether multinational enterprises are given more favorable tax treatment compared to domestic firms.

HYLKE VANDENBUSSCHE

■ foreign direct investment (FDI)

Foreign direct investments are defined as investments in which a firm acquires a majority or at very least a controlling interest in a foreign firm. Foreign investments not involving a majority or controlling stake are typically referred to as portfolio investments. Firms making foreign direct investments (FDI) are referred to as multinational enterprises (MNE) and the two terms are used somewhat interchangeably. A direct investment may involve creating a new foreign enterprise, often referred to as a greenfield investment, or acquiring an existing foreign firm (sometimes referred to as a brownfield investment, though that term is much less common; *acquisition* is the typical label).

Historically, there are three strands of literature that see the multinational and FDI in different ways: the international business tradition, the trade-theory tradition, and the macroeconomic tradition. This entry will focus heavily on the trade-theory tradition, where the biggest developments in the last twenty years have occurred.

The international business approach is very individual-firm oriented. It details the determinants of the decision of firms to go abroad and the mode they chose for doing so. In addition to FDI, the firm considers exporting, joint ventures, licensing or contracting with arm's-length foreign firms, and so forth. The international business literature has been far more interested than the other streams of literature in the choice-of-mode decision.

It is probably accurate to say that until the late 1980s the microeconomic trade-theory approach to FDI and the macroeconomic tradition were pretty much the same. These two traditions did not really distinguish between direct and portfolio investments: there was no real attempt to model the "D" in FDI. Both schools modeled FDI as the movement of homogeneous capital from locations where its return was relatively low to where its return is higher. The simple approach to capital flows had a natural intersection with Heckscher-Ohlin trade theory, in which factors are expensive where they are scarce and cheap where they are abundant. The consequence is the obvious hypothesis that capital should flow from capital-rich to capital-scarce countries.

There was no sense of individual firms in this literature, and certainly no modeling of mode choice. Even trade theory, with its better-developed sense of general-equilibrium than macroeconomics, was dominated by perfect-competition, constant-returns-to-scale models in which individual firms had no real meaning. But trade theory did have advantages over the international business approach in that it had a basic general-equilibrium structure that did at least give some predictions as to the pattern of capital flows we should observe.

Macroeconomics has more or less continued in the tradition of restricting analysis to aggregate capital flows generated by international rental-rate or cost-of-capital differentials. It is not easy to fit a rich structure for individual firms into macro models, and hence that stream of literature continues to make no real distinction between FDI and portfolio investments.

International trade theory, on the other hand, began to move sharply away from the macro approach in the 1980s, and to draw a clear distinction between FDI and portfolio investments. It began to move more toward the international business literature in that it included meaningful treatments of individual firms, yet the trade approach retained the general-equilibrium roots of its tradition. The split with macro seems to have been driven by some important statistical evidence that casts considerable doubt on the suitability of cross-country differences in the cost of capital as a driving and motivating force for FDI.

Troubling Statistics The first statistical difficulty confronting the traditional theory is that the high-income developed countries are not only the major source of FDI but also the major recipients. FDI does not primarily flow from capital-rich to capital-poor countries; it flows primarily from capital-rich to other capital-rich countries. Firms from high-income countries are mutually invading one another's markets. In addition, the FDI that does flow to developing countries is highly concentrated in the most advanced of those countries.

Many statistics are found in Caves (2007), Markusen (2002), UNCTAD, OECD, BEA, and other publications. One simple way to measure this source/recipient pattern is to simply compute the shares of total world FDI inward and outward stocks that are found in different countries or groups of countries. UNCTAD statistics for 2003 indicate that the developed countries accounted for 89 percent of the outward stock in this year, but also accounted for 69 percent of the inward stock. Of course, the developed countries also account for the overwhelming share of world income, so we can instead divide the inward share of a group by its share of total world income. This yields the results shown in table 1. The high-income countries are close to a share of inward FDI equal to their share of income. Developing countries are higher on this score, as the simple capital-scarcity macro approach would suggest, but it turns out that this is highly concentrated in the more advanced of the developing countries. The least-developed countries (a UN-defined group of 44 countries) have a share of inward FDI only slightly greater than their share of world income.

A second statistic that led to a rethinking of trade theory is that there is very often a disconnect between the act and amount of FDI and the sources of financing for new investments or acquisitions. There is much less systematic evidence on this point since published data rarely comment on the source of financing for individual foreign projects. Yet the international business literature documents a great variety of financing choices: retained earnings of the parent firm, equity or bonds issued in the parent-country market, equity or debt issued in the host-country market, or third-country financing. Apparently, many FDI projects in China are financed with Chinese capital, although systematic data are not known to this author. If we think of Chinese debt financing an American direct investment, we have in fact a portfolio and a direct investment flowing in opposite directions.

A third relevant statistic is that FDI is attracted to large markets. Inward FDI divided by GDP should not display any particular pattern in a simple cost-of-capital macro approach. The data shown in table 2 are from 1993 and thus somewhat dated (Markusen 2002), but there is no reason to think that the basic message has changed. They show that not only is FDI attracted to rich countries, it is clearly attracted to large markets.

A fourth statistic that called for a new approach to FDI is that a very large proportion of the actual output of FDI projects is for local sale in the host country. Firms were often replicating their home

Table 1
Share of world inward FDI stock divided by share of total world income

Developed countries	0.90
Developing countries	1.37
Least-developed countries	1.07

Table 2
Inward FDI per capita

Country group GDP per capita (US$)	Country group Size	Average inward FDI per capita (US$)
> 5000	Large	242
	Small	54
2500–5000	Large	46
	Small	32
1200–2500	Large	33
	Small	31
600–1200	Large	11
	Small	3

Table 3
Sales of foreign manufacturing affiliates
of U.S. multinationals, 2000 (shares in total sales,
sample of 39 countries for which BEA data is available)

	Local sales	Export sales to the U.S.	Export sales to to third countries
all countries	0.60	0.12	0.28
Ireland	0.13	0.16	0.71
Canada	0.57	0.38	0.05
Mexico	0.53	0.39	0.08

activities, goods or services, in foreign markets. These are now generally known as "horizontal" investments, although the term "market-seeking" is also used. The latter term emphasizes that the FDI is not motivated by cost-side considerations as it would be in a cost-of-capital-differential approach, but rather by the demand-side motive of serving the local market. Table 3 presents a few statistics from BEA data. Perhaps 60 percent local sales does not seem terribly high for the sample as a whole. But more interesting is the fact that only 12 percent of sales are back to the United States; 28 percent of the sales are to third countries, often referred to as "export-platform" production and sales.

Closer inspection of the data suggests that third-country sales are most important for affiliates located in large regionally integrated trade areas: the exports are destined for the other regional members. In an important sense, this represents horizontal production in which one location within the region is chosen. United States affiliates in Ireland, for example, export 71 percent of their total production to third countries, and apparently almost all of this is horizontal production destined for other European Union markets. For U.S. affiliates in Canada and Mexico, exports are similarly directed to other members of the North American Free Trade Agreement, and so the overwhelming portion of their exports are to the United States. Thus is it clear that the overwhelming portion of affiliate output is destined for local or regional sale. Note that Canada and Mexico

exhibit remarkably similar statistics in spite of the large difference in per capita income, and that local sales have shares close to the world average for U.S. affiliates. While many investments in Mexico are surely chosen to access cheap labor for production for the United States market, the general notion that multinationals are firms seeking cheap production abroad for sale back home is at best a minor phenomenon.

The consequence of these observations was that trade theory needed to move away from the old macro approach and adopt a firm-based approach, yet one still rooted in the general-equilibrium tradition. Trade theory began to think of and indeed measure FDI not in terms of the value of investments (inputs), but in terms of the outputs of foreign affiliates, the destinations for those outputs, and the trade patterns with the parent firm. But the old bias is still very evident in data sources: it is much easier to get data on FDI stocks and flows than on affiliate outputs, sales destinations, and intrafirm trade.

The International Business Approach As suggested earlier, researchers in the field of international business have produced a rich set of theory and empirical analysis, though little is formalized and few testable hypotheses emerge. Nevertheless, the newer formal models owe a great debt to these scholars. An early approach was by Dunning (1973) with his ownership-location-internalization (OLI) framework. Dunning suggested that three conditions must be met before a firm will want to establish an owned production facility. Subsequent researchers have assembled a great body of evidence, though very little of it formal econometric work, about the form that these advantages take.

The first condition is ownership advantage. Given a disadvantage relative to local firms in a host country, a foreign firm must own a propriety asset such as a superior product, production process, patent, trademark, or asset that gives it a compensating advantage over local firms in the host market. This focuses the theory on the assets of the individual firm and away from some general return to homogeneous capital. Caves (2007) has written much on this idea, using the term *intangible assets* to label these proprietary assets.

Empirical analysis established that multinationals tended to be firms that are intensive in knowledge-based assets (Markusen 2002) rather than physical capital. Multinationals are associated with patents, research and development (R&D) intensity, skilled white-collar and technical workers and engineers, new and complex products, and product differentiation variables such as advertising, trademarks, and brand names. Multinationals have a high value of intangible assets, which can be measured as a sort of Tobin's Q: the ratio of the market value of the firm to the book value of capital. There are good reasons why multinationality should be associated with knowledge-based assets, but a discussion of this is temporarily postponed.

But ownership advantage is not sufficient. For example, if the purpose of the investment is to serve local markets, then the firm can exploit its asset through exporting. The second condition is therefore location advantage. This is some factor that leads the firm to prefer to actually produce abroad rather than export. Location advantages tend to depend in large part on whether the purpose of the investment is to serve local markets or to export from the host country. For the first type, termed horizontal or market-seeking investments as noted earlier, location advantages are (1) a large host-country market to compensate for set-up costs and plant-level scale economies, and (2) trade costs in the form of tariffs or transportation costs (time as well as money) that make serving the host country by exports expensive. For investments that are more directed at using the host country as an export platform, termed vertical or resource-seeking investments, location advantages are more in the form of low input costs and low trade costs to get intermediate and final goods into and out of the country.

The third condition is internalization advantage. The firm must have a reason to own the foreign production facility rather than simply to license its asset or contract with a local firm to produce on its behalf. Internalization is often contrasted with its mirror image, outsourcing. These are the two alternatives to one decision: the firm must choose between internalizing and outsourcing.

Internalization advantages are the most abstract of the three. For some authors, the principal issue derives from properties of knowledge capital, which are discussed a bit more below. The firm needs to maintain tight control over knowledge-based capital or the value can be easily dissipated through copying and other forms of agent opportunism. Many threats of asset dissipation arise from the lack of strong legal institutions in host countries, such as intellectual property protection and contract enforcement. Other determinants of the internalization/outsourcing decision are familiar from more general discussion of the boundaries of the firm and are not focused on anything particularly international in scope (i.e., strictly domestic firms face decisions on what activities to outsource and which to internalize).

In what follows, we will focus on ownership and location issues in discussing both theory and empirical evidence. The goal is to explain the statistics presented earlier. Internalization is attacked with a very different set of tools and, to date, empirical evidence is scarce.

Early Trade-Theory Models Two very different papers appeared in 1984. Helpman (1984) is a model in which a firm can decompose a production process into a headquarters activity and a production activity. Headquarters and production have different factor intensities and firms can choose to geographically separate these activities. A multinational is a firm that has its headquarters in one country and a plant in the other; in other words, this is a model of vertical multinationals. There are no trade costs in the model and multinationals arise only when countries are sufficiently different in relative factor endowments (i.e., countries must be outside the factor-price-equalization set in the Edgeworth box). In particular, in this model multinationals cannot arise between identical countries, and there are no multiplant firms. Helpman's model is very much in the older tradition of factor-price difference driving FDI discussed earlier.

Markusen (1984) is a model in which there is also something like a headquarters activity and a production activity that can be geographically separated, but these activities do not have different factor intensities.

The whole focus of this model is different from Helpman's. The key idea in the Markusen paper is that headquarters activity, such as R&D, has a "jointness" or "public-goods" property, in that it can yield the full value of its productivity in two locations: adding a second production facility does not reduce the value of the R&D asset in the first location. A blueprint, formula, or procedure can be jointly and fully used in multiple locations. The focus of Markusen's paper is on multinational, horizontal or market-seeking firms that produce in two locations to exploit the value of their knowledge capital. Multinationals can arise between two identical countries, marking a clear break with the old capital-flows literature.

Subsequent Theoretical Developments Important refinements of the horizontal approach are in Horstmann and Markusen (1992) and Brainard (1993). These papers solve for equilibrium market structure between two countries and show that two-plant horizontal multinationals arise when firm-specific fixed costs (knowledge capital) are important relative to plant-level fixed costs, when trade costs are high, and when the two markets are large and similar in size. The result that FDI is expected between large, similar countries provided a theoretical underpinning for the empirical finding that most FDI occurs between large, high-income countries as discussed earlier.

The general-equilibrium structure of the problem was later fleshed out in several papers by Markusen and Venables (1998, 2000). Markusen and Venables use the world Edgeworth box. They concentrate on horizontal two-plant firms and do not consider vertical structures in which a single plant and headquarters are located in different countries. There can be single-plant national firms and two-plant multinationals located in each country, or four potential firm types in all.

They solve the model over a grid in the Edgeworth box, where countries different in size and/or in relative endowments occur at each point in the box (they are identical in the center of the box). Solutions indicate which types of firms are active in equilibrium (termed the "regime") and the pattern of foreign affiliate sales and exports. They show that affil-

iate production is most important when the two countries are similar in size and in relative endowments. The intuition is found by considering what happens when the two countries are quite dissimilar in either of these dimensions. If one country is quite large relative to the other, the dominant firm type will be single-plant firms located in that country serving the small country with exports: it does not pay to incur a plant-specific fixed cost in a small market. If the two countries are quite dissimilar in relative factor endowments, the dominant firm type will be single-plant national firms located in the country which is abundant in the factor used intensively in the multinational's industry.

An integrated treatment of horizontal and vertical multinationals was developed in Markusen's knowledge-capital model (Markusen 2002). Specifically, the model rests on three assumptions relating to knowledge-based assets. First, the services of these assets are easily used in foreign production facilities (transportability or fragmentation). Second, the production of knowledge-based assets is skilled-labor intensive (skilled-labor intensity). Third, knowledge-based assets can yield their full productivity in multiple locations at the same time (jointness). The first two properties support vertical firms while the third supports horizontal multiplant firms.

The contribution of this model is that it yields clear, testable predictions about how foreign affiliate production and trade should be related to the size, size differences, skilled and unskilled labor endowments, and trade and investment cost barriers for two countries. An important extension to include physical capital as a third factor and a third country is found in Bergstrand and Egger (2007).

Empirical Evidence Once again, a good deal of empirical evidence is found in Caves (2007) and Markusen (2002). Brainard (1997) gave convincing evidence for the first time that FDI is not closely related to factor endowments (further discrediting the simple cost-of-capital approach), but much more closely related to country similarity. The ratio of foreign affiliate production to home exports to the host market is increasing in trade costs, increasing in corporate scale economies, and decreasing in plant scale economies. Only that proportion of affiliate production that is destined for export is related to factor endowments, but that makes sense given the vertical motive for foreign production.

Carr, Markusen, and Maskus (2001) found strong support for the knowledge-capital model. In subsequent work, Markusen and Maskus (see Markusen 2002) found strong support for the horizontal model and virtually no support for a pure vertical model, and could not reject the pure horizontal model in favor of the more complex knowledge-capital model.

Combined with the Brainard paper, these results give strong confirmation to simple summary statistics that the vertical model, the most natural incorporation of the cost-of-capital approach, is a very poor fit indeed. Somewhat later and more sophisticated work by Braconier, Norbäck, and Urban (2006) has discovered more evidence in favor of vertical production, and has found it where the knowledge-capital model suggests it should be found. The addition of physical capital and a third country in Bergstrand and Egger (2007) clears up a number of issues. Finally, readers can find an empirical analysis of the horizontal model extended to heterogeneous firms in Helpman, Melitz, and Yeaple (2004).

The Way Forward There seems no clear direction to the research agenda at this time. Both theoretical and empirical work on multicountry models is needed. Most affiliate activity is directed at local markets as we have noted, and for this part of FDI studying bilateral relationships is fine. But the phenomenon of export-platform production is quantitatively important, and there are only a few papers on this topic. Competition among host countries for inward investment is also interesting and important for development economics.

Research integrating models of internalization/outsourcing into the ownership/location models would be valuable. There is some clear link in models that focus on knowledge capital: the same property that makes knowledge easy to transfer makes it easily dissipated through agent opportunism. There is much less of a link with some newer literature on the property-rights, hold-up approach.

While much has been done on country characteristics (size, endowments, trade and investment costs) as determinants of FDI, somewhat less has been done on the converse question: the effects of inward FDI on host countries. There certainly has been good work on the effect of inward FDI on local labor markets and local firms, but this literature remains disjoint from much of what is covered here. The relationship between host-country governments and multinationals deserves more work. Weak results on taxes as determinants of FDI may reflect the fact that, while multinationals don't like taxes, they value strong physical, educational, and institutional infrastructure that taxes bring.

A few papers have interfaced the so-called New Economic Geography with the theory of the multinational. It seems clear that results from the geography literature on the instability of diversified (or dispersed) equilibria in the presence of moderate trade costs break down when multinational firms are added: horizontal multinationals arise precisely when countries are similar and trade costs are moderate to high, and equilibria in the presence of horizontal multinationals are stable. But much more remains to be done. Similarly, the strategic-trade policy literature focuses almost exclusively on single-plant nationally-owned firms, yet it is precisely in those industries in which scale economies and imperfect competition dominate that we find multinationals.

Individuals working in theory would do well to revisit the international business literature as indicated above. That literature, while frustratingly informal and lacking in testable hypotheses, contains a great richness of insights and data that should be fertile ground for new theoretical ideas.

See also foreign direct investment: the OLI framework; internalization theory; knowledge-capital model of the multinational enterprise; multinational enterprises; outsourcing/offshoring

FURTHER READING

Bergstrand, Jeffrey H., and Peter Egger. 2007. "A Knowledge-and-Physical-Capital Model of International Trade Flows, Foreign Direct Investment, and Multinational

Enterprises." *Journal of International Economics* 73 (2): 278–308. Resolves some empirical puzzles by adding a third factor (physical capital) and a third country to the knowledge-capital model.

Braconier, Henrik, Pehr-Johan Norbäck, and Dieter Urban. 2005. "Reconciling the Evidence on the Knowledge-Capital Model." *Review of International Economics* 13 (4): 770–86. Finds evidence of vertical FDI, previously lacking, consistent with the knowledge-capital model by using new data and a new estimation strategy.

Brainard, S. Lael. 1993. "A Simple Theory of Multinational Corporations and Trade with a Trade-off between Proximity and Concentration." NBER Working Paper No. 4269. Cambridge, MA: National Bureau of Economic Research. Theory paper analyzing whether firms choose exporting or two-plant (horizontal) strategies in a two-country model, similar to Horstmann and Markusen (1992).

———. 1997. "An Empirical Assessment of the Proximity-Concentration Trade-off between Multinational Sales and Trade." *American Economic Review* 87 (4): 520–44. Important paper formally documenting for the first time that foreign affiliate sales are increasing in country similarity and not in factor-endowment differences: a death knell for the cost-of-capital approach.

Carr, David L., James R. Markusen, and Keith E. Maskus. 2001. "Estimating the Knowledge-Capital Model of the Multinational Enterprise." *American Economic Review* 91 (3): 693–708. Estimates and finds good support for Markusen's knowledge-capital model.

Caves, Richard E. 2007. *Multinational Enterprise and Economic Analysis.* 3d ed. Cambridge: Cambridge University Press. A rich set of theoretical ideas and empirical evidence; excellent background reading for both theoretical and empirical researchers.

Dunning, John H. 1973. "The Determinants of International Production." *Oxford Economic Papers* 25 (3): 289–336. Classic early paper in the international business tradition, contains the roots of the OLI approach.

Helpman, Elhanan. 1984. "A Simple Theory of Trade with Multinational Corporations." *Journal of Political Economy* 92 (3): 451–71. Early formal model of vertical FDI, single-plant firms that geographically separate headquarters and plant.

Helpman, Elhanan, Marc Melitz, and Stephen Yeaple. 2004. "Exports versus FDI with Heterogeneous Firms." *American Economic Review* 94 (1): 300–16. Heterogeneous-firm approach to horizontal affiliate production: more productive firms choose FDI over exporting.

Horstmann, Ignatius, and James R. Markusen. 1992. "Endogenous Market Structures in International Trade." *Journal of International Economics* 32 (1–2): 109–29. Theory paper analyzing whether duopolists choose exporting or two-plant (horizontal) strategies in a two-country model, similar to Brainard (1993).

Markusen, James R. 1984. "Multinationals, Multi-Plant Economies, and the Gains from Trade." *Journal of International Economics* 16 (3–4): 205–26. Early formal model of horizontal FDI in a model with identical countries: FDI supported by firm-level economies of scale due to joint-input nature of knowledge-based assets.

———. 2002. *Multinational Firms and the Theory of International Trade.* Cambridge, MA: MIT Press. Formal theory and empirical estimation of MNE models; concentrates somewhat on defining, developing, and estimating the knowledge-capital model.

Markusen, James R., and Anthony J. Venables. 1998. "Multinational Firms and the New Trade Theory." *Journal of International Economics* 46 (2): 183–203. General-equilibrium theory of horizontal production in an oligopoly framework where countries can differ in size and/or relative endowments.

———. 2000. "The Theory of Endowment, Intra-Industry, and Multinational Trade." *Journal of International Economics* 52 (2): 209–34. General-equilibrium theory of horizontal production in a monopolistic-competition framework; stresses the role of trade costs and relates results to the New Economic Geography.

JAMES R. MARKUSEN

■ foreign direct investment and exit of local firms

The exit of local firms refers to the discontinuing of operations by firms owned by local shareholders (i.e., not affiliates of foreign-owned multinationals, which represent foreign direct investment, or FDI). This cessation of activities might involve firms closing down completely and exiting the industry, or firms discontinuing their current operations but continuing activities in other guises (e.g., under a new name in the same or a different industry). The former situation is the one more frequently studied and is the focus of this entry. Empirical data show that firm exit (in the sense of complete shutdowns) is a fairly frequent phenomenon. In a comprehensive overview paper Caves (1998) provides evidence that in the United States around 7 percent of all firms shut down annually, accounting for about 3 percent of market share in the economy.

Economists have long debated whether there is a link between the large and growing activities of foreign multinationals and the exit of local firms in host countries (e.g., Lall 1978; McAleese and Counahan 1979). The question became even more topical at the end of the 20th century with the increasing concern about globalization and the fears this has sparked for domestic economic activity, in particular the jobs associated with it (Barba Navaretti and Venables 2004). There are three interrelated yet distinct parts to this question: first, whether there are differences in exit patterns between affiliates of foreign-owned multinationals and local firms; second, whether a foreign acquisition affects exit probabilities of the local takeover target; and third, whether the presence of foreign-owned multinationals affects, either positively or negatively, the exit and survival prospects of unrelated local firms.

Comparison of Exit in Foreign and Local Firms
When comparing the incidence of shutdown across foreign affiliates and local firms one may subscribe to one of three views. The first contends that affiliates of multinationals have shallower roots in the domestic economy than local firms and therefore are more likely to shut down production and move to another location, especially when the economy is hit by a negative shock (such as, for example, an economic downturn). A second perspective is that multinationals incur substantial costs for investing abroad, not all of which can be retrieved if they leave; hence, affiliates of multinationals are more likely than domestic firms to stay in the economy in order not to

lose the sunk investment costs. A third view contends that both affiliates of multinationals and local firms are purely profit-maximizing operations and, therefore, there is no strong case that either should behave differently from the other.

Analyzing these possible differences in the incidence or probability of exiting is hampered by a number of difficulties. Perhaps the most important of these is the issue of choosing the right comparison group. Affiliates of multinationals are, on average, quite different from the typical local firm—they are larger, more productive, more skill-intensive, and more technology-intensive. Firms that have these attributes are generally less likely to exit than others, irrespective of the nationality of their ownership. Then the question becomes whether one should compare the incidence of shutdown among foreign affiliates with that of an average local firm, or with that of a local firm that is as similar as possible to the average foreign affiliate.

A study by Görg and Strobl (2003a), using data for the Republic of Ireland, illustrates this issue. In a comparison of the total incidence of exit for all foreign affiliates and all local firms they find that local firms are, on average, significantly more likely to cease operations. This finding would, hence, support the optimistic view described earlier. It does not, however, take account of the fact that affiliates of foreign multinationals based in Ireland are, for example, larger and in more technology-intensive industries than the "typical" local firm and the difference in exit rates could be due to only these differences, rather than to the nationality of ownership per se. To deal with this issue, Görg and Strobl use an econometric technique that allows them to calculate the effect of nationality on the exit rate, abstracting from the effect of firm size and characteristics of the industry. When doing that, they find that affiliates of foreign multinationals are in fact more likely to exit than local firms. A similar analysis is undertaken by Bernard and Sjöholm (2003) for affiliates of foreign-owned multinationals in Indonesia, with results that are strikingly similar in qualitative terms, if not magnitude. Comparing foreign multinationals to a typical local firm shows that the former are less likely to exit. This difference can be explained by firm characteristics other than nationality, however. Once these are controlled for using econometric techniques, affiliates of foreign multinationals are found to be more likely to exit than a comparable local firm.

Foreign Acquisition and Exit These differences between affiliates of foreign multinationals and local firms raise the question of what would happen if a domestic firm were taken over by a foreign multinational. Would one expect these takeover targets to become more or less likely to face shutdown? Theoretically, the result could be either way. First, since multinationals are generally found to be more likely to exit, a change in ownership may also lead to a higher incidence of plant shutdown for the domestic takeover targets. Second, foreign acquisition may be a device to acquire market access, distribution channels, skills, and so on for a new foreign market entrant. Once these resources/capabilities have been ingested, the acquiring firm may divest itself of the acquired establishment and source its requirements from its plants elsewhere. Foreign acquisition may also lead to a lower threat of exit, however, if the foreign acquirer transfers technology, knowledge, or skills to the acquired plant and hence contributes to an improvement in its performance.

Empirical research into this issue poses some challenges, most important that of constructing a valid counterfactual. While one observes what happens to a local takeover target once it has been acquired by a foreign owner, the important question is what would have happened otherwise in order to identify the effect the acquisition has had. Of course, the latter scenario is unobservable as it did not materialize. Advances in statistical and econometric techniques allow researchers to deal with this problem in various ways, and most recent empirical work uses econometric techniques allowing one to essentially compare local takeover targets with a carefully chosen group of similar local firms that have not been taken over. Based on such econometric techniques, findings for the United States and the United Kingdom using data for the 1980s and 1990s suggest that a takeover by a multinational increases the chances that the takeover target will be closed (see Bernard and Jensen 2007; Girma and Görg 2004).

Impact of FDI on Exit of Local Firms The presence of foreign firms in an economy can also have an impact on the exit performance of unrelated local firms. The early pessimistic view is that foreign multinationals increase competitive pressure in the economy and therefore make it more difficult for local firms to survive, hence increasing the threat of shutdown for these firms. For a given market size, expansion of output by foreign affiliates attracts demand away from local firms. This shift will cause these domestic firms to cut their production, which, if they face fixed costs, will raise their average cost, reduce profitability, and therefore ultimately make them more vulnerable to shutdown. In fact, regardless of cost structure, increased production by foreign affiliates may lead to a reduction in output price (at least in the short run), which will reduce profitability for local firms and, thus, increase their exit threat.

Although this argument is still powerful, a more recent alternative view takes a more benevolent stance on foreign multinationals and asserts that foreign affiliates may transfer some of their technology to unrelated local firms (either voluntarily or involuntarily). This technology transfer allows local firms to improve their production processes and produce at lower average cost. Hence technology transfer can improve domestic firms' performance by lowering cost and increasing profitability and, thus, also lower the chance of shutdown. This positive effect provides a counterbalance to the possible negative influence through increased competition, and the net impact of foreign affiliates on the exit of local firms may hence be positive, negative, or neutral (the last if the positive and negative effects offset each other).

Empirical evaluation of this issue also is hampered by the challenge of constructing a valid counterfactual. One is able to observe what happens to a local firm in a given industry with a certain level of foreign affiliates operating in it; however, what is unobservable is what would have happened in the absence of these. Most recent empirical work uses econometric techniques to compare local firms in industries with different levels of presence of foreign affiliates, controlling for possible differences in other firm and industry characteristics in order to deal with this problem.

A study of Ireland by Görg and Strobl (2003b) finds that the presence of foreign affiliates has an exit-reducing effect only on local plants in high-tech industries, while it has no impact on local firms in low-tech industries. This suggests that in the former industries, domestic firms benefit from foreign firms through technology transfers that allow them to improve their performance and reduce the threat of exit. By contrast, if anything the results for firms in low-tech industries indicate that the negative and positive effects offset each other. Whether these findings hold for other countries is an issue for further research.

Policy Implications Foreign direct investment is an important feature of the globalized world economy. The impact of FDI on economic development, in particular the interplay between local firms and foreign affiliates of the countries involved, is an important issue for policymakers. Although studies have identified general trends and possible effects, it remains to be seen what lessons can be learned from these for particular economies at different levels of development.

See also agglomeration and foreign direct investment; exchange rates and foreign direct investment; footloose production; foreign direct investment and labor markets; foreign direct investment under monopolistic competition; foreign direct investment under oligopoly; outsourcing/offshoring; subsidies and financial incentives to foreign direct investment; transfer pricing

FURTHER READING

Barba Navaretti, Giorgio, and Anthony J. Venables. 2004. *Multinational Firms in the World Economy.* Princeton, NJ: Princeton University Press. Chapters 7 and 8 provide a textbook treatment of the effect of FDI on local firms, also looking at exit of local firms.

Bernard, Andrew, and Bradford Jensen. 2007. "Firm Structure, Multinationals, and Manufacturing Plant Death." *Review of Economics and Statistics* 89: 193–204. Looks empirically at firm exit in the United States and the role of multinationals and ownership change.

Bernard, Andrew, and Fredrik Sjöholm. 2003. "Foreign Owners and Plant Survival." NBER Working Paper 10039. Cambridge, MA: National Bureau of Economic Research. An empirical examination of differences in exit rates between foreign affiliates and local firms for Indonesia.

Caves, Richard E. 1998. "Industrial Organization and New Findings on the Turnover and Mobility of Firms." *Journal of Economic Literature* 36: 1947–82. A very comprehensive review of the research on firm entry and exit.

Girma, Sourafel, and Holger Görg. 2004. "Blessing or Curse? Domestic Plants' Survival and Employment Prospects after Foreign Acquisition." *Applied Economics Quarterly / Konjunkturpolitik* 50 (1): 89–110. Empirical study of effects of foreign acquisitions on exit of local takeover targets using UK data.

Görg, Holger, and Eric Strobl. 2003a. "Footloose Multinationals?" *The Manchester School* 71: 1–19. An empirical examination of differences in exit rates between foreign affiliates and local firms for Ireland.

———. 2003b. "Multinational Companies, Technology Spillovers, and Plant Survival." *Scandinavian Journal of Economics* 105 (4): 581–95. An empirical investigation of the impact of foreign multinationals on exit of local firms using data for Ireland.

Lall, Sanjay. 1978. "Transnationals, Domestic Enterprises, and Industrial Structure in Host LDC's: A Survey." *Oxford Economic Papers* 30 (2): 217–48. An early and very comprehensive survey of host country effects of foreign multinationals.

McAleese, Dermot, and Michael Counahan. 1979. "Stickers or Snatchers? Employment in Multinational Corporations during the Recession." *Oxford Bulletin of Economics and Statistics* 41: 345–58. An early discussion of the "footloose" nature of affiliates of foreign multinationals in host countries.

HOLGER GÖRG

■ foreign direct investment and export performance

The foreign direct investment–export link focuses on the role of foreign direct investment (FDI) in export performance. FDI represents international capital flows through which a firm in one country (the home) creates a subsidiary or acquires control over a business enterprise in another country (the host). The firm with FDI is thus a multinational enterprise (MNE), which must have firm-specific advantages (technology or brand name) and choose a host country with location advantages (cheap labor or growing markets). Export performance has many facets, including export volume, technological composition, growth rate, and global competitiveness. FDI plays a significant role in world exports. Broad estimates indicate that MNEs account for two-thirds to three-quarters of world exports, and foreign affiliates of MNEs account for more than one fifth of world exports and one third of developing country exports (UNCTAD 2002). The paucity of data, however, makes quantitative assessments of the effect of FDI on export performance difficult.

Theoretical studies generally identify two types of FDI: vertical and horizontal (Markusen 1995). A manufacturing MNE usually engages in three activities: firm activities producing headquarters services; upstream-plant activities producing components; and downstream-plant activities of assembling. Headquarters with firm activities are located in home countries, while cross-country relocation of downstream- and/or upstream-plant activities results in vertical and horizontal FDI.

Vertical (efficiency-seeking) FDI is associated with relocation of labor-intensive downstream-plant activities to host countries with cheap labor, while in horizontal (market-seeking) FDI, another set of production facilities (including both upstream- and downstream-plant activities) is built in host countries to serve local markets. Motivated by cheap labor and other resources, the vertical FDI firm may export capital-intensive components and headquarters services to its host-country affiliates for assembling, and ship finished products back to the home country or third-country markets (Helpman and Krugman 1985). Horizontal FDI tends to overcome trade barriers such as tariffs and transportation costs in order to maintain or expand market shares in host countries (Markusen 1984).

The sharpness of the distinction between the two types of FDI may be best explained by MNEs in semiconductors and automobiles. In the 1970s, U.S. chip firms made substantial investments in assembly and testing facilities in Southeast Asia, motivated by cheap labor there. Semiconductors were shipped from the U.S. design and manufacturing complexes to the assembly and testing facilities in Southeast Asia, and then shipped back to sales destinations in the United States and elsewhere. In contrast, Japanese automakers in the 1980s established production lines in the United States in order to avoid local protection threats by replacing existing exports with local production.

How Does FDI Affect Home-Country Exports?
FDI affects home-country export performance through direct effects on trade as well as indirect effects through various channels. The direct effects depend to a large extent on the type of FDI. Vertical FDI could enhance the home country's exports of intermediate products (parts and components) required for assembling. This intrafirm trade is called a complementary effect of exports. Horizontal FDI may lead to an increase in exports of capital goods and intermediate products in the short run, but its long-term impact turns out to be export reduction (so-called substitution effects).

Empirical evidence from developed countries (e.g., the United States, Japan, and Sweden) indicates the FDI-export link to be one of complements at country and industry levels, but of "substitution" at the product level (Blonigen 2001). When activities of foreign affiliates can be classified as vertical and horizontal, evidence is consistent with the theoretical prediction that vertical FDI complements exports and horizontal FDI substitutes for exports. FDI from high-income developing economies (e.g., Hong Kong, Korea, Singapore, and Taiwan) to other developing countries (e.g., China) has been found to be a contributory factor for expanding home-country exports (UNCTAD 2002).

In the long run, FDI may indirectly affect home-country exports by improving the competitiveness of parent companies; upgrading industrial structure; and creating spillovers to the rest of the home economy.

How Does FDI Affect Host-Country Exports?

Effects of FDI on the host country's exports may differ, depending on the MNE's motives. Horizontal FDI is oriented primarily to the host-country market, so it does not directly contribute to host-country exports. Vertical FDI directly boosts host-country exports, since output resulting from FDI is typically intended for export. Most vertical FDI is hosted in developing countries in labor-intensive industries such as textiles, garments, and home electronics. China, for example, attracted a significant amount of vertical FDI, which contributed 57 percent of its total exports in 2004 (Zhang 2006). While the overall impact is export-promoting, the real increase in host-country exports depends on the local content of value-added with exports. If local firms supply intermediate products to MNE affiliates, host-country exports would be much greater than in cases where the inputs are imported from outside the host economy.

A popular form of vertical FDI is located in export processing zones (EPZs), in which materials are imported duty free and transformed for exports, with strictly controlled trade with the rest of the host country. EPZs allow exploiting the location-specific assets of a host country while avoiding the restrictions imposed by its trade regime, providing good infrastructure, and offering fiscal incentives. Many countries (such as Costa Rica, China, Haiti, Mauritius, Bangladesh, Singapore, Malaysia, and Sri Lanka) have enjoyed spectacular growth in manufactured exports from EPZs. The most successful exports have been garments and semiconductors.

Theories and evidence suggest that FDI may have several potential mechanisms to influence host export performance. Its contribution may derive from additional capital, technology, and managerial know-how; training for the local workforce; and access to global and especially home-country markets. These resources and market access may complement a host country's own resources and capabilities, and may provide some of the missing elements for greater export competitiveness. The host country may build on these to enter new export activities and improve its performance in existing ones (UNCTAD 2002). Many studies emphasize the role of FDI in building host export competitiveness in manufacturing goods. Three positive effects of FDI may be identified: helping transfer of technology and new products for exports; expanding market access for exports; and building dynamic comparative advantages. On the other hand, some negative effects of FDI on host exports have been observed. FDI may (1) lower or replace domestic savings and investment; (2) transfer technologies that are low level or too complicated for the host country to absorb due to lack of human capital; (3) target primarily the host country's domestic market and thus not increase exports; (4) inhibit the expansion of indigenous firms that might become exporters; and (5) neglect the host country's dynamic comparative advantages by focusing solely on local cheap labor and raw materials (Zhang 2006).

While potential benefits of FDI to host exports exist, they do not automatically accrue. To what extent a host country can capture them depends largely on its own strategies and efforts. Opening up to FDI is only the first step, and host countries need to realize existing comparative advantages based on initial capabilities. For countries with weak industries and exports, FDI may well lead only to a short-lived boost in export performance. To build a more sustainable and dynamic export base, host countries have to use proactive policies, including selective liberalization to reconcile efforts to attract vertical FDI with the need to protect particular industries; attracting FDI by targeting investment conducive to export competitiveness and upgrading; and strengthening domestic enterprises, as well as the skills, capabilities, and institutions necessary for successful export-oriented strategy.

See also appropriate technology and foreign direct investment; export processing zones; intrafirm trade; knowledge-capital model of the multinational enterprise;

linkages, backward and forward; technology spillovers; vertical versus horizontal foreign direct investment

FURTHER READING

Blonigen, Bruce A. 2001. "In Search of Substitution between Foreign Production and Exports." *Journal of International Economics* 53 (1): 81–104. An empirical study of substitution- and complement-effects of FDI on home-country exports, using product-level data.

Helpman, Elhanan, and Paul Krugman. 1985. *Market Structure and Foreign Trade*. Cambridge, MA: MIT Press. Chapters 12 and 13 offer a central theoretical analysis of vertical FDI and its link to trade.

Markusen, James. 1984. "Multinational, Multiplant Economies, and the Gain from Trade." *Journal of International Economics* 16(3–4): 205–26. An important work on horizontal FDI.

———. 1995. "The Boundaries of Multinational Enterprises and the Theory of International Trade." *The Journal of Economic Perspectives* 9 (2): 169–89. A thorough review of the research on FDI and international trade.

United Nations Conference on Trade and Development (UNCTAD). 2002. *World Investment Report 2002: Transnational Corporations and Export Competitiveness*. New York: United Nations. Each year UNCTAD spotlights an important FDI issue; the 2002 report focused on empirical evidence about effects of FDI on exports in host countries, especially developing economies.

Zhang, Kevin Honglin. 2006. "The Role of FDI in China's Export Performance." In *China as the World Factory*, edited by Kevin H. Zhang. London: Routledge, 139–55. A comprehensive analysis of positive and negative effects of FDI on exports from China, a nation hosting the largest amount of FDI in the developing world and being globally the second largest exporter in 2007.

KEVIN HONGLIN ZHANG

■ foreign direct investment and innovation, imitation

Following successful innovation of a new process or product technology, production can be shifted abroad through a variety of channels: firms can license their technologies to foreign firms, undertake foreign direct investment (FDI), or may find that their technologies are transferred abroad through imitation by foreign firms. With FDI, the incumbent firm establishes a plant in another country, whereas with imitation, production in the other country is done by a rival firm (or firms).

FDI, innovation, and imitation each typically requires the investment of resources. Most innovation results from intentional efforts to develop new varieties of products, higher-quality levels of existing products, or lower-cost methods of production (process improvements). These efforts require firms to bear significant costs with an uncertain outcome. While there may be some products for which imitation is straightforward, in most cases imitation, like innovation, is also a costly and uncertain activity. Mansfield, Schwartz, and Wagner (1981) find that imitation costs average two-thirds of innovation costs for firms in the chemical, drug, electronics, and machinery industries. Undertaking FDI also incurs costs (prior to production), such as fixed costs of establishing new plants, adapting technologies to new economic environments, finding local suppliers, and the like.

Each of these activities—FDI, innovation, and imitation—must yield a reward in the form of an expected stream of profits sufficient to offset the initial costs or else firms would have little incentive to undertake them. Properly discounted, the total expected profits from an innovation must at least cover the costs of generating the innovation for firms to be willing to invest resources in the innovation. As the costs of a successful imitation tend to be lower than for the original innovation, the profits of a successful imitator can be lower (or shorter in duration) than for an innovator, but again imitators need to rewarded, through the expected profits from a successful imitation, for their imitation expenses. For FDI, the expected profits must rise by enough to compensate for the up-front costs of shifting technology abroad.

Additionally, these activities may be constrained by the availability of factors such as skilled labor. In countries where firms innovate, there must be enough resources for both R&D and production uses; in countries where firms imitate, there must be enough for imitation efforts, production by successful imitators, and production by multinational firms. Thus FDI, innovation, and imitation are all affected by incentives and resource availability—the two key factors that determine practically all economic activity.

How FDI Affects Innovation The costs of innovation need to be offset by the expected stream of profits from selling the product. As FDI is undertaken to enhance profits, it would seem that the opportunity to undertake FDI should accelerate innovation by enhancing the reward for innovation.

Suppose FDI involves shifting production to a lower-cost location. If the opportunity to shift production abroad arrives at a higher probability, then the higher profits under FDI should begin sooner, all else being equal. Glass and Saggi (1999), however, show that the effect of faster arrival of FDI opportunities on innovation can be essentially zero due to increased exposure to imitation. The faster arrival of higher profits under FDI is offset by a shorter duration of profits before imitation, when FDI opportunities are beyond the control of firms.

Why then are FDI opportunities commonly believed to stimulate innovation? Perhaps FDI occurs not in response to increases in opportunities to shift production abroad, but rather in response to other influences. Instead of a faster arrival of fixed FDI opportunities, suppose that FDI increases in response to variations in the underlying economic environment. For example, suppose the labor supply abroad increases to provide more labor for production there. In response, FDI increases to shift production from home to abroad, and innovation also increases, as shown in Glass and Saggi (2002). Other changes, such as a reduction in the difficulty of adapting technologies for production abroad, can also increase FDI and innovation. Crisuolo, Haskel, and Slaughter (2005) provide evidence that firms that are globally engaged do innovate more.

How FDI Affects Imitation By shifting production abroad, FDI typically generates technology spillovers through demonstration effects. More can be learned about a technology when it is produced locally than when only the final product can be seen. Although inspecting the final product can yield useful insights, full knowledge of the production process is hard to determine from the end result. When production occurs locally, however, workers at the multinational firm observe the production process firsthand. Workers who have been exposed to the technology, and perhaps specially trained, may leave the multinational to work for local firms or even start their own firms. Local suppliers of intermediates may also serve as sources of information. These knowledge flows act to lower the cost and difficulty of imitation. Hence, by reducing the cost of imitation, FDI should encourage imitation through incentive effects.

On the other hand, FDI vies with local production for local resources such as skilled labor. In some circumstances, FDI might deter imitation if multinationals bid up prices for scarce resources. Furthermore, when FDI is motivated by cost savings, multinationals have lower production costs than firms that export the good from elsewhere, so the profit margins earned when producing an imitation of a multinational's product should be less than that earned when producing an imitation of a product produced elsewhere. Due to the reduced profit margins for imitators, FDI could deter imitation. Glass and Saggi (1999) show that a faster arrival of opportunities to shift production abroad through cost-saving FDI can leave the aggregate rate of imitation essentially unchanged. So even though FDI makes imitation easier, there is no guarantee that FDI spurs local imitation.

How Innovation Affects FDI Multinational firms need to possess an ownership advantage in order to overcome the inherent difficulties of operating in multiple countries. Innovation yields the technological expertise that often provides the source of ownership advantage for multinational firms. As innovation is, in a sense, a necessary precondition for FDI, innovation should spur FDI.

Who is conducting the innovation matters, however. Doing more innovation should lead the innovating firm to do more FDI. But to the extent that innovation is being done by rival firms, FDI may be deterred. Innovation by rivals poses a risk that the profit stream that rewards innovation may be terminated (or reduced) by a successful innovation by another firm. In some industries, the existing leaders have significant advantages from successful past innovations and therefore have a greater incentive to innovate, whereas in other industries, firms are on more equal footing and innovation is spread across many firms. This distinction suggests that the relationship between innovation and FDI may differ across industries.

For the newest technologies, firms usually opt for FDI over licensing on account of large transaction costs that arise due to the presence of asymmetric information. At the moment when a new technology is first created, only the innovating firm is well informed about its key attributes. Thus transferring such technologies to independent firms in other countries via arm's-length contracts might be rather difficult since such firms would typically not have a reliable estimate of the value of the technology. Under such a scenario, the innovating firm might choose to undertake FDI by establishing a fully owned subsidiary as opposed to licensing the new technology to a foreign firm. By impeding arm's-length contracting, transaction costs can induce internalization on the part of an innovating firm.

Furthermore, such internalization might also be motivated by strategic considerations: a firm may be unwilling to share its newest technologies with foreign firms that could become future competitors. It may be difficult, or perhaps even impossible, to prevent a licensee from terminating the contract and undertaking independent production after it has mastered the new technology. A further worry is that a current licensee might use the technology to invent a future technology that would make it an even fiercer competitor. Both the transaction cost perspective and strategic considerations suggest that firms will typically transfer their newest technologies through FDI and relatively more mature, and less valuable, technologies through licensing and other arm's length arrangements. A wealth of econometric and case-study evidence supports this hypothesis.

How Imitation Affects FDI When FDI brings about higher profits through costs savings, imitation poses the risk that the enhanced profit stream under FDI will be terminated. Thus imitation would seem to deter FDI. To determine how imitation affects FDI incentives, however, Glass and Saggi (2002) have argued that, as multinationals need not be the only firms targeted by imitation, the relative risk of imitation for a multinational must be compared to the imitation risk of producing in the home country. Even though FDI lowers the cost of imitation, it also lowers the multinational's production costs and therefore the profit margin earned by an imitator targeting the multinational's product. So there is reason for both types of imitation to exist: easier imitation targeting multinationals and more difficult imitation (that is more richly rewarded in terms of profits) targeting products produced elsewhere. When imitators target technologies regardless of whether FDI has occurred, increased risk of imitation need not deter FDI if the imitation risk also increases for firms that produce back in their home countries. What matters is how much more exposed to imitation multinationals are relative to firms that export. Glass and Saggi (2002) demonstrate a tendency for the relative risk of multinationals to remain constant, so the increased risk of imitation for a multinational does not vary as many other parameters of the model change.

For example, if imitation becomes more difficult, the rate of imitation falls, which one might think would encourage FDI. But both imitation targeting multinationals and imitation targeting nonmultinationals decrease, and they decrease in equal proportion, so the relative imitation risk for multinationals is essentially unchanged. In addition, there are effects operating though the labor constraint: due to the increased difficulty of imitation, the labor needed for imitation can increase, even though imitation falls. The increased use of labor for imitation crowds out FDI, as there is less labor left for production by multinational firms. In this case, less imitation (due to increased difficulty) leads to less FDI.

Imitation can be thought to encourage FDI in some settings. Glass and Saggi (1998) construct a model with two types of FDI: FDI that transfers state-of-the-art technology and FDI using older technology. In that model, successful imitation of the older technology is required before FDI transferring state-of-the-art technology becomes feasible. The initial imitation is needed to establish a knowledge base in order for the technology transfer costs for the new technology to become reasonable. In this setting, although imitation of the latest technology could deter FDI, some initial imitation of older technologies is necessary for more advanced FDI to occur.

The impact of imitation on FDI can also depend on whether imitation is varied or whether imitation changes in response to other parameters of the model. Glass and Wu (2007) contrast the results for the effects of imitation on FDI when imitation changes on its own or in response to changes in other parameters of the model, as well as depending on whether imitations are quality improvements or new varieties, and whether innovations are done by leaders or rival firms (followers). Mostly, imitation and FDI move together in quality ladder models, except when innovations are done by followers. Increases in imitation may decrease FDI when innovations are new varieties (see Helpman 1993; Lai 1998). There are also models with R&D having decreasing returns to scale (see Dinopoulos and Segerstrom 2005; Sener 2006).

In sum, the interrelationships between FDI, innovation, and imitation are quite complex. Claims that may seem intuitively obvious, such as that innovation spurs FDI or even that FDI spurs innovation, need not be generally true. Similarly, FDI need not spur imitation and imitation need not always deter FDI. Given the many possible scenarios uncovered by theory, there is a great need for empirical work to sort out which outcomes are predominant. A better sense of what is happening in the data will lead to a better understanding of how imitation, FDI, and innovation matter to firms.

See also agglomeration and foreign direct investment; foreign direct investment under oligopoly; intangible assets; intellectual property rights and foreign direct investment; multinational enterprises; technology licensing; technology spillovers; trade-related investment measures (TRIMs)

FURTHER READING

Crisuolo, Chiara, Jonathan E. Haskel, and Matthew J. Slaughter. 2005. "Global Engagement and the Innovation Activities of Firms." NBER Working Paper No. 11479. Cambridge, MA: National Bureau of Economic Research. Evidence that globally engaged firms innovate more.

Dinopoulos, Elias, and Paul Segerstrom. 2005. "Multinational Firms and Economic Growth." Mimeo. University of Florida and Stockholm School of Economics. Compares effects of policies that encourage multinational firms to effects of globalization in the form of geographic expansion, in a scale-invariant growth model.

Glass, Amy J., and Kamal Saggi. 1998. "International Technology Transfer and the Technology Gap." *Journal of Development Economics* 55 (2): 369–98. A model of the connection between imitation, FDI, and innovation that distinguishes between the type of technology (new or old) transferred through FDI.

———. 1999. "Foreign Direct Investment and the Nature of R&D." *Canadian Journal of Economics* 32 (1): 92–117. Shows how exogenous increases in opportunities for cost-saving FDI affect imitation and innovation.

———. 2002. "Intellectual Property Rights and Foreign Direct Investment." *Journal of International Economics* 56 (2): 387–410. Models the interrelationships between imitation, FDI, and innovation when imitation is determined within the model and innovations are quality improvements.

Glass, Amy J., and Xiaodong Wu. 2007. "Intellectual Property Rights and Quality Improvement." *Journal of Development Economics* 82 (2): 393–415. Models the interrelationships between imitation, FDI, and innovation when imitation is not determined within the model and innovations are quality improvements; contrasts with other findings.

Helpman, Elhanan. 1993. "Innovation, Imitation, and Intellectual Property Rights." *Econometrica* 61 (6): 1247–80. Models the effect of imitation on FDI when innovations are new varieties.

Lai, Edwin L.C. 1998. "International Intellectual Property Rights Protection and the Rate of Product Innovation." *Journal of Development Economics* 55 (1): 133–53. Models the effect of imitation on FDI and innovation when innovations are new varieties.

Mansfield, Edwin, Mark Schwartz, and Samuel Wagner. 1981. "Imitation Costs and Patents: An Empirical Study." *Economic Journal* 91 (364): 907–18. Collects data on imitation cost and time relative to innovations.

Sener, M. Fuat. 2006. "Intellectual Property Rights and Rent Protection in a North-South Product-Cycle Model." Mimeo. Union College. Includes efforts by successful innovators to deter innovation and imitation by other firms.

Vernon, Raymond. 1966. "International Investment and International Trade in the Product Cycle." *Quarterly Journal of Economics* 80 (2): 190–207. The original product-cycle model with FDI.

AMY JOCELYN GLASS AND KAMAL SAGGI

■ foreign direct investment and international technology transfer

A technology gap separates developing countries from the developed world: from manufacturing processes to information technology provision in business, government, and higher education, poorer countries lag behind richer ones. One reflection of this gap is the high concentration of global research and development (R&D) in developed countries: in 2002, developed countries accounted for more than 90 percent of global R&D expenditures (UNCTAD 2005). The transfer of technology from developed to developing countries helps close the international technology gap and contributes to productivity growth in developing countries. Such technology transfer makes much economic sense, since it keeps poorer countries from having to spend already scarce resources on reinventing the wheel.

The results of R&D undertaken in developed countries are transferred globally through many channels, perhaps the most important of which is foreign direct investment (FDI)—investment projects whose ownership and control lie in the hands of overseas investors. The establishment of production facilities by foreign companies usually results in the introduction of new production processes and techniques to the local economy, making FDI a major channel of technology transfer. FDI also has come to play an increasingly important role in helping disperse R&D activities globally: during the period 1993–2002, R&D expenditures by foreign subsidiaries of multinational firms increased from $30 billion to $67 billion, representing a rise from 10 percent to 16 percent of global business R&D.

This article examines several questions related to international technology transfer. How do technologies originating in industrialized countries take hold in developing countries? What role does FDI play in this process? What benefits do developing countries enjoy from FDI? And how, if at all, can international organizations such as the World Trade Organization (WTO) facilitate the process of technology transfer?

International Technology Transfer and the Role of FDI While much FDI occurs between industrialized countries, developing countries are becoming increasingly important hosts for such investment flows. In fact, during 2001–5, average net FDI inflows equaled $754.3 billion, of which $212.4 billion (approximately 29 percent) went to developing countries. The global stock of FDI in 2004 stood at approximately $9 trillion with approximately 25 percent of it being in developing countries (UNCTAD 2005).

FDI is undoubtedly one of the primary channels of international technology transfer. It is well known that multinational activity occurs primarily in industries that are characterized by a high ratio of R&D to sales and by large shares of professional, scientific, and technical workers (Markusen 1995). In fact, a basic tenet of the theory of the multinational firm is that such firms rely heavily on their technology-based assets and well-established brand names to offset the logistical disadvantages of operating in multiple counties as well as to successfully compete with local firms that are usually more familiar with the local environment. In 1995, of all transactions in royalty and license fees, transactions within the same firm made up in excess of 80 percent, so most explicit trade in technology takes place within multinational firms (UNCTAD 1997).

Other private sector channels for technology transfer include technology licensing and joint ventures. With technology licensing, a licensee will pay royalties and fixed fees to a foreign licensor in exchange for the right to use its technology. Joint ventures, on the other hand, are typically organized as partnerships between foreign and local companies. Then there are the so-called indirect routes for technology transfer, which include international trade in goods and services and the movement of labor between countries. Another such route is the imitation or "reverse engineering" of technological products, which essentially involves taking them apart for analysis and then independently reproducing them—a practice that allows local entrepreneurs and companies to replicate products and technologies from abroad without paying any royalties or fees.

The usage of the word *transfer* in the phrase *technology transfer* conveys the impression that the process is smooth and costless. Such is hardly the case. The fact that developing countries lag behind the technology frontier merely creates the potential for technology transfer. For this process actually to occur, providers and acquirers of new technologies have to undertake deliberate and often significantly large investments. Substantial empirical evidence indicates that international technology transfer does not come cheap. Economists regard knowledge (and its application in the form of technology) as a nonrival good, meaning that it can be accessed by more than one person. The nonrival nature of knowledge does not mean, however, that it can be transferred free of cost. Rather, it simply implies that if two people are willing to pay the cost of adopting a new idea or a technology, they can do so without interfering with each other's decisions.

Analyses of FDI must always bear in mind one basic observation: multinational firms engage in the transfer of technology primarily to maximize profits and value for their stockholders. Thus any technology transfer activity that does not contribute to profit-making will typically not be attractive for a multinational company. For example, if transferring a technology runs the risk of strengthening a company's local rivals, the company should be expected to try to thwart the process of technology diffusion to some degree: it may choose not to invest locally and may simply export the product from its home market or may transfer only peripheral technologies as opposed to core ones.

Despite such concerns, FDI often generates benefits for both consumers and local companies in developing countries. Benefits to consumers include access to higher-quality goods or completely new goods that were not produced locally. Benefits to local companies include what is known as the "demonstration effect," in which local firms adopt a technology from overseas after observing its successful introduction by a multinational. People trained or previously employed by multinational firms can provide added benefit to local business by helping with technology transfer when they change jobs or start new firms.

Multinationals also engage in technology transfer to firms that either supply them or buy their products. An example can be found in Mexico's automobile industry. After the North American Free Trade Agreement (NAFTA) was ratified in 1992, U.S. car companies set up manufacturing plants in Mexico. Within five years this had led to hundreds of domestic producers of car parts and accessories springing up (Moran 1998). United States and other multinational corporations transferred technology to these Mexican suppliers, who, as a direct result, gained expertise in industry best practices and quality control. The Mexican story is by no means unique. A rich body of evidence indicates that Mexico's experience has been replicated across the world (Saggi 2002).

Policy Implications The earlier discussion suggests that the process of technology transfer via FDI may not always work smoothly. But does this necessarily create a role for government support or regulation of such activities? Historical experience of countries such as Japan, South Korea, and China suggests that many national governments perceive this to be the case. These countries have considerable experience in attracting—and regulating—private sector international technology transfer. Both Japan and South Korea have been deliberately selective in their choice of technology transfer method, preferring technology licensing over FDI. Their experiences have been studied in some depth. It is well known that during the 1960s and 1970s, Japan's Ministry of International Trade and Industry (MITI) limited competition between potential local buyers of foreign technologies to keep the prices they paid for it low. Furthermore, MITI never formally encouraged FDI and instead encouraged local companies to license technology from overseas. It even insisted that foreign firms share their technology with local firms as a precondition for doing business in Japan. South Korea presents a similar story. In fact, discouraging FDI while encouraging technology licensing was a central theme of South Korea's industrial policy.

There are several reasons why such countries may prefer technology licensing to FDI. They may share a fear that FDI may lead to a transfer of what are called "black box" technologies, in which local companies do not learn very much about how the technology was developed. Another perception is that FDI gives the foreign companies that supply the technologies a stronger bargaining position than the local ones receiving it. Governments also believe that FDI has fewer of what are called "spillover" benefits for local businesses, compared with technology licensing and joint ventures between local and foreign firms.

The evidence for these views remains quite thin, however. In fact, several studies have found that the opposite is true. For example, technology licensing may offer fewer opportunities for profit-making than is sometimes perceived. In addition, a licensee may need additional permission from the license holder to export the technology to a new country. Or it may need permission to make additional modifications or improvements. This shows that, if anything, technology licensing can carry a number of restrictions that may hamper technological development and growth of the licensee's businesses.

Because of these limitations, governments in many developing countries have come to adopt a more liberal approach to FDI than in the past. In fact, today most countries compete with one another to attract more FDI by providing a range of fiscal and other financial incentives. This is more relevant for manufacturing than for services, however. For example, in recent years, while China has been the biggest recipient of FDI in the world, its services sector has not been particularly open to FDI. This was, in fact, an important sticking point during China's negotiations regarding its entry into the WTO.

For international technology transfer to work well, policies need to take into account the needs of both buyers and sellers of foreign technology. As we have seen, the point of technology transfer from the perspective of developing countries is to save them from having to reinvent the wheel. At the same time, the costs of new technologies need to be kept low. From a policy point of view, this means that governments need to invest in education, infrastructure, and local expertise to adopt and adapt new technologies.

From the perspective of technology suppliers, transferring technologies to poorer countries comes with risks, which can be mitigated by appropriate (but not excessive) regulation. Historically, developing countries have not always appreciated the fact that suppliers of foreign technology need to profit from their endeavors. But today, the pendulum is in danger of swinging too far in the other direction. Developing countries may have become overeager to attract FDI into manufacturing, even while still restricting it in services. But this is problematic, as policies that favor one sector over another distort the flow of FDI relative to what would occur as a result of purely market forces. Few developing countries have comparative advantage in world-class manufacturing, and favoring the manufacturing sector can deprive the development of the service sector, leading to a misallocation to inward FDI as well as complementary domestic resources.

The Role of International Institutions Most international treaties at the United Nations level make some reference to the need for rich countries to help developing countries meet their treaty obligations by transferring technologies under favorable conditions. For example, Article 7 of the WTO's Trade-Related Aspects of Intellectual Property Rights (TRIPS) agreement notes that intellectual property protection should "contribute to the promotion of technological innovation and to the transfer and dissemination of technology, to the mutual advantage of producers and users of technological knowledge and in a manner conducive to social and economic welfare, and to a balance of rights and obligations." Article 66 of the same agreement commits developed countries to find ways to encourage international technology transfer to developing countries and to help improve their technological base.

Governments of industrialized countries are less enthusiastic about subsidizing technology transfer, however, in part because they are reluctant to interfere with what is now an activity dominated by the private sector. Their earlier pledges to transfer technology to help developing countries with international agreements on biodiversity and global climate change remained mired in debate at the end of 2007, as did discussion on concrete steps to implement Article 66 of TRIPS.

The WTO has a working group on trade and technology transfer, but through the end of 2007, it had focused primarily on information exchange between representatives of the group's member countries. And even here, the information provided had been little more than what is freely available in the academic literature.

The potential certainly exists for countries in the group with more experience, such as Japan and South Korea, to provide a mentoring role to less developed ones. Developing country members would benefit from practical case studies from Japan, for instance, that show its reasons for adopting certain technology transfer policies, and how these helped to strengthen local industry.

Poorer countries can also benefit from guidance on the structure of international technology transfer contracts, including, for instance, information on reasonable royalty rates, the conditions sellers of technology have been willing to accept, and the types of contract clauses that have proved helpful in encouraging local technological development.

It is a staple of today's development thinking that technology transfer from developed to developing countries is important for generating sustained economic growth. But historical experience shows that, to be innovators themselves, countries must first learn to absorb foreign technologies and adapt them to local conditions.

Because of government intervention, in several Asian countries technologies in the private sector were frequently transferred through technology licensing rather than FDI. This may have allowed some countries such as South Korea to obtain foreign technologies at relatively low prices. Although such policies are not necessarily the most desirable ones, they were more successful than the policies of countries such as India that focused on achieving self-reliance by fostering imitation and adoption of foreign technologies under a regime that protected local industries from foreign competition.

Today's multilateral trading system is a markedly different one, and it seems unlikely that developing countries can adopt the interventionist policies used by even Japan and South Korea, let alone India: several multilateral agreements of the WTO explicitly forbid governments from pursuing such policies. Furthermore, policies supporting technology licensing require an effective bureaucracy, which some of the poorest developing countries lack.

Developing countries are likely to maximize the benefits of technology transfer by investing more in local education and infrastructure development while giving multinational firms relatively unrestricted access to their markets. In particular, policies that favor one sector (such as manufacturing) at the expense of another (such as services) seem counterproductive. As an example, it is worth noting that the development and success of India's software sector has far outpaced its manufacturing sector despite the fact that the Indian government has always been rather keen to promote local manufacturing via the pursuit of a restrictive trade policy. In fact, it seems quite likely that the software sector succeeded because it was able to draw on India's investment in education (as evidenced by the fact that the Indian Institutes of Technology are considered on a par with the best universities in developed countries) and because the government did not (some would say it could not) restrict international trade in the sector.

In addition, governments in rich countries and international institutions such as the WTO have the potential to do more to encourage technology transfer. Similarly, the governments of advanced developing countries can play a more active role in sharing their own experiences of managing technology transfer from developed countries.

See also Agreement on Trade-Related Aspects of Intellectual Property Rights (TRIPS); appropriate technology and foreign direct investment; foreign direct investment and exit of local firms; foreign direct investment and innovation, imitation; foreign direct investment and labor markets; intellectual property rights and foreign direct investment; internalization theory; joint ventures; linkages, backward and forward; location theory; multinational enterprises; technology licensing; technology spillovers; trade-related investment measures (TRIMs)

FURTHER READING

Markusen, James R. 1995. "The Boundaries of Multinational Enterprises and the Theory of International Trade." *Journal of Economic Perspectives* 9: 169–89. A rigorous review of the economics of the multinational firm viewed from the perspective of international trade theory.

Moran, Theodore. 1998. *Foreign Direct Investment and Development.* Washington DC: Institute for International Economics. A rich discussion of the impact of FDI on economic development that draws on several recent national case studies.

Saggi, Kamal. 2002. "Trade, Foreign Direct Investment, and International Technology Transfer: A Survey." *World Bank Research Observer* 17: 191–235. A critical review of the economics literature on international technology transfer.

UN Conference on Trade and Development (UNCTAD). 1992–2005. *World Investment Reports.* New York: United Nations. Annual reports on global flows of FDI published by the United Nations Conference on Trade and Development.

KAMAL SAGGI

■ foreign direct investment and labor markets

Private cross-border capital inflows are made up of foreign direct investment (FDI) and portfolio equity and debt flows. *Direct* investments are defined as those which wield a significant influence on the management of the firm. FDI flows therefore comprise the financing of overseas greenfield investments (where new operational facilities are constructed from the ground up) and further expansions, and of cross-border mergers and acquisitions by multinational enterprises (MNEs). The total direct capital owned by nonresidents in a given country in a particular year constitutes the stock of FDI.

The regional and sectoral destination of FDI flows has changed substantially over the decades. At the outbreak of World War I, more than 80 percent of the foreign capital stock was located in developing economies, reflecting the importance of railway building, the extractive industries, and the colonial control of international trade at that time. In the early 21st century, by contrast, almost 80 percent of the global FDI stock is located in the developed world, and FDI is associated with a different range of activities. The transnationality of an industry today is associated with the sectoral importance of knowledge capital such as "patents, blueprints, formulae, managerial and work procedures, marketing knowledge, reputations and trademarks" (Markusen 1998). Knowledge spillovers are likely to be associated primarily with such knowledge-intensive industries. Within services—the sector which currently accounts for the bulk of the global FDI stock—the predominant subsectors are finance and business activities. Within manufacturing, the chemical industry is predominant, followed by motor vehicles and electronics. Primary activities account for only a small proportion of global FDI.

In discussing the labor-market effects of FDI, one clearly needs to distinguish between the effects on the host, or destination, economy and those on the home, or source, economy. The following two major subsections follow this distinction.

FDI and the Host-Economy Labor Market How might FDI affect the labor market of the host economy? Obviously, in the presence of unemployment, an FDI inflow might simply lead to new job creation, without further complications. If the inflow is large enough relative to the size of the economy, it might also bid up wages and improve the economy's terms of trade, generating gains even in the absence of market failures. For a small economy like Ireland, which had an unemployment rate of 17 percent before the substantial increase in export-platform FDI of the "Celtic Tiger" era of the 1990s and beyond, both of these considerations apply.

In general however, the matter is less straightforward, and indeed, cross-country growth regressions that attempt to isolate the effects of inward FDI yield inconclusive results. One problem with these studies is that they fail to distinguish between the different characteristics of FDI projects associated with import substituting and outward-oriented regimes. Case study investigations of FDI in the automotive and high-performance electronics industries in developing economies show that the effects depend very much on whether local subsidiaries are integrated into the parent firm's international sourcing networks (as under outward orientation) or whether they are oriented toward protected domestic markets. Foreign direct investment projects of the first type—motivated by "global sourcing" considerations—have been found to differ from "tariff-jumping" FDI projects of the second type in terms of the size of the local plant, its proximity to the technological frontier, the rapidity with which technology and quality control procedures are upgraded, and the general efficiency of the operations. In each case, the tariff-jumping FDI projects exhibit less desirable characteristics. Nor do they represent an effective infant-industry strategy, while many prominent domestic component producers in outward-oriented regimes are known to have originated as contract manufacturers to foreign plants (Moran, Graham, and Blomström 2005).

The cross-country studies on FDI also typically do not specify the precise microeconomic channels through which FDI might be thought to influence growth. Besides the direct first-round employment effects of an FDI project, second-round effects will arise through the impact of FDI on local firms, while third-round effects will arise through the impact on public-goods provision and expenditure of any increased tax revenues that might be associated with FDI.

MNE entry can crowd out local firms in the product market, though this outcome is less likely with export-platform FDI, while benefits can arise through the erosion of local monopoly power and the inducement to reduce internal inefficiencies. The investment might also raise the productivity of local firms through knowledge spillovers, deeper markets in specialized factors, and increased scope for backward and forward linkages between customer and supplier firms—the classic "Marshallian externalities."

In the labor market itself, while the short-term value of an FDI project will depend on the extent to which other jobs are crowded out, productivity growth and hence wage growth over the longer term may be higher in multinational firms. The characteristics of the jobs created are also important. If some interindustry wage differences are associated with industry rather than worker characteristics (as in efficiency-wage models, for example), an FDI-induced change in industrial structure can yield benefits in terms of increased wages. Labor-market volatility might also increase, however, because of the ease with which MNEs can switch activities across plants. The latter possibility, however, might also serve to make local labor markets more competitive.

In general, the second-round labor-market effects arise either because MNEs differ in a number of key aspects from the domestic firms they may replace or because FDI induces changes in the behavior of domestic firms.

All the international evidence suggests that MNEs on average are more productive than domestic firms—in terms of both output and value added per employee—and that they exhibit higher productivity growth. These findings are largely accounted for by the fact that MNEs are larger (in terms of output, employment, and value added), they invest more, and they use more intermediate inputs per employee than purely domestic firms. When these differences are controlled for, the productivity gap largely disappears, though the fact that some small element remains suggests that multinationality per se is associated with somewhat greater efficiency in terms of input usage. From a policy perspective, however, the fact that MNEs differ from local firms in these key characteristics is important in that it means that they bring to the host country a set of characteristics and techniques that would otherwise be difficult to establish locally.

The literature is virtually unanimous in its finding—from both developed countries such as the United States, the United Kingdom, and Ireland, and developing countries such as Côte d'Ivoire, Morocco, Venezuela, and Indonesia—that foreign firms pay higher wages than privately owned domestic firms (see, e.g., Aitken, Harrison, and Lipsey 1996; Harrison 1996; Scheve and Slaughter 2005). Part of the reason is undoubtedly that foreign MNEs employ more highly skilled labor than domestic firms do. It is difficult to determine whether this difference fully accounts for the wage differential as skills are often imperfectly measurable. There are a number of reasons, however, why MNEs might pay higher wages than domestic firms for equivalently skilled workers. MNEs may want to minimize the risk that their proprietary knowledge is dissipated through frequent labor turnover or they may wish to avoid excessive geographical disparities. Higher wages might also be required to compensate for perceived disadvantages such as greater employment volatility. Foreign firms also generally provide higher levels of training than domestic firms, resulting in higher subsequent wage growth.

Compared to the other topics discussed, little research has been carried out on the question of the relative volatility of employment in MNEs and domestic firms. Contrary to the presumption that MNEs might be more willing to switch activities across locations in response to wage pressures, the available research suggests that MNE employment levels are less affected by wage changes than is the case for domestic firms. This finding appears likely to arise because of the bundle of characteristics other than ownership per se that distinguishes them from local firms.

A recent study on Irish data adds a new element to the research on volatility. It finds that while the higher-technology MNE-dominated sectors exhibit faster employment growth than the traditional lower-technology sectors populated primarily by domestic firms, employment growth in the former sectors is also more volatile. The application of portfolio theory demonstrates however that the diversification resulting from the attraction of MNEs has allowed the aggregate manufacturing sector to grow more rapidly without a commensurate increase in overall volatility and risk (Barry and Kearney 2006).

We now turn to the question of whether and why FDI might induce changes in the behavior of domestic firms. Multinational and domestic firms interact in a number of ways, some beneficial and some harmful to the latter. The beneficial effects can arise through market transactions or via externalities while the adverse consequences arise through increased competition. The overall effect will determine the second-round employment consequences of foreign direct investment.

The transfer of proprietary assets from MNEs to domestic firms can take place via transactions deliberately negotiated between the parties, as in the case of technology licensing agreements or the provision of direct support for the upgrading of locally provided inputs, which is relatively common in developing countries. Alternatively, technology transfer can take place through externalities that do not bring any direct return to the MNE. Interactions between different firms can generate more knowledge flows than are contracted for. Indeed the inability to write complete contracts is a prime reason why MNEs frequently prefer to carry out such transactions internally. Even in this case, though, MNE employees who move to local firms will bring with them much of what they have learned in their earlier positions.

Pecuniary as opposed to technological externalities arise when the presence of MNEs leads to increased local investment in increasing-returns activities. There is widespread evidence that MNEs, by making use of local suppliers, have expanded both the quality and the output of the latter. MNE presence can also lead to an expanded provision of public goods such as infrastructure and education, investment in which might not be cost effective unless demand is sufficiently large. Enhanced provision of public goods clearly expands the development potential of the host economy.

MNEs also represent increased competition for domestic firms, however. If market structure is imperfectly competitive, local profit margins are reduced. In increasing-returns sectors, the reduction in market share can force local firms up their average cost curve and away from the minimum efficient scale level of output, possibly causing exit. These negative competitive effects can offset any favorable technological externalities for local firms but are nevertheless likely to be beneficial for the overall economy.

How do these two opposing forces play out in reality? The many empirical studies on the topic do not provide an unambiguous answer to the question. The message that does emerge, however, is that the likelihood of positive second-round employment effects depends on the size of the technological gap between MNEs and domestic firms, the extent of vertical linkages between the two, and the nature of competition in the industries concerned.

Earlier studies based largely on cross-section data almost always found MNE presence to be associated with higher domestic-firm productivity. This correlation might simply be a consequence of the fact that foreign firms tend to invest in higher productivity sectors. Hence more detailed analysis is required.

The importance of the technology gap between foreign and domestic firms is attested to in a number of ways. The gap is likely to be smaller in more developed economies. In line with this, a number of studies find that spillovers are concentrated in middle-income developing countries, with no evidence of such effects in the poorest developing countries. The type of technology and the amount imported by MNEs is also found to be greater in countries and industries where the local labor force is better educated. Beneficial effects on domestic firms are also found to be especially likely to occur when there are vertical linkages between local firms and MNEs, and particularly with upstream local suppliers.

While spillover effects appear strongest in technology-intensive sectors where local firms' capabilities are above a threshold level, competition effects appear to dominate in less technology-intensive sectors. Here, the entry of MNEs tends to lead to an initial decline in the profit margin of local firms, though these can bounce back in the event of competition-induced efficiency gains. A number of studies have also found that MNE presence helps local firms to break into new export markets.

FDI and the Source-Economy Labor Market
Similar questions arise in the case of source-economy labor markets. Here we are interested in the effect of *outward* direct investment (ODI) on employment, production, wages, and the skill mix of the economy, and on the productivity of the firms themselves.

The four channels through which source-economy effects arise are: (1) the redeployment of source-economy labor, if displaced by outward FDI, (2) increased imports of source-economy goods and services by the economies hosting increased FDI, (3) savings accruing to source-economy investors and customers if activities shift to lower-cost locations, and (4) profit repatriation by foreign affiliate companies. All of these will have knock-on effects on the labor market.

The short-term employment effect will depend on whether the overseas and domestic activities of the firm are complements or substitutes. The qualitative employment effects on the home base may differ between the short term and the longer term also, in that an ODI-induced expansion in the market share of the MNE can strengthen home-economy operations even if home activities appear to be substitutable for the firm's foreign operations in the short run. The counterfactual also should be taken into account, in that even if ODI leads to a contraction in home-location operations, the alternative to ODI may be the complete closure of these operations.

The question of whether home and host-economy activities are substitutes or complements is related to whether FDI is vertical or horizontal in nature. Vertical FDI entails the geographic fragmentation of the production process, while investments undertaken in order to gain an advantage in supplying local or regional markets are classified as horizontal. In general, vertical FDI (typically from developed to outward-oriented developing economies) is associated with complementarity between home and host activities. It might be thought that horizontal FDI (typically between developed economies) will be associated with substitutability as it can displace home exports. Foreign plants however frequently import inputs or other complementary products from the MNE's home base, and studies of U.S., Japanese, Swedish, and other European MNEs have found foreign-affiliate sales to be associated with an increase in the exports of the home-based parent MNE (see, e.g., Lipsey, Ramstetter, and Blomström 2000). Higher capital expenditures on the part of foreign affiliates of U.S. MNEs have also been found to be associated with higher U.S. investments by the parent companies (Desai, Foley, and Hines 2005). The overall implication is that home and foreign production are combined to generate final output at lower cost than would be possible without ODI. Thus production is ultimately increased in both locations. Even if this were not true at the level of the individual firm, labor-market flexibility can serve to ensure that the home economy remains at or close to full employment.

We now turn to the effect of outward FDI on the relative demand for skilled and unskilled labor. If firms in high-income countries fragment their production process and outsource labor-intensive stages to lower-wage countries, this outsourcing leads to a relative increase in the demand for skilled labor at home. Headquarters services are a particularly highly skilled segment, comprising R&D, design, marketing, finance, and strategic management. An increase in demand for such services will show up as an increase in the relative wages of more highly skilled labor, as has been seen in the developed world over recent decades.

The offshoring of unskilled-labor-intensive segments of the production process does entail real welfare losses for displaced workers, however. Evidence from the United States shows that about one-third of displaced workers will not have found a job one year after displacement, though most will have found new jobs after a further lag. Frequently, however, the new jobs found by such workers are at reduced wage levels. The types of workers who suffer most in the structural adjustment process are those of advancing age with low educational attainment, and those who have had a long period of tenure in the lost job (reflecting the depreciated value of their firm-specific and industry-specific skills). There is widespread agreement that public intervention to minimize dislocation resulting from structural change should be focused on providing the displaced with new skills and training and ensuring that they do not become detached from the labor market. While the economy gains in the long run, the adverse adjustment costs will be higher if labor-market rigidities hinder employment growth.

MNEs also establish foreign operations in order to source new technology, which tends to benefit both the companies themselves and the home economy. National productivity has been shown to be increased by outward investments in other R&D-intensive economies, while other research suggests that the international networks that MNEs establish can provide other home-based companies with links—through interaction with these firms—to innovation in other areas of the globe.

The evidence summarized here leads to generally positive conclusions. Inward FDI can yield positive benefits for domestic firms through externalities and other channels, while, to the extent that it causes exit of the least efficient incumbent local firms, this elimination of inefficient firms is itself associated with an increase in productivity and hence in wages.

In the case of outward FDI, foreign-affiliate output and employment are frequently complementary to parent-firm home activities and, even when they are not, ODI tends to boost domestic productivity so that home-economy wages rise even if new employment opportunities are located outside the original firm.

As in all cases of structural adjustment, labor-market flexibility is important to ensure that new employment opportunities materialize as existing jobs disappear. The benefits of structural adjustment frequently accrue to workers with different characteristics from those displaced in the adjustment process. Hence the discussion on labor-market interventions to deal with displaced workers raises issues similar to those encountered in the policy discussion on trade adjustment assistance (see, e.g., Baicker and Rehavi 2004; Kletzer 2004).

See also agglomeration and foreign direct investment; domestic content requirements; factor endowments and foreign direct investment; footloose production; foreign direct investment and tax revenues; location theory; outsourcing/offshoring; subsidies and financial incentives to foreign direct investment; technology spillovers; unions and foreign direct investment; vertical versus horizontal foreign direct investment

FURTHER READING

Aitken, Brian, Anne Harrison, and Robert Lipsey. 1996. "Wages and Foreign Ownership: A Comparative Study of Mexico, Venezuela, and the United States." *Journal of International Economics* 40 (3–4): 345–71. Shows that for Mexico and Venezuela, unlike in the case of the United States, there is no evidence of wage spillovers from foreign investment leading to higher wages for domestic firms.

Baicker, Katherine, and M. Marit Rehavi. 2004. "Trade Adjustment Assistance." *Journal of Economic Perspectives* 18 (2): 239–55. Presents a history of trade adjustment assistance and a discussion of the policy issues.

Barry, Frank, and Colm Kearney. 2006. "MNEs and Industrial Structure in Host Countries: A Portfolio Analysis of Irish Manufacturing." *Journal of International Business Studies* 37 (3): 392–406. Employs portfolio theory to analyze the characteristics of Ireland's stock of industries.

Desai, Mihir, C. Fritz Foley, and James R. Hines Jr. 2005. "Foreign Direct Investment and the Domestic Capital Stock." *American Economic Review* 95 (2): 33–38. Evaluates evidence of the impact of outbound foreign direct investment on U.S. domestic investment rates.

Görg, Holger, and David Greenaway. 2004. "Much Ado about Nothing? Do Domestic Firms Really Benefit from Foreign Direct Investment?" *World Bank Research Observer* 19 (2): 171–97. Survey of the literature on FDI spillovers.

Harrison, Anne. 1996. "Determinants and Effects of Direct Foreign Investment in Côte d'Ivoire, Morocco, and Venezuela." In *Industrial Evolution in Developing Countries*, edited by M. J. Roberts and J. R. Tybout. New York: Oxford University Press for the World Bank, 163–86. Côte d'Ivoire here emerges as an exception to the general finding that foreign firms pay higher wages than domestic firms.

Kletzer, Lori G. 2004. "Trade-related Job Loss and Wage Insurance: A Synthetic Review." *Review of International Economics* 12 (5): 724–48. Develops a set of stylized facts of trade-related job loss, with a focus on worker characteristics and labor market consequences.

Lipsey, Robert. 2004. "Home and Host Country Effects of Foreign Direct Investment." In *Challenges to Globalization: Analyzing the Economics*, edited by Robert E. Baldwin and L. Alan Winters. Chicago: University of Chicago Press, 333–79. Broad survey of the literature.

Lipsey, Robert, Eric Ramstetter, and Magnus Blomström. 2000. "Outward FDI and Parent Exports and Employment: Japan, the United States, and Sweden." *Global Economic Quarterly* 1 (4): 285–302. Studies the relationship between foreign-affiliate sales and parent-company exports and employment for Japanese, U.S., and Swedish multinational firms.

Markusen, James. 1998. "Multinational Firms, Location and Trade." *World Economy* 21 (6): 733–56. Sets out the "knowledge-capital" model of the multinational firm.

Moran, Theodore H., Edward M. Graham, and Magnus Blomström, eds. 2005. *Does Foreign Direct Investment Promote Development?* Washington, DC: Institute for International Economics. Includes discussion of the differences between FDI in protectionist and outward-oriented regimes.

Navaretti, Giorgio Barba, and Anthony Venables. 2004. *Multinational Firms in the World Economy*. Princeton, NJ: Princeton University Press. A summary of theory and evidence on FDI and multinational enterprises.

Scheve, Kenneth F., and Matthew J. Slaughter. 2005. "Foreign Direct Investment and Labour-Market Outcomes." In *The Internationalisation of Asset Ownership in Europe*, edited by Harry Huizinga and Lars Jonung. Cambridge: Cambridge University Press, 77–109. Broad survey of the literature.

FRANK BARRY

■ foreign direct investment and tax revenues

Does foreign direct investment (FDI) expand tax revenues? It is commonly believed that FDI enhances economic growth, both directly by increasing the stock of physical capital in the recipient economy, and indirectly by inducing human capital development and promoting technological upgrading. Based on evidence of positive effects of FDI on economic growth, international trade, and domestic investment (under certain conditions), it is then claimed that FDI also expands government tax revenues. The reasoning is that higher levels of economic activity generate higher levels of production, and consequently higher levels of government tax revenue, all else being equal. This perceived additional benefit of greater tax revenues has led host countries to expand their attraction packages to include firm-specific incentives such as tax holidays, tax breaks, and subsidies.

These potential benefits have given multinational corporations (MNCs) a strong bargaining position to negotiate favorable conditions for their entry into new markets. As a result, MNCs are often able to extract additional concessions in the negotiation process, in some cases even long-lived tax breaks and exemptions. Even if FDI has the potential to expand government tax revenues by enhancing economic growth, the fact that MNCs receive such tax incentives creates distortions that can contradict the main goals of tax policy. It can also affect the competitiveness of domestic firms and, consequently, influence the collection of tax revenues. Therefore, a direct link between FDI and economic growth does not necessarily translate directly to expanded government tax revenues.

The performance of government tax revenues is determined by three main aspects: *structural characteristics* (factors that influence the tax handles of an economy), such as income level, population size, the existence of informal or subsistence sectors, and the dependence on taxation of trade; *macroeconomic characteristics*, such as the governmental debt stance, the government's current and past budget position, and the degree of reliance on inflationary tax to generate revenue; and *external characteristics*, such as the terms of trade, exchange rate volatility, and the degree of trade liberalization of the economy. Changes in one or more of these factors can affect the performance of tax revenues; given that FDI can affect some of these factors, it can also potentially affect the collection of tax revenues. FDI's effect on government tax revenues in the host country may also differ from the effect on the source country.

FDI's Effect on the Source Country's Tax Revenues Even if FDI directs investment into foreign countries, the parent enterprises still maintain headquarter activities in the source country and thus generate tax responsibilities that affect the collection of tax revenues. Although FDI generates economic growth and spillovers in the countries that attract it, it mainly benefits the owners of the MNCs. Subsidiaries repatriate profits to their respective parent companies through dividends, interest, and royalty payments, which are taxed by the source country. In addition, most research and development is conducted in the source country, which generates significant taxable economic activity in the country of origin, thus again affecting the collection of tax revenues.

Most countries also offer relief from double taxation to MNCs participating in outward foreign investment. Some countries allow foreign tax credits to be applied to domestic tax liabilities, deductions of taxes paid to foreign governments from their tax liabilities, exemptions for the foreign earnings of their MNCs from domestic taxation, or some combination of the three. Although this relief from double taxation tends to lower the collection of tax revenues from production abroad, it protects the health of the MNCs of the host country.

Furthermore, since the performance of the MNCs affects the citizens of the source country—the owners of the firm—and MNCs bear the risk of expropriation that is inherent in foreign investment, there is an incentive for both the government and MNCs to protect and enhance the revenues from FDI through bilateral treaties. These treaties lower trade barriers, protect foreign investment, reduce tax rates abroad, and reduce tax uncertainty over the long term (Chisik and Davies 2004).

FDI's Effect on the Host Country's Tax Revenues FDI inflows are expected to fuel economic growth and generate higher levels of output in the host country. Conventional wisdom presumes that FDI would consequently increase government tax revenues. FDI can affect government tax revenues in a variety of ways: it can directly increase domestic taxes on income and goods and services if the higher levels of foreign investment increase production and employment; it can indirectly increase (1) taxes on international trade if the product is sold abroad or if imported inputs are used in the production process, (2) taxes on income and goods and services if it fosters greater activity in domestic firms participating in the production chain, and (3) overall taxes if higher or better incomes emanating from the previous points find their way back into the economy (multiplier effect); or it can affect the collection of tax revenues through the formalization of economic activity brought about by the existence or addition of foreign investment.

Although such considerations could have a positive impact on the collection of tax revenues, the intensive use of tax incentives to attract FDI may introduce potential distortion to this link, which can belie the conventional wisdom. In addition, although the greater economic activity brought about by FDI

should raise tax revenues in the long run, tax incentives tend to reduce tax revenues in the short run.

Since FDI goes hand in hand with trade liberalization—MNCs account for two-thirds of all cross-border sales—it is this area that has received the most attention. Trade tax revenues usually decrease with trade liberalization, and liberalization's effect on overall taxes depends on the efficiency of the transition toward domestic taxes (on goods and services), the resulting volatility of the exchange rate (and its effect on import and export bases), and the adjustment of exports and imports due to changes in the terms of trade.

FDI can also affect government tax revenues through formalization of the economy. Since greater foreign investment increases production in the formal sector, it also formalizes the production of domestic firms supplying inputs to the MNC, thus contributing to the collection of tax revenues. It also strengthens tax compliance of domestic companies by exposing them to the best business practices and corporate governance of the MNCs.

Although the potential impact of FDI on government tax revenues is considerable, empirical research in this area is almost nonexistent, with the exception of the work of Braunstein and Epstein (2004) and Vacaflores (2006). The former find that inward FDI has a negative impact on tax revenue in Chinese provinces—which is ameliorated by its positive impact on trade—while the latter shows that FDI has a positive impact on total tax revenues in Latin America, which is channeled through its impact on the main component, taxes on goods and services.

Despite this lack of conclusive empirical results, host countries are increasingly complaining about the tax evasion that tax treaties sometimes allow, the detrimental tax breaks that they were forced to give in the capitalization/privatization process, and the manipulation of intrafirm prices, all of which are perceived as detrimental to the tax collection of host countries.

Policy Implications The anticipation that a country's tax structure affects the MNC's choice to locate in a particular country has led most countries to adjust their tax system, making it more flexible to international firms, becoming in many cases even more attractive for MNCs than domestic firms. This subsidization of FDI through tax incentives brings to light the potential harm that greater foreign participation can inflict on domestic firms, as the partial or total crowding out of domestic firms increases the possibility that some domestic factors of production may lose with higher levels of FDI. Glass and Saggi (1999) show that if the impact of MNCs on the profitability of domestic firms is sufficiently negative, FDI may lower host-country welfare to a degree that the optimal policy toward FDI should instead be a higher level of taxation. So the degree of substitutability of production between domestic and foreign firms and/or complementarities in their production processes become important in the overall collection of tax revenues.

To better understand the overall effects of FDI, more needs to be known about the effects of FDI on government tax revenues. Theoretical studies suggest that this effect should be positive, at least in the long run once tax incentives have expired. However, the inherent adjustments in tax systems and potential impact on the performance of domestic investment require further research to establish the direction and magnitude of such effect more conclusively.

See also agglomeration and foreign direct investment; footloose production; foreign direct investment and labor markets; foreign direct investment under monopolistic competition; foreign direct investment under oligopoly; international investment agreements; intrafirm trade; location theory; trade-related investment measures (TRIMs); transfer pricing

FURTHER READING

Braunstein, Elissa, and Gerald Epstein. 2004. "Bargaining Power and Foreign Direct Investment in China: Can 1.3 Billion Consumers Tame the Multinationals?" In *Labor and the Globalization of Production: Causes and Consequences of Industrial Upgrading*, edited by Will Milberg. London: Palgrave Macmillan. An empirical analysis of the effects of FDI on economic growth, employment, investment, and tax revenues for Chinese provinces.

Chisik, Richard, and Richard B. Davies. 2004. "Gradualism and Tax Treaties with Irreversible Foreign Direct Investment." *International Economic Review* 45 (1): 113–39. Provides a concise description of tax treaties and their influence on tax rates for FDI.

Glass, Amy, and K. Saggi. 1999. "FDI Policies under Shared Factor Markets." *Journal of International Economics* 49 (2): 309–32. A study of the impact of MNCs (FDI) on the profitability of domestic firms, host-country welfare, and optimal tax policy.

Hanson, Gordon H. 2001. "Should Countries Promote Foreign Direct Investment?" United Nations Conference on Trade and Development, G-24 Discussion Paper Series No 9. Geneva: UNCTAD. A useful analysis of the impact of FDI on national welfare, with a practical summary of policies used to promote FDI.

Vacaflores, Diego E. 2006. "The Effect of Foreign Direct Investment on Tax Revenues in Latin America: Are the Facts in Accord with the Conventional Wisdom?" Texas State University Working Paper. San Marcos, TX. Examines the effect of FDI on tax revenue performance for a group of Latin American countries, for total tax revenues and its main components.

DIEGO E. VACAFLORES

■ foreign direct investment: the OLI framework

The OLI, or "eclectic," approach to the study of foreign direct investment (FDI), developed by John Dunning, has proved to be an extremely fruitful way of thinking about multinational enterprises (MNEs) and has inspired a great deal of applied work in economics and international business. In itself it does not constitute a formal theory that can be confronted with data in a scientific way, but it nevertheless provides a helpful framework for categorizing much (though not all) recent analytical and empirical research on FDI. This survey first summarizes the OLI paradigm and then uses it as a lens through which to review some of the highlights of this research, while also noting some important issues that it neglects.

OLI stands for ownership, location, and internalization, three potential sources of advantage that may underlie a firm's decision to become a multinational. Ownership advantages address the question of why some firms but not others go abroad, and suggest that a successful MNE has some firm-specific advantages that allow it to overcome the costs of operating in a foreign country. Location advantages focus on the question of where an MNE chooses to locate. Finally, internalization advantages influence how a firm chooses to operate in a foreign country, trading off the savings in transactions, hold-up, and monitoring costs of a wholly owned subsidiary against the advantages of other entry modes such as exports, licensing, or joint venture. A key feature of this approach is that it focuses on the incentives facing individual firms. This is now standard in mainstream international trade theory but was not at all so in the 1970s, when FDI was typically seen through a Heckscher-Ohlin lens as an international movement of physical capital in search of higher returns (see, for example, Mundell 1957).

Ownership Ownership advantages are key to explaining the existence of MNEs. A central idea is that firms are collections of assets, and that candidate MNEs possess higher-than-average levels of assets having the character of internal public goods. These assets can be applied to production at different locations without reducing their effectiveness. Examples include product development, managerial structures, patents, and marketing skills, all of which are encompassed by Helpman's (1984) catchall term *headquarter services*. Although this is clearly a multidimensional factor, it is common to model it in terms of a single index of firm productivity. The most sophisticated treatment along these lines is found in work on heterogeneous firms by Helpman, Melitz, and Yeaple (2004), which combines the simplest version of the horizontal motive for FDI (to be discussed later in this article) with the assumption that firms differ in their productivities. A potential firm must pay a sunk cost to determine its productivity, and when this is revealed, active firms sort themselves into different modes of production. Low-productivity firms produce only for the home market; medium-productivity firms choose to pay the fixed costs of exporting; but only the most productive firms choose to pay the higher fixed costs of engaging in FDI. These predictions are consistent with the evidence. As a further contribution, the paper derives from the model the prediction that industries with greater firm heterogeneity will have relatively more firms engaged in FDI and shows that this prediction is confirmed by the data. This work and others like it do not explore, however, why firm productivities differ in the first place. Prior investment in research and development (both process and product) and in marketing presumably account for the disproportionately greater productivity of most MNEs.

Location While international trade theory has tended to take ownership advantages for granted or else to model them in fairly obvious ways, rather more attention has been devoted to exploring alternative motives for MNEs to locate abroad. A key issue that has attracted much attention is the distinction between "horizontal" and "vertical" FDI. Horizontal FDI occurs when a firm locates a plant abroad in order to improve its market access to foreign consumers. In its purest form, this simply replicates its domestic production facilities at a foreign location. Vertical FDI, by contrast, is not primarily or even necessarily aimed at production for sale in the foreign market, but rather seeks to take advantage of lower production costs there. Since in almost all cases the parent firm retains its headquarters in the home country, and the firm-specific or ownership advantages can be seen as generating a flow of headquarter services to the host-country plant, there is a sense in which all FDI is vertical. Nevertheless, the distinction between market-access and cost motives for FDI is an important one.

The horizontal motive for FDI reflects what Brainard (1997) has called a "proximity-concentration trade-off": building a local plant saves on trade costs and so has the advantage of proximity; but it loses the benefits of concentrating production in the firm's home plant. Let $\pi^*(t^*)$ denote the operating profits that a potential MNE can earn from selling in a foreign market subject to per unit trade costs t^* (which can include both tariffs and transportation costs). These operating profits are decreasing in t^*: higher trade costs reduce operating profits. Constructing a local plant avoids the trade costs, leading to higher operating profits of $\pi^*(0)$; however, it requires an additional fixed cost f. Hence the trade-cost-jumping gain, the difference between the total profits from FDI, Π^F, and those from exporting, Π^X, equals:

$$\gamma(\underset{+}{t^*}, \underset{-}{f}) \equiv \Pi^F - \Pi^X = \pi^*(0) - f - \pi^*(t^*) \quad (1)$$

Thus FDI is encouraged relative to exports by proximity (lower trade costs t^*) but discouraged by the benefits of concentration (higher fixed costs f).

The vertical motive for FDI implies a very different view of the determinants and implications of FDI. Now the focus is on how a firm can serve its home market: either by producing at home, or by vertically disintegrating and moving its production facilities to a cheaper foreign location. Assuming for simplicity that each unit of output requires a single unit of labor, we can write the operating profits of serving the home-country market as $\pi(c)$, where c includes both factor costs and trade costs. If the firm remains a domestic firm and supplies its home market from its parent plant, where w is the local wage rate, it incurs no trade costs so its profits Π^D will equal $\pi(w)$. Alternatively, it can engage in FDI and locate a new plant in the host country, exporting all its output back to the source country and incurring a trade cost of t. In that case, it incurs a plant-specific fixed cost f as in the case of horizontal FDI, and earns operating profits of $\pi(w^* + t)$, where w^* is the host-country wage. The relative profitability of FDI is therefore:

$$\Pi^F - \Pi^D = \mu(w^* + t, w) - f$$
$$\text{where:} \quad \mu(\underset{-}{w^*} + t, \underset{+}{w})$$
$$\equiv \pi(w^* + t) - \pi(w) \quad (2)$$

Now the decision to engage in FDI depends on the trade-off between the benefits of concentration, on the one hand, and the cost savings from offshoring, on the other, where the latter are denoted by the term $\mu(w^* + t, w)$. This offshoring gain depends negatively on the host-country wage w^* and positively on the source-country wage w: the vertical motive for FDI attaches great importance to comparative costs of production. In addition, the gain is decreasing in the source-country trade costs t, implying plausibly that trade liberalization will encourage FDI.

Empirical studies of FDI have until recently tended to favor the horizontal over the vertical motive. For example, many case studies have shown that "tariff-jumping" has been important in many historical episodes. It has also been noted that the bulk of FDI is between high-income countries with relatively similar wage costs (though much of this is likely to be neither vertical nor horizontal FDI, but rather cross-border mergers and acquisitions, to be discussed further later). More formal econometric studies have shown that the horizontal motive provides a good explanation for FDI (see, for example, Brainard 1997; Markusen 2002). On the other hand, there is no clear evidence that FDI falls in importance with distance, as the horizontal model implies. In addition, more recent empirical work by Yeaple (2003b) and others, based on data at the level of individual firms, suggests that both motives are important. It is easy to see why this might be so even in the simple two-country case discussed above. If the foreign market is sizable, then the total gain from FDI as opposed to producing at home (in each case serving both domestic and foreign customers from a single plant) is given by the sum of (1) and (2) above: both trade-cost-jumping and offshoring gains have to be taken into account. More generally, with many countries there are additional reasons for FDI, and the two motives are likely to interact in complicated ways. For example, even for vertically integrated firms, proximity and concentration are not in conflict where serving a group of foreign countries is concerned. The reduction of trade costs between European countries in the 1990s encouraged American and Asian firms serving European markets to concentrate their production in European plants and so engage in "export-platform" FDI. Similarly, Yeaple (2003a) has shown that the horizontal and vertical motives may reinforce each other if a parent firm wishes both to serve foreign markets in similar high-income countries and to avail itself of lower production costs in low-income countries. In general, therefore, the pattern of location of foreign plants is likely to reflect the complex integration strategies of firms having both vertical and horizontal motives for engaging in FDI.

Internalization Internalization, the third strand of Dunning's taxonomy, is often seen as the most important; in the words of Ethier (1986), "Internalization appears to be emerging as the Caesar of the OLI triumvirate." Explaining why some activities are carried on within firms and others through arm's-length transactions is a major research topic for microeconomics as a whole, not just for the economics of FDI. A pioneering 1937 paper by Ronald Coase argued that the optimal scale of the firm, or the optimal degree of internalization, reflects a balance between the transactions costs of using the market and the organizational costs of running a firm. In recent decades, economists working in information economics have tried to endogenize these two sources of costs, emphasizing the inability of agents to write complete contracts. An early application of this approach to FDI was by Ethier (1986). In his model production requires prior research, the results of which can either be carried out within a vertically integrated firm (in the MNE case) or sold to downstream users. The end user must agree to purchase the research before its outcome is known, however. Ethier shows that a greater degree of uncertainty about the likely success of research efforts makes it more costly for the upstream and downstream firms to write a contract, which because of the complexity of the research process must necessarily be independent of the outcome. Hence more uncertainty raises the likelihood that production will be vertically integrated through MNEs. Moreover, the emergence of MNEs does not require international differences in factor prices, unlike other models of vertical FDI.

A different approach to endogenizing the internalization decision, though also relying on incomplete contracts, is taken by Antras and Helpman (2004). Following the Grossman-Hart-Moore property-rights approach to the problem of bargaining between a firm owner and a potential supplier/employee, ex post efficiency is greater when residual ownership rights are allocated to the party that contributes more to the final output. Embedded in a model of product differentiation and trade, this implies that more efficient firms and firms for which headquarter services are more important should exhibit internalization (the owner contracts with the supplier, who becomes an employee), while less efficient firms should exhibit arm's-length trade (the supplier remains a separate legal entity). In addition the model assumes that final-goods producers are located only in one country, the North of a two-country North-South model. Such producers are assumed to have a twofold choice: on the one hand, they have to choose between vertical integration, which solves the hold-up problem but at the cost of reducing incentives to the provider of the input, and an arm's-length relationship; on the other hand, they could locate their production in either country, trading off higher wages in the North against lower contract protection in the South. The full range of potential outcomes is shown in table 1, and Antras and Helpman show how heterogeneous firms will sort into these different modes, based on their productivity, on the share of headquarter services in the value of output, and on the differences in costs between home and foreign locations.

Cross-Border Mergers Both the OLI framework and the bulk of academic work on FDI until very recently have concentrated on the "greenfield" mode of FDI, where the parent firm constructs a new plant in the host country. Yet in reality the bulk of FDI, especially between developed countries, takes the form of cross-border mergers and acquisitions (M&As), in which the parent firm acquires a con-

Table 1
Taxonomy of location-internalization modes

	Location	
	Home	Abroad
Internal	Integrated national firm	FDI
External	Outsourcing	Offshoring

trolling interest in an existing host-country firm. (UNCTAD estimates suggest that M&As accounted for more than 80 percent of worldwide FDI in the 1990s.) The distinction matters, since recent research suggests that the determinants and implications of cross-border M&As are very different from those of greenfield FDI.

Domestic M&As have been extensively studied by scholars in finance and industrial organization, and these literatures suggest two principal motives for them. A "synergy" motive arises in any market where an acquired firm has assets that are complementary to those of the acquirer, whereas a "strategic" motive arises in oligopolistic markets (i.e., markets in which the number of competitors is small), since a firm gains from absorbing a rival and so increasing its own market power.

Postmerger synergies can arise from many sources, including cost savings via internal technology transfer, reductions of overhead and other fixed costs, and the integration of pricing and marketing decisions on differentiated products. In an open-economy context, a particularly plausible kind of synergy is between the "O" and "L" advantages of different firms: the superior productivity and international networks of an acquiring MNE, on the one hand, combined with the local knowledge and distribution network of a potential target firm, on the other. Nocke and Yeaple (2008) develop a model that captures this kind of synergy: a competitive international market for corporate assets allows firms to match with suitable affiliates. Their model predicts that efficient matching occurs: more efficient parent firms acquire more efficient targets. They also show, however, that the most efficient firms engage in greenfield FDI rather than in cross-border M&As, a result consistent with the evidence.

Mergers driven by synergies may be expected to raise world welfare, provided the synergies are realized in practice. By contrast, mergers driven by strategic considerations might be expected to reduce welfare since they increase concentration. Neary (2007) shows, however, that this intuition is incomplete for two reasons. First, in the absence of synergies, the only mergers that will occur in equi-

librium are those in which the acquirer can afford to buy out the target firm. This implies that the target firm must be considerably smaller, and therefore eliminating it is likely to enhance global efficiency. Second, in general equilibrium, the expansion of more efficient acquiring firms and the elimination of less efficient target firms puts downward pressure on wages, thus encouraging increased output and lower prices in all sectors. Hence mergers are likely to raise overall welfare, although income distribution shifts in favor of profits at the expense of wages. Neary's model also makes the positive prediction that mergers take place in the same direction as trade and therefore they are encouraged rather than (as in the horizontal model of greenfield FDI) discouraged by decreases in trade costs. In line with empirical evidence, cross-border mergers thus serve as "instruments of comparative advantage," encouraging more specialization and trade along comparative advantage lines.

The OLI Framework: An Overall Assessment
In conclusion, the OLI framework does not directly address one of the key issues that has dominated economists' thinking about FDI, the distinction between horizontal and vertical motives for locating production facilities in foreign countries. Nor does it address the increasingly important distinction between greenfield and M&A modes of engaging in FDI. Nevertheless it remains a helpful way of organizing thinking about one of the most important features of the world economy.

See also internalization theory; location theory; multinational enterprises

FURTHER READING

Antras, Pol, and Elhanan Helpman. 2004. "Global Sourcing." *Journal of Political Economy* 112 (3): 552–80. A pioneering model that shows how firms with different productivities will choose between locating production at home or abroad and keeping it within the firm or outsourcing it to a subcontractor.

Barba Navaretti, Giorgio, Anthony J. Venables, et al. 2004. *Multinational Firms in the World Economy.* Princeton, NJ: Princeton University Press. An invaluable overview of theoretical and empirical work on greenfield FDI.

Brainard, S. Lael. 1997. "An Empirical Assessment of the Proximity-Concentration Tradeoff between Multinational Sales and Trade." *American Economic Review* 87 (4): 520–44. A landmark paper in the empirical application of the horizontal model of FDI.

Dunning, John H. 1977. "Trade, Location of Economic Activity, and the MNE: A Search for an Eclectic Approach." In *The International Allocation of Economic Activity*, edited by Bertil Ohlin, Per-Ove Hesselborn, and Per Magnus Wijkman. London: Macmillan, 395–418. The first statement of the OLI approach, later refined and extended in many books and papers by the author and his collaborators.

Ethier, Wilfred J. 1986. "The Multinational Firm." *Quarterly Journal of Economics* 101 (4): 805–34. An important paper that models the internalization decision in a general-equilibrium model with incomplete contracts.

Helpman, Elhanan. 1984. "A Simple Theory of International Trade with Multinational Corporations." *Journal of Political Economy* 92 (3): 451–71. A pioneering exploration of vertical FDI, embedded in a Heckscher-Ohlin model with monopolistic competition.

Helpman, Elhanan, Marc Melitz, and Stephen Yeaple. 2004. "Exports versus FDI with Heterogeneous Firms." *American Economic Review* 94 (1): 300–16. Extends the horizontal model of FDI to allow for productivity differences across firms.

Markusen, James R. 2002. *Multinational Firms and the Theory of International Trade*. Cambridge, MA: MIT Press. An invaluable overview of the author's contributions, both alone and with coauthors, especially Horstmann and Venables. Emphasizes horizontal greenfield FDI.

Mundell, Robert. 1957. "International Trade and Factor Mobility." *American Economic Review* 47 (3): 321–35. A key reference in the Heckscher-Ohlin-inspired literature on FDI. An important step in the elaboration of the factor-endowments approach to trade flows. Through its emphasis on trade costs, it was a precursor of the horizontal view of FDI. However, its focus on sectors rather than firms, and its counterfactual prediction that FDI is mainly driven by international differences in rates of return, stand in contrast with the OLI approach, and have been abandoned in more recent work.

Neary, J. Peter. 2007. "Cross-border Mergers as Instruments of Comparative Advantage." *Review of Economic Studies* 74 (4): 1229–57. A model of cross-border mergers in general oligopolistic equilibrium, focusing on strategic motives.

———. 2008. "Trade Costs and Foreign Direct Investment." In *Foreign Direct Investment and the Multinational Enterprise*, edited by S. Brakman and H. Garretsen. Cambridge, MA: MIT Press, 13–38. An overview of recent work, highlighting that export-platform FDI and cross-border mergers can overcome the counterfactual prediction of the simple horizontal model that FDI should fall as trade costs fall.

Nocke, Volker, and Stephen Yeaple. 2008. "An Assignment Theory of Foreign Direct Investment." *Review of Economic Studies* 75 (2): 529–57. A model with monopolistically competitive firms, highlighting the synergy motive for cross-border mergers and acquisitions.

Yeaple, Stephen. 2003a. "The Complex Integration Strategies of Multinational Firms and Cross-Country Dependencies in the Structure of Foreign Direct Investment." *Journal of International Economics* 60 (2): 293–314. A model showing that vertical and horizontal motives can reinforce each other in a multicountry world.

———. 2003b. "The Role of Skill Endowments in the Structure of U.S. Outward Foreign Direct Investment." *Review of Economics and Statistics* 85 (3): 726–34. A careful empirical study using firm-level data which shows that U.S. outward FDI is driven by both vertical and horizontal influences.

J. PETER NEARY

■ foreign direct investment under monopolistic competition

Central questions in the study of foreign direct investment (FDI) are: Where do firms choose to locate their production? To what extent do firms become multinational and supply foreign markets through production by local subsidiaries rather than through trade? What are the associated levels of FDI and patterns of trade? Theories of FDI under monopolistic competition provide a framework to address these questions. They analyze firms' choices on where to locate production, and also endogenize the number of active firms operating in each country.

Monopolistic competition models typically focus on horizontal rather than vertical FDI. That is, they look at situations where FDI involves producing the same good (or at least undertaking the same stage of production) in several locations. This is in contrast to vertical FDI, where FDI takes the form of offshoring different parts of the production process, although a monopolistic competition framework has also been used to address this issue (for example, Helpman and Krugman 1985).

Theory There are three main elements in a model of monopolistic competition and FDI: equilibrium of the firm, equilibrium of the industry, and general equilibrium of the economy. This review focuses on the first two of these. Each firm has increasing returns to scale, typically modeled by two components: increasing returns at the level of the firm and increasing returns at the level of the plant. At the firm level, increasing returns may derive from the costs of headquarters operations or research and development (R&D); these can be represented by fixed cost F. Plant-level operations have increasing returns to scale, modeled by fixed costs associated with setting up a plant, P. Unit operating costs are typically assumed constant (equal to marginal costs), but contain two different components, production costs and costs of trading internationally, such as transportation costs or trade taxes.

The trade-off faced by firms is clear. If they supply all markets from a single country (and single plant) they save the fixed costs of setting up a new plant but incur additional trade costs. Conversely, FDI means paying for a new plant, but saving trade costs. This is sometimes referred to as the proximity-concentration trade-off. Firms' decisions depend on the levels of these various costs and—since fixed costs are involved—also on expected sales volumes.

Turning to the industry equilibrium, there is free entry and exit of firms, so the equilibrium number of firms in each country is determined by zero profit

conditions. Competition is imperfect and firms set a markup of price over marginal cost, thus covering their fixed costs. Imperfect competition is typically modeled via product differentiation, often using the Dixit-Stiglitz (1977) framework so that price-cost markups are constant. In the simplest cases all firms in the industry have identical cost and demand functions (e.g., Markusen and Venables 2000).

What equilibrium outcomes are possible? Suppose first that there are two countries of similar size and with similar factor prices. Then the two key parameters are trade costs and the plant fixed cost relative to the firm-level fixed cost, (P/F). If trade costs are low relative to P/F then each firm will operate in a single country (with just one plant) and export to the other country. There will be no FDI, but there will be large volumes of intraindustry trade. If the two countries are identical, intraindustry trade will be balanced; otherwise the larger country will be the net exporter of output from this sector, since trade costs tend to cause firms to locate in the larger market.

If trade costs are high relative to plant fixed costs (or to the ratio P/F), then firms substitute FDI for exports. In the case where the two countries are identical, there is two-way FDI, and each market is supplied by domestic firms and foreign affiliates. There is no trade in goods, although there is trade in services, in the sense that affiliates' earnings cover some of the firm-level fixed costs and can be viewed as payment for headquarters' services. If the two countries are of different sizes, equilibrium has the following pattern: the smaller country may be supplied only by multinationals, while the larger is supplied by both multinational firms and "national" firms producing in a single country. In a multicountry model country size should be interpreted to include the market access of each country. For example, a firm may use a small country as an export platform to supply a larger neighborhood (Ireland and the EU being the obvious example).

In the model sketched earlier, all firms based in one country have the same behavior, this property following from the assumption that they all have the same technologies and face the same demand functions. This has the unattractive consequence that no country will both export and have outward FDI in the same product. There are a number of ways of generalizing the model to get away from this stark result. One is to make firms within each country heterogeneous, and this approach has been pursued by Helpman, Melitz, and Yeaple (2004). All firms in a particular country face the same fixed costs, but there are now four such fixed costs incurred: by entry, by commencing production, by exporting, and by undertaking FDI. When the firm enters it learns its unit production cost (drawn from a distribution, and therefore varying across firms), and trade costs are a constant multiple of this. Each firm has to make three decisions. The first is whether to produce at all, or to exit; the second is whether or not to supply the foreign market; the third is whether to do so by exports or by FDI. Each of these decisions depends, in a natural way, on the level of the fixed costs associated with each activity relative to the per-unit cost.

The industry equilibrium, with free entry of firms, may now involve some firms exporting and others engaging in FDI. If there are two identical economies, then the following outcomes arise. Firms that commence production but have relatively high unit costs will produce only for the local market, neither exporting nor undertaking FDI. To see the reason for this, recall that the fixed costs of different activities are assumed to be the same for all firms, but the ability to cover these fixed costs depends on volume sold. High marginal cost firms will have small sales, and it is not profitable for them to incur the fixed costs of either exporting or FDI.

Firms with an intermediate level of unit costs will export but not undertake FDI, since the fixed costs of exporting are assumed to be less than those of FDI. Firms that have unit costs below some critical value switch from exporting to FDI, since they are able to sell at sufficient volume to cover the additional fixed costs. This critical value of unit costs is greater the higher are trade costs.

The model therefore predicts a size distribution of firms in each country, with firms engaging in a range of strategies—some selling just in their domestic market, some exporting, and the largest engaging in FDI. The volume of affiliate sales relative to exports will be larger the higher are trade costs. Country differences can be added to the model, with results similar to those in the simpler model outlined above.

One further empirical prediction comes from this model, that the volume of FDI relative to exports will be larger the greater the degree of heterogeneity among firms. The intuition is that, other things being equal, exporting is a strategy associated with the middle of the distribution of unit costs, and increasing the dispersion of this distribution empties out this middle relative to the tails.

Empirical Evidence A number of papers have conducted empirical investigations of the hypotheses outlined above. An early and influential study by Brainard (1997) looks at the exports and affiliate sales of U.S.-based firms to 27 countries and in 63 industries. Trade costs are measured by freight and insurance charges and by import tariffs. Plant scale economies are proxied by plant-level employment, and firm-level scale economies by total nonproduction workers (capturing headquarters activities). Industry measures of R&D and advertising intensity are used to capture internalization advantages. Brainard finds that the share of affiliate sales in total foreign sales (affiliate sales plus exports) increases with trade barriers, transportation costs, and firm-level scale economies, and decreases with plant-scale economies, offering support to the predictions of the monopolistic competition model. Helpman, Melitz, and Yeaple (2004) undertake a similar exercise, with an extended data set and including a measure of the dispersion of firm size (and thereby dispersion of operating costs). Their results confirm those of Brainard, and additionally they find that dispersion has a negative effect on exports relative to affiliate sales, consistent with the predictions of their model of FDI with heterogeneous firms.

Policy Issues Many countries seek to attract FDI in the belief that it brings both employment and beneficial spillover effects, either through productivity spillovers or by stimulating related sectors. But at the same time, entry of FDI to a sector may crowd out local firms, and many countries restrict FDI inflow to sensitive sectors in order to protect local firms. How do these forces balance out?

Models of FDI and monopolistic competition are well placed to address these issues, because they allow for changes in the number of firms operating in a country and industry, and because they can be used to analyze linkages between related sectors (Rodriguez-Clare 1996; Markusen and Venables 1999). Suppose that a multinational firm enters a "downstream" industry (production of a final good). Its initial impact on local competitors is negative and, if the industry is monopolistically competitive, some of the firms in this industry may exit. However, the multinational will use inputs and these generate "backwards linkages," that is, create demand for intermediate goods supplied by upstream industries. Adjustment in these upstream industries may involve entry of new firms, and this can create a positive feedback mechanism. If these new upstream firms produce new (or better) varieties of intermediate goods, then costs in the downstream industry will fall (a "forward linkage"). This is a pecuniary externality—the greater variety of intermediates benefits all firms in the downstream industry. It is then possible that entry of the multinational leads to a substantial increase in the industry's output—essentially, it acts as a catalyst for formation of a cluster of activity. Whether this outcome happens depends on a number of parameters of the model and is more likely the more the multinational sources its inputs from the local economy rather than from imports, and the greater are the potential pecuniary externalities—arising perhaps from variety effects, or also from direct knowledge spillovers or technological externalities.

These examples are illustrative of the rich set of possibilities that can be explored in models of FDI and monopolistic competition. There is potential for further work in several areas. For example, specification of sources of increasing returns needs to move beyond the simple characterization of fixed cost and constant unit cost. Richer modeling of firm heterogeneity would be desirable. A good deal of work needs to be done to further develop applications of the approach to policy, particularly in the context of understanding the contribution of FDI to the de-velopment of clusters of economic activity in developing countries and regions.

See also factor endowments and foreign direct investment; fixed costs and foreign direct investment; foreign direct investment and exit of local firms; foreign direct investment: the OLI framework; foreign direct investment under oligopoly; knowledge-capital model of the multinational enterprise; market size and foreign direct investment; monopolistic competition; outsourcing/offshoring; trade costs and foreign direct investment; vertical versus horizontal foreign direct investment

FURTHER READING

Barba Navaretti, Giorgio, Anthony J. Venables, Frank G. Barry, Karolina Ekholm, Anna M. Falzoni, Jan I. Haaland, Karen Helene Midelfart, and Alessandro Turrini. 2004. *Multinational Firms in the World Economy*. Princeton, NJ: Princeton University Press. Recent review of theory and empirical literature on FDI and multinational firms.

Brainard, S. Lael. 1997. "An Empirical Assessment of the Proximity-concentration Trade-off between Multinational Sales and Trade." *American Economic Review* 87 (4): 520–44. Finds that sales by overseas affiliates of multinationals relative to exports increase with high trade costs, low investment barriers, plant-level scale economies, and more similar countries.

Dixit, Avinash K., and Joseph E. Stiglitz. 1977. "Monopolistic Competition and Optimum Product Diversity." *American Economic Review* 67 (3): 297–308. The workhorse model of monopolistic competition.

Helpman, Elhanan, and Paul R. Krugman. 1985. *Market Structure and Foreign Trade*. Cambridge MA: MIT Press. A monograph on trade under imperfect competition.

Helpman, Elhanan, Marc J. Melitz, and Stephen R. Yeaple. 2004. "Export versus FDI with Heterogeneous Firms." *American Economic Review* 94 (1): 300–16. Employs the heterogeneous firm model to FDI and demonstrates the coexistence of firms that export and firms that undertake FDI.

Markusen, James R., and Anthony J. Venables. 1999. "Foreign Direct Investment as a Catalyst for Industrial Development." *European Economic Review* 43 (2): 335–56. Model of the effect of FDI on local firms that highlights how the profits of local firms can increase due to reduced input costs stemming from linkages to suppliers of intermediates.

———. 2000. "The Theory of Endowment, Intraindustry and Multinational Trade." *Journal of International Economics* 52 (2): 209–34. Model demonstrating that multinationals are more likely to form when countries are more similar in terms of their relative (and absolute) endowments, as the data indicates is the case.

Rodriguez-Clare, Andres. 1996. "Multinationals, Linkages, and Economic Development." *American Economic Review* 86 (4): 852–73. Model examining the conditions needed for linkage effects from FDI on the host country to be favorable.

ANTHONY J. VENABLES

■ foreign direct investment under oligopoly

An oligopoly is a concentrated industry in which only a few firms compete. The extreme case of oligopoly is duopoly, where just two firms exist in the market. The key qualitative characteristic of oligopoly is that there is significant interdependence between rival firms. Each firm is sufficiently large in relation to the overall product market for its actions (e.g., levels of research and development, plant investment, and pricing decisions) to have a significant effect on its rivals' profits.

Profit-maximizing firms in an oligopoly will recognize their interdependence and take account of the likely reactions of rival firms when making their own business choices. Accounting for strategic responses complicates the analysis of firm decision-making under oligopoly compared to monopoly and perfect or monopolistic competition, where firms typically act in isolation. Therefore, noncooperative game theory, which analyzes how independent, self-interested players behave in situations of mutual interdependence, is often used to predict the outcome ("equilibrium") of oligopolistic competition.

In an "international oligopoly," consumers are distributed over several countries, and a small number of firms populate the industry at a global level. Competition occurs on two levels: as well as producing output for each national product market, a key strategic decision for firms in an international oligopoly is the mode of market access. Firms choose whether to serve a given national product market through international trade (exports from a plant elsewhere) or local production. Foreign direct investment (FDI) is the name given to the funds that flow across national borders in order to establish production facilities abroad. A firm that undertakes FDI to set up plants outside its home country becomes a multinational enterprise (MNE), also known as a transnational corporation or a multinational corporation.

Empirical and Theoretical Points of Departure
Modern analysis of firms' plant location decisions in international oligopolies started with Stephen Hymer's famous PhD thesis, *The International Operations of National Firms* (submitted to MIT in 1960, but not published until 1976). Hymer began by noting that the predictions of the then-dominant theoretical approach to FDI flows, which treated FDI as an international flow of portfolio capital in a perfectly competitive global financial market, were strikingly contradicted by the data. In the traditional perspective Hymer critiqued, the rate of return to capital is given by its marginal product, which is itself a decreasing function of a nation's stock of capital relative to other factors of production. Therefore, the return to capital will tend to be low in capital-abundant (developed) countries and high in capital-scarce (developing) countries. Moreover, if capital is freely mobile internationally, then one would expect to observe FDI flowing from developed to developing countries.

Several representative features of the data (empirical "stylized facts") are strongly inconsistent with the traditional perspective. At the macro level, developed countries are the recipients of the majority of global FDI flows—as well as being the majority source, of course. Developing nations are left largely out of the global FDI loop. In this vein, Hymer observed in 1960 that the most popular locations for postwar U.S. outward FDI were Canada and the United Kingdom, both developed nations whose capital stocks survived the war much less depleted than those on the European continent. Moreover, two-way flows of FDI between pairs of countries ("cross-hauling") are common even at the industry level. Another robust and awkward empirical result comes from econometric studies of the macroeconomic determinants of FDI flows, which generally find little or no explanatory role for national measures of capital intensity or the return to capital. For excellent surveys of the empirical findings, see the introductory chapters of Barba Navaretti and Venables (2004), and Markusen (2002).

Hymer concluded that the traditional macroeconomic account of FDI flows under the assumption of perfect competition was inadequate, and that a microeconomic study of FDI—emphasizing the special characteristics of MNEs and the markets they inhabit—offered fresh hope. At the microeconomic level, Hymer and subsequent applied theorists highlighted two stylized facts for particular attention:

- MNEs are prevalent in relatively concentrated industries that seem to fit the theoretical category of oligopoly; and
- MNEs are most likely to be observed in industries where proprietary, knowledge-based assets (usually related to the production process or the product) are important. Moreover, within an industry, MNEs are generally the firms with the largest stocks of such assets. It seems intuitively obvious that industries where proprietary, knowledge-based assets are important should also be concentrated. The fixed costs of developing such assets generate significant economies of scale for incumbent firms, which means that there is only room for a few firms to operate profitably in the industry.

Moreover, because knowledge-based assets are nonrival within the firm (their so-called public good aspect), it is natural to expect multiplant firms to arise in industries where they are important. Of course, horizontal MNEs are a special case of multiplant firms, and Markusen (1984) examines their welfare consequences in a model where production requires both firm- and plant-level activities. The firm-level activity, which produces a joint input across all the firm's factories, might be research and development (R&D) investment. Markusen assumes a two-country world where each country hosts a single plant to produce the final good. The two plants may be owned by competing national firms or integrated within a single MNE. As Markusen shows, that organizational choice involves a trade-off between technical and allocative efficiency. Integrating the plants into a single MNE avoids duplication of firm-level activities and boosts profits, but it also creates a monopoly in the product market.

Dunning's popular OLI (ownership-location-internalization) framework suggests further reasons why FDI might be observed in knowledge-intensive industries. Given that a firm has chosen to produce abroad, Dunning argues that FDI is favored over licensing production to a foreign firm if the transactions costs of writing and enforcing contracts create sufficient "internalization advantages." The OLI approach also assumes that, in order to undertake FDI profitably, a firm must possess "ownership advantages" over its industry rivals (e.g., superior technology). We return to this point later.

Models of International Oligopoly Having established that knowledge-intensive industries are likely to be both oligopolistic and FDI-intensive, we now consider the direct relationship between FDI and oligopoly. The seminal early analysis of the implications of oligopoly for FDI behavior is Knickerbocker (1973). Knickerbocker documented follow-the-leader patterns in the data on firms' FDI behavior within given industries, most evident at intermediate levels of concentration. He claimed that tacit collusion lay behind this relationship: tacit collusion often leads to imitative, follow-the-leader behavior, and it naturally arises at intermediate levels of concentration ("loose-knit" oligopolies in his terminology). In contrast, if concentration is low, firms are too numerous to coordinate their activities; and if concentration is high (a "tight-knit" oligopoly), firms can coordinate to maximize industry profits and so surpass imitative behavior.

Graham (1998) uses game-theoretic techniques to formalize Knickerbocker's follow-the-leader story. In Graham's model, FDI is used as a threat to maintain collusion. In an international duopoly where the firms originate from different countries (and, for simplicity, international trade is ruled out), each firm tacitly agrees not to enter its rival's home market via FDI, thereby granting its rival a domestic monopoly. If one firm breaks the understanding by undertaking FDI, its rival reciprocates, thus producing follow-the-leader behavior. (Graham's theoretical framework is an infinitely repeated Prisoner's Dilemma game.)

The modern game-theoretic literature has suggested other direct linkages between oligopoly and FDI. If technology diffuses slowly, then incumbent firms have first-mover advantages over potential entrants into the industry. These can facilitate preemptive FDI to keep host-country product markets concentrated and deter entry by local firms. The mechanism is that, compared to international trade, inward FDI allows foreign industry incumbents to compete more aggressively with local entrants on host-country product markets. The possibility of preemption creates a strategic motivation for FDI in addition to considerations of demand and cost. (Formal models are presented by Markusen 2002, chapter 4; Motta 1992.)

In this preemption story, FDI sustains market power, whereas the *threat* of FDI is key under tacit collusion. Both scenarios seem quite intricate, however: Do firms really think like that? The results of the formal models of tacit collusion and preemptive FDI are also highly sensitive to assumptions: for example, if the local firm in the preemption setup described earlier could move before the foreign industry incumbent, then it could enter the host-country market to preempt inward FDI! Such fragility is, however, a common feature of game-theoretic models.

Recent game-theoretic analyses of international oligopolies have uncovered further reasons for the emergence of MNEs. In an important paper, Horstmann and Markusen (1992) use a symmetric two-firm, two-country framework to examine firms' choices between horizontal FDI and exporting. In the model, the firms originate from different countries, and competition takes place in two stages. First,

the firms choose between not entering the industry and entering either as a national firm or as a horizontal MNE. If it enters, a firm incurs a firm-specific fixed cost, which represents its headquarters and other joint-input activities such as R&D. Firms also incur a plant-specific fixed cost on each factory they establish. Therefore, choosing between entering as an MNE or a national firm (i.e., FDI versus exporting to the foreign market) involves a trade-off between fixed and marginal costs. FDI entails the fixed cost of an additional plant, but it allows the firm to "jump" the international trade cost that must be paid on exports. After having chosen the location of production, the firms compete (in Cournot fashion) on both national product markets. As is conventional, Horstmann and Markusen solve their model backwards to isolate its subgame perfect Nash equilibrium, thus capturing the idea that firms consider how their FDI choices will affect subsequent product-market competition.

Two results from the Horstmann-Markusen model are especially noteworthy. First, MNEs become more likely to arise in equilibrium as the firm-specific fixed cost rises relative to that for plants. This result echoes Markusen (1984): integrating national firms into an MNE economizes on firm-specific costs. Moreover, FDI cross-hauling occurs in equilibrium when the national markets are large enough to support the total fixed costs of two MNEs. This explanation of cross-hauling—reciprocal FDI flows—within a given industry is a major contribution because such flows are both empirically common and difficult to rationalize within other frameworks, such as OLI. Recall that a precondition for FDI in the OLI framework is that a firm possess "advantages" over its rivals. Therefore, FDI cross-hauling within an international duopoly suggests that firm A has advantages over B and B over A—clearly an impossibility.

A second key result from Horstmann and Markusen (1992) is their prediction on how changes in international trade costs affect firms' choices between horizontal FDI and exporting. Because the benefit of FDI to firms is the avoidance ("jumping") of trade costs, Horstmann and Markusen find that national firms tend to displace MNEs as trade costs fall. This prediction seems strikingly counterfactual, as we discuss later.

Markusen and Venables (1998) extend the analysis of firms' FDI decisions by allowing for entry into the industry and differences between the two host countries. They find that MNEs tend to displace national (exporting) firms in equilibrium as countries become more similar (both in size and in relative factor endowments), and as world income grows. These results fit the stylized facts well because a large proportion of global FDI flows between "similar" developed countries. Intuitively, similarities between the host countries encourage two-way FDI flows because they mean that MNEs from different countries are able to compete on similar terms.

A final area where oligopoly theory has been applied to FDI is in the analysis of horizontal cross-border mergers and acquisitions (M&As). Quantitatively, international M&As are more important in FDI flows than greenfield investment, the name given to the building of new production facilities abroad. Moreover, analysis of international M&As helps address a well-known paradox. As confirmed by Horstmann and Markusen (1992), intuition suggests that reductions in international trade costs should discourage FDI in favor of exports—and, within FDI, the share of vertical should grow because it involves some international trade, whereas horizontal FDI involves none. There has been dramatic growth in global FDI flows in recent decades, however, and the majority of FDI remains horizontal, despite the large reduction in international trade costs, due in part to ongoing trade liberalization.

Neary (2006) considers possible resolutions of this paradox. Unlike horizontal greenfield FDI, he shows that trade liberalization can increase the profitability of horizontal mergers. The profitability gain from a merger arises because it removes the competition that would otherwise have occurred between the participating firms. Moreover, competition in the global market is more intense, the lower are trade barriers. With high trade barriers, import competition is limited and, for example, isolated national firms can earn almost monopoly profits at home. Therefore, the profitability gain from reducing competition through merger/acquisition rises as trade costs fall, and we expect trade liberalization to encourage horizontal cross-border M&As.

Another potential resolution of the paradox is to allow for intrabloc trade liberalization, for example, the launch of the European Single Market or the North American Free Trade Agreement (NAFTA). These liberalizations might make horizontal inward FDI from the rest of the world to serve the whole bloc profitable, where previously inward FDI to serve primarily just one bloc member was not.

This survey has aimed to show how oligopoly theory can cast light on strategic motivations for FDI that are absent in other market structures. In the process, some empirical observations—such as FDI cross-hauling at the industry level—become easier to explain. Finally, we should note that although this survey has ignored policy issues, there are lively debates concerning oligopoly and FDI. One, for example, concerns whether large MNEs are able to "divide and rule" national governments and cause a "race to the bottom" in corporate taxes. Such controversies highlight what a fruitful area this is for further research.

See also factor endowments and foreign direct investment; fixed costs and foreign direct investment; foreign direct investment and exit of local firms; foreign direct investment: the OLI framework; foreign direct investment under monopolistic competition; knowledge-capital model of the multinational enterprise; market size and foreign direct investment; outsourcing/offshoring; trade costs and foreign direct investment; vertical versus horizontal foreign direct investment

FURTHER READING

Barba Navaretti, Giorgio, and Anthony J. Venables. 2004. *Multinational Firms in the World Economy.* Princeton, NJ: Princeton University Press. A recent and important monograph on multinational enterprises.

Dunning, John H. 1977. "Trade, Location of Economic Activity, and the MNE: A Search for an Eclectic Approach." In *The International Allocation of Economic Activity: Proceedings of a Nobel Symposium held at Stockholm*, edited by B. Ohlin, P.-O. Hesselborn, and

P. M. Wijkman, eds. London: Macmillan, 395–418. Definitive statement of the OLI framework.

Graham, Edward M. 1998. "Market Structure and the Multinational Enterprise: A Game-Theoretic Approach." *Journal of International Business Studies* 29 (1): 67–83. Very readable application of game theory to study of MNEs.

Horstmann, Ignatius, and James R. Markusen. 1992. "Endogenous Market Structures in International Trade (Natura Facit Saltum)." *Journal of International Economics* 32 (1–2): 109–29. Rigorous analysis of the FDI/exporting choice in an international duopoly.

Hymer, Stephen H. 1976. *The International Operations of National Firms: A Study of Direct Foreign Investment.* Cambridge, MA: MIT Press. The starting point of the modern theory of FDI.

Knickerbocker, Frederick T. 1973. *Oligopolistic Reaction and Multinational Enterprise.* Boston, MA: Harvard University Press. An important early work on FDI under oligopoly.

Markusen, James R. 1984. "Multinationals, Multiplant Economies, and the Gains from Trade." *Journal of International Economics* 16 (3–4): 205–26. A key early work on horizontal FDI.

———. 2002. *Multinational Firms and the Theory of International Trade.* Cambridge, MA: MIT Press. Survey of the author's contributions to the theory of FDI under oligopoly.

Markusen, James R., and Anthony J. Venables. 1998. "Multinational Firms and the New Trade Theory." *Journal of International Economics* 46 (2): 183–203. Extends Horstmann and Markusen (1992) to allow for country differences and entry into the industry.

Motta, Massimo. 1992. "Multinational Firms and the Tariff-Jumping Argument: A Game Theoretic Analysis with some Unconventional Conclusions." *European Economic Review* 36 (8): 1557–71. A formal model of pre-emptive FDI.

Neary, J. Peter. 2006. "Trade Costs and Foreign Direct Investment." CEPR Discussion Paper No. 5933. London: Center for Economic Policy Research. Addresses the empirical paradox of growing horizontal FDI flows in the presence of falling trade costs.

BEN FERRETT

■ foreign equity restrictions

A foreign equity restriction is a measure that imposes more stringent requirements on foreign investors than domestic investors and thereby influences decisions about where to invest and in what form. In some economies, such as Switzerland, private companies impose limits on foreign holdings of their own shares (Bailey, Chung, and Kang 1999), but in most cases foreign equity restrictions are the result of government policy.

The aim of regulatory restrictions on foreign equity ownership is to maintain the independence of domestic firms for reasons of sovereignty, national security, and economic stability. In particular, the measures are often intended to prevent the acquisition of controlling stakes in domestic companies by large multinational corporations, over which national governments and other stakeholders have little influence. Sectors that are frequently subject to foreign equity restrictions are telecommunications and media, air and maritime transportation, finance, public utilities, and defense electronics.

Resource Allocation Implications Foreign direct investment (FDI) is a form of international economic integration that can bring substantial gains to both investor and investment-receiver by fostering intrafirm trade and transactions in intangible assets, such as knowledge and product brands. Beyond the standard gains from trade, FDI inflows can provide dynamic spillovers from technology transfer and skill-building. These benefits are especially important in developing countries where advanced technology and managerial expertise are in short supply.

Barriers to FDI reduce or eliminate these benefits by distorting the allocation of capital among different economies, between foreign and domestic investment, among different sectors, and between temporarily held portfolio and longer-term direct investment. As a result, products and services may cost more than they would without the foreign equity restrictions and assets may not be used in the most productive way. The effects may manifest themselves through a variety of channels, such as higher prices, less consumer choice, lower capital stock, and lower productivity. The resulting costs of the foreign equity restrictions in terms of forgone economic welfare improvements have to be weighed against their noneconomic benefits in terms of sovereignty, security, and stability to arrive at an overall assessment of the rationale for such measures.

Types of Restrictions and Measurement Measures to control or influence FDI range from simple requirements that investments be registered and screened, with virtually automatic approval, to complete bans on foreign ownership in some sectors or countries. Restrictions also vary with respect to the level at which they are applied. For example, measures may affect market entry, ownership and control, or operations. Another classification of re-

strictions pertains to the way in which they are applied—for example, through legislation that clearly specifies ownership limits, or case-by-case assessments of whether entry will be allowed and the conditions that may apply (Hardin and Holmes 1997).

Assessing the relative prevalence and restrictiveness of different foreign equity restrictions presents major challenges, similar to those encountered when trying to measure other nontariff barriers. Relatively simple ways of summarizing the extent of foreign equity restrictions are based on counts of the number of measures in a sector or economy, or on indicators that reflect the proportion of investments covered by

Table 1
Coefficients on FDI restrictions (maximum 1.0)

Type of restriction	Scores
Foreign equity limits	
No foreign equity allowed	1
1 to 19% foreign equity allowed	0.6
20–34% foreign equity allowed	0.4
35–49% foreign equity allowed	0.3
50–74% foreign equity allowed	0.2
75–99% foreign equity allowed	0.1
no restriction but unbound	0.05
Screening and approval	
Investor must show economic benefits	0.2
Approval unless contrary to national interest	0.1
Notification (pre or post)	0.05
Other restrictions	
Board of directors/managers	
majority must be nationals or residents	0.1
at least one must be national or resident	0.05
must be locally licensed	0.025
Movement of people	
no entry	0.1
less than one year	0.075
one to two years	0.05
three to four years	0.025
Input and operational restrictions	
domestic content must be more than 50%	0.1
other	0.05
Total[a]	Between 0 and 1

Source: OECD, adapted from Hardin and Holmes (1997).
[a]If foreign equity is banned, then the other criteria become irrelevant, so that the index is at 1.0. It is possible that various scores sum to slightly more than 1.0 when foreign equity is not totally banned, and in such cases, the index is capped at 1.0.

barriers (Hoekman 1995). Although such frequency and coverage indexes have the advantages of simplicity and lack of arbitrariness, some measures are more constraining than others. It therefore seems desirable for analysts to attempt to weight different restrictions according to their significance, even though such a procedure entails some subjective judgments and possible errors (Golub 2003).

One weighting scheme that has been used by Organisation for Economic Co-operation and Development (OECD) researchers is shown in table 1. The overall restrictiveness of FDI barriers is derived for each industry and country, based on regulations in three areas: equity limits, screening and approval, and other restrictions. Area scores are added up to yield an overall indicator that ranges from 0 to 1. Equity limitations and screening are related to an investor's right of establishment, whereas measures affecting management structures, movement of people, and operational restrictions pertain to national treatment of established firms.

This line of analysis focuses on statutory restrictions, but many countries retain informal public or private barriers to foreign equity acquisition, which can in some cases be more restrictive than formal regulations. Nonformalized FDI impediments are by nature difficult to capture and compare, however.

Policy Reform Many economies have liberalized their foreign investment policies since the 1980s such that equity restrictions in manufacturing have virtually disappeared in OECD countries. Developing and emerging economies maintain on average more restrictive policies, but large variations across countries and sectors exist. While service sector privatizations have led to increased market openness in many economies, reforms have often involved limits on acquisitions by foreigners. Yet there are some notable differences between OECD and non-OECD countries. In particular, transportation and tourism are relatively less restricted in non-OECD countries, while electricity, wholesale and retail distribution, and finance are relatively highly restricted in non-OECD countries (Koyama and Golub 2006).

The general, broad-based trend toward removal of foreign equity restrictions suggests that policymakers have increasingly been persuaded of the merits of inward FDI over concerns related to sovereignty, security, and stability, as well as the partisan interests of entrenched lobbies. From an economic point of view, nondiscrimination between domestic and foreign investors is generally the best policy in the absence of a clear-cut market failure or threat to national interests. Neutrality involves both right of establishment for foreign firms and national treatment of such firms once they are established. Right of establishment signifies that there are no discriminatory obstacles to foreign greenfield investment or mergers and acquisitions, while national treatment involves nondiscrimination in conducting business (Golub 2003).

Progress toward liberalization of remaining restrictions can be facilitated by continued discussion in international forums on development of codes, guidelines, and best practices in areas with direct impact on public- and private-sector governance practices. Moreover, reforms do not necessarily have to involve the immediate and complete removal of foreign equity restrictions. In some cases, more direct measures that, for example, clearly specify quantity or value constraints on foreign investors' market access or operations will tend to achieve the policy goal at a lower cost than a regulation that tries to achieve the same objective but in a less direct and transparent way.

See also agglomeration and foreign direct investment; foreign direct investment (FDI); foreign market entry; international investment agreements; joint ventures; mergers and acquisitions; multinational enterprises; trade-related investment measures (TRIMs)

FURTHER READING
Bailey, Warren, Y. Peter Chung, and Jun-koo Kang. 1999. "Foreign Ownership Restrictions and Equity Price Premiums: What Drives the Demand for Cross-Border Investments?" *Journal of Financial and Quantitative Analysis* 34 (4): 489–511. Assesses the effects of foreign equity restrictions imposed by private companies on equity prices.

Golub, Stephen S. 2003. "Measures of Restrictions on Inward Foreign Direct Investment for OECD Countries." *OECD Economic Studies* 36: 85–115. Provides a discussion of the measurement of FDI restrictions and derives restrictiveness indicators for OECD countries.

Hardin, Alexis, and Leanne Holmes. 1997. *Service Trade and Foreign Direct Investment.* Canberra: Australian Productivity Commission. Analyzes a broad range of issues with respect to FDI restrictions in services sectors.

Hoekman, Bernard. 1995. "Assessing the General Agreement on Trade in Services." In *The Uruguay Round and the Developing Countries,* edited by Will Martin and L. Alan Winters. Washington DC: World Bank, 327–64. Analyzes the GATS partly based on frequency counts of foreign equity restrictions.

Koyama, Takeshi, and Stephen S. Golub. 2006. "OECD's FDI Regulatory Restrictiveness Index: Revision and Extension to More Economies." OECD Economics Department Working Papers No. 525. Paris: OECD. Provides estimates of FDI restrictiveness for more than 40 OECD and emerging economies.

PETER WALKENHORST

■ **foreign exchange intervention**

Foreign exchange intervention refers to the purchase and sale of currencies in the foreign exchange market by a country's monetary authority, such as its central bank. In many countries with managed exchange rates, intervention is used routinely to target the foreign exchange value of the country's currency. For example, a central bank with a currency whose value is dipping below its target range typically will sell some of its holdings of foreign currency in exchange for purchases of its own currency. This process reduces the supply of the country's own currency and thereby increases its value in the foreign exchange market.

In countries without exchange rate targets, foreign exchange intervention is used at times to try to influence other aspects of the foreign exchange market or to directly alter domestic macroeconomic conditions. Many central banks intervene in an attempt to dampen the volatility of the exchange rate, to slow the rate of change of the currency's foreign exchange

value, to calm disorderly markets, or to manage the official holdings of foreign exchange reserves. In a few countries, foreign exchange intervention is a standard tool for addressing important domestic macroeconomic concerns, such as the rate of inflation. Some of these domestic concerns may be linked only indirectly to the foreign exchange market itself. In principle, a monetary authority can use intervention to achieve any number of objectives.

When managing foreign reserves or influencing any aspect of the foreign exchange market is the objective of intervention, the monetary authorities face several choices in its implementation. Most important, a monetary authority must decide to what extent the foreign exchange intervention should be allowed to affect domestic monetary conditions. Foreign exchange intervention can be undertaken in tandem with offsetting domestic monetary operations. An intervention's effect on domestic monetary conditions thereby will be "sterilized"—that is, there will be no net direct effect on domestic monetary conditions. Alternatively, intervention can be undertaken by itself, without countervailing domestic operations. Such intervention is called "unsterilized" intervention.

A monetary authority must also choose how much information about its intervention to divulge to foreign exchange market participants. It may intervene in secret, it may reveal some of its information about intervention, or it may intervene openly. Finally, a monetary authority may choose to intervene in concert with others, in which case its intervention is said to be "concerted," or it may intervene unilaterally. The efficacy of foreign exchange intervention is thought to vary depending on these key aspects of its implementation—whether it is sterilized or unsterilized, secret or transparent, and unilateral or concerted.

Effectiveness of Foreign Exchange Intervention Intervention is quite effective in modifying the foreign exchange value of currencies when it is unsterilized. Since it is not offset by countervailing domestic operations, unsterilized intervention alters the amount of reserves in the banking system. When a central bank, for example, sells some of its foreign currency holdings, the reserves in the banking system decline correspondingly. Foreign exchange sales themselves are thus a form of monetary policy tightening. This type of intervention has a direct effect on the foreign exchange value of a country's currency: tighter monetary conditions strengthen a currency's foreign exchange value. Its effectiveness is apparent even for currencies with high turnover in deep markets. When exchange rate concerns dominate monetary policy, foreign exchange intervention is effective.

Sterilizing foreign exchange intervention means preventing it from bringing about a domestic monetary condition change—the very thing that would have the most direct effect on the currency's value. Therefore, in order for sterilized intervention to have an effect on the exchange rate, its effectiveness must come about through some other channel.

One important potential channel is known as the signaling channel. In this channel, intervention affects exchange rates when it signals a change in future monetary policy. In theory, such signals are credible (and intervention effective) only if intervention tends to be followed by consistent changes in monetary policy. Thus the signaling channel allows for an effect on exchange rates when the intervention, though initially sterilized, is expected ultimately to be unsterilized.

The microstructural approach to foreign exchange has recently provided other new insights into the efficacy of intervention. Microstructure models focus on the informational structure of foreign exchange markets. Because they are explicit about the informational structure, these models are well-equipped to show how an individual agent (such as the monetary authority) reveals its information when it initiates a transaction. This makes the microstructural approach particularly suitable both for understanding the role that intervention might play in coordinating exchange rate expectations and for sorting out some of the key aspects of the intervention's actual implementation. For example, microstructure models can provide precise answers to questions such as why intervention is carried out secretly, or why intervention, rather than an announcement, is used to convey information. The

intervention's optimal implementation is shown in these models to depend on the precise nature of the informational asymmetries in the market.

Practice of Foreign Exchange Intervention In most mature economies with floating exchange rates and open capital markets, intervention now occurs only infrequently. Although central banks engaged in more frequent unilateral and concerted intervention during some earlier periods, such as the 1980s, their intervention in the early 21st century was quite limited. For the central banks that issue the major international currencies, intervention—when it does occur—is usually small relative to the overall size of the foreign exchange market. It also typically takes the form of sterilized intervention. The only notable exception is the Bank of Japan, which has intervened frequently, and sometimes extensively. The European Central Bank and the U.S. Federal Reserve Board, for example, may let years go by without carrying out any intervention at all; and, when they do intervene, their intervention is sterilized routinely. Even the Bank of Canada, which had a policy of regular and automatic intervention until the mid-1990s, countenances intervention only in exceptional circumstances. For mature economies, extended central bank absence from the foreign exchange market is the norm.

The monetary authorities in many emerging economies, on the other hand, still intervene heavily in the foreign exchange market. In 2000–2006, the monetary authorities in China, in several of the oil exporting countries, and in a handful of emerging market countries sold off large quantities of their own currencies. In doing so, they accumulated immense holdings of foreign currency reserves.

Intervention among emerging market countries is most prevalent in those with exchange rate targets. Their intervention in some cases is unsterilized, and the corresponding changes in monetary conditions affect the exchange rate directly. In other cases, particularly where intervention occurs in a setting with significant barriers to capital mobility, it is sterilized. This combination of sterilized intervention and barriers to capital mobility is thought to enable a country to maintain a relatively weak exchange rate without engendering domestic inflation. It is also exactly this combination of sterilized intervention and capital controls that so frustrates the trading partners of a few emerging market countries and provokes accusations of excessive currency manipulation.

Research Challenges The practice of foreign exchange intervention has moved along in fits and starts. It has varied across both time and countries in nearly every way—in its objectives, in its implementation, and in its perceived effectiveness. This variation is mirrored in the dissonance of research on intervention, which as of the first decade of the 21st century provided little in the way of sure-footed guidance to monetary authorities. (In fact, the extent of any consensus arguably diminished since earlier decades, when a deeper skepticism about intervention prevailed.) Researchers face daunting empirical and theoretical challenges, and definitive conclusions remain a long way off.

On the empirical front, researchers face a scarcity of reliable, detailed data on actual intervention for all but a few countries. Foreign exchange market news reports have been used in lieu of actual intervention, but these reports have been found to be inaccurate. They can be used to measure—at best—only what the exchange rate response is to reports of intervention, not actual intervention. The reports are particularly unhelpful in exploring the role of secrecy in intervention. In addition, key pieces of intervention's implementation, such as whether or not it is sterilized or is concerted, often are not directly observable. This is problematic since theory tells us that intervention's effectiveness depends on these key pieces of its implementation. Moreover, intervention policy—even its objective—does not appear to be stable over time. This structural instability is generally, though not always, difficult to detect. When undetected, it means that atheoretical empirical studies are likely to conflate measures of effectiveness from different policy eras. Such conflated measures are difficult to interpret.

Empirical work on the intervention's exchange rate effectiveness also faces a serious simultaneity problem: foreign exchange intervention is carried out in response to changes in the exchange rate and in response to the conditions that affect the exchange rate. Thus intervention's effect on the exchange rate must be disentangled from the exchange rate's effect on intervention. Credible empirical studies must begin with plausible strategies to identify the effect of intervention by itself—and that is a tall order. The most common identification strategy has relied on assumptions about the timing of the effects: the strategy is to assume that intervention affects the exchange rate instantly, while the exchange rate affects intervention only slowly. Unfortunately, to the extent that monetary authorities "lean against the wind," their response to the exchange rate is automatic. Thus the assumption of a slow response is often rendered implausible and the problem of disentangling the effects reemerges.

Further complicating the empirical work are the important theoretical challenges to a clear understanding of foreign exchange intervention. For example, while some models provide good descriptions of the implications of asymmetric information, only a few address the source of the informational asymmetry. It is easy enough, at one level, to say that a monetary authority has privileged information about its own intervention objectives and about future monetary policy. However, that is a remarkably static explanation for work in a field that generally demands attention to dynamics. It calls for further explanation of why such an informational advantage might not erode over time. A dynamically consistent account of the informational asymmetry will pave the way for a more complete understanding of the role of foreign exchange intervention.

See also asymmetric information; capital controls; capital mobility; equilibrium exchange rate; exchange rate regimes; exchange rate volatility; fear of floating; impossible trinity; international reserves; money supply; new open economy macroeconomics; reserve currency; sterilization; vehicle currency

FURTHER READING

Dominguez, Kathryn M. E. 2003. "The Market Microstructure of Central Bank Intervention." *Journal of International Economics* 59: 25–45. Explores the intraday timing of intervention's effectiveness and the role of news reports of intervention.

Edison, Hali J. 1993. "Effectiveness of Central-Bank Intervention: A Survey of the Literature after 1982." *Special Papers in International Economics* 18: 1–68. International Financial Section, Princeton University. A benchmark review of the early literature on central bank intervention.

Popper, Helen, and John Montgomery. 2001. "Information Sharing and Central Bank Intervention." *Journal of International Economics* 55: 295–316. Models a novel source of the central bank's privileged information and is one of the few papers to examine explicitly some of intervention's welfare effects.

Sarno, L., and M. P. Taylor. 2001. "Official Intervention in the Foreign Exchange Market: Is It Effective and, If So, How Does it Work?" *Journal of Economic Literature* 39: 839–68. Updates Edison (1993), also explores intervention's role in addressing a coordination failure.

Vitale, Paolo. 1999. "Sterilized Central Bank Intervention in the Foreign Exchange Market." *Journal of International Economics* 49: 245–67. A classic microstructural approach to intervention's signaling role. Addresses the issue of secrecy when the central bank's target differs from the fundamentals.

HELEN POPPER

■ foreign market entry

Foreign market entry is an important strategy for multinational enterprises (MNEs) to expand their global reach and establish an international network of interdependent business units. Within this network, each subsidiary has a specific role, such as to provide access to local resources or markets. The design of an entry strategy has to match the needs and resources of the MNE with the opportunities and constraints in the local environment. Entry strategies are thus adapted to the local resource endowment, market demand, and institutional environment, though the degree of such adaptation varies across firms, industries, and locations.

Setting up a new business operation requires several strategic decisions, including the entry mode, location, timing, marketing, human resources, and logistics. Most scholarly research has focused on entry modes: export, contractual cooperation, or foreign direct investment (FDI). The FDI mode is further distinguished by the investors' share of equity ownership, and whether to build an operation from scratch, a greenfield project, or acquire an existing firm. These decisions are interdependent though economic analysts often prefer to analyze them ceteris paribus to generate more parsimonious theoretical models. Key parameters influencing the entry strategy vary with the objectives of the project; they are here illustrated primarily with a focus on market-seeking FDI.

Foreign entries are undertaken for a reason that is normally specified before the entry strategy is designed. The motives of FDI relate to the development and exploitation of resources of the MNE across its operations. Hence any specific entry decision cannot be viewed in isolation but has to be considered in relation to the overall strategic posture of the MNE. The MNE's global strategy thus sets the framework for specific foreign entries. This article considers the following aspects of foreign entry: entry mode, location, timing, marketing, human resource management, and logistics.

Entry Modes Foreign entry modes are classified in multiple ways. First, nonequity modes are distinguished from equity modes; the former include exports with and without trade intermediaries, as well as contractual forms of business such as licensing, franchising, outsourcing, and turn-key projects. Equity modes are distinguished by the ownership stake taken by the foreign investor: portfolio investment, joint venture (JV), and wholly owned subsidiary (Young, Hamill, Wheeler, and Davies, 1989; Welch, Benito, and Petersen 2007).

Portfolio investment involves the acquisition of a small equity stake as a financial investor, yet without influencing the strategy of the firm. Joint ventures are created by two or more partner firms each contributing resources and sharing the control of the operation. They are differentiated by ownership levels taken by the foreign investor; the higher the equity stake and the more dispersed the residual ownership the more the investor has control over the operation. Wholly owned subsidiaries provide the investor with full control.

Theoretical models of the choice of foreign equity focus on the internalization of transactions and control over operations (Buckley and Casson 1996; Brouthers and Hennart 2007). Transaction costs economics and internalization theory suggest that a JV would be chosen if three conditions are met: (1) the new business unit depends on resource contributions from two or more firms, (2) the transfer of these resources or the expected benefits for the investors are subject to high transaction costs, and (3) it is not feasible for the entire parent firms to be integrated into one firm, for instance because they are big relative to the envisaged project, or one of them is a state-owned enterprise.

High transaction costs are in particular likely to arise for investors who transfer intangible assets. This issue is particularly pertinent for MNEs because their ability to achieve competitive advantages in foreign markets is often based on the deployment of intangible assets. They face asymmetric information regarding the content, value, and usage of these assets, which are classic sources of market failures. Thus the more markets are characterized by information asymmetries, the more likely MNEs prefer to internalize an operation and establish a wholly owned subsidiary. Moreover, Kogut and Zander (1993), and other scholars, argue that knowledge to be transferred is often tacit and thus requires "learning by doing" and therefore an intraorganizational mode of transfer. This requirement provides an alternative explanation for why knowledge-intensive firms would abstain from licensing or JVs as modes of foreign entry. Thus the more MNEs compete on the basis of technology, brand names, or other intangible assets, the more likely they would enter foreign markets with wholly owned subsidiaries.

A different source of transaction costs is interdependence of business activities and thus high asset specificity. These transaction costs lead in particular to vertical JVs in industries that require large investments in assets specific to a business relationship, as in the mining and processing of certain natural resources.

Yet, transaction costs also depend on the institutional environment governing the market, notably the feasibility and cost of enforcing contracts. Where these institutions are weak, investors would abstain from relying on contracts; at the same time, local partners may be helpful in interacting with other local businesses in such contexts. Joint ventures may provide an avenue to operate in unfamiliar contexts, especially where market supporting institutions are weak.

A different distinction of investment modes concerns the make-or-buy decision, namely the establishment of a greenfield operation versus an acquisition of (a stake in) an existing company. This decision is primarily driven by the investor's need for local resources: an acquisition provides local organizationally embedded resources, such as human capital and networks with local authorities. A greenfield operation, in contrast, allows investors to create a new operation from scratch according to their own designs, and thus to replicate organizational procedures and practices. The greenfield option is preferred in particular by investors whose competitive advantages are grounded in the firm's organizational structure and culture. Acquisitions are preferred by those who need complementary local resources.

Location Location concerns both the choice of country to invest in and the selection of a specific site. For resource- or efficiency-seeking projects aiming to create an export platform, the primary concern is costs of production. Hence the key determinants for location decisions are the costs and quality of the local factor endowment. Entrants would consider the specific inputs that they require for their operations, including natural assets such as cost of the local workforce and natural resources and "created assets" such as intermediate goods, human capital, and infrastructure.

Created assets are often of primary concern in industrialized countries, but they are also of increasing importance in emerging economies. Created assets are often provided by other businesses, which is one cause of the agglomeration of FDI:

foreign entrants invest where a strong community of local and foreign-owned businesses already exists.

Market-seeking investors are primarily concerned with access to distribution channels and potential customers. They identify the relevant market and then seek a central location for sales, marketing, and distribution operations. In some industries, the actual production needs to be located close to the customer or the point of consumption, notably in service industries such as hotels and financial services, and for manufactured goods that face high transportation costs. Thus location decisions by market-seeking investors are a function of the expected market size and of transportation costs of bringing products to the customer. For consumer goods, market demand may be predicted based on demographic data such as per capita incomes and population size. For business-to-business operators, size and growth of the local customer industry are crucial. A special case is "follow-the-customer" entrants, which set up operations to best supply a specific customer, as commonly observed, for instance, in the automotive industry.

In addition to the primary considerations of factor costs and markets, location decisions are often moderated by the institutional environment. For instance, investors are concerned about regulation of the industry, political risk, and law enforcement, especially with regard to intellectual property rights. Moreover, they may prefer locations in cultural proximity because cultural differences between existing and new operations may reduce the efficiency of communication and coordination.

Location decisions may be made in two stages, first the country and then the site, but businesses may also compare alternative sites in different countries. The relevant parameters for both between-country and within-country location choice tend to be similar. MNEs may shortlist alternative sites and then negotiate with the pertinent national and local authorities in parallel. At this stage, investment incentives such as provision of specific local infrastructure or subsidies and financial incentives may tip the balance for a particular site, especially if competition for FDI is strong.

Timing of Entry Market-seeking foreign investors normally aim to be number one or two in their industry or market segment, especially if the industry tends toward oligopolistic market structures. Such market leadership may best be achieved by taking an early lead, or by taking over a local market leader (Lieberman and Montgomery 1988). Thus market-oriented investors often pursue first-mover advantages, while others enter the host country shortly after the first mover, aiming to challenge the first mover before its position is too strong.

Early entrants may attain a lead in building reputation and consumer loyalty, and in establishing relationships with major suppliers and customers. First movers may thus be able to lock their partners and customers into a relationship, and raise barriers to entry for later entrants. Moreover, first movers may build goodwill with local authorities, slide down the learning curve, and acquire unique local resources, such as distribution channels, local brands, and raw material sources.

Followers, on the other hand, may benefit from a less uncertain business environment, from observing the experiences of the first mover, and from customers and local authorities already familiar with the product and the practices of the industry. In particular, "fast seconds" may benefit from these advantages, while challenging the first mover before the market structure has stabilized. Empirical evidence suggests that first movers can maintain their leadership position if they continuously commit resources and focus on learning about the local environment. Yet evidence also points to many first movers who did not succeed in creating sustained market leadership.

Related to timing is the question of how fast to accelerate commitment to a market. In some industries, heavy up-front investment is required to establish a strong position in view of (potential) competitors, as for branded consumer goods, or because of the capital intensity of the industry, as for oil exploration. In other industries, a "platform strategy" may be appropriate as investors establish a small foothold from which to observe the local industry and to flexibly react to business opportunities if and when they emerge.

Marketing The marketing literature on foreign entry has focused on standardization versus local adaptation (Meyer and Tran 2006). A standardization strategy would use the same product, brand, and processes in all countries. Advantages of such a strategy include economies of scale in product development, production, and marketing. It is most likely to be appropriate in industries that are technology intensive and face little variation in consumer preferences. In contrast, a local adaptation strategy would emphasize localization of products to accommodate local needs and preferences. This may in particular include the creation or acquisition of local brands for the mass market. Such localization is important for instance in the food and beverage industry.

Standardization and localization are not exclusive, as MNEs may combine a high degree of standardization for their internal processes, such as product development and production, with adaptation of products and customer interfaces, notably marketing practices. Others pursue a multi-tier strategy and offer both an international product positioned in the premium segment and a local brand aimed at the mass market. Such a strategy allows synergies, for instance, in the use of distribution channels.

Human Resources and Logistics A foreign entry depends on qualified and motivated people to implement the strategy. Human resources management is particularly important to manage knowledge sharing within the organization, both to transmit key organizational practices to the new operation and to inform decision-makers at headquarters about the local business. Thus along with the establishment of a new subsidiary, expatriate managers have to be selected and prepared for their assignment, and local staff needs to be recruited and trained. Expatriates play a pivotal role in this process, as do training programs for local staff that may include learning by doing in other operations of the MNE. Other human resource management challenges include leadership of a workforce in a culturally different context and adaptation of systems for recruitment, performance assessment, and remuneration of local staff.

An important aspect of a foreign entry strategy that is little analyzed in the literature but of great importance for management practice is logistics. Lower labor costs are valuable for a business only if the products can be transported to the customer in good time at acceptable costs. Modern transportation infrastructure and information technology systems are designed to allow MNEs to optimize the integration of their internal operations as well as supplier relations. Specialist intermediaries offer services that may include not only warehousing, shipping, and door-to-door delivery but also processing of customer orders and identification of appropriate suppliers. A foreign entry often triggers changes in these systems, especially if it involves the relocation of production.

Interdependencies An entry strategy consists of many elements; entry strategy is, therefore, a multidimensional construct. Any decision has to take account of other dimensions. Take, for example, the choice of entry mode. If timing and speed of entry are crucial for an investor—as they are for those pursuing a first-mover advantage—an acquisition or a JV may offer quick market access. However, an acquisition poses greater challenges for the integration of the local operation with the global company in terms of, for instance, marketing, logistics, and human resource management. Thus foreign market entry decisions have to reflect the complex interdependence of multiple dimensions.

See also foreign direct investment: the OLI framework

FURTHER READING

Brouthers, K. D., and J. F. Hennart. 2007. "Boundaries of the Firm: Insights from International Entry Mode Research." *Journal of Management* 33 (3): 395–425. A critical review of the literature on ownership modes.

Buckley P. J., and M. C. Casson. 1996. "An Economic Model of International Joint Venture Strategy." *Journal of International Business Studies* 27: 849–76. A formal analysis of operation modes for different types of operations.

Kogut, B., and U. Zander. 1993. "Knowledge of the Firm and the Evolutionary Theory of the Multinational Corporation." *Journal of International Business Studies*

24 (4): 625–45. Foreign entry from the perspective of an evolutionary theory of the firm.

Lieberman, M. B., and D. B. Montgomery. 1988. "First Mover Advantages." *Strategic Management Journal* 9 (Special Issue: Strategy Content Research): 41–58. A classic paper on entry timing.

Meyer, K. E., and Y.T.T. Tran. 2006. "Market Penetration and Acquisition Strategies for Emerging Economies." *Long Range Planning* 39 (2): 177–97. An applied paper illustrating practical aspects of developing foreign market entries.

Welch, L. S., G.R.G. Benito, and B. Petersen. 2007. *Foreign Operation Methods: Analysis, Strategy, and Dynamics.* London: Edward Elgar. A new textbook.

Young, S., J. Hamill, C. Wheeler, and J. R. Davies. 1989. *International Market Entry and Development.* Hemel Hempstead, UK: Harvester Wheatsheaf. A classic, specialized textbook.

KLAUS MEYER

■ forward premium puzzle

Interest rates, the exchange rate, and the forward rate are all linked together by expectations and individual attempts to obtain the highest rates of return. The forward premium puzzle is closely related to the failure of uncovered interest parity (UIP) to hold, and the phenomenon of forward rate bias, which refers to the tendency for the forward exchange rate (the price of foreign currency agreed to today for a transaction some specific time in the future) to systematically mispredict the future spot exchange rate (the exchange rate in transactions in which one currency is directly exchanged for another). The puzzle is the finding that the forward premium—the gap between the spot exchange rate and the forward rate—usually points in the wrong direction for the subsequent actual movement in the spot exchange rate. Uncovered interest parity states that if the covered interest parity holds for a pair of currencies, then the forward discount, and hence the interest differential between the two countries, should be an unbiased predictor of the subsequent change in the spot rate, assuming that actors make guesses about the future

that are on average correct (what is sometimes termed "rational expectations"). The puzzle arises from the fact that, if market participants were risk neutral, the forward rate should equal the future expected spot exchange rate; yet when the forward rate suggests depreciation, typically the exchange rate appreciates, and vice versa.

The puzzle is of importance for what it suggests about the workings of international financial markets. To the extent that the puzzle reflects the failure of rational expectations to hold, then interest rate differentials will be poor guides to future exchange rate movements. In addition, the implied lack of market efficiency suggests a potential role for government intervention in foreign exchange markets. On the other hand, if the puzzle reflects the presence of a premium to compensate for the riskiness of specific currencies, then capital may not be so ready to migrate from one currency to another.

Explaining the Forward Premium Puzzle To fix concepts and terms, define the forward rate at time t for a trade to occur at time k as F_t^k and the spot rate at time t as S_t. Further, let the subjective expectation of the spot rate at time $t+k$, based on time t information, be defined as $\varepsilon_t(S_{t+k})$. Assume for the moment rational expectations, namely, $E_t(S_{t+k})$. Then one should expect:

$$S_{t+k} = F_t^k + \tilde{u}_{t+k} \qquad (1)$$

where the error term is an expectational error.

In reality, regression estimates do not obtain a regression coefficient of unity, although the point estimate is often not statistically significantly far from the posited value.

The forward premium puzzle can be identified by assuming that the error term is log normally distributed, so that (1) can be rewritten as:

$$s_{t+k} = \beta_0 + \beta_1 f_t^k + \tilde{u}_{t+k} \qquad (2)$$

where under the null hypothesis, $\beta_1 = 1$, and β_0 is allowed to equal some constant impounding some Jensens Inequality terms.

Notice that one can subtract the current log spot rate s_t from both sides, since under the null $\beta_1 = 1$. This yields:

$$s_{t+k} - s_t = \beta_0 + \beta_1(f_t^k - s_t) + \tilde{u}_{t+k} \qquad (3)$$

The left hand side of equation (3) is ex post depreciation, while the term in the parentheses is the forward discount (or the inverse of the forward premium).

The puzzle is that estimates of β_1 are not only different from the value of unity, and statistically significantly, but also that the coefficient estimates are typically *negative*. This suggests that agents could make substantial profits by arbitraging. To be concrete, individuals could borrow in the low interest currency and lend in the high interest currency, in a process termed "the carry trade." This well-known strategy can be highly profitable, although the profits are particularly vulnerable to sharp movements in the exchange rate.

This issue is linked up to uncovered interest parity in the following sense. If covered interest parity holds, then:

$$(f_t^k - s_t) = (i_t^k - i_t^{k^*}) \qquad (4)$$

Substituting this no-arbitrage-profits condition into (3), one finds that (3) can be rewritten as:

$$s_{t+k} - s_t = \beta_0 + \beta_1(i_t^k - i_t^{k^*}) + \tilde{u}_{t+k} \qquad (5)$$

The equation above is the regression used to test the joint null hypothesis of uncovered interest parity and rational expectations. The finding of a negative slope coefficient in equation (5) is equivalent to the finding of a negative slope coefficient in (3), for instances where covered interest parity holds.

Reasons behind the Puzzle A number of papers have investigated a wide variety of different econometric issues, but overall it appears that the negative slope coefficient cannot be entirely explained by the time series characteristics of the variables. Leaving aside these econometric issues, the forward premium puzzle might exist even when capital is perfectly mobile according to the covered interest parity criterion, either because of the invalidity of the rational expectations hypothesis or the existence of an exchange risk premium.

Estimates of equation (5) using values for k that range up to one year typically reject the unbiasedness restriction on the slope parameter. For instance, the survey by Kenneth Froot and Robert Thaler (1990) finds an average estimate for β of –0.88. Menzie

Chinn and Guy Meredith (2004) document that this result holds for more recent periods extending up to 2000. They also show that the bias decreases at longer horizons.

It is important to recall that uncovered interest parity, properly defined as relating to expected depreciation, is untestable. Estimation of the standard UIP regression equation relies on the rational expectations methodology embodied in equation (1). Of course, reliance on the assumption of rational expectations is by no means uncontroversial. In a number of papers, Kenneth Froot and Jeffrey Frankel (1989) demonstrate that the standard tests for UIP yield radically different results when one uses survey-based measures of exchange rate depreciation. They find that most of the variation of the forward discount appears to be related to expected depreciation, rather than a time-varying risk premium, thereby lending credence to UIP.

Menzie Chinn and Jeffrey Frankel (1994) document the fact that it is difficult to reject UIP for a broader set of currencies, although there is some evidence of a risk premium at the 12-month horizon. The authors interpret the differing results as arising from a wider set of currencies—they examine 17 currencies as opposed to the 5 or so examined by Jeffrey Frankel and Kenneth Froot (1987)—where the assumption of perfect substitutability of debt instruments is less likely to hold. As these authors have emphasized, rejection of the rational expectations hypothesis does not necessarily mean one accepts the proposition that agents are irrational. It may be that agents are constantly learning about the economic environment such that their forecasts are biased for long stretches of time.

Perhaps the most natural explanation for why the forward premium predicts the wrong direction of exchange rate movements is that a risk premium drives a wedge between expected changes and actual changes. However, the modeling of the risk premium has proven quite challenging. A standard model motivates the risk premium as a function of the correlation between relative returns on assets denominated in the two currencies, and the ratio of marginal utilities of consumption in the two respective countries. While the theory is quite straightforward, an implausibly high degree of risk aversion is necessary to rationalize the observed volatility of the risk premium. Some recent work has had success relying on different utility functions. For instance, Moore and Roche (2002) assume that the amount of utility that consumers gain from consumption depends in part on the amount of consumption undertaken in the previous period. This approach rationalizes the observed volatility with the seemingly small changes in consumption.

See also capital mobility; carry trade; foreign exchange intervention; interest parity conditions; monetary policy rules; peso problem; sovereign risk; sterilization

FURTHER READING

Alvarez, F., A. Atkeson, and P. J. Kehoe. 2002. "Money, Interest Rates, and Exchange Rates in Endogenously Segmented Markets." *Journal of Political Economy* 110 (1): 73–112. Offers risk-based explanations for the forward premium puzzle.

Baillie, R. T., and T. Bollerslev. 2000. "The Forward Premium Anomaly Is Not as Bad as You Think." *Journal of International Money and Finance* 19 (4): 471–88. Argues that there is a nonlinearity in the relationship between the spot rate and the forward discount. When the forward discount is large in absolute value, then the forward discount is likely to point in the right direction. When the forward discount is small, it is likely to point in the wrong direction, perhaps because transactions costs are large relative to potential gains.

Chinn, M. D., and J. A. Frankel. 1994. "Patterns in Exchange Rate Forecasts for 25 Currencies." *Journal of Money, Credit, and Banking* 26 (4) (November): 759–70. Assesses the characteristics of forecasts as measured by surveys of market participants.

Chinn, M. D., and G. Meredith. 2004. "Monetary Policy and Long Horizon Uncovered Interest Parity." *IMF Staff Papers 51* (3) (November): 409–30.

Engel, C. 1996. "The Forward Discount Anomaly and the Risk Premium: A Survey of Recent Evidence." *Journal of Empirical Finance* 3 (June): 123–92. Surveys the large literature concerned with modeling the risk premium.

———. 1999. "On the Foreign Exchange Risk Premium in Sticky-Price General Equilibrium Models." In *International Finance and Financial Crises: Essays in Honor of Robert P. Flood*, edited by Peter Isard, Assaf Razin, and Andrew Rose. Norwell, MA: Kluwer and IMF, 71–85. Offers a risk-based explanation for the forward puzzle.

Frankel, J. A., and C. M. Engel. 1984. "Do Asset Demands Optimize over the Mean and Variance of Returns? A Six Currency Test." *Journal of International Economics* 17 (3–4): 309–23. Examines the relationship between differential currency returns and the amounts of government bonds denominated in different currencies.

Frankel, J. A., and K. A. Froot. 1987. "Using Survey Data to Test Standard Propositions Regarding Exchange Rate Expectations." *American Economic Review* 77 (1): 133–53. Assesses the characteristics of forecasts as measured by surveys of market participants, and finds that these forecasts are typically biased.

Froot, K. A., and J. A. Frankel. 1989. "Forward Discount Bias: Is It an Exchange Risk Premium?" *Quarterly Journal of Economics* 104 (1): 139–61. Concludes that for the major currencies, the bias in forward rates is due to bias in exchange rate expectations.

Froot, K. A., and R. H. Thaler. 1990. "Foreign Exchange." *Journal of Economic Perspectives* 4 (3): 179–92. Surveys the literature on the forward discount.

Lewis, K. K. 1989. "Changing Beliefs and Systematic Rational Forecast Errors with Evidence from Foreign Exchange." *American Economic Review* 79 (4): 621–36. Incorporates Bayesian learning by agents about the economic environment such that their forecasts are biased for long stretches of time.

Lyons, Richard. 2001. *The Microstructure Approach to Exchange Rates*. Cambridge, MA: MIT Press. Appeals to institutional and microstructural factors to explain the presence of excess returns.

McCallum, B. T. 1994. "A Reconsideration of the Uncovered Interest Parity Relationship." *Journal of Monetary Economics* 33 (1): 105–132. Appeals to a monetary reaction function that responds to exchange rate changes, thereby making interest rates endogenous in an economic sense.

Moore, M. J. 1994. "Testing for Unbiasedness in Forward Markets." *The Manchester School* 62 (supplement): 67–78. Provides a statistical interpretation for why the forward rate is a biased predictor of the future spot exchange rate.

Moore, M. J. and M. J. Roche. 2002. "Volatile and Persistent Real Exchange Rates without the Contrivance of Sticky Prices." IDEAS. Web site of the Department of Economics, University of Connecticut. Available at http://ideas.repec.org/p/may/mayecw/n1160402.html. Incorporates a utility function with "deep habits" to explain the gap between the forward and expected future spot exchange rates.

Villanueva, O. Miguel. 2005. "FX Dynamics, Limited Participation, and the Forward Bias Anomaly." *The Financial Review* 40: 67–93. Provides econometric reinterpretations of McCallum (1994).

MENZIE D. CHINN

fragmentation

Fragmentation involves the decomposition of a production process into its constituent activities and the dispersion of those activities across national borders. It gives rise to cross-country production sharing and production networks. Under fragmentation, traded goods and services contain value added from more than one nation.

The ability to be "fragmented" into "production blocks," each capable of being carried out in a physically separate location, is in the first instance a matter of technology. Whether or not to take advantage of this facility, however, is an economic decision that depends on location-specific advantages, such as proximity to raw materials, factors of production, and markets. While the physical nature of production may remain largely unchanged, its organization undergoes significant transformation.

In addition to choosing locations for constituent activities, firms provide "service links" in order to facilitate communication and coordination and to allow for efficient and on-time transportation of parts and components within the network (Jones and Kierzkowski 1990). Hence, fragmentation will take place only where savings in production cost exceed the costs associated with service links.

When making their choices, firms must also determine whether to keep the dispersed activities under company management or to outsource them to independent contractors in so-called arm's-length relationships. The choice depends on economic as well as legal and institutional considerations; it involves trust, enforceability of contracts, and protection of intellectual property (Helpman 2006; Barba Navaretti and Venables 2004). A substantial proportion of cross-border production involves the foreign operations of the affiliates of multinational corporations, implying that a rising share of international trade is intrafirm trade.

Fragmentation, which has also been described as "breaking up the value-added chain," works particularly well between advanced and emerging economies and has grown rapidly in industries such as electronics, machinery, and textiles and apparel. Key factors facilitating this development have been reductions in trade restrictions and other barriers and cost-cutting innovations in transportation and communications technologies. The rapid spread of international production sharing is changing trade patterns, trade balance accounting, and the interaction between trade, the exchange rate, and other macroeconomic variables.

The spread of production sharing implies that traded products increasingly contain parts and components from more than one country. Hence domestic value added to a country's exports is often significantly less than the value of those exports. Chinese exports of electronic machinery, for example, incorporate imported components. Similarly, the imports of many countries contain components made in those countries. United States imports of automobiles from Mexico, for example, carry large amounts of U.S.-made components.

Production sharing gives rise to a new form of intraindustry trade, in which parts and components and finished products belonging to the same industry or sector pass back and forth among countries. This vertical intraindustry trade differs from the more traditional horizontal intraindustry trade of different varieties of the same end product.

Analytical Issues The term *fragmentation* was first used in this context by Jones and Kierzkowski (1990). Alternative terminology includes intra-product specialization and vertical specialization. The effects and implications of cross-border frag-mentation may be examined from a variety of theoretical perspectives, including Ricardian, Heck-scher-Ohlin (H-O), and imperfect competition (Arndt and Kierzkowski 2001). The first two are the workhorses of trade theory. In the Ricardian model, countries are differentiated by technology, so intra-product specialization among countries participating in production sharing is determined by location-specific technological know-how. Countries with limited technological development will engage in low-tech production, while more advanced compo-nents and assembly will be produced in countries possessing the necessary technologies.

In the Heckscher-Ohlin framework, differences in factor endowments provide the basis for special-ization, such that countries will specialize in activities that make intensive use of locally abundant factors of production. Labor-intensive component produc-tion and assembly will, therefore, be carried out in labor-abundant countries, other things being the same, while skill- and capital-intensive activities will be performed in more advanced countries. In that framework, fragmentation has effects on out-put, factor prices, trade, and welfare analogous to those associated with technological progress (Arndt 1997).

The factor-proportions view of vertical intra-industry specialization and trade is a key contribution of the H-O approach, which had been criticized in years past for its inability to explain horizontal specialization and trade. Indeed, it was this shortcom-ing that prompted the development of imperfect-competition models of international specialization and trade, in which consumers value variety and monopolistically competitive firms specialize in the production of variety. Intraindustry trade associated with production networks, on the other hand, con-sists of the movement across borders of parts, com-ponents, and end products belonging to the same industry.

Factor endowments, however, are not the only type of location advantage. Others include distance, border, country size, infrastructure, legal and finan-cial systems, and regulatory and other policies. The effects of these variables on trade in general have been studied with the aid of gravity models, which posit that trade between two countries will fall with dis-tance and the thickness of the border; that country size measured in various ways affects bilateral trade positively; and that strong and transparent legal and institutional structures, ample infrastructure, and protrade regulatory policies increase trade.

The gravity equation is now beginning to be employed in the context of production networks, for the purpose of which it must be amended in a variety of ways. There is, for example, more than one dis-tance to be accounted for. In addition to the distance between the importer and exporter of the final product, there is distance between countries sup-plying parts and components and the country in which the final good is assembled. Regional cluster-ing of supplier nations (as in Southeast Asia) is a distinct location advantage.

Foreign Direct Investment Production networks with developing economies typically require up-front capital formation, financed at least in part by inflows of foreign direct investment (FDI) and technology from advanced countries. Foreign investors erect production facilities and install infrastructure, bring in skilled workers, and transfer technology at levels of sophistication beyond those available in the country. While such activities violate several assumptions of the H-O model, that model is nevertheless useful in predicting the pattern of FDI flows.

The investment involved is vertical (VFDI), in-tended to support vertical or intraproduct speciali-zation. In a world of cross-border production frag-mentation, the H-O model predicts that VFDI will tend to flow from capital- and skill-abundant, labor-scarce countries to labor-abundant economies. The Ricardian model predicts that such flows will move from technologically advanced to technologically emerging economies.

As already noted, factor endowments are only one type of location advantage, and therefore cannot fully explain movements of FDI. Once again, the gravity model offers a way of accounting for additional location-specific considerations—including distance, country size, border effects, and various institutional and policy-related factors. The bulk of the existing empirical literature on FDI, however, covers periods dominated by horizontal foreign direct investment (HFDI), which prevails among advanced countries and which continues to be the dominant form of FDI.

According to this evidence, FDI responds positively to distance. The explanation lies in the fact that in horizontal specialization FDI is a substitute for exports. As distance and its costs increase, exports are replaced by on-site production for the local market and hence FDI flows rise. Vertical FDI, on the other hand, moves to support production sharing. Hence, when distance raises the costs associated with servicing a network, production sharing becomes unprofitable and FDI declines.

Multinational Companies While many multinationals go abroad to produce for the local market, an increasing number have become involved in production networks, a process in which affiliate operations play a key role. Often, the initial organizational structure follows a "hub-and-spoke" pattern, with affiliates in several countries trading directly with the parent company, but less with one another. As interactions become more sophisticated and infrastructure is developed, true networks evolve in which trade takes place among affiliates located in various countries, as well as between affiliates and local firms. This pattern is exemplified by Japanese multinationals operating in Southeast Asia (Kimura and Ando 2003).

Agglomeration of activities is important in this context, because it generates positive externalities. Clusters of multinationals operating in a given country or in several adjacent countries attract and train workers, improve access to finance and other services, and generate knowledge spillovers that raise productivity and reduce costs. The creation of such an environment benefits from supportive public policies and public investment in infrastructure. A classic example is Ireland and the electronics industry. Such an environment generates positive agglomeration effects, as workers with industry-specific skills migrate into the area and knowledge spillovers occur.

In this setting, local producers are encouraged to enter the industry as suppliers of goods and services to the multinationals. There is evidence that arm's-length trade is growing in Southeast Asia as foreign multinationals rely increasingly on local suppliers. For developing countries, this opens another path to industrialization.

Scale economies are important in production networks and are exploited by multinationals. Since neither the Ricardo nor Heckscher-Ohlin framework is capable of handling scale economies and externalities, the imperfect competition literature provides important insights. Scale economies come into play on both the production side and in the provision of service links among production blocks. If production of each part or component is concentrated in one location, for example, longer runs permit exploitation of internal scale economies at each location. Meanwhile, agglomeration and clustering of producers generate economies that are external to plant and firm.

In the provision of service links, the fixed costs associated with establishing a communications network can be spread over larger numbers of units and firms as the size of the network and the number of participating entities expand. Access to a service network encourages agglomeration of firms in a country or region. Where individual countries tend to be small, cooperative policies among countries are required to reap the benefits of agglomeration.

Productivity, Employment, and Wages The spread of fragmentation has sounded political alarm bells in advanced countries about jobs and wages not only in manufacturing, but in services industries, as "offshoring" of call centers, help desks, programming, and ticketing operations has proliferated. There is no doubt that jobs of workers whose functions are shifted to foreign locations are lost. But if cross-border sourcing of components raises competitiveness and lowers prices of final products or services, thereby increasing sales and thus output, then jobs will be created elsewhere in the industry or more generally in the economy.

With respect to wages, there are two concerns. First, production sharing with low-wage countries may exert downward pressure not only on the wages of workers whose jobs are lost, but on wages generally in a "race to the bottom." Second, it may change the wage distribution against low-skilled workers and widen the wage gap between skilled and unskilled workers.

The available evidence is mixed, in part because it is not easy to separate the effects of fragmentation from those of technological change and of other factors affecting employment and wages (Feenstra 1998). The outcome further depends on the sector in which fragmentation occurs, on the skill ratios in the affected industries, and on the relationship of each skill category to capital. In a framework in which fragmentation occurs in many industries, moreover, there will be "onshoring" as well as "offshoring," so that jobs lost in one sector must be balanced against jobs gained in others. Under such circumstances, the problem is mainly one of matching unemployed workers with emerging jobs. This is the familiar trade-adjustment problem.

Regional Integration In recent years, regional production sharing and trade in parts and components has grown rapidly. This growth has been facilitated by preferential trade liberalization. While production sharing is generally welfare-improving under free trade and in preferential trade areas (PTAs), rules of origin that restrict the movement of components from outside the PTA can introduce significant elements of trade diversion.

Production sharing is changing the nature of regional integration, in that it requires deeper integration than the removal of tariffs and other restrictions on the flow of goods and services. It calls for liberalization of investment and for the cross-border movement of persons, as well as harmonization of technical standards, regulatory policies, and dispute settlement procedures. To the extent that cross-border integration of production at the level of industries reduces asymmetries and promotes conver-

gence of business cycles, it helps pave the way for greater regional monetary cooperation, including monetary union.

When industries become linked across borders, production sharing tends to reduce the sensitivity of trade flows to exchange rate changes. Consider a depreciation of the Mexican peso against the dollar, which raises the price of imports of U.S.-made components for incorporation into passenger vehicles. When these vehicles are exported to the United States, the dollar's appreciation has an offsetting effect. Hence trade flows associated with production sharing are less sensitive to exchange rate movements than other types of trade. This has implications for intraregional exchange-rate arrangements (Arndt and Huemer 2007).

Fragmentation and Interdependence Production sharing allows countries to reap the benefits of increased specialization. In the context of standard trade theory, intraproduct specialization pushes out the production possibility curve and thereby allows countries to reach higher consumption frontiers. In this sense, its effects are analogous to those of technological progress and factor accumulation.

But it also links countries more closely to their trading partners and thereby reduces policy autonomy and increases interdependence. It goes well beyond trade in promoting economic integration by linking industries at the level of production. Countries are more open and thus more exposed to external shocks. A group of countries operating in a production network will experience similar shocks. As more industries become involved in networks, cross-country asymmetries decline. Business cycles tend to converge. The pressures—and incentives—for policy cooperation increase.

Fragmentation is an important feature of globalization. Products become internationalized, national markets are more closely linked to those abroad, economywide behavior patterns converge, and the domain of overlapping policy interests expands.

See also agglomeration and foreign direct investment; economies of scale; gravity models; Heckscher-Ohlin model; intrafirm trade; intraindustry trade; outsourcing/offshoring; Ricardian model; technology spillovers

FURTHER READING

Arndt, Sven W. 1997. "Globalization and the Open Economy." *North American Journal of Economics and Finance* 8 (1): 71–79. Derivation of key results of fragmentation in terms of the Heckscher-Ohlin Model.

Arndt, Sven W., and Alexander Huemer. 2007. "Trade, Production Networks and the Exchange Rate." *Journal of Economic Asymmetries* 4 (1): 11–39. Examines the effect of global production networks on the sensitivity of trade flows to exchange rates.

Arndt, Sven W., and Henryk Kierzkowski, eds. 2001. *Fragmentation: New Production Patterns in the World Economy.* Oxford: Oxford University Press. A collection of papers dealing with various aspects of fragmentation.

Barba Navaretti, Giorgio, and Anthony J. Venables. 2004. *Multinational Firms in the World Economy.* Princeton, NJ: Princeton University Press. A comprehensive study of the FDI, multinationals, and trade.

Deardorff, Alan V. 2001. "Fragmentation in Simple Trade Models." *North American Journal of Economics and Finance* 12 (2): 121–37. Provides a more formal assessment of the effects of fragmentation.

Feenstra, Robert C. 1998. "Integration of Trade and Disintegration of Production in the Global Economy." *Journal of Economic Perspectives* 12 (4): 31–50. Overview of theoretical and empirical issues related to fragmentation.

Helpman, Elhanan. 2006. "Trade, FDI, and the Organization of Firms." NBER Working Paper No. 12091. Cambridge, MA: National Bureau of Economic Research. A comprehensive overview of modeling multinationals.

Jones, Ronald W., and Henryk Kierzkowski. 1990. "The Role of Services in Production and International Trade." In *The Political Economy of International Trade*, edited by R. W. Jones and Anne O. Krueger. Oxford: Basil Blackwell, 31–48. Discussion of the role of service links in production networks.

Kimura, Fukunari, and Mitsuyo Ando. 2003. "Fragmentation and Agglomeration Matter: Japanese Multinationals in Latin America and East Asia." *North American Journal of Economics and Finance* 14 (3): 287–317. An empirical study of Japanese MNCs operating in the two regions with a focus on behavioral differences.

SVEN W. ARNDT

■ free trade area

A free trade area (FTA) is created by an agreement among a group of countries to eliminate trade barriers on most (if not all) goods between them. FTAs can be, and often are, regional and dictated by geographical considerations, such as the North American Free Trade Area, composed of the United States, Canada, and Mexico. They can also occur between countries that are far apart, as with the U.S.-Israel or U.S.-Singapore FTAs. Countries can belong to more than one FTA. The number of FTAs has increased rapidly since the early 1990s. For example, as of October 2007, the World Trade Organization (WTO) reported that approximately 110 notified (that is, officially existing) FTAs (excluding accessions) were active at that time.

In contrast to a customs union (CU), which sets a common external tariff, FTAs do not necessarily equalize their members' tariffs on nonmembers. With differences in tariffs, rules of origin (ROOs) prevent trade in a product from going through the country with the lowest tariff on it and then being shipped within the FTA, since a good is eligible for zero tariffs in the FTA only if it originates there and ROOs specify the conditions required for origin to be granted.

There are large differences in the effects of an FTA with and without ROOs. In the absence of ROOs, an FTA results in large changes in trade flows as trade seeks the lowest tariff entry point into the FTA. Goods are then transshipped to their final destination in the FTA. Of course this results in large tariff revenue transfer effects as this trade deflection transfers tariff revenue to the country with the lowest tariff entry point. As pointed out by Richardson (1995), this can result in a race to the bottom in setting tariffs. Moreover, in the presence of transshipment costs, such arbitrage may waste valuable resources: if such waste outweighs the positive effects of lower tariffs, an FTA without ROOs may even reduce welfare overall.

In the presence of ROOs, however, simple transshipment is not possible. Nevertheless, some trade deflection may still be possible. By shipping domestic production to its FTA partners and meeting domestic demand via imports, the low-tariff country can still attract trade to its ports.

The Legal Basis of FTAs Signatories to the General Agreement on Trade and Tariffs (GATT) accord most-favored-nation (MFN) status to one another. This means that they cannot offer anyone else a more favorable (lower) tariff. How then can FTAs, which are by their very nature discriminatory, be legal? The answer lies in Article XXIV of GATT, which explicitly allows FTAs and CUs as exceptions to this rule as long as substantially all trade is free among members, and trade barriers with nonmembers is not higher on average after the FTA or CU.

The Welfare Effects of FTAs Although one thinks of FTAs as liberalizing of trade, and trade liberalization as welfare improving, neither may be true. If one pictures an FTA as only reducing the tariff on each good to the lowest tariff set by any of the FTA members, one might be inclined to think that such an FTA is welfare improving. Even this is not necessarily so, however. The theory of the second best says that welfare could fall with liberalization if not all distortions are removed, and consequently, even in such a stylized setting, an FTA may reduce welfare.

The usual argument showing the possibility of welfare loss is Viner's (1950). If an FTA is formed with the high-cost supplier, what is called trade diversion occurs. The country imports from its higher-cost FTA partner rather than the lower-cost country outside the FTA, so the gain in consumer surplus or welfare from lower tariffs and resulting lower consumer prices could easily fall short of the loss in tariff revenue. Trade-diverting customs unions could reduce welfare, whereas trade-creating customs unions, those formed with the lowest-cost supplier, would raise welfare.

FTAs need not be liberalizing, since if ROOs are hard enough to meet, they will raise costs by enough that no firm will find it worthwhile to meet them in order to obtain zero tariffs. In this case, FTAs do nothing. It is even worse if ROOs are strict and raise costs a good deal, but are still worth meeting. In this case, even if prices fall a little, the loss from the cost increase due to ROOs, which wastes resources, and the tariff revenue forgone, could easily reduce welfare relative to that prior to an FTA.

Moreover, recent work in this area has shown that the goals of improved market access and welfare may well be in conflict. Ju and Krishna (2000) show that if the excess demand for exported goods does not respond to changes in the prices of imported goods, then any policy that increases imports must also reduce welfare. Anderson and Neary (2007) interpret these results in terms of the generalized mean and variance of tariffs. They show that welfare is negatively related and import volume is positively related to the generalized variance and this causes a tension in the two objectives.

Stepping Stones, Stumbling Blocks, or Building Blocks? Of significant policy relevance is whether FTAs help or hurt the chances of further liberalization along multilateral lines. Bhagwati (1991) has been a vocal opponent of FTAs, arguing that they dampen the enthusiasm of a country for nondiscriminatory reform such as the multilateral trade negotiations held under the auspices of GATT/WTO.

The first question to ask is why multilateral free trade should be seen as more desirable than bilateral free trade. After all, if an FTA is a microcosm of the whole world, then there is not much to gain from global free trade. This argument neglects two factors, however. First, increasing the size of the world does raise welfare when goods are differentiated (as larger economies have greater variety and therefore higher real income and welfare) or there are increasing returns to scale (as larger economies can better exploit economies of scale and therefore have lower prices and higher welfare). Second, bilateral arrangements are not usually of this form but tend to occur between similar countries first, extending to others later. This makes sense, as such FTAs are likely to face less resistance as they have little effect on factor prices and bring gains from reaping economies of scale and greater product variety.

Levy (1997) argues persuasively that, for political economy reasons, bilateral free-trade agreements can undermine political support for further multilateral trade liberalization. He uses a median voter model where agents have different endowments of capital, and where bilateral free trade could occur before multilateral free trade. With perfect foresight, no proposal that makes the median voter worse off than under multilateral free trade can occur. Thus if multilateral free trade is not possible directly, it cannot become so after a bilateral agreement. As a result, a bilateral agreement cannot be a stepping stone to multilateral free trade. It can, however, be a stumbling block. A free trade area has two effects in his model. It reduces the earnings of the relatively scarce factor in a country via standard Hecksher-Ohlin channels (since via trade, the relatively scarce factor in a country becomes in effect less scarce and so its price falls), and it raises the real income and, hence, welfare of all agents via increased variety. When the latter effect dominates, as it does if the FTA was among similar countries, a bilateral trade agreement makes most agents better off. But by doing so, it raises the reservation utility (the welfare under the status quo) for future multilateral agreements. Multilateral free trade would raise the gains to those with the most capital but reduce the gains to those with little capital, and as a result the median voter could be worse off with multilateral free trade. Thus, even if total welfare is highest under multilateral free trade, bilateral arrangements such as an FTA can prevent it from occurring.

A classic argument by Johnson (1967) is that multilateral reform would dilute existing preferences and therefore would provoke resistance by those adversely affected. For example, Mexican suppliers who are at an advantage under the North American Free Trade Agreement (NAFTA) would lobby against a reduction in the U.S. MFN tariff. Under the EBA (Everything but Arms) agreement of the European Union (EU), the poorest countries are allowed to export all goods other than arms to the EU market free of tariffs. If the EU reduced its MFN tariff, however, these preferences would be diluted and these poorest counties would lose their EU market to more competitive suppliers and would lobby hard against such liberalization on the part of the EU.

Limão (2006) has shown that there is evidence that such concerns are important. Using data on U.S. tariff reductions during the Uruguay Round of WTO negotiations, he shows that tariffs tended to be higher on goods that were traded in NAFTA. Moreover, as a result, the reciprocating tariff cuts tended also to be smaller.

Baldwin (2006) takes the opposing viewpoint. He argues that FTAs are building blocks for multilateral liberalization. He argues for a domino effect: once a group of countries form an FTA, then even if some countries stayed out of the FTA to begin with, once it is large enough, they would find themselves with so few trading partners that they would want to join! As a result, maybe there would be waves of integration: first a regional trading arrangement forms with a core group, then the next tier of countries joins, and so on. What happens more often, however, is that countries belong to many FTAs, and free trade is not a transitive relation. If A has an FTA with B and B has an FTA with C, this is not the same as A having an FTA with B and C. Goods from A will not have origin in B and therefore will not get zero tariffs when exported to C. Some exports from A via B to C could occur, however, with B's production being exported to C and B consuming A's products.

What, then, is the role of FTAs today and what can we expect in the future? Clearly, FTAs are here to stay. We cannot expect overlapping FTAs to do what multilateral free trade would, and there is empirical evidence that they act as stumbling blocks to global free trade. For these reasons, their proliferation is cause for concern. On the plus side, however, it is likely that their formation results in economic gains, both static and dynamic. Since FTAs may be possible (as sensitive sectors can be isolated via the use of restrictive ROOs) when multilateral free trade is not, it is as yet far from obvious what their net welfare effects are.

See also common market; customs unions; Free Trade Area of the Americas (FTAA); multilateralism; North American Free Trade Agreement (NAFTA); regionalism; rules of origin

FURTHER READING

Anderson, James E., and Peter Neary. 2007. "Welfare versus Market Access: The Implications of Tariff Structure for Tariff Reform." *Journal of International Economics* 71 (1): 187–205. Explains why the mean and the variance of tariffs matter in different ways for welfare and market access.

Baldwin, Richard E. 2006. "Multilateralizing Regionalism: Spaghetti Bowls as Building Blocs on the Path to Global Free Trade." *World Economy* 29 (11): 1451–1518. Discusses the possible positive effects of FTAs.

Bhagwati, Jagdish. 1991. *The World Trading System at Risk.* Princeton, NJ: Princeton University Press. A nontechnical introduction to the role of the WTO in the global economy.

Johnson, Harry G. 1967. *Economic Policies towards Less Developed Countries.* Washington DC: Brookings Institution. Outdated, but a classic.

Ju, Jiandong, and Kala Krishna. 2000. "Welfare and Market Access Effects of Piecemeal Tariff Reform." *Journal of International Economics* 51 (2): 305–16. Explores the trade-off between market access and welfare in the context of piecemeal policy reform.

Levy, Philip I. 1997. "A Political-Economic Analysis of Free-Trade Agreements." *American Economic Review* 87 (4): 506–19. An important early paper on the stepping stones versus stumbling blocks debate.

Limão, Nuno. 2006. "Preferential Trade Agreements as Stumbling Blocks for Multilateral Trade Liberalization: Evidence for the U.S." *American Economic Review* 96 (3): 896–914. Shows that the presence of an FTA seems to be correlated with reduced multilateral liberalization in goods traded in the FTA.

Richardson, Martin. 1995. "Tariff Revenue Competition in a Free Trade Area." *European Economic Review* 39: 1429–37. Looks at the incentives for tariff setting in an FTA.

Viner, Jacob. 1950. *The Customs Union Issue.* New York: Carnegie Endowment for International Peace. Old but still a classic.

KALA KRISHNA

■ Free Trade Area of the Americas (FTAA)

The United States and Latin America have long resisted what geography would seem to dictate: a special inter-American relationship built around open trade and investment flows. U.S. foreign policy has generally focused on other regions of the world—notably Europe and Asia—and eschewed regional favorites altogether in favor of a global reach. In Latin America, nationalists of the right and left have preferred to limit their dependence on U.S. power by diversifying their relations through stronger ties to Europe or other Latin American nations. Nevertheless, there have been periods in history when Latin America has reached out to the United States and the United States has responded affirmatively. The 1990s were one such period, and the centerpiece of such inter-American cooperation was the Free Trade Area of the Americas (FTAA).

The idea of a hemispheric free trade zone was not new when policymakers began to discuss it in earnest in the final decade of the 20th century. The goal can be traced back at least to Simón Bolívar (whose integrationist vision sometimes excluded but sometimes seemed to include North America), and it was discussed at the time of the founding of the Pan-American Union at the end of the 19th century. Presidents Ronald Reagan (1981–89) and George H. W. Bush (1989–93) made rhetorical references to the idea of a hemispheric free trade zone. However, this vague aspiration only became a concrete policy option when Latin American governments pressed a reluctant United States to take their free-trade agenda seriously. In 1990, it was Mexican president Carlos Salinas de Gortari who proposed a free trade accord to President Bush—the seed that became the North American Free Trade Agreement (NAFTA). It was the Chileans who pressed three successive U.S. administrations for a free trade agreement. It was the Latin Americans who proposed to the Bill Clinton White House that the United States convene a post-NAFTA meeting of hemispheric leaders to spread the spirit of NAFTA southward, and who insisted that the centerpiece of the subsequent 1994 Miami Summit be the Free Trade Area of the Americas (FTAA).

The Latin Americans had good reasons to pursue hemispheric integration. An FTAA would permit them secure access to the world's largest and most dynamic market, and would signal to investors a more stable policy environment and a warmer and more predictable business climate. A regional free trade alliance would focus national policy debates on the next stage of reforms (following on the controversial but generally successful Washington consensus financial stabilization programs) required to promote international competitiveness, including further market liberalization, effective regulation and competition policies, and modern infrastructure in, for example, telecommunications, energy, and transportation. Politically, Latin America's democratic leaders were looking to Washington to bolster their position against the ever-present authoritarian tendencies in Latin American polities.

For the United States, an FTAA would open markets for trade and investment, giving U.S. firms preferential access against competitors from Europe and Asia. It could help Latin American countries to lock in macroeconomic reforms, accelerate steps toward market liberalization, and enhance the legitimacy of still-fragile democratic governments. Furthermore, on issues from counternarcotics to counterterrorism, environmental protection to energy cooperation, free trade was widely understood as generating positive externalities or spillover effects in diplomatic negotiations. Countries linked together in an FTAA could also serve as useful allies in global forums, including in World Trade Organization (WTO) trade negotiations. At the same time, fearing job loss especially in low-wage goods, environmental destruction, and a broad-based lowering of social standards, in a "race to the bottom," powerful, contrary voices in the United States spoke out vociferously against a regional trade accord and accelerating globalization more generally. Still other critics questioned the value of focusing trade negotiations on Latin America, as opposed to larger markets in Asia and Europe, and the WTO.

From 1994 to 2005, hemispheric trade negotiations proceeded on three tracks. As follow-on to the Miami Summit and the launch of the FTAA nego-

tiations, an elaborate web of negotiating committees and working groups evolved into a network of as many as 1,000 officials. But, with a deadline of 2005, negotiations proceeded at a leisurely pace and repeated draft texts left the more contentious issues in brackets. The United States pressed for liberalization in manufacturing and services, while Brazil and other agricultural exporters focused on U.S. protectionism and fiscal subsidies in products such as sugar, beef, cotton, peanuts, and orange juice that undercut the competitiveness of Latin American producers. In 2002, on the eve of off-year elections, the U.S. Congress passed a farm bill that sharply increased such agricultural subsidies, embarrassing U.S. trade officials who for years had been chastising the Europeans and Japanese for protecting their domestic farmers at the expense of global efficiency and developing-country producers.

The two leading countries in the FTAA negotiations, the United States and Brazil, turned to the Doha Development Round of negotiations within the framework of the WTO to help resolve some of the agricultural issues. However, the global WTO seemed no more capable of cutting the Gordian knot of agricultural subsidies than did the regional FTAA forum.

As the Doha Round prospects dimmed and the FTAA negotiations stumbled, many countries turned to less ambitious, more manageable bilateral and subregional trade arrangements. Following NAFTA, the United States ratified similar agreements with Chile and Central America (CAFTA), and concluded negotiations with Panama, Colombia, and Peru (approved by the Colombian and Peruvian legislatures but by the end of 2007 the U.S. Congress had approved only the Peruvian accord). Trade-oriented Mexico and Chile negotiated numerous bilateral accords with other Latin American nations as well as with the European Union and a growing number of Asian nations.

As the FTAA negotiations slowed and the 2005 deadline approached, neither the United States nor Brazil was willing to tackle domestic protectionist interests to close the deal. The Bush administration became embroiled in Iraq and its domestic leverage declined, just as the Democrats in Congress became emboldened and, increasingly, fell under the influence of organized labor and other voices who demanded a new "fairer" approach to globalization. As the overall U.S. trade deficit ballooned, Democrats held proposed trade accords hostage, as leverage to overhaul other aspects of U.S. trade policy, and to better position the Democrats in upcoming elections. In Brazil, the 2002 election of Luiz Inácio Lula da Silva strengthened the nationalist forces in the powerful foreign ministry, Itamaraty, many of whose diplomats perceived the FTAA as strengthening the geopolitical position of the United States at the expense of Brazil's hegemonic aspirations in South America.

At the 2005 Summit of the Americas at Mar del Plata, Argentina, it became clear that political winds were shifting in South America. Argentine president and summit host Nestor Kirchner allied with Venezuelan president Hugo Chávez in adopting highly critical postures toward the FTAA. Emboldened by strong trade surpluses driven by the global commodity boom, the two outspoken Latin American leaders were critical of U.S. foreign policy and in particular President George W. Bush, attacking "neoliberalism" and the Washington consensus in favor of more state-directed, protectionist domestic economic policies. The 2001–2 crash of the Argentine financial system had embittered relations between Argentina and the United States and the International Monetary Fund (IMF), while the Kirchner administration focused more on domestic recovery than on international trade negotiations. In an overt challenge to the FTAA, Chávez launched his Bolivarian Alternative for the Americas (ALBA), and enlisted Cuba, Bolivia, and Nicaragua in what appeared to be mainly a series of foreign assistance and barter agreements, exchanging subsidized Venezuelan oil for trade and, in the case of Cuba, technical assistance. Kirchner helped Chávez pursue membership in the four-nation Mercosur—in part to offset the dominance of Brazil within the South American integration scheme—injecting that accord with a more ideological and anti-U.S. flavor.

Thus by 2007 the FTAA seemed to have reached a halfway point. A series of agreements links Canada, the United States, Mexico, the Central American nations, Chile and Peru, and possibly Colombia and Panama (pending U.S. congressional approval). NAFTA has facilitated dramatic increases in trade and investment flows and has generated a number of proposals to deepen the tripartite integration in areas such as infrastructure, energy, education, and immigration; politically, NAFTA weathered the challenge of the hotly contested 2006 presidential elections in Mexico. CAFTA has captured the imaginations of the Central American governments and private sectors; Sandinista leader Daniel Ortega, on regaining the Nicaraguan presidency in 2006, said his nation should take advantage of the market opportunities opened by CAFTA. The NAFTA and CAFTA nations faced the challenge of better integrating those accords (together with Chile and Peru, and possibly Colombia and Panama) to reduce inconsistencies and, possibly, create an umbrella governance mechanism. For its part, South America has become progressively fragmented by conflicting ideologies, economic policy preferences, and leadership styles, and none of the proposed integration schemes—the FTAA, Mercosur, ALBA—seems capable of bridging the divides. The promise, often voiced by Brazil, that Mercosur could serve as a stepping stone toward the larger FTAA, seems increasingly remote.

The future of the FTAA, therefore, remains uncertain. Has a historic opportunity been lost, or was the hemisphere simply experiencing a pause in the long march toward regional economic integration? One scenario, based on the coalescing of new domestic coalitions forming common cause against local vested interests, envisions a renewed push in the United States and Brazil to complete the deal. In such a scenario, other South American countries might want to avoid being left out and join the Brazilian-U.S. bandwagon, marginalizing Chávez and his ALBA. Alternatively, the hemisphere might become increasingly divided between a northern tier—NAFTA plus CAFTA—and a southern tier fractured by the simmering rivalries among Venezuela, Brazil, and Argentina, and the separate path chosen by an increasingly open, globalized Chile.

See also Andean Community; Central American Common Market (CACM); Central American–Dominican Republic Free Trade Area (CAFTA-DR); free trade area; International Monetary Fund (IMF); Mercosur; North American Free Trade Agreement (NAFTA); Washington consensus; World Trade Organization

FURTHER READING

Corrales, Javier, and Richard Feinberg. 1999. "Regimes of Cooperation in the Western Hemisphere: Power, Interests, and Intellectual Traditions." *International Studies Quarterly* 43 (March): 1–36. Traces the ups and downs of inter-American cooperation in the last 200 years, finding that major leaps forward in inter-American cooperation occur only when prointegration forces are strong in both the United States and leading Latin American countries. This oft-cited article was published before the deterioration in inter-American relations that transpired during the early 21st century.

Elliott, Kimberly Ann. 2004. *Labor Standards, Development, and CAFTA.* International Economics Policy Briefs 04-2. Washington, DC: Institute for International Economics. A balanced review of the arguments for and against including labor standards in international trade agreements.

Feinberg, Richard. 2002. "Regionalism and Domestic Politics: U.S–Latin American Trade Policy in the Bush Era." *Latin American Politics and Society* 44 (4): 127–51.

Argues that Latin Americans have sought to impose their free trade policy agenda on a reluctant United States and assesses the trade policies of the Bush administration and the divisions within the U.S. political system regarding trade with developing countries.

Jatar, Ana Julia, and Sidney Weintraub, eds. 1997. *Integrating the Hemisphere: Perspectives from Latin America and the Caribbean.* Washington, DC: The Inter-American Dialogue. A valuable collection of essays by leading Latin American economists explaining the trade policies of key countries and subregions.

Salazar-Xirinachs, Jose Manuel, and Maryse Roberts, eds. 2001. *Toward Free Trade in the Americas.* Washington, DC: Brookings Institution. Provides an overview of integration processes in the Americas at the turn of the millennium, identifies areas of convergence and divergence among the various regional trade agreements, and explores in detail the complicated, unresolved issues that eventually stymied FTAA negotiators.

Schott, Jeffrey J. 2001. *Prospects for Free Trade in the Americas.* Washington, DC: Institute for International Economics. Explores the rationales for inter-American economic integration and, while offering a generally optimistic assessment of prospects for the FTAA, also analyzes the serious obstacles to progress. Considers the debates and procedures in the U.S. Congress and the "readiness" of individual Latin American countries to participate in a hemispherewide free trade zone.

RICHARD FEINBERG

◼ gains from trade

The theory of international trade can be viewed as an application of positive economics (economics focused on establishing facts, in contrast with normative economics, which focuses on questions of policy). This theory seeks to determine the prices at which commodities are exchanged on world markets (the so-called terms of trade) and traces the causes of trade to comparative advantage, the principle by which a nation that opens to international trade is led to specialize in and export certain commodities and to import others. From the theory's inception in the early 19th century, economists showed an even stronger interest in the gains from trade, that is, the welfare implications of trade for the countries that participate in it. As Richard E. Caves (1960, 6) points out, "Classical international trade theory was concerned first of all with the gains from trade, and only occasionally with the analysis of international trade by means of a formal, determinate model." Aside from formal modeling, it remains true that gains from trade and causes of trade were closely linked by economists of the classical school because of their strong interest in economic policy. Their main reason for studying the causes of trade is that it benefits countries that engage in it. The intimate connection between trade and its welfare implications is captured in the titles that Jacob Viner assigned to the last two chapters of his magisterial *Studies in the Theory of International Trade*: "Gains from Trade: The Doctrine of Comparative Costs" and "Gains from Trade: The Maximization of Real Income." As Viner states, "Recognition of its 'welfare analysis' orientation is essential to the understanding and appraisal of the classical doctrine" (1937, 437).

Does international trade always benefit the countries that participate in it? Some observers, both economists and statesmen, have expressed skepticism about the existence of "gains" on a national level and believe they can carry a negative sign, in which case they should be labeled "losses from trade." Advocates for or against greater freedom of trade have argued with each other for centuries, and there is no reason to expect such arguments ever to cease. Although it is important to recognize these controversies over the benefits of free trade to the world as a whole, to a subset of countries that contemplate the creation of a free trade area, or to a single country, they can be fully addressed only from a multidisciplinary perspective that includes economic, political, sociological, environmental, labor, and other effects.

The gains from trade are important for understanding the world economy since the perception of what such gains (or losses) consist of has led for centuries to the implementation of trade policies such as trade restrictions (tariffs or quotas), or conversely the liberalization of trade adopted in the forum of bilateral or multilateral negotiations. The term *gains from trade* can apply to various types of economic agents not limited to nation-states, such as regions of a country (economic or geographic) or even smaller units such as firms or individuals. Since nations are regarded in this entry as the main agents of interest, a question immediately arises: If some groups or individuals gain from trade (or from the partial removal of trade restrictions) while others lose, does "the nation" gain or lose? This issue, which is considered in the next section, explains why trade and trade policies are such controversial issues at both the national and international level. Before examining how the gains from trade were described and quantified by pamphleteers, economists, and schools of economic thought since the early 18th century, it is helpful to set out how contemporary trade theorists define and measure them on the assumption that all individuals in a country are alike, or that any losers from trade are compensated.

Definitions of the Gains from Trade The gains from trade can be measured by either the *compensating variation* (CV) or the *equivalent variation* (EV). Their definitions given here can easily be generalized to economies with multiple commodities, but are best understood in the context of an economy with two commodities (good 1 and good 2). If the superscripts *a* and *t* refer to equilibrium values of variables in autarky (a term describing self-sufficiency or no trade) and free trade, the CV is the amount of income that would need to be withdrawn in an economy trading at the free trade prices (p_1^t, p_2^t) so that consumers can buy the same consumption bundle they chose under autarky, (c_1^a, c_2^a), rather than their preferred consumption bundle under free trade, (c_1^t, c_2^t). In algebraic terms,

$$CV = p_1^t c_1^t + p_2^t c_2^t - (p_1^t c_1^a + p_2^t c_2^a). \qquad (1)$$

The EV uses autarky prices rather than free trade prices as reference prices to measure the gain in welfare, so that

$$EV = p_1^a c_1^t + p_2^a c_2^t - (p_1^a c_1^a + p_2^a c_2^a). \qquad (2)$$

The EV can be interpreted as the amount of money that would have to be donated to consumers under autarky to allow them to purchase the same consumption bundle they choose under free trade. Since the consumption bundles (c_1^a, c_2^a) and (c_1^t, c_2^t) are valued at different relative prices in (1) and (2), the magnitudes of the CV and EV are usually different, and there is no reason to believe that either one is a superior measure of the gains from trade.

The CV and EV are illustrated in figure 1. If good 1 is plotted on the horizontal axis and good 2 on the vertical axis, DE is the concave production possibility frontier (PPF) that shows the output combinations that a neoclassical economy can produce with its given technology and factor endowments. If A is the point of equilibrium in autarky, the autarky price ratio is given by the slope of p^a, a line tangent to DE at A. If trade becomes possible at terms of trade given by the slope of line p^t, the production point moves from A to P, and the consumption point from A to C. The economy's comparative advantage in good 1 leads it to specialize partially in that commodity, and to export BP of good 1 in exchange for CB of good 2. For this reason, CBP is known as the economy's "trade triangle." The exports of good 1, BP or JK, equal production OK minus consumption OJ, and the imports CB of good 2 equal consumption CJ minus production PK (= BJ). If the exportable good 1 is the *numéraire*, or unit of account in which prices are measured, and AF is drawn parallel to p^t, the CV for the passage from autarky to free trade is FP. If CH is drawn parallel to p^a, the EV is GH, which usually differs in length from FP.

The CV and EV represent attempts to measure in terms of good 1 the "distance" between the consumption bundles C and A, or the enhanced welfare of consumers due to trade. A more intuitive way to recognize the existence of gains from trade is to note that the free trade consumption bundle C is located outside the PPF DE and is therefore unavailable to the economy in autarky (Corden 1984). Since C is chosen under free trade in preference to any point on

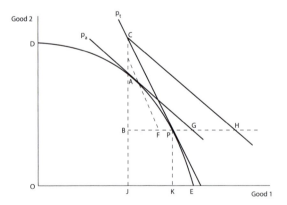

Figure 1

Gains from trade in a neoclassical economy

DE such as A, consumers are *potentially* better off under free trade since the gainers are always able to compensate the losers while remaining better off than in autarky (Samuelson 1939). In the absence of compensation, and in recognition of the fact that free trade usually produces both gainers and losers, a "social welfare function" is sometimes invoked that weights different persons' utilities according to the tastes of a dictator or decision-maker (benevolent or otherwise). The algebraic sum of these weighted utilities may be higher or lower than in autarky. Samuelson (1939) also made an observation, subsequently confirmed by other economists, that the gains from trade increase with the difference between the autarky and free trade price ratios. If these price ratios are identical, the economy remains in a state of autarky and there are no gains from trade.

If an economy trades according to its comparative advantage, does it always gain from trade? Leaving aside distributional issues, cases of foreign or colonial exploitation, "unequal exchange" and various distortions to which an economy may be subject (which are considered later), the answer is yes in the vast majority of cases. But there are exceptions where welfare under free trade is the same as in autarky, such as the case of an economy whose comparative advantage leads it to export a commodity it was not consuming before trade (Maneschi 1998a). Moreover when a large economy with a linear PPF attempts to trade with a much smaller one, it cannot fully specialize in its export commodity and faces terms of trade identical to its autarky price ratio, with zero gains from trade.

18th-Century Perspectives on the Gains from Trade In the 18th century, economists measured the gains from trade in accordance with what Viner calls the "18th-century rule," which postulates that "it pays to import commodities from abroad whenever they can be obtained in exchange for exports at a smaller real cost than their production at home would entail" (Viner 1937, 440), thus reflecting the benefits of trade as an indirect method of production. The earliest numerical example of the application of this "rule" was given by Henry Martyn (1701, 583): "If nine cannot produce above three Bushels of Wheat in *England*, if by equal Labour they might procure nine Bushels from another Country, to imploy these in agriculture at home, is to imploy nine to do no more work than might be done as well by three; . . . is the loss of six Bushels of Wheat; is therefore the loss of so much value." His numbers can be interpreted in terms of the two-commodity example of the previous section. In response to a cheaper overseas price of wheat (good 2), or terms of trade $(p_1/p_2)^t$ that exceed the autarky price ratio $(p_1/p_2)^a$, the economy tends to specialize in good 1. If $m_2 (= 9)$ bushels of wheat (good 2) are imported in exchange for x_1 units of good 1, balance of trade equilibrium requires that $m_2 = (p_1/p_2)^t x_1$. In autarky, x_1 units of good 1 are valued at $(p_1/p_2)^a x_1$, or 3 bushels of wheat. For every nine workers employed, the gains from trade (or *GT*) in terms of wheat are therefore

$$
\begin{aligned}
GT &= m_2 - (p_1/p_2)^a x_1 \\
&= [(p_1/p_2)^t - (p_1/p_2)^a] x_1 \quad\quad (3) \\
&= 9 - 3 = 6 \text{ bushels.}
\end{aligned}
$$

Martyn's numerical example is a rudimentary attempt to quantify the equivalent variation EV defined earlier, if it is expressed in terms of the importable good 2. If the economy is in a state of autarky, it would have to receive foreign aid amounting to 6 bushels of wheat for every nine of its workers in order for them to reach the same welfare level they would enjoy under free trade.

The 18th-century rule was used to characterize the gains from trade by writers such as the French economist and statesman A.R.J. Turgot and the author of *The Wealth of Nations*, Adam Smith. Smith applied it to trade between tribesmen, between town and countryside, and between two nations. For example, laying great emphasis on the importance of trade between town and countryside, Smith noted that "the inhabitants of the country purchase of the town a greater quantity of manufactured goods, with the produce of a much smaller quantity of their own labour, than they must have employed had they attempted to prepare them themselves" (1776, 376). Since Smith never attempted to illustrate his examples with numbers, Martyn's 1701 numerical illustration of the gains from trade stands out as a major analytical advance that was not equaled for more than a century, not even by someone as renowned as Smith (Maneschi 2002a).

The gains from trade were viewed in broader terms by the main French and British writers of the Enlightenment. Montesquieu and Voltaire praised commercial activity and luxury goods for their civilizing effects (*doux commerce*) and for promoting the power and military preparedness of nation-states. Smith's mentor and friend David Hume adopted similar views, observing that "commerce with strangers . . . rouses men from their indolence. . . . Imitation soon diffuses all those arts; while domestic manufactures emulate the foreign in their improvements, and work up every home commodity to the utmost perfection of which it is susceptible" (1752, 14). He later argued that "the encrease of riches and commerce in any one nation, instead of hurting, commonly promotes the riches and commerce of all its neighbours. Every improvement, which we have since [two centuries ago] made, has arisen from our imitation of foreigners. . . . Notwithstanding the advanced state of our manufactures, we daily adopt, in every art, the inventions and improvements of our neighbours" (1758, 78–79). Economists continue to maintain that trade encourages the international diffusion of technology, which may be one of its chief benefits. An international demonstration effect stimulates consumer demand for new commodities developed overseas and induces domestic firms to produce them. Hume also argued that the prosperity of neighboring nations promotes domestic prosperity instead of endangering it, as mercantilist writers had maintained.

In addition to using the 18th-century rule in various contexts, Adam Smith also took a broad perspective on the benefits of trade for producers as well as consumers (Maneschi 1998b). Consumers benefited not only from cheaper imports of staples but from the introduction of hitherto unknown commodities from Asia and the Americas. Europe's burgeoning market for manufactured exports allowed it greater scope for the division of labor and hence rising labor productivity. Another benefit that Smith emphasized was subsequently criticized by most classical economists: that trade offered a vent for surplus commodities produced over and above domestic needs. John Stuart Mill (1848, 579) called it "a surviving relic of the Mercantile Theory," since it implies that resources cannot be reallocated so as to avoid the "surplus" commodities whose existence Smith postulates. Smith also echoed Hume and French Enlightenment thinkers in praising trade for promoting economic interdependence. After arguing that "the discovery of America, and that of a passage to the East Indies by the Cape of Good Hope, are the two greatest and most important events recorded in the history of mankind," Smith observed that "by uniting . . . the most distant parts of the world, by enabling them to relieve one another's wants, to increase one another's enjoyments, and to encourage one another's industry, their general tendency would seem to be beneficial" (Smith 1776, 626).

David Ricardo's Twofold Gains from Trade In chapter 7 of his *Principles of Political Economy and Taxation*, Ricardo (1817, 132) claimed that international trade yields two distinct and coequal types of gain: "It is quite as important to the happiness of mankind, that our enjoyments should be increased by the better distribution of labour, by each country producing those commodities for which by its situation, its climate, and its other natural or artificial advantages, it is adapted, and by their exchanging them for the commodities of other countries, as that they should be augmented by a rise in the rate of profits." The first gain, the efficiency advantage arising from the reallocation of resources in accordance with comparative advantage, is unrelated to the second, a rise in the profit rate.

Ricardo quantified the first type of gain for two trading countries, England and Portugal, when he specified the amounts of labor embodied in each country's exports and the labor it would require to produce its imports:

England may be so circumstanced, that to produce the cloth may require the labour of 100 men for one year; and if she attempted to make the wine, it might require the labour of

120 men for the same time. England would therefore find it her interest to import wine, and to purchase it by the exportation of cloth. To produce the wine in Portugal, might require only the labour of 80 men for one year, and to produce the cloth in the same country, might require the labour of 90 men for the same time. It would therefore be advantageous for her to export wine in exchange for cloth. (Ricardo 1817, 135)

England thus saves $120 - 100 = 20$ men by importing wine instead of producing it, and Portugal saves $90 - 80 = 10$ men by importing cloth instead of producing it (Maneschi 2004). These gains from trade in terms of the labor each country economizes are another example of the "18th-century rule" cited earlier.

The second type of trade gain, incommensurable with the first, represents the increase in the rate of profit that trade may bring about: "It has been my endeavour to shew throughout this work, that the rate of profits can never be increased but by a fall in wages, and that there can be no permanent fall of wages but in consequence of a fall of the necessaries on which wages are expended. If, therefore, by the extension of foreign trade, or by improvements in machinery, the food and necessaries of the labourer can be brought to market at a reduced price, profits will rise" (Ricardo 1817, 132). This second type of gain depends exclusively on the import of commodities consumed by workers and is unaffected by that of luxury goods that do not enter the workers' consumer basket.

The increase in the profit rate achieved by trade was important for Ricardo since he had argued in previous chapters of the *Principles* that the pressure of population on land leads to diminishing returns at both the extensive and intensive margins of cultivation, to an increase in the price of "corn" (grains), to a rise in the money wage, and hence to a fall in the rates of profit and of capital accumulation. In the absence of trade or of technical change, the economy heads toward the stationary state. A trade-induced rise in the profit rate, resulting from the fall in the money wage when cheaper wheat is imported, reverses this trend by boosting the rate of capital accumulation. This "dynamic" gain from trade is additional to the "static" gain resulting from an improved resource allocation. Ricardo and the classical school thus closely associated trade with economic growth, and the gains from trade include those that affect an economy's trajectory over time. To judge from the frequency with which Ricardo referred throughout the *Principles* to the need for England to repeal the Corn Laws that held the price of grain artificially high, this second gain from trade was for him just as important as the saving of labor associated with the principle of comparative advantage (Maneschi 1992).

John Stuart Mill: Splitting the Gains from Trade When Ricardo postulated a trade equilibrium between England and Portugal, he stated each country's gains from trade but never explained how the terms of trade are determined. This task fell on the capable shoulders of John Stuart Mill, the son of James Mill, who had been one of Ricardo's closest supporters and disciples. John Stuart Mill pointed to reciprocal demand, the demand of each country for its trading partner's exports, as the force that determines the terms at which they trade (which he called the "terms of interchange"). His theory was first published in "Of the Laws of Interchange between Nations; and the Distribution of the Gains of Commerce among the Countries of the Commercial World," the first of his *Essays on Some Unsettled Questions of Political Economy* of 1844, and later in his *Principles of Political Economy* first published in 1848, which became the premier textbook of political economy in Great Britain. Mill argued that the gap between two countries' autarky price ratios, which reflect their respective comparative advantages, yields the range within which the terms of trade can settle, and that reciprocal demand determines where they settle within that range and hence how the gains from trade are split between them. According to Mill, "The produce of a country exchanges for the produce of other countries, at such values as are required in order that the whole of her exports may exactly pay for the whole of her imports. . . . So that supply and demand are but another expression for reciprocal demand: and to say that value will adjust itself so as to equalize demand with supply, is in fact to say that it will adjust itself so as to equalize the demand on one side with the demand on the other" (Mill 1871: 592–93).

The terms of trade favor a country more the closer they lie to the *other* country's autarky price ratio. If the terms of trade coincide with the country's own autarky price ratio, its gains from trade are zero and all gains go to its trading partner. As a corollary of this, Mill observed that large countries gain less from trade than smaller ones "since, having a greater demand for commodities generally, they are likely to have a greater demand for foreign commodities, and thus modify the terms of interchange to their own disadvantage" (1871, 604). A later neoclassical economist, Francis Edgeworth, referred to this finding as "Mill's paradox."

In addition to Mill, other classical economists such as Robert Torrens emphasized the role of reciprocal demand in yielding the terms of trade. Torrens went even further than Mill. Since a foreign country's tariff can turn the terms of trade and the gains from trade in its favor, Torrens demanded reciprocity in trade policy and advocated a defensive tariff. Other economists criticized him for abandoning his previous policy in favor of unilateral free trade (O'Brien 2004). Torrens's important insight gave rise to Francis Edgeworth's argument, expressed more precisely later by Charles Bickerdike, that a "large" economy (one that can affect its terms of trade) maximizes its gains from trade by levying an optimal tariff.

In another chapter of his *Principles*, Mill explored further the nature of the gains from trade by pointing to its "indirect effects, which must be counted as benefits of a high order," including "the tendency of every extension of the market to improve the processes of production." Foreign trade creates a demonstration effect akin to an "industrial revolution" by inducing people to work harder so they can import commodities they were previously not familiar with: "The opening of a foreign trade, by making them acquainted with new objects, or tempting them by the easier acquisition of things which they had not

previously thought attainable, sometimes works a sort of industrial revolution in a country whose resources were previously undeveloped for want of energy and ambition in the people." Moreover, "the economical advantages of commerce are surpassed in importance by those of its effects which are intellectual and moral. It is hardly possible to overrate the value . . . of placing human beings in contact with persons dissimilar to themselves, and with modes of thought and action unlike those with which they are familiar" (1871, 581). For Mill, as for other classical economists such as Smith and Ricardo, the dynamic benefits of trade ranked at least as high as the static benefits emphasized by the neoclassical school that followed them (Maneschi 1998c).

Mill is also remembered as the first orthodox classical economist who, breaking rank with his confreres, advocated the infant-industry argument for protection in carefully restricted circumstances. A "young and rising nation" (he may have had the United States or Germany in mind) should be willing to forgo some of its current gains from trade by protecting a new industry in which other countries have a "present superiority of acquired skill and experience. A country which has this skill and experience yet to acquire, may in other respects be better adapted to the production than those which were earlier in the field" (Mill 1871, 922). In other words, a country may have a *potential* comparative advantage in an industry, but this potential needs to be fostered by temporary protection for it to be realized (other advocates of the "creation" of comparative advantage starting with Alexander Hamilton are discussed in Maneschi 1998b, chapter 5). This policy does not contradict free trade as a policy goal once an industry has matured and can compete in world markets, since protection then can and should be removed. Whether countries have actually followed this exemplary behavior is of course another question.

Neoclassical Depiction of the Gains from Trade
The classical theory of comparative advantage was attacked as based on an incorrect theory of value by economists of the neoclassical school that emerged in the last quarter of the 19th century. The Austrian-

born Gottfried Haberler (1936) argued that the prices of commodities are based not on the classical labor theory of value, but on their opportunity costs as measured by the least-cost combination of the factors that produce them. Diagrammatically he represented them by the slope of a concave production possibility frontier (PPF) such as that shown in figure 1. On this basis, he generalized the Ricardian theory of comparative advantage while retaining some its main policy implications.

Haberler was unaware that, in a long footnote inconspicuously embedded in a textbook of economic principles, the Italian economist Enrico Barone (1908, 88–90) had used a nonlinear PPF to depict in general equilibrium terms the gains accruing to an economy as it passes from autarky to free trade. He thus anticipated similar diagrams presented some 25 years later by Viner, Abba Lerner, and Wassily Leontief (Maneschi and Thweatt 1987). Barone's diagram is shown in figure 2, where AB is the PPF showing all possible combinations of commodities A (on the vertical axis) and B (on the horizontal) that the economy can produce. The dashed curves, now known as community indifference curves (CICs), show the combinations of the two commodities that yield the same societal welfare level. Autarky equilibrium is at M, where the CIC curve 3 is tangent to the PPF. The autarky price ratio is given by the common tangent at M (not shown) to both the PPF and the CIC. If the economy is given the opportunity to trade at terms shown by the slope of the line PC, with a higher relative price of B, it tends to specialize in B. The production point moves from M to P, the consumption point from M to C. The trade triangle CQP shows that exports QP of B exchange for imports CQ of A. The CIC labeled "8," which the economy can attain in free trade and is tangent to CP at C, clearly yields a higher welfare than under autarky, and illustrates the gains from trade.

The Heckscher-Ohlin-Samuelson Theory and Beyond In the 20th century the theory of international trade was revolutionized by Swedish economic historian Eli Heckscher (1949) and his student Bertil Ohlin (1933), who traced the sources of comparative

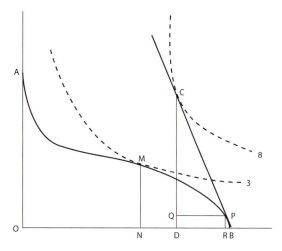

Figure 2
Barone's 1908 representation of the gains from trade

advantage to differences in relative factor endowments across countries and analyzed the effects of trade on income distribution. While Heckscher's intentions were reformist in nature, in the sense of modifying but not rejecting inherited trade theory, Ohlin aimed to overthrow the dated Ricardian theory and replace it with an explicitly neoclassical theory based on factor endowments. Both Heckscher and Ohlin noted that trade encourages the convergence of factor prices in the trading countries or regions. Ohlin, however, doubted that they could actually be equated and denied the possibility (as Haberler did before him) that a factor such as labor could be hurt by trade even if it is intensively employed in the import-competing industries whose prices are reduced by trade.

In a pathbreaking article, Wolfgang Stolper and Paul Samuelson (1941) showed that both Haberler and Ohlin were mistaken, since trade in fact can reduce the real wage of a factor such as labor if it is intensively used in the import-competing sector of the economy. Stolper and Samuelson proved this by stripping the Heckscher-Ohlin model down to two countries, two commodities, and two factors of production, thus obtaining results impossible to discern in the multicommodity, multifactor context of Heckscher and Ohlin. Samuelson (1948) complemented this paper by setting out the stripped-down Heckscher-Ohlin model in diagrammatic form and showing how factor endowments and factor intensities affect comparative advantage and the pattern of trade. He proved that factor prices are fully equalized by trade in specific circumstances. The Stolper-Samuelson and factor price equalization theorems are components of what became the Heckscher-Ohlin-Samuelson theory of trade, which revealed the ambiguity in the expression *gains from trade* when applied to a country: if some factors gain while others lose from trade, as the Stolper-Samuelson theorem predicts must happen, how can the "nation" be said to gain? Samuelson showed that it can do so since the gainers can compensate the losers and still be better off than in autarky. While this is an important finding, it is cold comfort to factors that lose from free trade if in reality they are not compensated.

All the models of trade discussed so far postulate perfect competition in product and factor markets. Their conclusions and associated gains from trade are modified if this assumption does not hold. After adopting the Heckscher-Ohlin-Samuelson model as the mainstream theory of trade after World War II, economists analyzed how various types of distortions in factor or commodity markets affect the direction of trade and the welfare conclusions drawn earlier, and how tax or trade policies can be designed to alleviate these distortions. Policies can sometimes be ranked in terms of first-best, second-best, and so on (Bhagwati 1971; Corden 1997). In the absence of offsetting policies, it can be shown that autarky may be preferable to free trade. Economic growth can be immiserizing (Bhagwati 1958) by causing the terms of trade to deteriorate to such an extent that consumers are worse off than before growth. An optimal tariff, however, can avert this outcome. Trade policy is thus crucial in determining the existence and size of the gains from trade.

Starting in the 1970s, economists developed a New Trade Theory based on imperfect or monopolistic competition or oligopoly (see, for example, Krugman 1990). In the models they developed, comparative advantage is dispensed with as the source of trade, its place taken by economies of scale. Even countries identical in all respects can be shown to gain from trade if they specialize in different manufactures and reap the associated economies of scale. The nature of the gains from trade was substantially enriched by the New Trade Theory, since consumers are shown to benefit not only from cheaper commodities but from a greater variety of them than is available in autarky. Moreover trade can provide a dynamic impetus by stimulating innovation, technical change, and learning by doing. Dynamic benefits from trade that include the availability of new commodities and new methods of production are reminiscent of those identified more than a century earlier by classical economists such as Hume, Smith, and Mill (Maneschi 2002b). Even Ohlin (1933) devoted chapter 3 of his book to economies of scale as a secondary cause of trade in addition to factor endowments. The "New" Trade Theory can thus boast of numerous distinguished precursors.

The gains from trade have figured prominently in discussions of the rationale for international trade since mercantilist times and have typically led economists to argue for trade liberalization except in cases where they wished to promote infant industries or exploit monopoly power by turning the terms of trade in a country's favor. Attempts to quantify the gains from trade began in 1701 with Henry Martyn and continued in 1817 with David Ricardo and in the 20th century with the calculation of the compensating and equivalent variations. Classical economists such as David Hume and John Stuart Mill also argued for a broader vision of the gains from trade that includes the dynamic benefits that can be realized from the imitation of foreign ideas and technical improvements. Beginning in the 1970s, the exponents of the New Trade Theory added the availability to consumers of a greater variety of commodities as another important gain from trade.

See also absolute advantage; comparative advantage; economies of scale; Heckscher-Ohlin model; infant industry argument; intraindustry trade; monopolistic competition; New Trade Theory; Ricardian model; terms of trade

FURTHER READING

Barone, Enrico. 1908. *Principi di economia politica*. Rome: G. Bertero. Contains the first diagram illustrating the gains from trade in a neoclassical economy.

Bhagwati, Jagdish N. 1958. "Immiserizing Growth: A Geometrical Note." *Review of Economic Studies* 25 (3): 201–5. An often-cited article proving that economic growth in a large country practicing free trade can make it worse off.

———. 1971. "The Generalized Theory of Distortions and Welfare." In *Trade, Balance of Payments, and Growth: Papers in International Economics in Honor of Charles P. Kindleberger*, edited by Jagdish N. Bhagwati et al. Amsterdam: North-Holland, 69–90. An important analysis of the impact on economic welfare of various economic distortions in open economies and a ranking of the policies that can offset them.

Caves, Richard E. 1960. *Trade and Economic Structure: Models and Methods*. Cambridge, MA: Harvard University Press. A comprehensive exposition of models of international trade and their welfare implications.

Corden, W. Max. 1984. "The Normative Theory of International Trade." In *Handbook of International Economics*, vol. I, edited by Ronald W. Jones and Peter B. Kenen. Amsterdam: North-Holland, 63–130. A noted trade economist surveys the welfare implications of international trade and of commercial policies.

———. 1997. *Trade Policy and Economic Welfare*. 2d ed. Oxford: Oxford University Press. An updated masterly survey of the welfare implications of trade and protection.

Haberler, Gottfried. 1936. *The Theory of International Trade*. Edinburgh: William Hodge. A comprehensive outline of neoclassical international trade theory and policy by one of its chief contributors.

Heckscher, Eli F. 1949. "The Effect of Foreign Trade on the Distribution of Income." In *Readings in the Theory of International Trade*, edited by H. S. Ellis and L. A. Metzler. Homewood, IL: Irwin, 272–300. First published in Swedish in 1919, the original and remarkably sophisticated presentation of the Heckscher-Ohlin theory of trade.

Hume, David. 1752. "Of Commerce." In *David Hume: Writings on Economics*, edited by E. Rotwein. Madison: University of Wisconsin Press, 1955, 3–18. An essay that stresses the importance of foreign trade for the power of the state and the happiness of its citizens.

———. 1758. "Of the Jealousy of Trade." In *David Hume: Writings on Economics*, edited by E. Rotwein. Madison: University of Wisconsin Press, 1955, 78–82. In the last of his economic essays, Hume emphasizes that free trade combined with openness to foreign ideas and technical improvements enhances economic prosperity.

Krugman, Paul R. 1990. *Rethinking International Trade*. Cambridge, MA: MIT Press. An anthology of articles based on the new trade theory by one of its most eminent exponents.

Maneschi, Andrea. 1992. "Ricardo's International Trade Theory: Beyond the Comparative Cost Example." *Cambridge Journal of Economics* 16 (4): 421–37. Although Ricardo was a pioneer of the theory of comparative advantage, he arguably placed greater emphasis on the dynamic benefits of foreign trade in raising the rates of profit and capital accumulation.

———. 1998a. "Comparative Advantage with and without Gains from Trade." *Review of International Economics* 6 (1): 120–28. Illustrates the fact that gains from trade are sufficient but not necessary for the existence of comparative advantage.

———. 1998b. *Comparative Advantage in International Trade: A Historical Perspective*. Cheltenham: Edward Elgar. An analysis of the genesis, evolution, and current significance of the concept of comparative advantage in the theory of international trade.

———. 1998c. "The Dynamic Nature of Comparative Advantage and of the Gains from Trade in Classical Economics." *Journal of the History of Economic Thought* 20 (2): 133–44. Argues that classical economists regarded comparative advantage as subject to change, and the gains from trade as dynamic in nature rather than static.

———. 2002a. "The Tercentenary of Henry Martyn's *Considerations upon the East-India Trade*." *Journal of the History of Economic Thought* 24 (2): 233–49. A celebration of the tercentenary of Martyn's pamphlet of 1701 that highlights his quantitative measure of the gains from trade.

———. 2002b. "How New Is the 'New Trade Theory' of the Past Two Decades?" In *Is There Progress in Economics? Knowledge, Truth, and the History of Economic Thought*, edited by S. Boehm et al. Cheltenham: Edward Elgar, 240–55. The new trade theory that emerged in the 1970s had remarkable anticipations in the classical school and in Ohlin's (1933) book.

———. 2004. "The True Meaning of David Ricardo's Four Magic Numbers." *Journal of International Economics* 62 (2): 433–43. A challenge to the conventional interpretation of the numerical example that Ricardo used to illustrate comparative advantage.

Maneschi, Andrea, and William O. Thweatt. 1987. "Barone's 1908 Representation of an Economy's Trade Equilibrium and the Gains from Trade." *Journal of International Economics* 22 (3/4): 375–82. Shows that the first diagram illustrating the gains from trade in a neoclassical economy was published by Enrico Barone in 1908.

Martyn, Henry. 1701. *Considerations on the East-India Trade*. In *Early English Tracts on Commerce*, edited by John R. McCulloch. Cambridge: Cambridge University Press, 1954, 541–629. The "reform mercantilist" Martyn's pamphlet supporting free trade and highlighting its gains.

Mill, John Stuart. 1871. *Principles of Political Economy*. Reprint of 7th ed. London: Longman, Green, 1920. First published in 1848, this became the most popular 19th-century textbook of British classical political economy.

O'Brien, Denis P. 2004. *The Classical Economists Revisited*. Princeton: Princeton University Press. A thorough analytical survey of the contributions of the classical school of economics.

Ohlin, Bertil. 1933. *Interregional and International Trade*. Rev. ed. Cambridge, MA: Harvard University Press, 1967. A comprehensive and literary elaboration of the Heckscher-Ohlin theory of trade.

Ricardo, David. 1817. *On the Principles of Political Economy and Taxation*. In *The Works and Correspondence of David Ricardo*, vol. I, edited by Piero Sraffa. Cambridge: Cambridge University Press, 1951. A fundamental contribution to classical economic theory containing a numerical illustration of comparative advantage and the gains from trade.

Samuelson, Paul A. 1939. "The Gains from International Trade." In *Readings in the Theory of International Trade*, edited by H. S. Ellis and L. A. Metzler. Homewood, IL: Irwin, 1949, 239–52. The first theoretical analysis of the gains from trade that can be realized by a country facing given world commodity prices.

———. 1948. "International Trade and the Equalization of Factor Prices." *Economic Journal* 58 (230): 163–84. Expounds and illustrates the Heckscher-Ohlin-Samuelson theory of trade.

Smith, Adam. 1776. *An Inquiry into the Nature and Causes of the Wealth of Nations*. Oxford: Clarendon Press, 1976. The most famous book of the founder of classical political economy.

Stolper, Wolfgang F., and Paul A. Samuelson. 1941. "Protection and Real Wages." In *Readings in the Theory of International Trade*, edited by H. S. Ellis and L. A. Metzler. Homewood, IL: Irwin, 1949, 333–57. An often-cited article establishing the Stolper-Samuelson theorem, one of the basic building blocks of the Heckscher-Ohlin-Samuelson theory of trade.

Viner, Jacob. 1937. *Studies in the Theory of International Trade*. New York: Harper. A magisterial survey of pre-classical, classical, and neoclassical trade theories.

ANDREA MANESCHI

■ gender

The global work force is largely female. First, at the international level, women make up about 50 percent of migrant workers—in Asia, even 75 percent—and their share is increasing. These are women from low-income countries, such as the Philippines and Sri Lanka, taking up jobs elsewhere in typically feminine occupations such as domestic work, child care, and nursing. The countries of destination are mainly Western, but also Arab countries, such as the United Arab Emirates. Second, at the national level, the majority of workers in export industries in developing countries is female. Together, these two levels of the global work force imply that more than 50 percent of workers in the global economy—that is, in globalized jobs—are women. This trend stands in striking contrast with the fact that universally, women's labor force participation is lower than that of men.

Female Employment in Export Manufacturing
The female share of employment in export manufacturing reached its peak in the 1970s and

1980s, in particular in countries that pursued an export-led growth strategy. These countries offered export processing zones (EPZs) to (foreign) investors with incentives such as tax holidays and limited enforcement of labor regulations. The countries include Mexico, Taiwan, and South Korea, but also low-income countries such as Bangladesh, Sri Lanka, and Mauritius, that all have shown female shares of export employment between 70 and 90 percent. Since the 1990s this share has declined, but remains above 50 percent for developing countries, whereas the female share in export manufacturing in countries that belong to the Organisation for Economic Co-operation and Development (OECD) has declined and is well below 50 percent. In developed countries, export employment has declined in labor-intensive sectors, which have moved to developing countries due to the wide availability of low-skilled labor and low wages there, as is predicted by the Heckscher-Ohlin model of international trade. Women in OECD countries have particularly lost jobs in female-intensive sectors such as textiles, garments, and leather products.

The high female shares of migration and export employment show that the world economy has provided new opportunities for women in the developing world to find jobs and earn an independent income. The reasons for the predominantly female employment in export industries in developing countries relate to perceived qualities of female labor as well as to labor market discrimination.

Women tend to be regarded by employers as more suitable for work in typical low-skilled jobs in export manufacturing production. This is also referred to as the "nimble fingers" view, which leads many employers in sectors such as garments, toys, microelectronics, and assembly to prefer female over male workers. The "nimble fingers" view of women workers values the typical skills required for detailed but repetitive tasks in mass production, which have not been acquired through formal education but through women's socialization (informal training in sewing for example). In addition, the "nimble fingers" perspective of female workers also extends to the perception of women workers as being socialized as more obedient and less militant than men, which is reflected in women's lower membership in trade unions.

Wage Discrimination Women are the preferred work force in industries that compete at the international level and experience a strong pressure toward cost reduction. Women are hired more often than men in such industries, because women's wages are lower than men's wages. This gender wage gap provides employers with a cost advantage, without much loss of productivity as long as women are hired only for low-skill jobs. Gender analyses of export employment indeed show that women are predominantly found in the lowest skill categories of production, both in wage employment and in subcontracted work, such as piece-rate home work. Econometric analyses have shown that countries with the highest ratio of export earnings to their gross domestic product also have the largest gender wage gaps, even when educational levels of women have moved close to those of men. The Asian tiger economies, the fast growing economies of South Korea, Taiwan, Hong Kong and Singapore, are prominent examples, suggesting that their export success has, at least in part, been built on wage discrimination against women.

Wage discrimination is not specific to export employment, but trade liberalization does tend to put wages in export sectors under pressure, as well as wages in import competing sectors. This makes it difficult to improve women's wages and to reduce the gap with men's wages without a loss in export earnings or a worsening of the competitiveness of domestic goods vis-à-vis imported goods. Moreover, gender norms in labor markets are strong and justify women's low wages on the basis of gender stereotypes. One was mentioned above, the "nimble fingers" view of women workers, in which women's skills are highly valued for export production but not rewarded in wages because the skills are perceived as "natural" and not part of women's formal human capital. Another gender norm that prevents women's wages from catching up with men's is the breadwinner bias in employers' decisions on payment: men are thought to deserve higher wages than women because of their traditional gender role as breadwinners. This norm, however, doesn't take into account that men's wages are often not sufficient to serve as a family wage and that globally there is an increase in the share of female-headed households, hence, an increase in the number of female breadwinners.

Women as the World's Flexible Work Force
Women are not only the preferred work force in wage employment for exports, but also make up the majority of flexible workers in the global production system. The informal economy, which is largely unregulated, with low or absent labor standards, is expanding. This is partly due to the outsourcing of production by multinational companies to local suppliers in global value chains—production processes with various layers of heavily competing suppliers for well-known brand names. Indeed, the global work force has been increasingly informalized, with women experiencing lower labor standards than men. Jobs in the global production system are increasingly subcontracted, flexible, and temporary. Women therefore find themselves increasingly working informally at the bottom of global value chains, outside the reach of labor laws, labor inspectors, and company codes of conduct.

The explanation for the increase in outsourcing rather than in-company production is, again, the cost pressure experienced by firms that try to survive in highly competitive low-wage sectors of the world economy. Large parts of production in these sectors are subcontracted and end up being done by flexible, irregular female workers in rented factories, small-scale workshops, or at home by individual workers. This process of global cost reduction through hiring cheap female labor is quite different from a process in which companies that are less vulnerable to global competition compete on the basis of productivity increases rather than cost reductions. Such a strategy requires investment in new technology and skills. Even though the educational gap between men and women is narrowing everywhere, and has disappeared in an increasing number of countries, it is men who benefit more often from the on-the-job

training and higher pay in such industries. This is exactly what is reflected in the figures referred to above, showing the defeminization of export employment in mature export industries. Employers prefer men for the higher skill jobs, believing that women would be less reliable workers because of maternity leave and possible career breaks when they have children. In addition, male workers' bargaining power is higher than that of female workers because of the male breadwinner norm and men's higher participation in trade unions. Women workers, therefore, remain at the lower end of export production.

The prospects for a reduction of the gender wage gap and improvement of working conditions are limited, despite women's increased levels of education, as long as labor market discrimination keeps women locked in low-skilled formal and informal employment in highly competitive global industries.

See also export processing zones; export promotion; fragmentation; Heckscher-Ohlin model; labor standards; migration, international; outsourcing/offshoring; social policy in open economies; trade and wages

FURTHER READING

Beneria, Lourdes. 2003. *Gender, Development, and Globalization: Economics as If All People Mattered*. New York: Routledge. This fine political economy study about the gender dimensions of globalization provides a comprehensive overview of the main issues, including such topics as labor standards, migrant workers, and unpaid work.

Grown, Caren, Diane Elson, and Nilüfer Çağatay, eds. 2000. *World Development* 28 (7) (Special Issue on Growth, Trade, Finance, and Gender Inequality). A rich collection of short papers that integrate gender analysis in macroeconomic analysis. Not all contributions to the special issue are about the world economy, but those that are present a variety of perspectives, ranging from formal models to econometric cross-country studies and policy-oriented papers.

International Working Group on Gender, Macroeconomics, and International Economics. Website available at http://www.econ.utah.edu/genmac. Salt

Lake City: University of Utah. Features working papers, discussions, and other sources of information on gender and trade.

Seguino, Stephanie. 2000. "Gender Inequality and Economic Growth: a Cross-Country Analysis." *World Development* 28 (7): 1211–30. A key publication that provides strong empirical evidence for the thesis that the success of export-led growth strategy largely depends on gender wage discrimination.

Standing, Guy. 1999. "Global Feminization through Flexible Labor: A Theme Revisited." *World Development* 27 (3): 583–602. An update of an earlier paper, showing that women make up the large part of the global work force, but under worse conditions and lower wages compared to men.

Staveren, Irene van, Diane Elson, Caren Grown, and Nilüfer Çağatay, eds. 2007. *The Feminist Economics of Trade*. London: Routledge. The first volume that brings together research on trade and gender. It analyzes not only gender impacts of trade but also shows how trade is affected by preexisting gender inequalities.

IRENE VAN STAVEREN

■ General Agreement on Tariffs and Trade (GATT)

From its creation in 1947 to its absorption into the newly created World Trade Organization (WTO) in 1995, the General Agreement on Tariffs and Trade—universally referred to as "the GATT"—was *the* multilateral agreement governing trade among a growing number of countries, including all of the major trading nations. As such, the GATT served two primary functions for its members. First, it provided a set of multilaterally agreed rules and disciplines governing selected policies affecting countries' trade in goods, in particular, tariffs and quotas on imports. The goal was to encourage international trade by imposing certain disciplines on countries' trade policies, thereby making future access to foreign markets more predictable. Second, it provided a forum for (1) the settlement of trade disputes among members, and (2) negotiations to further liberalize

trade, as well as to strengthen and extend the multilateral rules. Thus the GATT was both an agreement and an institution.

By any standard, the period 1948 to 1994 was an era of unparalleled economic prosperity for the world economy. Adjusted for inflation, output of goods and services grew at an average annual rate of 3.6 percent, with output per person increasing 2 percent a year (compared with an estimated 0.9 percent during 1820–1913). A key factor behind this rapid growth of output was the even more rapid expansion of world merchandise trade, which grew at an average rate of nearly 6 percent a year in real terms from 1948 to 1994. This meant that virtually every year saw a growing share of world production being traded across one or more borders.

It is widely accepted among trade specialists that GATT rules, in combination with periodic GATT-sponsored negotiations, played a major role in this expansion of world trade (Goldstein, Rivers, and Tomz 2006). The GATT has also attracted considerable interest from scholars and policy officials who believe a good case can be made that the GATT was the most successful of the postwar international economic institutions.

Origins of the GATT The immediate origin of the GATT was the UN draft charter for the stillborn International Trade Organization, often referred to as the "Havana Charter." Before going into this, however, it is useful to mention two earlier experiences with international commercial policies that influenced the drafters of the Havana Charter and thus the ultimate design of the GATT.

In the latter half of the 19th century, European treaties increasingly included a provision for most-favored-nation (MFN) trade status. Enshrined in trade agreements such as the Cobden-Chevalier Treaty of 1860 liberalizing trade between Great Britain and France, the MFN provision assured that trade was nondiscriminatory. This meant that trade benefits resulting from subsequent treaties were passed on to previous treaty partners through the promise that they would receive the lowest tariff rate granted to any trade partner. MFN created a multiplier effect for trade liberalization, leading to significantly lower barriers to trade throughout the continent (Curzon 1965).

More important, the drafters of the Havana Charter shared the experience of the Great Depression, when economic decline brought beggar-thy-neighbor policies, high tariffs, and depreciating currencies, as nations tried to protect their home markets. This, of course, only accentuated the general decline. The extent of the worldwide descent into virtually uncontrolled protectionism is evident from the 25 percent decline in the volume of world trade between 1929 and 1932 (minus 60 percent in dollar terms). By 1936 industrial production had recovered to a level 10 percent *above* its 1929 level, while the volume of world trade was still 15 percent *below* its 1929 level.

It was against this background that, in the closing years of World War II, American and British officials began laying plans for the postwar world economy. Among the most ambitious of those plans was the proposal for a new institution, to be called the International Trade Organization (ITO), that would be the third pillar—along with the International Bank for Reconstruction and Development (World Bank) and the International Monetary Fund (IMF), both already agreed to in 1944—underlying the postwar world economy. A preparatory committee established by the UN Economic and Social Council met in London in October–November 1946 to discuss a draft charter for the proposed ITO. That meeting also produced a resolution calling for a multilateral trade negotiation, to be held the following year in Geneva at the committee's second session and a recommendation that a "General Agreement on Tariffs and Trade," containing rules and disciplines to protect the value of the tariff concessions, be created.

The first full draft of the GATT, based primarily on text taken from the commercial policy section of the draft ITO charter, was produced at a January–February 1947 meeting in Lake Success, New York (Jackson 1969). Two concurrent negotiations began in Geneva in April, one focused on the draft ITO charter and another focused on reductions in tariffs and refinements in the accompanying draft GATT.

On October 30, 1947, 13 developed and 10 developing countries—accounting for more than three-quarters of world trade—signed the Final Act of the GATT containing (1) a schedule of concessions listing each government's agreed tariff reductions, and (2) rules and procedures regulating nontariff restrictions on trade—what Robert Hudec (1987) called a "code of behavior" for governments.

It was assumed that the ITO, whose charter was finalized in Havana in March 1948, would shortly come into force and that the GATT would come under its aegis. That option evaporated in 1950 when it became clear that the U.S. Congress would not ratify the Havana Charter. The provisional GATT became the framework for postwar commercial relations. Noting that the early GATT "was permeated by an atmosphere of impermanence," Richard Gardner (1956) described it as "a slender reed on which to base progress toward a multilateral regime."

The 23 participants in the Geneva trade negotiations were the GATT's first "contracting parties"—a term that emphasized both the contractual nature of the GATT and the fact that it was a "provisional agreement" and not a treaty-based organization. With a more or less steady increase in the membership over the period 1948–94, the number of contracting parties stood at 128 when the GATT was absorbed into the WTO in 1995, four-fifths of which were developing or least-developed countries.

Basic Principles Five basic principles—some explicit, some implicit—informed the rules and guided the activities of the contractual, rules-based GATT system.

Nondiscrimination. This principle embraces two elements. The better-known one is the most-favored-nation (MFN) clause, which prohibits a GATT member from discriminating between imports from other GATT members—any concession granted on a product from one contracting party "shall be accorded immediately *and unconditionally* to the like product originating in or destined for the territories of all other contracting parties" (Article I, emphasis added). Adherence to MFN both depoliticizes trade and ensures that a country buys its imports from the cheapest foreign source. Some exceptions were included in the GATT from the beginning, most notably for free trade areas and customs unions among small groups of countries. Later the contracting parties agreed to allow preferential treatment of imports from developing countries. By the early 1990s, with the rapid spread of preferential trading areas—especially free trade areas—many trade experts were openly questioning the relevance of the GATT's MFN provisions.

The second element of nondiscrimination is national treatment, which prohibits discrimination between imports and domestic products once the imports have entered the country. For example, a retail sales tax applied to imported TV sets but not to domestically produced TV sets would violate the national treatment principle (however, imposing a tariff on foreign-made TV sets as they enter the country is not a violation of national treatment).

Tariffs only. The GATT was not a free trade organization. Member countries were not required to participate in trade liberalizing negotiating rounds, and they were free to protect domestic producers by imposing restrictions on imported goods. If they did protect, however, they were required to use tariffs—rather than import quotas or other nontariff restrictions—to provide that protection. This made good sense. Not only is the level of protection provided by tariffs more transparent than nontariff protection, but tariffs are a less distorting (less inefficient) way of granting protection.

Consensus decision making. Although there were provisions for majority voting on a one-country, one-vote basis, the GATT developed a very strong tradition of making all decisions by consensus (defined as no country present at the meeting when the decision was taken formally objecting to the proposed decision). This often slowed the decision-making process, but—considering that many of the decisions resulted in legally binding obligations for all members—had important advantages, including adding to the intellectual and diplomatic "legitimacy" of the decisions.

Special treatment for developing countries. There were no special provisions for developing countries in the original GATT. In the 1950s the developing country members began demanding exemptions from GATT's rules and disciplines, to which was added, at the beginning of the 1960s, demands for special and more favorable treatment for their exports in the markets of other GATT members (Hudec 1987). Institutional changes reflecting these demands included special provisions for developing countries in GATT rules and procedures, the creation of a permanent Committee on Trade and Development, the Tokyo Round's "Framework Agreements," and technical assistance provided by the GATT Secretariat. Technical assistance aside, the extent to which these various developments actually benefited rather than harmed developing countries continues to be the subject of debate among trade experts.

Small Secretariat with a limited mandate. The member countries kept the Secretariat very small compared with the other major postwar international economic organizations (such as the World Bank and the IMF). Comparable figures for 1994 are not available, but in 1996, just after GATT's absorption into the WTO, the WTO Secretariat was in 16th place on the list of the 17 largest international economic organizations in terms of budget and number of staff members (Blackhurst 1998).

As for the Secretariat's limited mandate, consider, for example, the following: the Director-General could not initiate a dispute settlement case, no matter how blatant the rule violation; the Secretariat could not interpret GATT rules; the Secretariat was not allowed to report regularly on trade policy developments in member countries until 1977, 30 years after the GATT was signed; and the Secretariat was not allowed to have a formal Office of Legal Affairs until 1983, even though the GATT was based on contractual obligations. In essence, the Secretariat existed to service the meetings and other activities of the member countries. The popular way to describe this situation was to say that the GATT was a "member-driven" institution.

The explanation for the member-driven operation of the GATT and the Secretariat's very small size undoubtedly is the highly politicized nature of trade policies at the national level. Domestic politics meant that no government—and especially no developed country government—could be seen advocating a secretariat with any real independence and power. Some analysts argue that this was the secret behind GATT's success (Hudec 1993; Winham 1998).

Dispute Settlement A rules-based agreement is credible only if it includes effective dispute settlement procedures. In GATT's early years, working parties were created to handle disputes. Then in 1952 the contracting parties switched over to a "panel" system in which three (sometimes five) delegates from countries not party to the dispute evaluated submissions by the parties to the dispute and made recommendations or rulings, depending on the issue(s) at stake. The panel's final report was submitted to the GATT Council (a body representing all GATT members) for adoption by consensus, which meant that the country that "lost the case" could block the adoption of the panel report if it so desired. Odd as this may sound, the system worked—in the first three decades a substantial proportion of panel reports was adopted—because the contracting parties knew that if the dispute settlement system failed, the GATT would fail (blockage of panel reports emerged as a major problem only in the 1980s and was addressed in the Uruguay Round negotiations).

A defendant country that lost a case (and did not block the adoption of the panel's report) had three options: (1) withdrawal of the GATT-inconsistent measure(s), always the required and first-best option; (2) as an interim measure, pay compensation, generally by lowering one or more tariffs (on an MFN basis) on selected exports of interest to the winning plaintiff; or (3) if compensation was not paid, suffer retaliation by the plaintiff country, generally via a discriminatory increase in tariffs on items of export interest to the defendant country. The third option was possible only if it was authorized by the contracting parties—a very important proviso since it heavily modified the long-standing "right of unilateral reprisals" in international law. Although retaliation was authorized only once under the GATT, there is no doubt that countries' awareness of this option was crucially important in the enforcement of GATT rules.

In the early years there was a struggle between those countries that favored an approach to dispute settlement that was pragmatic and avoided undue "legalism" and those that favored a more judicial or legalistic approach. Over time the latter approach won out, as evidenced, for example, by the previously mentioned creation of GATT's first ever Office of Legal Affairs in 1983. In the course of providing other examples, Ernst-Ulrich Petersmann (1997) observes that this shift progressively transformed "the GATT into the most frequently used, and most effective, international system for the rule-oriented settlement of disputes among governments."

Beginning in the 1980s, the effectiveness and uniqueness of GATT's dispute settlement system acted as a magnet for issues outside GATT's area of responsibility. In two instances—the protection of intellectual property and the enforcement of workers' rights—proposals to extend GATT rules and dispute settlement (with trade retaliation a possibility) into new areas were motivated by the lack of effective enforcement mechanisms in the responsible international organizations, while in two others—trade in services (banking, insurance, and so forth) and protection of the environment—there was no effective international organization. Negotiations on these issues subsequently became key parts of the Uruguay Round (see below).

Negotiating Rounds Although the GATT was not a free trade organization, the underlying "ethos" included a strong belief by many members—including all the developed countries—that the pursuit of *freer* trade was an important goal for the organization. This is not surprising considering the high tariffs and widespread use of import quotas, inherited from the 1930s, that confronted the early GATT.

During the period 1947–94, GATT's contracting parties held eight rounds of trade liberalizing negotiations. Reciprocal reductions in tariffs—I'll reduce my tariff on radios if you reduce your tariff on corn—were the exclusive focus of the first five rounds and an important part of the agendas of the three later rounds. By 1994 the average tariff on manufactured goods entering the developed countries had been reduced from around 40 percent in the immediate postwar period to below 5 percent. Tariffs in many developing countries also started to come down beginning in the late 1960s and early 1970s as these countries adopted more outward-oriented development strategies.

Not only were tariffs reduced, but an increasing number were also "bound" under GATT rules. Binding a particular tariff, say the tariff on radios at 20 percent, meant that you were not permitted to increase it above that level (a lower tariff was okay). Raising it above 20 percent would put you in violation of your GATT obligations and risk a dispute settlement case. Binding members' tariffs was often as important as reducing rates since both increased the predictability of future market access and thus encouraged trade.

In the Kennedy Round (1964–67) anti-dumping measures were added to the agenda. Reflecting both the success in reducing tariffs and the increasing complexity of commercial relations, the Tokyo Round (1973–79) attempted, for the first time, to deal with a range of nontariff measures, including three—production subsidies, technical barriers to trade (for example, safety standards), and government procurement—that are applied not at the border but domestically in the importing country. The extent to which these initial steps "inside the border" signaled a turning point for the multilateral trading system was perhaps not fully appreciated at the time. Otherwise, little meaningful progress was made in the Tokyo Round, the principal achievement being a series of "codes" that were signed by a minority of the contracting parties, making them plurilateral rather than multilateral agreements.

The Uruguay Round It was not long before pressure to launch a new round began building as a result of both short-term concerns and medium-term goals. The former focused on the worsening trade relations among many of the leading traders in the early 1980s, caused in part by a sharp slowdown in the growth of world production and trade. Launching a new round, it was argued, would help governments to contain protectionist pressures, through the new round's standstill agreement (on new trade barriers) and the demonstration that governments

were dealing with the system's perceived shortcomings.

The medium-term goals behind the push for a new round, in turn, fell into two distinct categories. One was based on the widespread perception that the GATT system was in serious trouble and that something had to be done soon. Not only had the postwar liberalization momentum been lost, but even more ominously, the use of GATT-illegal discriminatory quantitative restrictions (often labeled voluntary export restraints, or VERs) by some of the major countries was spreading to ever more products, as was the use of trade-distorting production subsidies. Moreover, after seven rounds of negotiations, agricultural trade was still not subject to GATT's rules, and trade in textiles and clothing—a potentially important source of jobs and economic growth in many lower-income developing countries—remained heavily restricted by GATT-sanctioned quantitative restrictions.

The other medium-term goal stemmed from the belief on the part of many members—especially the developed countries—that after nearly 40 years the GATT needed to be updated to be able to deal effectively with the new realities of world trade and the policy frictions they engendered. A key part of this updating involved proposals for writing new GATT rules and disciplines to cover economic activities that had increased greatly in importance since the GATT was drafted. Attention focused on three areas: trade in services, the protection of intellectual property rights, and trade-related investment measures (for example, requiring foreign-owned firms to purchase a certain percentage of their inputs in the host country).

With growing support from the developed countries and many developing countries, momentum for launching a new round began accelerating in the early months of 1985. At the same time, a group of developing countries led by Brazil and India remained strongly opposed to a new round. Proposals to include "new areas" on the negotiating agenda—especially trade in services—also drew strong opposition from many developing countries. Eventually the countries favoring a new round won out, helped by a compromise whereby the services negotiations would be on the agenda but kept completely separate from the negotiations on goods.

GATT's eighth and final round of negotiations was launched in September 1986 at a meeting of the contracting parties in Punta del Este, Uruguay. The ministerial declaration launching the Uruguay Round gave the negotiators four years to complete their work. That target was missed when the December 1990 ministerial meeting in Brussels failed to resolve differences that had blocked agreement on a number of difficult issues, of which agricultural trade was by far the most high profile and politically charged. Negotiations continued and, finally, late in November 1993, GATT's new Director-General, Peter Sutherland, decided that there had been enough progress for him to give the negotiators a deadline of December 15 to wind up the round. The strategy worked. Describing the meeting of the Trade Negotiations Committee on December 15, John Croome (1995) observes, "At 7:30 in the evening, to huge applause, Sutherland brought down his gavel to signify approval of the Uruguay Round agreements. . . . It was, he suggested, 'a defining moment in modern economic and political history.'"

On a very general level, the principal achievements of the Uruguay Round can be summarized as follows:

- Agreement to create the World Trade Organization to replace the 1947 GATT provisional agreement.
- A major revision of the dispute settlement system. In a complete reversal of the practice under the GATT, panel decisions are now automatically accepted unless there is a consensus not to do so; this was coupled with the creation of an independent Appellate Body to hear appeals of panel decisions.
- Further liberalization of tariffs and nontariff restrictions on industrial products, and—for the first time—reductions in import barriers and other (domestic) interventions affecting agricultural trade.

- Creation of the General Agreement on Trade in Services (GATS)
- Creation of the Agreement on Trade-Related Aspects of Intellectual Property Rights (the TRIPS Agreement)

Trade ministers met in Marrakesh (Morocco) in April 1994 to sign the Uruguay Round Agreements, and the WTO began its existence on January 1, 1995.

What Became of the GATT? The original agreement, now referred to as GATT 1947, was phased out at the end of 1995. Within the WTO family of agreements, an updated version of the agreement—GATT 1994—is the umbrella treaty covering trade in goods.

The GATT played a key role in the economic prosperity of the second half of the 20th century. It also gave us the WTO, modeled on the GATT but with greatly expanded responsibilities in an increasingly globalized world economy. On both counts, we owe a great debt to the architects of the GATT and to the many national officials and Secretariat staff who—despite a very inauspicious beginning—made it work.

See also Agreement on Agriculture; Agreement on Trade-Related Aspects of Intellectual Property Rights (TRIPS); agricultural trade negotiations; anti-dumping; General Agreement on Trade in Services (GATS); labor standards; multilateralism; nondiscrimination; nontariff measures; quotas; special and differential treatment; tariffs; technical barriers to trade; textiles and clothing; trade in services; Uruguay Round; voluntary export restraints; World Trade Organization; World Trade Organization dispute settlement

FURTHER READING

Barton, John, Judith Goldstein, Timothy Josling, and Richard Steinberg. 2006. *The Evolution of the Trade Regime: Politics, Law, and Economics of the GATT and the WTO.* Princeton: Princeton University Press. An excellent interdisciplinary overview of the GATT regime and its transformation into the WTO.

Blackhurst, Richard. 1998. "The Capacity of the WTO to Fulfill Its Mandate." In *The WTO as an International Organization*, edited by Anne O. Krueger. Chicago: University of Chicago Press, 31–58. Although concerned mainly with the WTO, this paper by the former Director of Economic Research at both the GATT and WTO Secretariats (1985–97) includes a relatively detailed inside view of the operation of the GATT Secretariat.

Croome, John. 1995. *Reshaping the World Trading System: A History of the Uruguay Round.* Geneva: WTO Secretariat. An engaging, step-by-step, firsthand account by a former senior WTO official of the preparatory phase and the seven years of complex and wide-ranging negotiations.

Curzon, Gerard. 1965. *Multilateral Commercial Diplomacy.* Middlesex, UK: Michael Joseph. This early book on the GATT by an academic economist offers a careful analysis of how the GATT evolved from its inauspicious beginning as a strictly interim arrangement into an effective multilateral institution.

Gardner, Richard N. 1956. *Sterling-Dollar Diplomacy.* Oxford: Oxford University Press. A standard reference work on both the steps leading to the creation of the GATT and its activities in the early years.

General Agreement on Tariffs and Trade. 1985. *Trade Policies for a Better Future.* Geneva: GATT Secretariat. A report by seven independent world figures containing 15 recommendations for dealing with a variety of challenges facing the GATT in the first half of the 1980s. The report is generally credited with playing an important role in preparations for the Uruguay Round.

Goldstein, Judith, Douglas Rivers, and Michael Tomz. 2006. "Institutions in International Relations: Understanding the Effects of GATT and the WTO on World Trade." *International Organization* 61: 2. This article assesses the trade implications of membership in the GATT and provides empirical evidence that GATT membership increased trade for both developed and developing countries.

Goode, Walter. 2003. *Dictionary of Trade Policy Terms.* 4th ed. Cambridge: Cambridge University Press, World Trade Organization, and the Center for International Economic Studies (University of Adelaide). A nearly indispensable guide to the jargon-filled world of the GATT, the WTO, and other international economic organizations. The volume also covers various GATT/ WTO rules, newer issues, and developing country concerns.

Horn, Henrik, and Petros C. Mavroidis, 2001. "Economic and Legal Aspects of the Most-Favored-Nation Clause." *European Journal of Political Economy* 17 (2): 233–79. This article examines the merits of the theoretical rationales for MFN and tests them against the background of the current regulatory framework.

Hudec, Robert E. 1987. *Developing Countries in the GATT Legal System.* Aldershot, UK: Gower for the Trade Policy Research Centre (London). An excellent history, by a leading GATT legal scholar, of the GATT's evolving legal relationship with its developing country members, coupled with a critique of the relationship as it stood prior to the GATT's absorption into the WTO.

———. 1993. *Enforcing International Trade Law: the Evolution of the Modern GATT Legal System.* Salem, NH: Butterworth Legal Publishers. A standard reference work, by a leading GATT legal scholar, on the GATT legal system as it stood just prior to its major overhaul in 1995 as part of the Uruguay Round Agreements.

Irwin, Douglas A. 2005. *Free Trade under Fire.* 2d ed. Princeton: Princeton University Press. An excellent review of the case for free (freer) trade that also examines the various arguments for protection. Chapter 2 contains a nontechnical summary of the various ways trade liberalization stimulates economic growth.

Jackson, John H. 1969. *World Trade and the Law of the GATT.* Indianapolis, IN: Bobbs-Merrill. A standard reference work, by a leading GATT legal scholar, detailing the evolution of the GATT legal system during its first two decades.

League of Nations, Economic, Financial and Transit Department. 1942. *Commercial Policy in the Interwar Period: International Proposals and National Policies.* Geneva: League of Nations. A firsthand account of developments during 1918–39, with a focus on the many conferences and other international activities that were unable to prevent the catastrophic slide into worldwide protectionism and economic depression.

Petersmann, Ernst-Ulrich. 1997. *The GATT/WTO Dispute Settlement System.* London: Kluwer Law International. A very useful book by a leading GATT/WTO scholar that not only analyzes the GATT dispute settlement system (as well as that of the WTO), but also (a) places it in the broader context of international law and international organizations in general, and (b) uses several

concrete dispute settlement cases to illustrate GATT/
WTO law.

Winham, Gilbert R. 1998. "The World Trade Organization: Institution Building in the Multilateral Trade
System." *World Economy* 21 (3): 349–68. A political
scientist's view of the operation of the GATT and its
implications for the WTO.

World Trade Organization. 1999. *Guide to the Uruguay
Round Agreements.* Geneva: WTO Secretariat. In terms
of rhetoric and organization the official legal texts of the
Uruguay Round results are virtually incomprehensible
to the nonexpert. This book by WTO Secretariat staff
members presents the results in an authoritative but
understandable way that also makes it easy to get a good
sense of the overall package.

———. Website, http://www.wto.org. A comprehensive
user-friendly web site which, although focused on
the WTO, also includes material dealing with the
GATT, such as GATT documents and a list of the 128
GATT members at the time of its absorption by the
WTO.

RICHARD BLACKHURST

■ General Agreement on Trade in Services (GATS)

The General Agreement on Trade in Services
(GATS), an outcome of the Uruguay Round of
trade negotiations, contains the first set of multilateral rules for trade in services. It entered into force on
January 1, 1995, nearly fifteen years after it was first
put on the multilateral trade agenda at the initiative
of the United States (Feketekuty 1988). Developing
countries initially resisted negotiating services, but
today some, such as India, that have a growing stake
in services exports, are the main proponents. After
nearly twenty-five years of virtually continuous negotiations, the GATS has helped create a more secure, rule-based environment for services trade, but
it has so far failed to generate significant new trade
liberalization.

The Scope of the GATS The GATS is extremely
wide in scope and covers all measures affecting *trade
in services.* Instead of worrying about a precise defi-

nition of what a service is, GATS negotiators proceeded to list the entire range of services covered:

1. Business services
2. Communication services
3. Construction services
4. Distribution services
5. Educational services
6. Environmental services
7. Financial services
8. Health-related and social services
9. Tourism and travel-related services
10. Recreational, cultural, and sporting services
11. Transport services

As if this list were not long enough, there is a twelfth
residual category, "Other services not elsewhere
included."

Since the conventional definition of trade—
where a product crosses the frontier—would miss out
on a whole range of international transactions, the
GATS also takes an unusually broad view of trade,
which is defined (in Article I) to include four modes
of supply:

- *Mode 1—Cross-border*: services supplied
  from the territory of one member into the
  territory of another. An example is software
  services supplied by a supplier in one
  country through mail or electronic means to
  consumers in another country.

- *Mode 2—Consumption abroad*: services
  supplied in the territory of one member to
  the consumers of another. An example is
  when the consumer moves, for instance, and
  consumes tourism or education services in
  another country. Also covered are activities
  such as ship repair abroad, where only the
  property of the consumer moves.

- *Mode 3—Commercial presence*: services
  supplied through any type of business or
  professional establishment of one member
  in the territory of another. An example is an
  insurance company owned by citizens of
  one country establishing a branch in another country.

- *Mode 4—Presence of natural persons*: services
  supplied by nationals of one member in the

territory of another. This mode includes both independent service suppliers, and employees of the services supplier of another member. Examples are a doctor of one country supplying through his physical presence services in another country, or the foreign employees of a foreign bank. Note that the GATS does not apply to measures affecting natural persons seeking access to the employment market of a member, or to measures regarding citizenship, residence, or employment on a permanent basis.

Thus any measure affecting the supply of services through any of these modes is covered by the GATS. The inclusion of commercial presence as a mode extends the reach of the agreement to measures affecting foreign direct investment (FDI), and the inclusion of presence of natural persons (at the insistence of developing countries) to measures affecting the entry of foreign nationals, both of which have traditionally been a tightly controlled province of national governments.

The Rules of the GATS The major provisions of the GATS are summarized in table 1. The wide scope of the GATS contrasts with the gentleness of its rules. It is convenient to think of GATS rules as operating at two levels. First, there is a set of general rules that apply across the board to measures affecting trade in services; and second, there are the sector-specific commitments made by members, which determine the liberalizing impact of the agreement.

Key General Rules: The MFN Principle and Transparency Article II of the GATS constitutes a general obligation which is, in principle, applicable across the board by all members to all services sectors. Article II:1 of GATS states: "With respect to any measure covered by this Agreement, each Member shall accord immediately and unconditionally to services and service suppliers of any other Member treatment no less favorable than that it accords to like services and service suppliers of any other country." The GATS and its Most Favored Nation (MFN) obligation came into effect, however, before World Trade Organization (WTO) members were willing to completely eliminate discriminatory measures in services trade.

Table 1
Major provisions of the GATS
(article and main disciplines implied)

I	Definition. Trade in services covers all four modes of supply.
II	Most-Favored-Nation (MFN) obligation. Option to invoke exemptions on a one-time basis.
III	Notification and publication. Obligation to create an enquiry point.
IV	Increasing participation of developing countries. High-income countries to take measures to facilitate trade of developing nations.
V	Economic integration. Allows for free trade and similar agreements.
VI	Rules for domestic regulation. Requirements concerning the design and implementation of service sector regulation, including in particular qualification and licensing requirements.
VII	Rules on recognition of qualifications, standards, and certification of suppliers.
VIII	Monopolies and exclusive suppliers. Requires that such entities abide by MFN and specific commitments (Articles XVI and XVII) and do not abuse their dominant position.
IX	Business practices. Recognition that business practices may restrict trade. Call for consultations between members on request.
XIV	General exceptions. Allows measures to achieve noneconomic objectives.
XVI	Market access. Defines a set of policies that may only be used to restrict market access for a scheduled sector if they are listed in a member's specific commitments.
XVII	National treatment. Applies in a sector if a commitment to that effect is made and no limitations or exceptions are listed in a member's schedule.
XVIII	Additional commitments. Allows for any other specific commitment to be made on a sector-by-sector basis. To date these have been limited primarily to telecommunications, through the so-called Reference Paper.
XIX	Calls for successive negotiations to expand coverage of specific commitments (Articles XVI and XVII).
XXIX	States that annexes are an integral part of the GATS.

Specific sectoral sensitivities, such as a large number of bilateral agreements in maritime and road transport, that were revealed in the Uruguay Round raised the specter of wholesale sectoral exclusions from GATS as a means of avoiding the MFN rule. In order to prevent this, it was agreed to permit limited exemptions to MFN under GATS. Such exemptions, however, had to be taken at the time the negotiations were concluded and *in principle* were not meant to last longer than 10 years (that is, not beyond 2004) but at present they show no sign of disappearing.

Apart from services specified in individual MFN exemption lists, the only permitted departure from most-favored-nation treatment under the GATS covers preferential treatment among countries that are members of regional trading arrangements. The GATS rules on "Economic Integration," in Article V, are modeled on those in Article XXIV of the GATT. Article V:1 permits any WTO member to enter into an agreement to further liberalize trade in services with the other countries that are parties to the agreement, provided the agreement has "substantial sectoral coverage," eliminates measures that discriminate against service suppliers of other countries in the group, and prohibits new or more discriminatory measures. An approved agreement must be designed to help trade among its members, and must not result in an increase in the overall barriers faced by nonmembers in trading with the group within the respective sectors or subsectors (Article V:4). If the establishment of the agreement, or its subsequent enlargement, leads to the withdrawal of commitments made to nonmembers, there must be negotiations to provide appropriate compensation (Article V:5). Agreements that have been notified so far include the North American Free Trade Agreement; the European Communities; agreements between the European Union (EU) and the Slovak Republic, Hungary, Poland, the Czech Republic, Romania, Norway, Iceland, Liechtenstein, and Bulgaria (many of which became redundant upon accession of the countries concerned to the EU); and agreements between Canada and Chile and between Australia and New Zealand.

A related exception from the MFN rule, for the movement of natural persons, is permitted by Article V *bis* of the GATS. This allows countries to take part in agreements that establish full integration of labor markets. The only such agreement notified so far is the one involving Denmark, Finland, Iceland, Norway, and Sweden.

Specific Commitments on Market Access and National Treatment The GATS depends to a large extent on the specific commitments on market access and national treatment made by members. Both types of commitments are made for each of the four modes of delivery of service transactions.

Article XVI stipulates that measures restrictive of *market access* that a WTO member cannot maintain or adopt, unless specified in its schedule, include limitations on: (1) the number of service suppliers; (2) the total value of services transactions or assets; (3) the total number of services operations or the total quantity of service output; (4) the total number of natural persons that may be employed in a particular sector; (5) specific types of legal entity through which a service can be supplied; and (6) foreign equity participation (e.g., maximum equity participation). With the exception of (5), the measures covered by Article XVI all take the form of quantitative restrictions.

Three aspects of Article XVI are important. First, the Article XVI list does not include all measures that could restrict market access. Perhaps most significantly, fiscal measures are not covered. Thus, a member could maintain, without being obliged to schedule, a high nondiscriminatory tax on a particular service that severely limits market access. Second, Article XVI has been interpreted to cover both discriminatory and nondiscriminatory measures, that is, measures of the type "only five new *foreign* banks will be granted licenses" and also measures such as "only ten new [*foreign and domestic*] banks will be granted licenses." Finally, the limitations must be read as "minimum guarantees" rather than "maximum quotas," in other words, a country that has promised to allow five foreign banks entry is free to grant entry to more than five.

The other key pillar of the GATS is the *national treatment* obligation. Article XVII:1 states: "In the sectors inscribed in its Schedule, and subject to any conditions and qualifications set out therein, each

Member shall accord to services and service suppliers of any other Member, in respect of all measures affecting the supply of services, treatment no less favorable than that it accords to its own like services and service suppliers." Unlike Article XVI, Article XVII provides no exhaustive list of measures inconsistent with national treatment. Nevertheless, Article XVII:2 makes it clear that limitations on national treatment cover cases of both de jure and de facto discrimination. If domestic suppliers of audiovisual services are given preference in the allocation of frequencies for transmission within the national territory, such a measure discriminates explicitly on the basis of origin of the service supplier and thus constitutes formal, or de jure, denial of national treatment. Alternatively, a measure stipulating that prior residency is required to obtain a license to supply a service does not formally distinguish service suppliers on the basis of national origin, but it may de facto offer less favorable treatment for foreign suppliers because they are less likely to be able to meet a prior residency requirement than like service suppliers of national origin.

A member's specific commitments can be seen as the outcome of a two-step decision. Each member first decides which service sectors will be subject to the GATS market access and national treatment disciplines. It then decides which measures violating market access and/or national treatment respectively will be kept in place for each mode in that sector. Granting unrestricted market access with full national treatment would be equivalent to establishing free trade, and the flexible structure of rules reflects the desire of most governments to adopt a gradual and conditioned approach to opening up their markets. One result of this structure is that the GATS is not a particularly transparent or user-friendly instrument. More important, virtually all commitments made in the Uruguay Round were at best of a standstill nature, that is, a promise not to become more restrictive than already was the case for scheduled sectors (Hoekman 1996).

Doha Agenda and Beyond The negotiations under the Doha agenda show little sign of advancing services liberalization in the manner anticipated in the Uruguay Round. The best current offers of access in services do not even reflect the liberalization that has already taken place. The "request-offer" negotiating process, conducted first bilaterally and then pluriaterally, seems to have resulted in a low-level equilibrium trap where little is expected and less offered.

The WTO's Hong Kong Ministerial in December 2005 did identify the elements of a meaningful outcome in services. Such a package would have three elements. First was a promise not to impose new restrictions on trade in services. This would dispel the specter of protectionism that hangs over outsourcing of business services—which is producing huge cost savings in the North and ever-widening export opportunities for the South. Second was a commitment to eliminate barriers to FDI, either immediately or, in sectors where regulatory inadequacies need to be remedied, in a phased manner. The greatest benefits of securing openness to FDI, especially in infrastructure services, would accrue to the South while offering increased business opportunities to the North. Third was agreement to allow somewhat greater freedom of international movement for individual service providers (mode 4) in order to fulfill specific services contracts. Research, for example, by Winters et al. (2003) shows large potential benefits to both the North and the South from the liberalization of mode 4, as it offers a way to realize the gains from trade while averting social and political costs in host countries and brain drain losses for source countries.

For there to be a reasonable prospect of achieving these goals, more attention needs to be given to the regulatory context in which services liberalization takes place, in three ways. First, it may make sense to focus primarily on securing "national treatment," that is, ending all discrimination on the entry and operation of foreign services providers rather than on creating more intrusive disciplines. This will reassure regulators that multilateral commitments deprive them only of the freedom to discriminate and do not limit their freedom to regulate in any other way or to adopt policies that improve sector performance.

Second, it may be necessary to establish a credible mechanism to provide regulatory assistance to support liberalization commitments by developing countries. This will reassure developing country policymakers that regulatory inadequacies that could undermine the benefits of liberalization will be remedied before any market-opening commitments take effect.

Third, it should be possible to make temporary entry of foreign services providers conditional on the fulfillment of specific conditions by source countries. Immigration authorities in host economies must be assured that source countries will cooperate to screen services providers, to accept and facilitate their return, and to combat illegal migration.

In essence, these proposals suggest that it may be necessary for services negotiations to be complemented by broader cooperation. The assumption is that poorer developing countries would participate meaningfully in negotiations that offered an opportunity not merely to make binding commitments but also to mobilize assistance for regulatory reform. And migration authorities would engage constructively in negotiations that offered the opportunity not only to untie their hands, but also to secure assistance from source countries to deal with problems they cannot solve on their own.

See also Doha Round; financial services; nondiscrimination; temporary movement of natural persons; trade in services; World Trade Organization

FURTHER READING

Feketekuty, Geza. 1988. *International Trade in Services: An Overview and Blueprint for Negotiations.* Cambridge, MA: Ballinger. One of the first proposals for services negotiations at the WTO by one of the main protagonists.

Hoekman, Bernard. 1996. "Assessing the General Agreement on Trade in Services." In *The Uruguay Round and the Developing Countries*, edited by Will Martin and L. Alan Winters. Cambridge: Cambridge University Press, 88–124. The first and most comprehensive assessment of the GATS agreement and commitments.

Mattoo, Aaditya. 2005. "Services in a Development Round: Three Goals and Three Proposals." *Journal of World Trade* 39 (6): 1223–38. Proposals on how the GATS could become a more powerful catalyst for services trade reform.

Winters, L. A., T. L. Walmsley, Z. K. Wang, R. Grynberg. 2003. "Liberalizing Temporary Movement of Natural

Persons: An Agenda for the Development Round." *World Economy* 26 (8): 1137–61. Estimates the potential gains from the OECD countries allowing increased immigration.

AADITYA MATTOO

■ **generalized system of preferences (GSP)**
See special and differential treatment

■ **Gini coefficient**
See global income inequality

■ **Global Environment Facility**
The Global Environment Facility (GEF) grew out of an awareness in the 1980s of transboundary environmental problems and the accompanying recognition that efforts to improve matters would be costly (Sjöberg 1994). Launched in 1991 by the World Bank as an experimental facility, the GEF entered a three-year pilot program to test approaches and resolve competing governance schemes. Today it is the single largest grant-making institution for global environmental programs (Clémençon 2006). The GEF has allocated some $5 billion for more than 1,500 projects in 140 countries (GEF 2005). Because of its size, the GEF has great potential for affecting international environmental health, but as of 2007 its clearest results had been short-term, quantifiable projects such as those within the ozone program. The GEF's ability to work with populations around the world to create integrative, sustainable, long-term benefits will bolster its own position as an international environmental lender and promote the health of environments and communities worldwide.

Mission, Funding, and Change GEF projects are developed and financed through three implementing agencies: the World Bank, UN Environment Program (UNEP), and UN Development Program (UNDP). The World Bank is responsible for investments and mobilizing resources from the private sector. UNEP supports developing scientific and technical analysis, advancing environmental management in GEF financed activities, and managing the Scientific and Technical Advisory Panel. UNDP is responsible for building the human and institutional capacities that enable governmental agencies or nongovernmental organizations to take the actions necessary for global environmental protection. Executing agencies include regional development banks and a number of specialized UN agencies. GEF operations are coordinated by a Secretariat in Washington, DC.

The GEF provides concessional financing to cover the incremental costs necessary to achieve global environmental benefits. Incremental costs are calculated by subtracting the costs of any national or local benefit from the total cost of the project in order to provide financial incentives to create global environmental benefits. Cofunding is expected to cover the "national" benefits of the project. As such, GEF funding is intended to complement traditional development assistance by covering the additional costs or agreed incremental costs incurred when a development project also targets global environmental objectives. As one observer noted, "GEF assistance is not development 'aid' in the traditional sense, but the payment, by a certain group of donors, for the import of environmental services (cleaner air, biodiversity protection, etc.) provided by the South" (Jordan 1995, 306).

Today, the GEF promotes environmentally beneficial projects in developing countries through six focal areas: biological diversity, climate change, international waters, ozone depletion, land degradation, and persistent organic pollutants, as well as multifocal projects (see figure 1). The GEF acts as the financial mechanism for the following global conventions and international agreements: the UN Framework Convention on Biological Diversity, the UN Framework Convention on Climate Change, the Montreal Protocol, the UN Framework Convention on Combating Desertification, and the Stockholm Convention on Persistent Organic Pollutants.

In 2002, the GEF received $2.92 billion for the 2003–6 lending cycle, its largest financial allocation

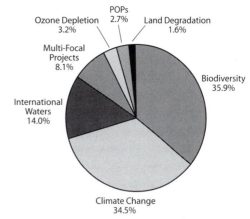

Figure 1

Distribution of GEF allocations by focal area. Source: GEF 2005.

up to that point in time. The United States is the largest single shareholder, supplying 20 percent of GEF financial contributions. However, since the GEF's first funding cycle, the United States has been holding down GEF funding levels. Most recently, it required the GEF to adopt a new resource allocation framework as a condition of continued U.S. financial support (Clémençon 2006).

Tackling Global Environmental Dilemmas and Achieving Results The GEF Evaluation Office independently monitors and evaluates GEF programs and projects. It periodically publishes its assessments in independent overall performance studies (OPS). The 2005 performance study (OPS3) emphasizes the challenge inherent in such evaluations: while some projects have quantifiable benefits and may be evaluated within immediate, short-term timeframes, most GEF projects are large and require long time frames to see results (GEF 2005b). The success of long-term projects hinges not merely on whether the GEF has completed a checklist of environmental goals, but also on whether the project is sustainable; projects must achieve financial sustainability by the time GEF funding ends (Clémençon 2006).

The Ozone Program is notable for its quantifiable, short-term benefits. Although not officially linked to the Montreal Protocol, the GEF has aided countries with economies in transition in achieving their obligations under the protocol. Consumption of ozone depleting substances (ODS)—chlorofluorocarbons, halons, carbon tetrachloride, and methyl chloroform—decreased by 99.8 percent from the 1980s to 2003 (GEF 2005b). Much of the success of this small-budget program is due to external factors such as economic slowdowns, but OPS3 finds that the GEF has essentially achieved its goal of eliminating the consumption and emission of ozone depleting substances in countries with economies in transition (GEF 2005b).

Other programs in the GEF portfolio may contribute to environmental benefits, but their success is dependent on long-term project sustainability and will not be quantifiable for decades. Instead, impacts can be measured in terms of socioeconomic and political achievements. The International Waters Program, which has no global convention to follow, has helped to foster open lines of communication and to jump-start regional cooperation among stakeholders and countries, in part by supporting the development of global and regional conventions (Clémençon 2006). Though less quantifiable than projects in the ozone area, the achievements of International Waters programs are nonetheless significant in terms of effecting positive environmental and socioeconomic conditions (GEF 2005b).

Likewise, GEF's energy efficiency portfolio has played an important role "in developing and transforming the markets for energy and mobility in developing countries" (GEF 2005b). The Climate Change Program has seen some socioeconomic and capacity-building impacts, but clear-cut environmental benefits remain blurry: while a particular Climate Change project may bring about carbon reduction, its effects are negligible in view of overall world emissions. One way to think about GEF interventions is that they may only be successful if they are replicable, lead to more funding, or build capacity that makes possible future policy development and implementation (Clémençon 2006). In this light, the success of the Climate Change projects has been limited.

The resources that GEF directs toward preserving biodiversity are notable. However, the impact of these resources remains ambiguous. The GEF's

contribution of more than U.S. $2 billion to biodiversity projects from 1991 to 2005 makes it the largest single benefactor of biodiversity (GEF 2005a). The GEF is thus highly influential for the future of the world's biodiversity, but one study reports that it is "difficult, if not impossible, to determine the impact GEF funding has had on the biodiversity it sought to protect" (Horta, Round, and Young 2002, 18). A recent assessment of some 34 biodiversity conservation projects found that in two-thirds of the projects, important outcomes were not sustained after project completion (Dublin, Volonte, and Braun 2004). The GEF's role in achieving the global goal of placing 10 percent of the world's land area in preservation should not be overlooked, and conservation within protected areas has been impressive, but biodiversity loss outside of protected areas continues unchecked (Clémençon 2006).

Since 1994, evaluations of the GEF have emphasized the necessity of a holistic approach that addresses the root causes of environmental problems (Horta, Round, and Young 2002; GEF 2002). The 2005 performance study (OPS3) echoes this call, specifically with attention to sustainability of natural conditions as well as political and social conditions. A biodiversity project, for example, may successfully establish a protected area in the short term, but the sustainability of that area is necessary in order to reduce biodiversity loss in the long term. Likewise, projects in the International Waters area are expected to take decades to establish the institutional and legal conditions to achieve improved water conditions (Gerlak 2004). Attention to the persistence of natural, political, and social conditions is key to the success of these projects.

In addition to sustainability, the 2006 performance study prescribes a more strategic vision and a clearer definition of performance indicators (GEF 2005b). Because of the complex nature of transboundary environmental projects, numerous agencies, organizations, and stakeholders lobby the GEF and a multiplicity of organizations offer guidance. Established in 2003, GEF's strategic priorities were intended to handle the proliferation of guidance coming from various global conventions and conferences but have actually increased guidance and broadened a strategic focus at the GEF (GEF 2005b). OPS3 envisions a synergistic, strategic approach with focused, coherent, and prioritized goals that could capitalize on areas where projects overlap, thus increasing efficiency. An approach that spans the focal areas as well as the various levels of landscape, ecosystem, country, and region will "allow GEF to fulfill its role as catalyst and facilitator of global environmental sustainability" (GEF 2005b, 4).

The halting or reversal of practices leading to the deterioration of the global environment exceeds the resources the GEF can provide. The GEF can, however, provide stimuli to catalyze local and governmental work toward mitigating environmentally harmful effects of various processes. On the learning curve of environmentally beneficial lending, the GEF has climbed quickly, especially within quantifiable, technical areas. While the learning curve at this point flattens out, the topography of complex, systems-oriented programs becomes unstable. The GEF's ability to navigate this terrain is imperative to its survival as the world economy's largest environmental lending organization and to its ability to affect the health of environments worldwide.

See also aid, international; multilateral environmental agreements; trade and the environment

FURTHER READING

Clémençon, Raymond. 2006. "What Future for the Global Environment Facility?" *Journal of Environment and Development* 15 (1): 50–74. Calls for a comprehensive look at the GEF as an institution and a consideration of the funds necessary to achieve its environmental objectives. In light of dwindling funds to the GEF's already modest resource base, this article seeks to stimulate discussion about fundraising and the future of the GEF.

Dublin, H., C. Volonte, and J. Braun. 2004. "GEF Biodiversity Program Study." *Monitoring and Evaluation Unity*. Washington, DC: GEF Secretariat. Program assessment by an independent expert and staff of the GEF Monitoring and Evaluation Unit; a major contribution to OPS3.

Gerlak, Andrea K. 2004. "One Basin at a Time: The Global Environment Facility and Governance of Transbound-

ary Waters." *Global Environmental Politics* 4 (4): 108–41. The first independent academic analysis of the International Waters program, this paper reveals broad trends in transboundary water governance, finding that the GEF has fared better with individual projects than with building capacity or enhancing the contractual environment.

Global Environment Facility (GEF). 2002. *Focusing on the Global Environment: The First Decade of the GEF*. Second Overall Performance Study (OPS2). Washington, DC: GEF. Assesses the extent to which the GEF has achieved its main objectives since restructuring in 1994 and policies adopted by GEF Council.

———. 2005a. "Achieving the Millennium Development Goals: A GEF Progress Report." *Global Environment Facility*. Washington, DC: GEF. Juxtaposes GEF environmental objectives with the UN Millennium Development Goals and draws important connections between human and environmental systems.

———. 2005b. "Overall Performance Study: Progressing Toward Environmental Results." Available online at http://www.gefweb.org/MonitoringandEvaluation/MEPublications/MEPOPS/documents/Publications_OPS3_E-book.pdf. The GEF's third overall performance study launches the fourth replenishment cycle of the GEF and assesses the extent to which the GEF has achieved, or moved toward achieving, its environmental objectives. OPS3 focuses its recommendations on synergistic, integrative strategies that bridge projects across both geographical and institutional levels.

———. 2006. www.gefweb.org. The GEF website provides a rich source for publications and documents by the GEF, as well as descriptions of the GEF's history, organizational scheme, financial contributions, participants, and stakeholders.

Horta, Korinna, Robin Round, and Zoe Young. 2002. "The Global Environment Facility: The First Ten Years—Growing Pains or Inherent Flaws?" *Environmental Defense and Halifax Initiative*. Washington, DC: GEF. Evaluates the first ten years of GEF operations, finding it a flawed mechanism in need of fundamental reform. Analyzes the successes and failures of the Small Grants Program.

Jordan, Andrew. 1995. "Designing New International Organizations: A Note on the Structure and Operation of the Global Environmental Facility." *Public*

Administration 73: 303–12. Traces the development of the GEF during the pilot phase and restructuring and examines issues likely to dominate a post-pilot phase GEF and sketches the broad potential of the GEF.

Sjöberg, Helen. 1994. "From Idea to Reality: The Creation of the Global Environment Facility." *Global Environment Facility*. Washington, DC: GEF. Documents the process leading up to the creation of the pilot phase of the GEF and examines the various proposals made and the negotiations which followed, leading up to the 1994 agreement on the new GEF.

ETHAN C. MYERS AND ANDREA K. GERLAK

■ global imbalances

Global imbalances are large and unsustainable mismatches in crucial macroeconomic variables in major countries or areas of the world economy. Among the most serious and persistent global imbalances in the early 21st century are (1) the large and unsustainable trade deficits of the United States and surpluses of China, Japan, and some other emerging Asian economies, (2) inadequate national savings of the United States and the excessive savings of China and Japan, (3) high unemployment rate of Europe and inadequate growth of Japan, and (4) dismal poverty and slow growth of some of the world's poorest countries in relation to the very high standards of living in advanced countries. Left uncorrected, these global imbalances can lead to serious economic problems in the countries and regions involved and for the world as a whole.

Persistent large U.S. trade deficits could lead to a collapse, or sharp depreciation, of the dollar, which in turn could result in higher interest rates and recession in the United States, and slower economic growth or recession in the rest of the world. Inadequate U.S. savings and excessive savings in China, Japan, and some other (mostly Asian) emerging market economies are leading to large capital inflows from these countries to the United States and a high level of U.S. international indebtedness; but a sudden sharp reduction in such capital inflows could inflict serious economic damage on the United States and

the entire world economy. High unemployment in Europe and slow growth in Japan due to their somewhat rigid or inflexible economies sharply reduce the economic growth of these economies and push them toward trade protectionism in a vain effort to protect labor and unproductive sectors from world competition, especially from China and other dynamic emerging Asian economies. Finally, dismal poverty and slow growth of some of the poorest countries, especially those of sub-Saharan Africa, lead to strife and political unrest in these countries and ethical conflicts and turmoil in the collective conscience of the rich countries.

Trade Imbalances between the United States and East Asia Table 1 shows the enormous and rapidly growing trade deficits of the United States, on the one hand, and the large trade surpluses of China and Japan, on the other hand, since the mid-1990s. The table shows that the U.S. trade deficit rose sharply from $191 billion dollars or 2.4 percent of the U.S. gross domestic product (GDP) in 1996 to $452 billion or 4.6 percent of the U.S. GDP in 2000, and $782 billion or 6.3 percent of U.S. GDP in 2005. Trade deficits in excess of 2 or 3 percent of GDP are deemed by most economists to be unsustainable in the long run and need to be corrected. Table 1 also shows that almost one half of the U.S. trade deficit is with China and the other emerging markets of East Asia and Japan, and it is against the currencies of these nations that the dollar is overvalued. The situation is different with respect to Europe and the euro. Since 2001 the dollar has depreciated substantially with respect to the euro. Overall, the large and rapidly increasing U.S. trade deficits are the result of extremely low and declining savings (table 2) of the United States and its more rapid growth relative to the euro area and Japan over the past decade.

Inadequate U.S. Savings Another serious global imbalance is given by the inadequate savings of the United States, on the one hand, and the excessive savings of China, Japan, and some other emerging Asian economics (sometimes referred to as a global savings glut). Table 2 shows that the savings rate of the United States declined from an average of 16.3

Table 1
Trade imbalances of leading industrial countries and areas, 1996–2005 (in billions of U.S. dollars)

Country/area	1996	1997	1998	1999	2000	2001	2002	2003	2004	2005
United States	−191.0	−198.1	−246.7	−346.0	−452.4	−427.2	−482.3	−547.3	−665.4	−782.7
US with respect to:										
Western Europe	−24.4	−24.2	−38.3	−58.4	−74.9	−77.1	−100.7	−116.4	−131.5	−146.4
Japan	−48.7	−57.3	−65.4	−74.8	−83.0	−70.6	−71.8	−67.8	−77.5	−84.7
China	−39.6	−49.7	−57.0	−68.7	−83.9	−83.2	−103.2	−124.1	−162.0	−201.7
Other Asia	−38.0	−41.3	−64.8	−81.0	−104.4	−90.2	−92.9	−100.0	−114.8	−83.2
Euro area	—	—	—	80.0	28.8	65.2	122.2	120.6	130.4	68.0
Japan	83.6	101.6	122.4	123.3	116.7	70.2	93.8	106.4	132.1	94.0
China	19.5	46.2	46.6	36.0	34.5	34.0	44.2	44.7	59.0	134.2

Source: Survey of Current Business, July 2006; IMF *International Financial Statistics Yearbook,* 2006.

percent of GDP in the period 1990–99 to 13.3 percent of GDP in 2005, or by 2.9 percentage points from 1991 to 2005, while U.S. investment rose from an average of 18.7 percent of GDP in the period 1990–99 to 20.0 percent of GDP in 2005, or by 1.5 percentage points from 1991 to 2005. As a result, U.S. net borrowing abroad (negative U.S. net savings) increased from an average of 2.4 percent of GDP in the period 1990–99 to 6.7 percent of GDP in 2005, or by 4.4 percentage points (−2.9–1.5 in net savings) from 1991 to 2005. The counterpart of the huge U.S. net borrowing was the large foreign net lending to the United States, primarily by Asian countries, with the euro area practically in savings-investment balance.

Most foreign lending to the United States during the 1990s took the form of foreign direct investments (FDI) attracted by high U.S. growth and profitability. During this period, an increasing amount of foreign capital flows to the United States took the form of foreign official purchases of U.S. government securities and accumulation of dollar reserves, mostly by Japan and Asian emerging market economies, especially China. By buying U.S. government securities and accumulating dollar reserves, Asian countries avoided a large depreciation of the dollar vis-à-vis their own currencies and hence a sharp reduction in their exports to the United States and to the rest of the world (which would result from Asian exports becoming much more expensive for consumers and businesses paying for them in depreciated dollars). Essentially, Asian countries thus followed an export-led growth strategy financed by lending large sums to the United States. This resulted in a dollar overvalued with respect to most Asian currencies and in a large and unsustainable U.S. trade deficit (the counterpart of the large U.S. net borrowing abroad).

Economists disagree over how long this process can continue. But a significant and rapid reduction in net foreign loans (capital inflows) to the United States could lead to a collapse of the dollar, higher interest rates in the United States, and a U.S. and world economic recession and crisis. There is a broad consensus among economists that the medium- and long-term solution to this problem is for the United States to adopt policies to stimulate domestic savings and curb its expenditures. This is not easy to do because, as most economists would agree, American consumers and firms have become accustomed to living with increasing levels of debt, and it is difficult to change this behavior. An increase in the U.S. savings rate would reduce the need for capital inflows, reduce or eliminate the dollar misalignment, and reduce U.S. trade deficits to sustainable levels. The United States, however, is hardly doing enough to overcome its savings-investment imbalance—a problem that could not, in any event, be easily or quickly solved. It has been suggested that China and other emerging market economies should increase domestic expenditures while Japan should restructure

Table 2
Savings, investments, and net savings in major economic areas, 1990–2005 (percent of GDP)

Country/area	Average 1990–99	Average 2000–03	2004	2005	Cumulative change 1991–2005 (percentage points)
United States					
Savings	16.3	15.5	13.4	13.3	−2.9
Investment	18.7	19.2	19.6	20.0	1.5
Net savings	−2.4	−3.7	−6.2	−6.7	−4.4
Euro area					
Savings	21.2	20.9	21.2	20.9	−1.0
Investment	19.8	20.7	20.5	20.9	0.7
Net savings	1.4	0.2	0.7	0.0	−1.7
Japan					
Savings	31.4	26.7	26.4	26.8	−7.6
Investment	29.0	24.0	22.7	23.2	−9.7
Net savings	2.4	2.7	3.7	3.6	2.1
China					
Savings	38.7	37.1	46.8	51.3	13.5
Investment	37.0	35.0	43.3	44.1	9.4
Net savings	1.7	2.1	3.5	7.2	4.1

Source: BIS, *Annual Report*, 2006.

its economy to further stimulate its growth. The International Monetary Fund through its new surveillance mandate may encourage the United States, China, and Japan to take cooperative steps to reduce their saving-investment imbalance to sustainable levels.

Structural Imbalances in Europe and Japan
Although savings and investment are in near balance in the euro area (see table 2), this part of the world faces a serious structural imbalance, which has kept its growth rate well below its potential and much lower than the growth rate in the United States since 1996 (see table 3). The restructuring that had taken place in the euro area during the decade from the mid-1990s to the mid-2000s clearly was inadequate, and its economy, especially its labor market, remained excessively rigid by the end of 2007. In addition, some economists argued that the euro area did not pursue the creation of a "new economy" sufficiently aggressively, and it thus was not able to harvest as much benefit as the United States did in the late 20th and early 21st centuries. From 1996 to 2005, the average annual growth rate was 2.0 percent for real (inflation-adjusted) GDP and 0.8 percent for labor productivity in the euro area, as compared with 3.3 percent and 2.2 percent, respectively, in the United States. This has kept the rate of unemployment much higher in the euro area than in the United States and contained European imports over the past decade.

Economists generally agree that the appropriate long-term policy for the euro area to overcome its imbalance would be to accelerate or speed up the restructuring of its economy and liberalize its labor markets, as well as encourage more rapid adoption and spread of new ICT (information and communications technology), and so stimulate labor productivity and growth of its economy. Strong labor opposition, however, has so far prevented European governments from introducing the deep structural reforms necessary. This may be understandable— Europe is proud of its high wages and generous social protection benefits, and it seems unwilling to compromise them. It is also difficult to introduce reforms

Table 3
Growth of real GDP and labor productivity, and unemployment rate, 1996–2005 (percentages)

Country/area	1996	1997	1998	1999	2000	2001	2002	2003	2004	2005	1996–2005 average
United States											
Real GDP	3.7	4.5	4.2	4.4	3.7	0.8	1.6	2.7	4.2	3.5	3.3
Labor productivity	1.8	2.1	1.9	2.4	1.9	0.9	2.8	2.7	3.1	2.1	2.2
Unemployment rate	5.4	4.9	4.5	4.2	4.0	4.7	5.8	6.0	5.5	5.1	5.0
Euro area											
Real GDP	1.4	2.6	2.7	2.9	4.0	1.9	1.0	0.7	1.8	1.4	2.0
Labor productivity	0.8	1.6	0.7	0.7	1.5	0.3	0.3	0.3	0.9	0.5	0.8
Unemployment rate	10.7	10.6	10.1	9.2	8.2	7.9	8.3	8.7	8.9	8.6	9.1
Japan											
Real GDP	2.6	1.4	−1.8	−0.2	2.9	0.4	0.1	1.8	2.3	2.7	1.2
Labor productivity	2.1	0.3	−1.1	0.6	3.2	0.9	1.4	2.0	2.1	2.3	1.4
Unemployment rate	3.4	3.4	4.1	4.7	4.7	5.0	5.4	5.3	4.7	4.4	4.5

Source: OECD, *OECD Economic Outlook,* June 2006.

and restructure labor markets when the economy is growing slowly. Furthermore, the benefits of restructuring generally come only over time, but most of the costs are paid up front. The longer the restructuring is delayed, however, the more the euro area falls behind the United States in real per capita income. In fact, after rapidly reducing the gap in real per capita income from more than 50 percent in 1950 to approximately 10 percent in the 1980s, the euro area average real per capita income slipped back to about 76 percent of U.S. income in 2005, widening the gap to 24 percent.

The Japanese imbalance is also structural and mostly internal in nature, thus requiring, for the most part, domestic policies to correct it. Specifically, Japan was in recession or slow growth for the entire decade of the 1990s, and by the end of 2007 still faced major structural imbalances. Domestic deflation rather than international disturbances was the primary cause of the large undervaluation of the yen with respect to the dollar and thus of the large Japanese trade surplus vis-à-vis the United States. By most yardsticks, Japan has a unique situation—it saves too much and consumes and invests domestically too little (see table 2).

Japan has followed three policies to correct its domestic deflation and structural imbalance. It has pursued a very powerful expansionary monetary policy, which has kept nominal interest rates at a practically zero level (with real rates negative because of domestic deflation). It has adopted an equally powerful expansionary fiscal policy (evidenced by an average annual budget deficit of 6.4 percent of GDP from 1996 to 2005 and 6.8 from 2001 to 2005—and a public debt equal to 172.1 percent of GDP in 2005). Finally, Japan has actively intervened in foreign exchange markets to prevent a further yen appreciation and a reduction of its exports. In fact, Japan's foreign exchange dollar reserves increased from about $120 billion in 1996 to $830 billion at the end of 2005. Yet, until 2004, Japanese growth remained very subdued. Despite the fact that growth resumed in 2004, remaining structural imbalances still kept Japan performing below its potential by 2007.

Dismal Poverty and Growing Global Inequality
Still another serious global imbalance in the world today is dismal poverty and slow growth of some of the world's poorest countries, especially those of sub-Saharan Africa. Table 4 gives the population and the per capita income of various countries or groups of

Table 4
Population and economic and health indicators, 1990–2004

Country/region	Population in 2004 (millions)	Income per capita		Infant mortality rate per 1,000 live births		Life expectancy at birth (years)	
		Dollars 2004	Growth rate 1990–2004 (% per year)	1990	2004	1990	2004
Low and middle income	5,344	1,502	2.2	69	59	63	65
Sub-Saharan Africa	719	600	0.3	111	100	49	46
East Asia and Pacific	1,870	1,416	6.4	43	29	67	70
of which, China	1,296	1,500	7.0	38	26	69	71
South Asia	1,448	594	3.6	86	66	59	63
of which, India	1,080	620	4.2	80	62	59	63
Europe and Central Asia	472	3,295	0.5	40	29	69	69
Middle East and N. Africa	294	1,972	1.1	60	44	64	69
Latin America and Caribbean	541	3,576	1.1	43	27	68	72
High-income economies	1,001	32,112	2.6	9	6	76	79
World	6,345	6,329	0.5	64	54	65	67

Source: World Bank, *World Development Report*, 2006; and *World Development Indicators*, 2006.

countries in 2004, as well as the growth in real per capita income from 1990 to 2004, and infant mortality and life expectancy in 1990 and 2004. The table shows that the average per capita income of all developing economies and former communist countries was only $1,502 in 2004 ($620 and $1,500 for India and China, respectively) as compared with $32,112 in high-income developed economies. Worse still, the average growth of real per capita income was close to zero in sub-Saharan Africa (as a result of drought, wars, rapid population growth, the spread of HIV, and the general failure of development efforts), only 0.5 percent in Europe and Central Asia (because of economic restructuring after the collapse of communism), and 1.1 percent in the Middle East (because of wars, political turmoil, and the sharp decline in petroleum prices during the 1990s).

The average growth of real per capita income was also very low (only 1.1 percent) in Latin America and the Caribbean between 1990 and 2004 because of political turmoil and failure in the development effort. Only in East Asia and the Pacific economies (and in particular, in China) did the real per capita

income increase very rapidly from 1990 to 2004. In South Asia, the growth of real per capita income, while not as spectacular as in East Asia, was very respectable, largely fueled by the economic revitalization of India. The table also shows that infant mortality is much higher and life expectancy much lower in low-income developing countries, especially in sub-Saharan Africa, than in high-income developed countries, but major improvements were made in both measures throughout the world from 1990 to 2004 (except, again, in sub-Saharan Africa). But the wide disparities in per capita incomes between rich and poor countries, especially the poorest developing countries, can be regarded as one of the most serious global imbalances in the world economy today.

An international economic system that has spread the benefits from globalization so unevenly can hardly be said to be functioning properly—not to mention equitably. And a world where millions of people starve not only is unacceptable from an ethical point of view, but also can hardly be expected to be peaceful and tranquil. The huge difference in standards of living between rich countries and the poorest ones certainly represents one of the most serious global imbalances in the world economy today.

See also balance of payments; Bank of Japan; conflicted virtue; dollar standard; European Central Bank; foreign exchange intervention; international financial architecture; International Monetary Fund surveillance; international reserves; liquidity trap, the; mercantilism; poverty, global; twin deficits

FURTHER READING

Bank for International Settlements (BIS). 2006. *Annual Report*. Basel: BIS. Report by the Bank for International Settlements on the world's financial and banking situation.

Campano, Fred, and Dominick Salvatore. 2006. *Income Distribution*. New York: Oxford University Press. Discusses how to measure changes in income distribution and income inequalities within and among nations.

de Rato, Rodrigo. 2005. "Global Imbalances and Global Poverty—Challenges for the IMF." Available at http://www.imf.org/external/np/speeches/2005/022305.htm. An analysis of the relationship between global imbalances and global poverty by the former managing director of the International Monetary Fund.

Eichengreen, Barry. 2004. "Global Imbalances and Lessons of Bretton Woods." NBER Working Paper No. 10497 (May). Washington, DC: National Bureau of Economic Research. Shows how global imbalances led to the collapse of the Bretton Woods System in the early 1970s and what can we learn from it.

Geitner, Timothy. 2006. "Policy Implications of Global Imbalances." Remarks at the General Financial Imbalances Conference at Chatham House, London (January 23). Available at http://www.ny.frb.org/newsevents/speeches/2006/gei060123.html. Proposals for correcting the global imbalances facing the world toward the end of the first decade of the 21st century by the president of the Federal Reserve Bank of New York.

International Monetary fund (IMF). 2005. "Global Imbalances: A Saving and Investment Perspective." *World Economic Outlook* (September). Washington, DC.: IMF, 91–124. Provides data on the saving-investment imbalance in the world economy and proposals for how to overcome it.

———. 2006a. *Annual Report*. Washington, DC: IMF. An analysis of the world's economic and financial situation by the International Monetary Fund.

———. 2006b. *World Economic Outlook* (September). Washington, DC: IMF. Provides a biyearly overview of the world economy by the International Monetary Fund.

OECD. 2006. *Economic Outlook* (June). Paris: OECD. A biyearly overview of the world economy by the Organisation for Economic Co-operation and Development.

Rajan, Raghuram G. 2005. "Global Imbalances—An Assessment." http://www.imf.org/external/np/speeches/2005/102505.htm. An evaluation of global imbalances facing the world toward the end of the first decade of the 21st century by the former chief economist of the International Monetary Fund.

Rogoff, Kenneth. 2006. "Global Imbalances and Exchange Rate Adjustment." *Journal of Policy Modeling* (August 2006): 695–99. An examination of how global imbalances could be eliminated or reduced by a coordinated approach by the world's major economies by the former chief economist of the International Monetary Fund.

Salvatore, Dominick. 2005. "Currency Misalignments and Trade Asymmetries among Major Economic Areas." *The Journal of Economic Asymmetries* 2 (1): 1–24. Shows how misalignments among the currencies of the major economies are the results of global structural imbalances and how to correct them.

———. 2006. "Twin Deficits in the G-7 Countries and Global Structural Imbalances." *Journal of Policy Modeling* (August): 701–12. Shows the relationship between budget deficits and current account deficits in the leading industrial economies.

United Nations. 2006. *Human Development Report*. New York: UN. Provides different measures of the standard of living of member nations by the United Nations.

World Bank. 2006a. *Annual Report*. Washington, D.C.: World Bank. An analysis of the world's economic and financial situation by the World Bank.

———. 2006b. *World Development Indicators*. Washington, D.C.: World Bank. A wealth of data on each country's economic and financial situation by the World Bank.

DOMINICK SALVATORE

■ global income inequality

Prevailing concerns about economic inequity in the world reflect many aspects of living standards and how they are distributed, and no single measure can hope to capture all those concerns. As conventionally measured, "inequality" and "poverty" are quite different aspects of income distribution, in that the former focuses on the (absolute or relative) disparities in income (or consumption), while the latter focuses on absolute levels of deprivation, which depend on the average levels of living in society as well as inequality.

Both poverty and inequality are closely related to a third concept, "social welfare," which aggregates welfare levels, which are taken to depend, at least in part, on income. (Differences in "income needs" may also play a role.) Poverty and social welfare are both sensitive to income changes at the bottom of the distribution: if everything else is held constant, as poverty rises, social welfare falls. They differ, however, in that standard measures of social welfare are also sensitive to changes at the top of the income ladder, whereas poverty measures typically are not. Inequality also relates to social welfare, since most social welfare functions have curvature properties that penalize higher inequality at any given mean income (Atkinson 1970).

Well-being itself has many dimensions, of course, and interpersonal aggregation is fraught with difficulties. Some people argue that the standard of living should be assessed in terms of capabilities—the set of "beings and doings" one is capable of enjoying—rather than income or consumption (see, for example, Sen 1985). This can be interpreted as an issue of how best to deal with interpersonal heterogeneity in income "needs."

There is not enough room in this entry to do justice to all these issues. The focus here is on global consumption and income distribution, and how they are changing.

Concepts, Methods, and Data Conceptual and methodological differences lie at the root of the ongoing debates about global inequality. There are significant differences in four main areas: the welfare indicator ("inequality of what?"), the definition of the distribution, the choice of inequality measure, and the appropriate data sources. Without some understanding of these differences, it is impossible to take an informed position in this debate.

Inequality of What? Standard practice has been to rank households by consumption or income per person. The consumption or income numbers that can be formed from most nationally representative large household surveys are reasonably comprehensive, in that they span the commodity space or all income sources (with imputed value for income in kind from production for one's own use or consumption). But they can hardly be considered complete metrics of welfare; access to subsidized health care or schooling is generally excluded, for example. Hence it is important to also look separately at key "nonincome" dimensions of welfare that capture the missing components. We will return to this topic, but for now we focus on the standard consumption or income measures available from surveys.

The choice between consumption and income is not a minor one, since inequality is generally lower for consumption than for income, due to consumption smoothing (whereby savings or borrowing are used to assure that living standards do not vary as much over time as incomes do). The consensus in the development literature is that consumption is both the conceptually preferable measure—given some degree of smoothing in the presence of intertemporal income variability—and more accurately measured in surveys. (Against this view, however, some scholars have argued that income may better reflect opportunities for consumption.)

The near-universal normalization by household size is also questionable. For example, it does not allow for economies of size in consumption (whereby two people can live more cheaply together than apart), and doing so can affect inequality and poverty comparisons, such as the claims often heard that larger households are poorer (Lanjouw and Ravallion 1995).

Naturally, household surveys measure expenditures in local currencies, which then have to be converted to a single currency. The basic choice is between market exchange rates, which measure international purchasing power in terms of traded goods, and purchasing power parity (PPP) exchange rates, which adjust for the fact that nontraded goods tend to be cheaper in poorer countries. Almost all researchers prefer PPPs, although there is more than one way to measure PPP exchange rates. The Geary-Khamis (GK) method used by the Penn World Tables (PWT) underestimates global inequality since the quantity weights used to compute the international price indexes give greater weight to consumption patterns in richer countries, which in turn results in an overestimate of expenditures in poorer countries. The Eltöte, Köves, and Szulc (EKS) method, which is the multilateral extension of the bilateral Fisher index, attempts to correct for this bias. (On the differences between the GK and EKS methods and implications for global poverty measures, see Ackland, Dowrick, and Freyens 2006. Since 2000, the World Bank's global poverty and inequality measures have been based on the Bank's PPPs, which use the EKS method.)

Although these are all difficult measurement issues, the main sources of the differences in existing numbers on the evolution of global poverty and inequality lie elsewhere.

What Distribution? There are three main—and very different—ways of defining the "world income distribution." The first is the distribution of country mean incomes, unweighted by population; we call this the "intercountry income distribution." This is of interest primarily to those who view the country, rather than the individual, as the main unit of interest. If gross domestic product (GDP) per capita is used as a measure of the country mean income, this concept corresponds closely to the macroeconomic literature on testing for international income convergence (see, e.g., Quah 1996; Pritchett 1997). The second distribution is that of country means, weighted by population—the "international income distribution." This places higher weight on more populous countries.

The third definition focuses on the distribution of *individual* incomes, across all people in the world. This is the "global income distribution," and for those concerned with the individual—rather than the country—as the fundamental unit of analysis, this third concept is clearly preferable. If inequality between rich Chinese (or Americans) and poor Chinese (or Americans) is rising, why should this not be counted as part of world inequality? The earlier literature focused on intercountry and international inequalities largely for data availability reasons. It is only since about the mid-1980s that household survey data have become available for a sufficient number of countries so as to enable a computation of global inequality. (These three measures—intercountry, international, and global—correspond, respectively, to inequality concepts 1, 2, and 3, as defined by Milanovic 2005. For decomposable measures, international income inequality corresponds to the between-country component of global inequality.)

What measure? A key conceptual distinction—too often ignored in applied work—is between *relative* and *absolute* measures of inequality. We consider relative measures first. One of the most popular inequality measures is the Gini index, which is constructed by summing income differences, expressed as a ratio to the mean, across all individuals in a population and then dividing it by the number of people. This measure has an intuitive interpretation: if two individuals are drawn at random, then the expected difference in their incomes, normalized by the mean, will be equal to twice the Gini index. The index can also be depicted graphically. If one orders the population from poorest to richest, and graphs the cumulative income share against the cumulative population share of each percentile (thereby obtaining the "Lorenz curve"), then the Gini index is twice the area between the Lorenz curve and the diagonal. There are many other inequality measures; a good overview can be found in Cowell (2000). Another popular measure is the mean log deviation, given by the average proportionate gap between mean income and actual income; this measure has some attractive properties, including decomposability into (population-weighted) between-group and within-group components (Bourguignon 1979).

These measures of inequality are designed to be *scale-invariant*, meaning that they do not change if every income in the distribution is multiplied by a positive constant. The resulting measure then depends solely on income *ratios*, in contrast to absolute measures, which depend on the absolute *differences* in incomes. If every person becomes 10 percent richer, then a relative measure of inequality does not change, even though the (absolute) gains to the rich are many times larger than those to the poor.

Many commentators on globalization appear to focus on absolute income differences rather than relativities. Being sensitive to differences rather than ratios, an absolute inequality measure would increase in our hypothetical scenario of a 10 percent rise in everyone's incomes. Though not often used in practice, an absolute version of the Gini index can be constructed by dropping the normalization of income differences by the mean, so that the measure is one-half of the mean difference in incomes of pairs of individuals.

It may well be the case that much of the debate about what is happening to inequality in the world is actually a debate about whether one thinks about "inequality" in relative or absolute terms (Ravallion 2004). Yet the choice between absolute and relative inequality measures is not a matter of right or wrong. They correspond to different procedures for aggregating gaps between incomes, and thus to different normative concepts of inequality. (Ravallion 2004 discusses this issue further and the implications of other conceptual distinctions, such as between vertical and horizontal inequality, for one's assessment of the impact of globalization on inequality.)

Other observers in the globalization debate focus more on absolute levels of living of the poor, rather than the gaps (whether absolute or relative) between the rich and poor. The measures of poverty found in practice reflect the absolute consumption or income shortfalls from some agreed minimum standard, the poverty line, which aims to have the same real value over time and (when relevant) space. Suppose again that all incomes increase by 10 percent. Relative inequality will remain the same and absolute inequality will have risen. But the incidence of absolute poverty will have fallen, reflecting the higher living standards of the poor. Although this entry focuses

mainly on global inequality, this would give an incomplete picture if we did not also look at what has been happening to global poverty.

What data sources? One might have guessed that there was general agreement on data sources, but that is not the case, and the choices made do matter. There are essentially two approaches. The first relies on secondary data sources, from existing data compilations such as the World Bank's *World Development Indicators*, and the second relies more heavily on primary sources, including unit-record data from household surveys.

A number of studies have used quintile shares or inequality measures derived from various inequality data bases as estimates of inequality in each individual country (examples include Bhalla 2002; Sala-i-Martin 2006). These shares are often derived from already grouped data (rather than from microdata), and they refer to different welfare concepts (income or consumption) and different recipient units (households or individuals). In order to increase the data coverage, the quintiles are pooled together without due attention to their comparability.

Another data issue is the choice between using national accounts (NAS) versus household survey means as the appropriate mean for the distribution. While GDP per capita numbers computed from NAS were traditionally used to construct intercountry and international distributions, household surveys have been the traditional tool for measuring poverty and inequality. The aggregates from these sources generally do *not* agree, and that is hardly surprising when one probes the way the numbers are generated. It seems that over relatively long time periods the two data sources tend to converge to a common ratio in most countries, but the remaining difference in levels can be sizable, and there are some notable short-term divergences (as documented by Ravallion 2003 and Deaton 2005).

Whether using quintile estimates from secondary data or original microdata, some authors rescale individual incomes in each country so as to have a mean corresponding to GDP per capita (from the NAS). They often argue that surveys do not capture a number of determinants of welfare, such as publicly provided goods. They also worry about income underreporting in these surveys.

There are problems with this rescaling method. On the one hand, it is not clear that the NAS data can provide a more accurate measure of mean *household* welfare than the survey data that were collected precisely for that purpose. On the other hand, even acknowledging the problems of income underreporting and selective survey compliance, there can be no presumption that the discrepancies with the NAS are distribution neutral; more plausibly, the main reasons why surveys underestimate consumption or income would also lead to an underestimation of inequality. For example, Banerjee and Piketty (2005) attribute up to 40 percent of the difference between the (higher) growth of GDP per capita and (lower) growth of mean household per capita consumption from household surveys in India to unreported increases in the incomes of the rich. Selective compliance with random samples could well be an equally important source of bias, although the sign is theoretically ambiguous; Korinek, Mistiaen, and Ravallion (2006) provide evidence on the impact of selective nonresponse for the United States.

Nor are the NAS always reliable. For instance, global inequality results depend crucially on China, but China's GDP per capita numbers are the subject of intense debate. Maddison (2003) and, to a lesser extent, Penn World Tables give significantly higher values for China's GDP per capita in the 1950s and 1960s than the official Chinese statistics. The differences have important implications for the estimation of global inequality.

For these reasons, there is a growing recognition that adjustment of household survey data by the NAS mean is probably undesirable (Deaton 2005; Bourguignon and Morrisson 2002; Anand and Segal 2008). The best current practices in measuring global inequality and poverty increasingly rely, to the maximum extent feasible, on nationally representative household survey data.

The Evolution of Global Inequality and Poverty Acknowledging these conceptual, data, and methodological caveats, what can be said about trends in the world distribution of income?

Bourguignon and Morrisson (2002) constructed a time series of world inequality estimates for the period from 1820 to 1992. For all but the last ten to twenty years of that series, disaggregated household survey data are not available for a large number of countries. Countries were grouped into 33 blocks, with block composition changing over time, depending on data availability (for details, see Bourguignon and Morrisson 2002). The distributions are constructed in such a manner that all the members of a block are assumed to have the same distribution as a country for which distribution data are available. The authors construct a distribution based on decile (and some ventile) shares, and on GDP per capita figures. Individuals are assumed to have the same incomes within tenths (or twentieths) of the distribution, where that income corresponds to the group's share of GDP per capita. This hybrid of the concepts discussed in the previous section was the compromise that allowed the authors to construct a long time series covering most of the 19th and 20th centuries. Given the long-run perspective of this exercise, however, it is likely that some of the problems discussed in the previous section were only moderately important. In particular, the estimated evolution of GDP per capita over such a long period is likely to be very strongly correlated with any measure of household welfare.

The main finding of the study is that world inequality rose almost continuously from the onset of the industrial revolution until the First World War. During that period, the Gini coefficient rose from 0.50 to 0.61. Although inequality was also rising within most countries for which data were available, the real driving force for this increase in global disparity was inequality *between* countries, that is, international inequality (see figure 1).

Between the two World Wars, and until around 1950, a decline in within-country inequality was observed, but the rise in inequality across countries continued apace and proved to be the dominant force. The world Gini coefficient rose further to 0.64. From the middle of the 20th century on, the rise of global inequality slowed, as Japan and parts of East Asia started growing faster than Europe and North

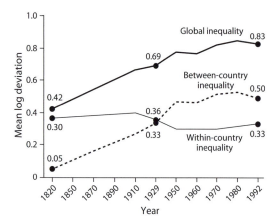

Figure 1

Inequality between and within countries. Source: Authors' manipulation of data from Bourguignon and Morrisson (2002).

America. This process became particularly pronounced after the takeoff of China in the 1980s. Broadly speaking, global inequality changes in the second half of the 20th century were much less significant than in the previous 130 years: there was certainly a reduction in the growth of inequality and, toward the end of the period, inequality may have started to decline.

When considering the last decades of the 20th century, however, better and more comprehensive data are available. Household survey data coverage, and the data's availability to researchers, increased dramatically in the 1980s and 1990s, and it became possible to construct not only intercountry and international inequality series based on a broader set of countries, but also real global income distributions, from the microdata.

Looking at the second half of the 20th century with these data, Milanovic (2005) and World Bank (2006) highlight two interesting regularities. First, even as (unweighted) intercountry inequality continued to grow between 1950 and 2000, international inequality began to fall. The disparate behavior in these two inequality concepts has been one of the reasons behind disagreements on globalization and inequality. The continuing rise in intercountry inequality (to which Pritchett 1997 refers as "divergence, big time") was due largely to slow

growth in most poor (and small) countries, relative to some middle-income and richer countries. The decline in international inequality, which refers to a population-weighted distribution, was due fundamentally to rapid growth in two giant countries that started out very poor: China and, to a lesser extent, India. As figure 2 suggests, once China and India are excluded from the international distribution, the post-1980 trend in that inequality concept changes dramatically and becomes much closer to the rising trend in intercountry inequality.

The second regularity is that the last two decades of the 20th century saw a resumption in the upward trajectory of within-country inequality, defined as the aggregate contribution of within-country inequality to total inequality. The rise in within-country inequality prevented the decline in international inequality (which began, slowly, around the 1960s) from translating immediately into a decline in global inequality. Recall that global inequality is the sum of (appropriately aggregated) within-country inequality and international inequality. Indeed, Milanovic (2002, 2005) finds that global income inequality between people was still rising between 1988 and 1993, but appears to have fallen between 1993 and 1998. This is confirmed by World Bank (2006), which extends Milanovic's data set by a couple of years.

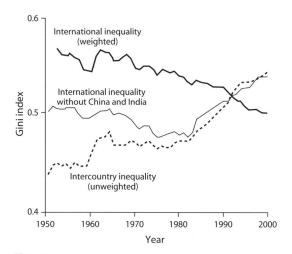

Figure 2

Intercountry inequality and international inequality. Source: Milanovic (2005).

The foregoing discussion has been about relative inequality. What about the competing concept of absolute inequality, which depends on the absolute gaps in levels of living between the "rich" and the "poor"? As figure 3 shows, the two concepts give rise to completely different trends for international inequality: whereas all relative inequality measures shown fall from 1990 on, all absolute measures record substantial increases. The difference is practically as important when considering global inequality. It would slightly increase and plateau when defined in relative terms and increase drastically when defined in absolute terms.

Recall that none of these measures tell us directly about the absolute standard of living of poor people. Has rising inequality reflected falling living standards for the world's poor? Using the longest available period of time with consistent series—1981–2004—the World Bank's latest estimates (reported in Chen and Ravallion 2007) show that the poverty rate for the developing world as a whole fell from 40 percent in 1981 to 18 percent in 2001, judged by the $1/day standard at PPP (figure 4). Here too measurement methods matter. Using secondary sources on inequality and NAS data on mean income, Sala-i-Martin (2006) finds that the global poverty rate fell from 13 percent in 1980 to 7 percent in 1998. By both methods, the poverty rate was almost halved over 1980–2000, although the levels are quite dif-

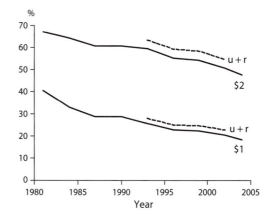

Figure 4

Incidence of absolute poverty in the developing world. This figure gives the estimated percentage of the population of the developing world living below $32.74 per month ("$1 a day") and $65.48 per month ("$2 a day") at 1993 consumption PPP. The lines u + r give the corresponding percentages when one incorporates an allowance for the higher cost of living in urban areas. Source: Chen and Ravallion (2007).

ferent. However, GDP includes much more than household consumption, and it is not clear why one would use the same poverty line when switching from household consumption from surveys to GDP from national accounts. Sala-i-Martin's estimates based on a $2/day line—to allow for the non–household consumption share of GDP—accord quite closely with the World Bank's estimates using $1/day.

While there is broad agreement that the world is making progress against absolute poverty, there are some important regional exceptions, notably much of sub-Saharan Africa over the 1980s and 1990s. It is also notable that a sizable share of the overall progress has been due to the success against poverty of just one country, China (Chen and Ravallion 2007).

Inequality in Other Dimensions Although this entry (and the broader debate) has focused on income inequality trends, there should be no presumption that it is the only inequality that matters. Indeed, from some perspectives, international disparities in health status and educational achievement may matter just as much (in addition to being instrumentally important in shaping income inequality and poverty). Since around 1930 there has

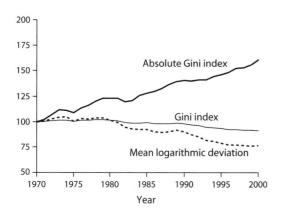

Figure 3

Absolute and relative inequality in the world. Source: Atkinson and Brandolini (2004).

been convergence in the intercountry and international distributions of life expectancy at birth (LEB). As mean world (weighted) LEB rose from 53.4 years in 1960 to 64.8 years in 2000, its distribution moved from bimodality to unimodality and the coefficient of variation fell from 0.233 to 0.194 (World Bank 2006). This heartening trend was partly reversed, however, during the 1990s, when LEB fell precipitously in some of the world's poorest countries, due largely to the spread of HIV/AIDS.

Educational inequality, measured by the distribution of years of schooling, has also fallen substantially since the 1960s. As mean years of schooling in the world rose from 3.4 in 1960 to 6.3 in 2000, the coefficient of variation fell from 0.739 to 0.461. (Note that inequality measures for variables like life expectancy or years of education have to be interpreted with care. Both variables are close to being bounded from above, and inequality tends to fall automatically when the mean increases.) This pattern of rising means and falling inequality in attainment was common to all regions of the world and, in addition, all regions also saw a reduction in gender disparities, as measured by the male to female schooling ratio (World Bank 2006).

Unfortunately, this reduction in *attainment* inequality has not always meant a reduction in the disparities in true educational *achievement*. Indeed, internationally comparable test score data suggest that these disparities remain strikingly large with, for example, the reading competence of the average Indonesian student in 2001 being equivalent to that of a student in the seventh percentile of the French distribution.

These changes in the distribution of health and education should be taken into account when assessing global inequality in a broad sense. While this entry provides only a very brief summary of the existing evidence along each dimension, a number of scholars have attempted to explore the correlations among the different dimensions. Because increases in longevity have been greater in poorer countries, for instance, Becker, Philipson, and Soares (2005) argue that inequality in measures of well-being that account for quantity, as well as quality, of life have been declining throughout the postwar period.

Another important aspect is the correlation of incomes over time, and the lack of mobility of countries in the international distribution. The persistence of poverty and income gaps across countries or individuals is not adequately represented by measures that are based on static snapshots of the global or international distribution of income. Relative income dynamics matter. Somehow, the severity of inequality, as observed at two different points of time, depends on whether individuals keep the same position or whether they switch. This is the reason for the attention given to the issue of convergence and the accompanying concept of intercountry inequality; for further discussion see Bourguignon, Levin, and Rosenblatt (2004), who analyze in some detail this issue of country mobility in the international distribution.

More work is needed to properly evaluate the extent of "global inequity" in all its dimensions and its evolution over time. Yet, despite the conceptual and methodological minefield inherent in measuring world income inequality and poverty, it is possible to reach agreement on some key stylized facts:

- Global income inequality was high in the early 19th century, but is even higher today.
- From the industrial revolution until roughly the middle of the 20th century, inequality rose in all three concepts of world income distribution: intercountry, international, and global.
- From around 1950 onward, although intercountry inequality continued to rise, (population-weighted) international inequality first stabilized and then declined. This reflects the catch-up of Asia with Europe and North America.
- Rising within-country inequality has attenuated the decline in global (interpersonal) inequality associated with growth in some of the poorest and largest countries, notably China and India. Nevertheless, global inequality appears to have fallen, or at least reached a high plateau, during the late 1990s.
- Although world inequality in the first few years of the 21st century has not yet been

properly analyzed, it seems likely that this trend has continued. Since 2002, the mean growth rate for low-income countries has been above the average rate for high-income countries, for the first time since the 1960s.

- Absolute income inequality in the world—the absolute gap between "rich" and "poor"—has been rising since at least 1970 and probably for a long time prior to that.
- Even so, the incidence of absolute poverty in the world as a whole has been falling since at least the early 1980s, though more rapidly in some periods and regions than others.
- Some large disparities in human development persist, although it is encouraging that global inequalities in health and education attainments have been falling overall. The scourge of HIV/AIDS has threatened this progress, with falling life expectancies in some of the poorest countries.

See also international income convergence; poverty, global

FURTHER READING

Ackland, Robert, Steve Dowrick, and Benoit Freyens. 2006. "Measuring Global Poverty: Why PPP Methods Matter." Mimeo. Research School of Social Sciences, Australian National University. Considers how differences in PPPs used affect calculation of global inequality.

Anand, Sudhir, and Paul Segal. 2008. "What Do We Know about Global Income Inequality?" *Journal of Economic Literature* 46 (1): 57–94. A critical assessment of methods and results of global inequality calculations.

Atkinson, Anthony B. 1970. "On the Measurement of Inequality." *Journal of Economic Theory* 2 (3): 244–63. Explores measures of inequality and their welfare implications.

Atkinson, Anthony, and Andrea Brandolini. 2004. "Global Income Inequality: Absolute, Relative, or Intermediate?" Paper presented at the 28th General Conference of the International Association for Research on Income and Wealth. August 22. Cork, Ireland. How standard results are overturned if instead of measures of relative inequality one uses absolute inequality.

Banerjee, Abhijit, and Thomas Piketty. 2005. "Top Indian Incomes, 1922–2000." *World Bank Economic Review* 19 (1): 1–20. Long-term evolution of income share of the very rich in India based on tax returns.

Becker, Gary, Tomas Philipson, and Rodrigo Soares. 2005. "The Quantity and Quality of Life and the Evolution of World Inequality." *American Economic Review* 95 (1): 277–91. How improvements in life expectancy and their lower dispersal across countries might imply less inequality across global citizens measured over their lifetime.

Bhalla, Surjit. 2002. *Imagine There's No Country: Poverty, Inequality, and Growth in the Era of Globalization.* Washington, DC: Institute for International Economics. Both global poverty and inequality are argued to be much lower than conventionally thought.

Bourguignon, François. 1979. "Decomposable Income Inequality Measures." *Econometrica* 47 (4): 901–20. Why decomposability (between recipients) matters for inequality measures and what are the measures that satisfy it.

Bourguignon, François, Victoria Levin, and David Rosenblatt. 2004. "Declining International Inequality and Economic Divergence: Reviewing the Evidence through Different Lenses." *Economie Internationale* 100: 13–25. Reviews the reasons why rigorous statistical analysis based on different definitions leads to contradictory conclusions about the evolution of global inequality.

Bourguignon, François, and Christian Morrisson. 2002. "Inequality among World Citizens: 1820–1992." *American Economic Review* 92 (4): 727–44. Calculates long-term trends in global inequality, both of income and income adjusted for life expectancy among countries.

Chen, Shaohua, and Martin Ravallion. 2007. "Absolute Poverty Measures for the Developing World, 1981–2004." Policy Research Working Paper No. 4211. Washington, DC: World Bank. Estimates poverty head counts using microdata from household surveys.

Cowell, Frank. 2000. "Measurement of Inequality." In *Handbook of Income Distribution*, vol. 1, edited by Anthony B. Atkinson and François Bourguignon. Amsterdam: North-Holland, 87–166. Measures of inequality, their characteristics, and the connection between inequality and welfare measurement.

Deaton, Angus. 2005. "Measuring Poverty in a Growing World (or Measuring Growth in a Poor World)." *Review of Economics and Statistics* 87 (2): 353–78. Issues in methodology of poverty and inequality measurement, especially the choice between survey-derived and national accounts mean income or consumption.

Korinek, Anton, Johan Mistiaen, and Martin Ravallion. 2006. "Survey Nonresponse and the Distribution of Income." *Journal of Economic Inequality* 4 (2): 33–55. How lower response among rich households biases measures of inequality and poverty.

Lanjouw, Peter, and Martin Ravallion. 1995. "Poverty and Household Size." *Economic Journal* 105 (433): 1415–35. How to correctly account for household economies of size and scale when measuring poverty.

Maddison, Angus. 2003. *The World Economy: Historical Statistics*. Paris: OECD Development Centre Studies. GDP and population statistics, often estimated and interpolated, for practically all countries of the world, and descriptions of main long-term trends of world economy.

Milanovic, Branko. 2002. "True World Income Distribution, 1988 and 1993: First Calculation Based on Household Surveys Alone." *Economic Journal* 112 (476): 51–92. Calculation of global inequality based mostly on microdata from household surveys.

———. 2005. *Worlds Apart: Measuring International and Global Inequality*. Princeton, NJ: Princeton University Press. How intercountry, international, and global inequality have evolved after the end of World War II up to the year 2000.

Pritchett, Lant. 1997. "Divergence, Big Time." *Journal of Economic Perspectives* 11 (3): 3–17. Intercountry income inequality was much less at the time of the industrial revolution than in the late 20th century.

Quah, Danny. 1996. "Empirics for Economic Growth and Convergence: Stratification and Convergence Clubs." *European Economic Review* 40 (6): 427–43. Discusses the shape of intercountry distribution of mean incomes under different scenarios regarding income convergence or divergence.

Ravallion, Martin. 2003. "Measuring Aggregate Economic Welfare in Developing Countries: How Well Do National Accounts and Surveys Agree?" *Review of Economics and Statistics* 85 (3): 645–52. Explores differences in the time path of the means calculated from household surveys and national accounts.

———. 2004. "Competing Concepts of Inequality in the Globalization Debate." In *Brookings Trade Forum 2004*, edited by Susan Collins and Carol Graham. Washington, DC: Brookings Institution, 1–38. How focus on absolute or relative measures of inequality affects our view of globalization.

Sala-i-Martin, Xavier. 2006. "The World Distribution of Income: Falling Poverty and . . . Convergence. Period." *Quarterly Journal of Economics* 121 (2): 351–97. Combines GDPs per capita and distributional data to make estimates of global poverty and inequality.

Sen, Amartya. 1985. *Commodities and Capabilities*. Amsterdam: North-Holland. Explores how welfare can be defined in terms of capacity to perform certain functions rather than solely in terms of access to goods.

———. 2001. "Ten Theses on Globalization." *New Perspectives Quarterly* 14 (4): 9–15. Inequality is at the core of the globalization debate even if globalization is not a zero-sum game.

Sutcliffe, Bob. 2003. "A More or Less Unequal World? World Income Distribution in the 20th Century." Working Paper Series No. 54. University of Massachusetts Amherst, Political Economy Research Institute. Published as "World Inequality and Globalization." *Oxford Review of Economic Policy* 20 (1): 15–37. A critical review of several studies of global inequality.

World Bank. 2006. *World Development Report: Equity and Development*. New York: Oxford University Press. Assesses global inequality in income, education, and health outcomes, and places it into the context of inequality of opportunity.

FRANÇOIS BOURGUIGNON, FRANCISCO FERREIRA, BRANKO MILANOVIC, AND MARTIN RAVALLION

■ **global production networks (GPNs)**
See commodity chains

■ **global public goods**
Whether people live in industrial or developing countries, whether they are poor or rich, their well-being, in large measure, depends on the availability of

a well-tuned balance between private goods, like food or clothing, and public goods, like peace and security, rule of law, communicable disease control, or financial stability. Many public goods have assumed a global dimension. They are global in that their benefits (and, as the case may be, their costs) span national borders, making an impact on countries in several regions and affecting not only present but perhaps also future generations.

Definition of Public Goods and Global Public Goods The classification of goods as private or public is based on their consumption properties. Goods that are made or left excludable and for which clear property rights can thus be assigned are referred to as private goods. It is up to its owner to decide how and by whom a private good can be used or consumed.

In contrast, public goods are nonexclusive in consumption. They are in the public domain, available for all. The term *good* in this context has no value connotation. People's preferences for these goods may vary widely, due to socioeconomic, political, cultural, and geographic factors. Some may perceive a public good such as financial stability as a top priority; and others may accord greatest importance to exploring new, drought-resistant crop varieties. Yet all face the same public goods, at the same provision level. As a result, the question of which public goods to provide, at which quantity, in what form, and at what net cost or net benefit to whom is often highly contested.

Moreover, in many—perhaps even most— instances, "publicness" and "privateness" do not constitute an innate property of the good. Rather, a good may be in the public domain, available for all to consume, for various reasons, including the following:

- Infeasibility of exclusion for technical or economic reasons (as in the case of the moonlight);
- Deliberate policy choice (as in the case of norms and institutions such as the regime of property rights);
- Policy neglect (as in the case of HIV/AIDS in poorer countries, which was allowed to linger and develop into a pandemic);

- Lack of knowledge and information (as in the case of chlorofluorocarbons, whose detrimental effect on the ozone shield was not recognized for a long time).

The publicness of a good in many instances reflects a policy choice. And so does globalness, which can be seen as a special dimension of publicness. From a worldwide perspective the creation of sovereign states has aspects of privateness, and reducing at-the-border or within-country policy barriers to free cross-border movements of goods, services, capital, and people—as has happened during recent decades as a result of often difficult and lengthy intergovernmental negotiations—entails reestablishing enhanced publicness.

The Link between Global Public Goods and Globalization Some global public goods such as the ozone layer or the moonlight are global-public by nature. Others would be most appropriately described as globalized national public goods. The globalization of hitherto essentially national public goods may occur for two main reasons. One is deliberate, intended harmonization of national public policy approaches and outcomes aimed at creating enhanced openness and interoperability of national physical and institutional infrastructure. Examples are the international civil aviation regime and the multilateral trade regime.

As openness progresses, national public policy domains become more closely interlocked. And as a result, a second, often unintended and also unaccounted-for process of national-public-good globalization sets in. Public effects or externalities now also move more easily across national borders—communicable diseases, contagion effects of financial crises, crime and violence, including terrorist threats.

Thus a growing group of globalized national public goods is joining the natural global commons and contributing to the increasing policy attention that global public goods are commanding today, nationally and internationally.

The Provision Path of Global Public Goods In order to understand the provision path of global public goods, it is useful, first, to examine how public goods are provided within the national context—and how this process has changed in recent decades.

Public goods and externalities are usually listed among the conditions associated with market failure and that may thus potentially justify state intervention. Many textbooks of public economics and public finance, therefore, refer to public goods also as state-provided goods. And indeed, some decades ago the state provided many goods directly and in full. In recent years, however, national borders have become increasingly open, the roles of markets and states have been rebalanced, and public-private partnering has increased. Today, public goods are often provided by multiple groups of actors—including governments, private business, civil society organizations, and private households and individuals.

Certainly, the state still exercises a certain amount of coercion (via regulation and taxation) to overcome the collective-action (free-riding) problems that often beset public goods precisely because they are public—available for all to consume once they exist. But its interventions are now geared less toward doing by itself what private actors won't do without adequate incentives, that is, direct intervention in the economy, and more toward creating incentives for other, nonstate actors to contribute to the provision of public goods.

If the provision of national public goods appears to be complex, the provision of global public goods is an even more complex process. Besides public and private actors it often also involves several—perhaps even, all—countries, and initiatives at the national as well as the international level.

The reason for the multilevel approach is that in many instances global public goods emerge as a result of a summation process: national public goods being provided in a concerted, harmonized fashion. For example, polio eradication requires immunizing the entire population in all countries. Of course, in order to achieve such concerted action across borders it is often important to have an international organization that oversees the implementation of the agreement to act. Thus global public goods may call for international cooperation *behind* national borders—within countries —and they may call for

international cooperation *beyond* national borders—at the international level. However, the bulk of the international cooperation required in order to support global public goods in many instances occurs at the national level.

In cases such as promoting the safety of air travel through airport security checks, the provision level of the good (air safety) depends on the contribution of the weakest link in the chain of providers. In these cases, it may, from a certain provision level onward, be more efficient for the other providers to find ways and means of encouraging the weakest-link actors to upgrade their contribution rather than improving provision levels at home. In such weak-link situations, corrective action at home may need to be complemented by interventions abroad. Yet, even in these cases, the bulk of international cooperation would most likely still consist of interventions within nations.

An exception arises in cases where the global public good follows a "best shot" production path. The invention of a vaccine is a case in point. Once the new vaccine technology has been found and formulated, it exists. To reinvent it would be inefficient. Yet, in order to release the new vaccine technology and permit its use, the inventors may want to be reimbursed for the research and development cost they incurred. If the vaccine in question is one that would primarily be of interest to the poor, the international foreign-aid community might decide to share the reimbursement costs and organize an international collective-action initiative for this purpose. In this case, international-level efforts may perhaps outweigh related national-level, private-sector initiatives.

Global challenges often need global responses. But "global" does not necessarily mean interventions only at the supranational level. Rather, it primarily means that governments in many countries have to act, individually as well as collectively, and in many instances also together with private and civil society actors—in concert, so that all the various inputs fit together and the global public good actually emerges.

At the national level, the state can intervene in a more or less direct, more or less coercive or incentivizing role to orchestrate the many contributions from the myriad of private and public actors who are often involved in the provision of public goods. However, the institution of the state has no equivalent internationally. Intergovernmental cooperation has to happen voluntarily. Hence a critical difference exists between the provision path of ("pure") national public goods and global public goods (including globalized national public goods). In international venues national governments are quasi-private actors: They tend to pursue national, particular interests.

One could thus expect that global public goods are severely underprovided. Indeed, several are, and it sometimes seems that the world is facing a lengthening list of global crises due to such underprovision—a crisis of global warming, intermittent financial instability, international terrorism, or new and resurgent communicable diseases. But then one also has to bear in mind that many global public goods are quite well provided, facilitating large streams of cross-border economic activity, sharing of information and knowledge, or the universalization of human rights and other norms such as those that help facilitate a good business climate.

The reason why quite a large number of global public goods are adequately provided despite the fact that intergovernmental cooperation has to happen voluntarily lies in the fact that different actors have different preferences for various public goods. Where their preference for a particular good is sufficiently strong, actors may in effect not free ride but reveal their preference—and pay for the provision of the good, irrespective of whether others may also enjoy it or not. Thus private business has often nudged governments into fostering the integration of markets. And civil society organizations have put pressure on governments to take action on global environment or gender concerns.

In the case of public goods generally, but certainly when it comes to global public goods, government failure or hesitation to act on these issues is often corrected by nonstate actors—either by way of private and voluntary provision of these goods (as the growing incidence of industry self-regulation signals) or by way of political advocacy and lobbying.

Policy Implications and Challenges The growing importance of global public goods has changed public policymaking in fundamental ways. It confronts policymakers with new tasks—to be met under new, changed conditions. As a result of greater economic openness, exclusive policymaking sovereignty is, in most countries, giving way to what might be called "responsive policymaking sovereignty." National policymaking increasingly takes into account not only national policy preferences but also external expectations (e.g., concerning rule of law or fiscal discipline) and global exigencies (e.g., the risk of global climate change).

As a result, it also appears that the role of the state is undergoing a fundamental change. The conventional Westphalian-type state that exercises exclusive policymaking sovereignty within its territorial boundaries is progressively giving way to the intermediary state, the hallmark of which is the blending of external and domestic policy expectations. Through this blending approach, states foster the globalization of national public goods and contribute what is expected of them in terms of delivery of national building blocks to global public goods.

The blending function of the intermediary state is evident not only from changes in budgetary allocations that echo global concerns (e.g., more resources devoted to fighting HIV/AIDS) but also from the use of new policy instruments geared to promoting, on the one hand, even further economic openness (e.g., through new investment laws), or on the other hand, new forms of national closure (e.g., through the introduction of "green" taxes to discourage border-transgressing pollution like greenhouse gas emissions).

Global public goods have changed the national toolkit of policymakers as well as conventional foreign policy. International cooperation beyond national borders is also changing from an essentially intergovernmental process to a multiactor process of public-private partnering. Similar to the change in the role of the state nationally, intergovernmental organizations are increasingly sharing the operational tasks of international cooperation with nonstate actors. Global markets are taking on tasks formerly performed by intergovernmental organizations. Examples are the emerging international carbon markets or also those for commodity-related futures and options markets. A variety of global public-private partnerships—established as either nonprofit or for-profit organizations—are today producing inputs into the provision of global public goods and making contributions to global equity concerns such as the development of poorer countries.

The Current Stage of the Debate on Global Public Goods Global public goods and their provision are a reality of growing importance. However, at present, this reality is frequently viewed through "old" conceptual lenses. International cooperation "practitioners" often view global public goods provision as foreign aid. The reason is that foreign aid or development assistance is a well-entrenched institution with existing policy and resource-mobilization channels. Thus when a global challenge like avian flu control requires financial support for a weak-link country that may lack requisite means for decisive and prompt corrective action, the richer industrial countries—the conventional aid donors—often use aid resources to provide such support. They do so, although this support is perhaps not being provided for ethical or moral reasons alone (i.e., because the recipient country is poor) but primarily in the "donors'" own, national self-interest—for efficiency rather than equity reasons.

Misperceptions occur not only on the practical-political side of global public goods provision but also on the academic, theoretical side. For the most part, mainstream public goods theory, and more broadly, public economics and finance theory are still based on the assumption of a closed, single economy. Thus current mainstream theory of public economics/finance may not always capture well the total provision path of global public goods. Its national-level focus may make it difficult for researchers to recognize that these goods call for a *concerted* provision of relevant national public goods and for limited yet critically important *complementary* international-level inputs like international agreements that often provide the framework for national-level policy harmonization.

A full understanding of how the provision of global public goods works at present and how it could work more effectively, efficiently, and equitably would require a broad perspective—a comprehensive examination of the overall provision path of these goods. It would involve rethinking a number of aspects of the current mainstream theory of public finance/economics. Much of this rethinking has so far been undertaken in respect to particular issues and is available in specialized journals and debates.

The time is now ripe for undertaking a synthesis of both the theoretical innovations and the lessons learned from various practical-political innovations that have been undertaken in order to respond to global challenges under the pressure of today's changed policy realities. An important question to explore in this context might also be whether an adequate understanding and management of the global economy would call for the creation of a new subfield within the domain of public finance/economics—the field of "global public finance."

See also aid, international; globalization; health and globalization; international policy coordination; social policy in open economies

FURTHER READING

Barrett, Scott. 2007. *A Guide to Understanding Global Public Goods.* New York: Oxford University Press. Prepared as a background study for the International Task Force on Global Public Goods (see www.gpgtaskforce.org), this work aims to make the concept of global public goods accessible to policymakers and the general public, and identifies policy options for correcting the under-provision of select global public goods that figure prominently on the international policy agenda.

Ferroni, Marco, and Ashoka Mody, eds. 2002. *International Public Goods: Incentives, Measurement, and Financing.* Washington, DC: Kluwer Academic and World Bank. Focuses on actions in the international arena to complement domestic efforts in addressing global challenges and addresses strategic and practical measures, with a special emphasis on financing international cooperation efforts in support of international—regional and global—public goods.

Kaul, Inge, and Pedro Conceição, eds. 2006. *The New Public Finance: Responding to Global Challenges.* New York: Oxford University Press. Recognizing that standard public economics and public finance theory has increasingly been adjusted to reflect the rebalancing of the roles of markets and states that has happened in recent decades but not yet to the greater openness of national borders, the authors of this volume explore how public finance has so far responded to globalization, notably the increased importance of global public goods and development concerns.

Kaul, Inge, Pedro Conceição, Katell Le Goulven, and Ronald U. Mendoza., eds. 2003. *Providing Global Public Goods: Managing Globalization.* New York: Oxford University Press. Building on the research and policy debates stimulated by the aforementioned book, this volume advances the concept of global public goods and deepens the discussion on the provision of these goods, covering both the negotiations or policymaking side of international cooperation as well as the operational side of cross-border collective action.

Kaul, Inge, Isabelle Grunberg, and Marc A. Stern, eds. 1999. *Global Public Goods: International Cooperation in the 21st Century.* New York: Oxford University Press. Introduces the concept of global public goods, explores its application to a variety of global concerns, and discusses the implications of the growing importance of global public goods for policymaking at the national and international levels.

Sandler, Todd. 2004. *Global Collective Action.* Cambridge: Cambridge University Press. Identifies the factors that promote or inhibit successful collective action at international levels for the growing set of global challenges associated with globalization. Because many of these concerns involve strategic interactions dependent on one's own and others' actions, the author examines these interactions in a simple but rigorous game-theoretic framework.

Sweden, Ministry for Foreign Affairs. 2001. "Financing and Providing Global Public Goods: Expectations and Prospects." Prepared by Keith Bezanson and Francisco Sagasti on behalf of the Sussex University Institute of Development Studies. Stockholm. A study of the idea of an effective and well-funded multilateral system for development. It recognizes that under conditions of glob-alization, development, including poverty reduction, and the provision of global public goods are two distinct yet closely linked endeavors.

www.gpgnet.net. The interested reader will find a comprehensive list of recently published contributions to the topic of global public goods, including academic studies, policy statements, and journalistic writings on the Knowledge Portal page. The Knowledge Portal classifies entries according to issue areas (e.g., climate stability, communicable disease control, or financial stability) and according to cross-cutting themes (like the concept of public goods and global public goods or the politics and financing of global public goods provision).

INGE KAUL

■ globalization

Globalization refers to a multidimensional process whereby markets, firms, production, and national financial systems are integrated on a global scale. These processes can range across a wide variety of affairs, but all point to the internationalization of everyday life. While we could speak of purely political or cultural aspects of this "shrinking of the world," the economic dimensions of globalization attract the greatest attention. Economic globalization centers on the material mechanisms connecting different countries, which then have political, cultural, and social consequences within and between states.

Some specific definitions of globalization take an overarching view of the economic ties comprising the phenomenon. For instance, the Organisation for Economic Co-operation and Development defines globalization as a process "by which markets and production in different countries become increasingly interdependent due to dynamics of trade in goods and services and then flows of capital and technology" (Stocker 1998). Others try to focus on more limited aspects of the economic contact across borders. Some, such as Richard Rosecrance (1999), prioritize the ease and volume of international flows of the factors of production themselves. For simplicity's sake, we can limit the discussion to three factors of production: land, labor, and capital. Land obviously is never mobile from one state to another, but the ability to move labor and capital over borders has fluctuated over time. Louis Pauly (1997) has observed that the opening up of financial markets since the early 1980s has focused scholarly attention on the fluidity of capital across borders. For many who study globalization, the integration of national financial systems, symbolized by the ease and speed at which capital can flow internationally, is the critical element of globalization.

Others emphasize the volume of goods in trade. Ronald Jones (2000), an economist, describes globalization in terms of rising interdependence—thus emphasizing the nature of the goods involved in trade, not merely the volume. This sort of interdependence involves a high degree of specialization and may also entail a fairly high level of integration of production across borders. While we can imagine ways in which factor flows involve single episodes of capital or labor flowing from one location to another (leaving each state different from before, but without a lasting relationship), the emphasis on trade suggests an evolving, intertwining connection. Since trade involves altering the mix of goods produced locally, and production in turn shapes how people work, where they live, and what they can consume, trade should be considered an essential part of globalization.

Given the many different definitions of globalization, scholars have employed a wide variety of indicators to measure this phenomenon. Some people recommend using the value of exports plus imports as a percentage of gross national product (GNP) as a measure. Others note that the nature of the goods being traded must be changing, to reflect the interdependent nature of the trade itself; this would require a measure that captures the changes in types of goods exported and imported over time. The pattern of flows of goods or factors is also important for distinguishing globalization from other phenomena such as bilateral or regional integration. For those interested more in factor flows, we would turn to measures of economic migration (such as percentage of the population born abroad) or of capital flows (again perhaps contrasted against a measure of

domestic economic activity—such as domestic savings or GNP).

Earlier Examples of Economic Globalization If we look at the evidence generated by any one of these indicators, we would discover that globalization is not a new phenomenon. The degree of the globalization of the world economy has fluctuated over time. For instance, during the decades between 1870 and 1914, national economies became much more tightly integrated than they had ever been before.

Economic globalization gained momentum in the late 19th century for several reasons. Technological advances in the early and middle part of the century reduced the cost of long-distance transportation. In particular, the harnessing of steam power made it possible to ship bulky commodities very far, very rapidly, at greatly reduced costs (O'Rourke 1997). Railroads penetrated deeply into the continents of North and South America, as well as Europe and Australia. Steamships shortened the time it took to cross oceans and also freed the ships to travel in directions other than the prevailing winds. The other important technological advance of this period involved communications. The development of the telegraph allowed people the first opportunity to send messages almost instantaneously over great distances. The ability to send information rapidly critically altered several aspects of the world economy. For instance, rapid communications helped individuals and firms select when and where to ship their goods. More important, better communications made it possible to integrate international production. Before the mid-19th century, the slow speed of communications made it difficult for producers to react to changes in distant markets or to seize new opportunities as they emerged.

Of course, policy decisions also determined why globalization accelerated in these years. The spread of liberal ideology in the middle of the 19th century led many states to lower their tariffs and to join the gold standard. By lowering their tariffs, they made it possible for firms and individuals to enter into international trade. These changes then triggered trade adjustment, as market forces pushed countries toward specializing in the types of goods they had a comparative advantage in producing. The gold standard had attributes that also supported economic globalization. By stabilizing exchange rates, the gold standard reduced uncertainties in international transactions. It also committed states to open flows of capital. Considering the high levels of international migration that also occurred in these decades, it is no surprise that many people argue the world's economy was more globalized in this era than in any other—capital and labor were both highly mobile across borders, as were all types of goods (i.e., both manufactured and agricultural products).

Economic globalization had risen and fallen in even earlier periods. In the 17th and 18th centuries, the expansion of the empires of European states caused the integration of their colonies' economies with those of the imperializing states. This economic integration was driven by mercantilism, however. Therefore, although parts of the world economy were linked together over vast distances, the type of integration was much more of the "hub and spoke" model than truly globalizing. In other words, we might observe the development of long-distance trade and the introduction of new commodities into international exchange (such as tobacco or chocolate), but the flow of goods often occurred within the political jurisdiction of a single authority rather than across the boundaries of states. Also, transportation and communication remained relatively slow.

Technological advances often triggered these earlier examples when globalization accelerated. The integration of the world's economy in the 16th and 17th centuries depended on earlier advances in navigation, the ability to construct more seaworthy ships, and map-making. These advances made it possible to introduce not only long-distance trade (as between Europe and Asia) in expensive items such as spices or precious metals but also to include bulky commodities such as timber or grain across shorter distances. While improvements in technology may permit globalization to proceed, by themselves improvements in technology cannot cause globalization. Some actor must seize the technology and utilize it; moreover, state policies must allow globalization to continue. Thus while technological ad-

vances create new opportunities for globalization, the impact of those opportunities is not felt evenly across the world.

Learning from These Earlier Eras of Globalization There are some important lessons to be learned from these earlier experiences with globalization. In the late 19th century, for instance, economic globalization triggered a greater integration of national economies, but various countries responded to this integration in quite different ways. Some countries grasped the economic opportunities present and used them to improve their economic welfare. In others, globalization sparked a political backlash.

As noted earlier, economic globalization initiates change. Some of these changes may appear fairly positive, but most involve reorganizing economic activity and consequently redistributing wealth within societies. Liberalizing trade is a perfect example. Liberalizing trade creates more wealth for society as a whole, but it also redistributes wealth within an economy. In the late 19th century, globalizing trade relations triggered both extreme efforts at adjusting production to exploit the opportunities present and also extreme efforts to shield national economies and societies from the pressures to transform themselves. Some states embraced liberalized trade, changed the goods they produced (and thus adopted new production techniques as well), and consequently reorganized the way people worked and lived. Countries such as Britain, Belgium, Sweden, and Denmark made great strides economically by industrializing and shifting to smaller-scale (but more capital-intensive) agricultural production. These changes were intimately tied not only to the creation and redistribution of additional wealth, but also to urbanization and dramatic changes in landholding patterns in rural areas. These transformations in turn created new political dynamics in these countries. The economic improvements that came with globalization can be linked with additional pressures for democratization and the transformation of political institutions.

On the other hand, some states were politically dominated by groups that feared globalization. In places such as Germany, the landed elite used their political advantages to defend their social and economic status. This meant separating the national economy from global ties. By blocking trade adjustment, the landed elite could continue to sell the goods they produced at prices above world market levels—but this undoubtedly proved a drag on other parts of the economy. The elites refused to share political power, since that would have led to a decline in their economic and social status as well. The elites' preference for protection led them to oppose democratization. Before leaping to the conclusion that protection and authoritarianism go hand in hand, however, one must consider other cases from the late 19th century. In France, the Third Republic's electoral rules gave great voice to the rural areas. Land reforms in the wake of the French Revolution had taken away land from large landholders and given it to peasants in small plots. Economic globalization proved more of a threat than an opportunity to these small farmers. Adjusting their production proved difficult, since they lacked the capital or technical skills to adopt new techniques. Their inability to compete in the global economy, coupled with their strong representation in the democratic institutions, led to overwhelming support for protectionism. In short, drawing on the experiences of a wide range of countries in the late-19th-century era of globalization, we can conclude that there is no simple relationship between the economic and political consequences of globalization. Depending on the economic and political context, globalization's impact varies.

Studying the Current Period of Globalization
The descriptions given earlier suggest that technological improvements may be a necessary (though not sufficient) cause for globalization to proceed. Different disciplines emphasize different dimensions of globalization but also pose quite varied questions about why it occurs or what its consequences are. This diversity can be observed by examining how separate disciplines address the issue.

For economists, the reasons for globalization often go unquestioned. Expansion of market relations makes perfect sense within standard economic frameworks. If markets are tools for generating greater utility for participants, then individuals and firms will seek to participate in ever wider markets. Economists may ask more questions about the consequences of this market integration—which is also their way to understand when and where opposition to globalizing forces arises. Depending on the aspects of economic globalization one selects, economists have developed models depicting how the increase in economic ties will affect domestic actors. While an expansion in the size and scale of the market generates growth and productivity gains, specialization triggers changes that redistribute wealth in important ways. Since most of these changes create both winners and losers, economists may therefore recommend that states participate in globalization and then adopt policies that compensate those who do not enjoy the benefits generated. Evidence also suggests that states that open themselves up to the world economy adopt higher levels of social policies to shield segments of the domestic economy from the buffeting caused by global economic forces (Rodrik 1997). On the whole, economists endorse globalization for the material gains it makes possible, although they recognize that it can also bring instability.

As the brief descriptions of previous examples when globalization accelerated make clear, globalization both is the result of policy choices shaped by politics and entails political consequences. Political scientists are interested in not only the consequences of globalization, but also why globalization has not proceeded in a clear, smooth trajectory over time. To understand why states choose to participate in economic globalization, political scientists begin with an economic model describing the likely economic gains and their distribution within the state, then use that information to inform their understanding of how interests align in political competition. Using models developed in political science to understand how institutions shape this competition over policy, political scientists can then explain why some states pursue the economic opportunities globalization offers (willingly making the domestic adjustments necessary) while other states forgo those economic opportunities.

Political scientists also question why globalization has proceeded in waves. While technological change may provide some insights into this pattern, political scientists also point to possible changes in the international political system. Markets require underpinnings to function effectively—one need only think of the importance of an accepted medium of exchange as an example. Most national markets function well because these infrastructural underpinnings are provided by a legitimate political authority. Yet the international system lacks a similar political authority. Instead it is composed of numerous actors claiming to be sovereign. Thus political scientists would emphasize the importance of powerful or leading states (or perhaps of actors within powerful states) who could provide and manage international institutions that make economic globalization possible. Although the technological changes of the mid-19th century triggered a great expansion in the flow of goods and factors of production across national boundaries in the pre–World War I period, that war disrupted many of those patterns. In the 1920s and 1930s, national policies undermined efforts to re-create a global economy—but many parts of the infrastructural underpinnings were also lacking. The United States and its allies made a conscious effort to create institutions fostering economic globalization after World War II.

It should come as no surprise that political scientists and economists are interested in globalization's impact on individual state's policies. On the one hand, many fear that integration into larger markets increases the pressures to be competitive. Globalization has therefore been viewed as a threat to states' freedom of choice on many different fronts. If one assumes that intervention in markets leads to distortions that reduce the competitiveness of domestic firms or individuals, or if one believes that governments are largely parasitic (i.e., not necessary), then one might believe in the "race to the bottom" thesis: the claim that economic globalization pressures states to deregulate markets more and more. However, there is little evidence of such a general trend. Instead, data suggest that states have responded to economic globalization in a variety of

ways, with some deregulating markets, but others introducing more government activity or services (Burgoon 2001). If the government can provide services that add to domestic actors' competitiveness, then globalization may trigger greater involvement in the economy, not less.

On the other hand, the pressures to compete also suggest ways in which government policies aimed at noneconomic goals may be adversely affected by globalization (Rudra 2002). Governments have increasingly sought to borrow funds to pay for their programs. Integration of national financial systems leads governments to borrow from foreign sources. Since their expenditures may target goals such as social or economic equality, without the aim of increased economic competitiveness, these states must be able to bear the weight of the debts they carry. Such pressures may be especially problematic for economically developing countries, since they may also wish to resist the global market's demands to specialize in nonindustrial production.

If we concentrate on international flows of the factors of production, the current period of globalization is striking for the speed and amount of short-term capital flows. Although high levels of capital were invested abroad in the late 19th century, this investment was largely long term (Williamson 1996). In the current period, the value of short-term speculative international investments now outweighs the value of goods in trade. Capital flows of this nature may deliver fewer benefits than the risks they also carry, especially for countries with few hard currency reserves. Therefore, many scholars have begun to question whether capital controls might be valuable—suggesting that we have reached the limits of globalization. Labor, on the other hand, does not flow very freely—and in the post–September 11 world, flows of labor are not likely to be freed up anytime soon.

Globalization and Identity Globalization can describe more than economic relations, of course. Since other dimensions of globalization can refer to communications or media, globalization is often also related to cultural changes. These aspects may trigger political responses on their own or interact with the politics sparked by economic globalization. Cultural issues may arise when we examine the nature of the goods crossing borders during globalization. If the goods include entertainment products (such as books, music, and films), these economic interactions can unleash strong forces on society.

This imagery was captured beautifully by the journalist Thomas Friedman in *The Lexus and the Olive Tree* (1999). Friedman's two images signify the pros and cons of globalization. The Lexus represents the greater wealth globalization makes possible. The olive tree represents culture—the way domestic actors are rooted. In Friedman's view, domestic actors want both: they desire continuation of their culture (with minimal outside influence) but also greater wealth. Friedman's symbols capture very well the test globalization presents to societies: how can a state ensure that its engagement in the global economic system brings more benefits than costs?

Challenges Ahead in the Study of Globalization Globalization presents several challenges for social scientists, but the greatest is undoubtedly how to model the impact of the many dimensions of globalization together. This requires multidimensional modeling, since trade and factor flows can each have different impacts. On top of these effects, we would want to add different domestic policies that might moderate the impact of increased immigration, international capital flows, or trade adjustment. A broader model would also need to integrate the politics of identity triggered by globalization. Only when we bring together different theoretical approaches from international and domestic politics, and from micro- and macroeconomics, will we have a better grasp on the broad phenomenon we call globalization.

See also anti-globalization; capital mobility; comparative advantage; exchange rates and foreign direct investment; foreign direct investment (FDI); migration, international; nontraded goods; social policy in open economies; trade in services

FURTHER READING

Burgoon, Brian. 2001. "Globalization and Welfare Compensation: Disentangling the Ties that Bind." *International Organization* 55 (3): 509–51. Examines the way domestic policies offset some of the risks economic openness creates.

Frieden, Jeffry. 1991. "Invested Interests: The Politics of National Economic Policies in a World of Global Finance." *International Organization* 45 (4): 425–51. A clear (and often-cited) examination of the domestic politics on international monetary policies.

Friedman, Thomas. 1999. *The Lexus and the Olive Tree*. New York: Farrar, Straus and Giroux. An easy to read, nonacademic discussion of the way economic globalization interacts with the politics of identity.

Garrett, Geoffrey. 1995. "Capital Mobility, Trade, and the Domestic Politics of Economic Policy." *International Organization* 49 (4): 627–55. Provides an overview of the arguments and evidence regarding the way economic globalization reorganizes domestic interests, and the consequences that has on politics.

Garrett, Geoffrey, and Peter Lange. 1996. "Internationalization, Institutions, and Political Change." In *Internationalization and Domestic Politics*, edited by Helen Milner and Robert Keohane. Cambridge: Cambridge University Press, 48–75. Maps out various ways to model the connections between the domestic and international political economies.

Hirst, Paul, and Grahame Thompson. 1999. *Globalization in Question: The International Economy and the Possibilities of Governance*. 2d ed. Cambridge: Polity Press. A classic textbook on globalization and global governance.

Jones, Ronald. 2000. "Private Interests and Government Policy in a Global World." Tinbergen Institute Discussion Paper TI 2000-051/2. Amsterdam, the Netherlands: Tinbergen Institute. An accessible economic analysis of economic openness.

O'Rourke, Kevin. 1997. "The European Grain Invasion, 1870–1913." *Journal of Economic History* 57 (4): 775–801. Concise example of how economic globalization affected the production and consumption of a single commodity in an earlier period of globalization, and the economic and political consequences that followed.

Pauly, Louis. 1997. *Who Elected the Bankers?* Ithaca, NY: Cornell University Press. Questions the responsibility and accountability placed on those who make international financial policy.

Rodrik, Dani. 1997. *Has Globalization Gone Too Far?* Washington, DC: Institute for International Economics. An economist's attempt to assess the impact of globalization.

Rosecrance, Richard. 1999. *The Rise of the Virtual State.* New York: Basic Books. Creatively explores the way technology is changing both the economic connections between states and also the way states relate to each other politically.

Rudra, Nita. 2002. "Globalization and the Decline of the Welfare State in Less-Developed Countries." *International Organization* 56 (2): 411–45. Presents evidence concerning the relationship between international openness and the capacity of economically developing countries to provide social welfare policies.

Stocker, Herbert. 1998. "Globalization and International Convergence in Incomes." In *Economic Effects of Globalization*, edited by John-ren Chen. Aldershot, UK: Ashgate, 97–115. An interesting contribution to an edited volume, both for its discussion of the definition of globalization and for the way in which it measures the results of liberalizing international economic policies.

Williamson, Jeffrey. 1996. "Globalization and Inequality Then and Now: The Late Nineteenth and Late Twentieth Centuries Compared." NBER Working Paper No. 5491. Cambridge, MA: National Bureau of Economic Research. A masterful overview of the domestic economic consequences of globalization in several cases drawn from the late 19th century.

MARK R. BRAWLEY

■ gold standard, international

The international gold standard was a grand experiment in decentralized monetary unification. From approximately 1880 to the start of World War I, many countries in Europe, North America, and the Southern Hemisphere spontaneously joined the gold standard—a monetary system in which the value of money is defined in terms of a given quantity of gold—during a time of free capital and labor mobility and low levels of protectionism. These countries were diverse in income levels and stages of economic development, but shared the belief that the conservative handling of money would ensure price stability, and that central banks should enjoy a high degree of independence from government.

The international gold standard was a decentralized process but had its own rules (McKinnon 1993). To begin with, paper money had to be convertible into a fixed weight of gold at an official price. Convertibility could be suspended under exceptional circumstances, such as wars or banking and financial crises. After a temporary period, however, convertibility would have to be reestablished at the original parity. Second, the expansion of the national money stock was limited by the stock of monetary gold. Third, gold and capital were free to move from country to country. Finally, monetary authorities were not to hamper the economic adjustment that was implied by gold flows; on the contrary, they were to reinforce this adjustment with appropriate policy actions.

Bilateral exchange rate parities were determined by the relative money prices of gold. As an example, in 1879 the official price of an ounce of gold was £4.252 in Britain and $20.67 in the United States. Parity between the dollar and the pound was, therefore, $20.67/£4.252 or $4.856 = £1.0. The exchange rate fluctuated around parity but was constrained by a band, of which the upper and lower edges—called the gold points—were defined by the transaction costs of shipping gold from one country to another. In practice, the bilateral bands of fluctuations were rather narrow. For the dollar-pound exchange market, the upper edge was estimated at $4.890 and the lower edge at $4.827. If the actual exchange rate were to move beyond $4.890, gold would flow from the United States to the United Kingdom; if the exchange rate were to fall below $4.827, gold would move in the opposite direction. The band of exchange rate fluctuations was and is a typical feature of fixed exchange rates.

Basic Principles The gold standard rested on a decentralized organization in which participants retained their own monetary authorities, their own fiscal autonomy, and their own political sovereignty; in essence, participating countries enjoyed monetary integration without fiscal and political integration. If properly functioning, the system ensured a common price level, the world price level, which was determined by the interaction of the global supply of and the global demand for money. The global supply of money was proportional to the stock of monetary gold; the global demand for money was the weighted sum of the national demands for money. The world price level would fall when real income rose relative to new flows of monetary gold. The latter would respond positively to the price of gold and productivity improvements in gold mining, and negatively to the world price level. As the price level rose, the stock of gold moved from monetary to industrial use. The decline in the stock of monetary gold reduced, in turn, the price level. For the world price level to be stable, the stock of monetary gold, inclusive of new flows, had to act as a buffer against the forces affecting the money market. But the stock of monetary gold, in fact, behaved too erratically to play this role (Cooper 1982, table 3), and prices, as we will see later, were not stable.

A country with a price level misaligned with respect to the world price level would face an adjustment process. The details of this process, known as the price-specie flow mechanism, were worked out by philosopher and economist David Hume in 1752. For example, a country experiencing a higher price level than the world price level would experience a balance-of-payments deficit. This deficit, in turn, would force a gold outflow and a proportional decline of the domestic monetary base. The money stock would decline in sympathy with the monetary base. With the economy running at capacity, the decline in the money stock would lower the domestic price level. The gold outflow in the deficit country would be directed toward countries with balance-of-payments surpluses and a lower price level than the world price level. In the surplus countries gold inflows would raise the monetary base and generate a process opposite to that in the deficit countries.

Under the assumption of fully utilized resources and price and wage flexibility, deficit and surplus countries would restore price level equilibrium symmetrically. To speed up adjustments, central banks were supposed to reinforce gold flows with appropriate policy actions. A gold outflow would

have to be followed with a rise in the discount rate (the interest rate a central bank charges to commercial banks and other financial intermediaries for loans of reserve funds), which would attract capital inflows and contract at the same time the domestic component of the monetary base and bank credit; the opposite for a gold inflow. In essence, the rules of the game prescribed a positive correlation between the foreign and the domestic components of the monetary base.

Basic Facts The practice of the gold standard differed somewhat from the theory. The system actually evolved into a gold reserve standard, with "senior" and "junior" currencies and financial centers and a periphery. The British pound was the "senior" currency and London the biggest and most sophisticated money and financial center in the world. The French franc and the German mark were junior currencies; Paris and Berlin, junior centers. All other countries were periphery, although with different degrees of closeness to the senior and junior centers. Foreign exchange reserves—that is, short-lived assets denominated in the currencies of the centers—grew more rapidly than gold reserves. The amount of international liquidity held in the reserve centers by far exceeded the total gold reserves held by these countries, in particular British official gold. The senior center and the two junior centers were net capital exporters, reassuring reserve holders that the centers were financially solid. All in all, there was a clear tendency for the gold standard to evolve into a gold reserve standard, economizing on gold.

The adjustment mechanism was not as symmetric as the theory claimed. Instead, a hierarchical structure was in place: the same action imparted different effects on the system depending on where it was initiated. The senior center had the largest impact; the junior centers had less and the periphery even less. Hierarchy, or asymmetry, did not imply that the actor located at a higher level of the pyramid was fully insulated from the effects of the actions taken by actors located at a lower level of the pyramid. Capital flows were more sensitive to changes in British interest rates than to interest rates in other countries. Increases in the Bank of England bank rate (the equivalent of the discount rate) tended to be followed by increases in the discount rates of other countries. Furthermore, if other countries were to match the British bank rate increase, capital would still flow to London.

To stem reserve outflows, and thus to prevent a convertibility crisis, other countries had to more than match the bank rate increase (Lindert 1969). Britain also reacted to interest rate changes initiated elsewhere, especially in the two junior centers. Some countries—Argentina, Bulgaria, Chile, Italy, Mexico, and Portugal—were so low in the hierarchy that were unable to compete in retaining reserves during rounds of bank rate increases and they had either to devalue their currencies or leave the standard altogether. The pressure on the periphery countries was especially intense during times of gold shortage, causing deflationary pressure and relatively high real interest rates.

The rule of reinforcing gold flows with appropriate changes in the discount rate was widely ignored. The typical pattern was an inverse correlation between the foreign and domestic component of the monetary base, evidence that central banks were sterilizing (compensating the effect of gold flows so as to leave the monetary base unaffected) gold flows to pursue domestic objectives (Nurkse 1944; Bloomfield 1959). The U.S. Federal Reserve system, as an example, sterilized gold movements for much of the 1920s. Even the Bank of England, at the center of the system, violated the rule, although less than other central banks. The sterilization of gold inflows by surplus countries, coupled with the pressure on deficit countries to raise interest rates and contract output, contributed to a deflationary bias in the system; see Keynes (1923, chap. 4).

The main achievement of the international gold standard was to stabilize the long-run inflation rate. For example, the average annual inflation rate in the United Kingdom from 1870 to 1913, measured with reference to wholesale prices, was –0.7 percent; in the United States, from 1879 to 1913, 0.1 percent (Bordo 1981, table 1). The money supply in the system was constrained by gold discoveries. Individual countries, on the whole, were committed to parity and were willing to undertake anti-infla-

tionary policies to restore that parity if they departed temporarily from it. The strategy of sticking to a course of action over time promised payoffs in terms of lower interest rates. In fact, countries that were stricter in the application of the standard enjoyed lower interest rates than countries with a sporadic commitment to convertibility.

The ex-post long-run stability of the price level did not mean, however, that price level uncertainty was low. The coefficient of variation of the inflation rate—calculated as the ratio of the standard deviation of the inflation rate to its mean—was approximately 3 times higher during the gold standard than in the interwar period and 12 to 14 times higher than post–World War II.

These short-run variations must have created considerable difficulty in the private sector in distinguishing price level changes from relative price movements. Furthermore, high short-run variability of the price level was made worse by a high degree of unpredictability of the adjustment period required for the price level to return to equilibrium level (Phinney 1932–33). The swings of the price level lasted up to 50 years. While it is true that prices in 1910 were practically the same as prices in 1850, people living in 1870 or in 1895 would have faced considerable uncertainty in predicting when prices would have returned to the 1850 level. One arrives at a similar conclusion by looking at the wholesale price indexes of four countries: the United Kingdom, Germany, France, and the United States from 1816 to 1913 (see Cooper 1982, table 2). Prices fell and rose dramatically over extremely long swings. For example, in the United States prices fell 45 percent from 1816 to 1849, rose 67 percent from 1849 to 1873, fell 53 percent from 1873 to 1896, and rose 56 percent from 1896 to 1913. The swings were somewhat smaller in the United Kingdom, Germany, and France.

The Gold Standard in the Interwar Period
World War I brought an end to the international gold standard. The Brussels Conference of 1920 and the Genoa Conference of 1922 tried to restore fiscal discipline, central bank independence, and the gold reserve standard. Despite the loss of its preeminent

position as the leading country of the international monetary system, the United Kingdom was a strong voice in the two conferences. On the other hand, the United States, anointed to replace the United Kingdom, decided not to participate at Genoa for reasons related in part to disputes over war debts and reparations (Eichengreen 1992, 11).

France strongly opposed the establishment of a gold reserve standard at the Genoa conference, seeing in this an attempt by Britain to reassert the dominance of the pound and London. What followed were a series of ad-hoc decisions without a common design. Germany returned to the gold standard in 1924 in the aftermath of its disastrous hyperinflation. Britain returned to the standard in 1925, and France in 1928. Prewar parities were set in Germany and Britain. The rules of the game dictated that, should a country leave the standard, it should reenter it at the old parity. This commitment was supposed to enforce credibility and prevent destabilizing speculation. In *A Tract on Monetary Reform*, John Maynard Keynes (1923) predicted that the return of Britain to prewar parity would be extremely deflationary: it overvalued the pound and created a deficit in the current account. Contrary to the hopes of the prewar parity advocates, the necessary downward price adjustment, especially of money wages, did not materialize; the adjustment fell primarily on production and employment.

France's new parity undervalued the French franc, causing a surplus in the current account. Furthermore, widespread speculation of a future appreciation of the French franc was responsible for large capital inflows. Consequently, international reserves exploded and the Banque de France sterilized the inflows of reserves with sales of domestic assets to prevent an appreciation of the franc. Saddled with large nongold reserves, the French were reluctant to give Britain the privilege of financing current account deficits with pound-denominated debt. The French opted to redeem reserves into gold, causing deflation in the "center" and easing the appreciation pressure on the franc. In terms of the implied rules of the game, France was no longer willing to accept the pre–World War I hierarchical structure.

Other countries as well were unwilling to cooperate. National policies became less internationally oriented as the Great Depression of the 1930s affected much of the industrial world. National political systems had become increasingly reluctant to tolerate the large swings in unemployment and cyclical movements that accompanied the commitment to parity, and the international gold standard eventually lost its appeal.

See also balance of payments; banking crisis; Bretton Woods system; commodity-price pegging; convertibility; currency crisis; foreign exchange intervention; international financial architecture; international liquidity; international reserves; money supply; quantity theory of money; sterilization; Triffin dilemma

FURTHER READING

Bloomfield, Arthur I. 1959. *Monetary Policy under the International Gold Standard*. New York: Federal Reserve Bank of New York. This study, together with that by Ragnar Nurkse, shows that during the gold standard central banks were pursuing domestic objectives in addition to convertibility.

Bordo, Michael D. 1981. "The Classical Gold Standard: Some Lessons for Today." *Review of the St. Louis Federal Reserve Bank* 63: 2–17. This article, written at the end of the worldwide inflation surge of the 1960s and the 1970s, reviews the record of the gold standard in providing stable prices and economic stability.

Cooper, Richard. 1982. "The Gold Standard: Historical Facts and Future Prospects." *Brookings Papers on Economic Activity* 1: 1–56. Reviews the economic record of the international gold standard especially with regard to the long swings in the price levels.

Eichengreen, Barry. 1992. *Golden Fetters. The Gold Standard and the Great Depression, 1919–1939*. New York: Oxford University Press. Explores the connection between the gold standard and the global economic crisis of the 1930s.

Hume, David. 1898 (1752). "On the Balance of Trade." In *Essays, Moral, Political and Literary*. London: Longmans, Green. This is the classic article on the so-called price-specie flow mechanism.

Keynes, John Maynard. 1923. *A Tract on Monetary Reform*. London: Macmillan. This is Keynes's famous study on the deflationary bias of the international gold standard.

Lindert, Peter H. 1969. "Key Currencies and Gold, 1900–1913." Princeton Studies in International Finance No. 24. Princeton, NJ: Princeton University. Presents evidence that the international gold standard had a hierarchical structure, with a center and a periphery.

McKinnon, Ronald I. 1993. "The Rules of the Game: International Money in Historical Perspective." *Journal of Economic Literature* 31: 1–44. Focuses on the rules of the game of the international gold standard and other monetary regimes.

Nurkse, Ragnar. 1944. *International Currency Experience.* Princeton, NJ: League of Nations. See description under Bloomfield, above.

Phinney, J. T. 1932–33. "Gold Production and the Price Level: The Cassel Three-Percent Estimate." *Quarterly Journal of Economics*, 47: 647–79. An early article showing that the price level during the gold standard was subject to long and uncertain swings.

MICHELE FRATIANNI

■ government procurement

Government procurement refers to state purchases of goods and services and to the leasing of capital equipment. The absence of any binding multilateral rules on government procurement practices is regarded as one of the most significant lacunae of the World Trade Organization (WTO) and its predecessor, the General Agreement on Tariffs and Trade (GATT). A plurilateral agreement on government procurement exists, but its membership is confined principally to industrialized countries. Many free trade agreements (FTAs) contain provisions on government purchases, and a nonbinding United Nations Model Law on Procurement of Goods, Construction, and Services adds to the uneven patchwork of international disciplines on public procurement matters.

Typically the objectives of government procurement policies are not just economic, such as obtaining "value for money." Often procurement policies seek to promote the well-being of certain societal groups, firms, regions, and industries. For example, small- and medium-size firms are the beneficiaries of such fa-voritism in many jurisdictions, including in the United States. State purchasers have plenty of means to attain these ends. Procurement procedures can be broken down into three distinct stages: namely, tendering procedures, evaluation of bids, and the notification of contract awards and associated review procedures. It is important to bear in mind that discrimination in a government procurement procedure can be both de jure (and, therefore, potentially transparent) and de facto (especially where state officials are given considerable discretion).

There is considerable uncertainty over the total value of government procurement of goods and services. The last attempt to compile a comparable cross-country dataset on state procurement expenditures was based on 1998 data (OECD 2001). On average, state expenditures on goods and services accounted for 7.6 percent of the national income of Organisation for Economic Co-operation and Development (OECD) nations. The total amount of government spending on goods and services in the industrialized world amounted to $1.795 trillion. The comparable numbers for the developing countries included in this OECD study were 5.1 percent and $0.287 trillion, respectively. Information concerning the ways in which governments discriminate against foreign bidders for state contracts is also hard to come by. However, the Trade Policy Reviews of the WTO do contain some useful information on the latter, yet no comprehensive database of procurement-related barriers to international trade has ever been prepared. It is quite likely that paucity of data has held back research on this subject.

Data limitations have not deterred theoretical analyses of the effect of public procurement discrimination on market outcomes and international trade. Although these analyses are almost always partial equilibrium in nature, in principle such discrimination could have general equilibrium effects (see Evenett and Hoekman 2006 for a discussion of the latter). As far as procurement discrimination in markets is concerned, the modern literature was started by Baldwin (1970) and Baldwin and Richardson (1972). They demonstrated that in a perfectly competitive market a procurement ban on foreign purchases by a state body will affect production levels, imports, and prices only if the quantity of goods demanded by that body exceeds total domestic supply at the moment the ban is imposed. If not, the procurement ban would merely induce a reshuffling of domestic and state purchasers between domestic and foreign suppliers. This finding, which other researchers have confirmed in alternative market structures, implies that not every discriminatory procurement policy reduces market access, so diminishing potential exporter interest in trade agreements that constrain such discrimination.

Many governments solicit bids for public contracts and consequently some analysts have examined the effect of discrimination against foreign bidders in an auction setting. McAfee and McMillan (1989) is the best known such analysis. They demonstrated that the introduction of a price preference, which inflates the foreign bids by a specified percentage before all of the qualifying bids are evaluated, can actually reduce the expected cost to the government of purchasing the good or service. The logic here is very similar to that of the terms-of-trade effects that can be induced by imposing a tariff on imports. Foreign firms partially absorb the price preference and so lower their (pre-preference-adjusted) bids. Domestic firms raise their bids but by less than the amount of the preference-adjusted foreign bids. If the distribution of foreign and domestic firms' costs is such that the probability of a foreign firm winning the contract is sufficiently high even after the price preference is imposed, then there are circumstances when the state's expected outlay falls. This result provides an efficiency-based rationale for the use of price preferences. Whether governments have the information necessary to optimally implement such price preferences is another matter. Moreover, retaliation by other trading partners may shift the calculus away from imposing price preferences.

From what is known about the international negotiations on public procurement matters at the WTO and the GATT it is not evident that these theoretical considerations have been given much weight. Instead the reluctance of some WTO members to develop multilateral disciplines on public procurement matters has been attributed to concerns that the objectives of procurement policies (including industrial policy goals) may not be effectively met using alternative government policy instruments, to defensive steps taken by the recipients of the rents created by current procurement discrimination, to the suspicion that certain political parties or campaigns are directly or indirectly funded through public procurement policies, and to the concerns that multilateral disciplines would be too costly or burdensome to implement. In fact, in 2004 WTO members decided not to start negotiating new multilateral rules to enhance the transparency of government procurement practices. Consequently, the only prevailing WTO agreement on government procurement is a plurilateral one, the negotiation of which was concluded in 1994. This agreement has 38 signatories (27 of which are members of the European Union). Having said this, 19 WTO members are observers to this agreement, 8 of which are negotiating to join this plurilateral accord. In addition to requiring steps that promote the transparency of the signatories' public purchasing policies and practices and introducing faster procedures for losing firms to challenge state procurement decisions, this plurilateral accord also bans—for agreed sectors—the use of price preferences. The obligations of the 1994 plurilateral agreement are binding on its signatories, and disputes can be subject to the WTO Dispute Settlement Understanding. Many other forms of discrimination, including those that may prevent bids outright by foreign firms or raise their costs, were not banned in the 1994 Agreement—suggesting that international disciplines in this area of government policymaking could be strengthened. The members of this plurilateral accord have sought its renegotiation, and in December 2006 a provisional agreement was reached (Anderson 2007).

It is important to appreciate that the WTO is not the only venue where international accords on public procurement matters have been developed. Binding obligations on these matters are frequently included in FTAs, in particular when an industrialized country is involved. In addition, the United Nations has developed a nonbinding Model Law on Procurement, Goods, Construction, and Services. In the years to come researchers may want to examine whether the spread of FTAs with public procurement provisions alters WTO members' positions on the desirability of negotiating corresponding multilateral provisions. Moreover, attention could be given to the relative impact of these binding and nonbinding international initiatives on the reform of national procurement practices in both developing and industrialized countries.

See also nontariff measures; World Trade Organization

FURTHER READING

Anderson, Robert D. 2007. "Renewing the WTO Agreement on Government Procurement: Progress to Date and Ongoing Negotiations." *Public Procurement Law Review* 16 (4): 255–73. An account of the agreement reached at the end of 2006 on revising the WTO's Government Procurement Agreement.

Baldwin, Robert E. 1970. *Nontariff Distortions of International Trade.* Washington, DC: The Brookings Institution Press. A classic introduction to nontariff barriers and of particular reference here to government procurement practices.

Baldwin, Robert E., and J. David Richardson. 1972. "Government Purchasing Policies, Other NTBs, and the International Monetary Crisis." In *Obstacles to Trade in the Pacific Area: Proceedings of the Fourth Pacific Trade and Development Conference,* edited by H. E. English and Keith A. J. Hay. Ottawa: School of International Affairs, Carleton University, 211–303. Another early analytical treatment of the effects of government procurement practices on trade flows.

Evenett, Simon J., and Bernard M. Hoekman. 2006. "Introduction." In *The WTO and Government Procurement,* edited by Simon J. Evenett and Bernard M. Hoekman. Cheltenham: Edward Elgar, vi–xxii. Includes all of the major legal, economic, and developmental papers that discuss the relationship between trade policy, trade agreements, government procurement policies, and international trade and economic performance more generally. The introduction to this volume contains a survey of the economic literature on the effects of procurement policies on national welfare and trade flows.

McAfee, R. Preston, and John McMillan. 1989. "Government Procurement and International Trade." *Journal of International Economics* 26 (3/4): 291–308. Contains an analysis of the effects of procurement discrimination against foreign bidders in an optimal auction setting.

Organisation of Economic Co-operation and Development (OECD). 2001. "The Size of Government Procurement Markets." *Journal of Budgeting* 1 (4). Available at http://www.oecd.org/document/63/0,3343,de_2649_201185_1845951_1_1_1_1,00.html. Contains statistics on the size of national procurement markets.

SIMON J. EVENETT

■ gravity models

Gravity models utilize the gravitational force concept as an analogy to explain the volume of trade, capital flows, and migration among the countries of the world. For example, gravity models establish a baseline for trade-flow volumes as determined by gross domestic product (GDP), population, and distance. The effect of policies on trade flows can then be assessed by adding the policy variables to the equation and estimating deviations from the baseline flows. In many instances, gravity models have significant explanatory power, leading Deardorff (1998) to refer to them as a "fact of life."

Alternative Specifications Gravity models begin with Newton's law for the gravitational force (GF_{ij}) between two objects i and j. In equation form, this is expressed as:

$$GF_{ij} = \frac{M_i M_j}{D_{ij}} \quad i \neq j \qquad (1)$$

In this equation, the gravitational force is directly proportional to the masses of the objects (M_i and M_j) and indirectly proportional to the distance between them (D_{ij}).

Gravity models are estimated in terms of natural logarithms, denoted "ln." In this form, what is multiplied in equation 1 becomes added, and what is divided becomes subtracted, translating equation 1 into a linear equation:

$$\ln GF_{ij} = \ln M_i + \ln M_j - \ln D_{ij} \quad i \neq j \qquad (2)$$

Gravity models of international trade implement equation 2 by using trade flows or exports from county i to country j (E_{ij}) in place of gravitational force, with arbitrarily small numbers sometimes being used in place of any zero values. Distance is often measured using "great circle" calculations. The handling of mass in equation 2 takes place via four alternatives. In the first alternative with the most solid theoretical foundations, mass in equation 2 is associated with the gross domestic product (*GDP*) of the countries. In this case, equation 2 becomes:

$$\ln E_{ij} = \alpha + \beta_1 \ln GDP_i + \beta_2 \ln GDP_j + \beta_3 \ln D_{ij} \quad (3)$$

In general, the expected signs here are $\beta_1, \beta_2 > 0$. However, the economics of equation 3 can lead to the interpretation of *GDP* as income, and when applied to agricultural goods, Engels's Law allows for *GDP* in the destination country to have a negative influence on demand for imports. Hence it is also possible that $\beta_2 < 0$.

In the second alternative, mass in equation 2 is associated with *both GDP and* population (*POP*). In this case, equation 2 becomes:

$$\ln E_{ij} = \varphi + \gamma_1 \ln GDP_i + \gamma_2 \ln POP_i + \gamma_3 \ln GDP_j + \gamma_4 POP_j + \gamma_5 \ln D_{ij} \quad (4)$$

With regard to the expected signs on the population variables, these are typically interpreted in terms or market size and are therefore positive ($\gamma_2, \gamma_4 > 0$). That said, however, there is the possibility of import substitution effects as well as market size effects. If the import substitution effects dominate, the expected sign is $\gamma_4 < 0$.

In the third and fourth alternatives, mass in equation 2 is associated with *GDP* per capita and with *both* gross domestic product *and GDP* per capita, respectively. In these cases, equation 2 becomes one of the following:

$$\ln E_{ij} = \tau + \delta_1 \ln (GDP_i/POP_i) + \delta_2 \ln (GDP_j/POP_j) + \delta_3 \ln D_{ij} \quad (5)$$

$$\ln E_{ij} = \mu + v_1 \ln GDP_i + v_2 \ln (GDP_i/POP_i) + v_3 \ln GDP_j + v_4(GDP_j/POP_j) + v_5 \ln D_{ij} \quad (6)$$

Since they involve the same variables, the parameters of equations 4, 5, and 6 are transformations on one another: $\gamma_1 = \delta_1 = v_1 + v_2$; $\gamma_2 = -\delta_1 = -v_2$; $\gamma_3 = \delta_2 = v_3 + v_4$; and $\gamma_4 = -\delta_4 = -v_4$.

Theoretical Considerations After being introduced by Tinbergen (1962), the gravity model was considered to be a useful physical analogy with fortunate empirical validity. Subsequently, however, connections have been made to key elements of trade theory. The standard assumption of the Heckscher-Ohlin model that prices of traded goods are the same in each country has proved to be faulty due to the presence of what trade economists call "border effects." Properly accounting for these border effects requires prices of traded goods to differ among the countries of the world. Gravity models have been interpreted in these terms.

Anderson (1979) was the first to do this, employing the product differentiation by country-of-origin assumption, commonly known as the "Armington assumption" (Armington 1969). By specifying demand in these terms, Anderson helped to explain the presence of income variables in the gravity model, as well as their multiplicative (or log linear) form. This approach was also adopted by Bergstrand (1985), who more thoroughly specified the supply side of economies. The result was the insight that prices in the form of GDP deflators might be an important additional variable to include in the gravity equations described above. Price effects have also been captured using real exchange rates (e.g., Brun et al. 2005).

The monopolistic competition model of New Trade Theory has been another approach to providing theoretical foundations to the gravity model (Helpman 1987; Bergstrand 1989). Here, the product differentiation by country-of-origin approach is replaced by product differentiation among producing firms, and the empirical success of the gravity model is considered to be supportive of the monopolistic competition explanation of intraindustry trade. However, Deardorff (1998) and Feenstra (2004) have cast doubt on this interpretation, noting the compatibility of the gravity equation with some forms of the Heckscher-Ohlin model and, consequently, the need for empirical evidence to distinguish among potential theoretical bases: product differentiation by country of origin; product differentiation by firm; and particular forms of Heckscher-Ohlin-based comparative advantage. In each of these cases, the common denominator is complete specialization by countries in a particular good. Without this feature, bilateral trade tends to become indeterminate.

Alternatively, there are other approaches to gravity-based explanations of bilateral trade that do not depend on compete specialization. As emphasized by Haveman and Hummels (2004), this involves accounting for trade frictions in the form of distance-based shipping costs or other trade costs, as well as policy-based trade barriers. Distance costs can also be augmented to account for infrastructure, oil price, and trade composition, as in Brun et al. (2005). The two approaches (complete versus incomplete specialization) can be empirically distinguished by category of good, namely differentiated versus homogeneous, as in Feenstra, Markusen, and Rose (2001).

Assessment Due to its log-linear structure, the coefficients of the gravity model are in terms of elasticities or ratios of percentage changes. These "unitless" measures are comparable across countries and goods and give us direct measures of the responsiveness of trade flows to the trade potential variables of equations 3–6. For GDP and distance, estimated elasticities tend to be close to 1.0 in value. For distance, comparison across groups of countries gives a measure of the degree of integration in the world economy. In addition to these standard variables, the coefficients of policy variables help us to understand the impacts of the represented policies on trade flows. It is also possible to obtain estimates of border effects independently of distance and other variables, as well as to investigate some issues in economic geography, as in Redding and Venables (2004). Despite some ambiguity regarding its theoretical foundations, then, the gravity model is an important empirical tool to help us understand trade and other economic flows in the world economy.

See also applied general equilibrium modeling; Heckscher-Ohlin model; intraindustry trade; monopolistic competition; New Trade Theory; partial equilibrium modeling; revealed comparative advantage

FURTHER READING

Anderson, James E. 1979. "A Theoretical Foundation for the Gravity Equation." *American Economic Review* 69 (1): 106–16. A first attempt to provide theoretical foundations to the gravity model.

Armington, Paul. 1969. "A Theory of Demand for Products Distinguished by Place of Production." *IMF Staff Papers* 16 (3): 159–76. The key contribution on product differentiation by country of origin.

Bergstrand, Jeffrey H. 1985. "The Gravity Equation in International Trade: Some Microeconomic Foundations and Empirical Evidence." *Review of Economics and Statistics* 67 (3): 474–81. A second attempt to provide theoretical foundations to the gravity model.

———. 1989. "The Generalized Gravity Equation, Monopolistic Competition, and the Factor-Proportions Theory in International Trade." *Review of Economics and Statistics* 71 (1): 143–53. An interpretation of the gravity model in terms of monopolistic competition.

Brun, Jean-François, Céline Carrère, Patrick Guillaumont, and Jaime de Melo. 2005. "Has Distance Died? Evidence from a Panel Gravity Model." *World Bank Economic Review* 19 (1): 99–120. A useful exploration of distance in gravity models.

Deardorff, Alan V. 1998. "Determinants of Bilateral Trade: Does Gravity Work in a Neoclassical World?" In *The Regionalization of the World Economy*, edited by Jeffrey A. Frankel. Chicago: University of Chicago Press, 7–22. A helpful review and assessment of the gravity model.

Feenstra, Robert C. 2004. *Advanced International Trade: Theory and Evidence*. Princeton, NJ: Princeton University Press. Chapter 5 of this book reviews the gravity model in light of trade theory and also delves into a number of key estimation issues.

Feenstra, Robert. C., James R. Markusen, and Andrew K. Rose. 2001. "Using the Gravity Equation to Differentiate among Alternative Theories of Trade." *Canadian Journal of Economics* 34 (2): 430–47. Tests the gravity model over differentiated and homogeneous goods, focusing on differences in estimated parameter values.

Haveman, Jon, and David Hummels. 2004. "Alternative Hypotheses and the Volume of Trade: The Gravity

Equation and the Extent of Specialization." *Canadian Journal of Economics* 37 (1): 199–218. Explores gravity model explanations both in terms of complete specialization such as in monopolistic competition models and incomplete specialization with trade frictions.

Helpman, Elhanan. 1987. "Imperfect Competition and International Trade: Evidence from Fourteen Industrial Countries." *Journal of the Japanese and International Economies* 1 (1): 62–81. A claim for monopolistic competition models of intraindustry trade using gravity model evidence.

Redding, Stephen, and Anthony J. Venables. 2004. "Economic Geography and International Inequality." *Journal of International Economics* 62 (1): 53–82. An application of the gravity framework to economic geography.

Tinbergen, Jan. 1962. *Shaping the World Economy: Suggestions for an International Economic Policy.* New York: Twentieth Century Fund. The first use of a gravity model to analyze international trade flows.

KENNETH A. REINERT

■ **greenfield investment**
See mergers and acquisitions

■ **Group of Seven/Eight (G7/G8)**
The Group of Seven/Eight (G7/G8) is an informal intergovernmental institution for the leaders of the world's most powerful countries to govern the global economy and promote the values of open democracy, individual liberty, and social advancement. It emerged in 1973 when the finance ministers of the United States, France, Britain, and Germany, soon joined by Japan, met secretly as a Group of Five (G5) in the library of the White House to discuss a replacement for the international monetary regime of gold-linked, fixed exchange rates, which had been destroyed by unilateral American action on August 15, 1971. When the finance ministers of France and Germany became leaders, they invited their counterparts in the G5 and Italy to Rambouillet, France, on November 15–17, 1975, to deal with the eco-

nomic stagflation and broader crisis of governability arising from the 1973 oil shock, the deadlocked Tokyo Round of trade negotiations, and security threats in the Middle East, Southern Europe, India, and Vietnam. They addressed economic growth, inflation and employment, international finance, trade, energy, and economic relations with the developing South and communist East.

At their subsequent summits, held for two or three days in late spring or summer every year, they added Canada in 1976, the European Community (later the European Union) in 1977, and the Russian Federation in 1998, to make it the G8. They have invited as partial participants the Soviet Union and then Russia since 1991; leading African and Middle Eastern democracies since 2001; China, India, Brazil, Mexico, and South Africa since 2003; and the executive heads of multilateral organizations such as the United Nations, the International Monetary Fund, and the World Bank starting in 1996.

The G5 finance ministers continued to meet on their own and with their leaders at the summit. In 1986 Italy and Canada were added to the finance ministers to form the G7, which soon replaced the G5 and was separated from the now leaders-only summit in 1998. Usually meeting four times a year, the G5/G7 finance ministers have had some significant achievements: the 1985 Plaza Accord, which produced a soft landing for the overvalued U.S. dollar, the 1987 Louvre Accord to manage the new exchange rate relationships, and action to contain the Asian-turned-global financial crisis that afflicted Thailand, Indonesia, South Korea, Russia, the United States, Brazil, Argentina, and Turkey from 1997 to 2001. Some see G7 finance performance as inherently harmful or declining during the globalization of the 1990s. Others highlight its continuing importance as a source of new ideas.

Other G7/G8 ministerial bodies were created, including one for trade in 1982 and one for development in 2002. In 1999, a broader Group of Twenty (G20) finance ministers and central bank governors of systemically important countries was created. At the official level, groups on energy proliferated in the 1970s. Two on macroeconomics arose in 1982. Many on financial crime, financial assistance to Russia, the Gulf States, development finance, Africa, terrorist finance, investment, and intellectual property have emerged since 1989.

The G7/G8 summit's economic agenda soon extended from macroeconomics into many specific microeconomic and social policy subjects. It also quickly embraced global issues such as migration, crime, drugs, and political-security subjects such as East-West relations, terrorism, proliferation of weapons of mass destruction, regional security, and the use of force. Its unique value has been in freely and flexibly addressing any and all issues, and integrating them in innovative ways. From its deliberations have flowed major new directions, such as redefining the relationship between inflation and unemployment. It has issued an expanding number of often ambitious collective commitments. Its members have generally complied at least partly with these commitments, especially in energy, trade, financial assistance to Russia, and debt relief for poor states.

The G7/G8 summit has made an effective contribution to global economic governance in several critical cases. In finance it mobilized the assistance necessary to sustain Russia's democratic revolution in the 1990s. In trade it provided a catalytic political push to launch multilateral trade negotiations in the Uruguay Round and Doha Development Agenda, and successfully conclude the overdue Tokyo and Uruguay Rounds. In energy it stopped the inflation and wealth redistributions brought by the second oil shock in 1979, although at the cost of a severe recession within the G7 and the default of several resource-rich developing states. In development, from the 1988 Toronto Summit to the 2005 Gleneagles Summit, it canceled the debt of the deserving poorest countries of the world and mobilized major new monies for development assistance. After the terrorist attack on the United States on September 11, 2001, it instituted an effective regime to control terrorist finance.

Some see G8 governance as propagating neoliberal values and perpetuating inequality between its rich Northern members and the poor developing South. Others regard it as an important source of political leadership and collective management, most clearly in its 1975 creation of a new monetary regime of managed floating exchange rates and its 1978 big package deal that integrated fiscal, monetary, trade, and energy concerns. Still others argue that it has emerged as the effective center of global governance in the post–Cold War, rapidly globalizing world, where even the most powerful economies are vulnerable to shocks that require concerted action to address.

The G7/G8 is increasingly reaching out to incorporate the growing economic powers of China, India, Mexico, Brazil, and South Africa more fully in its annual summit and ministerial processes. It is reaching down to involve business and civil society in its work. Although it still lacks any formal charter or secretariat, its comprehensive reach, freedom, flexibility, direct connection with leaders, and increasing inclusiveness enhance its relevance in guiding the global economy in the 21st-century world.

See also Doha Round; globalization; Louvre Accord; Plaza Accord; Uruguay Round

FURTHER READING

Baker, Andrew. 2006. *The Group of Seven: Finance Ministries, Central Banks, and Global Financial Governance.* New York: Routledge. An analysis of the discussions within the G7 finance ministers' forum.

Bayne, Nicholas. 2005. *Staying Together: The G8 Summit Confronts the Twenty-First Century.* Aldershot, UK: Ashgate. A detailed analysis of the G8 summit since 1998, offering a framework for assessing performance. It argues that G8 effectiveness is rising, due to the reforms instituted in 1998 and the G8's character as a club in which all members, not only the United States, now can and do lead.

Bergsten, Fred, and Randall C. Henning. 1996. *Global Economic Leadership and the Group of Seven.* Washington, DC: Institute for International Economics. An evaluation of the G7 finance ministers' forum, arguing that its performance has declined because its members mistakenly believe that globalization has now made markets, not their governments, the governors of the global economy.

Feldstein, Martin. 1988. "Distinguished Lecture on Economics in Government: Thinking about International Economic Coordination." *Journal of Economic Perspectives* 2 (spring): 3–13. The classic argument that G7 economic coordination is ineffective and even harmful, as G7 governments do not know the best targets or instruments to reach them any better than market players themselves.

Fratianni, Michele, Paolo Savona, and John J. Kirton, eds. 2005. *New Perspectives on Global Governance: Why America Needs the G8.* Aldershot, UK: Ashgate. A collection based on the U.S.-hosted summit in 2004, arguing that a newly vulnerable America needs, uses, and adjusts to the G8 to protect itself in a post–September 11 world.

Kaiser, Karl, John J. Kirton, and Joseph Daniels, eds. 2000. *Shaping a New International Financial System: Challenges of Governance in a Globalizing World.* Aldershot, UK: Ashgate. An examination of the G7/G8 response to the 1997–99 financial crisis, generally concluding that the G7/G8 was effective in the end.

Putnam, Robert D., and Nicholas Bayne. 1987. *Hanging Together: Cooperation and Conflict in the Seven Power Summits.* Rev. ed. Cambridge, MA: Harvard University Press. The classic description and systematic explanation of G7 summit performance, arguing that American leadership was a necessary condition for G7 success.

JOHN KIRTON

■ growth in open economies, neoclassical models

The neoclassical growth model is a widely used framework to study economic growth. The main focus of neoclassical growth theory is on explaining economic growth via the accumulation of factors of production, namely physical capital.

When economies are closed to foreign exchange, a central prediction of the theory is that among similar countries (those converging to the same steady-state, determined by factors such as the quality of institutions, overall level of education, government policies, etc.), the poorest should grow faster than the richest. This notion of *conditional convergence* is important because it suggests the existence of automatic forces that pull economies closer together. Several studies, relying on either cross-region or cross-country growth regressions, provide empirical support for conditional convergence. The assumption of closed economy is, however, very difficult to justify. A first problem is that, if conditional convergence holds among closed economies, the theory implies that foreign investors must be giving up extraordinary investment opportunities. Capital should actually be flowing across countries to arbitrage such return differences. A second problem is that many economies are in fact open. This includes South Korea, Taiwan, Hong Kong, and Singapore, the so-called East-Asian miracles that achieved very rapid and sustained postwar growth. Moreover, these are well-known examples of export-oriented growth. Open economy versions of the neoclassical growth model are able to deal successfully with both challenges.

Assumptions of the Theory Consider a typical economy, potentially open to trade with the rest of the world. The analysis rests on assumptions about the production technology and the preferences of individual consumers underlying saving behavior.

The economy produces a single homogeneous good, the model's counterpart to real gross domestic product (GDP) in the data. The technology available to produce this good is described by an aggregate production function—the maximum output that is technologically feasible for the economy as a whole to produce given the available factors of production. A common specification is the Cobb-Douglas production function, $Y_t = A_t K_t^\alpha L_t^{1-\alpha}$, where Y_t is the output (real GDP) in the current period, and K_t and L_t are the inputs, aggregate physical capital (all the plants and equipment) and aggregate labor (total number of workers), respectively. Capital may be accumulated over time; however, for simplicity, we assume L_t is constant at L. The parameter $0 < \alpha < 1$ captures the relative importance of capital in production. A_t is the level of technology, that is, the general knowledge available to society on how to produce. It captures how efficient an economy is in combining the available production inputs. Its determinants are not just narrowly technological but also more broadly institutions and government policies. Neoclassical theory is typically not explicit about these determinants; rather it assumes A_t grows at some constant rate common to all countries. For simplicity we assume here that A_t is constant at $A > 0$.

Since we are often interested in understanding the growth of real GDP per capita, rewrite the production function as $y_t = Ak_t^\alpha$, where $y_t = Y_t/L$ and $k_t = K_t/L$. This production technology has two important properties. First, since $\alpha > 0$, increasing k_t always increases production. Second, since $\alpha < 1$, increasing k_t becomes less productive when the scale of production, as proxied by k_t, is already large—a key property called decreasing returns to scale. The idea behind decreasing returns to scale is that, as k_t increases, each worker needs to operate more units of capital, and so capital becomes less productive—for example, some machines become idle sometimes, because there are not enough workers to operate all of them simultaneously.

The economy's residents have a preference for current versus future consumption. In addition, government policy such as capital income taxation influences individual saving behavior. For simplicity, we assume preferences and policy lead to a simple aggregate saving rule: national saving is a constant fraction of national income, or real gross national product (GNP). Real GNP is the residents' total income irrespective of origin—GDP plus the net income generated abroad.

The simple saving rule determines the level of saving in each period. However, the economy also needs to decide how to invest each period's saving, either domestically or abroad. We assume investors choose the option with the highest rate of return.

When today's saving is invested domestically, it will increase the capital stock tomorrow—assuming it takes one period to install new capital. Let's say capital tomorrow increases by one unit. The gross return from this investment is the extra production generated tomorrow by the additional unit of capital—what economists call the marginal product of capital, which in the present case equals $\alpha Ak_{t+1}^{\alpha-1}$. Because, due to wear and tear, capital

depreciates physically during production, the net return will be lower. With a rate of physical depreciation every period of $0 < \delta < 1$, only a fraction of the initial unit of capital survives production. The net return from investing domestically becomes $r_{t+1} = \alpha Ak_{t+1}^{\alpha-1} - \delta$. Importantly, because of decreasing returns to scale ($\alpha - 1 < 0$), a higher k_{t+1} lowers r_{t+1}: richer countries have a lower incentive to accumulate capital because they already have more of it.

Today's saving may instead be invested abroad. We assume there is a frictionless world credit market, where any economy can borrow or lend funds freely at the going world interest rate r_{t+1}^*. Suppose every economy is a small open economy, in the sense that their individual actions have a negligible effect on the world market. For simplicity, assume also that the world interest rate is constant at r^*. Picking the investment alternative yielding the highest return means comparing r^* with r_{t+1}.

So far, with a single homogeneous good being produced in every country, openness to trade only takes place in world credit markets. That is, all trade is intertemporal, involving only borrowing and lending—so far there is no scope for intratemporal trade in different commodities.

The Benchmark Case of a Closed Economy A closed economy has no access to world credit markets, so national saving is all invested domestically. Equivalently, domestic investment in physical capital must be financed through national saving.

Suppose the economy is relatively poor; in particular the current levels of capital and production are lower than their steady-state values. Because of decreasing returns to scale, r_{t+1} is high. With a high return, the saving rule generates enough investment to compensate for depreciated capital and still increase the capital stock tomorrow. Hence, the economy will be growing. However, the growth rate will diminish over time, since decreasing returns to scale reduce returns as capital grows. At some point, we reach a situation where the economy invests just the amount of resources needed to cover depreciation. At that point—the steady-state—capital and output per capita are constant over time, and the economy stops growing. In the more general case in which the rate of technological progress is positive (A_t grows over time), then GDP per capita would grow at this same rate in the steady-state.

Convergence to the steady-state from the initial level of GDP is only gradual. Convergence is not faster because domestic saving is insufficient to generate all the investment necessary to close the gap between the current and the steady-state levels of capital per capita.

Neoclassical growth theory views cross-country differences in growth rates as stemming from countries gradually converging toward their steady-states, starting from different initial levels. Poor countries, induced by higher returns, grow faster. As Lucas (1990) pointed out, this poses a quantitative challenge to the closed economy assumption. Rewrite the (gross) domestic return as $r_{t+1} + \delta = \alpha A^{1/\alpha} y_{t+1}^{(\alpha-1)/\alpha}$, using the definition of y_t. Consider now the actual experiences of the United States and Kenya through the lens of neoclassical theory. If both countries shared the same technology and differed only in their current position as they transit to a common steady-state, then

$$\frac{r^{KEN} + \delta}{r^{US} + \delta} = \left(\frac{y^{KEN}}{y^{US}}\right)^{(\alpha-1)/\alpha}$$

In 2003, the United States was about 30 times richer than Kenya. With $\alpha = 1/3$, as suggested by the data, then investing in Kenya would have earned a gross return $30^2 = 900$ times higher than in the United States! Even if we attempted to factor in the technological differences that do exist between Kenya and the United States, the return gap would still come out too high. The incentive for capital to flow from the United States into Kenya would be enormous, making it impossible to sustain the closed economy assumption.

Openness to Capital Flows The small open economy has free access to the world capital market, at the constant interest rate r^*. This interest rate reflects the overall return on capital in the rest of the world. Consider a scenario in which the economy is initially in autarky, and suddenly gains free access to the world credit market. Assume the domestic economy is poorer than the rest of the world. Due to decreasing returns to scale, domestic returns under autarky are higher than the world interest rate, $r_{t+1} > r^*$.

Faced with this return gap, foreign investors have an incentive to invest in the domestic economy. There will be a massive instant inflow of funds, which fuels domestic investment. As the stock of capital increases, r_{t+1} declines. The inflow of funds only ceases when $r_{t+1} = r^*$. The domestic economy reaches the steady-state instantly, and GDP automatically attains the level of rich countries. The economy forever becomes a net debtor in world markets, with external debt being serviced via the permanent increase in real GDP.

Differently from the closed economy case, convergence to the steady-state is extremely rapid. Convergence can be fast now, since investing in domestic production may be in part financed with foreign funds, and it does not have to rely only on domestic saving.

Slow Convergence with International Capital Flows Infinite convergence speeds are clearly counterfactual. Realistic convergence speeds obtain if the basic model is extended as in Cohen and Sachs (1986). First, we may relax the assumption that the domestic economy has unrestricted access to foreign funds. In order to finance domestic investment, assume foreign investors require residents to use a certain fraction of their own resources along with foreign funds. This might occur if foreign investors fear residents might default on their debt in the future. Cohen and Sachs (1986) have introduced such credit constraint in the basic model. Barro, Mankiw, and Sala-i-Martin (1995) have introduced a similar type of constraint in an augmented version of the basic model, where not only physical capital but also human capital is an input to production. They assumed that while foreign investors impose no constraints when financing the accumulation of physical capital, they are unwilling to finance the accumulation of human capital—that is, investment in education. The idea is that while physical capital may be offered as collateral on foreign borrowing, human capital cannot be—on default, physical capital is more easily repossessed by foreign investors than human capital. Since countries need to accumulate both physical and human capital in order to grow, a constraint on human capital accumulation is also a constraint on physical capital accumulation. Both types of constraint on borrowing generate realistic convergence speeds for credit-constrained economies.

Second, we may assume the existence of adjustment costs to investment in domestic capital. Suppose installing new capital entails costs that are higher than just the price of capital, and that these costs become much higher for very large investment rates. Then, the gap between r_{t+1} and r^* no longer determines by itself the incentives to invest: even if $r_{t+1} > r^*$, the effective return on domestic capital may well fall below r^* for large enough levels of investment. Economies will have to adjust slowly toward the steady-state, at realistic speeds.

Openness in Goods Markets To allow for trade in commodities, we need to extend the basic one-good model to multiple goods. Such a departure has been considered by Ventura (1997). Instead of the technology described previously, suppose real GDP is produced using two intermediate inputs—call them traditional and modern. Both are produced using capital and labor, but the modern commodity is more capital intensive. A closed economy behaves exactly as the basic one-good neoclassical growth model described above—the more general production technology leaves the convergence implications unaltered.

Suppose instead that both commodities are freely traded, while real GDP is nontraded, and capital and labor are immobile internationally. Due to free trade, commodity prices in the small open economy equal the corresponding world prices. With capital and labor perfectly mobile across the production of the two commodities, factor prices are also constant across countries sharing the same technology—an instance of the factor-price-equalization theorem. That is, even in the absence of international factor movements, wages and the returns to capital are indirectly pinned down by trade in goods, namely we get $r_t = r^*$.

If saving rates are constant, like before, then not only rich and poor countries wish to invest at the same rate, now they also enjoy the same return r^*. Since trade removes the poor countries' edge in terms of high returns, they stay poor relative to rich countries. There is neither (conditional) convergence nor divergence in world incomes: two economies with identical production technologies will forever stay different if they start out the growth process different. This stands in sharp contrast with both the closed economy implications and those of the basic one-good model.

Whether GDP actually converges or diverges across countries depends on the behavior of saving rates over time. If saving rates increase with the level of GDP, then incomes diverge over time. For convergence still to take place with trade, saving rates must decrease as a country develops.

The East-Asian Miracles Trade in goods also helps us understand the extraordinary growth experience of the East-Asian miracles. The basic one-good model, as well as the multiple-good model without trade, has trouble explaining very high growth rates, sustained over long periods of time: it requires not only high but also increasing saving rates, capable of defying decreasing returns to scale. A much more plausible explanation is that, because of trade-induced return equalization, economies may sustain very high growth rates by avoiding decreasing returns altogether. The performance of the East-Asian miracles may then be understood by the success of these economies at raising saving rates in the early 1960s, and their heavy reliance on exporting industries. Instead of meeting decreasing returns, the fast rates of capital accumulation were channeled to the modern capital-intensive sector. This sector expanded at the expense of the traditional one, its increased production heavily exported in exchange for traditional good imports. In a nutshell, the East-Asian miracles were successful by having the rest of the world absorb their high capital accumulation rates through manufacturing exports.

See also economic development; growth in open economies, Schumpeterian models; international income convergence; trade and economic development, international

FURTHER READING

Barro, Robert J., N. Gregory Mankiw, and Xavier Sala-i-Martin. 1995. "Capital Mobility in Neoclassical Models of Growth." *American Economic Review* 85 (1): 103–15. Argues that incorporating human capital reduces the rate of convergence in the open economy neoclassical model to a realistic level.

Barro, Robert J., and Xavier Sala-i-Martin. 2004. *Economic Growth*. 2d ed. New York: McGraw Hill. A comprehensive and authoritative, although technical, treatment of growth theory and evidence, starting from neoclassical models end extending beyond.

Cass, David. 1965. "Optimum Growth in an Aggregative Model of Capital Accumulation." *Review of Economic Studies* 32 (3): 233–40. A classic reference and one of the building blocks of the neoclassical growth model.

Cohen, Daniel, and Jeffrey D. Sachs. 1986. "Growth and External Debt under Risk of Debt Repudiation." *European Economic Review* 30 (3): 529–60. Argues that fear of default will deter large international capital flows, slowing the rate of income convergence.

Jones, Charles I. 2002. *Introduction to Economic Growth*. 2d ed. New York: W. W. Norton. Includes a very accessible exposition of growth facts and neoclassical growth theory.

Koopmans, Tjalling C. 1965. "On the Concept of Optimal Economic Growth." In *The Econometric Approach to Development Planning*. Amsterdam: North Holland, 1965, 225–300. A classic reference and one of the building blocks of the neoclassical growth model.

Lucas, Jr., Robert E. 1990. "Why Doesn't Capital Flow From Rich to Poor Countries?" *American Economic Review, Papers and Proceedings* 80 (2): 92–96. A short and accessible discussion of the international return equalization challenge facing neoclassical theory.

Ramsey, Frank. 1928. "A Mathematical Theory of Saving." *Economic Journal* 38 (152): 543–59. A classic reference and one of the building blocks of the neoclassical growth model.

Solow, Robert M. 1956. "A Contribution to the Theory of Growth." *Quarterly Journal of Economics* 70 (1): 65–94. A classic reference and one of the building blocks of the neoclassical growth model.

Ventura, Jaume. 1997. "Growth and Interdependence." *Quarterly Journal of Economics*. 112 (1): 57–84. Argues

that diminishing returns to capital is much less important to open economies, which helps explain the extraordinary growth of some east Asian economies.

RUI CASTRO

■ growth in open economies, Schumpeterian models

Schumpeterian growth is a particular type of economic growth generated by the endogenous introduction of product and/or process innovations. The term *endogenous* refers to innovations that result from research and development (R&D) investments undertaken by forward-looking, profit-seeking firms. The term *Schumpeterian growth* is named for Joseph Schumpeter, who described the evolution of capitalism through a process of "creative destruction." This process serves as the fundamental building block in models of Schumpeterian growth and captures the social costs and benefits that result from the endogenous destruction of old technologies by new ones: "Economic progress, in capitalist society, means turmoil. And . . . in this turmoil competition works in a manner completely different from the way it would work in a stationary process, however perfectly competitive. Possibilities for gains to be reaped by producing old things more cheaply are constantly materializing and calling for new investments. These new products and new methods compete with the old methods not on equal terms but at a decisive advantage that may mean death to the latter" (Schumpeter 1942, 42). Schumpeterian growth models are closer in spirit to Schumpeter's ideas than are other theoretical approaches to economic growth such as those that emphasize learning-by-doing, human capital accumulation, or physical capital accumulation as sources of economic growth.

The development of Schumpeterian growth theory started in the early 1990s, motivated by the divergence of national growth rates, Japan's challenge to the United States' technological leadership, and the inability of the neoclassical growth theory to account for the long-run causes of technological progress. The New Growth Theory has primarily focused on causes and effects of long-run technological progress, which is the sole determinant of long-run growth of income per capita. One of the most important insights of the New Growth Theory is the relationship between the economics of ideas and economic growth. Two inherent features of ideas are that they are *nonrival*: an operations manual for organizing a retail store can be used by many stores without any significant replication costs other than photocopying the manual, whereas consumption of an apple by a consumer precludes its consumption by another consumer. Ideas are also partially *excludable* in the sense that the owner of an idea can charge a fee for its use because he/she can restrict access to other users. For instance, Coca-Cola can restrict access to its formula, at least temporarily, by locking the recipe in a safe or by acquiring a patent.

Nonrivalry and partial excludability imply that ideas, which fuel the generation of technology, need to be produced only once, and involve a fixed cost and negligible marginal production cost. Consequently, the economics of "ideas" is necessarily related to the presence of increasing returns to scale and imperfect competition. In a general-equilibrium framework, temporary monopoly profits are essential to finance the R&D cost that occurs before manufacturing of new products (based on new ideas) takes place. Therefore, monopoly profits are not necessarily bad for society but provide incentives for firms to engage in risky R&D investments to discover new products or better processes. The New Growth Theory shifts its focus from competition in product-markets to intertemporal competition in the market for innovations. The latter determines the rate of product development, which generates long-run Schumpeterian growth and limits the duration of monopoly power in product markets.

One variant of Schumpeterian (R&D-based) growth theory focuses on economic growth generated by the introduction of better-quality products. These dynamic general-equilibrium models capture the process of creative destruction as follows: first, sequential and stochastic R&D races are typically used to formalize the entrepreneurial risk, uncertainty, and fixed cost that are inherent in the inno-

vation process; second, product obsolescence, which is based on the endogenous replacement of old, lower-quality goods by new, higher-quality ones, formalizes the Schumpeterian notion of creative destruction; and third, the assumption of patents granted to inventors of new goods formalizes the role of Schumpeterian temporary monopoly power that fuels technological change.

The presence of increasing returns and temporary monopoly power implies a divergence between the market and social optimum and leaves plenty of room for government intervention. In general, the welfare ranking between the social and market rates of Schumpeterian growth is ambiguous thanks to the presence of a few forces that create a divergence between social and private incentives to innovate. One force has been christened the *monopoly-distortion* effect. This force creates an incentive for overinvestment in R&D relative to the social optimum: firms are motivated by the instantaneous monopoly profit margin when engaged in R&D, which happens to exceed the increase in social value (measured by consumer surplus) generated by a typical innovation. Another countervailing force has been christened the *intertemporal-spillover* effect. This force creates a tendency for underinvestment in R&D relative to the social optimum: the social planner takes into account the fact that consumers benefit forever from an innovation. In contrast, being aware that their lives are finite (due to the process of creative destruction), private firms engaged in R&D discount the returns to innovation more than the social planner and invest less. This welfare ambiguity is present in both closed and open-economy Schumpeterian growth models.

First-generation models of Schumpeterian growth exhibit a counterfactual "scale-effects" property according to which more resources devoted to R&D are associated with a higher growth rate of total factor productivity (TFP), that is, output growth not accounted for by the growth in inputs, and the presence of a positive population growth rate must generate an unbounded (infinite) long-run growth rate of per capita income. In other words, according to these models, if R&D employment doubles, then the rate of product creation and the economy's growth rate must also double. Since 1950, however, R&D employment in the United States and other advanced countries has more than doubled without generating any significant acceleration in TFP growth.

Since the mid-1990s, growth theorists have developed a second generation of scale-free, Schumpeterian growth models that fall into two distinct categories depending on the way of removing the scale effects property. Semi-endogenous Schumpeterian growth models incorporate diminishing returns to the stock of knowledge that affects the productivity of R&D resources by assuming that, as technology becomes more complex, sustained growth in R&D resources is needed to maintain a given rate of TFP growth. In other words, easier inventions are discovered first, and as the set of technological opportunities diminishes over time, it becomes more difficult to discover new products. Semi-endogenous growth theory predicts that the long-run growth rate of TFP depends only on the rate of population growth, and therefore it is not affected by policy-related parameters. In other words, semi-endogenous growth theory generates exogenous scale-free long-run Schumpeterian growth.

The second category of R&D-based growth theory consists of fully endogenous and scale-free Schumpeterian growth models. This approach to the removal of scale effects builds on the insight that aggregate R&D effort becomes less effective either because it is spread among more product lines (as new varieties are discovered), or because incumbents who face a risk of going out of business raise barriers to frustrate the R&D effort of challengers. Fully endogenous Schumpeterian growth models maintain the assumption of constant returns to the stock of knowledge of earlier endogenous growth models and generate endogenous long-run growth. In other words, with the exception that the size of an economy—measured by its population level—does not affect long-run growth, these models share the same properties as earlier endogenous growth models. Although the evidence against the empirical validity of earlier endogenous growth models is convincing, the ongoing debate on whether semi-endogenous or

fully endogenous Schumpeterian growth models are more empirically relevant is inconclusive. The terms *earlier*, *semi*, and *fully* endogenous growth models will be used to refer to first-generation, scale-free exogenous, and scale-free endogenous Schumpeterian growth models, respectively, to conserve space and to clarify the exposition.

Economic Openness and Growth Open-economy models of Schumpeterian growth constitute the backbone of dynamic trade theory and complement traditional trade theory by focusing on the analysis of the economic forces that determine the generation and international transfer of technology. They provide valuable theoretical insights into the patterns of growth and trade, global income distribution and poverty, and the effects of economic policies on the performance of the global economy.

Earlier Schumpeterian growth models analyzed the nexus between trade patterns and long-run growth using a variety of approaches. They generated product-cycle trade, which is based on the observation that many products are first discovered in advanced countries and then their production shifts to less advanced countries as their technology is imitated, within a context of a high-wage innovating North and a low-wage noninnovative South, or within the context of two Northern economies facing equal factor prices but differing in their factor endowments. They also identified the economic determinants of sustained comparative advantage in high-technology industries: countries with higher comparative labor productivity in R&D activities, or countries that are abundant in factors used intensively in R&D, such as human capital, will export high-tech products to the rest of the world.

Schumpeterian models have also analyzed the determinants of growth in open economies. Earlier endogenous growth models identified three broad channels through which economic openness affects long-run growth. First, trade, by increasing the size of the market, raises the profitability of R&D investment and increases the long-run rate of innovation and growth in all trading countries. Second, economic openness, by facilitating the international exchange of information, increases the scope of knowledge spillovers, raises the productivity of researchers, and accelerates the rates of innovation and growth in the global economy. Third, trade openness, by reallocating economic resources across sectors and between R&D investment and manufacturing activities, affects the long-run rates of innovation and growth. This trade-induced "specialization" process, which is the major source of welfare gains in static models, has an ambiguous effect on long-run growth.

It should be noted, however, that the market-size-based effect of trade on growth can be traced to the scale-effects property of earlier endogenous growth models. Fully endogenous growth models predict more moderate effects of economic openness on growth. These effects operate through changes in relative prices and per capita reallocation of resources between R&D and manufacturing activities. For example, a reduction in international trade costs can accelerate the long-run rate of growth by increasing the flow of temporary monopoly profits and by shifting per capita resources from manufacturing production (that is, consumption) to R&D activities (that is, investment).

Globalization and Income Distribution Schumpeterian models of economic growth have provided valuable theoretical insights associated with the evolution of wage and income inequality within and across countries. The 1970s and 1980s witnessed an alarming rise in the demand for skilled labor and a decline in the demand for unskilled labor. These labor-market developments raised the relative wage of skilled workers in the United States and several developing countries and increased the unemployment rate of less-skilled workers in several advanced countries. Economic openness and skilled-biased technological change have been proposed as two competing explanations for the rise in the relative demand for skilled labor. In traditional trade theory, relative commodity prices represent the only channel that transmits the effects of trade openness on wages. The trade-based explanation for the rise in U.S. wage inequality has been rejected by evidence on U.S. relative prices, which have remained more or less constant during the period of rising wage inequality.

Unlike traditional trade theory, Schumpeterian growth theory views technological change as an endogenous process that could be affected by changes in the reward to innovation. The reward to innovation is proportional to the expected discounted profits associated with the discovery of new products. An increase in trade openness caused by a reduction in international trade costs can affect the profitability of R&D without necessarily causing any change in relative commodity prices. Under the reasonable assumption that R&D is a skilled-labor-intensive activity, Schumpeterian growth models predict that globalization increases the relative demand for skilled labor and accelerates the rate of technological progress. An increase in the relative demand for skilled labor can generate either a rise in the relative wage of skilled workers or a rise in the unemployment rate of less-skilled workers depending on the degree of labor-market flexibility. This novel mechanism has been formally established in the context of semi-endogenous and fully endogenous Schumpeterian models of economic growth.

The controversial issue of the dynamic effects of various components of globalization on the income gap between advanced (Northern) and poor (Southern) countries has drawn the attention of Schumpeterian growth theorists. An important strand of Schumpeterian models of North-South trade and growth has analyzed the income distributional effects of globalization-enhancing policies. The main insight of this literature is that any increase in the rate of imitation and/or decline in the rate of innovation reduces the North-South wage inequality measured by the Northern relative wage. In other words, faster international transfer of technology from North to South benefits Southern workers.

Government Interventions Schumpeterian models of economic growth have analyzed the long-run growth and welfare effects of a variety of government interventions. Policy instruments such as taxes and subsidies on R&D, production, and trade change relative product and factor prices and generate shifts in economic resources between consumption and R&D activities. In earlier and fully endogenous growth models, a policy-induced shift in per capita resources toward R&D activities accelerates permanently the rates of innovation and growth. In semi-endogenous growth models this resource shift generates a temporary (as opposed to a permanent) increase in the rate of innovation. In the presence of asymmetric industries and countries, dynamic general equilibrium forces can reverse the well-intended effects of several policy interventions. For instance, R&D subsidies may cause a country to export fewer R&D-intensive goods and import more of them; and industrial policies that subsidize manufacturing activities in high-technology sectors may have detrimental effects on global long-run innovation and growth because they could raise the costs of R&D by shifting resources away from R&D activities.

Several North-South Schumpeterian growth models have analyzed the dynamic effects of stronger protection of intellectual property rights (IPR). Stronger IPR protection, modeled either as an increase in patent length or as a reduction in the rate of Southern imitation, reduces the rate of international technology transfer from innovating North to imitating South, raises the North-South wage gap, and has an ambiguous effect on the rate of innovation and global Schumpeterian growth. Even if stronger IPR protection increases the rate of Northern innovation in the short run, it could reduce the welfare of Southern consumers and could raise the welfare of Northern consumers by shifting production from low-price South to high-price North. Consequently, North-South models of Schumpeterian growth are well fitted to provide useful policy recommendations regarding the intense debate surrounding the Agreement on Trade-Related Intellectual Property Rights (TRIPS), which was ratified by the members of the World Trade Organization in 1995 and calls for stronger Southern IPR protection.

See also Agreement on Trade-Related Intellectual Property Rights (TRIPS); North-South trade; technological progress in open economies

FURTHER READING

Aghion, Philippe, and Peter Howitt. 1998. *Endogenous Growth Theory*. Cambridge, MA: MIT Press. Provides a comprehensive analysis of endogenous growth theory.

Dinopoulos, Elias, and Peter Thompson. 1999. "Scale Effects in Schumpeterian Models of Economic Growth." *Journal of Evolutionary Economics* 9 (2): 157–85. Reviews available empirical evidence on the relationship between scale and growth, and attempts to develop Schumpeterian growth without scale effects.

Grossman, Gene M., and Elhanan Helpman. 1991. *Innovation and Growth in the Global Economy*. Cambridge, MA: MIT Press. Presents a coherent theoretical framework that integrates the variety-based and quality-based approaches of earlier Schumpeterian models of growth in open economies.

Schumpeter, Joseph. A. 1942. *Capitalism, Socialism, and Democracy*. New York: Harper and Row. This classic book provides a comprehensive treatment of the process of creative destruction.

Segerstrom, Paul S., T.C.A. Anant, and Elias Dinopoulos. 1990. "A Schumpeterian Model of the Product Life Cycle." *American Economic Review* 80 (5): 1077–91. This is the first model of Schumpeterian growth in open economies.

Romer, Paul M. 1990. "Endogenous Technological Change." *Journal of Political Economy* 98 (5, part 2): S71–S102. This seminal article developed the most influential and most widely cited closed-economy model of Schumpeterian growth.

ELIAS DINOPOULOS

Grubel-Lloyd index

See intraindustry trade

Gulf Cooperation Council

The Gulf Cooperation Council (GCC) was created in February 1981 by six Arab Gulf states: Bahrain, Kuwait, Qatar, Oman, Saudi Arabia, and the United Arab Emirates (UAE). The main motive for the creation of the GCC was to face the threat posed to the region's security by the Iran-Iraq war at that time. The aims of the GCC formation are to develop cooperation and integration among the member states on foreign and defense policies and to promote common interest in economic, social, and cultural affairs. A customs union that allows no tariffs or other barriers to trade among members (as in free trade areas) and harmonizes trade policies (such as setting of common tariff rates) toward the rest of the world was created between GCC members in January 2004.

Members of the GCC share common features such as religion, language, historical background, and social life. The GCC economies depend on similar natural resources and have a comparable structural base. The GCC members also share the same sociopolitical system in which the states, ruled by kings and princes, own most of the natural resources and the large public sector dominates all aspects of the economy.

The GCC population as of 2005 was approximately 36 million. Saudi Arabia has the largest population base compared to the other five members. Approximately 38 percent of the total GCC population is composed of expatriates with no permanent residence. The proportion of nationals out of the total population varies from one country to another. This ratio is very small in Kuwait, Qatar, and the UAE (35, 27, and 22 percent, respectively), compared to Bahrain, Oman, and Saudi Arabia (62, 78, and 72 percent). Even though the GCC fertility rate is among the highest in the world, their economic dependence on foreign labor is not decreasing.

GCC social indicators depict a very positive human development profile. Life expectancy is well above 70 years, infant mortality is far below the world average, and the population per physician is very low. However, fertility rates in most GCC countries are among the highest in the world, reflecting generous family allowances provided by governments in order to increase the population base. Finally, education spending has contributed to declining illiteracy rates.

Expatriates constitute the largest percentage of the labor force in GCC countries. Table 1 shows that approximately one-third of the total labor force in GCC countries are citizens while two-thirds are expatriates. The percentage of citizen labor force in the states of Kuwait and the UAE is less than 20 percent. Only in Saudi Arabia is the percentage of citizens in the labor force slightly greater than 50 percent of the total labor force. The greatest majority of GCC employees are working in the public sector, and the average wages and salaries of GCC citizens are almost three times higher than those of expatriates.

GCC economies depend entirely on the production of oil, and all economic sectors revolve around revenues generated by oil exports. The exploration for oil began in the Gulf region in 1945. The Gulf oil has been important in the global energy market for many reasons. First, the oil reserves of the GCC are huge in comparison to the world's total reserves. The GCC oil reserves constitute around 50 percent of the world total. Second, the GCC plays a significant role in the supply of oil to the world market. The share of the GCC in total world production is approximately 25 percent. Third, geological factors such as the location of the onshore oil fields close to the deep Persian Gulf, the flow of the oil toward the sea, and the ease of drilling have helped the GCC's oil to be produced relatively more cheaply than the rest of

Table 1
The GCC labor force in 2005 (thousands)

	Bahrain (%)	Kuwait (%)	Oman (%)	Qatar (%)	SA (%)	UAE (%)	GCC (%)
Citizens	145 (41.7)	327 (19.5)	205 (31.1)	41 (44.1)	3,469 (51.3)	450 (15.7)	4,637 (37.4)
Expatriates	203 (58.3)	1,349 (80.5)	454 (68.9)	52 (55.9)	3,289 (48.7)	2,411 (84.3)	7,758 (62.6)
Total	348 (100)	1,676 (100)	659 (100)	93 (100)	6,758 (100)	2,861 (100)	12,395 (100)

Sources:
   The Cooperation Council for the Arab States of the Gulf: Statistical Bulletin, 2006.
   Ministry of Planning in various GCC countries.

world's oil. Finally, the central geographical location of the Persian Gulf between the developed economies in the West and growing economies of East Asia has reduced transport costs and increased the significance of the GCC oil market.

Table 2 reveals that, at the end of 2005, oil reserves in GCC countries were approximately 470 billion barrels, oil products exceeded 15 million barrels per day, and oil revenue was approximately $187 billion. Saudi Arabia is the largest oil producer in the GCC countries, followed by Kuwait and the UAE. However, Qatar and Oman have much smaller oil reserves, and much less oil production and oil revenue, than these three members of the GCC. Bahrain seems to be losing its dependence on oil.

The petroleum and mining contribution to GDP in GCC countries constitutes 20 to 60 percent of total gross domestic product (GDP). This contribution is higher when oil prices rise. The contribution was the highest in Qatar (61 percent) and the lowest in Bahrain (22 percent) in 2005. The second most important economic activity is the services sector (wholesale and retail trade, transportation and communication, finance and insurance, real estate). The services sector contributes 20 to 30 percent of GDP. The contribution of the service sector in 2005 was 51 percent in Bahrain (which is no longer a major oil producer) and 15 percent in Qatar (which depends heavily on its production of oil and natural gas). The third most important sector is the government, which contributes 10 to 20 percent of GDP. The manufacturing sector plays a moderate

role in all members of the GCC. This sector contributes only 6 to 10 percent of GDP. The only exception is its contribution in the United Arab Emirates in 2005, which amounted to 14 percent. Contribution of the agricultural sector to GDP is negligible in most GCC countries and was only 4 percent in Saudi Arabia in 2005. The GCC members heavily subsidized the state-owned electricity, gas, and water sector.

The level of per capita income differs significantly among members of the GCC. Per capita income in the state of Qatar was the highest in 2005 ($39,101), while per capita income in Oman was the lowest ($9,939). Per capita income in all GCC members was approximately $14,346 in 2005.

The proportion of total expenditure on exports and imports constituted a significant proportion of GDP. Re-exporting is a major part of the Bahrain and UAE total exports (around 30 percent). The proportion of total expenditure on private consumption out of GDP is much lower than in countries with similar per capita income (around 35 percent) and is especially low in the state of Qatar (15 percent of GDP in 2005). Expenditure on public consumption was approximately 20 percent of GDP in the states of Kuwait, Oman, and Saudi Arabia in 2005.

The percentage of GDP devoted to gross fixed capital formation in the GCC countries varies from less than 15 percent in the case of Kuwait to 25 percent in the case of the UAE. The government carries out a large percentage of investment in these

Table 2

GCC oil production, revenue, and reserves in 2005

	Bahrain	Kuwait	Oman	Qatar	Saudi Arabia	UAE	GCC
Oil reserves (billion barrels/year end)	0.12	96.8	5.8	4.5	264.5	99	470.72
Oil production (thousand of barrels/daily)	36	2,318	816	792	8,958	2,518	15,436
Oil revenue ($M)	2,700	27,340	8,312	8,124	110,654	30,124	187,254

Sources:
  The Cooperation Council for the Arab States of the Gulf: Statistical Bulletin, 2006.
  Ministry of Planning in various GCC countries.

Table 3
Total trade and intratrade of members of the GCC Customs Union (1981–2005)

	1981			1989			1997			2005		
	Total trade (US$M)	Intra-trade (US$M)	% of intra-trade to total trade	Total trade (US$M)	Intra-trade (US$M)	% of intra-trade to total trade	Total trade (US$M)	Intra-trade (US$M)	% of intra-trade to total trade	Total trade (US$M)	Intra-trade (US$M)	% of intra-trade to total trade
Bahrain	8,471	3,750	44.3	5,849	1,427	24.4	10,468	1,415	13.5	18,283	2,564	14.0
Kuwait	23,161	878	3.8	17,425	677	3.9	23,011	1,055	4.6	34,516	1,654	4.8
Oman	6,695	560	8.4	6,620	3,352	50.6	12,509	2,325	18.6	19,165	3,437	17.9
Qatar	6,907	180	2.6	3,828	330	8.6	8,376	572	6.8	21,019	1,507	7.2
SA	148,472	3,371	2.3	49,537	2,721	5.5	89,135	5,446	6.1	155,412	6,993	4.5
UAE	30,604	1,494	4.9	26,034	1,354	5.2	54,231	2,988	5.5	114,613	6,078	5.3
All GCC members	217,403	10,233	4.7	109,293	9,861	9.0	197,910	13,801	7.0	363,008	22,233	6.1

countries. Public investment has been concentrated mainly in infrastructure and the oil sector, including petrochemical industries. Private fixed capital formation, on the other hand, was directed mainly to the construction sector and the (modest) manufacturing sector. Public investment is, to a great extent, autonomous of changes in demand and interest rates and is financed from government oil revenue. Private investment depends heavily on growth in private consumption, which is greatly affected by growth in government expenditure in the GCC countries. This suggests that total (public and private) investment in the GCC countries depends on lagged oil revenues.

The GCC countries depend heavily on the outside world for the supply of most of their needs (Metwally and Tamaschke 1980; Metwally and Daghistani 1987). This is because of the relatively weak productive capacity of these economies due to lack of resources, particularly labor, materials, and water. The downturn in oil prices after the end of 1982 resulted in a sharp reduction in GCC spending on imports (Metwally 1993). However, the proportion of GDP spent on imports of goods and services in 2005 (following the rise in oil prices) was approximately 40 percent. Moreover, available sta-

tistics suggest that the income elasticity of imports exceeds one in many GCC members (Metwally 2004a, b).

Many studies have developed econometric techniques and models to identify functional relationships in the GCC economies. Metwally (1987, 1993) attempted to examine the determinants of the external surplus or gap between exports and imports of the oil-producing members of the GCC. In spite of the sharp rise in oil prices during the 1970s, the GCC countries could not improve their external surplus per exported barrel. This indicated that the rise in oil prices was greatly matched by a larger increment in imports and by the fall in the volume of exports. Metwally tested the hypothesis that the external surplus balance varies inversely with GDP. In contrast to economic theory, the results showed that the external surplus is positively correlated with GDP in the case of GCC countries. The result was explained by the fact that total GDP in the GCC countries is dominated by oil revenues, which are owned by government and are not directly available for domestic expenditure. Thus an increase in oil exports would increase total GDP and add to the overall surplus. When non-oil income was used instead of total GDP, a significant negative correlation was obtained between non-oil income and the external surplus. Metwally also tested the interaction between the economies of the GCC and the rest of the world. The oil exports of the GCC responded favorably to the increase in the share of the Organization of the Petroleum Exporting Countries (OPEC) in world oil supply and the increase in world oil consumption. Finally, the marginal propensity to import out of non-oil income was extremely high in all GCC countries. This resulted in an "import trap," i.e., a tendency to increase imports even when the value of exports is declining (Metwally 1993; Metwally and Rammadhan 2000; Metwally 2003).

Table 3 gives data on total trade and intra-trade of members of the GCC customs union during the period 1981–2005. It is clear that the rise in oil prices resulted in higher rates of growth of intra-imports and intra-exports of most members of the GCC (Metwally and Alsowaidi 2005). Also, most commodities produced in GCC countries are not substitutes for commodities imported from outside countries. A rise in oil prices results in an increase in intra-exports due to improvement of domestic productive capacity through use of advanced technology. The analysis of Kaul, Metwally, and Perera (2007) suggests that intra-trade of most GCC members is strongly influenced by oil prices. The results also suggest that intra-exports of Qatar, Saudi Arabia, and the UAE are positively related to their intra-imports. These results also indicate that there are very significant feedback effects in intra-trade of Qatar, Saudi Arabia, and the UAE. An increase in these members' intra-imports results in an increase in their importers' incomes. However, there are no significant feedback effects in intra-trade of Bahrain, Kuwait, and Oman. These members might benefit from giving more attention to dynamic benefits of their customs union.

See also customs unions; migration, international; Organization of the Petroleum Exporting Countries (OPEC); petroleum; primary products trade; regionalism

FURTHER READING

Kaul, Nandini, M. M. Metwally, and Nelson Perera. 2007. "Feed-back Effects of Intra-trade between GCC Coun-
tries." *International Journal of Applied Business and Economic Research* 5 (1): 75–89. Reveals the existence of feedback effects between trade of some members and trade of others, but not between trades of all members of the GCC.

Metwally, M. M. 1987. "Determinants of the External Surplus of the Member States of the Gulf Co-operation Council." *Applied Economics* 19 (3): 305–16. Shows a significant negative correlation between the external surplus and non-oil income in each GCC member country.

———. 1993. "The Effect of the Decline in Oil Revenue on the Import Patterns of the Members of the Gulf Co-operation Council." *International Journal of Energy Research* 17 (5) (July): 413–22. Proves that the decline in oil revenue has resulted in a sharp rise in income elasticity of imports for all import groups in all GCC members.

———. 2003. "Impact of Price Elasticity of Exports on Terms of Trade: The Case of the GCC Countries." *Asia Pacific Journal of Energy* 13 (1) (June): 17–24. Proves that the faster the improvement in terms of trade of GCC countries, the lower the price elasticity of demand for oil.

———. 2004a. "Impact of Fluctuations in Oil Revenue on Investment in the GCC Countries." *Economia Internazionale* 57 (2): 173–89. Shows that the demand for investment in GCC countries was subject to structural shifts due to fluctuations in oil prices during the last quarter of the 20th century.

———. 2004b. "Determinants of Aggregate Imports of GCC Countries: Co-Integration Analysis." *Applied Econometrics and International Development* 4 (3): 59–76. Reveals that the downturn in oil prices resulted in a drastic reduction in the growth rates of imports of all the oil producers of the GCC.

Metwally, M. M., and Saif S. Alsowaidi. 2005. "Towards Unifying Monetary Policies in GCC Countries." *Global Journal of Finance and Economics* 2 (2): 149–62. Suggests that an application of a unified monetary policy for the integrated GCC countries could present difficulties.

Metwally, M. M., and A. I. Daghistani. 1987. "The Interaction between the Economies of the Member States of the Gulf Co-operation Council and the Industrialized Countries." *Indian Economic Journal* 35 (3): 51–59. Reveals that despite the large volume of financial reserves held by members of the GCC, their imports seem to depend on their export proceeds.

Metwally, M. M., and M. Rammadhan. 2000. "Impact of Fuctuations in Oil Prices on the Resource Balance of the GCC Countries." *Middle East Business and Economic Review* 12 (2): 1–9. Suggests that the resource balance of each GCC member is negatively correlated with non-oil income and positively correlated with growth in the world economy.

Metwally, M. M., and R. Tamaschke. 1980. "Oil Exports and Economic Growth in the Middle East and North Africa." *Kyklos* 33 (3): 499–522. Suggests that members of the GCC need to take more measures to exploit the investment opportunities generated by the growth in oil exports.

———. 2001. "Trade Relationship between the Gulf Cooperation Council and the European Union." *European Business Review* 13 (5): 292–96. Shows significant feedback effects in GCC countries that trade with the EU.

MOKHTAR M. METWALLY

■ health and globalization

Globalization interacts with health in several areas. Globalization directly affects economic outcomes, such as the level of income per capita, that may affect health outcomes, while health may affect the level or pattern of economic activities across countries. The dissemination of health-related know-how and internationally coordinated public health measures contribute to raising health standards globally. Increased movement of goods or people, however, also creates health risks arising from the dissemination of diseases or contaminated products.

Income, Inequality, and Health Higher income is associated with better health standards, both within and across countries. Cross-country studies find that aggregate health measures such as life expectancy are positively correlated with income per capita (see Pritchett and Summers 1996; Deaton 2004). The link between income and life expectancy appears to be strongest for low-income countries, but there also is more inequality in terms of health outcomes between these countries than among higher-income countries. Thus, although the potential health gains associated with higher incomes appear to be greatest in low-income countries, these countries are also where the impact of other factors on health outcomes is strongest, including (lack of) public health infrastructure or inefficiencies in the delivery of public health services, some of which, in turn, may also hold back improvements in income (Deaton 2004).

Rapid economic development is sometimes associated with an increase in income inequality, which may have implications for access to health services across income groups. Deaton (2003) points to the link between poverty and health outcomes, and finds little evidence for a role of inequality per se, however. Cross-country data on health care financing point to complex interactions between access to health care, poverty, and inequality. Financial sector development, and thus access to health insurance, is limited in many developing countries. Conversely, in developing countries the share of out-of-pocket expenditures in private health expenditure is higher, which implies that health risks are associated with higher risks to material living standards. For poor segments of the population, public health expenditure can compensate for the lack of health insurance, but the level of public health expenditures, their efficiency, and geographical access differ considerably across countries.

The correlation between increases in income and increases in life expectancy has motivated some studies trying to assess the contribution of each to improving living standards. Composite indexes, such as the Human Development Index of the United Nations Development Program, assign weights to measures of income, health, and possibly other indicators such as educational attainment. Some studies draw on microeconomic estimates of the valuation of mortality risks. Using this approach, Nordhaus (2002) suggests that the contribution of improved health to living standards has been of a magnitude similar to the contribution of improvements in gross domestic product (GDP) for the United States between 1900 and 1995, and Becker, Philipson, and Soares (2005) suggest that world health inequality has been declining even if incomes have not converged.

Knowledge Flows and Health Technologies International knowledge flows have played an important role in falling mortality rates across countries. Deaton (2004) asserts that health improvements in developing countries in the 20th century "ultimately came from the globalization of knowledge, facilitated by local political, economic, and educational outcomes," including applications of the germ theory of disease, DDT spraying against malarial mosquitoes, the use of antibiotics against tuberculosis, and oral rehydration therapy.

The prominent role of knowledge flows points to the value of international cooperation to facilitate and speed up the dissemination of health technologies, and to assist in their implementation, which is one of the key mandates of the World Health Organization (WHO). Recent examples of internationally coordinated health programs include the Measles Initiative, which reportedly succeeded in reducing global deaths from measles by 60 percent (and by 75 percent in sub-Saharan Africa) between 1999 and 2005, largely through mass immunizations and improvements in care. Another major international health campaign was the WHO's 3 by 5 campaign and related efforts to reduce the incidence of HIV/AIDS and to improve access to antiretroviral treatment in low- and middle-income countries.

A key factor in the global dissemination of health technologies is the legal framework for the protection of intellectual property rights, including the Agreement on Trade-Related Aspects of Intellectual Property Rights (TRIPS), which requires all World Trade Organization member countries to meet certain minimum standards for the protection of intellectual property rights, including patents. Patents allow pharmaceutical companies to recoup the costs of drug development by charging prices that far exceed production costs. Although most essential medicines (according to the WHO definition) are no longer protected by patents, patent protection can complicate access to medicines for relatively new diseases, such as HIV/AIDS. The experience with antiretroviral drugs to treat HIV/AIDS also involved numerous ways of facilitating access to these drugs in low-income countries, however.

Apart from its effect on the dissemination of medical know-how and drugs, the legal environment also has implications for the direction of research. As most of the profits from new drugs arise from sales in high-income countries, pharmaceutical companies direct their research efforts toward drugs for these markets, rather than drugs addressing health issues that are more prevalent in low-income countries.

Health, Growth, and the Location of Economic Activity While higher income can buy better health, the state of health can also have implications for income levels and affect the location of economic activities. Most directly, healthier people are also more productive. Fogel (1993), discussing the effects of nutrition on increased labor supply in Britain between 1800 and 1980, argues that improved nutrition contributed to an increase in the labor force participation rate, and that a higher intake of calories increased workers' productivity. Together, Fogel estimates that these two effects account for 30 percent of economic growth in Britain over the 19th and 20th centuries.

Conceptually related are attempts to estimate the impact of health on productivity, using data on aggregate macroeconomic outcomes and health indicators. Among the wave of empirical studies on sources of growth starting in the early 1990s, numerous authors have included some measure of health, usually the level of life expectancy. For example, Bloom, Canning, and Sevilla (2001) find that one additional year of life expectancy raises GDP per capita by 4 percent; and Cole and Neumayer (2006) discuss the link between various measures of morbidity and total factor productivity. These studies, however, are usually not able to clearly distinguish between level of life expectancy and growth rate effects and—in light of the large range of proxies for health status used—offer few insights into the nature of the link between health and growth.

In addition to its effects on productivity, health may affect economic development through its impact on the rate of population growth. The logic of this is already present in the basic Solow growth model, where higher population growth translates into a lower capital/labor ratio and thus lower output per capita. Along these lines, Acemoglu, Johnson, and Robinson (2006), studying the impact of declining mortality in the early 20th century, find that this has resulted in an increase in population growth and a slow-down in the rate of growth of per capita income. This effect has also played a role in explaining the limited impact of HIV/AIDS on economic growth in countries severely affected by the epidemic, as higher mortality translates to an increase in the capital/labor ratio; some studies, similarly, have illustrated the positive economic impact of health crises such as the Black Death and 1918 influenza epidemic on the incomes of survivors.

Another link between health and growth that has been intensively researched in recent years is the impact of health on institutional development. Acemoglu, Johnson, and Robinson (2003) highlight the role health conditions played in European colonial expansion. Where health conditions were hostile, Europeans set up extractive regimes with minimal investments of human resources and in institutional development, which tended to contribute little to the economic growth of the colonies. In environments more inviting to European settlers, European colonists were more likely to set up more egalitarian political and economic institutions that contributed more to the colonies' economic growth. The point of this institutional approach is that differences in health conditions have a persistent influence on economic outcomes through their impact on institutional development.

Although the evidence on the links between income and health suggests that health would improve with economic development, the link between globalization, development, and health may not be positive in all cases or for all regions or people involved. Specifically, health, environmental, and safety standards are generally less stringent in developing countries, which translates into a cost advantage for companies producing there. In a world of competitive markets, the stringency of health and other standards related to health may reflect legitimate societal preferences regarding the importance of

achieving certain health outcomes compared to other development objectives such as raising incomes or reducing poverty. Thus a government may accept lower health and environmental standards to attract investment and pursue its broader development strategy, and employees may accept health risks in return for higher salaries.

The most compelling arguments against trade based on differences in health and environmental standards across countries rest on asymmetric-information, incomplete-market, or moral arguments. The correct pricing of health risks requires that both sides understand the risks involved, a condition that often does not hold in employment relations in developing countries. Similarly, the absence of effective regulations or weak contract enforcement means that companies are not held accountable for negative externalities associated with their activities. For example, in the case of disposal of toxic waste, part of the costs of such processes may be—literally—"dumped" on the local population, with little or no accountability for the originator. From a moral perspective, certain production methods (frequently quoted examples are child labor and exports of toxic waste) may be regarded as morally questionable, which could motivate legal provisions in the source countries of exports, or—increasingly common—public campaigns by nongovernmental organizations targeting consumer behavior.

Health Risks Associated with the Movements of Goods and People One of the defining characteristics of globalization is an increasing intensity of trade in goods, which also has some implications for global health risks. Contaminated food and other supplies can amplify the spread of diseases globally, especially if long incubation periods are involved or the disease is new and the associated risks are not well understood. For example, one important channel of transmission of HIV in the early stages of the epidemic was the trade in contaminated blood products.

Most commonly, however, trade-related health risks are associated with contaminated food or other products for human consumption. One example is a spate of deaths in Panama in 2006 linked to drugs containing contaminated ingredients imported from

China. More frequently, health hazards associated with imported food arise from contamination with pesticides or industrial waste (e.g., in seafood) or bacteria such as salmonella.

Globalization complicates the task of ensuring food safety standards. First, national efforts to attain certain standards in food production need to be complemented by measures to ensure the quality of imported products, which could involve inspections of imported products at the port of entry, harmonization of standards, or measures to ensure that certain standards are met in the source countries (e.g., EU beef import requirements). At the same time, mass production of and increased trade in food and other products means that such products are sold over large regions and across borders. Effectively responding to a health emergency thus also requires the ability to trace products back to their origin and possibly recall affected products.

Globalization has also expanded the trade in illicit drugs. The United Nations Office on Drugs and Crime estimates that the value of the global market in illicit drugs was U.S. $90 billion in 2003, and that about 200 million people (5 percent of the world's population) consumed illicit drugs at least annually, and 110 million at least monthly. By far the most widely used drug is cannabis. The largest consumer market for illicit drugs is North America, accounting for about 44 percent of the world market, while the most important producing regions are Latin America for cocaine, and various Middle Eastern and Asian countries for opiates.

Apart from trade in goods, a second element of globalization is the increased intensity of the movement of people, including a massive increase in global air travel. Between 1950 and 2005, the number of air travelers increased by a factor of 60 (from 31 million to 1.9 billion), and the number of passenger kilometers multiplied by a factor of 123 (from 28 million to 3.4 billion). As a consequence, it is increasingly difficult to contain an infectious disease locally or regionally, an issue that has gained increased attention internationally following the SARS outbreak and in light of the risks attributed to avian flu. Similarly, the global spread of an epidemic such as the 1918 influenza would, under current conditions, occur much faster, allowing less time for preventive measures or for preparation of a health response, and might lead to bottlenecks in the availability of essential medicines.

See also access to medicines; globalization; global public goods; HIV/AIDS

FURTHER READING

Acemoglu, Daron, Simon Johnson, and James Robinson. 2003. "Disease and Development in Historical Perspective." *Journal of the European Economic Association* 1 (2–3): 397–405. An influential paper discussing the impact of disease on economic development in the long term.

———. 2006. "Disease and Development: The Effect of Life Expectancy on Economic Growth." NBER Working Paper No. 12269. Cambridge, MA: National Bureau of Economic Research. A discussion of the impact of increased life expectancy on growth in the early 20th century.

Becker, Gary S., Tomas J. Philipson, and Rodrigo R. Soares. 2005. "The Quantity and Quality of Life and the Evolution of World Inequality." *American Economic Review* 95 (1): 277–91. Discusses evolution of world inequality in terms of incomes and health outcomes.

Bloom, David E., David Canning, and J. Sevilla. 2004. "The Effect of Health on Economic Growth: A Production Function Approach." *World Development* 32: 1–13. Estimates the impact of health expenditures on economic growth.

Cole, Matthew A., and Eric Neumayer. 2006. "The Impact of Poor Health on Total Factor Productivity." *Journal of Development Studies* 42 (6): 918–38.

Deaton, Angus. 2003. "Health, Inequality, and Economic Development." *Journal of Economic Literature* 41: 113–58. Estimates the impact of poor health on worker productivity, controlling for differences in factors such as education levels and the use of capital.

———. 2004. "Health in an Age of Globalization." In *Brookings Trade Forum 2004*, edited by Susan Collins and Carol Graham. Washington DC: The Brookings Institution, 83–130. Both works by Deaton are good starting points for further reading on health and globalization.

Fogel, Robert W. 1993. "Economic Growth, Population Theory, and Physiology: The Bearing of Long-Term Processes on the Making of Economic Policy." *American Economic Review* 84 (3): 369–95. Nobel Lecture, also available online at http://nobelprize.org/nobel_prizes/economics/laureates/1993/fogel-lecture.html. Discusses the contributions of improved nutrition to health and economic growth in Britain over the 19th and 20th centuries.

López-Casasnovas, Guillem, Berta Rivera, and Luis Currais, eds. 2005. *Health and Economic Growth—Findings and Policy Implications.* Cambridge MA: MIT Press. A comprehensive resource about the affect of health on economic growth.

Nordhaus, William D. 2002. "The Health of Nations: The Contribution of Improved Health to Living Standards." NBER Working Paper No. 8818. Cambridge, MA: National Bureau of Economic Research. Compares contributions of health and growth to improving living standards.

Pritchett, Lant, and Lawrence H. Summers. 1996. "Wealthier Is Healthier." *Journal of Human Resources* 31 (4): 841–68. Another good starting point for further reading on health and globalization.

MARKUS HAACKER

■ Heckscher-Ohlin model

The Heckscher-Ohlin (H-O) model, which originated in Heckscher (1919) and Ohlin (1933) and was formalized and given narrower interpretation by Samuelson (1948), differs from the Ricardian theory of comparative advantage in two key respects. First, the Ricardian theory assumes only one factor of production, which robs it of any ability to address the internal income distribution effects of international trade. In contrast, the H-O theory allows for two factors of production, which opens the door to internal income distribution effects of trade. Second, whereas the Ricardian theory relies on the differences in technology across countries as the source of international trade, the H-O theory assumes the existence of the same technology everywhere and relies on the international differences in factor endowments as the basis of trade.

Because the H-O model allows economists to analyze the income distribution effects and plausibly gives a central role to intercountry differences in factor endowment rather than technology, which diffuses relatively rapidly internationally, it has come to serve as the main workhorse of trade theorists. The model leads to the conclusion that each country exports the goods that use its relatively abundant factor more intensively and such exports lead to a rise in the real and relative return to the latter. Symmetrically, the country imports products using its scarce factor more intensively, which lowers the real and relative return to the latter.

Recently, increased wage inequality in the rich countries as measured by skilled-to-unskilled wage has brought this model further to the center of the policy debate. Those favoring protection over free trade argue that just as the H-O model predicts, trade liberalization by skilled-labor-abundant rich countries has led to the rise in skilled-to-unskilled wage. Pro-free-trade economists argue, however, that the real culprit behind the phenomenon is technological advances in skilled-labor-intensive industries, which has led to a shift in demand in favor of skilled labor.

The Setting and Principal Results The following will largely focus on the strict two-factor, two-good, and two-country version of the H-O model, as formalized by Samuelson (1948). This version is narrower than originally conceived by Ohlin (1933) but is now widely used by trade economists. To formally outline the key assumptions and structure of the model, call the countries Home Country (HC) and Foreign Country (FC), products Corn (C) and Shirts (S), and factors Land (T) and Labor (L). Assume constant returns to scale in the production of each good. This means doubling the use of each factor in C doubles the output of C. The same holds true for S. Goods C and S require different technologies. Specifically, we assume that C is land intensive in the sense that at any given set of factor prices, the land-labor ratio in the production of C is higher than that in S: $T_C/L_C > T_S/L_S$. Here

T_C denotes the quantity of land employed in the production of C. A similar interpretation applies to L_C, T_S, and L_S. By implication, S is relatively labor intensive. Assuming both goods are produced in equilibrium and there is perfect competition in all markets, the H-O model leads to the following two theorems:

The Stolper-Samuelson (1941) theorem: An exogenous increase in the relative price of a good leads to an increase in the real and relative return to the factor used more intensively in that good and a decrease in the real and relative return to the other factor. For example, an increase in the price of C increases the real and relative return to land, which is used more intensively in the latter. It also leads to a decline in the real and relative return to labor, which is used more intensively in S.

The Rybczynski (1955) theorem: Holding the goods prices constant, an increase in the endowment of a factor leads to a proportionately larger increase in the output of the good using that factor more intensively and a decline in the output of the other good. For example, holding the goods prices constant, a 1 percent increase in the endowment of labor would raise the output of S, which uses labor more intensively, by more than 1 percent and lower the output of C.

Suppose we additionally assume that HC is land abundant relative to FC. Formally, using an asterisk to distinguish the variables associated with FC, $T/L > T^*/L^*$. The two countries have the same technology of production available. These two additional results follow:

The Heckscher-Ohlin theorem: The opening to trade leads each country to export the good using its abundant factor more intensively and to import the other good. For example, the land-abundant HC exports the land-intensive good C and imports the labor-intensive good S.

The Factor-Price Equalization theorem: Absent transportation costs, the opening to trade equalizes not only the goods prices but factor prices as well. That is to say, in a trading equilibrium, the HC ends up with the same real and relative wage and rental price of land as FC.

Deriving the Theorems Let us denote the wage by w and the rental price of land by r. The proportion of land to labor in C, T_C/L_C, depends on w/r. Specifically, as labor becomes more expensive relative to land, firms economize on the use of labor and employ land more liberally. In other words, as w/r rises, they raise the land-labor ratio. This relationship is shown by curve CC' in figure 1.

We assume that C is land intensive relative to S. This means that at each wage-rental ratio, C uses more land per unit of labor than S. In terms of figure 1, the line showing the land-labor ratio in S at different wage-rental ratios, SS', lies everywhere below CC'.

Represent the land-labor ratio of HC in figure 1 by T/L. We can then determine the range of possible wage-rental ratios in HC. At a sufficiently high relative price of C, the economy specializes completely in this product. In this case, the land-labor ratio in C coincides with the economy's land-labor endowment ratio, and the wage-rental ratio is given by $(w/r)_{min}$ in figure 1. At the other extreme, if the price of C is sufficiently low, the economy specializes completely in S, the land-labor ratio in S coincides with the economy's land-labor ratio, and the wage-rental ratio is given by $(w/r)_{max}$ in figure 1. At an intermediate price ratio, both goods are produced and the wage-rental ratio is between the two extremes.

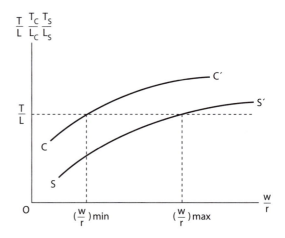

Figure 1

Factor prices and factor intensities

As we move from $(w/r)_{min}$ toward $(w/r)_{max}$, we increase the output of S and reduce that of C. With the wage-rental ratio rising during this movement, both sectors raise the land-labor ratio, and thus allow the labor-intensive sector S to expand.

Figure 2 shows the output changes just described using the construction of the production possibilities frontier (PPF). Given technology and factor endowments, MN shows the PPF of HC. The absolute value of the slope of the PPF at any point gives the opportunity cost of the product on the horizontal axis (C) in terms of the product on the vertical axis (S). The PPF is bowed out, which means that the marginal opportunity cost of each product in terms of the other rises as we expand the output of that product. For example, as we move from M toward N, the absolute value of the slope rises, meaning that the opportunity cost of C in terms of S rises with the rising output of C. This rising cost is the result of the imperfect substitutability between land and labor. To expand the production of C, which is land intensive, we must lower the land-labor ratio in each product. The more we substitute labor for land, the lower the marginal return to such substitution and the higher the marginal cost of further expansion.

Under perfect competition, production takes place at a point where the marginal cost equals the price.

Therefore, letting $(P_C/P_S)^0$ represent the relative price, the economy would produce at a point such as Q^0 in figure 2 where the price line is tangent to the PPF. The tangency ensures that the relative price equals the marginal opportunity cost of production.

Starting at Q^0, suppose we consider a small increase in the relative price of C. This would lead to an increase in the output of C and decrease in the output of S. At the original factor prices, the expansion of C would require more land per worker than S releases. This creates an excess demand for land and excess supply of labor. The return to land rises and that to labor falls. That is to say, a rising price of C, which is land intensive, is associated with a declining w/r ratio.

Let us plot these relationships in figure 3. In the right-hand panel, curve RS shows increasing supply of C relative to S as a function of the relative price of C, P_C/P_S. In the left-hand panel, curve RR' shows an inverse relationship between wage-rental ratio and the relative price of C. This latter relationship partially represents the Stolper-Samuelson theorem: it connects the goods prices to the relative factor prices. The representation is only partial since the Stolper-Samuelson theorem also relates the price change to the real factor returns.

To elaborate on how the Stolper-Samuelson theorem works, consider a move from autarky to free trade by HC. Suppose that the world relative price of C exceeds its autarky price. This means HC would export C and import S under free trade. As already

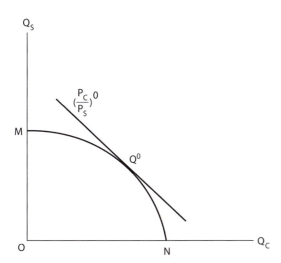

Figure 2
The production equilibrium

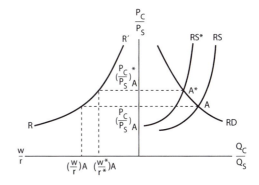

Figure 3
The Heckscher-Ohlin factor price equalization theorems

explained, the higher price of C brought about by trade would increase the output of C and lower the wage-rental ratio (see left-hand panel in figure 3). The income distribution within HC would move against workers and in favor of landowners. The critical question is whether the workers could still be better off in real terms due to the decline in the relative price of good S brought about by trade. The Stolper-Samuelson theorem answers this question in the negative: the wage declines not just in terms of good C whose price rises but also in terms of S whose price falls.

To see how this works, note that the firms employ workers up to the point where the wage equals the value of marginal product of labor. Denoting the marginal product of labor in C and S by MPL_C and MPL_S, respectively, we have

$$w = P_C . MPL_C = P_S . MPL_S \qquad (1)$$

Rearranging, this equation implies

$$w/P_C = MPL_C \text{ and } w/P_S = MPL_S \qquad (2)$$

That is to say, the purchasing power of the wage in terms of a commodity equals the marginal product of labor in that commodity. This purchasing power rises or falls as the marginal product of labor in the product rises or falls. A similar relationship applies to land: the purchasing power of rental income in terms of a good rises or falls as the marginal product of land in the production of that good rises or falls.

To determine what happens to the marginal product, recall that as C expands, the wage-rental rate falls, which leads to a decline in the land-labor ratio in each product. The decline in the land-labor ratio implies a decline in the marginal product of labor and a rise in the marginal product of land in terms of each product. It follows that the real return to labor falls and that to land rises in terms of each good. In effect, the decline in the wage is sharper than the decline in the price of good S, leaving the workers worse off even if they spend their entire wage income on that good.

Next, let us consider the effects of a change in the factor endowments at a given goods price ratio. To take a concrete example, let us increase the endowment of labor by 5 units. From curve RR' in figure 3, we know that as long as we hold the goods price

constant, the relative factor prices remain constant as well. Figure 1 then tells us that the land-labor ratios in the two goods must also remain unchanged. The economy must absorb the additional labor supply without altering the land-labor ratios. This constraint immediately rules out a simple-minded division of the additional units of labor between the two sectors without reallocation of land since such allocation would necessarily change the land-labor ratio in each product.

To see what kind of reallocations would be compatible with full employment at unchanging land-labor ratios, begin by placing the entire additional labor supply in the labor-intensive good S. To maintain the original land-labor ratio, this requires drawing land from C to work with the additional five units of labor in S. But since C must also maintain its original land-labor ratio, it would not release land without releasing labor. This means that S must absorb not just the 5 new units of labor but also those released by C as it releases land.

For concreteness, suppose the land labor ratio is 3 in C and 2 in S. Then each time C releases 3 units of land, it releases 1 unit of labor. But since the land-labor ratio in S is 2, it employs 1.5 units of labor for each 3 units of land. In other words, moving 3 units of land out of C allows S to absorb 1 unit of labor released by C plus a half unit out of the new 5 units. Therefore, if we move 30 units of land from C to S, the latter would absorb 15 units of labor that are exactly equal to the sum of the 10 units released by C and 5 new units. Full employment is achieved at unchanging land-labor ratios.

This example illustrates that a given expansion of the endowment of a factor leads to a proportionately larger expansion of the sector using that factor more intensively and a contraction of the other sector. We thus have the Rybczynski theorem, named after T. M. Rybczynski (1955), who first noted the result. The result is generalized in the sense that if both factors expand but the land-labor ratio declines, the output of the land-intensive good relative to the labor-intensive good falls as well.

The Rybczynski theorem is a key building block of the Heckscher-Ohlin theorem. Recall that we have assumed FC to be relatively labor abundant: $L^*/T^* > L/T$. An immediate implication of the Rybczynski theorem is that at any given price ratio, FC produces less C relative to S than HC. Therefore, denoting by Q_i the quantity of output of good i (i = C, S), we have $Q_C^*/Q_S^* < Q_C/Q_S$ at each price ratio. This is shown by the relative supply curve RS* in figure 3.

Assuming the relative demand depends only on the relative price and the consumers in HC and FC are identical, we can represent the demand in the two countries by a common demand curve RD in figure 3. The autarky equilibriums in HC and FC are then given by A and A*. It is straightforward that under autarky the land-intensive good C is cheaper in the land-abundant country HC and the labor-intensive good S is cheaper in the labor-abundant country FC. Therefore, when the two countries open to trade, each country would export the good that uses its abundant factor more intensively, just as the Heckscher-Ohlin theorem predicts (see above).

Finally, observe that, as the left-hand panel of figure 3 shows, under autarky the wage-rental rate is higher in the labor-scarce HC than in the labor-abundant FC. The opening to trade leads to a rise in the relative price of C in HC. This leads to a fall in the wage-rental rate there. The opposite happens in FC: the relative price of C declines there, which leads to a rise in the wage-rental rate. Therefore, the factor prices converge between the two countries. Assuming no transport costs, trade would equalize the goods prices. But as goods prices equalize, the wage-rental rate would equalize as well.

Given the same wage-rental rates in the two countries at the free-trade equilibrium, figure 1 tells us that the land-labor ratios across countries would also equalize for each product. This would then lead to the equalization of the marginal products and hence real factor prices of each product. Free trade would lead to the equalization of the relative and real factor returns internationally, as predicted by the factor price equalization theorem (see above).

Trade and Wages In the contemporary policy literature, the Stolper-Samuelson and factor price equalization theorems have played a crucial role.

Between the late 1970s and early 1990s, the real and relative wages of unskilled workers in relation to skilled workers in the rich countries declined. The ratio of skilled-to-unskilled wages, a measure of wage inequality, rose almost 30 percent in the United States. This period also coincided with a rapid expansion of trade between developed and developing countries. This led many to link the changes in the wages to the opening to trade via the Stolper-Samuelson theorem. If we think of the two factors in the H-O model as skilled and unskilled workers, the developed countries are importers of unskilled-labor-intensive goods. The H-O theory then predicts that opening to trade with the developing countries would push down the real and relative wages of the unskilled. In the spirit of the factor price equalization theorem, some observers have gone so far as to suggest that the wages of the unskilled in the developed countries may be pushed down to the levels prevailing in the developing countries.

Trade economists disagree with this diagnosis and argue that trade with the poor countries cannot explain the bulk of the increase in the wage inequality. They cite four reasons in support of their position.

- Trade works to lower the unskilled wage by lowering the relative price of unskilled-labor-intensive goods. But a study by Lawrence and Slaughter (1993) pointed out that the relative price of unskilled-labor-intensive goods had actually risen since the late 1970s. By itself this point is not decisive, however. In principle, trade may have lowered the relative price of unskilled-labor-intensive products but other factors such as sharply declining costs of skilled-labor-intensive products may have reversed this decline. Lawrence and Slaughter only looked at the ex post change in the prices but did not decompose them according to the sources of the change. Therefore, their analysis remains incomplete.

- Extra imports from the developing countries during the relevant period account for less than 2 percent of the total expenditure in the United States. This is the point made by Krugman (1995). He argues that such a small proportionate expansion of trade can simply not explain the large increase in wage inequality. This is a valid and important point.

- During this period, wage inequality rose in many developing countries as well. If the simple-minded Stolper-Samuelson theorem was driving the outcome, developing countries should have experienced a decrease in wage inequality. Given that they export unskilled-labor-intensive goods, the Stolper-Samuelson theorem should have driven their real and relative unskilled wages up. This did not happen.

- Technical change that shifted labor demand in favor of skilled labor and away from unskilled labor provides a far more compelling explanation for increased wage inequality in both rich and poor countries. Technological change has been concentrated in skilled-labor-intensive goods, and it has also moved progressively toward greater use of skilled labor. This change has shifted the demand in favor of skilled labor in both rich and poor countries and led to increased wage inequality in both regions.

The Heckscher-Ohlin model is the principal workhorse of trade economists. It shows that countries export goods that use their abundant factors more intensively and import goods that use their scarce factors more intensively. Given that imports bring goods that use the scarce factors more intensively, they lower the demand for and hence the returns to such factors locally. This conclusion has led to widespread claims that the imports of unskilled-labor-intensive goods from the poor countries have lowered real and relative wages of unskilled workers in the rich countries. Most trade economists disagree with this conclusion, arguing that a shift in technology in favor of skilled labor and away from unskilled labor is the true cause of the decline in the fortunes of unskilled workers.

See also comparative advantage; factor endowments and foreign direct investment; Ricardian model; specific-factors model; trade and wages

FURTHER READING

Bhagwati, Jagdish. 1964. "The Pure Theory of International Trade: A Survey." *Economic Journal* 74 (293): 1–84. Offers a careful survey of the development of the Heckscher-Ohlin theory along with other theories of international trade.

Heckscher, Eli. 1919. "The Effect of Foreign Trade on the Distribution of Income." *Ekonomisk Tidskrift* 21: 497–512. The original article to which the Heckscher-Ohlin theory is traced.

Krugman, Paul. 1995. "Growing World Trade: Causes and Consequences." *Brookings Papers on Economic Activity* 1: 327–62. Argues that the rise in volume of imports from the developing countries in relation to the total expenditure is too tiny to explain the large increase in wage inequality during the 1980s and early 1990s in the United States.

Lawrence, Robert Z., and Mathew J. Slaughter. 1993. "International Trade and American Wages in the 1980s: Giant Sucking Sound or a Small Hiccup?" *Brookings Papers on Economic Activity* 2 (Microeconomics): 161–226. Shows that the prices of unskilled-labor-intensive goods relative to skilled-labor-intensive goods rose during the phase that the unskilled wages fell in the United States.

Ohlin, Bertil. 1933. *Interregional and International Trade.* Cambridge, MA: Harvard University Press. First full-scale statement of the Heckscher-Ohlin theory in English by one of its two originators.

Panagariya, Arvind. 2000. "Evaluating the Factor-Content Approach to Measuring the Effect of Trade on Wage Inequality." *Journal of International Economics* 50 (1): 91–116. Offers a detailed analysis of the relationship of the factor content of trade to factor prices in the H-O model.

Rybczynski, T. M. 1955. "Factor Endowments and Relative Commodity Prices." *Economica* 22 (87): 336–41. Inaugurated the systematic analysis of the effects of the changes in factor endowments on outputs.

Samuelson, Paul A. 1948. "International Trade and the Equalization of Factor Prices." *Economic Journal* 58

(230): 163–84. Formalizes the Heckscher-Ohlin model and shows that trade would lead to the equalization of factor prices.

Stolper, Wolfgang, and Paul A. Samuelson. 1941. "Protection and Real Wages." *Review of Economic Studies* 9 (3): 58–73. Shows that in the H-O model, the owners of the scarce factor are left unambiguously worse off by imports.

ARVIND PANAGARIYA

▪ hedge funds

Hedge funds are broadly defined as private investment pools that are not available to the general public. They are more lightly regulated and have wider investment flexibility than public investment companies such as mutual funds, which pool money from many investors and invest in stocks, bonds, and other securities. Hedge funds can buy and sell securities in many financial markets, representing long and short positions, respectively. In addition, they can use leverage and derivatives, which are financial instruments whose value derives from some underlying asset or price.

The first hedge fund was started in 1949 by Alfred Winslow Jones, a financial journalist, who believed that this new investment style could deliver good returns with more stability than investments in stock mutual funds. The hedge fund industry has grown from 600 funds in 1990 to more than 8,500 in 2005. During the same period, total assets in hedge funds have grown from $40 billion to more than $1 trillion. This growth has been driven by the stable investment performance of the industry, especially when compared to the swings of the stock market. Because they pursue very active investment strategies, hedge funds are even more important than their asset size would suggest. As a result, hedge funds have become major players in international capital markets.

Types of Hedge Funds The hedge fund industry is much more heterogeneous than the mutual fund industry because of the greater latitude in investment style. Funds are typically classified into the following categories:

Global macro funds, which take positions in global markets (stocks, fixed-income investments, currencies, commodities);

Long/short equity funds, which buy and sell stocks;

Equity market neutral funds, where the long positions are exactly offset by short positions so as to create a zero, or neutral exposure to the stock market;

Arbitrage funds, which take long and short positions in securities such as fixed-income and convertible bonds;

Event-driven funds (merger arbitrage and distressed debt), which take positions driven by corporate events such as mergers, takeovers, reorganizations, and bankruptcies.

Long/short equity funds represent the largest sector of the industry, with approximately one-third of the funds.

Investment Strategy Consider a typical hedge fund, which has both long and short positions in stocks. Say the initial capital is $100. This represents the equity, or net asset value. The fund buys $100 worth of stocks and sells $50 worth of other stocks. Short-selling is achieved by borrowing a stock and selling it in the hope that its price will fall later, at which time the stock can be bought back and transferred to the lender. In such case, the borrower keeps the difference between the (higher) earlier sales price for the stock and the (lower) later purchase price. In the event that the stock price goes up, however, the borrower loses the difference between the (lower) earlier sales price and the (higher) later purchase price.

This type of investment strategy (short-selling) has two advantages relative to mutual funds, which typically are allowed to have long positions only. First, it allows the hedge fund manager the flexibility to buy assets that are viewed as undervalued, for example, and sell assets that are overvalued. In contrast, the manager of a long-only fund cannot implement a view that an overvalued asset is going to fall in price, because the manager cannot short the asset.

Second, it has less exposure to the direction of the stock market (called *directional exposure*) than a long-only position. Indeed, to "hedge" a bet can be defined as protecting against loss by taking a bet for a countervailing amount against the original bet. In hedge investing, the directional exposure to the market, also called *beta*, is reduced. As a result, the overall risk of loss is reduced as well. Hedge funds attempt to create risk-adjusted performance, also called *alpha*, without taking too much directional risk.

As an example, a manager could buy Google's stock because it is expected to go up by 25 percent, out of which 10 percent is due to the overall stock market and 15 percent to the company itself. The manager, however, is not confident about the direction of the stock market and is afraid the 10 percent expected profit on the market could turn into a loss. To hedge against a market fall, the purchase of Google is offset by a short position of the same size on the market. If the market falls by 10 percent, the transaction will create a profit of 15 percent minus 10 percent, for a 5 percent total gain on Google's stock, plus a gain of 10 percent on the stock market, for a total of 15 percent. Of course, if the market indeed goes up by 10 percent, the short position will lose 10 percent, leading to a net profit of 15 percent. Therefore, this hedge locks in a total profit of 15 percent irrespective of the market.

Another example of trading strategy that exploits inefficiencies in the market would be to identify two assets with similar characteristics, such as two long-term Treasury bonds with close maturities and similar interest rate risk. An *arbitrage* opportunity would arise if the bonds were to trade at sufficiently different prices. The hedge fund manager would then buy the cheap bond, say at $99, and sell the expensive one, say at $100. This position should create profits if the bond prices later converge. Even if successful, however, such strategy will produce only small profits, on the order of $1 per transaction (after taking into account the costs of making the transaction). To magnify profits, the hedge fund will typically use *leverage*. This involves the use of credit to increase the size of the position relative to the equity. For instance, the hedge fund with $100 in equity could be buying and selling $990 and $1,000 worth of bonds (using 10 percent equity and 90 percent credit), which will multiply the profit by a factor of 10.

This wider investment flexibility combined with hedging has proved successful. Hedge funds have generally performed well relative to other investments, especially when adjusting for risk. For fund managers, hedge funds provide greater remuneration than traditional investment funds. Typical investment management fees for mutual funds range from a fixed 0.5 percent to 2 percent of asset value. In contrast, hedge funds commonly charge a fixed 2 percent of assets plus 20 percent of positive returns.

Other categories of hedge funds include *multi-strategy funds*, which invest across the categories listed earlier, and *funds of funds*, which invest in individual hedge funds.

Investment Issues Hedge funds take risks in the expectation of high profits. Because of the leverage inherent in most hedge funds, this naturally leads to failures. Leverage increases the profits, but also the risks. In our previous example, a leverage of 10 transforms a profit of $1 into $10. On the other hand, a loss of $1 now becomes $10. In the limit, a very large loss of $10 becomes $100, wiping out the $100 equity. Indeed, hedge funds have a high rate of disappearance, from 5 to 11 percent per year. In most cases, this reflects an investment or operational failure that leads to the closing down of the fund. Mutual funds also fail, but less frequently.

Hedge funds present some specific problems not shared by mutual funds. Because hedge funds often invest in assets that are not traded on organized exchanges such as the New York Stock Exchange, some positions can be difficult to value. Thus the proper *valuation* of assets is a major issue for hedge funds. Assets that are not traded often are called illiquid.

Illiquidity explains the common practice of imposing a lockup period, which is the minimum amount of time during which investor money is to be held in the fund, and a redemption notice period, which is the time required to notify the fund of an intended redemption. Lockup periods average 3 months, and can extend to 5 years; redemption notice periods average 30 days.

Another problem with hedge funds is the *lack of transparency*. Because hedge funds follow proprietary trading strategies, they are generally reluctant to reveal information about their trading ideas or positions. Having no information about positions has serious disadvantages for investors. It becomes difficult to monitor the risk of the fund, to aggregate the risk profile of the fund with the rest of the investor's portfolio, or even to detect fraud.

Regulatory Issues The rapid growth of hedge funds has led to regulatory concerns on several issues. One is the *protection of investors*. Investors can lose money in hedge funds. Direct investment in hedge funds, however, is restricted to professional investors, such as wealthy individuals, pension funds, endowment funds, and other institutional investors. The general presumption is that such investors are conscious of the investment risk they take and can therefore fend for themselves. Also, hedge fund managers generally have significant personal investments in the fund, which partially aligns their interest with that of other investors.

Fraud is another concern. Fraud occasionally occurs in all investment activities, and there is no evidence that hedge fund advisors engage disproportionately in fraudulent activities. Even so, there have been some high-profile cases of hedge fund fraud which, combined with the rapid growth of the industry, have led regulators to look more closely at hedge funds.

Another issue is *protecting market integrity*. Market participants should not attempt to dominate or manipulate markets. Like other large investors, hedge funds are subject to rules against market manipulation.

Regulators also worry about the potential for *systemic risk*. Systemic risk arises when default by one institution has a cascading effect on other financial institutions (the first institution's default being of such a magnitude as to cause the failure of its creditors, which in turn default on their obligations to other institutions, and so on), thus posing a threat to the stability of the entire financial system. Indeed, the spectacular failure of the hedge fund Long-Term Capital Management (LTCM) in 1998 is said to have endangered the world financial system. LTCM was a hedge fund founded in 1994 by John Meriwether, the former head of bond trading at Salomon Brothers. The fund lost $4.4 billion in 1998, forcing the Federal Reserve Bank to organize a private bailout to avoid disruptions in financial markets.

The primary mechanism for regulating hedge fund risk is the discipline provided by creditors, counterparties, and investors. The leverage of the hedge fund industry is provided by counterparties such as banks and brokerage firms. It is in these lenders' best interest to make sure that loans to hedge funds are controlled and have sufficient collateral. Holding collateral can provide effective protection against default. The LTCM crisis revealed lax lending standards. Since then, however, the Counterparty Risk Management Policy Group (2005) has reported a general improvement in counterparty risk management practices.

Role of Hedge Funds Hedge funds have become important conduits of capital in international financial markets. Like any other speculator trading in the expectation of making profits, hedge funds enhance market liquidity by generating more trading activity, leading to deeper and more liquid markets. In addition, many hedge funds use relative value strategies, which buy underpriced assets and sell overpriced ones. These actions should help to push prices faster to their equilibrium values, which enhance market efficiency.

See also capital mobility; carry trade; hedging; speculation

FURTHER READING

Chan, Nicholas, Mila Getmansky, Shane Haas, and Andrew Lo. 2006. "Systemic Risk and Hedge Funds." In *The Risk of Financial Institutions*, edited by Rene Stulz and Mark Carey. Chicago, IL: University of Chicago Press, 235–330. A review of risk measurement issues and failure rates in the hedge fund industry.

Counterparty Risk Management Policy Group. 2005. *Toward Greater Financial Stability: A Private Sector Perspective*. New York: CRMPG. An evaluation of potential systemic risk problems in financial markets.

Edwards, Franklin. 1999. "Hedge Funds and the Collapse of Long-Term Capital Management." *Journal of Economic Perspectives* 13 (spring): 189–210.

Eichengreen, Barry, Donald Mathieson, Bankim Chadha, Anne Jansen, Laura Kodres, and Sunil Sharma. 1998.

Hedge Funds and Financial Market Dynamics. Washington, DC: International Monetary Fund. A review of the hedge fund industry, its role in the Asian currency crisis, and regulatory issues.

Financial Services Authority. 2006. *Hedge Funds: A Discussion of Risk and Regulatory Engagement.* London: FSA. Perspectives from a major regulator of hedge funds based in the United Kingdom.

Gupta, Anurag, and Bing Liang. 2005. "Do Hedge Funds Have Enough Capital? A Value-at-Risk Approach." *Journal of Financial Economics* 77 (July): 219–53. A detailed analysis of hedge fund risks.

Jorion, Philippe. 2000. "Risk Management Lessons from Long-Term Capital Management." *European Financial Management* 6: 277–300. The role of leverage and risk in the LTCM crisis.

PHILIPPE JORION

■ hedging

Hedging refers to the reduction of an existent risk by the elimination of exposure to price movements in an asset. Hedging stabilizes markets since it removes potential shocks to balance sheets that can destabilize the financial system. Also, if hedging is complete at the aggregate level, long and short positions can be matched with less price volatility. Those taking a short position want to sell an asset because they believe its price is going to fall, while those going long want to buy it since they expect a rise in the asset price. Unhedged short-term foreign borrowing played a major role in escalating the East Asian crisis of 1997–98.

Currency risk is hedged through contracts that protect the home currency value of transactions denominated in a foreign currency, removing the exposure to exchange rate fluctuations. The currency risk is transferred to another party who wants to take an exposure in opposite direction.

The value of a derivative hedging contract is based on the underlying basic spot exchange rate. Standardized contracts are available, or customized (over-the-counter, or OTC) contracts can be designed. An Indian exporter, for example, can sell the dollars due to him in the future on the dollar-rupee forward market, through a forward contract or an agreement to sell the dollars at a certain future rate for a certain price reflecting current prices. Hedging can also be accomplished informally, for example, if an exporter takes a foreign loan. Then if the home currency depreciates he will gain in export income but lose as the home currency value of his debt rises, so that his net exposure is low.

Hedging versus Speculation If the exporter does not sell the future dollars forward, thus entering into only one leg of a foreign currency transaction, he is speculating on a belief the rupee is going to depreciate. He may also take a short position on the rupee using derivative products. Speculation is the act of aiming to profit by betting on a predicted one-way price movement. Thus it is risk-taking, not risk-reducing. It is sometimes argued that since speculators buy when prices are low and sell when prices are high, rational speculative activity stabilizes markets. But this does not always follow, since speculators buy when there is a high probability of price appreciation and sell when the probability is low, and thus can cause cumulative movements.

Buying and selling currency in the spot market requires an initial cash payment. Forward contracts require no such initial payment, but can lead to a gain or a loss in the future transaction depending on changes in the exchange rate. Therefore, forward markets provide extra leverage to a speculator in comparison to spot markets. Options, another type of derivative, increase the leverage further since they confer a right but not an obligation to make a transaction. The option has an initial cost but then does not require buying or selling currency either in spot or in the forward market. Therefore it provides even higher leverage, at a price.

Incentives to Hedge Hedging does not necessarily rise with the availability of more market instruments, since the same derivative can be used for hedging or for speculation leveraging initial capital many times. Incentives to induce hedging are more important. Markets, instruments, and opportunities, with some restrictions on currency derivatives, existed in East Asia prior to the crisis, yet hedging was inadequate (Burnside et al. 2001).

Speculation dominates if there are aspects of the financial structure that encourage taking too much risk, such as lowering liability for promoters or managers; or if policy, such as one-way movement of exchange rates, creates opportunities for speculation. A firm's cost of borrowing is minimized if it is fully hedged so that bankruptcy does not occur. Since creditors normally set interest rates to cover expected default under bankruptcy, the risk-free interest rate is lower. So a fully hedged firm should get loans at lower rates. But if government guarantees the loan repayments and covers bankruptcy costs the incentive to hedge risks disappears (Burnside et al. 2001). Results are similar if laws make it difficult for creditors to recover loans.

If domestic interest rates are high, the high borrowing costs raise the opportunity costs of buying hedging instruments. Even if an importer holds a dollar deposit as an informal hedge, he sacrifices potential high domestic interest earnings. Similar considerations affect the hedging activities of banks.

Regulatory authorities sometimes put restrictions on derivative products that could facilitate hedging, in order to curb speculation. But with modern technology and regulation it is possible to distinguish between hedging and speculative foreign exchange market activities. Hedging transactions are charged lower margins on modern exchanges and their tax treatment also differs. If it is possible to monitor the use of derivatives it is not necessary to ban them.

Psychological factors also undermine rational hedging decisions. People prefer a sure gain, but they prefer an uncertain outcome with a small probability of a gain to a sure loss. Hedging involves a small sure loss or cost, and without it there is a small probability of a gain. Thus they are willing to forgo hedging and undertake more risk than is rational. But proper "framing" sensitive to psychological attitudes can reduce risk-taking behavior. An understanding that concentration on core business makes them more competitive and reduces volatility of profits may make firms more willing hedgers.

See also balance sheet approach/effects; currency crisis; financial crisis; hedge funds; speculation

FURTHER READING

Burnside, Craig, Martin Eichenbaum, and Sergio Rebelo. 2001. "Hedging and Financial Fragility in Fixed Exchange Rate Regimes." *European Economic Review* 45: 1151–93. Discusses the links between financial crises and failure to hedge.

Shefrin, Hersh. 2002. *Beyond Greed and Fear: Understanding Behavioral Finance and the Psychology of Investing*. Oxford: Oxford University Press. Applies psychology to analyze investor behavior.

Wang, Peijie. 2005. *The Economics of Foreign Exchange and Global Finance*. Berlin: Springer. A textbook treatment of hedging in currency markets.

ASHIMA GOYAL

■ HIV/AIDS

HIV/AIDS refers to the human immunodeficiency virus and the associated acquired immunodeficiency syndrome, which were first recognized as a global health issue in the early 1980s. In 2006, about 40 million people globally were living with HIV/AIDS, including 25 million in sub-Saharan Africa, and the epidemic claimed almost 3 million lives in that year. The international response has involved a rapid scaling-up of aid and an expansion of prevention and treatment programs, as well as the establishment of two specialized international agencies to deal with the epidemic—the Joint United Nations Program on HIV/AIDS (UNAIDS) and the Global Fund to Fight HIV/AIDS, Tuberculosis, and Malaria (GFATM).

Epidemiology and Demographics The most important modes of transmission of HIV are sexual contact with an infected person, sharing needles for injected drug use, mother-to-child transmission before or during birth or through breast-feeding, and transfusions of infected blood or blood clotting factors. HIV/AIDS is largely asymptomatic during the first years after infection. Over time, HIV/AIDS progressively damages the immune system, resulting in increased susceptibility to opportunistic infections (e.g., pneumonia, tuberculosis, and certain types of cancer) and, eventually, death. Antiretroviral treatment suppresses the virus and slows down the progression of the disease.

The region most affected by HIV/AIDS is sub-Saharan Africa; however, the high HIV prevalence rate of about 6 percent for the region masks very substantial differences in HIV prevalence across countries, ranging from less than 1 percent (e.g., in Senegal) to more than 20 percent in Botswana, Lesotho, Swaziland, and Zimbabwe (all data on HIV prevalence relate to the population ages 15–49, at end-2005). Although HIV prevalence appears to have stabilized in sub-Saharan Africa since around 2001, it has been spreading rapidly in Eastern Europe and Central Asia. Outside Africa, the country with the largest population of people living with HIV/AIDS is India.

Development Impact From an economic development perspective, the most direct impact of HIV/AIDS is the increase in mortality and consequent decline in life expectancy associated with it. For some of the most affected countries, it is estimated that HIV/AIDS has reduced life expectancy by more than 20 years. Development indexes such as the United Nations Development Program's Human Development Index, which combines measures of income, education, and health, suggest that HIV/AIDS has been the most significant single factor to adversely affect development in recent decades. Another consequence of the increase in mortality among young adults associated with HIV/AIDS is an increase in orphan rates, which are estimated to have reached 20 percent of the young population in some of the countries most affected by the epidemic.

The evidence regarding the macroeconomic impacts of HIV/AIDS is less clear. In light of the slowdown of the growth of the working-age population, there is a consensus that growth of gross domestic product (GDP) also slows as a consequence of HIV/AIDS. Studies applying a neoclassical growth model typically find that HIV/AIDS reduces GDP per capita through declining productivity and a fall in capital per worker that occurs as health-related spending lowers the national saving and investment rates. These effects are at least partly offset by the impact of increased mortality on the capital/labor ratio (mortality decreases the denominator, causing an increase in the overall ratio). The latter effect, however, partly dissipates if investment flows are sensitive to changes in the rate of return to capital.

On the microeconomic level, HIV/AIDS is associated with income losses (as household members become too sick to work and as working time is devoted to caregiving) and with increased health-related expenditures. Microeconomic data, largely from sub-Saharan Africa, therefore suggest an adverse impact of HIV/AIDS on incomes, consumption, and wealth of affected households. This is most pronounced during illness or around the time of death; households appear to partly recover later on. To understand the impact of HIV/AIDS on poverty or inequality, it is necessary to take a broader perspective, also covering households that may gain financially as they benefit from income opportunities associated with deaths in other households, most obviously when household members fill HIV/AIDS-related vacancies. Overall, the sparse evidence suggests that an increased volatility in incomes associated with higher mortality translates into an increase in poverty.

International Response On a global level, recognition of the health, humanitarian, and development challenges posed by HIV/AIDS has translated into an unprecedented effort to contain the epidemic and expand access to treatment. Important steps of the international response were the establishment of UNAIDS and the GFATM, and the United Nations General Assembly Special Session on HIV/AIDS (2004). In financial terms, the scale of the international response to HIV/AIDS has expanded very rapidly. Consistent estimates for HIV/AIDS-related spending are available for low- and middle-income countries only; for these, spending has increased from about U.S. $300 million in 1996 to about U.S. $9 billion in 2006, of which about U.S. $6 billion was financed by external aid. The most important funding agencies are the GFATM and the U.S. President's Emergency Plan for AIDS Relief.

National responses to HIV/AIDS depend on the state of the epidemic in a country. To various extents programs emphasize public prevention measures in schools and work places, prevention and awareness measures targeted at high-risk groups, strengthening the health care system, improvements in care for people living with HIV/AIDS, measures to mitigate the social impacts (including support for orphans), and programs to expand access to treatment.

The most effective prevention measures are those targeted at groups at high risk of contracting and passing on the virus, including promotion of condom use among sex workers and provision of sterile needles to injecting drug users. Those measures, together with the perceived impact of the epidemic, have been credited with increasing awareness and reducing risky behavior. Social attitudes, particularly toward men who have sex with men, or the illegal nature of some of the risky behavior such as injecting drug use, can complicate the implementation of prevention programs, however.

In the most affected countries in Southern Africa, the epidemic is generalized, and prevention efforts are geared toward raising awareness and reducing risk behavior across the population, especially among young adults, through the education system, media and advertising campaigns, and public endorsements by leading politicians. Although HIV prevalence has risen to double-digit levels in numerous countries in spite of these efforts, in 2005–6 many of the most affected countries reported increasing HIV awareness and somewhat falling prevalence rates among young adults.

The most significant development in the early years of the 21st century regarding the response to HIV/AIDS was the decline in the costs of antiretroviral treatment. In many developing countries, certain forms of antiretroviral treatment were available in 2007 at costs of around U.S. $300 annually, down from about U.S. $10,000 in 2000. This development reflected voluntary agreements with drug companies, often under the threat of compulsory

licensing to a local producer, and the fact that only a certain range of antiretroviral drugs was available at these low prices, which allowed for some market segmentation between industrialized and developing countries.

Falling prices of drugs and strong international financial support have contributed to a rapid expansion in access to treatment. UNAIDS reports that the number of people receiving antiretroviral treatment in low- and middle-income countries increased from 400,000 to 1.3 million between 2003 and 2005 (corresponding to a coverage rate of about 20 percent), with sub-Saharan Africa accounting for the bulk of the increase.

Continued spread of the disease and the longer survival of those already infected make the management of an increasing number of people requiring treatment the principal challenge in addressing the epidemic in the near future. Additional challenges include extending the gains made to countries with weaker public health systems, where progress in expanding access to treatment has been less pronounced so far, and managing the fiscal challenges and long-term commitments associated with the expansion in these health programs.

UNAIDS and the Global Fund The perception of HIV/AIDS as a threat to global health, beyond the capacity and expertise of any single international organization, resulted in the establishment of a unique institution, UNAIDS, in 1994. UNAIDS coordinates the HIV/AIDS-related activities of its cosponsoring organizations, which are 10 (initially 6) organizations under the UN system. Although a relatively small organization on an international scale (its annual operational budget amounted to about U.S. $58 million in 2006–7), it is also financing part of the activities of its cosponsors on HIV/AIDS, as well as interagency activities (U.S. $42 million annually in 2006–7). Moreover, cosponsors include all of their HIV/AIDS-related activities in UNAIDS's Unified Workplan, which brings the total of HIV/AIDS-related spending coordinated by UNAIDS to about U.S. $1.3 billion annually for 2006–7, about one-sixth of global spending on HIV/AIDS. Additionally, UNAIDS is a key provider of public information on the epidemic, including the annual Report on the Global AIDS Epidemic, which is the most important regular publication on HIV/AIDS.

The GFATM is primarily a funding agency. It receives about 95 percent of its funding from government sources. Grants typically underwrite comprehensive country programs, which are coordinated nationally, for several years. Between 2002 and end-2006, the GFATM disbursed U.S. $3.3 billion, of which U.S. $1.35 billion was disbursed in 2006. Of the accumulated grant portfolio, HIV/AIDS accounts for the lion's share (56 percent), followed by malaria (27 percent) and tuberculosis (15 percent). Although public institutions play the most important role as implementing agencies (accounting for about half of GFATM-supported funding), many of the national responses are implemented by nongovernmental organizations (about a quarter of funding) or by faith-based and academic organizations. Reflecting the burden of HIV/AIDS in the region, sub-Saharan Africa accounts for more than half of GFATM funding.

See also access to medicines; global public goods; globalization

FURTHER READING

Many key references are updated periodically and available online. Useful web sites are the ones of UNAIDS (www.unaids.org), including the annual Report on the Global AIDS Epidemic; the GFATM (www.theglobalfund.org); and the Global AIDS Program of the U.S. Centers for Disease Control and Prevention (www.cdc.gov/nchstp/od/gap/). The World Bank's website also includes much useful material, accessible from http://www.worldbank.org/aids. Other references include:

Beck, Eduard J., Nicholas Mays, Alan W. Whiteside, and Jose M. Zuniga, eds. 2006. *The HIV Pandemic—Local and Global Implications.* Oxford: Oxford University Press.

Canning, David. 2006. "The Economics of HIV/AIDS in Low-Income Countries." *Journal of Economic Perspectives* 20 (3): 121–42. An overview of key economic issues in the treatment and spread of HIV/AIDS in poor countries.

Haacker, Markus, ed. 2004. *The Macroeconomics of HIV/AIDS.* Washington, DC: International Monetary Fund. Available online at http://www.imf.org/external/pubs/ft/aids/eng/index.htm. A collection of essays addressing economic, social, and demographic challenges to economic development raised by the AIDS epidemic.

Jamison, Dean T., Richard G. Feachem, Malegapuru W. Makgoba, Eduard R. Bos, Florence K. Baingana, Karen J. Hofman, and Khama O. Rogo, eds. 2006. *Disease and Mortality in Sub-Saharan Africa.* Washington, DC: World Bank. Places the AIDS epidemic in the broader context of African health and disease.

MARKUS HAACKER

■ home country bias

Home country bias, or simply *home bias,* usually refers to a situation in which the proportion of foreign equities held by domestic investors in their portfolios is too small relative to the predictions of standard portfolio theory. The extent to which equity portfolios are concentrated in equities of the investor's domestic market is a notable feature of international portfolio investment and has remained an important yet unresolved empirical puzzle in financial economics since the 1970s (Levy and Sarnat 1970). Since portfolio theory is the foundation of asset pricing theory, the empirical evidence that investors may not optimize along objective risk-return trade-offs as portfolio theory predicts has important implications for our understanding of the way security prices are set.

Standard models of optimal international portfolio diversification imply that equity investors have not diversified internationally nearly as much as they should. If investors only care about the mean and the variance of the real return of their portfolio, one would expect investors, as a first approximation, to hold the world market portfolio of stocks. In empirical finance literature, home bias is essentially measured by the underweighting of foreign securities in portfolio allocation relative to market-capitalization weights. For example, by the end of 1989, Americans held roughly 94 percent of their equity portfolio in the U.S. stock market, even though the U.S. equity market comprises less than 48 percent of the global equity market (French and Poterba 1991). By the mid-1990s only about 10 percent of U.S. equity wealth was invested abroad, still much less than what it would have been had the U.S. investors held the world market portfolio (Tesar and Werner 1998). This phenomenon exists in other countries as well. A study based on worldwide equity fund holdings data in 1999 and 2000 documents the existence of home bias in every single country in its sample of 48 countries across the globe (Chan, Covrig, and Ng 2005). The literature has also shown that home bias exists not only among individual investors but also among institutional investors.

At the country level, the benchmark for measuring home bias is the share of equity of that country in the world market portfolio. For example, U.S. equity market capitalization accounts for about 50 percent of the world, and therefore the benchmark for U.S. portfolio diversification is 50 percent. At the individual level, the specific optimal mix depends on an individual's utility function, which should include factors such as risk aversion and investment horizon. Foreign holdings of all U.S.–based mutual funds (who are institutional investors) that invest in international stocks are considered foreign investment in the literature.

Possible Explanations of Home Country Bias
International financial markets offer a means for diversification across markets. Most investors do not fully exploit this risk-sharing opportunity, however, but instead hold large shares of their portfolios in domestic equities. Earlier studies in the literature mainly provide theoretical explanations for the home bias. One major explanation is that there are barriers to international investment such as governmental restrictions on foreign and domestic capital flows, foreign taxes, and high transaction costs associated with international investments (Errunza and Losq 1985). Many financial economists, however, have found that even though the barriers to international investment have fallen dramatically, foreign owner-

ship of shares is still extremely limited and much smaller than one would expect in the absence of these barriers. Home bias is prevalent even among investors with relatively low costs of transacting in financial markets such as institutional investors. Other explanations include investors' desire to hedge against inflation risk, deviations from purchasing power parity (Adler and Dumas 1983; Cooper and Kaplanis 1994), and the price uncertainty of human capital or other nontraded assets (Eldor, Pines, and Schwartz 1988; Stockman and Dellas 1989). By holding sufficient amounts of domestic assets, risk-averse investors may hedge against price uncertainty of the goods they consume, since the average return on the portfolio is high (low) when consumption becomes expensive (inexpensive). None of these factors, however, can fully explain the observed reluctance of investors to diversify their holdings internationally.

An alternative view attributes home bias to empirical mismeasurement of the home bias. Some researchers find that, after incorporating empirical uncertainty into the analysis, there may be no home bias because foreign diversification does not lead to a statistically significant improvement in portfolio performance, though the general validity of this thesis remains in doubt (Bekaert and Urias 1996; Pastor 2000).

As investor behavioral factors have been proposed to explain various anomalies in finance since the 1990s, familiarity has become the most dominant explanation of the home country bias puzzle. Familiarity is associated with a general sense of comfort with the known and discomfort with, or even fear of, the alien and distant, which adds a nonpecuniary dimension to the traditional risk-return trade-off emphasized by portfolio theory. Huberman (2001) finds that familiarity breeds investment, and paucity of international diversification is only one of the implications of this tendency to invest in the familiar. Familiarity can feed into the home bias puzzle through two channels: "pure" familiarity effect due to geographic proximity (such as language, culture, and distance) and, more important, information asymmetries caused by distance, which include low visibility of foreign firms, an inability to monitor the firms, and low credibility of financial information (Kang and Stulz 1997). Separating out pure familiarity effect from informational asymmetries, however, remains a challenge for the empirical literature. Some studies document that even within their foreign portfolios—however small these foreign holdings may be—investors prefer the stocks of foreign countries that are closer (Portes and Rey 2005) and whose equity markets are more, not less, correlated with their own (Chan, Covrig, and Ng 2005). Other studies find that familiarity-caused home bias is not only international, but also regional. For instance, U.S. investment managers exhibit a strong preference for locally headquartered firms in their domestic portfolios, where local investments reflect a true informational advantage (Coval and Moskowitz 1999). In addition, in Finland, there is evidence that investors are more likely to hold and trade stocks of Finnish firms that are located close to them, that communicate in their native language, and that have chief executives of the same cultural background (Grinblatt and Keloharju 2001).

Although the various factors just mentioned have been shown in the literature to explain the home bias to some extent, no single explanation seems to fully account for the extent of home bias. Nevertheless, attempts to explain home bias have helped raise questions to guide further studies on the issue.

Home Country Bias in Macroeconomics The home country bias also applies to real, not just financial, investments. Indeed, the oft-documented high positive correlation between a country's long-term savings rate and its investment rate suggests that money saved in a country is invested in that country rather than in the (possibly foreign) country that offers the best return. A closely related phenomenon is the so-called consumption home bias in macroeconomics, which refers to the lack of risk sharing observed in consumption co-movements across countries. Intuitively, the equity home bias puzzle and consumption home bias puzzle may be linked, yet home bias in equities is neither sufficient nor necessary for home bias in consumption (Lewis 1999). On the other hand, home bias in portfolio holdings and home bias in consumption may have some common causes such as various costs of international transactions (Obstfeld and Rogoff 2001). Further, understanding about the potential link between the two puzzles may rely on a better unified understanding of consumption and equity prices.

See also asymmetric information; balance of payments; capital flows to developing countries; capital mobility; Feldstein-Horioka puzzle; hedging; purchasing power parity

FURTHER READING

Adler, M., and B. Dumas. 1983. "International Portfolio Choice and Corporate Finance: A Synthesis." *Journal of Finance* 38 (3): 925–84.

Bekaert, G., and M. S. Urias. 1996. "Diversification, Integration, and Emerging Market Closed-end Funds." *Journal of Finance* 51 (3): 835–69.

Chan, K., V. Covrig, and L. Ng. 2005. "What Determines the Domestic Bias and Foreign Bias? Evidence from Mutual Fund Equity Allocations Worldwide." *Journal of Finance* 60 (3): 1495–1534.

Cooper, I., and E. Kaplanis. 1994. "Home Bias in Equity Portfolios, Inflation Hedging, and International Capital Market Equilibrium." *Review of Financial Studies* 7 (1): 45–60.

Coval, J., and T. Moskowitz. 1999. "Home Bias at Home: Local Equity Preference in Domestic Portfolios." *Journal of Finance* 54 (6): 2045–73.

Eldor, R., D. Pines, and A. Schwartz. 1988. "Home Asset Preference and Productivity Shocks." *Journal of International Economics* 25 (1–2), 165–76.

Errunza, V., and E. Losq. 1985. "International Asset Pricing and Mild Segmentation: Theory and Test." *Journal of Finance* 40 (1): 105–24.

French, K., and J. Poterba. 1991. "Investor Diversification and International Equity Markets." *American Economic Review* 81 (2): 222–26.

Grinblatt, M., and M. Keloharju. 2001. "How Distance, Language, and Culture Influence Stockholdings and Trades." *Journal of Finance* 56 (3): 1053–73.

Huberman, G. 2001. "Familiarity Breeds Investment." *Review of Financial Studies* 14 (3): 659–80.

Kang, J. K., and R. M. Stulz. 1997. "Why Is There a Home Bias? An Analysis of Foreign Portfolio Equity Ownership in Japan." *Journal of Financial Economics* 46 (1): 3–28.

Levy, H., and M. Sarnat. 1970. "International Diversification of Investment Portfolios." *American Economic Review* 60 (4):668–75.

Lewis, K. K. 1999. "Trying to Explain Home Bias in Equities and Consumption." *Journal of Economic Literature* 37 (2): 571–608.

Obstfeld, M., and K. Rogoff. 2001. "The Six Major Puzzles of International Macroeconomics Solved." In *National Bureau of Economic Research Macroeconomics Annual*, edited by B. Bernanke and K. Rogoff. Cambridge, MA: MIT Press, 339–90.

Pastor, L. 2000. "Portfolio Selection and Asset Pricing Models." *Journal of Finance* 55 (1): 179–223.

Portes, R., and H. Rey. 2005. "The Determinants of Cross-border Equity Flows." *Journal of International Economics* 65 (2): 325–51.

Stockman, A. C., and H. Dellas. 1989. "International Portfolio Nondiversification and Exchange Rate Variability." *Journal of International Economics* 26: 271–89.

Tesar, L., and I. Werner. 1998. "The Internationalization of Securities Markets since the 1987 Crash." In *Brookings-Wharton Papers on Financial Services*, edited by R. Litan and A. Santomero. Washington, DC: The Brookings Institution, 281–372.

FANG CAI

■ host country

See location theory

■ hot money and sudden stops

Hot money, also known as *mobile capital*, refers to short-term private capital that flows across borders into different markets in search of higher returns and can be easily reversed. Hot money consequently makes a country susceptible to "sudden stops." The sudden stop problem, first emphasized by Calvo (1998), refers to an abrupt cessation in foreign capital inflows and/or a sharp capital outflow concurrent with a currency/balance-of-payment crisis. Notable episodes of sudden stop crises are the financial crises

that hit Mexico in 1994, Thailand and Korea in 1997, Indonesia, Malaysia, and Russia in 1998, and Argentina in 2001.

There is a growing body of literature that attempts to define and measure sudden stops. One definition of a sudden stop is any episode in which two conditions are met: (1) there is a significant reversal of capital inflows (a decrease in the financial account of at least 2 standard deviations below the country-specific sample mean), and (2) the current account deficit is reduced in either year t or in $t+1$ (Calvo, Izquierdo, and Talvi 2006). Another definition of a sudden stop is an event in which a currency crisis and a current account reversal (an increase in the current account surplus of more than 3 percent of GDP) occur simultaneously (Hutchison and Noy 2006).

What leads to a sudden stop? Even after accounting for all macroeconomic fundamentals that may cause a capital outflow, a large unexplained component remains, which has been linked to herding behavior (Chari and Kehoe 2003).

Sudden Stops and Output Contractions Regardless of the exact definition, sudden stops lead to a large, though short-lived, negative impact on output growth that is substantially greater than the impact associated with a currency or financial crisis without a sudden stop. This abrupt reversal in foreign credit inflows, in conjunction with a realignment of the exchange rate, typically causes a sharp drop in domestic investment, domestic production, and employment. The recovery from these types of crises seems to be rapid, though it is usually not accompanied by full resurgence in capital inflows or by a recovery of domestic investment. There is evidence that sudden stops generally have a larger adverse impact on output in countries relatively closed to trade and with greater exchange rate fixity (Edwards 2004).

The question that follows is: What are the exact mechanics by which mobile capital leads to a financial crisis? The crisis-inducing nature of bank loans/debts is based on an open economy version of the bank panic model (Diamond and Dybvig 1983). Following some negative shock, depositors, concerned about the safety of their savings, attempt to withdraw en masse (which occurs because, given the "first-come-first-served" rule of deposit withdrawals, depositors all rush to withdraw their money before the banks fail). Since the banks' liquid asset/reserves (cash available for withdrawals) are often less than their potential obligations (demand deposits), they are forced into the premature liquidation of long-term investments. Given the partial irreversibility of investments, they obtain a lower return on liquidation. In the open economy, if the foreign currency revenues obtainable in the short term are less than the corresponding short-term potential foreign currency obligations, the banks are "internationally illiquid" (Chang and Velasco 1999), while creditors, such as foreign banks, are unwilling to roll over short-term interbank loans, especially for emerging markets. The sudden termination of bank finance that follows forces the abandonment of potentially solvent investment projects. This consequent decline in capital formation—indeed, capital destruction—leads to a sudden output/economic collapse.

The maturity mismatch story leading to a possible bad equilibrium in the event of a bank panic is well known, but there are many other possible channels of output contraction as well. Another prominent explanation relies on a "Fisherian" debt-deflation channel (Fisher 1933). In these models, deflation, triggered by an endogenous occurrence of a sudden stop when credit constraints become binding in high-debt states, leads to lower marginal returns to factors of production; this leads, through a debt-deflation amplification process, to a large decline in economic activity. The debt-deflation multiplier can be even more severe: firm bankruptcies may cause banks to become ever more cautious, reducing lending to other firms, and thus inducing a further fall in credit (Mendoza 2006).

Adverse balance sheet effects—an increase in liabilities that is not matched by a corresponding increase in assets, due to a combination of currency depreciation following a reversal in hot money and unhedged (uninsured) borrowing in foreign currency—are another channel through which sudden stops could adversely affect the real economy (Rajan and Shen 2006).

Importance of Financing via Foreign Direct Investment Economies that finance their current account deficits mainly through foreign direct investment (FDI) generally are less susceptible to sudden stops than are economies that experience high levels of hot money inflows. Thus, Hausmann and Fernández-Arias (2000) refer to short-term debt as "bad cholesterol" as it is motivated by "speculative considerations" such as exchange rate expectations. This type of financing is the first to exit in times of trouble. The resulting boom-bust cycle of capital flows in the 1990s inflicted great damage on many emerging economies.

Of course, short-term debt is not the only form of liquid liability. An alternative and more complete measure of illiquidity is mobile capital, or international capital markets, which refers to short-term bank loans plus portfolio investment in the form of equity and bond issues in offshore markets. Equity investment at least shares in the risk of falling market values, while long-term bond issues are less liquid. But FDI is seen as "good cholesterol" because it is bolted down and is relatively irreversible in the short run. It flows in because it is attracted by long-term prospects; it enhances the productive capacity of the country and produces the revenue streams necessary to cover future capital outflows (if they occur) without increasing the overall indebtedness of the economy.

Available summary statistics of private capital flows to developing economies suggest, consistent with conventional wisdom, that FDI has been the most resilient form of external financing (for instance, see Chuhan et al. 1996; Sarno and Taylor 1999). Empirical analysis suggests that emerging economies most prone to currency crashes tend to have a relatively smaller share of FDI in total capital inflows and a relatively higher share of short-term external debt (Frankel and Rose 1996). Other studies have confirmed that short-term indebtedness is a robust predictor of financial crises (Rodrik and Velasco 1999).

A potential criticism of the conventional view regarding differing degrees of stability of various capital flows is that complex interactions between

FDI and other flows are not taken into account. Therefore examining each flow individually, particularly during short periods of time (such as year-to-year variations) may not be a reliable indicator of the degree of risk of various classes of flows at best and could be highly misleading at worst (see Bird and Rajan 2002, and references cited there).

Contrary to popular belief, FDI itself, which is a form of external finance, is not "bolted down," though the physical assets it finances are. Foreign investors could use the physical assets as collateral to obtain a loan from banks and place the funds abroad. In other words, the foreign direct investor may hedge the firm's FDI exposure by borrowing domestically and taking short-term capital out of the country. Hence a firm may be doing one thing with its assets and a completely different thing with the manner in which it finances them. This appears consistent with the Malaysian capital flows data during the crisis where, as noted, portfolio outflows in 1997 sharply outweighed the cumulative inflows between 1980 and 1996. Apparently the portfolio outflows must have entered from some other account (such as FDI or bank loans) (Bird and Rajan 2002). Indeed, the distinction between portfolio and FDI flows in the balance of payments can be somewhat arbitrary, and the proportion of FDI flows in aggregate capital flows may be overstated. Small differences in equity ownership are unlikely to represent substantially different investment horizons.

All of this suggests that the casual presumption that the switch from hot money to FDI alone will automatically safeguard a country against sudden stops and output contractions should be viewed with a degree of caution.

See also balance of payments; balance sheet approach/effects; bubbles; capital controls; capital flows to developing countries; currency crisis; debt deflation; financial crisis; foreign direct investment (FDI); hedge funds; interest parity conditions; speculation; spillovers

FURTHER READING

Bird, Graham, and Ramkishen S. Rajan. 2002. "Does FDI Guarantee the Stability of International Capital Flows? Evidence from Malaysia." *Development Policy Review* 20 (2): 191–202. Examines the links between FDI and currency crisis with particular reference to Malaysia in 1997–98.

Caballero, Ricardo, and Arvind Krishnamurthy. 2004. "Smoothing Sudden Stops." *Journal of Economic Theory* 119 (1): 104–27. Describes various financial polices that can potentially prevent the occurrence of sudden stops.

Calvo, Guillermo. 1998. "Capital Flows and Capital-Market Crises: The Simple Economics of Sudden Stops." *Journal of Applied Economics* 1 (1): 35–54. The seminal work in the economic literature that describes sudden stop crises from a theoretical perspective.

Calvo, Guillermo A., Alejandro Izquierdo, and Ernesto Talvi. 2006. "Sudden Stops and Phoenix Miracles in Emerging Markets." *American Economic Review* 96 (2): 405–10. An empirical examination of the regularities of sudden stops, according to which gross domestic product typically recovers quickly following the crisis; this recovery, however, is not accompanied by resurgence of capital flows.

Chang, R., and A. Velasco. 1999. "Liquidity Crises in Emerging Markets: Theory and Policy." In *NBER Macroeconomics Annual 1999*, edited by B. Bernanke and J. Rotemberg. Cambridge, MA: MIT Press, 11–78. Develops a simple model to explain how short-term debt can lead to currency crisis.

Chari, V. V., and Patrick J. Kehoe. 2003. "Hot Money." *Journal of Political Economy* 111 (6): 1262–92. Develops a model of herd behavior to explain volatile capital flows.

Chuhan, P., G. Perez-Quiros, and H. Popper. 1996. "International Capital Flows: Do Short-term Investment and Direct Investment Differ?" Policy Research Working Paper No. 1507. Washington, DC: World Bank. Examines whether there are differences in FDI and short-term capital flows.

Diamond, P., and P. Dybvig. 1983. "Bank Runs, Deposit Insurance, and Liquidity." *Journal of Political Economy* 91 (3): 401–19. Develops a bank-based model on liquidity crises.

Edison, Hali, and Carmen Reinhart. 2001. "Stopping Hot Money: On the Use of Capital Controls during Financial Crises." *Journal of Development Economics* 66: 533–53. Evaluates the effectiveness of capital controls in preventing speculative reversal of hot money in emerging economies.

Edwards, Sebastian. 2004. "Thirty Years of Current Account Imbalances, Current Account Reversals, and Sudden Stops." NBER Working Paper No. 10276. Cambridge, MA: National Bureau of Economic Research. Examines the empirical evidence relating to sudden stops.

Fisher, Irving. 1933. "The Debt-Deflation Theory of Great Depressions." *Econometrica* 1 (4): 337–57.

Frankel, J., and A. Rose. 1996. "Currency Crashes in Emerging Markets: Empirical Indicators." *Journal of International Economics* 41 (3–4): 351–68.

Hausmann, R., and E. Fernández-Arias. 2000. "Is FDI a Safer Form of Financing?" Working Paper No.416. Inter-American Development Bank. Critically examines whether FDI is in fact a stable and safe source of financing.

Hutchison, Michael, and Ilan Noy. 2006. "Sudden Stops and the Mexican Wave: Currency Crises, Capital Flow Reversals, and Output Loss in Emerging Markets." *Journal of Development Economics* 79 (1): 225–48. Empirically defines what sudden stops are and measures the depth of the recessions that typically follow these crises.

Mendoza, Enrique G. 2006. "Lessons from the Debt-Deflation Theory of Sudden Stops." *American Economic Review* 96 (2): 411–16. Describes a set of dynamic, stochastic general equilibrium economic models that replicate many of the defining characteristics of sudden stop crises.

Rajan, Ramkishen S., and Shen Chung-Hua. 2006. "Why Are Crisis-Induced Devaluations Contractionary? Exploring Alternative Hypotheses." *Journal of Economic Integration* 18 (1): 1–24. Empirical investigation of the various factors that might lead a currency depreciation to be contractionary rather than expansionary.

Rodrik, D., and A. Velasco. 1999. "Short-term Capital Flows." NBER Working Paper No. 7364. Cambridge, MA: National Bureau of Economic Research. Examines the impact of short-term capital flows on currency crisis.

Sarno, L., and M. Taylor. 1999. "Hot Money, Accounting Labels, and the Permanence of Capital Flows to Developing Countries: An Empirical Investigation." *Journal of Development Economics* 59 (28): 337–64. Examines the permanence/durability of various types of capital inflows.

Williamson, John. 2005. *Curbing the Boom-Bust Cycle: Stabilizing Capital Flows to Emerging Markets.* Washington, D.C.: Institute for International Economics. This policy brief addresses many of the possible policy solutions to the sudden stop problem that has plagued financial markets in emerging markets for the past two decades.

ASHIMA GOYAL, ILAN NOY,
AND RAMKISHEN S. RAJAN